GEOPHYSICAL GLOBE

ROTHSTEIN/LOOK

AFGHANISTAN

ALBANIA

ALGERIA

ANDORRA

ARGENTINA

AUSTRALIA

AUSTRIA

BAHRAIN

BARBADOS

BELGIUM

BHUTAN

BOLIVIA

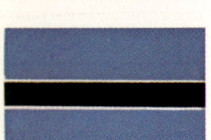
BOTSWANA

BRAZIL

BULGARIA

BURMA

BURUNDI

CAMBODIA

CAMEROON

CANADA

CENTRAL AFRICAN REPUBLIC

CEYLON

CHAD

CHILE

CHINA Communist

CHINA Nationalist

COLOMBIA · CONGO Brazzaville · CONGO KINSHASA · COSTA RICA

CUBA

CYPRUS

COWLES ENCYCLOPEDIA OF NATIONS

from Cowles Volume Library

COWLES EDUCATION CORPORATION

COWLES ENCYCLOPEDIA OF NATIONS

Managing Editor
ROBERT J. FELDMAN

Art Editor
JAMES T. ANDREWS

Assistant Editors
STEVEN P. DALBER, STEPHANIE L. DRANOFF,
M. T. v. GERLOFF, SARA DULANEY GILBERT, PHYLLIS G. ROSEN,
HILARY ROSS, JUDITH C. TARTELL

Editorial Assistants
SUZANNE L. RINGER, SIMONE Y. SONG, D. D. WHEELOCK

Published by
COWLES EDUCATION CORPORATION

DAVID C. WHITNEY
President and Editor

FRANCINE KLAGSBRUN
Executive Editor

RON GILBERT
Art Director

ROBERT F. HIRSCH
Production Manager

A division of
COWLES COMMUNICATIONS

GARDNER COWLES
Editorial Chairman

WILLIAM ATTWOOD
Editor in Chief

COWLES ENCYCLOPEDIA OF NATIONS

Copyright © 1968
by COWLES EDUCATION CORPORATION
A division of Cowles Communications
LOOK Building
488 Madison Avenue, New York, N.Y. 10022

All rights reserved. This volume may not be
reproduced in whole or in part in any form without
written permission from the publishers.

Published simultaneously in the United States and Canada.
Copyright under the International Copyright Convention.

Printed in the United States of America

Library of Congress Catalog Number 68-23249

PREFACE

Cowles Encyclopedia of Nations provides in a single, handy reference volume a survey of the world's nations, colonies, dependencies, cities, and geographic features. The 1,180 articles have been written and reviewed by leading authorities in the fields of geography, history, political science, anthropology, and economics. They contain up-to-date statistical information obtained from United Nations and official government sources.

The basic information you need about each of the world's more than 140 countries is presented clearly in every-day language. A brief sketch of U.S. geography, population, economy, and government also has been included for quick comparison with other countries. In addition there are articles on over 60 colonies and dependencies of foreign states—each organized in the same way as the country articles for parallel reference purposes.

Accompanying the articles on the world's countries and dependencies are concise, fact-filled articles on more than 330 major geographic features and over 640 key cities. Each of the city articles includes the up-to-date population figures.

The articles are illustrated with over 300 photographs, including full-color pictures of the world's outstanding natural features—the Nile, Angel Falls, Mount Everest, the Dead Sea. There are also full-color pictures of the flags of the nations and a special 64-page atlas prepared by the world-famous Rand McNally company. The entire volume is thoroughly indexed.

Cowles Encyclopedia of Nations provides ready-reference information for students, teachers, librarians, and businessmen who seek to keep up with the fast-changing world about us.

The Editors

CONTENTS

PART 1

Countries of the World	1
Afghanistan	1
Albania	2
Algeria	3
Andorra	4
Argentina	5
Australia	7
Austria	10
Bahrain	12
Barbados	13
Belgium	14
Bhutan	15
Bolivia	16
Botswana	17
Brazil	18
Bulgaria	21
Burma	22
Burundi	24
Cambodia	24
Cameroon	25
Canada	26
Central African Republic	35
Ceylon	35
Chad	36
Chile	37
China	39
Colombia	48
Congo (Brazzaville)	49
Congo (Kinshasa)	50
Costa Rica	51
Cuba	52
Cyprus	54
Czechoslovakia	54
Dahomey	56
Denmark	57
Dominican Republic	58
Ecuador	59
El Salvador	60
Ethiopia	61
Finland	62
France	64
Gabon	71
Gambia	72
Germany	73
Ghana	79
Greece	80
Guatemala	84
Guinea	85
Guyana	86
Haiti	87

Honduras	88
Hungary	89
Iceland	92
India	93
Indonesia	98
Iran	100
Iraq	101
Ireland	102
Israel	104
Italy	105
Ivory Coast	109
Jamaica	109
Japan	110
Jordan	113
Kenya	114
Korea	115
Kuwait	117
Laos	118
Lebanon	119
Lesotho	120
Liberia	120
Libya	121
Liechtenstein	122
Luxembourg	123
Madagascar (Malagasy Republic)	123
Malawi	124
Malaysia	125
Maldive Islands	126
Mali	126
Malta	127
Mauritania	128
Mauritius	128
Mexico	129
Monaco	132
Mongolia	132
Morocco	133
Muscat and Oman	134
Nauru	135
Nepal	135
Netherlands	136
New Zealand	137
Nicaragua	139
Niger	140
Nigeria	141
Norway	142
Pakistan	144
Panama	146
Paraguay	147
Peru	148
Philippines	149
Poland	150
Portugal	153
Qatar	154
Rhodesia	154
Romania	155
Rwanda	157
San Marino	158
Saudi Arabia	158
Senegal	159
Sierra Leone	160
Sikkim	161
Singapore	162

Somali Republic	162
South Africa	163
South Yemen	165
Soviet Union	166
Spain	175
Sudan	177
Swaziland	178
Sweden	179
Switzerland	181
Syria	182
Tanzania	184
Thailand	185
Togo	186
Trinidad and Tobago	187
Trucial Oman	188
Tunisia	188
Turkey	189
Uganda	191
United Arab Republic (Egypt)	192
United Kingdom	194
United States	204
Upper Volta	206
Uruguay	207
Vatican City	208
Venezuela	208
Vietnam	210
Western Samoa	213
Yemen	214
Yugoslavia	214
Zambia	217

PART 2

Colonies and Dependencies	218
Angola	218
Antigua	219
Bahamas	219
Bermuda	219
British Antarctic Territory	220
British Honduras	220
British Indian Ocean Territory	220
British Solomon Islands	220
British Virgin Islands	221
Brunei	221
Cape Verde Islands	221
Cayman Islands	221
Channel Islands	222
Christmas Island	222
Cocos Islands	222
Comoro Islands	222
Cook Islands	223
Dominica	223
Equatorial Guinea	223
Faeroe Islands	223
Falkland Islands	224
Fiji Islands	224
French Guiana	224
French Polynesia	224
French Southern and Antarctic Territories	225
French Territory of the Afars and Issas	225

Gibraltar	225
Gilbert and Ellice Islands	226
Greenland	226
Grenada	226
Guadeloupe	227
Hong Kong	227
Ifni	227
Isle of Man	228
Macao	228
Martinique	228
Montserrat	229
Mozambique	229
Netherlands Antilles	229
New Caledonia	230
New Guinea	230
New Hebrides	231
Niue	231
Norfolk Islands	231
Papua	231
Pitcairn Island	231
Portuguese Guinea	231
Portuguese Timor	232
Réunion	232
St. Helena	233
St. Kitts-Nevis-Anguilla	233
St. Lucia	233
St. Pierre and Miquelon	233
St. Vincent	233
Sao Tomé and Principe	234
Seychelles	234

South West Africa	234
Spanish Sahara	235
Surinam	235
Svalbard and Jan Mayen Islands	235
Tokelau Islands	236
Tonga	236
Turks and Caicos Islands	236
Wallis and Futuna Islands	236

PART 3

Natural Features 237

PART 4

Cities of the World 256

PART 5

Bibliography 290

PART 6

Atlas 291

PART 7

Index 355

CONTRIBUTORS

BAHLMAN, DUDLEY W. R., Ph.D. . . . Professor of History and Dean of the Faculty, Williams College. HISTORY: UNITED KINGDOM.

BARZANTI, SERGIO, Ph.D. . . . Associate Professor of Social Sciences, Fairleigh Dickinson University. GEOGRAPHY: EUROPE, MIDDLE EAST.

BROWN, LEON CARL, Ph.D. . . . Associate Professor of Oriental Studies, Princeton University. HISTORY: AFRICA.

BUSHNELL, DAVID, Ph.D. . . . Associate Professor of History, University of Florida. HISTORY: SOUTH AMERICA.

BYRNES, ROBERT F., Ph.D. . . . Distinguished Professor of History, Indiana University. HISTORY: EASTERN EUROPE.

CAREY, GEORGE W., Ed.D. . . . Associate Professor of Geography, Teachers College, Columbia University. GEOGRAPHY: CENTRAL AMERICA.

DUPREE, LOUIS, Ph.D. . . . Research Associate in Anthropolgy, American Museum of Natural History. Afghanistan.

EMBREE, AINSLIE T., Ph.D. . . . Associate Professor of History, Columbia University. HISTORY: INDIA.

ENNIS, THOMAS E., Ph.D. . . . Late Professor of Far Eastern History, West Virginia University. HISTORY: ASIA.

FISCHMAN, JEROME, Ph.D. . . . Associate Professor of History, Adelphi University. HISTORY: CENTRAL AMERICA.

HEIMSATH, CHARLES H., Ph.D. . . . Professor of South Asian Studies, School of International Service, The American University. HISTORY: BHUTAN, NEPAL, PAKISTAN, SIKKIM.

INABA, M. G., Ph.D. . . . Chairman, Department of Geography, Hofstra University. GEOGRAPHY: ASIA.

ISSAWI, CHARLES, M. A. . . . Ragnar Nurkse Professor of Economics, Columbia University. HISTORY: MIDDLE EAST.

JANOWSKY, OSCAR I., Ph.D. . . . Professor Emeritus of History, City College of the City University of New York; Visiting Professor of History, Brandeis University. HISTORY: ISRAEL.

KISH, GEORGE, Ph.D. . . . Professor of Geography, University of Michigan. GEOGRAPHY: EASTERN EUROPE.

KLINE, HIBBERD V. B., Jr., Ph D. . . . Professor and Chairman, Department of Geography, University of Pittsburgh. GEOGRAPHY: AFRICA.

KREN, GEORGE M., Ph.D. . . . Associate Professor of History, Kansas State University. HISTORY: EUROPE.

LEITH, JAMES A, Ph.D. . . . Associate Professor of French History, Queen's University, Ontario. HISTORY: FRANCE.

MELAMID, ALEXANDER, Ph.D. . . . Professor of Economics, New York University. GEOGRAPHY: MIDDLE EAST.

NOWELL, CHARLES E., Ph.D. . . . Professor of History, University of Illinois. HISTORY: ANDORRA, MALTA, PORTUGAL, SAN MARINO, SPAIN.

OLIVER, PETER N., A.M. . . . Lecturer, York University. HISTORY: CANADA.

ROTBERG, ROBERT I., D. Phil. . . . Associate Professor of History and Political Science, Massachusetts Institute of Technology. HISTORY: AFRICA.

ROWNEY, DON KARL, Ph.D. . . . Associate Professor of History, Bowling Green State University. HISTORY: SOVIET UNION.

SMITH, DAVID A., Ph.D. . . . Associate Professor of Geography, State University of New York at Buffalo. GEOGRAPHY: AUSTRALIA, NEW ZEALAND, WESTERN SAMOA.

THOMPSON, JOHN M., Ph.D. . . . Professor of History, Indiana University. HISTORY: SOVIET UNION.

WEBB, KEMPTON E., Ph.D. . . . Associate Professor of Geography, Columbia University. GEOGRAPHY: SOUTH AMERICA.

ZELINSKY, WILBUR, Ph.D. . . . Professor of Geography, Pennsylvania State University. GEOGRAPHY: CANADA.

ZOLBERG, VERA L., M.A. . . . Assistant Professor of Sociology and Anthropology, St. Xavier College. HISTORY: AFRICA.

COUNTRIES OF THE WORLD

AFGHANISTAN

Official name: Kingdom of Afghanistan
Area: 249,934 square miles
Population: (1966 est.) 15,960,000
Capital: Kabul (Pop., 1965, 449,000)
Language: Pashto, Dari
Religion: Islam
Currency unit: Afghani
National holiday: Independence day, May 27

Afghanistan, a landlocked, mountainous country in south Asia, is bordered on the north by the Soviet Union, on the east by China, on the south by Pakistan, and on the west by Iran.

THE LAND. Afghanistan is a high country, with an average elevation of about 6,000 feet above sea level. A great central mountain core dominates the landscape. In the east, the Hindu Kush ranges rise to more than 20,000 feet. The Koh-i-Baba and Paropamisus ranges, with elevations of 10,000 to 15,000 feet, fan out toward the west.

Near the western border the land drops to Seistan, a barren plateau at an elevation of 1,500 feet. East of Seistan are two deserts, the Dasht-i-Margo and the Registan.

Four major rivers flow from the central mountains through the country's major inhabited regions. The Amu Darya (Oxus) drains the hilly northeast and forms part of the border with the Soviet Union. The Hari flows west from the Paropamisus. The richest regions are the valleys of the Helmand and its tributaries, in the southwest, and the valley of the Kabul, which flows east to the Indus.

Afghanistan's climate is characterized by extremes. In the lower regions average temperatures range from over 115°F in summer to −10°F in winter. Mountain temperatures may vary by as much as 50°F in one day, although south of the mountains temperatures are more moderate. Winds are high throughout the country. Average precipitation ranges from 2 inches a year in the west to 12 inches in the east.

THE PEOPLE. Afghanistan's central position in Asia has given it a varied population. Over half the people are Pashtun, or Pathan, a tribal group related to the Persians and Indians. Their language, Pashto, is one of Afghanistan's official languages. Other major groups are the Hazara, who speak a mixed Persian-Turkish dialect, the Turkic-speaking Uzbek and Turkoman, and the Tajik, whose language is a dialect of Persian.

Almost all Afghanis live in rural villages, although by the mid-1960s urbanization was increasing. The major cities are Kabul in the east, Herat in the west, and Kandahar in the south.

ECONOMY. Afghanistan's economic life is based on farming and herding, although no more than 15 percent of the land can be cultivated and less than half of that is farmed. Mineral resources include coal, oil, gas, iron, salt, copper, gold, and lapis lazuli. Exploitation of these resources began only in the 1950s and 1960s.

Karakul sheep are Afghanistan's most valuable agricultural commodity, providing meat, milk, and fat for domestic consumption and skins for export. Goats, cattle, horses, donkeys, and camels are also raised. The leading crops are wheat, barley, and other grains; cotton; sugar beets; and a great variety of fruits and vegetables.

Leather processing, textile weaving, and flour milling are the only well-established manufacturing industries. The development of heavy industry began in the 1950s and 1960s with assistance from the United Nations, the United States, and the Soviet Union.

Projects have been initiated to develop hydroelectric resources, to expand transportation and communications facilities, and to improve education and health services.

Afghanistan's exports, valued at about $70.7 million in 1964–1965, include fresh and dried fruits, skins and hides, wool, cotton, and rugs. Fuel, fabrics, machinery, and metal and rubber products were among the $141.4 million worth of goods imported in 1964–1965. In the 1950s and 1960s the Afghan economy was supported by financial and trade assistance from the United States, the Soviet Union, and other countries.

GOVERNMENT. Afghanistan is a constitutional monarchy. The head of state is the padshah, or king. Under Afghanistan's 1964 constitution a prime minister appointed by the king chooses a cabinet, which requires the support of the lower house of parliament.

Members of the lower house are popularly elected to four-year terms. The upper house is partly appointed, partly elected, and partly chosen by provincial legislatures.

Afghanistan is a member of the United Nations.

HISTORY. Afghanistan lies at the crossroads of ancient Asian migration routes, and its early history is a story of invasions and conquests. The country has been inhabited since prehistoric times, but the first known settlers were Aryans, who passed through Afghanistan on their way to India in about 1500 BC.

By the 500s BC, Aryana, as the area was then called, was part of the Persian Empire. In 328 BC it was conquered by the Greek armies of Alexander the Great. After Alexander's death, it was divided between the Seleucid Empire of Persia, and Bactria, a kingdom in the east.

In the 100s BC these kingdoms fell before invasions from the north by nomadic tribes from central Asia, including the Yueh-chi. The Kushan dynasty of the Yueh-chi established a Buddhist empire centering on Afghanistan in the 100s AD. The Kushan empire was overthrown in the 400s by the White Huns.

Islam. At the end of the 600s and in the early 700s Arab armies invaded the country and converted the people to Islam. During the next several centuries many small kingdoms arose in Afghanistan, most of them ruled by Muslims. These kingdoms were dominated in the 900s by Turkic tribes, who made Afghanistan a center of culture and learning.

In the 1200s the Turkic kingdoms were destroyed by the Mongol armies of Genghis Khan. The Turkic-Mongol conqueror, Tamerlane, made Afghanistan part of his Asian empire in the 1300s. Two hundred years later Tamerlane's descendant, Babur, ruled the vast Indian Mughal (Mogul) Empire.

The Mughals lost most of Afghanistan to the Safavid rulers of Persia in the 1600s. But in the early 1700s Afghanistan asserted its independence and drove the Persians out. In 1747 the Afghan tribes jointly chose Ahmad Durrani of the Sadozay tribe as the first ruler of their newly united country. Many tribes were dissatisfied, however, and in the early 1800s rebellions toppled the dynasty.

Foreign Interference. Several civil wars were fought for control of the throne, leaving the country vulnerable to foreign invasion. For by the 1800s control of Afghanistan, long sought by Persia, also had become a goal of Russia and Britain, whose Indian territory bordered Afghanistan. In 1834 Dost Muhammad, a

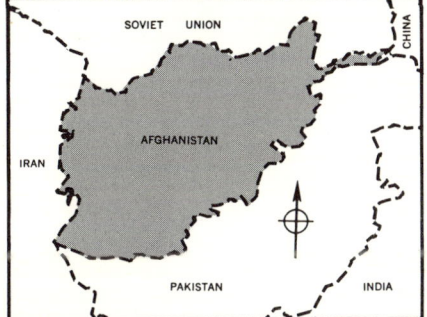

1

Barakzay tribal leader strongly opposed to foreign control, took the throne. To protect its position in India and the Near East, Britain sought to place a more friendly ruler in power. This led to an Anglo-Afghan war between 1839 and 1842.

The British captured Dost Muhammad, but could not put down a rebellion in the country and they withdrew. For the next 36 years Afghanistan's history was marked by civil war, Russian advances, Persian invasions, and, in 1878, by renewed war with Britain. In 1879, having won the war, Britain in effect made Afghanistan a buffer state between British and Russian imperialist ambitions.

In 1880 a new amir, Abd-ar-Rahman, came to the throne and cooperated with the British whenever it benefited Afghanistan. During his reign rebellious tribesmen were pacified and the present boundaries were set between Afghanistan, Russia, and British India. By the beginning of World War I, Britain was dominant in Afghanistan and the Russians and Persians had agreed to end their involvement there.

Afghanistan remained neutral during the war, but a spirit of nationalism developed and in 1919 nationalists led a war against Britain. Neither side was able to win the war, but the British allowed the country to conduct its own foreign affairs.

Modernization. After the war a new king, Amanullah, began to modernize the country. His reforms proved extreme, costly, and unpopular, and in 1929 he was deposed during a widespread tribal rebellion. Muhammad Nadir, a Pashtun leader, defeated rival contenders for power.

Under Nadir Shah and his successors Afghanistan was modernized very gradually. Many democratic forms and processes were introduced, the economy was developed, and the traditional society began to change as Western ideas penetrated the country.

—Thomas Ennis; M. G. Inaba; Louis Dupree

ALBANIA

Official name: People's Republic of Albania
Area: 11,020 square miles
Population: (1966 est.) 1,914,000
Capital: Tiranë (Pop., 1964 est., 156,950)
Language: Albanian
Religion: Islam, Orthodox Christianity, Roman Catholicism
Currency unit: Lek
National holiday: Liberation day, November 29

Albania, a small nation in southeastern Europe, lies along the western coast of the Balkan peninsula. It is bounded on the north and northeast by Yugoslavia, on the southeast and south by Greece, and on the west by the Adriatic Sea. Albania is separated from southern Italy by the narrow Strait of Otranto, at the entrance to the Adriatic. Albanians call their country *Shqiperia*, or "Eagle's land."

THE LAND. Albania is a mountainous land, and mountains cover more than two-thirds of the country. Level land is found only along rivers and near the coast. Albania's rivers are few and short, and they flow westward, to the Adriatic. Three large lakes lie astride Albania's borders—Scutari, in the northwest, and Ohrid and Prespa, in the east.

The climate along the coast is Mediterranean, with warm, dry summers and mild, damp winters. The vegetation there is of the *maquis* type—dry evergreen bushes and small trees. Further east the rainfall is considerably higher, and part of the original forest of oak, beech, and evergreens still stands.

THE PEOPLE. Almost all of the people are Albanians, but there is a small Greek minority in the south, along the Albanian-Greek border. About 1 million Albanians live across the border in Yugoslavia's Kosovo-Metohija region, and about 200,000 live in Greece. The population of Albania is increasing at a very rapid rate, estimated at more than 3 percent a year between 1958 and 1965.

The Albanians are divided into two main groups, each with its own dialect. The Ghegs live in the northern half of the country, and the Tosks live in the southern half. Most Albanians are Muslims. About 20 percent of the people are Orthodox Christians, and 10 percent are Roman Catholics.

ECONOMY. Albania's economy is controlled by the government, which directs economic life through a series of five-year plans. The government has sought to transform the country from an agricultural to an agricultural-industrial nation. Economic development has required support from abroad. Up to the early 1960s, Albania depended on the Soviet Union for economic and technical aid. Since then, it has depended on China.

Agriculture is the major employer of Albania's people, although there is little land that can be cultivated and soils are poor. Wheat and corn are the principal grain crops, and cotton, tobacco, and sunflowers are the main industrial crops. Large quantities of fruit are produced. Livestock includes cattle, goats, and sheep. Sheep are the most important.

Albania has considerable mineral resources, but the rough landscape makes it difficult to exploit them. The major minerals include oil, lignite, chromium, and copper. The country's fast-flowing rivers are used to provide hydroelectric power for industry. The basic industries process the nation's agricultural and mineral products.

In 1964 Albania's exports earned $60 million and its imports cost $98 million. The major exports are minerals and metals and agricultural products—fruit, wine, and tobacco. Imports consist largely of machinery and transportation equipment. Coking coal, required in metal processing, is also an important import. Abania trades heavily with China, but trade with Czechoslovakia, East Germany, and Poland is also important.

GOVERNMENT. Political life in Albania is dominated by the Communist party, officially called the Albanian Labor Party. The political bureau, or politburo, of the party's central committee determines national policy, and the first secretary of the Communist party is the key figure in the government.

The Albanian constitution provides for a popularly elected legislature of one house, the People's Assembly. Assembly candidates are nominated by the Albanian Democratic Front, which is controlled by the Communist party. The assembly chooses a small committee, or presidium, to act for it between its relatively short sessions.

The chairman of the presidium is the head of state. A council of ministers functions as a cabinet. It is headed by a chairman, who is equivalent to a prime minister.

HISTORY. Illyrian tribes from central Europe migrated into the area of present-day Albania in about 2000 BC. The region was called Epirus by the Ancient Greeks, who established colonies along the coast. In the 200s BC Pyrrhus of Epirus built a powerful state and in 280 invaded Italy. He was defeated, and internal unrest led to the disintegration of the state.

Roman Era. Rome conquered the Illyrian states by 167 BC, and the region became fairly prosperous from its geographic position astride Rome's trade routes to the East. Many Albanians became prominent in Roman life, and the towns generally became Roman in culture. In 395 the Roman

Empire was divided into eastern and western halves, and Albania became part of the Eastern, or Byzantine, Empire.

During the 400s AD a number of barbarian tribes invaded the region, and during the 600s and 700s Slavic peoples began to settle in the lowland areas. During the 800s and 900s the region was included in a Bulgarian state, but Byzantine rule was reestablished in 1018.

In 1054, a schism in the Christian church led to a new era of conflict. Normans and Crusaders, representatives of the Western, or Roman Catholic, church, invaded the country and fought against adherents of the Eastern, or Orthodox, church.

The decline of Byzantium in the 1100s was accompanied by the establishment of Albanian principalities, and in 1230 by the reimposition of Bulgarian rule. During the later 1200s, the Anjou rulers of Sicily established themselves in parts of Albania, and in the mid-1300s the region was included in a Serbian empire.

COUNTRIES OF THE WORLD

Ottoman Rule. The Ottoman Turks began the conquest of Albania in the 1300s, and by 1389 most of the country was under Ottoman control. Albania remained under Turkish control until 1912. There were many risings against Ottoman rule during the 1400s, and in 1443 a major rising was led by Gjergj Kastrioti (George Castriota), popularly known by his Turkish name, Skander, and title, beg ("Skanderbeg").

In 1444 a general assembly of Albanian notables created an Albanian league with Skanderbeg as president. The Albanian state collapsed after the death of Skanderbeg in 1468.

During the period of Ottoman rule, local officials, often Albanians, gained control of large areas, and they made these lands hereditary possessions. The population came to be divided into three main groups—Muslims, educated in Turkish; Orthodox Christians, educated in Greek; and Roman Catholics, educated in Italian.

In the 1800s the Ottoman Empire was near collapse, and Albania became a focal point for the ambitions of several states. Serbia and Montenegro, both part of present-day Yugoslavia, and Greece, staked out claims to Albanian lands.

In 1912 the first Balkan War was fought against Turkey by Bulgaria, Greece, Serbia, and Montenegro. The Greeks, Serbs, and Montenegrins planned to divide Albania among themselves. But the Albanians proclaimed their independence in the city of Vlorë in November 1912 and petitioned the great powers of Europe for recognition.

The powers agreed to the establishment of an autonomous Albanian state under the suzerainty of the Ottoman sultan, and set out the boundaries of the new state. The boundaries included only about one half the area and one half the people traditionally considered Albanian by the Albanians.

Independence. In 1913 the powers recognized Albania as an independent nation, but under a 10-year period of control by the powers. The new nation was to be a monarchy, and the powers chose a German prince, William of Wied, to head the new state. World War I broke out in 1914, and William left the country.

After the war, Italy, Serbia, Greece, and Montenegro all put forth claims to Albanian territories. But in 1920 Albania won recognition of its full independence and membership in the League of Nations.

The new Albanian government was weak. The country was poor, most of the people were illiterate, and neighboring nations interfered in the country's troubled politics. During the 1920s a regional chieftain, Ahmed bey Zogolli, or Achmed Zogu, emerged as the most powerful force in the government. He was briefly driven from the country in 1924 by a liberal rising, but regained power and in 1925 became president of Albania. In 1928 he transformed the government into a monarchy with himself as King Zog I.

During the 1930s, Italian influence became dominant in the economically hard pressed country, and in 1939 Italy moved to take full control of Albania. Italian troops were landed on Apr. 7, 1939, and on April 12 the union of Albania with Italy was proclaimed.

During World War II, Albania formed a part of the Italian empire. Traditionally Albanian areas in Yugoslavia (Kosovo) and in Greece (Cameria) were added to the puppet Albanian state. But Italian efforts to win Albanan support met with little popular success.

Communist Rule. In 1942 a national resistance movement, the National Liberation Front, was organized under Communist control. Although the Communist Party had been founded only in 1941, its leader, Enver Hoxha, was able to maintain leadership of the front and eliminate opposition from nationalist organizations. By the end of 1944, when German troops had been driven from the Balkans, the Hoxha group was in firm control of the country.

The Communist regime established in Albania had close ties with Yugoslavia, which had also come under Communist control. The Yugoslav Communist-led resistance movement had given significant aid to the Albanians during the war, but in 1948, when Yugoslavia and the Soviet Union split, the Albanians supported the Soviet Union.

Ties with the Soviet Union remained close until after the death in 1953 of the Soviet dictator, Joseph Stalin. The new leaders of the Soviet Union gradually moved to heal the breach with Yugoslavia, which again had become an enemy for the Albanians.

The development of a split in the Communist world between the Soviet Union and China in the early 1960s further troubled Soviet-Albanian relations. Despite its heavy dependence on Soviet economic aid, Albania supported China in the dispute.

—Robert F. Byrnes; George Kish

ALGERIA

Official name: Democratic and Popular Republic of Algeria
Area: 919,352 square miles
Population: (1966 est.) 12,150,000
Capital: Algiers (Pop., 1966, urban area, 943,142)
Language: Arabic, French
Religion: Islam
Currency unit: Dinar
National holiday: November 1

Algeria, a republic in northern Africa, is bounded on the north by the Mediterranean Sea, on the east by Tunisia and Libya, on the south by Niger and Mali, and on the west by Mauritania, Spanish Sahara, and Morocco. Algeria became independent in 1962 after more than a century of French rule.

THE LAND. Most of Algeria is part of the vast desert waste of the Sahara. A narrow northern zone, where the bulk of the people live, is dominated by two parallel east-west mountain chains—the Tell Atlas and the Saharan Atlas. Both are part of the massive Atlas Mountains, which stretch across northern Africa. The

MARKET IN ALGIERS, capital of Algeria.

Tell Atlas is a series of coastal mountains and valleys parallel to the Mediterranean Sea. The Saharan Atlas lies about 200 miles inland. Between the two ranges is a plateau area.

Most of the desert surface of southern Algeria is composed of rock and gravel, but there are some large sand areas. In the southeast are the Ahaggar Mountains, a volcanic rock mass that reaches above 9,600 feet. The Sahara region is sparsely populated.

In Algeria's coastal region, the winters are mild and rainy and the summers are hot and dry. The plateau region receives little rain. The Sahara is hot and dry and receives less than four inches of rain a year.

THE PEOPLE. Most of Algeria's rapidly growing population is Muslim of Arab-Berber stock. More than 1 mil-

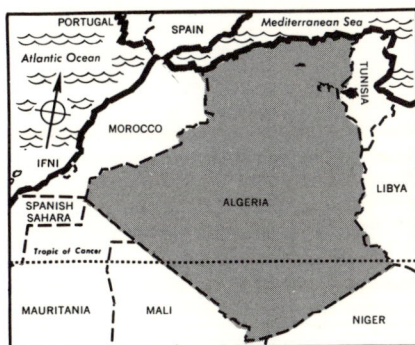

lion people of European origin left Algeria after independence was won in 1962. The Europeans had operated the most profitable and efficient farms and had filled most of the administrative, technical, and management positions. Their loss deprived the new nation of badly needed skilled personnel.

ECONOMY. Algeria has traditionally been an agricultural country, although there is relatively little good farm land. The bulk of its produce, which consists of wheat and barley and a variety of vegetables and fruits, comes from the region between the Tell Atlas and the Mediterranean.

In 1964 Algeria's imports cost $703 million and its exports earned $727 million. The most valuable Algerian export for many years was wine. The major exports today are petroleum and natural gas from rich fields discovered in the Sahara in the 1950s.

GOVERNMENT. Algeria's constitution provides for a national assembly and a president. A military coup overthrew the president in 1965, however, and governmental powers were assumed by a Revolutionary Council composed of army officers.

Algeria is a member of the United Nations and the Arab League.

HISTORY. The territory of present-day Algeria was invaded many times and dominated by many peoples before the country won its independence in 1962. Until the modern era, Algeria was often included in larger units that included parts of present-day Morocco and Tunisia.

The earliest known settlers were Berber-speaking peoples. The Phoenicians, who arrived in about 1200 BC, established control over part of North Africa. Their rule ended in 146 BC with the fall of Carthage to Rome.

Roman domination ended with invasions by Vandals in the 400s AD. In the 500s the region came under Byzantine rule. In the 600s the Arabs began to sweep through North Africa, and Algeria became part of the Arab-dominated Muslim world that stretched from Spain to Arabia.

Ottoman Era. In the early 1500s the Spanish, crusading against the Muslims who had withdrawn from Spain to North Africa, captured several Algerian cities. The inhabitants of Algeria appealed for help to a Muslim commander, Khayr-ad-Din, who drove the Spanish from Algiers in 1519. He offered allegiance to the Ottoman Empire in return for men and supplies. With Turkish aid, the Spanish were driven out of Algeria.

Algeria remained formally part of the Ottoman Empire until 1830. As an Ottoman province, its boundaries came to be roughly those of the modern Algerian state. Because of its great distance from Constantinople, Algeria became a Turkish regency in name only, and a Turkish *dey*, or governor, ruled the country almost as an independent state. The Turks held control of the coastal region, but the interior remained largely under traditional tribal rule.

French Rule. The French occupation of Algeria began in 1830. The Turkish dey quickly capitulated, but native Algeria, led by Abd al-Qadir (Abd-al-Kader), resisted. Not until 1847, when Abd al-Qadir was captured, did France secure control over most of Algeria.

Large numbers of French and other Europeans settled in Algeria soon after the defeat of Abd al-Qadir, and by 1900 Europeans made up 14 percent of Algeria's total population. The new settlers built up the Algerian economy, developing commercial agriculture for the French market. But the development basically served the needs of only the French Algerians, who gradually gained control of most of the best land.

By the early 1900s, the lack of economic opportunities and political inequalities created growing unrest within the Muslim majority. France attempted piecemeal reforms, but none succeeded in meeting the needs of the people.

Algerian desire for self-determination grew following World War II. In 1954 an armed rebellion against the French was begun by the National Liberation Front (FLN). The FLN slowly won the allegiance of most of the non-European Algerian population during a bitter struggle against the French in the years that followed.

Finally, in 1960, after a military effort that brought 500,000 French troops to Algeria and resulted in a series of French domestic political crises, French President de Gaulle agreed to negotiate with the FLN.

The two countries reached agreement only after months of bargaining. During that period part of the French army based in Algeria attempted a military coup against De Gaulle and a last-ditch terrorist campaign against a French withdrawal was waged by the European Secret Army Organization (OAS). On July 3, 1962, after 132 years of French rule, Algeria became independent.

Independence. The fruits of victory were almost lost in a near civil war that erupted immediately after independence was granted. Ahmed Ben Bella, a leader of the FLN who had been imprisoned in France since 1956, made a successful bid for power with the support of the FLN army.

By the end of 1962 Ben Bella had been elected premier by a newly formed national assembly, and he appeared to be securely in power. In June 1965, however, Ben Bella was deposed in a bloodless coup led by the army, and Houari Boumedienne, a military leader of the independence struggle, emerged at the head of a provisional military regime.

The emigration of most of Algeria's European population, which began when the country achieved independence, left Algeria stripped of its trained personnel and deepened the economic crisis that followed the years of civil war. Increasing production of Saharan oil and gas, however, somewhat brightened Algeria's economic future.

—L. Carl Brown; Hibberd V. B. Kline, Jr.

ANDORRA

Official name: Andorra
Area: 175 square miles
Population: (1966 est.) 11,000
Capital: Andorra la Vella
Language: Catalan
Religion: Roman Catholicism
Currency units: French franc, Spanish peseta

Andorra, one of Europe's smallest states, is a principality lying high in the eastern Pyrenees between Spain and France.

THE LAND AND PEOPLE. Andorra has a rugged landscape dominated by mountains rising from 6,500 to over 9,000 feet and cut by steep gorges. The climate is dry and rather mild.

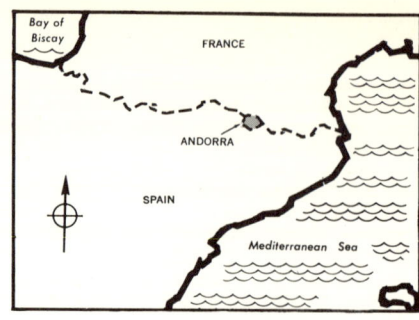

Andorrans are descendants of a people known to the ancient Romans. They speak Catalan, the language of Catalonia, a region in northeastern Spain. The population also includes Spanish and French minorities. Andorra la Vella, the capital, is the only large town.

ECONOMY. Although tiny, Andorra is quite prosperous. Its major natural resources are waterpower, from several lakes and the Valera River; small deposits of iron and lead; and timber. Only a small part of the land can be farmed. Rye, wheat, vegetables, and a valuable tobacco crop are grown, but Andorra depends on Spain and France for most of its food.

Tourism and trade contribute heavily to the economy. Andorra exports tobacco, cigarettes, and timber. Andorra's principal trading partners are Spain and France.

GOVERNMENT. Sovereignty over Andorra is exercised jointly by the Roman Catholic bishop of Urgel, in Spain, and by the head of the French state. Each is represented locally by a delegate called a *viguier*. Actual government is administered by a general council elected every four years by heads of households. The council chooses a nonmember as *syndic*, or chief executive.

HISTORY. Andorra's history as a state traditionally extends back to Charlemagne, who is said to have driven the Muslims from the region. The country gained semi-independent status in 1278, when the bishop of Urgel and the French counts of Foix assumed joint sovereignty over the "Valleys of Andorra," with the right to collect tribute.

The arrangement endured, but the counts were replaced by the princes and kings of Navarre, the kings of France, and then the presidents of France. Nominal tribute is still paid to the co-sovereigns.

Because of its small size and geographic isolation, Andorra escaped involvement in modern European wars, including the Spanish Civil War of 1936–1939. In the 1950s and 1960s, however, the increasing importance of the tourist trade led the principality to fuller involvement in European affairs.

In the early 1960s Andorra began to meet formally with other small European states, including Liechtenstein, Monaco, and San Marino, to discuss matters of mutual concern.

In 1967 French Pres. Charles de Gaulle paid a state visit to Andorra, the first visit by a French head of state since the 1200s.

—Charles Nowell

ARGENTINA

Official name: Argentine Republic
Area: 1,072,067 square miles
Population: (1967 est.) 23,031,000
Capital: Buenos Aires (Pop., 1960, urban area, 7,000,000)
Language: Spanish
Religion: Roman Catholicism
Currency unit: Peso
National holiday: Independence day, May 25

Argentina, a republic in the southern part of South America, is the second largest Latin American country in area and the third largest in population. It is bounded on the north by Brazil, Paraguay, and Bolivia; on the east by Brazil, Uruguay, and the Atlantic Ocean; on the west by Chile; and on the south by Chile and the Atlantic Ocean.

THE LAND. Argentina has four major land regions: the pampas, the North, the Andes, and Patagonia.

The pampas, great level plains, are divided into the Humid Pampa, in the east of Argentina's central region, and the Dry Pampa, in the west. The rich, black soil of the Humid Pampa makes it one of the most fertile agricultural areas in the world.

The pampas form the economic, political, and social heartland of the nation. The half circle around Buenos Aires, with a radius of 250 miles, includes only 24 percent of the country's total area but contains some 75 percent of the total population.

The North contains the semiarid, forested plains of the Chaco, the rolling hills and the floodplains of Mesopotamia, which lie between the Paraná and Uruguay rivers, and the Paraná Plateau.

The Andes region includes the "Monte," or foothill zone, with elevations below 2,500 feet, and the Andes cordillera (range) itself. In the northwest the cordillera reaches a height of 22,834 feet at Mt. Aconcagua, the highest point in the western hemisphere. The Argentine Andes are steep and have permanent snow caps. In the northwest the Andes are very dry, but in the extreme southwest they are covered by glaciers.

Patagonia is a dry, windswept plateau south of the Río Colorado. Rainfall ranges between 20 inches a year near the Andes and less than 8 inches along the Atlantic Coast. Patagonia's dryness is an obstacle to both farming and grazing, and it is sparsely populated.

THE PEOPLE. About nine out of every ten of Argentina's people are of European descent, and approximately one out of five Argentinians was born in Europe. In the 1800s a large number of Europeans, primarily Italians and Spaniards, emigrated to Argentina and their influence has made the country in many ways more European than Latin American. The dwindling indigenous population consists of small groups of Guaraní Indians in the north and Patagonian Indians in the south.

One third of the people of Argentina live in the metropolitan area of Buenos Aires, the capital. Population density decreases as one moves away from Buenos Aires, and other cities are small in comparison.

The larger provincial cities include Mar del Plata, about 250 miles from the capital, a beach resort; Rosario, the country's wheat exporting center, about 200 miles from Buenos Aires on the Río Paraná; Cordoba, an educational and commercial center in the heart of the country that has recently become important in manufacturing; and Tucumán, the major metropolis of northwestern Argentina and capital of the sugar-growing area.

ECONOMY. Agriculture is the chief source of income in Argentina. Most farming activity occurs in the Humid Pampa, where corn, wheat, oats, barley, and potatoes are grown. Argentina is a world leader in wheat, corn, and cotton production. Livestock raising, formerly the dominant economic activity, is now on a level with farming. Beef cattle are raised in the pampas, and sheep in Patagonia.

Mining had been limited mainly to copper, lead, and zinc, in the northwestern Andes, and coal in the Río Turbio area. Petroleum is now Argentina's major mineral resource.

Industry. After World War II Argentina made an effort to increase industrialization to broaden the base of its economy. Industrial development has been slow, however, and by the 1960s less than two fifths of the labor force was employed in industry, most of which is centered in Buenos Aires. The growth of heavy industry has been limited by inadequate mineral resources, especially coal.

Argentine industry is largely confined to the processing of food and agricultural products. Meat packing, flour milling, sugar refining, and wine making play an important role. Argentina also produces large quantities of cement, vegetable oil, soap, rubber goods, glass, pharmaceuticals, and chemicals.

Trade. In 1966 Argentina's imports were valued at $1,124 million and exports earned $1,593 million. By and

PAN AMERICAN AIRWAYS
PLAZA DEL MAYO, in Buenos Aires, capital of Argentina, faced by the presidential palace.

large Argentina trades its agricultural products for manufactured goods. Major imports include vehicles, machinery, petroleum, wood, chemicals, and manufactured iron and steel goods. Major exports are grain, meat and meat products, wool, and vegetable and linseed oil.

Argentina imports mainly from the United States, Brazil, West Germany, Italy, France, and Japan. Exports go primarily to Italy, the Netherlands, Britain, Brazil, West Germany, the United States, and Communist China.

GOVERNMENT. Argentina has been a republic since 1853, when its first constitution was drawn up. But democratic processes have frequently been disrupted by the military. Traditionally, the government has been headed by a popularly elected president, the head of state and chief executive. The legislative branch of government has included a senate chosen by provincial legislatures and a directly elected house of deputies.

Argentina is a member of the United Nations and the Organization of American States (OAS).

HISTORY. In the 1400s the Inca empire extended into the northern corner of what is now Argentina. Its drive south, however, was halted by Argentina's more primitive Indians, who were largely nomadic.

The first European to explore Argentina was the Spaniard Juan Díaz de Solís, who discovered the Río de la Plata in 1516. Exploration of the coast continued, and in 1536 an expedition headed by Pedro de Mendoza built a village on the site of present-day Buenos Aires. A majority of the early settlers, however, were Spanish colonists who crossed the Andes from Chile and Peru in the late 1500s.

The hostility of the Indians and the relative lack of precious metals at first made Argentina a neglected and sparsely settled part of the Spanish empire. It was not until the late 1700s that the colony acquired major economic importance as an exporter of cattle products, principally hides. In 1776 its capital, Buenos Aires, became the seat of the Spanish colonial viceroyalty of La Plata, which also included modern-day Bolivia, Paraguay, and Uruguay.

Independence. Argentinians acquired a new sense of their own power and importance in 1806 during the Napoleonic wars, when they expelled a British force that had seized Buenos Aires. Four years later, on May 25, 1810, they established an autonomous junta to rule during the captivity in France of Spain's King Ferdinand VII. Although independence was not formally declared until 1816, in practice the Argentinians had been self-governing since 1810.

Internal stability proved harder to achieve than independence. Not only were Argentine patriots unable to retain control over the outlying sections of the viceroyalty of La Plata, but within Argentina itself strong rivalry had developed between Buenos Aires and the inland provinces.

The capital favored a centralized government and was receptive to liberal reforms; the interior desired a federal system that would provide almost complete local autonomy and was politically conservative. For many years no really effective national administration could be established.

In the early 1820s, the liberal and centralist faction, the Unitarios, consolidated its control of the city and surrounding province of Buenos Aires under the leadership of Bernardino Rivadavia. The Unitarios encouraged immigration and investment, reformed the tax system, and restricted the influence of the Roman Catholic Church.

But they were unsuccessful when they tried to establish a centralized government over the entire country. The move provoked bitter Federalist resistance, which coincided with a war fought against Brazil over control of Uruguay (1825–1828).

Rosas Era. In 1829 the Unitarios lost even Buenos Aires, which came under the control of the wealthy rancher and Federalist leader, Juan Manuel de Rosas. Rosas ruled the Buenos Aires province as dictator from 1829 to 1832 and from 1835 to 1852. He brutally suppressed political opponents, repealed many of the reforms of the Unitarios, and governed in the interest of his own class of great ranchers.

Although his primary position was always that of provincial governor, Rosas joined with Federalist leaders of the interior to form a loose Argentine confederation. The confederation had no president or constitution, but Rosas was its unquestioned leader; it authorized him to direct defense and foreign relations for all the provinces.

Rosas fought a brief war with Bolivia in 1837–1838 and continually intervened in Uruguay's affairs. He also engaged in disputes with France and Britain, which resulted in a blockade of the Argentine coast from 1845–1848.

The European powers failed to humble Rosas, but eventually some of his own collaborators in the interior provinces turned against him. One of these, Gen. Justo José de Urquiza, formed a coalition with the Unitarios and in 1852, with aid from Brazil, drove Rosas from power.

Federalism. Urquiza sought to reorganize the government of Argentina, and in 1853 a new constitution providing for a federal system was adopted. The province of Buenos Aires at first remained outside the union, but it agreed to join in 1859. In 1862 its governor, Bartolomé Mitre, became the first president of a fully united Argentina, serving from 1862 to 1868. During his administration, Argentina joined Brazil and Uruguay in the War of the Triple Alliance against Paraguay (1865–1870), when Paraguayan troops ignored Mitre's refusal to allow them to cross Argentine territory.

Domingo F. Sarmiento, president from 1868 to 1874, was an ardent admirer of the United States and especially of U.S. educational methods. Sarmiento established a public school system that became the best in Latin America. Moreover, the nation experienced a period of rapid economic expansion during the latter 1800s and early 1900s. Argentina built up an elaborate railway network, attracted a flood of European immigrants, and became a major world supplier of meat and wheat.

Argentina's wealth was largely derived from the land, but there developed a large urban middle and working class, which gained its livelihood from commerce and transportation, public services, processing, and light manufacturing. Such groups had little voice in the Argentine government, which was dominated by the great landowners and allied business interests.

This ruling class was in many respects able and progressive, but it frequently stayed in power by irregular election practices and the use of arbitrary federal intervention in provincial affairs. The result was a gradual increase in political unrest, which found its most important expression in the Radical party, organized in the 1890s. The Radicals had special appeal for the middle class.

Enactment of an electoral reform law in 1912 finally opened the way for the Radicals to elect a president, Hipólito Irigoyen, in 1916. Once in power, the Radicals did not introduce any fundamental changes in social and economic policy, and Irigoyen, the first Argentine president ever chosen in a truly democratic election, was best known outside Argentina for his course of strict neutrality in World War I.

Irigoyen resigned in 1922, but was reelected in 1928. He was overthrown by a military coup in 1930, however, amid the crisis of the world economic depression.

This first revolutionary change of government in almost 70 years was followed in 1932 by the resumption of an outwardly constitutional government under a wealthy oligarchy similar to the one that had ruled prior to 1916. Another revolt occurred in June 1943, however, and led to the establishment of a military regime under Gen. Pedro Ramírez and later under Gen. Edelmiro Farrell, in which Juan D. Perón ultimately emerged as the leading figure.

Perón Dictatorship. The new regime was politically repressive, but through Perón's inspiration it gained working class support by expanding social security and other benefits. During World War II it continued the neutrality policy that it had inherited from the preceding administration, but with pro-Axis overtones. In March 1945, however, when the conflict was almost over, Argentina declared war on Germany and Japan.

Perón was briefly stripped of power in October 1945, but he scored an impressive victory early in 1946 in a free election and officially became president. Although opposition was never wholly suppressed, Perón's government was a dictatorship.

As president, Perón expanded his labor policy into a doctrine called *justicialismo*, which claimed to be a middle course of true social justice between the extremes of communism and capitalism. Workers received a steady stream of wage increases and benefits.

Perón also gave special encouragement to industry. His extravagant spending and economic favoritism, however, severely damaged grazing and agriculture and produced grave inflation. In addition, he quarreled with the Roman Catholic Church and alienated the army. Dissatisfaction with his policies steadily increased, and he was finally overthrown by a military coup on Sept. 19, 1955.

Contemporary Argentina. A series of provisional military governments ruled from 1955 until 1958, when the Radicals returned to power with the election of Dr. Arturo Frondizi to the presidency. His government was troubled by military interference, unrest in the ranks of labor, where *peronista* influence remained strong, and inflation and other economic problems inherited from the Perón regime.

Frondizi allowed the peronistas to enter candidates of their own in off-year elections in March 1962. When they won pluralities in a large number of provinces, antiperonista members of the military installed Senate leader José María Guido in the presidency.

In 1963 presidential elections were won by Dr. Arturo Illía, a Radical. The peronistas continued to be a disruptive force, however, and in 1964 Perón himself unsuccessfully tried to return to Argentina.

Peronista strength registered an increase in the 1965 congressional elections, and on June 28, 1966, the Illía government was overthrown by the military, which established a new regime headed by Gen. Juan Onganía.

—David Bushnell; Kempton E. Webb

AUSTRALIA

Official name: Commonwealth of Australia
Area: 2,967,909 square miles
Population: (1967 est.) 11,751,000
Capital: Canberra (Pop., 1966, urban area, 95,913)
Language: English
Religion: Anglicanism, Roman Catholicism, Protestantism
Currency unit: Dollar
National holiday: Australia day, January 26

Australia, an island-continent in the southern hemisphere, is bounded on the north by the Timor Sea and the Arafura Sea, on the east by the Coral Sea, the Pacific Ocean, and the Tasman Sea, and on the south and west by the Indian Ocean. Bass Strait separates the island of Tasmania from the Australian mainland.

The Commonwealth of Australia is composed of six states and two mainland territories. The states are New South Wales, Queensland, South Australia, Tasmania, Victoria, and Western Australia. The two internal territories are the Northern Territory and the Australian Capital Territory.

THE LAND. Australia contains some of the oldest and most stable portions of the earth's surface. It may once have formed part of an ancient continent known as Gondwanaland, consisting of Africa, parts of the Indian subcontinent, and Brazil, as well as Australia.

Regions. Australia has three main land regions—the Western Plateau, the Central Lowlands, and the Eastern Highlands.

The Western Plateau occupies approximately the western half of the continent. It has an average elevation of about 1,200 feet above sea level. It

EUCUMBENE DAM. One of the highest dams in the world, Australia's Eucumbene stands more than 381 feet high and is nearly half a mile thick at its base. Lake Eucumbene, the reservoir formed by the dam, contains eight times as much water as does Sydney Harbor.

is flat and monotonous for the most part, but there are some isolated mountain ranges, such as the Macdonnell and Musgrave ranges, which rise to almost 5,000 feet above sea level.

The Central Lowlands, lying east of the Western Plateau, have an average elevation of about 500 feet, although Lake Eyre, in the southern part of the region, lies about 40 feet below sea level. Marine sediments, laid down about 50 million years ago, cover much of the region.

Sedimentary rocks in the northern part of the Central Lowlands form the Great Artesian Basin, an important source of underground water in an area that receives very little rain. The Murray-Darling-Murrumbidgee Basin, Australia's most extensive river system, occupies the southeastern portion of the lowlands. The Great Australian Bight cuts into the southern coast, and the Gulf of Carpentaria cuts inland on the north.

The Eastern Highlands, sometimes known as the Great Dividing Range, are a collection of many mountain ranges and plateaus that run parallel to Australia's east coast. Among the ranges are the Australian Alps, Hunter Mountains, Blue Mountains, Liverpool Range, and Darling Downs. Mount Kosciusko, which rises more than 7,300 feet in the Australian Alps, is Australia's highest peak.

The island of Tasmania, about 130 miles from the Australian mainland, contains an extension of the Eastern Highlands. The highlands on Tasmania form a central plateau containing many natural lakes.

The Great Barrier Reef, a collection of islands, cays, and reefs, stretches for some 1,250 miles along the northern half of the east coast. Some parts of the reef are formed from the same rocks as the adjacent mainland; others are made up of the skeletons of millions of tiny coral polyps which have solidified into reefs and islands.

Climate. Australia's winter season extends from June through August, and summer from December to February. Winters are mild almost everywhere; summers are warm to hot. Precipitation is of greater concern in Australia than temperature, since much of the continent is deficient in rainfall.

The interior parts of the Central Lowlands and Western Plateau are extremely arid, and Lake Eyre is usually completely dry. The northern coastal region receives heavy seasonal rainfall. Australia's southwestern corner receives winter rain. The only area to receive year-round rain is the southeastern corner. Rainfall over most of the interior averages less than 10 inches a year.

Plant Life. Because of Australia's dryness, forest areas are composed of trees that are drought resistant. Forests occur only in the southeast and southwest and in isolated patches along the east coast. Almost half the continent is covered with semi-desert scrub or sand dunes. Another large portion has mixed grass and tree cover.

Australia's dryness, coupled with the continent's long isolation from the rest of the world, have led to the development of many unique species of plants and animals. Typically Australian are the eucalyptus and acacia types of plants, which together account for more than 1,000 different species. These plants, which may vary from low shrubs to tall trees, form the dominant non-grass vegetation.

Animal Life. The continent is also famous for its distinctive animal life, especially the platypus, kangaroo, wallaby, and koala. Rabbits, although not native to Australia, are so numerous that they have been labeled pests.

The kookaburra, emu, Australian lyrebird, and black swan are among the more famous of some 650 species of birds found in Australia.

THE PEOPLE. When the first European settlers arrived in Australia in the 1700s, they found an estimated 300,000 aborigines living there. The aborigines are related to small groups of people living in other areas of southern Asia.

Many of the aborigines died as a result of diseases introduced by the Europeans, and in 1961 there were only about 40,000 full-blooded aborigines living in Australia. There were, however, a larger number of people of mixed aboriginal and European origin. Most of the full-blooded aborigines live in the Northern Territory and in Western Australia.

About 95 percent of the Australian population is of British origin. After World War II Australia sought to double its immigration rate. Immigration restrictions were eased and over 665,000 people came to Australia between July 1947 and June 1966.

The population of Australia is unevenly distributed. More than 80 percent of the people live in urban areas that are, for the most part, on or near the coast. The interior of the continent has almost no permanent population.

Over half the people live in the capital cities of Australia's six states, and the capital cities are of vast importance in each of the states. Sydney, the capital of New South Wales, is the largest of Australia's cities and an important economic center. Melbourne, the capital and largest city of Victoria, is also a major economic center. Canberra, the national capital, is located in the Australian Capital Territory, approximately 180 miles south of Sydney.

ECONOMY. Although long famous for its agricultural products, wool, wheat, and cattle, Australia is also an important manufacturing nation. The smelting of iron and the production of machines, tools, and vehicles today constitute the largest group of Australian manufacturing industries. By 1948 the value of Australia's manufacturing production had surpassed the value of its agricultural output, and by 1963 manufacturing contributed 28 percent of the country's gross domestic product.

Manufacturing is concentrated in the southeastern corner of the continent. Sydney is a major industrial center, with clothing, metal, machinery, and food processing plants. Melbourne also has many industries, and its neighboring cities of Geelong and Broadmeadows are major centers of the automobile industry.

Agriculture. Agriculture accounted for 14 percent of the gross domestic product in 1963, as compared with 29 percent in 1950. Although the range of products is very great, wheat, wool, and meat continue to dominate the agricultural part of the economy.

Wheat is produced mainly in a crescent-shaped area beginning in New South Wales, running southwestward through Victoria and South Australia, jumping the Great Australian Bight, and continuing through the southern portion of Western Australia to the Indian Ocean.

Cattle are raised in all of the Australian states, although Queensland accounts for more than one third the national total. Sheep are also found in all of the states, although New South Wales and Victoria account for well over half of the country's total. In many cases wheat and sheep or cattle are raised in the same area. Other agricultural products include sugar cane, grapes and wine, fruits and vegetables, and dairy products.

Mining. Mining is important to Australia's economy. In recent years the mining industry has been dominated by coal, lead, zinc, copper, gold, and iron ore. The principal coal producing state is New South Wales, especially the Hunter Valley. Lead and zinc come primarily from New South Wales and Queensland.

Copper is mined in several places, including Queensland, the Northern Territory, and Tasmania. Most of the gold comes from Western Australia. Whyalla, in South Australia, and Yampi Sound, in Western Australia, are the principal producers of iron ore.

Transportation. Australia is well served by modern road, rail, and air networks. The greatest density of roads is in the southeast.

Australian railroad tracks were built to three different widths, and this has created problems in shipping goods from one part of the continent to another. But a program of rebuilding many of the lines to a standard gauge was well underway by the mid-1960s.

Trade. In 1966 Australia's imports were valued at almost U.S.$3,200 million and exports earned slightly more than U.S.$3,000 million. Wool is the most valuable single export item, accounting for about 30 percent of the total income from merchandise exports. Other important exports are wheat, flour, and meat. Australia's major imports include chemicals and fertilizers, petroleum products, paper products, and fabrics, as well as machinery.

Australia's main trading partners include Britain, New Zealand, the United States, and Japan.

GOVERNMENT. Australia's federal system of government is patterned on the governments of Britain and the United States. The nominal head of the Australian government is the British Queen, who is represented by a governor-general. Actual executive power is wielded by a cabinet, headed by a prime minister, responsible to the national legislature.

Legislative power is vested in Parliament. Parliament has two houses—the 60-member Senate, with 10 senators elected from each of the 6 states to 6-year terms, and the House of Representatives, popularly elected to a 3-year term.

The British sovereign also appoints individual state governors. Each state has its own parliament to deal with local matters. The organization of the state parliaments varies from state to state, according to the various state constitutions.

Australia is a member of the Commonwealth of Nations, and close ties are maintained with Britain and other Commonwealth countries. Australia is also a member of ANZUS, a defense pact linking Australia, New Zealand, and the United States, and of the South East Asia Treaty Organization (SEATO). Australia was a charter member of the United Nations, and it plays an active role in UN affairs.

HISTORY. The original settlers of Australia were aborigines, who came to the continent about 12,000 years ago from Southeast Asia. These people lived at an extremely primitive level, with very little in the way of material culture, but with a highly developed ability to survive in a hostile natural environment.

In the 1600s Portuguese, Spanish, and Dutch navigators explored the southern hemisphere. In 1606 a Spanish commander, Luis Vaez de Torres, sailed through the strait which now bears his name off the northeastern tip of the mainland. In the same year Willem Jansz explored the region around the Gulf of Carpentaria.

Abel Tasman discovered the island of Tasmania in 1642. In 1770 Captain James Cook made extensive explorations of the continent's east coast, and landed at Botany Bay in southeastern Australia. He later sailed north, landed on an island off the northeastern tip of Australia, and claimed the eastern part of the continent for England.

Settlement. Britain made the first settlement in Australia in 1788, when 11 ships under the command of Capt. Arthur Phillip landed at Botany Bay. The 1,030 people carried by the ships included 726 convicts. A settlement was made at Port Jackson, which eventually became the great city of Sydney. Britain established a second colony in 1803-1804 in Tasmania.

The early history of the settlements was dominated by the convict system, and by the struggle of the free settlers to establish their rights as Englishmen. The colony's first economic objective was agricultural self-sufficiency, and when a convict's time expired, he was encouraged to set up a small farm.

Farming did not provide an exportable surplus, however, and free officers in the colony set up a profitable business in rum. The colony's governors unsuccessfully tried to put an end to the rum trade, and in 1808 the officers forcibly ousted Gov. William Bligh, who had tried to end the rum trade.

Lachlan Macquarie, governor from 1809 to 1821, energetically reorganized the community and ended the officers' power. He emphasized agricultural development and convict rehabilitation. He developed aesthetically appealing public buildings, useful roads, and a bank. The colony's population increased considerably, but London recalled Macquarie and rebuked him because of claims that he had overstepped his official authority.

By 1796 Merino sheep had been introduced into the colony, and wool soon became an important industry and changed Australia's economic base. The dynamic wool industry spread rapidly after the 1820s and

COUNTRIES OF THE WORLD

provided an export commodity that has since been basic to the Australian economy. With the industry's spread over the continent's usable land, businessmen and free workingmen came to settle.

Because sheep farming requires broad fields and a small work force, each colony tended to develop a single urban center, usually near a port. In 1829 settlers founded Perth, in Western Australia; in 1835, Melbourne, in the Port Phillip district of what was then New South Wales; and in 1836, Adelaide, in South Australia. Except for Western Australia, the new colonies were for free men only.

The early 1800s were also marked by further efforts of the former convicts to establish their civil rights and of the colonies to achieve self-government. Many of the free colonists and the authorities were unwilling to grant political rights to the large number of ex-convicts and feared the end of the convict system, which provided cheap labor.

Nevertheless, many Australians and Englishmen strongly attacked the convict system on the grounds that it morally damaged Australian society, it had ceased to be a punishment for English criminals, it did not rehabilitate the prisoners, and it unfairly competed with free labor. Britain ceased sending convicts to New South Wales in 1840, to Tasmania in 1853, and to Western Australia in 1868.

Self-rule. Progress toward self-rule developed as the number of free colonists grew. In 1850 the British Parliament passed the Australian Colonies Government Act, which allowed the Australian colonies to organize legislatures. The act formed the Port Phillip district of New South Wales into the separate colony of Victoria, and provided for the separation of Queensland from New South Wales in 1859. Western Australia waited until 1890 for responsible government, however.

In 1851 gold was discovered in eastern Australia, and the ensuing gold rush brought a rapid rise in the population, which grew from some 400,000 in 1850 to 1,146,000 in 1860. Australians faced both an economic struggle to develop an economy diverse enough to allow for the successful assimilation of an increasing population and a political struggle for stability.

Economic development involved the investment of both government and private capital. Industrialists invested earnings from the wool industry in wheat, sugarcane, irrigation, dairy farming, gold mining, and base metal mining.

Cities expanded and the government built railways in each colony. Victoria and New South Wales developed at faster rates than the other parts of Australia. Base metal mining stimulated the Tasmanian economy, but Western Australia stagnated until the development of gold mining there in the 1890s and the later development of wheat and wool.

In the 1890s, in the midst of a world-wide financial depression, a serious shipping, shearing, and mining strike erupted in Australia. The ef-

AUSTRALIAN NEWS AND INFORMATION BUREAU

SYDNEY HARBOR, showing the modern terminal wharves and the elevated Cahill Expressway. Berthed at the overseas passenger terminal, seen at the left, is the S.S. Canberra.

fects of the strike were intensified by a tremendous drought, which reduced the numbers of sheep and cattle. At that time trade unions grew in importance, and the first politically oriented labor parties emerged.

Recovery from the depression of the 1890s was reasonably quick, largely the result of rising export prices. The government extended the railway system, and wheat farming and sheep raising expanded. In the 1890s the government established free, compulsory state schools. The number of universities grew, and authentically Australian schools of painting and writing appeared.

Commonwealth. In 1897–1898, a convention met to draft a federal constitution. In 1900 Britain accepted a federal, political framework for Australia, and the Commonwealth of Australia came into being on Jan. 1, 1901.

A significant development between 1901 and the outbreak of World War I was the political impact of the Labor party, organized in 1891. Trade unions saw the need for political support for social welfare legislation, but the Labor party, representing the trade unions, entered federal politics reluctantly. It felt the best prospects for success lay in influencing the state governments.

In 1902 the Labor party allied itself with Alfred Deakin, who became prime minister, although Labor's views were more socialistic than Deakin's. Labor supported a White Australia position; that is, they wanted to keep out Orientals, whom they feared as cheap labor. Deakin also convinced Labor of the need for a high protective tariff.

By 1910 the Labor party held a majority of seats in the House of Representatives, but implementation of the full Labor program was frustrated by the electorate's refusal to approve necessary constitutional changes.

At the outbreak of World War I, Australia was weak in manufacturing. After foodstuffs and raw materials, its major export for war was manpower. Of a total population of about 4 million, Australia mobilized some 400,000 men and sent 332,000 volunteers overseas. The men served in the Middle East and in France. The federal government increased its authority over the states during the era of war preparation.

In 1915 William Morris Hughes, leader of the Labor party, became prime minister. Hughes advocated conscription for overseas service, but a popular referendum twice defeated his attempts. A rift developed within the party following the defeat, and Hughes and his colleagues broke from the Labor party. Hughes organized a National War Government, and his followers formed the Nationalist party, politically opposed to the Labor party.

Interwar Era. Hughes represented Australia at the peace conference at the end of World War I. He sought punitive measures against Germany and heavy reparations for Australia. Hughes also fought successfully a League of Nations proposal to establish racial equality and thereby compromise the White Australia policy.

After the war the Commonwealth came under the rule of a coalition of the Nationalists and a new group, the Country party. The Country party was formed in 1918 by farmers who felt that rural areas were not adequately represented.

War production over, the government emphasized land industries, but although men and money were forthcoming, the markets failed. There was a postwar recession, exports declined, and tremendous imports left companies without means to finance purchases. The rural industries, except for wool, had to be supported by high, government-fixed domestic prices.

The world-wide depression of the 1930s hit Australia hard because of the sharp drop in prices for its exports—foodstuffs and raw materials. Labor regained federal power in 1929 but lost in 1931, unable to master the depression situation. Former Nationalist and Labor party members formed the United Australia party to meet the results of the depression with sound finance.

In the 1920s there had been a concentration on material development and a lack of experimentation. In the 1930s, however, activity in painting, literature, and education all showed a renewed vitality.

World War II. At the opening of World War II, Australia's industrial war potential was considerable. The prime minister, Robert Gordon Menzies, prepared Australia for war. He assisted Britain with supplies and food, increased war production, and raised an army. The country became a heavier exporter of foodstuffs and raw materials than it had been during World War I. Its manpower was also greater.

Australians early realized the great importance of war developments in the Pacific. From 1939 to the bombing of Pearl Harbor by the Japanese in 1941, Australians anxiously watched developments in the Pacific. At the same time they sought to organize their industrial war potential and deployed their armed forces in North Africa.

Because of Britain's inability to provide for Australia's security in the Pacific, ties with the United States were fostered. In 1940 a representative was sent to Washington, and a U.S. representative went to Canberra. When Singapore fell to the Japanese in 1942, a course was set for Australian-U.S. collaboration.

The Australians elected the Labor party to office in 1941. Labor confirmed the steady growth of federal power, worked to diversify the economy, and stressed industrialization and social welfare.

Contemporary Australia. In 1949 the Labor party lost to Robert Gordon Menzies. Menzies led a coalition of the Country party and the Liberal party, which had supplanted the United Australia party in 1944. The Menzies government kept the emphasis on manufacturing growth but also looked to develop land industries to provide basic exports. The government strengthened ties with the United States through U.S. capital investment in Australia.

Federal responsibility was extended to include internal transportation, water resource development, and higher education. The government maintained control over state finances and relaxed immigration restrictions. The national product rose sharply, and Australians acquired a new affluence.

Menzies retired in 1966, and the Liberal party leader, Harold Holt, became prime minister. Holt continued the policy of cooperation with the United States and strongly supported the U.S. position in the Vietnam conflict.

Prime Minister Holt lost his life in a swimming accident in December 1967, and in January 1968 John Gorton was chosen to succeed him as leader of the Liberal party and as prime minister. Gorton pledged to continue Holt's program.

—David A. Smith

AUSTRIA

Official name: Federal Republic of Austria
Area: 32,371 square miles
Population: (1966 est.) 7,290,000
Capital: Vienna (Pop., 1965 est., 1,640,100)
Language: German
Religion: Roman Catholicism
Currency unit: Shilling
National holiday: October 26

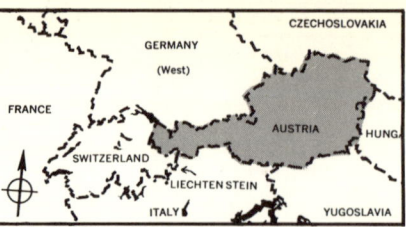

Austria, a landlocked nation in central Europe, is bounded on the north by Germany and Czechoslovakia, on the east by Hungary, on the south by Yugoslavia and Italy, and on the west by Switzerland and Liechtenstein. Although Austria today is a small republic, it was once the center of the mighty Holy Roman and Austro-Hungarian empires, and Vienna was a cultural and intellectual capital of the world.

THE LAND. Austria is a mountainous land. The Austrian Alps run west to east from the Swiss border and occupy nearly all of central and southern Austria. Aside from a few prosperous valleys, the Alps are rugged and barren, with many ice-covered peaks rising above 10,000 feet.

North of the Alps lies the crescent-shaped Alpine Foreland, a hilly area that grades into a forested plateau region between the Danube River and the Czech border. In the northeastern corner of the plateau is the fertile and heavily populated Vienna basin. The navigable Danube crosses northern Austria on its way to the Black Sea, and its many tributaries thread the country.

The Austrian climate varies greatly from region to region. For the country as a whole, the average temperature in January is 22°F, and in July 64°F. The Alps, however, are much colder in winter and cooler in summer than the rest of Austria. Rainfall averages between 30 and 40 inches a year.

THE PEOPLE. The people of Austria are almost entirely German-speaking, but there are some who speak other languages, including Croatian, Czech, and Slovene. Over 90 percent of the people are Roman Catholic, and about 6 percent are Protestant. There is a small Jewish minority.

The most densely populated areas are on the northern and southern edges of the Alps, especially along the Danube River in the north. Vienna, in the northeast, is Austria's largest city, with over 20 percent of the country's total population. The mountainous central part of the country is sparsely settled.

THE ECONOMY. Austria is a prosperous nation. Industry is the most important part of the Austrian economy, contributing more than 40 percent of the national product in the mid-1960s.

PAN AMERICAN AIRWAYS
AUSTRIA'S ALPINE SCENERY attracts thousands of tourists to the country each year.

SCHOENBRUNN CASTLE, originally built for Emperor Leopold I (1658–1705) by the baroque architect Johann Bernhard Fischer von Erlach, was reconstructed in its present form by Empress Maria Theresa (1740–1780) after plans by the architect Nicolas Pacassi.

An important factor in industrial growth has been the availability of water power. Austria's hydroelectric power potential has been greatly developed, and large quantities of electricity are exported to neighboring nations. Austria's moderate mineral resources include iron, oil, magnesite, lead, and copper.

Since World War II, industry has shifted from the production of luxury articles to the manufacture of iron and steel, metal goods, aluminum, chemicals, and forest products.

Agriculture and forestry are important in the economy. Dairying is the leading farm activity, and wheat, corn, barley, oats, sugar beets, and potatoes are the principal crops.

Trade, mainly with West Germany and other western European nations, is vital to Austrian prosperity. In 1966 the country imported $2,328 million worth of goods and exported goods valued at $1,684 million. Imports consist mainly of machinery, foodstuffs, vehicles, electrical equipment, and textile raw materials. Exports include iron and steel, machinery, wood and wood products, and textiles. Tourism is an important source of income.

GOVERNMENT. Austria is a federal republic made up of nine provinces. A president, elected to a six-year term, is head of state. He appoints the chancellor, or prime minister, who heads the cabinet. The chancellor and cabinet are responsible to the lower house of the legislature. Members of the lower house are popularly elected; those of the upper house are chosen by provincial legislatures.

By the 1955 treaty restoring its sovereignty, Austria may possess only defensive weapons and must maintain neutrality in world affairs. It is a member of the United Nations and the Council of Europe.

HISTORY. The Danube Basin was an important roadway for peoples migrating from the east many centuries ago. The Romans established military posts in the area, but by the 400s AD migrating Germanic tribes had forced the Romans out of the region. By about 800 the area had become part of the empire of Charlemagne, who made it the eastern kingdom, the "Ostmark" or "Osterreich," of his realm.

In 1282 Austria, then part of the Holy Roman Empire, became a possession of the Hapsburg family. The Hapsburgs, Holy Roman emperors for 400 years, ruled Austria for over 600 years. Through the strength of their dynasty the country achieved a position of leadership in Europe during the 1500s, 1600s, and 1700s. During that time Austria was the center of a Hapsburg empire that controlled territory throughout Europe.

The Empire. In 1804, two years before the Holy Roman Empire was dissolved, the Hapsburg Francis II declared himself emperor of Austria and Austria itself became an empire. In the following 50 years, the Austrian Empire, led by its foreign minister, Prince von Metternich, played a major role in the complex series of military and political alliances that characterized European affairs during the Napoleonic and post-Napoleonic eras.

The Austrian Empire included Galicia, Bohemia, Hungary, northern Italy, and part of the Balkan peninsula, and the many different and often restless nationalities that lived in those regions. Austria's government was highly centralized and conservative.

In the 1840s and 1850s liberal and nationalist revolutions broke out in the Austrian Empire. These rebellions weakened the government's power and led to reforms that only partly satisfied the empire's subject peoples —particularly the Croatians, Czechs, and Hungarians. Austria's loss of absolute control over its people weakened its international position.

In 1867 the many separate German states were united under Prussia, Austria's rival in German politics. The German union excluded Austria. The unification of Germany forced Austria, in order to retain some internal stability and international power, to make the restive Hungarian region of the empire an equal partner with the German part. The two states were joined in the Dual Monarchy of Austria-Hungary in 1867.

Creation of the Dual Monarchy, controlled by the Germans of Austria and the Magyar people of Hungary, left the Slavic subject peoples in Bohemia and the Balkans dissatisfied. The discontent of the Slavs was an important cause of World War I, which began when a Slav from Serbia assassinated Archduke Francis Ferdinand, the heir to the Austro-Hungarian throne. Austria-Hungary declared war on Serbia, and was joined by Germany.

The German allies were defeated, and at the end of the war in 1918 the Hapsburg empire lay in ruins. In 1918 the emperor abdicated and was replaced by a provisional government. The provisional assembly declared its desire to unite with Germany, but the Allied powers prohibited Austrian-German unification by the Treaty of St. Germain (1919).

The Allies divided much of Austria's old territory among Italy, Hungary, a restored Poland, and the new states of Czechoslovakia and Yugoslavia. The treaty also proclaimed Austria a republic.

The First Republic. In 1920 a permanent government was formed, and its members drafted a constitution. Austria, now a small, overwhelmingly German-speaking nation, was made a federal state with a president as chief of state and a cabinet led by a chancellor. A two-house legislature was elected democratically.

Two political parties dominated the republic—the Christian Socialists and the Social Democrats. The Christian Socialist party drew its principal support from the wealthy landowners and manufacturers, the clergy, and the farmers. It favored some form of authoritarian government. The Social Democrats represented mainly the urban workers and followed a socialist program. A small, nationalistic faction favoring union with Germany grew rapidly in size and power during the 1920s.

The first republic faced serious difficulties from its earliest years. In 1920 the government had to use force to prevent parts of the country from seceding and joining Germany. Pressure for unification with Germany, or *Anschluss*, was to plague the republic continually. The Austrian economy was weak. It avoided total collapse only by receiving financial grants from the League of Nations between 1922 and 1925.

Party politics created the most severe problems, however. In 1926 a serious conflict opened between the Christian Socialist national government and the Social Democrats. The Social Democrats governed the province that included the capital city, Vienna, where one quarter of the country's population then lived.

In Vienna the Social Democrats had financed experimental social welfare programs for the workers by heavily taxing the rich. The conservative

Christian Socialists objected strongly to these programs. The conflict, centered in Vienna, led to frequent riots. Each party had its own private army, and the riots were usually bloody.

A new Christian Socialist national government elected in 1929 set the restoration of order as its primary goal. It outlawed the bearing of arms and banned the political parties. In 1930 it signed a treaty of friendship and protection with Benito Mussolini's fascist government of Italy.

To strengthen Austria's economy the government in 1931 tried to enter a customs union with Germany. Both countries gave up the attempt when the World War I Allies protested. Without the agreement, the Austrian state bank collapsed. The League of Nations granted funds again in 1932 on the condition that Austria would form no economic union of any kind for 20 years.

The financial crisis had seriously weakened the national government, which proved unable to handle the continuing political conflicts. The National Socialist (Nazi) party's growing power in Germany inspired the Austrian nationalists. They held demonstrations in Austria and in 1932 nearly succeeded in taking over the government of one province. The nationalists' strongest opposition came from the Social Democrats, and the conflict between the two parties grew violent.

Dictatorship. A Christian Socialist cabinet formed in 1932 by Chancellor Engelbert Dollfuss determined to restore order. In 1933 Dollfuss dissolved parliament and restricted the rights of free speech, press, and assembly. He tried to ban the Austrian Nazis in 1933, but when Germany strongly objected, he turned his attack on the Social Democrats.

After 1934 an undeclared civil war raged between the nationalists and the socialists, and Dollfuss lost the support of the working class when he destroyed a new Social Democratic housing project in Vienna. In a last effort to restore order, Dollfuss rewrote the constitution and made himself a dictator. The chancellor's aim was to make Austria strong enough to prevent a German conquest.

Austria's international situation became desperate, as Germany's growing power threatened Austria's very existence. In 1934 Dollfuss entered an alliance with Hungary and Italy, despite the provisions of the treaty of St. Germain. He hoped to gain Italy's support against Germany, where Adolf Hitler's Nazi party had come to power in 1933. On July 25, 1935, however, Austrian Nazis assassinated Dollfuss in an attempt to take over the government. Germany was unable to aid the Austrian Nazis because of a military threat from Italy, and Austria won one more chance for independence.

Dollfuss' associate, Kurst Schuschnigg, who succeeded him as chancellor in 1934, continued the dictatorship. He relied even more heavily on Italy for military and economic aid. Schuschnigg, too, hoped that with order at home and Italy's aid abroad, Austria could escape conquest by Germany. Domestic disorder continued, however, and Italy's effectiveness as a protector decreased rapidly as Mussolini and Hitler drew closer.

In 1938 Hitler forced Schuschnigg to recognize the Austrian Nazi party and to admit a Nazi, Arthur Seyss-Inquart, to the cabinet. Increased Nazi activity followed and brought more violence to Austria. The Christian Socialist government could not control the Nazi outbreaks alone, and Schuschnigg attempted to unite with his party's old rivals, the Social Democrats. The Social Democrats, however, refused to join him.

Anschluss. In a last effort to save Austria, Schuschnigg tried to show the world that Austrians did not want to join Germany. He planned an election in which the citizens would vote for either independence or union. By the chancellor's arrangement, a "yes" vote for independence would have been easy to cast; a "no" vote almost impossible.

Hitler responded to this plan with an ultimatum. Austria must either accept Nazi rule peacefully, or face military conquest. Hitler then began massing troops on the Austrian border. Schuschnigg resigned, and Seyss-Inquart, the Nazi minister of the interior, replaced him as chancellor. In March 1938, Seyss-Inquart announced Austria's union with Germany and invited the German army into the country. The *Anschluss* had been accomplished.

The Allies, who had the treaty right to oppose the German occupation of Austria, did not protest. They hoped to avoid a second war by letting Hitler take Austria. In 1939, when World War II did begin, Austria, as part of Germany, shared Germany's fate. The early years of victory ended in 1945 with the defeat of the Axis, the German allies.

Contemporary Austria. After the war, the Allies treated Austria as a liberated country rather than as a conquered enemy. But Austria was divided into four zones, each occupied by one of the major Allied powers—the Soviet Union, Britain, France, and the United States.

The democratic constitution of 1920 was restored, and the Socialist and the People's parties, the more moderate successors of the prewar Social Democratic and Christian Socialist parties, formed a coalition government. The coalition avoided the destructive political conflicts of the first republic, and, with Allied aid, Austria rebuilt and expanded its economy.

Austria was not fully independent, however, until a final peace treaty with the Allies was signed. Peace negotiations were hampered by the Soviet Union, which wanted large war damage payments from Austria and which was unwilling to withdraw its occupation troops. Finally, in 1955, Austria once more became independent with the signing of the Austrian State Treaty.

Austria grew steadily stronger economically and politically. In 1966 Chancellor Josef Klaus' People's Party won an election by enough votes to allow a one-party government to replace a coalition cabinet for the first time since the war.

—George M. Kren

BAHRAIN

Official name: Bahrain
Area: 231 square miles
Population: (1966 est.) 193,000
Capital: Al Manama (Pop., 1959, urban area, 61,700)
Language: Arabic
Religion: Islam
Currency unit: Dinar

Bahrain is a tiny, oil-rich island nation in the Gulf of Bahrain, an inlet of the Persian Gulf between the Qatar peninsula and the Saudi Arabian coast. The country's major islands are Bahrain, the largest, Sitra, Al Muharraq, Umm an Nasan, Jidda, and Hawar.

THE LAND AND PEOPLE. All of the islands are deserts with an extremely hot and humid climate. Almost no rain falls on them, and their only water comes from a few underground springs. Cities developed around these springs, and in the mid-1960s about two-thirds of Bahrain's people lived in two major cities, Al Manama, on Bahrain Island, and Muharraq.

Native Bahrainis are Muslim Arabs, and they constitute about 80 percent of the population. There are also Arabs from other countries, Iranians, Indians, and European oil workers.

ECONOMY. Oil is the small country's principal natural resource and chief export. In 1966 more than 3.1 million metric tons of oil were pumped from beneath Bahrain's deserts and coastal waters. A refinery on Bahrain Island processes oil from Bahrain and from Saudi Arabia. Royalty fees paid by oil companies have financed educational and medical programs, communications and power development projects, and agricultural modernization programs.

Dates, grain, vegetables, and citrus fruits are raised in the islands' oases. Trade passing through Al Manama, one of the best ports in the Persian Gulf, is an important source of income. Pearling, once the mainstay of the economy, is still of some significance.

GOVERNMENT. Bahrain is ruled by a sheikh, who is a hereditary monarch with absolute power. He heads a government council formed of members of his family and appointed cabinet members.

A British political agent advises the government, and Britain is responsible for the country's foreign affairs and defense.

COUNTRIES OF THE WORLD

HISTORY. Bahrain's islands may have been inhabited as early as 3000 BC, and they were known to the ancient Greeks. Their strategic location for trade and rich beds of pearl oysters attracted several conquerors. In 1507 Portugal occupied the islands and held them until 1602, when the Persians conquered them.

In 1782 Arab tribes seized power and founded the Khalifa dynasty. In 1820 Bahrain entered into treaty relations with Britain, and in 1861 the two countries concluded a treaty of protection for Bahrain.

The discovery of oil in 1932 brought Bahrain sudden international importance and radically changed the islanders' traditional way of life. Iran laid claim to the islands and protested the British presence there.

In the mid-1950s and mid-1960s Bahraini pan-Arab nationalists incited anti-British riots and called for union with other Arab states. But the Khalifa dynasty maintained its control, and Bahrain remained under British protection. But British plans to withdraw from the Persian Gulf by 1970 led Bahrain to draw closer to Saudi Arabia. In 1968 they agreed to build a causeway linking Bahrain Island to the Arabian mainland.

—Charles Issawi; Alexander Melamid

BARBADOS

Official name: Barbados
Area: 166 square miles
Population: (1966 est.) 245,000
Capital: Bridgetown (Pop., 1960, 11,452)
Language: English
Religion: Anglicanism, Protestantism
Currency unit: East Caribbean dollar
National holiday: November 30

Barbados, a small island nation at the extreme eastern end of the West Indies, lies about 300 miles north of Guyana, on the South American mainland. Barbados achieved its independence in 1966 after some 300 years of British control.

THE LAND. Barbados is a triangular-shaped island about 20 miles long and 14 miles across at its widest point. Most of the island is a low-lying plateau, but there is a small highland area in the northeast. There are good beaches along the western and southwestern coasts.

Barbados has an adequate supply of fresh water, but there is little natural vegetation. The climate is comfortable. Temperatures range between 70°F and 87°F, and the trade winds blow across the island all year.

THE PEOPLE. Most of the island's people are of African origin. Persons of mixed African and European background make up about 17 percent of the total, and those of European origin represent about 3 percent.

The island is densely populated, and population growth creates serious economic and social problems.

ECONOMY. Sugar is the basis of the economic life of Barbados. Sugarcane is grown on about 80 percent of the cultivatable land, and sugar and sugar products—rum and molasses—account for approximately 80 percent of export earnings. Yams, peas, beans, and corn are grown for local food needs.

PAN AMERICAN AIRWAYS
THE HARBOR AT BRIDGETOWN, capital of Barbados, is a sight familiar to many tourists.

The government has worked to diversify the economy. Light industry has been growing, and other activities, such as fishing, have been promoted. Tourism is an important source of income.

GOVERNMENT. The head of state is the British monarch, represented on the island by a governor-general, the nominal chief executive. Actual executive powers are exercised by a prime minister and cabinet. The prime minister is normally the leader of the majority party in the legislature.

The legislature, or parliament, has two houses, the Senate and the House of Representatives. The 21 members of the Senate are appointed by the governor-general. Twelve are named on the advice of the prime minister, 2 on the advice of the leader of the opposition party, and 7 to represent religious, economic, and other interest groups. The 24 members of the House of Representatives are popularly elected.

Barbados is a member of the United Nations, the Commonwealth of Nations, and the Organization of American States (OAS).

HISTORY. Arawak Indians lived on Barbados until about 100 years before the arrival of the first British voyagers in 1625. An English merchant group had won control of the island by 1629, but during the English civil wars of the 1600s the English government took direct control. In doing so, the British granted the islanders the Charter of Barbados, which provided for government by a governor, council, and elected assembly, and taxes levied only with the consent of the inhabitants.

British Rule. Barbados was a prosperous island. Coffee, tobacco, cotton, and other crops were grown for export, and cassava and corn were raised for local needs. In the late 1600s sugar became the major crop, and large numbers of African slaves were brought to Barbados to work on sugar plantations.

The abolition of slavery in 1834 had little effect on the island's economic, social, or political life. Prosperity continued until late in the 1800s, when home-grown sugar beets began to meet Europe's sugar needs, and the world price of sugar dropped.

The economy revived in the early 1900s as a result of British financial aid, improvements in sugar production, and the beginnings of the export of labor. Many Barbadians went to Central America to work on the construction of the Panama Canal. They were able to send money home, and many saved enough to buy small farms on their return.

The emigration of Barbadians to Panama ended in 1913, but World War I led to a great demand for sugar. Prosperity continued until the onset of the world economic depression of the 1930s.

Federation. Political progress was rapid after World War II, and universal suffrage was introduced in 1951. Political parties were formed during the postwar years, and elections held in 1951 were won by the Barbados Labor Party (BLP), led by Grantley Adams.

In 1958 Barbados became a member of the short-lived Federation of the West Indies, which united ten of Britain's West Indian and Caribbean territories, and Adams became the federation's prime minister. Adams' BLP lost elections held in Barbados in 1961. The victor was the Democratic Labor Party, led by Errol Barrow, which had been formed in 1955 by dissident BLP members.

Independence. The Federation of the West Indies began to break up in 1962, when Jamaica and Trinidad withdrew to become independent nations. In 1965 Barbados decided to seek its own road to independence, and on Nov. 30, 1966, Britain granted the island its freedom.

Prime Minister Barrow quickly brought the new country into the United Nations and the Commonwealth of Nations. In 1967 Barbados became a member of the Organization of American States (OAS).

—Robert J. Feldman

BELGIUM

Official name: Kingdom of Belgium
Area: 11,781 square miles
Population: (1966 est.) 9,528,000
Capital: Brussels (Pop., 1965 est., urban area, 1,065,900)
Language: Flemish, French
Religion: Roman Catholicism
Currency unit: Franc
National holiday: Independence day, July 21

Belgium, a small nation in western Europe, is bounded on the north by the Netherlands, on the east by West Germany and Luxembourg, on the south by France, and on the west by the North Sea.

In 1922 Belgium and Luxembourg formed an economic union that abolished the customs frontier between them. The union was dissolved in 1940, but was reestablished in 1945. In 1948 a customs union went into effect linking Belgium and Luxembourg with the Netherlands, which is known as the Benelux Customs Union. Full economic union of the three countries has existed since 1960.

THE LAND. Most of Belgium consists of low-lying plains. In the southeast, however, the country is quite hilly, and this highland pasture zone—the Ardennes—is rather sparsely settled. The main rivers in Belgium are the Schelde, the Sambre, and the Meuse.

Belgium has little variation in climate. Its mild winters and cool summers are characterized by light rainfall, high humidity, and partial cloudiness. In the southwest, however, the higher elevations cause somewhat cooler summers and distinctly colder winters, and the precipitation is much heavier.

THE PEOPLE. Belgium can be nearly evenly divided linguistically, and, to a certain extent, culturally, by an east-west line. In the north are Flemings, who make up about 55 percent of the population. They speak Flemish, a language closely related to Dutch. In the south, French-speaking Walloons are dominant. Brussels is bilingual. Flemish and French are the official languages, and both are used for highway signs, public announcements, and official documents. Belgium is overwhelmingly Roman Catholic.

The population is relatively stable, having increased on the average by only 0.6 percent a year between 1958 and 1966. Population is densest in the central district and sparsest in the southeastern quarter of the country. Belgium is highly urbanized. Its major cities include Brussels, Antwerp, Liège, Charleroi, Ghent, and Louvain.

ECONOMY. Belgium is primarily an industrial nation, and, although it is small, it ranks high among European nations in the manufacture of such products as refined copper, pig iron, steel, and textiles. Belgium's only important mineral is coal, and this vital industrial requirement has been the basis of much of the country's industry.

Industry. The western cities, of which Ghent is the largest, specialize in textiles and food processing. Antwerp's industries, with access to the endless variety of raw materials unloaded at its great port, range from diamond cutting to smelting and shipbuilding.

Brussels concentrates on a wide variety of light industries. The coal-rich Sambre-Meuse area contains the country's heavy industry. Metallurgy and metal fabrication are important, and cement, glass, chemicals, rubber goods, and paper are all produced there in large quantities.

Agriculture. Although agriculture plays a secondary role in Belgium's economic life, employing only a small share of the labor force, the country's farms meet about 80 percent of domestic food requirements and provide an important share of raw materials for industry.

Trade. International trade is of great importance to the country, and Belgium has a sizable merchant fleet. Antwerp, on the River Schelde, is one of Europe's busiest ports. Belgium and Luxembourg trade as a unit, and in 1966 their exports earned $6,811 million, and their imports were valued at $7,054 million.

Major exports include iron and steel products, machinery, chemicals and pharmaceuticals, and textiles. Major imports include textiles, chemicals, machinery, and petroleum. Exports go chiefly to the Netherlands, West Germany, France, the United States, Britain, Italy, and Switzerland. The principal suppliers of imports are West Germany, France, the Netherlands, the United States, and Britain.

GOVERNMENT. Belgium is a constitutional monarchy. The king is head of state. Executive power is exercised by the king and his ministers. No act of the king is effective, however, unless countersigned by a minister. Ministers are appointed by the king from among the members of the majority party in parliament, and they are responsible to parliament. Since World War I the government has been headed by a prime minister, who coordinates national policy.

Legislative power is exercised by the parliament, which consists of two houses, the Senate and the Chamber of Representatives, and by the king, who sanctions and promulgates the laws. Members of the Chamber of Representatives are popularly elected on the basis of proportional representation. The Senate includes 46 members chosen by local government councils, 109 directly elected members, and 23 chosen by their fellow senators.

Belgium, in addition to inclusion in Benelux, belongs to the European Communities, the United Nations, and the North Atlantic Treaty Organization (NATO).

HISTORY. The Belgae, or Belgians, were one of the Gallic tribes conquered by Julius Caesar in the first century BC, and the area that is now Belgium became part of the Roman Empire. Roman occupation was followed by invasions of Franks between the 200s and 400s AD. After 476 Belgium was ruled by the Merovingians, and later it became part of Charlemagne's empire (800–843).

During the Middle Ages Belgium existed as a group of duchies, which in 1384 came under the control of the dukes of Burgundy. Belgium passed to the Hapsburgs through marriage in 1477 and subsequently became part of the Holy Roman Empire. On the resignation of the Holy Roman Emperor Charles V in 1556, Belgium, along with the Netherlands, passed to Philip II of Spain.

The northern provinces of the Netherlands, or Holland, formed the Union of Utrecht and declared their independence in 1581. But the provinces that constitute modern Belgium continued to be ruled by Spain and then by Austria (1713) until conquered by France in 1792.

Belgium became part of Napoleon's empire in 1801. The Congress of Vienna (1814–1815), which redrew the map of Europe after Napoleon's defeat, united Belgium with Holland in the Kingdom of the Netherlands.

The union failed to take into consideration the difference in character between the two regions, however. Holland was Protestant, Germanic, agricultural, and commercial, whereas Belgium was Roman Catholic, French-oriented, and industrial. Holland favored a policy of free trade, and Belgium sought high tariffs to protect its industry.

Independence. In 1830 the Belgians revolted. King William I sent Dutch troops into Brussels to suppress the revolution, but they were unsuccessful. A provisional government was established, and Prince Leopold of Saxe-Coburg-Gotha was elected king. Within a year, after several conferences, the Great Powers recognized

BELGIAN GOVERNMENT INFORMATION CENTER

BRUGES, capital of Belgium's West Flanders province, derives its name from the Flemish word, *brug*, which means bridge.

the independence of Belgium and in 1839 guaranteed its neutrality.

Under Leopold I, who ruled from 1831 to 1865, Belgium's economy expanded rapidly, and under Leopold II (1865–1909) Belgium acquired a vast empire in Africa. By the end of the 1800s Belgium had transformed itself from an oligarchy governed by a small middle class to a democracy based on universal suffrage with very advanced social welfare programs.

Belgian neutrality was violated by Germany during both World War I and World War II. German troops first entered Belgium on Aug. 4, 1914, after Germany repudiated the treaty guaranteeing Belgian neutrality. The resulting destruction and death toll were enormous, and the country was plundered to the extent that the people were reduced to starvation.

Belgian war damage amounted to more than $7 billion, and the tremendous cost of reconstruction after the war caused a rapid rise in the national debt, inflation, and other financial problems that were to plague the country for almost 20 years. Economic problems increased demands for social legislation, and popular dissatisfaction was expressed politically. As a result, the interwar period was characterized by a series of short-lived governments.

During World War II the Germans attacked Belgium on May 10, 1940, and on May 28, King Leopold III surrendered to avoid further bloodshed. It was felt, however, that his early surrender had weakened Allied strategy. The patriotic feelings of many Belgians were outraged, and Leopold was deposed. The second German occupation was far worse than the first. Material damage was more extensive and many more lives were lost.

After World War II the Belgians voted on Mar. 12, 1950, to recall King Leopold to the throne. Socialist opposition proved so bitter, however, that Leopold abdicated on June 16, 1951, in favor of his son, who became King Baudouin.

Contemporary Belgium. Early during the postwar period, Belgium recognized the need for economic cooperation among the nations of Europe. It was a founding member of the European Monetary Agreement (1950), the European Coal and Steel Community (1951), and the European Economic Community (1958). In 1957 Belgium, along with five other nations, signed the treaty establishing the Common Market.

One of the main concerns of the government during the 1950s was the increasing political unrest in the mineral-rich Belgian Congo. Independence was granted to the Congo on June 30, 1960, and the loss of this important market and source of raw materials dealt a severe blow to the Belgian economy. The government initiated an austerity program to offset the loss, but the program was met by a series of strikes and antigovernment demonstrations.

The austerity program also contributed to a revival of the long-standing hostility between French and Flemish-speaking Belgians. Each claimed the government exhibited economic favoritism toward the other.

Demonstrations aimed at bringing about an official linguistic, if not political, division, between Wallonia and Flanders occurred in 1961 and 1962. In November 1962 the legislature passed a bill making Flemish the official language in the north and French the language in the south. But Flemish-Walloon animosity continued, and in 1968 led to the resignation of the prime minister and cabinet.

In 1967 Belgium met with the Netherlands and Luxembourg to discuss extending the integration of their countries beyond the field of economics, hoping thus to encourage closer cooperation among the other members of the European Community.
—George M. Kren

BHUTAN

Official name: Kingdom of Bhutan
Area: 18,000 square miles
Population: (1966 est.) 750,000
Capital: Thimbu
Language: Dzongkha
Religion: Buddhism
Currency unit: Indian rupee

Bhutan is a small kingdom on the northeastern border of the Indian subcontinent. It is bounded on the north by China, on the east and south by India, and on the west by Sikkim. India manages Bhutan's foreign affairs and is responsible for its defense.

THE LAND. Bhutan is no more than 190 miles long and 90 miles wide, but it has three distinct geographical zones. Within 20 miles of its northern border is a wild and snowy region, where peaks of the eastern Himalayas tower to almost 25,000 feet. A central zone, about 40 miles wide, ranges in elevation from 3,500 feet to 10,000 feet and is forested with evergreens. The southern region, which grades into the valley of the Brahmaputra River, is low and mostly covered with dense semitropical forest.

Several Himalayan rivers flow south through Bhutan. The most important are the Amo Chu, the Ma Chu, and the Manas.

Bhutan's climate varies with elevation. In the north, where alpine tundra conditions prevail, the cold is extreme, and glaciers fill the higher valleys. The central zone is temperate, and rainfall averages 40 to 60 inches a year. The southern region has a semitropical climate—heat and humidity are extreme, and up to 300 inches of rain may fall in a year.

THE PEOPLE. Bhutan's population is concentrated in the river valleys of the temperate central region. Approximately 70 percent of the people are Bhotia, a Tibetan-speaking people. A Nepali minority makes up about 20 percent of the population, and there is a small group of Mongols. Bhutanese are Mahayana Buddhists.

ECONOMY. Agriculture is the basis of Bhutan's economy. Bhutan's forests are valuable, and there are deposits of gypsum and limestone, but these remained unexploited in the mid-1960s. Farms are concentrated in the rich river valleys, and although small, they produce a surplus of food. The major crops are rice, corn, barley, and millet. Fruits and vegetables are also raised.

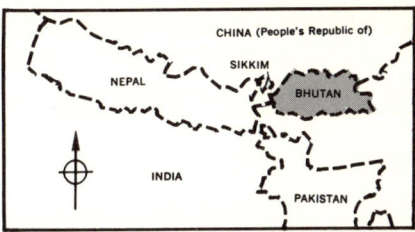

Yaks, goats, and ponies are herded. Traditional handicrafts include weaving, woodworking, and metalworking.

In the 1950s and 1960s development projects were undertaken jointly with India to begin exploiting the country's natural resources, especially its vast hydroelectric potential.

Bhutan exports grains, wax, lac (the base for lacquer), and musk (a perfume base). Almost all of its trade is with India. By treaty, India makes an annual contribution to Bhutan of 500,000 rupees—about $66,000 at the 1968 rate of exchange.

GOVERNMENT. Bhutan is a monarchy ruled by a hereditary maharaja, or king. He is limited by no constitution, but there is an advisory council of elected village headmen and appointed officials.

HISTORY. Little is known of Bhutan's early history. In the 1500s Tibetans conquered the Mongol tribes that inhabited the land and settled there. Tibetans governed Bhutan and placed it under the spiritual authority of the Dalai Lama of Tibet. In the 1700s China conquered Tibet and assumed control over Bhutan jointly with the Dalai Lama, but the country actually was governed by local tribal chieftains.

In 1774, after several raids by Bhutanese hill tribesmen on British India, the British East India Company forced Bhutan to grant it trading privileges through the important Himalayan passes that Bhutan controlled. But the raids continued, and in 1865 British troops subdued the hill tribesmen and annexed Bhutan's eastern region, which included the major passes.

In 1885, after years of feuding among the tribal chieftains, one leader, Ugyen Wangchuk, gained dominance over all the tribes. He cooperated with the British and by 1907 had established himself as the maharaja of Bhutan. During the early 1900s China tried unsuccessfully to reassert control over the country, but in 1910 an Anglo-Bhutanese treaty recognized Bhutan's sovereignty. Its foreign affairs were to be managed by Britain, which also agreed to pay compensation for the territory annexed in 1865. Bhutan remained largely isolated from the rest of the world for half a century.

The Chinese Communist conquest of Tibet in 1950 greatly increased Bhutan's strategic importance to China and India. India, which in 1949 had agreed to assume Britain's responsibilities in Bhutan, lent technical and financial assistance for the development of Bhutan's economy. During the 1950s and 1960s Bhutan's society and government began to be modernized, and the country began to participate more fully in the affairs of the modern world.
—Charles H. Heimsath; George Inaba

BOLIVIA

Official name: Republic of Bolivia
Area: 424,162 square miles
Population: (1967) 3,801,000
Capital: Sucre (Pop., 1965 est., 58,400)
Language: Spanish
Religion: Roman Catholicism
Currency unit: Peso
National holiday: Independence day, August 6

Bolivia, a landlocked country in west-central South America, is bounded on the north and east by Brazil, on the west by Peru and Chile, and on the south by Argentina and Paraguay. Lake Titicaca, on the Peru-Bolivia border, is the largest lake in South America.

THE LAND. The basic natural division of the country is between Lowland Bolivia and Mountain Bolivia. The lowlands, or Oriente, in the east, occupy about 70 percent of the country. Mountain Bolivia includes four regions—the Altiplano, the Western Cordillera, the Northeastern Cordillera and Yunga Zone, and the Eastern Bolivia Highland.

Lowland Bolivia. The lowlands are sparsely inhabited, although pioneer activity begun in the 1950s attracted a number of people from the overpopulated upland areas. The humid, tropical condition of the north, situated within the southern part of the Amazon Basin, contrasts with the southeastern Chaco, which has frosts as well as temperatures of over 100°F. Rainfall can vary as much as 25 inches a year from an average of 38 inches.

Mountain Bolivia. The core of Mountain Bolivia is the vast central plateau of the Bolivian Andes, the Altiplano (literally, "high flat area"). The Altiplano, averaging 12,000 to 13,000 feet above sea level, is composed of a series of high and gently rolling basins surmounted here and there by snow-capped mountains. The region is cool and dry in the south but more humid in the north.

The Western Cordillera, separating Bolivia from Chile, is a long series of dry slopes among which are several extinct volcanoes. The Northeastern Cordillera, or Cordillera Reál, forms the edge of the Altiplano. Its streams have carved steep valleys in the course of their rapid descent to the broad Beni River system, which empties into the enormous Amazon River. Also known as the Yungas (semi-tropical mountain valleys), the area has a large population and supplies food to the highland communities.

The remaining area of Mountain Bolivia is the Eastern Bolivia Highland, or the Puna, a sloping region connecting the Northeastern Cordillera with the plains. The important regional centers of Cochamba, Sucre, and Tarija provide markets for the corn, wine, and fruit grown in the area.

THE PEOPLE. Over half of the people of Bolivia are Indians. A small percentage of the population is of European descent. The remainder of the people are mestizo, of mixed Indian and European origin.

The Indians in the Lake Titicaca area speak Quechua, the Inca language, but the majority of the Andean

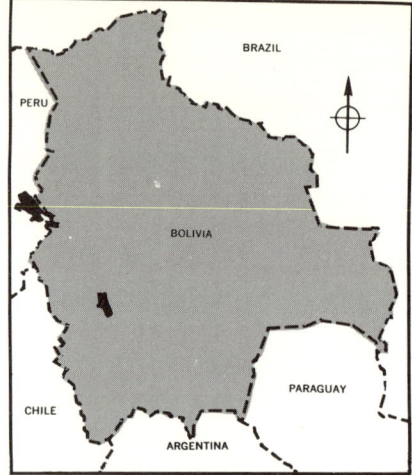

Indians speak Aymara. Most of the mestizo and white population is found in the eastern valley towns of the Yungas and in the south.

La Paz, lying more than 12,000 feet above sea level, is the social, political, and economic center of the country and occupies the position formerly held by Sucre, which is still the administrative capital of Bolivia. The population of La Paz in 1965 was estimated at more than 360,000.

Bolivia's second largest city is Cochabamba, the focus of the road and rail routes that link Mountain Bolivia with the lowlands. It is also the center of a populous farming area.

Other important cities include Santa Cruz, the capital of the mineral-rich department of Santa Cruz; Oruro, which refines half the tin produced in the country; Potosí, in the center of the tin mining region; and Tarija, one of the oldest cities in Bolivia.

ECONOMY. Bolivia's economy is based on mining. The country depends on the export of its mineral resources, particularly tin, to earn the foreign exchange necessary to import essential goods. Bolivia is the second largest tin-producing country in the world, and in 1966 production was 25,920 metric tons. There are also large deposits of lead, copper, silver, and oil.

Approximately three out of every four workers are engaged in agriculture, but farm production meets only about 75 percent of Bolivia's food needs. The Altiplano, where most of the people live, is ill-suited for agriculture. Nevertheless, some barley, wheat, corn, beans, and potatoes are grown there. Coffee is a major crop and is produced in the Yungas, where sugarcane is also grown.

Industry is limited and mainly produces simple consumer goods for domestic needs. La Paz is the country's manufacturing center. The lack of an adequate transportation system has been a major obstacle to economic growth. The cost of building roads and railroads over the steep, mountainous terrain is extremely high.

Bolivia usually imports more than it exports, and the resulting deficit has been met by foreign economic aid, principally from the United States. In 1965 Bolivian exports were valued at $110 million, and imports cost $126 million.

Minerals are Bolivia's major export, and foodstuffs and manufactured goods make up the bulk of imports. Bolivia exports primarily to the United States and Britain. Most imports come from the United States, although Japan is increasingly important as a supplier of imports.

GOVERNMENT. The chief executive and head of state is the president, who is popularly elected to a four-year term of office. The Congress consists of the Senate and the Chamber of Deputies. Senators are elected to six-year terms and deputies to four-year terms.

Bolivia is a member of the United Nations and the Organization of American States (OAS).

HISTORY. The Andean portion of what is now Bolivia was long a center of advanced Indian civilization. It formed part of the Inca empire from the 1300s to the 1500s. The Inca empire was overthrown by the Spanish in 1533, and in 1538 an expedition led by Gonzalo and Hernando Pizarro conquered Bolivia.

In 1559 Bolivia became part of the Spanish colonial viceroyalty of Peru and was known as Upper Peru. It later became important to Spain as a supplier of precious metals, especially silver. Spanish rule was harsh, and from 1661 to 1780 there were many Indian uprisings.

Independence. In 1809, after Napoleon had conquered Spain, the people of the city of La Paz deposed the Spanish authorities and established a junta under the leadership of Pedro Domingo Murillo. Murillo was soon overthrown by the Spanish, and attempts by Argentine patriots to liberate Bolivia from the south met with failure. Nevertheless, scattered guerrilla activity against Spain continued.

In December 1824, Simón Bolívar's forces, under the command of Antonio José de Sucre, won a decisive victory at Ayacucho, Peru, that set the stage for the final defeat of the Spanish in Bolivia the following year. Bolivians were then faced with the alternatives of joining Argentina, of joining Peru, or becoming a separate nation. An assembly in 1825 chose independence for the country and adopted the name Bolivia.

The Early Republic. Antonio José de Sucre was elected Bolivia's first president in 1826. His administration was enlightened but brief. Unrest among his own troops combined with an invasion by Peru forced him from power in 1828. Sucre was succeeded by Andrés Santa Cruz, who remained in office until 1839. For roughly the next 50 years government consisted largely of a rapid succession of dictatorships.

One recurring feature of the mid-1800s was the interference in each other's affairs by Bolivian and Peruvian military dictators. From 1835 to 1839 Santa Cruz united both countries in a confederation, but a war with Chile brought about its collapse. Bolivia again fought Chile in the War of the Pacific (1879–1884), which resulted from Chilean designs on the nitrate deposits controlled by Bolivia and Peru in the Atacama desert along the Pacific coast. Bolivia was defeated and lost its portion of the Atacama desert, which included Bolivia's only outlet to the sea.

Modernization. Bolivia began to modernize rapidly in the early 1900s under presidents Ismael Montes (1904–1909; 1913–1917) and Eleodoro Villazón (1909–1913). Railroads were constructed, industries developed, and tin mining greatly expanded. During World War I Bolivia remained neutral until 1917, when it broke off diplomatic relations with Germany.

In the late 1920s an old boundary dispute with Paraguay over the Chaco region was renewed. War broke out in 1932, and in 1935 Bolivia was defeated. The final settlement, negotiated in 1938, gave three-fourths of the disputed territory to Paraguay. The land lost was not valuable, but the humiliation of defeat caused widespread bitterness against the nation's traditional ruling class, and participation in the struggle awakened many Bolivians to the modern world.

Dissatisfaction with the traditional social, economic, and political domination by Bolivians of European descent coupled with economic difficulties brought on by the world economic depression of the 1930s resulted in a rapid turnover of governments.

New political parties arose with programs aimed at modernizing the country and improving the condition of the masses of the people. One of these, the National Revolutionary Movement (MNR), came to power in 1943 with a program calling for sweeping economic and social reforms.

Contemporary Bolivia. The MNR was overthrown in 1946 before it could accomplish a great deal, but it staged a successful uprising in 1952 after its leader, Victor Paz Estenssoro, had been cheated of his victory in a presidential election. The MNR managed to consolidate its position and carried out a series of reforms that included nationalization of the tin mines and distribution of large private estates among the Indian peasantry.

The MNR incurred huge deficits in operating the tin industry, and the drastic land reforms resulted in a sharp drop in production. Severe food shortages in the cities followed. Only massive U.S. aid kept the government functioning and saved many Bolivians from starvation. Nevertheless, progress was made in expanding education and in developing the fertile but sparsely populated eastern lowlands.

Paz Estenssoro himself remained in power from 1952 until 1956, when he resigned in favor of a party colleague, but he returned as president in 1960. After a period of strikes and rioting, especially in the tin mining region, he was overthrown in 1964 by the military, and a junta took power.

The new regime was committed to carrying out much the same objectives as the Paz Estenssoro administration. In 1965, the junta promised free elections, and in the following year Gen. René Barrientos Ortuño, who had been one of the junta leaders, was elected president.

—David Bushnell; Kempton E. Webb.

BOTSWANA

Official name: Republic of Botswana
Area: 219,915 square miles
Population: (1967 est.) 593,000
Capital: Gaberones (Pop., 1965 est., 4,200)
Language: English, Tswana
Religion: Traditional religions, Christianity
Currency unit: South African rand
National holiday: Independence day, September 30

Botswana, a republic in southern Africa, is bordered on the northeast by Rhodesia, on the east and south by South Africa, and on the west and north by South West Africa. A large, sparsely populated country, Botswana was the British protectorate of Bechuanaland before receiving its independence in 1966.

THE LAND. The Kalahari Desert occupies most of central and western Botswana. This dry region, covered with sand, grass, and thorn bush, has no rivers. The land in eastern Botswana is well-watered and fertile. The Okavango River flows into northern Botswana and forms an area of swamps and marshes. The Molopo and Limpopo rivers run along the southern border.

Northern Botswana has a tropical climate. Further south, the climate is generally hot and dry. The north receives an average of 27 inches of rain a year, but the south receives less than 9 inches.

THE PEOPLE. Most of Botswana's people are Bantu-speaking Africans. There are eight principal tribes in Botswana, each with its own traditional tribal area. The Bamangwato is the largest tribal group. Eighty percent of the people live in villages in the eastern part of the country.

ECONOMY. Cattle are the basis of Botswana's traditional economic life. Most of the people are herdsmen, and livestock contributed some 85 percent of the value of exports in the mid-1960s. Some minerals, including gold and manganese, are also exported. The basic food crops of Botswana include corn, sorghum, and peanuts.

Botswana's economy is closely linked with South Africa's. South Africa levies and collects Botswana's customs duties, and in return Botswana receives a fixed share of South Africa's customs revenue. Botswana also uses South African currency, the rand.

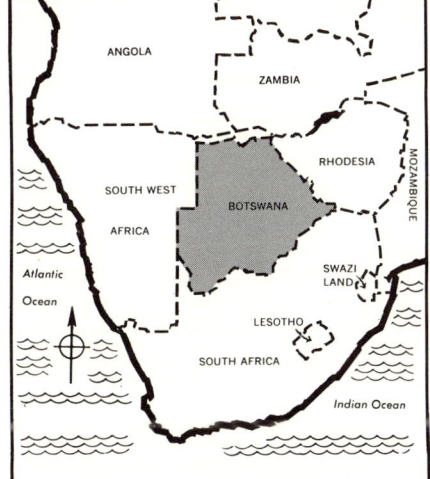

GOVERNMENT. The head of state and chief executive of Botswana is the president, who is elected along with the legislature, the National Assembly. Assembly candidates must indicate their choice for president, and the presidential candidate with the greatest number of supporters elected to the assembly becomes president. A House of Chiefs, composed of members of the eight dominant tribes, serves as an advisory body to the National Assembly.

HISTORY. Botswana's dry, thornbush grassland attracted few immigrants until the early 1800s, when Tswana-speaking people entered the area. The Tswana were driven from the Transvaal, in present-day South Africa, by invading Zulus. In the years following, there were tribal wars and conflicts with Boer pioneers from the Transvaal.

British Rule. In 1885 the British placed present-day Botswana under their protection. They viewed the area as economically useless, but strategically important because it served as an access route to the north, which was then unoccupied by whites. The land served also as a wedge between the Germans, then in South West Africa, and their Boer allies, in the Transvaal.

In 1895 the British government incorporated the land south of the Molopo River into the Cape Colony, later a part of South Africa. The British instituted indirect rule in the protectorate, allowing the Botswana chiefs to retain their authority under the protection of the British Crown. The protectorate became economically dependent upon South Africa, into which the British assumed Bechuanaland would eventually be incorporated.

The protectorate progressed slowly until after World War II, when political change became rapid, spurred by the development of nationalism in other parts of Africa. A serious issue arose in 1948, when Seretse Khama, chief of the Bamangwato tribe, married a white Englishwoman. Although a tribal council had approved the marriage, the British refused to allow him to return to the country until 1956, after he surrendered his claim to the chieftaincy.

Independence. A constitution promulgated in 1960 allowed elections for a legislative assembly, and Seretse Khama became the country's leading political figure. He founded the Bechuanaland Democratic Party and became an advocate of moderation.

Early in 1965 the capital was moved from Mafeking, in South Africa, to Gaberones, and in March general elections were held. Seretse Khama's party won an overwhelming majority of seats in the new legislature, and Seretse Khama became the first prime minister. Britain granted the country its independence on Sept. 30, 1966, and Seretse Khama became Botswana's first president.

—Hibberd V. B. Kline, Jr; Gary A. Weissman

BRAZIL

Official name: Republic of Brazil
Area: 3,286,470 square miles
Population: (1967) 85,655,000
Capital: Brasília (Pop., 1965 est., 200,000)
Language: Portuguese
Religion: Roman Catholicism
Currency unit: Cruzeiro
National holiday: Independence day, September 7

Brazil, South America's only Portuguese speaking nation, covers almost half the South American continent and contains nearly half its people. Brazil borders every country in South America with the exception of Chile and Ecuador. It is bounded on the north by Colombia, Venezuela, Guyana, Surinam, and French Guiana; on the northeast and east by the Atlantic Ocean; on the south by Uruguay; and on the west by Argentina, Paraguay, Bolivia, and Peru.

THE LAND. Brazil has a widely varied landscape, but there are two major types of terrain: the broad lowlands of the northern third of the country, which include the Amazon Basin, and the Brazilian Highlands, which consist of low plateaus and mountains.

Brazil's land surface is unusual in that the highest areas lie just behind the Atlantic coast, and most of the rivers flow toward the interior, where they eventually empty into the Amazon River or the Paraná-Paraguay river systems.

Major Regions. Brazil has five major land regions: the North, the Northeast, the East (the coast), the South, and the Central West.

The North, which includes more than half the nation's land area, has less than 10 percent of its total population. The area's few inhabitants live mainly within the floodplains of the Amazon River and its numerous tributaries. Since the 1950s, the exploitation of jute, cacao, tropical hardwoods, medicinal plants, oil-bearing nuts, and black pepper has improved the economic situation of the North. A number of Japanese immigrants have settled in the North, particularly in the Amazon Delta.

The Northeast is a region of great physical diversity. A wet, tropical, coastal plain is separated from desert, or *sertão*, by a dry forest area, the *agreste,* which forms a narrow zone between the two. Droughts have always afflicted the desert, and it is only within the last two or three decades that the building of reservoirs and the development of drought-resistant forage plants for cattle have lessened the effects of the dry periods.

The Northeast is the poorest area of Brazil. Few farmers own land and the general level of productivity is extremely low. Modern agricultural techniques are still alien to the traditional thinking of most farmers of the Northeast. In the 1960s the Brazilian government began a large-scale development program in the area.

The Eastern region contains the states of Minas Gerais and Bahia. Minas Gerais is agricultural in the south and west and pastoral in the north. The areas near the city of Rio de Janeiro are devoted to dairy products. The region's western area is one of Brazil's principal food-producing zones, supplying both Rio de Janeiro and São Paulo, the country's largest cities. Belo Horizonte, the capital of Minas Gerais, is a leading manufacturing center, and has numerous metallurgical industries.

The South contains over one third of the nation's population although it constitutes only 10 percent of Brazil's total area. It is Brazil's richest and most productive region and received the major portion of European immigrants. The South is composed of a series of plateaus which rise abruptly from the sea and dip slightly in the west to the lower basin of the Paraná River. It is the center of coffee production and is also important for its forests, which provide softwoods.

The Central West, the fifth region, includes almost 22 percent of the total area, but is occupied by only 3 percent of the country's population. It is an area of extensive grasslands with scattered trees, known as *campo cerrado,* or savanna. These *cerrados* occupy high plateaus at elevations of between 2,000 and 3,000 feet and are dry for most of the year.

In the south, it snows during the winter months in the highest areas, but usually the snow does not stay on the ground for more than a day. The vast western central interior of Brazil experiences sporadic showers three to four months a year, from November through March or April, followed by a dry season during which the scrub vegetation turns brown.

THE PEOPLE. Brazil's population is composed of three main stocks: Indians, descendants of the original inhabitants; whites, descended from Portuguese and other European colonists; and Negroes, brought as slaves from Africa by the Portuguese in the 1500s.

The bulk of the population is concentrated along the coast in a strip extending approximately 250 miles inland. The few remaining pureblooded Indians live within the remote interior, particularly in the Amazon Basin. Negroes live primarily in the Northeast, especially near the coast, where once there were many sugar plantations.

The major cities of Brazil are on or near the coast. The largest city is São Paulo, which had almost 5 million inhabitants in 1965. Rio de Janeiro, the capital of Brazil until 1960, is the country's second largest city, with almost 4 million people in 1965. Rio remains the artistic and cultural center of the country, although it has been superseded in economic importance by São Paulo.

The capital, Brasília, in the Central West, is a model of modern architecture and city planning. It is designed to link the heavily populated coast with the still underdeveloped interior.

ECONOMY. Historically, Brazil's economy has depended heavily on the export of one commodity at a time. Sugar was the mainstay in the 1500s and 1600s, minerals, gold, and diamonds in the 1700s. In the mid-1800s coffee became Brazil's most important product. Although the coffee boom declined, the country has continued to rely heavily on the export of coffee for foreign exchange.

Brazil is rich in natural resources, including a vast, largely untouched

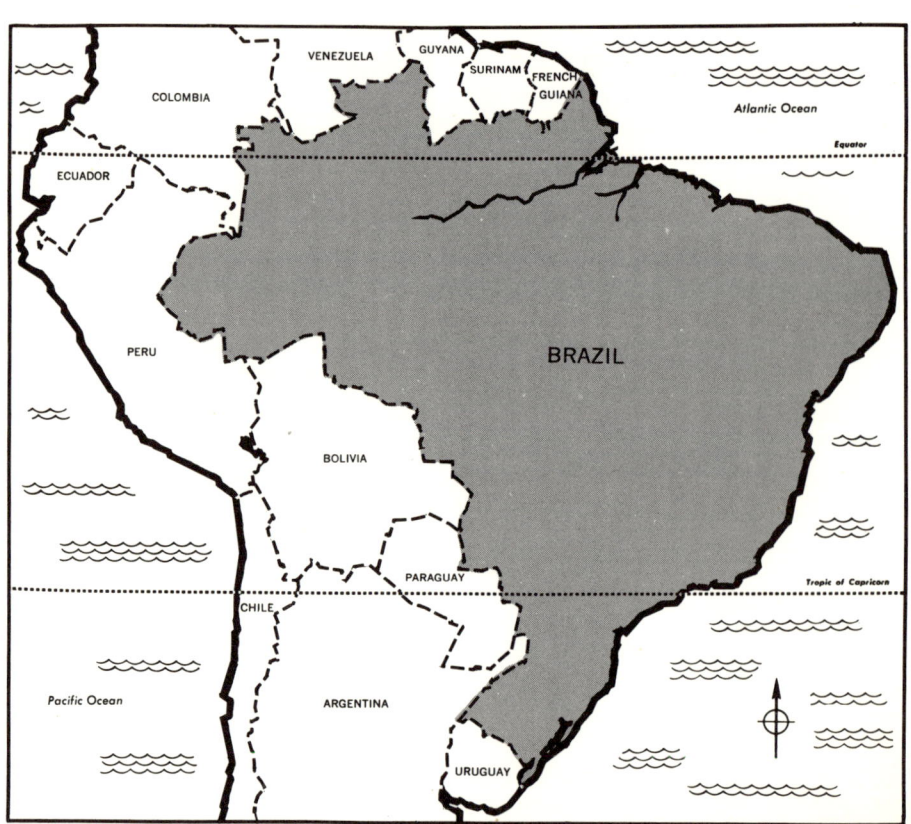

HARBOR OF RIO DE JANEIRO. The rock rising 1,270 feet above the sea is Sugarloaf.

supply of minerals. Their distribution in relation to the distribution of population and markets, however, is poor. Brazil's potential for hydroelectric power is enormous, but many sites, such as the Iguaçu falls, are too far from inhabited areas to prove useful.

Mining has changed from the production of gold and diamonds to exploitation of iron ore and manganese. Coal is mined in southern Brazil, principally in Santa Catarina, but it is of poor quality. The iron ore and coal are consumed in the various iron and steel mills located at Volta Redonda, on the route between Rio de Janeiro and São Paulo, and in Minas Gerais.

Agriculture. Agriculture employs about 3 out of every 5 workers, and 90 percent of Brazil's exports are derived from agriculture. But the productivity of the farm worker is less than half that of the industrial worker, and only 2 percent of the land was cultivated in the mid-1960s.

In addition to coffee, Brazil produces much of the world's cacao and considerable amounts of sugar, vegetable oils, and tobacco. Brazil is also a world leader in cotton production.

Industry. Since World War II there has been an accelerated growth of both light and heavy industry, centered primarily in the state of São Paulo. The major Brazilian industries produce textiles, iron, steel, motor vehicles, and foodstuffs.

Transportation. The transportation situation in Brazil has changed markedly since World War II. The physical integration of the country is being accomplished by building roads to the cities of the interior. Airlines have also come to serve the entire country. As a result, physical isolation, one of the primary barriers to development, is rapidly being overcome.

Trade. In 1966 Brazil's exports earned $1,742 million and its imports cost $1,496 million. Coffee normally makes up about half the value of Brazil's exports. Other major exports include cacao, sugar, pinewood, iron and manganese ores, and cotton. Brazil imports large quantities of manufactured goods, machinery, fuels, vehicles, industrial raw materials, and foodstuffs.

Brazil exports chiefly to the United States, Argentina, West Germany, and the Netherlands. Imports come largely from the United States, West Germany, Venezuela, and Argentina.

GOVERNMENT. Brazil was proclaimed a republic in 1889, but democratic processes have often been disrupted. The military overthrew the constitutional government in 1964 and in 1967 put into effect a new constitution.

The 1967 constitution strengthened the central government considerably, changing Brazil from a federal union of states into a centralized republic. It vested executive powers in the president, no longer elected by popular vote but chosen indirectly, by the congress. Strong powers were given to the president, including the right to appoint state governors and declare legislation initiated by him law if not passed by congress within 30 days.

The congress, consisting of the Senate and the Chamber of Deputies, continued to be elected by popular vote, but the franchise was restricted to those able to read and write.

Brazil is a member of the United Nations and the Organization of American States (OAS).

HISTORY. In 1494 Spain and Portugal, rivals in the establishment of colonies, signed the Treaty of Tordesillas, which granted Portugal all the territory east of a north-south line that extended from the mouth of the Amazon River to the São Paulo coast, neither of which had then been discovered. Thus, in 1500, when the Portuguese explorer Pedro Alvares Cabral claimed Brazil for the Portuguese crown, the claim was incontestable.

Brazil was at first overshadowed by Portugal's Asian and African possessions. It had no great Indian civilization or readily apparent mineral wealth, and early Portuguese contacts consisted mainly of sporadic expeditions to obtain dyewood and to trade with the Indians. Other Europeans, however, especially the French, began frequenting the Brazilian coast for the same reasons, and the rivalry spurred Portugal into taking more effective possession of the vast land.

Colonial Administration. In 1534, Portugal carved Brazil into a series of "captaincies," under proprietary governors called "captains donatary," who were authorized to colonize and rule in the name of the king. In 1549 Portugal also sent out a royal governor-general to the city of Salvador, on Brazil's northeast coast, to exercise general jurisdiction over the entire colony.

Gradually, from the mid-1500s through the 1600s, sugar plantations worked by African slaves took root in the northeastern coastal belt. The export of sugar yielded huge profits and became the backbone of Brazil's economy. It was basically sugar that enticed the Dutch to carve out a short-lived colony in northeastern Brazil in the second quarter of the 1600s. Farther south, there arose a more varied agricultural and grazing economy which relied on Indians and mestizos rather than on Negro slaves for labor.

At the same time, some settlers, especially those of São Paulo, ranged far and wide through the interior seizing Indians to work as slaves and searching for gold. In the process they pushed the boundaries of the colony far to the west of the zone allotted to Portugal by the Treaty of Tordesillas. In the late 1600s they found gold and diamonds in the region of Minas Gerais.

In the 1700s population growth and the increased importance of the south with its gold and diamond deposits brought a number of administrative changes. The last vestiges of the powers of the captains donatary, already largely superseded by royal officials, were eliminated, and in 1763 the capital was transferred from Salvador to Rio de Janeiro. It was also at that time that the first agitation for independence, which drew inspiration from the revolutions in France and the United States, began to occur.

In 1789 in Minas Gerais a militia subaltern nicknamed Tiradentes, meaning "toothpuller," headed a conspiracy against the government. The Tiradentes conspiracy was easily suppressed, but it set a precedent for later attempts.

Brazil's status was altered without a struggle early in 1808, when Prince Regent Dom João and the Portuguese court arrived on Brazilian soil in flight from the armies of Napoleon. Rio de Janeiro became the temporary capital of the Portuguese empire, and Brazil obtained many of the advantages of independence. Moreover, Dom João lingered in Brazil even after Portugal was evacuated by Napoleon's forces. When he did return to Portugal in 1821, he left his eldest son, Pedro, in Brazil as regent, and advised him to become an independent monarch if a final separation of the two countries should prove unavoidable.

The Empire. The eventuality feared by Dom João became a reality in 1822, when the Portuguese government attempted to return Brazil to a subordinate position within the empire. A resistance movement developed, and on Sept. 7, 1822, Pedro declared Brazil independent. On Dec. 1, 1822, he was crowned Emperor Pedro I of Brazil.

Although Brazil was organized as a limited, constitutional monarchy, Pedro I was unable to work smoothly with the parliament. His government's popularity also suffered because of an unsuccessful war with Argentina over control of Uruguay and dislike of Pedro's numerous Portuguese advisers. In 1831 the emperor was forced to abdicate in favor of his infant son, Pedro II. From then until 1840 Brazil was governed by a series of regencies chosen by parliament.

The regency period was marked by outbreaks of republicanism, regional separatism, and general political turmoil, but the monarchy survived. Demands for regional autonomy were partially met by the Additional Act of 1834, which amended the constitution to grant limited self-government to the provinces.

Pedro II. In 1840 Pedro II was declared of age, and he began performing his duties personally. During his reign of almost 50 years, Brazil attained a high degree of political freedom and stability. Brazil's two political parties, the Conservatives and the Liberals, peacefully alternated in power under prime ministers chosen from first one and then the other.

Pedro II wielded substantial personal power, but civil liberties were guaranteed even to the small republican minority. However, the monarchy was slow to deal with the problem of Negro slavery. The slave trade had been outlawed by a treaty signed with Great Britain in 1827, but it continued in practice until the mid-1800s.

Slavery itself was completely ended only in 1888. The fact that slavery was abolished without compensation alienated the slave-owning aristocracy. By that time, moreover, the monarchy had also begun to weaken in other ways.

In the 1870s a serious clash with the Roman Catholic Church had occurred as a result of government interference with an anti-Masonic campaign launched by a group of bishops. Brazil's participation in the war of the Triple Alliance against Paraguay (1865–1870), although it ended in victory, added little to the empire's prestige.

Nevertheless, after the war the army aspired to a greater role in Brazilian life, and thus came into conflict with the civilian-minded emperor and his ministers. Finally, republicanism increased steadily after 1870. The aging Pedro II still retained great personal popularity, but there was no serious resistance on his behalf when a military coup led by Marshal Manoel Deodoro da Fonseca overthrew the monarchy in 1889.

The Republic. In 1891 the new Brazilian republic adopted a federal constitution modeled after that of the United States. The first two presidents, however, were military officers, and both showed arbitrary tendencies that provoked wide unrest. The first president to serve a full term was a civilian from São Paulo, Prudente José de Moraes Barros (1894–1898). His administration was harassed by military upheavals and by a revolt in the back country of northeastern Brazil led by a religious fanatic, Antônio Conselheiro. But when Barros left office, the republic appeared to be firmly established.

Subsequent administrations until 1930 were mostly controlled by a narrow oligarchy representing the large and wealthy states of São Paulo and Minas Gerais. Nonetheless, constitutional forms were generally maintained.

During the mid-1800s coffee had replaced sugar as Brazil's chief crop and major export. Coffee production steadily increased until in the early 1900s serious overproduction appeared. The government then began to restrict coffee planting and later to buy up surplus stocks, hoping to support coffee prices. Meanwhile a great rubber boom had swept the Amazon basin, only to collapse on the eve of World War I in the face of Asian competition.

The economy recovered with the wartime and early postwar demand for Brazilian products, but slumped with the later return to normal conditions. The 1920s were characterized by serious social and economic unrest.

The world economic depression of the 1930s caught Brazil in a highly vulnerable position because of its heavy dependence on coffee as an export. The government was unable to halt a disastrous drop in coffee prices. Moreover, the economic crisis coincided with an attempt in 1930 by the outgoing president, Washington Luís Pereira de Souza, to assure the election of Julio Prestes as his successor. Prestes won, but a revolution by the military installed the more popular opposition candidate, Getulio Vargas, in the presidency.

The Vargas Era. Although he had condemned undemocratic practices of the previous regime, Vargas himself ruled by decree, which provoked demands for a return to constitutional procedures and an uprising in São Paulo in 1932. The revolt failed, however, and Vargas remained in power as dictator.

From the beginning Vargas recognized the need for social and economic reforms. On assuming office, he initiated labor legislation, supported labor unions, and expanded educational facilities and social services in the larger towns and cities. He also encouraged industrialization in an attempt to diversify the economy, and with foreign financial assistance began the creation of a Brazilian steel industry.

In World War II Vargas sided with the Allies and sent Brazilian troops to fight in Italy. Toward the end of the war Vargas found himself subject to increasing public pressure to observe in Brazil the democratic principles for which he was ostensibly fighting abroad. He therefore began to modify his dictatorship and promised free presidential elections in 1945.

Fearing that Vargas would go back on his word, the military ousted him from office in October 1945. The 1945 elections were won by Enrico Gaspar Dutra, who took office on Jan. 1, 1946. In September a new constitution completed the restoration of political freedom and representative government.

In 1951 Vargas returned to the presidency by popular election. His new administration, however, was characterized by blatant corruption and demagoguery. Vargas did create a government petroleum monopoly, Petrobras, which was designed to save Brazil from exploitation by foreign oil interests. Nonetheless, he was generally unable to solve Brazil's postwar economic problems.

An attempt by men close to the president to assassinate an opposition publisher brought forth a new move by the military to oust Vargas. Rather than resign as demanded he committed suicide in August 1954.

Contemporary Brazil. After a period of political confusion, Juscelino Kubitschek took office as president for the next full term (1956–1961). Kubitschek's main accomplishments were the creation of a new capital city, Brasília, located near the geographic center of the country, and the building of highways and hydroelectric works.

To finance these and other expenditures, Kubitschek issued vast amounts of paper money. By doing so he added to an inflationary spiral that had begun before his presidency. Economic growth nonetheless continued.

Jânio da Silva Quadros was elected president in 1960. His government resumed diplomatic relations with the Soviet Union and decorated the Argentine-born Cuban guerrilla expert Ernesto "Ché" Guevara. In general, Quadros proved to be a highly erratic leader, and he resigned in less than a year. The military unsuccessfully tried to prevent Vice President João Goulart from succeeding him because of Goulart's strong leftist leanings.

Under President Goulart (1961–1964), inflation increased. Much was said about fundamental social reforms, including agrarian reform, but little was accomplished. In March 1964, a new military coup ousted Goulart.

A provisional military government had some success in slowing the pace of inflation. It conducted a wide-spread purge of prominent politicians, and gained control of the congress by barring opponents. Gen. Humberto Castello Branco was elected president by the purged congress on Apr. 11, 1964.

On Oct. 3, 1966, Marshal Artur da Costa e Silva was elected by congress as Castello Branco's successor. In December 1966 Castello Branco had pushed through congress a new constitution providing for the consolidation of federal power and the election by congress of the president, who was granted semi-dictatorial powers. The new constitution went into effect on Mar. 15, 1967, when President Costa e Silva took office.

—David Bushnell; Kempton E. Webb

BULGARIA

Official name: People's Republic of Bulgaria
Area: 42,823 square miles
Population: (1966 est.) 8,257,000
Capital: Sofia (Pop., 1965, urban area: 793,300)
Language: Bulgarian
Religion: Orthodox Christianity
Currency: Lev
National holiday: National liberation day (Anniversary of the socialist revolution in Bulgaria), September 9

The People's Republic of Bulgaria, a nation in southeastern Europe, occupies the northeastern corner of the Balkan peninsula. It is bounded on the north by Romania, on the east by the Black Sea, on the south by Turkey and Greece, and on the west by Yugoslavia.

THE LAND. Mountains and plains alternate in Bulgaria to form four major geographical regions. In the north is the Danube Basin, a low, fertile plateau crossed on the north, at the Bulgarian-Romanian boundary, by the Danube River.

At the eastern end of the Danube Basin is the Dobruja, a large limestone plateau region. To the south of the basin, arching southeastward from Bulgaria's northwestern corner to the Black Sea, are the Balkan Mountains (the Stara Planina), ranging from 3,000 feet to over 7,000 feet in elevation. The entire southwestern corner of the country is also mountainous, with the Rila, Pirin, and Rhodope ranges rising to over 9,000 feet.

Between the two mountainous regions, in central Bulgaria, is the basin of the Maritsa River. At its eastern end, the basin widens and opens into the Black Sea. At its western end is the heartland of Bulgaria, the Sofia Basin. The basin is one of the great crossroads of the Balkan peninsula, connected by river valleys to the Danube on the north, the Morava River in Yugoslavia on the west, and with the Aegean Sea on the south.

The Bulgarian climate varies from region to region. The Danube plateau has cold, snowy winters and hot summers. The Maritsa basin, further south, is protected by the mountains to the north and has milder winters. The mountains throughout the country tend to have harsher weather, with yearly variations in temperature and rainfall.

THE PEOPLE. Nearly 90 percent of the people are Bulgarians. They speak Bulgarian, a south Slavic language, and use an alphabet similar to the Russian. The larger minority groups include Turks, Macedonians, Romanians, Armenians, and Gypsies. Most of the people belong to the Bulgarian Orthodox Church, an independent Eastern Christian body. Islam is the largest minority religion.

Population is densest in the Sofia Basin, especially around Sofia, the capital, which is a rapidly growing industrial center as well as the administrative and intellectual heart of the country. Other large urban centers are Plovdiv in the Maritsa valley; Varna and Burgas, the leading Black Sea ports; and Ruse, the largest Danubian port.

ECONOMY. Bulgaria's economy, traditionally based on agriculture, became increasingly industrialized in the 1950s and 1960s under the direction of the Communist party, which came to power during World War II.

The country has a good supply of natural resources. They include low-grade coal, useful for generating electric power, as well as uranium, petroleum, iron ore, lead, zinc, copper, and manganese.

Rich soil, especially in the Danube and Maritsa basins, is also a vital resource, and in 1965 agriculture contributed one-third of the national product. Bulgarian agriculture is almost entirely collectivized.

Wheat and corn are the leading cereal crops, occupying about 75 percent of the total cultivated area. Rye, barley, and oats are also important. Tobacco is the leading industrial crop, and Bulgaria is one of the world's largest producers of the Oriental type of tobacco. Sunflowers, sugar beets, cotton, and soybeans are also grown in substantial quantities. Because of its climatic advantages, including an early spring, the Maritsa basin is known for such specialty crops as early vegetables and fruits and especially for rose oil, pressed from rose petals and used as a base for perfumes.

Livestock is grazed on mountain pastures. Fishing and forestry are of importance.

Industry expanded greatly during the 1950s and early 1960s, and in 1965 contributed 45 percent of the national product. The leading industries include metal working, oil refining, iron and steel production, machinery manufacture, chemical production, and the production of electricity. The traditionally important light industries, including textiles and weaving, leather tooling, woodworking, and tobacco processing, thrive on a smaller scale.

Bulgaria's international trade increased greatly in the 1950s and 1960s, and in 1966 imports cost $1,474 million and exports earned $1,305 million. Farm products, especially tobacco, are the leading exports, and clothing, fruits, and ship parts are also important. Leading imports are machinery, fuel, minerals, metals, and other raw materials.

Over 75 percent of Bulgaria's trade is with other communist countries, but by the mid-1960s trade had increased with western Europe, especially with Italy, West Germany, and Britain.

Tourism also increased rapidly during the early 1960s. The most popular tourist attractions are the Black Sea beach resorts.

GOVERNMENT. The Communist party dominates Bulgarian political life. At the head of the party is a central committee, whose political bureau, or politburo, determines national policy. The first secretary of the party is normally the key figure in government.

The constitution formally vests governmental powers in the popularly elected National Assembly. But assembly candidates are nominated by the Fatherland Front, a mass organization controlled by the Communist party. The National Assembly elects an executive committee, or presidium, to function for it between its short sessions. The chairman of the presidium is the official head of the state. The assembly also elects a council of ministers, or cabinet, and its chairman, the prime minister.

Bulgaria is a member of the United Nations and the Warsaw Pact, a military alliance of communist-dominated European nations.

HISTORY. Bulgaria's location has made the country subject to competing Slavic, Byzantine, Ottoman Turkish, and West European influences, and Bulgaria's history has been marked by frequent conquest and domination by foreign powers. Present-day Bulgaria was part of the Roman Empire by the middle of the first century AD. By the 500s a variety of Slavic tribes had settled in the region.

In the 600s the Bulgars, a warlike people from the northern shores of the Black Sea, conquered the Slavs and settled in the territory. By the 700s the Bulgars had organized a state, the first Bulgarian Empire, and for the next 100 years they resisted conquest by the Byzantine Empire. In 817 a Bulgarian-Byzantine treaty established peace between the two nations.

During the mid-800s, under Emperor Boris, the Bulgarian Empire reached its height. Boris consolidated his power by putting down rebellious nobles, and his armies conquered new territory. During that time the Bulgars were converted to Christianity. In the late 900s Bulgarian territory began to fall to Byzantine armies, and by 1018 the entire nation had been conquered.

During the 1100s, when the Byzantine Empire had begun to disintegrate, a second Bulgarian empire was established. By the 1200s it had become a great power.

Ottoman Rule. The brief period of brilliance and expansion of the second empire was followed by 500 years of rule by the Ottoman Turks. Under the Ottomans, Bulgaria was isolated from both the Western and the Slavic worlds. Ottoman control of the country was complete, and only those Bulgarians who became Muslims could achieve positions of authority. But the life of the peasants—the bulk of the population—was probably no more difficult than under Bulgarian rulers.

During the second half of the 1800s, Bulgarian nationalism became an active force. The Ottoman Empire had

become weak, and Bulgarians were able to assume greater control over their own affairs. They established a national school system, an active press, and an independent Bulgarian church. In 1876 a revolt against the Turks was crushed with vicious ferocity. This provided Russia, an enemy of the Ottomans, with an excuse to go to war with Turkey in 1877.

Independence. Russia was victorious, and in 1878 the Treaty of Berlin granted independence to the principality of Bulgaria, the northern section of present-day Bulgaria. The southern two-thirds, known as Eastern Rumelia, received independence separately. The area remained the center of international political and territorial disputes, however, until 1885, when the two regions were united as Bulgaria.

The new nation was governed by nationalist leaders until 1908, when Prince Ferdinand proclaimed it a kingdom. In the years between 1886 and 1912, Bulgaria made substantial economic and political progress under a democratic constitution. Domestic progress was continually jeopardized by territorial quarrels, however. Bulgaria claimed Macedonia from Serbia and Greece, Thrace from Greece and Turkey, and southern Dobruja from Romania.

These territorial disputes led in 1912 to the first Balkan War, which Bulgaria and its Balkan allies won against Turkey. In the second Balkan War, in 1913, Bulgaria lost territories to its former allies, Greece and Serbia, and to Romania and Turkey. When Germany and Austria promised the return of these territories, Bulgaria sided with them in World War I. Germany and its allies lost the war, and the 1919 treaty of Neuilly forced Bulgaria to cede still more territory—to Yugoslavia, Greece, and Romania.

The losses embittered Bulgaria's domestic politics and foreign relations during the decades between the two world wars. Relations with Greece and Yugoslavia were especially uneasy, and border disputes were frequent. Resentment within Bulgaria led to the loss of many social and economic gains. Premier Aleksandr Stamboliski, the effective political leader of the time, instituted many reforms, but his methods were unpopular and aroused further resentment.

In 1923 a militant nationalist organization, IMRO (Internal Macedonian Revolutionary Organization) helped overthrow the Stamboliski government. IMRO played a large part in precipitating a series of government crises during the next ten years. After a decade of disorder, the military seized control in 1934.

A second coup staged by the king took place in 1935. The king suspended the constitution and made himself a dictator. Bulgaria's continuing territorial ambitions and close trade ties with Germany brought it into World War II on the German side in 1941.

Communist Rule. Toward the end of the war, in September 1944, the Soviet Union declared war on Bulgaria, and within a week Soviet forces had occupied the country. In 1945 elections were held under communist rule, and a government dominated by the communist-controlled Fatherland Front came to power. In 1946 Georghi Dimitrov, long prominent in the international communist movement, became prime minister.

Bulgarians voted in 1946 to abolish the monarchy, and a socialist republic was proclaimed. A constitution establishing a people's republic was adopted in 1947, and by the end of 1947 communist rule was absosolute. The nationalistic Bulgarian communists who had organized the republic gradually were replaced by those controlled from the Soviet Union.

During the late 1940s and early 1950s industries were nationalized and farms were collectivized. The government concentrated on ending Bulgaria's traditional dependence on agriculture and transforming the country into an industrial state. During the 1950s Bulgaria grew increasingly dependent politically and economically on the Soviet Union.

In the early 1960s, when other Soviet bloc countries began to move away from Soviet domination, Bulgaria's ties with the Soviet Union remained close. In 1960, however, diplomatic relations with the United States, which had been severed in 1950, were resumed, and during the 1960s trade and diplomatic contacts were expanded with Western Europe.

Progress was made toward industrialization, but the general standard of living remained low. Moreover, in the drive to industrialize, agriculture had been neglected. A farm crisis in the early 1960s led in 1963 to rationing and in 1964 to the encouragement of private farming.

In 1962 Todor Zhivkov, first secretary of Bulgaria's Communist party since 1957, was named premier as well. In 1965 an alleged plot by a pro-Chinese Communist group to overthrow the government was thwarted. The attempted coup was followed by a purge of the party and a reorganization of the government.

—Robert F. Byrnes; George Kish

BURMA

Official name: Union of Burma
Area: 261,787 square miles
Population: (1966 est.) 25,246,000
Capital: Rangoon (Pop., 1966 est., 821,800)
Language: Burmese, English
Religion: Buddhism
Currency unit: Kyat
National holiday: Independence day, January 4

Burma, an independent nation in Southeast Asia, is bounded on the northeast by China, on the east by Laos and Thailand, on the south by the Andaman Sea, and on the west by the Bay of Bengal, Pakistan, and India. Burma received independence from Britain in 1948 as a union of Burma proper and the Shan, Chin, Kachin, Kayah, and Karen states.

THE LAND. Burma is a diamond-shaped country with a long, narrow extension stretching southward into the Malay Peninsula. The Tenasserim coast, in the south, and the Arakan coast, to the north, are rocky and steep. The central coast is shallow

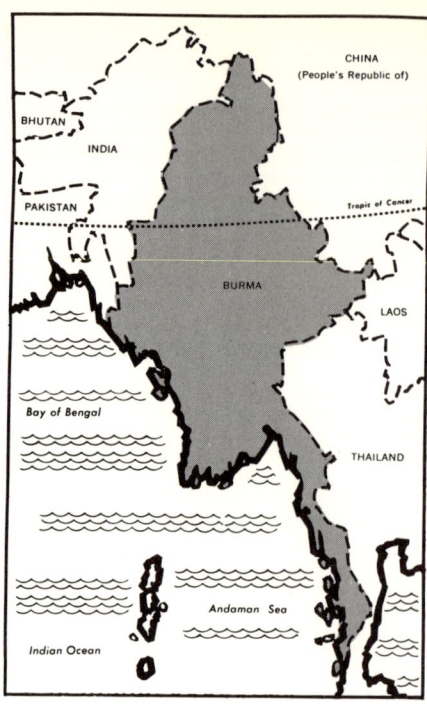

and filled with sandbars. Many small islands dot the long coastline.

Along the coast the densely forested Arakan mountain range rises more than 10,000 feet and extends into a region of hills in the country's northwest corner. Central Burma is a low basin through which flows the Irrawaddy River and, east of a low range of hills, the Sittang River. In the east is the hilly Shan Plateau, about 3,000 feet in elevation, threaded by the Salween River and its tributaries.

The Irrawaddy River dominates Burma's terrain. It rises in the far north and flows southward for approximately 1,400 miles before entering the Gulf of Martaban at the head of the Andaman Sea. It is navigable for about 875 miles inland, and it leaves a deposit of rich soil in its valley and delta. The delta is 150 miles wide and extends about 180 miles inland from the sea.

Burma has a tropical climate. Average winter temperatures range from 70°F along the coast, where humidity is very high, to 60°F in the interior. Summer temperatures rise above 100°F. In southwestern and northeastern Burma, monsoons are common and rainfall is generally heavy—about 80 inches a year in the northeast and up to 200 inches in the southwest. Tropical forests cover these wet regions. Central Burma is a treeless, grassy plain that receives only about 25 inches of rainfall a year.

THE PEOPLE. The people of Burma are divided into a number of traditional tribal and language groups. The dominant people are the Burmans, who speak Burmese, a Sino-Tibetan language, and use an alphabet similar to that of Sanskrit. The larger minority groups are Chin, Shan, and Kachin peoples of the hill regions, and the Karen of lower Burma.

Population is densest in the river valleys. Rangoon and Mandalay are the largest of the country's few cities.

COUNTRIES OF THE WORLD

ECONOMY. Burma is a country with rich natural resources. Over half of the country is forested, and there are valuable stands of teak and ironwood. Burma's mineral riches include petroleum, lignite, lead, tin, tungsten, copper, iron, nickel, zinc, silver, gold, jade, amber, and rubies. All are mined to some extent but none has been fully exploited.

Burma's most valuable resource is its soil, which is extremely fertile in the river valleys. The economy is dominated by agriculture, which contributed one-third of the national income in the early 1960s. The chief crop is rice, which is grown on approximately two-thirds of the cultivated land, mostly in the rich, moist delta region. Rice is also grown on irrigated land in the drier central region, where peanuts, millet, beans, cotton, and tobacco are also raised. Fishing is important along the coast.

Most of Burma's few industries are concerned with the processing of agricultural goods or the extraction of such natural resources as timber and oil. Although industrialization increased during the late 1950s and early 1960s, manufacturing is limited to the production of such light consumer items as textiles and cigarettes.

International trade is second only to agriculture in economic importance, and contributed 20 percent to the national product in the early 1960s. In 1966 exports earned $193 million, and imports cost $160 million.

Rice and teak are the chief exports. Oil, rubber, and cotton are also important. Finished goods and machinery must be imported. India, Japan, Indonesia, Pakistan, Britain, and Ceylon receive most Burmese exports. Britain, Japan, China, India, West Germany, and the United States are the main sources for imports.

GOVERNMENT. Burma's 1948 constitution provided for a parliamentary democracy with a president as head of state and with executive powers exercised by a prime minister and a cabinet responsible to a popularly elected legislature. In 1962 the military overthrew the constitutional government and established a Revolutionary Council to govern Burma.

Burma is a member of the United Nations.

HISTORY. The easy migration and invasion routes along the Sittang and Irrawaddy river valleys have helped make Burma's history turbulent. The earliest known settlers were the Pyu, probably a Tibetan people, who had moved into the region by the late 600s. In the late 700s, a more powerful people, the Mon, settled in the delta region of lower Burma and in the 800s conquered the Pyu.

The Burmans. The Burman people immigrated from northeastern Tibet during the 900s. They came in such large numbers that they were able to occupy all of central and southern Burma and parts of Siam, and they soon dominated the entire region. At first the Burmans were divided into many small clans, but in the mid-1000s one clan chieftan, Anawrahta, united all the Burmans into one empire.

The Burmans conquered the Mon and adopted much of their culture, which was focused on warfare and religion. The king was deified, and many great temples were built in their fortress-like capital, Pagan, in central Burma.

In 1287 Pagan fell to the Mongols, and the empire collapsed. The Mongols took over central Burma, the Mon reestablished their southern kingdom, and a newly powerful people, the Shan, established a group of states in the northeastern hills. The Shan led the Burmans in resistance to the Mongols and drove them out of the region in the early 1300s.

Once more the region was divided among numerous rulers, and for the next several centuries the Shan, the Burmans, and the Mon competed for control of Burma while holding off attacks from Chinese, Laotian, and Siamese invaders. During the 1500s a Burman dynasty briefly united the kingdoms.

In the late 1500s and the 1600s, the Portuguese, Dutch, and English all attempted to establish trading posts in Burma. But the almost continuous warfare in the country contributed to the failure of the trading colonies and discouraged the Europeans.

In the 1750s a powerful Burman dynasty arose under Alaungpaya, who reunited the kingdoms and conquered portions of India and Siam. The destruction wrought by centuries of violence and the stagnation created by an archaic system of government had weakened the country, however, and it was unable to meet a strong challenge from British merchant interests.

British Rule. Between 1824 and 1826 the British drove the Burmese out of northeastern India and occupied the Arakan and Tenasserim coasts. The Burmese refused to grant trading privileges to the British, and by 1886 the British had conquered all Burma and made it a part of British India.

Burma's economy and government were modernized under British rule. Burma became the world's greatest exporter of teakwood, and the Irrawaddy delta became one of the world's largest producers of rice. Missionaries, especially from the United States, began working in Burma's upland areas, and many of the hill peoples were converted to Christianity and brought into contact with the modern world.

Many Burmese resented the British and the Indians, who had come to play a prominent role in economic affairs. After World War I a wave of nationalism led to strikes, riots, and, in 1931, to a brief but large-scale rebellion. The British introduced democratic forms of government in the 1920s and 1930s, and in 1937 granted a constitution separating Burma from India and permitting a good deal of self-government.

By the beginning of World War II, Burma had a prosperous economy and a fairly stable political system, but Japanese occupation in 1942 and British reconquest in 1944 caused great economic destruction.

Independence. After the war a group of nationalists who had organized an anti-Japanese army and a political network during the occupation led a drive for independence. As the Anti-Fascist Peoples Freedom League (AFPFL), they emerged as the dominant political party after the British granted Burma its independence in 1948.

Violent political disputes and tribal rebellions kept the nation in disorder from 1948 until 1952, when the Burmese government, under Prime Minister U Nu, succeeded in restoring its authority. Some social and economic gains were made during the 1950s, but corruption and lack of skills slowed progress. Moreover, the national government was too weak to

LOOK MAGAZINE

BURMESE BUDDHIST MONKS IN PRAYER. Most of Burma's people are Buddhists, and Buddhism exerts a strong influence on Burmese cultural and political life.

cope with the demands of the minorities for greater autonomy or with communist-led insurrections.

In 1958, faced with dissension within the ruling AFPFL, conflict among Burma's other parties, and the imminence of rebellion and civil war, U Nu asked Gen. Ne Win to take power. Army rule brought a measure of peace to the country, and elections in 1960 restored civilian government under U Nu.

In 1962, with a rebellion among the Shan and a threat of total civil war, Ne Win led an army coup and again took control of the government. The army governed through the Revolutionary Council. In 1963 and 1964 most large businesses were nationalized and the repatriation of many Indians and Pakistanis was ordered.

The Revolutionary Council adopted a neutralist policy in international affairs, attempting to steer clear of alignment with either East or West. In 1967, despite Burma's neutralist position, Communist China broke relations with the Burmese government.
—M. G. Inaba

BURUNDI

Official name: Republic of Burundi
Area: 10,747 square miles
Population: (1966 est.) 3,274,000
Capital: Bujumbura (Pop., 1965 est., 71,000)
Language: Kirundi, French
Religion: Roman Catholicism
Currency unit: Franc
National holiday: Independence day, July 1

Burundi, a small, densely populated highland country in central Africa, is bordered on the north by Rwanda, on the east and south by Tanzania, and on the west by the Democratic Republic of the Congo. Burundi was united with present-day Rwanda as the Belgian-administered UN trust territory of Ruanda-Urundi until 1962, when it became independent.

THE LAND. Plateaus, lying at elevations of between 2,500 and 3,500 feet, cover most of Burundi. The Great Rift Valley, which stretches along Burundi's western boundary, is bordered by peaks that rise above 7,000 feet. The country's land surface is badly eroded, and soil erosion is a basic problem almost everywhere in Burundi. The climate is temperate throughout the year.

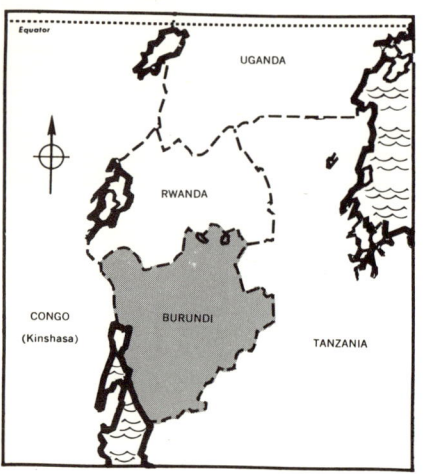

THE PEOPLE. Two tribal groups are dominant in Burundi, the Hutu and the Tusi, or Watusi. The Hutu, comprising about 85 percent of the population, are mostly farmers. The Tusi, who make up about 15 percent of the total, are traditionally herdsmen and warriors. The Tusi long dominated the Hutu and provided the country's rulers.

ECONOMY. Burundi is chiefly an agricultural country, and coffee is the main export. Cotton and rice are also grown.

GOVERNMENT. In 1966 Burundi's constitutional monarchy was overthrown, and a republic proclaimed. Governmental powers were assumed by a 12-member National Revolutionary Committee.

HISTORY. The Tusi, who probably came south from the area of Ethiopia, overran Burundi and Rwanda in the 1500s. A Tusi aristocracy headed by a *mwami*, or king, established its rule, and the Hutu became a subject people.

In 1890 Germany seized the area of present-day Burundi and Rwanda, which became known as Ruanda-Urundi. Belgium occupied the region in 1916 during World War I, and after the war Ruanda-Urundi became a Belgian mandate under the League of Nations. Ruanda-Urundi became a UN trust territory in 1946.

Burundi became independent on July 1, 1962. Moderate Tusi and Hutu formed the National Union and Progress Party (UPRONA), which became the majority party in Burundi. Mwami Mwambutsa IV, who had come to the throne in 1915, became chief of state.

Rivalry among factions within the government caused political instability in the period following independence. Premier Pierre Ngendandumwe was assassinated by extremists in January 1965. His successor, Joseph Bamina, was ousted by the king in July 1965, and in September the king appointed Léopold Biha premier.

In July 1966, the king's son, Prince Charles, seized power from his father and ousted Premier Biha. Charles appointed Michel Micombero premier. In September 1966, the prince was proclaimed Mwame Ntare V. Two months later the army, led by Micombero, overthrew the king and declared Burundi a republic.
—Hibberd V. B. Kline, Jr.;
Vera L. Zolberg

CAMBODIA

Official name: Kingdom of Cambodia
Area: 69,898 square miles
Population: (1966 est.) 6,320,000
Capital: Phnom Penh (Pop., 1962, urban area: 403,500)
Language: Cambodian (Khmer), French
Religion: Buddhism
Currency unit: Riel
National holiday: Independence day, November 9

Cambodia, a kingdom in southeast Asia, is bounded on the north by Thailand and Laos, on the east and south by Vietnam, and on the west by the Gulf of Siam and Thailand.

THE LAND. Cambodia occupies the mountain-rimmed basin of the lower Mekong River. At the center of the basin, only a few feet above sea level, is Tonle Sap, a lake that serves as an overflow basin for the floods of the Mekong. It has an area of about 1,000 square miles and a depth of 5 feet during the dry season, but increases to four times that area and ten times that depth during the rainy season.

Cambodia's highest point, in the Chaîne des Cardamomes along the southwest border of the basin, is only slightly under 6,000 feet. Separated from the Cardamomes by a narrow lowland corridor in the northwest is the Dang Raek plateau, over 2,000 feet high, which rims the basin on the north. East of the basin, the Moi plateau rises to between 1,500 and 4,000 feet.

Cambodia has a tropical climate, with rainy summers and dry winters. Year-round temperatures range from 70°F to 100°F, and the humidity is high. An average of 60 inches of rain a year falls in the basin, and the mountains receive about 80 inches a year.

THE PEOPLE. Cambodia's population is quite homogeneous. Most of the people are Khmers, or native Cambodians. They are Theravada Buddhists and speak Khmer, or Cambodian. There are minorities of Vietnamese, Chinese, and Chams—Muslims of Indonesian origin—as well as some small tribal groups in the hills.

Population is concentrated around the shores of Tonle Sap. About one-tenth of Cambodia's people live in or near the capital, Phnom Penh.

ECONOMY. The Cambodian economy is underdeveloped, but the country can support itself. Natural resources include valuable hardwood forests, iron ore deposits, and rich soil, especially in the central basin. Agriculture is the mainstay of the economy, and the chief crop is rice. Livestock is raised, and cotton, tobacco, pepper, beans, kapok, and rubber are grown. Fishing is second in importance only to farming, and Tonle Sap and the Gulf of Siam yield abundant catches.

Cambodia has few major industries other than traditional handicrafts and rice processing. In the early 1960s, with foreign technical and financial aid, a hydroelectric development project was initiated and some industrialization was undertaken. By the mid-1960s, cigarette plants, a rubber tire factory, paper mills, sawmills, and textile mills were in operation.

The country depends on foreign trade for many commodities. In 1966 Cambodian exports earned $67 million, and imports cost $111 million. Rice and rubber are the only important exports, and transportation equipment, machinery, and textiles are imported.

Most Cambodian trade is with neighboring Asian countries and with France. Almost all of Cambodia's trade passes through the modern port of Sihanoukville, on the Gulf of Siam, which was built with French aid in the early 1960s.

GOVERNMENT. Cambodia is a constitutional monarchy. Its constitution provides for a monarchy limited by a cabinet that is responsible to the parliament. It requires that the more powerful lower house of parliament be popularly elected and that the upper house be elected by limited suffrage to represent certain groups. Another representative body, the National Congress, holds semiannual meetings in which all Cambodians may participate directly.

During the early 1960s the former king, Prince Norodom Sihanouk, assumed more direct control as chief of state but did not rule absolutely.

HISTORY. Cambodia's history extends back at least as far as the 100s AD, when the Kingdom of Funan, in southern Cambodia, was established. It gained power over territory in present-day Thailand, Malaya, Vietnam, and Laos. During the 500s, the kingdom of the Chenla, to the north, overthrew the Funan empire.

By about 800, the Khmers, inhabitants of southern Cambodia who may have been descended from Indians, united with the Cham, an Indonesian people of the northern Malay peninsula. They conquered the Chenla and established an empire centered at Angkor, on the plain northeast of Tonle Sap. Their culture was predominantly Indian and their religion similar to Hinduism.

For the next 400 years Khmer god-kings ruled an empire that included large areas of southeast Asia. Their rice-growing civilization was quite advanced, and evidence remains of great temples, roads, irrigation projects, and public buildings. Khmer power declined during the 1300s. In 1431 the Siamese conquered and sacked Angkor, and the Khmer kings retreated to the region near Phnom Penh.

During succeeding decades, the Khmers fought several disastrous wars with their former subject peoples, the Cham, the Thais, and the Vietnamese, and lost much of their territory. By the mid-1800s, when French colonists began to settle in Indochina, Cambodia was a minor principality plagued by dynastic disputes and in danger of being divided between the Siamese and the Vietnamese.

French Control. In 1863 France made Cambodia a protectorate. Except for preventing its partition, the French generally ignored Cambodia. They fostered little social or economic change and allowed the Cambodian monarchy to continue to function. During the 1930s Cambodian nationalism began to grow, and it turned into anti-French feeling during World War II, when Vichy France allowed Japan to use bases in Cambodia and permitted Thailand to occupy Cambodian territory.

In 1945 Japan took direct control of the Cambodian government, but Prince Norodom Sihanouk proclaimed his country's independence. In 1953 the French, having allowed Cambodia complete internal self-government, turned control of the military over to the Cambodians. In 1954 Vietnamese communist forces invaded Cambodia, joining anti-French guerrillas who had been active there since 1945. A Geneva conference held late in the year ended the fighting, and the troops were withdrawn along with all remaining French troops.

Independence. In 1955 King Sihanouk abdicated in favor of his parents and assumed the title of prince. He consolidated the nation's political strength and founded a political party, the Peoples' Socialist Community, which dominates Cambodia's political life. In 1960, when Sihanouk's father died, the prince was elected chief of state. He was chosen to lead a council to act as regent for his mother.

The country concentrated on social and economic development and remained at peace despite violent conflicts raging in neighboring Southeast Asian nations. In the early 1960s, however, when the Vietnam war intensified, Cambodia feared for its safety and sought international guarantees of its independence and neutrality.

Although Cambodia did not become directly involved in the Vietnam war, eastern Cambodia was used as a military staging area. In 1965 Cambodia severed relations with the United States after the bombing of a Cambodian village. In 1967, as the border situation worsened, Prince Sihanouk assumed special powers and took firmer control of the government.

—M. G. Inaba

THE RUINS OF ANGKOR remain as a symbol of the rich heritage of Cambodia's people.

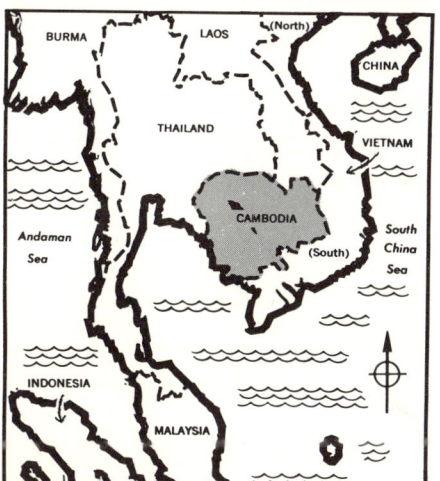

CAMEROON

Official name: Federal Republic of Cameroon
Area: 183,568 square miles
Population: (1966 est.) 5,229,000
Capital: Yaoundé (Pop., 1965 est., 101,000)
Language: French, English, African languages
Religion: Christianity, Islam, traditional religions
Currency unit: Franc CFA (African Financial Community)
National holiday: Independence day, January 1

Cameroon, a federal republic in western Africa, is bordered on the northeast by Chad, on the east by the Central African Republic, on the southeast by the Congo (Brazzaville), on the south by Gabon and Equatorial Guinea (Río Muni), and on the west by the Atlantic Ocean and Nigeria. Cameroon is a federation of two former UN trust territories—one French-administered, now East Cameroon, and the other under British control, West Cameroon.

THE LAND. Cameroon has a varied landscape. In the north are broad grasslands. In the center of the country is the Adamawa Plateau, with elevations of between 2,600 and 5,000 feet above sea level. In the south is a densely forested plateau averaging 2,000 feet in elevation. The volcanic Mt. Cameroon, which rises over 13,300 feet, is near the coast. The coastal region is forested and marshy.

The climate throughout the country is hot and humid. Some regions in the south receive as much as 180 inches of rain each year.

THE PEOPLE. Many different tribes live in Cameroon. Bamileke, Kirdi, and Fulani peoples live in central and northern Cameroon. Bantu-speaking people inhabit parts of southern Cameroon. Some pygmies live in the forests of the south. Cameroon's largest cities include Yaoundé, the capital, and Douala, the major port.

ECONOMY. Cameroon has a variety of resources and products. Cacao, coffee, cotton, and bananas are grown. Forestry provides an important source of revenue. Mineral resources are limited, but in the 1960s exploitation of bauxite deposits was begun.

A large aluminum factory has been built at Edéa, in the west, where there is a major hydroelectric power station. But industrial development elsewhere has been hampered by a lack of power, although small, local hydroelectric plants have been built in various parts of the country. A 20-year economic development program was begun in 1961 to improve the standard of living and ensure a stable economy.

In 1965 imports cost $152 million and exports earned $139 million. The chief exports are cacao and coffee. Cameroon imports manufactured goods, machinery, transportation equipment, chemicals, and petroleum products.

Cameroon maintains close economic relations with France, and it has a customs union with some of its neighbors.

GOVERNMENT. The federal government of Cameroon is headed by a president and a vice-president, both popularly elected to five-year terms. Legislative powers rest with the Federal National Assembly. The assembly includes one representative for every 80,000 people. The assembly elected in 1964 had 50 members, 40 from East Cameroon and 10 from West Cameroon. Assembly members are directly elected to five-year terms.

Cameroon is a member of the United Nations and the Organization of African Unity (OAU).

HISTORY. Cameroon was the original home of the agricultural Bantu-speaking people, who swept westward across central Africa in prehistoric times. Between the 1600s and 1800s, the Portuguese and British established trading posts in the area. In 1884 Germany established the Kamerun protectorate, which covered approximately the same area as the present-day republic.

After World War I the German protectorate was divided into separate French and British mandates under the League of Nations. The two mandates later became UN trust territories. France acquired the larger share of the former German territory. Britain acquired two disconnected land areas, one in the north, inhabited by Muslim Fulani with a feudal system closely allied to that of northern Nigeria, and a part of the southwest, a humid, tropical rain forest area with Bantu-speaking inhabitants.

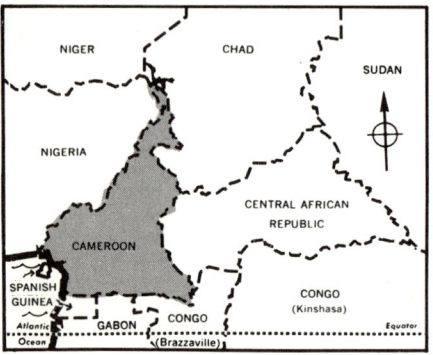

France administered its territory as part of the Federation of French Equatorial Africa. East Cameroon received internal autonomy from France in 1958, and full independence in 1960 under the administration of Ahmadou Ahidjo. Britain administered its territory with Nigeria, using local chiefs in the administration and permitting some representation in Nigerian assemblies.

In 1961, in a UN-sponsored plebiscite, the northern region expressed the desire to remain with Nigeria, but the southern region voted to join the Republic of Cameroon. A federal republic was formed on Oct. 1, 1961, with Ahidjo as president and John Ngu Foncha, prime minister of the former British region, as vice-president.

—Hibberd V. B. Kline, Jr.;
Vera L. Zolberg

CANADA

Official name: Dominion of Canada
Area: 3,851,809 square miles
Population: (1967 est.) 20,441,000
Capital: Ottawa (Pop., 1965 est., urban area: 482,000)
Language: English, French
Religion: Roman Catholicism, Protestantism, Judaism
Currency unit: Dollar
National holiday: Dominion day, July 1

Canada occupies all of the northern half of North America with the exception of Alaska in the northwest and the Danish island of Greenland to the northeast. Canada is the world's second largest nation in area, but it ranks far lower in population. The enormous area of the country and its relatively small population have at times brought into question Canada's very existence as a separate nation in North America.

Few countries have been so deeply affected by their geography as has Canada. The vast, rock-strewn Canadian Shield, which covers the northeastern half of the country, and the harsh climate in the north created a pattern in which three-quarters of the population live within 200 miles of the U.S. border. But the habitable regions—the Maritime area, the St. Lawrence Valley, the prairies, and the Pacific slope—are separated from each other by formidable land barriers, and each of the regions is more closely linked geographically with U.S. areas to the south than with other parts of Canada.

The major forces helping to preserve a separate Canadian nation have been historical and cultural. These include the military and diplomatic protection provided Canada by membership in the British Empire and later in the Commonwealth of Nations, the determination of most English-speaking Canadians to retain their British heritage, and the French-speaking Canadians' fear of assimilation by the numerically overpowering culture of the United States.

Within Canada, however, the problem of establishing and maintaining a national identity has been complicated not only by the influence of the United States, but also by the division between English and French Canadians. The existence of these two distinct and often competing cultural groups has been a source of dissension throughout Canada's modern history.

THE LAND. A northerly location and continental dimensions are basic elements in Canadian geography. From the northern tip of Ellesmere Island, in the Arctic Ocean, to southernmost Ontario, thrust deep into the Great Lakes region, Canada extends for a distance of some 2,800 miles, most of it within Arctic and subarctic regions. At its widest, Canada extends 3,200 miles from east to west and stretches across seven time zones.

This huge area is divided into ten provinces and two territories. Newfoundland, New Brunswick, Prince Edward Island, and Nova Scotia—the Maritime Provinces—lie along the Atlantic coast. The provinces of Quebec and Ontario occupy the southeast. Manitoba, Saskatchewan, and Alberta —the Prairie Provinces—lie in the center of the country. British Columbia is on the Pacific coast. The Northwest and the Yukon territories lie in the north and northwest.

The country is fringed with islands along its three ocean shorelines. To the east, in the Atlantic, lie Newfoundland, Cape Breton Island, Prince Edward Island, and Anticosti. To the north, in the Arctic Ocean, there stretches a vast archipelago containing some 20 large islands, of which Baffin and Ellesmere are the largest and most rugged. The mountainous, deeply indented Pacific coast is rimmed by rocky islands, including Vancouver Island and the Queen Charlotte and Alexander archipelagos.

Landscape. The country's dominant physical feature is the Canadian Shield, a great mass of ancient rock that covers roughly the northeastern half of the country. At its southern end it reaches the north shore of Lake Superior and extends into the United States in northern Minnesota and the Adirondack section of New York. The shield is a low plateau that rises to a fringe of hills and mountains in the east along the Labrador coast and in the south to the Laurentian Highlands overlooking the Gulf of St. Lawrence.

The center of the shield is a depressed basin, most of which is occupied by the broad, shallow Hudson Bay. The shield reflects the most obvious effects of glaciers that covered virtually all of Canada during the Pleistocene Period, from about 1 million to 10,000 years ago. Except for thin patches of poor soil and two major pockets of sedimentary material, in the Ontario-Quebec Clay Belt and around Quebec's Lake St. John, the shield's surface is largely ice-scoured, boulder-strewn rock marked by a maze of swamps, lakes, and streams. Although its agricultural resources are extremely meager, the Canadian Shield is one of the world's greatest sources of minerals and waterpower.

To the south and east of the shield is a zone of plains reaching from the Gulf of St. Lawrence to the Arctic Ocean. The southern Ontario and Quebec segment of the plains, which includes the Great Lakes and the St. Lawrence Valley, is small in area,

COUNTRIES OF THE WORLD

Canada

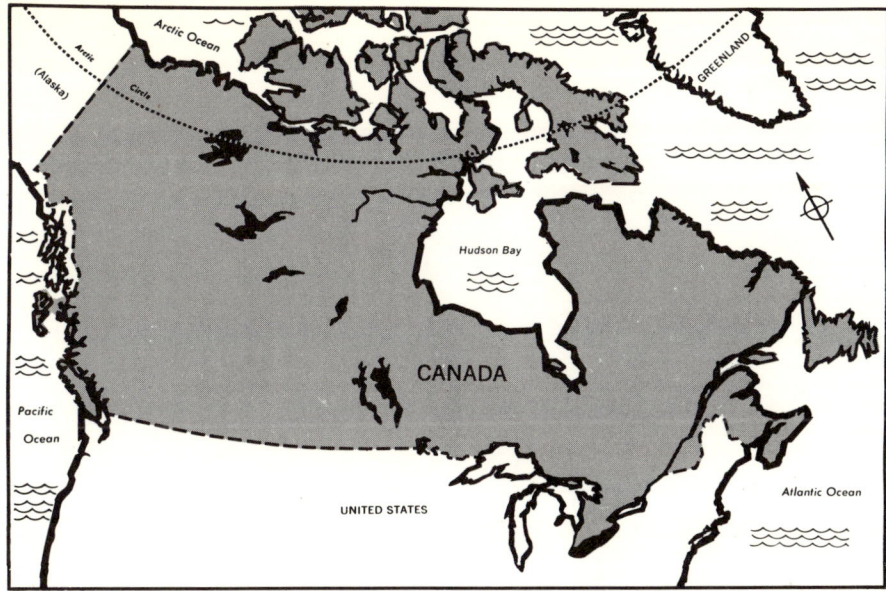

CANADA'S MAPLE LEAF FLAG (NATIONAL FILM BOARD)

but enjoys some of Canada's best climate and forms the economic heartland of the nation. As the Prairie Region, the plains zone extends westward into southern Manitoba, Saskatchewan, and Alberta. This belt of plains contains some of the best Canadian soils as well as the country's principal reserves of petroleum, natural gas, and coal. The plains extend further north as the Mackenzie Valley of the Northwest Territory, a less developed area containing oil and coal.

Westward to the Pacific and the Alaska border lies the extremely mountainous Cordilleran Region. This region contains three major divisions—the Canadian Rockies on the east, the Coastal Ranges on the west, and, between them, a high, deeply dissected plateau drained by the Columbia, Fraser, and other westward-flowing rivers. There are some important deposits of metallic ores in British Columbia.

In southeastern Canada, an upland belt lies between the narrow St. Lawrence lowland and the Atlantic Ocean. This Appalachian system, extending northeast from New England, is a zone of hills and low plateaus and is deeply indented by the sea. The mineral wealth of the east is moderate in comparison with that of the west.

Climate. Low temperatures and a short or sometimes nonexistent growing season have been major hindrances to Canada's economic development. The frost-free season exceeds 120 days only in southern Ontario and Quebec and in southern and coastal British Columbia. But even in the Great Lakes-St. Lawrence inland water system, ice impedes navigation for four or five months each winter.

In the Prairie Region, along the U.S. border, a moderately long, warm to hot summer combines with rather low precipitation, 15 to 20 inches a year, to bring about a natural grass cover. This region and the British Columbian "rain-shadow" to the east of the humid Coastal Ranges are the only areas in Canada in which drought is common. Further eastward in southeastern Canada, greater precipitation—30 to 50 inches a year—generates a rich, mixed forest cover.

Further north, as the temperature drops, both prairie and mixed forest give way to a vast, continent-wide belt of spruce, fir, and pine. This, in turn, thins out gradually until finally a treeless, truly Arctic tundra is reached. Winters are so long and bitterly cold (*average* January temperatures may be as low as –30°F) that only the topmost layers of the earth thaw during the few weeks of summer, and there is a permanently frozen subsurface, or "permafrost."

Icebergs are a major hazard off the Labrador coast, Hudson Bay is ice-jammed for as many as nine months of the year, and only rarely can ships force their way through the nearly permanent icefields bordering Canada's Arctic coast.

THE PEOPLE. Canada's people are of varied origins, for Canada has been one of the major destinations for the great European migrations of recent times. About 30 percent of the total population is of French origin. Although concentrated strongly in Quebec, French Canadians live in all the provinces and are particularly numerous in Ontario and New Brunswick. About 44 percent of Canada's people are of British origin—Irish, Scot, and Welsh, as well as English. They are widely distributed outside the French-speaking region.

Other important groups—Germans, Italians, Ukrainians, Dutch, Scandinavians, Poles, and Russians—are represented in Ontario, the Prairie Provinces, British Columbia, and the city of Montreal. They have been partly or wholly assimilated into the English-speaking community. Approximately 120,000 Canadians are of Asian descent—mostly Chinese and Japanese. Once almost entirely confined to British Columbia, they have begun to migrate eastward.

Some 220,000 Indians and Eskimos were counted in the 1961 census. About three-quarters of them live on government-administered reservations. Religious life is also highly varied. About 45 percent of the population is Roman Catholic. Most live in Quebec, but all the other provinces have large Roman Catholic minorities. The major Protestant denominations—United Church, Anglican, Presbyterian, Lutheran, Baptist, Mennonite, and Pentecostal—are well represented outside Quebec, as are Greek Orthodox and Ukrainian Catholics. Canadian Jews are concentrated in the larger cities.

Distribution. The distribution of population is extremely uneven. Some 90 percent of all Canadians live within 10 percent of the country's area, a long, narrow, fragmented strip of territory along the southern boundary. In addition to being quite narrow, the populous region is split into four physically and socially isolated areas of settlement.

In the west, there is a relatively dense urban and rural settlement in southern British Columbia, especially within the Fraser and Columbia valleys. This is separated by the rugged Rocky Mountains from the thinly, but continuously, settled Prairie zone bounded on the east by the Canadian Shield and on the north by a forested zone of poor soils.

Canada's main concentration of population and wealth lies several hundred miles to the east in the lowlands wedged between the Canadian Shield, the Great Lakes, and the Appalachian uplands. This Canadian "heartland" is sharply divided culturally between a French-speaking, Roman Catholic Quebec and an English-speaking, ethnically and religiously diverse Ontario. Lastly, the Maritime area of settlement is isolated from the St. Lawrence–Great Lakes region by the Gaspé uplands and U.S. territory.

North of the main population belt, settlement is limited to a few areas such as Alberta's Peace River Valley, the Clay Belt, the Lake St. John basin, and various mining districts. Much of the Arctic is uninhabited. The total population of the Yukon and Northwest territories was only some 27,000 in the mid-1960s.

Growth. Canada's population has been growing rapidly, more so than that of almost any other economically developed nation. Between 1958 and 1965 the rate of increase was 2 percent a year. The government encourages the immigration of people with skills needed for the development of Canada's resources. Most of the increase has occurred in the relatively prosperous portions of Ontario and Quebec and in the two western provinces of British Columbia and Alberta.

Impressive growth has been limited almost wholly to cities and suburbs. By the early 1960s some 70 percent of the population was officially classified as urban and almost 45 percent lived in the 17 largest metropolitan areas. Among the relatively small number of large cities, two giants dwarf all others — Montreal, with more than 2.3 million people in its metropolitan area in 1965, and Toronto, with over 2 million.

ECONOMY. Canada is one of the most prosperous of the world's nations. In good part, this results from the combination of a small but highly skilled and well-educated population, rich natural resources, and the availability of investment capital from Europe and the United States.

Resources. Canada has abundant mineral and power resources. With thousands of miles of developed rivers and streams, the country is one of the world's leading producers of hydroelectric power. Waterpower produces approximately 80 percent of Canada's output of electricity, which in 1966 totaled nearly 160 billion kilowatt hours.

Large reserves of petroleum, gas, and coal lie in the Prairie Provinces. The Maritime Provinces also have important coal deposits.

Iron ore, copper, lead, zinc, nickel, cobalt, uranium, radium, and other metallic ores are mined in the shield. The western mountains are rich in zinc, lead, copper, gold, nickel, and silver.

In addition to these resources, forests cover almost 2 million square miles of Canada, and Canadian rivers and coastal waters are well stocked with fish.

Agriculture. Poor soils and harsh climate limit Canada's agricultural area, and in 1966 only some 7 percent of the land was under cultivation. Two regions are quite fertile—the prairies and the St. Lawrence lowlands.

Agriculture is the mainstay of the Prairie Provinces, where wheat and other small grains are grown in enormous quantities. Flaxseed, hay, sugar beets, cattle, and sheep are also major sources of farm income. Southern Quebec and Ontario produce grains and vegetables as well as meat and dairy products.

The Great Lakes region of Ontario raises the greatest variety of crops. Corn, tobacco, fruits, and vegetables are added to the usual grain, hay, and root crops. In southern British Columbia vegetable-growing, dairying, berry-farming, bulb-raising, and cattle herding are all important. In the Maritimes general farming is profitable only in a few localities, but fruit farms prosper.

Manufacturing. Manufacturing makes the largest contribution to Canada's economy, accounting for more than one quarter of the gross national product in 1966. Pulp and paper milling, ore processing, and oil refining are the leading industries. The processing of meat, grains, milk, and other farm products is also important.

Plants manufacturing machinery, vehicles, electrical equipment, chemicals, and textiles are concentrated in the urban centers of southern Ontario and Quebec. Many are affiliates of U.S. corporations.

Extractive Industries. The fur trade is still carried on in large sections of northern Canada. Forest industries continue to expand in areas with easy access to markets, and Canada is a major producer of pulp and paper.

Mining is increasing with further exploration, improved transportation, and rising world demand. Iron ore production rose sharply in the early 1960s with the development of mines in Labrador and north of Lake Superior.

Fishing remains important to the economies of Newfoundland and Labrador, but it is less significant than in earlier years. Newfoundland, for example, has started major forest and mineral industries. Deep sea fishing, especially for salmon, is important in coastal British Columbia.

SORTING LOGS in British Columbia to feed the country's key pulp and paper industries.

Tourism. Tourism is an increasingly important source of income. Throughout the nation, during the early 1960s tourist and recreation facilities were being developed rapidly for Canadians and for European and U.S. visitors.

Transportation. The Canadian economy depends upon a transport system capable of coping with enormous distances and bad weather. Canada's highway network is adequate only within the well-populated regions. The Trans-Canada Highway runs from the Atlantic to the Pacific, and the Alaska Highway links Canada's northern and southern boundaries.

Much of Canada's freight travels by rail, on the government-owned Canadian National and the private Canadian Pacific, or by boat. Canada has many good natural harbors, especially along the Great Lakes-St. Lawrence system, but many ports are closed by freezing weather during most of the winter.

Trade. Canadian economic well-being depends heavily upon international trade. In 1966 the country's exports were valued at just over $9,500 million and its imports cost slightly more than $9,000 million.

Major Canadian exports include paper, newsprint, wheat, lumber, wood pulp, nickel and nickel products, aluminum, copper, uranium, petroleum, iron ore, asbestos, synthetic rubber, plastics, machinery, and whisky. Imported goods include petroleum and coal for eastern Canada, raw sugar, bauxite, coffee, cotton, rubber, fruits, and a broad range of industrial products.

Most of Canada's trade is with the United States. Britain, once Canada's principal market, ranked second in the 1960s.

GOVERNMENT. Canada, a federation of ten provinces, is a parliamentary democracy. Although it is an independent nation, Canada is a member of the Commonwealth of Nations and recognizes the British monarch, or the Crown, as head of state. A governor-general represents the Crown in Canada and is the nominal chief executive.

A prime minister, normally the leader of the majority party in the parliament, is the functioning chief executive of the national government. He heads a cabinet responsible to the House of Commons, the lower house of parliament. Members of the House of Commons are popularly elected to a normal term of five years. Members of the upper house, the Senate, are nominated by the prime minister and appointed for life by the governor-general.

A lieutenant-governor appointed by the governor-general in council with the prime minister formally leads the government in each province. Actual provincial executive power is in the hands of a prime minister, or premier, and cabinet responsible to the provincial legislature.

The legislatures are unicameral in every province but Quebec, where the assembly has two houses, and all are popularly elected. Federally appointed commissioners and small elected councils govern the Yukon Territory and the Northwest Territories. The Dominion government has direct authority over many territorial matters, however.

Canada is a member of the United Nations. It has close ties with Britain and with other members of the Commonwealth. Canada is also a member of the North Atlantic Treaty Organization (NATO).

HISTORY. The history of Canada has been called a story of challenge. First, New France, as the French possessions in North America were called, struggled for survival against the wealthier British colonies to the south, in the present-day United States. Then, after the British conquest of New France in 1763 and the American Revolution, British Canada began its own long struggle against the powerful military, economic, and cultural forces exerted by the United States. While struggling to maintain itself as a nation, Canada has also struggled to establish a national identity, to be Canadian.

Early Exploration. The first Europeans to reach America were the Vikings, who came in the 1000s by way of Iceland and Greenland. The extent of Viking penetration of the continent and the fate of Viking settlements have remained uncertain. Norse sagas and maritime traditions preserve much knowledge of those early discoveries and a map of "Vinland," published in the 1960s, indicates that they explored Newfoundland, at the least.

It was not until the late 1400s that English, French, Spanish, and Portuguese ships began to cross the Atlantic. The first voyages were undertaken by John Cabot in 1497 and 1498. With permission of England's King Henry VII, Cabot sailed on behalf of a group of English merchants who wished him to find a Northwest Passage to the Orient. No shortcut to the riches of Asia was found, but Cabot's party did discover the great North Atlantic fishing banks near the Gulf of St. Lawrence.

The fame of the fisheries spread among Europe's seafaring nations, but by the end of the 1500s the fishermen of England and France were taking the greatest advantage of the fishing banks. The main catch was cod, and as the fish had to be dried, fishermen built storehouses and dwellings on the shore. The fishermen began to trade with Indians eager to exchange their fur clothing for European trinkets. This sideline soon proved enormously profitable. It led to the founding of posts devoted to the fur trade, and the demand for furs gradually lured trappers deeper into the continent. Fish and furs became the two great staples of the Canadian economy.

In 1534 and 1535 Jacques Cartier undertook exploratory voyages on behalf of France's King Francis I. On his second voyage, Cartier discovered the mighty St. Lawrence River. He sailed up the St. Lawrence as far as the Iroquois villages then located on the sites of the present-day cities of Quebec and Montreal.

As a result of Cartier's voyages, France attempted to colonize the area near Quebec in 1541–1543. The failure to discover hoped-for treasures of gold and jewels discouraged the French, and their first attempt to found a colony in Canada failed. Cartier's efforts were not in vain, however, for his voyages established a clear title for later French claims to the whole area of the St. Lawrence gulf and valley.

New France. During most of the remainder of the 1500s internal religious and political struggles distracted France from further efforts to colonize Canada. Fishing and fur trading continued, however, and the popularity of beaver hats in France spurred the fur trade.

When Henry IV became king of France in 1589, stability began to return and important commercial interests looked to Canada for fur to meet the continuing European demand for fur clothing. Henry IV was personally interested in resuming the exploration and settlement of Canada, and he used the interest of French merchants in the fur trade to accomplish his ends. In 1599 the merchants of Honfleur received the first of a series of royal monopolies of the fur trade.

The French controlled New France through these monopolies until King Louis XIV took direct control in 1663. A monopoly of the fur trade in a particular region was granted to a company in return for its undertaking settlement and missionary work. This policy succeeded in planting French colonies in North America, but the hostility of the Iroquois, the lack of interest in settlement among the monopolists, and the harshness of the climate led to their failure and to the revocation of the monopolies.

Much of the credit for the colonization that was achieved belongs to Samuel de Champlain (c.1567–1635). Soldier, geographer, and fervent Roman Catholic, Champlain was the true founder of New France. He surveyed the explored territories for possible settlement sites, and after the original coastal colonies had failed he persuaded the monopolists to concentrate on developing the St. Lawrence Valley. The energy and initiative with which he guided the destinies of New France from 1608, when he founded a trading post at Quebec, until his death in 1635 were responsible for the colony's survival in the face of the same obstacles to which earlier settlements had surrendered.

NATIONAL FILM BOARD

SHIPPING FREIGHT at St. John, New Brunswick, in southeastern Canada's Maritime region.

Other forces also worked to insure success. The religious zeal of the Catholic Counter-Reformation in France soon spread to Canada. The enthusiasm of the Jesuit and other religious orders to convert the Indians led to the establishment of missions and kept the colony active.

In 1627 Cardinal Richelieu, the chief minister of Louis XIV, organized a new monopoly, the Company of New France, also known as the Company of One Hundred Associates. It assumed direction of the colony and permitted only Catholics to come to New France.

The church founded and conducted the colony's social and educational institutions and in 1642 established a mission and hospital for the Indians on the site of what is now Montreal. But the zeal of the missionaries alone could not maintain the colony, even though many new settlements were being founded.

By 1663 New France faced grave problems. The fur trade did not encourage settlement. It depended on single men rather than on families, and in fact the fur companies had established only about two thousand people in the colony. In addition, the Iroquois were a constant threat. Thus the colony remained little more than a fur-trading station dependent on France for almost all its supplies.

Royal Rule. At that critical moment, Louis XIV, having firmly established his power in France, initiated an entirely new policy designed to turn the colony into a source of strength for the crown. The Company of New France was persuaded to surrender its monopoly in 1663, and Louis XIV assumed personal control through his finance minister, Jean Baptiste Colbert.

Government was placed in the hands of three officials, each directly responsible to the king. A governor was to direct military affairs, especially defense against the Indians; a bishop was to direct the church; and an *intendant*, a new official in Canada, was to regulate economic and judicial matters. All three officials sat on a supreme council that included five other appointed members. The council handled administration and acted as a court of appeals. This government endured until the loss of the colony in 1763.

In 1665 the king ended the immediate threat from the Indians by sending more than a thousand well-trained soldiers to Canada. A revival of the fur trade soon followed the victories over the Indians. The first intendant was Jean Talon, who served from 1665 to 1672. His bold plans transformed the colony. Encouragement of immigration and rewards for early marriage helped raise the population from about 3,000 in 1666 to almost 7,000 by 1673.

Social organization in New France was a modification of that in the mother country. Colonial strength resulted from social changes made possible or necessary by the conditions of pioneer life. France's feudalistic seignorial system of landholding was reorganized.

Some of the rigid restrictions on the peasants were relaxed to allow them more freedom from their seigneur, or landlord. As semi-independent small farmers, the peasants became a source of social stability. Agriculture began to prosper, and the long, narrow farms fronting on the St. Lawrence gave New France the appearance of a continuous village with a single street, the river. Law was based on the French code, but it included statutes passed by the council and decrees made by the intendant.

Talon tried to make the colony less dependent on the fur trade, and he promoted lumbering, fishing, shipbuilding, hemp-growing, brewing, tanning, and the mining of potash. He was only partially successful in this, however, and trade with France and the French West Indies never reached substantial proportions. By the end of the 1670s, royal interest in the colony had waned once more and New France was again forced to rely on its own resources.

The fur trade and rivalry with the expanding British colonies to the south pushed the French ever deeper into the interior of North America. Louis Joliet and the Jesuit missionary Father Jacques Marquette explored the Mississippi area in 1673. The Sieur de la Salle explored the Ohio River in 1669 and the Mississippi River in 1682, claiming the entire Mississippi Valley, "Louisiana," for France.

By 1700 French possessions stretched north to Hudson Bay, west beyond Lake Superior, and south to the Gulf of Mexico. But this great territorial expansion contributed to the fall of New France, for the area was large and had few French settlers.

French-British Rivalry. Conflict between Britain and France for dominance in Europe had started in 1689 and continued with only occasional periods of peace until 1763. The French-British conflict also involved the American colonies. The vast territories of France were held in spite of the colony's small population and economic weakness.

New France in the 1750s had only about 60,000 inhabitants, whereas the population of the wealthier British colonies approached 2 million. But New France relied on the ability of a united colony organized along military and authoritarian lines to mobilize swiftly its entire strength.

French ability to win Indian support, the warlike qualities of the French nobility and militia, and French pride, daring, and vigor long enabled New France to withstand British power in North America.

French expansion received its first check in 1713, when the Treaty of Utrecht gave Britain Newfoundland, Acadia (Nova Scotia), and Hudson Bay. Although New France made an impressive recovery from this setback, British numerical and naval superiority in the New World made final defeat inevitable.

The tide turned in favor of the British in 1758, and in 1759 British Gen. James Wolfe defeated Commander Louis Montcalm on the Plains of Abraham. This led to the fall of Quebec, the strategic center for French power in America. The Treaty of Paris, signed in 1763, brought the struggle of empires to a close. France surrendered its mainland possessions in North America and formally transferred Canada to Britain.

British Canada then included the Atlantic Coast maritime region, part of which England had possessed before the treaty; "Canada," part of the present-day Quebec and Ontario provinces, won under the treaty; and the Northwest Territories, north and west of Hudson Bay. Britain also had access, if not absolute title, to the largely unsettled wilderness between the Great Lakes and the Pacific.

British Canada. Britain was faced with the problem of governing a French-speaking community in the British Empire. In the Proclamation of 1763, Britain announced the goal of assimilating the French into British culture. To increase the English-speaking population, Britain sought immigrants from the 13 American colonies. The government promised

BRITISH TAKING THE CITY OF QUEBEC in 1759, from an old print by an unknown artist.

English law and institutions to all colonists and rule by Protestants, not by Catholics.

The expected heavy immigration did not occur, however, and British officials began to doubt the wisdom of turning Canada into a typically British colony at a time when the other British colonies in North America were becoming increasingly rebellious. Sir Guy Carleton, who governed Canada for much of the critical period between 1766 and 1796, avoided enforcing the assimilation policy. He had come to see Canada as a strategic outpost for England and as a potential source of manpower for subduing the American colonies if they should rebel.

The assimilation policy was officially abandoned by the Quebec Act of 1774 in a move to win the loyalty of the French Canadians. The act guaranteed the continuance of French civil law along with English criminal law, the maintenance of the French seigniorial system of landholding, the admission of Catholics to public office, and the right of the Church to collect tithes.

The act also extended the boundary of Quebec south to the Ohio River. American colonists felt that this provision was meant as punishment, although it was not so intended.

At the outbreak of the American Revolution, the American colonies hoped to win both Quebec and Nova Scotia to their cause, and the British looked to Quebec for military support. Both sides were disappointed.

French Canadians were weary of war and, with few exceptions, remained neutral. Nova Scotia, although inhabited by many recent immigrants from New England, was still economically dependent on trade with England and was intimidated by the great British naval and military base at Halifax. The American Revolution found little active support there, either.

The only major battles of the revolution fought on Canadian soil occurred in 1775, when American forces attacked Montreal and Quebec. The American colonists moved an army under Richard Montgomery toward Quebec to meet a second American force led by Benedict Arnold. Although Montreal fell to Montgomery's army, Quebec withstood the American siege. In the spring, when ships of the British navy sailed up the St. Lawrence, the Americans retreated.

The boundary agreed upon at the close of the American Revolution in the Treaty of Paris (1783) affected Canada as much as the United States. Most Canadians believed it a surrender of their interests. It abandoned much of the Ohio territory, on which the fur trade depended, and it left undetermined Canada's southern boundary west of the Mississippi. But the war had brought new settlers to Canada—some 40,000 Loyalists from the United States.

In Nova Scotia, nearly 30,000 Loyalists swelled the original population, transforming the region into a fiercely loyal British colony. To assist the immigrants, the British government assigned a liberal portion of land to each family. On Aug. 16, 1784, New Brunswick, where the largest number of Loyalists had settled, was formed from the western part of Nova Scotia. It became the most loyally British and the most conservative province in Canada. West of the Maritimes, the Loyalists settled in three main areas: along the upper St. Lawrence; on the north shore of Lake Ontario; and on the Niagara peninsula.

The Loyalists throughout Canada soon claimed the right to have an elected assembly, and in 1791 the British Parliament passed the Constitutional Act establishing representative government in the Canadian colonies. The act also divided the colony of Canada into two separate sections—Upper Canada and Lower Canada.

Upper Canada, now the province of Ontario, was where most of the Loyalists had settled. Lower Canada, now the province of Quebec, lay nearer the mouth of the St. Lawrence and had remained predominantly French. Each had an appointed governor, a legislative council chosen by the governor, and an elected assembly. In Upper Canada, English common law formed the basis for government. Lower Canada retained much of the old French civil code.

The resolve of the Loyalists to remain British was tested in 1812 by the renewal of war with the United States. Although the war achieved little for either England or the United States, it had some important results for Canada. Canadian nationalism, as distinct from loyalty to England or to France, began to be felt as French and English Canadians fought side by side and, with the help of British regulars, fought off a U.S. invasion.

The war also reinforced Canadian conservatism, and for decades afterward forces of social and political reform could be greatly weakened by an accusation that they were American-inspired.

Until 1867 Upper and Lower Canada and the Maritime Provinces developed as separate units, but all were experiencing rapid social change, commercial expansion, and population growth. After the Napoleonic Wars, hard times in Britain drove immigrants to British America and the population level rose from under 500,000 in 1815 to 2.5 million in 1850. This rapidly transformed the colony from a comparative wilderness into a region of settled communities.

Fur, the chief industry of the wilderness, was no longer the basis of Canadian economic life. New activities were making important contributions to Canada's growth — lumbering and grain-growing in Upper and Lower Canada, and lumbering, shipbuilding, and fishing in the Maritimes.

Improved transportation became a necessity, and a program of canal-building, centered on the St. Lawrence River and its tributaries, was undertaken to tap the trade of the U.S. west. Although in the 1830s Canada completed the Welland Canal, which joined Lake Erie to Lake Ontario, the U.S. Erie Canal system easily maintained its superiority over the St. Lawrence route.

A world-wide depression in 1837 dealt a heavy blow to Canadian prosperity. Canada's economy was weakened further when Britain removed its protective trade system in the 1840s. Economic despair was reflected in the Annexation Manifesto requesting union with the United States, which was signed by numerous merchants in 1849 but never acted upon.

In the 1850s, railway-building helped bring renewed prosperity to British North America. The Reciprocity Treaty, signed in 1854, established freer trade between Canada and the United States and opened new markets for Canadian produce.

Canadian-American relations had already been improved by settlement of old boundary disputes in the 1840s. The Webster-Ashburton Treaty of 1842 set the line between New Brunswick and Maine at its present position, and the Oregon Treaty of 1846 set the U.S.-Canadian boundary west of the Mississippi along the 49th parallel.

During the 1800s Canada matured politically as widely separated struggling pioneer settlements grew into robust provincial societies. For several years after the War of 1812 the governments of Upper and Lower Canada were dominated by small, powerful groups called "family compacts" or "cliques." They controlled the legislative councils, the colonial cabinets.

The compacts often won popular support and adopted reasonably progressive policies, but too often they used their power to promote their own interests. Reform groups demanded that power be concentrated in the popularly elected assemblies. The political situation in Lower Canada was further complicated by an ethnic struggle. The ruling clique was almost entirely British, and the opposition, which controlled the assembly, was primarily French.

Robert Baldwin, a member of the legislature of Upper Canada, led the drive to obtain responsible government, with the executive responsible to the majority in the elected assembly. The local compacts opposed this threat to their power. They were supported by the British Colonial Office, which feared that responsible government would reduce the governor to a mere agent of the local assembly and would have almost the same effect as granting independence.

To these political grievances were added the severe financial crisis in 1837 and general economic hardship caused by widespread crop failures. Discontent led in 1857 to rebellions in Upper and Lower Canada.

The rising in Upper Canada involved only the more radical reformers, led by the Upper Canadian legislator William Lyon Mackenzie, and was primarily a protest against rule by the compacts. The rising was quickly suppressed, and the majority of the population remained loyal to the government.

In Lower Canada the revolt was more widespread, particularly among the French Canadians, who resented what they felt was unjust treatment by British officials. There, the untrained rebel forces were soon routed by British regular troops. The rebellions caused friction along the U.S. border and resulted in several ill-organized raids on Canada by misinformed American patriots. The uprisings dealt the British government a severe blow and in 1838 led to the dispatch of the Earl of Durham, John George Lambton, to report on unrest in the colonies.

Responsible Government. Lord Durham's *Report on the Affairs of British North America* (1839) was a denunciation of rule by compacts. The report recommended the institution of responsible government, a clear division between imperial and local functions, and the union of Upper and Lower Canada. But these were only partially put into effect by the British Parliament's Union Act of 1840.

The Canadas joined in 1841 to become the Province of Canada. Durham had intended the union of Upper and Lower Canada to solve the French-British cultural conflict by assimilating French Canadians into British culture. The proposal for a united legislative assembly was carried out, but the attempted assimilation did not succeed. The Union Act gave each equal representation in the legislature, despite their unequal populations, and the idea of two distinct sections was kept alive.

Responsible government began in 1848. It came first to Nova Scotia, which had not been disturbed by the rebellion. A few months later the Province of Canada followed. Robert Baldwin, the attorney general of Upper Canada, joined Louis H. Lafontaine, a prominent French Canadian, to form a government. But Canadian politics continued to be plagued by sectional strife based on historical and cultural differences. With each section stubbornly opposed to the other, Canada could make little progress.

The French-Canadian element, because of its solidarity, had great political strength. It campaigned for objectives of its own, such as separate Roman Catholic schools, and against the programs of the more liberal element.

By the early 1850s Upper Canada, then called Canada West, had a larger population than Canada East, the predominantly French-Canadian portion of the union, but each had equal representation in the assembly. George Brown, publisher of the Toronto *Globe* and a Liberal member of the Canadian parliament from Canada West, led the campaign to end what was called "French domination" by achieving representation on the basis of population.

French Canadians responded by staunchly supporting Brown's opponents in the Conservative Party. As a result, there were three changes of government between 1861 and 1864. The sections were so evenly balanced that the deadlock would only have continued after another election.

Confederation. To break the stalemate, the Liberal and Conservative parties formed a coalition to promote the union of all the British North American colonies. At that same time the Maritime Provinces had planned a conference to discuss a limited union among themselves, and delegates from Canada East and Canada West attended the meeting, held in September 1864.

At another meeting held at Quebec City the following month, the Canadas won over the Maritimes to their plan of union. Both Canada and the Maritimes faced common problems, which Confederation was expected to solve. In Canada, the agricultural frontier had reached its limits and a stronger political authority was needed to promote settlement of the western plains, an area already threatened by U.S. expansionism.

Moreover, the nation had a great need for railroads and other major transportation facilities. Projects of such vast proportions could be handled and financed more easily by a centralized government than by the individual provinces. In the Maritime Provinces prosperity based on the timber trade, wooden-ship building, and fishing was threatened by the new economy based on coal and steel.

When the United States showed its determination to cancel the Reciprocity Treaty of 1854, all Canadians became aware of the need for a united country to resist U.S. economic pressure and to seek new markets. Other external pressures also made a united front desirable. During the U.S. Civil War most Canadians favored the South. Fear of attack by Union armies led many to support Confederation as a defense against U.S. invasion.

British support made Confederation almost inevitable. The British government realized that a united British North America could take more vigorous defensive measures against U.S. pressure and, in addition, could relieve the mother country of much of the colonies' financial burden. Britain therefore used all its influence and power to bring about confederation and it pressured the reluctant Nova Scotia and New Brunswick into joining the union. Nevertheless, Newfoundland and Prince Edward Island refused to join.

The Dominion. The British North America Act of 1867 united Canada East and Canada West with New Brunswick and Nova Scotia to form the Dominion of Canada. Canada East became Quebec province, Canada West became Ontario, and Nova Scotia and New Brunswick retained their former boundaries and provincial organization. Ottawa, in Ontario but near the Quebec border, was chosen as the dominion capital.

In response to the French Canadians' desire to protect their language and religious rights, the new dominion was a federal and not a unitary state. In contrast with the U.S. example, however, the central government, not the provinces, received all powers that the constitution did not specifically grant to one or the other.

The aim of the planners was to create a strong central administration that would control most of the important functions of governing the dominion. The new dominion combined the British parliamentary form of government with the U.S. principle of federalism in a government that still remained subordinate to Britain.

John A. Macdonald, the dominion's first prime minister, and his Conservative Party dominated the political history of Canada from Confederation until 1891. Macdonald's task was to build a nation. His first great achievement was to prevent Nova Scotia's attempted withdrawal from Confederation in 1869 by granting needed economic assistance to the province.

In foreign affairs, Macdonald ably represented Canadian interests in negotiations between Britain and the United States that resulted in the Treaty of Washington of 1871. The treaty resolved a U.S.-Canadian dispute over fishing rights in the waters off Nova Scotia. It also set the boundary between Washington state and British Columbia firmly at the 49th parallel in accordance with the Oregon Treaty of 1846.

During Macdonald's ministry, three new provinces entered Confederation. In 1869 the Hudson's Bay Company sold its rights in the West to the Canadian government, but before the transfer was completed the largely French-Indian, or *métis* population of the territory of Red River, led by Louis Riel, rose in protest.

The *métis* feared for the survival of their cultural and property rights if they were forced into Confederation. Macdonald negotiated with Riel and sent troops to nearby Fort Garry to enforce order. Red River entered Confederation on July 15, 1870, as the province of Manitoba.

On July 1, 1871, British Columbia, on the Pacific coast, attracted by generous offers of economic aid and the promise of a transcontinental railway, entered Confederation and completed the rapid expansion of the new Dominion from coast to coast. This milestone was followed on July 1, 1873, by the addition of the Atlantic coast colony of Prince Edward Island, where a financial crisis had overcome earlier opposition to Confederation.

Macdonald's Conservative government, implicated in a railway scandal, lost to the Liberals in 1873. The Liberals' period in office, under Alexander Mackenzie, coincided with an international economic depression. The Liberal government appeared helpless in the face of the crisis, and in 1878 Macdonald was returned to power.

Macdonald's platform in the 1878 election race promised a "national policy" to rebuild the economy. It proposed high protective tariffs, increased railway building, and a stepped-up immigration program. A protective tariff instituted after the election became a central feature of Canadian economic policy, and the Canadian Pacific Railway, with the help of generous government grants, was completed to the Pacific in 1885.

Unfortunately, the expected immigration, without which the railway and the tariff could be of little value, failed to materialize. In addition, the return of world economic depression in the 1880s led to the stagnation of the Canadian economy, which was vulnerable because of its heavy dependence on exports.

Disunity. At that critical time, Canada once again faced old problems. The last two decades of the 1800s were

THE PARLIAMENT BUILDINGS of the Dominion of Canada, in Ottawa, the nation's capital. The buildings house Canada's federal legislature, the Parliament, which has two houses—the Senate, or upper chamber, and the House of Commons, or lower chamber.

marked by the renewal of bitter cultural conflicts between French-speaking Roman Catholics and English-speaking Protestants. This conflict and a strong movement for provincial rights challenged the centralizing policies of Macdonald's nationalism.

In 1885 the *métis* and Indians again joined behind Louis Riel in a second and more serious rebellion, this time in the Northwest Territories. Riel was executed in 1885, and French Canadians blamed his death on political pressure from Ontario Protestants, who sought revenge for Riel's execution of a Protestant during the 1869 revolt.

A new wave of anti-British feeling swept Quebec, and in 1886 the province elected a fiery French-Canadian nationalist, Honoré Mercier, as premier. French Canadians began to turn away from a national government controlled by British votes and toward their own provincial government for protection of their rights.

The English-speaking provinces also experienced strong localist sentiment. Opposition in Manitoba and the Maritimes to Macdonald's centralizing nationalism probably originated in economic depression. Wealthy Ontario, led by the Liberal Premier Oliver Mowat, also challenged the centralist policies of the Conservatives in power at Ottawa.

At the Interprovincial Conference of 1887 the premiers of five of the seven provinces passed resolutions attacking federal interference in provincial matters. Under attack, Macdonald's government partially abandoned such federal policies as the disallowing of laws passed by provincial legislatures.

Provincial power also was enhanced by a series of decisions handed down by the judicial committee of the Privy Council in England, the empire's highest court. By 1896 the central government retained little of the great power provided it by the constitution of 1867.

Macdonald won his last election in 1891, defending his "national policy" against the Liberal's advocacy of provincial rights and of unlimited reciprocity with the United States. His death later in 1891 removed the leading figure in Canadian politics.

Macdonald's Conservative successors were unable to cope with renewed economic depression in the 1890s or with the continuing quarrel between French- and English-speaking Canadians. In 1896 the nation turned to the Liberal Party and its distinguished leader, the French Canadian Wilfrid Laurier.

Laurier Administration. Laurier was dedicated to achieving harmony among the different elements of Canada's population. To reduce cultural conflicts, he advocated stronger provincial rights, and he reconciled many of the conflicts between French- and English-speaking Canadians.

World prosperity enabled the Liberals to succeed on the basis of economic policies introduced by Macdonald's Conservatives. Two new transcontinental railways were constructed with government aid, opening new forest lands and exposing untapped mineral wealth.

Settlers from the United States and Europe moved to the Canadian west in response to an imaginative immigration program. The planting of new types of early-maturing grain and the development of mechanized farming made possible a great wheat boom in the early 1900s. On Sept. 1, 1905, Saskatchewan and Alberta provinces, formed from part of the Northwest Territories, entered Confederation. Canada was filled with an unprecedented sense of self-confidence.

An equally important feature of Laurier's administration was his attitude toward a growing sentiment in Britain for a stronger, more unified empire. Laurier recognized Canada's great need for British support to balance U.S. influence, but he was fully aware of the danger to Canada's national unity and independence in the new British imperial policy. At a series of Imperial Conferences Laurier gradually won a measure of world recognition of Canadian independence without seriously affronting the imperialist element within Canada.

Laurier dealt less successfully with the controversial question of imperial defense. Pressure had been put on him from both Canada and Britain to contribute to the imperial navy, but French Canadians opposed the move. When Laurier attempted to compromise by building a separate Canadian navy, Ontario Conservatives attacked him for doing too little and French Canadians condemned his policy as a surrender to imperialist interests.

Laurier also lost popularity over the Reciprocity Agreement of 1911 that he had negotiated with the United States. Had it been passed, the agreement would have greatly lowered tariffs on goods traded with the United States, but the nation's Liberal manufacturers opposed the agreement. Opposed by French Canadians, Nationalists, some Liberals, and the Conservatives, Laurier lost the election of 1911, and Robert Borden, a Conservative, became prime minister.

World War I. Prime Minister Borden was soon faced by the outbreak of World War I. Canada responded to the war quickly. Over 600,000 men were mobilized, and more than 400,000 went overseas. About 40,000 of them did not return. Canadian farms supplied food for British armies, and Canadian industries provided equipment. French Canadians, however, were not as enthusiastic in their support of the war as were English-speaking Canadians.

A coalition government of Liberals and Conservatives that included no French Canadians called for compulsory military service. The French-speaking population objected, often violently, to being forced to submit to a conscription act of an all-British government. Quebec blamed the Conservative Party for the draft act, and for decades afterward the party was weak in that province.

Interwar Era. After its war effort, Canada was in a position to assert its independence within the British Empire. At the Imperial War Conference of 1917 Prime Minister Borden insisted upon full autonomy for Canada and the right to an equal voice in foreign affairs and imperial defense.

The conference passed a resolution drafted by Borden and Gen. Jan Christiaan Smuts of South Africa, which for the first time officially used the term "Commonwealth." The resolution laid the basis for what was soon called the "dominion status" of certain former colonies of the British Empire.

At the end of the war, Canada signed the Treaty of Versailles, and on Borden's insistence Canada's parliament ratified the treaty separately from Britain. Largely through Borden's efforts, Canada and the other British dominions received the right to sit as independent members of the League of Nations.

Borden's health forced him to retire in 1920, and his successor, Arthur Meighen, was defeated in 1921 by the Liberals led by Mackenzie King. King, Laurier's successor as leader of the Liberals continued and extended Borden's policies of autonomy. In 1931 Canadian independence received legal and constitutional acceptance by the British Parliament in the Statute of Westminster.

Prime Minister King demonstrated a political skill that demoralized opposition parties and an administrative ability that attracted strong leaders to the federal government. King was a sincere social reformer who moved Canada slowly and cautiously towards a system of social welfare.

King introduced old-age pensions, family allowances, and unemployment insurance. In many areas, however, the central government was unable to take action. Responsibility for education, labor relations, highway building, and other government services rested upon the individual provinces.

The constitution had given the federal government the wider powers of taxation, and the provinces—especially those in the poorer Maritime and Prairie regions—found it difficult to maintain the services for which they were constitutionally responsible.

Economic Crisis. The world economic depression of the 1930s worsened the economic problems caused by this imbalance of power and responsibility. The wheat-exporting Prairie Provinces were financially crippled, and the high tariff remedy of the Conservatives, in power under Prime Minister Richard Bennett from 1930 to 1935, was of little help.

Facing an election in 1935, Bennett suddenly introduced his "new deal," consisting of national marketing, wages and hours legislation, and an employment and social insurance law. But the Conservatives were overwhelmingly defeated in 1935, and in 1936 the courts declared the programs unconstitutional.

Mackenzie King's Liberals were returned to power in 1935 and they sought a solution to the depression and to the imbalance between federal taxing power and provincial responsibilities.

In 1937 the federal government appointed the Royal Commission on Dominion-Provincial Relations, which in 1940 recommended that the central government be given the authority to deal with the country's more pressing social needs and that it pay the poorer provinces a series of "adjustment grants" to enable them to maintain the less urgent remaining services. The richer provinces—Ontario, British Columbia, and Alberta—rejected these proposals. World War II provided a temporary solution, however, by allowing the federal government greater power.

Contemporary Canada. Canada entered World War II on Sept. 10, 1939, and Canada's war effort was intense. The country raised $12 billion and completely mobilized its industrial and human resources. Canada emerged from the war with increased prestige and with a new willingness to play its role in the international organizations of the postwar world. After the war the dominion government negotiated temporary agreements with the provinces that included adjustment grants similar to those of the rejected program.

Louis St. Laurent, a French Canadian, succeeded Mackenzie King as prime minister in 1948. The Liberal Party continued its political dominance over the Conservatives as well as over two new protest parties born in the 1930s—the socialist Cooperative Commonwealth Federation and the Social Credit Party. In 1949 Canada gained its tenth province when Newfoundland entered Confederation.

Renewed immigration, rapid industrialization, increased urbanization, and a booming economy created a high standard of living and a stable political situation. Canadians, aided by heavy foreign investment, opened new mining frontiers, developed new oil fields, initiated vast hydroelectric projects, and with the United States began construction of the St. Lawrence Seaway in 1954.

Canada, a founding member of the North Atlantic Treaty Organization (NATO), also played an active role in the United Nations as a "middle power," balancing between the two mighty power blocs of East and West. Under Lester Pearson's guidance as minister of external affairs, Canada took a full share of international responsibilities, including heavy participation in military action with UN forces in Korea.

During the 1950s and 1960s Canada moved ever closer to the United States economically, culturally, and militarily. Many Canadians feared the loss of their national identity as their economy grew more dependent on the United States for markets, imports, and capital. Unrest caused by the increasing speed of movement into the U.S. orbit contributed to a political upheaval in 1957 that swept the Conservatives into power after 22 years of Liberal government.

Economics also played a part in the defeat of the Liberals. Although the country as a whole was enjoying prosperity, not all regions shared in the economic boom. The poorer Atlantic coast and the grain-growing areas in the west had both turned to Conservative provincial governments before the national election. Moreover, Liberal foreign policy was greatly criticized, particularly when the Canadian government sided with the United States in the UN against British action in the 1956 Suez Canal crisis.

John Diefenbaker, a Conservative, became prime minister in 1957, and he offered the country a plan for national development apart from the Canadian-U.S. partnership promoted by the Liberals. Skillfully using Canadian fear of excessive U.S. influence, Diefenbaker represented a resurgence of Canadian national feeling. He presented an attractive alternative to a government many felt had been too long in office.

In power from 1957 to 1963, the Conservatives made substantial achievements. These included enormous wheat sales to communist countries, extended social welfare measures, new tax agreements with the provinces, and the passage of a bill of rights for Canadians. Conservative popularity waned, however, as an economic recession developed. Exports declined, and unemployment rose.

The Conservatives proved themselves particularly inept in foreign affairs. They antagonized Britain by opposing its plans to enter the European Common Market, and irritated the United States by lengthy indecision on an offer to provide nuclear weapons for Canadian forces. In addition, Conservative failure to understand or cope with a new surge of French-Canadian nationalism weakened the government in Quebec.

In 1963, after a bitter campaign, Lester Pearson's Liberal Party returned to power, but without a clear majority in the House of Commons. The Liberals again failed to win a solid majority after another election in 1965, and they were prevented from taking effective action on many important issues.

In 1964 and 1965, despite partisan political quarrelling and several governmental scandals, Canada made progress in reforming parliamentary organization, in further extending social welfare programs, and in insuring the conservation of the nation's vital natural resources. In 1964 parliament decided on a new national flag, a single maple leaf on a field of white and red, to replace the former modified British flag. The change, achieved only after much debate, symbolized Canada's independent nationhood.

In Canadian-U.S. affairs, meetings between Prime Minister Pearson and Pres. Lyndon B. Johnson led to the formation of a joint commission to study the relationships of the two nations and the negotiation of new trade agreements.

Centennial. As Canada celebrated the centennial year of confederation in 1967 with "Expo '67," a world's fair at Montreal, it maintained its position as a middle power in the world and was experiencing tremendous prosperity at home. But many of the same problems that had plagued the nation since its earliest years remained unsolved.

Conflict between French-speaking and English-speaking citizens still smoldered, and a small group of separatists even argued for an independent French-speaking state. The conflict was aggravated in 1967 by France's Pres. Charles de Gaulle's open support for a "free Quebec." Nonetheless, in 1968 a French Canadian, Pierre Elliot Trudeau, was chosen to succeed retiring Prime Minister Pearson.

The relationship between the federal government and the provinces also remained a matter of dispute. Various new proposals were put forth for increasing government services to the poorer provinces without restricting their provincial rights. At the same time, the wealthier western provinces objected to some of the more progressive federal activities in the provinces and turned to conservative leaders.

Canadians still feared domination by the U.S. dollar, and businessmen and politicians debated the effects of foreign investment and U.S. economic influence. But they conceded the contribution of U.S. investment to Canadian prosperity.

Despite its unresolved problems, Canada continued the struggle to maintain its independent existence and to forge a unique, Canadian national identity.

—Peter Oliver; Wilbur Zelinsky

CENTRAL AFRICAN REPUBLIC

Official name: Central African Republic
Area: 239,534 square miles
Population: (1967 est.) 1,459,000
Capital: Bangui (Pop., 1964, urban area, 126,602)
Language: French, Sangho and other African languages
Religion: traditional religions
Currency unit: Franc CFA (African Financial Community)
National holiday: Independence day, December 1

The Central African Republic, a landlocked country in central Africa, is bounded on the north by Chad, on the east by Sudan, on the south by the Congo (Kinshasa) and the Congo (Brazzaville), and on the west by Cameroon. Before receiving its independence from France in 1960, the territory was known as Ubangi-Shari because of its location near the Ubangi and Shari (Chari) rivers.

THE LAND. The Central African Republic lies on a plateau with an average elevation of 2,000 feet above sea level. In the east are mountains with heights ranging up to almost 4,600 feet. There are forests in the south, but savanna woodlands and grasslands cover most of the country. Tributaries of the Shari River, in the north, and of the Ubangi River, to the south, flow through the country.

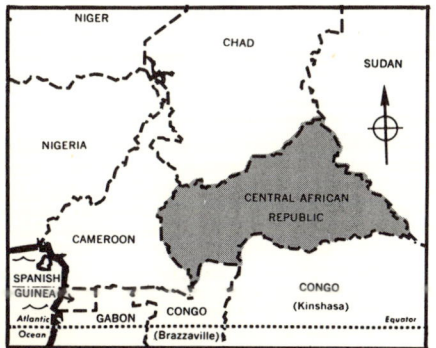

Because of the altitude, the climate is quite mild. Temperatures average between 70°F and 80°F.

THE PEOPLE. The Central African Republic is a sparsely populated country inhabited by peoples of the Mandjia-Baya, Banda, M'Baka, and Zande tribes. The people are mostly farmers. A few thousand Europeans live in Bangui and in other smaller towns.

ECONOMY. The Central African Republic traditionally has been an agricultural country. The main crops are cassava, cotton, and coffee. In the early 1960s diamond mining became important, and by 1965 diamonds accounted for half of the country's exports.

In 1966 imports were valued at $35 million and exports earned $31 million. The Central African Republic is a member of a customs union that includes Cameroon, Chad, the Congo (Brazzaville), and Gabon.

GOVERNMENT. Until 1966 the Central African Republic had a presidential form of government. The president was elected by universal suffrage to a seven-year term of office. Legislative power was vested in a popularly elected, 50-member National Assembly. In 1966 army officers seized control, overthrew the president, and abolished the National Assembly.

The Central African Republic is a member of the United Nations and of the Organization of African Unity (OAU).

HISTORY. Little is known of the early history of the present-day Central African Republic. The French entered the region in the mid-1800s and gave it the name Ubangi-Shari. They met with little opposition from the tribesmen who live there.

In 1899 France permitted private companies to develop the region. Company abuses led to loss of life from forced labor and disease, and loss of capital because of inefficient management. In 1910 France united Ubangi-Shari with present-day Chad, the Congo (Brazzaville), and Gabon in the Federation of French Equatorial Africa.

In 1946 France reorganized the administration and introduced territorial assemblies. Barthelemy Boganda, a political leader in Ubangi-Shari, created the Movement for the Social Evolution of Black Africa (MESAN). Boganda was elected to the territorial assembly in 1952, and by 1956 MESAN had won all the seats in the territorial assembly.

Ubangi-Shari voted to join the French Community in 1958 as an individual member, thus ending the federation of Equatorial Africa. Boganda became the nation's first premier. Ubangi-Shari changed its name to the Central African Republic. Boganda was killed in an airplane crash in 1959, and the assembly elected Boganda's cousin and political associate, David Dacko, president of the republic. Complete independence came on Aug. 13, 1960. Dacko dissolved all opposition parties in 1962, leaving MESAN the sole legal political party.

In 1966, the army chief of staff, Col. Jean Bedel Bokassa, deposed Dacko and assumed the position of chief of state.

—Hibberd V. B. Kline, Jr.; Vera L. Zolberg

CEYLON

Official name: Dominion of Ceylon
Area: 25,332 square miles
Population: (1966 est.) 11,491,000
Capital: Colombo (Pop., 1963, 510,947)
Language: Sinhalese, Tamil, English
Religion: Buddhism, Hinduism
Currency unit: Rupee
National holiday: Independence day, February 4

Ceylon is an island nation lying off the southeastern tip of India. It is separated from India by the Gulf of Mannar and Palk Strait. The Bay of Bengal lies off Ceylon's east coast, and the Indian Ocean lies to the south.

THE LAND. Ceylon's coastline is low and sandy except for the area around the Jaffna Peninsula, in the north, and at Trincomalee, in the east. Both have excellent natural harbors. In the interior of southern Ceylon, mountainous highlands rise from the coastal plain to a peak of over 8,000 feet. The north is largely a flat plain with an elevation only slightly above sea level.

Ceylon has a tropical climate, with average year-round temperatures ranging between 80°F and 100°F. It is cooler in the mountains. Humidity is high throughout the country, but especially in the southwest, where as much as 200 inches of rain a year may fall. About 50 inches falls yearly on the rest of the country.

THE PEOPLE. More than two-thirds of the people of Ceylon are Sinhalese, and speak Sinhalese, an Indic language. Most are Buddhist. Almost one-quarter of the people are Tamils, a people of southern Indian origin who speak Tamil, a Dravidian language. Most Tamils are Hindus. The Tamils are divided between "Ceylon Tamils," those who have been Ceylonese for many generations, and "Indian Tamils," the descendants of Indian laborers brought to the island in the 1800s.

Smaller minorities include Muslim Arabs, "Burghers"—descendants of Dutch colonists, Eurasians, Muslim Malays, and Veddas, descendants of the island's first settlers. Relations among the various groups have not always been good, and there have been bitter conflicts between the Sinhalese and the Tamils.

The population is concentrated in the southwestern corner of the island and in places along the coasts. The population is growing at a rapid rate, 2.6 percent a year between 1958 and 1965.

ECONOMY. Ceylon's economy is based almost completely on agriculture, and the soil is Ceylon's most important natural resource. There are deposits of graphite and precious gems. The leading crops, tea, rubber, coconuts, and spices, are grown on large plantations. Tea is grown in the highlands, rubber in the wet lowlands, and coconuts in drier coastal regions. Small farms produce rice and vegetables. Fish are abundant off the coasts.

Ceylon's few industries are mainly concerned with processing tea, rubber, and coconuts. Manufacturing increased during the 1960s, and there are factories producing textiles, cement, soap, and other consumer items. In 1967 construction began on an oil refinery.

PICKING TEA IN CEYLON. Tea is one of Ceylon's major crops and an important export.

Ceylon relies heavily on foreign trade for many commodities. In 1966 its exports earned $357 million and its imports cost $426 million. Tea, rubber, and coconut products make up more than 90 percent of exports. The major imports include foodstuffs, petroleum products, fertilizers, textiles, and machinery. Ceylon trades mainly with India, Britain, the United States, and China. Technical and financial aid from the United States, Britain, and west and east European countries is important to Ceylon.

GOVERNMENT. Ceylon has a parliamentary system of government. The British monarch is head of state, and is represented in Ceylon by a governor-general. Actual executive power is wielded by a prime minister and cabinet responsible to parliament. Ceylon's parliament has two houses. Members of the lower house are popularly elected. The upper house is partly appointed by the governor-general and partly elected by the lower house.

Ceylon is a member of the United Nations and of the Commonwealth of Nations.

HISTORY. Ceylon's first known inhabitants were a primitive people, the Veddas. In the 500s BC they were conquered by the Sinhalese, an Aryan people from northern India. The Sinhalese established a kingdom in the north central portion of the island, constructing irrigation works to enable them to grow rice in the dry region. By the 200s BC Sinhalese civilization was quite advanced, and its culture, centered on Buddhism, had produced many magnificent temples, especially in the capital at Anduradhapura.

The kingdom was subjected to repeated attacks and invasions by peoples from southern India, and it was conquered in the 900s AD by the Chola empire. The Chola were driven out in the 1000s, but some Chola cultural influences remained. During the 1000s Arab traders began to stop at Ceylon, and some settled on the island.

Between the 1200s and the 1400s the island was attacked repeatedly by Malay and Chinese adventurers, as well as by Indians. In the 1300s the Hindu Tamil people of southern India invaded Ceylon and settled in the northern part of the island, forcing the Sinhalese to the south.

European Influence. In the 1500s Portuguese traders arrived in Ceylon, drawn by the high quality of the cinnamon that the islanders grew. They destroyed the Tamil kingdom and established control over the coastal regions of Sinhalese territory. The Sinhalese retreated to the highland interior, around Kandy. In 1638 traders of the Dutch East India Company arrived.

By 1658, aided by the king of Kandy, the Dutch had driven out the Portuguese and taken over the spice trade. The Dutch exerted little control over the island's government. During the 1600s and 1700s the Sinhalese Kingdom of Kandy underwent a cultural revival and grew in power, controlling some smaller islands in the Indian Ocean.

In 1796 the British replaced the Dutch in the coastal areas, and in 1802 made them a crown colony. By 1815, with the aid of some of the Kandyans, the British took control of the entire island, including Kandy. The British expanded the area of cultivated land, planted tea and rubber, and improved irrigation facilities in the drier north. They established schools and introduced Western forms of government.

In 1931 Ceylon was granted limited self-government. Parliamentary elections were held in 1947, and on Feb. 4, 1948, Ceylon was granted sovereignty as an independent member of the Commonwealth of Nations.

Independence. Independent Ceylon concentrated on developing its economy and improving the lot of its people through social welfare programs. From the mid-1950s to the mid-1960s Ceylonese politics were dominated by the socialist Sri Lanka Freedom Party (SLFP). S. W. R. D. Bandaranaike, leader of the SLFP, was prime minister from 1956 until his assassination in 1959. Under his widow, who became prime minister in 1960, the country followed strongly socialist policies, and many businesses were nationalized. The government's methods were unpopular, and it fell in 1964.

Under the more moderate United National Party (UNP) elected in 1965, the socialist program continued, but encouragement was given to private business in an effort to speed economic growth. The UNP government concentrated on uniting the many factions of Ceylon's society.

Rioting broke out in 1966 when the government introduced legislation permitting the official use of the Tamil language in Tamil areas, but the legislation was passed. A graver problem, the citizenship of Indian Tamils, was resolved in 1967, when an agreement was ratified by which India agreed to repatriate some Indian Tamils and Ceylon agreed to grant citizenship to the rest.

—Thomas E. Ennis; M. G. Inaba

CHAD

Official name: Republic of Chad
Area: 495,752 square miles
Population: (1966 est.) 3,361,000
Capital: Fort-Lamy (Pop., 1964 est., urban area, 99,000)
Language: French, Arabic, Sara
Religion: Christianity, Islam, traditional religions
Currency unit: Franc CFA (African Financial Community)
National holiday: Independence day, January 11

Chad, a large, landlocked republic in central Africa, is bounded on the north by Libya, on the east by Sudan, on the south by the Central African Republic and Cameroon, and on the west by Nigeria and Niger. The country derives its name from Lake Chad, which is located on its western border.

THE LAND. Most of Chad is a vast plain. The northern region of the country forms part of the Sahara. Grasslands cover central and southern Chad. The country's lowest point is the dry Bodele Depression, in north-central Chad. In the extreme north is the Tibasti Massif, with elevations of about 11,000 feet. The country's most important rivers are the Shari and the Logone.

Northern Chad is hot and dry and receives less than 10 inches of rain a year. The climate in the south is more tropical, and rainfall averages about 40 inches a year.

THE PEOPLE. Chad is a sparsely populated country. The composition of Chad's population differs in each part of the country. Arabs and Hamitic people live in the north. People of the Sara tribe, the largest tribal group in Chad, live in the south.

Most of the people are either farmers or herdsmen. Chad's major cities are concentrated in the southern part of the country. They include Fort-Lamy, the capital, and Moundou.

ECONOMY. Chad's economy depends on agriculture. The people grow cotton, millet, and peanuts. Cattle are raised in some parts of the country. There is practically no mineral production, and the country's few industries are hampered by a lack of transportation facilities.

In 1966 exports were valued at $24 million and imports cost $32 million. The most important export is cotton. Chad imports petroleum, textiles, machinery, and transportation equipment. Most trade is with France.

GOVERNMENT. Chad has a presidential system of government. Executive power is vested in the president. Legislative power is held by a popularly elected National Assembly. The National Assembly votes on the presidential candidate proposed by the country's sole legal political party, the Chad Progressive Party. The people then vote for or against the candidate. The president holds office for an indefinite term.

Chad is a member of the United Nations and of the Organization of African Unity (OAU).

HISTORY. The area that is now Chad was for many centuries an important crossroads. From about 200 BC to AD 1000, its inhabitants maintained close contacts with the peoples of the Nile Valley, with whom they shared a fairly similar culture.

Christianity flourished in central Chad in about 300 AD. Later, nomadic peoples from Darfur, in Sudan, overran Chad, dispersed the indigenous inhabitants, and created an empire known as Kanem in the region near Lake Chad. In the 1000s Islam penetrated the area. From about that time the peoples of Chad strengthened their commercial ties with the Mediterranean coast.

In the period from about 1000 to 1600 there were a number of violent internal and foreign wars. As a result of those conflicts, the Kanem empire moved its center to Bornu, on the southwestern side of Lake Chad in what is now northern Nigeria.

Both the sultanate of Bagirmi and the Wadai empire became powerful in Chad, and maintained their control until the late 1800s. At that time Rabeh, a warlord and slave trader from Sudan, gained control of Chad.

The French, who had established themselves in Chad in the 1890s, defeated Rabeh in 1900 and proceeded to conquer all of Chad. The present boundaries of Chad were established in 1913, and in 1920 Chad became a member of the Federation of French Equatorial Africa.

During World War II Chad supported Free France and contained important Allied bases. Postwar politics were at first largely controlled by the French. After 1958, however, African leaders rapidly gained prominence. France gave Chad its independence in August 1960, and François Tombalbaye became the country's first president.

—Hibberd V. B. Kline, Jr.;
Robert I. Rotberg

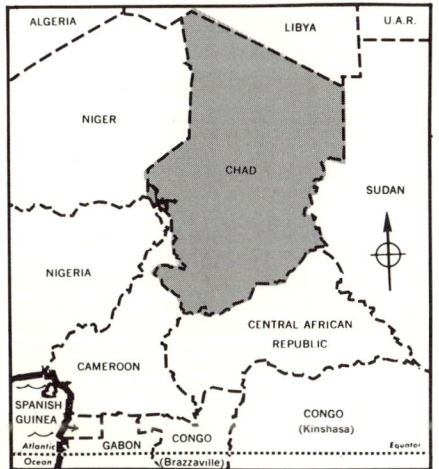

CHILE

Official name: Republic of Chile
Area: 292,256 square miles
Population: (1966 est.) 8,750,000
Capital: Santiago (Pop., 1965 est., urban area, 2,248,400)
Language: Spanish
Religion: Roman Catholicism
Currency unit: Escudo
National holiday: Independence day, September 18

Chile is a long, narrow country on the western coast of South America. It stretches 2,650 miles from north to south, but averages only 100 miles in width. The country has imposing natural boundaries. On the north the Atacama Desert separates Chile from Peru; on the northeast and east the Andes separate the country from Bolivia and Argentina; on the south the Drake Passage separates Chile from Antarctica; and on the west is the Pacific Ocean.

THE LAND. The highest mountain in the western hemisphere, Mt. Aconcagua (22,834 feet), lies on the Chile-Argentina border. The Chilean Andes form a single mountain range in the east, and there is a low coastal mountain range in the west. A central valley nearly 500 miles long nestles between the two parallel ranges.

Northern Chile, the desert region, is very dry, and there are weather stations there that have no record of rain ever having fallen. The region has rich mineral resources. The central valley has a mild climate, with a winter rainy season and summer drought. It is the heartland of the country. Almost 90 percent of the people live there, and it produces most of the country's domestic food supply.

Southern Chile is wet and heavily forested. The land is said to resemble Switzerland because of its high, snow-capped mountains and glacial lakes. Temperatures average in the low 50°s F. In the extreme south, at the end of the continent, are Patagonia and Tierra del Fuego. The area has steep slopes, heavy rainfall, low temperatures, and high winds. It is very sparsely populated.

THE PEOPLE. Approximately 25 percent of Chile's population is of European descent. Most of the rest is mestizo, of mixed Spanish and Indian heritage.

About 100,000 Araucanian Indians live in the forests of south-central Chile. Changos live along the northeastern frontier and are employed in the mines. Groups of nomadic Fuegians inhabit Tierra del Fuego.

A dominant trend in Chile is the movement of people from the rural areas to the urban centers. The capital, Santiago, has sizable suburbs, as does Valparaiso, the principal port, which had a 1964 population of over 270,000. The country's third major city is Concepción, located in the center of Chile on the Bío-Bío River. Smaller cities such as Talcahuano, Puerto Montt, and Punta Arenas, the most southerly city, are important ports.

ECONOMY. Chile is largely dependent on the exploitation of its mineral resources, which are found primarily within the Atacama Desert. In 1965,

for example, copper, iron ore, and nitrates made up four-fifths of the total value of Chilean exports.

Chile has long been a world leader in copper and nitrate production, but in the early 1960s iron ore replaced nitrates as the country's second most important export. In 1965 Chile ranked third in world copper production and tenth in the production of iron ore. Iodine, a by-product of nitrate, has also become an important export, and by the mid-1960s Chile was producing 75 percent of the world's supply.

Agreements with foreign mining companies provide for a portion of the profits to remain in Chile, and the income has aided the development of the entire economy.

Only a fraction of Chile's total land area is suitable for cultivation, and only a small part of that is used. Chile's Central Valley is the main agricultural region. The principal crops are wheat, barley, and oats. Livestock raising is also important, but neither cattle nor crop production is adequate for Chile's needs, and foodstuffs must be imported.

Chile is one of the most industrialized countries in South America. The Huachipato steel plant, inaugurated in 1951, meets almost all Chile's requirements. Chile also manufactures a variety of consumer goods for domestic consumption including textiles, medicines, shoes, paper, and cement. Major industrial centers are in the provinces of Santiago, Valparaiso, and Concepción.

In 1966 Chile's exports were valued at $878 million and imports cost $755 million. Major exports are copper, iron ore, nitrates and iodine, fish meal, beans, lentils, wool, and paper. Principal imports include industrial raw materials, industrial and agricultural machinery and equipment, vehicles, petroleum, and consumer goods.

Most exports go to the United States, Britain, West Germany, the Netherlands, and Japan. Imports come largely from the United States, Argentina, West Germany, and Britain.

GOVERNMENT. Chile is a republic with a strong tradition of constitutional government. The head of state and chief executive is the president, who is popularly elected to a term of six years and is not eligible for reelection.

Legislative power is vested in the National Congress, which consists of a Senate and Chamber of Deputies. The Senate has 45 members, but the number of members of the Chamber of Deputies, which is based on the size of the population, varies. Senators and Deputies are directly elected, senators to a term of eight years and deputies to a term of four years.

Chile is a member of the United Nations and the Organization of American States (OAS).

HISTORY. During the 1400s, the northern part of Chile had come under the influence of the Inca empire. The extent of Inca control is not known, but it did not extend to the warlike Araucanian Indians who lived in the southern forest region. The Spaniards, under Pedro de Valdivia, conquered Chile in 1541 but were unable to defeat the Araucanians, who were not completely subdued until the late 1800s.

In the more open central portion of Chile Spain created a stable agricultural colony, and Chile was part of the Viceroyalty of Peru until the 1800s.

The first move toward independence was made in September 1810, when Chileans established an autonomous junta to rule during the absence of the Spanish king, Ferdinand VII, who was held prisoner by Napoleon. The patriot regime was suppressed in 1814 by loyalist forces from Peru.

The Spanish were finally defeated in 1817–1818 by the army of José de San Martin, which crossed the Andes from Argentina. San Martin's Chilean comrade-in-arms, Bernardo O'Higgins, was made provisional ruler of Chile with the title of Supreme Director.

Independence. O'Higgins gave Chile a generally sound and progressive administration. Nonetheless, he antagonized Chile's powerful class of wealthy landowners by his efforts at mild social reform and his concentration of authority in his own hands. In 1823 he was forced to resign. Chile was then plunged into a brief period of turmoil during which rival political factions battled for control.

In 1830 the Conservatives came to power under the leadership of Diego Portales. Although he never assumed the presidency, Portales nonetheless created a strong centralized government while holding various cabinet posts. Portales was assassinated in 1837 while organizing a military campaign against a confederation of Peru and Bolivia, which he believed posed a threat to Chile. Chile won the war and broke the confederation in 1839.

An Era of Growth. From the 1840s through the 1880s, Chile made notable social and material progress, although those who benefited most were the upper and middle classes. Educational facilities were expanded, religious toleration and the abolition of entailed estates were peacefully achieved. Economic development was aided by the extension of railway and coastal steam navigation, and by the final subjugation of the Araucanians.

From 1879 to 1883 Chile fought Bolivia and Peru in the War of the Pacific, which began as a dispute over Bolivia's treatment of Chilean nitrate interests in the Atacama region. Chile won the war and annexed the nitrate-producing provinces of Peru and Bolivia. A Chilean nitrate boom followed and lasted until the development of synthetic nitrates during World War I.

Commerce, manufacturing, and coal and copper mining grew during the same period. This progress was accompanied by the rapid growth of an urban and mining proletariat, whose poor working conditions led to serious unrest in the early 1900s.

Call for Reforms. Chile had moved toward a system of constitutional rule in which the legislative branch established its supremacy over the executive. Confirmation of this trend was assured by a civil war in 1891, in which an attempt by Pres. José Manuel Balmaceda to reassert presidential authority was defeated. Congress was controlled by parties representing the landed aristocracy and the allied urban upper class, and little was done to improve the conditions of Chilean labor.

Chile remained neutral during World War I. The economy was stimulated by the wartime need for nitrates, but was badly hurt when prices dropped after peace was declared. Social and political dissatisfaction on the part of the middle and working classes increased and resulted in the election in 1920 of Arturo Alessandri, who had run on an ambitious reform platform. Once in office, however, Alessandri had little success in carrying out his program and was forced to resign.

From 1924 to 1932 constitutional government was severely shaken. There were numerous changes of administration and even a mild dictatorship from 1927–1931 under reform-minded Gen. Cárlos Ibañez. Nevertheless, Chile emerged from this period of turmoil with a start in labor legislation and a new constitution designed to end congressional domination of the executive.

Alessandri, allied with both Conservatives and Liberals, returned to the presidency in 1932 and successfully restored the pattern of constitutional government. He was succeeded in 1938 by Pedro Aguirre Cedra, whose Popular Front administration drew support from both socialists and communists, although Aguirre Cedra himself was from the generally moderate Radical party.

The Popular Front sponsored additional benefits for labor, including government medical programs and low-cost housing. It collapsed during World War II, and for the following 20 years Chile was ruled by a succession of middle-of-the-road and right-of-center administrations.

Contemporary Chile. Despite a high degree of political freedom and stability, and a seemingly impressive body of social legislation, Chile still had not really solved its social problems. Almost nothing had been done for the landless rural masses, and the standard of living of urban workers did not keep pace with overall national economic gains.

Persistent inflation became a major problem, and in the late 1950s a vigorous socialist-communist alliance showed signs of growing political strength. This was counterbalanced by the rapid rise of the Christian Democratic Party, which called for fundamental changes in social structure—including land redistribution—while rejecting both communism and traditional capitalism.

The Christian Democrats finally gained power in 1964, when their leader, Eduardo Frei Montalva, was elected president. Frei set about effecting basic changes in Chile's economic and social life under the slogan "revolution within liberty and law." His program called for part ownership by the government of the copper mines and included a broad agrarian reform program.

—David Bushnell; Kempton E. Webb

CHILEAN STEEL PLANT at Talcahuano, near the important industrial city of Concepción.

CHINESE SAMPANS dock in the harbor at Shanghai, near modern office buildings.

AGRICULTURE IN COMMUNIST CHINA still depends heavily on human labor. Despite the country's rapid industrialization, agriculture remains the prime factor in the economy.

CHINA

COMMUNIST CHINA
Official name: People's Republic of China
Area: 3,692,000 square miles
Population: (1966 est.) 710,000,000
Capital: Peking (Pop., 1957 est., 4,010,000)
Language: Chinese
Currency unit: Yuan

NATIONALIST CHINA
Official name: Republic of China
Area: 13,886 square miles
Population: (1967 est.) 13,142,000
Capital: Taipei (Pop., 1964 est., 1,085,100)
Language: Chinese
Currency unit: New Taiwan dollar
National holiday: National Day, October 10

China, an ancient land of East Asia, is one of the world's largest nations and contains nearly one quarter of the world's people. Since 1949 two governments have claimed to represent China's people—one, the People's Republic of China, a communist state controlling the mainland of China; and the other, the Republic of China, occupying Taiwan, or Formosa, an island off the mainland's east coast.

The Republic of China, or Nationalist China, is recognized as the legal government of China by the United States and represents China in the United Nations. The People's Republic of China, called Communist China or Mainland China, is recognized by the Soviet Union and the world's communist-ruled nations as well as by many other countries, including Britain and France.

Mainland China is bounded on the north by the Mongolian People's Republic and the Soviet Union; on the east by North Korea, the Yellow Sea, the East China Sea, and the Formosa Strait; on the south by British Hong Kong and Portuguese Macao, the South China Sea, North Vietnam, Laos, Burma, India, Bhutan, Sikkim, and Nepal; and on the west by India, Pakistan, Afghanistan, and the Soviet Union. Many of the boundaries are disputed. The large island of Hainan off China's southern coast is controlled by the mainland.

The Republic of China, on Taiwan, is bordered on the north by the East China Sea, on the east by the Philippine Sea, on the south by the South China Sea, and on the west by the Formosa Strait. The P'enghu archipelago (the Pescadores Islands) in the Formosa Strait are controlled by the republic.

THE LAND. China is an immense country, and only the Soviet Union and Canada are larger in area. Mainland China's length from east to west is approximately the same as that of the United States, and its range from north to south is equivalent to that from Puerto Rico to Labrador.

China's 4,000-mile-long coastline is deeply indented and dotted with small islands. The North China coast is flat and shallow, the South China coast is steep and rocky. The North China coast has few harbors, but there are many good harbors along the south coast.

The huge area of Mainland China is divided into 21 provinces, five autonomous nationality regions, and two municipalities—Peking, the capital, and Shanghai. The autonomous regions are more than administrative units. Each of the five—Kwangsi-Chuang, Tibet, Sinkiang-Uighur, Ningsia-Hui, and Inner Mongolia—contains a majority of non-Chinese people, and each has a history and culture different from China's.

Nor are the provinces merely administrative subdivisions. There is a cultural connotation to the units, which have recognizable dialects, if not individual languages, and customs, social patterns, and traditions, within the larger framework of Chinese culture. Identification with provincial birthplace and the banding together of provincial compatriots have long characterized Chinese society.

Regions. Geographically, it is conventional to divide Mainland China into five regions—China Proper, Manchuria, Tibet, Sinkiang, and Mongolia. China Proper, the region south of the Great Wall and east of Tibet, occupies a third of the land. It is the geographical and historical core of the country, containing the bulk of the population and the roots of Chinese civilization.

The other four regions comprise what is often called Outer China. Manchuria, northeast of China Proper, is more sparsely populated and contains rich mineral deposits. Tibet, in the southwest, lies high in the Himalayas and has a very small population. Sinkiang, in the northwest, is arid and inhabited mainly by Uighur peoples. The Mongolian region, Inner Mongolia, north of China Proper, is arid and peopled primarily by Mongols.

Uplands. Highlands dominate China's terrain. High mountains thrusting eastward from the southwest include the Himalayas and their foothills, the Thanglha Ri, the Kunlun, the Astin Tagh, and the Nan Shan, with many peaks over 20,000 feet.

These mountain systems and the high, barren plateau of Tibet in their center form the world's most formidable land barrier, separating the Hindu civilization of South Asia from the Chinese civilization of East Asia. The eastern edge of these mountains also contains the sources of China's two great rivers, the Yangtze and the Hwang Ho, the Yellow River.

Between this mountainous mass and a northern spur, the towering Tien Shan in Sinkiang, is the Takla Makan, a desert lying about 8,000 feet above sea level. The center of the Dzungarian Basin in northern Sinkiang is also desert, separating the Tien Shan from the Altai mountains, which mark the Sinkiang-Soviet-Mongolian border.

Arid, flat or rolling highlands continue across the northern rim of China. They include the Alashan desert, bordered on the south and east by the

Ala mountains; the Ordos desert, east of the Alashan desert; and the eastern fringe of the Gobi desert, bounded on the east by the Greater Khingan range, which marks the western edge of Manchuria.

South and east of these barriers of towering mountains and barren deserts, China Proper and Manchuria are crisscrossed by less formidable highlands that follow two major sets of intersecting structural areas, one trending northeast to southwest and the other intersecting it from east to west.

The northeast-southwest axis is marked in the east by the Fukien Massif of hills along the southeast coast, the rounded mountains of the Shantung and Liaotung peninsulas, and the Manchurian highlands bordering Korea in the northeast. The central portion of this axis is formed by the Greater Khingan range in Manchuria and the Wut'ai and Luya ranges in Shansi province further south.

This line is a major physical and cultural division of eastern Asia. To the west of it elevations are from 3,000 to 6,000 feet higher than to its east. The west is arid, the east is humid; the western economy is based upon pastoral activities, the eastern on sedentary agriculture. Following the axis west of this core section are the Ala Shan.

The series of east-west trending chains is represented at the far north by the Lesser Khingan mountains, at the southern edge of Mongolia by the Yin Shan, and in the far south by the Nan Ling mountains, a series of hills and low mountains between the Yangtze and the Hsi rivers. By far the most important mountains of the east-west axis are those of the Ch'in Ling, which bisect China Proper.

The Ch'in Ling has a physical and cultural significance similar to that of the north-south Khingan divide. South China, below these mountains, is generally warm and humid whereas north China tends to be cold and dry.

Lowlands. China's few major lowlands and plateaus lie in China Proper and Manchuria, among the intersecting lines of highlands. In the northeast the Manchurian Plain, about 130,000 square miles in area, is bounded by the Khingan mountains, the East Manchurian Highlands, and the Gulf of Liaotung. It is drained by the Sungari River in the north and the Liao River in the south. Its grasslands contain some of China's most fertile soils.

The flat and fertile North China Plain, also about 130,000 square miles in area, is essentially a giant compound delta of the Hwang, the Huai, and the Yangtze rivers. The loess plateau is a dissected region in North China. About 120,000 of its 200,000 square miles is covered with loess, a deep layer of loose dust and silt. It is watered by the Hwang Ho, to which its dust imparts a yellow color.

The 100,000-square-mile Yangtze Basin contains lakes Tungt'ing and P'oyang, which serve as natural reservoirs for the Yangtze River. The basin is rich with alluvial soils. The mountain-ringed Szechwan basin on the upper Yangtze River includes about 75,000 square miles of rolling terrain.

The most important region in south China, the Canton lowlands, is the compound delta of the Hsi, Pei, and Pearl rivers, bordering on the South China Sea. Although only some 3,000 square miles in area, it is a key agricultural, industrial, and commercial center.

Rivers. Almost all of China's rivers, which are concentrated in the eastern portion of the country, flow east or south toward the sea. The most important in the south is the Hsi, formed by the Yu, the Li, and other streams flowing from the eastern Tibetan foothills.

The Yangtze rises in the east Kunlun mountains and twists some 3,200 miles through south-central China, passing through deeply etched gorges in Szechwan and emptying into the East China Sea at Shanghai.

The Hwang Ho rises near the Yangtze and flows north along a winding course, making a great bend northward around the Ordos desert and on eastward between Shansi and Honan provinces. It empties into the Gulf of Chihli, an inlet of the Yellow Sea.

Both the Huang and the Yangtze are subject to frequent and vicious floods and sudden changes of course, but both supply the water and the soil to raise food for the huge concentration of people in their valleys.

Climate. Most of Mainland China lies within the temperate zone, but the climate varies greatly from region to region. Manchuria has a subhumid continental type of climate. Winters there are long and severe. A mild growing season lasts for about 5 months, and rainfall is generally less than 20 inches a year.

Northwestern China, the region bordering Mongolia, has a semi-arid to arid climate. Precipitation is under 20 inches a year and frequently less than 10 inches. Winters are long and severe, and the growing season is less than 200 days.

North China, the southern portions of Manchuria, the loess highlands, and the northern half of the North China Plain form a transitional region between the arid continental north and the humid subtropical south. The growing season ranges from 150 to 225 days, and the annual precipitation averages 15 to 30 inches.

Within the Yangtze lake region and the delta of the Yangtze Basin, the summers are hot and humid and the winters are generally mild. The frost-free period is 225 to 280 days. Precipitation averages 45 to 80 inches a year with the peak rainy period in June and July.

South China, except in its higher elevations, is a warm and humid region. The frost-free period is 300 to 365 days. There is no dry period, and average annual precipitation varies from 50 to 80 inches. Along the coast typhoons bring high winds and heavy downpours from July to October. In the far south, including Hainan Island, the climate tends toward the tropical.

Climatic conditions in southwest China are intermediate between those of subtropical China and Tibet. Temperatures are generally mild. Precipitation ranges from 40 to 60 inches a year, with the peak period coming during the summer season.

Much of Tibet above 16,000 foot elevations has a tundra-type climate with less than 4 inches of precipitation yearly. Temperatures average about 10°F in January and 45°F in July.

Large parts of Sinkiang and Mongolia are occupied by midlatitude continental deserts. Precipitation is extremely limited, and many areas in the two regions receive less than 5 inches of rain a year.

Taiwan. Nationalist China's island of Taiwan is also mountainous. Its major range, the Chungyang, runs from north to south in the eastern third of the island. It contains many peaks over 10,000 feet high, and its highest peak, Yü Shan, is more than 13,000 feet high. To the east, across a narrow rift valley, a coastal range rises to a maximum of 7,000 feet and then drops sharply into the sea. Many rivers flow east and west from the Chungyang.

To the west of the mountains the land slopes to a fertile coastal plain that is the heartland of the island. It is only some 25 miles at its widest, but its width is being extended by continuous sedimentation along the shallow west coast. The west coast contains the island's best harbors.

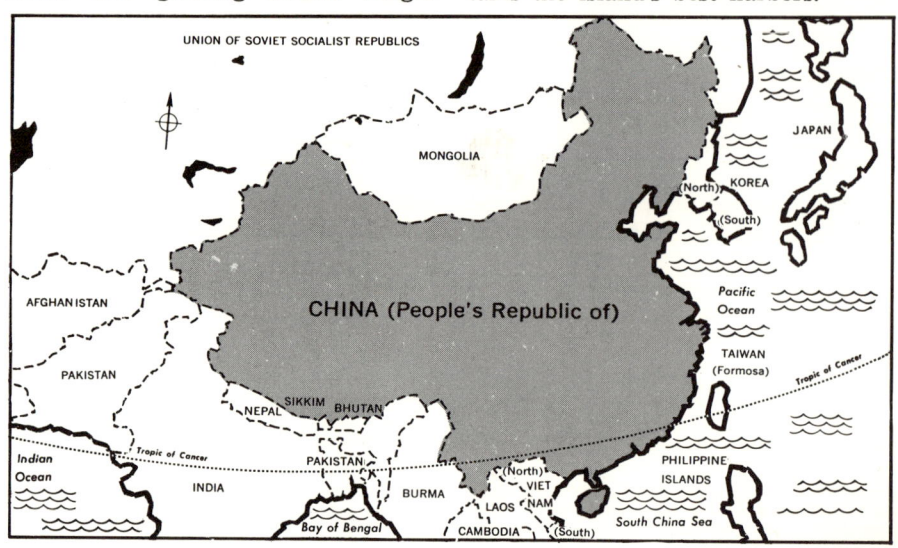

Taiwan's climate is semitropical. Annual precipitation varies from 50 inches in the mountains to 200 inches on the coasts. During winter, from October to April, north to northeast winds bring much rain to the northern areas. In summer, the winds are chiefly from the south and southwest, and it is during this period that most of the south receives its maximum rain. From May to November, the island may be struck by typhoons.

Temperatures in the lowlands rarely drop below 60°F. The higher elevations are colder, and the higher peaks have prolonged snow cover.

THE PEOPLE. With a 1966 population estimated by the United Nations at 710 million and by the U.S. census bureau at between 760 and 894 million, Communist China contains approximately one-quarter of the world's people. Its rate of population growth was estimated by the UN at 1.5 percent a year in the 1950s and 1960s, representing a tremendous numerical increase each year.

About 90 percent of the people live in the eastern third of China, where population density averages more than 500 people per square mile. Over the years, many thousands of Chinese have emigrated, largely from South China, and formed large communities in Southeast Asia and elsewhere throughout the world.

Although many ethnic groups make up China's population, more than 90 percent of the people are of the Han group, the people commonly considered "Chinese." The Han have great cultural unity and share the same written language, but they speak innumerable regional dialects of Chinese.

The Cantonese dialect, for example, is widely spoken in the south, and the Peking dialect, or Mandarin, is the national language (*Kuo-Yü*) and is taught in the schools throughout China. Most people adhere to a Chinese religious pattern that is a combination of Buddhism, Taoism, Confucianism, and animism.

About 6 percent of China's people are non-Han Chinese. They belong to more than 50 different ethnic groups that live in the areas surrounding China Proper. The Chuang, a Thai-speaking people in southeastern China, are the largest minority. The Yi, also in the south, is another large group. Along the western and northwestern frontiers Tibetans, Uighurs, and Mongols are in the majority, and the Manchu peoples, related to the Mongols, are concentrated in the northeast.

Taiwan. Taiwan was settled by Chinese from Fukien and Kwantung provinces during the period from the 1600s to the 1900s. There was a large influx of people from all parts of the mainland in the late 1940s and early 1950s. There are also small numbers of aborigines who come from Polynesian stock.

Taiwan is densely populated, with over 900 people per square mile in 1966. A very high rate of population growth slowed to a still rapid 3.4 percent a year increase between 1958 and 1965.

ECONOMY. China has traditionally been an agricultural land, and this remains true for Mainland China despite considerable industrialization since the advent of the communist regime in 1949.

Natural Resources. Exploration and development of the mainland's mineral resources was not undertaken on a large scale until the 1950s and 1960s. The country has oil, iron ore, and coal in Manchuria, Sinkiang, and in the central Yangtze basin.

There are also large supplies of tungsten, antimony, manganese, tin, bauxite, copper, mercury, molybdenum, lead, and zinc. Magnesite, sulfur, bismuth, mica, and graphite deposits are also worked, mostly in Manchuria. The extent of mineral resources in remote regions is unknown.

Agriculture. Farming occupies about 80 percent of the population, and in 1965 agriculture contributed one-half of the national product. The poor climate, rough terrain, and inadequate soils or water prohibit farming in much of China. With an estimated 270 million acres, or about 11 percent of China's total area, under cultivation, there is less than half an acre of farm land per person.

The major growing regions are in Manchuria, the North China Plain, the Lower Yangtze basin and delta, the Szechwan basin, the Wei and Fen river valleys, the Han river valley, the Canton delta, and the lower Hsi valley. Most of these are both dependent upon floods for soil and water and endangered by heavy flooding.

During the 1950s the communist government initiated a program of total collectivization of agriculture. Most farm households were organized into communes, and private property was virtually eliminated. The project was a failure, however, and in the early 1960s most of China's peasant farmers had returned to more traditional patterns of living. China's farmers remained organized into local cooperatives, however.

The chief crops are wheat, raised chiefly in North China and Manchuria, and rice, grown mainly in the Yangtze basin and South China. Other important crops include barley, millet, kaoliang, soybeans, cotton, tobacco, and tea. There is little livestock raising, but there is some fishing off the coasts and in the rivers.

Industry. The communist regime of Mainland China has emphasized the development of heavy industry and transportation, and by 1965 industry contributed an estimated 26 percent of the national product of Communist China. China's traditional industries, such as textiles, continued to play an important role in the economy.

Industrial development advanced rapidly in the 1950s with financial and technical aid from the Soviet Union. But attempts to move ahead too rapidly created serious problems in the late 1950s. The economy had recovered by the early 1960s, but political and social upheavals associated with the Red Guard movement in the mid-1960s again slowed development.

By the mid-1960s, however, Chinese manufactured goods could be found in the markets of Southeast Asia, and many nations looked at Communist China as a potential competitor.

Trade. Agriculture provides about two-thirds of Mainland China's exports, although precise trade figures are not available. Textiles, minerals, light manufactures, and parts for machinery are also exported. Foodstuffs, machinery, and industrial raw materials are major imports.

Communist China's trade was once solely with communist countries, especially the Soviet Union. By the mid-1960s, however, about two-thirds of the Mainland's trade was with non-communist nations, notably Japan, the Southeast Asian countries, France, Britain, and Canada.

Taiwan. The Republic of China had more success in moving from an agricultural to an agricultural-industrial economy in the 1950s. By the mid-1960s it was a very prosperous country with one of the highest per capita incomes in Asia.

The island's mineral resources are limited. Coal is mined in the north, and there is some petroleum, natural gas, sulfur, and salt.

The island's chief natural resource is the water power of streams that rush from the Chungyang mountains. Between 1958 and 1965 the production of electricity rose sharply, from 2.7 billion kilowatt hours (kwh) in 1957 to 6.6 billion kwh in 1965.

Agriculture continued to play an important role in the economy, however, contributing over 26 percent of the domestic product in 1965 and employing a little more than half the labor force. As only one-quarter of the island's land can be cultivated, farming is intensive and two or three crops a year are raised on the same land.

Rice is the major crop, and the staple of the diet. Sugarcane, raised primarily for export, is second in importance. Sweet potatoes, soybeans, tea, peanuts, and fruits are also significant items.

Industry contributed 24 percent of the island's domestic product in 1965. Most of the industry, developed with large-scale foreign aid, especially U.S. aid, consists of light manufacturing. Food processing is the most important industry, but textiles, machinery parts, glass, and rubber goods are also leading products.

Taiwan has a rather poor balance of trade. In 1966 imports cost $623 million and exports earned only $536 million, but the gap was closing. Sugar, fruit, textiles, and light manufactures are exported. Foodstuffs, machinery, fuels, and textile fibers are imported. The United States and Japan are Taiwan's leading trading partners.

GOVERNMENT. The government proclaimed for Communist China in 1949 and embodied in a constitution in 1954 is a People's Republic, which is democratic in form but in fact dominated by the Communist party.

Supreme legislative and executive power is vested in the National People's Congress, which is elected every four years. The congress chooses a standing committee to act for it between its short yearly sessions. The congress also elects a state council, or cabinet, led by a prime minister, to administer the government, and a Chairman of the Government, who acts as head of state.

The actual seat of power is the Chinese Communist party's Political Bureau, or Politburo, of the party's Central Committee. It determines national policy, and its chairman is usually the key figure in the government. Only party-supported candidates are elected to public office, although party membership is not required for election. Most important government posts are held by party leaders.

A "cultural revolution" launched in 1966 to reorganize and "purify" Chinese society turned into a mass upheaval that disrupted the Chinese social order, economy, and established patterns of government.

Taiwan. Taiwan has a republican form of government. The island has two elected legislatures—one theoretically for all China, and one "provincial" assembly for Taiwan affairs.

The executive branch of government is quite strong. It consists of a president and vice president elected by the National Assembly and a premier, or prime minister, appointed by the president and responsible to the assembly. The Kuomintang, or Nationalist party, is the island's dominant political organization.

HISTORY. China has a long continuous history. Remains of prehistoric "Peking man," found in North China, date back as far as 1 million years and indicate that this early man was probably an ancestor of the modern Chinese. The valley of the Yellow River on the North China Plain was the site of one of the earliest human societies, which developed its own, unique culture.

First Dynasties. Heroic legends tell of a Hsia dynasty founded by an emperor Yü in 2205 BC. There is no concrete evidence of its existence, however, and the first documented Chinese dynasty is the Shang, or Yin. Exact dates of ancient Chinese events are often disputed, but the Shang dynasty was founded in 1766 or 1523 BC on the North China Plain.

Remains of the Shang dynasty show that the basis for the present-day Chinese language already had been formed, and the early characters are similar to those in use in modern China. The Shang controlled many smaller principalities on the North China Plain. One of these, the western kingdom of the Chou, under its king, Wu, overthrew the Shang in 1122 or 1027 BC.

The Chou. The Western Chou (1122–771 BC) is the first dynasty for which a quantity of detailed records exist. Early Chou kings expanded their rule from the North China plain northward to the Liaotung peninsula, southward to the Yangtze valley, and westward to the Himalayan foothills.

Although control of this area was actually divided among many petty states, often in conflict with each other, the Chou dominated them all and was the most influential state for about 300 years.

During the early Chou period society came to be organized along a feudalistic pattern, with wealth based on land ownership and the economy based on agriculture. Warrior-nobles formed the upper class, and village peasant society was communal.

In the 700s BC an eastern branch of the Chou took the throne. The Eastern Chou (770–256 BC) held little power over the nobles and China was actually a federation of states. But during 500 years of Eastern Chou rule, China experienced its classical age of culture and considerable prosperity.

Agricultural and military technology improved, canals were built, a money economy developed, population grew, contact was made with western Asian countries, and trade prospered. Art, music, and literature all flourished, but the Eastern Chou is known primarily for its philosophers. Indeed, so many philosophies, ethical codes, and religions developed during the later Chou that it is known as the era of the "One Hundred Schools."

The Philosophers. Three of the most important philosophers who founded schools of thought between 600 and 300 BC were Lao Tzu, Confucius (K'ung-fu-tzu), and Hsüntzu. Lao Tzu, probably in reality several writers, in the *Way of Power (Tao Te Ching)* taught that there was a natural order to the universe of which man was a part. Man could fulfill himself by achieving balance and harmony within himself and with his environment.

Confucius and his student and interpreter Mencius (Mengtzu) laid the foundation for much of China's subsequent social order, moral code, and political development. Confucius taught that leaders could rule through good example, education, moderation, and justice.

The Confucian idea that man could find fulfillment through self-discipline and brotherly love extended to all of society. And the paternalistic, well-ordered, well-educated, and mutually cooperative society that he envisioned stood as the ideal Chinese state for many centuries.

Hsüntzu laid the basis for the "legalist" school of thought, which provided the philosophical foundation for an authoritarian state led by an absolute ruler and ordered by strict laws. The states which followed the legalist pattern were feudalistic and militaristic.

The Ch'in. One state that benefited directly from the legalist doctrine was the Ch'in. It was the westernmost of the many warring states under Chou influence, and it rose to power in the 300s BC. The Ch'in grew prosperous with an excellent system of irrigation, which made agriculture more productive, and a strong central government, which contributed to social stability and military strength.

The Ch'in made alliances with warlike nomadic "barbarian" (non-Chi-

GREAT WALL OF CHINA extends 1,500 miles across the country's northeastern border region.

nese) states beyond the fringes of Chou civilization and extended its territory north of the Chou. The Ch'in conquered all of the Chou subject states, and in 256 BC Ch'in armies crushed the Chou.

The Ch'in dynasty gave China its name and marked the first Chinese empire. The Ch'in ruler adopted the title Shih Huang-ti, or "First Emperor," in 221 BC. Ch'in administrators unified the formerly warring states and centralized the government.

The Ch'in emperors extended Chinese rule south to modern Canton and west across the plateau of Yünnan. By linking short walls built earlier, the First Emperor built the Great Wall to keep out invaders from the north, the only exposed frontier.

The centralized government of the Ch'in depended heavily on the central ruler, and when the First Emperor died in 210 BC and the succession was disputed, China was once more plunged into political chaos. In 206 BC Liu Pang, a leader from the Ch'in territory of the Wei valley, became the first emperor of the Han dynasty (206 BC–AD 220).

The Han. The Han emperors worked from the firm political, social, and territorial base laid by the Ch'in. They built an empire that was, with Rome, one of the world's greatest states.

Early Han rulers consolidated the power of the central government over national affairs and successfully beat off attempted invasions by the "barbarians." Han administrators maintained political order by giving all governmental responsibility in distant regions of the empire to the vassals of the emperor.

By the beginning of the reign of Wu Ti, in 141 BC, China's social organization and political system were strong enough for the country to expand its territory and further develop its cultural life. Wu Ti conquered territory almost equal to that of modern China—excluding only mountainous Tibet, Manchuria, and the coastal area around Shanghai, but including northern Korea and part of Indochina.

Thus China had a route north of the Kunlun Mountains into western Asia and then to the Mediterranean. The Chinese traded with the Romans and received artistic and cultural influences from the west.

China grew prosperous under the later Han emperors, who introduced state monopolies and the licensing of certain commodities and state control of parts of the economy. Trade expanded, and roads, canals, and irrigation works were built. Education widened, and Confucianism, with its ideals of discipline, balance, and moderation found expression in all aspects of Chinese society and culture.

In about 8 AD a government official, Wang Mang, usurped the throne. He attempted wide-scale land reform to improve the lot of the peasants and to increase tax revenue. He nationalized landed estates and instituted fiscal reforms that were unpopular with the great landowners. In 23 rebel lords sacked the palace and killed Wang Mang.

The Han dynasty was restored, and although it made some subsequent territorial gains it had lost power to local lords. The lords had been the government's main source of money and manpower, and the dynasty had to compensate for their loss by taxing the peasants more heavily.

Peasant rebellions and fighting between rival lords were frequent in the 100s AD. Professional armies moved into local areas to keep the peace and soon came under the control of the local lords.

Three leaders of these armies grew to such power that they divided the empire into three semi-independent kingdoms—the Wei, the Wu, and the Shu Han. Imperial power disintegrated, and the last Han emperor died in 220.

The Six Dynasties. For the next 370 years China was merely a collection of petty states, most of them at war with one another, and none able to dominate the others. The period was known as the era of the "six dynasties," as six houses in succession managed to gain the throne, but none actually ruled China.

The Chinese had to face both invasion from the north by nomadic non-Chinese peoples and the challenge of strong non-Chinese cultural influences from the south and west. In the 300s and 400s nomads conquered China's northern frontier region, although the natural mountain and desert barriers prevented them from penetrating further. Many northern Chinese migrated southward, and during the 300s and 400s they spread their culture into Southeast Asia.

While military invasion from the north disrupted China, the spread of Buddhism, the Indian religion from the south, altered China's traditional social base. Confucianism had fallen from favor because of the failure of the Han dynasty, which had been built upon it. Taoism also grew in strength and soon rivaled Confucianism in importance.

The Sui. By about 550 one dynasty, the Sui, had emerged dominant among the Chinese kingdoms in the south. In the late 500s and early 600s Sui rulers, allied with Turkic-speaking people, led the reconquest of the northern territories held by the barbarians, who by then had absorbed Chinese culture. During the brief Sui dynasty (589–618) the central government was restored to its former power, the Great Wall was rebuilt, and the economy was put on its feet again.

In trying to expand Chinese territory the Sui met disastrous defeats at the hands of the Koguryo people of Korea in the north and Turkic tribes in the west. Following these defeats, a rebellion toppled the Sui.

A brief period of turmoil followed the end of the Sui. Li Yüan, a Sui bureaucrat of Chinese and "barbarian" descent, with the support of Turkic tribes from central Asia became emperor of China in 618, founding the T'ang dynasty (618–907).

The T'ang. The 300-year T'ang era was one of China's most brilliant. In the 600s T'ang rulers consolidated their control of the government and made China's borders secure against further invasion by forming an alliance with the powerful, warlike Uighurs. T'ang government was efficient, economical, and more just to all classes.

Agriculture and trade prospered. Chinese thinkers assimilated Buddhism, Taoism, and Confucianism and developed a unified philosophical base for society. Under the T'ang, poetry, painting, sculpture, scholarship, and science flourished and attracted artists and scholars from other lands.

T'ang peace and prosperity were interrupted in the mid-700s by a revolt led by An Lu-shan, a "barbarian" who commanded some Chinese armies. The rising resulted in a bloody civil war and caused the emperor to flee his capital, Ch'ang-an. Thus weakened, the empire was open to attack by its neighbors, and the late 700s were marked by invasions by such peoples as the Uighurs and Tibetans.

In the 800s the empire disintegrated into political anarchy once more, and in the 900s effective power was divided among many rival warriors. The Khitan Mongols, a newly powerful northern tribe, seized present-day Mongolia, Manchuria, and Korea from China.

The Sung. The Sung dynasty (960–1279), which finally won the competition for power in 960, led China into the modern age. Sung leaders reformed the military and reorganized the government by creating a large, well-salaried, honest, and efficient civil service. They won the support of the masses by reducing taxes, by abolishing the traditional forced labor, by providing loans to farmers, and by initiating public works projects.

The arts and sciences continued to advance, spurred by the widespread use of printing. The Sung empire was not a strong military state, however. By 1234 the north had fallen before the Mongols, who had begun in the 1100s to conquer an empire that eventually included all of Asia north of India.

The Yüan. In 1260 Kublai Khan, a leader of the Mongols, established the Yüan dynasty (1271–1368) in northern China. By 1279 the dynasty controlled the entire country, and China was a subdivision of the Mongol empire. Although Chinese cultural development was slowed or suspended during the 100 years of Mongol rule, Kublai Khan expanded and developed the Chinese economy.

He improved agricultural techniques, built roads, established a postal system and instituted a system of public relief and care for the aged and indigent. He greatly extended Chinese trade with other Asian states and with Europe. One European adventurer, Marco Polo, from Venice, visited Kublai Khan's court, and his reports excited European interest in the empire.

Despite rule by non-Chinese, central China retained its traditional culture and social organization and remained remarkably unified. In the 1300s Chinese antagonism to foreigners sparked rebellions against the Mongols. These rebellions and rivalries among the Mongols themselves led to the disintegration of the Yüan dynasty in the late 1300s.

The Chinese leaders of the rebellion against the Mongols competed among themselves for the throne. Chu Yüan-chang, a Buddhist from northwestern China, emerged dominant and in 1368 established himself as the first emperor of the Ming dynasty (1368–1644).

The Ming. By 1382 Ming rulers had driven the Mongols out of China Proper, and by the 1400s they had regained control of all but the western third and the northern fringe of present-day China. In 1421 Yung-lo moved the capital from Nanking, where it had been since the founding of the dynasty, to Peking, where a walled "forbidden city" became the center of imperial rule.

The Ming emperors proclaimed China supreme in all the world, and indeed China wielded great power throughout Asia. From its Asian neighbors China demanded tribute, either token or actual, that indicated that China was superior to the tributary states. China also gained the right to approve the rulers of the tributary states. In return for this recognition of China's pre-eminence, China gave financial aid and military protection to the tributary states.

Under rules of conduct established by China, the empire opened diplomatic relations with neighboring states. Ming expansion of foreign contacts improved Chinese prosperity and influenced the country's cultural growth.

For the first time large numbers of Christian missionaries and Western merchants visited China. Chinese literature and art flourished, but in the 1600s the Ming declined. Corruption paralyzed the government and left it incapable of managing the affairs of the empire.

Opposition to the dynasty arose from many groups, which formed into rival parties. In the 1630s a bandit, Li Tzu-ch'eng, gained control of northern China, and his rebellion soon spread. He gained the support of many groups in society, won control of most of China, and soon conquered Peking.

Added to this rebellion was an external threat from the Manchus, a non-Chinese people who lived in the region northeast of China proper. Manchu society was based on farming and herding, but the Manchus had been strongly influenced by China, and their culture was quite similar to that of China. In the 1500s they began expanding their territory, building alliances with their non-Chinese neighbors, streamlining their government, and strengthening their military organization.

By the 1640s the Manchus had begun to invade China and were poised to attack Peking just as a Chinese army was preparing to drive out the rebel forces of Li Tzu-ch'eng. The Manchus joined the government troops in defeating the rebels and then used their position of power to establish the Ch'ing dynasty (1644–1912).

The Ch'ing. Much of the first 100 years of the Ch'ing dynasty was spent in putting down resistance by supporters of the Ming and in subduing the non-Chinese neighbors of China and annexing their territory.

By about 1800 the Ch'ing had expanded to the boundaries of present-day China, and beyond, to Taiwan in the east, across Mongolia and coastal Siberia in the north, and to Tibet in the west. These non-Chinese areas were administered by governors under the control of Peking.

The Manchus ruled China with Chinese assistance. They did not attempt to replace Chinese customs, rather, they continued the political and economic policies of their Ming predecessors, maintaining strict state control over all areas of Chinese life. Chinese culture and scholarship continued to flourish in the traditional pattern through the 1700s.

Chinese society remained too stable, in fact, and tradition permitted little progress or modernization. The end of the 1700s brought unprecedented problems to China. The Western world was beginning to take an active interest in the Far East, and European states were beginning to establish trading colonies in the nations around China.

The Portuguese in the 1500s were the first to trade with China, and they were followed by the Dutch and the British. The British East India Company established a trading station at Canton in the late 1600s and throughout the 1700s carried on a brisk trade in tea through Canton.

At the same time as this new factor was posing a threat to traditional Chinese society, Chinese leadership entered a decline. The Ch'ing rulers became mired in fruitless military activity, and their court became riddled with corruption. Chinese prosperity began to wane as the population level began to soar and the traditional economy could not support it.

Western Impact. At the turn of the century rebellions broke out throughout China, caused by hardship and poverty and directed at the lax government administration. As the old ways were proving to be inadequate, new ideas flooded China. Western merchants and settlers brought with them Western technology and science. Western missionaries brought Western ideals of culture along with Christianity.

Unable to meet these challenges, the Ch'ing rulers tried to frighten them away. They banned Christian missionaries and literature, and they refused contact with western diplomats and merchants. Western pressure only grew stronger.

By the early 1800s the British East India company virtually controlled Canton, China's major port, on the Pearl River. In addition to the tea trade, the British carried on a brisk, illegal trade in opium. The narcotic was grown in British India.

Peking banned the opium trade in the early 1800s, partly because the habit was becoming so widespread that it seriously endangered the health of China, and partly because it was too costly and placed too great a strain on China's silver supply.

A deeper reason for Peking's attempts to control the opium trade with Britain was its anger that foreigners should not only not violate their status as guests in the country by breaking its laws, but should refuse to pay tribute to the emperor as other foreign nations did. This was only the first of many Western blows to China's pride.

The Ch'ing rulers attempted to enforce their prohibition of the opium trade in 1839 by seizing and burning a shipment of opium. British warships moved into Canton harbor, and the British occupied the river forts to force the Chinese to continue the trade, and, necessarily, admit British military superiority. Negotiations began between British and Ch'ing representatives, but no agreement was reached.

The Ch'ing cut off all legal trade with Britain, blockaded river mouths and harbors, and finally attacked British-held posts. China's rulers gained little support from the people of Canton, who, despite a growing anti-foreign sentiment, liked their ineffectual, corrupt Manchu rulers even less.

The British defeated the poorly armed and trained Ch'ing forces, and the government finally agreed to British demands. In the Treaty of Nanking of 1842 China ceded Hong Kong, an island at the mouth of the Pearl River, to the British and opened five other ports to foreign trade. The Ch'ing relinquished their claim to superiority and much of their right to control foreign traders. Finally, they granted a low import tariff and paid an indemnity to the British.

In 1844 another treaty granted extra-territorial rights to foreign nations in the treaty ports—foreigners were not subject to Chinese law. Under pressure from missionaries, Christianity was granted official toleration in 1845. Although merchants and missionaries were not permitted outside the treaty ports, Chinese who traded with the merchants and were converted by the missionaries spread Western influence.

China was humiliated. It was no longer supreme even within its own boundaries. China was revealed to be technologically backward and unable to meet the Western challenge, and the empire was thus opened to further intrusion and insult from abroad. Moreover, the Ch'ing dynasty was revealed to the Chinese people to be too weak even to handle its domestic problems or to put down rebellion.

Rebellions. In 1850 an insurrection broke out in Kiangsi, where floods and crop failures had aggravated problems caused by government mismanagement. Led by a religious mystic with the aid of a military officer, a large force of rebels marched toward Peking, conquering the territory along their route. This, the Taiping Rebellion, nearly succeeded in overthrowing the Ch'ing.

The rebels founded the Taiping kingdom in southeastern China, but they were unable to administer it. After approximately 14 years of destructive civil war, the rebellion was finally put down.

Southeastern China was not the only restless part of the country. Rebellions broke out throughout China in the 1850s. In 1853 the Nien began 15 years of terror and plunder in the north-central provinces of Anhwei, Kiangsu, Shantung, and Shansi. The army and the capital were too busy with the Taiping and foreign intrusions to suppress them.

In 1855 Muslims in southwestern Yünnan rebelled and set up a separate Muslim state, and non-Chinese Miao tribesmen in neighboring Kweichow province opened a 26-year rebellion. The destruction of years of violence set China's economy back still more.

Treaty System. Problems raised by the presence of foreigners worsened. Canton, where most of the Westerners were concentrated, was especially rebellious because of its resentment at the British conquest in the Opium War. Friction between the Cantonese and the foreigners grew so intense that in 1857 and 1858 French and British troops, using the need to protect their interests as an excuse, seized and occupied the city.

In settlement of this conflict, the treaties of Tientsin opened more ports to foreigners, legalized the importation of opium, permitted the establishment of European diplomatic missions at Peking, allowed missionaries and traders to enter the interior of the country, and exacted further indemnities from the Chinese.

The Ch'ing rulers, giving the matter second thought, refused to admit foreign ambassadors to Peking. In reprisal, British and French armies stormed Peking in 1860 and burned the summer palace.

Having thus proved the weakness of the imperial government, the British and French saw an advantage in maintaining a weak dynasty, which they could control, and they assisted the Ch'ing rulers in putting down the bloody rebellions throughout the country. The Ch'ing remained on the throne, but they and China were dependent on the Westerners who flooded the once isolated empire after 1860.

By 1890 China had established formal diplomatic relations with Britain, France, Russia, the United States, and other nations. With foreign aid, cable and rail lines were laid connecting China with the "outside world," and the building of a navy was begun. Friction between China and the foreigners did not lessen, however, and ranged from the persecution of missionaries to protests over Japanese involvement in Taiwan and Korea, a tributary of China.

The imperial government still made no major attempts to reform its administration or modernize its economy and society, and China continued to be humiliated as it became more and more subservient to the foreign powers.

Renewed Conflict. In 1874 the Ch'ing proved unable to prevent Japan from invading Taiwan, and they avoided losing the island only through Western diplomatic maneuvers. In the 1880s France, ostensibly in retaliation for the killing of French citizens, occupied Indochina, part of the traditional Chinese tribute system, and forced China to recognize France's position there. In 1887 Portugal was granted Macao, a port near Hong Kong.

Relations with Japan, which had made a rapid transition from its traditional ways to the technological and political sophistication of the 1800s, grew tense. Korea, long a tributary of China, slipped into Japanese control in the 1860s and 1870s, when China refused to take responsibility for Korean actions and later did not protest Japan's recognition of Korea as an independent state.

In 1885 both China and Japan agreed to withdraw their troops from Korea, but continuing intrigue and growing Korean nationalism led in 1894 to war between Korea and China and to a Sino-Japanese war.

By early 1895 Japanese troops had all but destroyed China's army and navy. Further humiliation was added in 1895 by the Treaty of Shimonoseki, by which China was forced to recognize Korean independence, cede Taiwan, the Liaotung Peninsula, and the Pescadores to Japan, pay a huge indemnity, and open more ports to foreigners.

This defeat was a final blow to the pride and patience of many Chinese. Chinese intellectuals realized that a revolution was needed to force China out of its traditional ways and into modern ways if the country was to survive the competition from the technologically advanced nations of the world.

Although a young emperor sat on the throne, actual power rested with his aunt, the dowager empress, Tz'uhsi, who had ruled for him when he was an infant and who had ruled as regent for much of the reign of the previous emperor, her son. The dowager empress was extremely conservative and held to an archaic ideal of China's grandeur.

Reform Efforts. In 1894 Dr. Sun Yat-sen (Sun Wen) organized one of the earliest secret revolutionary societies whose goal was the overthrow of the Ch'ing. After the Treaty of Shimonoseki in 1895, reformers who had been demanding modernization voiced their demands even more loudly.

Students organized "study societies" such as the "society for the study of self-strengthening," to develop theories of reform. Philosophers reinterpreted Confucianism to permit modernization and reform within Chinese traditional ideology. It seemed that even quite radical reform programs would be adopted.

K'ang Yu-wei, a reformer with a positive program for modernizing China, convinced the emperor that reforms were necessary. In 1898 the emperor gave the reformers the power to enact reform measures. In the so-called "One Hundred Days of Reform," edicts were issued to make the schools effective for all classes, remove extra-territorial rights, develop China's natural resources, improve agricultural technology, better national health, expand trade, begin industrialization, and modernize the police and the military.

Conservative opposition to these projected programs was immediate. The dowager empress supported the conservatives, and in September 1898 she had the emperor imprisoned, revoked the reform edicts, and placed conservatives in power.

Foreign Encroachments. While China's domestic policies were in upheaval, Chinese entanglements with foreign powers grew more complex. In 1896 China and Russia concluded a secret treaty by which Russia guaranteed to defend China from attack in return for the right to build and manage a railway across Manchuria to the Russian city of Vladivostok.

The concession to Russia was followed by a commercial treaty with Japan and in 1897 by commercial concessions to Britain. Germany, hoping for equal benefits, used the murder of Germans in China as a pretext for seizing Kiaochow Bay in 1897. It forced China to grant Germany a 99-year lease on the bay and the right to operate mines and build railroads in Shantung.

The other European powers were quick to demand similar favors. Britain gained exclusive rights to much of China's inland river trade, and Russia forced the granting of a 25-year lease on the southern tip of the Liaotung Peninsula. France gained the 99-year lease on Kwangchow Bay, Japan gained a guarantee of prominent influence in Fukien province, and Britain was granted Kowloon, on the mainland across from Hong Kong.

The reactionaries who had come to power with the defeat of China's attempts at domestic reforms hoped to restore China to its position of isolation. Thus, in 1899 when Italy sought concession of a port, the demand was rejected violently. An anti-foreign militia was organized in Eastern China called the "Righteous and Harmonious Fists," or "Boxers."

The Boxer Rebellion. The Boxers sought to drive foreigners and foreign influence out of China by violence. The Boxers received the support of the empress dowager, and by 1900 they were at the core of Peking mobs that attacked foreigners and foreign diplomatic missions. The uprising also sparked anti-foreign incidents elsewhere in China.

In response to the Boxer rising, Germany, Russia, and a joint force of Western European allies attacked China, occupied areas in many provinces, and seized Peking. The empress dowager and the government fled. In 1901 the Boxer Protocol ended the fighting. It exacted further indemnities, apologies, and trade, territorial, and diplomatic concessions from China.

That China was actually divided into foreign "spheres of influence"—regions in which one nation held dominant influence—was pointed out by the United States, which had no sphere of influence in China. The United States urged that an "Open Door" be left for other nations to trade with China.

New Reforms. The utter failure of the conservatives' methods forced the dowager empress to allow some reforms. In 1902 imperial edicts were issued to expand education, modernize the army, and reform the economy.

These reforms were too little, too late, and too slow in materializing for the more radical Chinese reformers. Moreover, opponents of the regime felt that no reform program could be effective without bringing under Chinese control the foreigners who held vital portions of the nation's economy.

In 1905 Sun Yat-sen, who had been seeking support from Chinese throughout the world for his campaign against the Ch'ing dynasty, united in Japan many Chinese reform societies into one revolutionary organization, the T'ung-meng hui, or United League.

Government-sponsored reform continued at a slow pace. Preparations begun in 1906 for the institution of constitutional government were hindered in 1908, when both the dowager empress and the emperor died. The regent for the infant heir to the throne was a conservative, who dismissed the liberal reformers in the government and appointed conservative Manchus as the chief ministers. The meeting of a parliament was put off until 1913.

Republican Revolution. This stalling increased the restlessness of the revolutionaries, who by 1910 had established a network throughout China. The spark that ignited the revolution was the discovery of the revolutionary headquarters by government police in October 1911. Within a month, most of the country had risen against the Manchus.

A truce was signed in December between the rebels and the government, and a revolutionary provisional assembly met in Nanking. It elected Dr. Sun Yat-sen president of China. In February 1912 the Manchus acknowledged defeat. The abdication of the boy emperor was announced, and the assembly proclaimed the Republic of China.

Yüan Shih-K'ai was elected provisional president of the republic in February 1912. A provisional constitution was adopted which would have made the national assembly the supreme organ of government, and a dispute immediately began between President Yüan, who wanted to head a strong executive, and the assembly. Opposition parties grouped around this issue.

Liang Ch'i-ch'ao formed the Progressive party, which supported Yüan's government. Sun Yat-sen led the Kuomintang (KMT), or Nationalist party, which favored parliamentary supremacy. Thus, in disarray within a month of its formation, the republic began to disintegrate.

The first elected parliament was convened in April 1913. A loan received by Yüan from Britain, France, Russia, and Japan, which would serve to finance his drive for increased power, caused his opponents to lead a second revolution. It was quickly suppressed, and Kuomintang leaders were forced to flee to Japan.

Yüan, who was formally elected president of the republic in October 1913, consolidated his power by expelling Kuomintang members from the parliament and then by dissolving parliament itself in January 1914. In place of the constitution, which was to have been ratified by the parliament, Yüan governed under a "constitutional compact," which he announced in 1914 and which gave him a 10-year term as a powerful president.

The establishment of the republic did not lessen the financial and political power wielded by foreign nations, however, and Chinese political instability left China even more unprepared to cope with foreign interference. When World War I broke out in 1914, China became the diplomatic and occasionally the military battleground for Russia, Japan, and Germany.

Nor was the war the only source of violence in China. A successful rebellion broke out in 1915 in Yünnan, led by Yüan's opponents in response to Yüan's assumption of the title of emperor. Yüan died in 1916, shortly after he had renounced the imperial title. He was succeeded by Li Yüan-hung.

Li restored the constitution, but in 1917 military leaders rebelled and restored the Ch'ing dynasty for two weeks. In July 1917 Sun Yat-sen established a military government in the south, with its capital at Canton.

With China itself divided, the end of World War I also found Manchuria in the hands of Japan and Mongolia under Russian domination. The Versailles Treaty, which ended the war, allowed Japan to retain Shantung, and China refused to sign the document.

At the Washington Conference in 1922, the Allied powers agreed to reconsider their demands for extraterritorial rights, to respect China's territorial integrity, and to assist China in the formation of a stable government. A Sino-Japanese treaty was arranged, by which Japan was to withdraw from Shantung.

This official end to foreign intervention came too late, however. No one government led China, and in 1920 the country was plunged into open civil war among warlords—military leaders who held sway over districts, even provinces—while in the larger cities, anti-foreign mobs rioted.

Kuomintang. In 1924 a Kuomintang congress met to plan the party's future. It accepted communists as members and employed Soviet advisors to train members in military and political tactics. Sun Yat-sen died in 1925, and leadership of the Kuomintang passed to Chiang Kai-shek. Dr. Sun's wife, Soong Ch'ing-ling, supported a radical left-wing of the nationalist movement, however.

With Soviet aid, Chiang suppressed the warlords and gained control of northern China. Soon, however, a split opened between the conservative nationalists, led by Chiang, and the radicals and communists. The radicals and communists established a government at Wuhan, and the nationalists set up a government at Nanking.

After a brief reconciliation, the two factions split widely apart. In 1927 Mao Tse-tung, a Communist party leader, organized a peasant uprising in Hunan province. When the uprising was suppressed, the communists retreated into the interior and organized an anti-Kuomintang revolutionary army. In June 1928 Chiang and a purged Kuomintang captured Peking and proclaimed a single government for the whole of China with its capital at Nanking.

Since the revered Dr. Sun had recommended that a strict, authoritarian regime strengthen the country before democracy was introduced, a strong central executive was established under Chiang and the now moderate-conservative Kuomintang. From 1928 to 1930 the Nanking government consolidated its international position by negotiating treaties recognizing Chinese sovereignty.

The Kuomintang did not rule all of China, however. Warlords had risen to power again in the north, and communists controlled the southwest.

In 1931 Japan invaded and occupied Manchuria. Chiang's government was able to put up little effective resistance, and in 1932 Japan proclaimed Manchuria independent as Manchukuo (Manchu-nation), with a puppet government headed by the former Ch'ing emperor of China.

Japan used Manchukuo as a base for further military operations in China and by 1933 had gained control of Jehol province and claimed the provinces of the North China Plain for Japan.

Late in 1934 Mao Tse-tung and his communist followers began a "Long March" from the south, where the pressure of government forces had made their position untenable. They walked 5,000 miles into Shensi province in the northwest. The march, accomplished over difficult terrain and under almost constant attack by government troops, took nearly a year.

Communist losses were heavy, but the survivors formed a tightly knit, dedicated unit. In late 1935 the communists established a government headed by Mao at Yenan, in Shensi.

Chiang, without control of the entire nation, felt unprepared to go to war against Japan, although it was apparent that Japan was preparing for total war with China. In 1936 Chiang was kidnapped by nationalists who attempted to force him to postpone internal struggles to meet the threat posed by Japan. After his release, Chiang concluded a truce with the communists, and the nationalists and communists formed a united front against Japan.

War with Japan. In 1937 Japan opened a major offensive against China. Japanese troops met surprisingly strong resistance from both communist and nationalist forces, but by 1939 they had conquered and occupied the eastern third of China, the country's heartland. From this large mainland base, Japan entered World War II.

During the war the British, Soviet, and U.S. governments aided the Chinese by sending supplies through western China. In 1943 Britain and the United States abrogated all treaties giving them special rights in China and promised President Chiang that they would force Japanese restitution of Chinese territories after the war.

During the Japanese occupation, however, the communist forces gained widespread popular support and won control of most of the northeast. The nationalist regime, having been pushed inland, made the city of Chungking its capital. It was weakened by internal division and corruption, and was separated from the vital coastal areas from which it had drawn its support. Late in the war Soviet troops occupied Manchuria and stripped the industrially developed area of its machinery.

When the war ended in 1945, civil war again broke out between the nationalists and the communists. A U.S. mission led by Gen. George C. Marshall tried without success to mediate the conflict.

The communists won most of the battles and in 1949 captured the nationalists' restored capital, Nanking, and proclaimed the People's Republic of China from Peking. Chiang Kai-shek and his government fled to the

COUNTRIES OF THE WORLD

China

island of Taiwan, where they established themselves at Taipei.

Communist Regime. The outbreak of the Korean war (1950–1953) aided the communist government. It rallied popular support against the U.S. and UN forces and gained prestige by successfully repelling an invasion across the Yalu River and pushing back the U.S.-UN forces led by Gen. Douglas MacArthur.

By 1952 the Communist party had consolidated its control of the mainland, and in 1953 it announced the first five-year economic plan to industrialize China. However, plans for enacting the program were not drawn up until 1955.

With aid from the Soviet Union, Communist China's strong central government and well-disciplined party, backed by a strong army, made great strides in repairing the damage done by years of warfare. The communist government collectivized agriculture and worked for the rapid industrialization of China.

In 1956 the government called for a "Great Leap Forward," which aimed at replacing family and village life with communal life and which hoped to have each citizen participate in all phases of the economic development program.

But the first plan and the subordination of agriculture to industrial growth proved to be disastrous mistakes. Combined with floods and poor initial organization, they caused a great decline in crop production. Moreover, industrialization did not proceed at the pace the communist planners had hoped, and it was not until the early 1960s that China's economy seemed based on a firm foundation.

In foreign affairs Communist China concentrated on extending its influence throughout eastern and Southeast Asia. Communist Chinese troops had aided North Korean forces in the Korean war and supported communist guerrilla bands in Laos, Vietnam, Cambodia, and elsewhere. Also, despite its own need for food and funds, the communist government sent foreign financial and technical aid to other nations.

China's progress toward stability, prosperity, and prestige was interrupted in the mid-1960s by events stemming from an ideological conflict that had been growing between the Soviet Union and China since the mid-1950s. The dispute became an open break in the early 1960s.

The Chinese government declared itself ideologically purer than the Soviet Union, and made the Soviet Union and its leaders the target of abuse. By the mid-1960s the two nations had ended most contacts and were in open competition for the leadership of the world communist movement.

Chairman Mao carried his ideological campaign further in 1966 by proclaiming a "proletarian cultural revolution" to purge China of "revisionist," or regressive, tendencies. The movement, spearheaded by Red Guards, as the pro-Mao activists were called, grew into an orgy of anti-Western, anti-Soviet violence.

Schools were closed, agricultural and industrial production interrupted, and the government's administrative machinery disrupted. Nonetheless, China successfully continued its research and development programs in atomic weapons, and exploded its first thermonuclear device.

Taiwan. In 1945, when the nationalists took over the government of Taiwan, they were faced immediately with difficulties in governing the island. Descendants of the mainland Chinese who had settled Taiwan in the 1600s regarded themselves as native Taiwanese, different from the mainland peoples. And some had hoped for complete independence for Taiwan after the Japanese withdrew.

Japan had made the island a colony after winning it from China in 1895, and although Japanese rule improved the economy considerably, it was oppressive and unpopular. The island had become a strategic base for Japan's military operations, and during World War II Japanese bases on the island were heavily bombed by Allied forces.

The sufferings of the Taiwanese under alien rule, their unmet demands for independence, and the ineptitude and harshness of the Nationalist government after 1945 combined to create severe friction between the Taiwanese and the mainlanders. The situation worsened, and in 1947 the Taiwanese rebelled. The revolt was crushed ruthlessly.

When the nationalists lost to communist forces on the mainland in 1949, they moved their government, their army, and some 3 million of their citizens to Taiwan. There, President Chiang proclaimed a government of all China and declared his intention to return to the mainland.

In 1950 Communist China declared Taiwan to be a part of its territory and announced its intention to reclaim it. The U.S. Navy protected the island and prevented any mainland invasion attempt. Both sides have a claim to the island, for in the peace treaty that Japan signed in 1951, it relinquished all its claims to Taiwan without ceding it to any particular state.

Taiwan's history in the 1950s and 1960s was shaped by the claim of both Chinas to be the sole representative of the Chinese people. Because of the rivalry, low level military activities continued between the two Chinas in the 1950s and 1960s, flaring up into several major crises—the battle for the tiny offshore islands of Quemoy and Matsu in the late 1950s, and the large-scale buildup of communist and nationalist troops on facing coasts in the early 1960s.

The division radically affected the nation's foreign affairs as well. Taiwan committed itself to maintaining its position in the noncommunist world as the sole legal government of China, and it refused to deal officially with any nation that recognized Communist China.

The United States not only protected the island with U.S. naval forces, but gave the nationalists their main diplomatic support, trained the nationalist army, and provided the aid that made possible Taiwan's economic growth. Taiwan was frequently used as a symbol of the larger conflict between the United States and the communist world, and Taiwan benefited greatly from U.S. interest in limiting the spread of communism in Asia.

Taiwan's growing prosperity helped to ease the friction between the native Taiwanese and the mainland-dominated government. But the movement for Taiwanese independence continued.

The Kuomintang claim to all China affected Taiwan's domestic politics in other ways. Full-scale national elections were postponed until the return to the mainland, and the republic's affairs remained in the hands of the National Assembly, which elects the president. Twice it amended the constitution to permit President Chiang to be reelected.

No party other than the Kuomintang was active in Taiwan until 1960, when opposition leaders attempted to form the China Democratic party. Direct and indirect suppression by the Nationalist government, consisting only of Kuomintang members, caused the collapse of the new party. Its role was taken by politicians calling themselves "independents" who managed to win several contests for local and provincial offices in the 1960s.

In the early 1960s the Kuomintang moved to strengthen its control over Taiwan politics in response to this widening of opposition activities. In 1966 the National Assembly greatly increased the powers of the presidency, at the same time promising that elections would be held for the assembly on Taiwan.

The advanced age of President Chiang, the center of the nationalist movement for over 50 years, led in the early 1960s to speculation over Taiwan's future. The appointment of President Chiang's son, Chiang Kuo, as minister of defense in 1965, however, seem to indicate a continuance of Chiang's policies.

—Thomas E. Ennis; M. G. Inaba

U.S. ARMY

NATIONALIST CHINESE airmen overhaul an aircraft engine at air cadet training school.

COLOMBIAN INDIAN FARMERS. Agriculture employs about half of Colombia's people.

COLOMBIA

Official name: Republic of Colombia
Area: 439,512 square miles
Population: (1966 est.) 18,650,000
Capital: Bogotá (Pop., 1964, 1,697,311)
Language: Spanish
Religion: Roman Catholicism
Currency unit: Peso
National holiday: Independence day, July 20

Colombia is unique among the South American nations in facing both the Caribbean Sea and the Pacific Ocean. Colombia is bordered on the north by the Caribbean, on the east by Venezuela and Brazil, on the south by Peru and Ecuador, and on the west by the Pacific Ocean and Panama.

THE LAND. The country is crossed by three distinct ranges of the Andes, which create serious barriers. Most of the country's people and economically important areas lie in scattered valleys, separated not only by the Andes but also by climate and different ways of life.

Physical Regions. Colombia has two main land regions—the Andes, in the west, and the lowlands, in the east. The Andean region is a continuation of the broad Andes mountain system which runs almost the entire length of the western side of the South American continent. The Colombian Andes fan out in an east-west direction in the southwest to form three separate ranges: the Cordillera Occidental, the Cordillera Central, and the Cordillera Oriental.

The Cordillera Central has peaks that rise more than 18,000 feet above sea level. The cordilleras Occidental and Oriental are somewhat lower. The Cordillera Oriental widens in the north and forms a narrow plateau in the vicinity of Bogotá. The Magdalena River separates the Cordillera Oriental from the Cordillera Central, and the Cauca River separates the Cordillera Central from the Cordillera Occidental. Both rivers flow northward and empty into the Caribbean Sea.

The eastern lowlands drain into the Amazon and Orinoco river systems. The southern section of the region is tropical rain forest and is sparsely populated. The northern section consists of savannas, or *llanos*. Although flooded for a large portion of the year, it is suitable for livestock raising.

Climatic Zones. Climate in Colombia varies with altitude. The lower areas, from sea level to about 3,000 feet, comprise the *tierra caliente*, or hot country. It has average temperatures of from 75°F to 85°F, and tropical crops such as rice and bananas are grown there.

The *tierra templada*, or temperate country, lies between 3,000 and 6,500 feet above sea level. It has year-round temperatures of 65°F to 70°F, and coffee flourishes on the Andean slopes of the region.

The third level is the *tierra fría*, or cold country, between 6,500 and 10,000 feet above sea level. Wheat, maize, and fruit are grown there. Above 10,000 feet but below the 15,000-foot snow line the land is unsuitable for cultivation and is devoted to pasturing livestock.

THE PEOPLE. About 70 percent of the Colombian population is mestizo, of mixed Spanish and Indian descent, and mulatto, mixed Negro and white. Whites constitute about 20 percent of the total and are concentrated in the major cities. Negroes make up less than 7 percent of the population and live mainly along the Caribbean and Pacific coasts. Indians represent about 3 percent of the population.

Most Colombians live in the Andean valleys. Bogotá, the capital, lies more than 8,500 feet above sea level. Cali, in the fertile Cauca Valley, is a market point for agricultural products and an industrial center. It had a population of almost 638,000. The city of Medellín, located in the Cordillera Central, is the center of the coffee and textile industries. It had a 1964 population of almost 773,000.

Barranquilla, on the Caribbean coast, is the country's largest port. It had a population of approximately 500,000 in 1964. Cartagena, one of the oldest South American cities, is Colombia's foremost tourist center. It is also the shipping point for petroleum and petroleum products from a large local refinery. In 1964 it had more than 242,000 inhabitants.

ECONOMY. Agriculture is the most important part of Colombia's economy. Although only 2 percent of the nation's total land area is cultivated, about half the population is employed in agriculture. Coffee is the chief crop, and Colombia relies heavily on its export to earn foreign exchange. Other major commercial crops are bananas, sugarcane, tobacco, cotton, and cacao. Cattle are also important and are raised on the *llanos* of the country's eastern lowlands.

Colombia is rich in mineral resources, and mining plays an important role. Petroleum is the country's second most valuable export, and in 1966 Colombia ranked third among South American oil producers. Colombia leads South America in gold production and is the world's most important source of emeralds.

Although by the mid-1960s industry was not highly developed, it has been growing. Manufacturing is largely devoted to textiles and food processing, but beverages, shoes, steel, and a variety of chemicals are also produced. The growth of both industry and mining, however, is hampered by a lack of capital for investment, poor transportation facilities, a small domestic market, and political instability.

In 1966 Colombian exports were valued at $508 million and imports cost $673 million. Coffee accounts for about 65 percent of the value of all exports. Other exports include petroleum, bananas, tobacco, cotton, and sugar. Chemicals, machinery, steel products, paper, and vehicles are the country's main imports. Colombia's major trading partner is the United States. Other important trading partners are West Germany, Britain, Spain, and Sweden.

GOVERNMENT. Colombia is a constitutional republic. The chief executive and head of state is the president, who is popularly elected to a term of four years. He may not serve consecutive terms.

The Congress is composed of the Senate and the House of Representatives. Senators serve for four years, and representatives for two.

Colombia is a member of the United Nations and the Organization of American States (OAS).

HISTORY. Before the Spanish Conquest in the 1500s, the high Andean region of Colombia stretching northeastward from Bogotá was the home of the Muiscas, a Chibcha-speaking American Indian people who had evolved a stable agricultural society and were highly skilled at goldwork. They were easily subdued by the Spaniards, who began exploring the Caribbean coast as early as 1500.

Spanish Era. The first permanent Spanish communities were established at Santa Marta in 1525 and Cartagena in 1533. Santa Marta later served as the base for an expedition under Gonzalo Jiménez de Quesada that moved inland to conquer the Muiscas and resulted in the founding of Bogotá in 1538.

To the west, the Spaniards discovered what was to become the chief gold-producing area of their empire, and Cartagena, on the Caribbean coast, became the principal naval base of the Spanish Main. Nonetheless, most of Colombia remained virtually uninhabited throughout the Spanish colonial period. Its few people were engaged chiefly in raising cattle and growing crops for local consumption.

Colombia's struggle for independence began in 1810, when local leaders deposed the Spanish authorities and established a number of juntas, ostensibly to rule in the absence of Spain's King Ferdinand VII, who was held captive by Napoleon. Spanish armies reoccupied the principal regions of the country in 1815–1816, but in 1819 Simón Bolívar returned from Venezuela and decisively routed the Spanish forces at the battle of Boyacá.

Independence. In the same year, 1819, the former Viceroyalty of New Granada—which included modern Colombia, Panama, Venezuela, and Ecuador—was organized by the leaders of the independence movement into the republic of Gran Colombia. Bolívar was elected president, but he left to continue the war against Spain and turned over the government to his vice president, Francisco de Paula Santander.

Santander proved an able administrator, but was harassed by separatist movements in Venezuela and Ecuador. Not even the return of Bolívar could prevent the final dissolution of the republic of Gran Colombia in 1830.

In 1831 the territory of modern Colombia and Panama was established as the Republic of New Granada. Santander became its first elected chief executive in 1832. Soon, however, a long and often violent struggle began between Liberals and Conservatives over church policy and constitutional organization.

Era of Conflict. During the 1850s and 1860s, the Liberals established freedom of worship and separation of church and state, but they also seized church lands, abolished monastic orders, and placed restrictions upon the Roman Catholic clergy. Politically, they carried the concept of states' rights to such extremes that the national government itself was often rendered ineffective.

The Liberals' extreme approach to local autonomy and their church policy brought a strong reaction against them in the 1880s. Although originally a Liberal, President Rafael Núñez joined forces with the Conservatives to adopt a rigorously centralist constitution in 1886 and removed the major restrictions placed upon the church.

The policies of Núñez did not end internal strife. Liberals fought to undo his work by launching civil wars, the longest and bloodiest of which raged from 1899 to 1902. This war, plus the secession of Panama in 1903, shocked the leaders of both parties into laying aside at least some of their former bitterness.

Civil wars abruptly ceased, and for nearly 50 years Colombia enjoyed relative stability and constitutional government. Meanwhile, economic growth continued. The production of coffee increased and new commodities, such as bananas and petroleum, and the beginnings of manufacturing, especially of textiles, served to broaden the base of the economy.

Reforms. Until the Liberal administration of Alfonso López (1934–1938), however, neither party had given much attention to the great majority of Colombians, who remained illiterate, impoverished, and beyond the reach of modern health facilities and social services. To deal with this problem López launched a program that included labor reform and social welfare legislation.

Although his program was generally moderate, it aroused strong opposition from wealthy Colombians. At the same time, it aroused among the working class hopes that could be only partially satisfied. Colombia thus faced a new period of strife in which inherited political rivalries were aggravated by new social and economic conflicts.

Tensions reached a climax on Apr. 9, 1948, when the leftist Liberal leader Jorge E. Gaitán was assassinated in Bogotá and his followers staged an orgy of rioting in protest. A year later, inter-party relations broke down entirely, and violence spread to large areas of Colombia. Beginning as a struggle between Liberals and Conservatives, it often degenerated into banditry.

Contemporary Colombia. A dictatorship by Gen. Gustavo Rojas Pinilla, from 1953 to 1957, brought a slight decline in civil strife but failed to stop the violence, which in the decade following Gaitán's death claimed roughly a quarter million lives. The violence of the 1950s and the growing unpopularity of the Rojas regime led Liberal and Conservative leaders to cooperate once again.

After joining to overthrow the dictator in May 1957, the two parties created a National Front coalition government. The terms of the coalition agreement provided for the alternation of Liberals and Conservatives in the presidency and the division of other offices on a 50-50 basis for a 16-year period. Under the National Front, violence decreased but did not completely disappear.

A new approach was made to the nation's fundamental social and economic problems, including efforts at agrarian reform. But Colombia's difficulties were compounded by an extremely high rate of population increase, large-scale migration to the cities, and a sharp drop in the world price of coffee, which limited the financial resources available for carrying out reform programs.

Popular dissatisfaction was reflected in the loss of support for both traditional parties in elections held in 1966. Many Colombians abstained from voting and others backed the forces of ex-dictator Rojas Pinilla, which made strong gains. Nonetheless, the Liberal party candidate, Carlos Lleras Restrepo, was elected president by a safe majority.

—David Bushnell; Kempton E. Webb

CONGO (Brazzaville)

Official name: Republic of Congo
Area: 132,047 square miles
Population: (1966 est.) 850,000
Capital: Brazzaville (Pop., 1962, urban area, 136,200)
Language: French, African languages
Religion: Christianity, traditional religions
Currency unit: Franc CFA (African Financial Community)
National holiday: National day, August 15

The Congo (Brazzaville), a republic in central Africa, is bordered on the north by the Central African Republic, on the east and southeast by the Congo (Kinshasa), on the southwest by the Cabinda region of Angola and the Atlantic Ocean, on the west by Gabon, and on the northwest by Cameroon. The Congo, formerly a territory in French Equatorial Africa, received its independence from France in 1960.

THE LAND. The Congo has a varied geography. Along the coast is a relatively cool and practically treeless plain. Farther inland is the wet and forested Mayombé Escarpment, which is cut by the Kouilou River. The Niari Basin, a region of woodlands and grassy plains, lies east of the escarpment.

To the north of the escarpment are the grassy Batéké plateaus. There are swamps along the Sangha River in the northern part of the country. The Congo and Ubangi rivers border the Congo on the east.

The Congo has a hot, tropical climate. The coastal area, cooled by ocean currents, has generally lower temperatures than the rest of the country.

Congo (Kinshasa)

THE PEOPLE. There are many different ethnic groups in the Congo. The Bacongo people make up almost half the population. Other important groups are the Vili, the Batéké, the M'Bochi, and the Sangha.

Most of the people live in rural areas. The country's major cities include Brazzaville, the capital and major river port, and Pointe Noire, a port city on the Atlantic Ocean.

ECONOMY. The economy of the Congo is based largely on agriculture, and about 60 percent of the people are farmers. Bananas, manioc, peanuts, rice, tropical fruits, and corn are grown for local consumption. Forestry is very important to the Congo's economy. The Congo is poor in mineral resources, apart from large potash deposits near Pointe Noire, and there is little industry.

The Congo has a well-developed transportation system. The Congo-Ocean railroad links Brazzaville and Pointe Noire, and the Congo and Ubangi rivers provide excellent water routes for the Congo and neighboring countries.

In 1966 imports cost $70 million and exports were valued at $43 million. The Congo imports machinery and consumer goods. The major exports include diamonds mined in neighboring countries and timber.

GOVERNMENT. The Congo has a modified presidential system of government. The chief of state is the president, chosen by an electoral college composed of members of the national legislature and local government councils. The chief executive is the prime minister, responsible to the legislature, the National Assembly. Assembly members are popularly elected to five-year terms.

The Congo (Brazzaville) is a member of the United Nations and of the Organization of African Unity (OAU).

HISTORY. The Balali people, an offshoot of the Bacongo kingdom centered in nearby Angola, overran the M'Bochi and Vili people living in the present-day Congo many centuries ago. Portuguese explorers had begun trading with these people in the 1400s. The original trade in gold and ivory was replaced by the slave trade. British, Dutch, and French companies joined the trade until slaving was abolished in the 1800s.

French Rule. The French explorer Pierre Savorgnan de Brazza reached the area in 1873, and signed an agreement with the Batéké king. The French obtained European recognition of their influence over the region of the present-day Congo at the Berlin Conference on African Affairs in 1884.

The French called the area Middle Congo. In 1910 France joined Middle Congo with present-day Gabon, Chad, and the Central African Republic to form the Federation of French Equatorial Africa.

France gave private companies control of developing the country, but company rule was harsh. Africans were deprived of legal rights, and in the 1920s African political dissatisfaction was expressed in the rise of various local religious sects. The most important sect was the Matswa movement among the Bacongo.

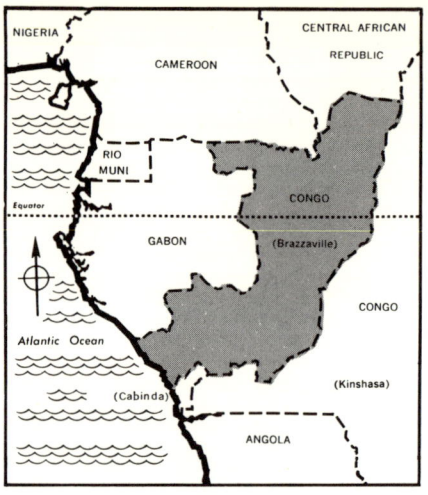

Middle Congo supported Free France during World War II. In 1944, in gratitude for their support, France held a conference to discuss colonial reforms in Brazzaville. Shortly after, Middle Congo became an overseas territory within the French Union, and many political parties developed, largely along tribal lines.

Independence. In the mid-1950s Fulbert Youlou became the dominant political figure in the country. Youlou, a Bacongo and a Roman Catholic priest, had gained the support of the Matswa movement. In 1958 Middle Congo agreed to join the French Community and changed its name to Republic of Congo. In 1959 Youlou became the first president, and the Republic of Congo became independent on Aug. 15, 1960.

Youlou attempted to establish a one-party state, but in 1963 his opponents staged a successful coup, and Alphonse Massamba-Debat became president under a new constitution.
—Hibberd V. B. Kline, Jr.; Vera L. Zolberg

CONGO (Kinshasa)

Official name: Democratic Republic of the Congo
Area: 905,562 square miles
Population: (1966 est.) 15,986,000
Capital: Kinshasa (Pop., 1966 est., 507,868)
Language: French, African languages
Religion: Christianity, Islam, traditional religions
Currency unit: Zaire
National holiday: Independence day, June 30

The Democratic Republic of the Congo, a nation in central Africa, is bordered on the north by the Central African Republic and Sudan, on the east by Uganda, Rwanda, Burundi, and Tanzania, on the south by Zambia and Angola, and on the west by the Congo (Brazzaville) and the Cabinda region of Angola. The country was a colony of Belgium until 1960, when it received its independence.

THE LAND. Tropical grasslands and forests are typical of most of the Congo's landscape. The interior of the country is a vast plain with swamps in some places. There are highlands along the eastern border, including Mount Ruwenzori, which has an elevation of about 16,800 feet. There are also highlands in the south.

There are many lakes along the Congo's eastern border, including lakes Albert, Edward, Kivu, Tanganyika, and Mweru.

The Congo River flows through part of the northeastern Congo and along the western border. The wide, navigable lower part of the river drops nearly 1,000 feet between Kinshasa and the sea. The Ubangi and Kasai rivers are the main tributaries of the middle Congo River. The climate throughout the country is tropical.

THE PEOPLE. Most of the Congo's indigenous population is Bantu-speaking. Many different groups of people, including the Bacongo, Lulua, and the pygmies, live in the Congo. About one-third of the people are Christian, a small number are Muslim, and most of the remainder follow traditional tribal religions.

In 1966 the Congo renamed its cities that had Belgian names. Leopoldville, the capital, became Kinshasa, and the important city of Elisabethville was renamed Lubumbashi. Stanleyville became Kisangani.

ECONOMY. Since independence in 1960, the economy of the Congo has been seriously disrupted by political instability and civil wars. The Belgians had developed the country's rich mineral resources and had built railroads to complement river navigation. Most of the technically trained Belgians left during the political disorder following independence.

The Congo's mineral riches include copper, cobalt, zinc, gold, and diamonds. In 1965, 288,600 metric tons of copper ore, about 8,400 metric tons of cobalt ore, 117,400 metric tons of zinc ore, and 72,850 ounces of gold were mined. Diamond production in 1965 reached 26.6 million carats, more than half the world's total.

There is little industry in the Congo apart from the processing of minerals and agricultural products. Most of the Congo's people are engaged in subsistence farming. The main crops are corn, millet and sorghum, peanuts, coffee, and fruits.

In 1965 imports cost $320 million and exports were valued at $330 mil-

lion. The Congo's main exports include copper, cobalt, diamonds, tin, palm oil, and coffee. The main imports are foodstuffs, petroleum products, transportation equipment, and textiles.

GOVERNMENT. A constitution promulgated in 1967 established a presidential system of government. Executive power is vested in a president elected to a seven-year term. Legislative power is held by a National Assembly elected to a five-year term. The constitution called for the establishment of a two-party system.

The Congo is a member of the United Nations and of the Organization of African Unity (OAU).

HISTORY. Many different tribal peoples have lived in the vast region of the present-day Congo. Among the earliest inhabitants were the pygmies and the Bacongo peoples. Portuguese sailors reached the region in 1482, but the area remained largely unknown until the late 1800s. Between 1874 and 1877 the British explorer Henry Stanley explored the area. In 1884 Belgium's King Leopold II obtained European recognition of a Congo Free State at the Berlin Conference on African Affairs.

Colonial Rule. Between 1885 and 1908 Leopold's agents used unscrupulous methods to secure labor to exploit the Congo's rubber and ivory resources. Mistreatment of the people created an international scandal, and in 1908 Leopold turned over control of the area to the Belgian parliament.

From then until 1960, large companies controlled the economy, Roman Catholic missionaries with government subsidies controlled education, and Belgian administrators ran the government.

Under Belgian rule there was economic advancement, and a high literacy rate was achieved. But there was little secondary education and no higher education until the founding of Lovanium University in 1954.

The administration encouraged vocational training and the breaking of tribal ties, but did not allow the inhabitants to gain political experience. Early African political expression took the form of national religious sects. After World War II, however, Belgium slowly liberalized its colonial rule.

In 1954 the Bacongo people, led by Joseph Kasavubu, demanded political rights and autonomy from the rest of the country. From then on the tempo of political change greatly accelerated. In 1955 Belgium discussed a plan for citizenship, but in response to growing African pressure, Belgium announced in January 1960 that independence would be granted June 30.

Independence. The country held elections in the midst of turmoil. Parties were hastily organized by almost every ethnic group, and the elections failed to produce a clear majority for any single party or group. Patrice Lumumba, leader of the National Congolese Movement, which won the most seats in the assembly, became prime minister, or chief executive, of the new republic. His closest election rival, Joseph Kasavubu, became president, or head of state.

Lumumba's government faced both a mutiny in the army and the flight of most of the country's European technicians and administrators. The Congo's richest province, Katanga, under the leadership of Moise Tshombe, seceded from the new republic in July 1960.

Lumumba then appealed to the United Nations for aid in restoring order. A military coup, led by Col. Joseph Mobutu, overthrew Lumumba in September 1960, and he was assassinated in February 1961.

In July 1961 Kasavubu designated Cyrille Adoula as prime minister, but the new government could not stabilize the situation. In 1963 UN forces finally ended Katanga's secession. In June 1964 Adoula resigned, and in July Tshombe became prime minister despite the objections of many African states, which saw him as a tool of European mining interests.

In August 1964 a newly adopted constitution vested increased powers in the president, and Tshombe showed signs of wanting the office. In October 1965 Kasavubu claimed that Tshombe had violated constitutional procedures and ousted him from office. Evariste Kimba was appointed prime minister in Tshombe's place.

In November 1965 army chief of staff Joseph Mobutu ousted both Kimba and Kasavubu and named himself president. In 1966 Mobutu took over all legislative powers from parliament, and in 1967 he proclaimed a new constitution providing for a strong presidential system of government. Mobutu also instituted needed economic reforms.

—Hibberd V. B. Kline, Jr.; Vera L. Zolberg

COSTA RICA

Official name: Republic of Costa Rica
Area: 19,575 square miles
Population: (1966 est.) 1,486,000
Capital: San José (Pop., 1965 est., urban area, 339,100)
Language: Spanish
Religion: Roman Catholicism
Currency unit: Colón
National holiday: Independence day, September 15

The Republic of Costa Rica, a small country in Central America, is bounded on the north by Nicaragua, on the east by the Caribbean Sea and Panama, and on the south and west by the Pacific Ocean.

THE LAND. Costa Rica has three major regions: a Caribbean coastal plain, a mountainous central area, and a Pacific coastal plain.

The Caribbean coast is rainy and covered with tropical evergreen forests and swamps. The central region, which has a temperate climate, consists of high flat basins formed by three mountain ranges—the Cordillera de Guanacaste, the Cordillera Central, and the Cordillera de Talamanca. The *Meseta Central,* or central plateau, the largest basin of the region, lies between the Cordillera de Guanacaste and the Cordillera de Talamanca.

The Pacific coastal plain, a region of tropical forests and savanna, has alternating wet and dry seasons.

THE PEOPLE. With the exception of a relatively small Negro population concentrated in the Caribbean coastal area, Costa Ricans are almost all of European, largely Spanish, descent. Most people live in the Meseta Central, the site of San José, the industrial and cultural center as well as the capital of the country.

Costa Rica has a very high population growth rate, estimated at more than 4 percent a year between 1958 and 1965.

ECONOMY. Costa Rica's rapid rate of population increase creates serious economic problems. Although the total national income increased considerably between 1960 and 1965, population growth absorbed most of the gain, and living standards rose but little.

In 1963 Costa Rica entered the Central American Common Market, and agricultural production, the main source of national income, and manufacturing expanded rapidly. By the mid-1960s Costa Rica had become the most industrialized nation of Central America. The most important industrial products are foodstuffs, cotton, textiles, synthetic fibers, and pharmaceuticals.

In 1966 Costa Rica's exports earned $138 million and its imports cost $179 million. Coffee, bananas, cacao, abaca, cotton, and cattle are the major agricultural exports. Other exports are fish, lumber, gold, and manganese.

Costa Rica's economic progress is heavily dependent on foreign aid and investment. Through the Alliance for Progress the United States has helped finance Costa Rica's efforts to industrialize further.

GOVERNMENT. Costa Rica has a presidential form of government. The head of state and chief executive is the president, who is popularly elected to a four-year term of office. Legislative powers rest with the unicameral Legislative Assembly, which is also popularly elected to a four-year term.

Costa Rica is a member of the United Nations, the Organization of American States (OAS), and the Organization of Central American States.

HISTORY. Columbus discovered Costa Rica in 1502 on his last voyage to America. Expecting to find gold, he named it *Costa Rica,* or rich coast. Disappointed treasure hunters who followed him stayed only long enough to pillage the land. The first permanent European settlement was established in 1564 at Cartago, on the Meseta Central, by Juan Vásquez de Coronado.

Costa Rica was part of the Spanish colonial province ruled by the captain general of Guatemala. When Agustín de Iturbide proclaimed Mexico's independence from Spain in 1821, the Spanish Captain General Gabino Gaínza declared Central America independent. In 1822 Gaínza was overthrown and the region was annexed to Mexico.

Iturbide fell in 1823, and Costa Rica joined Guatemala, El Salvador, Honduras, and Nicaragua to form the United Provinces of Central America. Dissatisfaction with Guatemala's domination of the union soon developed, and in 1839 Costa Rica withdrew from the federation and became a separate nation.

Independence. Braulio Carrillo, a dynamic president, who served from 1834 to 1837 and again from 1838 to 1842, promoted the cultivation of coffee, which became a major export, and subdivided many large estates, thus increasing the number of small landholders.

In 1842 Carrillo's dictatorial methods led to a successful revolt under the leadership of Francisco Morazán. Morazán was himself shortly overthrown, and a period of anarchy followed. Order was finally restored in 1849.

In 1870 Tomás Guardia overthrew the government and dominated national affairs until his death in 1882. He modernized the economy and increased unity, partly through a vast program of railroad construction.

Under Pres. Bernardo Soto (1885–1890), free compulsory education was established and in 1889 the first free elections were held. Costa Rican support of democratic principles was expressed in public hostility to a coup in 1917 led by Federico Tinoco Granados, and his regime lasted for less than two years.

Conflict with Panama over Coto, a border region on the Pacific coast, dominated foreign affairs during the 1920s and 1930s. Costa Rica invaded the Panamanian-occupied territory in 1921, and the United States pressured Panama to accept Costa Rican control of Coto. The issue was finally settled in 1941, when both countries agreed to redefine their common boundary.

Contemporary Costa Rica. In 1948 a communist-supported attempt to elect fraudulently former president Calderón Guardia over the moderate Otilio Ulate was frustrated by rebels under the leadership of José Figueres. The Figueres victory was followed by 18 months of rule by a junta. During that period many progressive social reforms were enacted into law. Otilio Ulate was inaugurated in 1950 after Figueres restored civilian rule.

At the end of Ulate's term in 1953, Figueres was elected president. Figueres, a liberal, was a severe critic of Latin American dictators, in particular of Pres. Anastasio Somoza of Nicaragua. Early in 1955 a Nicaraguan-instigated rebellion broke out, but the rebels were crushed.

Francisco Orlich, a supporter and friend of Figueres, was defeated in the 1958 election by Mario Echandi Jiménez, a conservative. In 1962, however, Orlich won the presidency and, a year later, brought Costa Rica into the Central American Common Market. The resulting economic progress led to greater political stability and unity.

Economic growth continued under Pres. José Joaquín Trejos Fernández, elected in 1966 as the candidate of a coalition that included Ulate, Echandi, and Calderón Guardia.

—George W. Carey; Jerome Fischman

CUBA

Official name: Republic of Cuba
Area: 44,218 square miles
Population: (1967 est.) 8,033,000
Capital: Havana (Pop., 1965 est., urban area, 1,543,900)
Language: Spanish
Religion: Roman Catholicism
Currency unit: Peso
National holiday: Independence day, May 20

Cuba, the largest island in the Greater Antilles, occupies a strategic position dominating the sea lanes that link the Atlantic Ocean, the Caribbean Sea, and the Gulf of Mexico. The island lies about 100 miles southeast of the United States, from which it is separated by the Straits of Florida. There is a major U.S. naval base in southeastern Cuba, at Guantanamo Bay.

A revolutionary government was established in Cuba in 1959 under the leadership of Dr. Fidel Castro Ruz. Under Castro's leadership, Cuba became closely tied to the communist bloc of nations.

THE LAND. Cuba is made up largely of level or rolling land. There are only three mountain areas—all small. The Sierra Maestra and associated highlands lie in the extreme southeast and reach a maximum elevation of about 6,500 feet. The heavily eroded, limestone Sierra de los Organos, with a maximum elevation of some 2,500 feet, is in the dry and barren northwest. The Trinidad Mountains, rising less than 4,000 feet, are on the south coast, east of Cienfuegos.

The island has two rainy seasons, one in summer and one in winter. Hurricanes frequently occur in the fall and winter.

THE PEOPLE. The people of Cuba are largely of Spanish, African, and mixed origins. More than half the population lives in urban areas. The major cities include Havana, the capital; Camaguey, a center of the sugar industry; and Santiago, a major port.

The rate of population increase is high, but there has been a heavy emigration since the early 1960s, when the Castro government launched a socialist program. Many of the émigrés settled in the United States. They included large numbers of professional people, managerial personnel, and technicians.

ECONOMY. Cuba is a rich country, and it is among the most economically developed nations of Latin America. The island has rich soils and considerable mineral wealth. There are abundant deposits of iron ore, chromite, manganese, nickel, cobalt, and copper ore. There is also some petroleum, although not enough to meet the country's needs. There is a good transportation system, with an excellent road and rail network and a number of well equipped ports.

Cuba has long been one of the world's leading producers of sugar, and is also known for its tobacco, which is grown in the region east of the Sierra de los Organos. Coffee is produced in southeastern Cuba. Other important crops include henequen, sweet potatoes, citrus fruits, vegetables, and pineapple.

LOOK MAGAZINE

MODERN BUILDINGS RISE ABOVE THE SLUMS in Havana, Cuba's capital and largest city.

COUNTRIES OF THE WORLD

Cuba 53

FIDEL CASTRO in the Sierra Maestra in 1957.

Manufacturing is significant and growing. Sugar processing is the most important activity, but Cuba is on a par with several European countries in the production of several types of goods—synthetic fibers, for example. Steel and power consumption are also high. But industry has been hampered by a shortage of technicians and parts since the Castro revolution.

In 1965 Cuba's exports earned $686 million and its imports cost $865 million. Sugar represents about 85 percent of export earnings. Tobacco; ores, especially nickel; and chemicals are also significant exports. Imports consist largely of machinery and transportation equipment, foodstuffs, and manufactured goods.

Before the establishment of the Castro regime, the United States was Cuba's major trading partner. By 1965 the Soviet Union had replaced it. China and other communist-controlled countries are also important trading partners.

GOVERNMENT. Cuba has traditionally been a republic with democratic institutions. But the country has experienced long periods of dictatorship. The constitution of 1940, which was suspended in 1959, provided for an elected president and a legislature of two houses. The upper house, the Senate, included 54 members elected to four-year terms, and the lower house had 140 members, half of whom were elected every two years.

Dr. Castro instituted a dictatorship under his personal control. The head of state was still nominally the president, but power rested in Castro's hands as prime minister and first secretary of the Communist Party of Cuba, or PCC, from its initials in Spanish.

The United Party of the Cuban Socialist Revolution (PURSC), formed in 1962 by the merger of Cuba's old Communist party with Castro's Integrated Revolutionary Organizations (ORI), was renamed the Communist Party of Cuba in 1965. Castro's followers remained the dominant group. In 1967 Castro promised that Cuba would have a new, "socialist," constitution by 1970.

Cuba is a member of the United Nations.

HISTORY. Christopher Columbus claimed the island of Cuba for Spain in 1492, on his first voyage to the new world. At that time the island was inhabited by Arawak Indians. The Arawak had been weakened by raids by the warlike Carib Indians and they were soon enslaved by the Spanish.

Spanish Rule. Under the leadership of Gov. Diego Velázquez, Cuba became an important base for Spanish exploration and conquest of the American mainland. Cities were built and slaves were brought from Africa to replace the fast-disappearing Arawak as a source of labor. The island grew rich from sugar and was the object of pirate raids during the 1500s and 1600s. During a war with Spain in the 1700s the British briefly gained control of Havana.

Cuba remained aloof from the general struggle for independence from Spanish rule that occupied the mainland during the early 1800s. Although in 1812 a slave revolt was led by José Aponte, Spanish rule remained secure, based on capable administrators, loyal troops, and an aristocracy that feared the loss of its wealth should relations with Spain be changed. Resentment against Spain developed by the mid-1800s, however, as Spanish rule became increasingly corrupt.

The first serious attempt to organize an independence movement was made by Narciso López, a veteran of the mainland independence struggles. López was captured and executed, but his death served to strengthen Cuban nationalism. In 1868 a group of Cuban patriots, including Carlos Manuel de Céspedes, drew up the *Grito de Yara*, or "Cry of Yara," a call for independence. The new movement fought a bitter ten-year struggle, the Ten Years' War (1868–1878), which ended in a truce.

Resentment against Spanish rule intensified in the early 1890s, when the island was struck by an economic depression and North American tariff restrictions were raised against Cuban tobacco and sugar exports. In 1895 a new rebellion broke out, sparked by the poet and journalist José Martí, Cuba's national hero.

The rebel forces were led by men such as Máximo Gómex, Antonio Maceo, and Calixto García. The Spanish colonial troops were commanded by Gen. Valeriano Weyler. Within a short time, Weyler had the rebellion under control, and he launched a bitter campaign of repression, during which many thousands of Cubans died of mistreatment.

U.S. Rule. The Spanish repression kindled cries in the United States for support of the Cubans, and in 1898 war broke out between the United States and Spain after the U.S. battleship Maine blew up in Havana harbor. The Spanish-American War lasted but 100 days. Spain gave up Cuba, but instead of granting Cuba independence, the United States sent forces to occupy the island, remaining until 1902.

During the U.S. occupation, Cuba benefited from improved sanitary conditions and public education was extended. Yellow fever was wiped out after a Cuban doctor, Carlos Finlay, discovered that it was carried by a mosquito. But Cuban resentment grew as the United States continued to refuse to withdraw its troops.

The United States set as a condition for withdrawal the inclusion in the Cuban constitution of the Platt Amendment. The amendment provided the United States with naval bases in Cuba, including a base at Guantanamo Bay, and allowed the United States to intervene if it felt Cuban sovereignty threatened.

Independence. The Cuban constitution was promulgated in 1901, and in 1902 a conservative, Tomás Estrada Palma, became Cuba's first president. Liberal opposition and popular unrest led to the resignation of Estrada in 1906, and U.S. forces were again landed in Cuba.

In 1909 José Gómez, a liberal, was elected president. Instability continued, and in 1917 U.S. troops again returned. In 1925 Gen. Gerardo Machado won the presidency, and changed the constitution to maintain himself in power. Machado instituted an era of tyranny that lasted until 1933, when he was toppled by an army revolt led by Sgt. Fulgencio Batista.

Batista remained in control of Cuba until 1944, when he unexpectedly allowed fair elections. Dr. Ramón Grau San Martín, once an associate of Batista but by then a bitter political foe, was elected president. Grau was succeeded in 1948 by Carlos Prío Socarrás. In 1952 Batista again seized power and gradually instituted a repressive regime that became increasingly unpopular.

Castro Revolution. In 1953 a young law-school student, Fidel Castro, and his brother, Raúl, led a revolt against Batista. On July 26, the rebels unsuccessfully tried to seize the Moncado army base in Santiago. Captured, but later pardoned in a general amnesty, the Castros went into exile.

In 1956 Castro returned with a small band of followers that included an Argentinian, Ernesto (Ché) Guevara. They succeeded in reaching the rugged Sierra Maestra, and gradually their strength grew as students and peasants from Oriente Province joined them. Large-scale fighting broke out in 1958, and on Jan. 1, 1959, Batista fled the country.

Castro took power on a wave of popular support, but his popularity quickly waned at home and abroad. Former associates broke with him over communist influence in the new government, and in 1960 a socialist program was launched with the nationalization of much of the economy. Hundreds of thousands of Cubans fled, most of them finding refuge in the United States.

U.S. property was among that seized, and the United States retaliated by reducing sugar imports from the island. In 1961 Cuba signed a trade agreement with the Soviet Union, and Castro announced his acceptance of Marxist-Leninist doctrine.

U.S. diplomatic relations with Cuba were severed in 1961, and in that year the United States sponsored an invasion of Cuba by a force of Cuban exiles. The force landed at the Bay of Pigs, and was soon destroyed. In 1962 Castro exchanged the survivors of the invasion for needed foodstuffs and medical supplies from the United States.

A new crisis in Cuban-U.S. relations occurred in 1962, when U.S. Pres. John F. Kennedy charged that Soviet missiles were being installed in Cuba. A blockade of Cuba was announced by the United States, and the Soviet Union agreed to dismantle the missile bases.

Castro attempted to spread his form of revolution throughout Latin America, and Cuban-supported insurrections broke out in many countries. In 1962 the Organization of American States (OAS) suspended Cuba's participation in the work of the organization. Prominent among the Cuban revolutionaries active in promoting Castro-type revolutions in other countries was Ché Guevara, who lost his life fighting with a rebel band in Bolivia in 1967.

—George W. Carey; Jerome Fischman

CYPRUS

Official name: Republic of Cyprus
Area: 3,572 square miles
Population: (1967 est.) 614,000
Capital: Nicosia (Pop., 1964, urban area, 103,000)
Language: Greek, Turkish
Religion: Orthodox Christianity, Islam
Currency unit: Pound
National holiday: Independence day, October 1

Cyprus, an independent island republic in the eastern part of the Mediterranean Sea, lies about 40 miles south of Turkey.

THE LAND. The island of Cyprus is mountainous. Two ranges rim the coasts—the Kyrenia Mountains in the north and the Olympus Mountains in the south. A wide, fertile plain occupies the center of the island. Summers are hot and dry, and winters are cool with occasional rain.

THE PEOPLE. About four-fifths of the Cypriots are Greek Christians, and about one-fifth are Turkish Muslims. The island's population is concentrated in the central plains, especially around Nicosia, and along the southern coast, in the port cities of Limassol and Famagusta.

ECONOMY. Copper, asbestos, and iron mined in the Olympus Mountains are among Cyprus' principal exports. Vegetables, oranges, and wines produced for the European market are also important. Wheat, olives, and carobs (a cattle fodder) are grown. The island has not developed any heavy industry, but there are many light-manufacturing plants.

Tourism is encouraged by the government and has been an important source of income. In 1966 Cyprus' exports earned $78 million and its imports cost $154 million.

GOVERNMENT. Cyprus' constitution, adopted at the time of independence, established a republic with government posts divided proportionally between the Greek and Turkish communities. The president was to be a Greek-speaking Christian, the vice president, a Turkish-speaking Muslim. The parliament was also divided —70 percent Greek and 30 percent Turkish.

Cyprus is a member of the United Nations and of the Commonwealth of Nations.

HISTORY. People have lived on Cyprus since before 4000 BC. The ancient Greeks traded with Cyprus and established colonies on the island. From about 800 BC to modern times, Cyprus was ruled by whatever nation dominated the adjacent seas. Phoenicians, Assyrians, Persians, Romans, Byzantines, Arabs, Crusaders, and Venetians all occupied the island.

In 1571 the Ottoman Turks conquered Cyprus and held it until 1878, when Britain took control. During the period of Ottoman rule a Turkish-speaking Muslim minority developed alongside the original Greek-speaking Christian majority. In 1914, at the beginning of World War I, Britain formally annexed Cyprus from the Ottoman Empire, an ally of Germany. In 1925 the island became a British crown colony.

During the years of Venetian and Ottoman government the island had undergone an economic and cultural decline, but as a British colony it experienced a revival. With this revival came an awakening of national consciousness and a rising demand on the part of Greek Cypriots for union with Greece, *Enosis*, a demand Turkish Cypriots opposed. In 1955 Greek Cypriots began a guerrilla war against the British.

Independence. In 1959, after years of bloody fighting, an agreement signed by Britain, Greece, and Turkey granted Cyprus independence with strict safeguards for the rights of the Turkish minority and for British military interests.

Archbishop Makarios, head of the Cypriot Orthodox Church and leader of the Greek community, became president, with a Turkish Cypriot leader as vice president. Increasing friction between the Greek and Turkish communities soon paralyzed the new government, however.

At the end of 1963, a dispute arose over a proposed constitutional change that would have reduced the power of the Turkish minority. Turkish officials withdrew from the government, and civil war broke out between the two communities. Turkey and Greece became involved in the conflict and came close to war over Cyprus.

In 1964 a UN force arrived on the island and secured a ceasefire, but the United Nations failed to achieve a permanent solution to the island's communal problem. Fighting again erupted in late 1967, and Greece and Turkey were again drawn into the conflict. Despite the crisis, the Greek Cypriot administration held elections in 1968, and Archbishop Makarios was reelected president.

—Charles Issawi; Alexander Melamid

CZECHOSLOVAKIA

Official name: Czechoslovak Socialist Republic
Area: 49,370 square miles
Population: (1966 est.) 14,240,000
Capital: Prague (Pop., 1965 est., 1,023,000)
Language: Czech, Slovak
Religion: Protestantism, Roman Catholicism
Currency unit: Koruna
National holiday: Liberation day, May 9

The Czechoslovak Socialist Republic is a landlocked nation in east-central Europe. It is bounded on the north by Poland, on the east by the Soviet Union, on the south by Hungary and Austria, and on the west by West Germany and East Germany.

The country consists of three historic regions—Bohemia, or Czeçy, in the west, Moravia in the center, and Slovakia in the east. These regions were united in 1918 to form Czechoslovakia.

THE LAND. Uplands dominate Czechoslovakia's terrain. In Bohemia, the western third of the country, the rolling plateau of the Bohemian Quadrangle is rimmed with mountains. The Bohemian Forest in the southwest, the Erz (Ore) Mountains in the northwest, and the Sudeten range in the north all rise above 4,000 feet, and the hills of the Czech-Moravian Uplands (Ceskomoravská Vysočina) form the eastern limit of the plateau. The Elbe River and its tributaries drain the entire region. Flowing northwest, the Elbe provides a route to the North Sea.

Moravia, in central Czechoslovakia, is a wide passageway of river valleys and low hills drained by the Morava and Oder rivers. The Morava flows south toward the Danube River, which provides access to the Black Sea. The Oder flows north toward the Baltic.

Higher mountains rise in Slovakia, the eastern third of the country. The Carpathian range reaches a peak of more than 8,000 feet. From this mountainous core a series of lower ranges, hills, and plateaus descends toward lowlands in the southeast.

Czechoslovakia's climate is moderate, with temperatures averaging about 70°F in summer and 20°F in winter. Between 20 and 40 inches of rain fall each year, most of it in the winter.

THE PEOPLE. Slightly less than two-thirds of the people are Czech, and just under one-third are Slovak. There are small groups of Hungarians, Ukrainians, Germans, and Poles. Czech and Slovak, the official languages, are West Slavic tongues.

Slovaks are concentrated in the east, Czechs in the center and west. Friction between the two groups has created serious problems.

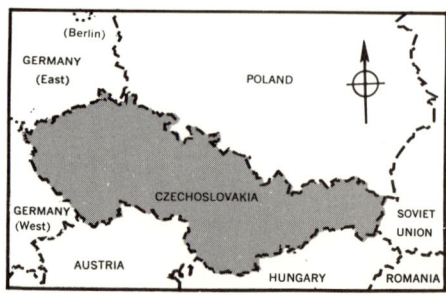

COUNTRIES OF THE WORLD

Population is densest in central Bohemia, especially around Prague, the capital, largest city, and cultural and economic center of the country.

ECONOMY. Czechoslovakia is one of the most prosperous countries in eastern Europe. Its prosperity stems largely from industry, which is based on the country's location along many excellent transportation routes, its industrious and skilled population, and its rich natural resources.

Mineral resources include large deposits of brown coal, more limited amounts of hard coal, and uranium. There are also smaller deposits of antimony, mercury, graphite, glass sands, silver, iron ore, lead, and zinc.

Agriculture. Although there is rich soil, agriculture is limited to the lowland areas and contributed only 13 percent to the national product in 1965. Most of the land is cultivated by collective farms. The limited amount of good farmland is partially compensated for by the use of advanced agricultural techniques.

Wheat, rye, barley, oats, sugar beets, and potatoes are the leading crops. Meadows and fields devoted to fodder crops support large herds of livestock.

Industry. Czechoslovakia is one of eastern Europe's most industrialized nations, and in 1965 industry contributed 65 percent of the national product. All large-scale industries and businesses are operated by the government.

Chemicals, iron and steel, heavy machinery, and electricity are the country's major products. Traditional light industries, including leather working, glass making, textile weaving, brewing, and food processing, still thrive but have declined in importance as heavy industry expanded during the 1950s.

Industrial activity is concentrated around Prague and Plzen, in central Bohemia, Brno, in central Moravia, and Bratislava, in southwestern Slovakia on the Danube.

Trade. In 1966 imports cost $2,729 million, and exports earned $2,745 million. Iron, steel, machinery, and chemicals are the leading exports, and fuel oil, raw materials, and foodstuffs are imported. The Soviet Union is the country's leading trading partner, followed by other eastern European states. In the early 1960s, trade was expanded with some western European, Asian, and African countries.

GOVERNMENT. The Communist party dominates political life. At the head of the party is a central committee, whose presidium, or executive committee, determines national policy. The first secretary of the central committee is the key political figure in the country.

A constitution places executive power in a president, who is chosen for a five-year term by the popularly elected 300-member National Assembly. The president appoints a cabinet of ministers. Candidates for the assembly are chosen by the National Front, a mass organization controlled by the Communist party.

Czechoslovakia is a member of the United Nations; the Warsaw Pact, a military grouping of European communist-controlled states; and the Council for Mutual Economic Assistance (COMECON), which attempts to coordinate economic programs within the Soviet bloc.

PETER SPRAGUE
PRAGUE'S CHARLES BRIDGE, a city landmark, was built by King Charles IV in 1357.

HISTORY. Czechoslovakia came into existence as a single independent state in 1918. Prior to that, the history of the Czechs of Bohemia and Moravia and that of the Slovaks differed, but each was characterized by domination by other nations.

The basins of the Elbe, Oder, and Morava rivers, protected by the surrounding mountains, had been settled by Slavic peoples by the 500s. By the 600s some tribal and geographical distinctions had been made between Czechs, Moravians, and Slovaks.

Moravia developed most quickly, and by the end of the 800s Moravian princes ruled an empire that included Slovakia and parts of present-day Austria and Hungary. Moravian subjects became Christians during the 800s. In the early 900s, the Moravian empire was conquered by the Magyar people of Hungary.

Hungary ruled Slovakia and the eastern part of old Moravia for 1,000 years, until the defeat of Austria-Hungary in World War I. The Czech tribes of Bohemia were gradually united during the 800s and 900s. By the end of the 900s one leader ruled Bohemia and western Moravia.

In the 1000s the kingdom of Bohemia became part of the Holy Roman Empire, but its military power and political strength was great enough to permit the state a great deal of independence. Its wealth, prestige, and cultural and political leadership reached a peak in the 1300s, when Prince Charles of Bohemia became Holy Roman emperor.

Hapsburg Rule. During the 1400s, especially after the execution in 1415 of a Bohemian religious reformer, John Hus, conflict within Bohemia and between Bohemia and the empire led to a gradual decline in the kingdom's prestige. In 1526 a Hapsburg of Austria was elected king of Bohemia, and in 1547 the Bohemian crown became the hereditary possession of the Hapsburgs, who ruled Bohemia together with Austria and Hungary. Hapsburgs also ruled the Holy Roman Empire.

The Bohemian nobles resented the Hapsburg king. Not only because he was not Czech, but also because he was a Roman Catholic and during the late 1500s many Bohemians had become Protestants. In 1618 the Bohemian nobles rebelled. The rebellion raged for two years, until 1620, when the Bohemians were defeated at the battle of White Mountain, near Prague.

Through the 1600s and 1700s Bohemia was included in the Hapsburg Holy Roman Empire, which was succeeded by the Hapsburg-ruled Austrian Empire. Catholic German rule impoverished Bohemia and crushed Czech spirits and Czech prospects. In the early 1800s the pan-Slav movement developed in Bohemia and Slovakia, and in 1848 it contributed to a Slavic revolt against the German-speaking Austrians.

The rebellion was put down by 1849, but the movement gained strength as Austria lost power to Prussia and gradually relaxed its rule. In 1867 Austria's reception of the Magyars of Hungary into an equal partnership in a dual Austrian-Hungarian monarchy served to spur the Slavic independence movement. By the last decades of the 1800s, Austria-Hungary's encouragement of industrialization in Bohemia had made the Czechs among the most prosperous people of Europe.

Austria-Hungary went to war with Serbia in 1914, and World War I began. The Czechs were economically, emotionally, and politically ready to take advantage of the turmoil the war caused in Austria-Hungary. Czech and Slovak soldiers surrendered independently to the Allied armies and fought against Austria-Hungary, thus winning support for their independence movement in the Allied countries.

During the war Tomáš Masaryk, the leader of the Czech national movement, and Slovak leaders agreed to unite in a new country and formed a provisional government. After the war the Allies recognized the provisional government as the representative of the Czech and Slovak peoples, and in

1918 Czechoslovak independence was proclaimed.

Independence. The new state was formally recognized in 1919 in the Treaty of St. Germain. A democratic constitution was adopted, and Masaryk became the first president. He was succeeded in 1935 by his associate, Eduard Beneš.

Czechoslovakia was the most promising new parliamentary democracy in Europe, and in many ways Czechoslovakia more than fulfilled its promise. It became the most democratic and prosperous country in eastern Europe.

Although equal status had been granted to Czechs and Slovaks, the new state was based largely on Czech political and economic leadership centered in Prague. The Slovaks, after 1,000 years of rule by Hungary, were not as advanced as the Czechs politically or economically.

Friction between Czechs and Slovaks mounted over political, economic, religious, educational, and social issues. To these difficulties was added the dissatisfaction of a sizable German minority included in the new state. The Germans, concentrated in the strategic Sudeten region of northwestern Czechoslovakia, resented rule by Czechs and Slovaks, whom they had dominated for centuries. They charged discrimination and claimed that they had no effective voice in government.

The problems of Czechs and Slovaks and of Slavs and Germans might have been solved if Adolf Hitler and the Nazi party of Germany had not taken advantage of the German minority's dissatisfaction. Suffering the effects of the world economic depression of the 1930s and excited by Hitler's brand of German nationalism, Sudeten Germans served as German agents within Czechoslovakia. Their complaints and Hitler's diplomatic and military pressures created an international crisis that led in 1938 to the Munich agreement.

Britain and France agreed at Munich to the division of Czechoslovakia and the transfer of one-third of its population and its vital defenses to Germany. Poland and Hungary also took areas they had long claimed. In return, Hitler promised to leave untouched the remainder of Czechoslovakia. In 1939, despite Munich, German troops occupied the rest of Czechoslovakia.

During the war, a major Czechoslovakian resistance movement was organized in which Czechoslovakian communists played a prominent role. In 1944–1945 Soviet troops liberated Slovakia, Moravia, and most of Bohemia from the Germans. U.S. forces liberated western Bohemia in 1945, but the Soviets insisted that Soviet troops be allowed to free the capital, Prague. This gained for the Soviet Union the bulk of the prestige associated with the country's liberation.

Communist Rule. The presence of Soviet troops and the desire of President Beneš and other Czechoslovak leaders to cooperate with the Soviet Union allowed the communists to make their leader, Klement Gottwald, prime minister. The communists also gained control of the key departments of defense, which controlled the army, and of interior, which controlled the police.

In elections held in 1946, however, the Communist party received only 38 percent of the votes. In 1948, because of Soviet refusal to allow Czechoslovakia to receive U.S. economic aid under the Marshall Plan, it seemed likely that the communists would receive even fewer votes. In 1948, before elections could be held, the communists staged a successful coup d'etat. They took control of the government and made Czechoslovakia part of the Soviet bloc.

During the 1950s the communist-controlled government nationalized all large-scale business and industry and collectivized agriculture. The government concentrated on developing Slovakia and on building up heavy industry in Bohemia. Czechoslovakia became one of the most productive states in the Soviet bloc, and its industry contributed heavily to Soviet economic aid projects in Africa and the Middle East.

But inefficient state management led to a sharp decline in Czechoslovakian output in the late 1950s and early 1960s. In 1965 the party reorganized its economic control programs and established a new management plan emphasizing profits and wage incentives. In 1967 economic reforms were carried still further, and in 1968 leading party and government posts were filled by more liberal communists.

—George Kish; Robert F. Byrnes

DAHOMEY

Official name: Republic of Dahomey
Area: 43,483 square miles
Population: (1966 est.) 2,410,000
Capital: Porto-Novo (Pop., 1964 est., 69,500)
Language: French, African languages
Religion: Christianity, Islam, traditional religions
Currency unit: Franc CFA (African Financial Community)
National holiday: Independence day, August 1

Dahomey, a republic in west Africa, is bounded on the east by Nigeria, on the south by the Atlantic Ocean, on the west by Togo, and on the north by Upper Volta and Niger. Dahomey, a former French territory, received its independence in 1960.

THE LAND. Most of Dahomey lies at an elevation of less than 1,000 feet above sea level. Dahomey has a narrow, sandy coastline. Behind the coast are marshes and lagoons. The mainland begins in a low-lying clay plain, which is intensively cultivated. There are grasslands in the north.

A low dividing ridge crosses the country at its greatest width. Rivers south of the ridge drain into the sea. To the north they are tributaries of the Volta and Niger rivers.

The climate in the coastal region is hot and wet. In the north it is dry from November to June, and rainy from June to November.

THE PEOPLE. The population of Dahomey includes many ethnic groups. The Fons live in the southern part of the country. The Nagots live in western Dahomey and in the districts of Porto-Novo and Abomey. The Baribas live in the north. Other ethnic groups

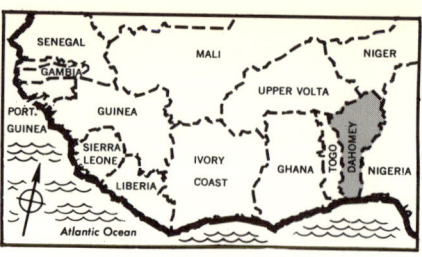

are the Peuhls, the Sanbas, the Azios, and the Adjas. There is a small European population.

Dahomey is densely populated, and numbers of men emigrate to neighboring countries in search of work.

Most people live in rural areas. The port of Cotonou is Dahomey's largest city and economic center. Porto-Novo, the capital, is the second largest city.

ECONOMY. Dahomey's economy depends on agriculture. Most of the people are farmers who grow corn, coffee, peanuts, and millet. Fishing provides an additional source of income for the people of the coastal region. Livestock are also raised. Although there are deposits of iron, gold, and chromite, mineral resources are not exploited to any great extent. There is little industry, but handicrafts are important.

In 1965 exports earned $14 million and imports cost $34 million. Exports consist largely of oil palm products. Imports include foodstuffs, motor vehicles, machinery, petroleum products, and cotton fabrics. Most trade is conducted with France.

GOVERNMENT. Until 1965 Dahomey elected a president and vice-president, each to a five-year term. The president served as chief of state. The vice-president held actual executive power. Legislative power was vested in a single-chambered National Assembly, which consisted of 42 members. In 1965 the army took power.

Dahomey is a member of the United Nations and of the Organization of African Unity (OAU).

DAHOMEAN WEAVER working on a tapestry.

COUNTRIES OF THE WORLD

HISTORY. Many rich and highly organized kingdoms existed in the area of present-day Dahomey. The most famous was the Fon kingdom of Abomey, whose ruler had conquered other coastal states by the early 1700s.

Portuguese traders came to what is now Porto-Novo in the 1600s. With the rise of the slave trade the English, Dutch, Spanish, and French also came to the area. European slave companies dealt largely with the foreign minister of the kingdom of Abomey.

French Rule. In 1851 the French established themselves at Cotonou, and in 1890 hostilities broke out between France and Abomey. In 1890 France established a protectorate over the area and exiled the king, although France continued to use tribal chiefs in administering the region. The boundaries of Dahomey were defined by 1898, and in 1904 Dahomey became part of the Federation of French West Africa.

Local conflicts dominated Dahomey's politics after World War II. In 1947 France introduced a territorial assembly, and Sourou-Migan Apithy, a southern leader, and Hubert Maga, a northerner, were elected to the French National Assembly. But regional movements did not solidify into a single national organization.

France granted Dahomey internal autonomy in 1957, and Apithy was elected prime minister. In 1958 Dahomey voted to become a member of the French Community.

Independence. France granted Dahomey its independence in August 1960. Several parties merged, and Maga was elected president. Party unity did not last, however, and a military coup overthrew Maga in October 1963.

The army set up a provisional government which, although headed by Col. Christophe Soglo, also included Maga, Apithy, and Justin Ahomadegbé. In January 1964 the people elected Apithy, the sole candidate, president and Ahomadegbé premier. In November 1965 Soglo ousted Apithy and Ahomadegbé, and assumed executive power the following month.

—Hibberd V. B. Kline, Jr.;
Vera L. Zolberg

DENMARK

Official name: Kingdom of Denmark
Area: 16,629 square miles
Population: (1966 est.) 4,797,000
Capital: Copenhagen (Pop. 1965, urban area: 1,377,605)
Language: Danish
Religion: Protestant
Currency unit: Krone
National holiday: Birthday of the king, March 11

Denmark, a small kingdom in northern Europe, lies between the North Sea, to the west, and the Baltic Sea, to the east. Its only land boundary is with West Germany, to the south. Denmark consists of the Jutland peninsula, four main islands—Fyn, Sjaelland, Lolland, and Bornholm, and 478 smaller islands, 99 of which are inhabited. The self-governing Faeroe Islands and Greenland are dependencies of Denmark.

Denmark occupies a strategic position in northern Europe controlling the Kattegat and the Skagerrak, the waterways that connect the Baltic Sea with the North Sea. The narrow Sound, the only easily navigable waterway between the Kattegat and the Baltic, passes between Sjaelland and Sweden and is the major route for shipping between the Baltic and North seas.

COPENHAGEN'S NYHAVEN, where centuries-old buildings face the four-block-long canal.

THE LAND. Denmark has a long, deeply indented coastline with many fine harbors. Almost all of Denmark is low plains. The highest point, on hilly East Jutland, is less than 600 feet above sea level. There are many small lakes and streams throughout Denmark.

Denmark's climate is generally mild and moist. Average temperatures range from about 32°F in January to 62°F in July, and rainfall averages about 24 inches a year in the east, and about 30 inches in the west. In the western part of the country, winters are slightly warmer, summers cooler, fog more frequent, and the humidity higher.

THE PEOPLE. The Danish population is quite homogeneous. Danish is the universal language, and 97 percent of the Danes belong to the Danish Lutheran Church.

Overall population density is high, but the rate of population growth is low. The most heavily populated regions are northern Fyn, East Jutland, and eastern Sjaelland, especially the Copenhagen area, where almost 20 percent of the population lives. Western Jutland, which is rather barren, is sparsely settled.

ECONOMY. Denmark's prosperity is based on its very efficient farming, light industry, and commerce. There are few mineral resources other than building stone, sands, and clays.

Over half of Denmark's land is cultivated. Agriculture employs about 25 percent of the population, and in 1965 it contributed 11 percent to the national product. Farms are small and privately owned, but farmers are organized into cooperative societies for purchasing, for processing and marketing their produce, and for improving production.

Dairying and the production of meat, especially pork, are the most important farm activities. Cereals, particularly barley, account for about 50 percent of the cultivated land. Fishing is also an important activity.

Manufacturing contributed 30 percent to the Danish national product in 1965, and between 1960 and 1965 industrial output increased at a rapid rate. The leading industrial products are processed foods, furniture, textiles, pharmaceuticals, chemicals, china and glassware, light machinery, and machine parts. Tourism is an important source of income. Shipping is a major activity, and in 1966 Denmark's fleet totalled almost 3 million gross registered tons.

Denmark generally has a slightly unfavorable balance of trade. In 1966, for example, exports earned $2,454 million and imports cost $3,003 million. The deficit is usually covered by such "invisible" items as shipping and tourism.

Denmark's leading imports are heavy machinery, petroleum products, motor vehicles, iron and steel products, textiles, and foodstuffs. The major exports are meat and meat products, fish and fish products, dairy products and other processed foods, and machinery. Most Danish trade is with Great Britain, the western European countries of the European Economic Community, and the United States.

GOVERNMENT. Denmark is a constitutional monarchy with a hereditary king as head of state. A prime minister and a State Council wield executive power and are responsible to the parliament, the Folketing. The parliament has one house and is popularly elected. Greenland and the Faeroe Islands are represented in the Folketing.

Denmark is a member of the United Nations, the North Atlantic Treaty Organization (NATO), and the Nordic Council, an association of the Scandinavian states.

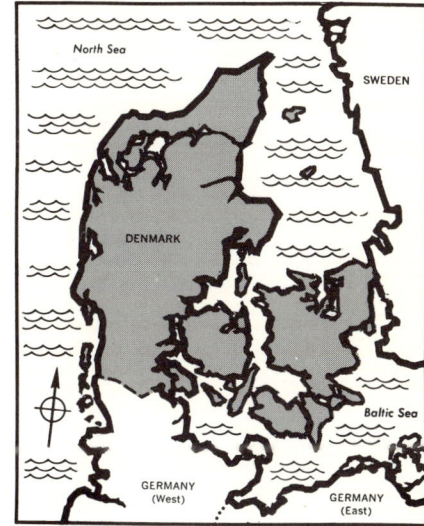

HISTORY. Archeological evidence indicates that the region of present-day Denmark has long been inhabited by man. Primitive civilization may have existed there as early as 10,000 years ago, and beginning about 2500 BC a society based on agriculture developed in the area. Early Danish peoples may have included the Cimbri and Teutons, warlike tribes described by Roman histories as inhabiting the region in the first century BC.

By the 800s AD, Danish Vikings had developed a society with a complex social organization. The Viking period, between about 800 and 1050, was turbulent. Scandinavian adventurers —raiders, merchants, and eventually settlers—visited the Caspian Sea, Iceland, Greenland, and possibly even North America. During the 900s Christianity was introduced into the region, and by about 1035 it had become the dominant religion.

The inhabitants of Denmark remained divided into separate communities until about 950, when one chieftain, Harold Bluetooth, began uniting the tribal kingdoms. The consolidation continued gradually until the 1000s, when King Canute (1014–1035) ruled a single Danish kingdom. Canute also expanded his power over England and Norway, but this Anglo-Scandinavian empire did not survive his death.

By the mid-1200s a highly organized, semi-feudal society had developed, with a strong central monarchy limited by a council of royal advisors firmly based on a middle class of farmers and artisans. During the 1200s and 1300s Denmark extended its control over territory in the Baltic area, Norway, and Sweden.

Union. By 1388 both Norway (with its possessions—the Faeroe Islands, Greenland, and Iceland) and Sweden were united under the Danish crown. This union survived, at least in form, for over a century. At the beginning of the Protestant Reformation in the early 1500s, Scandinavia was torn by religious disputes and social conflicts. As a result, Sweden in 1523 asserted its independence, but Norway remained under Danish rule.

Wars with Sweden were frequent well into the 1600s. A peace settlement was finally reached in 1660, by which Denmark surrendered to Sweden the southern part of the Scandinavian peninsula. In the same year, the monarchy became absolute as the result of a rebellion among townsmen and the clergy in support of the throne. Led by several strong rulers, Denmark-Norway regained lost territory from Sweden and rebuilt its strength.

In the 1700s, however, the monarchy weakened and a form of parliamentary government was introduced. Many other liberal reforms followed, and industry and trade expanded. During the Napoleonic period of the early 1800s, the monarchy of Denmark-Norway allied itself with France against England and Sweden, and as a result of the defeat of Napoleon, Denmark lost Norway to Sweden.

Nationalism and Reform. After the Napoleonic wars a nationalist and liberal movement developed in Denmark that was directed toward rebuilding and reforming the country. Representative local government was introduced in the 1830s, and in 1849 a constitution was adopted that limited the monarchy, created a national assembly, and guaranteed civil liberties.

The Danish nationalist movement was partly responsible for attempts to bring under Danish rule the duchies of Schleswig and Holstein, at the southern end of the Jutland peninsula. Although the duchies had once been ruled by Danes, all but the predominantly Danish northern section of Schleswig was German in language and loyalty, and the German states disputed Danish claims to the territory. The conflict led to two Danish-German wars, one in 1848–1850 and the second in 1864. A peace settlement in 1864 forced Denmark to relinquish all claims to the duchies.

The latter half of the 1800s was an era of continuing reform in Denmark. The cooperative movement was organized, and broad social welfare measures were introduced. The constitution underwent several revisions, and by 1914 Denmark had a fully democratic parliamentary government.

Modern Denmark. Denmark remained neutral during World War I. In 1918 Iceland was granted independence, but it remained united with Denmark under the Danish crown. In 1920, in a plebiscite required by the Treaty of Versailles, the Danes of Schleswig voted to rejoin Denmark.

During the 1920s Denmark entered agreements with other Scandinavian states for mutual aid and defense, and in 1926 Denmark began complete disarmament. During the 1930s Denmark had marked success in repairing the damage done by the world economic depression. Advanced social legislation was passed that remained in effect long after the depression had ended.

Denmark again proclaimed its neutrality at the beginning of World War II, but in April 1940 German forces invaded and occupied the country. King Christian X refused to go into exile or to yield to the Germans, and the Danes governed themselves until 1943, when the Germans assumed direct control. In 1944 Iceland severed its ties with Denmark and proclaimed itself an independent republic.

The Danish resistance movement was strong throughout the war. It successfully sabotaged German facilities and helped almost all of Denmark's Jews to escape German persecution. In 1945 the country was liberated.

Denmark's economy had been badly damaged during the German occupation, but by the early 1950s, prosperity had returned. In 1953 a new constitution was adopted. It removed Greenland from colonial status, and it substituted a unicameral for a bicameral legislature.

Danish politics in the 1950s and 1960s were complex, and the existence of a large number of political parties made majority governments rare. In 1968 Denmark's voters swung to the right, and 15 years of government by Social Democratic-led coalitions came to an end. A new right-of-center government headed by Hilmar Baunsgaard took over from Social Democrat Jens Otto Krag.

DOMINICAN REPUBLIC

Official name: Dominican Republic
Area: 18,816 square miles
Population: (1967 est.) 3,889,000
Capital: Santo Domingo (Pop., 1966 est., 560,600)
Language: Spanish
Religion: Roman Catholicism
Currency unit: Peso
National holiday: Independence day, February 27

The Dominican Republic occupies the eastern two-thirds of the Caribbean island of Hispaniola. The western third of the island is occupied by Haiti. Hispaniola is situated between Cuba on the west, Jamaica on the southwest, and Puerto Rico on the east.

Santo Domingo, the country's capital, was founded in 1496 by Bartholomew Columbus and is the oldest permanent European settlement in the Western Hemisphere.

THE LAND. The Dominican Republic has four mountain ranges, which lie roughly parallel to each other. The narrow Cordillera Septentrional is the northernmost range. The Cordillera Central, with peaks over 10,000 feet, is the backbone of the country. To the south are the Sierra de Neiba and the Sierra de Bahoruco.

The Cibao plain, the largest lowland in the republic, separates the Cordillera Septentrional from the Cordillera Central. In the eastern part of the plain is the humid and rich Vega Real, which is drained by the Río Yuna in the east and by the Río Yaque del Norte in the northwest.

Southwest of the Cordillera Central is the San Juan Valley, and south of the Sierra de Neiba lies the Cul de Sac, a semi-arid lowland area watered by Lake Enriquillo. A broad Caribbean coastal plain is the site of Santo Domingo.

The climate of the Dominican Republic is generally subtropical. Extremes in temperature do not often occur, and rain is abundant in most areas. The higher inland regions, however, are cooler, and rainfall is greatest on the slopes facing northeast, toward the trade winds.

THE PEOPLE. Most Dominicans are mulatto, of mixed white and Negro origin, but there are white and Negro minorities. The Vega Real and the Caribbean coastal plain are the most heavily populated regions.

ECONOMY. Fertile soil and a favorable climate have made agriculture and stock raising the principal economic activities. Sugar, cacao, coffee, tobacco, and bananas are grown for export. Meat and dairy products are also exported.

There is a great variety of mineral resources, and gold, silver, copper, iron, and bauxite are mined for export. Textiles and lumber are manufactured mainly for domestic use.

In 1966 exports earned $137 million and imports cost $159 million. Sugar and sugar products, such as molasses and rum, make up about 50 percent of all exports. The major imports are machinery, textiles, iron and steel products, and petroleum products.

Civil conflict in 1965 resulted in serious reductions in the volume of the

Dominican Republic's trade. As a result, the country faced serious economic problems and was forced to rely heavily on foreign economic aid.

GOVERNMENT. The head of the government is the president, who is popularly elected to a four-year term of office. He is assisted by a cabinet, whose members are appointed by him. Legislative power rests with the Legislative Assembly, whose members are also elected to four-year terms.

The Dominican Republic is a member of the United Nations and the Organization of American States (OAS).

HISTORY. Christopher Columbus discovered the island of Hispaniola in 1492 and claimed it for Spain. In 1697 Spain ceded the western third of Hispaniola to France, and in 1795 it also surrendered the eastern two-thirds of the island, Santo Domingo. Spain regained Santo Domingo in 1809 with British and Dominican help.

Independence. In 1821 the middle class rebelled against Spain and proclaimed the country's independence. But in 1822 Haitian forces occupied Santo Domingo, and for 22 years Dominicans suffered under oppressive Haitian rule. In 1844 the Dominicans expelled the Haitians and established the Dominican Republic with Pedro Santana as president.

During the following years, a fierce power struggle between Santana and Buenaventura Báez and the continued fear of Haitian aggression threatened the existence of the republic. To protect the state and maintain himself in office, President Santana in 1861 proclaimed the reannexation of the Dominican Republic to Spain with himself as governor-general. Spanish forces occupied the country, but sporadic uprisings, called the War of Restoration, forced the withdrawal of the Spanish troops in 1865.

Under Báez's intermittent rule, from 1865 until 1878, the country continued to be poor and backward and accumulated large foreign debts. In 1869 Báez negotiated a treaty of annexation with the United States. Although the measure was supported by Pres. Ulysses S. Grant, it was rejected by the Senate.

In 1882 Ulises Heureaux gained the presidency and ruled the country until he was assassinated in 1899. Although he greatly increased the foreign debt, he maintained internal peace, launched public works programs, and developed industry.

U.S. Role. With the death of Heureaux, violence and disorder again erupted. In 1905 Pres. Theodore Roosevelt, fearing aggression by foreign nations demanding repayment of loans, agreed to place Dominican customs duties under the control of U.S. collectors, who would use the customs revenues to pay the foreign debts. In addition, U.S. loans reassured both foreign creditors and Dominicans.

Political instability continued, however, and in 1911 President Ramón Cáceres was assassinated and a military government installed. Peace was temporarily restored in 1912 by a U.S. mission, and in 1914 by U.S. supervision of elections.

Further difficulties in 1916 led Pres. Woodrow Wilson to send troops and to establish a U.S. military government in the Dominican Republic. Although material improvements were made during the occupation, Dominicans resented foreign rule. The occupation forces were withdrawn in 1924, but U.S. control of Dominican customs continued until the 1940s.

Trujillo Regime. Horacio Vásquez was elected president of the republic in 1924. When he attempted to remain in power indefinitely, his government was overthrown in 1930 by Rafael Leonidas Trujillo Molina. Trujillo ruled the country, directly or indirectly, until he was assassinated in 1961.

Trujillo achieved political stability and economic progress at the expense of civil liberties. Dominicans had the highest per capita income of any of the small Caribbean republics, the budget was balanced, and debts were paid. The expansion of industry and public works projects broadened the economy and raised the standard of living.

Nonetheless, no opposition was tolerated and Trujillo, supported by the army, ruled by means of a system of terror. In 1960 the Trujillo regime was censured by the Organization of American States (OAS) for trying to assassinate Pres. Romulo Bétancourt of Venezuela.

Trujillo was assassinated in 1961, and the army and the bureaucracy, both controlled by the Trujillo family and their supporters, seized power. But they were forced out when the United States threatened to intervene.

Search for Stability. A provisional council of state governed until 1962, when elections were held. Juan Bosch, a popular intellectual and a member of the Dominican Revolutionary Party, became president.

Seven months later the military deposed Bosch and established an army-backed civilian triumvirate, headed by Donald Reid Cabral, which initiated considerable economic reforms. On Apr. 24, 1965, however, civil war broke out between government forces led by Gen. Elías Wessin y Wessin and Bosch supporters under Col. Francisco Caamaño Deñó.

Pres. Lyndon B. Johnson, fearing communist infiltration of the pro-Bosch faction, sent troops to the republic. After bitter fighting, a military occupation of U.S. and OAS forces was established. Despite the condemnation by some Latin American countries for this violation of the non-intervention provisions of the OAS charter, an OAS-sponsored provisional government headed by Dr. Héctor García-Godoy was formed.

Elections were held in June 1966, and Joaquín Balaguer, a former puppet president under Trujillo, defeated ex-President Bosch. The U.S. and OAS forces were withdrawn by September 1966, and the country set about restoring its war-shattered economy and developing democratic processes.

—George W. Carey; Jerome Fischman

ECUADOR'S SAN FRANCISCO CATHEDRAL

ECUADOR

Official name: Republic of Ecuador
Area: 109,483 square miles
Population: (1966 est.) 5,326,000
Capital: Quito (Pop., 1965 est., 401,811)
Language: Spanish, Quechua
Religion: Roman Catholicism
Currency unit: Sucre
National holiday: Independence day, August 10

Ecuador, a republic in northwestern South America, is bordered on the north by Colombia, on the east and south by Peru, and on the west by the Pacific Ocean. Ecuador's territory also includes the Galapagos Islands, situated about 600 miles from the mainland.

THE LAND. Ecuador has three major geographical zones: the coastal lowlands in the west, the Andes, and the eastern lowlands.

The Andes in Ecuador form two parallel chains: the Cordillera Occidental and the Cordillera Oriental. The mountains of these ranges, which have elevations of between 10,000 and 20,000 feet above sea level, are frequently volcanic. The ranges are highest in the north, where there are three towering, dormant volcanoes—Chimborazo, Cotapaxi, and Sangay.

Between the ranges is nestled a long trough, with an elevation of between 6,000 and 9,000 feet. This trough is composed of a series of interconnected mountain basins cut by rivers flowing west to the Pacific or east to the Amazon. Over three-fourths of the population lives within this central valley region. Livestock, poultry, grains, and vegetables are produced there, mainly for local consumption. Cotton and sugarcane are also cultivated in the lower basins.

The Cordillera Occidental descends abruptly to a warm coastal plain that is 40 to 50 miles wide. The northern

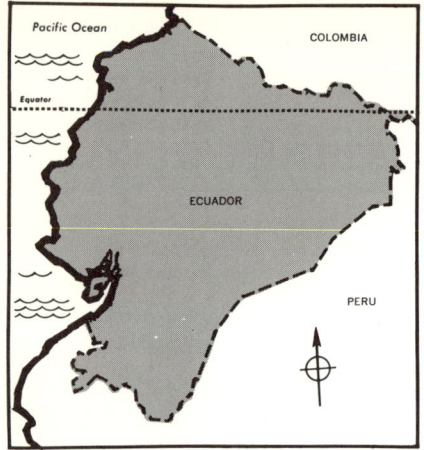

part of the plain is well watered and forested, but the southern region is semi-arid and grades into the desert of the Peruvian coast.

The coastal plain is crossed by rivers, the most important of which is the Guayas, which flows south and empties into the Gulf of Guayaquil. It is in this region that Ecuador's banana, coffee, and cacao plantations are found.

The eastern lowlands form a humid, tropical area that is almost uninhabited, except for the primitive Jivaro Indians.

THE PEOPLE. Most of the people of Ecuador are Indian or mestizo, of mixed Indian and European origins. About 10 percent of the population is of European origin, and some 10 percent is Negro. The Indians live mainly in the Andes, and the mestizos are concentrated in the Andes and in the coastal areas. The Europeans, largely of Spanish descent, live primarily in the large cities, particularly Quito and Guayaquil, and the Negroes live mainly along the coast.

The capital, Quito, lies at an elevation of about 9,500 feet above sea level. The chief commercial center and largest city is Guayaquil, located on the warm coastal plain. It had a 1965 population of over 650,000. Guayaquil sends out about 75 percent of Ecuador's exports and receives about 90 percent of all imports. It is linked with Quito by a narrow-gauge railroad, the country's major rail line.

ECONOMY. Agriculture is the mainstay of Ecuador's economy and employs most of the country's labor force. Bananas, coffee, and cacao have been the chief crops since World War II. Although some petroleum is produced, there is no large-scale mining industry. Manufacturing, with the exception of textiles, is limited.

Ecuador's exports and imports for 1964 were each valued at $148 million. Ecuador's major export is bananas. Other important exports are coffee, cacao, fish products, rice, sugar, and balsa wood. Ecuador also exports "Panama hats," so named because they were shipped through the Panama Canal. Ecuador's imports consist primarily of manufactured goods—machinery, motor vehicles, chemicals, textiles, and paper.

Ecuador's major trading partner is the United States, which supplies about half its imports and buys about half its exports. Ecuador also trades extensively with West Germany and Belgium.

GOVERNMENT. Ecuador is officially a republic, but it has a long tradition of political upheaval and coups d'etat have been frequent. Traditionally, the head of state and chief executive is a popularly elected president. Legislative powers have rested with a congress consisting of a senate and chamber of deputies.

Ecuador is a member of the United Nations and the Organization of American States (OAS).

HISTORY. Present-day Ecuador was originally the Indian kingdom of Quito. The Incas, however, conquered Quito and incorporated it into their empire. After the Spanish conquest of Peru by Francisco Pizzaro in 1533, an army led by one of his captains, Sebastián de Belalcázar, conquered Ecuador and in 1534 established the city of San Francisco de Quito on the site of the ancient Indian capital. At first Ecuador was part of the Spanish colonial Viceroyalty of Peru, but after 1740 it belonged to the Viceroyalty of New Granada.

During the Spanish American struggle for independence in the early 1800s, Quito was one of the first cities to establish an autonomous government, or junta (August 1809). This junta was quickly suppressed by forces loyal to Spain.

A second patriot government created in 1810 was also suppressed. In 1820, however, the port of Guayaquil threw off Spanish rule. Two years later, the rest of Ecuador was liberated with the help of one of Simón Bolívar's lieutenants, Antonio José de Sucre, who decisively defeated the Spaniards at the battle of Pichincha.

Independence. After gaining its freedom, Ecuador joined with Venezuela and Colombia to form the republic of Gran Colombia. But separatist feeling was strong, and in 1830, with the dissolution of Gran Colombia, Ecuador became an independent republic.

Ecuador's first president was Gen. Juan José Flores, another of Bolívar's lieutenants and a Venezuelan by birth. Flores remained a dominant figure until 1845, serving twice as president (1830–1835, 1839–1845) and keeping control of the army even during the four years he was out of office. His last administration was followed by 15 years of political instability. Some attention, however, was given to liberal reforms—slavery, for example, was completely abolished in 1854.

A new era began in 1860 with the election of Gabriel García Moreno as president. From then until 1875 he exercised firm control over Ecuador. García Moreno launched an ambitious public works program and expanded the school system, but his rule is remembered chiefly for its close alliance with the Roman Catholic Church, to which García Moreno gave wide control over both education and cultural life.

García Moreno was assassinated in 1875, and during the following two decades political anarchy reigned. In 1895 Ecuadoran Liberals, led by Gen. Eloy Alfaro, gained control of the government. Over the next few years they attempted to weaken the influence of the church and enacted a series of laws that included the legalization of divorce and the granting of religious freedom. In addition, the completion in 1908 of a railroad from Guayaquil to Quito was a major step toward the modernization of the country.

Various factions of the Liberal party generally remained in control until the mid-1940s, despite numerous coups and periods of political chaos. During the period 1925–1948, for example, Ecuador had more than 20 presidents or chiefs of state, and none completed a normal term of office.

Contemporary Ecuador. An undeclared border war with Peru broke out in 1941. The conflict was settled by the Rio de Janeiro Protocol of 1942. Under its terms Ecuador was forced to give up most of its claims to territory in the Amazon basin, Ecuador's Eastern Region. In 1961 Ecuador unilaterally denounced the agreement, however, and renewed its claims.

In 1956 Camilo Ponce Enríquez was elected president. He was the first Conservative to hold the office in 60 years. He was succeeded in 1960 by José María Velasco Ibarra, a political independent with demagogic tendencies, who had broad popular support and had been president three times previously. In 1961 a series of violent anti-government demonstrations broke out, and Velasco Ibarra resigned in favor of Vice President Carlos Julio Arosemena Monroy.

Arosemena was overthrown by a military junta in 1963. In March 1966 the junta was replaced by an interim civilian president, Clemente Yerovi Indaburu. The Yerovi administration held elections for a constituent assembly, which convened in November and chose a civilian, Otto Arosemena Gómez, as provisional president of Ecuador.

—David Bushnell; Kempton E. Webb

EL SALVADOR

Official name: Republic of El Salvador
Area: 8,260 square miles
Population: (1966 est.) 3,037,000
Capital: San Salvador (Pop., 1963 est., 281,-122)
Language: Spanish
Religion: Roman Catholicism
Currency unit: Colón
National holiday: Independence day, September 15

The Republic of El Salvador is the smallest and most densely populated of the Central American states. It is bounded on the north and east by Honduras, on the southeast by the Gulf of Fonseca, on the south by the Pacific Ocean, and on the northwest and west by Guatemala.

THE LAND. The backbone of El Salvador is formed by two volcanic mountain ranges, which run parallel to the Pacific coast. Between the two ranges is a large, high plateau with rich volcanic soils. The plateau is the most densely populated region of the country. There is a narrow plain along the Pacific coast. The Río Lempa, cuts El Salvador in two and pro-

UNITED NATIONS

THE SQUARE IN IZALCO, in western El Salvador, lies in the shadow of Izalco Volcano.

vides hydroelectric power and water for irrigation.

The climate of El Salvador is tropical, but the heat is modified by elevation. Rainfall is heavy from May to October and slight from November to April. There are frequent earthquakes and volcanic eruptions.

THE PEOPLE. Most of the people are mestizo, of mixed European and Indian origin, but there are white and Indian minorities. The population is growing at a very rapid rate, estimated at 3.4 percent a year between 1958 and 1965.

ECONOMY. Agriculture is El Salvador's main source of income and the source of most of the country's exports. Coffee, cotton, sesame, and balsam are grown for export, and corn, sorghum, beans, rice, sugarcane, and fruits are raised largely for domestic consumption. Cattle raising is also important.

Mineral resources include gold, lead, zinc, mercury, sulfur, gypsum, alum, limestone, iron, and coal. The major manufactured products are cement, refined sugar, cotton textiles, coffee concentrates, and henequen bags for the coffee industry.

In 1966 El Salvador's imports cost $220 million and its exports earned $192 million. Coffee and cotton are the major exports. Other exports include gold, silver, and balsam. The chief imports are machinery, chemicals, textiles, wheat, and petroleum products. El Salvador is a member of the Central American Common Market.

GOVERNMENT. The constitution of El Salvador provides for a system of checks and balances similar to that of the government of the United States. Executive power is vested in a president, who is popularly elected to a five-year term. Legislative power rests with the Legislative Assembly, which has a single house, or chamber. Assembly members are popularly elected to two-year terms.

El Salvador is a member of the United Nations, the Organization of American States (OAS), and the Organization of Central American States.

HISTORY. In 1524 Pedro Alvarado led an expedition southeast from Guatemala into El Salvador to continue the Spanish conquest of the area. In 1525 Alvarado founded San Salvador de Cuscatlán.

As a Spanish colony, El Salvador was part of a province under the control of the captain-general of Guatemala. The province, including El Salvador, declared its independence from Spain on Sept. 15, 1821.

Soon after, Augustín de Iturbide, who had been crowned emperor of Mexico, sent troops to El Salvador and incorporated the country into his empire. In 1822, however, the government in El Salvador petitioned to be included in the United States as a sovereign state, but the U.S. Congress rejected the appeal.

In 1823 Iturbide's empire fell and El Salvador joined the other Central American states to form the United Provinces of Central America. In 1828 El Salvador, prompted by the threat of Guatemalan dominance within the federation, withdrew and in January 1841 independence was proclaimed.

Independence. The history of the republic has been turbulent. During the 1800s, there were frequent presidential successions and revolutions reflecting factional strife between liberals and conservatives. Internal unrest was complicated by foreign aggression and the country's participation in numerous wars. The period from 1900 to 1930 was relatively peaceful, however. The coffee industry grew and the country prospered.

In 1931 Gen. Maximiliano Hernández Martínez seized power, ruling until 1944. Although he instituted one of the most brutal regimes in the country's history, the period was one of the most prosperous for El Salvador.

Contemporary El Salvador. The overthrow of Martínez in 1944 was followed by a new period of political instability. In 1945 Gen. Salvador Castañeda Castro became president. Castro was removed from office at the expiration of his term in 1948, however, when he tried to alter the constitution to retain power indefinitely.

Castro was replaced by a junta, and in 1950 Maj. Oscar Osorio, a member of the junta, was elected president. His administration grew increasingly autocratic, and in 1956 a follower of his, Lt. Col. José Mariá Lemus, was chosen president.

Lemus ruled until 1960, when he was deposed by a military-civilian junta, which promised democratic reforms including free elections in 1962. In January 1961, however, a military directorate seized control of the government. In elections, held in 1961, Lt. Col. Julio Adalberto Rivera, a member of the directorate, was the only candidate.

Although Rivera's government depended on the military, there were some political reforms. Local elections held in 1964 and 1966 were free from military interference, and in 1967 Col. Fidel Sanchez Hernández was chosen president.

—George W. Carey; Jerome Fischman

ETHIOPIA

Official name: Empire of Ethiopia
Area: 471,776 square miles
Population: (1966 est.) 23,000,000
Capital: Addis Ababa (Pop., 1965 est., 560,000)
Language: Amharic, English
Religion: Coptic Christianity, Islam
Currency unit: Dollar
National holiday: Birthday of the emperor, July 23

Ethiopia, an ancient kingdom in east Africa, is bordered on the north by the Red Sea, on the east by the French Territory of the Afars and the Issas (French Somaliland) and the Somali Republic, on the south by Kenya, and on the west by Sudan. The former Italian colony of Eritrea was incorporated into Ethiopia in 1962.

THE LAND. Most of Ethiopia is occupied by the Ethiopian Highlands, a region formed of tremendous thicknesses of volcanic lava split by deep gorges and canyons. The Great Rift Valley divides the highlands along a line running southwest from the east-central part of the country.

A large mountain mass northwest of the Great Rift Valley rises more than

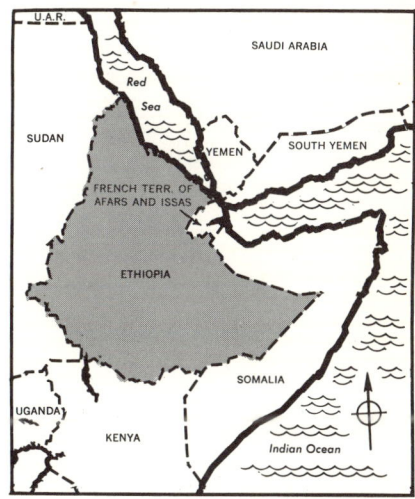

15,000 feet. There is a plateau in the southeast with elevations above 10,000 feet. In the northern part of the country, near the Red Sea, is a low-lying desert region, the Danakil Depression.

There are many rivers and lakes in Ethiopia. At the western end of the Rift Valley is the Omo River, which drains into Lake Rudolf, along the border with Kenya. Lake Tana, near the center of the Ethiopian Highlands, is the source of the Blue Nile. The Takkaze River, another Nile tributary, originates near the eastern slope of the highlands. The Awash River in the eastern end of the Rift Valley flows northeast through a dry plain to its final destination in Lake Abbe.

Ethiopians distinguish three major natural regions—the Kolla, the Woina Dega, and the Dega. The Kolla is a zone of desert plants, dry shrubs, and savanna grasslands with elevations up to 6,000 feet. The Woina Dega reaches elevations between 6,000 and 8,000 feet and is well cultivated. The Dega is a region of mountain grasslands lying above 8,000 feet.

THE PEOPLE. There are many ethnic groups in Ethiopia. Among the most important are the Amhara, Tigrean, and Galla peoples. The Amhara people live in the central highlands, and the Tigrean people live in the northern part of the country.

Both the Amhara and Tigrean peoples are Coptic Christians, and they form the ruling groups in Ethiopia. Some Galla people are Muslim, some are Christian, and some are pagan. They live in the south and also in parts of central Ethiopia.

Most of the people are farmers. Ethiopia's major cities include Addis Ababa, the capital, and Asmara, in the northern part of the country.

ETHIOPIAN COPTIC PRIESTS celebrating the Feast of the Timkat in Addis Ababa.

ECONOMY. Ethiopia's economy depends on agriculture, and the most important crop is coffee. Most farmers, however, are engaged only in producing basic food crops, and about one-half the farmland is planted in grains.

Although Ethiopia has deposits of gold, platinum, and other minerals, mining is poorly developed, partly due to the high costs of overland transportation. Industrial production greatly increased in the 1960s, and the country has textile and food processing plants. Ethiopia's many rivers provide a potential source for hydroelectric power, vital to further industrialization.

In 1966 imports cost $152 million and exports earned $112 million. Coffee is Ethiopia's major export. Ethiopia's major imports include petroleum products, textiles, transportation equipment, and machinery. Ethopia's main trading partners are the United States, Italy, and Japan.

GOVERNMENT. Ethiopia is a constitutional monarchy. Supreme political power is vested in the emperor. A constitution promulgated in 1955 provides for a bicameral parliament consisting of a Senate and a Chamber of Deputies. Senators are appointed by the emperor. Deputies are elected by universal suffrage to four-year terms. An appointed Council of Ministers, or cabinet, is responsible to the emperor.

Ethiopia is a member of the United Nations and of the Organization of African Unity (OAU).

HISTORY. Ethiopia is one of the world's oldest kingdoms, and the historical and archaeological records of Ethiopian culture go back to about 500 BC. The present-day rulers claim descent from the Queen of Sheba, whose descendents ruled over the ancient Semitic-speaking Sabaean people, whose origins are in southern Arabia.

Ethiopia was under Semitic influence until 324 AD, when the emperor Azana was converted to Christianity. Muslims invaded Ethiopia in the 600s. The Muslims converted the Galla people and pushed the Amhara people to the highlands, where they remained cut off from the rest of the world until the early 1500s.

In the 1400s Portugal sent an expedition to Ethiopia. In 1527 Muslims overran Ethiopia, but with the aid of Portugal, Ethiopia expelled the Muslim sultan in 1541. Portuguese Jesuits came to Ethiopia and tried to bring the Ethiopian Christians into the Roman Catholic Church. In 1632 the emperor, Fasilidas, expelled the Jesuits.

Political unrest, poor relations with Britain, and religious wars marked the period until 1887. At that time Italy attempted to gain territory in Ethiopia. Italy proclaimed Ethiopia a protectorate in 1889, and in 1895 the Italian army invaded Ethiopia. Italy was defeated at the Battle of Adua in 1896, but retained the coastal region of Eritrea.

Modern Ethiopia. In 1916 Ras Taffari became the regent for the Empress Zauditu. He succeeded to the throne at her death in 1930, and took the name Haile Selassie I.

In 1935 Italy, then under the rule of Benito Mussolini, renewed its claims on Ethiopia and invaded the country.

The emperor unsuccessfully appealed to the League of Nations for help, and the Italians were victorious. In 1936 Italy united Ethiopia, Eritrea, and Italian Somaliland to form Italian East Africa.

In 1941 English and Ethiopian troops defeated the Italian occupation forces, and Haile Selassie returned to the throne. In 1950 the United Nations approved the federation of Eritrea with Ethiopia, and in 1962 Eritrea was integrated fully into Ethiopia.

In 1960 the Imperial Guard revolted against Haile Selassie in protest against a lack of social and political reforms. The army, loyal to the emperor, suppressed the rising. In the following year, the emperor appointed some younger men to high posts and increased educational opportunities. Fighting broke out between Ethiopia and the Somali Republic in 1961, 1964, and 1967 because of a disputed border between the two countries.

—Hibberd V. B. Kline, Jr.;
Vera L. Zolberg

FINLAND

Official name: Republic of Finland
Area: 130,119 square miles
Population: (1967 est.) 4,664,000
Capital: Helsinki (Pop., 1965 est., urban area, 651,988)
Language: Finnish, Swedish
Religion: Protestantism
Currency unit: Markka
National holiday: Independence day, December 6

Finland is a republic in northern Europe. It is bounded on the north by Norway, on the east by the Soviet Union, on the south by the Gulf of Finland, and on the west by the Gulf of Bothnia and Sweden. The Åland Islands, between the Baltic Sea and the Gulf of Bothnia, are Finnish.

THE LAND. The name Finland means "land of fens and marshes," and much of Finland is quite low and swampy. Ten percent of the land area is occupied by about 50,000 lakes, most of which are concentrated in the central third of the country. The southwestern third of Finland lies on a low coastal plain. Elevations rise to above 1,000 feet only in the northern third of the country where densely forested uplands extend into the barren Lapland region of the far north.

About one-third of Finland lies north of the Arctic Circle, but the sea moderates the climate, especially in the south. Finland has long, cold winters and short, warm summers. Snow covers the ground for from four months of the year in the south to almost eight months in parts of the north. Rainfall averages about 30 inches in the southwest and decreases generally toward the north.

THE PEOPLE. Finland is rather sparsely populated. Population is concentrated in the southwestern third of the country, especially along the coast near Finland's largest cities, which include Helsinki, the capital, Turku, and Tampere.

The majority of the people speak Finnish, a language related to Estonian and Hungarian. Swedish is a second language, spoken by fewer than 10 percent of the people. Most Finns are

COUNTRIES OF THE WORLD

Lutheran, but there are Orthodox Christian, Jewish, and Roman Catholic, as well as other Protestant groups.

The semi-nomadic Lapps of the far north make up about 5 percent of the population. They remain generally isolated from Finnish life.

ECONOMY. Finland's economy is based on the exploitation of its rich forest and mineral resources, especially copper. Almost two-thirds of the country is forested, and deposits of copper, nickel, lead, zinc, and iron are mined. Abundant water is available for power.

Manufacturing contributed 28 percent to the national product in 1965, with wood and paper products the principal manufactured goods. Copper smelting and iron and steel production are also important. Shipbuilding and shipping are valuable industries, and the Finnish fleet in 1966 totaled over 1 million gross registered tons.

Agriculture is of decreasing importance in Finland, but in the mid-1960s agriculture and forestry together em-

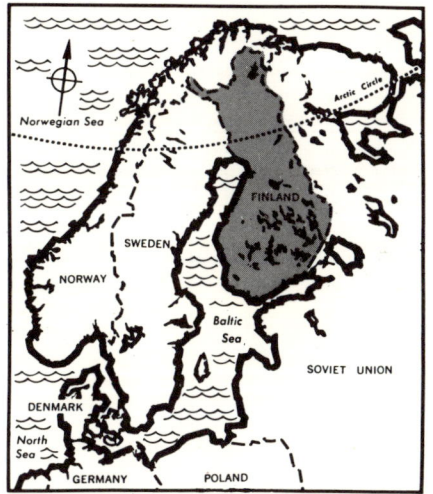

ployed approximately 30 percent of the labor force and contributed about 20 percent to the net domestic product. Only about 8 percent of the land is under cultivation, and farming is confined almost entirely to the south. Dairying is the main activity, and such hardy crops as hay, fodder, and cereals are grown. Minks and foxes are raised for their fur, and coastal fishing is prosperous.

The Finnish economy depends heavily on foreign trade, which increased sharply in value during the 1950s and 1960s. In 1966 exports earned $1,505 million and imports cost $1,726 million. Much of the trade deficit is made up by shipping and other invisible items.

Finland's exports include paper and wood pulp, timber and wood products, machinery, and transportation equipment. The major imports are heavy machinery and vehicles, finished consumer goods, fuels, chemicals, and foodstuffs. Most of Finland's trade is with Great Britain, West Germany, the Soviet Union, and Sweden.

GOVERNMENT. Finland is a republic, with a president as head of state. Executive power is wielded by a prime minister and cabinet responsible to the parliament. Members of the parliament, which has one house, are popularly elected to four-year terms.

HELEN BUTTERFIELD
FINLAND IN WINTER. The midwinter sun shines only six hours a day in Finland.

Finland is a member of the United Nations and the Nordic Council, an association of the Scandinavian nations.

HISTORY. Finland contains archeological evidence of human settlement as early as the Stone Age, over 50,000 years ago. Modern Finland was settled by people who migrated from the eastern Baltic region in about 100 AD. For many centuries they lived in a tribal society based on hunting, trapping, and fur trading.

In the 1100s Sweden conquered the Finnish tribes and converted them to Christianity. The Finns absorbed a great deal of Western culture through Swedish influence and with Sweden adopted Lutheranism in the 1500s. For most of the 600 years that Sweden controlled Finland, the Swedes and the Russians competed for control of the Baltic region, and Finland was often their battleground.

Finally, in 1808, during the Napoleonic wars, Sweden lost Finland to Russia. Emperor Alexander of Russia made Finland an autonomous grand duchy and allowed it to govern itself. The Finns enjoyed a great deal of autonomy throughout the 1800s. Beginning in 1894, however, rising Russian nationalism resulted in the loss of Finnish home rule and threatened Finnish national identity.

Independence. Finland took advantage of the turmoil caused in Russia by the 1917 revolutions and proclaimed its independence. In January 1918 civil war broke out in Finland between the communists and socialists, called the Reds, and conservative factions, called the Whites. Aided by German troops, the Whites won and established a republic.

Occasional fighting with Russia over territorial issues continued through 1919, but in 1920 the Soviet government ceded to Finland an ice-free port. Finland joined the League of Nations in 1920 and in 1921 was given sovereignty over the Åland Islands, which were to retain an autonomous government.

In the 1920s and 1930s the Finns labored to establish a stable society, and the country passed advanced social and economic reform legislation. But the young republic had difficulty in striking a balance between the extremes of the right and left. During the 1930s several attempted right-wing coups shook the government, and in 1937 a socialist coalition government came to power and banned extreme rightist organizations.

In the 1930s the Soviet Union put forth claims to Finnish territory, and in 1939 Soviet armies invaded Finland. The Finns put up a strong resistance, but in 1940 they were forced to surrender about 16,000 square miles of territory in southern Finland.

Between 1941 and 1944, during World War II, Finland renewed the struggle with the Soviet Union. But under the peace settlement it lost more territory and was forced to pay heavy reparations.

A 1947 peace treaty confirmed the reparations debt, which Finland paid by 1952, and limited the size of the Finnish army. In 1948 the Soviet Union and Finland signed a long-term mutual assistance treaty.

During the 1950s and 1960s Finland's foreign policy was strongly influenced by the powerful presence of the Soviet Union, and Finland was able to make few decisions fully independent of Soviet pressures. The Soviet Union also influenced Finnish domestic affairs.

During the postwar era, while trying to maintain the security of its borders, Finland concentrated on expanding its economy. A socialist coalition won elections in 1966 and initiated projects designed to improve Finland's economic situation.

FRANCE

Official name: French Republic
Area: 211,206 square miles
Population: (1966 est.) 49,400,000
Capital: Paris (Pop., 1962, urban area, 7,369,387)
Language: French
Religion: Roman Catholicism
Currency unit: Franc
National holiday: Bastille day, July 14

France, the largest country in western Europe, is bounded on the north by the English Channel, Belgium, and Luxembourg; on the northeast by West Germany; on the east by Switzerland and Italy; on the south by the Mediterranean Sea and Spain; and on the west by the Bay of Biscay, an arm of the Atlantic Ocean. Corsica, an island lying about 100 miles southeast of the Mediterranean coast, is also part of France.

France occupies a central position in western Europe and for centuries has played an important role in European affairs. Its intellectual and cultural life have been outstanding and have had a major influence on other countries.

THE LAND. The surface of France is quite varied. The interior consists largely of plains and low plateaus and includes the Northern French Lowlands, the Breton Massif, the Aquitaine Basin, the Rhone-Saône valley, and the Mediterranean plain. With the exception of the Massif Central, an extensive highland area in the south central part of France, the upland and mountain regions are found on or near the borders of the country.

The Alps, in the southeast, separate France from Italy. The Jura and Vosges mountains in the east run along France's boundaries with Switzerland and Germany. The Pyrenees form France's boundary with Spain in the south, and in the north the Ardennes cross the border with Belgium.

France's major rivers are the Seine, the Loire, the Garonne, and the Rhone. The Rhine River forms part of the eastern border with Germany.

Climate. Most of France has a maritime climate, with cool winters and mild summers. The southern coast has a typical Mediterranean climate, with hot, dry summers and mild, rainier winters. The greatest seasonal variations in temperature occur in the east and in the highland areas.

THE PEOPLE. France has one of Europe's most homogeneous populations. There is a strong feeling of cultural unity, and France has been troubled very little by minority unrest.

French is the universal language, and more than 95 percent of the people are Roman Catholic. Breton, Flemish, German, Catalan, and Basque are spoken in the border areas by relatively few people. The only substantial linguistic minority is the German-speaking population in Alsace.

In the early 1960s there were hundreds of thousands of foreign workers employed in French industry. Algerians formed the largest single group. Other large groups were from Italy, Portugal, and Spain.

Long comparatively stable, France's population increased between 1958 and 1964 at an annual rate of 1.3 percent, somewhat above the European average. France's population is fairly evenly distributed throughout the country. Only a few areas, such as the high Alps and parts of the infertile Landes district, near the Spanish border, are sparsely populated, and only a few industrial areas are densely settled.

Paris, the capital, is by far the largest city. Other major cities, with the 1962 populations of their urban areas, include the industrial city of Lyon, 885,944; France's principal seaport, Marseille, 807,500; the seaport and industrial center of Bordeaux, 462,171; the manufacturing and marketing center of Toulouse, 329,044; and Nice, 310,063.

ECONOMY. France's economy moved ahead briskly during the late 1950s and early 1960s, sharing fully in the remarkable economic resurgence of western Europe. Membership in the European Coal and Steel Community and the European Economic Community, the EEC or Common Market, has given a tremendous impetus to French industrial and agricultural growth.

Part of this economic growth has been the result of the revamping of much of the nation's transportation and communications system, and heavy investments in the modernization of French mines and factories during the early and middle 1950s.

Strong governmental direction of the economy under a series of formal development plans also contributed greatly to France's economic growth. The plans involve close cooperation between government and private business and have been successful in channeling resources and balancing economic growth. The fifth plan covered the period 1966–1970.

Natural Resources. France's mineral endowment is varied and, by European standards, moderately rich. There are major deposits of iron ore in Lorraine and bauxite, from which aluminum is made, in the southeast. France leads Europe in the production of these minerals. There are many coal fields scattered throughout the country, but mining them is expensive and much of the coal is of modest quality.

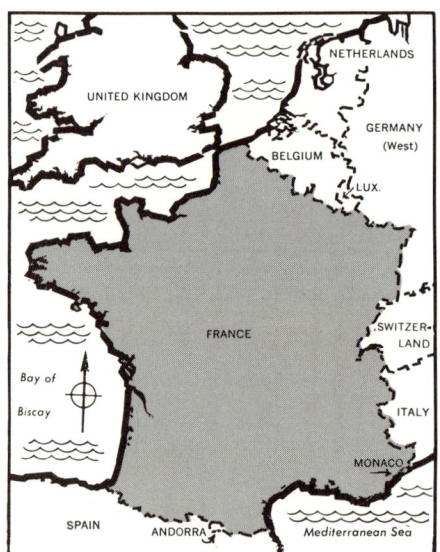

TRANS WORLD AIRLINES

EIFFEL TOWER, in Paris' Champs de Mars, is for many a symbol of Paris and France.

Securing adequate coal, particularly coke, has long been a problem of the French economy. However, the country has benefited by the rapid development in the late 1950s and the 1960s of huge French-controlled North African oil and natural gas deposits. Other mineral resources of importance are lignite sulfur, and potash.

The abundant water power of the Alps, Pyrenees, and Massif Central place France second in Europe in developed hydroelectric capacity. The country's forests and coastal fisheries also yield substantial harvests. In 1964 France ranked third in Europe in lumber production and in 1965 ranked sixth in fish catch.

Agriculture. France leads Europe in agricultural production and exports more farm products than any other European country. France has several natural features that have contributed to its success in agriculture. It has large tracts of fertile soils; in fact, one half of the European Economic Community's farmland is in France. France is also fortunate in having a climate well suited for the production of a variety of crops.

Although one-fifth of France's labor force is in agriculture, which is high for so important an industrial nation, French agriculture is highly mechanized. Great increases in the use of fertilizers, improved farm practices, and progress in consolidating fragmented individual holdings have further raised productivity and made farming more efficient, particularly in northern France. The extension of irrigation works in the dry-summer Mediterranean region have greatly increased production there.

France produced 14,270 thousand metric tons of wheat in 1965, by far the most wheat of any European country, and it ranks high in the production of meat, milk, oats, and barley. France vies with Italy as the world's leading wine maker, producing 1.8 million gallons in 1965. Other important agricultural items include corn, sugar beets, cheese, butter, and a great variety of fruits and vegetables.

Industry. France is one of the world's most important industrial nations, and French industry produces many different products. In 1965 France ranked second in Europe in the production of cement and radio and television receivers, and third in the production of iron and steel, paper, synthetic rubber, and motor vehicles. France is Europe's leading primary aluminum producer, and ranks high in the production of textiles, in shipbuilding, and in coke manufacture.

France's manufacturing is concentrated in five major industrial regions: Le Nord, Paris, Lorraine, Alsace, and Lyon–St. Étienne. The region of Le Nord, situated along the Belgian border in the midst of France's extensive coal fields, is the country's leading textile-producing area. Metal manufacture, metal fabrication, and chemical production are also important industries in Le Nord. The region's major urban center is Lille; others are Tourcoing, Roubaix, and Valenciennes.

Paris and its suburbs form France's most important industrial district. The city's large reservoir of highly skilled workers, concentrated market with high buying capacity, and position as France's government and chief cultural center have led to the development of a great variety of industries.

Especially important there are those industries characterized by their small consumption of raw materials and their high value, producing such items as scientific instruments and machine tools. Paris is the major center of the important French automotive industry and of a host of enterprises specializing in luxury articles such as jewelry, fine furniture, and perfumes—items often called "Paris goods." Paris is also world renowned for the manufacture of women's clothing.

Lorraine's manufacturing is concentrated along the Moselle valley from Nancy, its chief city, in the south to Thionville, in the north, where it extends west to include Longwy, near the Luxembourg border. The district is the site of Europe's leading iron mines and produces more than three-fourths of France's iron and steel. Some coal is brought from eastern Lorraine, but most of it is imported from nearby West Germany. Chemicals, particularly fertilizers, are also important.

Alsace is a leading textile district. The French side of the Rhine valley houses most Alsatian industry. Mulhouse is the leading manufacturing city in the south, Strasbourg in the north. The cotton textile industry, however, is scattered throughout the hilly Vosges country in central and western Alsace. The fertilizer industry, based on large potash deposits near Mulhouse, is also important.

The Lyon–St. Étienne district, which possesses coal and metals, is located at the juncture of the Rhone and Saône rivers. It produces textiles and chemicals, particularly fertilizers, are also steel and metal fabrication.

Other manufacturing centers outside the five major industrial regions are Marseille, Toulouse, Grenoble, Bordeaux, Nantes, Clermont-Ferrand, and Le Havre.

Transportation. France has an excellent transportation network. There are about 25,000 miles of railroad track, about a fifth of which is electrified. The road network is about 500,000 miles long and extends to all parts of the country. Air transportation is also highly developed, and Paris' Orly and Le Bourget airports are among Europe's busiest.

Navigable inland waterways are vital to France's economy, and there are more than 3,000 miles of both navigable rivers and canals. French flag vessels carry two-thirds of the goods entering and leaving French ports, and at the beginning of 1963 the French merchant fleet included 5,260,-000 gross registered tons.

Trade. In 1966 France's exports were valued at $10,898 million and its imports cost $11,875 million. France's major exports include steel, chemicals, perfumes, transportation equipment, foodstuffs, pottery and glassware, natural and synthetic rubber, and textiles. The principal imports include petroleum products and fuels, ores, raw textiles, and machine tools.

France's principal trading partners are West Germany, Belgium, Luxembourg, Italy, Algeria, the Netherlands, Switzerland, Britain, and the United States. About two-fifths of France's foreign trade is with its European Economic Community partners. France has made a determined effort to develop trade with Eastern Europe, the Soviet Union, Communist China, and the developing countries of Asia, Africa, and Latin America.

GOVERNMENT. France is a democratic republic. The head of state and chief executive is the president, who is directly elected to a seven-year term. The president appoints a prime minister and council of ministers, or cabinet, as well as all other civil and military officials.

The constitution grants the president the right to dissolve the powerful lower house of the legislature, the National Assembly, after conferring with the prime minister, and the right to call new elections. In the event of a national emergency, the president may assume all executive and legislative powers.

Legislative authority is vested in the parliament, which consists of the National Assembly and the Senate. The stronger of the two houses is the National Assembly, whose 487 deputies are popularly elected to four-year terms. The 274 members of the Senate are elected by regional and city electoral colleges to nine-year terms.

France was once master of a vast overseas empire. In 1958, under the constitution of the Fifth Republic, French territories were offered the choice of becoming independent, becoming overseas departments of France, or keeping their dependent status.

In 1966 the overseas departments of France were Martinique, Guadeloupe, Réunion, and Guiana. French dependencies included New Caledonia, French Polynesia, the French Territory of the Afars and Issas formerly

FRENCH EMBASSY PRESS AND INFORMATION DIVISION

THE LAND AND THE PEOPLE. The grape harvest in the Champagne country *(left)* and the peaceful Normandy countryside *(above)* reflect traditional aspects of French life today.

French Somaliland), the Comoro Archipelago, Saint-Pierre and Miquelon, the Southern and Antarctic Territories, and the Wallis and Futuna Islands.

France is a member of the French Community, a loose confederation of French overseas territories and former colonies, and the European Communities. It is also a member of the United Nations and the North Atlantic Treaty Organization (NATO).

HISTORY. France, which was known in ancient times as Gaul, was inhabited by Celtic tribes when Julius Caesar led his Roman legions into the region in 58 BC. By 51 BC Caesar had brought all of Gaul under his control. The Romans introduced the Latin language, and, later, Christianity to the Gauls.

For over 200 years the region was prosperous, and had a distinctive Gallo-Roman culture. By the 200s AD, however, Gaul was beset by political and economic upheavals as the Roman Empire began to disintegrate. The Gallo-Romans could not prevent the infiltration of Teutonic tribes, and in the 400s Visigoths, Franks, and Burgundians established themselves in various parts of Gaul.

The Merovingians. In the late 400s the Franks set out to conquer all of Gaul. They were led by Clovis I, the first of the Merovingian kings, who ruled from 481 to 511. By the end of the 400s Clovis had succeeded in conquering Gaul and western Germany. By converting to Christianity, and forcing his army to do the same, Clovis won the support of the Christian Celts. Nonetheless, Clovis was unable to create a permanently unified state, and his sons divided his lands among themselves after his death.

During the 500s and 600s rival Merovingian rulers quarreled with each other, and the high degree of civilization that the Gauls enjoyed under the Romans drastically declined. The Merovingians were weakened by civil war and were led by ineffectual leaders, called *rois fainéants*, or do-nothing kings.

In the 600s the Carolingians, who were the royal stewards of the Merovingians, assumed most of the royal authority. In 732 the Carolingian, Charles Martel, thwarted Muslim invaders at Tours—halting the Muslim threat to France and enhancing the prestige of his house. But Charles did not depose the Merovingians, who continued as nominal rulers of the Franks until 751, when Charles' son, Pepin the Short, seized the throne.

The Carolingians. Pepin's son, Charlemagne, or Charles the Great, who ruled from 768 to 814, won control of most of western Europe. He created a powerful empire, which he administered efficiently. Charlemagne was a patron of learning, and scholars from all of western Europe came to his capital, Aachen. Charlemagne cooperated closely with the Church, and in 800 Pope Leo III crowned him emperor of the Romans. His coronation marked the birth of the Holy Roman Empire.

The strength of the Carolingian empire was dependent upon the genius of Charlemagne. His son, Louis the

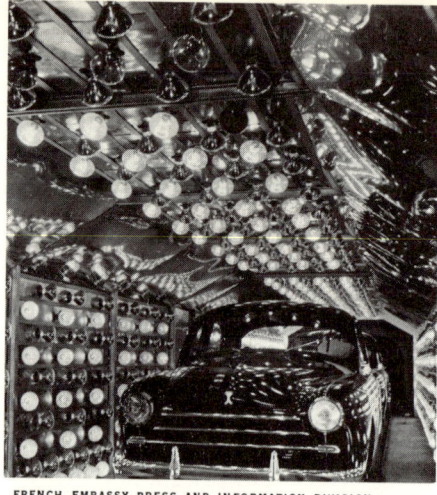
AUTOMOBILES drying under infrared lights. Autos are a major French export.

Pious (r.814–840), was incapable of maintaining a strong hold over the kingdom. The centralized administration collapsed, and Louis' three sons struggled among themselves for supremacy. In 843 they finally settled their differences and signed the Treaty of Verdun, which divided the Carolingian empire into three parts.

The eastern region, Germany, was awarded to Louis the German; the western region, France, went to Charles the Bald; and the middle strip, which included northern Italy and Alsace-Lorraine, was given to Lothair I, who also retained the title of Holy Roman Emperor. The partition of 843 marked the beginnings of modern France and Germany.

Throughout the Middle Ages France remained a separate kingdom, except for the period from 884 to 887, when Charles the Fat briefly reunited the Carolingian empire. Carolingian rule declined rapidly in the 800s and 900s. New barbarian invasions shook Europe, and political power fell into the hands of feudal lords. Economic life shrank and became centered on the self-sufficient manor.

The Capetians. The Carolingian dynasty died out in 987, and the powerful nobles chose Hugh Capet as king. Hugh Capet reigned from 987 to 996, and the Capetian kings—Hugh and his descendants—brought authority and prestige to the French crown. The Capetian kings of the 900s and 1000s had limited power and did not even control the royal domain of the Île de France, a narrow strip of land running from just north of Paris to just south of Orléans.

The Capetians gradually extended their domain and built a strong monarchy. Louis VI (the Fat; r.1108–1137), coerced the feudal lords who owed him allegiance into accepting his sovereignty and organized his domain into administrative districts (*prévôtés*) and appointed royal officers (*prévôts*) to govern them. The *prévôts* were loyal to the throne and effectively executed the king's will.

Unfortunately, Louis VI's son, Louis VII (r.1137–1180), lacked his father's political wisdom. King Henry II of England had acquired by inheritance, diplomacy, and marriage the "Angevin empire," consisting of the huge counties and duchies of Normandy, Poitou, Guyenne, Gascony, Anjou, Maine, and Touraine. Before his death Louis VI had arranged the marriage of his son to Eleanor of Aquitaine to assure France Eleanor's duchy of Aquitaine.

Finding Eleanor incompatible, Louis asked the pope to dissolve the marriage. Henry seized the opportunity to add Aquitaine to his Angevin empire and married Eleanor shortly after Louis received an annulment. The Angevin empire then surrounded the Île de France.

Louis VII's son, Philip Augustus (r.1180–1223), was determined to regain the territory lost to England and unify all of France with himself as absolute monarch. Philip succeeded in wresting control of Normandy, Anjou, Maine, Poitou, and Touraine from the English between 1202 and 1204.

To carry royal power to his newly acquired territories, Philip replaced the feudal *prévôtes* with larger administrative districts (*bailliages*) governed by royal agents (*baillis*). After a crusade against the Albigensians (1208–1213), the French crown acquired the huge fiefs of the counts of Toulouse in the south.

During the reign of Louis IX (r. 1226–1270) the royal court began to evolve into a central bureaucracy. Louis established a high court of justice, known as the *parlement*, and reorganized the royal treasury into a more workable body of government.

Under Philip IV (the Fair; r.1285–1314) the crown developed new sources of revenue from indirect taxes on commerce, money payments from nobles in place of military service, and taxation of the clergy. Philip proposed this last measure without securing papal approval, thus defying a papal bull of 1296 that prohibited rulers from levying taxes on the clergy.

A bitter feud ensued between the French monarch and Pope Boniface VIII, and in 1302 Boniface promulgated the most emphatic declaration of papal supremacy in the Middle Ages in the bull, *Unam sanctam*. Philip then summoned an assembly of the Estates General, which was made up of the nobility, clergy, and bourgeoisie (the middle class of the towns), to secure their support for his ecclesiastical policies. With their backing, the French monarch determined to limit papal interference.

At the death of Boniface in 1305, Philip effected the election of a French prelate as pope. This pope, Clement V, was induced by Philip to establish his residence at Avignon, on the border of France. For over 70 years—an era called the "Babylonian Captivity"—the popes reigned from Avignon under the supervision of the French monarchs.

The Valois Kings. The Capetian line expired in 1328, and the throne passed to one of Philip's nephews, Philip VI (r.1328–1350), who was the first of the Valois dynasty. Under the Valois royal power continued to grow, despite some major setbacks.

In 1337 the right of Philip VI to the throne was challenged by his distant cousin, Edward III of England. This led to a long, complex dynastic conflict from 1337 to 1453 known as the Hundred Years' War. During this war the French crown also faced a revolt of French peasants, the *Jacquerie* of 1358; a Parisian insurrection; and bitter civil strife among powerful French nobles, particularly between those of Armagnac and Burgundy.

In 1420 Henry V of England, who had defeated the French at Agincourt in 1415, forced the Valois king, Charles VI, to disown his own son and make Henry the heir to the French throne. However, the dauphin, as the French heir to the throne was known, fought back. With the help of Joan of Arc, who escorted him to Reims, where in 1429 he was crowned Charles VII (r.1422–1461), he managed to drive the English out of all of France except Calais by 1453.

During the Hundred Years' War the French kings had begun to create a more effective army by placing it under royal control, supporting it with royal funds, and selecting its officers. They also obtained a special direct tax on land, called the *taille*, which they did not give up at the end of the conflict.

Louis XI (r.1461–1483) inherited a monarchy that had almost absolute power and that was no longer threatened by foreign intervention. Louis destroyed the power of the remaining feudal lords and brought most of present-day France under royal control. Louis continued to reinforce the strength of the monarchy, and sought ways to ally the throne with the growing middle class. He appointed advisers from among the bourgeoisie and paid them generously for their support.

Louis XI's son, Charles VIII (r. 1483–1498), introduced a French policy of expansion abroad with campaigns in Italy. Although they were unsuccessful, they succeeded in stimulating French interest in Renaissance culture. Charles' cousin, Francis I (r.1515–1547), continued the Italian campaigns and initiated French support of German Protestants as a means of weakening the rival Hapsburg dynasty, which controlled Spain, the Holy Roman Empire, and the Lowlands (present-day Belgium and the Netherlands).

Henry II (r.1547–1559) won a foothold in Lorraine by seizing the bishoprics of Toul, Metz, and Verdun from the Holy Roman Emperor Charles V. The French also captured Calais, the last English possession in France, and ended the Italian wars.

Religious Conflict. After Henry's death, his three sons ruled France in succession—Francis II (r.1559–1560), Charles IX (r.1560–1574), and Henry III (r.1574–1589). During most of that period, the queen mother, Catherine de Médicis, dominated French political life.

Catherine and her sons were unable to maintain royal control in the face of Calvinism, rivalry between the powerful Catholic Guise and Protestant Bourbon families, and the intervention of Hapsburg Spain in French affairs.

The Huguenots, as the French Calvinists were called, created the greatest problems for the three Medici monarchs. During their reigns the royal army was intermittently engaged in a fierce civil war with Huguenot forces.

The struggle reached its bloodiest point in 1572, when Catherine incited Parisian Catholics against a large assemblage of Huguenots gathered in the capital to attend the wedding of Margaret of Valois, Catherine's daughter, and the Huguenot, Henry of Bourbon, King of Navarre. The Massacre of St. Bartholomew's Day ensued, resulting in the death of many Protestants.

The leadership of the Huguenots fell to Henry of Navarre, who had successfully escaped the massacre, and when the Valois line ended in 1589 amid the confusion of civil and religious strife, Henry returned to Paris to ascend the throne as Henry IV (r.1589–1610), the first of France's Bourbon kings.

Bourbon Rule. The Bourbons made France a relatively centralized state and a world power. Henry IV took several steps to bring order to divided France. He became a Roman Catholic to consolidate his position as king, but in 1598 he issued the Edict of Nantes, which gave the Huguenots religious rights and political guarantees. He defeated or bought off rebellious nobles and rebuilt the economy.

After initial difficulties, his successor, Louis XIII (r.1610–1643), was able to continue the expansion of royal power by delegating authority to Cardinal Richelieu. Richelieu, an important force from 1624 to 1642, crushed rebellious Huguenots while allowing them religious privileges; forced the nobles to demolish fortifications that did not protect the frontiers; developed the technique of sending out royal inspectors, or *intendants*, to supervise local administration; and ruthlessly suppressed conspiracies against the regime.

Outside France, the cardinal intervened in Germany's religious conflict, the Thirty Years' War, on the side of the Protestant princes to prevent the consolidation of Hapsburg power.

After Richelieu's death in 1642, Cardinal Mazarin carried on his work, surviving a series of revolts—called the *Fronde*—by the nobility and *parlements*, who sought greater participation in government.

Mazarin also brought the Thirty Years' War to an end in 1648 with the Peace of Westphalia. This settlement strengthened the French foothold in Lorraine and won France most of Alsace. Although the Austrian Hapsburgs had conceded defeat, the Spanish Hapsburgs continued to fight until 1659, when they yielded some territories in the Pyrenees and the Lowlands.

Louis XIV. With the death of Mazarin in 1661, Louis XIV (r.1643–1715) began to rule France personally. By that time France was already the most unified,

FISHING AND CHEESE MAKING have long been important. Brittany's fishermen *(left)* continue to sail the oceans, and the cheese makers near Rouen *(above)* still produce Camembert.

MONT-SAINT-MICHEL rises on a rock-island base between Britanny and Normandy.

most populous, and wealthiest state in Europe. Louis, known as "the Sun King," further strengthened the power of the monarchy and reinforced French hegemony in Europe.

Louis excluded the great nobles from his councils in favor of reliable middle class officials, domesticated the troublesome aristocracy in his splendid palace at Versailles, silenced opposition from the *parlements*, used *intendants* to enforce his will in the provinces, and avoided convening the Estates-General.

Jean Baptiste Colbert, his controller general of finance, encouraged the development of industry with favors and protection; the Marquis de Louvois, minister of war, reorganized the army; and the Marquis de Vauban, a military engineer, improved military fortifications. In North America, French explorers and soldiers built an empire extending from the St. Lawrence River and the Great Lakes to the mouth of the Mississippi River on the Gulf of Mexico.

The work of modernizing France was only half-completed, however. The tax system remained riddled with exemptions and inequities; internal customs barriers still impeded commerce outside of central France; and underneath the royal superstructure lay a confusion of local administrative organs, courts, and laws inherited from the past.

Louis, moreover, weakened French economic life when he revoked the Edict of Nantes in 1685, suppressing the remaining Protestant rights. This led to the emigration of thousands of Huguenots, large numbers of whom were merchants, manufacturers, and craftsmen.

Finally, Louis' wars, inspired primarily by a desire for glory, drained French resources and made his reign unpopular. As a result of the first three wars (War of Devolution, 1667–1668; Dutch War, 1672–1678; and War of the League of Augsburg, 1688–1697) France acquired bits of the Spanish Netherlands, the Franche-Comté, in east-central France, and Alsace.

After the War of the Spanish Succession (1701–1714), however, waged against a Grand Alliance of European powers, France had to recognize English claims to Newfoundland, Nova Scotia, and Hudson Bay territory in North America; and although one of Louis' grandsons became Philip V of Spain, the Spanish and French were thrones never to be united.

Decline of the Monarchy. In the 1700s the French monarchy began to lose its power and prestige. Louis XV (1715–1774) preferred private pleasure to the tasks of government. French intellectuals of the Enlightenment, a contemporary philosophic movement characterized by its emphasis on the idea of universal human progress, campaigned for social and political reform.

Although their ideas influenced large numbers of the bourgeoisie and many European monarchs, including Catherine the Great of Russia and Frederick of Prussia, the most famous "enlightened despots" of the period, Louis XV chose to ignore them. Ministers quarreled, necessary reforms were defeated, and the *parlements* repeatedly challenged royal authority on behalf of vested interests.

France also became involved in several new wars. The War of the Polish Succession (1733–1735) assured France of eventual acquisition of the rest of Lorraine, but the War of the Austrian Succession (1740–1748) ended in stalemate. Finally, the Seven Years' War (1756–1763), fought after a "diplomatic revolution" in which France became allied with its old rival, Hapsburg Austria, resulted in the loss of French Canada to the British.

Louis XVI (r.1774–1792) was a well-intentioned ruler, but he, too, lacked determination. Early in his reign he was faced with the problem of the public debt, swelled by war costs and aid to the American rebels against England. The antiquated tax system could not provide enough funds to balance the budget, and the nation faced bankruptcy.

A series of reform ministers who saw the need to tax the upper classes were dismissed. Finally, as the crisis mounted, a program was proposed that would force the aristocracy to assume their share of the tax burden. They rebelled, maintaining that the Estates-General alone had the authority to approve new taxes. In 1789, hopeful of consolidating their position, the aristocracy compelled the king to summon the Estates-General for the first time in 175 years.

The Revolution. The aristocratic rebellion finally sparked the French Revolution. The middle-class representatives of the third estate took over the Estates-General and renamed it the National Constituent Assembly. They then destroyed the remnants of feudalism, swept away antiquated laws and local institutions, guaranteed certain basic civil rights, and created a constitutional monarchy with a fairly democratic legislative assembly.

The revolutionaries antagonized many Frenchmen when they seized church property to gain revenue and proceeded to turn the church into a government department with elected priests paid by the state and virtually detached from Rome. The revolution also produced economic disorder and high prices, which kept the country unsettled. Even more serious for the new constitutional monarchy was the public distrust of Louis XVI and his queen, Marie Antoinette.

Even before the constitution went into effect in the autumn of 1791, the royal family had tried to escape the country. The leaders of the legislative assembly became convinced that reactionary European rulers were allying against them and on Apr. 20, 1792 they declared war on Austria, inaugurating the wars of the French Revolution, which were to last until 1815. When it became clear that the king and queen sympathized with the enemy, the monarchy was overthrown by a Parisian insurrection on August 10.

The First Republic. On Sept. 21, 1792, a new revolutionary assembly, the National Convention, announced the establishment of the First Republic. The convention delegates, elected by universal manhood suffrage, were republicans and they proceeded to draft a republican constitution. In the convention, the radical Jacobin party, which was allied with the Parisian populace, gradually defeated the moderate Girondists.

A reign of terror occurred in 1793–1794, when the Jacobin leaders of the convention formed a Committee of Public Safety to conduct the government. Faced with foreign invasion, serious threats of counterrevolution, and grave economic problems, the committee created a "revolutionary government" designed to crush its enemies and prepare the way for the establishment of a democratic republic.

This revolutionary government, led by Maximilien de Robespierre, featured a centralized dictatorship, a single party, a police regime, a dictated economy, and attempts at mass propaganda. Thousands of Girondists and counterrevolutionaries, as well as Louis XVI and Marie Antoinette, were executed.

To win the war—which had expanded by the spring of 1793 to include Prussia, Sardinia, Britain, the Dutch Republic, and Spain—the government drafted the entire able-bodied male population. With the largest army ever organized in Europe, the French Republic turned the tide of war in its favor.

The Directory. In July 1794 Robespierre was overthrown by the more moderate members of the convention. A reaction against the terror followed, culminating in 1795 in the establishment of a conservative republic called the Directory, because executive authority was shared by five directors.

Under the Directory (1795–1799), France experienced ineffective and unstable government at home, but enjoyed marked military success abroad. France won control over Belgium, the Rhineland, and much of Italy. In 1799 Napoleon Bonaparte, the Republic's most successful general, overthrew the Directory and proclaimed himself consul. In 1802 he made himself consul for life, and in 1804, emperor. Each change was approved by the people in a plebiscite.

Napoleonic Era. Within France Napoleon created a political system that was an amalgam of the old monarchy and the Revolution. He made himself a hereditary, divine-right ruler and formed a new aristocracy composed of those who served the state well. He made peace with the Roman Catholic Church in 1801 in a concordat with the pope, although he did not return the clergy's confiscated lands.

Napoleon issued a new civil law code, usually known as the Code Napoléon, which assured all citizens equality under the law. He introduced a tax system that was more efficient and equitable than that of the Old Regime and instituted administrative reforms that gave France a highly organized and centralized bureaucracy.

Abroad, France absorbed Belgium, Holland, the Rhineland, and part of Italy. Napoleon set up puppet states in western Germany, Switzerland, Italy, and Poland, and forced Austria, Prussia, and Russia into an alliance. However, failure to crush Britain either militarily or economically, a costly war in Spain, and a disastrous campaign in Russia led in 1814 to Napoleon's defeat by a European coalition. Napoleon's attempt to regain control—known as the Hundred Days—ended in his final defeat at Waterloo, Belgium, in 1815.

Restoration. Under the terms of the peace agreement concluded at the Congress of Vienna in 1815, France's territory was reduced to what it had been in 1792 and the Bourbons were restored to the French throne. The Bourbons could not restore the Old Regime, however, and in 1814 Louis XVIII (r.1814–1824) issued the Constitutional Charter to win the support of the bourgeoisie and the peasants. It guaranteed basic liberties and created a constitutional monarchy modeled on the British system.

The king headed a chamber of peers whom he appointed and a chamber of deputies chosen by a small electorate. The "ultra-royalists" in the chamber of deputies, who opposed the liberalism of the king, were not discouraged, for their leader was the count of Artois, the brother of Louis and heir to the throne. When he succeeded Louis as Charles X (r.1824–1830), he immediately made it clear that he wished to reestablish the prerevolutionary order.

Charles chose reactionary ministers, granted indemnities to the nobles whose lands had been confiscated during the revolution, and entrusted public education to the clergy. The chamber, dominated by the liberal bourgeoisie, tried to stop the king's actions.

Charles dissolved the chamber and called for new elections, but the majority of the electorate failed to support his policies. He retaliated by promulgating the July Ordinances, which restricted the freedom of the press, reduced the size of the electorate, and again dissolved the chamber of deputies.

Fearing that the ordinances were a prelude to a coup d'état, liberal intellectuals incited the Parisians to revolt in the July Revolution of 1830. Charles abdicated, and a constitutional monarchy was established. A cousin of the deposed ruler, Louis Philippe, duke of Orléans, became the new king.

The July Monarchy. To the disappointment of the republicans, the liberal middle class, and the workers, the "July Monarchy," as Louis' reign was called, proved to be as opposed to social and economic reforms as the previous regime. At first Louis Philippe mollified the republicans and liberals by upholding the Constitutional Charter of 1814 and extending the right to vote.

But the revolution had merely shifted the power from one small group to another—the upper middle class, or *haute bourgeoisie*, had replaced the nobility. Like their aristocratic predecessors, the bourgeoisie refused to widen voting privileges, and they used their newly acquired power to develop industries and businesses for their own material gains.

Many groups opposed the "July Monarchy." The "Legitimists" wanted Charles X or his grandson, the duke of Bordeaux, restored to the throne, and the republicans wanted universal suffrage and a republic. The workers demanded better working conditions and a voice in the government.

The workers joined with the republicans, both groups believing that only a radical change in the country's political structure could bring about improved social conditions. On Feb. 22, 1848, rioting broke out in Paris, and two days later Louis abdicated. Although the liberals were willing to place Louis' grandson on the throne, the republicans demanded a republic.

The Second Republic. A provisional government headed by the poet Alphonse de Lamartine and the journalist Louis Blanc was established. Blanc, strongly in favor of social reform, established National Workshops to provide jobs for the unemployed. He was unable to provide enough work for everyone, however, and in the ensuing dissension dissolved the workshops. The closing of the workshops was followed by rioting, which was finally suppressed by the army.

In November 1848 an assembly completed the drafting of a new constitution, which provided for a legislature of one house and a president with strong powers to be elected by universal suffrage. In December 1848 the first presidential election under the Second Republic was held. The vote made Louis Napoleon, a nephew of Napoleon Bonaparte, president, and revealed that the country as a whole, especially the French peasantry, was much more conservative than the vocal Paris populace.

Second Empire. Louis Napoleon overthrew the republic in 1851 and established an empire the following year, becoming Emperor Napoleon III. Under the Second Empire France enjoyed rapid economic growth, but in the 1860s Louis Napoleon's free trade policies and meddling in Italian affairs brought about opposition.

THE ARC DE TRIOMPHE, in Paris, covers the tomb of France's "unknown soldier."

To gain popularity, Napoleon liberalized his regime and initiated an aggressive foreign policy. But his indecisiveness and military ineptness resulted in a series of national humiliations. Napoleon III was also incapable of halting the rising power of Prussia.

On July 19, 1870, with French international prestige and military strength at its lowest point, the Prussian Chancellor Otto von Bismarck provoked Napoleon into a disastrous conflict, the Franco-Prussian War. When news reached Paris on Sept. 2, 1870, that Napoleon III had surrendered to the Germans at Sedan, the Parisians demanded a republic be proclaimed.

The Third Republic. On Sept. 4, 1870, the Third Republic was born. A provisional government of national defense raised an army to try to prevent the Germans from occupying the city of Paris, but the Parisians were defeated after a four-month siege. Under the terms of the peace treaty negotiated between Bismarck and Adolphe Thiers, the head of the National Assembly, France was forced to cede Alsace and part of Lorraine to Germany and to pay a huge indemnity.

Before the treaty was signed the Third Republic was confronted by an insurrection in Paris, which evolved into a civil war. Unwilling to concede defeat to the Prussians, the Parisians drove the French government troops out of the capital in March 1871 and formed their own municipal regime—the Paris Commune. Civil war raged for two months until the supporters of the National Assembly managed to suppress the commune.

Although the Third Republic started badly, it survived until 1940. The republic, headed by Thiers, was provisional at first since a majority of deputies in the National Assembly favored a monarchy. But the monarchists were divided between supporters of the Bourbon and Orleans lines, and gradually the voters turned to conservative republican candidates. By 1879, when Jules Grévy was chosen president, the republicans controlled all branches of government.

During the Third Republic there was a rapid change in cabinets—more than 50 before World War I. Since presidents did not call elections when ministries were voted out, deputies were not afraid to overthrow a cabinet. More important, France did not develop large, disciplined political parties such as those in Britain. Instead, after a century of ideological conflict, there was a multitude of small parties.

This system, which continued into the Fourth Republic, was not as unstable as it seemed, however. Changing ministries were composed of many of the same men who represented coalitions of center parties. Also, behind the shifting ministries stood the Napoleonic administrative structure, with its centralized bureaucracy.

The republic weathered a number of crises—such as a threatened coup in 1889 and the Dreyfus Affair in the late 1890s. In 1894 Alfred Dreyfus, a Jewish army officer, was convicted of treason. Later evidence pointed to his innocence, but the army refused to reopen the case. Monarchists, conservatives, and militarists opposed reopening the case, wishing not only to stand behind the army but to disgrace the republic. The country was bitterly divided.

In 1898 the case was reopened, and the following year Dreyfus was pardoned. In 1906 he was fully exonerated. Thus the Dreyfus Affair ultimately discredited the monarchists and strengthened the republic.

The Third Republic proved politically radical but socially conservative. Republicans led by Jules Ferry restricted the role of the church in education, and the schools were to turn out loyal republicans. An anticlerical movement culminated in the absolute separation of church and state in 1905, ending Napoleon's 1801 concordat with the Roman Catholic Church.

In social welfare legislation, however the republic lagged behind Germany and Britain. The Radical Socialists, who held the balance of power in the chamber before World War I, proved radical in name only.

France had a large conservative bloc of voters composed of peasants and small merchants. The working class was still too small and divided to exert any real pressure on the government, and the workers did not give united support to the Socialists, who spoke for them in the chamber.

Industry expanded, but not as rapidly as in other nations, and the population barely increased at all. Yet French trade grew considerably as a result of extensive colonial expansion in Africa and Southeast Asia (Indochina). By 1914 France's colonial empire was second only to Britain's.

To protect its colonial interests and to secure its position against Germany, France strengthened its army and navy, formed an alliance with Russia in 1894, and entered the Entente Cordiale with Britain in 1904. Rather than risk losing a vital ally, France supported Russia in the Balkan crisis that precipitated World War I.

World War I. In August 1914 German troops drove westward through Belgium to invade France, and soon most of Europe was involved in the conflict. Britain supported France, and the United States entered the conflict on their side in 1917. For four years most of the fighting on the western front was done in northeastern France, costing the lives of over 1 million French soldiers and untold physical damage.

Although the Allies eventually defeated Germany, France still faced a powerful German state, and after the 1917 Bolshevik Revolution Russia was lost as an ally. Under the terms of the Treaty of Versailles (1919) France was granted a 15-year occupation of the Rhineland, which was to be permanently demilitarized.

Germany was disarmed, and France was given Alsace-Lorraine. France also received the coal mines of the Saar for the duration of the 15-year occupation, large war reparations, and some former German colonies. The period from 1919 to 1925 was marked by labor unrest and serious inflation, and French foreign policy was based on a tough line against Germany. France occupied the Ruhr in 1923 to force reparation payments from Germany, and in 1921 formed an alliance with Poland.

Interwar France. From 1925 to 1932 France pursued a more conciliatory German policy, although France allied itself with the nations of the Little Entente—Czechoslovakia, Romania, and Yugoslavia. The Locarno treaties of 1925, guaranteeing the Versailles frontiers and providing for arbitration of disputes, seemed to ensure European stability. At home, prosperity obscured the need for social legislation, although a modest social security system was approved. The world economic depression of the 1930s and the rise of Adolf Hitler in Germany ended this quiet interlude.

Unemployment, growing insecurity, and a succession of ineffective ministries gave rise to extreme right-wing groups, who were as militant, antirepublican, and antidemocratic as their prototypes in Italy and Germany. In 1934, when the government was alleged to be involved in a financial scandal, the rightists staged anti-parliamentary riots.

In response to the right-wing threat, the Socialist, Radical Socialist, and Communist parties formed a political bloc, known as the Popular Front, which came to power in 1936. The Popular Front's premier, Léon Blum, promised moderate reforms well within a capitalistic economic system.

Blum won parliamentary approval to establish collective bargaining, a 40-hour work week, paid vacations, closer government control over national financial affairs, nationalization of the arms industry, and cultural programs for the lower classes. But Blum's government lasted only a year, and in 1938 France returned to economic and social conservatism under Premier Edouard Daladier.

With its finances exhausted, lacking British support, preoccupied with internal politics, and with an influential right-wing sympathetic to Germany's Nazi dictator, Adolph Hitler and Italy's Fascist dictator, Benito Mussolini, France avoided taking action against the growing aggressiveness of Nazi Germany.

France failed to halt German rearmament in 1935, remilitarization of the Rhineland in 1936, or the annexation of Austria and the dismemberment of Czechoslovakia in 1938. A Nazi-Soviet nonaggression pact in 1939 nullified an undeveloped alliance with the Soviet Union and left France without a powerful ally on Germany's east.

World War II. In 1939 World War II began with Germany's attack on Poland. France was economically stagnant, politically divided, and militarily unprepared. In May 1940 France collapsed before the German *blitzkrieg*, and on June 22 an armistice was signed with the Nazis.

Northwestern France was occupied by the Germans. In the southeast the Germans set up a puppet government headed by Marshal Henri-Philippe Pétain, which was known as the Vichy regime after the town that was its capital.

Gen. Charles de Gaulle and a handful of Frenchmen escaped to London and formed the French Committee of National Liberation (the Free French). At first the committee functioned to recruit Frenchmen to continue the fight against Germany, but eventually it took the form of a provisional government ready to take control of France after the defeat of Germany.

FRENCH EMBASSY PRESS AND INFORMATION DIVISION

NUCLEAR POWER PLANT, at Chinon, illustrates France's industrial and technological progress.

COUNTRIES OF THE WORLD

After four years of German occupation and government by the Vichy regime, France was liberated in August 1944 by Allied forces, which included contingents of the Free French under General de Gaulle. During the immediate post-liberation period De Gaulle presided over a provisional government, but he resigned in 1946 because of communist and socialist opposition to a constitution providing for a strong executive.

After the resignation of De Gaulle, a coalition of communists, socialists, and members of the MRP (the Catholic Popular Republican Movement) carried through various social reforms and nationalized the country's most important power, transportation, and banking facilities.

The Fourth Republic. Soon after the establishment of the Fourth Republic in 1946, however, the coalition broke up over ideological differences and Cold War tensions. Power once again was given to the center parties—the Socialists, the MRP, and the Radicals, and France once more returned to social and economic conservatism.

During the late 1940s France was beset by inflation, strikes, and foreign exchange problems. Nevertheless, the French economy was modernized and production increased with the help of U.S. aid under the Marshall Plan, which was inaugurated in 1947.

The most serious problem facing the Fourth Republic was the struggle to maintain the French colonial empire. France waged a losing war in Indochina from 1946 to 1954, when it was forced to withdraw. A few months later France was engaged in a costly war against nationalists in Algeria, where there were many French settlers.

Finally, weakened by the old pattern of changing ministries, the Fourth Republic was destroyed in 1958 by an attempted coup led by French soldiers and settlers in Algeria determined to forestall an agreement with the nationalists.

The Fifth Republic. De Gaulle returned to power as head of France's Fifth Republic, which placed extensive powers in the hands of the president, and in 1962 he recognized Algerian independence. Meanwhile, France had granted independence to most of its other African dependencies.

During the first decade of the Fifth Republic France enjoyed stability and prosperity, and played an ambitious role in foreign affairs. De Gaulle worked to build France into a major power free from the constraint or influence of other nations, particularly the United States, and foreign policy was directed toward that end.

France developed its own nuclear atomic force and refused to participate in an international atomic test-ban treaty in 1960. It recognized Communist China in 1964, and in 1966 withdrew all French troops from allied command and ordered NATO headquarters, military bases, and troops from France. Despite reduced support in presidential elections held in 1965 and in legislative elections in 1967, De Gaulle retained control of France's future.

—James A. Leith

UNITED NATIONS
GABONESE FISHERMEN on the beach near Libreville, the capital of the West African country.

GABON

Official name: Gabon Republic
Area: 103,346 square miles
Population: (1966 est.) 468,000
Capital: Libreville (Pop. 1964, urban area, 45,909)
Language: French, African languages
Religion: Christianity, Islam, traditional religions
Currency unit: Franc CFA (African Financial Community)
National holiday: August 17

Gabon, a republic in west Africa, is bordered on the north by Spanish Equatorial Guinea (Río Muni) and Cameroon, on the east and south by the Congo (Brazzaville), and on the west by the Atlantic Ocean. Gabon was a French territory until 1960, when it received its independence.

THE LAND. Most of Gabon is covered by wet tropical forests. Inland from a coastal plain is the edge of the African Plateau, called the Crystal Mountains in the north and the Mayombé Mountains in the south. In the southeast is the Batéké Plateau, a region of grasslands. Gabon's principal river is the Ogooué. The climate throughout the country is hot and humid.

THE PEOPLE. There are many different tribal groups in Gabon, most of which are Bantu-speaking. The Fang, who migrated from the north in the 1800s, form the largest group. There are also peoples of the Eschira, Okande, and Adouma tribes.

Gabon is thinly populated. Most of the people live in rural areas, and the major city is the capital, Libreville. Port Gentil is Gabon's major port.

ECONOMY. The economy of Gabon is based largely on mining and forestry, although most of the people are engaged in subsistence farming. Manioc, corn, and bananas are the country's main crops.

Gabon is rich in minerals. The country has some of the world's largest deposits of manganese and iron ore. In 1965 Gabon produced over 637,000 metric tons of manganese ore, about 11 percent of the world total. Uranium, petroleum, and natural gas are also produced. Gabon's forest areas provide wood products of great value.

In 1966 exports earned $100 million and imports cost $66 million. Gabon exports wood and wood products and minerals, and imports foodstuffs and manufactured goods. Gabon is a member of a tariff union with the countries of the Central African Republic, Chad, and the Congo (Brazzaville).

GOVERNMENT. Gabon has a presidential system of government. Executive power is vested in a president popularly elected to a seven-year term. Legislative power rests with a unicameral National Assembly. The assembly has 47 members elected by universal suffrage to five-year terms.

Gabon is a member of the United Nations and of the Organization of African Unity (OAU).

HISTORY. Little is known of the early history of the Gabon area. In the 1400s Portuguese explorers established trade relations with the Loango kingdom. The original trade in gold dust, ivory, palm oil, and wood soon gave way to slaving. Several European countries joined in the slave trade, but France became predominant.

French Rule. Slave trading was abolished in the early 1800s, and in 1849 France established a center for freed slaves at Libreville. In 1899 France began granting concessions to private companies to develop the region. Company abuses led to depopulation, depletion of resources, and loss of capital. In 1910 Gabon became part of French Equatorial Africa.

Political activities before World War II were confined mainly to groups in Libreville, religious cults, and Fang tribal societies. After the war, France liberalized its colonial system, and in 1946 created the French Union. Gabon was permitted to establish territorial assemblies and to elect deputies to the French National Assembly. Jean-Hilaire Aubame, representing the northern Fang people, was elected to the French assembly.

Self-Rule. France granted Gabon internal self-government in 1957. Leon M'Ba, representing the southern Fang and other groups in his party, the Gabonese Democratic Bloc (BDG), became prime minister of a coalition government that included Aubame's Gabonese Social and Democratic Union (UDSG).

Gabon became a member of the French Community in 1958, but broke its ties with French Equatorial Africa, from which it had long desired to secede because of its own wealth.

Gabon became independent on Aug. 17, 1960, and M'Ba was elected president. Early in 1964 a military coup threatened the regime, but the French intervened in support of M'Ba. In elections held in April 1964 M'Ba's party won a majority of seats in the National Assembly, and M'Ba continued as president until his death in 1967. He was succeeded by Bernard-Albert Bongo, a political associate.

—Hibberd V. B. Kline, Jr.;
Vera L. Zolberg

GAMBIA

Official name: The Gambia
Area: 4,361 square miles
Population: (1966 est.) 336,000
Capital: Bathurst (Pop. 1964, urban area, 42,104)
Language: English, African languages
Religion: Islam, traditional religions
Currency unit: Pound
National holiday: Independence day, February 18

The Gambia, a small independent nation in West Africa, is bordered on the north, east, and south by Senegal, and on the west by the Atlantic Ocean. The Gambia received its independence in 1965 after a century and a half of British control.

THE LAND. The Gambia is dominated by the Gambia River, which flows through the narrow country from east to west for a distance of over 200 miles. Mangrove swamps line the river for about 150 miles inland from the ocean. Beyond the swamps the land is grassy with patches of sandy soil. Sandstone plateaus cover the region farthest from the river.

The Gambia receives about 40 inches of rain a year. The rainy season lasts from June to October.

THE PEOPLE. Several different peoples live in the Gambia. Among the larger groups are the Mandingo, Wolof, and Fulani, most of whom are Muslims.

The Gambia's major city, Bathurst, is on St. Mary's Island at the mouth of the Gambia River.

ECONOMY. The Gambia's economy depends on agriculture. The main crop is peanuts, and in 1964–1965 the Gambia produced about 114,000 metric tons of peanuts. The people grow sorghum and rice for local consumption. The Gambia has few mineral deposits and little industry. Livestock grazing is hindered by the prevalence of disease caused by the tsetse fly.

In 1965 the Gambia's imports cost $16 million and its exports earned $14 million. Peanuts accounted for about 95 percent of the value of exports. The Gambia imports rice, wheat, sugar, petroleum products, motor vehicles, and manufactured goods.

GOVERNMENT. The Gambia has a parliamentary system of government. The British Queen is head of state and is represented by a governor-general, who serves as nominal chief executive. Actual executive powers rest with a prime minister and cabinet responsible to the legislature, the House of Representatives. The legislature has 32 popularly elected members and 4 members elected by local chiefs.

The Gambia is a member of the United Nations and the Organization of African Unity (OAU).

HISTORY. Little is known about the early history of the Gambia. A Carthaginian, Hanno, may have sailed up the Gambia River in the 500s BC. During the 900s AD, the Gambia region was probably a distant outpost of the empires of Ghana and Mali.

In the 1400s the Portuguese explored the Gambia region and traded with the people there, as did Dutch, English, and French merchants in the following years. Between the 1500s and the 1700s, slaves from the area were transported to America.

By the 1700s the British and French had established trading posts and forts at the mouth of the Gambia River. British and French merchants competed vigorously throughout the 1700s for control of trade with the Gambia, but in 1783 the Gambia was awarded to Britain by treaty.

British Rule. Throughout the 1800s British merchants trading on the Gambia River resisted proposals that the Gambia should become part of French-controlled Senegal. The Gambia was ruled from the British Crown Colony of Sierra Leone until 1843, when the Gambia was made a crown colony. The two colonies once again were administered jointly for a brief period, from 1866 to 1888, but after 1888 the Gambia remained a separate entity.

In 1889 Britain and France agreed on the present boundaries of the Gambia, which Britain had been acquiring piece by piece from tribal chiefs since the early 1800s.

After World War II Britain faced the problem of Senegalese demands for the Gambia. Senegal wanted the Gambia in order to round out its own boundaries and to eliminate smuggling between the two countries. The Gambians had mixed feelings about union with Senegal. They realized that their country could not be economically successful, but there were significant differences in language and culture between the two countries.

Self-Rule. Out of the differences of opinion created by possible unification with Senegal, Dawda Jawara formed the Progressive People's Party, which won elections held in 1960 and 1962.

In 1963 the Gambia became self-governing with Jawara as prime minister. He led the Gambia to independence in February 1965, without the issue of its future relations with Senegal having been resolved.

—Hibberd V. B. Kline, Jr.;
Robert I. Rotberg

GAMBIA'S PRIME MINISTER, Dawda Jawara, addresses villagers during an election campaign.

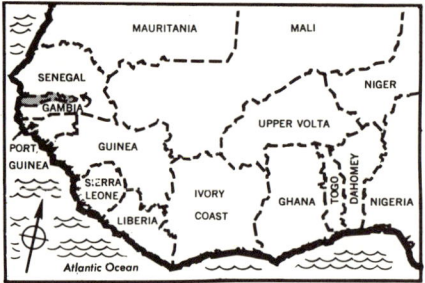

GERMANY

WEST GERMANY
Official name: Federal Republic of Germany
Area: 95,743 square miles (excluding West Berlin: 186 square miles)
Population: (1966 est.) 57,458,000 (excluding West Berlin: 2,191,000)
Capital: Bonn (Pop., 1965 est., 141,700)
Language: German
Religion: Protestant, Roman Catholic
Currency unit: Deutsche Mark

EAST GERMANY
Official name: German Democratic Republic
Area: 41,661 square miles (excluding East Berlin: 156 square miles)
Population: (1966 est.) 15,988,000 (excluding East Berlin)
Capital: East Berlin (Pop., 1966 est., 1,079,000)
Language: German
Religion: Protestantism, Roman Catholicism
Currency unit: Mark

Germany is a divided nation in north-central Europe. German territory is bounded on the north by the North Sea, Denmark, and the Baltic Sea; on the east by Poland and Czechoslovakia; on the south by Austria, Liechtenstein, and Switzerland; and on the west by France, Luxembourg, Belgium, and the Netherlands.

After World War II Germany was divided among the four major Allied powers—Britain, France, the United States, and the Soviet Union. Its capital city, Berlin, was also partitioned into four zones. Each zone was occupied by one of the Allied powers. Pre-World War II territories of Germany lying east of the Oder and Neisse rivers were placed under Polish administration. East Prussia, a separate territory on the east coast of the Baltic, was annexed by the Soviet Union.

In 1949 the Soviet zone was established as the German Democratic Republic, with the eastern sector of Berlin as its capital, and the other Allies merged their three zones into the Federal Republic of Germany. The line separating East Germany, as the communist sector is called, from West Germany, the noncommunist sector, runs an irregular course south from Lubeck, on the Baltic Sea, to Adorf, on the Czechoslovakian border.

THE LAND. The political division of Germany is arbitrary, for East and West Germany form a geographical unit containing two distinct and strikingly different regions—northern Germany, low and flat, and southern Germany, hilly and of complex relief. The North German Plain, south of a low, sandy northern coastline, is low and dotted with swamps and lakes especially in the northeast. Toward the interior are hummocks and low hills.

The elevation begins to rise in central Germany, the *Mittelland*, a region of uplands with plateaus and low mountains broken by broad river valleys. These uplands rise into the Bohemian forest, the Black Forest, and the Bavarian Plateau until, near the southern border, the Alps reach almost 10,000 feet.

Several major European rivers cross Germany. The Rhine, with its tributaries, including the Main and the Moselle; the Ems; the Weser; and the Elbe all flow through central Germany into the North Sea. The Oder crosses eastern Germany and empties into the Baltic. The Danube and the Inn drain southern Germany and flow toward the Black Sea.

Germany's climate is temperate. Warm ocean currents moderate the cold of the far north, and high elevations counteract warmer tendencies toward the south. Winter temperatures average below 20°F in the south and about 30°F in the north. Summer temperatures average in the mid-60s throughout the country. Rainfall is moderate, averaging about 30 inches for the country as a whole and generally decreasing toward the south.

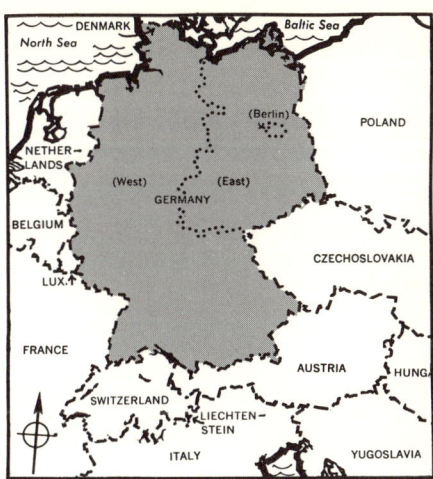

THE PEOPLE. The population of both Germanys is quite homogeneous. German is the universal language. A majority of the people are Protestant, with Lutherans forming the largest community. Roman Catholicism ranks second. There are no major minority groups. A large Jewish community that lived in Germany before World War II was destroyed by the Nazi regime.

During the 1950s and early 1960s, West Germany received a steady flow of refugees from East Germany. The western population was also swollen by an influx of foreign workers, mostly from southern Europe, who were attracted by West Germany's manpower shortage. As a result of the migrations, West Germany, in 1965 was one of the most crowded nations in Europe.

West Germany is highly urbanized, but with many small cities rather than a few large metropolitan centers. The largest cities are Hamburg, in the north, and Munich, in the south. Divided Berlin is the largest city in all Germany.

GERMANY'S LANDSCAPE includes the mountains of Bavaria *(left)*, whose peaks tower over high valleys, and the rolling banks of the Rhine River *(above)*, which hold terraced vineyards.

The East German population density is much lower, in part because of a steady migration to the west. In the 1950s and 1960s urbanization was rapid, but East Germany's largest cities, Dresden and Leipzig, are smaller than many West German cities.

ECONOMY. Both East and West Germany are prosperous countries, although West Germany is by far the wealthier of the two. Germany's prosperity is based on a long tradition of industry and on a highly skilled, well-disciplined, and industrious labor force. Industry makes the greatest contribution to the German economy.

The economies of both Germanys expanded rapidly during the 1950s and 1960s. In West Germany, the expansion consisted of rebuilding and developing industries destroyed in World War II, to become the leading industrial nation in Europe. In East Germany, the expansion consisted largely of developing new industries, to become the most industrialized of the east European countries other than the Soviet Union. Both Germanys concentrate on heavy industry.

Germany has some excellent farmland, especially in the river valleys of the *Mittelland*, but agriculture is of much less importance than industry in both East and West. It contributes a greater proportion of the East German national product than the West German.

International trade is of more importance in the economy of West Germany than in that of East Germany. West Germany is fully integrated into the western European economy through the Common Market. East Germany's economy is tied to that of other communist-dominated eastern European countries through their economic alliance, the Council for Mutual Economic Cooperation (COMECON).

West Germany. West Germany's principal natural resource is high-grade hard coal. There are also deposits of petroleum, potash, iron, copper, and zinc, and water power is abundant. The leading West German industries are iron and steel production, mining, chemical manufacture, machinery and vehicle production, shipbuilding, and power production. The older light industries of textile weaving, brewing, food processing, and precision tool manufacture still prosper, however.

West German industry is concentrated in the Saar and the Ruhr regions near the western border, on the northern plain, and in the middle Rhine valley.

West Germany is Western Europe's leading producer of rye and potatoes. Wheat, barley, and sugar beets are also important crops. Tobacco, nuts, and fruits—especially wine grapes—are grown in the lower Rhine valley. Dairy cattle and other livestock, particularly pigs, are important.

West Germany is the second-ranking trading nation in the world. In 1966 its exports earned over $20,000 million and its imports cost just over $18,000 million. Machinery and equipment, automobiles, and chemicals are the leading exports, and foodstuffs and raw materials are imported. Most West German trade is with other Western European countries and the United States.

East Germany. East Germany's main natural resource is lignite, of which it is the world's leading producer. Uranium, cobalt, iron, copper, potash, and zinc are also available, and water power is abundant. All East German industry is nationalized, and the state has concentrated on developing heavy industry. Iron and steel production, mining, machinery and vehicle production, chemical manufacture, shipbuilding, and power production are the main industries.

All East German agriculture is collectivized. Wheat, rye, barley, sugar beets, and potatoes are the leading crops. Livestock, especially pigs, are raised, and dairying is also important to the economy.

East Germany has a generally favorable balance of trade. In 1966 both exports and imports were valued at about $3,000 million. Machinery and vehicles, textiles, and chemicals are the leading exports, and foodstuffs and raw materials are imported. Most East German trade is with other communist-dominated Eastern European countries, particularly the Soviet Union.

GOVERNMENT. The Federal Republic of Germany is a democracy; the German Democratic Republic is a totalitarian state.

West Germany. West Germany is a federal union of 10 *lander,* or states. The city of West Berlin has close political ties with West Germany. A president is head of state. Actual executive power rests with a chancellor, or prime minister, who is elected by the *Bundestag,* the larger house of the legislature. He and the cabinet he leads are responsible to the legislature.

Members of the *Bundestag* are popularly elected to four-year terms. Members of the *Bundesrat,* the smaller, less powerful upper house, are chosen by the governments of the individual *lander* for indefinite terms. Representatives of West Berlin sit as members of the West German legislature.

The Federal Republic is a member of the European Communities and the North Atlantic Treaty Organization (NATO).

East Germany. Political life in the German Democratic Republic is dominated by the East German Communist party, officially called the Socialist Unity Party. The politburo, or political bureau, of its central committee determines national policy, and the first secretary of the party is usually the key figure in the government.

The East German constitution provides for a popularly elected legislature. Candidates for the legislature are nominated under party control. The legislature chooses a council of

ASSEMBLY LINE turning out auto parts reflects Germany's highly industrialized economy.

MUNICH PARADERS celebrate *Oktoberfest,* a traditional Bavarian festival held in autumn.

COUNTRIES OF THE WORLD

state to act for it between its short sessions, and the chairman of the council serves as head of state. Actual executive power rests with a council of ministers, or cabinet, and its chairman, who is equivalent to a prime minister.

Most noncommunist countries do not recognize the Democratic Republic. It is a member of the Soviet-controlled Warsaw Pact, a military grouping of east European states.

HISTORY. Political division is not new to Germany. With no major natural boundaries save the Alps, the territory has been open to invasion from east, north, and west. In ancient times there were many small, tribal states, all subject to easy conquest. Among the earliest settlers were the Teutons, a Germanic people.

The territory was divided among several Teutonic tribes—the Franks, the Saxons, and the Thuringians—led by elective kings. Beginning in the 200s AD, other Germanic peoples from the east settled in the area—notably the Goths and the Burgundians. The Romans made several unsuccessful attempts to conquer the Germanic tribes, but no single ruler gained control of the entire region until the 300s, when the Huns swept across the land.

Both the Huns and the Vandals, who followed soon after, were migratory, warlike peoples whose main goal was conquest, and their rule over the settled tribes was brief. It was only the Franks, who settled in the Rhine valley in the late 300s, who attempted to unite permanently the Germanic peoples.

Frankish Kingdom. The Franks expanded westward from the Rhine into Gaul, driving out the Roman legions stationed there. They adopted Christianity and won the support of the popes, whose power by the 500s was greater than that of the Roman emperors. They defeated the other Germanic tribes and in 732 they fought off a Muslim invasion of Europe.

The Franks reached the height of their power under Charles the Great, or Charlemagne, who became king in 768. Under Charlemagne, the Franks controlled a vast territory ranging from Central Italy on the south to the Baltic Sea on the north and from the Pyrenees on the west to the Elbe River on the east. Charlemagne accepted the role of protector of the popes, and in 800 he was crowned emperor in Rome, an act that laid the religious and political foundations for the later Holy Roman Empire.

The unity Charlemagne achieved did not long survive him. Several decades of disunity followed his death in 814, and in 843 the Treaty of Verdun divided his territories into three parts. The eastern, predominantly Teuton, portion, between the Rhine and the Elbe Rivers, went to Louis the German, and became the core of modern Germany.

The Saxons. The tribal loyalties and ambitions born before Charlemagne's time had not been forgotten. Each major tribal unit had formed a country, and the dukes and princes who led them vied for control of the German throne. By the early 900s one Teuton clan, the Saxons, had emerged dominant. Its first ruler, Henry the Fowler, extended German territory to the Oder River and defended it against attacks from Magyar and Slavic peoples to the south.

A Saxon king, Otto I, in 962 was given the crown of Italy and became the first Holy Roman Emperor as a reward for aiding the pope. The Holy Roman Empire revived, at least in name, the old Roman Empire and gave to Germany the empire's prestige as well as the support of the papacy. As Holy Roman Emperor, Otto gained control over the German dukes and princes, who were willing to support a prestigious empire that was growing in size and power.

By about 1030, the Holy Roman Empire was a prosperous feudal nation with thriving towns and vigorous trade. Henry III, who became emperor in 1039, probably held more actual power than any other. He brought all

DUISBURG, GERMANY, where the Rhine and Ruhr rivers join, has Europe's larger river harbor.

of the mightiest princes—his rivals for power—into submission and he maintained tight control of the church, introducing many needed reforms.

Henry was the last emperor with such power, however. After his death in 1056 a regent ruled for his young heir, and the period of the regency was fatal for the strength of the German throne. Both the church and the nobility had become dissatisfied with their lack of power. By the 1070s the pope and the emperor were in open conflict over the distribution of political and religious power. The local princes sided with the papacy to reduce the strength of the emperor.

The conflict continued into the mid-1200s, and although both emperors and popes won victories, the final result of the struggle was a great loss of power for both. The empire disintegrated into a state of anarchy in the 1250s. For a 20-year period known as the "Great Interregnum" no one man ruled Germany, although many tried. Moreover, as each faction grew in power—the princes, the dukes, the bishops, and the towns—a tradition of disunity was firmly established, and it became even harder to consolidate political power.

It was only in 1273, at the insistence of Pope Gregory X, who feared the growing power of France, that the German princes elected one of their number to be Holy Roman Emperor. Their choice was Rudolf of the House of Hapsburg in Austria, which was then a minor princely house. Rudolf took steps to insure the continuance on the throne of members of his family, and later Hapsburg emperors became powerful.

The Hapsburgs. During the Middle Ages, the Hapsburg emperors added to the territory under their control, but the unification of the German states did not follow the Hapsburg rise to power. The German emperor was an elected king by tradition and by a law enacted in 1356. As he could rule only with the consent of the princes who elected him, the German emperor constantly had to make concessions to them, and he was unable to rule as firmly as a hereditary monarch could.

Because of the weakness of the central government, the German states were less an empire than a federation dominated by the stronger states. Nearly constant competition for power kept the German states in turmoil from the 1300s to the 1800s, but the Hapsburg family remained the dominant power through the 1700s. An important factor in German decentralization was the growth in importance and size of the German towns during the Middle Ages.

Administrative and economic policies initiated during the 1100s had encouraged the development of the towns. By the middle of the 1300s, these policies, coupled with a renewed interest in the arts and an expanding economy, had transformed many towns into "free cities"—large, autonomous units free from the control of local princes. From the middle of the 1200s to the middle of the 1400s, the influence of German cities rivaled that of German princes.

Despite the fragmentation of the Holy Roman Empire, it reached the height of its power and size in the early 1500s under Emperor Charles V, who, by inheritance and marriage, ruled Spain, Portugal, Belgium, and the Netherlands as well as the German states. It was during his reign, however, that religious controversy flared, contributing to the final disintegration of the empire. In 1517 Martin Luther, an Augustinian monk, called for reforms in the Roman Catholic Church.

Reformation. The Lutheran "reformation" attracted many more radical social, political, and religious reformers, and they became a threat to both the church and the empire. Charles V led a diet, or council, at Worms in 1521 to try Luther. The council banned the spread of any new doctrines. The reformers continued, however, encouraged by power-seeking princes, who adopted their reforms as a means of opposing the emperor.

The progress of the Reformation was speeded by Charles' involvement in a series of wars with France. In Germany, disputes among the proliferating Protestant sects and between Protestants and Roman Catholics led to a series of religious wars, which were ended in 1555 by the Peace of Augsburg.

The peace settlement marked the final collapse of the emperor's real power. It granted to each prince within the empire the right to determine the religion of his subjects. In 1556 Charles abdicated, leaving his Spanish possessions to his son Philip, and his German dominions to his brother, Ferdinand.

The Peace of Augsburg had not finally settled the religious disputes, and it had only aggravated Germany's political confusion. In 1618 fighting began again in the war that was to earn the name of the Thirty Years' War. At first the war was confined to the Roman Catholic–Protestant conflict, but almost immediately the old issues of prince versus emperor, and federation versus empire, were renewed.

The war spread and eventually involved most of continental Europe as well as England and Sweden. The Peace of Westphalia, which settled the war in 1648, formalized German disunity by giving the local princes more power than the emperor. Each of the 300 separate German states received the right to conduct its own diplomacy, determine the religion of its people, and vote on the emperor's rights to collect taxes, raise an army, or conduct foreign policy.

Germany's enemies, notably France, gained from German fragmentation, which greatly diminished its international power. Between the mid-1600s and mid-1700s, France led Europe, and the only real power left to the Holy Roman Empire was that which its Hapsburg emperors derived from their own vast personal territories. Austria continued as leader and protector of the German states, defending them, for instance, from the onslaught of the Ottoman Turks in the 1600s.

Rise of Prussia. During the latter half of the 1600s, however, Prussia, known then as Brandenburg, began to grow from a small duchy into the most powerful state in Germany. Prussia's ruling Hohenzollern house increased the territory within its domain and, at the same time, established an efficient, centralized administration to control it. The army, officered by the nobility, became the central institution of the state.

Decisive in Prussia's ascendency to power within Germany was the succession to the throne in 1740 of Frederick II, called the Great, a man of driving force and shrewd statesmanship. Immediately upon assuming the throne he invaded Silesia, a large and wealthy Austrian territory.

The wars precipitated by the invasion of Silesia engulfed most of Europe for 15 of the next 23 years. Finally, in 1763, Prussia won the disputed Silesian territory, which doubled Prussia's population and natural resources. Germany was then polarized between northern Germany, dominated by Prussia, and southern Germany, led by Austria.

Prussia's rapid rise to power had been due in large part to Frederick the Great, and after his death in 1786, the system he had built could not function effectively. Thus in 1806, when the French armies of Napoleon were conquering Europe, Prussia offered little resistance and fell to Napoleon after the Battle of Jena.

Napoleonic Era. By 1806 Napoleon controlled most of the German states, which he organized into the Confederation of the Rhine, and he persuaded the Austrian emperor, Francis I, formally to dissolve the Holy Roman Empire. In 1809 Austria itself yielded to the French, and Napoleon's troops occupied all of Germany.

The French occupation ended in 1813, however, after Austria reluctantly joined forces with Prussia and Russia in a war of liberation that pushed Napoleon's armies west of the Rhine. But the fairly brief French occupation had wrought changes in Germany more significant than the formal dissolution of the Holy Roman Empire.

Germany was still a loose collection of states, but the Napoleonic Confederation of the Rhine had reduced their number and the Congress of Vienna, held in 1815 after Napoleon's defeat, accepted the reduction by creating the Germanic Confederation, a loose grouping of 38 independent German states.

Prussia, represented at Vienna by the liberal statesman Baron Heinrich Stein, had pressed for a more unified Germany, but the congress encouraged the autonomy of the states as sought by the Austrian foreign minister, Prince Klemens von Metternich. Metternich's leadership led to tightened monarchial control over the social, political, and economic life of Austria. This "Metternich system" dominated the south German states.

In Prussia, too, the movement for reform—which before 1815 had resulted in tax and administrative reforms and the abolition of serfdom—began to lag as reactionary forces triumphed over liberalism throughout Germany.

The Napoleonic wars had awakened democratic and nationalistic movements that the German governments

LUFTHANSA

HARBOR OF BREMEN, an important port of entry and the principal seat of German import and export trade. Once a free port, Bremen joined the German Customs Union in 1888.

felt must be repressed. Under the leadership of Austria's Metternich, the German states imposed tight controls on all civil liberties, especially on the activities of the universities. These controls only spurred the liberals and nationalists, and in 1848 they rebelled against Metternich's reactionary government.

Risings of 1848. Inspired by a similar revolution in Paris, large numbers of Austrians, mostly in Vienna, organized and demanded a constitution. Metternich fled Austria, and the emperor granted a constitution and abdicated in December 1848.

The rebellion had spread from Vienna to the Hapsburg's Hungarian and Slavic subject peoples, who demanded the establishment of independent Slavic and Magyar states. The Slavs organized a Pan-Slav Congress to lead their nationalistic movement. A new Austrian emperor, Francis Joseph I, concentrated on crushing the rebellions in Hungary and the Slavic areas, ignoring the more peaceful rebellion among the Germans.

The rebellious Germans were demanding not only political and social liberties, but the political union of Germany. Most German states elected liberal local governments, which in turn elected liberal representatives to a national assembly which met in Frankfurt in May 1848 to establish a republic. In 1849 the assembly drafted a democratic constitution for a unified German state and elected Prussia's ruler, Frederick William IV, emperor of the new nation.

Some of the states opposed the new organization, however, and Austria, which with Russia's help had quelled the Hungarian and Slavic revolutions in early 1849, refused to join the unification movement, which would have forced it to give up its non-German territories.

Frederick William IV, unwilling to accept the throne from an elected assembly, refused the imperial crown, and by 1850 the old constitution of the Germanic Confederation had been readopted and the unification and reform efforts of the assembly had failed. Austria was once more able to impose a superficial calm on Germany after putting down the 1848 rebellions, but it could not stem the movement for unification.

Unification. In 1844 Prussia had encouraged unification by organizing a customs union, the *Zollverein,* among more than half the German states, excluding Austria. The unification efforts gathered strength after 1862 under the leadership of Otto von Bismarck, Prussia's chief minister, who followed a stern policy of "blood and iron" in leading Germany to European dominance.

Bismarck centralized and strengthened Prussia's government and pressed the development of the army and expansion into new territory. Prussia annexed the two predominantly German duchies of Schleswig and Holstein, which Denmark claimed. Austria aided Prussia to drive out the Danes, but Bismarck's subsequent attempt to control Holstein angered Austria, and war between the two was only narrowly averted.

War did break out between them for seven weeks in 1866 after the Diet of Frankfurt, at which Bismarck had pressed for federal reform. In the Seven Weeks' War Prussian forces easily defeated Austria, and in 1867 a constitution was adopted for a new confederation excluding Austria and several south German states.

Constitutionally a federal state, the new North German Confederation was actually under Prussian control. Austria, having lost control of Germany, was forced to admit Hungary as an equal partner in a dual monarchy, and Austrian history diverged from that of Germany.

German Empire. Prussia quickly became the greatest power in Europe and roundly defeated France in 1870–1871 in a war over dynastic claims to the throne of Spain. Prussia forced France to accept a harsh and humiliating settlement—France ceded the industrially rich territories of Alsace and Lorraine, paid a large indemnity, and supported a German army of occupation.

Now the leader of all Europe, Bismarck also succeeded in 1871 in bringing the south German states except Austria into the North German Confederation. He became the first chancellor of this German Empire.

The new Prussian state was a curious mixture of democratic and authoritarian institutions. Advanced social welfare laws existed side-by-side with legislation curbing the Roman Catholic Church and suppressing the socialists. Both the central government and the 25 states comprising the union had monarchial forms of government.

Each state enjoyed a large degree of autonomy, although the federal government, or *Reich*, was empowered to administer a common communications system, maintain an army, and conduct foreign affairs. In addition to the *Kaiser*, or emperor, the federal government had a legislature with two houses—the *Bundesrat*, where the states received representation, and the *Reichstag*, where the people were represented through a system of universal manhood suffrage.

The economic growth of the new empire was astounding. In 1860, for example, German steel production did not even equal that of France; by 1900 it exceeded that of both England and France combined. By 1900, moreover, German naval power rivaled that of Great Britain, the traditional "mistress of the sea."

Germany's political prestige also grew, a result not only of its strengthened economic and military position but also of the capable leadership of the "iron chancellor." Bismarck consolidated Germany's continental position by arranging alliances in 1882 with Austria-Hungary and Italy, in the Triple Alliance, and in 1887 with Russia.

Bismarck fell from power in 1890, when the young emperor, William II, who opposed his authoritarian measures and his diplomatic techniques, decided to conduct German diplomacy personally.

Under William, Germany followed a policy of aggressive imperialism which divided Europe into two opposing camps—pro-German and anti-German. William antagonized Britain by enlarging the German navy, enraged his ally Russia by competing with it for territory in the Near East, and made no attempt to improve relations with France, which had been poor since the acquisition of Alsace-Lorraine.

German aggressiveness drew France and Britain, traditional enemies, closer together. In the Entente Cordiale of 1904 the two settled several long-standing disputes and united in opposition to Germany. In 1905 William tested the Entente by openly urging independence for the French protectorate of Morocco.

The Entente proved solid, and in 1906 France and Britain led the Algeciras Conference of European powers, which berated Germany for its insult to France. In 1907 Russia, Germany's former ally, entered the British-French alliance, forming the Triple Entente. In 1911 Germany precipitated a second "Moroccan Crisis" and was again rebuked.

World War I. The European powers were able to settle the incidents of 1905 and 1911 peacefully, but crisis followed crisis in the Balkan region. Bulgaria and Turkey, having lost territory in Balkan wars in 1912 and 1913, joined Germany, Austria-Hungary, and Italy to form the alliance of Central Powers in opposition to the Triple Entente.

In 1914 a crisis caused by the assassination of Archduke Francis Ferdinand, heir to the Austrian throne, led to World War I. Bosnia, where the assassination occurred, was an Austrian territory, but as the assassin was Serbian, and as Serbia had led Pan-Slav activity in Bosnia, Austria threatened reprisals against Serbia. Germany supported Austria and Russia backed Serbia.

Both sides misjudged the seriousness of the situation, and the war that resulted involved the allies of Germany and Russia and eventually all of Europe as well as the United States, Japan, and the Middle East. Germany had predicted that the war would be short, and had based its military strategy on that prediction. But the war lasted four years, and Germany was unable to maintain the strength of its forces.

In 1918, with defeat imminent, rebellions broke out in the German territories, resulting in the abdication of the emperor and the declaration of a German republic. The peace settlements exacted huge reparations payments; confiscated German overseas possessions and non-German-speaking European territories, including Alsace and Lorraine; and disarmed the country.

Weimar Republic. A republic was formally established in July 1919, when the Weimar Constitution was adopted. The new German state faced difficulties from its establishment, especially in dealing with the humiliation of the dictated peace and in bearing the heavy burden of reparations, which led to inflation and a currency collapse.

The lack of a tradition of unity

and of parliamentary democracy provided a shaky foundation for the new government, made more unstable by attacks from communists on the extreme left and authoritarian nationalists on the extreme right.

In 1929, just as the government had begun to solve its economic and political problems and had begun to be reintegrated into Europe by joining the League of Nations, the worldwide economic depression struck. Unemployment rose and with it came widespread resentment against the existing German government. The heavy victories of extremist parties in elections held in 1930 reflected the growing popular discontent.

On the left, the communists scored heavily, and on the right, Adolf Hitler's National Socialist, or Nazi, party, gained enough seats to become the second largest party in the *Reichstag*. In 1932 elections, the Nazis became the largest single party in the *Reichstag*, and in 1933 Adolf Hitler was appointed chancellor.

Nazi Era. Hitler came to power partly by heading a highly organized political party, but also because the brand of nationalism that he preached was attractive to the Germans—humiliated by defeat in the war, impoverished by the depression, and fearful for their property in the face of communism.

He promised to create a revitalized, strengthened Germany—a Germany stronger than the First Reich, the Holy Roman Empire, or the Second Reich, Bismarck's empire. He assured Germans that they were capable of greatness because they were descended from the strong, pure, "Aryan race" of Teutons, and he directed their hostility toward the Jews and non-Germans, especially the Slavs.

Although the Nazi Party received only 44 percent of the vote in elections held in late 1933, Hitler proclaimed that the elections had made him the spokesman of all Germany. The *Reichstag* granted him dictatorial powers and suspended the constitution. Germany was transformed from a federal state into a highly centralized state. The office of president was abolished, and Hitler assumed all powers of state.

EAST BERLIN lies beyond the Brandenburg Gate, divided by a wall from the city's western half.

Economic policy was determined by the central government, and unemployment was reduced by public works projects and massive rearmament. All opposition parties were banned and strict censorship was imposed. The legal system was reorganized to place the needs of the state above accepted standards of justice, and concentration camps were opened to imprison Hitler's "convicted" political opponents.

The camps came to be used primarily for the imprisonment and murder of Jews, as anti-Semitism became an increasingly important part of the Nazi program. Jews were forbidden to teach, hold office, attend universities, or engage in many businesses, and non-Jews were ordered to ostracize them and to boycott Jewish businesses. Between 1935 and 1945 Hitler's regime killed some 6 million European Jews.

At the basis of Hitler's foreign policy was hostility to the conditions imposed on Germany by the Versailles treaty system that ended World War I. In 1933 Germany ended its membership in the League of Nations. Hitler abrogated German agreements to remain neutral, and in 1935 began openly to rearm the country.

In 1936 and 1937 Germany entered into treaties with Japan and Italy. Italy, led by the Fascist dictator Benito Mussolini, became an especially close ally, forming one half of the "Rome-Berlin Axis." One common feature of these treaties was their declaration of opposition to communism, but in 1939 Hitler entered a nonaggression pact with the communist government of the Soviet Union.

Hitler also refused to obey the territorial limits set by the Versailles settlement. Using the desire to unite all German-speaking peoples as an excuse, Hitler annexed Austria in 1938 and in 1939 he took part of Czechoslovakia. The World War I allies did not strongly object to his actions, hoping to appease him and prevent a second world conflict.

World War II. Until 1939 Hitler had gained territory and allies bloodlessly, but in that summer he demanded that the Free City of Danzig, within Poland's borders, be "restored" to the Reich. When he was refused, Germany invaded Poland and occupied Danzig. Britain and France, bound by treaty to protect Poland and realizing that Hitler could not be appeased, declared war on Germany on Sept. 3, 1939.

The major German offensive against the west began in 1940, when German troops overran the neutral states of Denmark, Norway, the Netherlands, and Belgium, and invaded France. In June, 1941 German armies broke the nonaggression pact and invaded the Soviet Union.

In December 1941 the United States entered the war against Hitler, and in 1942 Soviet troops began a counteroffensive. Before the tide turned in favor of the Allies, Hitler controlled

NÜRNBERG COURTROOM was the scene of German war crimes trials held after World War II.

by conquest or alliances almost all of continental Europe as far east as Moscow and territories in North Africa and the Middle East.

The main Allied counteroffensive began in June 1944, when British, Canadian, and U.S. troops landed on the beaches of Normandy. By September 1944 the Allies had reached the German border. When Soviet troops reached the outskirts of Berlin from the east in May 1945 and the fall of the city seemed imminent, Hitler committed suicide. The Germans surrendered, and the war was over.

Occupation. The leaders of the four major allied nations met at Potsdam, Germany, in July 1945 and agreed to partition Germany into four zones of occupation. The Soviet Union occupied the portion east of the Elbe River and the United States, Britain, and France divided the territory to the west.

Portions of Germany east of the Oder and Neisse rivers were placed under the administration of Poland, which was dominated by the Soviet Union. The Allies also divided Berlin into four occupation zones and established the Allied Control Council to coordinate the occupation.

The Soviets did not cooperate with the other members of the council, and in 1948, after several policy disputes with the Soviet Union, France, Britain, and the United States merged their sectors and gave the new zone a large measure of self-government.

Later in the same year, elections were held in western Germany and a federal constitution was agreed upon. The Soviet Union responded in October 1949 by establishing the Soviet zone of occupation as the German Democratic Republic.

Germany was thus divided again. The Soviet Union tried to force the Allies to leave Berlin and to allow unification on Soviet terms by blockading Berlin in 1949, but a massive airlift broke the blockade.

Britain, France, and the United States maintained nominal control over West Germany until 1955, when the Federal Republic of Germany became fully sovereign. In 1955 the Soviet Union recognized the sovereignty of the German Democratic Republic, in the east.

Divided Germany. In the early 1950s both Germanys concentrated on repairing the destruction wrought by the war, and both worked to develop and expand their industry. By the mid-1960s West Germany had become one of the world's leading industrial nations. Its political recovery paralleled its economic recovery.

Under the leadership of Konrad Adenauer and his Christian Democratic party, West Germany became integrated into Western Europe as a staunch ally of the west. A resurgence of extreme right-wing nationalism in the mid-1960s disturbed the government and led in 1966 to the formation of an alliance of the Christian Democrats and their traditional opponents, the Social Democrats. Willy Brandt, leader of the Social Democratic party, joined the cabinet led by the Christian Democratic chancellor, Kurt Kiesinger.

East Germany made somewhat slower progress in rebuilding its economy. Although it had become relatively prosperous by the early 1960s, the general standard of living of its people remained low. It became fully integrated into the economy of the Soviet bloc and its industry became a vital factor in the economies of other Soviet-bloc states.

Despite its progress, the East German regime remained dependent on the Soviet Union for its existence as a sovereign state. In 1953, for example, Soviet troops and tanks were required to put down an antigovernment rising in East Berlin.

East Germany demonstrated some independence of Soviet policies, however. Both Wilhelm Pieck, a German communist leader who was president of East Germany until his death in 1960, and party secretary Walter Ulbricht, who in 1960 formally assumed the additional duties of chief executive, refused, for example, to follow the program of "de-Stalinization" of Soviet Premier Nikita Khrushchev in the late 1950s.

West Germany refused to recognize the existence of East Germany and refused to give up its support of West Berlin. The western half of the city, whose economic progress made a striking contrast to the rather drab eastern sector, became a showcase of western prosperity, and an important escape point for Germans fleeing the eastern zone. In 1961 the East Germans built a wall separating the two sectors to stem the flow of refugees.

The wall emphasized the depth of the postwar political division of Germany. No way was found to achieve reunification of the country, as neither side could agree to the conditions for negotiations demanded by the other.
—George Kren

GHANA

Official name: Republic of Ghana
Area: 92,099 square miles
Population: (1966) 7,945,000
Capital: Accra (Pop. 1964, urban area, 557,348)
Language: English, African languages
Religion: Christianity, Islam, traditional religions
Currency unit: Cedi
National holiday: Independence day, March 6

Ghana, a republic in western Africa, is bordered on the north by Upper Volta, on the east by Togo, on the south by the Gulf of Guinea, an arm of the Atlantic Ocean, and on the west by the Ivory Coast and Upper Volta. Ghana was formed in 1957 by the union of the former British colonies of the Gold Coast and Ashanti, the British protectorate of the Northern Territories, and British Togoland.

THE LAND. Grasslands and forests occupy much of Ghana's land. The Volta River and its principal tributaries, the Black Volta, White Volta, and Oti, drain all of northern Ghana and about half of the south. Extensive grassy plains and isolated hills are typical of the Volta Basin landscape. The south and west of Ghana is hilly and forested.

In the southeast the Volta River flows between the Akwapim Hills and the Togo Mountains. At that point there is a large dam and power plant, at Akosombo. The climate throughout the country is tropical.

THE PEOPLE. Many Ghanaians are Akan-speaking people, mainly Fanti along the coast and Ashanti further inland. The Ga people, who are related by culture and language to the Ashanti, live around the city of Accra. In the north are the Moshi-Dagomba people.

UNITED NATIONS
GHANAIAN TRIBAL CHIEF attending a ceremony marking the inauguration of a fellow chief.

GHANAIAN STUDENTS in the library of the Institute of Public Administration, at Achimeta.

Most Ghanaians are farmers. Ghana's major cities include the capital, Accra; Kumasi; and the ports of Tema and Takoradi.

ECONOMY. Ghana's economy depends heavily on agriculture. Ghana is a major producer of cacao, and in 1965 Ghana produced over 415,000 metric tons of cacao. Yams, rice, cassava, and grains are basic food crops. Tropical wood and wood products from forests in south and west are important to Ghana's economy.

Ghana also has rich mineral deposits. In 1965 Ghana produced almost 2.3 million carats of diamonds, about 288,000 metric tons of manganese ore, more than 760,000 troy ounces of gold, and 309,000 metric tons of bauxite, from which aluminum is made. Ghanaian industry has developed gradually since the time of independence and is centered around Accra and the nearby port of Tema.

In 1966 Ghana's imports cost $352 million and its exports earned $244 million. The major exports are cacao, gold, diamonds, manganese, timber, and aluminum. Ghana imports manufactured goods, machinery, food, and chemicals. The country's major trading partners are Britain, the United States, and western Europe.

GOVERNMENT. In 1966 a military coup overthrew Ghana's government and a 12-member National Liberation Council took power. Before the coup executive power was vested in a president and a cabinet responsible to the legislature. The president was elected to a five-year term by members of the legislature. Legislative power was held by the National Assembly, which consisted of 104 directly elected members and 10 specially elected women members.

Ghana is a member of the United Nations, the Commonwealth of Nations, and the Organization of African Unity (OAU).

HISTORY. Ghana is named after a medieval empire in western Africa. In 1471 Portuguese explorers encountered the Fanti people, who were then migrating southward. In the years that followed several European countries engaged in trade for gold, ivory, and slaves supplied by the Ashanti through Fanti middlemen.

British Rule. The British and the Ashanti waged wars throughout the 1800s. In 1874 the British finally achieved victory and formed the coastal area of Ghana into the Gold Coast Colony. In 1896 Britain exiled the Ashanti king, Prempeh I, and in 1901 the British established the Colony of Ashanti, which included the interior region north of the Gold Coast Colony.

In the same year, 1901, the Northern Territories, the region north of Ashanti, became a British protectorate. The German colony of Western Togoland became a British mandate under the League of Nations after World War I, and was administered together with the Gold Coast.

In the 1920s railroads were built and cocoa became an important export. A new class of educated Africans formed trade unions, professional associations, and cultural groups, and began to contest the power of traditional chiefs, through whom Britain administered the country.

After World War II, Ashanti representatives were given seats in the colony's legislative council, which had been established at the beginning of colonial rule, and in 1946 the council acquired an African majority.

In 1947 Dr. J. B. Danquah organized a nationalist movement, the United Gold Coast Convention (UGCC). Kwame Nkrumah broke away from UGCC in 1949 and founded the Convention People's Party (CPP). Riots broke out in 1950 in support of Ghanaian independence, and Nkrumah was arrested for his role in the disturbances.

Nkrumah's party won elections held in 1951, and he was released to become a member of the government. In 1952 he became prime minister. Although the CPP won elections held in 1954 and 1956, newly formed regional parties challenged its power. Several of these parties merged into the National Liberation Movement, which called for a federation of regions rather than a unitary state.

Independence. In March 1957 the Gold Coast, Ashanti, the Northern Territories, and British Togoland became independent as the nation of Ghana. Ghana became a republic in July 1960, and Nkrumah was elected president. Nkrumah became a leader in Pan-African affairs.

The CPP remained dominant, but strong political opposition developed. The regime became increasingly authoritarian, and its opponents resorted to plotting and an attempted assassination of the president.

In January 1964 Nkrumah acquired dictatorial powers. He ran the country into debt, and his regime was accused of corruption. While on a trip to Communist China and North Vietnam in February 1966, the National Liberation Council, headed by Lt. Gen. J. A. Ankrah, overthrew Nkrumah's government. Nkrumah found asylum in Guinea, where he was named honorary president.

Ankrah pledged his government to revive the economy and to repay the external debts built up by the Nkrumah government. Ankrah proposed a new constitution that would eventually return Ghana to a two-party system.

—Hibberd V. B. Kline, Jr.;
Vera Zolberg

GREECE

Official name: Kingdom of Greece
Area: 50,944 square miles
Population: (1966 est.) 8,614,000
Capital: Athens (Pop., 1961, urban area, 1,852,700)
Language: Greek
Religion: Orthodox Christianity
Currency unit: Drachma
National holiday: Independence day, March 25

Greece, the southernmost state of the Balkan peninsula, is a mountainous country with many small peninsulas that jut out into the Mediterranean Sea. Almost one-fifth of the total land area consists of islands, the largest of which are Crete, Rhodes, Lesbos, Chios, and Sámos. Mainland Greece is bordered on the northwest by Albania, on the north by Yugoslavia and Bulgaria, and on the northeast by Turkey. To the east is the Aegean Sea; to the west, the Ionian Sea; and to the south, the open Mediterranean.

THE LAND. The surface of Greece is mainly rough and hilly, and there is very little flat land. The rugged Pindus Mountains dominate the landscape of western mainland Greece from the northern border to the southern coast. Plains are few and lie mostly along the eastern coast. They are isolated by

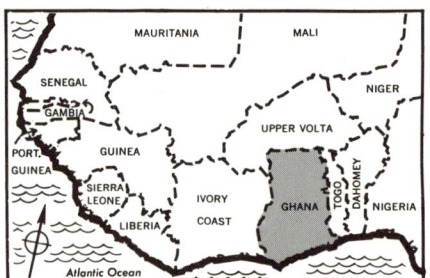

intervening highlands. Rivers are short and usually dry in summer.

The climate varies from region to region. In general, the south and east have hot, dry summers, and mild, moist, windy winters. In the north and west winters are rather cold, summers are hot, and rainfall is more abundant than in the south and east.

West of the mainland are the Ionian Islands. To the east, in the Aegean, are the Cyclades, Sporades, Dodecanese, and other island groups.

THE PEOPLE. Almost the entire population of the country is Greek, but there are small minorities of Bulgarians, Turks, Slavs, and Albanians in the border areas.

Population is densest along the eastern coast, in the Athens region, in the major towns of Macedonia in the north, and on a few of the islands. The southern Peloponnesus and the more mountainous interior are sparsely populated. Greece has traditionally had a high rate of emigration, and Greeks have settled throughout the world.

ECONOMY. Greece is not a prosperous country. Agriculture, which employed about half the labor force in 1961, is the mainstay of the economy, despite the fact that less than 30 percent of the land is suitable for cultivation.

The country has a variety of minerals, including iron and iron pyrites, lignite, lead, zinc, bauxite, emery, chromium, manganese, and oil. They are present only in very small amounts, however, and facilities are lacking to exploit them fully. Supplies of lignite and oil are inadequate for fuel needs, and, despite impressive gains in hydroelectric production during the early 1960s, energy shortages persist.

Greece's generally poor soils are suitable for only a limited variety of crops. In the south and along the coasts, the most important crops are olives and grapes. Some cotton and tobacco also are grown. In the interior and the northeast, grains and tobacco predominate. In the rugged but wet northwest, sheep and goat-herding are the main occupations, and corn is raised extensively.

In 1966 Greece's imports cost more than $1,000 million and its exports earned only slightly more than $406 million. The expenditures of tourists in Greece, more than $100 million in 1964, and the remittances of Greeks abroad partially offset the large deficit.

The chief exports are tobacco, fruits, cotton, wine, olives and olive oil, and mineral ores. The main imports are machinery and vehicles, lumber, textiles, manufactured consumer goods, foodstuffs, chemicals, and petroleum. Greece's leading trading partner is West Germany, followed by the United States and Britain.

GOVERNMENT. Greece is a constitutional monarchy. Under the 1952 constitution the king was empowered to appoint a premier, or prime minister, for an indefinite term. The premier and his cabinet were responsible to a popularly elected unicameral parliament. The constitutional system was overthrown in 1967, however, and a military government took power.

HISTORY. Modern Greece has roots in the Classical Greek civilization that flourished on the Hellenic peninsula in ancient times. Between about 800 BC and 300 BC, the Greeks developed a culture that laid the foundation for much of later Western civilization.

In 338 BC Greece was conquered by its northern neighbor, Macedonia, and Greek culture was spread throughout Macedonia's vast Middle Eastern and Mediterranean empire, which eventually came under the control of Rome. Rome, too, absorbed many Greek artistic and intellectual achievements.

In 285 AD the Roman Empire was divided, and Greece became part of the eastern section, ruled from Byzantium. In 330 Byzantium, renamed Constantinople, became the capital of all that remained of the Roman Empire. As a part of this Byzantine Empire, the Greeks were still the cultural and intellectual leaders of the eastern Mediterranean.

While western Europe struggled with the disorder produced by barbarian invasions, the Orthodox Christian, Graeco-Roman civilization of the eastern empire maintained its stability. Greek cultural influence was dependent on Byzantine political strength, however, and the eastern empire was unable to withstand the onslaught of a new power in Asia Minor, the Ottoman Turks.

In the 1000s, the Turks began to attack the Byzantine Empire. Over a period of 400 years they conquered Byzantine territory bit by bit, until in 1453 they captured Constantinople itself.

Ottoman Rule. The Greeks did not fare badly under the Ottomans. They enjoyed some self-government, and Greeks in Constantinople, called Phanariots, filled many high positions in the Ottoman administration. The Turks did not force the Greek Christians to convert to Islam, although those who did enjoyed a higher status in the Muslim society.

For the most part, the Ottoman government ignored Greeks living outside Asia Minor, and in many cases neglected them. What remained of Classical Greek culture decayed, and the people of Greece sank into poverty.

The Greeks were far from content under Turkish rule, however. In the 1700s those who still lived in the Hellenic peninsula began to develop a feeling of national pride and a desire for independence. Moreover, in the 1700s the Ottoman government began to loosen control over its more distant territories.

The Greek economy, exhausted since Roman times, began to revive, and Greek trade, industry, and shipping expanded. At the same time self-government began to develop on the local level. The spirit of nationalism swept Europe in the early 1800s, and Greek nationalism took the form of a desire for full freedom from Turkey and included the goal of uniting all Greek-speaking people into one nation.

Independence. The Greek struggle for independence began in 1821, when Alexander Ypsilanti, a leader of a secret revolutionary organization, *Hetairia Philiké*, or Society of Friends, led a revolt in the Phanariot-governed principalities of Moravia and Walachia, part of present-day Romania.

LUFTHANSA

ACROPOLIS OF ATHENS, site of the Parthenon and other masterpieces of classical Greek art.

Ypsilanti had hoped for aid from neighboring Russia, but he received no support and was defeated. Uprisings also broke out in the south of Greece, however, and continued despite severe Turkish reprisals.

By 1822 the rebellion was countrywide, and the Greeks declared their independence. Over the next few years Greek guerrilla forces won control of much of their territory from the Ottoman Turks. In 1825, however, Turkey gained the support of Egypt, nominally a part of the Ottoman Empire. The untrained Greek guerrillas could not stand up against the power and organization of the Turkish-Egyptian army, and the Greeks steadily lost the land they had won.

The rebels would have met total defeat if they had not received help in 1827 from Britain, France, and Russia. All three had interests in the Balkans, and all three opposed Turkish domination of the region. The European nations agreed to join in finding or forcing a solution to the war. They tried to impose an armistice and urged Turkey to grant independence to Greece.

When the Turks refused, the European powers ordered a blockade to enforce a truce and to prevent the Turkish forces from receiving supplies. In enforcing the blockade, ships from Britain, Russia, and France destroyed most of the Egyptian fleet when it tried to bring troops and supplies into the port of Navarino in October 1827.

In 1828 Russia declared war on Turkey, and by so doing aided the Greeks. Although the war grew out of a Russo-Turkish territorial dispute, Russia also saw an advantage in weakening Turkey by driving the Turks from Greece.

Russia defeated Turkey in August 1829, and the Treaty of Adrianople, which ended the war, contained a provision granting independence to Greece. Turkey agreed to accept the London Protocol of March 1829, in which the three European powers decided that Greece—which then included only the Peloponnesus, the Cyclades, and Central Greece—would be an autonomous state under a king to be chosen from among the royal families of Europe.

The Greeks, however, already had a government. In 1827 they had chosen an assembly and elected a president, Ioannes Kapodistrias. He was assassinated in 1831, however, and Greece then accepted the powers' choice of a Bavarian prince, Otto, as king.

A New Nation. The new state faced great problems. Many Greeks wished to continue fighting to liberate territory that was inhabited by Greeks but not governed by Greece. The economy, severely damaged by the revolution, was weak—there was little manufacturing and agricultural techniques were old-fashioned and inefficient. A sense of local pride hindered administration by a national government.

Otto's attempts to solve these problems led to a highly centralized, bureaucratic government that was too clumsy to be effective and too complex for the people to deal with. In addition, the European powers still had great influence in Greek politics.

In 1843 two political factions, one supported by the British and one by the Russians, rebelled against the king. The rebels demanded a constitution

GREEK BOYS WHITEWASHING THE STREETS in Mykonos, one of the Cyclades islands.

and an elected assembly. Otto agreed to these demands and established a constitutional monarchy. The new system worked almost as poorly as absolute rule had, and in 1862 Otto was deposed.

In the following year a Danish prince was named king as George I of Greece (r.1863–1913). The Greeks had selected another leader, but accepted the powers' choice of George when Britain gave Greece the Ionian Islands, which had been a British protectorate.

George's attempts to transform Greece into a country governed by the most advanced parliamentary institutions were only partly successful. The Greeks' lack of education and their inexperience with parliamentary government resulted in a rapid turnover of governments.

The first leader to have any success in establishing an efficient Greek government was Eleutherios Venizelos, who became prime minister in 1910. Venizelos won a strong majority in parliament in 1911 and passed a revised constitution that allowed for more stable parliamentary government.

Venizelos reorganized and simplified the bureaucracy and reduced the power of the army in government affairs. During his first years in office the educational system was broadened and large estates were divided among small farmers.

Expansion. During the reign of George I, Greece made many additions to its territory. The European powers exerted great efforts to prevent this expansion from resulting in a clash with Turkey that could lead to a general European war. In 1881 the powers forced Turkey to yield most of Epirus and Thessaly to Greece as part of the settlement of the Russo-Turkish War of 1877.

In 1896 Greece, trying to aid a rebellion in Crete against Turkish rule, did go to war against Turkey, and was soundly defeated. But Britain, France, and Russia forced Turkey to evacuate Crete, which was then occupied by the

THESSALY'S CRAGGY PEAKS shelter many Christian monasteries, such as this one at Meteora.

three powers and by Italy. Crete successfully rebelled in 1905, and in 1908 declared its union with Greece. The European alliance withdrew its forces the following year.

Greece entered another territorial war before World War I. In the spring of 1912 Premier Venizelos made an alliance with Bulgaria, and in the following fall Greece and Bulgaria—with its ally, Serbia—declared war on Turkey over conflicting territorial claims. Greece and its allies won this First Balkan War, and in 1913, by the Treaty of London, Turkey gave up its claims to Crete and ceded Macedonia to the Balkan allies.

Another Balkan War in the summer of 1913, fought by Greece, Serbia, and Romania against Bulgaria, determined which state would receive what part of the territory. By the Treaty of Bucharest, Greece gained part of Macedonia and another section of Epirus.

In World War I, Premier Venizelos urged Greek intervention on the side of the Allies (Britain, Russia, and France). King Constantine, who had come to the throne after his father's death in 1913, preferred to remain neutral. It was not until 1917, after an Allied ultimatum forced Constantine to yield the throne to his son, Alexander, that Greece entered the war against Germany.

Greek troops fought primarily in the Balkans, and at the end of the war the Treaty of Sèvres gave Greece eastern Thrace, the Turkish islands in the Aegean, and a mandate to occupy a part of Turkey's mainland. Turkish nationalists opposed the treaty, however, and in 1920 a Greek army invaded Turkey, only to meet disastrous defeat in 1922. King Constantine, who had regained the throne after Alexander's death in 1920, was forced to abdicate again.

Search for Stability. Constantine's son became king as George II, but his government was forced out of office in 1923 by a powerful faction that favored a republican form of government. In 1924 this faction formed a revolutionary government that proclaimed Greece a republic. The republic was a failure. The leaders of the new government could not agree on policy, and after a rapid succession of governments, George II was restored to the throne in 1935.

Greece's extreme political instability left the nation helpless in the face of serious problems. The greatest difficulties were economic. Weak industry, unproductive agriculture, and an extremely high birth rate kept the people in poverty. The world economic depression of the 1930s was particularly severe for Greece because of its dependence on exporting such costly items as wine and olive oil.

In 1936 King George appointed Gen. Ioannes Metaxas as premier after a parliamentary election gave no party a majority. Metaxas dissolved the parliament and made himself dictator. His fascist-like regimentation of society was unpopular, but he relieved some of the country's economic problems.

World War II ended the Metaxas dictatorship, but brought enormous economic, social, and political problems. The Greeks successfully fought off an Italian invasion attempt in 1940, but in 1941 German forces conquered the country and occupied it until 1944.

During the war George Papandreou, a leader of the Greek parliament, formed a government-in-exile. After the war, however, his government remained in office for only three months, in 1945. Its rivals for power were two opposing political organizations formed during the war.

A communist-led resistance group had political and economic control of the countryside, and a right-wing royalist faction dominated parliament. An election in 1946 restored the monarchy, but by the time King George returned a few weeks later, a civil war had broken out between the right and the left.

Greece's desperate political and economic troubles inflamed the war, which continued with support from

GREEK FISHERMEN REPAIRING THEIR NETS on Thasos, an island in the northern Aegean Sea.

Yugoslavia for the communist guerrillas and with U.S. aid for the government forces. In 1947 Yugoslavia withdrew military assistance from the rebels and the United States gave large-scale financial and military aid to the country under the Truman Doctrine. By 1949 Greek government troops were able to subdue the rebels.

King Paul took the throne after his brother George's death in 1947. He built a constitutional monarchy that was able to maintain a fairly stable government despite occasional political clashes. When he died in 1964, his son succeeded him as Constantine II.

Contemporary Greece. Between 1963 and 1967, Greece endured almost continual government crises. No one party succeeded in winning a majority in parliament, and premiers were forced to rely on weak coalition cabinets. George Papandreou, head of the Center Union party, led coalition cabinets in 1963, 1964, and 1965, when he resigned in a dispute with the king.

The caretaker premiers who followed had to rely on Papandreou for much of their support. In March 1967 Papandreou withdrew the support of the Center Union from the government, causing its fall.

King Constantine appointed Panayotis Canellopoulos, leader of the conservative National Radical Union party, premier. Canellopoulos, a personal and political rival of Papandreou, formed a one-party cabinet and dissolved parliament in April 1967 to permit his government to last until scheduled elections could be held in May. But in April a group of army officers led a coup that took power from the civilian authorities.

The military leaders of the coup maintained that their takeover had saved the country from a leftist rebellion planned by Andreas Papandreou, son of George Papandreou. Many prominent political leaders were imprisoned, and intellectual and cultural life was subjected to censorship.

The colonels stated that their purpose was to "purify" Greek government and society—they hoped to restore the country to "traditional morality" and to revive the spirit of nationalism. They suspended many civil liberties and imposed direct government control over the politically and socially important Greek Orthodox Church.

In November 1967 King Constantine attempted to overthrow the junta, but he failed and went into exile. The colonels strengthened their hold on the army by purging officers believed loyal to the king, and in 1968 won diplomatic recognition for their government from the United States and other countries.

—George Kren

GUATEMALA

Official name: Republic of Guatemala
Area: 42,042 square miles
Population: (1966 est.) 4,575,000
Capital: Guatemala City (Pop., 1964 est., 577,100)
Language: Spanish
Religion: Roman Catholicism
Currency unit: Quetzal
National holiday: Independence day, September 15

Guatemala, the largest republic in Central America, is bordered on the west and north by Mexico; on the east by British Honduras, the Gulf of Honduras (an arm of the Caribbean Sea) and Honduras; and on the south by El Salvador and the Pacific Ocean.

THE LAND. Guatemala is a mountainous land. The Central American Cordillera, which lies roughly parallel to the Pacific coast, includes the highest peak in Central America, the volcanic Mt. Tajumulco, 13,812 feet above sea level.

A narrow plain borders the Pacific coast. Inland from the plain are the central highlands, which include about

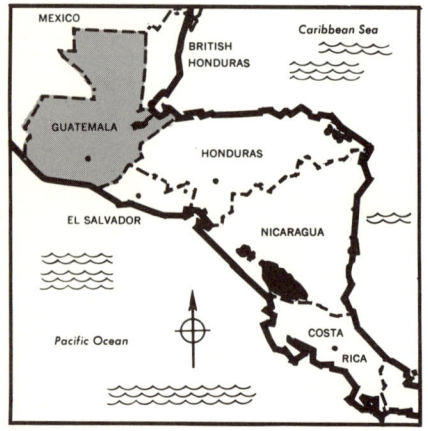

OPEN AIR MARKET in the plaza of Chichicastenango, a village in Guatemala.

a fifth of the country's land area. In the southeast are the Caribbean lowlands. In the north is the Petén district, a sparsely settled forest region containing about a third of the country's area.

The Caribbean lowlands are hot and rainy. The Pacific coast has dry winters and wet summers. The central highlands have a cool, dry climate.

THE PEOPLE. More than half of Guatemala's people are of American Indian stock, descendants of the Mayas, and about 30 percent are *ladino*, or mestizo, of mixed Indian and European background. A small minority, perhaps 10 percent of the population, claims unmixed European descent. Most of the people live in the highlands, where Guatemala City is located.

The population is increasing at a very rapid rate, estimated at more than 3 percent a year between 1958 and 1967. This rapid rate of increase places heavy strains on the economy, for more and more goods, more housing, and more jobs must be provided every year.

ECONOMY. Guatemala is an agricultural country, and in 1966 agriculture contributed 28 percent to the national product. Approximately 60 percent of the population is directly dependent on agriculture for its livelihood, and three crops—coffee, cotton, and bananas—contributed more than 60 percent of total export earnings in the mid-1960s.

Agriculture is concentrated in the central highland valleys and the narrow coastal plains. The main commercial crops are coffee, cotton, sugarcane, and bananas. The major food crops include corn, rice, wheat, and beans. Livestock include cattle, sheep, and pigs.

Forests cover about 40 percent of the country's land, and forest resources are increasingly exploited. The country's mineral resources include antimony, chromium, lead, and zinc, but only salt is produced in appreciable quantities.

Industry became the most rapidly growing part of Guatemala's economy in the mid-1960s, and by 1965 industry contributed 16 percent of the national product. The most rapidly growing industries include chemicals and textiles. Food processing is also important to the country.

In 1965 Guatemala's exports earned $187 million and imports cost $229 million. Coffee is the most important export, representing more than 40 percent of 1965 earnings. Cotton, meat, sugar, bananas, chicle, and essential oils such as citronella are also valuable exports. Manufactured goods are of growing importance. Imports include foodstuffs, petroleum products, machinery and vehicles, and manufactured goods.

Guatemala is a member of the Central American Common Market, and the country's trade increasingly has been directed to fellow market members, especially El Salvador. In 1965 about 20 percent of Guatemala's trade was within the market area, but the United States remained the country's most important trading partner, taking 37 percent of exports and supplying 43 percent of imports.

GOVERNMENT. Guatemala has a long tradition of political upheaval and of dictatorial rule. The country's third constitution in 20 years was promulgated in 1965.

The 1965 constitution vested executive powers in a president and vice-president. Legislative powers rest with the Congress, which has but one house of 55 members. The president, vice-president, and congressmen are popularly elected to four-year terms of office. If no presidential candidate wins a majority of votes, the Congress chooses the president.

Guatemala is a member of the United Nations and the Organization of American States (OAS). The country has engaged in a long-standing dispute with Britain over British Honduras, which is claimed by Guatemala.

HISTORY. Long before the Spanish conquest of Central America in the 1500s, most of present-day Guatemala was part of the great Mayan civilization, which flourished in the area between 300 and 800 AD. Mayan civilization had declined as a result of internal dissension, and in 1524 Spanish forces led by Pedro de Alvarado conquered the area.

The region became part of the Spanish colonial captaincy-general of Guatemala, which included much of Central America. In 1543 the capital of the captaincy was established at Antigua, a city near present-day Guatemala City. Antigua was destroyed by an earthquake in 1773, and soon after Guatemala City became the capital.

Independence. On Sept. 15, 1821, following Mexico's successful independence struggle, Guatemala was peacefully separated from Spain and joined to the Mexican Empire of Augustín de

COUNTRIES OF THE WORLD

Iturbide. Quickly dissatisfied with Mexican control, Guatemala joined El Salvador, Honduras, Costa Rica, Nicaragua, and Chiapas (now part of Mexico) in the United Provinces of Central America. The United Provinces were torn by internal conflicts, and in 1838 the federal system collapsed.

Guatemala became a sovereign state in 1839 under the leadership of Rafael Carrera, who remained the country's strong man until his death in 1865. Carrera had the complete support of the Indians, and his conservative policies won the support of the upper classes and the army. He made Guatemala a republic in 1847, and in 1851 he was elected president. He assumed the presidency for life in 1854. Conservatives remained in power until a liberal revolt in 1871.

Guatemala was ruled by a liberal dictator, Justo Rufino Barrios, from 1873 to 1885. His administration was characterized by great progress in railroad construction, educational reforms, and encouragement of foreign investment. In an attempt to reestablish the Central American Federation under his leadership, he launched a war against Guatemala's neighbors and was killed in battle.

Manuel Estrada Cabrera gained control of the country in 1898. During his administration, the United Fruit Company, a U.S. firm, entered Guatemala and began to play an influential role in Guatemalan politics. Estrada Cabrera was toppled from power in 1920.

Jorge Ubico Castañeda ruled Guatemala from 1931 to 1944. He led the country through the world economic depression of the 1930s, but his despotic rule provoked widespread dissatisfaction. He was removed from power by the military, which attempted to replace him with Federico Ponce.

PAN AMERICAN AIRWAYS
THE CATHEDRAL OF SAN JOSÉ in Antigua, a city that was once the capital of Guatemala.

But student riots and a general strike forced the military to allow free elections and grant a new constitution.

Modern Guatemala. The "revolutions" of Oct. 20, 1944 raised the hopes of many Guatemalans for a new era of social reform. Serious inequalities in the distribution of wealth and income plagued the country. A small number of wealthy people had controlled economic and political life, and the mass of the people had little land and lived in poverty.

Dr. Juan José Arévelo was overwhelmingly elected president, and he launched a program that included support for trade unions and the introduction of social security programs. Although opposition from the privileged minority threatened his administration, he became one of the few presidents to complete his term of office. In 1951 he was peacefully succeeded by Col. Jacobo Arbenz Guzmán.

Arbenz attempted to continue the reforms. He initiated an extensive land reform program and restricted the activities of the United Fruit Company. His administration was charged with being communist dominated, and in 1954 an armed force led by Col. Carlos Castillo Armas and supported by the United States invaded Guatemala from Honduras and toppled Arbenz.

Castillo Armas took control and promulgated a new constitution in 1956. Castillo Armas was assassinated in 1957, and in 1958 Gen. Miguel Ydígoras Fuentes became president. Attempts at moderate reform won Ydígoras the enmity of the conservatives, who thought he was going too far, and of the left, which felt he was not going far enough.

In 1963 the military overthrew Ydígoras and Col. Enrique Peralta Azurdía was placed in power. Peralta's administration abrogated the 1956 constitution. Considerable economic growth was achieved under Peralta's rule, and in 1964, bowing to popular pressure, a constituent assembly was convened to draw up a new constitution. The new basic law, promulgated in 1965, outlawed communist and other totalitarian groups.

Elections were held in 1966, but the military split into two major factions and a civilian candidate, Julio César Méndez Montenegro, led the *Partido Revolucionario* (PR—Revolutionary Party) to victory. The PR won 30 of the 55 seats in Congress, and since no candidate had won a majority of votes in the presidential contest, the Congress elected Méndez president.

Inaugurated on July 1, 1966, Méndez moved to further economic diversification and to expand social development programs. He took the lead in promoting the further integration of the Central American nations through the Central American Common Market.
—George W. Carey; Jerome Fischman

GUINEA

Official name: Republic of Guinea
Area: 94,909 square miles
Population: (1966 est.) 3,608,000
Capital: Conakry (Pop., 1964 est., urban area, 175,000)
Language: French, African languages
Religion: Islam, traditional religions
Currency unit: Franc
National holiday: Independence day, October 2

Guinea, a republic in western Africa, is bounded on the north by Portuguese Guinea, Senegal, and Mali, on the east by Mali and the Ivory Coast, on the south by Liberia and Sierra Leone, and on the west by the Atlantic Ocean. Guinea was a territory of France until 1958, when it declared its independence.

THE LAND. The landscape of Guinea is varied. There is a wide, rainy coastal plain, but further inland the land is drier and has elevations of more than 3,000 feet above sea level. In the central part of the country is the mountain region of Fouta Djallon. From the mountains the land descends to the east into the drainage basins of the Senegal and Niger rivers. There are grasslands and forests in the east.

Temperatures vary throughout the country. In the coastal region temperatures average about 80°F. The Fouta

PAN AMERICAN AIRWAYS
LAKE ATITLAN, in southwestern Guatemala, lies at an elevation of about 4,700 feet.

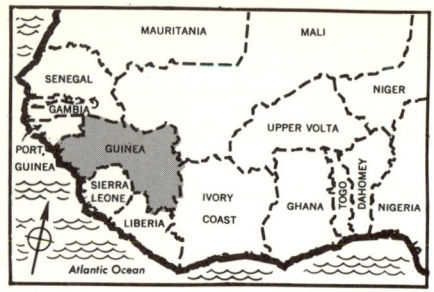

Djallon is relatively cool. Temperatures range over 80°F in the region north and east of the Fouta Djallon.

THE PEOPLE. There are many different ethnic groups in Guinea. The larger groups are the Fulani, Malinke, and Susu. A majority of the people are Muslim.

Most of the people live in rural areas. Guinea's largest city is the capital, Conakry, situated on Tombo Island off the mainland of Guinea. Conakry is also Guinea's major port.

ECONOMY. Guinea's economy depends largely on agriculture. Bananas, coffee, palm products, and peanuts are the chief cash crops. The basic food crops are manioc, fruits, millet, and rice.

Mining, especially of bauxite, is increasing in importance in Guinea. The country has abundant hydroelectric power, which is used in processing bauxite into alumina, enriched bauxite. In 1965 almost 2 million metric tons of bauxite were produced, more than six times the amount produced at the time of independence in 1958. Diamonds and iron ore are also mined.

In 1964 Guinea's imports cost $49 million and its exports earned $43 million. Guinea's main imports are petroleum products, cement, and sugar. The chief exports are bauxite and alumina, iron ore, diamonds, bananas, and palm kernels.

GOVERNMENT. Guinea has a presidential system of government. Executive power is vested in a president, who is popularly elected to a seven-year term. Legislative power rests with a 75-member National Assembly. Assembly members are popularly elected to five-year terms.

Guinea is a member of the United Nations and the Organization of African Unity (OAU).

HISTORY. Little is known of the early history of Guinea. Beginning in the 1400s the peoples of Guinea were in regular commercial contact with European sailors and merchants. They also had connections of long standing with trade across the Sahara.

Islam penetrated what is now Guinea, and many of the Fulani of upper Guinea became Muslims. In the early 1700s Muslims in the Fouta Djallon region revolted against their pagan rulers and created a state of their own.

The French began to acquire portions of Guinea in the 1800s. The indigenous peoples fought against these acquisitions, but they were largely unsuccessful. Samori ibn Ture, a warrior who assembled his own army and ruled much of upper Guinea, fought a frequently victorious guerrilla war against the French in the 1880s and 1890s. By 1898, however, French armies had forced Samori into exile.

French Rule. In 1895 Guinea became a part of French West Africa, and was subject to direct rule from France. In the Muslim area of Fouta Djallon, however, France initiated a system of indirect rule. Schools and hospitals were provided in both the coastal and interior areas.

The peoples of the coastal region, particularly those of Conakry, became thoroughly acquainted with French culture. A railway was built which linked Conakry to Kankan, in upper Guinea, by 1925. The railway thus made possible the export of tropical products.

In 1946 Guinea became a territory within the French Union, but Guinea was the only French territory that refused to join the newly formed French Community in 1958. In October 1958, under the leadership of Sékou Touré, claimed as a descendant of Samori and a prominent trade unionist, Guinea became independent.

Independence. At the time of independence, France withdrew financial and administrative help, causing a serious crisis in Guinea. In July 1961 Guinea joined with Ghana and Mali to found a short-lived union.

Even after the breakup of the union, Guinea continued to follow a pan-African policy. In 1966, after the overthrow of Ghana's government, Touré named former Ghanaian president Kwame Nkrumah honorary president of Guinea.

—Hibberd V. B. Kline, Jr.;
Robert I. Rotberg

GUYANA

Official name: Guyana
Area: 83,000 square miles
Population: (1966 est.) 665,000
Capital: Georgetown (Pop. 1960, urban area, 148,391)
Language: English
Religion: Hinduism, Christianity, Islam
Currency unit: Dollar
National holiday: Independence day, May 26

Guyana, a small country on the northeast coast of South America, is bounded on the north by the Atlantic Ocean, on the east by Surinam (Dutch Guiana), on the south and southwest by Brazil, and on the west by Venezuela. Guyana received its independence from Britain in 1966, after more than 150 years as the colony of British Guiana.

THE LAND. Guyana's land surface consists of a low coastal plain that rises gradually into the heavily faulted Guiana Highlands. The coastal plain varies between 10 and 40 miles in width. Although it represents only 3.5 percent of Guyana's total land area, it is the home of 90 percent of the population. The coastal plain is the only area suitable for agriculture, and the country's two main crops, sugarcane and rice, are raised there.

South of the coastal plain is an inland forest region, which covers 86 percent of Guyana. The inland forest contains great quantities of commercially valuable wood, but transportation is poor and the region has remained largely unexploited. Guyana also has about 8,000 square miles of grassland savannas, located primarily in the southwestern interior and off the northeast coast.

Guyana has four major rivers—the Essequibo, Demerara, Berbice, and Courantyne—as well as a number of small rivers, but they are generally navigable only from about 40 to 100 miles upstream. Further inland the irregularity of the highland terrain creates numerous falls and rapids, which have hindered access to the interior.

Guyana has a humid tropical climate. The coastal plain is cooled by the northeast trade winds and has an average temperature of 80°F, but the savannas and inland forest have somewhat higher temperatures. Annual rainfall ranges from about 80 inches on the coast to about 100 inches in the interior. The coast has two rainy seasons, from April to August and from November to January.

THE PEOPLE. About 50 percent of the population is descended from East Indian laborers who came to work on the sugar plantations in the mid-1800s. About 31 percent is descended from Negro slaves. Twelve percent is mixed. The remainder consists of indigenous Indians (Amerindians), Chinese, and Portuguese and other Europeans.

The diversity of Guyana's people is reflected in their religious beliefs. Some 30 percent of the population is Hindu, 15 percent Muslim, 35 percent Protestant, and 15 percent Roman Catholic.

ECONOMY. The economy of Guyana is based on agriculture and mining. The chief agricultural product is sugar, which constitutes about one-fourth of Guyana's exports. Rice has become an important crop and in 1965 made up about 14 percent of the country's exports. Coconuts, coffee, cocoa, citrus, and other fruits are grown largely for domestic consumption.

Guyana's most important mineral is bauxite, from which aluminum is made. In 1966, 3,348 million metric tons of bauxite were produced. Manganese has been discovered in the northwest, at Matthews Ridge, and large-scale mining operations began in 1960. Small amounts of gold and diamonds are also mined.

In 1965 Guyana's exports were valued at $97 million and its imports cost $104 million. Major exports are sugar, bauxite, rice, fish, uncut diamonds, manganese ore, rum, and wood. Principal imports are foodstuffs, petroleum products, textiles, iron and steel products, machinery, transportation equipment, and chemicals. Guyana trades primarily with Britain, Canada, the United States, and Trinidad and Tobago.

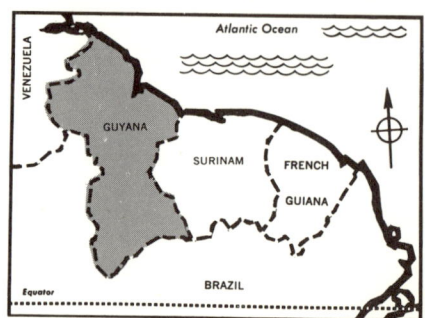

GOVERNMENT. Guyana has a parliamentary system of government. The British monarch is the head of state and is represented in Guyana by a governor-general. Executive power is exercised by a prime minister and cabinet. The prime minister is normally the leader of the majority party in the legislature.

Legislative power is vested in the unicameral House of Assembly, whose 53 members are elected directly under a system of proportional representation.

Guyana is a member of the Commonwealth of Nations and the United Nations.

HISTORY. The Guyana coast was one of the first parts of South America to be discovered by Europeans. There was no immediate attempt at colonization, but the legend of the golden land of El Dorado and tales of fabulous riches to be found further inland led to the exploration of the interior by Sir Walter Raleigh, who led expeditions in 1595 and 1617.

During the 1600s the Dutch, French, and English established small settlements along the coast. For 200 years different parts of the Guianas passed back and forth among the three powers, and it was not until the Congress of Vienna in 1814–1815 that the Guianas were formally divided into British, French, and Dutch areas.

British Rule. The economy of British Guiana was based on sugar, which was raised on large plantations worked by Negro slaves. During the early 1800s there was a great deal of unrest among the slaves, partly fostered by abolitionists in England. Slavery was abolished in 1833, and the economy suffered when the former slaves drifted off into the unsettled backlands and established themselves as small farmers.

Efforts were made to find an alternative labor force, and East Indians were eventually brought to work on the sugar plantations under a system of indentured labor. By 1883 they constituted one-fourth of the population. Sugar production rose in step with East Indian immigration, but friction began to develop among groups of different backgrounds.

The British kept the colony under tight political control and allowed only a few wealthy Guyanese to have some voice in its government. Serious discontent, however, did not become evident until the 1900s. There was some minor labor unrest as a result of the world economic depression of the 1930s, but it did not reach major proportions until after World War II.

In 1949 Cheddi Jagan, of East Indian origin, established the People's Progressive Party (PPP) to work for social and economic reforms, and to achieve self-government. Britain granted the colony a constitution providing for a good deal of autonomy in 1953. The PPP won elections held in April 1953 under the new constitution, but in October Britain suspended the constitution, charging the PPP was under strong communist influence.

In 1955 the PPP split along ethnic lines. Forbes Burnham led most of the Negro members into a new party, the People's National Congress (PNC).

New elections were held in 1961 under a new constitution, and the PPP returned to power. But communal violence and fear of Jagan's left-wing connections led the British to intervene once more.

Independence. Elections were held under a system of proportional representation in 1964, and the People's National Congress, with the support of a small conservative party, the United Force, gained control of the government. Britain granted Guyana independence on May 26, 1966, and Forbes Burnham became the country's first prime minister.

—David Bushnell; Kempton E. Webb

HAITI

Official name: Republic of Haiti
Area: 10,714 square miles
Population: (1966 est.) 4,485,000
Capital: Port-au-Prince (Pop., 1960 est., 240,000)
Language: French, Creole
Religion: Roman Catholicism
Currency unit: Gourde
National holiday: Independence day, January 1

The Republic of Haiti occupies the western third of the island of Hispaniola in the Greater Antilles. The Dominican Republic occupies the eastern two-thirds of the island. Hispaniola is bounded by the Atlantic Ocean on the north and by the Caribbean Sea on the south. Cuba lies to the west, and Puerto Rico to the east.

THE LAND. Haiti is a mountainous country. The principal ranges are the Massif du Nord, in the north; the Montagnes Noires, in the center; the Montagnes du Trou d'Eau, the Chaine des Matheux, and the Massif de la Selle, all in the southeast; and the Massif de la Hotte, in the south.

Between the mountains is a system

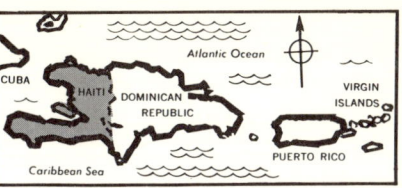

of plains and valleys. Among the most important are the Cul-de-Sac in the south, where Port-au-Prince is situated, the Plaine du Nord in the northeast, the Plaine de l'Artibonite in the center, and the Plaine Centrale in the east. Haiti's most important river is the Artibonite.

Haiti has a tropical climate, but temperatures are modified by altitude, rainfall, and sea winds.

THE PEOPLE. Haiti's people are mainly of African Negro origin, but about 10 percent of the population is mulatto, of mixed African and European background. The mulattoes dominated Haitian political, economic, and social life for many years.

Most of the people live in the mountain valleys, but transportation facilities through the mountains are poor and the cities lie along the coasts.

ECONOMY. Agriculture is the main source of income, and most of the people are poor farmers who work very small plots of land in the mountain valleys. The leading cash crops are coffee, cacao, and sugarcane. Sisal, essential oils, and castor beans are also important export crops. Cotton, bananas, tobacco, fruits, and rice are grown as well.

Manufacturing industries produce cotton textiles, soap and pharmaceuticals, sisal rope and plastics, furniture and building materials, foodstuffs, and molasses and rum.

Bauxite is mined for export, and there are deposits of other minerals, including copper, manganese, gold,

MARDI GRAS IN HAITI. The pre-Lenten festival is celebrated with costumes, masks, and floats.

silver, iron, tin, and coal. Tourism has been a major source of income.

In 1965 Haiti's exports earned about $37.5 million and its imports cost $37.7 million. The major exports include coffee, sugar, bauxite, and sisal. Imports include machinery and vehicles, petroleum products, and manufactured goods.

A major barrier to economic development is the increasing pressure of people on the land. Only about one-third of the country's land can be cultivated, and it is estimated that there are some 1,500 persons per square mile in the agricultural areas. Although the government instituted programs to encourage industrial development and increase agricultural production, Haiti in the mid-1960s remained one of the world's most underdeveloped nations.

GOVERNMENT. Haiti has a long tradition of political instability and of dictatorial rule. The country is formally a republic headed by a president. In 1961 Dr. François Duvalier was elected to a six-year term of office, and in 1964 had himself proclaimed president for life. A legislature with one house of 58 deputies was also elected to a six-year term in 1961. Haiti is a member of the United Nations and of the Organization of American States (OAS).

HISTORY. Christopher Columbus discovered the island of Hispaniola in 1492 during his first voyage to the New World. The peaceful Arawak Indian inhabitants called the island Haiti, "land of mountains," but Columbus named it Española, which later became Hispaniola.

Columbus described the Arawak in a letter to the Spanish monarchs as "timid, full of fear, and lovable." Nonetheless, the Indians were soon subjected to severe exploitation by Spanish colonists, and by the end of the 1500s the Arawak had been almost completely exterminated.

Although Spain claimed the entire island, Spanish settlements were concentrated in the east, and French and English pirates were able to establish themselves on the western coast. The French eventually drove out the English, and in 1697 Spain ceded the western end of the island to France, which called it St. Dominique.

French Rule. The French established sugar and tobacco plantations, importing slaves to work the land. They gradually succeeded in building a flourishing colony in which many mulattoes prospered and became slaveholders themselves. But social class rivalry was intense, and the slaves were kept in the worst possible conditions.

In 1791, sparked by the French Revolution in Europe, civil war broke out in Haiti. Toussaint L'Overture, a former slave, led the Negroes in a victorious revolt. He forced the French to abolish slavery in 1793, and in 1801 became head of an autonomous government. He successfully expelled Spanish and British forces that attempted to intervene, but in a struggle to achieve complete independence from the French he was captured and sent to prison in France, where he died.

Independence. Jean Jacques Dessalines, another former slave, assumed leadership of the struggle and ultimately led a Negro army to victory. Independence was declared on Jan. 1, 1804, and Dessalines proclaimed himself governor-general for life. He was later crowned Emperor Jacques I. His despotic rule over a war-ravaged country ended with his murder in 1806.

Two states emerged in Haiti following Dessalines death, and there began a struggle for power between Henri Christophe, in the north, and Alexandre Pétion, in the south. Christophe ruled as a benevolent despot from 1811 to 1820, and the north made considerable economic progress. Pétion's rule in the south during the same period had disastrous results.

North and south were reunited in 1820 under the rule of Jean Pierre Boyer, who had succeeded Pétion in the south in 1818 and then extended his rule to the north when Christophe committed suicide. Boyer ruled ineffectively until 1843, when he was exiled. At that time the inhabitants of Santo Domingo, in the eastern part of the island, broke away and established the Dominican Republic.

U.S. Intervention. The next 70 years were marked by almost constant misrule, misery, and revolution. Dictators rapidly succeeded each other, and Haiti fell into a state of chaos. In 1915 U.S. marines landed in Haiti. The U.S. occupation was ordered by Pres. Woodrow Wilson, who feared that Haiti's political and economic breakdown and recurring violence would spread throughout the Caribbean.

Although considerable progress was made during the occupation, Haitians expressed continued resentment of foreign interference. Under Pres. Herbert Hoover, a U.S. commission met with leading Haitian citizens to discuss withdrawal of U.S. troops; by 1934, under the administration of Pres. Franklin Roosevelt, evacuation of the marines was completed.

Modern Haiti. Following the end of the U.S. occupation, several enlightened mulatto leaders ruled Haiti. In 1946, however, the Negroes revolted and restored leadership to the "authentiqué," the Negro. The government changed hands many times during the next several years, and disorder and misery increased. Then, in September 1957 François Duvalier, a physician, was elected president.

"Papa Doc," as Duvalier became known, established an oppressive dictatorship. Duvalier's rule rested in large part on his secret police, popularly called the *tonton macoute* (Haitian Creole for "bogeyman").

Duvalier became involved in disputes with the United States, which led to the withdrawal of U.S. aid in 1963, and with his neighbor, the Dominican Republic. Relations with the Dominican Republic improved in 1966, after the election of Joaquín Balaguer as that country's president. Duvalier also came into conflict with the Roman Catholic Church, but relations with the church improved in 1966, when a Haitian was inaugurated archbishop.

—George W. Carey; Jerome Fischman

HONDURAS

Official name: Republic of Honduras
Area: 43,277 square miles
Population: (1967 est.) 2,445,000
Capital: Tegucigalpa (Pop., 1965 est., 170,500)
Language: Spanish
Religion: Roman Catholicism
Currency unit: Lempira
National holiday: Independence day, September 15

Honduras, the second largest of the Central American republics, is bounded on the north by the Caribbean Sea; on the east by Nicaragua; on the south by the Gulf of Fonseca, an arm of the Pacific Ocean, and El Salvador; and on the west by Guatemala. Honduras includes the Bay Islands, or Islas de la Bahía, which lie off the north coast.

THE LAND. Honduras is a mountainous country. The Central American Andes dominate the landscape, running from northwest to southeast. The highlands are cut through by fertile river valleys, the largest of which is the valley of the Río Ulúa.

A fertile, well-watered plain stretches inland from the Caribbean coast. The plain is narrow in the west, near the border with Guatemala, and broad in the east, along the border with Nicaragua. The eastern part of the plain is known as the Mosquito Coast. There is another, smaller lowland region along the Pacific coast.

The Caribbean lowlands have a hot, humid tropical climate. The Pacific coastal region has wet summers and dry winters. The uplands have a pleasant, temperate climate.

THE PEOPLE. Most Hondurans are mestizo, of mixed Indian and European origin. There are some Indians, whites, and Negroes.

The population of Honduras is increasing at a very rapid rate, estimated at 3.3 percent a year between 1958 and 1964. This rapid rate of growth places heavy strains on the economy, for more food, housing, and jobs must be found each year.

ECONOMY. Honduras is an agricultural land. In the mid-1960s, two out of every three working people were employed in agriculture and agriculture contributed one half the national product. The chief crops raised for export are bananas, coffee, and cotton. Bananas are the country's most valuable export, and in 1965, 917,000 metric

tons of bananas were produced. Sugarcane, corn, sorghum, beans, and rice are grown for local food needs.

Honduras has rich forest resources, and lumbering is an important economic activity. The country also has considerable mineral resources, including gold, silver, lead, and zinc. But there is little manufacturing, and the major products of Honduran industry are consumer goods, such as clothing.

A government development plan covering the years 1965–1969 was designed to diversify the economy. A program of road building to provide links between the various parts of the country was begun, and Honduras began to tap the rich hydroelectric power potential offered by its rivers.

In 1965 Honduras' exports earned $129 million and imports cost $122 million. Exports consist almost entirely of agricultural products and raw materials. The major exports are bananas, coffee, cotton, wood, and minerals. Imports consist largely of manufactured goods, machinery and transportation equipment, chemicals, and foodstuffs.

Honduras is a member of the Central American Common Market (CACM), and its foreign trade is increasingly with fellow market members, especially El Salvador. Nonetheless, the United States remains the country's major trading partner, buying almost 60 percent of exports and providing over 45 percent of imports in 1965.

GOVERNMENT. Honduras is officially a republic with democratic institutions. But there is a strong tradition of political instability and of military interference with constitutional processes.

Constitutional government was overthrown by the military in 1963, and a junta composed of military men took power. A 64-member constituent assembly was elected in 1965, and it chose as president of Honduras the leader of the junta.

HISTORY. Christopher Columbus reached the area of Honduras in 1502, on his final voyage to the New World. But it was not until 1524 that the first Spanish colony was established. The American Indian inhabitants fiercely resisted the Spanish conquest, and the Indian chief Lempira is regarded as a national hero for his bravery in the struggle against the Spanish.

In 1539 Honduras was included in Spain's captaincy-general of Guatemala. Silver was discovered in the 1570s, and an influx or prospectors led to the founding of Tegucigalpa.

Independence. Following Mexico's achievement of independence in 1821, the Central American region proclaimed its independence of Spanish rule. The area was annexed to Augustín de Iturbide's Mexican empire, but after Iturbide's fall in 1823 it regained its freedom. Honduras then formed part of the United Provinces of Central America, which also included Costa Rica, El Salvador, Guatemala, and Nicaragua.

By the late 1830s the federation was divided by bitter rivalries among its members, as well as by divisions within the member states. In 1838 Honduras withdrew to become a separate nation, and in 1841 Francisco Ferrara became the country's first constitutional president.

During the later 1800s and early 1900s, Honduras struggled to remain independent in the face of threats posed by its neighbors, particularly Guatemala and Nicaragua. Rafael Carrera, dictator of Guatemala from 1838 to 1865, unseated liberal regimes in Honduras, and in 1885 Justo Rufino Barrios of Guatemala unsuccessfully attempted to restore the Central American federation by force.

In 1841 Britain gained control of the Bay Islands, withdrawing only in 1859. From 1871 to 1874 Honduras was at war with Guatemala and El Salvador, and in 1906 Honduras and El Salvador fought Guatemala.

By 1912 the troubled political situation led Pres. William Howard Taft to send troops to protect U.S. business interests in the country, mainly the United Fruit Company. U.S. forces intervened again in 1919 and in 1924.

Modern Honduras. Honduras achieved a measure of stability under the rule of Tiburcio Carías Andino, who ruled from 1933 to 1948. During that period economic progress was made, roads were built, and schools and hospitals were opened.

In 1948 Carías Andino gave the presidency to Juan Marval Gálvez, who permitted the organization of trade unions, a free press, and open political debate. He retired in 1954, a year marked by a 10-week strike against the United Fruit Company.

Elections were held in 1954. No candidate won a majority of the votes, and Julio Lozano Díaz assumed the presidency. He was overthrown in 1956 by a bloodless coup, and an army-supported junta took power.

The junta held elections for a constituent assembly in 1957. The assembly drafted a new constitution and chose Dr. Ramón Villeda Morales president. Villeda brought Honduras into the Central American Common Market and worked to raise the standard of living of the people.

In 1963 the military toppled the Villeda government and a junta again took power. Col. Oswaldo López Arellano, leader of the junta, called for the election of a new constituent assembly in 1965, and the assembly elected him president.

—George W. Carey; Jerome Fischman

HUNGARY

Official name: Hungarian People's Republic
Area: 35,919 square miles
Population: (1967 est.) 10,212,000
Capital: Budapest (Pop., 1965 est., 1,944,000)
Language: Hungarian
Religion: Roman Catholicism, Protestantism
Currency unit: Forint
National holiday: Anniversary of the liberation, April 4

The Hungarian People's Republic, a nation in central Europe, occupies the middle basin of the Danube River. It is bounded on the north by Czechoslovakia, on the northeast by the Soviet Union, on the east by Romania, on the south by Yugoslavia, and on the west by Austria.

THE LAND. Most of Hungary is flat land less than 600 feet in elevation. The lowlands fall into two main areas, the Lesser Hungarian Plain and the

Greater Hungarian Plain, divided by the Central Hungarian Uplands.

In the northwest lies the fertile, triangular Lesser Hungarian Plain, drained by tributaries of the Danube.

The Greater Hungarian Plain occupies the southeastern half of the country and is crossed on the west by the Danube. West of the Danube, the Greater Hungarian Plain is characterized by rolling land that rises gradually towards the south, culminating in the Mecsek uplands in the southernmost part of Hungary. East of the Danube the plain is almost completely level, drained toward the south by tributaries of the Danube, and dotted with lakes.

The central uplands consist of several ranges of hills and low mountains. West of the Danube, in the region known as Transdanubia, are the mineral-rich Bakony and Vértes ranges. East of the Danube, in the north-central part of the country, are the higher, heavily forested, Börzsöny, Cserhát, Mátra, and Bükk ranges, which reach a height of over 3,000 feet near the northern border.

The Danube, Hungary's largest river, forms part of the boundary between Hungary and Czechoslovakia and cuts through the Hungarian upland. The Danube's two most important tributaries in Hungary are the Drava in the south and the Tisza in the east. Lake Balaton, along the southwestern edge of the central uplands, is Hungary's largest lake.

Hungary's climate varies from region to region. For the country as a whole, summer temperatures average 71°F and winter temperatures average 31°F. About 25 inches of rain falls each year. The greater plain tends to be hotter and drier, and the uplands somewhat colder and wetter than the average.

THE PEOPLE. Over 95 percent of the population is Magyar, or Hungarian. The Hungarian, or Magyar, language is similar to Estonian and Finnish, and is unrelated to any of the languages spoken in neighboring countries. About two-thirds of the people are Roman Catholic, and most of the rest are Protestant. There are small minorities of Germans, Slovaks, Serbs and Croats, and Romanians.

About 40 percent of the people are urban-dwellers and half of these live in the capital, Budapest, which is the political, cultural, economic, and intellectual center of the country. Other important cities are Miskolc, an industrial center in the northeast, Debrecen, an eastern university town, Pécs, near the center of an important southern mining district, and Szeged, a southeastern city known for its textiles and food products and especially for its strong paprika.

ECONOMY. The Hungarian economy, traditionally based on agriculture and light industry, became industrialized under the communist regime that took power in 1947. Industrialization was based largely on development of the country's natural resources.

Natural Resources. Bauxite, found mainly in the western part of the central upland, is the most important mineral, and Hungary is one of the world's largest producers, mining over 1.4 million metric tons in 1966. Uranium is mined in the southwest, and there are deposits of iron ore and manganese.

Coal is Hungary's prime source of energy, but the reserves are mostly of low quality, consisting largely of brown coal and lignite. A dam on the middle Tisza River is the major hydroelectric installation. There is oil in the southwest, and some natural gas is produced.

Agriculture. Hungary's soil is quite rich and is especially suitable for raising grains. Corn, the leading crop, and wheat, barley, and rye represent about half of the total crop acreage. Potatoes, sugar beets, sunflowers, and tobacco are the main industrial crops. Warm summers enable Hungary to produce table and wine grapes, fruit, and vegetables. Almost all agriculture is collectivized.

Industry. In 1966 industry contributed over half of the national product. Under the communist regime, there has been a distinct shift from light to heavy industrial production, and by 1960 heavy industry accounted for two-thirds of the value of output and nearly two-thirds of industrial employment.

Iron, steel, chemicals, heavy construction machinery, railroad equipment, and small ships are the main products of heavy industry. Light industries still prosper and produce wool, cotton, and synthetic textiles, and flour and sugar. Budapest is Hungary's major industrial center.

Trade. Hungary generally has a favorable balance of trade. In 1966 exports earned nearly $1,600 million and imports cost just over $1,500 million. Raw materials, farm products, processed food, and some machinery are exported, and raw materials, textiles, and machinery are imported.

Hungary is integrated into the economy of the Soviet bloc through COMECON, the Council of Mutual Economic Assistance, an association of communist countries. Most of Hungary's trade is with other East European countries, but it also trades with Western Europe and Britain.

GOVERNMENT. Political activity in Hungary is dominated by the country's Communist party, officially called the Hungarian Socialist Workers Party. The political bureau, or politburo, of its central committee determines national policy, and its first secretary is usually the key figure in the government.

The Hungarian constitution places supreme governmental power in a one-house legislature, the National Assembly. All candidates for assembly seats are sponsored by the Communist party, and all legislation is proposed by the party.

The assembly elects a presidential council to act for it between sessions, and to serve collectively as head of state. Actual executive power rests with a cabinet, the council of ministers, appointed by the assembly with party approval. The council is led by a prime minister.

Hungary is a member of the United Nations and of the Warsaw Pact, a Soviet-led military alliance of eastern European communist states.

HISTORY. The Hungarian plains and the Danube valley lie along a major ancient European migration route and offered good settlement sites for early European peoples. The territory, known to the Romans as Pannonia, was inhabited by a succession of Germanic and Slavic tribes and by the Huns between about 1000 BC and the 800s AD. In the late 800s the Magyars, a people from the Ural Mountains, arrived on the Pannonian plains and conquered and mixed with the Slavic peoples settled there.

The Magyars were a semi-nomadic and warlike people. Under their leader, Prince Árpád, they expanded their territory at the expense of nearby Germanic and Slavic kingdoms. In 955 they were defeated by the Germans, and the Magyars, by then a mixture of Magyar, Slavic, and Germanic peoples, retreated to territory in the Danube basin and settled into an agricultural way of life.

The Hungarian Kingdom. By the end of the 900s the Magyars had developed a stable government and a well-organized feudal society. In 997 Stephen, a descendant of Árpád, became Hungary's first king. Stephen established strong ties with western, rather than eastern, Europe and with the Roman Catholic Church.

During Stephen's reign, the Magyars became Christian. Stephen began what was to be a long struggle to weaken the great nobles and centralize Hungary's government. During Stephen's reign, Hungary's territory was greatly expanded.

Several decades of dynastic warfare followed Stephen's death in 1038, but order was restored in 1077, when Ladislas, also of Árpád's line, became king. For the next 150 years Hungary's territory grew, its prosperity increased, and its ties with the west strengthened.

Hungary was unable to resolve the conflict between the king and the nobles, however. The nobles' feuds and rebellions against the king threatened the stability of the nation and left the country unprotected, as the nobles were responsible for its defense.

In 1241 Mongol armies swept across Hungary, meeting little opposition. The destruction they wrought was repaired, but by the end of the 1200s no solution had been found to the dispute between the king and the nobles. Their rivalries for power permitted a foreigner, Charles of Anjou, to take the throne in 1308.

Hungary's new rulers also held thrones in other countries, and as a result of the foreign involvements of Charles and his descendants during the 1300s and early 1400s Hungary became increasingly active in the diplomatic affairs of Western Europe.

Hunyadi. In the early 1400s the Ottoman Turks posed a threat to Europe, and Hungary assumed the role of protector of the west. Between 1437 and 1456 Hungarian armies led by a powerful nobleman, János Hunyadi, blocked attempted Turkish invasions of Europe.

Hunyadi's son, Matthias, became king of Hungary in 1458 and led the country to its peak of greatness. He broke the power of the great nobles, organized an efficient centralized administration, and introduced the art and learning of the Renaissance into Hungary.

In an attempt to become leader of a united central Europe that could crush the Ottoman Turks, Matthias conquered territory in Bohemia, where he was named king, and in Silesia, Moravia, and Austria. At his death in 1490 Hungary was the most powerful state in western Europe. Matthias' successors were weak men. They lost most of his political and territorial gains, and they took no action against the Turks.

Ottoman Era. In the early 1500s the Turks began to move toward Hungary, and in 1526 they overwhelmed the country. Although the Turks were the nominal overlords of all Hungary, in fact the country was divided in three parts.

Northern and western Hungary was ruled by the Hapsburgs of Austria, who succeeded to the throne of Hungary in 1526. In the northeast, the principality of Transylvania grew so powerful that it was independent in all but name. The Turks controlled central Hungary.

Throughout the country there was turmoil. The Magyars resented Austrian and Turkish rule; Hungary's Slavic peoples resented the Austrians, the Turks, and the Magyars; and the Magyar nobility was split between those who had gained power by supporting the Turks and those who fought against the Turks and the pro-Turkish Magyars.

To these frictions was added religious strife arising from the Protestant Reformation. The Hungarians were unable to resolve their differences or to throw off Turkish rule.

Austrian Rule. In 1686 Austria's armies drove the Turks out of the region, and Austria assumed complete rule over the Magyar and Slavic peoples of Hungary. Austria did little to rebuild the country, which was still laboring under an outmoded feudal structure and which had been ravaged by years of warfare. Austrian rule at first was harsh and autocratic, and was unpopular with all Hungarians.

The Austrian rulers of the latter half of the 1700s were more liberal, however. They improved the economy and expanded the educational system, which in turn stimulated efforts for more radical reforms. Organizations were formed by democratic, progressive nationalists, and in the late 1700s and early 1800s, inspired by the French Revolution, they led demands for social, economic, and governmental reforms.

The Austrian emperor, with the support of the conservative Hungarian nobility, refused the demands and harshly repressed the movement. Repression only intensified the revolutionary spirit. In 1848, when liberal, democratic rebellions were breaking out all over Europe, Hungarian nationalistic reformers led an uprising against the Austrian Empire and demanded independence as a democratic state. The emperor yielded, the Hungarian nobles fled, and a republican government was established.

The new regime abolished the country's feudal, social, and economic organization, but the republic was short-lived. In 1849, under orders from a new emperor, Austrian and Russian troops crushed the republic, and Hungary once more became a subject state. The old order could not be restored by force, however, and Hungary remained the most independent of all of Austria's territories.

The Dual Monarchy. After 1848 Austria steadily lost power to Prussia, and in 1867 Prussia organized a union of German states that excluded Austria. The Hungarians took that opportunity to demand independence. In the same year, 1867, Austria and Hungary arrived at a compromise by which the Dual Monarchy of Austria-Hungary was formed.

The two states shared control of foreign policy, finance, and defense. Hungary, however, was a self-governing state that ruled Slavic subjects as well as Magyars. The Slavs resented Magyar rule, which was no better than Austrian rule had been.

Austria-Hungary had joined the series of alliances creating the Central powers, and in 1914 entered World War I. In 1918 Hungary went down to defeat with its allies. When defeat was imminent, a rebellion broke out in Hungary, and in November 1918 a republic was proclaimed. But in 1919 the Communist party assumed control. Communist rule was overthrown at the end of 1919 by monarchists, who chose Admiral Miklós Horthy as regent in 1920.

The Regency. In June 1920 the Hungarian government signed the Treaty of Trianon, which officially ended World War I for Hungary and which stripped Hungary of much of its territory and power. Under the treaty, Hungary ceded almost three-quarters of its land and two-thirds of its population to Austria, Romania, and the new states of Czechoslovakia and Yugoslavia. In 1921 Hungary's king, who attempted to return, was exiled.

The regency remained in power throughout the 1920s and 1930s. It was a conservative and authoritarian government, and all efforts at reform were stifled. Hungarian foreign policy was based on opposition to the Treaty of Trianon, and the government sought to recover the lands and peoples lost under the treaty.

HUNGARIAN RISING OF 1956. Citizens of Budapest rally on a tank in front of the Parliament building situated in the main square of the nation's capital and largest city.

The regency was bitterly hostile to the "Little Entente" of the new Slavic states and to their western patron, France. It was equally hostile to the Soviet Union, because of the brief but violent and destructive communist dictatorship of 1919.

The government of the regency thus was attracted by the political and territorial aims of Adolf Hitler of Germany and Benito Mussolini of Italy. Despite strong opposition within Hungary from monarchists, communists, and democratic liberals, right-wing nationalists prevailed in the government. In 1934 Hungary entered a political and economic alliance with Italy and Austria and moved closer to the National Socialist (Nazi) government of Germany.

In 1939 and 1940 Adolf Hitler restored to Hungary parts of its former territories in Romania and Czechoslovakia. In November 1940 Hungary formally allied itself with the Axis powers, although Hungarians did not fight in the war at first.

The Germans used the country as a base to delay Soviet advances into Central Europe, and in 1944 took direct control of the government. In the winter of 1944–1945 Soviet troops invaded and occupied Hungary, and when the war ended they were in firm control of the country.

Communist Rule. After the war a Control Commission of representatives of the Allied nations directed Hungary's government. The Soviets used their position on the commission to assist Hungary's minority Communist party to come to power. In 1948 a communist dictatorship with close ties to the Soviet Union was established under the leadership of Mátyás Rakosi. The Communist regime did not enjoy wide support and used repression and terrorism to stay in power. Communist efforts to transform the basis of Hungary's economy from feudalistic agriculture to state-owned heavy industry were inefficient and seriously damaged the country's economic life.

Economic, political, and social grievances fanned Hungarian nationalism and desire for independence from Soviet control. After the death of the Soviet dictator Joseph Stalin in 1953, the Hungarian Communist party split between advocates of continuing tight controls over all aspects of life and those seeking a more moderate, national course.

In October 1956 demonstrations against the government erupted and led to a popular rising. The revolution had wide support, even from the communist prime minister, Imre Nagy, but it was crushed by Soviet troops and tanks.

Janos Kadár became prime minister and first secretary of the Communist party. In 1958, after a secret trial, Nagy was executed. The Hungarian Communist party, which had disintegrated during the revolution, was completely reorganized.

The methods used by Kadár to consolidate power were repressive, but when the government's position was more secure Kadár began to relax controls and allowed an increasing measure of freedom. Under Kadár's administration economic programs were reorganized to achieve greater efficiency and a better balance between agriculture and industry.

Some free enterprise was permitted, consumers and producers were given a greater voice in the economy, and trade with noncommunist countries was expanded. The general standard of living rose, and by the mid-1960s Kadár's regime was among the least repressive of the governments of Eastern Europe.

In 1965 Kadár relinquished the role of prime minister to Gyula Kállai, although Kadár retained the more powerful post of first secretary of the Communist party. Jenö Fock became prime minister after elections held in 1967, which were the first in which "opposition" candidates were allowed to participate.

—Robert F. Byrnes; George Kish

HYDRO-ELECTRIC POWER STATION for the Sog and Laxa river project in Iceland.

ICELAND

Official name: Republic of Iceland
Area: 39,768 square miles
Population: (1966 est.) 195,000
Capital: Reykjavik (Pop., 1965 est., urban area, 89,400)
Language: Icelandic
Religion: Lutheranism
Currency unit: Króna
National holiday: Anniversary of the establishment of the republic, June 17

Iceland is an island republic in the North Atlantic Ocean, less than 200 miles southeast of Greenland. The Arctic Circle just touches the northern tips of Iceland.

THE LAND. Iceland is a forbidding land, with a rugged, barren terrain. The island is quite mountainous, with a central core of highlands rising above 5,000 feet. Glaciers cover large areas, and many swift rivers rush down from the glaciers.

Iceland is of volcanic origin, and some volcanoes are still active. Hot springs are common in the volcanic areas. In the early 1960s two new volcanic islands rose in Iceland's coastal waters.

The island's northerly climate is moderated by a section of the Gulf Stream that warms its coasts. Average temperatures range between 30°F and 52°F throughout the year. Almost 50 inches of rain a year falls in the southern lowlands. The mountains are much wetter, but the far north receives only an average of 15 inches.

THE PEOPLE. Iceland is rather sparsely settled, but its population is growing rapidly. In the mid-1960s it had one of the highest birthrates in Europe, almost 25 per 1,000 inhabitants. The interior of the island is almost entirely uninhabited, and most of the people live along the coast, especially in the southwest around Reykjavik, where almost 40 percent of Icelanders live.

Iceland's population is quite homogeneous. Almost all the people are Scandinavian in origin, and Icelandic, a Scandinavian tongue, is the universal language. Over 95 percent of the population is Lutheran.

ECONOMY. Despite its barrenness, Iceland is a moderately prosperous country with an economy based almost entirely on fishing and trade. The chief natural resources are its rushing rivers, which provide hydroelectric power, its thermal springs, and its geographic position near rich fishing banks and along a major route between Europe and North America.

Less than 1 percent of the land is cultivated, and only hay, root crops, and other hardy crops can be grown. Grazing land is available and dairying is of some importance.

Fishing and related activities make the greatest single contribution to the Icelandic economy. Cod and herring, from coastal waters and from the Grand Banks near Canada, are the chief catches. Fishing and fish processing constitute the bulk of Iceland's industrial activity. Salted, dried, frozen, and canned fish, and fish meal and oils are the country's main products.

During the 1950s and 1960s Iceland investigated other resources and developed new industries, in an effort to end its economic dependence on a single commodity. Major new industries, supported largely by private investment, included a huge aluminum plant and a vast power project in southwestern Iceland.

Other newer industries include textile milling, book production, chemical manufacture, and shipbuilding. Many of the farms, businesses, and industries in Iceland are organized in cooperatives.

Trade is vital to the Icelandic economy. In 1966 exports earned $141 million and imports cost $159 million. Fresh and processed fish and fish products accounted for over 90 percent of the country's exports in the mid-1960s. Raw materials, foodstuffs, machinery, manufactured goods, petroleum products, and ships must be imported. Most of Iceland's trade is with Great Britain, the United States, West Germany, the Soviet Union, and the Scandinavian countries.

GOVERNMENT. Iceland is a republic, with a president as head of state. Actual executive power rests with a prime minister and cabinet responsible to the legislature. Members of the bicameral legislature, the *Althing*, are popularly elected. The Althing chooses one-third of its members to sit as an upper house; the remaining two-thirds forms the lower, more powerful, house.

Iceland is a member of the United Nations, the North Atlantic Treaty Organization (NATO), the Council of Europe, and the Nordic Council.

HISTORY. Iceland was settled in the late 800s by Norwegian Vikings. Immigration increased through the 900s, with settlers coming from the British Isles as well as from Norway. By the end of the 900s, the descendants of these first settlers had established their own system of representative government, with a constitution, a court system, and the Althing.

The yearly Althing, the meeting of chieftains and popular representatives, soon became the social and cultural center of Icelandic life, as well as the country's legislature and supreme court. In 1000 the Althing adopted Christianity as the religion for the entire country. During the 900s and 1000s, Vikings from Iceland made many voyages of exploration. They discovered and settled Greenland and visited North America.

Dissension among the Icelanders during the early 1200s led to the breakdown of government, and in 1262 Iceland joined with Norway and submitted to the rule of the Norwegian king. Although the island remained nominally self-governing, government under Norwegian rule was centralized and by the mid-1300s Iceland was ruled by an absolute monarch. In 1387, when Denmark and Norway were united, Iceland came under the rule of the Danish crown.

Danish Rule. Between the 1300s and the 1700s the island was struck by many natural disasters, including volcanic eruptions, plague, and floods. Denmark did little to alleviate the resulting famine and poverty. Moreover, during the 1600s and 1700s, trade monopolies and other commercial regulations served Danish rather than Icelandic interests.

In the early 1800s, when Iceland had begun to recover from the effects of the natural disasters, a spirit of nationalism spread through the island and led to demands for independence. The first step toward increased autonomy was the restoration of power to the Althing in 1843.

In 1854 Denmark relaxed its trade restrictions and Iceland's economy began to improve. In 1874 Iceland was granted a new constitution, which provided for Icelandic self-government under the supervision of a Danish minister. The island became completely self-governing in 1904.

Independence. After World War I Iceland demanded the self-determination that had been granted to other nations by the Treaty of Versailles. In 1918 a Danish-Icelandic treaty recognized Iceland's independence within a personal union with the Danish crown, and Denmark remained responsible for Iceland's foreign affairs and defense.

During the 1920s and 1930s Iceland was generally isolated from the rest of the world. During World War II, however, Iceland was of great strategic importance as an Allied air and naval base. After its occupation by Germany in 1940, Denmark was unable to handle Icelandic affairs, and in 1944 Iceland proclaimed itself a sovereign republic.

During the 1940s and 1950s Iceland concentrated on expanding and balancing its economy. The island began to participate more fully in world affairs, and it became increasingly dependent on international trade agreements and defense pacts. It was also an important link on international air travel routes as well as being a strategically important NATO base manned by the United States.

In 1951 the United States agreed to manage Iceland's defense, as Iceland has no military establishment, but domestic and international political conflicts led to the withdrawal of most U.S. troops in the early 1960s.

In 1958 Iceland extended the limits of its territorial waters from four miles to 12 miles, leading to international protests from fishing nations. In 1961 Britain, most affected by the new limits, agreed to recognize them.

Economic expansion began to flag in the mid-1960s, and elections held in 1966 reflected an increase in the strength of the left-wing Progressive and Social Democratic parties.

INDIA

Official name: Republic of India
Area: 1,175,579 square miles (excluding Kashmir)
Population: (1967 est.) 511,115,000 (excluding Kashmir)
Capital: New Delhi (Pop., 1966 est., 314,400)
Language: Hindi, English
Religion: Hinduism, Islam, Christianity
Currency unit: Rupee
National holiday: Anniversary of the proclamation of the republic, January 26

The Republic of India occupies most of the southern appendage of the Eurasian land mass known as the subcontinent of India. The country is bounded on the north by Nepal, Sikkim, Bhutan, and China; on the east by Burma, East Pakistan, and the Bay of Bengal; on the south by the Indian Ocean; and on the west by the Arabian Sea and West Pakistan.

Before it became independent in 1947, India was part of British India, which included most of the subcontinent. In 1947 the subcontinent was divided. Predominantly Muslim areas in the north became the nation of Pakistan, and the bulk of the subcontinent, predominantly Hindu, became the nation of India.

A number of semiautonomous princely states in the subcontinent were given the freedom to join either Pakistan or India. The Hindu ruler of predominantly Muslim Kashmir, one of the largest and richest of the states, acceded to India. Pakistan protested the act and insisted that the people of Kashmir be allowed to express their view in a plebiscite. India refused, and warfare broke out.

The United Nations arranged a cease fire, but the status of Kashmir, partly occupied by Pakistani forces and partly incorporated into India, remained a sore point in Indian-Pakistani relations. In 1964 Indian Kashmir had an estimated population of 3,729,000.

THE LAND. India, approximately one-third the size of the United States, stretches about 2,000 miles from north to south. It has three major land regions: the Himalayas and associated mountain ranges in the north, the Indus-Ganges-Brahmaputra plain in north-central India, and the Deccan Plateau in the south.

Land Regions. The Himalayas extend from east to west for 1,500 miles, broken only by gaps produced by the Indus and Brahmaputra rivers. The mountains range from 150 to 200 miles in width, from north to south. In many places the mountain system consists of three parallel ranges.

The Great Himalayas are the northernmost chain and the highest, with many peaks exceeding 20,000 feet above sea level. The Lesser Himalayas are the middle range, with the highest elevations averaging 12,000 to 15,000 feet. The third and southernmost range, the Outer Himalayas, overlooks the Gangetic plain. Average elevations in the Outer Himalayas are 3,000 to 4,000 feet.

The Indus-Ganges-Brahmaputra Plain, which lies between the Himalayas and the Deccan Plateau, is formed by hundreds of feet of fine sediment laid down by three rivers and is one of the largest alluvial plains in the world. Two of these rivers, the Indus and the Brahmaputra, originate on the northern side of the Himalayas. The Ganges, the third river, originates on the southern side of the Himalayas. It flows directly eastward and joins the Brahmaputra.

The Deccan Plateau, which forms the triangle-shaped peninsular portion of the Indian subcontinent, is bounded by the Vindhya–Satpura mountains in the north. Running southwest to northeast for about 800 miles, they rise from 1,500 to over 4,000 feet.

The plateau tilts eastward toward the Bay of Bengal. It is bounded along the Arabian Sea coast by the Western Ghats and along the Bay of Bengal by the Eastern Ghats. The Western Ghats rise abruptly to elevations of 3,000 feet with some peaks reaching 4,700 feet. Near the southern tip of the peninsula, the Western Ghats have peaks of over 8,000 feet.

The Eastern Ghats have an average height of 1,500 to 2,000 feet. The inner areas of the plateau average 1,000 to 3,000 feet in elevation, with some hills rising to 4,000 feet.

The northern edge of the plateau is drained by a series of rivers flowing northward to the Gangetic plain. The Narbada-Tapti river system in the northwestern portion of the plateau drains westward into the Gulf of Cambay. The major rivers of the plateau rise on the eastern flanks of the Western Ghats, flow eastward across the plateau, and drain into the Bay of Bengal. The largest of these rivers are the Godavari, Krishna, and the Cauvery.

Climate. The Himalayas shield the Indian subcontinent from the main body of the Eurasian land mass. As a result, the climate of the subcontinent is unique. In winter, high pressure systems in the Punjab region produce winds that move down the Gangetic plain into the Bay of Bengal. Winters are generally dry in most of the subcontinent.

During March, April, and May, there is little air movement and the subcontinent begins to heat up, creating low pressure conditions in the north. By the end of May or the beginning of June, the summer monsoons arrive, bringing rain into the Ganges valley.

Rainfall varies considerably. On the Ganges-Brahmaputra Delta, in the Khasi and Chittagong hills, Assam, the southern zone of the Himalayas, and along the Malabar coast, the total may exceed 80 inches a year. In the northeastern portions of the Deccan, along the southeast coast, and in parts of the Western Ghats and the Punjab, the total ranges from 40 to 80 inches. In Kathiawar and the western half of the Deccan, the annual rainfall is 20 to 40 inches.

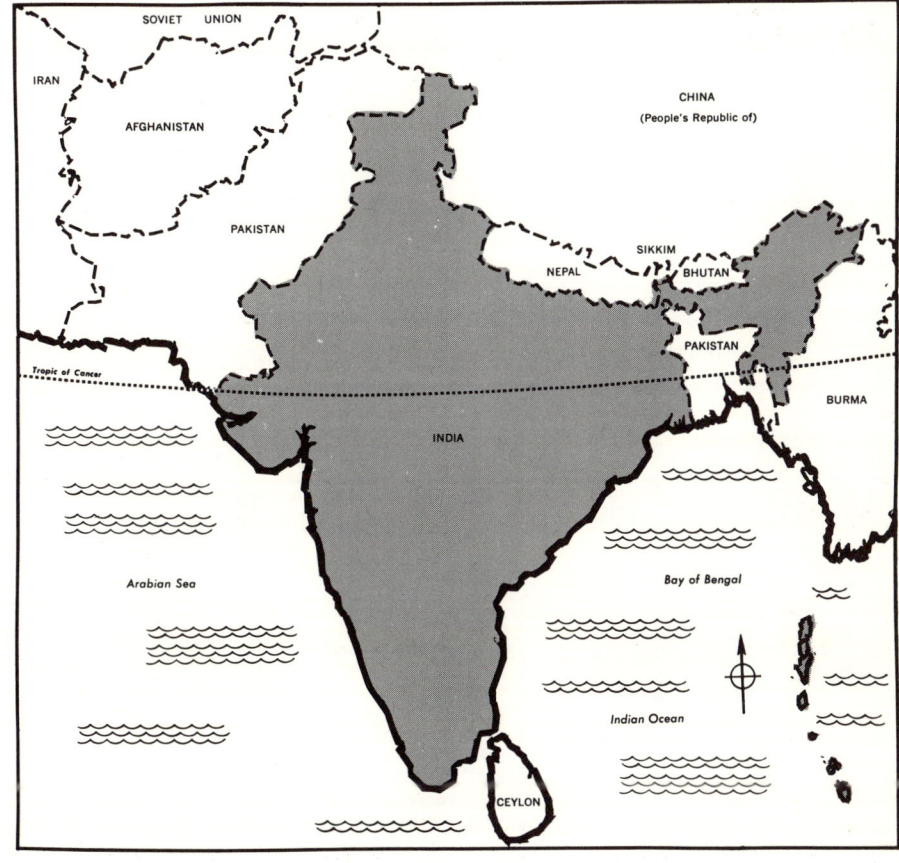

In the southern half of the country, temperatures are tropical and vary little from month to month. In northern India, however, the annual range is considerable. In January the average temperature in the north may be 30°F lower than in the south.

THE PEOPLE. India has a varied population. The majority of Indians, however, belong to either Indo-Aryan or Dravidian language groups. The tall, light-skinned people who live mainly in northern India speak Indo-Aryan languages. The people of southern India mostly speak Dravidian languages. Tribal people such as the Khasis, Nagas, Bhils, and Santals, who live in the Himalaya regions, speak a number of languages, many of which are neither Indo-Aryan nor Dravidian.

Fourteen major languages are spoken in India, and these are broken up into hundreds of dialects. The Indo-Aryan languages include Hindi, Urdu, Assamese, Bengali, Gujarati, Kashmiri, Marathi, Oriya, Panjabi, and Rajasthani. The main Dravidian languages are Kannada, Malayalam, Tamil, and Telugu. Hindi is the official national language although English is still used in government and is the common means of communication among educated Indians.

The vast majority of Indians are Hindus, but India has one of the world's largest Muslim communities. In addition, there are about 10 million Christians, 7.5 million adherents of Sikhism, and 2 million followers of Jainism.

India is second only to China in population. In 1965 the average population density was 413 persons per square mile, but there is great geographic variation in the distribution of population. Most Indians live in the Gangetic lowlands and the coastal areas. There, rural population densities approach 2,000 persons per square mile in the more crowded districts. Average population densities of the 17 states of India range from a high of 1,131 persons per square mile in Kerala to a low of 58 in Nagaland.

India's population is increasing at a very rapid rate, and rapid population growth places a heavy burden on the nation's economy. The government has embarked upon a family planning program in an attempt to sharply reduce the rate of population increase.

Although only approximately 30 percent of India's population is urban, in the mid-1960s there were 110 cities with populations of more than 100,000. Eight of those had populations of over 1 million—Bombay, Calcutta, Delhi, Madras, Hyderabad, Ahmedabad, Bangalore, and Kanpur.

ECONOMY. India has great economic problems. There is not enough arable land or industry to support the country's huge population, and unemployment and underemployment are high. In 1951 the government launched the first of a series of five-year plans to double per capita yearly income—from about $55 to $100—by 1977.

India's first five-year plan, covering 1951–1956, concentrated on increasing agricultural production and electric power resources. The second plan, 1956–1961, emphasized rapid industrialization through the development of heavy industry. The third plan, 1961–1966, provided for expansion of both food and industrial production, and gave special attention to family planning and population control. The fourth plan emphasized the same objectives as the third plan.

Natural Resources. India has most of the mineral resources required for industrial expansion. It has one of the largest high-grade iron ore reserves in the world as well as large deposits of coal. Among the more common industrial raw materials, the most serious deficiencies appear to be petroleum, lead, zinc, nitrogen, sulphur, and phosphates.

Agriculture. About 70 percent of India's working population is engaged in agriculture. Living in small villages, working farms that average two acres per family, and using age-old cultivation techniques based on human or animal power, the average Indian farmer is the model of inefficiency. He is seldom able to provide his household with more than a bare subsistence.

It is estimated that roughly 50 percent of India's total area is cultivated. The chief hazard to Indian agricultural development is lack of water, and much of the Indian government's effort to improve agriculture is in the field of irrigation.

India produced 93 million tons of food grains in 1964–1965, which represents a substantial increase over the annual levels of the 1950s. The kind of grain grown—whether rice, wheat, barley, corn, or the indigenous jowar, raggee, or bajra—depends upon the local climate and availability of water. Cash crops include tea, coffee, sugarcane, tobacco, jute, cotton, spices, and tropical fruits.

India has one of the largest livestock populations in the world, but most of the animals are undernourished and diseased. The Hindu religion prohibits the eating of beef, and the Indian constitution prohibits the slaughter of cattle. The government recognizes the impediment that the livestock situation creates in the country's economic development. It has adopted programs to improve veterinary services and animal breeding and marketing of dairy products.

UNITED NATIONS
BOATS ON THE GANGES RIVER, at Banaras, in northern India.

Industry. As of 1964 industrial production contributed less than one-fifth of the domestic product. The Indian government is seeking ways to develop manufacturing and increase its role in the economy.

Manufacturing in India can be divided into two groups. The first group consists of handicraft industries organized on a household or guild basis. They are small, producing light consumer goods and utilizing traditional techniques. The second group is made up of modern factory industries.

The chief industry is the manufacture of cotton and silk textiles, but the Tata iron and steel mills are the largest in Asia. India is also an important producer of chemical fertilizers, sulfuric acid, drugs and pharmaceuticals, dyestuffs, and plastics. There is also an expanding automotive industry.

In 1964 India had an installed electric generating capacity of 8.4 million kilowatts, and this capacity is increasing quite rapidly with government construction of large-scale hydroelectric plants.

Trade. Since India achieved independence in 1947 imports have exceeded exports. In 1966 India's imports cost $2,751 million and its exports earned only $1,608 million. India's leading exports are jute products, cotton piece goods, tanned hides and skins, tea, iron ore, pepper, nuts, and tobacco. The chief imports include food grains, machinery, mineral oils, motor vehicles, and chemicals. India's major trading partners are the United States and Britain.

GOVERNMENT. India is a democratic republic and has a parliamentary system of government. The head of state is the president. He is elected to a five-year term by the members of the national and the state legislatures. Effective executive power is exercised by a prime minister, who is normally the leader of the majority political party.

Parliament consists of two houses, the *Rajya Sabha* (Council of States) and the *Lok Sabha* (House of the People). The Council of States consists of up to 250 members, who are indirectly elected to six-year terms. The House of the People may have up to 525 members. Of these, 500 may be direct-

VILLAGE CHIEFS of Faridabad township meet to plan for community development.

ly elected to five-year terms by universal suffrage from territorial constituencies in the states; up to 25 representatives of the Union Territories may be chosen according to laws passed by parliament.

Unlike the Council of States, which is a permanent body, the House of the People can be dissolved by the president, and new elections called, if the prime minister loses the support of a majority in parliament.

The organization of India's 17 state governments is similar to that of the federal government. Each has a legislature and an administration headed by a governor, who is appointed by the president.

In emergency situations the federal government has extraordinary power over the states. Parliament can, under special circumstances, take over the power of the state legislatures. India also has ten Union Territories, governed by the president through an administrator appointed by him.

India is a member of the Commonwealth of Nations and the United Nations. It has played a prominent role in international affairs as a leader of the nonaligned nations—those countries seeking to avoid identification with either of the world's two great power blocks, the Eastern, or communist, group of states led by the Soviet Union, and the Western, or noncommunist nations, led by the United States.

HISTORY. Evidence of the first permanent village settlements in India, dating from about 3000 BC, is found in the hilly areas of southern Baluchistan. Some time after the appearance of these settlements a great urban civilization developed in the Indus Valley, which lasted from about 2500 to 1500 BC. It is probable that this civilization was related to the great river valley civilization that had already appeared in Mesopotamia, but there is little evidence of direct borrowing.

An extraordinary cultural uniformity is observable in Indus civilization throughout its thousand years of history, suggesting some form of strong, central political control. The Indus people had a system of writing, but the script has not been deciphered and very little is known of their beliefs or ideas.

The Indus civilization was apparently destroyed by invaders in about 1500 BC. Nothing certain is known of these invaders, but they may have been a group of the Aryans, a wandering, pastoral people. Between 2000 and 1500 BC, the Aryans spread from their homeland, which may have been in southern Russia, to Europe, Mesopotamia, and India. Aryan migrations into India probably extended over several centuries after about 1500 BC.

The Aryans spoke an Indo-European language from which classical Sanskrit and the modern languages of northern India, such as Hindi, Bengali, Marathi, and Gujarati, are descended. The Aryans gradually advanced from northeastern India through the Punjab, down into the Gangetic plain. By 900 BC they had probably begun to penetrate the Deccan Plateau.

During this long period of expansion the Aryans subjugated the native inhabitants, whom they referred to contemptuously as *dàsas* (dark spirits). These people were a dark-skinned race who may have been related to the Indus Valley people or to the Dravidians, the people of southern India.

The conquest of new lands and contact with the original inhabitants led to profound changes in the Aryan way of life. The Aryan tribes settled in permanent communities and began to cultivate the land. By the 600s BC the tribal communities were being absorbed into small kingdoms, which had hereditary monarchs and capital cities.

Changes also took place in the Aryan religion. The relatively simple rites and ceremonies of the *Rigveda*, the most ancient of the Aryan religious texts, gave way to elaborate sacrificial rituals that exalted the role of the Brahmans, or priestly class. At the same time use of magic and the worship of various deities not known in the earliest Vedic traditions became part of the religion of the Aryans.

These two movements—emphasis on the importance of the Brahmanic priesthood and absorption of religious practices from many sources—transformed the older Aryan cult into Hinduism, the religious structure that colored the later history of India.

The First Empires (600 BC–AD 300). By the 600s BC a number of small kingdoms had appeared in northern India, the most important of which were Kosala, between the Ganges and the Nepal mountains, and Magadha, south of the Ganges in modern Bihar. In the 500s BC this area of the Gangetic plain also produced Buddhism and Jainism, two great religions that denied the authority of the old Vedic scriptures and the supremacy of the Brahmanic priesthood.

By the beginning of the 300s BC Magadha, ruled by the Nandas, had become the dominant power in the Gangetic plain. In about 322 BC the Nanda dynasty was overthrown by a young adventurer, Chandragupta Maurya, who ruled until about 298 BC. Chandragupta embarked on a policy of conquest that brought under his control most of northern India, including part of modern Afghanistan, and much of southern India.

The Maurya empire was ruled from the splendid capital of Pataliputra (modern Patna). Asoka (r.273–232 BC), Chandragupta's grandson, extended the empire by conquering Kalinga, the coastal region of modern Orissa and Andhra Pradesh. After that acquisition, however, he turned his back on territorial expansion and sought to make Buddhist ethics the guiding force for a kingdom of righteousness.

On rock walls and pillars all over the kingdom he had engraved the principles of conduct that his people were to follow. In these edicts he emphasized honesty, obedience to parents and teachers, religious toleration, and service to others.

Asoka's espousal of Buddhism helped its spread throughout India and Ceylon. The beginning of the Buddhist shrines that were to provide many of the great masterpieces of Indian art date from Asoka's reign. Neither at that time nor later did the majority of the Indian people become Buddhists, but for 500 or 600 years Buddhism tended to be the religion of kings and merchants. In addition to its effect on artistic creativity, Buddhism made important contributions to philosophy.

The Mauryan empire disintegrated soon after Asoka's death in 232 BC, when foreign invaders entered from the northwest. Among the invaders of the Mauryan empire were the people known as Sakas, or Scythians, whose kingdoms were first established by the generals of Alexander the Great in Bactria, and the Kushan, a Central Asian people.

Of all the invaders the Kushans were the most influential. They established a strong kingdom in northern India in the first century AD that lasted for nearly 200 years. Their greatest king, Kanishka (r.c.78–c.110 AD), supported Buddhism, and during his reign missionaries carried Buddhism to Central Asia. From there it was eventually transmitted to China and other parts of East Asia.

In most of southern India Mauryan control had probably never been very strong, and in the extreme south three kingdoms—the Chola, the Pandya, and the Chera—had existed independently during Asoka's reign. These three kingdoms, with periods of decay and obscurity, continued to exist up to the 1100s AD. Following the disintegration of the Mauryan empire, the history of southern India tended to be quite separate from that of the north. From the first century BC to about 200 AD, most of Deccan was controlled by the Satavahanas, who ruled from Andhra Pradesh.

Guptas and Rajputs (300–1200 AD). After the downfall of the Kushan no empire developed in northern India until the 300s, when the Guptas, a family from the Magadha region (modern Bihar), built up a powerful new kingdom. Under Samudragupta (r.c.330–c.375) and his son Chandragupta II (r.c.375–c.413), the dynasty's power spread all over northern India. The principal cities of the empire were Pataliputra and Ujjain.

The Gupta period was an age of great activity in literature, the fine arts, religion, science, and philosophy. Its intellectual and artistic accomplishments reflected a prosperity and state of material well-being perhaps never again matched in India's history. During this golden age, Buddhism and Jainism remained important, but Hinduism, which had developed its characteristic social laws and devotional rituals, had become dominant.

The intellectual and religious achievements of the Gupta age remained the great heritage of Indian civilization during the centuries of invasions and political unrest that followed its decline at the end of the 300s. A Central Asian people, the Huns, invaded northern India in the 400s, and while their empire was short-lived, it destroyed the power of the Guptas.

Attempts were made in the following century, notably by Harsha (r.606–647) to recreate a single political authority in northern India, but none of these efforts was particularly successful. By the 800s northern India was split up into many kingdoms ruled by Rajputs, who claimed to trace their origins to the ancient ruling families of Rajasthan, but who may have been descendants of invaders who were accepted into Hinduism as members of the warrior class.

The greatest of the Rajput kingdoms was that of the Pratiharas. The Pratiharas and the other Rajput kings were almost always at war with one another. While this may have prevented them from uniting against enemies, it did lead to the growth of a martial spirit and an emphasis on heroic action that helped to preserve the society when it was later threatened.

Developments in Southern India. During the period of Gupta and Rajput ascendancy in northern India, southern India was controlled by various regional kingdoms. The Chalukyas, who ruled from Badami in the western Deccan, were dominant from about 600 to 750 AD. Their major enemies were the Pallavas, whose capital was Kanchipuram. The Pallavas ruled from the 300s until the end of the 700s, when they were overthrown by the Chola kings of Tanjore.

The Cholas maintained control of all the territory south of the Tungabhadra River from about 850 to 1200, when they were superseded by the revived power of the Pandyas at Madura. The later Chalukya of the Deccan were also destroyed during the 1100s, and their kingdom was divided among the Hoysalas of Mysore, the Yadavas of Devagiri (modern Daulatabad), and the Kakatiyas of Warangal.

The southern kingdoms were the centers of cultural and religious movements of great importance. Most of the rulers were great builders, and they adorned their kingdoms with magnificent temples and palaces. The Pallavas were responsible for the series of rock–carved temples at Mamallapuram and the great temple complex at Kanchipuram. The Cholas built numerous temples, of which the most famous is that at Tanjore, and decorated them with stone and bronze sculpture.

A religious movement of great vitality underlay this outburst of temple building. Out of the synthesis of Aryan and Dravidian cultures had come a new Hindu devotional sect that emphasized the worship of three great deities, Brahma, Siva, and Vishnu. This new movement, aided by the support of kings, brought to an end the flourishing Buddhist and Jain communities of southern India.

Muslim Dominance (1200–1700). The first impact of Islam on India came in 712, when Arab control was established over Sind, the lower Indus Valley. The Rajput kings of northern India prevented their further expansion. The next Islamic intrusion came not from the Muslims of the Middle East, but from Afghan Turks who had established their power at Ghazni (now part of Afghanistan).

The Ghaznavids made numerous raids into India throughout the 1000s, but actually ruled only the territory west of Lahore. A change came when a new dynasty of Afghan Turks from Ghor defeated a confederacy of Rajput kings in 1192 at Taraori. The Indian defeat was probably due not only to internal divisions among the Rajput kings, but to the superior military techniques of the Turks as well.

The Turks established a sultanate at Delhi and from there gradually extended their control over all northern India. Under Ala-ud-din Khalji (r.1296–1316), the Turks conquered southern India. This new empire, the greatest in India since that of the Mauryas, began to disintegrate under the Tughluq dynasty, which came to power after Ala-ud-din's death.

This process of disintegration was hastened by the invasion of Tamerlane in 1398. He made no attempt to establish his authority, but his raids weakened the control of the sultanate in northern India.

By 1500 the Delhi sultanate held only parts of the Punjab and the Gangetic plain. But permanent changes had been effected in the pattern of Indian civilization by 300 years of Muslim occupation. A large Muslim minority had been created, and Islamic ideas and values had begun to influence Indian life. This influence was never very great as far as the masses of the people were concerned, and orthodox Hinduism remained quite unchanged.

A new group of invaders entered India in 1526, led by Babur, a Turkish chieftain who had founded a kingdom at Kabul after having been driven out of his homeland in Turkistan. Because one of his remote ancestors was the Mongol conqueror Genghis Khan, his family came to be referred to as Mughals, or Moguls. He defeated the Delhi sultan at Panipat in 1526, and made himself master of the Gangetic plain up to Patna.

On his death in 1530 he was succeeded by his son Humayun, who was driven out of India in 1540 by Sher Shah, an Afghan chieftain. Humayun recovered Delhi in 1555, but he died the following year. He was succeeded by his son Akbar (r.1556–1605), the real founder of the Mughal empire. Akbar pursued an aggressive policy of expansion that brought all of northern India under his control.

Akbar's reign is one of the most vital in Indian history, for he initiated policies that had a lasting influence. At the very beginning of the conquests, the Muslims had been faced with the problem of the proper treatment of the Hindus. A compromise had been effected that allowed them to practice their religion, but they were subjected to discriminatory taxes and laws and many rulers showed their orthodoxy by destroying Hindu temples.

Akbar enunciated a policy of universal toleration, the most obvious sign of which was the abolition of the *jizya*, the discriminatory tax. Some of the highest officers in the army were Hindus, and Akbar made marriage alliances among the Rajputs. His interest in Hindu culture led to a synthesis of Indian and Islamic artistic forms, which in turn created a new flowering in music, literature, painting, and architecture.

His support of an eclectic religion, the Din-i-Ilahi, which drew upon Hindu metaphysics, lent credence to the charge made by orthodox Muslims that he had abandoned Islam. Akbar also instituted far-reaching administrative reforms. One of the most important of these was the expansion of the revenue system initiated by Sher Shah. Akbar ordered a careful survey of all cultivated land and reformed the system of taxation.

Akbar's successors, Jahangir (r.1605–1627) and Shah Jahan (r.1628–1658), continued his policy of consolidation and expansion. During Shah Jahan's reign the Muslim kingdoms of the Deccan were brought under imperial control. Shah Jahan was also a great builder. The Taj Mahal and the Pearl Mosque at Agra, and the palace and Great Mosque at Delhi, are among the great monuments of his reign.

Shah Jahan's son, Aurangzeb, (r.1658–1707) reversed the religious policy initiated by Akbar. As a devout Muslim he looked with disfavor on the growing power and prosperity of the Hindus, and as a statesman he probably questioned the possibility of holding the empire together without the loyalty of a Muslim ruling class. The discriminatory taxes were reimposed on the Hindus, the building of new temples was forbidden, and an attempt was made to replace Hindu government officials with Muslims.

Aurangzeb also embarked on a policy of territorial expansion that brought all of India, except the extreme southern tip, under Mughul control. For 20 years he battled the Marathas of southern India under their great leader Sivaji.

Aurangzeb's vast empire began to crumble within a generation of his death. Rebellions broke out everywhere in the Mughul empire, and a series of weak successors to the throne were unable to control the administration effectively. In 1739 northern India was invaded by Nadir Shah of Persia. By 1750 the empire was reduced to the territory around Delhi, and regional kingdoms had been established throughout India.

Western Dominance and Unification. The Marathas were the most important of the regional powers that emerged from the wreckage of the Mughul empire. By 1760 they controlled all of central India and much of the south. Their expansion was checked in 1761 with their defeat at Panipat by a combined Mughul and Afghan army, and further halted in the 1780s by the rising power of the English East India company.

The English had been in India since 1600 as traders, but the company became important as a political power only after the decline of Mughul power. In 1757 the company interfered in a succession dispute over the throne of Bengal. By 1765 the company was in effective control of Bengal's resources, which it used to pay for the cost of expansion. By 1820 it was the paramount power in India, and within the next 30 years all of India was brought under its control.

From 1784 on the British government had a decisive voice in the selection of the chief officials of the company. In 1857 an uprising, generally known as the Great Mutiny, occurred in northern India. It was instigated by the company's Indian soldiers but was abetted by other groups in the population who had special grievances against the new power, such as rulers who had been dispossessed of their lands.

The rebellion was crushed, and the company lost its power to rule. A new administration was created, directly responsible to the British crown.

The new administration directly ruled Bengal, Bombay, Madras, the Punjab, and the United Provinces (modern Uttar Pradesh). Indirect control was exercised over the remaining two-fifths of the territory through about 600 Indian princes. Although these rulers had internal autonomy, they had no control over their relations with other states. Overall supervision was exercised by a governor-general through his representatives in the individual states.

The political unity achieved in the 1800s was made possible by a number of factors. The development of modern communications and transportation brought all India under the immediate control of the central government through telegraphs, railways, and steamships.

Improved communications also made possible the strategic location of the army. Although smaller than that of previous empires, it had the advantage of modern techniques and the new forms of discipline developed in Europe in the 1700s and 1800s.

Although all army officers were British, many enlisted men were Indian. An efficient civil service was also created for the first time. A uniform legal system introduced Western ideas and methods of jurisprudence. Finally, English was the language used not only in administration but in higher education. Colleges and universities gave Indians a common means of communication as well as a common knowledge of Western thought.

The Rise of Nationalism. The emergence of a nationalist movement in the late 1800s was the direct result of political unification. Educated Indians became aware simultaneously of the Western tradition of political freedom, the dependent state of their own country, and the glory of their past history. The nationalist movement had its formal beginnings in 1885 with the founding of the Indian National Congress by Allan Octavian Hume and a small group of Indian intellectuals.

The Congress at first asked only for a measure of representative government that would allow Indians to share with the British the administration of the country. This moderate demand was rejected by a radical group in the Congress, led by Bal Gangadhar Tilak, who argued that freedom was not something for the British to give but for the Indians to take as their birthright.

The nationalist movement, with its demands for responsible government and a larger degree of independence, was complicated by Hindu-Muslim relations. Muslim leaders argued that responsible government based on direct popular representation would mean that Muslims, who constituted 25 percent of the population, would be a permanent minority ruled by Hindus. This led to the founding in 1906 of the Muslim League to look after Muslim interests.

The British responded to the demands of the nationalists in 1909 through the Morley-Minto Reforms. They allowed the direct election of a number of Indians to provincial legislatures under a restricted property franchise and gave the Muslims separate electorates to ensure them adequate representation. The Indian National Congress denounced this as an attempt by the British to continue their hold over India by turning one religion against another.

The next response to nationalist demands came in 1919, when a new constitution, known as the Montagu-Chelmsford Reforms, increased the power of the elected representatives in the provinces and widened the franchise. Indian political leaders were disappointed with the constitution, for they felt the British had, through the control of finance, kept all the important sources of power in their own hands.

The Indian National Congress, under the leadership of Mohandas K. Gandhi, passed a resolution in 1920 condemning the new system of government and began a campaign of nonviolent noncooperation. This became the characteristic method of the Congress in its struggle against the British from that time on.

Gandhi's great achievement was making the demand for independence a mass movement through the use of terminology and symbols drawn from traditional Indian religion and culture rather than from Western political thought. His chief lieutenant was Jawaharlal Nehru, who appealed to the intellectuals of India as well as to the country's masses.

Gandhi's successful use of traditional Hindu religious symbols and cultural terms tended to alienate the Muslims, who increasingly argued that when freedom came, provision should be made for the Muslims to control their own destinies. Muhammad Ali Jinnah emerged as the leader of the Muslims. The Government of India Act of 1935 granted Indians a further measure of responsible government, but it failed to satisfy the nationalists. On the outbreak of World War II in 1939, the Congress leaders who had been elected to major political offices in elections held in 1937 resigned their posts on the grounds that India had been drawn into the war by Britain without their consent. They started a campaign in 1942 demanding that the British quit India at once, and the Congress leaders, including Gandhi and Nehru, were jailed for the duration of the war.

In 1945 a new Labor government in Britain entered into negotiations with the leaders of the Congress and the Muslim League. Jinnah insisted that Nehru's demands for British withdrawal and the election of a constituent assembly to decide the future of the country would leave the Muslims without any protection against the Hindu majority.

Jinnah's demand for some form of separate homeland for the Muslims was rejected by the Congress leaders until 1947, when outbreaks of violence between Hindus and Muslims, and growing support for Jinnah from all sections of the Muslim population, convinced the Congress that the creation of a separate Muslim state was the only solution to the problem.

Independence. On Aug. 15, 1947 British rule ended in India. A Muslim state, Pakistan, was formed from territories in the west and east, with Jinnah as governor-general and Liaqat Ali Khan as prime minister. The remainder of British India became the Dominion of India, and the new state inherited British India's organization and international obligations and rights. Nehru became prime minister and Lord Mountbatten was made governor-general.

With partition, violence flared along the border, particularly between West Pakistan and the Indian part of Punjab, as Hindus fled to India and Muslims to Pakistan. Estimates of the number killed in two months of bloodshed are as high as half a million. The two governments finally succeeded in stopping both the riots and killings.

The bitterness of the communal struggle led on Jan. 30, 1948, to the assassination of Gandhi by a member of a Hindu extremist organization. Nehru then became leader of the new India.

Many issues remained, and combined with the memory of violence on both sides and dislike by most Indians of the fact of partition, have strained relations between the two countries. These issues include such things as the use of the water of the Indus river system for irrigation, payment of compensation for property left behind by refugees, and, above all, disputes over Kashmir.

The Indian states, which had treaty relations with the British crown but were not part of British India, were given the right to join either India or Pakistan in 1947. Most of the states made their decisions on the basis of geographical contiguity, but Kashmir, one of the largest, refused to make a decision. Its ruler, Maharaja Hari Singh, was a Hindu, with a reputation for bad relations with his subjects, most of whom were Muslim.

When the maharaja refused to make any commitment about the state's future, Muslim tribesmen from the Pakistan side of the border invaded his territory and moved toward the capital of Srinagar. The maharaja called for Indian help, but the government said they could not take action unless he agreed to join India.

The maharaja agreed to accede to India and the Indian army entered Kashmir. At the end of 1947 India appealed to the United Nations on the grounds that Pakistan had invaded Kashmir.

On Jan. 1, 1949, a cease-fire was arranged by the United Nations along the lines occupied by both sides, and general agreement was given for holding a plebiscite to determine the wishes of the people of Kashmir. The plebiscite was not held because of the inability of India and Pakistan to agree on prior conditions.

On Jan. 26, 1950, India adopted a new constitution by which it became a sovereign republic but remained a member of the Commonwealth of Nations. Universal suffrage created an electorate of 176 million, about one-half of whom voted in the first election, which was held in 1952.

In 1952 and in elections in 1957 and 1962, the Indian National Congress won a majority of seats in the national legislature. Jawaharlal Nehru, as head of the Congress party, remained prime minister until his death in 1964.

Contemporary India. Relations with China became of crucial importance in 1959, when the Peking government asserted direct control over Tibet. The Indian government attempted, without success, to get the Chinese to accept the existing Indian-Chinese borders as defined during the era of British rule, and there was an increasing number of incidents along the remote Himalayan frontier.

In October 1962 the Chinese began what the Indians regarded as unprovoked aggression by sending troops into areas of Ladakh and the North-East Frontier Agency, which India claimed had been acknowledged as its territory in the 1800s. Indian troops were forced to withdraw in a number of strategic areas.

Although China refused to negotiate, it withdrew its troops to the approximate positions held before the October movements. India began to expand its defense forces, and accepted military aid from both the Western countries and the Soviet Union.

Relations between Pakistan and India worsened during this period as Pakistan agreed to negotiate a treaty with China in May 1962. The treaty defined a part of the frontier west of the Karakorum Pass held by Pakistan but claimed by India.

A new quarrel broke out in April 1965 over the boundaries between the two in the Rann of Kutch, a desolate territory on the western coast. India insisted that the boundaries established in the early 1900s by the British were binding. Pakistan asserted that they should be redefined since the existence of two independent countries altered the situation. Fighting broke out, but a truce was arranged in June 1965.

At the end of August 1965 fighting again erupted between the two nations, this time along the border between Indian- and Pakistani-controlled Kashmir. The intervention of the UN Security Council brought about a cease fire in September.

In January 1966 Lal Bahadur Shastri, India's prime minister since the death of Nehru in 1964, and Pres. Ayub Khan of Pakistan, at the invitation of Soviet Premier Aleksei Kosygin, went to Tashkent, in the Soviet Union, to settle the Kashmir problem.

The outcome of the conference was the Tashkent Agreement, a pledge taken by both Pakistan and India to move their troops back to positions held before the fighting. Several hours after he signed the agreement, Prime Minister Shastri died.

Indira Gandhi, the daughter of Nehru and an important figure in the Congress party, succeeded Shastri as prime minister. In elections held in February 1967 Mrs. Gandhi's party barely won the majority necessary to keep her in office. The elections revealed that the power of the Congress party, although still the largest party in India, was dwindling. The Communist party, the second ranking party in India, gained a substantial number of seats in parliament.

In May 1967 India reaffirmed its status as a secular state with the election of a Muslim, Zakir Husain, to the presidency. He succeeded Pres. Sarvepalli Radhakrishnan, who had declined to seek another term.

—Ainslee T. Embree; M. G. Inaba

INDONESIA

Official name: Republic of Indonesia
Area: 575,896 square miles (excluding West Irian, 159,376 square miles)
Population: (1966 est.) 107,000,000 (excluding West Irian, 800,000)
Capital: Djakarta (Pop. 1965 est., 3,500,000)
Language: Bahasa, Indonesian
Religion: Islam
Currency unit: Rupiah
National holiday: Independence day, August 17

The Republic of Indonesia, a southeast Asian island nation, occupies the Malay Archipelago. It lies between Asia and Australia and separates the Indian Ocean from the Pacific Ocean.

The archipelago is separated from the Asian mainland, to the north, by the Strait of Malacca and the South China Sea. In the northeast the Sulu Sea and the Celebes Sea lie between Indonesia and the Philippines. The Pacific Ocean lies to the east. On the south, the Arafura and Timor seas separate Indonesia from Australia. The Indian Ocean is to the southwest of Indonesia.

Indonesia consists of over 3,000 islands and stretches some 3,000 miles from east to west and some 1,500 miles from north to south across the equator. The islands are divided into three main groups—the Greater Sundas, in the west; the Lesser Sundas, in the south; and the Moluccas, in the east.

The Greater Sundas include Indonesia's largest and most important islands—Java, Sumatra, Kalimantan (Borneo), Bali, and Sulawesi (Celebes). The western part of New Guinea, West Irian, is also part of Indonesia.

The islands are separated by many seas and straits, some of which, like the Java Sea, are shallow and studded with reefs, but others, like the Banda Sea, are quite deep.

THE LAND. A typical Indonesian island consists of a core of high mountains and hills ringed by coastal plains. The islands are divided into three geologic regions. The largest islands, in the northwestern portion of the archipelago, are outcroppings of the Sunda Shelf, a submerged extension of the continent of Asia. The southeastern islands are part of the Sahul Shelf, the continental shelf of Australia and New Guinea.

Between these two stable geologic regions lies a third region still in formation. It is marked by a semicircular band of some 300 volcanoes, of which 60 are considered active.

Indonesia has an equatorial climate moderated by the influence of the sea. Temperatures are high, but not excessively so, and stable throughout the year, usually ranging between 75°F and 90°F. Rainfall is generally heavy, between 40 and 100 inches a year.

THE PEOPLE. Indonesia is one of the world's most populous nations and in 1966 ranked fifth among the nations in population. Almost two-thirds of the people live on Java, which accounts for only one-tenth of the country's area. Population is extremely dense near Djakarta, the capital.

The two next largest Indonesian cities are also on Java—Surabaja, the leading port, and Bandung, a cultural and educational center. Parts of Sumatra and Bali are also heavily populated, but elsewhere population is sparse.

Most Indonesians are Malays, but the population is divided into many ethnic and cultural groups that speak numerous dialects. Approximately 90

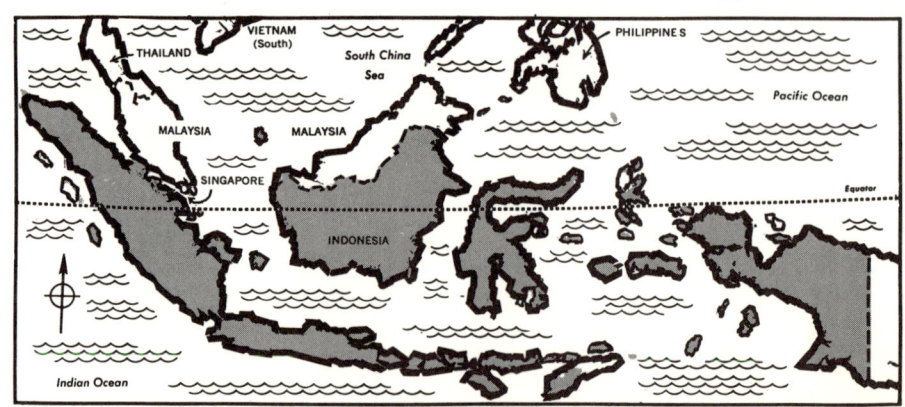

INDONESIAN RICE TERRACES climb the hillsides to increase the amount of usable farmland.

percent of Indonesians are Muslim, and most of the rest are Hindu, Christian, and Buddhist. There are Chinese and Arab minorities.

ECONOMY. Although it is extremely rich in natural resources, Indonesia is a poor country, largely as a result of economic mismanagement and political instability. The largest reserves of petroleum in the Far East are in Sumatra, Borneo, Java, and Ceram, and in 1966 Indonesia produced over 23 million metric tons of oil.

Indonesia is also a leading world producer of tin, mining nearly 13,000 metric tons in 1966. Tin deposits are found mostly on three small islands—Bangka, Belitung (Billiton), and Singkep.

There is also bauxite on Bintan, sulfur and manganese on Java, nickel on Celebes, and abundant iron ore and low-grade coal in Sumatra, Java, and Borneo. In addition to their rich resources, the islands are covered by valuable forests, which provide teak, sandalwood, bamboo, resins, camphor, and oils.

Most of Indonesia's resources are undeveloped, however, and agriculture is the mainstay of the economy. The equatorial climate permits year-round farming. Agricultural products raised primarily for export include cinchona, rubber, coffee, tea, copra, palm oil, kapok, sisal, tobacco, sugar, cocoa, indigo, and pepper and other spices. The basic food crops include rice, corn, sweet potatoes, peanuts, soy beans, bananas, manioc, and a variety of vegetables.

Mining and food processing are the major industries. Manufacturing is limited largely to handicrafts and the production of some light consumer goods, mostly in factories on Java.

Indonesia's economy traditionally relies heavily on the earnings of exports. In the late 1950s and early 1960s the country's international trade was damaged by its political instability, and although the trade balance remained favorable, the value of exports declined steadily.

In 1966 imports cost $583 million and exports earned $679 million. Rubber, petroleum, tin, copra, tea, coffee, and forest products are the chief exports. Textiles, machinery, foodstuffs, chemicals, and iron and steel are imported. Malaysia, Singapore, the United States, Britain, Japan, West Germany, Mainland China, Australia, and the Soviet Union are the country's major trading partners. Indonesia relies heavily on foreign financial aid.

GOVERNMENT. Although Indonesia's independence constitution of 1950 established a parliamentary form of government, representative institutions functioned effectively for only a brief period in the mid-1950s.

The constitutional system provides for a president as chief of state and vests executive power in a prime minister and cabinet responsible to a popularly elected legislature of one house. For the first few years of independence the president was the dominant figure in the government and he appointed the parliament until 1955, when the first parliamentary elections were held.

Political instability led to the dissolution of the parliament in 1960, and a new governmental system called "Guided Democracy" was introduced. This system was based on a 1945 pre-independence constitution that gave the president great power. The president again appointed members of the parliament, which was made part of a larger body, the People's Consultative Assembly, which was also appointed by the president.

"Guided Democracy" ended in 1966, when a military government took power. The military established a 5-man presidium, or governing council, at the head of a large cabinet and retained the People's Consultative Assembly. In 1967 the congress appointed the leader of the military group as acting president to serve until elections could be held. Indonesia is a member of the United Nations.

HISTORY. Indonesia has been inhabited since prehistoric times, and remains of one of the earliest forms of man have been found on Java. By the 100s BC, Malay people had developed on the islands of the archipelago simple societies based on fishing, agriculture, and seafaring. In the 100s AD Indian peoples began to come to the islands, first as traders and then as settlers. The Malays were strongly influenced by Indian culture.

Early Kingdoms. By the 500s and 600s many small Indian-Malayan Buddhist and Hindu kingdoms had been established on the islands, and there developed a variety of cultures and societies. They built up a vigorous trade with nearby island and mainland states, and with India and China.

The first of these kingdoms to achieve significance beyond its own island territory was Srivijaya, on Sumatra. It developed a high Buddhist culture and an advanced civilization, and by the 800s it controlled an empire that included part of the Malay peninsula as well as most of the Indonesian islands.

In the 1100s internal conflicts and threats of attack from the mainland weakened Srivijayan control over the islands, and a new kingdom centered at Majapahit, on Java, gained power. After leading a defense of the islands against an attack by the Mongols in the late 1200s, the Javanese kingdom became the dominant influence in the archipelago.

In the 1300s and 1400s Muslim Arabs began to settle in Indonesia, and by the late 1400s Islamic influence had weakened the older Hindu and Buddhist kingdoms, so that by the early 1500s there was no single powerful state governing Indonesia. In the 1400s and 1500s European traders began visiting the islands, attracted by the fame of the spices, woods, and other goods of the "East Indies" and the "Spice Islands," as Indonesia was called.

European Control. The Portuguese were the first Europeans to establish trading posts in the islands. By the mid-1500s they held military control over most of the islands, and they attempted to convert the islanders to Christianity. The islanders were unable to drive out the conquerors, but they did resist them. Islam spread rapidly through the islands as one weapon against the Europeans.

Portugal held a virtual monopoly of the islands' trade by 1580, when Spain acquired the Portuguese crown. Spain's European rivals, especially England and the Netherlands, redoubled their efforts to break the monopoly after 1580. The Dutch won out with the assistance of Muslim islanders, and they gained a foothold on the islands.

In 1602 the Dutch formed the Dutch East India Company, and during the 1600s it drove out the Portuguese and other European traders and soon subdued the islanders. The Dutch trading center of Batavia, on western Java, grew into a prosperous center for the rich trade of the islands. The Dutch were joined in the 1700s by Chinese immigrants, whose plantations first developed the islands' agricultural potential and who began investing in the colony's business.

Dutch Rule. In 1798 the Netherlands government took direct control of the colony from the East India company. The company's government had grown corrupt and inefficient, and the Netherlands needed the islands as a naval base during the Napoleonic wars. Moreover, the colony had proved even richer than expected. In the early 1800s the French and the British briefly occupied the Netherlands East Indies, but the Dutch resumed control in 1816.

During the 1800s the Dutch reaped great riches from the colony through a system of state-regulated privately owned plantations. The Europeans' concentration on producing export crops to the exclusion of subsistence crops led to frequent famines and to the misuse and depletion of the islands' resources.

Although the Dutch encouraged and educated some islanders and did not prohibit them from owning their own businesses or farms, the majority of Indonesians were illiterate, poor, and powerless. And although colonial regulations protected native workers from mistreatment, most of them were severely exploited.

In the early 1900s Indonesian nationalist movements grew out of the resentment of colonial inequities. Led by Dutch-educated Indonesian intellectuals, the movements grew rapidly. In 1916 these groups succeeded in obtaining from the Dutch a *Volksraad*, or people's council, in which Indonesians could participate. The council had little authority, however, and did not satisfy the nationalists.

As the nationalists grew stronger and more active in the 1920s and 1930s, they met with repression. Their leaders were jailed and the colony's limited social welfare and educational programs were curtailed.

In 1942, during World War II, Japanese forces invaded Indonesia, quickly crushed the Dutch defenses, and occupied the islands. The Japanese encouraged Indonesian nationalism by allowing the Indonesians to participate in the occupation government. One government leader, Achmed Sukarno, had founded the National Indonesian Party, one of the country's major nationalist organizations.

Indonesian leaders who opposed the Japanese established a government-in-exile in Australia. There they outlined a plan for a gradual postwar separation of Indonesia from the Netherlands.

In 1945, three days after the Japanese surrender, Sukarno and Muhammad Hatta, another nationalist leader, proclaimed the independence of the Republic of Indonesia.

Independence. Several years of political conflict and warfare followed, with Sukarno's government fighting not only the Dutch, who attempted to reestablish their control, but more conservative nationalist groups as well. In 1949 the Netherlands yielded sovereignty over the islands.

An independent federal union was established, loosely united with the Netherlands. Dissatisfaction with this organization led in 1950 to the abolition of the federal state and the creation of the centralized Republic of Indonesia, which included all the islands.

The new country was faced from the start with the problem of unifying a large number of islands with a variety of cultures and no tradition of unity. It tried to solve this problem with a strong central government. Between 1950 and 1955, Sukarno, the nation's first president, held great power, appointing all local officials and all members of parliament.

The country held its first elections in 1955 for both a parliament and a constituent assembly, which was to draft a permanent constitution. Of Indonesia's 29 political parties, the communists emerged from the elections as one of the four strongest, along with two Muslim parties and Sukarno's Nationalist party.

The army objected to the influence of the communists on the government, and in 1958 army officers on Sumatra rebelled, sparking an uprising that spread to Sulawesi and many smaller islands. The rebellions were not quelled until 1961.

Between 1957 and 1959 Dutch property was seized and Dutch businesses harassed, and all Dutch citizens were ordered out of Indonesia. The resulting economic crisis compounded the problems created by the rebellion and left the government very weak. Moreover, the constituent assembly was unable to agree on plans for a new constitution. In 1959 it was dissolved and a government reorganization was begun.

By 1960 the country was under a system that Sukarno called "Guided Democracy"—a government, parliamentary in form, but with an executive so powerful that popular participation was effectively stifled—but dissension among the islanders did not end. Conflicts with the Dutch also continued, with Indonesia demanding sovereignty over the Netherlands New Guinea colony, called West Irian by the Indonesians. In 1963 the Netherlands agreed to surrender the territory.

Contemporary Indonesia. In 1963 a new, more violent dispute erupted out of the opposition of the Sukarno government to the establishment of the nearby Federation of Malaysia, formed by the union of four former British colonial areas—Malaya, Singapore, Sarawak, and Sabah (North Borneo).

A "Crush Malaysia" campaign soon became the prime concern of the Indonesian government. Border fighting was frequent, and in 1965 Indonesia announced its withdrawal from the United Nations after Malaysia was admitted to membership.

Hostility to Malaysia was one aspect of Sukarno's general opposition to all European involvement in southeast Asia. In 1965 Indonesia nationalized all foreign-owned businesses in the country, and although it officially remained neutral in foreign affairs, the government strengthened its ties with Communist China as its opposition to western nations stiffened.

Indonesia's Communist party grew in power, and in October 1965 attempted to seize the government. The coup attempt was crushed by the army, and thousands of Indonesian communists were killed in the aftermath. Many thousands of Indonesia's Chinese residents were murdered or driven from their homes. Some of Sukarno's top aides were convicted of complicity in the communist plot.

The army officially took control of the government in 1966, and Lieutenant General Suharto became prime minister. Sukarno retained the post of president until March 1967, when the Peoples' Consultative Assembly dismissed him and appointed Suharto acting president until elections could be held.

The military government concentrated on rebuilding the economy, ravaged by years of violence and political upheavals. It reestablished normal relations with western nations and relations with Communist China deteriorated. It established friendly diplomatic relations with Malaysia and resumed Indonesia's membership in the United Nations.

—Thomas E. Ennis; M. G. Inaba

IRAN

Official name: Empire of Iran
Area: 636,296 square miles
Population: (1966 est.) 25,500,000
Capital: Teheran (Pop., 1963 est., 2,317,000)
Language: Persian
Religion: Islam
Currency unit: Rial
National holiday: Birthday of the shah, October 26

Iran, an oil-rich nation in the Middle East, is bounded on the north by the Soviet Union, on the east by Afghanistan and Pakistan, on the west by Iraq and Turkey, and on the south by the Gulf of Oman and the Persian Gulf.

THE LAND. Central Iran lies on a great plateau which has an average elevation of 4,000 feet above sea level. It contains two barren, salty deserts—the Dasht-i-Kavir and the Dasht-i-Lut. West and south of the pleateau are the rugged Zagros Mountains, and to the north the Elburz range rises to over 18,000 feet above sea level. Narrow, fertile lowlands skirt the country's seacoasts.

Iran's climate varies from region to region. Rainfall averages only 12 inches a year for the country as a whole, but the pleateau receives less than 5 inches and the mountains and northern coasts may receive as much as 40 inches annually. In the central deserts summer temperatures rise above 115°F, but the mountain areas are cooler both in summer and in winter.

THE PEOPLE. Population is concentrated on the lower mountain slopes and in the coastal regions. Ancient Iran was settled by tribes that migrated into the region from Europe.

The country's population also includes Arabs, Jews, Armenians, and nomadic Kurds, Baluchi, Turkoman, and Bakhtiari.

ECONOMY. The wealth of Iran is derived from oil, but farming and herding are the occupations of most Iranians. The bulk of the cultivated land is in the moist northwest, where wheat and barley are the leading crops. Corn, rice, sugar beets, tea, tobacco, and fruits are also raised. Cotton thrives on the edges of the plateau, and goats, sheep, and camels are grazed in semi-desert areas. Fishing prospers on the Caspian coast.

Industry increased in economic importance in the 1950s and 1960s. Most of Iran's industries process agricul-

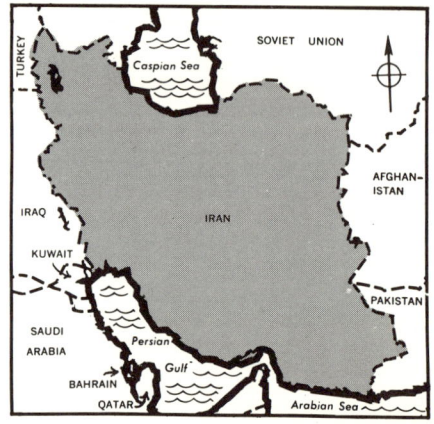

ISFAHAN, IRAN, is famed for its royal mosque, built by Shah Abbas I in the 1500s.

tural products, producing cotton and wool textiles, dried fruits, cigarettes, vegetable oils, and leather. Carpet weaving is an ancient craft that is still important.

Revenues from oil production and refining constitute the largest single portion of Iran's national income. A government-owned company and several international companies pump the oil. In 1966 production totaled more than 100 million metric tons.

GOVERNMENT. Iran is a constitutional monarchy, with a shah, or king, as hereditary head of state. A prime minister appointed by the shah acts as chief executive, and with his cabinet is responsible to the lower house of parliament.

Members of the *Majles,* or National Assembly, the lower and more powerful house of parliament, are popularly elected to a normal term of four years. The upper house is the Senate, one-half of which is elected and one-half appointed by the shah to a two-year term. Although the shah is subject to the will of parliament, he does have constitutional authority to dissolve parliament and assume absolute control of the country in times of emergency.

Iran is a member of the United Nations and of the Central Treaty Organization (CENTO).

HISTORY. The modern history of the Middle East began in Iran in 1908, when the region's first oil was found there. In ancient times, too, Iran—or Persia—was important as the core of the great Persian Empire, which ruled the entire Near East in the 500s and 400s BC. Alexander the Great conquered the empire in the 300s BC, and his successors were defeated by Parthians in the 200s BC. It was not until the 200s AD that Persians regained control of their land, under the Sassanian dynasty.

Sassanians ruled until 641, when they were overthrown by Arab armies that converted the Persians to Islam. Seljuk Turks replaced the Arabs as rulers in the 1000s, and they in turn were overthrown by the Mongols in the 1200s. When the Mongol empire disintegrated in the 1500s, Persians again took control and rebuilt and reunited the country.

Under Nadir Shah, who ruled in the 1700s, the Persians drove out invading Afghans and went on to conquer Afghanistan and part of India. Civil war followed Nadir Shah's death in 1747 and caused the loss of all the newly conquered territory. The Qajar faction emerged dominant from the civil wars and founded a dynasty that ruled until the 1920s.

Although Persia remained sovereign during the 1800s and early 1900s, it was subject to the competing economic and political influences of Russia and Britain. In 1905 a rebellion broke out among Persians who objected to the weak shah's dependence on these foreign states, and in 1906 the shah yielded to the rebel's demands for a constitution and an elected assembly.

Riza Shah. Foreign interference increased after the discovery of oil in 1908, however, and in 1921 Riza Pahlavi, an army officer, led a coup that drove the pro-British shah into exile. In 1923 Pahlavi became prime minister, and in 1925 the Majles proclaimed him shah.

Riza Shah began the modernization of Persia. During his reign, communications, education, and industry were expanded and the judiciary, military, and all of society began to be reordered on a western pattern. Britain retained its influence only as operator of the Iranian oil fields.

During World War II Iran declared itself neutral, but Britain and Russia occupied the country. In 1941 the Allies forced Riza Shah to yield the throne to his son, Muhammad Riza.

Contemporary Iran. After the war a strong Iranian nationalist movement developed, with the ending of foreign control as its primary goal. Muhammad Mossadegh, a leader of the nationalists, became prime minister in 1951 and ruled as a dictator.

During Mossadegh's ministry the British-owned oil fields were nationalized. Iran was unable to market the oil without foreign help, however, and the country faced financial ruin. In 1953 the shah removed Mossadegh from office and had him arrested.

Oil production began again in 1954 under the direction of British, U.S., French, and Dutch companies that shared the profits with Iran. Oil revenues were spent on programs of social and economic reform, and during the 1950s and 1960s the pace of industrialization and modernization was speeded. By 1967 Iran was able to end U.S. economic aid programs, although U.S. military assistance continued.

In 1967 Iran climaxed a two-year celebration of its 2,500 years as a nation with the official coronation of Muhammad Riza.

—Sergio Barzanti; Alexander Melamid

IRAQ

Official name: Republic of Iraq
Area: 173,258 square miles
Population: (1966 est.) 8,338,000
Capital: Baghdad (Pop., 1965, 1,745,328)
Language: Arabic
Religion: Islam
Currency unit: Dinar
National holiday: Anniversary of the revolution and the establishment of the republic, July 14

Iraq, an Arab republic in the Middle East, lies in the valleys of the Tigris and Euphrates rivers. It is bordered on the north by Turkey, on the east by Iran, on the south by Kuwait, Saudi Arabia, and a neutral zone jointly administered with Saudi Arabia, and on the west by Syria and Jordan.

THE LAND. The high Zagros Mountains rim Iraq on the north and east. The western and southwestern regions are desert. Central Iraq consists of a "lower plain," in the southern part of the Tigris-Euphrates valley, and an "upper plain," a rolling, hilly region in the northeast of the country.

About 5 inches of rain falls yearly on the lower plain, and the upper plain receives about 15 inches of rain a year. The rest of the country is quite dry. Summer temperatures in Iraq's desert areas often climb above 120°F, but averages for the country as a whole range from about 50°F in winter to 95°F in summer.

THE PEOPLE. The population is concentrated in the river valleys. Most Iraqis are Arab, but the population also includes a large Kurdish minority in the northeast. Bedouin tribes live in the southwest.

ECONOMY. Iraq's economy is based on oil production and agriculture. Oil is the most valuable resource, and almost no other minerals are mined. The country's rivers provide water for irrigation.

Farmers in the fertile central plain grow barley, wheat, rice, tobacco, cotton, and dates. Sheep are raised on the upper plain and on the fringes

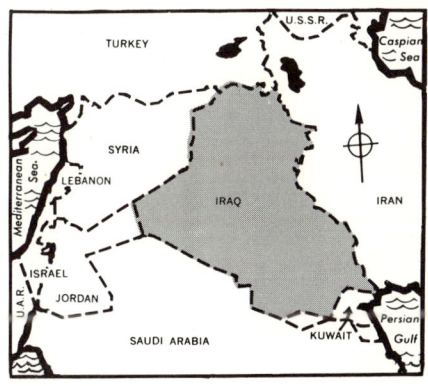

BAGHDAD, IRAQ, has many large mosques.

of the desert. Large-scale irrigation and flood control programs were undertaken in the 1950s and 1960s to create more usable farm land.

Oil production began in 1927 and by the mid-1960s remained Iraq's only major industry. Over 68 million metric tons of oil were pumped in 1966. The richest fields are at Kirkuk, Mosul, and Basra. The government owns one oil company, but the largest firms are internationally owned and pay royalty fees to Iraq. Iraq's other industries are mostly small in scale, producing building materials, textiles, carpets, cigarettes, dried fruits, and leather goods.

The country's chief export is oil, which accounted for all but a small portion of the $882 million earned by exports in 1965. Barley, dates, wool, and cotton are also exported. Imports, which cost $450 million in 1965, include foodstuffs, machinery, iron, and steel.

GOVERNMENT. A provisional constitution adopted in 1964 provided for a president as head of state and a premier, or prime minister, appointed by the president as chief executive. The constitution also provided for a popularly elected legislature.

HISTORY. Modern Iraq is the site of ancient Mesopotamia, "the land between the rivers," where the oldest known civilization—that of the Sumerians—flourished in about 3000 BC. Other great empires—Babylonia, Assyria, and Persia—followed Sumer in the "fertile crescent" between the Tigris and the Euphrates rivers.

In 750 AD, Arab Muslims conquered the region and converted the people to Islam. Arab rule continued until 1258, when Mongol armies devastated the country. Iraq made little recovery under the Ottoman Turks, who took power in 1638 and ruled the area until World War I.

After the war Britain received a League of Nations mandate over Iraq. In 1921 Iraqis chose as king Emir Faisal of the Arabian province of Hejaz, and in 1924 the country was proclaimed a constitutional monarchy.

Independence. In 1932 the League of Nations recognized Iraq's sovereignty by admitting it as a full member. Faisal died in 1933 and was succeeded by his son Ghazi, who reigned until his death in 1939. Ghazi's young son and heir, Faisal II, was a minor, and a regent ruled in his name.

Iraq's modern history has been turbulent. During the 1930s minority groups rebelled against the new government, and nationalists fought against the presence of British personnel and troops. During 1941 a pro-Nazi group briefly controlled the government, but it was overthrown, and Iraq supported the Allies in World War II.

Faisal II came of age in 1953, but in 1958 army officers led by Gen. Abdel Karim Qasim overthrew the government, assassinated King Faisal, and proclaimed Iraq a republic. Qasim became premier, but was killed in February 1963 during another coup, in which Abdel Salaam Arif took power.

Contemporary Iraq. After the unsuccessful attempt to form a federation with the United Arab Republic (U.A.R.) and Syria, Arif in November 1963 split with the pan-Arab leaders in power in the U.A.R. and Syria. In the following year a new constitution took effect that favored a close alliance, but not a merger, with the U.A.R.

Arif died in an accident in 1966, and his brother, Abdel Rahman Arif, became president. Several attempted coups in 1965 and 1966 resulted in a series of governmental reorganizations, but the army remained in control.

A major domestic problem between 1961 and 1966 was a rebellion among the Kurds, who wanted to establish an independent Kurdish state. A 1966 settlement granted the Kurds self-government within their own region. Abroad, Iraq participated in the 1948-1949 and 1967 Arab wars against Israel, and the republic tended to follow the policy of the U.A.R. in international affairs.

Iraq made gradual social progress in the 1950s and 1960s. Oil revenues financed the expansion of educational and health services, the improvement of communications and transportation facilities, and agricultural reforms. The country as a whole, however, did not undergo a swift modernization or radical westernization, and most Iraqis continued to live according to ancient customs.

—Sergio Barzanti; Alexander Melamid

IRELAND

Official name: Republic of Ireland (Irish Republic)
Area: 27,135 square miles
Population: (1966 est.) 2,884,000
Capital: Dublin (Pop., 1966, urban area, 647,336)
Language: Irish, English
Religion: Roman Catholicism
Currency unit: Pound
National holiday: St. Patrick's Day, March 17

The Republic of Ireland, or Eire, is an independent country that occupies the southwestern five-sixths of the island of Ireland, one of the two main British Isles. The northeastern sixth of the island makes up Northern Ireland, which is part of the United Kingdom. The North Atlantic lies to

COUNTRIES OF THE WORLD

the west and south, and the Irish Sea to the east, separating Ireland from Britain.

THE LAND. Ireland is an old, low, glaciated plateau with few elevations above 2,000 feet. There is a central plain, opening more widely on the east, fringed by higher and more rugged land, especially in the north and southwest. Drainage is a problem, and much of Ireland is covered by odd-shaped lakes, marshes, and peat bogs.

The combination of damp, acid soils, a very damp climate, and uncertain drainage has restricted forest growth and greatly limited the variety of agriculture. More than a third of Ireland is classified as moor and heath, although there are sizable tracts of excellent grassland suitable for raising livestock.

The climate is dominated by maritime influences. Winters are mild, and summers are quite cool. The humidity is high, rain is abundant and frequent, and it is often cloudy or foggy. Dublin has a temperature range of only 20°F, with August averaging 62°F and January 42°F.

THE PEOPLE. The Irish people are culturally quite homogeneous. Irish, a Celtic Indo-European language related to Gaelic, is the official first language and is spoken in the southern and western coastal regions of Cork, Kerry, Mayo, and Donegal. English, however, is universally spoken, and official documents are printed in English and Irish. About 94 percent of the population is Roman Catholic. Most of the remainder is Anglican or Protestant.

Ireland's population declined steadily from the late 1840s until the 1960s. In the 1840s potato diseases began to attack the country's principal crop, and famine precipitated a flood of emigrants to North America and other areas. A high rate of celibacy and a low birth rate contributed to the decline in population, a trend reversed only in the 1960s.

Dublin, the capital, is by far the largest city, and one-fifth of the entire population of Eire resides in the Dublin area.

ECONOMY. Ireland is predominantly agricultural. In the mid-1960s farmers constituted more than one-third of the labor force and agricultural products made up more than half of the total value of exports. Most farms are small, less than 30 acres in size.

The economics of the industrial, agriculturally deficient British and the nearby, largely agricultural Irish have become highly complementary, and the Irish economy has been geared toward meat and dairy exports to Britain. Recent developments, however, are changing this. The Irish are emphasizing raising wheat and sugar beets in an attempt to reduce imports, and the country is making an intensive effort to industrialize.

Ireland's exports in 1966 were valued at $680 million, and its imports at $1,044 million. Tourism and the remittances of Irish abroad help to fill the gap. Exports consist chiefly of agricultural products. Major exports include livestock, meat, dairy products, eggs, beer, stout, and Irish whiskey. The principal imports are machinery, electrical goods, textiles, coal, vehicles, grain, mineral oils, and fats.

Ireland's leading trading partner is Britain, which in 1965 received about 70 percent of exports and provided about 50 percent of imports. Ireland also exports to the Benelux countries and West Germany and imports from the United States, West Germany, France, and the Netherlands.

GOVERNMENT. Ireland is a republic. The head of state is the president, who is elected to a term of seven years. Executive powers are wielded by a prime minister, who is usually the leader of the majority party in the House of Representatives. He is appointed to a five-year term by the president, on the recommendation of the House of Representatives.

Legislative power is vested in the Parliament, which includes the House of Representatives, elected on the basis of proportional representation, and the Senate, which is partly elected and partly appointed by the prime minister.

HISTORY. In the 300s BC, the Celts crossed from Europe to Ireland and easily defeated the indigenous population. The Celts divided the country into a number of small kingdoms.

Ireland lived in isolation until the 400s AD, when St. Patrick landed on the island to spread Christianity among the generally pagan populace. Christianity quickly took hold, and a brilliant scholarly tradition was begun at newly founded monasteries, which became widely known centers of learning and culture.

In the 800s the island was invaded by the Northmen, or Vikings, who raided the land periodically. They were not defeated until 1014, when a great Irish king, Brian Boru, routed them at Clontarf, near Dublin.

In 1167, King Henry II of England invaded Ireland upon the invitation of a deposed Irish king, Dermot MacMurrough. The Irish were defeated, and in 1171 Henry established his personal rule over the country.

English Rule. In time, England relaxed its control, partly because its attention was almost totally given to the Hundred Years' War (1338–1453) with France and to the internal Wars of the Roses (1455–1485). A considerable degree of autonomy had gradually been obtained by the local aristocracy, and the era is known as the period of "aristocratic home rule." Direct English control was actually reduced to an area around Dublin known as the Pale.

It was not until 1494, under the first of the Tudors, Henry VII, that English power was reestablished throughout the island. During the Tudor dynasty, the major issues that were to poison relations between the two countries—religion, land ownership, and home rule—began to arise. Henry VIII broke with the papacy in 1534 and attempted to eradicate Roman Catholicism from Ireland.

Mary I, Henry's daughter, tried to force the assimilation of the Irish by confiscating the lands of the Irish lords who refused to conform and distributing them to English settlers. Elizabeth I continued this system,

IRISH TOURIST OFFICE
ASHFORD CASTLE, in County Mayo, stands on the northeastern shore of Lough Corrib.

which came to be known as "plantation," and excluded the Irish from any significant role in the administration.

A great rebellion—known as the "Tyrone Wars"—finally broke out in 1597, and its leaders became two of the most celebrated Irish heroes—Hugh O'Neill, earl of Tyrone, and Hugh O'Donnell. After a series of victories, they were finally defeated in 1601 by the English at Kinsale.

Under England's Stuart king, James I, Scottish settlers were given lands in Ulster. As a result, a new rebellion started in 1641, when the Ulstermen massacred many of the usurpers of their lands. Terrible revenge was taken in 1649 by England's Puritan dictator, Oliver Cromwell. The population of the town of Drogheda in eastern Ireland was slaughtered, and most of the land still remaining in Irish hands was confiscated.

Conditions were better under Charles II, and they improved greatly under James II, who was a Roman Catholic. The Glorious Revolution of 1688, however, soon removed him from the throne, and he was finally defeated on Irish soil at the battle of the Boyne in 1690.

Eventually the Penal Laws—a series of laws first formulated under James I that sought to reduce the power of the Irish—were made more stringent, and economic measures ruinous to the Irish nation were enacted. Tension mounted steadily.

It was only in 1798, however, that a major revolution, led by Wolfe Tone, was attempted. The effort failed, and England then deprived Ireland of its own parliament. In 1800 Ireland was united to England and allowed representation in the English Parliament.

The Period of Union. A great disaster, the "potato famine," struck the island in 1845, causing about 1 million deaths in a few years. A massive emigration then began, directed chiefly to the United States.

Emigrants living in the United States founded the Fenian Society to continue the struggle against Britain. In 1873 the Home Rule League was formed in Ireland. Its outstanding figure was Charles Stewart Parnell, a brilliant and extremely popular leader.

Later, a more active movement, the Sinn Féin, came to the fore. On Easter Monday, 1916, in the middle of World War I, several hundred of its members rose in Dublin, but the rebellion was put down by British troops. In the following years, another organization, the IRA (Irish Republican Army) harassed the British.

Free State and Republic. After the war, the Sinn Féin triumphed in elections held in 1918, winning most of the Irish seats in the British Parliament. These candidates refused to go to England, however, and instead set up their own parliament in Dublin, declaring Ireland an independent republic.

A period of political upheaval followed, during which the British tried to maintain order by pouring troops into the country. But in 1922 Britain recognized the Irish Free State and granted it dominion status. The six northern, predominantly Protestant, counties of Ulster chose to remain part of the United Kingdom. The new situation provoked profound and violent dissension among the Irish.

Under Prime Minister (later president) Eamon de Valera, a new constitution was promulgated in 1937, whereby the sovereign country of Ireland, or Eire, was proclaimed. In 1948 the last ties with the British Commonwealth were cut and Ireland proclaimed itself a republic on Apr. 18, 1949. Eamon de Valera again became prime minister in 1951, as a result of the republic's first general elections. Ireland became a member of the United Nations in 1955.

De Valera lost to John A. Costello in 1954, but became prime minister again in 1957. In 1959 he resigned to become president, and Sean Lemass was appointed prime minister. Lemass was re-appointed in 1961 and 1965. De Valera was reelected president in 1966, but Lemass retired in favor of Finance Minister Jack Lynch.

—Sergio Barzanti

ISRAEL

Official name: State of Israel
Area: 7,992 square miles
Population: (1967 est.) 2,669,000
Capital: Jerusalem (Pop., 1965 est., 191,700)
Language: Hebrew and Arabic
Religion: Judaism, Christianity, Islam
Currency unit: Pound
National holiday: Independence day, May 15

Israel, a republic established in 1948 in the land of ancient Palestine, lies on the eastern coast of the Mediterranean Sea. A bitter war between Israel and the Arab states of the Middle East accompanied the proclamation of the State of Israel in 1948.

The boundaries set in 1948–1949 by truce agreements left the new state bordered on the north by Lebanon, on the east by Syria and Jordan, on the south by the Gulf of Aqaba, on the southwest by the Sinai region of the United Arab Republic (U.A.R.), and on the west by the Mediterranean Sea and the Gaza Strip, a small area once part of Palestine, under U.A.R. administration.

Israel's 1948–1949 boundaries were disputed by the Arab states and defended by Israel until 1967, when a new Arab-Israeli war erupted. In the 1967 campaign Israeli forces occupied the Sinai Peninsula and the Gaza Strip, the Syrian border area, and that part of Jordan lying west of the Jordan River, including all of the ancient city of Jerusalem, which had been divided between Israel and Jordan.

THE LAND. Israel is a small, irregularly shaped country with a varied landscape. A narrow, fertile plain borders the Mediterranean. In central Israel, the hilly Judaean plateau rises east of the coastal plain. In the north rise the highlands of Galilee, a region of rolling hills and rich valleys. Near Israel's eastern border the land drops sharply into the valley of the Jordan River. The wedge-shaped, barren Negev desert, in the south, occupies more than half of Israel's land area.

The Jordan, Israel's principal river, flows along the northeastern border into Israel's largest freshwater lake, the Sea of Galilee, and on into the Dead Sea. Smaller streams thread the northern and central portions of the country, but only dry river beds are found in the southern regions.

The southern desert receives almost no rain, but rainfall in the northern and central areas averages 20 inches a year, most of it falling during the winter and spring. In the desert, average summer daytime temperatures climb to about 100°F and winter temperatures average 65°F. Temperatures along the coast and in the hills average 80°F in summer and 45°F in winter.

THE PEOPLE. Between 1948, when Israel became a state, and 1966 more than 1 million Jews from many parts of the world poured into this neglected land. In 1948 Israel's population of about 1.5 million included only about 655,000 Jews, who were living largely as pioneers. By 1966 the total had reached more than 2.6 million, of which over 2.3 million were Jews. The remainder consists mostly of Christian and Muslim Arabs. During and after the 1948–1949 Arab-Israeli war, most Arabs fled Israel and took refuge in neighboring Arab states.

Population is concentrated in the more fertile and temperate northern and central regions of Israel. The two largest cities, Haifa and Tel Aviv-Jaffa, are on the coast. Jerusalem, the capital, lies in the center of the Judaean Hills.

ECONOMY. The people of Israel have worked hard to meet the challenge of a harsh land. In an area that a few decades ago had only a subsistence agriculture, Israelis have developed manufacturing industries and have increased agricultural production to feed an expanding population and to export produce.

Israel's desert lands hold a great variety of mineral resources. Potash and salts are obtained from the Dead Sea, copper is mined in the southern Negev, and stone is quarried in the center of the country. Israel has some oil and natural gas, but not enough to meet its needs.

Agriculture. Although agriculture occupies only one-sixth of the population, the land is intensively cultivated. In areas that once were swamps or deserts, farmers use every available piece of land and every drop of water to raise their crops. About one-third of the cultivated land is irrigated.

Citrus fruit, grown on the coastal plain, is the most important farm product and is one of Israel's principal exports. Grains, tobacco, grapes, olives, and other fruits are grown in Galilee. Farmers on the fringes of the Negev raise cotton and dates. Nomadic herdsmen graze goats and sheep in the Negev, and dairy farming prospers in the north and on the plain.

Industry. Manufacturing contributes 25 percent of Israel's income. The refining of domestic oil and of crude oil shipped to Haifa is the country's most important heavy industry. Others include chemical production, metal processing, and machinery manufacturing. Israelis work in many light industries, including diamond polishing, textile weaving, glass making, food processing, and wine making.

Many industries and farms are operated as cooperatives or collectives. Most of Israel's factory, farm, and office workers belong to *Histradrut*, the leading national labor union, which provides a wide variety of social and economic services.

Trade. Israel exports fruit, machinery, textiles, chemicals, and building materials. The value of these exports in 1966 was over $475 million. The country imported over $810 million worth of raw materials, food, machinery, and other goods in 1966.

Most of Israel's trade is with the United States and western European countries. Grants and loans from the United States, reparations payments from West Germany, technical aid from the United Nations, and contributions from private groups and individuals around the world help to support the Israeli economy.

GOVERNMENT. Israel is a parliamentary democracy. The chief of state is a president, who is elected every five years by the parliament, or *knesset*. With the advice of the *knesset*, the president appoints a prime minister to act as chief executive. The prime minister and the cabinet he chooses are responsible to the parliament.

Members of the *knesset*, which has one house, are popularly elected to a normal term of four years. Participation in government is open to all Israeli citizens, including non-Jews.

Israel is a member of the United Nations.

HISTORY. Although the state of Israel is new, the land is ancient. In about 2000 BC wandering tribes of Hebrews appeared in "Canaan," later called Palestine. Perhaps 500 years later a group of Hebrews was conquered and enslaved by the Egyptians.

After 1200 BC Hebrews once again inhabited Palestine and developed a society based on herding and agriculture. Over the next 1,000 years there developed the Hebrew culture and religion that produced the Hebrew bible, the Old Testament; gave root to Christianity; and contributed its part to the foundation of Western civilization.

Despite the strength and importance of their culture, the Jews were never powerful militarily or politically. In the 900s BC the Hebrew kingdom split in two—the kingdom of Israel in the north and the kingdom of Judah (the source of the word Jew) in the south. By 586 BC both kingdoms had been conquered and most Jews were in exile in Babylonia. Fifty years later Babylon fell and the Jews were permitted to return to Palestine.

Those who returned settled in southern Palestine and rebuilt Jerusalem. They were free from foreign domination only briefly, however. Palestine became in turn a province of Persia (538–332 BC), of Alexander (332–323 BC), of Egypt (323–198 BC), and of the Syrian Seleucid dynasty (198–168 BC).

The Jews were able to maintain their own society and culture, however, and it was during the period

ISRAEL'S HEBREW UNIVERSITY is situated in Jerusalem, the nation's capital.

after the Babylonian captivity that the Hebrew bible was compiled from earlier and contemporary writings.

In 168 BC the Jews successfully rebelled against the Seleucids, only to be subjugated in 63 BC by the Romans. In 70 AD the Jews tried to throw off Roman rule, but they were crushed and their capital city, Jerusalem, was destroyed.

The Diaspora. Many Jews left Palestine and scattered throughout the world in what was called the *diaspora,* or the dispersion. Palestine remained in the hands of the Romans and their successors, the Byzantines, until the 600s. Then, the armies of a new religion, Islam, made Palestine part of a vast Arab empire.

Four hundred years later, the Seljuk Turks conquered Palestine but were soon challenged by the Christian Crusaders, who penetrated the country. Finally, Egypt drove out the crusaders and held Palestine until it became a part of the Ottoman Turkish empire in the 1500s. Palestine remained Turkish until the end of World War I.

Many of the dispersed Jews had never been completely accepted into the societies in which they had settled. Often they were victims of prejudice and persecution, but they maintained their religion, their culture, and the hope that they would one day return to Palestine, or "Zion."

Zionism. During the 1800s a Zionist, or nationalist, movement arose, and small groups of Jews returned to Palestine as pioneers. The first Zionist Congress was held in 1897 at Basel, Switzerland, under the leadership of Theodore Herzl, an Austrian Jew.

The congress greatly strengthened the efforts of the early idealistic pioneers and formulated the Basel Program, which called for the settlement of Jews in Palestine and the creation of a homeland there for the Jewish people. Zionism as an international, mass movement included both religious idealists and political nationalists, and it won the support of many non-Jews.

The Zionists tried to persuade Turkey to allow mass settlement of Jews in Palestine, but the request was refused. In 1917, during World War I, Britain's foreign secretary, Arthur Balfour, publicly announced Britain's support for the Zionist program.

This "Balfour Declaration" pledged to facilitate "the establishment in Palestine of a national home for the Jewish people" without injuring the non-Jewish population already there. Britain occupied Palestine during the war. In 1922 the League of Nations gave Britain a mandate over Palestine —which included both present-day Israel and Jordan—which obliged the fulfillment of the Balfour pledge.

British Mandate. The Zionists were well organized. They established organizations to encourage immigration, handle finances, set up political structures, and plan agricultural and industrial development. The Jewish community developed alongside the traditional Arab society, but Jewish immigration and land purchases and the pioneer spirit of the Jews encountered Arab resistance.

The British sought to appease the Arabs by restricting Jewish activity. Finally, in 1939–1940, they drastically limited Jewish immigration and land purchases to keep Jews a minority in Palestine. The Arabs were not satisfied, however.

During World War II the Palestinian Arab leader, the Mufti of Jerusalem, cooperated with the Germans. The Jews supported the British in the war, and a Jewish brigade fought in the Middle East and in Europe.

Jews did defy the British effort to close Palestine to refugees from Nazi countries, and many Jews entered Palestine despite British opposition. Opinion in the non-Arab world began to turn against Britain. By the end of the war the deadlock over Palestine was complete. Britain, unable to find a solution satisfactory to all sides, submitted the dilemma to the United Nations in February 1947.

Statehood. In November 1947 the UN voted to terminate the British mandate and to partition Palestine into an Arab state, a Jewish state, and a multinational enclave in Jerusalem. The British left Palestine by May 15, 1948, and an Israeli government immediately took power, and was soon recognized by most non-Arab states.

Desultory fighting had broken out in Palestine immediately after the UN partition resolution, and on the heels of the British withdrawal the Arab states of the Middle East, united in the Arab League, invaded Israel. The Israelis drove the invaders out, and in 1949 the UN negotiated separate armistice agreements between Israel and the Arab states. But no final peace treaty was signed, and a formal state of war continued.

The Arabs refused to recognize Israel and employed tactics of encirclement, noncommunication, economic boycott, and border harassment. Several times this tension flared into widespread conflict. When Egypt began a military buildup on Israel's frontier in 1956, Israel invaded Egyptian territory. The Israelis were defeating Arab forces when the UN forced them to withdraw.

The Suez Canal had been closed to Israeli shipping and remained closed. In 1967 the United Arab Republic announced the blockade of the Gulf of Aqaba, Israel's only outlet to the south, and other Arab states threatened Israel's borders. Fighting broke out, and Israel quickly routed the Arab armies.

Israel opened the Gulf of Aqaba, encamped on the east bank of the Suez Canal, and occupied Jordan's part of Jerusalem and the land west of the Jordan River, as well as the Syrian heights, which had dominated Israel's northern border. The UN again arranged a ceasefire, but was still unable to achieve a permanent solution to the conflict between the Arab states and Israel.

—Oscar Janowsky; Alexander Melamid

ITALY

Official name: Italian Republic
Area: 116,304 square miles
Population: (1966 est.) 51,962,000
Capital: Rome (Pop., 1965 est., 2,484,737)
Language: Italian
Religion: Roman Catholicism
Currency unit: Lira
National holiday: Anniversary of the republic, June 2

Italy, a republic in southern Europe, is bounded on the north by Switzerland and Austria; on the east by Yugoslavia and the Adriatic and Ionian seas; on the south by the Mediterranean Sea; on the southwest by the Tyrrhenian Sea; and on the northwest by the Ligurian Sea and France.

The country is a boot-shaped peninsula measuring about 750 miles in length and averaging about 125 miles in width. Its territory includes two large islands—Sicily, lying just off the toe of the boot, and Sardinia, lying 130 miles off the southwest coast —as well as a number of smaller islands. Of these the most important are Elba, Capri, Ischia, Capraia, Giglio, and the Lipari Islands.

Although Italy was not politically unified until 1870, it has since Roman times made important contributions to the cultural and intellectual life of Europe.

THE LAND. Much of Italy is hilly or mountainous, and the amount of land suitable for agriculture is limited. The Alps run along the entire northern border. In the northeast they curve south to form the Apennines, which extend down through the peninsula into the toe of the boot and across to Sicily. The only sizable plain is the valley of the Po River, in the north, although there are coastal plains and numerous interior basins.

Italy's major rivers are the Po, the Adige, the Arno, and the Tiber. Many shorter streams originate in the Apennines and flow toward the Adriatic or Tyrrhenian coasts.

Italy's climate is varied. The north has a continental climate, with warm summers and cold winters, which are often accompanied by heavy snowfall in the more mountainous regions. Southern Italy has a typically Mediterranean climate, with hot, dry summers and mild, rainy winters.

Rainfall varies, generally decreasing toward the southeast. The north averages over 30 inches a year, but parts of Apulia, at the heel of the boot, receive less than 15 inches.

THE PEOPLE. The country is densely settled. Overpopulation has long plagued Italy and has led to a heavy outflow of Italians to the rest of Europe and to many other parts of the world. The Italian birthrate is no longer one of the highest in Europe, and the rate of population increase, counting emigration, is less than 1 percent a year. This modest rate of increase is manageable for the present-day Italian economy.

Italian is the nearly universal language. There are a few small linguistic minority groups, the largest being the German-speaking population of the South Tyrol, in the north along the Austrian border. More than 99 percent of the people are at least nominally Roman Catholic.

Italy is traditionally urban, and over half of the population lives in cities and towns. According to 1964 estimates four cities—Rome, Milan, Turin, and Naples—had more than 1 million inhabitants and 30 other Italian cities had populations of more than 100,000.

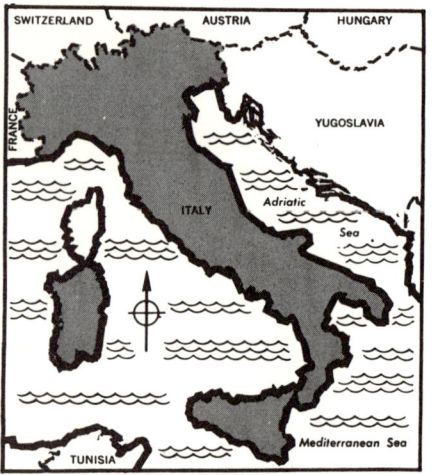

FLORENCE'S PONTE VECCHIO, on the Arno River, is crowded with jewelry and leather shops.

ECONOMY. Before the mid-1950s, the Italian economy was largely dependent on agriculture and tourism. Although both are still important, their relative weight in the economy has declined in the wake of industrial expansion in the mid-1950s and early 1960s. A rapid growth of industry accompanied Italy's participation in the European Economic Community, and the gross domestic product almost tripled between 1953 and 1965.

An important factor in the Italian economy is the tremendous difference in the standard of living between the north and south. The north is highly industrialized and has the country's more fertile farmland, which is the most intensively cultivated in southern Europe. The south is heavily populated and suffers chronically from high unemployment. It is much poorer and far less developed, having little industry and small, inefficient farms.

In 1950 the government established the Fund for the South, an ambitious program for land reclamation and industrial development. In 1967 the government initiated a five-year program for economic development that included a $524 million yearly allotment for the industrialization of the south.

Natural Resources. Italy is poor in natural resources. Sulfur and mercury are mined in quantity and large amounts of limestone and marble are quarried. Aside from these, and modest deposits of coal, petroleum, and natural gas, there are no major minerals. The shortage of fuels has led Italy to tap the large water power resources of the Alpine zone, and in 1964 the country led Western Europe in installed hydroelectric capacity.

Agriculture. Agriculture employs about one-fourth of the labor force, although increasing numbers of farm workers are being absorbed by industry. In recent years production has improved with land consolidation, increased mechanization, and improved agricultural methods.

The Po Valley, which has an extensive irrigation system, raises all the nation's rice, most of its wheat, and three-fourths of its corn. Yields per acre compare favorably with those of northwestern Europe and rank among the world's highest. The region also supports large numbers of cattle and produces substantial quantities of wine.

Southern Italy grows a variety of vegetables, fruit, and nuts. Among the most important of these are olives, peas, beans, grapes, citrus fruits, and almonds. Livestock is also raised in the south, but sheep and goats are more numerous than cattle.

Industry. The government plays an important role in Italian industry. Three state-owned holding companies —the Industrial Reconstruction Institute, the National Hydrocarbons Agency, and the National Power Authority—control a major part of the country's industrial capital. Government holdings are heavily concentrated in iron and steel, engineering, telecommunications, shipbuilding, shipping, petroleum, gas, and electric power.

Most of Italy's industry is concentrated in the northwestern part of the Po Valley, particularly in the triangle formed by the cities of Milan, Turin, and Genoa. Textiles, refined and fabricated metals, machinery, vehicles, and electrical equipment are the most important manufactures. Food processing, based on the varied harvest of the region, is also a major industry.

Trade. Italy's exports in 1966 earned $8,031 million and its imports cost $8,571 million. Italy's main exports are textiles, vehicles, electrical equipment, machinery, chemicals, fruits and vegetables, and wine. Principal imports include iron and steel, petroleum, coal, chemicals, foodstuffs, timber and paper products, and raw cotton and wool.

The nation's most important trading partners are West Germany, the United States, France, the Benelux countries, Britain, and Switzerland.

Government. Italy is a democratic republic with a parliamentary form of government. The chief of state is the president, who is elected to a seven-year term by the legislature. The president has the power to dissolve the legislature and call for new elections. He also nominates the prime minister, who must be approved by the legislature.

The prime minister chooses the ministers who form his cabinet from among the members of the legislature. The prime minister and cabinet are responsible to the legislature.

The legislature, or parliament, consists of the 630-member Chamber of Deputies and the 315-member Senate. Both chambers are directly elected on the basis of proportional representation to five-year terms. The Senate also includes 5 lifetime members and former presidents of the republic. Legislation may originate in either house and must be passed by a majority of both.

Italy belongs to the European Economic Community, the North Atlantic Treaty Organization (NATO), and the United Nations.

HISTORY. Italy has been inhabited since very early times, and traces of Paleolithic and Neolithic cultures have been found throughout the peninsula. In about 2000 BC a group of people closely related to the ancient Greeks entered Italy from the north and gradually established themselves throughout the peninsula.

Approximately 1,100 years later the Etruscans came from Asia Minor, settled in north-central Italy, and subjugated the local inhabitants. In the 700s and 600s BC the Greeks colonized parts of southern Italy and Sicily. They dominated the area to such an extent that it was known as *Magna Graecia*, or Greater Greece.

In 388 BC Rome, an insignificant city-state that until 100 years earlier had been dominated by the Etruscans, gained control of the surrounding area of Latium. By 270 BC the Romans had conquered all of Italy, and the history of Italy from the 200s BC to the 400s AD is largely the history of Rome and the Roman Empire.

In the 400s Italy was invaded by peoples from central and eastern Europe, including the Visigoths, Ostrogoths, Heruli, and Huns. In 476 the last Roman emperor in the west, Romulus Augustus, was deposed by Odoacer, a Heruli chieftain. Odoacer ruled until 493, when he was killed by Theodoric, king of the Ostrogoths. Theodoric established a kingdom that lasted until 553, when Italy was conquered by the emperor of the east, who ruled from Byzantium.

The Byzantines were unable to defend Italy, and in 568 it was invaded by the Lombards. The Lombards gained control of most of the peninsula except Rome, Ravenna, and Naples. Furthermore, in 726 Pope Gregory II, who had quarreled with the Byzantine emperor over ecclesiastical matters, declared Rome independent.

Rome's independence was continually threatened by the Lombards, and the popes began to turn to the Carolingian kings of the Franks for help. In 756 Pepin subdued the Lombards and forced them to cede part of central Italy to Pope Stephen II, creating the nucleus of the Papal States.

Pepin's son Charlemagne deposed the last Lombard king in 774, and in 800 Charlemagne was crowned Emperor of the Romans by Pope Leo III. Italy was ruled by the Franks until 887, when the Carolingian empire disintegrated.

A century of turmoil followed, during which Muslims established themselves in southern Italy and Sicily. Order was restored in 962 with the coronation by Pope John XII of Otto I of Saxony as emperor of Italy and Germany. This union of Italy and Germany marked the beginning of the Holy Roman Empire.

The German emperors, who were mainly concerned with domestic affairs, rarely visited Italy, and the northern and central parts of the country were ruled by warring feudal lords. In the south the Normans wrested Sicily from the Muslims and Apulia and Calabria, at the tip of the peninsula, from the Byzantines. The Normans established the Kingdom of the Two Sicilies.

City-states. During the 900s cities began to develop, particularly in north-central Italy, and by the 1000s and 1100s they had become independent communes. The Italian cities prospered as a result of the Crusades and increased trade with the Muslim world. Venice and other cities in the north became Europe's market places and banking centers.

Strong rivalries existed between these cities and prevented even partial national unification. By the end of the 1200s Italy was divided into several hundred city-states. In the 1300s and 1400s several republics, such as Genoa and Venice, and the ruling princes of a number of other cities, including the Medici of Florence, the Visconti and Sforza of Milan, and the Este of Ferrara, grew extremely rich and powerful.

There was constant warfare among the city-states, and Italy became prey to its more powerful neighbors. But the era of the city-states saw the development of the Renaissance, and the intellectual and artistic works of the Italian Renaissance remain even today as a symbol of cultural greatness.

The descent of Charles VIII of France into Italy in 1494 began the Italian Wars, which arose over rival French and Spanish claims to the throne of the Kingdom of Naples. The wars did not end until 1559, when the Treaty of Cateau-Cambrésis was signed. The treaty recognized Spanish supremacy in Italy, and marked the end of independence for most of the Italian states.

Foreign Domination. The wars of the Spanish Succession (1701–1713) and of the Polish Succession (1733–1735) increased foreign domination of Italy. At the end of the War of the Austrian Succession, which lasted from 1740 to 1748, the only independent states left were the declining republics of Venice, Genoa, and Lucca; the Papal States; and the Kingdom of Sardinia, established in 1720 under the house of Savoy.

Although divided and under foreign domination, Italy during the 1700s enjoyed enlightened rule. The rulers of Italy, inspired by the principles of rationalism, which emphasized the idea of universal human progress, embarked on a program of government reform.

By about 1790, however, the French Revolution had caused a reactionary spirit. Nonetheless, many Italians had become familiar with progressive ideas, and when the French emperor, Napoleon Bonaparte, won Lombardy from the Austrians in 1796, a movement for independence and unity developed and spread throughout the peninsula of Italy.

Under the protection of Napoleon several republics were created. In 1799 Napoleon was driven out of Italy by Russian and Austrian armies of the Second Coalition, formed the previous year between Russia, Britain, Austria, Portugal, and the Ottoman Empire. But Napoleon returned in 1801 and was crowned king of Italy in 1805.

The government of Napoleon was one of enlightened despotism. Although the Italians had little political freedom, many economic, administrative, and educational reforms were carried out.

The Napoleonic empire collapsed in 1814, and the Congress of Vienna, which met to redraw the map of Europe, restored the old regimes in Italy. Austrian influence was dominant in the peninsula. By and large the restoration was reactionary, and most of Napoleon's reforms were repealed.

Risorgimento. Many Italians, especially those of the middle class who had benefited the most under Napoleonic government, realized how advantageous a strong central government could be. This realization, the memory of the earlier reform governments of the 1700s, the recent republican experiments, and a growing feeling of nationalism, all contributed to the development of the *risorgimento*, or resurgence, and the desire for a united and independent Italy.

Some of the more daring patriots joined secret societies, whose aim was to overthrow the existing governments. The most important of these societies was the Carbonari. The Carbonari staged a revolution in Naples in 1820 which overthrew the monarchy there and set up a constitutional government. But Austrian troops defeated the rebels the following year.

The Carbonari also led a number of less successful revolutions—in Piedmont in 1821 and in Modena, Parma, and the Papal States in 1831–1832. Soon after the failure of these uprisings the Carbonari began to decline. It was largely replaced by *Giovine Italia*, Young Italy, founded in 1831 by Giuseppe Mazzini, a former member of the Carbonari.

Mazzini believed that God's will was an independent Italy that would take the lead in the spiritual and political regeneration of Europe. During the 1840s and 1850s Mazzini incited numerous revolts throughout Italy, all of which were unsuccessful.

Unification. Italian unification was finally brought about by Count Camillo Benso di Cavour, prime minister of the Kingdom of Sardinia. Cavour understood that foreign aid was needed to free Italy from Austrian domination. In 1858 Cavour met

THE ROMAN COLOSSEUM, as seen through the Arch of Titus.

secretly with Napoleon III of France at Plombières and promised him Nice and Savoy in return for military assistance against the Austrians.

War broke out in 1859 and the Austrians were defeated, but the Sardinians gained only Lombardy. Meanwhile, however, Tuscany, Modena, Parma, and Romagna had declared their independence and formed provisional governments. Under the sanction of Napoleon III plebiscites were held in March 1860 and the four states voted for union with Sardinia.

In May 1860 Giuseppe Garibaldi, a nationalist leader, landed in Sicily with 1,000 volunteers. By September he had won not only Sicily but Naples as well. Sardinian troops then marched into the Papal States, but France intervened on behalf of the pope.

Nonetheless, the Kingdom of Italy, excluding Rome, was proclaimed in 1861 under Victor Emmanuel, the king of Sardinia. In 1870 French troops were withdrawn from Rome when war broke out between France and Prussia, and the Papal States and Rome were added to the new kingdom.

The Kingdom of Italy was a constitutional monarchy with a parliamentary form of government. The two major political forces were the Right, which was conservative, and the Left, which was radical. From 1860 to 1876 the government was controlled mainly by the Right. A highly centralized government was formed, which set about establishing national armed forces, restoring the country's finances, modernizing the transportation system, encouraging industry, and improving agriculture.

This program was continued and expanded by the Left, which held power from 1876 to 1891. The right to vote was extended, elementary education was made compulsory, administrative and legal reforms were instituted, and the army and navy were strengthened.

Expansion. In the late 1800s and early 1900s many Italians felt that the acquisition of colonies was necessary to Italy's international prestige, and Italy embarked on a program of colonial expansion in Africa. In 1885 Italy began the occupation of Eritrea, and in 1889 southern Somaliland was obtained. Territory in present-day Libya was added to Italy's African possessions in 1912. These colonies, for the most part desert, proved to be a heavy drain on Italy's economy.

In 1882 Italy, with Germany and Austria-Hungary, formed the Triple Alliance against France. A year earlier France had occupied Tunisia, where there was a large Italian population. The Triple Alliance was renewed in 1887, 1891, 1902, and 1912.

World War I broke out in July 1914 and Italy proclaimed its neutrality in the conflict, which ranged the Central Powers, led by Germany and Austria-Hungary, against the Allied Powers, led by Britain, France, and Russia. Italy maintained that it was not bound by the terms of the Triple Alliance inasmuch as Austria was an aggressor.

Within Italy feelings were divided as to whether the country should remain neutral throughout the course of the conflict. Many Italians felt that they should not let the war end without trying to secure territory in the Balkans and firmly establish the border with Austria, which was open to question.

To secure these ends Italy began negotiations with Austria. The Austrians proved evasive, and on Apr. 26, 1915 Italy concluded the secret Treaty of London with the Allies. In the event of Allied victory, the treaty promised Italy Trentino, the south Tyrol, Istria, Gorizia, Gradisca, and the city of Trieste, some of the Dalmatian Islands, sovereignty over the Dodecanese Islands, part of Germany's African colonies, and the seaport of Adalia on the coast of Asia Minor.

Italy declared war on Austria-Hungary in May 1915 and in August 1916 declared war on Germany. Italian troops fought the Austrians and Germans along the northern frontier for four years with varying degrees of success. In 1918 they held firm against a major offensive launched in June and in November won a decisive victory at Vittorio Veneto.

Fascism. At the 1919 Versailles Peace Conference which ended the war, Italy won little of what it had been promised. The resulting popular discontent, together with postwar social and political unrest, contributed to the development of an extreme nationalistic movement, Fascism, led by Benito Mussolini. Fascism was embraced primarily by discontented members of the lower middle class.

On Oct. 28, 1922 the Fascists staged a march on Rome. King Victor Emmanuel III, rather than use the military to put down the revolt, asked Mussolini to form a government. Mussolini was named prime minister and gradually created a dictatorial regime. Parliament became his puppet, and in 1938 the lower house, the Chamber of Deputies, was replaced by the Chamber of Fasces and Corporations, whose members were appointed by the Fascist party.

Fascist foreign policy was imperialistic. In defiance of the League of Nations, Mussolini invaded Ethiopia in October 1935, and following the conquest of Ethiopia, Victor Emmanuel assumed the title of emperor of Ethiopia. In 1937 Italy withdrew from the League of Nations, and in 1939 Italy conquered Albania and Victor Emmanuel was named its king.

Mussolini also supported fascist movements abroad. He aided Gen. Francisco Franco in the Spanish Civil War of 1936–1939 and supported Adolf Hitler in Germany's annexation of Austria and Czechoslovakia. Finally, on May 22, 1939, he concluded an alliance with Germany, establishing the Rome-Berlin Axis.

World War II. Following the outbreak of World War II in September 1939, Mussolini declared Italy's neutrality. But in June 1940, when France was on the verge of defeat, he invaded southern France, bringing Italy into the war. The Italian troops were ill-prepared and were soon demoralized by disaster after disaster. General discontent grew as the war continued, and German troops moved into Italy.

On July 25, 1943 the king dismissed Mussolini as head of the government, and a new government was formed by Marshal Pietro Badoglio. The Allies invaded Sicily in July and August 1943, and in September Italy surrendered. Mussolini proclaimed a "social republic" in the German-controlled north, which lasted until the country was completely liberated in 1945.

On May 9, 1946 Victor Emmanuel abdicated in favor of his son, who became King Humbert II. But the monarchy had lost its popularity as a result of its cooperation with Mussolini, and a referendum held in June made Italy a republic. A new constitution was adopted in 1947, and in 1948 Luigi Einaudi became president.

Republic. Italy soon developed three major political parties—the Christian Democrats, led by Alcide de Gasperi; the Socialists, led by Pietro Nenni; and the Communists, led by Palmiro Togliatti. From 1945 to 1953 the government was headed by Prime Minister Alcide de Gasperi.

De Gasperi developed programs for the reconstruction of war-torn Italy and cooperated closely with other nations of western Europe and the United States. Italy joined the United Nations in 1955 and in 1957 became a founding member of the European Economic Community.

De Gasperi's government fell in 1953, and a succession of Christian Democrats headed right-center coalition governments until 1962. In 1962, to strengthen the government, Christian Democrats joined with the Socialists to form a coalition, known as the "opening to the left."

In October 1967 parliament approved renegotiation of the Concordat of 1929, which determined Italy's relations with the Vatican, in answer to popular demand for less church involvement in state affairs. Under the terms of the Concordat, Roman Catholic religious doctrines are taught in public schools and marriage is governed by church law, which effectively forbids divorce in Italy.

—Sergio Barzanti

COUNTRIES OF THE WORLD

IVORY COAST

Official name: Republic of Ivory Coast
Area: 124,504 square miles
Population: (1966 est.) 3,920,000
Capital: Abidjan (Pop., 1963 est., urban area, 250,800)
Language: French, African languages
Religion: Traditional religions, Islam, Christianity
Currency unit: Franc CFA (African Financial Community)
National holiday: First Monday in August

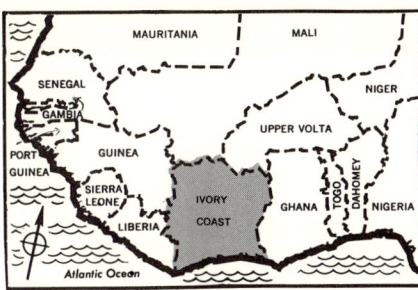

The Ivory Coast, a republic in western Africa, is bordered on the north by Mali and Upper Volta, on the east by Ghana, on the south by the Atlantic Ocean, and on the west by Liberia and Guinea. The Ivory Coast was a territory of France until 1960, when it received its independence.

THE LAND. The surface of the Ivory Coast is relatively flat. There are plantations along the eastern part of the country's coast, beyond which are tropical rain forests. There are forests along the western part of the coast. North of the forest is a savanna region. There are mountains in the west and northwest with elevations above 5,000 feet.

Three almost parallel rivers flow from north to south—the Sassandra in the west, the Bandama, and the Comoé in the east. The Cavalla River flows along part of the Ivory Coast's western border.

The Ivory Coast has a hot, tropical climate. The coastal region receives an average of about 80 inches of rain each year, and the northern part of the country receives an average of about 50 inches yearly.

THE PEOPLE. There are many ethnic groups in the Ivory Coast. The most important are the Baule, Senufo, Agni, and Kru. Most of the people are farmers. The Ivory Coast's largest city and major port is Abidjan, the country's capital.

ECONOMY. The Ivory Coast's economic life depends heavily on agriculture. The country's most important crops are coffee, cacao, pineapples, and bananas. Although most of the Ivory Coast's land is undeveloped, in 1964-1965 the country was the world's third largest producer of coffee and the fourth largest producer of cacao. Large quantities of bananas and pineapples are also produced.

The basic food crops are yams, manioc, and rice.

The Ivory Coast is becoming an important fishing country; in 1965 the catch was 58,500 metric tons. The Ivory Coast is also breeding cattle resistant to disease carried by the tsetse fly.

The Ivory Coast has rich forest resources, and wood and wood products are valuable exports. There are deposits of diamonds and manganese in the country. Although the Ivory Coast is not highly industrialized, light industry has been developing.

In 1966 imports cost $265 million and exports earned $310 million. The country's major imports are machinery, petroleum products, and consumer goods. Exports include coffee, cacao, bananas, timber, and pineapple. The Ivory Coast in 1959 joined with Dahomey, Upper Volta, and Niger, and in 1966 with Togo, for mutual economic cooperation.

GOVERNMENT. The Ivory Coast has a presidential system of government. Executive powers are vested in a president, who is popularly elected to a five-year term. Legislative power is held by an 85-member National Assembly. Assembly members are elected by universal suffrage to five-year terms.

The Ivory Coast is a member of the United Nations and the Organization of African Unity (OAU).

HISTORY. The important Muslim city of Kong in the north of the present-day Ivory Coast dates from the 1000s as a caravan trade center. African kingdoms in the southeast of the country date from the time of the expansion of Ashanti people from present-day Ghana in the 1700s and 1800s.

French Rule. France had contacts with the Ivory Coast in the 1600s and 1700s. In 1893 France established the Ivory Coast Colony, and in 1904 the colony was made a part of the Federation of French West Africa. But the total conquest of the area was not completed until the end of World War I.

There was little freedom of political expression for Africans until after World War II. At that time Felix Houphouët-Boigny founded the Ivory Coast Democratic Party (PDCI), a local section of the African Democratic Rally. The PDCI rapidly became the dominant political force in the country.

In 1946 the colony became a territory within the French Union. With support from French communists and the French administration, Houphouët-Boigny was elected to the French National Assembly.

He gained fame in the assembly for his law abolishing forced labor. France then attempted to suppress the PDCI, and as a result many regional parties sprang up. In 1950 Houphouët-Boigny broke with the communists and adopted a pro-French policy. He rebuilt his party, benefiting from prosperity created by a coffee boom and from French aid.

Independence. From 1956 to 1959 Houphouët-Boigny was a member of successive French administrations. In 1958 his country voted overwhelmingly to become an autonomous member of the French Community.

The Ivory Coast became independent on Aug. 7, 1960, and Houphouët-Boigny was unanimously elected president of the republic. All opposition parties were silenced, and the PDCI became the country's sole legal political party.

—Hibberd V. B. Kline, Jr.;
Vera L. Zolberg

JAMAICA

Official name: Jamaica
Area: 4,411 square miles
Population: (1966 est.) 1,839,000
Capital: Kingston (Pop., 1960, urban area, 376,520)
Language: English
Religion: Anglicanism, Protestantism, Roman Catholicism
Currency unit: Pound
National holiday: First Monday in August

Jamaica, an island nation in the West Indies, lies 90 miles south of Cuba in the Caribbean Sea. Jamaica received its independence in 1962 after more than 300 years of British control.

THE LAND. Jamaica is a mountainous island. A central mountain axis runs from west to east, reaching elevations above 7,000 feet in the Blue Mountains, in the east. There is a narrow coastal plain in the north and a wider coastal plain in the south, where Kingston, the capital and chief port, is located.

The climate varies with elevation. Temperatures throughout the year average in the low 80°s F in the plains, but it is much cooler in the mountain areas. The mountains also affect the distribution of rain. The slopes facing northeast receive the heaviest rainfall, about 200 inches a year. The southern coast is blocked off from rain-bearing winds and receives little rain.

THE PEOPLE. Most Jamaicans are of African and of mixed African and European descent. There are also people of Chinese, East Indian, European, and Near Eastern origins.

Jamaica is a densely populated island. In the cultivable areas, there is an average of more than 2,000 people per square mile. Many Jamaicans migrated to other countries, particularly to the United States and Britain, in search of work.

Immigration restrictions, however, have reduced the possibilities of employment abroad. Thus the country constantly must find more jobs for its growing population, which increased at the rate of almost 2 percent a year between 1958 and 1965.

ECONOMY. Agriculture and mining are the mainstays of the Jamaican economy, and they form the basis for the island's developing industry. The country has rich soils and produces valuable tropical crops, and Jamaica is one of the world's major sources of bauxite, from which aluminum is made. The island also earns a great deal of money from tourism, and resorts such as Montego Bay, on the northwest coast, are popular.

The most valuable export crops are sugarcane and bananas. In 1965 the island produced 497,000 metric tons of sugar and 318,000 metric tons of bananas. Sweet potatoes, rice, and corn are important food crops. Other crops include coffee, citrus fruit, cacao, ginger, pimento, cassava, and tobacco.

Jamaica's mineral resources include gypsum as well as bauxite, but bauxite is the most valuable product of the island. In 1966 bauxite production exceeded 9.2 million metric tons.

Industry is based on processing agricultural and mineral products. Sugar and sugar products, alumina (enriched bauxite ore), and cement are all produced. Oil refining is an important activity.

In 1966 Jamaica's exports earned $229 million and imports cost $321 million. The major exports are bauxite and alumina, which account for about half of all export earnings, and foodstuffs, especially sugar and sugar products—rum and molasses. Jamaica trades mainly with Britain, the United States, and Canada.

GOVERNMENT. Jamaica has a parliamentary system of government patterned on that of Great Britain. The head of state is the British monarch, who is represented by a governor-general. Executive powers are wielded by a prime minister and cabinet responsible to the parliament. The prime minister is normally the leader of the majority party in the parliament.

The parliament has two houses, a 21-member Senate and a 53-member House of Representatives. Senators are appointed by the governor-general—13 on the advice of the prime minister and 8 on the advice of the leader of the opposition party. House members are popularly elected to a term of five years.

Jamaica is a member of the United Nations and the Commonwealth of Nations.

HISTORY. Christopher Columbus claimed Jamaica for Spain in 1494, during his second voyage to the New World. The island, called Xaymaca by its Arawak Indian inhabitants, became a Spanish colony in 1509. Under Spanish rule, the Arawak were exterminated and slaves were brought from Africa to provide labor for the colony.

Britain captured Jamaica in 1655. During the British conquest, many of the slaves fled to the mountains, where they developed a distinct culture. Known as Maroons, they successfully fought off the British for more than 100 years. Jamaica had become a haven for pirates, but piracy was suppressed after 1670, when British control was officially recognized in the Treaty of Madrid.

British Rule. Jamaica became a prosperous colony, thriving as the major slave market of the Western Hemisphere and as a producer of tropical produce, especially sugar and coffee. The slave trade was abolished in 1807, and slavery itself was ended in 1838, after a serious slave revolt. Before the island could recover from the loss of slave labor, Britain in 1846 removed its protective colonial tariff and the plantation economy was ruined.

Economic hardship and misgovernment combined in 1865 to provoke a Negro rising at Morant Bay. The rebellion quickly spread throughout the island and was suppressed only after a bitter struggle marked by violent excesses by both sides.

In 1866 Jamaica was made a crown colony and Sir John Peter Grant was sent from Britain as governor. He initiated political, economic, and social reforms and introduced the cultivation of bananas, which soon became an important export. The colonial administration introduced by Grant lasted into the 1900s.

Self-government. World War II led to an economic depression. The conflict cut Jamaica's trade and virtually eliminated tourism. But political progress became rapid. In 1944 the island received a large measure of self-rule, and in 1945 universal suffrage was introduced.

Jamaican politics had come to be dominated by two figures—Alexander Bustamante, leader of the Jamaica Labor Party, and Norman Manley, leader of the People's National Party. Both parties rested on trade-union support. Bustamante won elections held in 1945 and in 1949, but Manley was victorious in 1955.

In 1958 Manley brought Jamaica into the Federation of the West Indies, which united several British Caribbean and West Indian territories. Jamaicans voted in 1961 to withdraw from the federation, and in 1962 general elections were held in Jamaica.

Independence. Bustamante was returned to power in April, and on Aug. 6, 1962 he led the island to independence. Although no longer led by Bustamante, the Jamaica Labor Party was again victorious in elections held in 1967.

—George Carey; Jerome Fischman

JAPAN

Official name: Japan
Area: 142,727 square miles
Population: (1967 est.) 99,920,000
Capital: Tokyo (Pop., 1965, urban area, 10,-869,800)
Language: Japanese
Religion: Buddhism, Shintoism
Currency unit: Yen
National holiday: Birthday of the emperor, April 29

Japan, an island nation in the northwest Pacific Ocean, is separated from the Soviet Union and Korea on the Asian mainland by the Sea of Okhotsk, to the north, and by the Sea of Japan and the Korea Strait, to the west. The Soviet island of Sakhalin lies 26 miles north of Japan, and the Soviet Kuril Islands lie 10 miles to the northeast. The East China Sea separates Japan from Mainland China on the southwest.

THE LAND. The Japanese archipelago consists of over 3,000 islands and extends 1,400 miles from northeast to southwest. But 98 percent of the area lies within the four major islands of Honshu (87,300 square miles); Hokkaido (30,300 square miles); Kyushu (16,200 square miles); and Shikoku (7,200 square miles).

Most of the country is mountainous, with only about 15 percent of the land sufficiently level for cultivation. The country's limited plains areas are concentrated on Honshu.

Many of the mountains are folded ranges upthrust from the Pacific floor. Japan is crossed by seven principal volcanic chains containing 192 major volcanoes, 58 of which are active. An average of four seismic shocks a day are recorded. Volcanic masses produce the highest peaks in the country. Mt. Fuji, a dormant volcano on Honshu, has an elevation of 12,389 feet. Associated with this intense vulcanism are thousands of natural springs.

All of Japan's rivers are short and swift with greatly varying water levels. Only three rivers exceed 200 miles in length—the Shinano and the Tone on Honshu, and the Ishikari on Hokkaido. The Inland Sea, bounded by Honshu, Shikoku, and Kyushu, serves Japan as a major waterway. It is about 250 miles long and is connected with the Pacific Ocean by the Kii and Bungo Straits and with the East China Sea by the Shimonoseki Strait.

The coastline of the Sea of Japan has few indentations and consequently has few good harbors. The western and southern Kyushu coasts, however, are remarkably indented and have many offshore islands. The southern coast of Honshu contains Japan's most important harbors and ports, such as Tokyo, Yokohama, Nagoya, Osaka, and Kobe. Three famous bays—Sagami, Suruga, and Ise—lie between Tokyo Bay and the Inland Sea.

Climate. Japan's climate, subtropical in the south and cooler in the north, is generally mild and pleasant. The average mean January temperature is 45°F in southern Kyushu and 14°F in Hokkaido. August is usually the hottest month of the year, with a mean of 81°F in the south and 69°F in the north.

Western Hokkaido, eastern Honshu, and the Inland Sea region receive 40 to 60 inches of rain a year. In central Honshu and along the Sea of Japan 100 to 120 inches of rain is not uncommon. In most parts of the country maximum precipitation occurs in early summer.

THE PEOPLE. The Japanese are a Mongoloid people with an admixture of Malay and Caucasoid stocks. The only large minority group consists of about 600,000 Koreans. There are small groups of Chinese and Europeans. Japanese is the national language, and Buddhism and Shintoism, the latter indigenous to Japan, the principal religions. There are about 700,000 Christians, mostly members

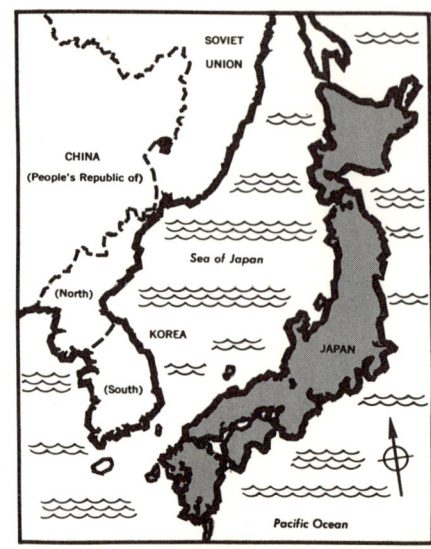

JAPAN'S HIGH-SPEED RAIL LINE links Tokyo to other key cities by 125-mile-per-hour trains.

of various Protestant denominations.

With a population about half that of the United States in a land smaller than California, Japan in 1967 had a population density of almost 700 people per square mile. Because the country is mountainous and largely unsuitable for agriculture, the number of people per square mile of arable land was close to 5,000. The Japanese, however, have succeeded in reducing population growth to the lowest rate of any Asian nation—1 percent a year between 1958 and 1965.

The 1965 census listed seven urban areas with populations of over 1 million. All are industrial centers on the island of Honshu—Kitakyushu (1,042,388); Kobe (1,216,666); Kyoto (1,365,007); Nagoya (1,935,430); and Tokyo (10,869,800).

ECONOMY. Japan's rate of economic growth since the end of World War II has been extraordinary. The economy expanded at an average annual rate of about 11 percent between 1947 and 1952. Although growth slowed down for a few years when postwar reconstruction was completed and the Korean War (1950–1953) ended, the average annual rate of increase was about 10 percent from 1955 to the mid-1960s.

In 1966 Japan's gross national product reached $97.3 billion, the fifth largest in the world. Per capita income is by far the highest of any Asian country, although still low by West European standards.

Natural Resources. Japan has a large variety of mineral resources but the deposits are small and inadequate for Japan's advanced level of industrial development. Coal is the main mineral resource, but most of it is of low grade and unfit for coking. Coking coal has to be imported, as do other basic industrial materials such as oil and bauxite, from which aluminum is made.

Minerals in which domestic production is sufficient are lead, zinc, arsenic, bismuth, pyrite, sulfur, limestone, gypsum, barite, silica, feldspar, and dolomite. Vanadium, chromium, molybdenum, tungsten, titanium, tin, manganese, mercury, antimony, and iron ore are also produced, but large imports are still required to meet the economy's needs.

Japan's mountainous terrain and abundant rainfall help make the country the fourth largest producer of hydroelectricity in the world. Japan also has rich forests and coastal fisheries.

Agriculture. The position of agriculture has been declining steadily since World War II. It contributed 21 percent to the gross domestic product in 1953 and only 12 percent in 1965. In 1965 about one-quarter of the labor force was employed in agriculture, but only about 20 percent of the farm households in Japan were entirely dependent on agriculture for their income.

The average Japanese farm of about 2.5 acres is intensively cultivated. Such techniques as fertilizers, irrigation, multiple cropping, and terracing place Japan's crop yields per acre among the highest in the world.

About half the cultivated land is used for the production of paddy rice, the staple of the Japanese diet. Barley, wheat, potatoes, pulses, vegetables, and fruits are also grown. Since World War II Japan's silk industry has become less important, and in the mid-1960s there were only about 432,000 acres of mulberry orchards. Livestock raising is limited by the lack of land, but some cattle, pigs, and poultry are raised.

Fishing. Fish ranks second to rice in the Japanese diet and is the principal source of protein. Japan's fish catch in 1965 reached almost 7 million metric tons, the second largest in the world. Japanese coastal waters contain a great variety of fish because of the mixing of two major ocean currents off the coast, the warm Kuro Shio from the south and the cold Oya Shio from the north.

The sardine catch leads in both volume and value, although herring and mackerel are important in northern waters. In addition to coastal fishing, Japan has a large fleet which goes to distant fishing grounds in the north and south Pacific.

The Japanese government has promoted a shallow sea culture of raising fish (chiefly prawn, sea bream, and yellowtail), which led to a 25 percent rise in total fish production between 1961 and 1964. Fish production in Japan not only provides a major food item but is also important for oil, meal, and fertilizer.

Forestry. About two-thirds of Japan is covered by productive forests, which are the source of building materials, fuel, paper, and other articles. The forests are also important in stabilizing the soils and the water runoff in this mountainous country.

Oak, laurel, and bamboo grow in southern Japan. A mixed forest including maple, ash, birch, cypress, and pine is found in central Japan. And conifers such as spruce, fir, and hemlock grow in mountain areas in northern Japan.

Industry. Despite its limited natural resource base, Japan is one of the world's major industrial nations. From the end of World War II until 1959, Japan was engaged in reconstructing and reorganizing its war-devastated industries. By 1960 the emphasis was on expanding heavy industry.

In the mid-1960s improvements in technology and production, rather than expansion, were emphasized. The petrochemical and electronics industries, in particular, began to create new products for industry and for the consumer.

In 1966 Japan ranked first in world production of rayon and acetate fabrics. It ranked second as a producer of zinc, woolen fabrics, synthetic rubber, jute yarn, plastics, resins, and tires. Japan ranked third in the production of cement, aluminum, iron alloys, and crude steel; fourth in the production of cotton fabrics; and fifth in refined and smelter copper.

Japan is also a major producer of automobiles, ships, cameras, sewing machines, electric generators, machinery for textile production, aircraft, precision machinery, and chemicals.

An important development since World War II has been Japan's rise as a producer of electronic equipment such as television sets, transistors, transistor radios, tape recorders, and computers. Over 73 percent of Japan's electrical-machinery exports consists of electronic products.

Japan in 1965 ranked fourth in the world in electric energy production. Installed capacity in 1965 was 41 million kilowatts (kw), about 40 percent of which was hydroelectric. Three-quarters of Japan's waterpower potential had been developed by the mid-1960s and many large hydroelectric installations had been built.

Because of the small size of Japan's rivers, most of the stations have small capacities and are the "run-of-stream" type, which is based upon natural flow rather than impounded water. The greatest concentration of hydroelectric stations is found in central and northern Honshu.

Since the mid-1950s thermoelectric power has been emphasized, and in 1962 more power was produced by this means than by water resources. The generation of electric power through nuclear energy has begun in Japan, with 2 million kwh produced in 1964. Atomic power output by 1980 is estimated at 8 million kwh.

Trade. Deficient both in arable land and natural resources, Japan is heavily dependent upon foreign trade. In 1966 it was the world's sixth largest trading nation, with imports costing $9.5 billion and exports earning $9.7 billion.

Raw materials, foodstuffs, and fuel are Japan's principal imports, especially cereals, sugar, raw cotton and wool, iron ore, bauxite, copper ore, coking coal, crude rubber, and crude petroleum. Almost all of Japan's exports are manufactured goods, such as textiles, particularly cotton and synthetic fabrics, chemicals, iron and steel and other metal products, automobiles, radios, textile and leather machinery, ships, and scientific instruments.

Japan's most important trading partner is the United States, which in 1965 accounted for about 30 percent of both exports and imports. Canada and Australia are other important trading partners.

GOVERNMENT. Japan is a constitutional monarchy with a parliamentary system of government. The emperor is the symbol of the state, and executive power is wielded by a prime minister and cabinet responsible to the legislature, the Diet. The prime minister, chosen by the Diet from among its members, appoints the cabinet ministers, at least half of whom must be members of the Diet.

The Diet is composed of the House of Representatives, whose 486 members are elected to four-year terms, and the House of Councillors, with 250 members elected to six-year terms. One hundred Councillors are elected by the nation at large, and the other 150 members are elected from constituencies.

Japan is a member of the United Nations.

HISTORY. Although the first inhabitants of Japan were ancestors of the modern Ainu, a Caucasoid people, archeological evidence indicates that most of the early Japanese were Mongoloid invaders from Korea, who first appeared in Japan in about 200 AD. They brought with them a bronze and iron civilization and founded the Japanese state.

Early Japan was ruled by numerous clans, one of which, the Yamato, gained supremacy by the 200s or 300s. From the Yamato descended the Japanese royal family, although Japanese tradition maintains that the Sun Goddess of the Yamato chiefs is the progenitor of the imperial family.

Chinese Influence. Contact with the advanced civilization of China, which began in about 550 with the introduction of Buddhism into Japan, revolutionized Japanese culture. Eager to learn from their powerful neighbor, the Yamato sent an official embassy to China in 607, a practice which lasted until the 800s. Japanese scholars returning from the embassies helped introduce Chinese ideas and institutions into Japan.

For the first time the Yamato chief conceived of himself as an emperor as well as Shinto high priest. A complex centralized administration in the Chinese manner was established and Chinese-style cities were built. Nara was built as the capital in 710. It was replaced by Kyoto in 794. Less successfully imitated by the Japanese were China's provincial administration and land distribution systems, which were strongly opposed by the clans.

Such cultural borrowings as Buddhism and Buddhist art were the most enduring. Attempts to adapt the Chinese writing system to the Japanese language were largely unsuccessful and made writing unnecessarily difficult. After 200 years of imitation a native Japanese culture began to emerge, and in 838 the last Japanese embassy was sent to China.

A brilliant Japanese court life developed which came to be dominated by the Fujiwara family. The Fujiwara gained control over the imperial family through intermarriage, and from about 850 on its head acted either as regent or as civil dictator.

While the Fujiwara dominated the court in the 900s and 1000s, real power came to reside in the provincial knights. Of all these military families, the Minamoto emerged the most powerful in 1185. Its chief, Yoritomo, settled in Kamakura and gave himself the title of shogun, or generalissimo.

Kamakura Era. By appointing its men as estate managers throughout the country, the Kamakura group was able to control both peasants and court nobles, whose incomes came from the Kamakura-managed estates. Kamakura became the only real central government in Japan, and the institution of the shogunate lasted until 1867.

Upon Yoritomo's death, the Hojo family assumed power, ruling through a puppet shogun from the Fujiwara family and then from the royal family.

By the late 1200s the Kamakura system had begun to disintegrate, although Kamakura soldiers were able to repel Mongol invasions ordered by Kublai Khan in 1274 and 1281. The Japanese were aided by a typhoon called *kamikaze*, or divine wind, which was supposed to protect the land from foreign invaders.

The Kamakura system collapsed as loyalties to the chief lessened and as increasing numbers of knights decreased the number of lucrative positions available. In 1331 a retired emperor, Daigo II, led a revolt against Kamakura, beginning a 200-year period of political disorganization. During this period of political collapse, however, commerce and manufacturing prospered and trade with China expanded.

From China Japan imported Southeast Asian and Indian products as well as Chinese goods, and by the 1500s Japan was exporting not only raw materials but such manufactured products as swords and fans. The East China Sea trade was soon dominated by Japanese sailors.

Political reunification came in the late 1500s when Oda Nobunaga, a feudal lord, seized Kyoto in 1568 and became ruler of central Japan. His successor, Hideyoshi, assumed power in 1582 and reunited the entire country. He attempted an invasion of Korea in 1592, but was repulsed by Chinese forces. Hideyoshi was succeeded in 1598 by Tokugawa Ieyasu, who took the title of shogun in 1603.

Tokugawa Era. Tokugawa and his successors created a political system which remained unchanged for 250

ACTOR YAMASHINA SHIOJURO as a samurai.

years. The price of stability and peace, however, was an oppressive and reactionary government. To achieve social stability, four classes were created—warrior-administrator, peasant, artisan, and merchant. Members of the aristocracy of warriors were called *samurai*, and their emblem was a long and a short sword worn at the side.

While repressive domestically, the Tokugawa were even more extreme in their foreign relations, which had become important with the arrival of Europeans in the Far East. The first Europeans to reach Japan were Portuguese sailors who landed in 1542, and in 1549–1551 St. Francis Xavier, a Jesuit missionary, introduced Christianity to Japan.

Japanese officials, regarding Christianity as a political menace associated with European expansion in east Asia, banned all Christian missionaries in 1587. The Spanish and Portuguese were expelled, and in 1638 Japanese were forbidden to go abroad. The construction of oceangoing vessels was also prohibited. But Chinese merchants were allowed to trade at Nagasaki and the Dutch were permitted to maintain a trading post on a small island in Nagasaki harbor.

By the 1800s the isolation of Japan had become anachronistic, and in 1853 U.S. Commodore Matthew C. Perry arrived in Tokyo Bay with a letter from Pres. Millard Fillmore asking for the establishment of trade relations. For the first time in 600 years the emperor was asked his opinion.

Although the emperor wanted no foreigners in Japan, the Tokugawa had no choice but to sign a trade treaty when Perry returned in 1854. In 1858 a full commercial treaty with the United States was signed, and similar agreements with European countries followed. Foreign businesses were established in Yokohama, which soon became a major world port.

Meiji Restoration. The Tokugawa regime lost national confidence by negotiating a treaty with a foreign power, and in 1867 the new shogun voluntarily surrendered control of the country to the emperor. This return to royal rule was called the Meiji Restoration. In 1868 the capital was moved to Tokyo.

A period of rapid modernization followed the emperor's return to power. Although a constitution establishing a Diet with two houses was promulgated in 1889, the electorate was small (universal manhood suffrage was not introduced until 1925) and government was carried on by a small, competent group of oligarchs.

Japanese students, sent abroad to study Western science and government, returned home to create a modern army, navy, and civil service. Aware that rapid modernization required a technically competent citizenry, the government set up a system of universal education in which technical skills useful to the government were taught. Both the schools and a conscript army employed techniques of political indoctrination, glorifying military prowess and the Japanese nation. Thus a nationalistic, technically skillful population was created.

The government controlled public utilities and to some degree directed business and industry, which expanded rapidly due to the combination of Western technology and cheap labor. With a strong army and navy, and a large industrial complex, Japan was ready to test itself as a world military power.

Expansionism. A quarrel with China over Korea provoked the Sino-Japanese war of 1894–1895, which was easily won by Japan. In 1902 Japan signed a Treaty of Alliance with Britain, confirming its newly achieved international status. Clashes of interest with Russia over Korea and Manchuria finally produced the Russo-Japanese war of 1904–1905, a war won by the Japanese after a series of stunning victories on land and on sea. Korea was annexed in 1910.

In 1914 Japan, as Britain's ally, declared war on Germany in World War I. Seeking to take advantage of the situation, Japan in 1915 presented to China the Twenty-one Demands, calculated practically to transform China into a Japanese protectorate.

But China's territorial integrity was preserved by decisions made at the Washington Conference of 1922. Japan agreed to give up its wartime territorial acquisitions and to limit its navy, in return for the promise that no Anglo-American naval bases would be built east of Singapore or west of Hawaii. Japanese-American relations deteriorated, however, after the United States moved to exclude Japanese immigrants in 1924.

The democratic, progressive elements which had grown up in Japan in the 1920s were gradually eliminated by the military, and a policy of armed expansionism was shaped. This aggressive posture was aggravated by the world economic depression of the 1930's, which proved disastrous to Japan's foreign trade.

To maintain its economy and large population, Japan was desperately in need of foreign markets where it could obtain supplies and sell its exports. With the depression, Japan became subject to the will of other nations' tariff policies.

By the 1930s many Japanese, especially the militarists, were eager to engage in a policy of colonial expansion to obtain sources of raw materials and markets. This culminated in the invasion of Manchuria in 1931. Full-scale war with China started in 1937.

World War II. Meanwhile, in 1936, Japan had signed with Germany the Anti-Comintern Pact. Finally, in 1940, the Rome-Berlin-Tokyo Axis was established. To break the economic blockade set up by the Western nations, especially the United States, in protest against Japanese aggression, Japan attacked without warning at Pearl Harbor on Dec. 7, 1941.

After many important initial Japanese successes, the United States and its allies counterattacked. By 1943 Japan was in retreat. Yet Japan did not surrender until Aug. 14, 1945, after the United States dropped the world's first atomic bombs on the Japanese cities of Hiroshima and Nagasaki.

Japan was occupied by U.S. forces under the command of Gen. Douglas MacArthur and attempts at a thorough democratization of the country were started. Emperor Hirohito disclaimed his divinity, and in 1946 suffrage was extended to women and a new constitution was promulgated.

Contemporary Japan. Economic recovery was slow after the destruction wrought by the war. But the rapidly changing international situation provoked sharp modifications in U.S. policy in regard to Japan. The dismantling of large financial-industrial groups was discontinued in 1948 and reparations from capital equipment were almost abandoned.

The real turning point came with the outbreak of the Korean War (1950–1953). Japan enjoyed great benefits from its strategic position and its industries were given a tremendous push by the "special procurements" for U.S. armed forces. By the end of 1951, Japanese industrial production was equivalent to that of prewar years.

Important political advantages also derived to Japan from the new situation: it regained its independence following the signature of a peace treaty at San Francisco on Sept. 8, 1951. On the same day the United States concluded a security pact with Japan.

Since the peace treaty, Japan has been ruled by conservative governments which have maintained friendly relations with the West. The Liberal Democratic Party (LDP) and the Japan Socialist Party (JSP) came to dominate Japanese politics.

Eisaku Sato of the LDP became prime minister in 1964, and the LDP received almost 49 percent of the vote in 1967 legislative elections. Together with a 5 percent independent vote, the LDP held a majority in the House of Representatives.

In November 1967 Prime Minister Sato and U.S. Pres. Lyndon B. Johnson met in Washington and discussed the status of the Bonin and Ryukyu Islands, under U.S. administration since 1945. The United States agreed to consider the early return of the Bonin Islands to Japan and announced that the status of the Ryukyu Islands would be reviewed.

—Sergio Barzanti; M. G. Inaba

JORDAN

Official name: Hashemite Kingdom of Jordan
Area: 37,737 square miles
Population: (1966 est.) 2,040,000
Capital: Amman (Pop., 1966 est., 330,000)
Language: Arabic
Religion: Islam
Currency unit: Dinar
National holiday: Independence day, May 25

The Hashemite Kingdom of Jordan is bordered on the north by Syria, on the east and south by Saudi Arabia, and on the west by Israel. Jordan has a short coastline on the Gulf of Aqaba, at the extreme southern tip of the country.

THE LAND. Most of Jordan is barren land. Almost the entire eastern half of the country is desert, partly covered by salt or lava. In the west a hilly region separates the desert from a wide, deep gorge that runs the length of the country. The Jordan River flows through the northern part of this gorge, from the Sea of Galilee into the salty Dead Sea.

South of the Dead Sea the gorge is a dry river bed, the Wadi al Araba. West of the Jordan River is the fertile Judaean Hill region, which was seized from Palestine in 1948 and occupied by Israel in 1967.

In the western uplands, Jordan's climate is mild, with average temperatures of from 45°F to 76°F and from 15 to 25 inches of rainfall a year. Almost no rain falls in the desert, where summer temperatures rise above 120°F.

THE PEOPLE. Almost the entire Jordanian population is Arab. In 1965 it included more than 688,000 Arab refugees who had fled Palestine during the 1948–1949 Arab-Israeli war. Population is densest in the northwestern hills and valleys.

ECONOMY. Jordan is a very poor, arid country, with little surface water, infertile soils, and few exploitable resources. Potash and phosphates, mined around the Dead Sea, are its most important minerals. Some marble, gypsum, manganese, and ceramic clays are also mined, and there are untapped reserves of copper, iron, sulfur, and silicon.

Only about 10 percent of Jordan's land is suitable for cultivation, and only part of that was being farmed in the 1960s. The best growing regions are in the moist northwest, but even there some irrigation is necessary. Barley and wheat are the main crops. Beans, tobacco, and citrus and other fruits grow in the Jordan valley, and grapes, dates, figs, olives, and nuts are raised in the drier areas. Goats, sheep, camels, and horses are raised.

Natural phosphates, vegetables, and fruits are the most important of Jordan's exports, which were valued at $36 million in 1966. The country imported $187 million worth of goods in 1966, primarily foodstuffs, petroleum, pharmaceuticals, textiles, and machinery. Most trade is with the United States, Britain, West Germany, and the Arab states. The United States, Britain, and the United Nations contribute heavily to the support of the Jordanian economy.

GOVERNMENT. Jordan is a constitutional monarchy. The hereditary head of state is a king who wields great authority over all branches of government. He appoints the prime minister and other members of the cabinet and may dismiss them at will.

The ministers are also responsible to the lower house of the National Assembly, the House of Representatives, which is elected every four years by male citizens. Members of the upper house, the Senate, are appointed by the king.

Jordan is a member of the United Nations and the Arab League.

HISTORY. The area of Jordan is believed to have been inhabited since prehistoric times, and it was part of the land of the ancient Hebrews. As a part of Syria, the region was occupied by a succession of Middle Eastern empires. The last was the Ottoman Empire, which controlled the country from the 1500s into the 1900s.

After World War I Jordan became part of a new Syrian kingdom, which came under French control. In 1922 the League of Nations gave Britain a mandate over Palestine and Transjordan, as the territory between the Jordan River and Saudi Arabia was called. In 1923 Transjordan gained semi-independent status within the mandate area.

Emír Abdullah ibn Hussein, an Arabian ruler, governed with British advice. He was the first of the *Hashemite* ("of Hashem," or "Hussein") dynasty. For the next 20 years the country moved toward independence with British assistance. Transjordanian troops aided the Allies in World War II, and a treaty signed in 1946 with Britain established Transjordan's sovereignty. Britain retained great influence, however.

In 1948–1949 Transjordan participated in the Arab war against the newly proclaimed state of Israel. Abdullah annexed a portion of Palestine just west of the Jordan River and changed the country's name from Transjordan, "across the Jordan," to Jordan.

Contemporary Jordan. King Abdullah was assassinated in 1951, and his son and heir, Talal, was judged incompetent. Talal's son, Hussein, came to the throne in 1952. Hussein sought British aid in meeting the country's pressing economic and social problems. But the presence in the country of a large number of Palestinian refugees demanding renewed war with Israel to allow them to return to their homes led to political instability.

Anti-Western riots in 1955 and 1956 forced the departure from the country of all British personnel and an end to British assistance. In 1957 and 1958 King Hussein himself barely avoided being deposed during a government upheaval.

In the early 1960s Jordan's domestic politics remained relatively calm, but the monarchy's position was precarious. Pan-Arab sentiment fostered by the United Arab Republic (Egypt) looked to the establishment of a republic and a resumption of the Arab-Israeli war.

In 1967 the Arab-Israeli conflict again broke into open warfare, and Israeli forces swept through Jordan's defenses. When the conflict ended, the west bank of the Jordan River was occupied by Israel, and Jordan was faced with economic ruin.

—Alexander Melamid; Charles Issawi

KENYA

Official name: Republic of Kenya
Area: 224,960 square miles
Population: (1967 est.) 9,948,000
Capital: Nairobi (Pop., 1962, urban area, 314,760)
Language: English, Swahili and other African languages
Religion: Traditional religions, Christianity, Islam
Currency unit: Shilling
National holiday: Independence day, December 12

Kenya, a republic in eastern Africa, is bordered on the north by Sudan and Ethiopia, on the east by the Somali Republic and the Indian Ocean, on the south by Tanzania, and on the west by Uganda.

Kenya received its independence from Britain in 1963.

THE LAND. Kenya has a varied landscape. The land is low in both northern Kenya and eastern Kenya behind the coast. Except for the area around Mombasa, the eastern and northern regions are too dry for intensive settlement. Lake Rudolf extends into northern Kenya. In the southeastern part of the country the land is flat and dry. There is a highland region in the west and southwest.

The highland terrain is extremely varied. The Rift Valley cuts through the highlands. There are also lakes and volcanic peaks, including Mt. Kenya, which has an elevation of over 17,000 feet. Lake Victoria borders Kenya's southwestern corner. The highland region receives abundant and reliable rainfall, and temperatures are moderate.

THE PEOPLE. Africans make up about 97 percent of Kenya's population, and Europeans, Asians, and Arabs account for the remaining 3 percent. Kenya's people belong to many different tribes. The largest tribes are the Kikuyu, Luo, Baluhya, Masai, and Kamba. The Kikuyu people have played an important role in Kenya's political history.

Kenya's largest city is its capital, Nairobi. Mombasa, on the Indian Ocean, is the country's major port.

ECONOMY. Kenya's economy is based largely on agriculture. The highlands have become the mainstay of the country's economy. Many crops are grown on European-owned plantations, including coffee, tea, and sisal.

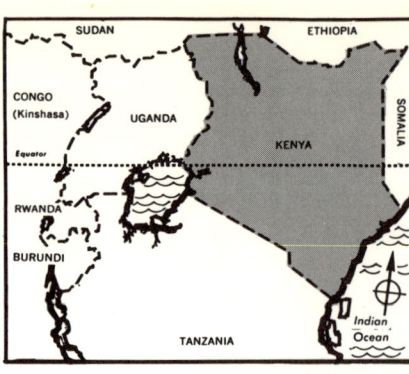

Kenya is the world's largest producer of pyrethrum, a vegetable ingredient used in certain insecticides. In 1964–1965 about 6,000 tons of pyrethrum were produced. The staples of the country, produced by Africans and Europeans, include corn, wheat, vegetables, dairy products, and meat.

Although Kenya is apparently not well-endowed with mineral resources, the country is a major producer of soda ash. The Kenyan government has made efforts to develop the country's industry and has encouraged tourism, based largely on safaris from Nairobi to see the country's varied wildlife.

In 1966 imports cost $315 million and exports earned $168 million. Kenya's main imports are machinery, petroleum, food, and fabrics. Exports include coffee, tea, sisal, pyrethrum, and petroleum products. The country's main trading partners are Britain, the United States, West Germany, the Netherlands, and Japan.

With a well-built seaport at Mombasa and connecting railroads and roads, Kenya is the principal handler of Uganda's trade. Kenya, Uganda, and Tanzania cooperate closely in the fields of communications, technical services, trade, and economic development.

GOVERNMENT. Kenya has a presidential system of government. Executive power is held by a president, who is popularly elected to a five-year term. Legislative power is vested in a 175-member House of Representatives. House members are popularly elected to five-year terms.

Kenya is a member of the United Nations, the Organization of African Unity (OAU), and the Commonwealth of Nations.

HISTORY. Starting in the 700s the peoples of present-day Kenya traded with the Arabs, mainly for slaves. By the 1600s Turks and Portuguese had joined the trade, but in the early 1800s Britain outlawed slaving.

British Rule. In 1887 the Sultan of Zanzibar, who had nominal control of the region, granted the British East African Company control over all of present-day Kenya in return for a fixed sum of money. Britain declared the area a protectorate in 1895. In the same year Britain began building a railroad from Mombasa to Uganda with the aid of Indian laborers.

To make the railroad pay for itself by transporting agricultural products, the British government encouraged Europeans to settle and farm in Kenya by offering long-term land leases in the highlands. Britain set up reserves

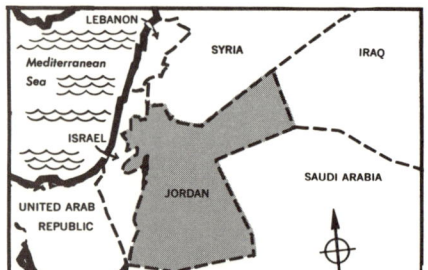

KENYA'S PORT CITY OF MOMBASA
UNITED NATIONS

of land for Africans displaced by European settlers south and north of the highlands.

Britain established a legislative council in the region in 1907. In 1920 all but the coastal area became a crown colony. The coastal region became the Kenya Protectorate.

Nationalism. In 1938 the highland region, which became known as the "white highlands," was officially closed for settlement to all but Europeans. The European community came to dominate political affairs. Meanwhile, the African population, especially the Kikuyu people, was increasing and crowding the reserves. Many Africans were forced to seek work in the new cities. Although an African was nominated to the legislative council in 1944, power remained in the hands of the white settlers and unrest grew among the Africans. Educated Kikuyu, such as Harry Thuku and Jomo Kenyatta, created African political organizations in the 1940s.

Starting in 1952 the Mau Mau, a movement of militant Kikuyu trying to gain independence for Kenya, terrorized the country. Britain declared a state of emergency. In the years of terrorism, 13 Europeans and 19 Asians were killed, but 9,597 Africans were killed, 7,811 of whom were listed as Mau Mau. Kenyatta was imprisoned and exiled as presumed leader of the uprising. The Mau Mau danger came to an end in 1956.

After the Mau Mau uprising, British policy in Kenya changed. In 1957 Britain permitted a limited number of Africans to vote for the first time, and in 1960 Britain promised that Kenya would be an independent country ruled by Africans. Constitutional changes gave more representation to Africans and ended white-settler power. Britain opened the highlands to African settlement and provided African farmers with loans to buy land.

With liberalization, new political parties emerged. The Kenya African National Union (KANU), made up of the larger ethnic groups—the Kikuyu, Luo, and Kamba peoples—favored centralized government. The Kenya African Democratic Union (KADU), representing the many smaller groups, favored regional autonomy.

Independence. In June 1963 Britain granted Kenya internal self-government. Kenya became fully independent within the Commonwealth of Nations on Dec. 12, 1963, with Kenyatta, leader of KANU, as prime minister. One year later Kenya became a republic and Kenyatta became the country's first president.

In 1964 the leaders of KADU dissolved their party, leaving Kenya a one-party state. In 1966 the Senate was dissolved and all Senate members were given seats in the House of Representatives.

—Hibberd V. B. Kline, Jr.;
Vera L. Zolberg

KOREA

SOUTH KOREA
Official name: Republic of Korea
Population: (1967 est.) 29,784,000
Area: 38,004 square miles
Capital: Seoul (Pop., 1966, 3,800,000)
Language: Korean
Religion: Buddhism, Ch'ondogyo, Christianity
Currency unit: Won
National holiday: Independence day, August 15

NORTH KOREA
Official name: Democratic People's Republic of Korea
Area: 46,568 square miles
Population: (1966 est.) 12,400,000
Capital: Pyongyang (Pop., 1960 est., 653,100)
Language: Korean
Religion: Buddhism, Ch'ondogyo, Christianity
Currency unit: Won

Korea is a divided nation occupying the Korean Peninsula in northeastern Asia. The peninsula was divided at the end of World War II at the 38th parallel, a division reaffirmed in 1953 after a ceasefire ended the Korean conflict. The Democratic People's Republic of Korea, or North Korea, occupies the northern half of the peninsula, and the Republic of Korea, or South Korea, occupies the southern half.

North Korea is bounded on the north by China and the Soviet Union, on the east by the Sea of Japan, on the south by South Korea, and on the west by Korea Bay. South Korea is bounded on the north by North Korea, on the east by the Sea of Japan, on the south by the Korea Strait, which separates the peninsula from Japan, and on the west by the Yellow Sea.

THE LAND. Mountains dominate the Korean peninsula, especially in the north, where branches of China's Chang-pai range rise over the northern border. In the northeast the Taebaek Mountains rise sharply from the east coast to over 8,300 feet.

The Taebaeks extend south along the eastern coast, but they do not rise over 5,600 feet in the south. From the Taebaek range, spurs radiate to the west and southwest, gradually descending into highlands that extend almost to the Yellow Sea coast.

Many narrow, winding rivers thread Korea's hills. The Yalu and the Tumen mark North Korea's northern border. Farther south the major navigable streams are the Ch'ongch'on, the Naktong, the Han, and the Taedong. Almost all of these drain south or west. The southern and western coasts are deeply indented and dotted with islands.

The South Korean climate is temperate, with mild winters and hot summers. In the north, the winters are long and severe. Average yearly rainfall ranges from 60 inches along the southwestern coast to 25 inches in the northern interior.

THE PEOPLE. Almost all of the people of the Korean Peninsula are Korean. They speak Korean, and the rate of literacy is very high. Although there are slight regional variations in language and culture, the only significant minority is a small number of Chinese. Korean religions include Buddhism, Confucianism, Christianity, Shamanism, and Ch'ondogyo, a religion that originated in Korea.

South Korea is much more densely populated than North Korea. In 1966 the South Korean population was over 29 million, and the North Korean population was about 12.4 million. Population is concentrated on the western and southern coasts. Seoul, the south's capital and largest city, and Pyongyang, the north's capital and only large city, are both in the west. Pusan, South Korea's second largest city and most important port, is on the southern coast.

ECONOMY. Both North and South Korea have expanding economies. The north is by far the richer in natural resources, with deposits of iron ore, copper, lead, zinc, pyrites, tungsten, graphite, coal, and magnesite. Water power is abundant and there are many acres of forests. A northern climate and the rough terrain limit agriculture, although rice, barley, maize, sorghum, and wheat are grown. Fishing is important, as is forestry.

The main manufactures are steel, chemicals, cement, and machinery. Agriculture is collectivized, and industry is nationalized. Almost all North Korean trade is with the Soviet Union and Communist China.

South Korea has only a small share of the peninsula's mineral resources, although some iron, coal, tungsten, copper, graphite, and kaolin are extracted. It does have most of the peninsula's cultivable land, however.

Agriculture is the mainstay of the South Korean economy, contributing over 40 percent of the national product in 1965. Rice is the main crop. Barley, wheat, cotton, fruits, vegetables, and mulberry trees are also cultivated. Fishing thrives, and forestry is also important, but many forests have been depleted.

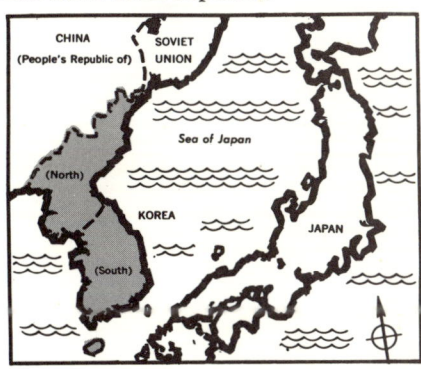

116 Korea

There are few heavy industries in South Korea, but light industry grew rapidly in the 1950s and early 1960s. Textiles, processed foods, clothing, paper, and other consumer items are the leading products. South Korea relies heavily on U.S. technical and financial aid to develop and support its economy, and from 1946 through 1966 U.S. nonmilitary aid totaled more than $4,348 million.

South Korea has a very unfavorable balance of trade. In 1966, for example, imports cost $716 million and exports earned only $250 million. Silk textiles, fish, and tungsten and iron ores are the leading exports. Chemicals, cereal grains, sugar, raw cotton, petroleum, textile yarns, transportation equipment, and machinery are imported. Japan, Hong Kong, and the United States are Korea's chief trading partners.

GOVERNMENT. Both North and South Korea have highly centralized governments led by strong executives. In North Korea the Communist party, officially called the Korean Workers Party, dominates political life. Its central political committee determines national policy and its chairman is usually the key figure in North Korea's government.

A constitution adopted in 1948 vests supreme power in a popularly elected legislature, the Supreme People's Assembly, but the party nominates all candidates for the assembly. The assembly elects a presidium, or governing council, to act for it between its short sessions. The president of the presidium is head of state. The assembly elects a presidium, or govern- and cabinet, officially responsible to it.

South Korea's 1962 constitution established a republican form of government. The president, popularly elected every four years, is the central figure in the government and wields strong executive power. He presides over an appointed administrative cabinet that includes a prime minister, who serves as the assistant to the president. A popularly elected legislature of one house exercises legislative power.

HISTORY. Korea was settled more than 3,000 years ago, probably by peoples from Manchuria or northern China. They lived by hunting, fishing, and herding, and over many centuries developed a culture unique to the peninsula. Although many legends exist about civilizations that grew up in the Korean Peninsula in the 2000s and 1000s BC, the first known state of any significance was the kingdom of Wiman Choson, which was founded in the 190s BC.

It was destroyed in the early 100s BC by the Chinese and replaced by four Chinese colonies. Only one of these, Lolang, or Nangnang, in the northwest, survived Korean rebellions. Lolang grew prosperous on trade with China and Japan and became the source of Chinese influence on the peninsula.

By the end of the 300s AD three native Korean kingdoms had developed—Koguryo in the north, Paekche in the southwest, and Silla in the southeast. Koguryo destroyed Lolang and tried to conquer the other two Korean kingdoms, which united and successfully resisted Koguryo. Silla grew in power under the strong leadership of a political and military elite, and in the 600s, with aid from China, it conquered Paekche and Koguryo.

Silla ruled a unified peninsula for almost 250 years, a period considered the golden age of Buddhism. The government was efficiently run, society was well organized and peaceful, trade prospered, the arts flourished, and Buddhist culture and learning took firm root. By the 800s, however, Silla's kingdom began to collapse, and society was divided into three warring factions—king, aristocracy, and peasantry.

Disorder led in 935 to the establishment of a new dynasty, the Koryo, from whose name Korea is derived. The Koryo restored order by establishing a centralized, bureaucratic government. The new government did nothing to remedy the inequitable division of land and power that had split Korean society, however, and civil disorders continued.

A military group seized power in the 1100s, but it also broke up into factions, and Koryo became too weak to defend itself. In the 1250s it surrendered to invading Mongol armies. Korea suffered greatly under the Mongols, but by the late 1300s it was independent again, under the Yi dynasty.

Yi Dynasty. The Yi dynasty was founded by an army general, who gave the kingdom its ancient name, Choson. Once more the central government was reorganized.

The era of the Yi dynasty is considered the golden age of Confucianism in Korea. Confucian emphasis on learning produced an elite of scholars and was responsible in the 1400s for the development of an alphabet for the Korean language. The Korean alphabet eventually was blended with the Chinese writing system. Confucian ethics served to widen the divisions within the traditional social and economic order, and factionalism severely weakened the country.

In the 1590s Japanese troops invaded Korea on the way to attack China, and defending Chinese troops were sent into Korea. Before both armies withdrew, Korea had been devastated. It had barely begun to recover when, in the 1620s and 1630s, it was overrun by Manchu armies that conquered all of China and established the Ch'ing dynasty in China.

The Yi remained in power, but they had little left to rule. Poverty and disorder reigned, and the country was totally dependent on China for support and protection.

New Influences. The total destruction of the old social and economic orders and the weakening of traditional values left Korea open to new influences. Christian missionaries began to visit the country in the 1600s, and by 1800 they had won many converts and had introduced "Western learning" and ideals into the peninsula.

Also by the 1800s, a new middle class of craftsmen and merchants had replaced the old feudal landlords as the dominant and most prosperous group in society. Trade with Japan

SOUTH KOREAN FARMER. Agriculture is the mainstay of South Korea's economy.

thrived, and the appearance of trading ships from Western nations in the 1800s promised even greater prosperity for the merchants.

The Korean government tried unsuccessfully to maintain traditional society by repressing "Western learning" and banning foreign trade. Moreover, by the mid-1800s China had lost much of its power and was unable to serve as Korea's protector or as its agent in foreign affairs. By the late 1800s Korea was open to many foreign influences and was forced into involvement in world affairs.

Foreign Rivalries. Japan and China vied for political, commercial, and diplomatic control of Korea. To back its position, China invited the United States, Britain, Germany, Italy, France, and Russia to enter into trade and diplomatic relations with Korea, and in the 1800s Korea became a diplomatic battleground for the world's great powers. The government was sharply divided into rival factions and extremely unstable.

In protest against domestic disorder and international interference in Korea, there developed a conservative and antiforeign, nationalistic religious movement called Tonghak, or "Eastern learning," which was later called Ch'ondogyo. In 1894 it led a rebellion to demand the withdrawal of all foreigners from the country.

The government requested aid from China in quelling the rebellion. Japan then sent troops into Korea to "protect" Japanese interests, precipitating a Sino-Japanese war that ended in 1895 in victory for Japan. Japan forced China to relinquish all claims to Korea, and promised to "guarantee" Korean sovereignty.

Russia, with interests and influence in Korea second only to those of China, challenged Japanese dominance over Korean affairs. Russo-Japanese rivalry led to war between the two in 1904. The treaty ending the war in 1905 recognized Japan's dominant position in Korea, and in 1910 Japan annexed Korea, making it a colony.

Japanese Rule. Korea was ruled despotically, and Japan was concerned only with economic exploitation of the land and the people. The Japanese developed the country's industries and resources by using forced labor, they gave the best land and jobs to Japanese, and they tried to impose Japanese culture on the people of Korea.

Japan's rule was bitterly resented, and an independence movement soon developed. Although the independence movement was able to do little against the Japanese, the leaders it developed dealt with the World War II Allies who were fighting Japan—China, Britain, the United States, and the Soviet Union.

Divided Land. In 1945 Soviet and U.S. troops liberated the peninsula from the Japanese. To facilitate acceptance of the Japanese surrender and to prepare the country for independence, the two agreed to divide their authority in Korea at the 38th parallel. U.S. and Soviet representatives could not agree on the formation of a provisional government for a reunited country, or on the withdrawal of their troops, and the matter was turned over to the United Nations.

In 1947 the United Nations called for elections in Korea under UN supervision. But when elections were held in 1948, UN observers were not permitted in the northern zone. In the south, a constituent assembly was elected and a constitution adopted. Syngman Rhee, a leader of the independence movement, was elected president.

In the northern zone a government was established on the Soviet pattern. It was dominated by a newly formed Communist party. In China, the Chinese Communist party had just won a long civil war and established a communist government there that greatly influenced the affairs of North Korea.

The division of the country added to the difficulties it faced in recovering from years of war and colonial rule, and Korea became a focus of the worldwide confrontation between the United States and the Soviet Union.

In 1949, feeling that South Korea could stand on its own, the United States withdrew most of its troops from the southern zone. In 1950 North Korean troops invaded South Korea, and the United Nations Security Council was called into immediate session. When fighting continued even after a UN call for a ceasefire, the UN asked for an international armed force.

The United States, later followed by 15 other nations, immediately sent troops to South Korea. The U.S.-UN troops drove the North Koreans back, only to face an attack by Chinese Communist troops. Negotiations for an armistice began in 1951 and continued, along with the fighting, until July 1953, when fighting was formally stopped and a ceasefire line was set at the 38th parallel. The 38th parallel remained heavily armed and guarded.

Contemporary Korea. While dealing with continuing military threats, both Koreas devoted their energies to developing strong governments and rebuilding their economies. In the north both the government and the economy were centralized under the control of the Communist party, and North Korea repaired the damages of the war and continued to develop its heavy industry.

North Korea received support and maintained friendly relations with both the Soviet Union and Communist China, but it remained cut off from the noncommunist world.

The south, with fewer resources, made slower economic progress. It received support from the United Nations, the United States and other Western nations in improving its agriculture and developing light industries. But inexperience with democracy made political stability difficult to achieve under the south's democratic constitution. President Rhee assumed strong powers and was accused of governing autocratically and undemocratically.

In 1960 Rhee won a fourth presidential term in elections that his opponents charged were dishonest. Antigovernment riots broke out, and Rhee resigned, leaving a caretaker government in power.

In 1961 a military group seized power and established a dictatorship, led by Gen. Chung Hee Park. Voters elected a constituent assembly that drafted a new constitution in 1962, and in elections held in 1963 Park was elected president.

South Korean politics remained turbulent, but in 1967 Park was re-elected with a minimum of disorder. Strengthening its ties with the noncommunist world, Park's government established official relations with Japan in 1965, and sent troops to aid U.S. and South Vietnamese forces in South Vietnam.

Korea again became a focus of world attention in 1968, when North Korea seized a U.S. intelligence ship, claiming it had violated North Korea's territorial waters.

—Thomas E. Ennis; M. G. Inaba

KUWAIT

Official name: State of Kuwait
Area: 6,178 square miles
Population: (1966 est.) 491,000
Capital: Kuwait (Pop., 1965, 99,609)
Language: Arabic
Religion: Islam
Currency unit: Dinar
National holiday: National day, February 25

Kuwait is an oil-rich Arab sheikhdom on the west coast of the Persian Gulf. It is bordered on the north and west by Iraq, on the east by the Persian Gulf, and on the south by Saudi Arabia and a neutral zone jointly administered with Saudi Arabia.

THE LAND AND PEOPLE. Kuwait's surface is level desert broken only by a single ridge of hills and a few small oases. The climate is extremely hot, and almost no rain falls.

Native Kuwaitis are Arabs but there are large minorities of Indians, Iranians, and non-Kuwaiti Arabs, as well as European and U.S. oil workers. The largest cities—Kuwait, the capital, and Al Ahmadi, the oil port—are on the coast.

ECONOMY. Oil is Kuwait's only important natural resource. An estimated one-fifth of the world's proved oil reserves lie beneath Kuwait's land and off its coasts. Water, however, is scarce. Water is imported and seawater is desalted. Most of the land is not suitable for cultivation, but fruits and vegetables are grown in oases, and in the 1950s and 1960s large areas of desert were irrigated to provide more farmland.

Kuwait's major industry is oil production. In 1966 the tiny country was the world's fifth largest producer of crude oil, pumping over 114 million metric tons. In 1965-1966 taxes and royalties paid by the foreign operating companies that exploit the oil totaled more than $500 million.

Much of the oil money is used to finance social welfare programs and economic development projects. By the mid-1960s Kuwait's industries included chemical production, food canning, and the manufacture of building materials.

Kuwait's major export is oil, but processed foods, leather goods, building materials, and other manufactures are also exported. Imports include vehicles, foodstuffs, and raw materials.

GOVERNMENT. Kuwait is a constitutional monarchy in which the ruler, a sheikh, exercises great power. The sheikh appoints a council of ministers and a prime minister. A national assembly elected every four years by male citizens proposes legislation for the sheikh's approval and may override his veto.

Kuwait is a member of the Arab League and the United Nations.

HISTORY. Kuwait was first settled in the early 1700s by Arab peoples from the interior of Arabia. It grew prosperous as a trading center and a pearl fishery. Attacks from Saudi Arabia in the late 1700s impoverished the country, but by the end of the 1800s the economy had recovered.

In 1899, after attempts by the Ottoman Empire to annex Kuwait, the country signed a treaty of protection with Britain. By that treaty and a later agreement, Britain assumed responsibility for Kuwait's foreign affairs and defense.

The beginnings of full-scale oil production in 1946 radically changed the way of life of the people of Kuwait. Within 20 years the country had become a wealthy welfare state.

Kuwait gained full independence in June 1961, when the 1899 protective treaty with Britain was canceled and replaced by a treaty of friendship. Within the month, Iraq announced its intention of annexing Kuwait, which it claimed as Iraqi territory. British troops were sent to protect Kuwait, and later an international force of the

Arab League replaced the British troops. Arab League forces remained in Kuwait until the threat from Iraq ended in 1962. The dispute was not finally settled until 1963, however, when new leaders seized power in Iraq.

Since 1962 the Kuwait Fund for Arab Economic Development has been a major source of funds for development projects in other Arab lands, and in 1967, after renewed Arab-Israeli hostilities caused severe economic problems in many Arab states, Kuwait increased its aid to these Arab lands.

—Charles Issawi; Alexander Melamid

LAOS

Official name: Kingdom of Laos
Area: 91,429 square miles
Population: (1966 est.) 2,700,000
Capital: Vientiane (Pop., 1962 est., urban area, 162,297)
Language: Lao, French
Religion: Buddhism
Currency unit: Kip
National holiday: Constitution day, May 11

Laos, a small kingdom in Southeast Asia, is bordered on the north by China, on the east by Vietnam, on the south by Cambodia, and on the west by Thailand and Burma.

THE LAND. Laos is a long, narrow country, broader in the north and with a southern panhandle that narrows to little more than 50 miles in width. In the northern region sandstone and limestone plateaus are deeply etched by the Mekong River and its tributaries. In the center of this region is a lowland area where the Mekong meets the Ou and Seng rivers.

The country has its highest elevation, over 9,000 feet, in the Plain of Jars, east of the Mekong. In the south the Mekong forms most of the western boundary. East of its broad, low valley rise the foothills of the Annam mountains. At the southern tip of the country is the high Bolovens Plateau.

Laos has a tropical climate, with high humidity and year-round temperatures averaging between 80°F and 90°F. There are some regional variations. On the lowlands frost is unknown and rainfall is just sufficient for rice growing. In the uplands temperatures may be considerably lower and rainfall higher. Monsoons occur from May to October.

THE PEOPLE. About half the people of Laos are Lao, a branch of the Tai people of southern China, who speak Lao. There are various other peoples who have their origins in present-day China, such as the Miao, and there is a small group of Kra, the aboriginal inhabitants of Laos. Most Laotians are Buddhist.

Laos is sparsely populated. Ninety percent of the population lives in rural areas, and there is no large metropolis. Vientiane, the administrative capital, is the largest city. Luang Prabang, the royal capital, ranks second, with a much smaller population.

ECONOMY. Laos is a poor country with an undeveloped economy and an unskilled, largely illiterate labor force. It is thought to have deposits of

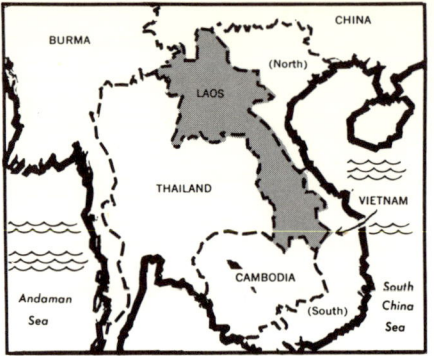

iron ore, manganese, gold, coal, and copper, but these have not been explored. Tin, gypsum, salt, and limestone are mined in small amounts.

Almost all of the country is forested with potentially valuable timber, and the soil is very rich, especially in the valleys of the Mekong River and its tributaries.

Subsistence agriculture dominates the economy. In the lowlands the major crop is paddy rice, but yields are very low, only 500 to 600 pounds per acre. In areas where irrigation is not possible, upland rice, corn, and sweet potatoes are produced.

Vegetables, spices, and some fruits, including bananas, mangoes, and pineapples, are grown throughout the country. Cotton is widely raised, and there is some commercial tobacco farming around Vientiane.

Many upland tribes still follow the "slash and burn" form of farming. These farmers clear the forest by cutting down the smaller trees and burning the refuse. In the fields thus cleared, they plant a variety of crops for a few seasons and then abandon the field to the forest to start over again at another clearing. When all the land within a certain radius of the village has been exploited, the people migrate to a new area.

Foreign trade is of little importance in the economy, and the balance of trade is very poor. Exports earned $1 million and imports cost $33 million in 1965. The main exports are tin, coffee, soy beans, leather, and forest products such as wood, cardamom, benzoin, and lac. Petroleum, manufactured goods, and foodstuffs are imported. Laos relies heavily on technical and financial aid from abroad.

GOVERNMENT. Laos is a constitutional monarchy with a king as head of state. A council of ministers, headed by a prime minister, is responsible to a popularly elected legislature of one house. Laos is a member of the United Nations.

HISTORY. The aboriginal Kha people of Laos were joined in the mid-1200s AD by the Lao, one tribe of the Tai peoples who fled the Mongol invasion of south-central China and settled the northern edge of the Indochinese Peninsula. They established many small kingdoms that were in almost constant competition for control of the entire region.

Lan Chang. In the mid-1300s Fa-Ngum, ruler of a kingdom centered in Muang Swa, on the upper Mekong River, conquered most of the kingdoms of Laos and northern Siam and united them in the empire of Lan Chang, or Lan Xang, the "Land of a Million Elephants." The culture and religion of India, transmitted through tribes south of Laos, heavily influenced Lao culture. Fa-Ngum adopted Buddhism and made his capital a center of Buddhist culture.

His son, Sam Sene T'ai, consolidated the kingdom and established an efficient administration. By the late 1300s Lan Chang was a powerful, peaceful kingdom that had grown prosperous as a producer of forest products and as a center of trade in Southeast Asia.

During the 1500s attacks by two powerful neighbors of Laos—Annam, to its east, and Siam (Thailand), to its west—weakened Lan Chang and lowered its prestige. During this period the Lao capital was moved south, to Vientiane, and Muang Swa was made a temple city and renamed Luang Prabang.

Civil Strife. In the late 1500s Laos was torn by violent dynastic struggles that left it poverty stricken and defenseless against tribal rebellions and attacks by Annam and Siam. By the early 1700s, this civil strife had split Laos into two rival states, one ruled from Luang Prabang and the other from Vientiane.

Neither state could regain the former power, prosperity, and prestige that the unified kingdom had enjoyed, and each sought the aid of Siam, Annam, and Burma in conquering the other. As a result, Laos continued to be torn by conflict throughout the 1700s, and by the early 1800s Siam had conquered both kingdoms and had annexed Laos.

During the 1800s European explorers, traders, and missionaries began to visit Laos. Although Laos itself, with few riches and no access to the sea, held little attraction for the Europeans, competition was keen among the European states for control of all the territory in Southeast Asia.

French Control. By the late 1800s only Siam, which included Laos, separated British Burma from French Cambodia. The British wanted Siam to remain independent, and the French wanted to gain control of Siam. In 1893, in an effort to hold off French conquest, Siam ceded to France all its territory east of the Mekong, which included most of Laos. In 1904 most of the remainder of present-day Laos became French.

France governed Laos as part of French Indochina, which also included Cambodia and the Vietnamese regions of Annam, Cochin China, and Tonkin. Unlike the rest of French Indochina, Laos did not resist French rule. The Lao had seen so much war that a peaceful conquest did not affect them, and the French did much to improve conditions.

The French imposed peace on the warlike Lao tribes and kingdoms, and they allowed Lao leaders to participate in the government. They modernized the government, abolished slavery, and brought education and medical care to the Lao. The French also attempted to develop the country's natural resources and improve its economy, but the world economic depression of the 1930s hindered any real economic progress.

Japan occupied all of Indochina from 1941 to 1945, during World War II, and during the Japanese occupation, Lao nationalism began to grow. A "Free Laos" government was organized and it took over when the Japanese withdrew. After the war the French made an unsuccessful attempt to reestablish their control. In 1947 the Lao adopted a constitution establishing a monarchy and a parliament. In 1949 Laos became an independent state within the French Union.

Opposition to the French was quite violent elsewhere in Indochina. In Vietnam open war, supported by communist forces, was raging against the French, and in 1953 the communist-supported Vietminh forces of Vietnam invaded Laos. In 1954 the French gave up the struggle in Vietnam.

Independence. A peace conference held at Geneva later in 1954 officially ended the war and recognized Laos as a sovereign state. Lao independence and neutrality were guaranteed by all the participants in the Geneva Accords, including the United States, France, the Soviet Union, and Communist China.

Political and economic chaos reigned in Laos between 1954 and 1960, as the governments that came to power were too unstable to deal with the many factions within Laos or to repair the social and economic damage of years of warfare. In addition, communists from Vietnam recruited and organized a rebel army, the Lao People's Liberation Army, originally called the Pathet Lao.

In 1960 a conflict between neutralist and anticommunist politicians caused a government crisis that precipitated a civil war between the Pathet Lao and government troops. Fighting continued even after a ceasefire was arranged in 1961. In 1962 an international conference at Geneva established a coalition government for Laos consisting of pro-Western, neutralist, and procommunist factions. A neutralist, Souvanna Phouma, became premier.

The coalition soon disintegrated, however, leaving Souvanna Phouma as sole executive. Fighting erupted again, with the Pathet Lao in control of most of northern Laos. The Laotian People's Liberation Army received heavy support from Communist China and North Vietnam.

In 1964 the Laotian government began receiving military aid from the United States, and the fighting remained stalemated. Political disputes within Laos further worsened the condition of the country.

In addition to its own internal conflicts, Laos became involved in renewed warfare in neighboring Vietnam. U.S. and Vietnamese planes bombed Lao territory used by the North Vietnamese for supply, transport, and invasion bases.

In 1967 Lao government troops engaged in direct combat with North Vietnamese forces for control of a range of hills in northeastern Laos. In elections held in 1967, Souvanna Phouma's government was reelected, but the Lao Patriotic Front, the political arm of the Pathet Lao, boycotted the elections.

—Thomas E. Ennis; M. G. Inaba

LEBANON

Official name: Republic of Lebanon
Area: 4,015 square miles
Population: (1966 est.) 2,460,000
Capital: Beirut (Pop., 1964 est., 700,000)
Language: Arabic
Religion: Christianity, Islam
Currency unit: Pound
National holiday: Independence day, Nov. 22

Lebanon is an independent republic at the eastern end of the Mediterranean Sea. It is bordered on the north and the east by Syria, on the south by Israel, and on the west by the Mediterranean.

THE LAND. Mountains cover more than half of Lebanon. The Lebanon Mountains run through the center of the country, and the Sharqi, or Anti-Lebanon, chain extends along the eastern border. A narrow, fertile plain lies between the coast and the Lebanon Mountains, and the Bekaa, a fertile plateau, lies between the Lebanon and the Sharqi ranges. Lebanon's major river, the Litani, flows through the Bekaa.

Lebanon's climate is mild and moist. Average temperatures range from 50°F in winter to 80°F in summer, and yearly rainfall averages between 30 and 50 inches.

THE PEOPLE. The Lebanese people are largely Arab. Approximately half the population is Christian and half is Muslim. There are many separate sects within each community. The largest are the Maronite Christians and the Sunni Muslims.

The population is concentrated in port cities along the coast, especially Beirut, Tripoli, and Sidon. Heavy emigration, primarily to North and South America, has characterized the Lebanese population since the 1860s, and there are almost as many Lebanese living abroad as in Lebanon. Many emigrants maintain economic and social ties with Lebanon and contribute to the country's economic and cultural life.

ECONOMY. Lebanon's economy is more diversified than that of many other Middle Eastern nations. Agriculture, industry, and trade are all important. The country has no major exploitable mineral resources except for some deposits of iron ore.

Agriculture occupies about half of the labor force and in 1965 contributed approximately 17 percent to the country's national product. The leading crops are grains, tobacco, olives, and citrus and other fruits. Sheep, pastured in the mountains, and timber forests, in central Lebanon, are also of economic importance.

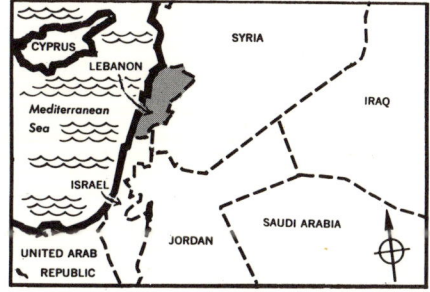

The availability of a well-educated and skilled labor force and the development of the country's great hydroelectric resources enabled Lebanon's industry to expand rapidly in the early 1960s. Lumber and food processing, textile weaving, oil refining, and cement production are the leading industries. Income from tourism is also important.

International trade and finance are vital to the Lebanese economy. They contributed about one-third of the country's income during the early 1960s. Lebanon is a leading banking center, and Lebanese ports handle a large share of the trade passing through the eastern Mediterranean.

In 1965 Lebanese exports earned $85 million and imports cost $482 million. The main exports are agricultural products, and the major imports include machinery and vehicles, textiles, and manufactured consumer goods.

GOVERNMENT. Lebanon is a republic in which power is divided between Christians and Muslims. A Christian president, elected by a unicameral parliament, is head of state. A prime minister, who is a Muslim, and a cabinet are responsible to the parliament. Members of parliament are popularly elected under a system of confessional representation by which each religious group elects a number of representatives in proportion to its membership. Lebanon is a member of the United Nations and the Arab League.

HISTORY. Lebanon is an ancient land. In its forests grew the Cedars of Lebanon mentioned in the Old Testament, and its excellent ports have made it a vital trading center since ancient times. Before 2000 BC the area was the home of the Canaanites, or Phoenicians, who were the leading traders of the ancient world, and in the 800s BC it was conquered by the Assyrians.

Lebanon's history has been closely associated with that of Syria, but Lebanon was set apart by the strong influence of Christianity. Because of its proximity to Palestine, Phoenicia was the site of some of the earliest Christian communities, and by the 300s AD it was entirely Christian. A small group of Lebanese Christians escaped Muslim armies that conquered and converted most of Syria-Lebanon in the 600s AD. Their descendants became the Maronites—Arab Christians affiliated with the Roman Catholic Church.

Ottoman Era. In the 1500s the Ottoman Empire conquered both Lebanon and Syria, but Lebanon was allowed a great deal of autonomy. This relative freedom and the country's commercial importance placed Lebanon in an advantageous position that it maintained through the 1800s. In addition, the presence of a large number of British and French missionary schools and colleges made it a center for Arab intellectual development in the 1800s.

During the period of Ottoman rule, Lebanese Christian and Muslim communities expanded, and the two occasionally came into conflict. In 1860 a revolt by Christian peasants against Muslim overlords touched off widespread religious strife, eventually leading to civil war. Britain and France intervened and forced Turkey to give Lebanon an autonomous government that divided power between the Christians and the Muslims.

Independence. After the defeat of the Ottoman Empire in World War I, France received a League of Nations mandate over Lebanon. In 1926 the French created a republican government, but the Lebanese demanded complete independence. In 1941, following Germany's defeat of France in World War II, a free Lebanese government proclaimed the country's independence of the German-controlled Vichy French administration.

A treaty recognizing Lebanon's sovereignty was signed in 1943 by Lebanon and the Free French government. In 1945 Lebanon was admitted to the United Nations as an independent nation and it also joined the Arab League. All foreign troops had left the country by 1946, and in 1947 parliamentary elections were held.

A high rate of literacy, experience with representative government, and continuing vigorous trade made the early republic stable and prosperous. During the 1950s and 1960s Lebanon strengthened its economy and expanded social welfare and development programs.

Lebanon followed a moderate course in foreign affairs and came into conflict with more extreme pan-Arab nationalist groups in neighboring states. In 1958 the Lebanese government accused the United Arab Republic (Egypt) of inciting a widespread rebellion. Civil war was ended only with the landing of U.S. troops. Relations with Syria, too, became tense during conflicts over trade policies and border defenses.

In general, however, Lebanon attempted to maintain strict neutrality in conflicts among the Arab states. Although Lebanon lent diplomatic and economic support to the Arab side in the Arab-Israeli war of 1967, it did not become deeply involved and was not seriously harmed by the conflict.

—Sara Gilbert; Charles Issawi

LESOTHO

Official name: Kingdom of Lesotho
Area: 11,716 square miles
Population: (1966 est.) 860,000
Capital: Maseru (Pop., 1966, urban area, 18,000)
Language: English, Sesotho
Religion: Christianity, traditional religions
Currency: South African rand
National holiday: Independence day, October 4

Lesotho, a republic in southern Africa, lies entirely within the borders of the Republic of South Africa. Lesotho, formerly known as Basutoland, received its independence from Britain in 1966.

THE LAND. The Drakensberg Mountains occupy most of Lesotho. The mountains reach elevations of about 11,000 feet above sea level, but they have areas of grassland and alpine pasture. Lowlands, in the west, occupy about one-quarter of Lesotho. The Orange River and its tributaries flow through the country. Rainfall averages about 28 inches a year.

THE PEOPLE. Almost the entire population is made up of Africans of the Basuto tribe. Most of the people live in the lowlands. About 70 percent of the people are Christian. Many thousands of Basutos are employed in the Republic of South Africa because Lesotho cannot support its population. Lesotho's major city is its capital, Maseru.

ECONOMY. Lesotho's economy is based on subsistence agriculture, livestock raising, and the earnings of workers employed in South Africa. The chief crops are corn, beans, sorghums, peas, and wheat. Cattle, sheep, and goats are raised throughout the country, and hides, wool, and mohair are produced.

There are only a few small industries in the country. Mineral deposits, except for diamonds, have not been discovered. In 1967 one of the world's largest diamonds, more than 600 carats, was found in Lesotho.

In 1965 imports cost about $24.5 million and exports earned over $6.5 million. Lesotho imports food, machinery, manufactured goods, and petroleum products. Exports include wool and mohair, diamonds, and foodstuffs. Most of Lesotho's trade is with the Republic of South Africa, with which Lesotho has a customs union. Lesotho receives financial aid from Britain.

GOVERNMENT. Lesotho has a parliamentary system of government. The head of state is the king. The prime minister, appointed by the king, holds actual executive power. The prime minister is ordinarily the leader of the majority party in the National Assembly.

Legislative powers are held by a parliament, consisting of a Senate and National Assembly. The Senate is composed of 22 tribal chiefs and 11 members nominated by the king. The 60 members of the National Assembly are popularly elected to five-year terms.

Lesotho is a member of the Commonwealth of Nations and the United Nations.

HISTORY. The Basuto nation emerged in the early 1800s from the union of Sotho and other Bantu-speaking peoples under the leadership of a northern chief, Moshesh. Moshesh had successfully defended these peoples from raiding Zulu and Matebele bands.

The newly organized nation ran into conflict with the Boers, Dutch farmers migrating northward from the Orange Free State. The conflicts led Moshesh to sign a treaty of friendship with the British governor of Cape Colony. In 1868 Britain declared a protectorate over present-day Lesotho to prevent seizure of the country by the neighboring Orange Free State.

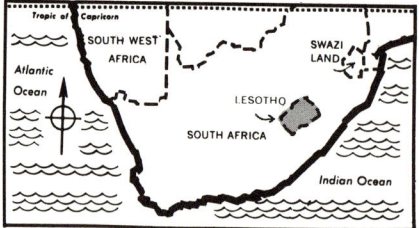

British Rule. In 1871, a year after the death of Moshesh, the British gave control of Basutoland to Cape Colony. Between 1880 and 1882 Cape Colony troops waged the Gun wars, a series of military campaigns, to disarm Basutoland's inhabitants who had rebelled against Cape Colony rule. The effort failed, and Cape Colony abandoned the territory. In 1884 Basutoland became a British High Commission Territory.

The British administered the territory through a resident commissioner who rarely acted contrary to the wishes of the paramount chief. Basuto traditional law endured under British rule.

Basutoland's economic affairs were tied to South Africa, and until 1948 Britain assumed that South Africa would eventually incorporate Basutoland. Union with South Africa was unacceptable to Basutoland, however, because of South Africa's policy of apartheid, or rigid separation of the races.

Nationalism. In the 1950s the Basutoland African Congress, an African nationalist organization, campaigned for Basutoland's independence. The Congress also sought support from Britain and the United Nations to lessen Basutoland's economic dependence on South Africa.

In 1964 Britain abolished the High Commission, and appointed a representative to Basutoland. On Oct. 4, 1966 Basutoland became an independent member of the Commonwealth. The new nation, renamed Lesotho, was led by the Basuto paramount chief, Moshoeshoe II. In 1967 the king accepted the role of a constitutional monarch, and Prime Minister Leabua Jonathon acquired greater executive powers.

—Hibberd V. B. Kline, Jr.;
Gary A. Weissman

LIBERIA

Official name: Republic of Liberia
Area: 43,000 square miles
Population: (1966 est.) 1,090,000
Capital: Monrovia (Pop., 1962, 80,992)
Language: English, African languages
Religion: Christianity, Islam, traditional religions
Currency unit: U.S. Dollar
National holiday: Independence day, July 26

Liberia, a republic in western Africa, is bordered on the north by Guinea, on the east by the Ivory Coast, on the south by the Atlantic Ocean, and on the west by Sierra Leone. Liberia declared itself a sovereign nation in 1847.

THE LAND. Most of Liberia is occupied by hills and low uplands. The country has a rocky coastline, beyond which are swampy plains. In the north, along the border with Guinea, are the grass-covered Nimba Mountains, with elevations of about 4,500 feet. The Lofa, St. Paul, St. John, and Cess rivers flow through the country.

Liberia is one of the rainiest areas in western Africa. The rainy season extends from May through October. Rainfall averages more than 140 inches a year in the coastal region and over 100 inches a year in the interior of the country.

COUNTRIES OF THE WORLD

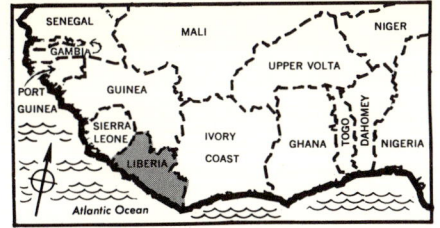

THE PEOPLE. There are two distinct population groups in Liberia—the Americo-Liberians, descended from Negroes brought to Liberia from the United States during the 1800s, and the tribal peoples, who form the majority of Liberia's people. Liberia's indigenous tribes include the Kru, Mandingo, Gola, Vai, and Kissi.

The major cities of Liberia are Monrovia, Buchanan, and Harper, all of which are ports.

ECONOMY. Liberia's economy is based on subsistence agriculture, mining, and rubber growing. The people raise cassava, rice, palm fruit, and bananas for local consumption.

Liberia exported only palm oil products, coffee, and cassava until 1926, when the Firestone Rubber Company established rubber plantations in Liberia and loaned the government capital for development. In the 1960s other private companies established rubber plantations in Liberia, and in 1965 over 52.6 million tons of rubber were exported.

Liberia is a major producer of iron ore, and in 1965 over 10 million metric tons of ore were exported. There are iron ore deposits in the Bomi Hills, some 45 miles northwest of Monrovia, in the Nimba Mountains, and in other places.

In the 1950s a railroad built from Monrovia to the ore deposits at Bomi Hills made possible the export of high-grade iron ore. Ore mined in the Nimba Mountains travels by rail to Buchanan for export.

Liberia also has deposits of many other minerals, including gold, diamonds, and lead.

In 1965 Liberia's imports cost $104.5 million and exports earned over $130 million. Liberia's main imports are food, fuels, and machinery. The main exports are iron ore and natural rubber. Most trade is conducted with the United States, West Germany, Britain, and Italy. Liberia receives economic assistance from the United States.

GOVERNMENT. Liberia has a presidential system of government. Executive power is held by a president, who is popularly elected to an initial eight-year term and is eligible for reelection to four-year terms.

Legislative powers rest with a Senate and a House of Representatives. The Senate is composed of 18 members elected by universal suffrage to six-year terms. The house has 52 members popularly elected to four-year terms.

Liberia is a member of the United Nations and the Organization of African Unity.

HISTORY. Europeans began establishing trading posts in Liberia in the 1400s. In 1822 the American Colonization Society began to settle freed slaves from the United States in Liberia. Malaria killed most of the original colonizers, but several new groups followed. They negotiated treaties with the native tribes, until consolidation of the land was completed in 1838.

Agents of the American Colonization Society administered the region until July 26, 1847, when Liberia declared its independence. Most world powers quickly recognized the new nation's independence, but the United States withheld recognition until 1862. Liberia established a government modeled after that of the United States.

In the early 1900s Liberia was faced with a financial crisis when the world-market price for its coffee dropped. Liberia sought the aid of foreign countries. In 1926 the Firestone Rubber Company leased large land areas from Liberia which provided the country with an important source of revenue. In the 1930s a League of Nations study of labor conditions uncovered widespread forced labor which resulted in the resignation of Liberia's president, Charles D. B. King.

During World War II U.S. soldiers built the first roads into the interior, and in 1948 the first modern port opened at Monrovia, built with U.S. money.

William V. S. Tubman was elected president in 1943 for an eight-year term. Tubman was reelected in 1951, 1955, 1959, 1963, and 1967 without much opposition to his True Whig Party, the governing party in Liberia for over 100 years.

Tubman ended the Firestone company's monopoly by inaugurating an open-door policy to international investment, thus beginning the development of the country's rich resources of iron ore. Tubman has also had some success in bringing tribal Liberians into the modern economy.
—Hibberd V. B. Kline, Jr.; Vera L. Zolberg

LIBYA

Official name: Kingdom of Libya
Area: 679,362 square miles
Population: (1967 est.) 1,738,000
Capitals: Tripoli (Pop., 1964, 213,506); Benghazi (Pop., 1964, 137,295)
Language: Arabic
Religion: Islam
Currency unit: Pound
National holiday: Independence day, December 24

Libya, a kingdom in northern Africa, is bordered on the north by the Mediterranean Sea, on the east by the United Arab Republic (Egypt) and Sudan, on the south by Chad and Niger, and on the west by Algeria and Tunisia. Libya is made up of three historic regions—Tripolitania in the northwest, Cyrenaica in the northeast, and the Fezzan in the southwest.

THE LAND. Libya is almost entirely desert. Less than 2 percent of the land is cultivated, and less than 1 percent is forested.

The Gulf of Sidra (Sirte) divides Libya's Mediterranean coast into two major segments, northern Tripolitania in the west and northern Cyrenaica in the east. There are oases in the coastal region separated from each other by sand dunes and salt marshes. There are highlands beyond the coast, including the Jabal Nafusah in Tripolitania and the Al Jabal al Akhdar in Cyrenaica.

THE LIBYAN DESERT is being held back by the planting of thatch grass from Tunisia.

The Sahara has many landscapes, three of which are important in Libya—upland bare rock surfaces, as in the Hammadah al Hamra in southern Tripolitania; gravel-covered plains, as in the Sarir Tibasti in the south; and areas of extensive sand dunes, as in the Idehan Marzug in the Fezzan and the Sand Sea of Calanscio of northeastern Cyrenaica.

There are few oases in southern and eastern Libya. Oases are more common in the southwestern Fezzan, where they are usually formed by springs and wells in valleys and at the foot of escarpments.

Libya does not have any year-round rivers, but there are dry water routes in many parts of the country. There are deep, salty lakes in Libya, the largest of which is Arrashia, in Cyrenaica. Rainfall averages about 14 inches a year along the Mediterranean coast. There is virtually no rainfall in the desert regions.

THE PEOPLE. Most of the people in Libya are Arabic-speaking Muslims of mixed Arab and Berber origin. There are also some Berber-speaking peoples in northern Libya and in the desert region. Italians form the largest European community in Libya.

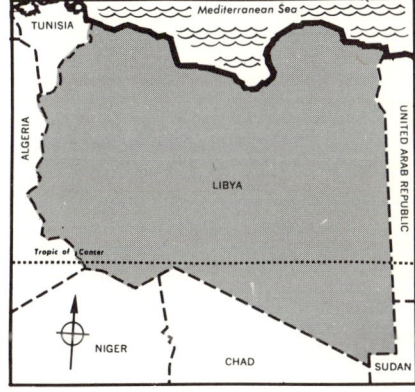

Libya is one of Africa's least densely populated countries. Only at oases in the Sahara and near the borders of the Mediterranean Sea is permanent human habitation possible. Many of the people are nomads, who must move about in the desert in search of grazing land for their flocks. Most of the cities and towns are concentrated in the coastal region. Libya's largest cities are Tripoli and Benghazi.

ECONOMY. The modern economy of Libya is based on oil production. The traditional economy is based on dates and other produce of the coast and oases, flocks and herds raised by the nomads, the catch of Mediterranean fishermen, and the handicrafts of urban dwellers.

Since 1959 economic life has been almost completely altered by the production of petroleum, particularly from the Zelten and Dahra fields, both of which have pipelines leading to the Gulf of Sidra. In 1966 Libya produced more than 72 million metric tons of petroleum.

The majority of the population is engaged in subsistence farming. Barley, date palms, citrus fruits, and peanuts are grown, mostly in the coastal region, where there is sufficient rainfall for crops. Date palms are also grown in the desert oases. Sheep, camels, and goats are raised by nomads, mainly in Cyrenaica.

Libya's industry centers on the production and processing of its oil and its agricultural products. There are canneries in Tripolitania that process fish caught in the coastal waters.

In 1966 Libya's imports cost $405 million and exports earned $995 million. The country's main imports are chemicals, manufactured goods, textiles, iron and steel, and machinery. Although Libya's chief export is petroleum, hides, and skins, peanuts, and fruits are also exported. Most trade is conducted with France, West Germany, Italy, the Netherlands, and Britain.

GOVERNMENT. Libya is a constitutional monarchy. The king is head of state and executive power is vested in him. The king appoints a prime minister, who serves as head of government.

Legislative power is exercised by the king in conjunction with a parliament. Parliament consists of the Senate, with 24 members appointed by the king to eight-year terms, and the House of Representatives, in which there is one deputy for every 20,000 inhabitants. House members are popularly elected to four-year terms.

Libya is a member of the United Nations, the Organization of African Unity, and the Arab League.

HISTORY. Libya's three main regions have had a separate existence for most of the country's history. Even after the Arab conquest of the region in the mid-600s, Cyrenaica was administered for the most part from Egypt, and Tripolitania was administered by dynasties in northwestern Africa. The Fezzan has also had its own distinctive history. Regional differences are still important in modern-day Libya.

Ottoman Era. Libya came under the rule of the Ottoman Turks in the 1500s. For over a century, from 1711 to 1835, a local dynasty, the Qaramanli, controlled Tripoli. In the early 1800s the United States fought against the bey, or governor, of Tripoli, whose pirates were raiding U.S. ships.

European nations united to eliminate piracy in the Barbary States—Tripoli in Libya plus Algiers and Tunis to the west—thus cutting off one of the major sources of government revenue. The Qaramanli regime declined, and the Ottoman government reestablished direct control of Tripoli in 1835.

Italian Rule. In the mid-1800s a Muslim leader, Muhammad bin Ali al-Sanusi, created the Sanusian religious brotherhood, which soon became the most important social and political force in Cyrenaica and the Fezzan. In 1911 Italy wrested control of Libya from the Ottoman Empire after a short war and the Sanusiya served as the focal point of resistance to Italian colonialism.

During World War II major battles were fought in Libya. The North African campaigns virtually wiped out the Italian colonial settlements, and after the war a defeated Italy was stripped of its colonies. A deadlock over which major power should assume trusteeship for Libya led to the decision to give the former colony complete independence.

Independence. The Sanusiya had cooperated with the Allied powers in fighting the Axis, and it was the strongest political force in Libya. The Sanusian chief, Idris, grandson of the order's founder, became king when Libya attained independence in December 1951.

From 1951 to 1963 Libya was a federal state composed of its three major regions. In 1963 Libya became a unified state.

—Hibberd V. B. Kline, Jr.;
L. Carl Brown

LIECHTENSTEIN

Official name: Principality of Liechtenstein
Area: 61 square miles
Population: (1965 est.) 19,000
Capital: Vaduz (Pop., 1961 est., 3,514)
Language: Alemannic
Religion: Roman Catholicism
Currency unit: Swiss franc
National holiday: January 23

Liechtenstein is a very small independent principality located on the border between Austria and Switzerland. It extends no more than 16 miles from north to south and 7 miles from east to west.

THE LAND. The Alps dominate the country's landscape in the east, rising to over 8,000 feet. Western Liech-

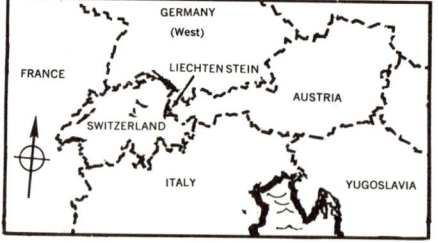

tenstein lies in the valley of the Rhine River, which flows along the country's western border. Winters are long and cold, but summers are mild.

THE PEOPLE. Liechtenstein's population is concentrated in the Rhine Valley, where Vaduz, the capital and only large town, is located. The people speak Alemannic, a Germanic dialect. More than 90 percent of the population is Roman Catholic. During the 1950s and 1960s large numbers of foreign workers, mostly from southern Europe, swelled the population.

ECONOMY. Liechtenstein's economy was once based almost entirely on agriculture, but by the mid-1900s industry had become the main source of income. Cattle, dairy foods, corn, fruit, and potatoes are the leading farm products.

Liechtenstein's hydroelectric power resources, good transportation facilities, and skilled labor force combine to attract industry. Liechtenstein's major manufactured products include precision instruments, small machine parts, pharmaceuticals, and false teeth. Textiles, ceramics, leather goods, and processed foods are also produced.

A large portion of the country's income consists of registration fees paid by foreign companies which incorporate in the principality because of its favorable tax policies. The sale to collectors of postage stamps also contributes to the economy, as does tourism, which increased greatly during the 1950s and 1960s.

Liechtenstein has a favorable balance of trade, as its exports earn a great deal and it must import only a few items. It trades heavily with western Europe and the United States, and it has a customs union with Switzerland.

GOVERNMENT. Liechtenstein is a constitutional monarchy ruled by a prince of the house of Liechtenstein. A head of government, an assistant head, and two councilors, all appointed by the prince, are responsible to a 15-member, popularly elected parliament. Switzerland represents the country's interests abroad.

HISTORY. In ancient times, Liechtenstein's territory was part of the Roman province of Rhaetia. During the 1300s and 1400s the Holy Roman Empire's county of Vaduz and barony of Schellenburg were united under a single count, and by 1712 this feudal state had come into the possession of the Liechtenstein family.

In 1719 the Holy Roman Emperor granted the fief to the family as the Principality of Liechtenstein, and at the dissolution of the Holy Roman Empire in 1806 it became fully independent. Since then, to secure protection, diplomatic representation, and trade advantages, it has become associated with a succession of other states, including those of the Flemish Confederation, the German Confederation, and Austria-Hungary.

In 1919, after Austria-Hungary's defeat in World War I, Switzerland agreed to represent Liechtenstein abroad. In 1921 Liechtenstein established a democratic form of government, adopted Swiss currency, and entrusted postal and telecommunications services to Switzerland. In 1924 the two countries formed a customs union.

Liechtenstein avoided involvement in World War II. The country concentrated on developing its economy, and by the mid-1960s its people enjoyed a high level of prosperity. During the 1960s Liechtenstein began to meet formally with other small European states to discuss matters of mutual concern.

—Sergio Barzanti

LUXEMBOURG

Official name: Grand Duchy of Luxembourg
Area: 998 square miles
Population: (1966 est.) 335,000
Capital: Luxembourg (Pop., 1965 est., 78,721)
Language: Letzeburgesch (Luxembourgish), French, German
Religion: Roman Catholicism
Currency unit: Franc
National holiday: Grand Duke's birthday, June 23

Luxembourg, one of the smallest countries of Europe, is bordered on the north and west by Belgium, on the east by West Germany, and on the south by France.

In 1922 Luxembourg and Belgium formed an economic union that abolished the customs frontier between them. The union was dissolved in 1940, but was reestablished in 1945. In 1948 a customs union went into effect among Luxembourg, Belgium, and the Netherlands, which is known as the Benelux Customs Union. Full economic union of the three countries has existed since 1960.

THE LAND. The southern third of Luxembourg is part of the Lorraine Plateau and consists of rolling plains. The northern two-thirds of the country is part of the Ardennes and is hilly and wooded. Its principal river is the Sauer.

Luxembourg has a cool, temperate, rainy climate. Winters are mild and summers cool, with summer temperatures averaging 60°F. Precipitation averages about 30 inches a year.

THE PEOPLE. Luxembourgers are a mixture of nationalities—primarily French, Dutch, German, and Belgian. The official languages are French and German, but Letzeburgesch, a Germanic dialect, is the national language. More than 95 percent of the people are Roman Catholic. The only important urban center is the capital, Luxembourg.

ECONOMY. The mainstay of Luxembourg's economy is the iron and steel industry. There are large iron ore deposits in southwestern Luxembourg, and there is coal nearby in Germany. This combination has made Luxembourg one of western Europe's major iron and steel producers. Other important industries include distilling and tanning.

About one-fifth of the labor force is employed in agriculture, which is the major occupation in the hilly, sparsely settled, northern two-thirds of the country. Livestock is raised, and the principal crops are potatoes, wheat, barley, and wine grapes. Domestic production meets most of Luxembourg's food needs.

The iron and steel industry provides about 85 percent of Luxembourg's exports. Major imports include fuels, motor vehicles and parts, machinery, and a variety of manufactured goods. Luxembourg's major trading partners are Belgium, West Germany, France, and the Netherlands.

GOVERNMENT. Luxembourg is a constitutional monarchy with a grand duke as chief of state. Executive power is exercised by the grand duke and the Council of Government. The council, or cabinet, is headed by a minister of state, or prime minister. Legislative power rests with the Chamber of Deputies, which is directly elected to a term of five years. The Council of State, an advisory body of elder statesmen appointed by the grand duke, deliberates on proposed legislation and expresses its opinion on other matters referred to it, but its decisions can be overruled by the Chamber of Deputies.

In addition to being part of Benelux, Luxembourg is a member of the European Economic Community, the United Nations, and the North Atlantic Treaty Organization (NATO).

HISTORY. The name Luxembourg is derived from the castle of Lützelburg, the seat of Count Siegfried I, under whose sway several lands were united in the 900s. The size of the country gradually increased under a series of able rulers. In 1308 Count Henry of Luxembourg became Holy Roman Emperor. In 1354 his grandson, Emperor Charles IV, expanded Luxembourg's territories considerably and made it a duchy.

Luxembourg was conquered by Philip the Good of Burgundy in 1443. In 1477 it passed to the Hapsburgs through marriage, and in 1555 Philip II of Spain received it from Charles V as part of the Low Countries. Luxembourg was conquered by Louis XIV and ruled by France until 1697, when it was restored to Spain.

It was ruled by Austria from 1714 until 1795, when it again came under French rule. Luxembourg was annexed to the French Republic and subsequently became a part of the Napoleonic empire. At the Congress of Vienna (1814–1815) Luxembourg was made a grand duchy, ruled by William I, who was also king of the newly created Kingdom of the Netherlands.

Luxembourg was associated with Belgium when it seceded from the Netherlands in 1830, but in 1839 part of the country merged with Belgium and the rest remained an independent grand duchy under the personal rule of the Netherlands' king.

Lacking economic ties with the Netherlands, Luxembourg became associated with the German states, and in 1866, upon dissolution of the German Confederation, Luxembourg was neutralized, and the crown passed to Grand Duke Adolphe of Nassau.

Modern Luxembourg. Luxembourg was invaded by the Germans in 1914, at the outbreak of World War I, and it remained under German occupation throughout the war. Luxembourg's neutrality was violated again in World War II, when German troops occupied the Low Countries in 1940. Grand Duchess Charlotte and the cabinet carried on a government-in-exile in London and Montreal, Canada. The country was liberated in 1944.

In 1945 Luxembourg became one of the charter members of the United Nations. In 1949 the country abandoned its traditional position of neutrality and became a member of the North Atlantic Treaty Organization (NATO). Luxembourg and five other European countries formed the European Coal and Steel Community in 1952, and in 1958 the country became a member of the European Common Market and Euratom.

In 1964 Grand Duchess Charlotte, who had reigned since 1919, abdicated in favor of her son, Grand Duke Jean.

—Sergio Barzanti

MADAGASCAR

Official name: Malagasy Republic
Area: 226,658 square miles
Population: (1966 est.) 6,200,000
Capital: Tananarive (Pop., 1965 est., 321,654)
Language: Malagasy, French
Religion: Christianity, traditional religions
Currency unit: Franc CFA (African Financial Community)
National holiday: Proclamation of the republic, October 14

The Malagasy Republic is an island nation in the Indian Ocean, some 240 miles off the southeastern coast of Africa. Its territory consists of the large island of Madagascar and several small, adjacent islands. Madagascar received its independence from France in 1960.

THE LAND. Madagascar is about 1,000 miles long and 360 miles at its greatest width. Most of the island is dominated by a great interior highland, which has an average elevation of about 4,000 feet above sea level.

The highlands contain deep canyons and volcanic mountains, with elevations as high as about 9,400 feet. Steep cliffs border the highlands, especially in the east. The island's major rivers are the Mangoky, Betsiboka, and Mania.

Easterly winds, which blow all the year on the eastern cliffs, bring heavy rains to eastern Madagascar, but it is dry to the west of the cliffs and in the south.

THE PEOPLE. Madagascar's indigenous population is made up of 18 different ethnic groups. The largest is the Hova, or Merina, who live mainly in the central highlands and are important in the political life of the country. The Betsileo people also live in the central highlands.

Other important groups include the Betsimisaraka, in east-central Madagascar; the Sakalava, in the western part of the island; and the Bara, a

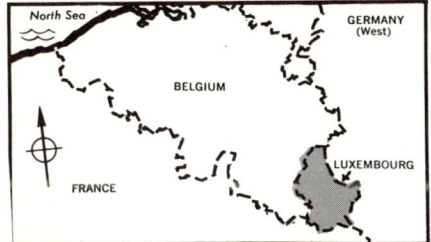

pastoral people who live in southern Madagascar.

The country's largest city is its capital, Tananarive, which is situated in the highlands.

ECONOMY. The economy of Malagasy has suffered because of its isolation. Madagascar's economy is based on agriculture. Coffee, vanilla, rice, sugar, and cloves are the principal crops. Although mineral resources are not well developed, Madagascar is a major producer of graphite. The island also has deposits of mica. There is little industry.

In 1967 Madagascar's imports cost $145 million and exports earned $104 million. The country's major imports include manufactured goods, especially textiles and iron and steel, machinery, petroleum products, and food. Major exports include coffee, vanilla, sugar and tobacco. Most trade is conducted with France, West Germany, and the United States. Malagasy receives economic assistance from France.

GOVERNMENT. Madagascar has a presidential system of government. Executive power rests with a president, elected by universal suffrage to a seven-year term.

Legislative powers are held by a 107-member National Assembly and a 54-member Senate. Assembly members are popularly elected to five-year terms. In the Senate, 36 members are elected by provincial electoral colleges and 18 members are appointed by the president. Senators serve six-year terms.

The Malagasy Republic is a member of the United Nations and the Organization of African Unity.

HISTORY. Arab traders established small, feudal principalities along the Madagascar coast as early as the 1000s or 1100s. In the 1500s and 1600s Dutch, French, and British merchants established trading and supply posts on the island as part of their routes to India. Buccaneers established a short-lived republic on the island in the 1700s.

During the 1500s and 1600s the indigenous peoples were involved in civil wars. Confederations and military commands were established on the island, but most collapsed because of internal strains or the rebellion of subjugated peoples. In the central plateau, however, the Hova people gradually expanded the area under their control.

In the early 1800s a Hova king, Radama I, brought European advisers to his court, welcomed missionaries, and instituted education in the Malagasy language. Later rulers played the British and the French off against each other. In 1890 French claims to Madagascar were recognized by Britain, and in 1896 Madagascar became a French colony. France abolished the Hova monarchy and exiled the Queen. By 1904 the French had established their control over the entire island.

Modern Madagascar. Short-lived nationalist movements emerged briefly during World War I and again in the 1920s. In 1947 discontent over land confiscation and the periodic imposition of involuntary labor led to a serious revolt. France suppressed the revolt and took steps to develop Madagascar's economy, but at the same time it prohibited political activity.

In 1956 France changed its policy and permitted political activity in all French African colonies. Of the several political parties that emerged in Madagascar, the nationalist Social Democratic Party (PSD) won most local elections.

In October 1958, under the leadership of the PSD headed by Philibert Tsiranana, Madagascar became an autonomous republic within the French Community. Tsiranana became head of a provisional government formed in 1958, and in May 1959 he was elected president. In June 1960 the country became independent as the Malagasy Republic. Tsiranana was re-elected president in 1965.

—Hibberd V. B. Kline, Jr.; Gary A. Weissman

MALAWI

Official name: Republic of Malawi
Area: 46,066 square miles
Population: (1966 est.) 4,035,000
Capital: Zomba (Pop., 1966, 19,000)
Language: English, African languages
Religion: Christianity, Islam
Currency unit: Pound
National holiday: Independence day, July 6

Malawi, a republic in southern Africa, is bordered on the north and northeast by Tanzania, on the southeast, southwest, and south by Mozambique, and on the west by Zambia. Malawi, formerly called Nyasaland, received its independence from Britain in 1964.

THE LAND. Most of Malawi is occupied by mountains and plateaus. Because of its rugged terrain, Malawi has been described as "Switzerland without snow." The Great Rift Valley runs through Malawi in a north-south line. Lake Nyasa, or Malawi, which stretches along the eastern border, lies in the valley. The Shire River, the lake's outlet, flows southward into Mozambique.

West of the lake the land climbs steeply to a plateau with elevations between 4,000 and 7,000 feet. The Shire Highlands are south of Lake Malawi. East of the Shire River is Mt. Mlanje, which has an elevation of about 9,800 feet.

The lake region of Malawi has a generally hot, humid climate. Temperatures throughout the rest of the country vary with differences in altitude.

THE PEOPLE. Most of Malawi's people are Bantu-speaking. The largest groups, the Nyanja and Yao, live mainly near Lake Malawi. The Nyanja are descendants of early inhabitants of Malawi. There are also communities of Europeans and Asians.

Zomba, in southern Malawi, and Lilongwe and Blantyre, in the central part of the country, are Malawi's largest cities.

ECONOMY. The economy of Malawi is based on agriculture. Malawi's resources cannot support its population, and many workers find employment in nearby countries. Basic food crops include corn, millet, cassava, peanuts, and rice. Commercial crops include cotton, tobacco, and tea.

There is no mining or manufacturing of any significance in the country. The Shire Highlands is the key economic region of the country. In 1963 construction was begun on a hydroelectric plant on the Shire River. Malawi's landlocked position and its limited transportation system have slowed economic development.

In 1966 Malawi's imports cost $75.8 million and its exports earned $48.6 million. The major imports are manufactured goods, especially textiles and iron and steel, chemicals, petroleum products, and machinery. Exports include cotton, tobacco, tea, and peanuts. Most of Malawi's trade is with Britain and Rhodesia. Malawi receives economic aid from Britain.

GOVERNMENT. Malawi has a presidential system of government. Executive power is held by a president, who is elected to a five-year term. Legislative power is held by a National Assembly elected to a five-year term. Fifty of the assembly's members are elected by universal suffrage, and five are appointed by the president.

Malawi is a member of the United Nations, the Commonwealth of Nations, and the Organization of African Unity.

HISTORY. Malawi owes its name to the Malawi, or Maravi, people who entered the area in the 1500s. Portuguese explorers in the mid-1500s believed them to be the rulers of a vast empire. The western shore of Lake Malawi became a popular route for Bantu-speaking immigrants entering central Africa from the north, and by the 1800s the area's dense population made it a favorite target for Arab slave-raiders.

European interest in present-day Malawi originated in the 1870s, after the explorations of David Livingstone and other Scottish missionaries who were anxious to put an end to the slave trade. In 1889 missionary pressure for governmental action against the Arab slave traders and the threat of Portuguese occupation led Britain to declare the area the British Central Africa Protectorate.

Cecil Rhodes' British South Africa Company financed the region's administration in the early years of the protectorate, but a dispute over political control led the British government to accept complete responsibility for the territory. In 1907 the name of the area was changed to Nyasaland.

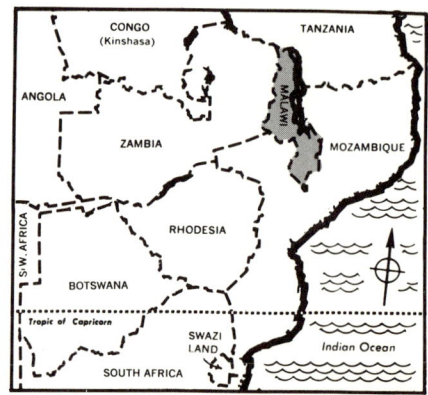

Nationalism. African nationalist movements developed early in Nyasaland, organized by politically conscious laborers returning from work in the mines of Northern Rhodesia (present-day Zambia), Southern Rhodesia, and South Africa. Because of resentment of British colonial policies and fear of federation with the Rhodesias, nationalists formed the Nyasaland African Congress in 1944.

In 1951 the Congress leadership demanded self-government for Nyasaland. Two years later, however, against African sentiment, Britain joined the two Rhodesias and Nyasaland into the Federation of Rhodesia and Nyasaland.

The nationalists, under the leadership of Dr. Hastings Banda, attracted wide support denouncing the federation. Britain finally agreed to an African elected majority in the Nyasaland legislative council, and in elections held in 1961 Dr. Banda's Malawi Congress Party won an impressive victory.

Independence. Britain formally dissolved the federation in 1963, and on July 6, 1964 the country became independent with Banda as its prime minister.

In 1966 Malawi became a republic, and Banda became the first president. In 1967 Malawi signed a trade agreement with South Africa, despite South Africa's policy of apartheid and the opposition of other African countries.

—Hibberd V. B. Kline, Jr.;
Gary A. Weissman

MALAYSIA

Official name: Malaysia
Area: 128,400 square miles
Population: (1966 est.) 9,725,000
Capital: Kuala Lumpur (Pop., 1963, 1,258,894)
Language: Malay, Chinese
Religion: Islam, Buddhism
Currency unit: Dollar
National holiday: National day, August 31

Malaysia, a federal state in Southeast Asia formed in 1963, includes Malaya, on the southern end of the Malay peninsula, and Sarawak and Sabah, on the island of Borneo. Singapore was a member of the federation between 1963 and 1965. West Malaysia, on the Malay Peninsula, and East Malaysia, on Borneo, lie more than 400 miles apart, separated by the South China Sea.

West Malaysia is bordered on the north by Thailand, on the east by the South China Sea, on the south, across the narrow Johore Straits, by Singapore, and on the west by the Strait of Malacca. East Malaysia is bordered on the north by the South China Sea, on the east by the Sulu Sea, on the south by Indonesia, and on the west by Indonesia and the South China Sea. The British protectorate of Brunei forms an enclave in Sarawak.

THE LAND. West Malaysia consists of a narrow central core of low, jungle-covered mountains rimmed by swampy mineral-rich coastal plains. East Malaysia has a mountainous interior and a narrow border of swampy coastal plains. Small islands lie off the coasts of both West and East Malaysia. Of the many rivers that thread Malaysia,

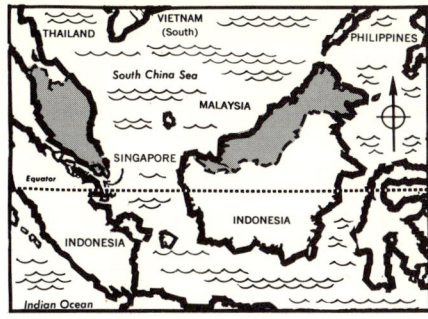

the most important are the Pahang, in West Malaysia, and the Rajang, in East Malaysia.

The Malaysian climate is equatorial. The year-round temperature averages 80°F, and an annual average of 100 inches of rain falls on the country as a whole.

THE PEOPLE. The Malaysian population is quite varied. Just under half of the people are Muslim Malays, who speak Malay. Slightly more than one-third are Chinese. The Chinese are primarily urban; the Malays are predominantly rural. Indians and Pakistanis make up about 10 percent of the population, and the remainder consists of a variety of native islanders, mostly in east Malaysia.

Population is concentrated in the coastal regions. It is densest in the western half of West Malaysia, where the country's largest cities are located —Kuala Lumpur, the federation's capital, Ipoh, and Georgetown, a port city on Penang Island in the Malacca Strait. Malaysia's population is growing at a rapid rate, estimated at 3 percent a year between 1958 and 1965.

ECONOMY. Malaysia has a prosperous and growing economy, due largely to its wealth of natural resources, especially rubber and tin. Malaysia is the world's leading producer of natural rubber, with an output of almost 1 million metric tons in 1965. Most rubber comes from West Malaysia.

Malaysia's abundance of high-grade tin ore, concentrated on the west coast of the Malay peninsula, has made it the world's largest producer of tin, mining 70,000 metric tons in 1966. Forests cover more than 75 percent of Malaysian territory and are one of the country's most valuable resources, supplying timber, palm oil, pepper, hemp, and coconut products. Bauxite, iron ore, and petroleum are also found in Malaysia.

Rubber processing and tin smelting are the country's major industries. In an effort to lessen its economic dependence on two commodities—rubber and tin—which fluctuate sharply in value, the government in the mid-1960s encouraged the development of diversified manufacturing industries.

Very little of Malaysia's cultivable land is devoted to subsistence crops. Rice paddies, concentrated in the coastal lowlands, account for most of the farmland, and the country's farmers raise less than half of the rice they need. Fish, the other staple of the Malaysian diet, are abundant off the coasts.

Malaysia has a favorable balance of trade, with West Malaysia making a much larger contribution to the country's trade than East Malaysia. In 1966 imports cost about $1.1 billion, of which West Malaysia accounted for $860 million, and exports earned nearly $1.3 billion, of which West Malaysia accounted for more than $1 billion.

Rubber and tin represent over half the value of exports, which also include timber and other forest products. Foodstuffs (mainly rice), textiles, and machinery are imported. Britain, the United States, Singapore, and Japan are Malaysia's chief trading partners.

GOVERNMENT. Malaysia is a constitutional monarchy. The Paramount Ruler, or king, is elected to a five-year term by the sultans of the states of West Malaysia. He serves as chief of state and as Muslim religious leader. Actual executive power is wielded by the federation's prime minister and cabinet, who are responsible to a parliament.

The Senate, the upper house of parliament, is partly elected by the state legislatures and partly appointed by the king. The larger, more powerful House of Representatives is popularly elected. Parliament shares legislative power with the state legislatures.

Each member state has a parliamentary government, with a legislature of one house. The member states of the federation are quite powerful.

Malaysia is a member of the United Nations and of the Commonwealth of Nations.

HISTORY. The territory of present-day Malaysia was inhabited in ancient times by Malay peoples who lived in many small coastal kingdoms and whose economies were based on fishing, farming, and trading. From the 800s to the 1200s they were controlled by the Sumatran Buddhist Srivijayan empire, and in the 1300s by the Javanese Hindu kingdom of Majapahit.

In about 1400 a Malay ruler founded the state of Malacca, on the western coast of the peninsula. Its capital, the port city of Malacca in the center of the eastern shore of the Strait of Malacca, soon became the most important trading center in Southeast Asia. During the 1400s Arab traders and missionaries converted the ruler and the people of Malacca to Islam. The state became a center for the spread of Islam throughout the area.

Malacca's port interested European nations that were establishing colonies in Southern Asia in the late 1400s. In 1511 Malacca fell to the Portuguese, but in 1641 the Portuguese were ousted by the Dutch. The Europeans did not develop the territory or attempt to bring all of Malaya under their authority. Malacca gradually declined in importance except as a stopping-off point on the sea route between Asia and Europe.

British Role. In 1795 Britain took Malacca from the Dutch. In 1826 it was consolidated with the British settlements at Penang, at the northern end of the Strait of Malacca, and with Singapore, at the southern end of the peninsula, to form the Colony of the Straits Settlements.

In the mid-1800s an English adventurer, James Brooke, gained control of Sarawak in northwest Borneo. In

1881 a British chartered company took over what is now Sabah in north Borneo. Thus an arc of British influence developed across the northern edge of the island world at the same time that Dutch influence was slowly growing in what is now Indonesia. The Dutch and the British formally apportioned sovereignty over the island world by treaties in 1824 and 1891.

After the opening of the Suez Canal in 1869, Southeast Asian trade became more profitable and important, and competition increased among European states for territory in the region. Also in the late 1800s the wealth of Malaysia's tin mines was realized, and the tin industry there grew prosperous and attracted the interest of the British.

By 1914 Britain had concluded treaties making protectorates of the sultanates on the Malay peninsula. Once the British presence guaranteed their security, Chinese miners poured into Malaya. These workers formed the nucleus of the states' large Chinese minority.

Malaya soon was the world's leading producer and exporter of tin. In the early 1900s the British also developed rubber plantations on the peninsula. The rubber industry was manned largely by Indian labor, and the Malay states soon ranked as the world's leading producer of rubber.

By the 1920s, with a well-ordered government under British administration and a prosperous economy run by Chinese and Indian labor, Malaya was economically, politically, and socially unique in Southeast Asia. The great alien immigration that had left the native Malays and their sultans a bare majority in their own land inhibited the development of nationalist movements.

Malayan nationalism was finally awakened during World War II, when the country was occupied by Japanese forces. Under Japanese direction the Malayans were largely self-governing, and a desire for full independence followed liberation from the Japanese.

In 1948, after two years of an unsatisfactory trial union, the protected Malay states were united to form the Federation of Malaya. In June 1948 guerrilla fighting broke out, instigated by Chinese communists with the support of part of the Malayan Chinese population. Rivalries and conflicts between the Chinese and the Malays within Malaya helped to keep the war going. With the aid of British troops, the federation government gradually defeated the guerrillas.

Independence. In 1957 Malaya was granted full independence under a constitution that attempted to balance carefully the power of the Chinese and the Malay portions of the population.

In 1961 the self-governing British colony of Singapore proposed union with Malaya as a step to ensure its economic position. Malaya agreed on condition that the British colonies on Borneo, with their predominantly Malay population, be admitted to the union to balance Singapore's heavily Chinese population.

In 1963 the union took place, creating the Federation of Malaysia, with Tunku Abdul Rahman as leader of the new state. The inclusion of the Borneo states aroused the opposition of two neighboring states, Indonesia and the Philippines. Each claimed territory in East Malaysia.

The Philippines suspended diplomatic relations, and in 1963 Indonesia began a "Crush Malaysia" campaign. The campaign led to open fighting between 1964 and 1966, when the fall from power of Indonesia's President Sukarno ended Indonesia's opposition to the federation.

Nor did the inclusion of the Borneo states of Sabah and Sarawak balance the power of Singapore's Chinese to the satisfaction of the Malays. In 1965 Singapore reluctantly withdrew from the federation. —M. G. Inaba

MALDIVE ISLANDS

Official name: Maldive Islands
Area: 115 square miles
Population: (1966 est.) 101,000
Capital: Male (Pop., 1965, 11,202)
Language: Maldivian
Religion: Islam
Currency unit: Rupee

The Maldive Islands is an independent island nation occupying an archipelago about 400 miles southwest of Ceylon. The archipelago lies between the Arabian Sea and the Indian Ocean.

THE LAND AND PEOPLE. The country is formed of some 2,000 islands grouped into 12 distinct atolls, or island groups. Most of the islands are very small and low-lying, and only about 220 are inhabited.

The Maldivians are an amalgam of peoples from Ceylon, India, Southeast Asia, the Middle East, and Africa. They speak a language similar to Elu, or old Sinhalese, the language of ancient Ceylon. Almost all the people are Muslim. Population is densest near the center of the group, on Male Atoll, which is the site of the capital and largest city, Male.

ECONOMY. The economy of the Maldive Islands is based on fishing and coconuts. In addition to coconut palms, some fruits and millet are grown. Fishing is the main activity, and dried bonito, called Maldive fish, is the country's chief product. Coconuts are processed for their oil, fibers, and other products.

Dried fish and coconut products are ported. The country relies heavily on Rice and other necessities must be imported. The country relies heavily on foreign assistance, primarily from Britain.

GOVERNMENT. The Maldive Islands is a constitutional monarchy. A sultan, or king, is elected for life. The popularly elected legislature, the Majlis, has one house. A prime minister appointed by the sultan with the consent of the Majlis heads the government.

The country is a member of the Commonwealth of Nations and the United Nations.

HISTORY. The Maldive's have been inhabited by peoples of the Indian Ocean region for many centuries. They had strong ties with the island of Ceylon and were long required to pay tribute to the kings of Kandy, in Ceylon. During the 1500s the islands were under the nominal control of Portugal, and during the 1600s they were under Dutch rule.

Britain made Ceylon a crown colony in 1789 and assumed indirect authority over the Maldive Islands. In 1887 the islands became a British protectorate. During World War II, Britain built an important air base on Gan Island, in the southern Addu Atoll.

The 1950s were years of great unrest for the islands. In 1953 the national assembly abolished the sultanate and proclaimed a republic, but in 1954 an insurrection resulted in the restoration of the sultanate. British attempts to reactivate its air base on Gan led to clashes between those opposing and those favoring the British presence in the islands. Moreover, the government was unable to deal with the islands' severe food shortage.

Discontent led in 1959 to an insurrection in Suvadiva, south of Male. A rebel leader declared Suvadiva a republic and requested aid from Britain. Britain granted the aid, arousing strong anti-British feeling in Male. In 1960 the Suvadiva rebellion ended and the British were allowed to reopen their air base.

During the early 1960s the Maldivian government and Britain negotiated the islands' future, and in 1965 a treaty between Britain and the Maldive Islands granted full sovereignty to the country. Britain was allowed to retain control of the Gan Island base and agreed to provide financial and technical aid to relieve the new nation's pressing economic problems. —Sara D. Gilbert

MALI

Official name: Republic of Mali
Area: 463,950 square miles
Population: (1967 est.) 4,745,000
Capital: Bamako (Pop., 1965 est., urban area, 165,000)
Language: French, African languages
Religion: Islam
Currency unit: Franc
National holiday: Independence day, September 22

Mali, a republic in western Africa, is bordered on the north by Algeria, on the east by Niger, on the southeast by Upper Volta, on the south by the Ivory Coast and Guinea, and on the west by Senegal and Mauritania. Mali, long a French territory known as the Soudan, was joined with Senegal from 1959 until 1960 as the Mali Federation. It declared its independence in 1960.

THE LAND. Most of Mali is flat, with areas of low plateaus. The vast desert wasteland of the Sahara occupies the northern third of the country. In the northeast is a mountain region.

The Niger River flows through southern Mali, and the Sénégal River flows from southwestern Mali. The desert region is hot and dry, but the southern part of the country is cooler.

THE PEOPLE. There are many different ethnic groups in Mali. The largest are the Mandingo (including the Bambara, who number over 1 million), Sarakolle, Fula (Fulani), and Malinke. Tuareg live in the desert region. Most of Mali's people are Muslim.

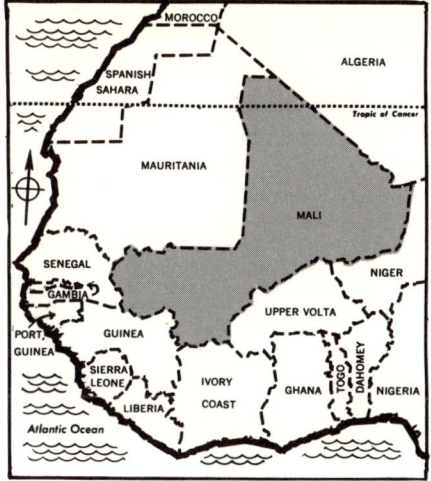

The country's largest cities are Bamako, Mopti, Ségou, and Tombouctou (Timbuktu). All are near the Niger River or its tributaries.

ECONOMY. The economy of Mali is based on agriculture. Millet, rice, and corn are the basic food crops. The principal commercial crops are peanuts and cotton. Fish from the Niger River are an important export. Cattle, sheep, and goats are raised, mainly in central and northern Mali.

The Niger River valley is the most productive region in Mali. There is a large irrigation project on the upper part of the river, and the land near the lower Niger is fertile.

There is little mining, although there are deposits of salt, bauxite, phosphates, manganese, zinc, copper, and gold. There is also little industry, and industrial development is hampered by the country's inaccessibility.

In 1965 imports cost $43 million and exports earned $16 million. Major imports include manufactured goods—especially textiles, iron and steel, and machinery—and sugar. Peanuts, live animals and hides, raw cotton, and fish are Mali's major exports. Most trade is conducted with neighboring countries and with France and the Soviet Union.

GOVERNMENT. Mali has a presidential system of government. Executive power is vested in a president, who is elected to a five-year term. Legislative power is held by the National Assembly. The 80 members of the assembly are elected by universal suffrage to five-year terms.

Mali is a member of the United Nations and the Organization of African Unity (OAU).

HISTORY. In the early 1200s Sundiata, a powerful leader of a group of Mandingo people, defeated Sumanguru, ruler of the Susu people, and created the Mali empire. By the 1300s this empire stretched from the Gambia River to what is now the northwestern border of Nigeria. The people of Mali traded gold from the upper Niger and Sénégal River regions for the salt of the Sahara and luxury goods from northwestern Africa.

In the early 1300s, the old kingdom of Mali's most illustrious ruler, Musa, extended the empire from Niger to the southern Sahara. In the late 1400s the ruler of old Mali was overthrown by the king of the new state of Songhai. The Songhai kings governed the vast area once loyal to Musa until 1591, when a Moroccan army crossed the Sahara and defeated the Songhai. The Moroccan army was not strong enough to control the entire empire, and the territory broke up into smaller city-states.

During the 1800s two Muslim reformers, Ahmadu Lobo and Al-hajj Umar, created Islamic theocracies in the region. The creation of the Islamic states was one phase of a wave of religious revivalism that swept tropical Africa south of the Sahara.

French Rule. France at that time was extending its colonial rule southward from northern Africa, and Al-hajj Umar's state clashed with French forces. By 1880 France had emerged victorious, and in 1895 France formed the colony of the Soudan, which it administered as part of French West Africa. In 1946 this area became a territory, and in 1958 the territory became an autonomous member of the French Community.

In 1959 France joined the Soudan with Senegal to form the Mali Federation, and in June 1960 the federation became an autonomous member of the French Community. Two months later Senegal withdrew from the federation, and on Sept. 22, 1960, the former Soudan withdrew from the French Community and proclaimed itself the Republic of Mali.

Independence. Modibo Keita became the first president of the new republic. In 1963 relations with Senegal were normalized, and work was begun to rehabilitate the railroad linking Mali to the port of Dakar, in Senegal.

—Hibberd V. B. Kline, Jr.;
Robert I. Rotberg

MALTA

Official name: Malta
Area: 122 square miles
Population: (1967 est.) 319,000
Capital: Valletta (Pop., 1965 est., 17,679)
Language: Maltese, English
Religion: Roman Catholicism
Currency unit: Pound
National holiday: Independence day, September 21

Malta is an island nation in the Mediterranean Sea about 60 miles south of Sicily. The country includes the islands of Malta, Comino, and Gozo, and two uninhabited islands.

THE LAND. The Maltese islands are rather flat and consist of limestone rock sparsely covered with a thin layer of soil. There are few trees and no rivers or lakes.

The climate is semitropical, with mild winters and hot summers. An average of 20 inches of rain a year falls on the islands, but the amount varies greatly from year to year.

THE PEOPLE. The Maltese are a Mediterranean people who speak a Semitic language. The population is almost entirely Roman Catholic. Malta's population density is extremely high—about 2,600 persons per square mile in 1967. Emigration, especially since the end of World War II, has been high and directed mainly to Australia, Britain, and Canada.

ECONOMY. Malta is in the process of developing its economy. Its only resources are its people, its geographic location, and the limestone of its rocks.

Agriculture contributed only about 8 percent to the country's domestic product in 1965. Potatoes, tomatoes, grapes, and wheat are the leading crops. Fishing is important.

Industrialization began on Malta in the early 1960s. Manufactures, which accounted for 19 percent of the domestic product in 1965, included textiles, rubber products, and gloves. Processed farm products, especially wine, are also important. Construction and ship repair are Malta's most valuable industries. The main dockyard was long an important British naval installation.

Malta's imports cost about $98 million in 1965 and exports earned only about $24 million. The leading exports are potatoes, wines and processed foods, textiles, and cut flowers. The leading imports are textiles, machinery, foodstuffs, and consumer goods.

GOVERNMENT. Malta is a parliamentary democracy. The head of state is the British monarch, who is represented by a governor-general. Executive power is exercised by a prime minister and cabinet responsible to parliament. The popularly elected parliament has one house.

Malta is a member of the Commonwealth of Nations and the United Nations.

HISTORY. Malta, called Melita in ancient times, and its small sister island, Gozo, were inhabited in prehistoric times by people whose great stone monuments are still in existence. An important refuge for ships following Mediterranean trade routes, the islands were visited by early Phoenicians and Greeks, and in the 200s BC they passed under Carthaginian rule. Malta became a Roman possession in 216 BC. During the first century AD the Maltese adopted Christianity.

After the dissolution of the Roman Empire, Malta passed successively to the Byzantine Empire, the Arabs, Sicily, the kingdom of Aragon, and then to the united kingdoms of Aragon and Castile. In the early 1500s the Holy Roman emperor received Malta from Spain by inheritance, and in 1530 he granted it to the Order of the Hospital of St. John of Jerusalem.

The knights, who served as protectors of religious pilgrims, regarded Malta as an outpost for the defense of Christianity. They withstood attacks by the Muslim Turks, including a long siege in 1565. The island under the knights was supported and protected by the nations of Europe, and it grew prosperous from Mediterranean trade.

The military strength and effectiveness of the order declined during the 1600s and 1700s, and in 1798 Napoleon Bonaparte of France occupied Malta. Two years later, with the aid of the Maltese, a British force drove out the French, and the Maltese requested permanent British protection. In 1814 Malta became a British crown colony and a vital British naval base.

British Rule. The islanders had partial self-government during the 1800s. They were self-governing during the 1920s and 1930s, but two issues sharply divided the island—the choice of Maltese or Italian as an official language and church-state relations. The conflict grew so bitter that Malta's home rule was abolished in 1936.

During World War II, Malta had great strategic value. It withstood heavy German and Italian air bombardments and was a base for the Anglo-U.S. invasion of Sicily in 1943. In 1942 Britain awarded the George Cross to the Maltese people for their bravery during the bombardments.

Independence. After the war the country worked to achieve sufficient unity to allow restoration of complete internal self-government, which it received in 1962. Maltese and English were made the official languages, and Roman Catholicism was declared the official religion of Malta. In 1964 the British granted the country full independence.

Malta concentrated on expanding its economy to end its dependence on the British naval base, which had been its major source of income and which was being closed down. In 1966 a serious Anglo-Maltese conflict arose when Britain announced plans to withdraw its defense forces from the island, but a compromise was reached.

—Charles Nowell

MAURITANIA

Official name: Islamic Republic of Mauritania
Area: 397,955 square miles
Population: (1966 est.) 1,070,000
Capital: Nouakchott (Pop., 1965 est., 15,000)
Language: Arabic
Religion: Islam
Currency unit: Franc CFA
National holiday: Independence day, November 28

Mauritania, a republic in western Africa, is bounded on the north by Algeria, on the east by Mali, on the south by Senegal, and on the west by the Atlantic Ocean and the Spanish Sahara. Mauritania received its independence from France in 1960.

THE LAND. About two-thirds of Mauritania is desert. In the west long lines of sand dunes are separated by broad lowlands. In the north and east rocky desert surfaces are common. There is cultivated land in the southwest, near the Sénégal River, which flows along the country's southwestern border. The climate of Mauritania is generally hot and dry.

THE PEOPLE. Most Mauritanians are nomadic Moors, people of mixed Berber and Arab stock. Negro Muslims live in southern Mauritania, mainly near the Sénégal River, and Tuareg people live in the central part of the country. Mauritania's largest cities are Kaédi, Fort Gourand, Port Étienne, and Nouakchott, the capital.

ECONOMY. Mauritania's economy is based on livestock breeding and agriculture. Sheep, cattle, goats, and camels are raised, mainly in central and northern Mauritania. The only considerable area of cultivated land is in the Chemanna, the Mauritanian part of the Sénégal River valley.

The basic foodcrops are millet, dates, rice, and corn. Acacia trees, the source of gum arabic, are grown in the central part of the country. Fish from the Sénégal River also provide an important source of income.

There is an extremely rich deposit of iron ore at Fort Gouraud, in western Mauritania. In 1963, to export the ore, a 400-mile railroad was built linking Fort Gouraud with Port Étienne, on the Atlantic Ocean. Valuable copper and oil deposits have also been discovered.

In 1964 imports cost $15.7 million and exports earned $45.8 million. The country's major imports are manufactured goods, machinery, and food stuffs. Major exports include live animals, fish, iron ore, copper, and gum arabic. Most trade is conducted with France, the Congo (Brazzaville), the United States, and West Germany.

GOVERNMENT. Mauritania has a presidential system of government. Executive power is held by a president, who is popularly elected to a five-year term. Legislative power is held by a 40-member National Assembly. Assembly members are elected by universal suffrage to five-year terms.

Mauritania is a member of the United Nations and the Organization of African Unity. Mauritania has strong ties with Morocco, based on common backgrounds in religion and language, but relations between the two countries have been complicated by Moroccan claims to Mauritania.

HISTORY. In about the 800s a confederation of nomadic Berbers entered Mauritania from the north and forced the existing Negro population southward. The Berbers adopted Islam in the 900s, but retained many of their traditional beliefs. In the 1000s they united to form the Almoravids (al-Murabitun), which quickly became a powerful religious and political force.

The Almoravids overran Morocco, western Algeria, and Muslim Spain. Their leaders founded the famous city of Marrakech, in Morocco, and established a dynasty which lasted almost 100 years. A branch of the Almoravids went south and conquered the empire of Ghana in 1076. Starting in the 1300s nomadic Arabs migrated into Mauritania, and the region gradually became Arabized.

In the 1800s the French established their control over areas to the north, Morocco and Algeria, and to the south, Senegal and present-day Mali. In the early 1900s, France began to occupy Mauritania. In 1903 it became a French protectorate, and in 1920 a colony, part of French West Africa. But effective French control over the entire country was not achieved until 1934.

In 1946 Mauritania became a territory in the newly formed French Union, and in 1958 an autonomous member of the French community. On Nov. 28, 1960, France granted the country its independence. In 1961 Mokhtar Ould Daddah became Mauritania's first president, and in 1966 he was reelected president.

—Hibberd V. B. Kline, Jr.;
L. Carl Brown

MAURITIUS

Official name: Mauritius
Area: 790 square miles
Population: (1967 est.) 774,000
Capital: Port Louis (Pop., 1965 est., urban area, 129,700)
Language: English, French, Creole
Religion: Hinduism, Islam, Christianity
Currency unit: Rupee

Mauritius is an island nation in the Indian Ocean, about 500 miles east of the island of Madagascar. The country's territory includes the island of Mauritius, Rodrigues Island, and the smaller islands of the Agalega and Cargados Carajors archipelagos.

THE LAND. The islands of Mauritius are volcanic in origin, and Rodrigues rises sharply from the sea. On Mauritius, a 2,200-foot central plateau is rimmed by rocky mountains. Many rivers and streams flow down from the mountains. Rodrigues is mountainous and barren except for some fertile valleys. The Agalega islands are low and fertile, and the Cargados Carajos islands are little more than rocky reefs.

The country's climate is semitropical, with hot summers, cool winters, and high humidity. Rainfall is heavy —from 50 to 200 inches a year on all the islands. Cyclones are a frequent danger, especially between December and April.

THE PEOPLE. The population density of Mauritius is very high—almost 1,000 persons per square mile on Mauritius and Rodrigues in 1966. The population continued to grow rapidly in the 1950s and 1960s, at a rate of 3 percent a year. Malaria, which once slowed population growth, was eliminated in the late 1940s, and population growth soared. In the 1960s family-planning measures were introduced in an effort to reverse the trend.

The people of Mauritius are of varied origins, and the population is rather sharply divided along ethnic lines. Between 65 and 70 percent of the population is Indo-Mauritian, of Indian background; under 5 percent is Sino-Mauritian, of Chinese descent; and about 30 percent, called the "general population," is of European, African, and mixed origins.

English is the official language, but Creole, a French dialect, is the common tongue. Chinese, Hindi, French, and Arabic are also spoken. Slightly less than half the population is Hindu, about 30 percent is Christian, and some 15 percent is Muslim.

COUNTRIES OF THE WORLD

ECONOMY. Mauritius depends almost completely on sugar. During the early 1960s efforts were undertaken to diversify the economy, because of the dangers of a single-crop economy. The island has valuable forest resources, but exploitation of the forests was not begun until the mid-1960s.

The chief crop is sugarcane, grown on over 90 percent of Mauritius' cultivated land in 1965. Tea is the only other important crop, but in the early 1960s, under a program of agricultural diversification, increased acreage was devoted to tobacco, food crops, and livestock, including dairy cattle. Fish catches are abundant.

Sugarcane processing is the leading industry, with sugar and molasses the principal products. Related industries include making fiber bags for the sugar. Newer industries include cigarette-making, tea production, soap manufacture, brewing, and brickmaking.

In 1966 exports earned almost $71 million and imports cost just under $70 million. Sugar accounted for almost 90 percent of exports in 1965, although the percentage declined from the previous year as tea, tobacco, and other goods gained in importance. Foodstuffs, fuels, fats, chemicals, and manufactured goods must be imported. Mauritius relies on British aid to implement its economic development projects.

GOVERNMENT. Mauritius has a parliamentary form of government, with the British monarch as head of state. Actual executive power is wielded by a prime minister and a cabinet responsible to a popularly elected legislature.

HISTORY. Mauritius has been known for many centuries to Arab and Malay sailors, who probably first used it for shelter before 1000. Portuguese sailors landed on the island in the 1500s, but they did not establish settlements. The Dutch, who named the island Mauritius for their ruler, Prince Maurice, attempted to establish a colony but failed.

No successful settlement was made until 1715, when the French East India Company claimed the island for France and renamed it Ile de France. The French began sugar cultivation, using slave labor, and the colony grew prosperous.

In 1767 the French government took control from the company and made the island a naval base for use in France's struggle with Britain for control of India. Britain captured the island in 1810, and in 1814 the Treaty of Paris, which ended the Anglo-French wars, awarded the island to Britain.

British Rule. The island, renamed Mauritius, was Britain's main source of sugar during the 1800s. Few Britons settled there, however, and French cultural influence remained strong. In 1833 Britain abolished slavery on Mauritius, and indentured workers, mostly from India, were brought to work the sugar plantations.

The economy grew increasingly dependent on sugar, which was subject to damage by cyclones and drought and to sharp fluctuations in world market prices.

After 1886 limited home rule was granted to Mauritius. The islands moved gradually toward fuller self-government, led most frequently by the Indo-Mauritians, who had become the dominant political force on the island.

Independence. Seewoosagur Ramgoolam, a leader of the independence movement, was elected the country's first premier after self-government was granted in 1964. In 1967 the Legislative Assembly, dominated by his party, voted to request full independence from Britain. Britain agreed to grant Mauritius its independence effective Mar. 12, 1968.

—Sara D. Gilbert

MEXICO

Official name: United States of Mexico
Area: 761,604 square miles
Population: (1967 est.) 45,671,000
Capital: Mexico City (Pop., 1966 est., 3,287,334)
Language: Spanish
Religion: Roman Catholicism
Currency unit: Peso
National holiday: Independence day, September 16

Mexico, a republic at the southern end of the North American land mass, is bounded on the north by the United States, on the east by the Gulf of Mexico, on the southeast by British Honduras and Guatemala, and on the south and west by the Pacific Ocean.

THE LAND. The physical geography of Mexico is very complex, partly due to the fact that it is formed by both North American and Central American land structures. North American landforms end in the volcanic region south of Mexico City. The mountains of Oaxaca, which lie west of the Isthmus of Tehuantepec, together with all the highlands to the south are Central American.

Eastern Mexico, north of Oaxaca, consists of a coastal plain. This plain is broad near the U.S. border, where it forms a continuation of the Texas Gulf coastal plain, but narrows sharply south of Veracruz, ending with Mt. San Martin, the beginning of the Tabasco coastal lowlands and marshes.

West of the coastal plain are the eroded valleys and peaks of the Sierra Madre Oriental, whose elevations exceed 13,000 feet above sea level. The Sierra Madre Oriental forms the eastern border of the Central Plateau, which is subdivided into a northern and southern region by the Sierra de Zacatecas. The southern region of the Central Plateau contains Mexico City and most of the country's people.

The Sierra Madre Occidental forms a barrier of chasms, canyons, and arid pocket valleys between the central plateau and the narrow Pacific coastal plain. These mountains are so rugged that in Jalisco the land plunges 5,000 feet into the Pacific within a distance of only 275 miles. Only one pass through this range is used extensively for transportation, and Guadalajara, Mexico's second largest city, is located at that strategic point.

A cordillera of volcanic mountains extends from east to west across Mexico south of Mexico City. Peaks like Popocatépetl, over 17,880 feet, and Iztaccíhuatl, over 17,340 feet, are scenically striking, but form a barrier that isolates the southern plateau region from the Balsas Valley to the south.

The Sierra Madre del Sur, to the southwest, forms a barrier between the Balsas Valley and the very narrow Pacific coastal plain. This range runs eastward into Oaxaca and forms a tangled mountain knot west of the Isthmus of Tehuantepec.

The Central American portion of Mexico includes the Tabasco lowlands, the limestone plateau of the Yucatán Peninsula, and the mountain and plateau system of Chiapas, which extends into Mexico from northwestern Guatemala.

The peninsula of southern California is an extension of the coastal range of California and lies across the Gulf of California from northern Mexico.

Climate. As the surface of Mexico is complex, so is the climate, which varies with altitude and wind pattern. Mountain slopes facing the prevailing winds receive more rainfall than the leeward slopes. The highlands are cooler and have less variation in temperature than the lowlands.

Along the western coast of the peninsula of lower California are cold, upwelling Pacific waters which chill the air masses passing over them, inhibiting rainfall. Thus, much of the north and northwest of Mexico is desert. The eastern coastal plain, on the other hand, receives much moisture south of Tamaulipas, where the trade winds encounter the Sierra Madre Oriental.

THE PEOPLE. Approximately 75 percent of the people of Mexico are mestizo, of mixed European and Indian ancestry. About 10 percent of the population is of European descent—primarily Spanish. The remaining 15 percent of the Mexican population is Indian.

Spanish is the official language, but more than 2 million Mexicans speak Indian languages. These fall into more than 30 major linguistic groups and range from Nahautl, or Aztec, and Otomi, which are spoken by large groups of people, to tribal languages spoken by only a few family groups.

The overall Mexican population density of 57 people per square mile is not great, but more than 50 percent of the people live within the Central Plateau, which represents only 14 percent of the national territory. Mexico's population is increasing at a very rapid rate, 3.4 percent a year between 1958 and 1965. But the economy has been developing fast enough to absorb the increase.

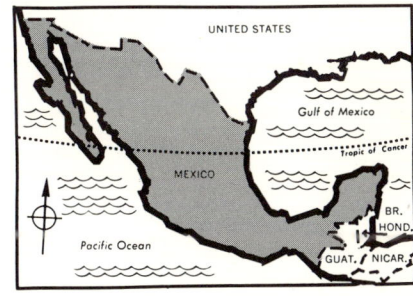

The country's capital, Mexico City, is one of the world's major urban centers. Unlike most major cities in the Western Hemisphere, it is located inland, with no river access to the ocean.

This also is true of Mexico's largest cities, including Guadalajara, which had a 1966 estimated population of 1,105,900; Monterrey, 849,700; Ciudad Juaréz, 415,600; and Puebla, 349,500. Tampico and Veracruz, located on the Gulf of Mexico, are the principal seaports. Mazatlán is the most important seaport on the Pacific coast.

ECONOMY. Mexico has an expanding economy. Between 1960 and 1965 the gross domestic product rose at an annual average rate of 6 percent. While the economy as a whole has been developing steadily, this rise is largely due to the increasingly important role played by industry.

Natural Resources. Mexico is rich in natural resources. It is one of the world's leading producers of silver and ranks high in the production of antimony, graphite, sulfur, mercury, lead, zinc, copper, and gold. The country also mines quantities of iron ore, cadmium, molybdenum, tungsten, manganese, arsenic, and bismuth.

Mexico has an abundance of coal, oil, and natural gas. Production of natural gas increased over 50 percent between 1960 and 1966.

Agriculture. About half of Mexico's labor force is engaged in agriculture, which contributed 17 percent of the gross domestic product in 1965. Agricultural production has been increasing rapidly and more than doubled between 1953 and 1965. This increased production is largely the result of government irrigation projects.

A major share of Mexican farming is devoted to the production of basic food crops such as corn, wheat, beans, and rice. Commercial crops, which are also important, include sugarcane, cotton, coffee, and henequen, a fiber plant.

Industry. The growth of industry has been steady. The contribution made by industry to the gross domestic product rose from 27 percent in 1950 to 32 percent in 1965. In recent years the government has made a concerted effort to develop the manufacture of chemicals, synthetic fibers, plastics, industrial machinery, and automobiles.

In spite of major advances in these areas, Mexico's most important industries are textiles, food processing, and beverages. The country also produces cement, iron and steel, and a variety of consumer goods.

About 40 percent of Mexico's industry is concentrated in the area around Mexico City. Monterrey and Guadalajara are also important industrial centers.

Trade. In 1966 Mexico's exports earned $1,222 million and its imports cost $1,605 million. Mexico usually imports more than it exports, but tourism helps to make up the gap. The country's chief exports include cotton, sugar, coffee, fish, wheat, and metals. Principal imports are chemicals, machinery, appliances, and transportation equipment. Approximately half of Mexico's trade is with the United States.

UNIVERSITY OF MEXICO LIBRARY. The library's murals show themes from Mexico's past.

GOVERNMENT. Mexico is a federal republic composed of 29 states, 2 territories, and a Federal District, in which the capital, Mexico City, is located. The head of state and chief executive is the president, who is directly elected by popular vote to a six-year term. He may not serve more than one term. The president is assisted by a cabinet appointed by him.

Legislative power is vested in the Congress, which consists of the Senate and the Chamber of Deputies. The Senate has 60 members, who are elected to six-year terms. The members of the Chamber of Deputies are directly elected to three-year terms. Senators and deputies may not serve two consecutive terms.

Mexico is a member of the United Nations and the Organization of American States (OAS).

HISTORY. Before Columbus discovered the New World in 1492, Mexico was the site of the greatest Indian civilizations on the North American continent.

The civilization of the Mayas, which was at its height from about 300 BC to 800 AD, was centered in Guatemala and southern Mexico. The Mayas built great cities and were skilled at astronomy and mathematics. They also developed a calendar that was probably more accurate than the one used in Europe at the time, and they had a well-developed system of writing.

In the 800s the Mayas, for unknown reasons, abandoned their cities and reestablished themselves in the Yucatán peninsula. Gradually, however, the Mayas became weakened by attacks made on them from the north by the Toltec Indians of the Central Plateau. By the 1400s Mayan civilization was in decline.

The Toltecs, whose capital was in the Valley of Mexico in the Central Plateau, were subjugated in the early 1400s by the Aztecs, whose original homeland is unknown.

The Aztecs built an empire ruled from their capital, Tenochtitlán, founded in 1325 near the site of present-day Mexico City. Nearly invincible, Tenochtitlán was constructed upon a group of islands in the middle of Lake Texcoco and connected to the mainland by a series of causeways.

In 1517–1518 the Spanish governor of Cuba sent two expeditions to investigate rumors of the existence of mainland civilizations rich in gold. Both expeditions retreated to Cuba after brief and bloody encounters with the Indians. In 1518–1519 Hernán Cortés, undaunted by the failures of his predecessors, undertook the conquest of Mexico with fewer than 600 men.

The conquest of the Aztec empire was accomplished primarily by the skillful use of horses and guns, which terrified the Indians who had never seen them before. In addition, the Indians believed that the light-skinned, bearded Spaniards riding on horses were gods, and Cortés was allowed to enter Tenochtitlán. He captured Montezuma, the Aztec emperor, and by the mid-1500s all Mexico had been subdued.

Spanish Rule. Following the Spanish conquest, the Indians were reduced to the level of slaves. They were forced to work in the mines or on the estates of the Spaniards. Gold and silver were taken from the land with unceasing zeal.

In 1535 Mexico City became the capital of the viceroyalty of New Spain, which included a large part of Central America as well as Mexico. The immediate subordinates of its governor, or viceroy, were the *peninsulares*, Spaniards born in Spain. Native-born Spaniards, known as Creoles, were not permitted to hold high government office.

During the colonial period the Creoles grew to resent the privileged position of the *peninsulares*. Discontent also surged among the rapidly growing population of mestizos, those of mixed Spanish and Indian parentage. The successful American and French revolutions of the late 1700s further increased native resentment of Spanish injustice and exploitation.

In 1808 Napoleon Bonaparte of France conquered Spain and imprisoned Spain's king, Ferdinand VII, thus leaving Mexico without a legitimate ruler.

Struggle for Independence. On Sept. 16, 1810 a Creole priest in the town of Dolores, Miguel Hidalgo y Costilla, issued the famous "Cry of Dolores," in which he denounced the injustices of the Spanish government and cried out for social reform. With Indian support, Hidalgo and his followers were able to dominate southern Mexico.

The Creoles would not support Hidalgo's social revolution, which threatened their own position, and without Creole support the revolt could not succeed. Hidalgo was defeated and executed. The struggle was renewed by another priest, José María Morelos, a mestizo, but he too was eventually defeated and executed, in 1815.

Hope for independence lay dormant until 1820, when Ferdinand VII, who had been restored to the Spanish throne after Napoleon's armies were expelled from Spain, was forced by internal pressures to approve a new liberal constitution. Mexican Creoles feared that the liberal reforms would weaken their position in Mexico and they aligned themselves with the struggle for independence.

Independence. In 1821 Gen. Augustín de Iturbide led another revolution. He declared Mexico independent and established himself as emperor Augustín I. In 1823 he was overthrown by Antonio López de Santa Anna, another ambitious general, who proclaimed a republic. Santa Anna remained the dominant political figure in the new republic until 1855. For most of those years he was either president or dictator, although he was intermittently overthrown.

In 1836 the territory of Texas, which had been settled largely by people from the United States, declared its independence. Santa Anna attempted to prevent the secession, but after an initial victory at the Alamo he was decisively defeated at the battle of San Jacinto, in April 1836. The United States annexed Texas in 1845, which angered the Mexicans, who had never recognized Texan independence.

War broke out between Mexico and the United States in 1846. Mexico was defeated, and under the terms of the Treaty of Guadalupe Hidalgo (1848) Mexico was forced to cede a large section of land north of the Río Grande to the United States. The land lost included New Mexico and California, as well as Texas. In 1853 Santa Anna, short of government funds, sold the Mesilla Valley to the United States in the Gadsden Purchase. This final loss of territory gravely insulted the Mexicans.

Revolution and Reform. Shortly afterward, bands of guerrillas gathered in the mountains and stormed the capital, demanding liberal reforms. Led by Juan Álvarez and Benito Juárez, the rebels declared their intention to institute many reforms for the good of the people of Mexico. They planned to assert civilian control over the church and the military; to eliminate sharp class distinctions by breaking up large estates and distributing land among the peasants; and to unite the country to prevent further losses to the United States.

In 1855 Santa Anna was overthrown by the rebels and Alvarez became acting president. Various edicts outlining the reforms were issued from Mexico City, and in 1857 a new constitution, which provided for a more liberal and democratic government, was adopted. The Liberals were staunchly opposed by the army, the church, and the upper classes. The ultimate result was civil war lasting from 1858 to 1860, when Benito Juárez led his Liberal forces to a costly victory.

During the war Mexico had become deeply indebted to Spain, Britain, and France. In 1861 Juárez, faced with national bankruptcy, suspended payment on these debts. A combined army of French, Spanish, and British troops invaded Mexico in December 1861 to force payment. Napoleon III of France seized this opportunity to conquer the country. A Mexican victory at the battle of Puebla in May 1862 only temporarily halted the French advance, and with reinforcements the French won control in 1863.

In 1864 Napoleon declared Maximilian, an Austrian prince, Emperor of Mexico. In 1867, under diplomatic pressure from the United States, which objected to French intervention, France withdrew its troops. Maximilian, under the erroneous impression that he had popular support, refused to leave the country and was captured and shot. Juárez returned as president and held office until 1872.

Díaz Era. Juárez and his successor, Sebastián Lerdo de Tejada, attempted to enact liberal reforms, but in 1876 the government was overthrown by Porfirio Díaz, who ruled as dictator from 1876 to 1911. Under his rule the upper class again enjoyed prosperity, foreign investments multiplied, and the government budget was balanced. The Indians and the growing working class were neglected, however. The slogan, "Mexico, mother of foreigners, stepmother of Mexicans," expressed the growing popular resentment.

Discontent with Díaz's rule culminated in revolution in 1910. In an interview with a U.S. news correspondent, Díaz expressed the view that Mexico was prepared for a democratic election. Although his comments were intended to be read only in the United States, translations of his statement reached Mexico. Francisco Madero, a Creole from northern Mexico, challenged Díaz to hold free elections, and Díaz was forced to uphold the declaration he had made.

The elections were rigged, however, and Madero was imprisoned after his defeat by Díaz. Resentment surged throughout the country, and the people revolted. In the north, Francisco ("Pancho") Villa and Pascual Orozco led armies of peasants in rebellion. In the south, Emiliano Zapata and an army of Indians raided large estates. In May 1911 Díaz was forced to flee from the country.

Civil Strife. Francisco Madero became the popularly acclaimed president in November 1911. His term of office brought some extension of democratic institutions, but no sorely needed economic and social reforms. The Indians and workers remained dissatisfied and once again revolted. In 1913 Madero unwisely enlisted the support of Gen. Victoriano Huerta, who betrayed Madero and had him assassinated.

Huerta ruled as dictator until 1914, when revolutionary movements erupted throughout Mexico. Venustiano Carranza, Álvaro Obregón, and Pancho Villa led the revolutionary movements in the north. In the south, an army of peasants was again led by Emiliano Zapata. Huerta's army was defeated and he fled to the United States.

Peace was not restored to Mexico, however, for the victorious troops then fought among themselves for control of the government. Villa and Zapata seized Mexico City, while Carranza and Obregón held Vera Cruz. With promises of extensive liberal reforms, the Obregón forces triumphed. In 1917 Carranza became president and a liberal constitution was drawn up.

Reform Era. The constitution protected labor, limited church authority, and provided for the division of large estates into the ancient Indian communal land system, known as the *ejido*. The constitution was not implemented, however, and when Carranza tried to choose his own successor, he was overthrown by Obregón. In September 1920 Obregón was elected president, and during his four-year term a modest, but solid, program of reforms was initiated.

In 1924 Gen. Plutarco Elías Calles was elected president. Disputes with the church and with foreign investors plagued his administration. In 1928 Obregón was again elected, but was assassinated before taking office. From 1928 to 1934 a series of puppet presidents, controlled by Calles, ruled Mexico. During this period the strongly reformist *Partido Nacional Revolucionario* (PNR), or National Revolutionary Party, was formed and came to dominate Mexican politics.

In elections held in 1934, the PNR candidate, Lázaro Cárdenas, was elected to the presidency. Under the Cárdenas administration, reforms demanded during the revolution were enacted. Millions of acres of land were distributed to the *ejidos* and schools, hospitals, and roads were constructed. In 1938 both the U.S. and British oil industries were nationalized.

Contemporary Mexico. In 1940 Manuel Avila Camacho was elected president. Although Camacho made no innovations during his own term of office, he consolidated the gains that had already been made. In 1942, after German submarines had sunk Mexican tankers, Mexico declared war on the Axis. Mexico contributed strategic raw materials to the war effort. Mexicans enlisted in the United States armed forces, and a squadron of the Mexican air force was sent to the Pacific. In 1945 Mexico became a charter member of the United Nations.

Postwar administrations basically followed the domestic policies of President Camacho and focused on increasing food production and developing transportation. Pres. Adolfo Ruiz Cortines (1952–1958) greatly extended Mexico's farmland through irrigation projects. Under Adolfo López Mateos (1958–1964) Mexico's educational system was expanded.

In 1964 Gustavo Díaz Ordaz was elected president. During his administration, on Oct. 28, 1967, Mexico signed a treaty with the United States which settled a century-old border dispute. Under the terms of the treaty the United States ceded to Mexico the territory known as El Chamizal, 437 acres of land lost by Mexico when the Rio Grande changed its course in 1864.

—George W. Carey; Jerome Fischman

MONACO

Official name: Principality of Monaco
Area: 368 acres
Population: (1966 est.) 23,000
Capital: Monaco
Language: French
Religion: Roman Catholicism
Currency unit: French franc
National holiday: November 19

Monaco is a tiny principality on the French Riviera. It is bounded on the north, east, and west by France and on the south by the Mediterranean Sea.

THE LAND AND PEOPLE. Monaco is set into steep cliffs surrounding an excellent harbor. Its climate is mild and rather dry.

There are three sections in the principality—Monte Carlo, La Condamine, and Monaco-Ville, which lies atop a rocky promontory jutting into the Mediterranean.

A majority of the people are from other European countries, and in the mid-1960s only slightly more than one-tenth of the people were native Monagasques. French is the official language, and Roman Catholicism the predominant religion.

ECONOMY. Tourists, attracted by Monaco's scenery, beach resorts, and gambling casino, are the major source of Monaco's income. The sale of postage stamps to collectors is important, and the country also has light industries producing pharmaceuticals, precision tools, and luxury consumer items.

Monaco has no income tax, and it long served the wealthy as a refuge from taxes.

GOVERNMENT. Monaco is governed by a prince, who is assisted by a small appointed cabinet. An elected council shares legislative power with the prince. France is responsible for Monaco's foreign affairs and defense, but the principality maintains consulates and missions throughout the world.

HISTORY. The ancient Phoenicians, Greeks, Carthaginians, and Romans all used Monaco's harbor. In the 600s and 700s Monaco was occupied by the Lombards, who built a fortress on its rocky promontory. In the 800s the fortress fell to the Saracens.

Monaco became part of the Holy Roman Empire, and in the 900s Monaco was granted to a leading family of Genoa, which later took the name Grimaldi. The Grimaldis did not exercise their rights over the territory until the late 1200s, when they were driven from Genoa as a result of political feuds.

The tiny state was in constant danger of being overwhelmed by its larger neighbors. With its fortress and its excellent harbor and port facilities, Monaco was coveted by Genoa, Savoy, Florence, France, and Spain. Monaco managed to maintain its independence, however, and in 1512 the right of the Grimaldis to rule Monaco was formally acknowledged by the king of France.

After the French Revolution, in 1793 France annexed the principality. The sovereignty of the Grimaldis was restored in 1814, and in 1815 the Treaty of Vienna made Monaco a protectorate of the Kingdom of Sardinia. In 1861 the principality once more came under the protection of France. In 1911 Monaco adopted a constitution ending the absolute rule of the princes.

During the early 1900s, the principality developed into a fashionable resort, well-known for its gambling casino. In the mid-1900s Monaco moved to broaden and modernize its economy by developing light industry. Prince Rainier III, who took the throne in 1949, married a U.S. actress, Grace Kelly, in 1956.

—Sergio Barzanti

MONGOLIA

Official name: Mongolian People's Republic
Area: 604,249 square miles
Population: (1966 est.) 1,140,000
Capital: Ulan Bator (Pop., 1962 est., 195,300)
Language: Mongolian
Religion: Buddhism
Currency unit: Tugrik
National holiday: People's revolution day, July 11

Mongolia is both a geographical region and a nation. The region, in east-central Asia, lies between Siberia and northern China. It is divided between Inner Mongolia, south of the Gobi, part of China, and Outer Mongolia, an independent nation officially called the Mongolian People's Republic.

The Mongolian People's Republic is bounded on the north by the Soviet Union and on the east, south, and west by Communist China.

THE LAND. Much of Mongolia occupies the grassy, rolling Mongolian Plain, which ranges in elevation from 3,000 to 6,000 feet. Mountains in the north and west rise to between 5,000 and 11,000 feet. Along the southwestern border the Altai range towers over 12,000 feet. In the south and southeast, the Mongolian Plain slopes into the barren desert of the Gobi Depression, which extends into Inner Mongolia.

All of Mongolia's principal rivers flow northward, toward the Soviet Union. They include the Selenge and the Orkhon, which empty into Lake Baykal, and the Kerulen, an important tributary of the Amur River.

Mongolia's climate is generally dry and is characterized by long, cold winters and short, cool summers. Precipitation increases from south to north, ranging from less than 5 inches to 15 inches a year.

THE PEOPLE. The population is almost entirely Mongol, divided into a number of groups, of which the Khalkha is by far the largest. They use an alphabet similar to the Russian. There are minorities of other Mongols, and some Russians and Chinese. Lamaist Buddhism is the dominant religion, but its practice has been restricted since the 1930s.

Over half of the population is rural, and some is semi-nomadic. Population is concentrated in the northern half of the country. About 25 percent of the people live in Ulan Bator, the capital, in east central Mongolia.

ECONOMY. Livestock herding, the Mongol's traditional way of life, remains the mainstay of the country's economy. But by the mid-1900s settled agriculture had increased and industrialization had begun, and an increasing proportion of the population was sedentary.

The country's huge herds of sheep, goats, cattle, horses, and camels provide most necessities, including food, clothing, shelter, and transport, as well as goods for export. The principal crops are grain, potatoes, and some vegetables. Agriculture is collectivized.

Mongolia mines coal, copper, gold, iron, and petroleum. The country's considerable hydroelectric capacity is being developed, and manufactures include building materials, textiles, and processed foodstuffs.

Mongolia exports farm and animal products and some metal ores. Consumer goods, raw materials, and machinery are imported. Mongolian trade is primarily with communist countries, especially with the Soviet Union.

GOVERNMENT. Although Mongolia is constitutionally a republic in which supreme power is vested in a popularly elected assembly, the Khural, political power actually rests with the country's Communist party, officially called the Mongolian People's Revolutionary Party.

The party proposes all candidates for the Khural, and its political bureau, or politburo, sets national policy. The party first secretary is the key figure in the government. The chief of the presidium, a council elected by the Khural to govern between its short sessions, serves as a collective head of state.

Mongolia is a member of the United Nations and the Council for Mutual Economic Assistance (COMECON), a Soviet-led economic alliance of communist states.

HISTORY. The early Mongols were divided into many rival nomadic tribes. They lived by herding and raiding neighboring tribes and states, and by the beginning of the 1200s, the Mongols held the territory all around the Gobi.

Expansion. The first leader to unite the Mongol tribes was Timujin, who in 1206 became Genghis Khan, the "very mighty king." He led the Mongols in the conquest of northern China, eastern Russia, and the Islamic lands of the Near East. The Mongol's small but skilled mounted army conquered quickly, and the Mongols destroyed much of the conquered lands.

After Genghis Khan's death in 1227 his son, Ogotai, led the Mongols across Hungary and Poland as far west as Vienna. Ogotai's death in 1241 forced the Mongols to retreat to elect a new khan. Kublai Khan, their choice, conquered all of China and Korea and controlled much of Southeast Asia.

The Mongols proved less skillful at governing than at conquering, however, and in eastern Europe and the Middle East effective Mongol rule ended as soon as the Mongol armies were withdrawn. In China, where the Mongols had established the Yüan dynasty, government corruption eroded Mongol authority and scattered revolts broke out in the Chinese provinces.

Decline. After Kublai Khan's death in 1294 the empire was divided, with the East Asian portion coming under the Mongol-Chinese Chin dynasty. In the late 1300s, under Tamerlane, a second Mongol empire briefly ruled western Asia. But Mongol power and influence had declined greatly, and the Mongols were gradually pushed back to the Mongolian Plain.

In the 1500s Lamaist Buddhism spread to Mongolia and soon became a powerful force. Buddhist monasteries came to hold much of the land, and a large proportion of the male population became monks.

In the 1600s Inner Mongolia came under the control of the Manchus, who conquered China in 1644 and established the Ch'ing dynasty. Despite Mongol resistance, the Manchus had conquered almost all of Outer Mongolia by the 1680s, and Mongolia became a province of China. In the early 1700s Russia began to exert a strong influence on northwestern Mongolia.

Apart from its contacts with China and Russia, during the 1700s and 1800s Mongolia remained isolated from the outside world. Mongolians came to resent their Chinese administrators, who governed the region as though it was a colony, and Chinese settlers, who appropriated grazing land for farm use.

Autonomy. Manchu power had declined by the early 1900s and Japan and Russia agreed to share influence in Mongolia, with Japan controlling eastern Inner Mongolia and Russia dominating Outer Mongolia. In 1911 a revolution in China overthrew the Manchu dynasty and the people of Outer Mongolia, with Russian support, toppled the Chinese provincial government and proclaimed the autonomy of Outer Mongolia. The Mongolians chose a lama, the *hutukhtu*, or "Living Buddha," as nominal ruler.

The country was far from independent, however. China did not recognize Mongolia's autonomy, and it remained under the protection of Russia. In 1919, during the upheaval accompanying the fall of the monarchy in Russia, China resumed rule over Mongolia. By 1921 Soviet troops had occupied Outer Mongolia, however, and in 1924, when the reigning hutukhtu died, Mongolia became the

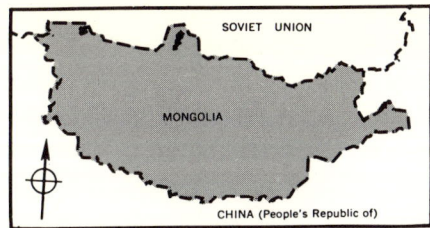

Mongolian People's Republic, the first state to follow the communist pattern of government established in Russia.

People's Republic. During the 1920s and 1930s the government promoted radical and rapid economic and social change. The economic power of the Chinese in Mongolia was destroyed, and the power of the Buddhist lamas was crushed. All opposition to government programs was suppressed.

Inner Mongolia had remained a Chinese province, and in the 1930s it was occupied by Japanese forces. Japanese occupation posed a threat to the Mongolian People's Republic, and in 1939 Soviet and Mongol troops drove the Japanese from the border area.

The Mongolian People's Republic participated briefly in World War II. In 1945, as part of the war settlement, the people of Outer Mongolia voted in a referendum to be independent of China, and in 1946 China, under Chiang Kai-shek, recognized Outer Mongolia's independence. In 1950, after a communist government had been established in China, the Chinese communists and the Soviets agreed to guarantee the independence of the Mongolian People's Republic.

In the late 1950s Mongolia began to expand its diplomatic and commercial contacts with the west, and in 1961 Mongolia became a member of the United Nations. In the early 1960s, when a split developed between Communist China and the Soviet Union, Mongolia sided with the Soviets. In 1966 Mongolia and the Soviet Union reaffirmed their close relations in elaborate ceremonies accompanying the signing of a 20-year treaty of friendship, protection, and aid.

—Thomas E. Ennis; M. G. Inaba

MOROCCO

Official name: Kingdom of Morocco
Area: 171,835 square miles
Population: (1967 est.) 14,140,000
Capital: Rabat (Pop., 1965 est., 355,000)
Language: Arabic
Religion: Islam
Currency unit: Dirham
National holiday: Independence day, March 3

Morocco, a kingdom in northern Africa, is bounded on the north by the Mediterranean Sea, on the east by Algeria, on the south by Spanish Sahara, and on the west by the Atlantic Ocean. Between 1912 and 1956 Morocco was divided into a French zone, two Spanish zones, and the international zone of Tanger (Tangier). In 1956 Morocco became a sovereign state.

THE LAND. The western end of the Atlas Mountain system dominates Morocco. In the north the Rif Atlas runs parallel to the Mediterranean Sea. The Middle Atlas, which has elevations of over 10,900 feet, and the Grand Atlas, which has elevations of over 13,600 feet, run through central Morocco. The Anti-Atlas, in the southwest, borders the desert region of the Sahara, which stretches along eastern and southern Morocco.

The Moroccan Meseta, or plateau, lies on the Atlantic side of the Grand Atlas and Middle Atlas. It is irrigated in places, as at Marrakech, and crossed by rivers leading into lowland plains. The Moulouya River and valley are east of the Middle Atlas.

The Grand Atlas and Middle Atlas intercept rain-bearing winds, which bring moisture to the north and west, and cause hot, desert conditions in the south and near-desert conditions in the east.

THE PEOPLE. The Moroccans are descended from Berber-speaking peoples, possibly the original inhabitants of the area, and from later Arab settlers. Most of the people are Muslim. There is a small Jewish population in the country, and there are small communities of Europeans, mainly French and Spanish.

Morocco's major cities include Rabat, the capital; Casablanca, an industrial and commercial center and port; Fes (Fez); Marrakech; and Tanger (Tangier).

ECONOMY. The economy of Morocco is based primarily on agriculture. The basic food crops are wheat and barley, wine grapes, citrus fruits, and vegetables. With the aid of foreign capital, particularly from France, Morocco has become an important source of seasonal fruits and vegetables for Western Europe. Large irrigation projects have been developed to increase agricultural production. Sheep and goats are raised in the mountains.

Morocco has deposits of several minerals. Phosphate rock, used in the production of fertilizers, is the most important, and in 1965 over 9.8 million metric tons of phosphate rock were produced. Iron ore, manganese, cobalt, and zinc are also mined. There are a number of small industries in the country. Cement, superphosphates, Moroccan leather, flour, sugar, and other products are produced.

In 1966 imports cost $477 million and exports earned $429 million. The major imports are petroleum products, food, manufactured goods, especially iron and steel and textiles, and machinery. Exports include live animals, fish, fruit, vegetables, phosphates and fertilizers, iron ore, and leather. Most trade is conducted with France, West Germany, the United States, and Spain.

GOVERNMENT. Morocco's 1962 constitution vested executive powers in the king, the head of state, and legislative power in the popularly elected House of Representatives and the House of Counsellors, elected by local authorities and various interest groups. In June 1965 the king took all executive and legislative powers.

Morocco is a member of the United Nations, the Organization of African Unity, and the Arab League.

HISTORY. The earliest known inhabitants of present-day Morocco were Berber-speaking peoples. In the 1200s

BC Phoenicians landed on the Moroccan coast and established trading posts in the region. In the 100s AD Rome established a province in northwestern Morocco. Roman domination came to an end in the 400s with the invasion of the Vandals.

In the early 700s Muslim armies invaded Morocco, and the Berber-speaking peoples gradually adopted Islam. In the late 700s most of the country united under Idris, a member of the 'Alid family. His son established the city of Fez.

In 1056 Berber-speaking tribes formed a powerful religious and political force, the Almoravids. The Almoravids founded the city of Marrakech in 1062, and established a dynasty which ruled Morocco until 1147. The Almohads, another Berber confederation, defeated the Almoravids and established a dynasty which lasted until 1269. The Marinid dynasty succeeded the Almohads.

In 1544 Morocco came under the rule of another 'Alid dynasty, the Sa'dis, and in 1664 yet another branch of the 'Alid, the Filalis, or 'Alawites, assumed control.

European Control. Although only about seven miles from Europe, Morocco did not come under European rule until the 1900s. In the early 1900s Britain, Spain, France, and Germany competed for control of Morocco. In 1912 the Moroccan sultan was forced to sign the Treaty of Fez with France, and most of Morocco became a French protectorate. In the same year Spain obtained control of a region in the north and one in the south. In 1923 the city of Tangier became an international zone.

From 1912 to 1925 Louis Lyautey ruled French Morocco as resident-general. He brought security to most of the country and established good relations with the Moroccans, based on respect for the monarchy and the traditional Moroccan way of life.

In 1921 a leader in the Rif Mountains, Abd al-Krim led a rising against the Spanish, and then fought a combined Spanish and French force. He was defeated in 1926. After 1925 the government of French Morocco was more centralized and the European population in Morocco steadily increased.

Nationalism. Moroccan nationalism began to develop in the late 1920s. In 1927 France placed Muhammad bin Yusuf (Muhammad V) on the throne, believing he would act favorably to France. The French assumption appeared valid when in 1930 Muhammad signed the Berber *Dahir*, which downgraded the importance of Islamic law. After that, however, Muhammad responded to the appeals of the nationalists.

By the time of World War II he was cautiously cooperating with them while maintaining favorable relations with France. In 1953 France forced Muhammad to abdicate in order to end his nationalist activity. He went into exile, but as a result nationalist disturbances intensified. In 1955 France accepted the necessity of dealing with Muhammad, and he returned to Morocco in triumph.

Independence. Negotiations quickly led to independence for French Morocco, achieved on Mar. 2, 1956. By agreements in April 1956 and April 1958 the Spanish zones were granted independence, and in October 1956 Tangier was incorporated into Morocco.

Muhammad V died in 1961, and his son Hasan II succeeded him. In 1962, with the adoption of its first constitution, Morocco became a constitutional monarchy. In June 1965 Hasan took over all executive and legislative powers because of opposition he faced in parliament from the major political parties.

—Hibberd V. B. Kline, Jr.;
L. Carl Brown

MUSCAT AND OMAN

Official name: Sultanate of Muscat and Oman and Dependencies
Area: 82,000 square miles
Population: (1966 est.) 565,000
Capital: Muscat (Pop., 1960 est., urban area, 6,208)
Language: Arabic
Religion: Islam
Currency unit: Persian Gulf Indian rupee

Muscat and Oman, an Arab sultanate in the southeastern corner of the Arabian peninsula, occupies a strategic position at the mouth of the Persian Gulf. The country is bordered

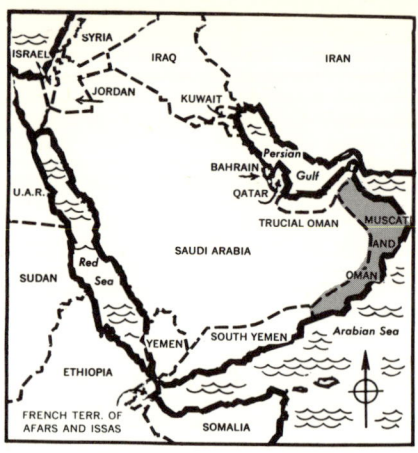

on the northwest by the Trucial Coast, on the north by the Gulf of Oman, on the east and south by the Arabian Sea, on the southwest by South Yemen, and on the west by Saudi Arabia. The borders of Muscat and Oman are largely undefined, and some are disputed.

THE LAND. A narrow plain skirts the country's 1,000-mile coastline. The northwestern portion of the plain, the Batinah, is quite fertile. Rugged mountains rise sharply to nearly 10,000 feet above the plain. In the interior is a low, barren plateau, the eastern end of the vast Rub al Khali, or "Empty Quarter," of the Arabian Peninsula. The climate throughout the country is hot and dry.

THE PEOPLE. The native people are Arab, but there are Indian, Iranian, and Negro minorities. Population is concentrated in three main regions—Muscat, on the northeast; Oman, in the mountains; and Dhofar, on the Arabian Sea coast.

ECONOMY. Muscat and Oman's economic life is based on farming, herding, and trading. The only major mineral resource is oil, which was discovered in 1964 in sufficient quantities for production.

Dates, grown on the Batinah and in mountain valleys, are the leading crop. Coconuts, cereals, and citrus fruits are also grown. Large herds of camels are raised in the interior, and there is good fishing off the coast. There is little industry.

Trade is important. The main port is Matrah, on the Gulf of Oman. Dates are the chief export, with India, Pakistan, and the Persian Gulf states the leading markets. Foodstuffs, cement, textiles, and vehicles are imported, primarily from Britain, India, and Pakistan.

GOVERNMENT. Muscat and Oman is ruled by the sultan of Muscat. The province of Oman has some autonomy under its own ruler, but Muscat has sovereignty over the region.

HISTORY. Arab peoples have inhabited Muscat and Oman for many centuries. Because of its strategic position at the mouth of the Persian Gulf, the land attracted conquerors seeking control of the gulf. In 1508 the Portuguese occupied Muscat, and during the following century they competed for control of the region with the Ottoman Turks, who had captured several areas.

MOROCCO'S ISLAMIC HERITAGE is reflected in architecture and the dress of the people.

By 1650 the native Arabs had driven out both the Portuguese and the Turks. Arab control was not secure, however, until 1737, when the Ahmad Ibn Said dynasty fought off a Persian invasion.

During the 1700s and 1800s the sultanate extended its control over parts of southern Iran and eastern Africa. In the later 1800s, however, internal political disputes divided the region between coastal Muscat and interior Oman. The power of both declined, and foreign territories were lost.

In 1891 Muscat granted special privileges to Britain in return for British protection. Close ties with Britain were reaffirmed several times in the 1900s by treaties of friendship. In the mid-1950s British-led troops helped the sultan of Muscat put down a rebellion in the interior. Following this conflict, the United Nations acknowledged Muscat's sovereignty over Oman.

The traditional way of life of the people of the country faced new challenges in the late 1960s as the exploitation of oil resources brought increased prosperity and drew world attention to Muscat and Oman.

—Charles Issawi; Alexander Melamid

NAURU

Official name: Nauru
Area: 8 square miles
Population: (1966) 6,056
Capital: Nauru
Language: Nauruan
Religion: Christianity

Nauru, a small, isolated coral island in the South Pacfic Ocean, is located about 30 miles south of the equator, northeast of the Solomon Islands. It was made a UN Trust Territory in 1947 and placed under the joint control of Britain, Australia, and New Zealand, with Australia as administrator. The trustees granted Nauru its independence Jan. 31, 1968.

THE LAND AND PEOPLE. Nauru is ringed by coral reefs. The island consists of a narrow coastal plain encircling an upland region, most of which is occupied by phosphate-bearing rock. The climate is hot and humid throughout the year.

Native Nauruans are a mixture of Micronesian and Polynesian stocks. Most are Christian. Chinese and other foreign workers and European administrators and managers make up about half the population.

ECONOMY. The island's economy is almost totally dependent on phosphate mining, although coconuts and other fruits and a few vegetables are raised on the coastal plain. The production of phosphates is Nauru's chief industry, and the island is one of the world's leading producers of phosphate rock, mining over 1.7 million metric tons in 1964–1965.

The mining and export of the rock is managed by Britain, Australia, and New Zealand, under Nauruan and UN supervision. Royalties and other fees are paid to the Nauruans. As a result, the islanders have one of the highest standards of living in the world, pay no taxes, and enjoy free education and medical services.

Phosphates are the only exports, and food, machinery, and consumer goods are imported. Most trade is with Australia, New Zealand, and Britain. In the early 1960s efforts began to diversify the economy in preparation for the predicted depletion of the phosphate deposits in the 1990s.

GOVERNMENT. Nauru's government is headed by a president, who is chosen by a popularly elected legislative assembly from among its members.

HISTORY. Nauru was discovered in 1798 by a British explorer, but for over a century it remained a beachcombers' refuge and a minor source of copra. In 1888 possession passed to Germany.

In 1900 Nauru was found to be rich in phosphate rock, the basis of a fertilizer then coming into extensive use in Australia and New Zealand. By agreement with the Germans, phosphate mining was undertaken by an Australian-based British company.

After World War I, in 1919, Nauru was made a League of Nations mandate entrusted to Britain, but Australia administered economic and political affairs. Phosphate production was shared by Australia, New Zealand, and Britain. Occupied by the Japanese in World War II, the island was reoccupied in 1945 by Australian troops.

Following the war it became a UN Trust Territory under joint Australian, British, and New Zealand authority, but with Australia administering the island for the three. In 1964, as exhaustion of the phosphate rock was foreseen, Australian and Nauruan officials discussed relocating the islanders, but the Nauruans wished to remain on Nauru.

In 1966 the UN General Assembly recommended that the trustee nations make the island habitable again when the phosphate was depleted by replacing all soil that had been removed with the rock. The UN also recommended independence for Nauru, and the island became an independent nation on Jan. 31, 1968.

NEPAL

Official name: Kingdom of Nepal
Area: 54,360 square miles
Population: (1966 est.) 10,294,000
Capital: Katmandu (Pop., 1961, 122,507)
Language: Nepali
Religion: Hinduism and Buddhism
Currency: Rupee
National holiday: National day, February 18

Nepal is a small kingdom in the Himalaya Mountains in South Asia. It is a landlocked country bounded on the north by the Tibet region of China and on the east, south, and west by India.

THE LAND. Nepal can be divided into three distinct geographical regions, each extending east to west. The Great Himalayas dominate the northern region, an area of spectacular alpine scenery with many of the world's tallest mountains.

There are eight peaks with elevations of over 26,000 feet, and Mt. Everest, on the Nepal-Tibet border, with an elevation of 29,028 feet, is the tallest mountain in the world. Elevations in the northern region generally exceed 20,000 feet, and the lower portions of this region are forested. The climate is extremely cold and rather dry.

The second region, in central Nepal, is also mountainous. Elevations range from 4,500 in the valley bottoms to 10,000 feet. Most of the lower slopes and valleys are cultivated.

The most important part of the central region is the Katmandu Valley, the heart of the country. Only 18 by 15 miles in area and surrounded by high mountains, it contains Nepal's main towns—Katmandu, the capital, Patan, and Bhadgeon. The valley is well-watered, receiving about 58 inches of precipitation annually, and has a moderate climate.

The third region, called the terai, is a narrow belt 10 to 20 miles wide next to the Indian border. Much of the terai is heavily wooded. Its climate is hot and humid, with rainfall averaging 60 inches a year. Winters can be quite pleasant, however.

Many rivers flow from the Himalayas through Nepal, including the Kosi, the Trisuli, the Baghmati, the Gandak, and the Karnali.

THE PEOPLE. Nepal's population is concentrated in the central region, especially the Katmandu Valley, and in the southern region, the terai. The north is sparsely populated.

The Nepalese are descendants of Mongols and peoples of northern India. They are traditionally divided along tribal lines, with the Gurkha the dominant group. The minority Newar and Sherpa peoples are Mongol-Tibetan. The Nepalese speak Nepali and a variety of hill dialects. Buddhism and Hinduism are the major religions.

ECONOMY. The Nepalese economy is based on agriculture, but the country is rich in natural resources. Nepal's mineral resources include deposits of copper, iron, sulfur, coal, hematite, and bauxite. But in the 1960s they remained virtually untapped because of Nepal's isolation and lack of transportation facilities.

There are many acres of valuable forests, especially in the south, where the hardwood sal tree is the most valuable commercial timber. Because of its many rapid rivers, Nepal has a large hydroelectric potential.

The country's best farmland is in the south, where farmers grow rice, jute, mustard, tobacco, wheat, linseed, and some sugarcane. The south produces a surplus of cereal grains. The majority of farmers in the central region eke out a subsistence existence by intensively cultivating small, terraced plots of irrigated land.

Rice is grown in the warm season and wheat and vegetables in the dry, cool months. Corn, millet, and legumes are grown on the hillsides. A few cows are kept for milk.

Herding is the main activity of the Sherpa, in the north, who graze sheep, goats, and yaks on the Himalayan slopes. Wheat and barley are grown in the valley bottoms of the north.

An important source of income and foreign exchange traditionally has been the service of Gurkha soldiers in the British and Indian armies.

Nepal relies on financial and technical assistance from many nations and from the UN for development.

Nepal's international trade is limited. The main exports are rice, jute, wool, timber, linseed, and hides. Textiles, fuels, medicines, footwear, and industrial raw materials are imported. Most trade is with India.

GOVERNMENT. Nepal is a constitutional monarchy, with a king as chief executive and head of state. The king appoints a council to advise him and he chooses a council of ministers from among the members of the Panchayat, the legislative assembly. Most members of the Panchayat are elected to five-year terms by local and regional panchayats, and some are appointed by the king.

Nepal is a member of the United Nations.

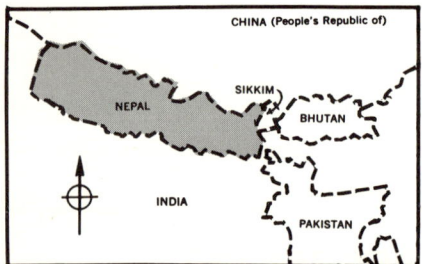

HISTORY. The earliest inhabitants of the Katmandu Valley were the Newars, who lived under a tribal form of government and developed a religion and customs representing a blend of Buddhism and Hinduism. In the first centuries AD the valley came under the rule of Indian kings, who consolidated Indian influence in Nepal in the form of the Hindu religion and culture and monarchial government.

When the last of the dynasty of Indian kings, the Malla, began to weaken in the 1400s, the country returned to tribal government. In the 1500s a western Nepalese principality, Gurkha, gained strength under the Shah dynasty, whose most famous ruler, Prithvi Narayan, conquered the Katmandu Valley in 1769 and created the modern Nepalese state.

Expansionism. Combining fierce military ambition with an unusual talent for administration, Prithvi Narayan extended his rule eastward to Darjeeling, now in India, and his descendants expanded Nepalese hegemony to the east as far as Kashmir and to the south into present-day India. Nepalese expansion led to conflicts with Tibet and India.

Two Nepalese invasions of Tibet, in 1788 and 1791, brought retaliation from China, which had gained suzerainty over Tibet. A Chinese army crossed the Himalayas and approached the Katmandu Valley. Nepal was forced to withdraw from Tibet and to pay tribute to China. The payments ceased in 1908.

Nepalese expansionism turned southward and confronted the British, who were extending their control of India northward in the Ganges Valley. The Nepalese refused to negotiate with the British and permitted frequent raids into the Indian plains.

The British were able to subdue the Nepalese marauders and reach a settlement with Nepal in 1816, in the Treaty of Sagauli. The treaty established Nepal's boundary with India and gave Britain a deciding influence in Nepalese foreign relations. Gurkha soldiers began to be used by British armies.

Rana Rule. Struggles for power in the early 1800s weakened Nepal and in 1846 resulted in the establishment of rule by the prime ministers, the Ranas. This pattern of government continued until 1951. Rana rule, supported by the army and the British in India, was marked by conspiracies and assassinations within the extended Rana family and the isolation of Nepal from modernizing influences.

In the 1900s in India Nepalese intellectuals began to aspire to advancement for their country, and this led to a movement supported by the titular ruler, King Tribhuvana, to unseat the Ranas. After India achieved independence in 1950, the Nepalese National Congress, modeled on the Indian Congress party, led a reform drive which was backed by the new government in India.

The Ranas responded with legislative concessions in 1950, but revolts broke out and with Indian encouragement King Tribhuvana was able to end Rana power in 1951. The political and administrative turmoil accompanying the downfall of the Ranas lasted for 8 years, while the country was held together by the newly found power of the king. Tribhuvana died in 1955 and was succeeded by his son, Mahendra.

Contemporary Nepal. King Mahendra experimented unsuccessfully with various political leaders and party coalitions in the 1950s. But none seemed able to unify the country or introduce needed reforms. Meanwhile, Chinese power was increasing in Tibet, and the security of Nepal, as well as India, was threatened. In 1959 the king promulgated a new constitution giving himself supreme executive powers but also providing for a legislature.

In an unprecedented election in 1959, 43 percent of the electorate voted, a considerable achievement in a country of hundreds of semi-independent village settlements. B. P. Koirala, of the Nepalese Congress, took office as prime minister with a program calling for land reform, more efficient administration, and the development of a more active foreign policy.

King Mahendra overthrew the Koirala government at the end of 1960 and introduced direct royal rule. The king's action did not lead to dictatorship, but rather to a new delegation of authority to village councils in what the king called "democracy from below" and to a resurgence of popular support for the monarch.

The king attracted a progressive body of supporters in the government with a program directed toward modernization of the still largely traditional society and economy. He also pursued an active policy in foreign relations, including a state visit to the United States in 1967.

—Charles H. Heimsath; M. G. Inaba

NETHERLANDS

Official name: Kingdom of the Netherlands
Area: 12,990 square miles
Population: (1967 est.) 12,597,000
Capital: Amsterdam (Pop., 1965 est., 864,900)
Language: Dutch
Religion: Protestantism, Roman Catholicism
Currency unit: Guilder
National holiday: Birthday of the queen, April 30

The Netherlands, a small nation in western Europe, is bounded on the north and west by the North Sea, on the east by West Germany, and on the south by Belgium. The Frisian Islands separate the mainland from the open sea in the north.

In 1948 a customs union went into effect linking Belgium, Luxembourg, and the Netherlands, which is known as the Benelux Customs Union. Full economic union of the three countries has existed since 1960.

THE LAND. The Netherlands consists mostly of low plains, although there are some hilly sections in the east. Much of the land along the coast lies below sea level. It is protected by dikes and kept dry by drainage and pumping systems. The Dutch have a much higher percentage of reclaimed land than any nation in Europe, and systematic land reclamation continues.

The climate is maritime, with cool summers, mild winters, and high humidity. Rainfall is ample and reliable.

THE PEOPLE. The Netherlands is one of the most densely settled of the world's developed nations, with some 970 people per square mile. The population is densest in the western half of the country. The largest city in the Netherlands is Amsterdam. Other major cities include Rotterdam, The Hague, Utrecht, Eindhoven, and Haarlem.

The population is homogeneous. There are no large ethnic minorities, although religious differences have been the basis of past friction. About 40 percent of the population is Roman Catholic, and 40 percent is Protestant. Most of the rest profess no religion. Dutch is the universal language.

ECONOMY. The Netherlands is located along the heavily trafficked North Sea coast, and commerce is a mainstay of the Dutch economy. The Dutch merchant fleet is one of Europe's largest, and Rotterdam is the continent's leading port.

The mineral resources of the Netherlands are limited. There is some coal in the extreme south, in Limburg, and there are deposits of good ceramic clays. In 1960 Europe's largest natural gas field was discovered in the northeastern province of Groningen.

Most land in the Netherlands is suited for agriculture, and about 70 percent of the land is used for crops or grazing. Dutch agriculture uses intensive and highly efficient methods, and yields per acre and per animal are among the highest in the world.

Industry has expanded greatly since 1950, and by the mid-1960s about 40 percent of the labor force was engaged in manufacturing. Major industrial products include steel and other finished metals, transportation equipment, machinery, chemicals, refined petroleum, radios, textiles, ships, and a wide variety of processed foodstuffs. The chief industrial cities are Rotterdam, Amsterdam, Utrecht, Eindhoven, Limburg, and Groningen.

In 1967 exports earned $7,288 million, and imports cost $8,338 million. About 70 percent of the Netherlands' exports consist of industrial products, and 25 percent consist of agricultural produce and foodstuffs. Industrial exports include chemicals, refined petroleum, metal and electrical goods, and textiles. Major imports are industrial raw materials, which make up about one third of the total; foodstuffs; fuels; and a variety of consumer goods.

The Netherlands' chief trading partners are West Germany, Belgium, Luxembourg, the United States, Britain, and France.

GOVERNMENT. The Netherlands is a constitutional monarchy. The sovereign is head of state, but executive power is exercised by a prime minister and cabinet. The prime minister must normally be able to command a majority of votes in the legislature.

Legislative power is held by the States-General, which consists of two houses. The upper house is called the First Chamber, and its members are chosen by provincial legislatures for six-year terms. Members of the lower house, the Second Chamber, are directly elected and serve four-year terms.

The Netherlands is a member of the European Communities, the United Nations, and the North Atlantic Treaty Organization (NATO).

Surinam, or Dutch Guiana, and the Netherlands Antilles are the remains of a once vast overseas empire controlled by the Dutch.

HISTORY. When Roman legions led by Julius Caesar first advanced into the Netherlands in 57 BC, the area was inhabited by Celtic and Germanic tribes. The region south of the Rhine became a part of the Roman Empire, and remained so until 400 AD, when the Netherlands came under the control of the Franks. The Netherlands were part of Charlemagne's empire from 800 to 843. After the breakup of the empire, they emerged as a group of duchies, most often under the control of German princes. After 1384 they were ruled by the dukes of Burgundy.

Mary of Burgundy married the future Holy Roman Emperor Maximilian I in 1477, and in 1493 the Netherlands became part of the Holy Roman Empire. After the resignation of Emperor Charles V in 1555, the empire was divided, and the Netherlands passed to Philip II of Spain.

During the second half of the 1600s, many of the Dutch accepted Calvinism. Philip, a devout Roman Catholic, saw the suppression of Protestantism as a paramount goal and introduced the Inquisition into the Netherlands. Religious persecution intensified the existing conflict between the Dutch and Spaniards. In addition to religious freedom, the Dutch desired economic independence and self-government, and they strongly resented foreign rule.

Independence. In 1579 the seven northern provinces formed the Union of Utrecht, and two years later they proclaimed their independence. A bloody civil war was fought until 1609, when a twelve-year truce was signed. Under the leadership of William of Orange the Dutch Netherlands thus achieved their *de facto* independence.

At the end of the truce, Spain resumed the war, but the Dutch were more than able to hold their own, and in 1648 the Treaty of Westphalia formally recognized the independence of the United Netherlands. The southern provinces continued to be ruled by Spain and then by Austria until the end of the 1700s.

During the 1600s the Dutch nation reached its political and cultural height. The Dutch established a colonial empire, and for a brief time the Netherlands was the leading commercial power in Europe. Dutch supremacy was broken by a series of wars with England (1652–1654; 1665–1667), which soon reduced the Netherlands to the status of a second-rate power.

During the second half of the 1600s, the Dutch were also engaged in trying to stem the expansionist tendencies of France under King Louis XIV. Although successful, they were never able to recover from the strain of the effort, and after the War of the Spanish Succession (1702–1713) the Dutch economy declined.

In 1795 the Netherlands were conquered by France and made into the puppet state of the Batavian Republic. In 1810 the Dutch were incorporated into the Napoleonic empire. After the defeat of Napoleon, the Congress of Vienna (1814–1815) restored independence to the Netherlands.

Union. The Congress of Vienna also joined the Austrian and former Spanish provinces with the Dutch Netherlands to create the Kingdom of the Netherlands, which was intended to serve as a bulwark against future French expansion. But the union between Belgium and Holland was short-lived.

Holland was Germanic in orientation, Calvinistic in religion, and favored a policy of free trade, whereas Belgium was French in orientation, predominantly Roman Catholic, and sought high tariffs to protect its growing industry. In 1830 a revolution broke out in Belgium which eventually resulted in the separation of the two countries.

Modern Netherlands. The Netherlands remained neutral in World War I, but was invaded by the Germans during World War II. It suffered greatly during German occupation. Queen Wilhelmina escaped to London, where she led a government in exile. After the liberation in 1944 she was restored to her throne. In 1948, after a reign of 50 years, she abdicated in favor of her daughter, Juliana.

During the postwar period, the Netherlands lost a large portion of its colonial possessions. A nationalist rebellion broke out in Indonesia in 1945, and in 1949 the Dutch granted the country its independence. In 1954 the American colonies of Dutch Guiana and the Netherlands Antilles gained internal self-government, but they remained in the kingdom as equal partners of the Netherlands. In 1962 Netherlands New Guinea (West Irian) was transferred to Indonesia.

The Netherlands has played a prominent role in bringing about closer ties among the countries of Western Europe. In 1967 the Netherlands met with Belgium and Luxembourg to discuss extending the integration between their countries beyond the field of economics, hoping thus to encourage closer cooperation between France, West Germany, and Italy, the other members of the West European Community.

—George M. Kren

NEW ZEALAND

Official name: New Zealand
Area: 103,740 square miles
Population: (1967 est.) 2,726,000
Capital: Wellington (Pop., 1966, urban area, 167,844)
Language: English
Religion: Anglicanism, Protestantism, Roman Catholicism
Currency: Dollar
National holiday: New Zealand day, February 6

New Zealand, an independent nation in the South Pacific Ocean, lies some 1,200 miles southeast of Australia, from which it is separated by the Tasman Sea. New Zealand is made up of two main islands, North Island and South Island, and several smaller islands, including Stewart Island and the Chatham Islands.

THE LAND. New Zealand is a relatively mountainous country. The Southern Alps extend along the length of South Island, and there are 28 peaks with elevations over 10,000 feet above sea level. The highest peak, reaching an elevation of 12,349 feet, is Mount Cook, in the west-central part of South Island. The eastern part of South Island contains several areas of level land at fairly low elevations, notably the Canterbury and Southland plains. Cook Straight separates North Island from South Island.

North Island has four volcanic peaks with elevations of over 6,000 feet, the highest of which is Ruapehu, with an elevation of 9,175 feet. Among the larger lowland regions of North Island are the Waikato-Thames Plain and Manawatu-Horowhenua Coastal Plain.

There are many rivers on the islands, including the Waikato, Wanganui, and Rangitaiki on North Island, and the Waitaki, Oreti, and Clutha on South Island.

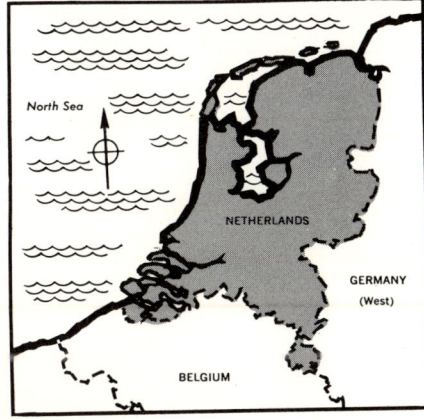

NEW ZEALAND'S SOUTH ISLAND is mountainous, and many of the mountains extend to the sea.

COUNTRIES OF THE WORLD

Climate. New Zealand has a damp, mild climate, which is strongly influenced by the small size of the islands in relation to the vastness of the surrounding ocean. The waters surrounding the country tend to moderate its temperatures, so that the winters are relatively mild and the summers comparatively cool.

Only a limited area of South Island receives less than 20 inches of rain a year, whereas many parts of both North and South islands receive over 50 inches of rain a year. The greatest rainfall occurs in the western part of South Island, where some areas receive over 200 inches a year.

THE PEOPLE. Over 90 percent of New Zealanders are of British descent. There are also small numbers of Europeans of other origins. The Maori, a people of Polynesian stock, migrated to New Zealand from the Pacific islands beginning in the 900s. In 1965 Maoris made up over 7 percent of the population.

New Zealand has a rapidly growing population, and between 1958 and 1965 the rate of population growth was 2.1 percent a year. About two-thirds of the people live on North Island. The New Zealanders are largely urban dwellers, and two cities, Auckland and Wellington, with their suburbs, accounted for over 25 percent of the population in 1965.

ECONOMY. New Zealand is primarily an agricultural country. At one time all of North Island and most of South Island were forested. In the 1800s European settlers cleared large areas to establish farms, and today only about 20 percent of New Zealand is forested. In many places the removal of natural cover resulted in erosion or the growth of tussock grasses.

Agriculture. The country's mild climate and its grasslands provide excellent conditions for pastoral industries. Sheep are raised in most parts of the country, and in 1965 there were more than 53.7 million sheep in New Zealand.

Sheep on South Island are raised primarily for their wool, and sheep on North Island are raised for wool and mutton. On South Island sheep are grazed on large ranges in the mountainous central region. There are two sheep-rearing regions on North Island, one extending along the entire east coast and the other running from Auckland to Wanganui.

Dairying is also an important agricultural industry in New Zealand. Most of the dairying is confined to North Island, in the areas north and south of Auckland, and in the southwestern corner of the island. The principal products are butter and cheese.

Although the sheep and dairy industries dominate New Zealand agriculture, many other products and crops are produced in significant quantities. In the eastern and southern coastal regions of South Island, wheat, oats, barley, and turnips are grown. Fruits and vegetables are grown mainly on North Island and on the northern tip of South Island.

Mining and Manufacturing. New Zealand is not an important mining country, but enough coal is mined to meet local needs in most years and some gold is produced. Because of a lack of major mineral resources and a limited home market, New Zealand has not developed a great number of manufacturing industries.

Aside from the processing of agricultural products, such as butter and cheese making, canning and freezing vegetables, and leather and wool preparation, most manufacturing is based on imported raw materials. Auckland is the principal manufacturing center, with automobile assembly, woodworking, textile, brewing, and light engineering plants. Christchurch has automobile assembly plants.

Trade. In 1967 imports cost over U.S. $955 million and exports earned over U.S. $933 million. The major imports are petroleum, textile yarn and fabrics, iron and steel, and machinery. The major exports are meat, dairy products, and wool. Most trade is conducted with Britain, the United States, Australia, Canada, and Japan.

GOVERNMENT. New Zealand has a parliamentary system of government. The head of state is the British Queen, who is represented in New Zealand by a governor-general. Actual executive power is vested in a prime minister and cabinet responsible to the legislature. Legislative power is held by an 80-member House of Representatives. House members are popularly elected to three-year terms.

New Zealand is a member of the United Nations and the Commonwealth of Nations. It is also a member of the Southeast Asia Treaty Organization (SEATO); the Tripartite Security Treaty (ANZUS), with Australia and the United States; and ANZAM, a defense agreement with Australia and Britain.

HISTORY. The Maori migrated to New Zealand between the 900s and 1300s. In 1642 the Dutch navigator Abel Tasman sighted the islands of New Zealand, but they were not visited by Europeans again until 1769, when Capt. James Cook accurately charted the coasts.

Only after European settlement in Australia in the late 1700s and early 1800s did Europeans develop an interest in New Zealand. From the 1790s to the 1840s Europeans exploited New Zealand's timber, seals, whales, and flax and established a port of call at the Bay of Islands, on North Island.

Missionaries worked among the Maoris, while Britain sought to maintain order on the islands and stimulate trade without assuming governmental responsibility. Perhaps 2,000 Europeans then lived in New Zealand.

British Rule. In 1840 settlement began in earnest. In that year the British signed the Treaty of Waitangi with the Maoris. By this treaty Britain extended its sovereignty over New Zealand and promised protection of Maori land rights and equality in a biracial society. In 1841 New Zealand became a crown colony.

In quick succession, settlements were made at Wellington, Auckland, and at Nelson, Dunedin, and Christchurch on South Island. The British settlers intended to develop an economy based on crop production, but sheep grazing and wool production proved more feasible and profitable.

South Island was dominant until about 1910. There were few Maoris there and the land was reasonably accessible. North Island had many Maoris and was heavily wooded. In 1852 Britain granted New Zealand a constitution providing for a loose federation of six provinces, and in 1856 a parliamentary system of government was established.

Federal Government. Gold was discovered in the 1860s on South Island, and gold rushes brought men and capital. In that same decade North Island was preoccupied with wars between Maori tribes and settlers over land. The Maoris were defeated in 1872 and after that time many Maoris refused to cooperate with the government.

The Maori population declined from about 100,000 in 1840 to 40,000 at the end of the 1800s. After that time, however, under educated Maori leadership, the Maoris developed into an influential minority, and by 1960 they numbered some 150,000.

Aside from problems arising from conflicts between the central and provincial governments and relations with the Maoris, New Zealand concerned itself with social and economic development. The effective power for this development rested with the provinces. In 1876, seeking to effect a national development program, Sir Julius Vogel, the prime minister, dissolved the provinces.

Centralization. Vogel's development program included borrowing funds in Britain, railroad construction, encouraging immigration, and opening up land for individual purchase to encourage diversified agricultural production. The program was not entirely successful, however. Borrowing became difficult, the railroad system was left incomplete, immigrants could not acquire closely held lands, and economic diversification did not materialize.

New Zealand stagnated in the 1880s and people left the island. Technological changes solved New Zealand's problems, however, as the introduction of refrigerated shipping made possible the export of meat and dairy products to Britain. This development diversified pastoral exports and triggered a rapid growth of dairying on North Island.

In 1891 the Liberal party, supported by small farmers and city workers, came to power. Prime Minister Richard Seddon launched a program of social and economic experimentation. The government introduced land reforms, compulsory labor arbitration, and social services. Trade unions grew in importance. Reforms, along with technological changes and improved export prices, provided a system which benefited the common man, farmers in particular. In 1907 Britain granted New Zealand dominion status.

Dominion. Seddon had died in 1906, and in 1912 the Liberal party was defeated. Between 1912 and 1935 a more conservative government, supported mainly by North Island farmers, remained in office almost constantly.

The power of the farmers confirmed New Zealand's role as a supplier of dairy products, meat, and wool to Britain, to which it was also politically and culturally loyal. New Zealand soldiers aided the British in World War I. After the war, land industries predominated, and factories chiefly processed farm produce.

Politically important in the years from 1916 to 1935 was the rise of the Labor party, supported by a growing industrial working class. In 1931 the Labor party's strength provoked Seddon's followers and the farmer party to form a coalition. But in 1935 Labor came to office and held power continuously for 14 years.

The world economic depression of the 1930s had hit New Zealand hard. The Labor government arranged guaranteed prices for farmers, and took control of exports and imports, foreign exchange, and banking. It emphasized the redistribution of income, elaborated a social security system, and promoted factory industries to balance the economy. In effect, the government sought to socialize national income rather than the means of production.

Contemporary New Zealand. In 1939 New Zealand entered World War II, collaborating with the United States in the Pacific and with Britain in Europe and Africa. After the war New Zealand continued to collaborate with the United States in defense and political affairs.

In 1949 the National party, emphasizing a program of private enterprise, defeated Labor, and Sydney Holland became prime minister. The National party further advanced the social welfare policies introduced by the Labor government.

Holland retired in September 1957, and Keith Holyoake became prime minister. Three months later elections were held and the Labor party, led by Walter Nash, was victorious. But in 1960 the National party, led by Holyoake, was returned to power and was reelected in 1963 and 1966.

—David A. Smith

NICARAGUA

Official name: Republic of Nicaragua
Area: 50,000 square miles
Population: (1966 est.) 1,715,000
Capital: Managua (Pop., 1965 est., 262,000)
Language: Spanish
Religion: Roman Catholicism
Currency unit: Córdoba
National holiday: Independence day, September 15

Nicaragua, the largest of the Central American republics, is bounded on the north by Honduras, on the east by the Caribbean Sea, on the south by Costa Rica, and on the west by the Pacific Ocean.

THE LAND. Most of Nicaragua is occupied by the Central American Cordillera of the Andes, which extends in a north-south direction through the center of the country. The cordillera separates the wide Caribbean coastal plain, known as the Mosquito Coast, from a narrow Pacific coastal plain.

A long, narrow depression runs diagonally across Nicaragua from the Gulf of Fonseca in the northwest into Costa Rica. This depression contains two large lakes, Lake Nicaragua and Lake Managua. Lake Nicaragua, about 100 miles long and 45 miles wide, is one of the largest bodies of fresh water in Central America.

The mountains to the west of the depression are actively volcanic, and eruptions and earthquakes are a constant hazard in the area.

Nicaragua has a hot climate. Temperatures seldom drop below 75°F, although it is generally cooler in the central mountain region. Rainfall is moderate on the Pacific coast and in the mountains. It is extremely heavy, however, along the Caribbean coast, where some places receive as much as 200 inches a year.

THE PEOPLE. Over 70 percent of the people of Nicaragua are mestizo, of mixed Indian and European ancestry. About 15 percent are of European descent. The remainder of the population is composed of the indigenous Mosquito Indians and Negroes from the West Indies.

Much of Nicaragua is thinly settled. The Mosquito Indians and most of the Negroes live in the Caribbean coastal plain. The bulk of the population is concentrated along the Pacific coast and in the area around Lake Nicaragua and Lake Managua. It is in this area that Nicaragua's three largest cities—Managua, León, and Granada—are located.

ECONOMY. Nicaragua is predominantly an agricultural nation, although the government has been attempting to diversify the economy.

Nicaragua is rich in minerals. Mining is confined mainly to gold, silver, and copper, but there are deposits of iron, bauxite, antimony, tungsten, mercury, and manganese.

About half of Nicaragua is covered with forests, and timber, including mahogany, pine, cedar, rosewood, and balsa, is an important export. Rubber is also an important forest product.

Agriculture. Agriculture employs about 60 percent of the labor force. A major share of the country's crops are raised in the west, where extensive tracts of fertile soil are ideal for mechanized farming, but a large percentage of Nicaragua's arable land is not cultivated.

Corn, beans, rice, and sugarcane are raised for domestic consumption. Cotton, coffee, and sesame are the leading commercial crops. Tobacco, cacao, and fruits are grown, and cattle are important in the west.

Industry. Nicaraguan industry is almost entirely limited to food processing and the manufacture of a few consumer items for local consumption. The largest industry is sugar refining. Factories produce cement, insecticides, cigarettes, soap, liquor, and clothing.

Trade. Nicaragua's exports in 1967 earned $146 million and imports cost $204 million. Major exports are cotton, coffee, copper, oilseeds (cotton and sesame), meat, and timber. Principal imports include machinery, transportation equipment, chemicals, textiles, and foodstuffs. Most of Nicaragua's trade is with the United States, Japan, and West Germany.

GOVERNMENT. Nicaragua is a republic. The head of state and chief executive is the president, who is directly elected to a four-year term. Congress consists of the Senate and the Chamber of Deputies, whose members are directly elected to four-year terms on the basis of proportional represen-

tation. In addition, all former presidents are appointed to the Senate as members for life.

Nicaragua is a member of the United Nations and the Organization of American States (OAS).

HISTORY. Nicaragua was discovered in 1502 by Christopher Columbus on his last voyage to the New World, but it was not explored until 1522, when Gil González Dávila led an expedition from Panama. In 1524 the Spanish founded the cities of León and Granada in the western lowlands, and except for sporadic raids by English pirates during the latter half of the 1600s, the colonial period in Nicaragua was peaceful.

Independence from Spain was won in 1821, but Nicaragua was annexed to the Mexican Empire. When the Mexican Empire collapsed in 1823, Nicaragua joined the United Provinces of Central America, which included El Salvador, Honduras, Guatemala, and Costa Rica. In 1838 Nicaragua left the United Provinces and declared itself independent.

Sovereignty. As a sovereign nation, Nicaragua suffered from intense rivalry between Liberals, centered in León, and Conservatives, in Granada, who battled for political control of the country. In 1856, when the Conservatives gained power and attempted to establish a strong and stable government, the Liberals invited an adventurer from the United States, William Walker, to help oust the Conservative administration.

With a following of approximately 60 men, Walker managed to capture control of Nicaragua and install himself as president. The U.S. financier, Cornelius Vanderbilt, who feared that a steamship monopoly he held would be restricted by Walker and the Liberals, took an active role in Nicaragua's politics.

Vanderbilt helped organize an invading army recruited in neighboring countries, and after only one year in office, Walker was forced to flee. In 1860 he was captured in Honduras and executed. Following Walker's death, tension between Liberals and Conservatives was temporarily abated and Nicaragua enjoyed peace and prosperity under several consecutive Conservative administrations.

Zelaya Era. A revolution by Liberal forces in 1893 brought José Santos Zelaya to power. Zelaya moved the capital from León to Managua, promoted railroad construction, brought the Indians of the east coast under the government's jurisdiction, and promoted agricultural development. Zelaya also involved Nicaragua in revolutions in neighboring Central American countries.

In 1909 Zelaya executed two U.S. engineers, whom he maintained were implicated in a plot to overthrow his government. The United States severed diplomatic relations with Nicaragua, weakening the prestige of the Zelaya administration. The Conservatives rebelled, forcing Zelaya to resign.

U.S. Intervention. For several years political and economic conditions in Nicaragua were in a chaotic state. In 1912 the United States sent marines to restore order at the request of provisional Pres. Adolfo Díaz.

In the same year Díaz was elected president, and in 1914 Nicaragua signed the Bryan-Chamorro Treaty with the United States. The treaty gave the United States the right to construct a trans-isthmian canal through Nicaragua and to establish military bases on both coasts. Except for a brief period in 1925, the U.S. marines remained in the country until 1933.

Contemporary Nicaragua. In 1936 Gen. Anastasio Somoza, commander of the U.S.-trained National Guard, established himself in the presidency and assumed dictatorial powers. His administration was characterized by economic development and political repression. During World War II Somoza actively cooperated with the United States.

In 1947 Leonardo Arquello was elected president, but Somoza had him removed from office. Victor Manuel Roman y Reyes was then selected by a constituent assembly to occupy the presidency. Roman y Reyes died in May 1950, at which time Somoza again became president. Somoza was assassinated in September 1956, and his son, Luis Somoza Debayle, was appointed acting president for the duration of his father's term. The following year he was elected president.

Luis Somoza's administration, contrary to expectations, proved to be less oppressive than that of his father. Civil liberties, freedom of the press, and political opposition were permitted.

In 1963 René Schick Gutiérrez was elected president. Schick died in 1966, and Congress elected Lorenzo Guerrero Gutiérrez to finish his term. In 1967 Gen. Anastasio Somoza Debayle, the brother of Luis Somoza, was elected president.

—George W. Carey; Jerome Fischman

NIGER

Official name: Republic of Niger
Area: 489,000 square miles
Population: (1967 est., 3,546,000)
Capital: Niamey (Pop., 1962 est., 40,172)
Language: French, African languages
Religion: Islam, traditional religions
Currency unit: Franc CFA (African Financial Community)
National holiday: Proclamation of the republic, December 18

Niger, a republic in western Africa, is bounded on the north by Algeria and Libya, on the east by Chad, on the south by Nigeria and Dahomey, and on the west by Upper Volta and Mali. Niger was granted its independence from France in 1960.

THE LAND. Most of Niger is flat. In the north there is desert and in the east there are scrubby and grassy lowlands. In north-central Niger a great mass of volcanic mountains known as the Aïr (Azbine) rise to elevations of almost 6,000 feet. Lake Chad lies at the southeastern corner of Niger. The Niger River flows through southwestern Niger.

Niger's climate is hot and dry. Half of Niger receives less than four

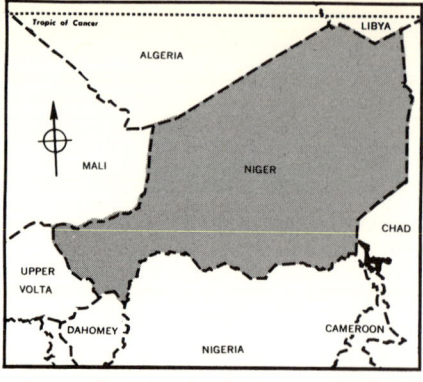

inches of rain each year. Rainfall averages about 20 inches a year near the border with Nigeria.

THE PEOPLE. There are four main ethnic groups in Niger—the Hausa, Dyerma, Fulani (Fula), and Tuareg. The greatest concentration of people is in the southern part of the country, especially near the Niger River. Most of the people are Muslim. Niger's largest cities are Niamey, the capital, and Zinder.

ECONOMY. The economy of Niger is based on agriculture. The basic food crops are millet, sorghum, rice, beans, and wheat, and the main commercial crops are peanuts, cotton, and tobacco. Most of the cultivated land is near the border with Nigeria. Cattle, sheep, and goats are raised in most parts of the country.

Tin and tungsten are mined in the Aïr Mountains. There are also small deposits of salt, oil, and copper. The country's industry is poorly developed.

In 1965 imports cost $38 million and exports earned $25 million. The main imports include sugar, petroleum products, machinery, and manufactured goods, especially textiles. Niger's major exports are live animals, peanuts and peanut oil, and vegetables. Most trade is conducted with France, Nigeria, the Ivory Coast, and the Netherlands. Niger has close economic ties with Dahomey, the Ivory Coast, Togo, and Upper Volta.

GOVERNMENT. Niger has a presidential system of government. Executive power is held by a president, who is popularly elected to a five-year term. Legislative power rests with a 50-member National Assembly, which is also popularly elected every five years.

Niger is a member of the United Nations and the Organization of African Unity (OAU).

HISTORY. Much of what is now western Niger was part of the Songhai empire, which flourished from the 1400s to the late 1500s, when it was conquered by a Moroccan army. During the same period, the city-states of the Hausa people in southern Niger maintained their independence from foreign domination. In the north the nomadic Tuareg roamed the arid fringe of the Sahara. All of these peoples traded with North Africa, and the city of Zinder was a center for trade caravans.

In the early 1800s the Hausa region was engulfed in revolution. Usuman dan Fodio, a Fulani Muslim cleric, proclaimed a holy war against the Hausa ruling class of Gobia, one of the more important city-states. He voiced long-existing religious and social complaints of the subjects of the Hausa rulers.

The war lasted from 1804 to 1810, by which time nearly all the Hausa states had come under Fulani rule. In time, all of southern Niger and northern Nigeria owed allegiance to Fulani overlords.

French Rule. The power of the Fulani rulers, and of the Tuareg, was broken by the French, whose army conquered what is now Niger between 1890 and 1914. Beginning in 1895 Niger was administered as part of French West Africa. After World War II Niger became a territory within the French Union.

In 1958 the Niger Progressive Party, led by Hamani Diori, won an overwhelming majority of seats in the territorial assembly. In that year Niger became an autonomous member of the French Community. The assembly soon dissolved all opposition parties.

Independence. On Aug. 3, 1960, Niger became independent and Diori became president. There has been organized opposition from outside the country to Diori's one-party system, and several attempts to overthrow his government have been made. Nonetheless, Diori was re-elected president in 1965.

—Hibberd V. B. Kline, Jr.; Robert I. Rotberg

NIGERIA

Official name: Republic of Nigeria
Area: 356,669 square miles
Population: (1966 est.) 58,600,000
Capital: Lagos (Pop., 1963, 665,246)
Language: English, African languages
Religion: Islam, traditional religions
Currency unit: Pound
National holiday: Independence day, October 1

Nigeria, a republic in western Africa, is bounded on the north by Niger, on the east by Chad and Cameroon, on the south by the Gulf of Guinea, an arm of the Atlantic Ocean, and on the west by Dahomey. Nigeria was granted its independence by Britain in 1960.

THE LAND. Most of Nigeria is occupied by plains or low rolling hills. There are tropical forests and mangrove swamps along the coast. The Niger River, which flows through south-central Nigeria, forms a large delta where it reaches the ocean.

There are grassy savannas in central Nigeria, north of the junction of the Niger and Benue rivers. In the north-central part of the country is the Bauchi Plateau, which has an elevation of almost 6,000 feet above sea level. There is grassland and desert in the far north. The Adamawa Mountains are in the southwest.

The climate of Nigeria is hot and humid. Some areas in the south receive as much as 150 inches of rain each year.

THE PEOPLE. Nigeria is one of the most populous countries in Africa. There are four main ethnic groups in Nigeria—the Yoruba, Ibo, Hausa, and Fulani (Fula). The Fulani and Hausa peoples are predominantly Muslim and are concentrated in northern Nigeria. The Yoruba live mainly in the west, and the Ibo in the east.

The country's largest cities include Lagos, the national capital, which is on an island off the southwestern coast; Ibadan and Ogbomosho, in the southwest; and Kano, in the north.

ECONOMY. Nigeria's economy is based largely on agriculture. Peanuts, oil palm products, cacao, cotton, and rubber are the leading commercial crops. The basic food crops include yams and corn. Nigeria has rich forest resources, and timber is exported. Fish from the Niger River provide an additional source of food. Cattle are raised mainly in the northern part of the country.

Nigeria also has rich mineral resources. There are vast petroleum deposits, mainly in the Niger delta, and in 1966 over 1.7 million metric tons of petroleum were produced. There are also reserves of natural gas, coal, tin, and columbite.

Nigerian industry developed greatly after independence was achieved in 1960. Textiles, cement, plywood and timber, and automobiles are produced. A large dam has been planned for the Niger River to provide the country with hydroelectric power. The transportation system is well developed, and railroads link Port Harcourt, Kano, and Nguru.

In 1966 exports earned $792 million and imports cost $718 million. The main exports are cacao, palm products, peanuts and peanut oil, rubber, crude petroleum, and tin. Major imports include petroleum products, fabrics, iron and steel, machinery, cereals, and chemicals. Most trade is with Britain, West Germany, the Netherlands, and the United States.

GOVERNMENT. The 1963 constitution of Nigeria provided for a federal government and governments for the country's four regions—Eastern, Western, Northern, and Mid-Western.

Federal legislative power was held by a House of Representatives and a Senate. House members were popularly elected and Senate members were appointed from the regions. The federal legislature elected a president to serve as head of state. Executive power was wielded by a prime minister and cabinet.

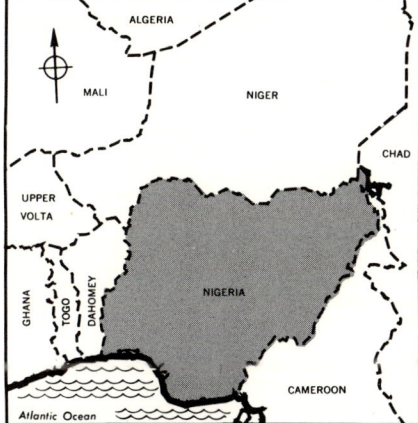

Each region had its own legislature consisting of a popularly elected House of Assembly and a House of Chiefs. The people elected a governor, who appointed a provincial prime minister. Executive power was exercised by the prime minister.

In 1966 the constitution was suspended and a military council took executive and legislative powers. The four regions were abolished, and in their place the council established 12 states.

Nigeria is a member of the Commonwealth of Nations, the Organization of African Unity (OAU), and the United Nations.

HISTORY. The many peoples of Nigeria have a rich heritage. In about the 1100s the Yoruba people settled in western Nigeria, and in the north Hausa people established agricultural states. In the 1200s the Hausa were converted to Islam by the Fulani people, who came from eastern Africa. In the early 1800s a Fulani leader, Usuman dan Fodio, conquered the Hausa city-states and replaced the Hausa dynasties with Fulani emirs.

Portuguese traders came to Nigeria in 1472, and Portugal and other European countries shared in the lucrative slave trade that developed. The British penetrated the area beginning in 1807 to halt the slave trade. Lagos was occupied by Britain in 1861, and the United Africa Company, later known as the Royal Niger Company, opened the Niger Valley to trade. In 1885 the Oil Rivers Protectorate was set up in the coastal region.

British Rule. The British government took over direct administration of the protectorate in 1891, and by 1893, with the addition of a region beyond the coast, formed the Niger Coast protectorate. In 1900 it became the protectorate of Southern Nigeria. In the same year the territory of the Royal Niger Company became the protectorate of Northern Nigeria. In 1903 the emirates of the north came under British control.

The protectorates were united in 1914, and after World War I the former German colony of Cameroon was added as a mandate under the League of Nations. In 1939 southern Nigeria was divided into the Eastern and Western provinces.

Nigerians had begun to seek greater freedom before World War I, but nationalist movements tended to be regional. Most prominent were the Northern Peoples' Congress (NPC) led by Sir Ahmadu Bello, the Action Group in the Western region led by Chief Obafemi Awolowo, and the National Council of Nigeria and Cameroons (NCNC) led by Dr. Nnamdi Azikiwe. After World War II regional legislatures and elections were introduced.

In 1954 the first national elections were held, and the NPC and NCNC obtained the most votes. Eastern and western Nigeria became self-governing in 1957, but the north, which was less developed, did not achieve self-government until 1959.

Independence. On Oct. 1, 1960 Nigeria became an independent nation. In 1961 a UN plebiscite was held in the British Cameroons, and the Northern Cameroons voted to become part of Nigeria, which then consisted of three regions—Eastern, Western, and Northern Nigeria. On Oct. 1, 1963 Nigeria became a republic and Azikiwe was elected president by the federal Parliament. Abubakar Tafawa Balewa became prime minister. In the same year, the Mid-Western region was formed.

In January 1966 there was a military coup and Balewa was assassinated. Gen. Johnson Aguiyi-Ironsi of the Eastern region proclaimed himself head of state. In July 1966 Aguiyi-Ironsi was assassinated and Yakubu Gowon of the Northern region became head of state.

In May 1967 Eastern Nigeria voted to secede and declared itself the Republic of Biafra. Gowon took full power as head of the national government. He proclaimed a state of emergency and moved to end the secession by force.

—Hibberd V. B. Kline, Jr.;
Vera L. Zolberg

NORWAY

Official name: Kingdom of Norway
Area: 125,182 square miles
Population: (1967 est.) 3,784,000
Capital: Oslo (Pop., 1965 est., 483,196)
Language: Norwegian
Religion: Lutheranism
Currency unit: Krone
National holiday: Constitution day, May 17

Norway, a kingdom in northern Europe, occupies the entire western side of the Scandinavian Peninsula. It is bounded on the north by the Arctic Ocean, on the east by Sweden, on the northeast by the Soviet Union and Finland, on the south by the Skagerrak and the North Sea, and on the west by the Norwegian Sea, an arm of the North Atlantic Ocean.

THE LAND. Norway is a long, narrow country described as being "all mountains and sea." It is almost totally devoid of plains. Most of the terrain is rugged and mountainous, but there is a high, hilly plateau region in the center of the country.

A mountainous ridge follows the border with Sweden. It rises to about 8,000 feet in the south-central region, and steep slopes plunge into the Skagerrak along the coast.

Norway's long coastline is penetrated by almost innumerable deep, sheltered, navigable inlets, or fjords, and is protected from the open sea by a fringe of islands. Many lakes lie scattered throughout Norway, and many rivers and streams rush down from the mountains.

More than one-third of the country lies north of the Arctic Circle, and two arctic islands, Jan Mayen and Spitsbergen (Svalbard), are part of Norway.

Norway's climate is varied. The south has a temperate marine climate, with cool summers, mild winters, and much cloudiness. The warm North Atlantic drift keeps the entire coast ice-free all the year. In the north and in the higher elevations the climate is colder and more severe. Precipitation is plentiful, particularly in the mountains.

THE PEOPLE. Norway has one of Europe's smallest populations, and in 1966 there were about 30 persons per square mile. The population is increasing very slowly, less than 1 percent a year between 1958 and 1965.

The interior and the northern two-thirds of the country are sparsely inhabited, and most of the people live along the southern coast, where Norway's main cities, Oslo, Bergen, and Trondheim, are located.

Almost all of the people are Norwegian. Norwegian is the universal language and Evangelical Lutheranism is the established religion. In the far north there is a minority of about 20,000 semi-nomadic Lapps, who have their own language and culture. There is also a small Finnish minority in the north.

ECONOMY. Norway's economy traditionally was based upon merchant shipping, fishing, forestry, and agriculture. In the 1900s the country began to expand its industry by developing and utilizing its natural resources.

Norway's most valuable resource is its enormous water power, which is easy and inexpensive to harness for electricity. Norway also has a modest endowment of minerals, including pyrites and some iron, copper, zinc, molybdenum, and nickel. Forests cover about one-quarter of the land and provide the basis for important wood pulp and paper industries.

Commercial fishing, though of less importance than formerly, still prospers, and forestry is important in the economy.

Merchant shipping, always important in Norway's economy, contributed about one-eighth of the national product in 1965. Norway has one of the world's largest merchant fleets, over 16 million gross registered tons in 1966. Income from the fleet accounts for about one-third of the country's foreign exchange earnings.

Agriculture. Less than 5 percent of Norway's land is cultivable, and in 1965 agriculture contributed only 9 percent to the domestic product. But agriculture employed about 20 percent of the labor force and met a large part of the country's food requirements. The major emphasis is on livestock raising and dairying. Hardy grains, potatoes, and some fruits and vegetables are also grown.

Manufacturing. Norwegian industry received a tremendous boost in the 1950s and 1960s from the rapid development of hydroelectric power, which almost doubled in output between 1957 and 1965. In 1965 manufacturing contributed 27 percent of the national product. Among the newer industries made possible by cheap and abundant electricity are the electrometallurgical and electrochemical industries. Major industrial products include ships, machinery, and vehicles. Lumber and pulp and paper mills are also important, and fish processing plants produce some of Norway's major exports.

Trade. Earnings from shipping and tourism help to make up for Norway's poor balance of international trade. In 1966 imports cost $2,746 million and exports earned only $1,736 million.

Major imports are ships and boats, machinery, petroleum products, textiles, and foodstuffs. Metals and ores, pulp and paper, and fish and fish products are the leading exports. Sweden, Britain, West Germany, the United States, and Denmark are Norway's major trading partners.

GOVERNMENT. Norway is a constitutional monarchy, with a king as head of state. Actual executive power is wielded by a prime minister and cabinet responsible to the parliament.

The parliament, called the *Storting,* is popularly elected every four years. It elects one-quarter of its membership to sit as an upper house, the *Lagting.* The remainder of the *Storting* is called the *Odelsting.* Most legislative actions are taken by the united *Storting.*

Norway is a member of the United Nations, the Council of Europe, the North Atlantic Treaty Organization (NATO), and the Nordic Council, an association of the Scandinavian nations —Norway, Sweden, Denmark, Finland, and Iceland.

HISTORY. Archeological evidence indicates that man lived in Norway as early as 8,000 years ago. Beginning about 7,000 years ago, a variety of wandering tribes from the north and south appeared in Scandinavia. Germanic tribes, the main forebears of the present Norwegian people, had established themselves in the land by about 500 BC.

For the next 1,000 years, during the eras of the Roman Empire and the barbarian migrations, tribal groups in Norway shifted and resettled, competing for dominance over the entire region.

During the 800s AD the tribal communities were gradually united, and Harold Fairhair (Harald Haarfager) became Norway's first king. The united tribes began to expand their territory, and from the late 800s through the early 1000s, Norwegian Vikings explored the shores of Britain, Ireland, the Faroe Islands, Iceland, Greenland, and probably North America.

During several brief intervals in the late 900s and early 1000s the country was under Danish rule, but Norwegian kings always regained control, and by the mid-1000s the monarchy was quite strong.

COUNTRIES OF THE WORLD

Early Kingdom. Through the efforts of King Olaf Tryggvesson and King Olaf Haraldsson in the late 900s and early 1000s Christianity was introduced into Norway. As the church gained influence, it challenged royal power and was supported by members of the growing land-owning aristocracy.

Civil wars filled the period between the mid-1100s and the mid-1200s, but the strength of the monarchy was maintained, and the 1200s marked the high point of Norwegian power and prosperity. Between 1217 and 1263, during the reign of King Haakon IV, Iceland and Greenland were added to the realm. Norwegian art and literature flourished, and King Magnus VI sponsored a codification of law for the entire country in the 1270s.

This era of greatness was short-lived, however. In the mid-1300s the Black Death killed half of Norway's population and crippled the country. The merchants of the German Hanseatic League gained a firm grip on Norwegian economic life. Moreover, the Norwegian royal succession became entangled with that of Sweden and Denmark.

In 1380 King Olaf V, the last of Harold Fairhair's dynasty, became king of both Norway and Denmark. When he died in 1387, his mother, Queen Margaret of Denmark, combined the thrones of both kingdoms. In 1397 Sweden was added to form the Kalmar Union, which was dominated by Denmark.

Norway was the weakest member, and its territory, prestige, and autonomy declined steadily in the 1400s. The union was frequently torn by internal struggles, and in 1523 Sweden broke away.

Danish Union. Norway remained linked with Denmark, as part of a kingdom ruled and administered by Danes. With Denmark, Norway became Lutheran in 1536. Norway shared Danish wars, including a series of territorial and dynastic struggles with Sweden between the 1560s and the 1720s.

The Norwegians did enjoy some economic benefits from Danish rule, however, between 1588 and 1648. King Christian IV reformed the administration of Norway and initiated the development of Norwegian resources. Absolutists who ruled Denmark-Norway after 1660 stimulated Norway's economy by expanding exports and founding new towns.

Modest but steady economic growth continued through the 1700s and helped to lay the basis for the development of a Norwegian national consciousness. In 1807 Denmark granted Norwegian requests for a national assembly. Norway's sufferings during the Napoleonic wars, in which Denmark sided with France, stimulated Norwegian nationalism. In 1814 Sweden, which had opposed Napoleon and had won a victory over Denmark, forced Denmark to cede Norway.

Swedish Union. The Norwegians rose in protest and refused to recognize Swedish rule. They convened a national assembly, which adopted a liberal constitution in May 1814, and they elected the Danish prince Christian Frederick as their king.

NORWEGIAN INFORMATION SERVICE
NORWAY'S LANDSCAPE is dominated by mountains stretching the length of the country.

The crown prince of Sweden invaded the country and succeeded in taking the Norwegian throne, however. Nevertheless, the Norwegians, by their resistance, secured a great deal of autonomy before they would accept union with Sweden. Norway was granted an elected *Storting*, and was proclaimed indivisible and independent; it was joined in personal union with the Swedish crown. The *Storting* ratified the union in 1815.

During the 1800s Norway underwent a national renaissance. Scholarly and scientific activities widened, and arts and letters flourished. The economy of Norway-Sweden improved steadily during the 1800s.

As their strength increased, Norwegian liberal intellectuals grew restless under rather arbitrary kings. Sweden granted concessions, including a system of free education, complete religious freedom, expansion of voting rights, and, in 1864, a new liberal constitution.

The reform movement accelerated in Norway after the passage of the constitution. In the late 1880s a parliamentary system of government was introduced, based on universal manhood suffrage. In the 1890s Norwegian demands for complete independence grew, led by Johan Sverdrup. The economies of both countries were booming, with Norway's merchant fleet as the basis of the prosperity.

Renewed Independence. As Norway's international trade expanded, the Norwegian *Storting* requested permission to handle Norway's consular affairs under its own flag. When the Swedish king refused, the Norwegian *Storting* declared Norway independent in June 1905. Norway elected the Danish prince Charles to be king as Haakon VII. Sweden accepted Norway's declaration of independence in October 1905.

Norway was well prepared for independence by its material progress, political activism and social reforms of the late 1800s. Democratic reform continued in Norway after independence. The royal veto over the *Storting* was abolished, the vote was extended to women, and social welfare programs were initiated.

Norway remained neutral in World War I, but its vital merchant fleet was severely damaged. After the war the nation suffered an economic depression which was itensified by the world economic depression of the 1930s.

Economic and social reforms initiated during the 1920s and 1930s included the formation of cooperative enterprises, the institution of national collective bargaining, and the expansion of social welfare legislation under the leadership of Liberal, Labor, and left-wing farmers' party governments. A Labor government elected in 1935 was successful in ending Norway's economic crisis by expanding government participation in the economy.

In 1940, during World War II, Germany invaded Norway, and despite stiff Norwegian resistance Nazi troops conquered and occupied the country. The Germans governed Norway through a puppet minister, Vidkun Quisling. The exiled King Haakon rallied resistance to the Germans, and the Norwegian home front played a prominent part in Norway's liberation from the Germans in 1945.

The nation had suffered severe economic damage during the war, and a Labor government elected in 1945 instituted an austerity program which, by the early 1950s, had restored many of the losses.

Contemporary Norway. Norway participated actively in postwar international affairs. In 1945 it became a charter member of the United Nations and a Norwegian, Trygve Lie, became the first secretary general of the UN. In 1948–1949, when its neighbors pressed for a Scandinavian defense union, Norway joined NATO, but it encouraged the social, economic, and cultural unity of the Scandinavian nations and in 1952 joined the newly formed Nordic Council.

Sharing a common border with the Soviet Union, Norway has had to be circumspect in its foreign policy during the era of the Cold War between the Soviet Union and the United States, but it remained anti-Communist in domestic politics and tended to be pro-Western in international affairs. In 1957 King Haakon died and was succeeded by his son, Olav V.

During the 1950s and 1960s Norway concentrated on expanding and modernizing its economy and developing its natural resources, particularly its water power. The growth of industry was not rapid enough to support Norway's broad social welfare programs, and in the early 1960s the economy began to falter. The Labor government, which had introduced most of the social welfare programs during nearly 30 years in power, bore the brunt of popular dissatisfaction.

In 1965 Labor was voted out of office and was replaced by a coalition of more conservative parties. In its first years in office the coalition government tried to stabilize the economy. In 1967, to strengthen its international economic position, Norway applied for admission to the European Common Market.

PAKISTAN

Official name: Islamic Republic of Pakistan
Area: 365,529 square miles (excluding Jammu and Kashmir)
Population: (1967 est.) 107,258,000 (excluding Jammu and Kashmir)
Capital: Islamabad; interim capital: Rawalpindi (Pop., 1961, 340,175)
Language: Bengali, Urdu, English
Religion: Islam, Hinduism
Currency unit: Rupee
National holiday: Pakistan day, March 23

Pakistan, a republic in South Asia, was created in 1947 from predominantly Muslim regions of British India. It consists of two distinct geographic parts, East Pakistan and West Pakistan, separated by nearly 1,000 miles of Indian territory. West Pakistan, centered on the Indus River Valley, has an area of more than 310,000 square miles, and East Pakistan, in the Ganges River delta, has an area of approximately 55,000 square miles.

West Pakistan is bounded on the north by Afghanistan and China, on the east by India, on the south by the Arabian Sea, and on the west by Iran. East Pakistan is bordered on the north, west, and east by India, on the southeast by Burma, and on the south by the Bay of Bengal. There are boundary disputes with India, and both Pakistan and India claim Kashmir, a region at the northern tip of the Indian subcontinent, and each has occupied a portion of it.

THE LAND. The two regions of Pakistan are quite dissimilar. Most of East Pakistan, the smaller region, is low, level, and swampy, and is drained by the Ganges and the Brahmaputra rivers. The only upland areas are found along the margins of the Khasi hills in the northeast and in the Chittagong hills in the southeast.

East Pakistan has a subtropical climate, with rainfall averaging between 70 and 90 inches a year and as much as 200 inches falling annually in the northeast. Temperatures remain in the 80s°F.

West Pakistan can be divided into five separate geographic regions. Baluchistan, in the southwest, is an arid region of mountains and valleys. The Makran Coast forms a narrow corridor connecting the Indus valley with Iran. The Northwest Frontier is a subhumid mountain and hill region whose many mountain passes, including the Khyber Pass, historically have been the gateways to the Indian subcontinent.

Punjab, in the upper Indus valley, is the traditional economic, political, and cultural heart of Pakistan. Sind, a desert region, occupies the lower Indus valley and the southeastern corner of the country.

The mighty Indus River and its many tributaries flow through the eastern part of the region and empty into the Arabian Sea. In contrast with the east, West Pakistan is arid, with an average annual rainfall of about 20 inches. Temperatures vary widely between cold winters and hot summers.

THE PEOPLE. The population is not evenly divided between East and West Pakistan. Although it occupies almost 85 percent of the nation's total territory, West Pakistan has less than 50 percent of the population. The country's two largest cities, Karachi and Lahore, are in West Pakistan, however.

Pakistanis are varied in background and language. Urdu is the national language of West Pakistan and Bengali the language of East Pakistan, but a number of regional languages are also spoken, especially in West Pakistan. About 90 percent of Pakistanis are Muslims, and about 10 percent are Hindus. Most Hindus live in East Pakistan.

ECONOMY. Faced with the dual problem of modernizing its economy and building a separate economic system from one formerly joined with India, Pakistan has made economic progress, especially in the 1960s. Despite the initiation of major industrialization, in the mid-1960s agriculture remained the dominant factor in the economy.

Industrial development has been hindered by the country's scarcity of natural resources. Its limited supplies of minerals are concentrated mainly in West Pakistan and include modest deposits of chromite, low-grade coal, oil, iron ore, limestone, gypsum, and rock salt. Large reserves of natural gas discovered in the early 1960s in both East and West Pakistan constitute an important resource for industry.

Pakistan's soil suffers from a high salt content and aridity in the west and waterlogging from floods and poor drainage in the east. The Indus Valley is fertile, however, and productive when irrigated.

Agriculture. In the mid-1960s agriculture contributed about half of the domestic product and occupied over two-thirds of the labor force. Pakistan's major food crops are rice, grown in the east, and wheat, grown in the west. Other crops include millet, corn, and barley.

The principal commercial crops are jute, cotton, tea, sugarcane, and tobacco, all of which are valuable as exports and as industrial raw materials. Livestock-raising is important, especially in the west, and oxen, buffalo, sheep, and goats are raised.

Most Pakistani farmers cultivate small plots of land. Traditional agricultural methods are primitive and inefficient, and the improvement of irrigation, farming techniques, and the quality of crops is a major goal.

Manufacturing. In the mid-1960s manufacturing and mining contributed about 11 percent to the domestic product. In 1952 the government established the Pakistan Industrial Development Corporation to expand the production of cotton textiles, processed jute, refined sugar, cigarettes, cement, paper, fertilizers, chemicals, and steel.

An indicator of Pakistan's industrialization is the production of electricity, which rose from 129 million kilowatt hours (kwh) in 1948 to 950 million kwh in 1957, and quadrupled between 1957 and 1966, when 3.9 billion kwh were produced. In 1967 the giant Mangla Dam, one of a series in Pakistan's hydroelectric-irrigation development projects, was opened on the Jhelum River.

Trade. Rapid expansion of exports in the 1950s and 1960s did little to improve Pakistan's unfavorable balance of trade, for imports expanded even more than exports. In 1966 imports cost $900 million and exports earned $601 million.

Jute and cotton, dependent on weather and subject to sharp fluctuations in world-market prices, are the leading exports. Hides, tea, and wool are also exported. The major imports are wheat, iron and steel, machinery, and consumer goods. Most trade is with Britain, The United States, West Germany, Japan, and India.

GOVERNMENT. Under its 1962 constitution Pakistan is a federal republic led by a strong executive, the president. Legislative power is vested in a National Assembly. East Pakistan and West Pakistan each has a powerful provincial assembly and is administered by an appointed governor. The president and the members of the national legislature are elected by a body of some 120,000 popularly elected local officials called "basic democrats."

Pakistan is a member of the United Nations, the Central Treaty Organization (CENTO), the Southeast Asia Treaty Organization (SEATO), and the Commonwealth of Nations.

HISTORY. Although Pakistan shared India's history until 1947, its existence as a separate Muslim state is rooted in the early history of northern India. Islam began to influence northern India in the early 600s, when Muslim sailors from Arabia visited the coast of Sind, at the mouth of the Indus. Muslim conquerors ruled Sind from the 600s, and spread Islam there.

In the 1000s Muslims from Afghanistan began extending their rule over territory in northwest India, and until the 1800s Afghans, Turks, Arabs, and finally the Mughals (or Moguls), ruled all or part of northern India, establishing many small kingdoms and princely states that at times were unified into empires. In addition to their religion, the Muslims brought Persian and Arabic art, literature, learning, and customs, to produce a way of life different from that of Hindu India to the south.

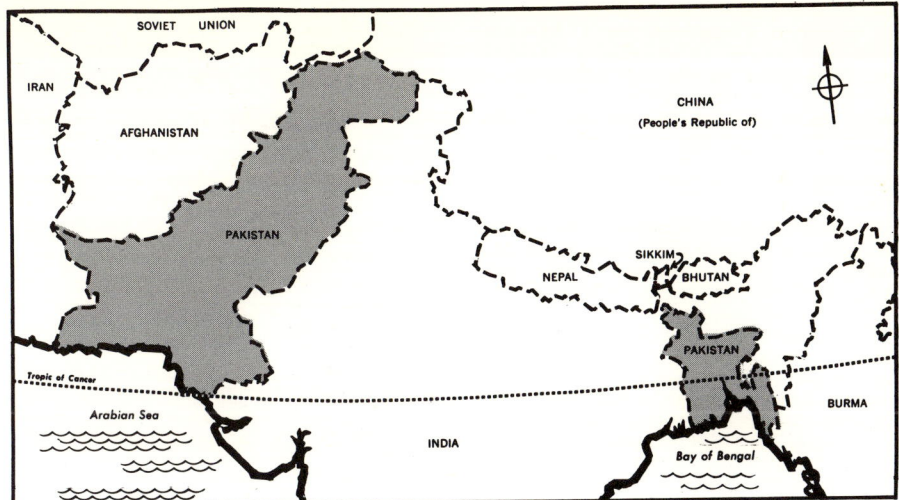

Britain began extending its influence over India in the 1700s. By the early 1900s the British controlled most of the Muslim territories, and by the mid-1800s, with the addition of Punjab and Sind, the British were in firm command of all of India.

In the late 1800s, when Indian leaders began to demand a stronger voice in their country's government, Muslims made up about one-quarter of India's population. The Indian National Congress, formed in 1885 to work for gradual measures of self-government, spoke for all India and included prominent Muslims. Its composition, however, was predominantly Hindu.

Muslim Autonomy. The positive movement toward autonomy for Indian Muslims began soon after the Indian nationalist movement was organized, and in part as a result of its organization. Sir Sayyid Ahmad Khan and other Muslim leaders argued that there was a distinct Muslim "nation" in India which should not be submerged in the Hindu majority as, they contended, would happen if the British left the country and fully representative government was introduced.

While urging Muslims to advance their relatively backward condition through education and commerce, Sir Sayyid recommended that they not participate in the activities of the Indian National Congress. Muslim fears of Hindu domination deepened at the turn of the century, when a strong movement developed in India for the revival of Hinduism and the creation of a nation based essentially on Hindu traditions and culture.

Muslim League. In 1906 Muslims founded the All India Muslim League to press for special protection and advantages for Muslims. Although its overall goal, self-government for India, was the same as that of the National Congress, the two organizations could not agree on a plan for dividing power and protecting Muslim interests.

In 1909 the British responded to Indian demands for self-government by permitting the election of members of the legislative council. The reforms satisfied the Muslims' plea for representation by providing separate electorates for them. But the limited franchise and weak powers of the legislature were a bitter disappointment to both Hindu and Muslim nationalists.

After World War I Mohandas K. Gandhi assumed the leadership of the Congress with a program designed in part to unify India's Hindus and Muslims for a great struggle to overthrow British rule. Gandhi and many leading Hindu members of the Congress argued that Muslim fears of Hindu domination were groundless and a result of British efforts to divide and rule.

Rioting between Hindus and Muslims in the 1920s and 1930s as well as continued sponsorship of a Hindu revival widened the split within the nationalist movement. The final blow to unity came in 1937, when the Congress gained control of most provincial legislatures popularly elected on a broadened franchise. The Muslim League believed that the policies of these Congress majorities discriminated against Muslims.

It was after 1937 that Muhammad Ali Jinnah, a former Indian Congress leader and advocate of Hindu-Muslim unity, began a drive for the creation of a separate Muslim state. By 1940, under Jinnah's leadership, the Muslim League resolved that a Muslim state should be created when India was given independence.

In 1946 negotiations took place for a transfer of power to Indians, but the Congress and the League could not agree on terms for establishing an interim government, or for drafting a constitution for the new state. The British had strongly supported a unified India, but they had also sponsored separate religious electorates and encouraged Muslim ambitions.

Partition. In 1947, when the Hindu-Muslim stalemate could not be broken, Britain acquiesced in Muslim demands for a separate state. It was to consist of all contiguous areas with Muslim majorities in British India. Bengal and the Punjab were divided and the princely states adjacent to Pakistan were to be given the choice of joining one or the other of the new states.

On Aug. 15, 1947 Pakistan was created an independent nation within the British Commonwealth. Muhammad Ali Jinnah became Pakistan's first governor-general.

Partition created serious problems for both India and Pakistan. Communal rioting, especially in the Punjab, killed thousands. The economies of the two countries were disrupted by the migration of millions of Muslims to Pakistan and millions of Hindus to India.

More lasting internal problems plagued the government of Pakistan. Separation of Muslim majority areas from India implied the creation of a state governed according to Islamic principles, but many Pakistanis urged that traditional religious ideals could not determine the policies of a modern state. Split on this fundamental issue, the government of the new state had a difficult start.

The cultural difference between the eastern and western parts of the new state also caused much antagonism and sharpened struggles for political power. In addition, Pakistani political leadership faltered after the death in 1948 of Jinnah and the assassination in 1951 of Liaqat Ali Khan, Pakistan's first prime minister. Delays in formulating a constitution extended the period of governmental instability.

The Republic. A republican constitution was finally adopted in 1956. But years of political turmoil had severely weakened the economy, and the decentralized federal system established by the constitution could do little to solve the country's economic problems.

Relations with India, bitter after decades of religious conflict, grew especially hostile in the mid-1950s over the issue of Kashmir. India gained control of the bulk of Kashmir, but the region has a Muslim majority, and Pakistan argued that Kashmir should be made part of the Muslim state. This dispute worsened Pakistan's internal political and economic situation.

In 1958 a group of military leaders under Gen. Muhammad Ayub Khan took control of the government. They revoked the constitution, dissolved the legislatures, banned political parties, and imposed martial law. Ayub assumed the title of president, and in 1960 he was elected in an indirect vote under his own system of "basic democracies." Under this system locally elected officials choose national leaders.

The government took firm control of economic activity and initiated modernization programs which improved the economy. In 1962 a new constitution was adopted, and martial law was gradually lifted and civil rights restored. In 1965 President Ayub Khan won re-election by a large majority. The country's economy continued to improve in the mid-1960s under government development programs using aid from abroad.

In 1965 the dispute over Kashmir again broke into open warfare. Bitter fighting lasted three weeks, until a stalemate was reached. At an international conference at Tashkent, in the Soviet Union, an Indian-Pakistani truce was signed, but no lasting solution to the dispute was achieved.

—M. G. Inaba

PANAMA

Official name: Republic of Panama
Area: 29,762 square miles (including the Canal Zone)
Population: (1967 est.) 1,329,000 (excluding the Canal Zone)
Capital: Panamá (Pop., 1966 est., 343,700)
Language: Spanish
Religion: Roman Catholicism
Currency unit: Balboa
National holiday: Independence day, November 3

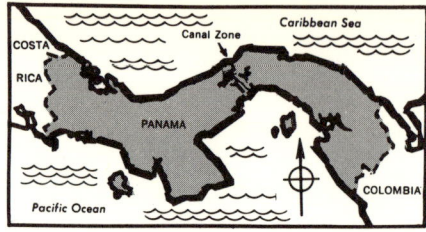

Panama, a Central American republic situated on the Isthmus of Panama, is bounded on the north by the Caribbean Sea, on the east by Colombia, on the south by the Pacific Ocean, and on the west by Costa Rica. The Panama Canal cuts through the country at its narrowest point. The canal runs through the Canal Zone, a strip of land 5 miles wide on each side of the canal, leased to the United States by the Panamanian government in 1903.

THE LAND. Panama's land surface is mostly hilly and mountainous. The highest mountains rise in the west, near the Costa Rican border, and are volcanic. The highest peak is Chiriquí Volcano, 11,410 feet above sea level. These mountains gradually slope down toward a hilly central lowland, which separates them from jungle-covered highlands in the east. It is through this lowland that the Panama Canal runs.

The only other significant lowlands are plains along the Caribbean and Pacific coasts. The Caribbean plain, along the north coast, is extremely rainy. Tropical evergreen rain forests predominate. The Pacific plain, along the south coast, has a wet and a dry season, producing semi-deciduous forest mingled with savanna.

Panama's climate varies with elevation. The lowlands have a tropical climate, with an average annual temperature of about 80°F. Temperatures in the mountains range from 50°F to 66°F.

THE PEOPLE. The people of Panama are largely mestizo, of mixed European and Indian parentage, but there are small groups of whites, Negroes, and Indians. The overwhelming majority of the population is Roman Catholic. Spanish is the national language, although English is widely understood.

Colón, near the northern end of the canal, and Panamá, at its southern end, are the country's major seaports and urban centers. Outlying areas are sparsely settled, especially the region east of the Canal Zone.

ECONOMY. The economy of Panama is largely based on providing goods and services for the Canal Zone. In recent years the government has sought to lessen Panama's dependence on the canal and diversify the economy by increasing agricultural production and expanding industry.

Panama has rich natural resources, but they are mostly unexploited. Only small quantities of gold, silver, and manganese are mined. Limestone is quarried and it supplies the cement industry. Panama also has valuable timber and an abundance of fish in its coastal waters.

Only a fraction of Panama's arable land is cultivated, and farms traditionally are small and primitive. Rice and corn are the basic food crops, but a variety of fruits and vegetables are also grown. Bananas are by far the most important commercial crop. Coconuts, cacao, sugarcane, and coffee are also significant.

Panama has very little industry. Small factories produce cement, shoes, soap, soft drinks, alcoholic beverages, furniture, and clothing. There is also some food processing and a variety of home handicraft industries. In 1961 a large oil refinery was built near Colón.

Trade. In 1966 Panama's exports were valued at $89 million and imports at $215 million. Most of the gap is made up by income from the Canal Zone and fees from the registry under the Panamanian flag of vessels of world shippers.

Panama's chief exports are bananas, petroleum products, fish—especially shrimp—sugar, and coffee. Principal imports include petroleum, machinery, motor vehicles, textiles, chemicals, and foodstuffs. The bulk of Panama's trade is with the United States.

GOVERNMENT. Panama is a democratic republic. The president, who is directly elected to a term of four years, is the head of state and chief executive. Legislative power is vested in the National Assembly, whose members are directly elected to four-year terms.

Panama is a member of the United Nations and the Organization of American States (OAS).

HISTORY. Panama was discovered in 1501 by Rodrigo de Bastidas. In 1502 Christopher Columbus explored the Caribbean coast and claimed the territory for Spain. Further explorations led to the establishment of settlements along the Caribbean coast. In 1513 Vasco Núñez de Balboa crossed the isthmus and discovered the Pacific Ocean, thereby putting the western coast within Spanish reach.

In 1519 the small village of Panamá, on the Pacific coast, was made the capital of the isthmus. The Spanish explorer Francisco Pizarro used Panama as the base for expeditions to Peru in 1531. The cities of Nombre de Dios and, later, Portobelo became the ports through which gold and silver were shipped to Spain.

During the late 1600s and the 1700s Spain entered a period of political and economic decline and the importance of Panama began to wane. In 1751 Panama lost its autonomy and became part of the viceroyalty of New Granada, which included present-day Colombia.

In 1821 Panama gained independence from Spain and joined with Colombia, Ecuador, and Venezuela to form the Republic of Gran Colombia. Gran Colombia was dissolved in 1830, but Panama remained part of Colombia. A spirit of Panamanian nationalism began to grow, however, and political relations with Colombia deteriorated as Panamanians grew to fear that their interests might be sacrificed.

Independence. In 1903 the Colombian government refused to ratify the Hay-Herrán Treaty, which would have permitted the United States to build a canal through the Isthmus of Panama. Fearing that the United States would build the canal through Nicaragua instead, the Panamanians revolted and declared their independence from Colombia. U.S. Pres. Theodore Roosevelt insured the success of the revolt when he ordered a U.S. warship to prevent Colombian troops from entering the isthmus.

On Nov. 6, 1903, three days after the revolution began, the United States recognized an independent Panamanian government. Panama's newly formed government leased the Canal Zone to the United States in perpetuity for a payment of $10 million and an annual payment of $250,000.

Panama became prosperous as a result of the Panama Canal, but political unrest developed during the world economic depression of the 1930s. Panama sided with the Allies in World War II and in 1945 became a charter member of the United Nations.

Contemporary Panama. During the mid-1950s opposition to U.S. sovereignty over the Canal Zone began to grow. In November 1959 anti-United States demonstrations broke out in Panamá and Colón. Tension was further increased by Washington's announcement of its interest in constructing a new sea level canal in another part of Central America.

In January 1964 Panamanian students led violent anti-United States riots, which resulted in the breaking off of diplomatic relations between the United States and Panama. Diplomatic relations were resumed in April 1964, and the two countries agreed to negotiate their differences.

In June 1967 the negotiators drafted a new treaty, which provided for Panamanian sovereignty over the Canal Zone and a joint board to govern the canal itself.

—George W. Carey; Jerome Fischman

PANAMA'S SAN BLAS ISLANDS, lying in the Atlantic, are peopled by American Indians.

PARAGUAY

Official name: Republic of Paraguay
Area: 157,047 square miles
Population: (1967 est.) 2,161,000
Capital: Asunción (Pop., 1962, 305,160)
Language: Spanish, Guaraní
Religion: Roman Catholicism
Currency unit: Guaraní
National holiday: Independence day, May 14

Paraguay, a small landlocked republic in South America, is bounded on the north by Bolivia, on the east by Brazil, and on the south and west by Argentina.

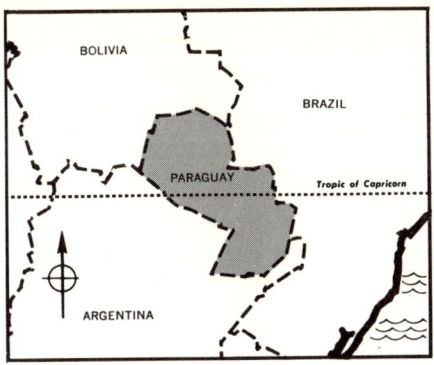

THE LAND. The Paraguay River, which flows down from Brazil and joins the Paraná River in the southwestern corner, at the Argentine border, divides Paraguay into two contrasting regions. The western region, or Chaco Boreal, is a hot, parched wasteland, partially covered with scrub forest. The eastern region consists of fertile plains, grasslands, and dense forests.

In the extreme east is the heavily forested Paraná Plateau, which ranges in altitude from 1,000 to 2,000 feet above sea level. In the northern part of the plateau the forests give way to grasslands or savannas. West of the plateau are rolling, grassy plains.

Climate. Because of its location within the interior of the continent, Paraguay experiences wider temperature fluctuations than almost any other part of South America. Summer temperatures average about 80°F, but temperatures over 100°F are fairly common. Winter temperatures average 55°F.

Annual rainfall varies, although it is generally quite dry in the west and becomes progressively wetter towards the east. The average annual rainfall at Asunción, on the Paraguay River, is 62 inches, but near the Brazilian border it increases to about 80 inches.

THE PEOPLE. The overwhelming majority of the people are of mixed Guaraní Indian and Spanish ancestry. Although the admixture of Spanish blood in the population is small, there are few pureblooded Indians left in Paraguay and they mostly inhabit the remoter regions of the Chaco. There are also small numbers of foreigners who have settled in agricultural communities. They include Germans, Japanese, Italians, Brazilians, Argentines, and Canadian Mennonites.

The official language is Spanish but Guaraní is spoken almost universally. Most Paraguayans belong to the Roman Catholic Church.

About 96 percent of the people live in the eastern region, which represents 40 percent of the national territory, and about 75 percent of the people live within 100 miles of the capital of Asunción. Most of the country's economic activity is also located within the same radius.

ECONOMY. Paraguay's economy is based on agriculture and forestry, and these activities account for almost all the country's exports.

Paraguay has deposits of manganese, iron, copper, kaolin, mica, talc, and bauxite, but the only two minerals mined are limestone and salt. The country's most important natural resource is its forests, which yield valuable hardwoods and a variety of other products. Two of the most important forest products are tannin, used in tanning, dyeing, making ink, and medicine, and yerba maté from which a tea-like beverage is made.

Agriculture. Although 70 percent of the people are engaged in agriculture, only a fraction of Paraguay's arable land is cultivated. Farming methods are primitive and most farmers raise only enough to feed their own families.

Food crops include manioc, corn, sugarcane, sweet potatoes, rice, and citrus and other fruits. The country's most important commercial crops are cotton, tobacco, coffee, and oilseeds.

Cattle have long been an important source of income, and meat products are Paraguay's most valuable export. Cattle are raised chiefly in the area between the Paraguay and Paraná rivers, in Concepción near the northwestern border, and in the Chaco.

Industry. Paraguay is one of the least industrialized countries in South America. The nation's few industries are limited to the processing of its agricultural products and the manufacture of a small number of consumer goods and construction materials such as soap, matches, glass, cement, and bricks.

Trade. Paraguay's exports in 1966 earned $49.4 million and imports cost $49.5 million. The major exports are meat, woods, tobacco, cotton, tannin, and coffee. Imports include machinery, wheat, iron and steel products, transportation equipment, fuel oil, and chemicals.

Paraguay exports primarily to Argentina, the United States, Britain, the Netherlands, and Spain. Most imports come from the United States, Argentina, West Germany, and Britain.

GOVERNMENT. Paraguay is a republic. The head of state and chief executive is the president, who is directly elected to a term of five years. He is assisted by a cabinet, which he appoints.

The legislative branch of government consists of the House of Representatives, with 60 members, and the Senate, with 30 members.

Paraguay is a member of the United Nations and the Organization of American States (OAS).

HISTORY. Paraguay was discovered in 1524 by Alejo García, a Portuguese explorer. Two years later Sebastian Cabot explored the Paraná and Paraguay rivers for Spain, and in 1537 a permanent Spanish settlement was made at Asunción, on the Paraguay River.

Spanish Rule. In 1609 the Jesuits arrived in Paraguay to convert the Guaraní Indians. The Jesuits were highly successful in their missionary work and they founded more than 30 *reducciones*, which were self-sufficient, autonomous mission communities. Between 150,000 and 200,000 Indians lived and worked within this system.

The Jesuits were not popular with the Spanish colonists, who wanted the Indians to work for them and who resented the competition from mission agricultural produce. In 1767 Spain expelled the Jesuits from South America, and the *reducciones* collapsed.

In 1776 Paraguay was incorporated into the newly formed Viceroyalty of Río de la Plata, which included present-day Argentina and was governed from Buenos Aires. In 1810 the Argentinians rebelled against Spain and set up a junta, or government council, at Buenos Aires. Paraguayans refused to recognize this government, but the following year they threw off Spanish rule and established a junta of their own at Asunción.

Independence. In 1814 one of the members of the junta, Jośe Gaspar Rodríguez de Francia, took over the government and became president. Francia exercised strong autocratic control, aided both by an internal spy network and by the superstitious reverence that he managed to inspire in the common people. He followed a policy of political isolation, which protected Paraguay from outside influences and encouraged economic self-sufficiency.

Francia died in 1840, and in 1844, after a brief period of transition, his nephew, Carlos Antonio López, became president. López made education free and compulsory, built roads, and loosened Francia's policy of isolation. But whereas Francia had been personally honest, López and his family profiteered at the nation's expense. When López died in 1862 his son Francisco Solano López immediately became president.

The central feature of the regime of Francisco Solano López was the War of the Triple Alliance, which pitted Paraguay against Argentina, Brazil, and Uruguay. In 1864 López attacked Brazil, ostensibly because of Brazil's interference in the affairs of Uruguay. Also at stake was López's ambition to expand Paraguayan influence and territory at the expense of Argentina and Brazil, with whom Paraguay had long-standing territorial disputes.

In 1865 the conflict expanded into a general war. Paraguay was victorious at first, but the overwhelmingly superior resources of the allies assured Paraguay's eventual defeat. In 1870 López was killed and the war ended. The devastation from the war was tremendous. Paraguay's population had fallen from approximately 1 million to about 220,000, of whom fewer than 30,000 were adult males. Paraguay also lost some territory, but rivalry between Argentina and Brazil prevented Paraguay's complete dismemberment.

Modern Paraguay. Recovery was slow and political conditions were unstable. Between 1870 and 1932 Paraguay had 29 presidents. Nonetheless, Paraguay made some economic progress in these years. Foreign capital and enterprise, much of it from Argentina, assisted the nation's development, and a number of small immigrant colonies were established.

In 1932 Paraguay fought a war with Bolivia over the Gran Chaco, a semi-wasteland lying between the two countries. Paraguay, with the benefit of superior leadership and shorter lines of communication, defeated Bolivia. A truce was declared in 1935, and under the treaty signed in 1938 Paraguay gained possession of three-fourths of the disputed territory.

Gen. José Félix Estigarribia, the commander of Paraguay's forces during the Chaco War, became president in 1939. He was killed in an airplane accident and was succeeded by Higinio Morínigo. General Morínigo soon evolved a strong dictatorship, but was forced out of office by a revolt in 1948.

In 1954, following a series of short-lived governments, the army under Gen. Alfredo Stroessner took over the government. Running without opposition, Stroessner was elected to the presidency later that year. Stroessner was reelected in 1958, 1963, and 1968.

Stroessner established a rigid dictatorship. Over the years his rule became less harsh, however, and he gave the country stability and relative prosperity. In 1968 opposition candidates were permitted to enter the presidential race, although Stroessner easily won a third term.

—David Bushnell; Kempton E. Webb

PERU

Official name: Republic of Peru
Area: 496,224 square miles
Population: (1967 est.) 12,385,000
Capital: Lima (Pop., 1961, urban area, 1,436,231)
Language: Spanish, Indian languages
Religion: Roman Catholicism
Currency: Sol
National holiday: Independence day, July 28

Peru, a republic on the west coast of South America, is bounded on the north by Ecuador and Colombia, on the east by Brazil and Bolivia, on the south by Chile, and on the west by the Pacific Ocean.

THE LAND. Peru is a country of striking diversity. Within its borders are humid tropical lowlands, in the east; ice covered peaks, in the Andes; and rainless coastal desert, in the west. The country has three main geographic regions: the coastal desert, or *costa*; the Andean highlands, or *sierra*; and the eastern Andean slopes and Amazon lowlands, or *montaña*.

The coastal zone extends from Ecuador to Chile and is generally less than 30 miles wide. It is extremely dry. Winds blowing in from the ocean are chilled by the cold Peru, or Humboldt, Current and yield no moisture. The only oases are the valleys of 50 or 60 seasonal rivers that drain the western slopes of the Andes. These rivers flow from June to November and provide water for irrigation.

The Andean highlands consist of a broad altiplano, or plateau, which lies between 10,000 and 15,000 feet above sea level, and is surmounted by moun-

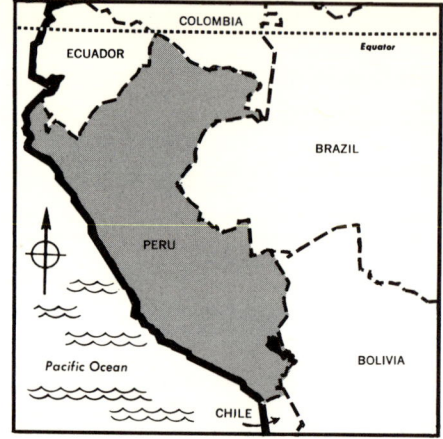

tain peaks. The grassland vegetation of the altiplano, known as *puna*, provides good pasturage for livestock, and the mountain valleys contain Peru's most fertile land.

The *montaña* is part of the Amazon Basin and is covered with tropical forest and jungle. Although it constitutes 60 percent of the nation's territory, it is very thinly populated. Development of the area has been impeded by its physical isolation.

Climate varies from region to region. The climate on the coast is dry and temperate. Temperatures in the *sierra* vary with altitude from temperate to frigid and most of the area is fairly dry. The *montaña* is hot and humid, with temperatures in the 70°sF and 80°sF, and rainfall often exceeds 100 inches a year.

THE PEOPLE. About half of the population is Indian and most of the remainder is mestizo, of mixed Indian and Spanish ancestry. About 10 percent is of European origin. Spanish is the official language but it is spoken by only about half of the population. The Andean Indians speak either Quechua or Aymara, and the Amazon tribes of the *montaña* have their own Indian languages. Roman Catholicism is the state religion.

Peru's principal city is Lima, the capital, which is the largest and most important city on the Pacific coast of South America. Other major urban centers, with their 1961 census populations, include Arequipa, 135,358; Callao, 155,953; and Trujillo, 100,130.

ECONOMY. Peru's economy is based largely on agriculture and mining, and the Peruvian Andes are rich in minerals. Although the country has deposits of a wide variety of minerals, copper, iron, zinc, and lead are the mainstays of the mining industry. There are important oil fields in the northwest.

Fish abound in Peru's offshore waters. In 1965 the country's fish catch of almost 7.5 thousand metric tons was the world's largest, and fish meal is a leading export.

The forests of the *montaña* cover more than half the country's territory. Although still largely unexploited, they produce valuable quantities of cedar, mahogany, and other tropical hardwoods as well as rubber, leche caspi (used in making chewing gum), jute, and a variety of medicinal plants.

Agriculture. Agriculture employs approximately half the labor force and is the backbone of the Peruvian economy. It contributed 20 percent of the gross domestic product in 1964. But there is a lack of well-watered arable land and farming methods are often inefficient. As a result, Peru cannot raise enough food for its own use and foodstuffs must be imported.

Potatoes and corn are the major food crops and are raised in the *sierra*, which has 60 percent of the country's cultivated land. Large quantities of rice and beans are also grown. The leading commercial crops are sugarcane and cotton, which are grown in the coastal valleys and in the *montaña*. The *montaña* also produces coffee, tobacco, cacao, fruit, and nuts.

Peru has very few cattle, and meat and dairy products must be imported. Sheep, vicuñas, and alpacas are raised in the southern Andes and their wool exported.

Industry. Peruvian industry is limited largely to the processing of agricultural products, smelting and refining, and the manufacture of a variety of domestic consumer goods. The most important of these include textiles, beverages, footwear, leather goods, construction materials, paper and cardboard, chemicals, pharmaceuticals, and synthetic fertilizer.

Trade. In 1966 Peruvian exports earned $774 million and imports cost $833 million. The country's major exports are fish meal, cotton, sugar, iron ore, copper, lead, zinc, and silver. Principal imports include machinery, transport equipment, foodstuffs, chemicals, and pharmaceuticals. Major trade partners are the United States, West Germany, Japan, and Britain.

GOVERNMENT. Peru is a republic. The head of state and chief executive is the president, who is directly elected along with two vice-presidents to a six-year term. The president cannot serve consecutive terms. Legislative power is vested in the Senate and Chamber of Deputies. Members of both houses, whose numbers vary, are also elected to six-year terms.

Peru is a member of the United Nations and the Organization of American States (OAS).

HISTORY. Before Christopher Columbus reached the New World in 1492, Peru was the center of a great American Indian civilization, that of the Inca. In about 1200 the Incas began to move out from their original homeland in the southern Peruvian Andes and subjugate neighboring Indian peoples living in the highlands and on the coast.

By the late 1400s the Incas had established an empire that stretched along the western coast of South America from Ecuador to Chile. This vast empire was joined together by an intricate network of roads and was ruled from the city of Cuzco, high in the Andes of southern Peru.

In 1531 a small army of Spaniards led by Francisco Pizarro invaded Peru. Despite their small numbers the Spanish easily conquered the Incas, who were weakened and divided by civil war and terrified by the guns and horses of the Spaniards. By 1533 Cuzco had fallen.

Spanish Rule. In 1542 the Spaniards transformed what had been the Inca empire into the Viceroyalty of Peru, ruled from Lima, which Pizarro had founded in 1535. Rich deposits of precious metals, particularly silver, made Peru for many years the most prized of Spain's American colonies.

In the 1700s Peru's importance was diminished by the creation of the viceroyalties of New Granada, in 1717, and Río de la Plata, in 1776. Internal tranquility was shaken by a number of Indian uprisings, the most serious being that of Tupac Amaru, between 1780 and 1783. Nevertheless, during the first years of the 1800s when Spain's other South American colonies were seeking independence, Peru remained a loyalist stronghold.

It was not until 1820, when the Argentine leader José de San Martín, who had already defeated the Spaniards in Chile, landed with an Argentine-Chilean army of liberation, that the Peruvian struggle for independence began in earnest. San Martín captured Lima and a year later, on July 28, 1821, declared Peru independent. But Spain's power was not finally broken until December 1824, when the forces of Simón Bolívar, who had replaced San Martín, routed the Spanish at the battle of Ayacucho. The independence of Peru marked the end of Spain's empire in South America.

Independence. For nearly 20 years after gaining independence, Peru was controlled by a succession of military dictators, or *caudillos*, including Luis José Orbegosa, who drew Peru into a short-lived confederation with Bolivia from 1836 to 1839.

In 1845 the presidency was assumed by Gen. Ramón Castilla, who, except for a brief interval from 1851 to 1854, ruled the country until 1862. Castilla brought about the abolition of Negro slavery and a reduction in the special privileges of the church, developed Peru's guano and nitrate sources, and provided the country a large measure of stability.

The 10 years following Castilla's regime were marked by a growing public debt, political corruption, and internal disorder, all of which were intensified in 1865–1866 by a brief war with Spain, which sought redress for the mistreatment of Spanish citizens in Peru. Chile, Ecuador, and Bolivia came to the aid of Peru, and the Spanish ultimately withdrew.

Dissatisfaction with the military in Peruvian politics increased. As a result, in 1872 Manuel Pardo, a civilian, who represented a coalition of landed aristocrats and financial and commercial interests, was elected president. Pardo aided higher education, sought to reduce the size and influence of the army, and tried to improve the economy. He was hindered in his efforts by a decline in the important guano industry, which was only partially offset by increased nitrate production in the southern coastal province of Tarapacá.

Through an alliance that Pardo had made with Bolivia in 1873, Peru became involved in the War of the Pacific, from 1879 to 1883, which resulted from a dispute between Bolivia and Chile over the Atacama nitrate fields. Chile was victorious and under the terms of the peace treaty Peru was forced to yield its nitrate province of Tarapacá as well as to permit Chilean occupation of the adjoining provinces of Arica and Tacna. Peru was left bankrupt and exhausted.

Modern Peru. Peru did not fully recover until the early 1900s. Progress was especially notable during the second administration of Augusto B. Leguía y Salcedo, which stretched from 1919 to 1930. Leguía managed to bolster the economy by securing foreign loans and investments. He also built large-scale public works.

Leguía was relatively popular until 1930, when the world economic depression cut off the inflow of foreign capital and reduced the earnings of Peruvian exports. He was then overthrown by Col. Luis Sánchez Cerro, who remained in power until 1933, when he was assassinated. Under his successor, Oscar Benavides, in office until 1939, Peru gradually recovered from the depression.

Nevertheless, the Indian population of the Andean region received little direct benefit from the progress that had taken place. Control of Peruvian society remained in the hands of a small, wealthy minority and protest movements arose. One of these was the *Alianza Popular Revolucionaria Americana* (APRA—American Popular Revolutionary Alliance) founded by Victor Rául Haya de la Torre.

APRA's original program was Indianist, socialistic, and extremely hostile to foreign capital. During the 1930s, APRA became the strongest political movement in Peru, but it was distrusted by the military and repeatedly frustrated in its efforts to gain power even though it gradually became more conservative.

The moderately leftist and prodemocratic *Partido de Acción Popular* (PAP—Popular Action Party), founded and led by Fernando Belaúnde Terry, ultimately had more success. Belaúnde was elected president in 1963 and sponsored agrarian reforms and supported other measures beneficial to the Indians, while seeking to effect a larger degree of popular participation in government. He also put special emphasis on the development of the *montaña*. But Belaúnde was hampered by the high cost of his programs and by his inability to obtain solid support from the Congress.

—David Bushnell: Kempton E. Webb

PHILIPPINES

Official name: Republic of the Philippines
Area: 116,000 square miles
Population: (1967 est.) 34,656,000
Capital: Quezon City (Pop., 1965 est., 482,400)
Language: Filipino, English, Spanish, indigenous languages
Religion: Roman Catholicism
Currency unit: Peso
National holiday: Independence day, June 12

The Philippines is an independent island nation in the Pacific Ocean, some 450 miles off the southeastern coast of China. The country's nearest neighbors are Taiwan, about 65 miles to the north, and Indonesia, approximately 150 miles to the south. The Philippines received its independence from the United States in 1946.

THE LAND. There are more than 7,000 islands within the Philippine archipelago, but the 11 largest islands account for 94 percent of the country's total land area. The largest islands are Luzon (40,420 square miles) and Mindanao (36,537 square miles). Each of the remaining islands is less than 6,000 square miles in area.

Most of the islands are hilly or mountainous with only limited areas of level land. In the northern half of Luzon, the principal island, there are several mountain ranges running from north to south. The Sierra Madre range runs parallel to the northeastern coast, and the Central Cordillera forms the spine of the island. Between the two ranges is the Cagayan Plain, one of the two sizable lowlands on Luzon.

The other major lowland is the Central Plain, between the Central Cordillera and the Zambales Mountains, in western Luzon. Most of southeastern Luzon is made up of discontinuous mountains and volcanoes, including Mt. Mayon, which reaches an elevation of over 8,200 feet. Manila Bay juts into southwestern Luzon.

The Philippines has a warm, even temperature the year round. Average monthly temperatures at sea level range from 76°F to 84°F. Although it is cooler at higher altitudes, temperatures below 60°F rarely occur. Typhoons strike the Philippines every year. Most of the Philippines receives at least 60 inches of rain a year, and some regions, up to 125 inches.

THE PEOPLE. Most people in the Philippines are of Malay stock, but there are also people of Chinese, American, and Spanish origin. The Philippines has a rapidly growing population, and between 1958 and 1965 the rate of increase was 3.3 percent a year.

The population is unevenly distributed. Luzon, Cebu, Negros, Bohul, Leyte, and Panay are the most heavily populated islands. The largest city is Manila, on Luzon, which had a 1965 population estimated at 1,356,000.

ECONOMY. The economy of the Philippines is based on agriculture, and almost 60 percent of the labor force is dependent upon agriculture for its livelihood. About one-third of the land is arable, and about three-quarters of that is devoted to domestic food crops.

Rice occupies almost one-half of the cropped land. Corn and coconuts are also important crops. Other crops of some significance include root crops, fruits, nuts, sugarcane, abaca, tobacco, ramie, kapok, and rubber.

The yields per acre in the Philippines are among the lowest in Asia. The low productivity of Philippine agriculture stems largely from poor farm management, inadequate use of fertilizers, poor seeds, and lack of incentive on the part of the farmers, many of whom are tenant farmers.

The number of persons engaged in fishing is second only to the number in agriculture. Fish ranks second to rice in the Filipino diet, and fishing is becoming an increasingly important industry. In 1965 the fish catch exceeded 685,000 metric tons.

Forests cover about 40 percent of the country and are among the most important resources of the Philippines. *Luan*, commonly called Philippine mahogany, is one of the most important commercial woods. There are vast pine forests in the high mountains of northern Luzon.

Various minerals are mined in the Philippines, including gold, iron ore, copper, and chromite. The country lacks adequate supplies of mineral fuels, although some coal is mined on the islands of Cebu and Mindanao.

Before independence in 1946, industry was confined largely to processing agricultural products. Since independence, the government has promoted industrialization. A number of consumer goods industries have been established or expanded and some heavy industry has been established. There are iron and steel works, oil refineries, and assembly plants for automobiles and trucks.

In 1966 imports cost $957 million and exports earned $838 million. The main imports are machinery, cereals, transportation equipment, iron and steel products, and petroleum. The major exports are copra, sugar, wood, copper, and iron ore. Most trade is conducted with the United States and Japan. The Philippines receives economic aid from the United States.

GOVERNMENT. The Philippines has a presidential system of government. Executive power is vested in a president, who is popularly elected to a four-year term. Legislative power is held by a congress consisting of a Senate and House of Representatives. Senators are popularly elected to six-year terms, and members of the House are popularly elected to four-year terms.

The Philippines is a member of the United Nations and the Southeast Asia Treaty Organization (SEATO). In 1966 agreement was reached on the formation of a Southeast Asian regional association with Malaysia, Indonesia, and Thailand.

HISTORY. Ferdinand Magellan visited the Philippines in 1521 and claimed the islands for Spain. In 1571 Miguel López de Legazpe, a Spanish soldier, established the first Spanish settlement in the Philippines. Legazpe extended Spanish control over Cebu, Leyte, Mindanao, Panay, and central Luzon. In 1571 he took possession of Manila and made it the capital of the territory.

Long before the Spanish conquest, the Philippines traded with China. Later, Spanish galleons brought silver to Manila from the port of Acapulco, in Mexico, to trade with the Chinese for luxury goods, and Manila became an important trading center.

Under Spanish rule, Christianity and Western legal concepts and customs were introduced into the Philippines, and a centralized government was established. In the 1800s resentment against Spanish rule grew, and by the end of the 1800s the Filipinos had staged a number of revolts.

In 1896 José Rizal, a leading Filipino patriot, was executed for his part in uprisings that broke out in that year. His death spurred the revolutionary movement. Spain promised to grant Filipino representation in Madrid and to permit wider autonomy for the islands. Spain failed to keep these promises, however, and the Filipinos, led by Gen. Francisco Makabulas, offered strong resistance to Spanish rule.

U.S. Rule. In April 1898 the United States declared war on Spain, after the U.S. battleship *Maine* was destroyed in Havana harbor, in Cuba, which was also under Spanish rule. By that time the Filipinos were battling hard against the Spanish in the Philippines. In August 1898 U.S. forces occupied Manila, and in the Treaty of Paris, signed on Dec. 10, 1898, Spain ceded the Philippines to the United States for $20 million.

In 1899 a war of insurrection against the United States was led by Emilio Aguinaldo, head of the anti-Spanish rebellion of 1896. The United States put down the rising, and in 1901 Aguinaldo was captured.

Between the summer of 1900 and the summer of 1901 the islands were administered by a military governor and the Taft Commission, established by Pres. William McKinley and headed by William Howard Taft. In July 1901 this system became a civil government, headed by Taft. Plans were made to establish a legislature, to be made up of an elected assembly, or lower house. In 1907 the first elections were held for the assembly.

In 1934 Pres. Franklin D. Roosevelt signed the Tydings-McDuffie Act, stipulating that independence was to be granted the Philippines in 1946. Under the terms of the act, the Philippines in 1935 became a self-governing Commonwealth headed by an elected president, and Manuel Quezon was chosen the first president.

On Dec. 7, 1941 Japanese forces struck the islands, and on Jan. 2, 1942 Manila was occupied by the Japanese. Valiant defensive battles were fought on Bataan peninsula and Corregidor, an island in Manila Bay, but the Philippines were forced to surrender in May 1942.

Japan established a puppet government in the Philippines, in which many Filipinos served. Quezon established a government-in-exile in Washington, D.C., and Americans and Filipinos organized a large-scale guerrilla movement to fight the Japanese in the Philippines.

After the Japanese invasion in 1941, many landlords fled to Manila. During the war, the Japanese started a reign of terror, supported by some of the landlords who arrested peasant leaders and union organizers and turned them over to the Japanese for execution.

Early in the war the peasant farmers struck back by creating an army, the Hukbalahap, commonly called Huk, led by Luis Taruc. The Huks rallied the rural population and killed some 25,000 Japanese and their Filipino supporters.

On Oct. 20, 1944 U.S. troops, supported by Filipino guerrillas, landed on the island of Leyte, and on Feb. 23, 1945, after a fierce three-week battle, the Allied forces took Manila.

Independence. On July 4, 1946 the Philippine Islands became independent and Manuel Roxas became president. The new government faced the problem of rebuilding the country's war-ravaged economy. Another problem facing the new government was the rebellion of the Huk, which became a communist-dominated group.

Under the leadership of Pres. Ramón Magsaysay, who was elected in 1953, the Huk rebellion was suppressed. In 1957 Magsaysay was killed in a plane crash and was succeeded by Carlos García. In 1961 Diosdado Macapagal became president. He was defeated by Ferdinand Marcos in 1965. In 1967 there was a resurgence of Huk strength in central Luzon, and Huks staged attacks against government forces.

—Thomas E. Ennis; M. G. Inaba

POLAND

Official name: Polish People's Republic
Area: 120,665 square miles
Population: (1967 est.) 31,944,000
Capital: Warsaw (Pop., 1965 est., 1,249,100)
Language: Polish
Religion: Roman Catholicism
Currency unit: Zloty
National holiday: National liberation day, July 22

Poland, a communist-controlled nation in Eastern Europe, is bounded on the north by the Baltic Sea, on the east by the Soviet Union, on the south by Czechoslovakia, and on the west by East Germany.

Following World War II Poland underwent major territorial changes. In 1945, as a result of the Potsdam Agreement among the leading Allied Powers—Britain, the Soviet Union, and the United States—the country lost nearly 45 percent of its territory, in the east, to the Soviet Union. In compensation Poland was given German lands east of the Oder and Neisse rivers. Permanent determination of the German-Polish frontier, however, was to be decided by a future peace treaty.

THE LAND. The greatest part of Poland is level to rolling lowland, although there are local variations in relief. In the north, near the Baltic coast, the soil is sandy, and sand dunes, some of which are several hundred feet high, dominate the landscape. To the south of the coastal zone a belt of low hills studded with lakes stretches from west to east across the country.

Central Poland is a flat plain and the only noticeable relief features are deeply cut river valleys. The Vistula, Poland's largest and longest river, crosses the eastern part of this plain and flows north to the Baltic. The Warta and the Noteć rivers cross the plain in the west to join the Oder, which flows north along the western border. South of the central plains, low plateaus and rolling hills stretch from the upper course of the Oder eastward to the Polish-Soviet frontier.

Southern Poland is mountainous. To the west lies the Sudeten Range, to the east, the Carpathian Mountains. The two mountain systems are separated by the uppermost valley of the

Oder River, which is known as the Moravian Gate.

Most of Poland has a distinctly continental climate, characterized by wide yearly temperature variation. Winters are cold and snowy, and summers are warm and dry.

THE PEOPLE. Before World War II Poland was a state with substantial minorities—Byelorussians, Germans, Jews, and Ukrainians. After World War II it became largely homogeneous.

The former religious and linguistic minorities were either exterminated during the wartime German occupation, or were forced to leave Poland after 1945. The Byelorussians and Ukrainians had been concentrated in the eastern regions annexed by the Soviet Union. The population is now nearly all Polish-speaking and Roman Catholic, although there are small Greek Orthodox and Protestant communities.

Warsaw, Poland's capital, suffered greater destruction during World War II than almost any other city in Europe. Warsaw had more than 1 million people in 1939, but in 1945 it had only about 20,000 inhabitants living in bombed-out ruins.

Other major cities include Łódź, which is primarily industrial, and Kraków, which was untouched by the war and is full of monuments to Poland's past. Gdańsk (Danzig), at the mouth of the Vistula, on the Baltic, is Poland's first port for freight traffic. Nearby Gdynia specializes in passenger traffic.

ECONOMY. Before World War II Poland was primarily an agricultural country. As a result of the Potsdam Agreement in 1945, however, Poland gained industrial areas in Silesia in the west and lost farmland in the east, and thus emerged with the resources for a more balanced economy.

The government has made intensive efforts to industrialize the country, and economic development has been fairly steady. But despite overall gains the standard of living remained relatively low, and in the mid-1960s serious shortages remained in areas such as housing and quality consumer goods.

Natural Resources. Coal is Poland's most valuable mineral resource, and its major source of energy. Polish coal deposits, located largely in Upper and Lower Silesia, the middle and upper valley of the Oder River, are the third largest in Europe. In 1965

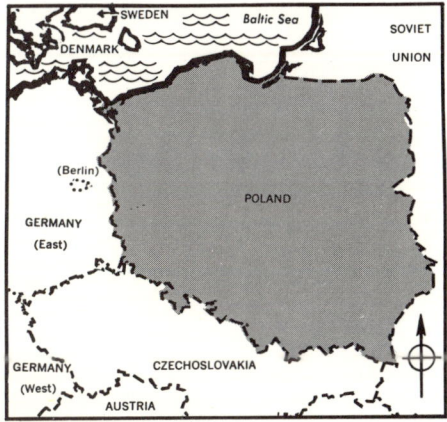

KRAKÓW, POLAND, served as the capital of that nation from 1320 to 1609. Seen in the picture above is the former Royal Castle, the *Wawel*, now the city residence of the president.

Poland was the world's fifth largest coal producer.

Upper Silesia's coal deposits are the most extensive, but are short on coking coal, necessary for steel making. Lower Silesia (the middle Oder valley) produces high-grade coking coal. Poland has little iron ore but possesses large deposits of sulfur, lead, zinc, rock salt, and copper, as well as some nickel, gold, and arsenic.

Agriculture. Polish agriculture differs fundamentally from that in most other communist-controlled countries, for little land is collectivized. Nearly nine-tenths of Poland's agricultural land is privately cultivated. Farms are generally small, averaging between 8 and 30 acres. Animal power is still widely used in farming, although agricultural machinery is being produced in increasing quantities.

The government has encouraged the raising of livestock, with an emphasis on pigs and sheep. Poland produces enough meat to fill domestic needs, and meat and meat products are important exports.

Rye is the principal crop, but large quantities of wheat, barley, and oats are also grown. Potatoes are grown for food, fodder, and the making of alcohol.

Industry. Industry expanded greatly following World War II and in 1965 contributed 51 percent of the gross domestic product. Poland's largest industrial center is located in Upper Silesia, near the country's major coal deposits.

Although occupying only a small area, Upper Silesia had six cities with more than 100,000 people in the mid-1960s. The largest, Katowice, is one of Europe's principal industrial centers. Iron and steel, heavy machinery, and chemicals are the main products of Upper Silesian industry. Fifty miles to the east of Katowice is Poland's newest steel center, Nowa Huta, which is supplied with coal from Silesia and iron ore from the Soviet Union.

A second, smaller industrial center is in Lower Silesia, around the cities of Wrocław, Wałbrzych, and Jelenia Góra. This area contains mostly light industry and produces some consumer goods. Łódź, in central Poland, is the nation's leading textile center. Poznań, in the west, and Warsaw account for a substantial portion of the output of machinery, cars and trucks, and chemicals. The city of Szczecin, at the mouth of the Oder, is Poland's leading shipbuilding center.

Trade. In 1967 Poland's exports earned $2,640 million and its imports cost $2,521 million. Poland's chief exports include coal, meat, and ships. Principal imports are petroleum, cotton, iron ore, wheat, and metalworking machinery. Poland trades mainly with the Soviet Union, Czechoslovakia, and East Germany.

GOVERNMENT. The Polish Communist party, officially known as the Polish United Worker's Party, dominates political life. The politburo, or political bureau, of the party's central committee determines national policy and the party's first secretary is usually the most powerful figure in the government.

Under the constitution supreme authority is vested in the *Sejm*, or parliament. Members of the Sejm are directly elected to four-year terms. The Sejm elects the 15-member Council of State, which exercises legislative functions and acts as a collective head of state, and the Council of Ministers, which performs executive functions.

Poland is a member of the United Nations and the Warsaw Pact, a military alliance of Communist states headed by the Soviet Union.

HISTORY. The Poles were originally one of several Slavic tribes that settled between the Oder and Vistula rivers before the 700s. During the 900s they joined with neighboring peoples to fight off a series of invasions by Germanic tribes and became unified under the Piast dynasty.

In 966 one of the early Piast rulers, Prince Mieszko accepted Christianity. Mieszko's successors expanded Polish domains, especially to the east. In 1138, with the death of Boleslav III, Poland entered a period of political disintegration that was worsened by attacks from the Mongols.

Under Casimir the Great (r. 1333–1370), however, Poland revived. Casimir strengthened the central government, consolidated Polish territory, developed agriculture, and constructed roads and bridges. In 1364 he founded the University of Kraków, one of the oldest institutions of higher learning in Eastern Europe.

On the death of Casimir in 1370 the Piast dynasty died out and the crown passed to Louis I of Hungary, Casimir's nephew. Louis was succeeded by his daughter Jadwiga, who in 1386 married Ladislas Jagello of Lithuania. Under the Jagellons, cultural activity reached a peak and Poland greatly extended its territory, which by the mid-1500s stretched from the Baltic to the Black Sea.

The Jagellon dynasty ended in 1572 with the death of Sigismund Augustus, and for 200 years the succession to the Polish throne was contested by the various ruling houses of Europe. The succession was further complicated by the fact that the king was elected by the Polish parliament, which was composed of the nobility.

Any noble could block any measure by his one vote. This practice, known as the *liberum veto*, not only made the election of a new monarch extraordinarily difficult, but almost paralyzed the central government.

Partition. In 1764 a pro-Russian Polish nobleman, Stanislas Poniatowski, was made king through pressure exerted by Russia. This interference by Russia was resented by the Polish nobles, who rebelled in 1768. Russian troops crushed the rebellion, but Prussia and Austria feared that Russia would absorb Poland to their disadvantage. As a result, in 1772, the three countries agreed to partition Poland. Russia, Prussia, and Austria annexed territories adjoining them, and Poland lost approximately one-third of its land.

Alarmed, the Poles sought to strengthen their government and institute various reforms. Russia, however, invaded Poland again in 1793 and the country was once more partitioned, with Russia and Prussia each annexing more land. A third partition by Russia, Prussia, and Austria took place in 1795, and Poland was wiped off the map.

In 1807 Napoleon I of France created the Grand Duchy of Warsaw out of the Polish territories that had been annexed by Prussia. Although nominally independent, the Grand Duchy was really a puppet state. After Napoleon's defeat, the Congress of Vienna, held in 1814–1815, divided the Grand Duchy among Russia, Prussia, and Austria. Thousands of Polish intellectuals left the country for other nations in Western Europe, where they kept the spirit of Polish nationalism alive.

Life for Poles in the three territories varied. In Russian Poland, despite some persecution, Poles took part in Russian national life. In Austrian Poland, the Poles gained important political privileges and frequently held posts in the Austrian government service. In Prussian Poland, the Poles were politically oppressed but became strong economically.

Throughout the 1800s, however, all Poles sought to rid themselves of foreign rule. Uprisings in Russian Poland took place in 1830 and 1863 but were brutally crushed.

Independence. At the turn of the century the movement for independence gained momentum. In 1917, during World War I, Polish political leaders from Austria and Russia formed the Polish National Committee in Paris, which was recognized by the Allies as the spokesman for Polish independence. When U.S. Pres. Woodrow Wilson enunciated his Fourteen Points in 1918, he called for an independent Poland. Meanwhile, inside Poland, a group was organized under the leadership of Józef Piłsudski, a Polish officer.

The Central Powers were defeated in 1918, and Piłsudski established an independent Polish government in Warsaw. Under the terms of the Treaty of Versailles in 1919, Poland regained most of Polish territory from Prussia and much of Upper Silesia. The region around the Lithuanian city of Vilna, which both countries claimed, was granted to Lithuania in 1920 but seized by Poland in 1922.

Poland gained access to the sea through the Polish Corridor, a narrow strip of land that cut through Germany to the port of Danzig, which was made a free city under the supervision of the League of Nations. Poland's claim to territories in the east, however, soon resulted in a clash with the Soviet Union.

The Allies had suggested a border between Poland and the Soviet Union based on ethnic lines, with the non-Polish territories in the east going to the Soviet Union. This suggested border, known as the Curzon Line, was rejected by the Poles, and in 1920 fighting broke out between Poland and the Soviet Union. A peace treaty signed at Riga in 1921 made Poland's frontier much the same as it had been before the partition in 1795.

Interwar Era. In 1921 Poland adopted a democratic constitution that provided for a parliamentary form of government. The new republic, lacking a strong executive and subject to the conflicting demands of many different political parties, was unable to deal effectively with the myriad problems caused by bringing together territories that had been parts of other states for more than 100 years, and large minorities of other nationalities, including Ukrainians, Byelorussians, and Germans.

In 1926 Józef Piłsudski headed a military coup that overthrew the existing government and established himself as dictator. On his death in 1935 a group of army colonels continued the dictatorship.

World War II. The rise to power of Adolf Hitler in Germany, the disintegration of the League of Nations, and the collapse of the various efforts within Europe to establish regional security arrangements led, on Sept. 1, 1939, to World War II. The war began with a German invasion of Poland from the west, and two weeks later the Soviet Union invaded from the east. The Poles fought bravely, but were quickly overwhelmed. A government-in-exile was established in London, and Polish units fought with the Allies throughout the war.

In April 1943 the Soviet government broke relations with the Polish government in London, and in July 1944 created the Polish Committee of National Liberation on conquered Polish territory. In January 1945 the Soviet Union reorganized the committee as the government of Poland.

British and U.S. efforts to ensure the active participation of democratic groups in this government and to guarantee free elections in Poland were unsuccessful, and after controlled elections in January 1947 a communist government was firmly in power.

Communist Rule. The history of Poland under Communism followed that of the other states of Eastern Europe, with the destruction of rival political groups, the purge of the Communist party itself, rapid industrialization, forced collectivization of agriculture, a mass indoctrination effort, and complete control of the army and internal security police by the Soviet Union.

This pattern was broken in the summer of 1956, however, when riots for "bread and freedom" in Poznań sparked a successful revolt against Soviet rule. Władysław Gomułka, a former head of the Polish Communist party who had been ousted in 1948 and later imprisoned for opposing certain Stalinist policies, was made first secretary of the party. Stefan Cardinal Wyszyński, the ranking Roman Catholic churchman, was released from detention.

All Poland united to resist Soviet pressure, and Gomułka was able to win a wide measure of freedom for his country to allow it to pursue a Polish rather than a Soviet "road to socialism." The Polish army was placed under Polish officers, and the terms of Polish-Soviet trade were revised in Poland's favor. Collectivization was almost completely abandoned, industry was decentralized to some degree, and more attention was given to the production of consumer goods.

Most important, the Poles were given more freedom, and the country was allowed more independence in foreign relations, including increased contact with Western nations. This led to an artistic and cultural revolution, which frightened the Gomułka regime and led to a gradual reimposition of controls over freedom of expression.

Poland's problems remained serious, however. The country continued to be troubled by a disaffected intellectual class, a bitter struggle between the Communist regime and the hierarchy of the Roman Catholic Church, a severe housing problem, and the economic inefficiency and weaknesses caused by a large bureaucracy and an absence of incentives.

—Robert F. Byrnes; George Kish

COUNTRIES OF THE WORLD

PORTUGAL

Official name: Republic of Portugal
Area: 35,510 square miles
Population: (1966 est.) 9,335,000
Capital: Lisbon (Pop., 1965, 822,000)
Language: Portuguese
Religion: Roman Catholicism
Currency unit: Escudo
National holiday: Day of Portugal, June 10

Portugal, a republic occupying the western part of Europe's Iberian peninsula, is bounded on the north and east by Spain and on the south and west by the Atlantic Ocean. The Madeira islands and the Azores, lying respectively, about 1,000 and 750 miles to the southeast in the Atlantic Ocean, are administered as integral parts of Portugal.

THE LAND. Portugal has three major geographic regions. In the northeast the western fringe of the high tablelands of central Spain produces a fairly rugged terrain. Narrow mountain ranges rise to elevations of more than 3,000 feet above sea level and extend almost to the Atlantic. In the west is a broad coastal plain, which widens toward the south. The southeast is covered by low, rolling hills, mostly under 650 feet in elevation.

Portugal's principal rivers are the Douro in the north; the Tagus, which divides the country almost equally into northern and southern regions; and the Guadiana in the southeast. The wide, protected mouth of the Tagus gives the city of Lisbon one of the world's finest natural harbors.

Portugal has a temperate maritime climate. Winters are generally mild, except in the highland areas where they are cold and snowy. Summers are warm in the north and hot in the south. North of the Tagus rainfall is abundant, averaging nearly 30 inches annually, but it decreases toward the southeast and is less than 20 inches along the southern coast.

THE PEOPLE. Portugal has no significant minority groups. Portuguese is the universal language, and the overwhelming majority of the people are Roman Catholic.

The population is concentrated in the north along the coast from the region of Setúbal to the Spanish border, and is especially dense in the lower Tagus and the lower and middle Douro river valleys. The country is sparsely settled south of the Tagus and along the entire eastern border.

Portugal has the highest birth rate in Europe next to Iceland. Substantial emigration, however, keeps the average net population increase down to about 0.7 percent a year.

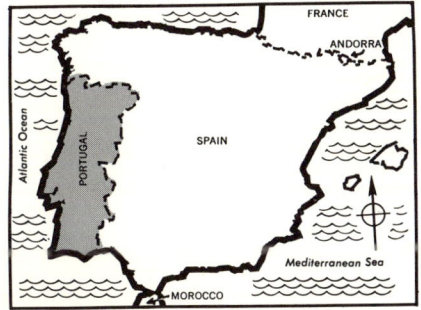

Portugal's population is mostly rural and in the mid-1960s there were only two cities with more than 100,000 inhabitants—Lisbon and Porto, the second largest city, at the mouth of the Douro River.

ECONOMY. Portugal is one of Europe's poorest countries. In 1965 annual per capita income was estimated at $340. The economy is improving, however, and the country's gross domestic product rose at an annual average of 6.2 percent between 1960 and 1965.

Natural Resources. Portugal has few important mineral resources. The most important mineral mined is wolframite, from which tungsten is produced. Some coal, copper, iron, pyrites, tin, lead, and kaolin—a fine white clay used for ceramics—are also mined.

Approximately 25 percent of Portugal is forested and forest products constitute one of the country's major exports. Portugal ordinarily supplies 50 percent of the world's cork. Other important forest products include turpentine, rosin, and timber.

Fish, particularly tuna and sardines, are an important source of income. In 1965 Portugal's fish catch amounted to 554,000 metric tons and fish constituted the country's leading export.

Agriculture. Portugal is an agricultural country, and in 1965, 42 percent of the labor force was engaged in agriculture, one of the highest percentages in Europe. Portugal's major agricultural product is wine, and the country is known for its port and Madeira.

Fruits and nuts, produced in the south, are also important exports and include oranges, lemons, figs, grapes, and almonds. Olives are grown throughout the country and rice, the principal cereal crop, is raised in the Tagus river valley.

Industry. Industry is largely undeveloped, although in the mid-1960s improvements in the transportation system, increased hydroelectric capacity, and foreign loans spurred hopes for more rapid industrialization.

Portugal's most important industries are textiles and food processing. Also manufactured are tile, tobacco, glass, pottery, and cement. Heavy industry is almost nonexistent, although a steel mill opened in 1961 at Seixal, near Lisbon.

Trade. In 1966 Portugal's exports earned $620 million and imports cost $1,023 million. The deficit is largely made up by tourism, emigrant's remittances, and earnings from Portugal's overseas provinces.

Portugal's major exports include fish, wine, agricultural produce, and cork. Principal imports are manufactured goods, machinery, transportation equipment, coal, petroleum, chemicals, and cotton and other raw fibers.

The country's chief trading partners are West Germany, Britain, the United States, and France.

GOVERNMENT. Portugal is officially a corporative republic but it has had a dictatorship since 1932, when Dr. António de Oliveira Salazar became premier and concentrated power in his own hands.

Under the constitution, the president is elected to a seven-year term by an electoral college composed of members

CASA DE PORTUGAL
PORTUGUESE BOAT, with painted prow.

of the National Assembly, the Corporative Chamber, and representatives from overseas legislatures. The president appoints the premier and a cabinet, which are responsible to him.

The legislature consists of the National Assembly, whose 130 members are directly elected to four-year terms. There is also an advisory group, the Corporative Chamber, which is made up of representatives from various commercial, industrial, religious, and cultural groups.

Following World War II the status of Portugal's overseas possessions was changed from "colonies" to "provinces." The Portuguese overseas provinces are the Cape Verde Islands, Portuguese Guinea, St. Tome and the Principe Islands, Angola, Mozambique, Portuguese Timor, and Macao.

Portugal is a member of the United Nations and the North Atlantic Treaty Organization (NATO).

HISTORY. The history of Portugal is inseparable from that of Spain until the 1000s. In 1055 Ferdinand I of León and Castile began to reconquer from the Muslims, or Moors, the northern part of present-day Portugal and organize it as a country. In 1094 Ferdinand granted the Country of Portugal to Henry of Burgundy, who had distinguished himself in the campaign against the Muslims.

Afonso Henriques of the Burgundian dynasty became count in 1128 and declared Portugal independent of Castile. In 1143, in the Treaty of Zamora, Castile formally recognized Portuguese independence, and Afonso Henriques was proclaimed king.

Afonso continued to push the Muslims southward, and in 1147 he captured Lisbon and established a frontier on the Tagus River. Afonso's immediate successors, Sancho I, Afonso II, and Sancho II, extended Portugal to its present boundaries, which were attained in 1249.

Avís Dynasty. Afonso's direct descendants reigned until 1385, when John I of Avís seized the throne and successfully defended Portugal against Castilian invasion. During the 1400s the Portuguese kingdom consolidated its power and began to expand overseas.

Under the direction of Prince Henry the Navigator (1394–1460), the third son of King John I, Portugal discovered and colonized the Madeira Islands, the Azores, and the Cape Verde Islands, and explored far down the west coast of Africa.

John II (r.1481–1495) further advanced Portuguese exploration, and in 1488 Bartholomeu Dias reached the Cape of Good Hope. During the reign of Manuel I (r.1495–1521) the Portuguese sailed to India, discovered Brazil, and began to establish a vast empire through the acquisition of territories in the East Indies and Southeast Asia.

During the 1500s the Eastern trade brought great profits for a time, but holding such extensive territories proved difficult and eventually the empire proved a disastrous drain. Reckless spending, persecution of the Jews, who were prominent in banking and finance, and the introduction of the Inquisition further weakened the small kingdom.

Bragança Dynasty. In 1580 the Portuguese throne fell vacant and was seized by Philip II of Spain. Philip and his son and grandson ruled for 60 years, during which time Portugal was little more than a conquered province. The kingdom regained its independence in 1640, when the Portuguese revolted and elected John of Bragança to the throne, but most of Portugal's Eastern empire had been lost to the Dutch and the English.

The 1700s brought a revived prosperity, largely due to the trade and newly discovered wealth of Brazil. In the mid-1700s the country was ruled by the Marquis of Pombal, a powerful minister of Joseph Emanuel (r.1750–1777).

Although he was often ruthless, Pombal sought to strengthen the monarchy, develop trade and agriculture, and reorganize the army and navy. He also attempted to break the power of the church and nobility in order to weaken class differences. The Braganças proved unable to cope with the international problems raised by the French Revolution of 1789, and in 1807 the country was conquered by Napoleon I of France.

The Braganças fled to Brazil and did not return until 1822, seven years after Napoleon's final defeat at the battle of Waterloo. In the same year Brazil declared its independence and Portugal was beset by a series of political and constitutional struggles that lasted until the mid-1800s.

The reigns of Peter V (r.1853–1861) and Louis I (r.1861–1889) brought some measure of political calm. Portugal attempted to balance the budget and reduce poverty, but little progress was made and discontent with the monarchy grew.

The reign of Carlos I (r.1889–1908) brought no improvement. The king was financially extravagant and licentious. Popular discontent increased and Carlos was assassinated in 1908. His son Manuel II was also financially irresponsible and following an insurrection in Lisbon in 1910, he was forced to flee the country. Portuguese leaders immediately proclaimed a republic but political conditions remained extremely chaotic and a total of 18 revolutions took place during the next 16 years.

Republic. During World War I Portugal fought on the side of the Allies, but the government was continually threatened by pro-German factions, which made several attempts to seize power.

In 1926 a junta of military officers, headed by Gen. António Oscar de Fragoso Carmona, seized power. In 1928, unable to handle economic problems, the generals appointed a professor of economics, António de Oliveira Salazar, finance minister. In 1932 Salazar became premier, or prime minister, and soon established a dictatorship. Although he did not assume the presidency, he arranged for the successive election of figureheads while firmly holding power himself.

Portugal remained neutral in World War II, but provided Britain with raw materials from its African possessions and the right to establish a military base in the Azores. In 1946 Portugal attempted to join the United Nations, but the Soviet Union vetoed its proposed membership and the country did not gain admittance until 1955.

During the late 1950s and in the 1960s Portugal was troubled by problems with its overseas possessions. In 1961 India seized Portugal's Indian territories of Goa, Damão, and Diu, and nationalist rebellions broke out in the African territories of Angola, Mozambique, and Portuguese Guinea. Despite increasingly open internal opposition, as well, Salazar remained at the center of power in the Portuguese government.

—Charles E. Nowell

QATAR

Official name: Sheikhdom of Qatar
Area: 8,500 square miles
Population: (1966 est.) 71,000
Capital: Doha (Pop., 1963 est., 45,000)
Language: Arabic
Religion: Islam
Currency unit: Qatar/Dubai dinar

Qatar, an oil-rich Arab sheikhdom, occupies the Qatar Peninsula on the southern shore of the Persian Gulf, which borders the country on the north, east, and west. To the south are Saudi Arabia and Trucial Oman. The land boundaries are undefined.

THE LAND AND PEOPLE. The Qatar Peninsula is a low plain, thinly covered with sand. The climate is hot and dry, and rainfall is less than 4 inches a year. The people of Qatar are of Arab stock. The population also includes Arabs from neighboring states and European and U.S. oil workers.

ECONOMY. Oil is Qatar's only natural resource, and the country has almost no cultivable land. Fishing, pearl diving, and the herding of goats and camels, the main means of livelihood before the discovery of oil, continue to contribute to the economy of Qatar.

Oil production, begun in 1949, is the country's only industry. In 1966 the wells at Dukhan, in western Qatar, and those off the coasts produced almost 14 million metric tons of oil. Foreign companies operate the fields and pay large royalty fees to Qatar's sheikh, who spends much of the in-

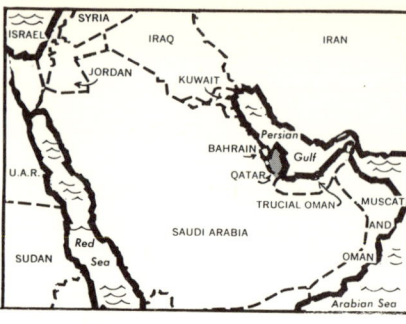

come on social and economic development programs.

In addition to oil, Qatar exports some pearls. Food, machinery, textiles, as well as raw materials must be imported.

GOVERNMENT. Qatar is under the absolute rule of a hereditary sheikh. By treaty, Britain manages Qatar's foreign relations and provides for its defense.

HISTORY. Qatar has been inhabited by Arab peoples for many centuries. The sheikhs of Qatar were compelled to pay tribute to sheikhs of Bahrain for protection and support until 1872. In 1868 Qatar entered into the first of a series of treaties with Britain, which was then building a strong position in the Persian Gulf. Between 1872 and 1914, however, the Ottoman Turks maintained a fort in Qatar and controlled the country.

In a treaty signed in 1916 Qatar's sheikhs granted Britain special diplomatic and commercial rights in return for protection. The discovery of oil in 1939 brought wealth and international importance to the sheikhdom, and since World War II Britain has encouraged the development of Qatar's independence.

—Charles Issawi; Alexander Melamid

RHODESIA

Official name: Rhodesia
Area: 150,333 square miles
Population: (1967 est.) 4,530,000
Capital: Salisbury (Pop., 1965 est., urban area, 325,000)
Language: English, African languages
Religion: Anglicanism, Presbyterianism, Roman Catholicism, traditional religions
Currency unit: Pound

Rhodesia is a British dependency in southern Africa that proclaimed its independence in 1965. The Rhodesian unilateral declaration of independence (UDI) was considered unconstitutional by Britain. Rhodesia is bordered on the north by Zambia, on the east by Mozambique, on the south by South Africa, and on the west by Botswana and South West Africa.

THE LAND. Most of Rhodesia is occupied by a level plateau that has an elevation of over 3,000 feet above sea level. The higher portions of the plateau are in the east. In east-central Rhodesia are the Inyanga Highlands, with elevations of about 8,500 feet.

The only extensive lowlands are in the southeast, near the Limpopo River and its principal tributary, the Shashi. The Zambezi River flows along part of the northern border, and many other rivers flow through the country. Kariba Lake is in northwestern Rhodesia.

The lowlands are hot and dry, but temperatures on the plateau above 3,500 feet are moderate. Rainfall is confined to the period from October to April.

THE PEOPLE. About 95 percent of the people are of African origin, and about 5 percent are of European background. Most of the Europeans are of British or South African origin.

The Africans are mostly Bantu-speaking, and mainly of the Shona (Mashona) tribe in the east and the Ndebele (Matabele) in the southwest. The Ndebele are related to the Zulu people of South Africa. Many of the Africans are Christians.

The major cities are Salisbury, the capital, and Bulawayo.

ECONOMY. Agriculture is important in the Rhodesian economy. The basic crops are corn and grains. The major commercial crops are tobacco and sugar, which are grown mainly on European-owned farms. Cattle and sheep are raised in most parts of the country.

Rhodesia has rich mineral resources, particularly gold, asbestos, and chromium ore. Industry is more highly developed than in most African countries, and a wide range of products is manufactured.

In 1965, after Rhodesia declared its independence, Britain called for economic sanctions against Rhodesia, and British trade with Rhodesia was virtually cut off. Soon after, the UN Security Council requested member countries to impose economic sanctions on Rhodesia. Most member nations, including the United States, joined the embargo.

In 1965, before sanctions were imposed, imports cost $335 million and exports earned $442 million. In 1966 imports cost $236 million and exports earned $293 million. The country's major exports are tobacco, asbestos, gold, and chromium ore. The major imports are machinery, transportation equipment, textiles, iron and steel products, and fertilizers.

GOVERNMENT. The 1961 Rhodesian constitution provided for a parliamentary system of government. The British queen was head of state, and nominal executive power was vested in her representative, the governor-general.

Actual executive power was held by a prime minister and cabinet responsible to the legislature. Legislative power was held by a 65-member Legislative Assembly popularly elected every five years. Fifteen seats in the assembly were reserved for Rhodesian Africans.

After independence was declared, the new government replaced the governor-general with an "officer administering the government," but kept the general framework of the 1961 constitution.

HISTORY. In about 1000 AD Bantu-speaking tribes from central Africa drove off the aboriginal Bushmen living in the region of present-day Rhodesia. They established trade relations with Arabs of the eastern coast of Africa and, through them, with Indian sea traders.

The Bantu-speaking people founded the Zimbabwe civilization, which left imposing stone ruins. In the 1400s another Bantu-speaking people, the Shona, expelled or absorbed their predecessors and built the Monomotapa empire, which was based on gold mining.

In the 1600s Portuguese from Mozambique ravaged the African states in the Zambezi valley, and the Monomotapa empire collapsed. The Portuguese imposed their overlordship on the Shona, and destroyed the trade between Africa and India. By the 1800s the power of the Portuguese had declined, and in the early 1800s the Matabele subjugated the Shona.

British Control. Matabeleland lay in the path of British expansion northward from Cape Colony in South Africa, and in 1888 the Matabele king accepted British protection over the area. He also granted to Cecil Rhodes, for whom Rhodesia is named, a monopoly over mining rights for his British South Africa Company. Rhodes then organized the white occupation of the territory. The Matabele rebelled in 1893 but were defeated.

The company administered Southern Rhodesia until 1923, when the white settlers voted for autonomy under British rule and Southern Rhodesia became a crown colony. Southern Rhodesian whites persistently pressed for confederation with Northern Rhodesia (now Zambia) and Nyasaland (now Malawi). Because Southern Rhodesia was under white-settler control, Africans in Northern Rhodesia and Nyasaland vehemently protested against any such association.

Nonetheless, in 1953 Britain established the Federation of Rhodesia and Nyasaland, but on Dec. 31, 1963 the federation was dissolved. Northern Rhodesia and Nyasaland became independent, and Southern Rhodesia remained under British control as the self-governing colony of Rhodesia.

UDI. The Rhodesian government pressed for independence, but Britain refused, insisting on assurances of adequate representation for the country's African majority. Despite Britain's position, Prime Minister Ian Smith declared Rhodesia independent on Nov. 11, 1965. Britain declared the act illegal and refused to recognize Smith's government.

—Hibberd V. B. Kline, Jr.;
Gary A. Weissman

ROMANIA

Official name: Social Republic of Romania
Area: 91,699 square miles
Population: (1967 est.) 19,287,000
Capital: Bucharest (Pop., 1965 est., urban area, 1,382,000)
Language: Romanian
Religion: Orthodox Christianity, Roman Catholicism, Protestantism, Judaism
Currency unit: Leu
National holiday: Liberation day, August 23

Romania, a communist-controlled country in southeastern Europe, is bordered on the north and northeast by the Soviet Union, on the east by the Black Sea, on the south by Bulgaria, and on the west by Yugoslavia and Hungary.

THE LAND. The land surface of Romania is dominated by the great arc-shaped mountain system formed by the Carpathians and the Transylvanian Alps. The Carpathians run from the northwest to the southeast, where they meet the Transylvanian Alps. The Transylvanian Alps run across the country from the southeast to the southwest, ending at the Danube River.

West and north of these mountains lies Transylvania. This triangular plateau is drained by the Mures and Somes rivers, which flow northeast toward Hungary. The Transylvanian plateau is separated from the Hungarian plain by the low Bihor Mountains. Beyond the Bihor, Romania controls a long, narrow strip of the Hungarian plain.

The region between the Carpathians and the Prut River, which forms the border with the Soviet Union, is known as Moldavia. The area between the Transylvanian Alps and the Danube is Walachia. Between the Danube and the Black Sea lies the Romanian portion of the Dobruja Plateau.

The Danube is Romania's largest river, although for much of its course it forms the border with Bulgaria and Yugoslavia. The Oltul and Siret, which cross the lowlands of Walachia and Moldavia, are the Danube's most important tributaries.

Most of Romania has a continental climate with hot, dry summers and cold, windy, snowy winters.

THE PEOPLE. Romanians represent about 86 percent of the total population. Approximately 9 percent of the population is Hungarian and 2 percent is German. Other small minority groups include Ukrainians, Gypsies, Russians, and Yugoslavs (Serbs and Croatians). The minorities are concentrated in western and west-central Romania.

The Romanian language, which is derived from Latin, belongs to the Romance group. Its vocabulary, however, contains substantial borrowings from the Slavic languages.

The population is predominantly rural, and only about 30 percent of the people live in urban areas.

Bucharest, the capital, is the country's political, artistic, and intellectual center. It is a large sprawling metropolis and contains only a few relics of its long history. The second largest city is Cluj, in Transylvania.

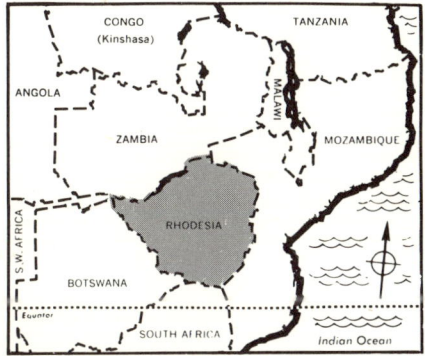

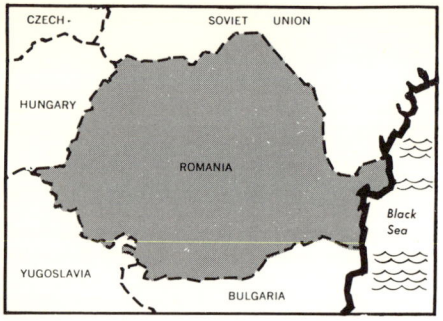

Timișoara, in the southwest, and Brasov, in eastern Transylvania, are important regional trade centers. Ploiești is the oil center of Walachia. Iasi, in Moldavia, is known for its university.

ECONOMY. Before World War II Romania was largely an agricultural nation, but under the communist regime great emphasis has been placed on industrial development.

Natural Resources. Oil is Romania's most important resource, and in 1966 Romania ranked second among European oil producers, producing more than 12.8 million metric tons. The principal oil fields are located along the southern and eastern flanks of the main mountain system, in Walachia and Moldavia.

Romania also has major deposits of natural gas near its oil fields and in Transylvania. The production of natural gas has been growing rapidly and it doubled between 1957 and 1964. In 1966 Romania produced 18,612 million cubic meters of natural gas, making it the fourth largest producer in the world. In addition, Romania mines iron, manganese, gold, silver, and uranium.

Agriculture. Most of Romanian agriculture is collectivized. In 1961 more than 84 percent of the country's cultivated land was controlled by collective and state farms. Cereals are the country's major crops. The most widely grown cereal is corn, which is used for both food and animal feed. Wheat ranks second and together with maize accounts for two-thirds of the country's crop acreage.

Potatoes, fodder, crops, and sunflowers—an important source of vegetable oil—are also grown. The best farmland is in Moldavia and Walachia. Little livestock is raised, although some sheep are pastured in the central uplands.

Industry. Although Romanian industrialization has been rapid, it has been directed toward the development of heavy industry rather than the production of consumer goods. In 1966 Romania produced almost 3.7 million metric tons of steel, almost ten times as much as in 1948.

Substantial progress has also been made in the production of iron, machinery, and chemicals, as well as in nonferrous metallurgy. Textiles and food processing are the most important light industries.

The country's chief industrial centers are Bucharest, Ploesti, Brasov, Timisoara, Resita, and Hunedoara.

Trade. In 1966 Romanian exports earned $1,186 million and imports cost $1,213 million. The country's chief exports include electric motors, petroleum products, window glass, wood products, ball bearings, and transformers. Major imports include automobiles, iron ore, finished rolled metal, coking coal and industrial coke, and industrial equipment.

About one-third of Romania's trade is with the Soviet Union. Other important trading partners are West Germany, Czechoslovakia, East Germany, Italy, and France.

GOVERNMENT. Political life in Romania is dominated by the Romanian Communist Party, and the party's leading role is written into the constitution. Under the constitution the legislature, the Grand National Assembly, is the supreme organ of state. Its 465 members are popularly elected to four-year terms.

The assembly meets for only a few days a year, however, and when not in session its functions are carried out by the Council of State, which is elected by the assembly from among its members. The president of the council is Romania's chief of state. The assembly also appoints a council of ministers to carry out executive functions.

Romania is a member of the United Nations and the Warsaw Pact, a military alliance of communist countries headed by the Soviet Union.

HISTORY. During the 300s BC, what is now Romania was settled by the Dacians, a people related to the Thracians in Greece. In about 60 BC the Dacians were united by Burebistas. The Roman Emperor Trajan conquered the Dacian kingdom in 105–106 AD and in 107 made it a Roman province. Roman rule lasted until 271, when the Emperor Aurelian, who was faced with the threat of barbarian invasions and various problems within the empire, withdrew Roman troops together with a substantial part of the population.

For the following 700 years Romania was swept by successive waves of barbarian invaders, including the Visigoths, Huns, Lombards, Avars, Slavs, and Magyars. These invasions all but obliterated the original Dacian population.

During the 1200s two principalities, Moldavia and Walachia, emerged. The principalities were prevented from gaining power, however, by the strength of their neighbors, Poland, Hungary, and the Ottoman Empire. By the 1500s the Moldavian and Walachian princes were reduced to paying heavy tribute to the Ottoman Turks.

For a brief period during the late 1500s, Michael the Brave of Walachia succeeded in defeating the Turks and uniting the two principalities. But on his death in 1601 the Turks regained control of the area. Early in the 1700s Moldavia and Walachia allied themselves with Peter the Great of Russia in his campaign against the Turks, but the joint effort failed.

Phanariot Rule. The Turks appointed Phanariots, wealthy Byzantine Greeks, to the thrones of Moldavia and Walachia. The Ottoman sultan usually sold the throne to the highest bidder, and the Phanariot princes sought to

WHEAT HARVEST on a Romanian collective.

extort enough money from the populace to show a profit over their original investment. The Phanariot period was one of misery for the Romanians.

From 1802 to 1812, as the result of wars between the Russians and Turks, the principalities were occupied by the Russians. The Peace of Bucharest in 1812 restored Ottoman control, but the Moldavian province of Bessarabia remained in Russian hands.

In 1821 revolts against the Phanariots took place in Moldavia and Walachia. Although the revolts failed, the Turks replaced the Greeks with native princes. In 1829, as a result of the Russo-Turkish War of 1828–1829, the Russians once again occupied the principalities.

Autonomy. Russia withdrew in 1834, and Moldavia and Walachia were granted autonomy under Ottoman suzerainty. During the following 14 years the principalities made progress in education, agriculture, and trade.

In 1848 Romanian intellectuals staged revolutions in Moldavia and Walachia to secure social and political reforms. The revolt in Moldavia was quickly put down, but in Walachia the rebels established a republic. The Russians and Turks both intervened to suppress the republican government, and the princes were restored under an arrangement whereby they were elected to seven-year terms of office.

After the Crimean War (1854–1856), in which Russia was defeated by the British, French, Sardinians, and Turks, it was decided that a commission would determine the future status of the principalities. Elections were held in 1857, and Moldavia and Walachia voted for union under one prince. But the Convention of Paris, held in 1858, decided that the principalities were to have a central control commission but separate legislatures and separate princes. Both Moldavia and Walachia then elected the same prince, Alexander Cuza.

In 1861 the principalities succeeded in having their union recognized by the Turks and the European powers, and in 1862 they established a single legislature and cabinet. Cuza, however, proved to be unpopular and in 1866 he was forced to abdicate.

Independence. Cuza was replaced by Charles of Hohenzollern-Sigmaringen, who reigned as Carol I. After the Russo-Turkish War of 1877–1878, in which Romania sided with Russia, the Turks were forced to recognize Romanian independence, which was recognized internationally by the Treaty of Berlin in 1878. In 1881 Carol became Romania's first king.

In the years following independence Romania was governed by a conservative and authoritarian landowning class that allied the country and its economic and political development with Germany and Austria-Hungary. Nonetheless, the desire to gain Transylvania and Bukovina from Austria-Hungary led Romania to enter World War I on the side of the Allies in 1916.

Romania emerged from the war having gained not only those two territories but also Bessarabia, from the Soviet Union, and eastern Banat, from Austria-Hungary, which had a large Magyar (Hungarian) population.

In the postwar period the government remained conservative and authoritarian. In the 1930s the world economic depression brought financial hardship to the Romanians and especially to the peasantry. Dissatisfaction was expressed politically and the Romanian Communist Party and the strongly pro-German fascist Iron Guard grew in strength.

Dictatorship. In 1938 several factors, including a mounting agricultural crisis and a need to control the power of the Iron Guard in the face of increasing pressure from Nazi Germany, led King Carol II to establish a royal dictatorship. Nonetheless, in 1940 Germany and Italy forced King Carol to cede Transylvania to Hungary and southern Dobruja to Bulgaria in an agreement known as the Vienna Award. The Romanians were outraged and the king was forced to abdicate.

Carol was succeeded by his son Michael, and the government was taken over by Gen. Ion Antonescu, the former prime minister under Carol, who had strong Iron Guard leanings and who continued to maintain a dictatorship.

During World War II Romania was occupied by the Germans and participated in Germany's campaign against the Soviet Union. In August 1944 King Michael overthrew Antonescu's dictatorship and entered the war on the side of the Allies. Romania restored Bessarabia and Bukovina to the Soviet Union, which in turn nullified the Vienna Award.

Communist Rule. Following World War II, despite the presence of an Allied Control Council in the country, the Soviet Union managed to take control of Romania. King Michael abdicated in December 1947 and Romania was proclaimed a People's Republic. By 1952 nationalist communist leaders had been replaced by pro-Soviet Romanian communists.

A constitution modeled after that of the Soviet Union was adopted, and Georghe Georghiu-Dej, the first secretary of the Communist party, became president of the State Council. Under the communist regime agriculture was collectivized and forced industrialization took place. Georghiu-Dej died in 1965 and was succeeded as first secretary by Nicholai Ceausescu.

In the mid-1960s Romania began to take an international position that was increasingly independent from that of the Soviet Union. The government refused to cooperate fully with the Soviet-dominated Council of Mutual Economic Assistance (COMECON), and Romania increased its trade with Western Europe.

Romania also proclaimed its intention to pursue its own industrialization policies, abolished Russian as a required language in the schools, and revived many national traditions. In 1967 Ceausescu also became the head of state.

—Robert J. Byrnes; George Kish

RWANDA

Official name: Republic of Rwanda
Area: 10,169 square miles
Population: (1967 est.) 3,306,000
Capital: Kigali (Pop., 1959, urban area, 4,273)
Language: Kinyarwanda, French
Religion: Roman Catholicism, traditional religions
Currency unit: Franc
National holiday: Independence day, July 1

Rwanda, a landlocked republic in eastern Africa, is bordered on the north by Uganda, on the east by Tanzania, on the south by Burundi, and on the west by the Congo (Kinshasa). Rwanda was joined with present-day Burundi as Ruanda-Urundi until 1962, when it received its independence from Belgium.

THE LAND. Rwanda is composed mainly of hills and uplands. A continuous chain of mountains with elevations above 6,500 feet runs along Rwanda's western border. An eroded plateau slopes eastward from the mountains. In the north there are active volcanoes in the Virunga Mountains, which reach an elevation of over 14,700 feet. The Kagera River drains Rwanda's plateau. Lake Kivu is in western Rwanda.

There are two wet and two dry seasons each year. In most places between 40 and 60 inches of rain falls during the wet seasons.

THE PEOPLE. There are three ethnic groups in Rwanda—the Hutu, the Tusi ("Watusi"), and the Twa. About 86 percent of the people are Hutu, 13 percent are Tusi, and about 1 percent are Twa. Until recently the Hutu, traditionally farmers, were dominated by the Tusi under a feudal system. The Twa people, pygmy forest-dwellers, are probably descendants of Rwanda's original inhabitants.

Rwanda had a population density of over 300 persons per square mile in 1965, and population pressure on the land is great. The rate of population growth is high, 3.1 percent a year between 1958 and 1965.

There are few towns or cities in the country, and the largest urban center is Kigali, the capital.

ECONOMY. Rwanda's economy is based on agriculture. The basic food crops are beans, corn, and sweet potatoes, and the basic cash crop is coffee. Cattle are numerous and are a symbol of both wealth and social position.

Soil erosion and drought are constant problems throughout the country. Belgium instituted a ten-year economic development plan in 1952, and new drought-resistant crops were introduced.

Although Rwanda has deposits of cassiterite, tungsten, and other minerals, the country's resources have not been fully developed, and there is little industry.

In 1965 exports earned about $13.6 million and imports cost about $18 million. Rwanda's main exports are coffee, tin, and tungsten. Imports include foodstuffs, textiles, machinery, chemicals, and petroleum products. Most trade is conducted with Belgium, Luxembourg, the United States, Uganda, and West Germany.

GOVERNMENT. Rwanda has a presidential system of government. Executive power is held by a president, who is popularly elected to a four-year term. The president is assisted by a council of ministers, equivalent to a cabinet. Legislative power is held by the 47-member National Assembly. Assembly members are popularly elected to four-year terms.

Rwanda is a member of the United Nations and the Organization of African Unity.

HISTORY. The Tusi people, who probably came from Ethiopia, invaded Rwanda in the 1500s. They established themselves as a ruling aristocracy, headed by a mwami, or king, over the agricultural Hutu people of the region.

In 1894 the first European, Graf von Goetzen, a German, reached the kingdom, and in 1899 Germany established a protectorate over the region. Germany administered the area as part of German East Africa until World War I. After the war the former protectorate became a mandate of Belgium under the League of Nations. Belgium administered the region jointly with present-day Burundi as Ruanda-Urundi. In 1946 the area became a UN trust territory.

Belgium permitted little African political activity and until the 1950s supported traditional Tusi rule over the Hutu majority. At that time Africans organized political parties along ethnic lines, and the Party of the Hutu Emancipation Movement (PARMEHUTU), composed mainly of Hutu people, opposed the Tusi-dominated National Rwandan Union (UNAR). Tension between the Hutu and the Tusi led to civil war in 1959. The Hutu ended Tusi dominance, and large numbers of Tusi fled to neighboring countries.

In elections held in 1961 PARMEHUTU won an overwhelming victory. The Belgium trusteeship was ended on June 28, 1962, and Rwanda was declared an independent republic on

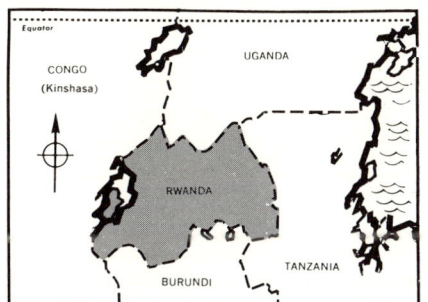

July 1, 1962. Grégoire Kayibanda of PARMEHUTU became president.

Kayibanda initiated a policy of reconciliation and appointed Tusi ministers to his cabinet. But in 1963 fighting again broke out between Tusi and Hutu. Many Tusi were massacred, and many fled the country. Kayibanda was reelected in 1965.

—Hibberd V. B. Kline, Jr.;
Vera L. Zolberg

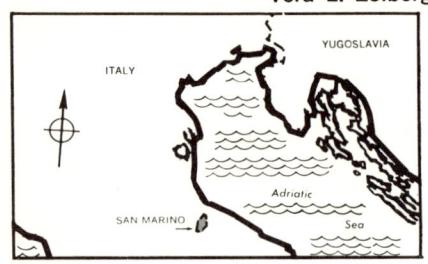

SAN MARINO

Official name: Republic of San Marino
Area: 23.6 square miles
Population: (1966 est.) 18,000
Capital: San Marino (Pop. est., urban area, 3,817)
Language: Italian
Religion: Roman Catholicism
Currency unit: Italian lira
National holiday: Anniversary of the foundation of San Marino, September 3

San Marino is a tiny republic in the north of the Italian Peninsula and is entirely surrounded by Italy.

THE LAND. San Marino consists almost entirely of one mountain, the three-peaked Mt. Titano, which rises over 2,700 feet. Several rivers rush down the mountain. The most important rivers are the Fumicello and the San Marino.

San Marino's climate is mild, with rather cold winters and warm summers. Rainfall is moderate.

THE PEOPLE. Almost all of San Marino's population is of Italian descent. Roman Catholicism is the religion of all but a few, and the people speak Italian.

Most of the population is concentrated in 12 towns lying around the base and on the peaks of Mt. Titano. The largest town, Borg Maggiore, is on one peak of the mountain. The capital, San Marino, is on the highest peak.

ECONOMY. San Marino is a moderately prosperous country. Its chief natural resources are building stone, which is quarried, farm and pasture land, and magnificent scenery, which attracts many tourists.

Farming is the main occupation. Grapes and wheat are the leading crops, and dairying is important. San Marino's industries produce textiles, paper, leather goods, pottery, bricks, cement, wine, and candy. Tourism and the sale of postage stamps contribute heavily to the country's income. San Marino has a customs union with Italy and uses Italian currency.

San Marino's international trade is modest, and is almost entirely with Italy. It exports building materials, foodstuffs, wine, and hides, and imports manufactured consumer items.

GOVERNMENT. San Marino is a republic. Legislative power is vested in a 60-member assembly, the Grand and General Council, which is popularly elected every five years.

Twice yearly the council appoints from among its members two regents who, with the Council of State, or cabinet, wield executive power. San Marino is represented diplomatically abroad by Italy.

HISTORY. According to tradition, San Marino was founded in the 300s AD by Marinus, a Christian stonemason from Dalmatia who was fleeing from religious persecution. Marinus is said to have been later made a saint, San Marino. The earliest document definitely establishing San Marino's existence as an independent commune, however, is dated 885. San Marino was apparently self-governing at that time.

San Marino's rugged terrain and its political and economic insignificance protected it from destruction by medieval invaders of Italy and helped to keep it generally aloof from violent political and religious feuds that disrupted Italy during the 1200s and 1300s.

In the 1400s and 1500s San Marino avoided incorporation into the Papal States and was able to expand its territory somewhat. In the 1500s it was controlled for a brief period by the powerful Italian Borgia family, but in 1549 Pope Paul III proclaimed its sovereignty.

When Napoleon I of France conquered Italy in the late 1700s, he spared the tiny republic. When the many states of Italy were united in 1861, San Marino did not join the new nation. In 1862 it entered a customs union with Italy, and in 1879 San Marino and Italy signed a treaty of friendship.

San Marino entered World War I as an ally of Italy, and in the 1930s, when Benito Mussolini led the fascist government of Italy, San Marino adopted a fascist form of government. In World War II, it proclaimed its neutrality and was a haven for refugees, but it was bombed by Allied planes and suffered damage from ground fighting.

After the war, in the late 1940s, a communist-socialist coalition government was elected and held power until 1957, when the more conservative Christian Democratic party took control. Elections held in 1964 gave the Christian Democrats a majority in the assembly.

—Charles Nowell

SAUDI ARABIA

Official name: Kingdom of Saudi Arabia
Area: 869,970 square miles
Population: (1966 est.) 6,870,000
Capital: Riyadh (Pop., 1965 est., 225,000)
Language: Arabic
Religion: Islam
Currency unit: Rial
National holiday: September 23

Saudi Arabia is an oil-rich Arab kingdom occupying the bulk of the Arabian Peninsula. It is bounded on the north by Jordan, Iraq, Kuwait, and two neutral zones, one administered jointly with Iraq and one shared with Kuwait. It is bordered on the east by the Persian (or Arabian) Gulf, Trucial Oman, and Muscat and Oman; on the south by Muscat and Oman, South Yemen, and Yemen; and on the west by Yemen and the Red Sea. Many of the boundaries are not demarcated.

THE LAND. Most of the surface of Saudi Arabia is barren. A narrow, infertile plain, the Tihama, lies along the western coast. To its east the Hejaz mountains, in the north, and the Asir mountains, in the south, rise sharply to 11,000 feet. These treeless, sandstone and lava mountains slope into an interior plateau, which consists of two desert regions—An Nafud, in the north, and the Rub al-Khali, in the south.

The interior plain occupies about 90 percent of the country's area and is largely uninhabited. Along Saudi Arabia's eastern border rolling coastal plains slope into the Persian Gulf.

Saudi Arabia has no rivers—only wadis, dry river beds where rainfall may collect. Underground water is tapped by wells.

The climate is hot and dry. Summer daytime temperatures often climb to over 125°F in most of the country, but nights, especially in the desert, can be quite cold. In the mountains and along the eastern coast the average year-round temperature is more moderate, 80°F. Rainfall is rare, and the deserts may go for years without any rain.

THE PEOPLE. Almost all Saudi Arabians are Arabic-speaking Muslims. Population is clustered around its few oases, watered by underground springs, where such large towns as Mecca, Jidda, Riyadh, Hofuf, and Medina developed.

Nomadic Bedouin tribesmen have long roamed the deserts. Government programs have been directed toward settling the nomads in areas where irrigation can make sedentary life possible.

ECONOMY. Saudi Arabia's wealth is based on oil. Oil is the country's most important natural resource, and oil production is the major industry. Oil operations are centered in the eastern part of the country. The principal refinery is on the east coast, at Ras Tanura. Saudi Arabia produced 7 percent of the world's oil in 1967 and is believed to have 10 percent of the world's oil reserves.

Income from fees, taxes, and royalties paid by the foreign companies that hold exploitation rights exceeded $800 million in 1967. Oil revenues are used to provide free education and health care for Saudi Arabians, government expenses, and domestic improvements including industrialization and agricultural expansion and modernization.

Most of the people of the country live as farmers or herders. The country's only major crops are grains, citrus fruits, and dates, which are grown in oases. Sheep, goats, and camels graze in the deserts. There is some pearl diving and fishing along the coasts. Money spent in the country by Muslim pilgrims to the holy cities of Mecca and Medina is the second most important source of Saudi Arabia's income.

Saudi Arabia's prosperous international trade is based on oil. In 1963-1964 imports cost $282 million and exports earned $1,175 million. Oil is the main export. Foodstuffs, building materials, textiles and clothing, machinery, and chemicals are imported. Saudi Arabia sells oil throughout the world, but Japan is the largest single customer. The United States, Western European countries, and other Middle Eastern states are the kingdom's main sources of imports.

GOVERNMENT. Saudi Arabia is an absolute monarchy with a king who serves as political and religious leader of the country. The king appoints a cabinet and an assembly, but he may overrule them. Saudi Arabia is a member of the United Nations and the Arab League.

HISTORY. Saudi Arabia became a nation in 1926, but Arabia has been inhabited since ancient times by Arab herdsmen and traders and was the site of several ancient kingdoms. Muhammad, the prophet, was born in the trading city of Mecca in 570 AD, and the city became an important center of the Muslim religion.

During the century following Muhammad's death in 632 Muslim armies conquered North Africa and the entire Middle East and Muslim power extended into Spain. Religious disputes and competition for power soon brought disorder to Arabia, however. It was divided into two major sheikhdoms—Nejd in the interior of the peninsula and the Hejaz in the west—and many petty states.

Parts of Saudi Arabia were conquered in the 1200s by the Egyptians and in the 1500s by the Ottoman Turks. The conquerors were most interested in the Hejaz, because of the importance of controlling the Muslim holy city of Mecca, its capital.

Wahhabis. In Nejd in the 1700s a Muslim sect whose goal was to reform and purify Islam was founded by Muhammad Ibn Abd al-Wahhab. His followers, the Wahhabis, allied with Muhammad ibn Saud, a ruler of part of Nejd.

Saud's successors carried Wahhabism to the Persian Gulf and by 1806 had conquered the Hejaz from the Sharifs, the rulers of Mecca who controlled the Hejaz. But Saud's Wahhabis were driven back into the interior of Nejd by Turkish and Egyptian troops. In Nejd they lost power to the rival sheikhdom of al-Rashid.

Nearly 100 years later, in 1902, Saud's descendant, Abd al-Aziz Al Saud, conquered Nejd's capital, Riyadh, from the Rashids. By 1913 he had defeated the Rashids and had driven the Ottomans from most of central Arabia.

In 1916 Saud's rival for power, Sharif Hussein of Mecca, led a pan-Arab revolt against the Turks that carried his sons to the thrones of the new Arab states of Iraq and Transjordan (present-day Jordan). After World War I uneasy relations between the Husseins and the Saudis led to warfare in 1924. The Saudis captured the Hejaz and forced out the Husseins.

In 1926 Abd al-Aziz united Nejd and the Hejaz and two small dependencies, Asir and Hasa, into a Wahhabist state. He proclaimed himself king of the entire region, which he named Saudi Arabia in 1932.

Modern Saudi Arabia. Under Abd al-Aziz the modernization of Arabia began, and the discovery of oil in 1938 greatly speeded up the process by providing a source of income for the government. Large-scale oil production began in 1945, after World War II. Oil revenues made possible social changes which promised to affect radically Saudi Arabian life, but the country maintained internal political and social stability.

Abd al-Aziz' son, Saud, succeeded him as king in 1953, but in 1964 he was replaced by his half-brother, Faisal.

The United Arab Republic (U.A.R.), led by Gamal Abdel Nasser, favored rapid, radical social reform in the Arab states, and thus came into conflict with the traditionalist, conservative royal House of Saud. The U.A.R. and Saudi Arabia became the principal rivals for the leadership of the Arab world. In 1966 King Faisal formed the Islamic Alliance with the leaders of Jordan and Iran to counter the U.A.R.'s influence. In a civil war that erupted in Yemen in 1962, Saudi Arabia and the U.A.R. supported and supplied opposing factions, but Nasser and Faisal agreed in 1967 to withdraw their aid and support from the contending Yemen factions.

Saudi Arabia did unite with its Arab rivals in opposing the state of Israel, however. Faisal supported President Nasser's blockade of the Gulf of Aqaba in 1967 but did not participate directly in the resulting Arab-Israeli war.

—Charles Issawi; Alexander Melamid

SAUDI ARABIA'S PROPHET'S MOSQUE, a Muslim shrine, is in the city of Medina.

SENEGAL

Official name: Republic of Senegal
Area: 75,750 square miles
Population: (1966 est.) 3,580,000
Capital: Dakar (Pop., 1961 est., urban area, 374,700)
Language: French, African languages
Religion: Islam, Christianity, traditional religions
Currency unit: Franc CFA (African Financial Community)
National holiday: Independence day, April 4

Senegal, a republic in western Africa, is bordered on the north by Mauritania, on the east by Mali, on the south by the Republic of Guinea and Portuguese Guinea, and on the west by the Atlantic Ocean. The Gambia, a small, independent nation, forms an enclave in Senegal, stretching inland from the Atlantic coast. Senegal proclaimed its independence from France in 1960.

THE LAND. Senegal is occupied mostly by lowlands with elevations below 650 feet, and sandy plains are typical of most parts of the country. Senegal lies largely in Africa's Sahelian zone, a region of sparse grass and spiny trees.

There are plateaus in the southeast with elevations up to about 1,640 feet, and swamps and tropical rain forests in the southwest. The Cape Vert Peninsula, Senegal's westernmost point, protrudes into the Atlantic Ocean.

Four major rivers flow through the country—the Sénégal in the north, the Gambia and Saloum in central Senegal, and the Casamance in the south.

Temperatures are moderate in most parts of the country. Some regions in southern Senegal receive as much as 60 inches of rain each year. The peninsula receives about 24 inches a year.

THE PEOPLE. There are many tribal groups in Senegal. The largest groups are the Wolof; the Fula, or Peul; the Serer; the Mandingo; and the Tukulor. Most of the people are Muslims. There is a small number of non-Africans, who are mainly Europeans, Syrians, and Lebanese.

Dakar, located on the peninsula, is Senegal's largest city. Other large cities are Kaolack, Saint Louis, and Thiès.

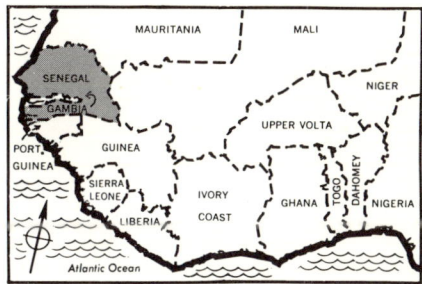

ECONOMY. The economy of Senegal is based on agriculture. The basic food crops are millet, sorghum, and rice. Peanuts are the main commercial crop, and in 1965 over 1.1 million metric tons of peanuts were produced. Fishing is also important in the Senegalese economy.

Senegal has rich phosphate deposits, and in 1965 over 1 million metric tons of phosphate were produced. Industry is centered in Dakar and is well developed. Peanuts, phosphates, and fish are processed for export.

In 1966 imports cost $161 million and exports earned $149 million. The main imports are textiles, machinery, and foodstuffs. The leading exports are peanuts, peanut oil, and phosphates. Most trade is conducted with France, Cambodia, West Germany, and the United States. Senegal receives economic aid from France.

GOVERNMENT. Senegal has a presidential system of government. Executive power is held by a president, who is popularly elected to a four-year term. Legislative power is held by an 80-member National Assembly. Assembly members are also popularly elected to four-year terms.

Senegal is a member of the United Nations and the Organization of African Unity.

HISTORY. Between about the 400s and 200s BC the peoples of what is now Senegal traded by sea with the Carthaginians. During the next millennium they traded with the merchants of ancient Ghana and Mali.

Portuguese sailors visited the shores of Senegal during the 1400s, and beginning in the 1500s French, Dutch, and British merchants came to the region. In the late 1600s the French established settlements at Saint Louis and on Gorée Island, near the Cape Vert Peninsula.

Under a succession of energetic colonial governors, the French tried to transform Senegal into a profitable outpost of their empire. But few Frenchmen could be induced to settle there, and wars with Britain over control of the area were costly. Britain conquered Senegal in the 1750s and administered the area in union with the Gambia as the Crown Colony of Senegambia.

French Rule. By the 1800s France had gradually reestablished its control over most of the country. Only at that time did the French alter the indigenous way of life. From 1854 to 1865, under the aggressive governor Louis Léon César Faidherbe, the French subjugated the people living between Saint Louis and Gorée Island, and successfully asserted their authority over the peoples living on both banks of the Sénégal River.

The Senegalese opposed the French at every turn. Muslims along the Sénégal River, many of whom had become subject to a Fulani-ruled empire in the 1700s, unsuccessfully fought the French. In the interior, al-hajj 'Umar, a Muslim reformer who had created Islamic states in the region in the 1800s, temporarily halted the French advance.

By 1890, however, nearly all of the Senegalese had begun to acknowledge France's might.

In 1904 Dakar became the capital of French West Africa. The more important schools and hospitals of French West Africa were located there, and Senegal's coastal region became the most westernized part of French West Africa.

In 1946 Senegal became a territory within the French Union. In elections held in 1951 and 1957 Léopold Senghor, a French-educated poet, led the Senegalese Progressive Union to victory. In 1958 Senegal became an autonomous member of the French Community.

Independence. In 1959 France joined Senegal with present-day Mali to form the Mali Federation, which became an autonomous member of the French Community in June 1960. On Aug. 20, 1960 Senegal withdrew from the federation and proclaimed its independence. Senghor became Senegal's first president, governing the country together with the prime minister, Mamadou Dia.

In 1962, after an unsuccessful attempt by the prime minister to overthrow Senghor, the country adopted a new constitution providing for a strong presidential system of government. In 1963 relations with Mali were normalized.

—Hibberd V. B. Kline, Jr.;
Robert I. Rotberg

SIERRA LEONE

Official name: Sierra Leone
Area: 27,699 square miles
Population: (1967 est.) 2,439,000
Capital: Freetown (Pop., 1966 est., 148,000)
Language: English, African languages
Religion: Islam, Christianity, traditional religions
Currency: Leone
National holiday: Independence day, April 27

Sierra Leone, a republic in western Africa, is bordered on the north by Guinea, on the east by Liberia, and on the south and west by the Atlantic Ocean. Sierra Leone received its independence from Britain in 1961.

THE LAND. Sierra Leone has a varied landscape. In the northwest a mountainous peninsula extends into the Atlantic Ocean. Inland from the peninsula and in other places along the coast there are swampy plains. Further inland the plains rise to plateaus.

There are forests and grasslands in the north and east. In the northeast are the Loma Mountains, with a peak elevation of over 6,390 feet. Many rivers flow through the country, including the Rokel and the Moa.

Sierra Leone has a tropical climate, and the peninsula is one of the rainiest parts of western Africa, receiving about 145 inches of rain each year.

THE PEOPLE. There are some 20 tribal groups in Sierra Leone, the largest of which are the Mende and the Temne. The Mende live mainly in the south and the Temne live in the north. There are also several thousand Creoles, descendants of freed slaves who came to Sierra Leone in the 1700s and 1800s.

The Creoles live mainly in and near Freetown, the country's capital and largest city. Bo, Kenema, and Makeni are also major urban centers.

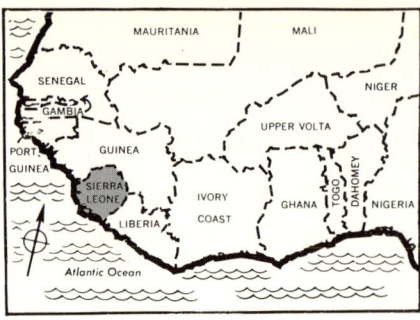

ECONOMY. The economy of Sierra Leone is based on agriculture. The basic food crops are rice and cassava. Palm kernels, cacao, kola nuts, ginger, and coffee are important commercial crops. Fishing is also an important source of income for the people along the coast.

Sierra Leone has rich mineral resources, and the country is one of the world's major producers of diamonds, which are dug from river gravels. Iron ore, another important export, is shipped from the port of Pepel, near Freetown. There are also deposits of chromium ore and bauxite, from which aluminum is made.

In 1966 imports cost $100 million and exports earned $83 million. The principal imports are foodstuffs, petroleum products, textiles, and machinery. The major exports are diamonds, iron ore, and coffee. Most trade is conducted with Britain, the Netherlands, West Germany, and Japan.

GOVERNMENT. Sierra Leone's 1961 independence constitution provided for a parliamentary system of government with the British queen as head of state, represented by a governor-general. Actual executive power was vested in a prime minister responsible to the legislature.

Legislative power was held by the House of Representatives, which consisted of 62 popularly elected members and 12 paramount chiefs chosen by the tribal chiefs. All legislators were elected to five-year terms.

In March 1967 the military seized control of the government, and an eight-man National Reformation Council assumed executive and legislative powers.

Sierra Leone is a member of the United Nations, the Commonwealth of Nations, and the Organization of African Unity.

HISTORY. The Portuguese explorer Pedro da Cintra visited Sierra Leone in 1462 and gave the area its name, which means Lion Mountain. The course of Sierra Leone's modern history was affected by the proclamation in 1772 by Britain's Lord Chief Justice William Mansfield that slavery was never acknowledged by law; consequently, slaves held in England were set free.

In London and in other British cities freed slaves found it difficult to obtain employment, and they constituted a source of embarrassment to the British government. The government gave its support to a plan of a private company, the Society for the Abolition of Slavery, to ship the freed slaves to Africa.

In 1788 the first shipload of freed slaves settled in present-day Sierra Leone. First by purchase and later by force, they acquired land and built villages near what later became Freetown. In 1791 the Sierra Leone Company began administering the settlement. New groups of freed slaves came to Sierra Leone from Nova Scotia and Jamaica.

British Rule. In 1808 the coastal area became a British crown colony. The colony grew in wealth and importance, new settlements were made along the coast, and the settlers began to increase their trade contacts with the tribes of the interior. The settlers also took more and more tribal land. In the early 1800s the number of settlers was increased by the addition of slaves freed at sea by a British patrol stationed in Freetown.

In 1896, in a move to prevent French territorial expansion, the British government established a protectorate over the interior. The two regions—the colony and the protectorate—were administered separately until 1924. British administrative policy during the 1930s and 1940s helped to integrate the peoples of the protectorate with those of the colony. It also worked to eliminate the antagonism between the descendants of the settlers, the Creoles, and the Africans of the interior.

At first the peoples of the coast felt superior because of their higher educational attainments, but the growth of indigenous political movements reversed this. In 1951 Milton Margai, a Mende physician from the protectorate, led the Sierra Leone People's Party to an important electoral victory over the combined opposition of the parties loyal to two Creoles, Dr. H. C. Bankole-Bright and I. T. A. Wallace-Johnson.

Independence. Margai strengthened his position in elections in 1957, and when Sierra Leone became independent on Apr. 27, 1961, he became the first prime minister. Milton Margai died in 1964, and his half-brother, Albert Margai, who had been finance minister, became prime minister.

In March 1967 elections were held for the House of Representatives in the midst of criticism caused by Albert Margai's attempts to establish a one-party state. The elections were contested by two main parties—Margai's Sierra Leone People's Party and the All People's Congress led by Siaka Stevens.

On the basis of early election returns, the governor-general appointed Stevens prime minister. Disturbances broke out almost immediately. The military seized control of the government and established a National Reformation Council headed by Lt. Col. Andrew Juxon-Smith to run the country. —Hibberd V. B. Kline, Jr.; Robert I. Rotberg

SIKKIM

Official name: Sikkim
Area: 2,744 square miles
Population: (1966 est.) 180,000
Capital: Gangtok (Pop., 1961 est., 6,848)
Language: Lepcha, Nepali, English
Religion: Buddhism, Hinduism
Currency: Indian rupee

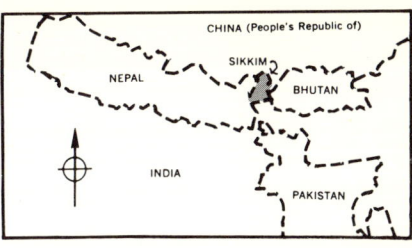

Sikkim is a small principality in South Asia lying high in the Himalayas. It is a protectorate of India. Sikkim is bordered on the north by the Tibet region of China, on the east by Bhutan, on the south by India, and on the west by Nepal. The small country lies astride important routes over the Himalayas connecting Tibet and India.

THE LAND. Sikkim is a mountainous country. The Singalila Range rises on its western border, and the Chola Range rises on the east. Between these border mountains there is a succession of ranges and valleys generally trending north to south.

Elevation increases toward the north, with the highest peak, Kanchenjunga, rising to 28,168 feet in the northwestern corner of the country. At least three other peaks are known to be over 20,000 feet. The Natu La and the Jelip La over the Chola Range are important passes to and from Tibet. The Tista River flows south from the Himalayas across Sikkim.

Sikkim's climate varies with elevation. In the lower regions of the south, temperatures are subtropical; in the central valleys and plateaus, they are moderate; and in the high regions of the north, they are arctic. The line of perpetual snow is reached at about 17,000 feet. Precipitation is abundant, with an annual average of 137 inches of rainfall at Gangtok, the capital, in the center of the country.

THE PEOPLE. Sikkim's population consists of three main elements—Nepalese, Bhotias, and Lepcha. The Nepalese, who constitute a majority, are concentrated in the higher altitudes. The Bhotias, of Tibetan extraction, live mainly in the central plateaus. The Lepcha, believed to be Sikkim's earliest inhabitants, are found in the lower valleys.

The Nepalese are Hindu, but although they are in the majority, Lamaist Buddhism, the religion of the Bhotia and the Lepcha, is the official religion.

ECONOMY. Farming and herding are the major occupations in Sikkim. Livestock is grazed on summer pastures on the plateaus at elevations of between 12,000 and 15,000 feet. Corn, millet, fruit, legumes, and potatoes are raised on terraced fields near the center of the country at elevations of from 4,500 to 6,500 feet. At lower elevations in the southern valleys rice is grown wherever irrigation is possible.

There is no modern industry in the country. Cottage industries produce items such as clothing and household utensils and supply most of the peoples' requirements. There is some trade across the Indian border exchanging manufactured items for potatoes, fruit, and various other agricultural products.

In the 1960s, with aid from India, Sikkim began to improve its transportation system and to modernize its economy.

GOVERNMENT. Sikkim, a protectorate of India, is ruled by a hereditary maharajah with the advice of an Indian official. Also advising the maharajah is a state council. Two-thirds of the council members are elected, with representation divided proportionally among Sikkim's three ethnic groups. India is responsible for Sikkim's foreign affairs, defense, and communications.

HISTORY. Sikkim has been inhabited for many centuries, but little is known of its early history. It was long used as a trade route between India and Tibet, and because of its strategic position it has been ruled by Nepal, Tibet, and China. Its Lepcha people became Buddhists in the 1500s, and its ruling dynasty was founded in the 1600s.

Britain extended its influence from India into Sikkim in the 1800s, during wars against Nepal and Tibet. In 1890 Britain made Sikkim a protectorate, and responsibility passed to India in 1947, when India became independent. A treaty signed in 1950 reaffirmed Sikkim's status as a protectorate.

The British encouraged Nepalese to settle in Sikkim, and by the mid-1900s the Nepalese were in the majority. Their demands for a larger share in the government of the country became Sikkim's major political problem. They were granted a majority of the seats on the advisory council in 1960 and their voting rights were expanded in 1961.

Maharajah Gyalsay Palden Thondup Namgyal, who had married an American, came to the throne in 1963. He concentrated on modernizing Sik-

SIERRA LEONE WORKERS panning for alluvial diamonds along a river bank.
UNITED NATIONS

kim's political and economic life while maintaining its social stability.

Sikkim's strategic position between India and China endangered it in the early 1960s, when border warfare between India and China erupted. In 1967 fighting broke out again between Indian and Chinese troops on Sikkim's borders.

—Charles H. Heimsath; M. G. Inaba

SINGAPORE

Official name: Republic of Singapore
Area: 224 square miles
Population: (1967 est.) 1,956,000
Capital: Singapore (Pop., 1967 est., 1,956,000)
Language: Malay, Chinese, Tamil, English
Religion: Islam, Christianity, Buddhism, Hinduism
Currency unit: Dollar
National holiday: August 9

Singapore is a small island republic lying off the southern tip of the Malay Peninsula in Southeast Asia. It became a sovereign state in 1965 after two years as part of the nation of Malaysia. Before joining Malaysia, it had been a British possession for some 150 years.

Singapore is separated from West Malaysia on the north, east, and west by the narrow Johore Strait. To the south, the Riao Islands of Indonesia lie across the Singapore Strait.

THE LAND. The nation of Singapore consists of the large island of Singapore and some 40 low-lying islets within 10 miles of its eastern and southern shores. On Singapore Island, a coastal plain surrounds a central plateau that has a peak of 581 feet. Once swampland and jungle, most of the island has been cleared for farming and building.

Singapore's climate is hot and humid. The average year-round temperature is about 81°F and an average of 96 inches of rain falls each year.

THE PEOPLE. Singapore is very densely populated, with over 7,500 persons per square mile in 1965, and the rate of population growth is high, 3 percent a year between 1958 and 1966. Approximately two-thirds of the people live in the capital and largest city, Singapore, on the southern coast of Singapore Island.

The people are of many backgrounds. About three-quarters of Singapore's people are of Chinese descent. Malays and Indonesians make up some 14 percent, about 8 percent are of Indian and Pakistani origins, and there are small groups of Europeans and people of mixed ethnic backgrounds.

Malay is the national language, and Malay, Chinese, English, and Tamil, an Indian language, are official languages. Many Chinese adhere to Confucianism, Taoism, and Buddhism. Most of the Malays and Pakistanis are Muslim, the Indians are largely Hindu and Sikh, and there are many Christians.

ECONOMY. Singapore's prosperity is based on its location on important sea routes between the Indian Ocean, the South China Sea, and the Pacific, and on its large, industrious population. Singapore is the commercial and financial center of Southeast Asia, and a large share of the region's trade passes through its large, excellent harbor.

There is little agricultural land, but in the 1960s the government initiated agricultural development programs and reclamation projects to create new farmland. Rubber is the chief crop, and coconuts, vegetables, fruits, and tobacco are raised. Dairying is important, and pigs and chickens are raised for domestic use and export.

Industry. Singapore's industry traditionally has been based on processing Southeast Asia's natural products, especially tin, rubber, spices, copra, coffee, and timber. These industries still prospered in the 1960s, as did Singapore's important shipyards.

In the 1960s the government encouraged the development of new industries to broaden the base of the economy. Hydroelectric power stations, iron and steel mills, an oil refinery, chemical plants, textile mills, clothing factories, and dairy processing plants were among the new facilities opened in the 1960s. Many of them are located in a large industrial park at Jurong, west of Singapore city.

Trade. Commerce, especially transshipment trade, remained the major factor in Singapore's economy, however, as the country processed Asian goods for export and distributed imports to Asian market centers.

In 1966 Singapore's imports were valued at $1,328 million, and its exports were valued at $1,102 million. Over half of the totals were transshipped goods. Rubber, petroleum products, tin, wood products, spices, and some finished goods are exported. Machinery and vehicles, foodstuffs, and finished consumer goods are the main imports.

Malaysia, Indonesia, Japan, Britain, the United States, and Communist China are Singapore's principal trading partners.

GOVERNMENT. Singapore is a republic with a parliamentary system of government. The head of state is the president, who is chosen by a popularly elected legislature, or parliament. Executive powers are exercised by a cabinet, headed by a prime minister, responsible to the parliament. The parliament has one house with 51 members elected under a system of compulsory universal suffrage.

Singapore is a member of the United Nations and the Commonwealth of Nations.

HISTORY. Singapore had become an important commercial center by the 1100s AD. In 1377 Singapore city was destroyed by Java, and it lost its trading importance. In 1819 Sir Stamford Raffles, an agent of the British East India Company, established a trading post on the island. Commerce flourished, and in 1824 the British bought Singapore and the adjacent islands.

British Rule. In 1826 Britain established the "Straits Settlements," combining Singapore with two former rival trading centers, Malacca and Penang. In 1867, as their prosperity and importance increased, the settlements were raised to the status of a crown colony.

The opening of the Suez Canal in 1869 and the development of steamships increased Europe's trade with the Far East, and further bolstered Singapore's prosperity. In the late 1800s profitable tin smelting and rubber processing were added to the island's trading activities.

In the 1920s the British established a major naval base at Singapore, and in the 1930s an air base. In 1942, during World War II, Japan captured Singapore and occupied it until the British recaptured it in 1945. In 1946 Singapore was separated from Penang and Malacca and made a separate crown colony.

In the 1950s Singapore moved toward self-government, and in 1959 it was granted full internal autonomy. The major political force in the country became the largely Chinese People's Action Party.

Independence. In 1963 Singapore joined the new nation of Malaysia, formed of Malaya, Sabah (North Borneo), and Sarawak. Singapore's dominant economic position and its Chinese majority led to friction between it and Malaysia's federal government. As a result, in 1965 Singapore reluctantly withdrew from the federation and became a sovereign state.

The nation concentrated on expanding its economy and on maintaining a policy of friendly relations with Malaysia and its other Asian neighbors. In 1967 it joined with Malaysia, Indonesia, Thailand, and the Philippines to form the Association of Southeast Asian Nations (ASEAN), an organization for economic, social, and political cooperation.

—Sara D. Gilbert; M. G. Inaba

SOMALI REPUBLIC

Official name: Somali Republic
Area: 246,201 square miles
Population: (1966 est.) 2,580,000
Capital: Mogadiscio (Pop., 1966 est., 170,000)
Language: Somali
Religion: Islam
Currency unit: Shilling
National holiday: July 1

The Somali Republic, an independent country in eastern Africa, is bordered on the north by the French Territory of the Afars and Issas (French Somaliland) and the Gulf of Aden, on the east by the Indian Ocean, on the south by Kenya, and on the west by Ethiopia. The Somali Republic was formed in July 1960 by a union of the former Italian Somalia Protectorate and British Somaliland.

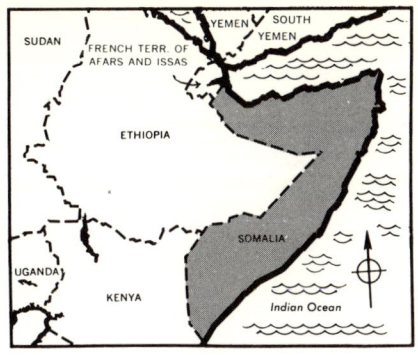

THE LAND. Most of the Somali Republic is occupied by a featureless, high plain. In some places, especially in the north, high limestone cliffs border the plain. Near the eastern coast the plain is sandy, and gives way inland to low hills and ridges.

In the northeastern part of the country, the Somali Peninsula juts into the Indian Ocean. Near the peninsula are the Carcar Mountains, which have an average elevation of 3,000 feet. The country's main rivers are the Giuba (Juba) and the Shabali (Scebeli).

Although the southwestern part of the country receives about 20 inches of rain each year, semiarid and arid conditions prevail in most of the Somali Republic. The northern part of the country receives less than 10 inches of rain each year.

THE PEOPLE. The Somali Republic has a relatively homogeneous population. Most of the inhabitants are Somali, a people of mixed Ethiopian, Arab, and Indian ancestry. Bantu-speaking people live in the southern part of the country.

The Somali Republic's largest city is its capital, Mogadiscio (Mogadishu), which is on the Indian Ocean.

ECONOMY. The Somali Republic's economy is based on herding, and camels, sheep, and goats are raised in most parts of the country.

The basic food crops are corn and sorghum, and the main cash crop is bananas, which are grown mainly on irrigated plantations in the southern part of the country. In 1965, 140,000 metric tons of bananas were produced. Sugarcane and a variety of fruits are also grown.

Although there are small canneries and leather tanneries, industry is poorly developed. The Somali Republic has deposits of iron ore, gypsum, beryl, and columbite, but mineral deposits have not been fully exploited. A five-year plan was begun in 1963 to develop transportation, communications, agriculture, and industry.

In 1965 imports cost about $49.5 million and exports earned about $33.2 million. The main imports are rice, petroleum products, textiles, and machinery. The main exports are bananas, live animals, and hides and skins. Most trade is conducted with Italy, the Soviet Union, and Kenya.

GOVERNMENT. The Somali Republic has a parliamentary system of government. Legislative power rests with the 122-member National Assembly. Assembly members are directly elected under a system of universal adult suffrage to five-year terms. The head of state is the president, who is elected by the assembly to a six-year term. Executive powers are exercised by a prime minister responsible to the legislature.

The Somali Republic is a member of the United Nations and the Organization of African Unity.

HISTORY. In about the 900s the Galla people, who were originally from Ethiopia, migrated into what is now the Somali Republic and pushed the indigenous agricultural Bantu-speaking peoples southward. Between the 1200s and 1300s the Somali peoples displaced the Galla.

Arabs and Persians made settlements on the northern coast between the 800s and 1500s, and helped make Islam the dominant religion. In the early 1800s the sultan of Zanzibar obtained control of the southern part of the country.

The Protectorates. Egyptians occupied the area of the Somali Republic between 1874 and 1885. The Egyptian occupation was ended when Britain established a protectorate over the northern part of the country. Under the terms of agreement made with the sultan of Zanzibar, Italy established the Protectorate of Somalia in the south in 1889.

Between 1900 and 1920 both the British and the Italians fought a rebellion led by a Muslim religious leader, Sayyid Muhammad Abdulla Hassan, whom they called the "Mad Mullah."

In the 1920s and 1930s the fascist government of Italy maintained firm control of the south and encouraged settlement by Italian colonists. Italy used the region as a staging base to attack Ethiopia in 1934. After World War II broke out, Britain took over the administration of the Italian protectorate in 1941.

Postwar politics centered on reuniting the Somali people. Haja Muhammad Hussein, leader of the Somali Youth League (SYL), a nationalist movement he had founded in 1943, called for unification of the two protectorates under a single UN trusteeship.

In 1949, however, the UN General Assembly voted to return southern Somalia to Italy as a trusteeship for a ten-year period so that Italy could prepare the region for independence. In 1956 elections were held in the Italian trust area, and Abdullaha Issa of the SYL became the first prime minister of Somalia.

In 1954 a British-Ethiopian agreement granted the Haud area of Ogaden in the western part of the country to Ethiopia, but the Somali people retained the right to graze their cattle on the land. A legislative council was created in British Somaliland in 1957, and on June 26, 1960 Britain granted the former protectorate its independence.

Independence. On July 1, 1960, after the Italian trusteeship had ended, the Italian and British regions were united to form the Somali Republic. Aden Abdullah Osman was elected president by the parliament, and he appointed Abdi Rashid Shermarke prime minister.

At the time of independence Ethiopia withdrew the rights of the Somali to graze cattle in Ogaden. Both the Somali Republic and Ethiopia claimed the area, and fighting broke out in 1963. Fighting also broke out with Kenya over disputed land.

Members of all political parties united in the Somali National Congress to deal with the territorial claims of the Somali Republic to land in Ethiopia, northern Kenya, and French Somaliland (the present-day French Territory of the Afars and Issas). In 1964 a new government was formed, and Hussein became prime minister.

Border fighting with Kenya broke out again in 1966 and 1967. In July 1967 the National Assembly elected Shermarke president, and he appointed Muhammad Ibrahim Egal prime minister.

—Hibberd V. B. Kline, Jr.;
Vera L. Zolberg

SOUTH AFRICA

Official name: Republic of South Africa
Area: 471,445 square miles
Population: (1967 est.) 18,733,000
Capital: Pretoria (Pop., 1960 est., urban area, 422,600)
Language: English, Afrikaans, Bantu languages
Religion: Protestantism, Roman Catholicism, traditional African religions
Currency: Rand
National holiday: May 31, Republic day

The Republic of South Africa, an independent country in southernmost Africa, is bordered on the north by South West Africa, Botswana, and Rhodesia; on the east by Mozambique, Swaziland, and the Indian Ocean; on the south by the Indian Ocean; and on the west by the Atlantic Ocean. Walvis Bay, located on the Atlantic coast of South West Africa, is a part of South Africa. Lesotho lies completely within the borders of South Africa.

SOUTH AFRICAN RAILWAYS
SOUTH AFRICA'S CAPE TOWN is the country's second largest city and its chief port.

South Africa

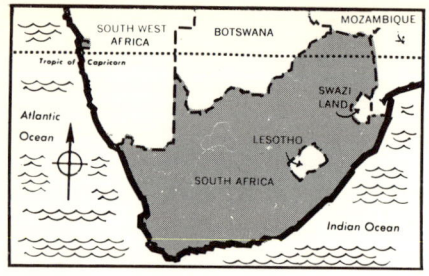

Between 1910 and 1961 South Africa was a union of four provinces—Cape Province in the west, Orange Free State in the central part of the country, Transvaal in the northeast, and Natal in the east. On May 13, 1961 South Africa withdrew from the British Commonwealth because its policy of apartheid, the rigid separation of the races, was unacceptable to other Commonwealth countries. On May 31, 1961 South Africa became a republic.

In 1963 the government established the Transkei, an area near Port Elizabeth in South Africa, as a partially self-governing homeland, or "Bantustan," for Negro Africans.

THE LAND. Most of South Africa is occupied by a plateau, which slopes inward from its rim. The most striking feature of the landscape is the Great Escarpment, which borders the plateau in an almost unbroken line running southward from the northeastern corner of the country, rounding the southern coast, and continuing northward on the western side of the country. The upper edge of the escarpment is over 5,000 feet above sea level.

South Africa's highest point is in the east, where the Drakensberg, a mountainous region, reaches an elevation of over 11,400 feet above sea level.

Between the oceans and the foot of the Great Escarpment is a coastal zone about 100 miles wide. This region consists of greatly eroded, steplike landforms cut by streams and valleys, especially in the wetter, eastern side of the country. In the south these steps give way to long, low mountains known as the Cape Ranges, some of which reach the sea in peninsulas.

Cape Agulhas, the southernmost point of Africa, separates the Atlantic Ocean on its west from the Indian Ocean on its east. The most famous point on the Atlantic coast is the Cape of Good Hope.

Most of the plateau is drained by the Orange River and its principal tributary, the Vaal. Both rivers flow westward from the Great Escarpment. The Augrabies Falls are at the head of a deep canyon leading to the Atlantic Ocean at the point where the Orange River leaves the surface of the plateau. The northern half of the Transvaal is drained by the Limpopo River, which forms the border with Rhodesia.

Climate. Rainfall in South Africa is much heavier on the east coast and on some parts of the Cape Ranges than on the plateau surface. Half of the country receives less than 20 inches of rain a year, and water-supply problems are common, particularly in the west.

The climate is moderate in most parts of the country. Northern and eastern Transvaal are tropically hot, but most of South Africa has cool winters with occasional frost.

THE PEOPLE. The South African population is legally divided into four distinct groups—"Bantu," or Negro; white; "Colored," those of mixed origins; and Asian. In mid-1967 Negro Africans made up 68 percent of the South African population; whites, 19 percent; Coloreds, 10 percent; and Asians, 3 percent.

Most of the Negro Africans are Bantu-speaking peoples. Among the main tribal groups are the Xhosa, Zulu, and Sotho. About two-thirds of the Negro Africans live either on farms owned by whites or on reserves established by the government.

A majority of the whites are Afrikaners, Afrikaans-speaking people descended from Dutch, German, and French Huguenot settlers. Most of the remainder of the whites are of British descent. The Coloreds are descended largely from the indigenous Hottentots, Malays, and white settlers. The Asians are largely of Indian origin.

The major cities of South Africa include Johannesburg, in the Transvaal, a major commercial center and industrial city; Cape Town, in Cape Province, South Africa's legislative capital and major port; Durban, in Natal, the Indian Ocean outlet for the Transvaal and the center of the English-speaking and Indian business communities; Pretoria, in the Transvaal, South Africa's administrative capital and major industrial center; and Port Elizabeth, in Cape Province, an industrial city and port.

ECONOMY. South Africa has the most highly developed industrial economy of any African country. Economic development has been made possible largely by South Africa's rich mineral resources, especially diamonds and gold.

Negro African labor plays an essential part in South Africa's growing economy. Although Negro Africans form the bulk of unskilled labor in industry, agriculture, and mining, they are generally barred from the skilled labor force. The whites are the most economically prosperous group in South Africa. Although Coloreds and Asians are economically better off than the Negro Africans, they are not as prosperous as the whites.

Agriculture. Between 1945 and 1964 over 40 percent of the population was engaged in agricultural occupations. Agriculture employs a considerable proportion of Afrikaners and most Negro Africans. Crop production, however, is restricted by limited rainfall and poor soil in most parts of the country.

The basic food crop of the Negro African population is corn. Fruits, especially citrus and grapes, are the most important commercial crops and are grown mainly in the region inland from Cape Town. Cattle and sheep are raised, and wool and hides are important exports.

Mining and Manufacturing. Manufacturing developed rapidly after World War II, and in 1965 it accounted for 22 percent of the national product. Mining provides the capital and supports the markets required for economic growth. Iron, steel, cement, machinery, and a great variety of consumer goods are produced.

South Africa has rich mineral resources, and it is one of the world's largest producers of diamonds and gold. In 1965 over 5 million metric carats of diamonds were produced, mainly from mines in Kimberly and Pretoria. South Africa produced over half the world's supply of gold in 1965. Gold comes from mines in the Witwatersrand, in the northern part of the country, and from Odendaalsrus, in central South Africa. Waste materials at the gold mines are reprocessed to yield uranium.

South Africa also has vast resources of coal and iron ore. The shortage of petroleum products is partially relieved by a coal distillation process yielding liquid fuels.

Trade. In 1966 South Africa's imports cost $2,300 million and its exports earned $1,700 million. The leading imports are iron and steel, machinery, petroleum and petroleum products, textiles, plastics, coffee, and tea. The leading exports are diamonds, gold, fruits, and wool.

Most of South Africa's trade is with Britain, the United States, West Germany, and Japan. In 1967 South Africa signed a trade agreement with Malawi, its first with an African country. But its share in the developing African market is jeopardized by its racial policies, which are unacceptable to most African nations and to many other nations.

GOVERNMENT. South Africa is ruled by a white minority. The right to vote is limited to whites over 18 years of age. In Cape Province Coloreds and Asians over 21 years of age with certain educational and income or property qualifications have limited voting rights. In the Transvaal and Orange Free State, Coloreds and Asians cannot vote. Members of parliament must be white.

South Africa has a parliamentary system of government. Nominal executive power is held by a president, who serves as head of state. The president is elected to a seven-year term by an electoral college. Actual executive power is held by a prime minister and cabinet responsible to the legislature.

Legislative power is held by a parliament with two houses—the Senate and the House of Assembly. There are 54 members in the Senate, 43 of whom are elected by an electoral college made up of members of parliament and members of councils in the provinces and in South West Africa. One senator is appointed by the president to watch over the interests of the Coloreds of Cape Province. Ten are appointed by the president to represent the interests of nonwhites. All senators serve five-year terms.

There are 170 members in the House of Assembly, who serve five-year terms. Of these, 160 are elected to represent whites, six to represent South West Africa, and four to represent the Coloreds of Cape Province.

South Africa is a member of the United Nations.

COUNTRIES OF THE WORLD

HISTORY. Bantu-speaking peoples from northern Africa came to South Africa in the 1400s or 1500s, destroying or intermarrying with the indigenous Hottentots.

In the 1480s a Portuguese explorer, Bartholomeu Dias, rounded the Cape of Good Hope. But permanent European settlements were not made in South Africa until 1652, when the Dutch East India Company founded Cape Town as a supply base for voyages to the East Indies. The base developed into the Cape Colony, composed of Dutch settlers who supplied food for passing ships. Because cash crops would not grow well in the poor soil, the farmers, called Boers, turned to hunting and cattle raising.

Pushing eastward, the Boers repeatedly clashed with the Bantu-speaking peoples over grazing land, water, and cattle thefts. By the end of the 1700s, Boer pressure on the Bantu-speaking peoples' already crowded land gave rise to a powerful military organization led by Chaka, chief of a Bantu-speaking clan called Zulu. In the early 1800s Zulu forces made widespread destructive attacks on the Europeans and on other African peoples in southern Africa.

British-Boer Conflict. The British seized control of the colony in 1795. They stimulated the economy and extended the government to the frontier. Britain abolished slavery in 1834, and in 1836 it returned to the Bantu-speaking peoples territory captured from them by the Boers.

The Boers, irritated by the liberal racial policies and the new legal institutions of the British, undertook a mass migration to the east known as the Great Trek. During the migration, the Boers destroyed the Zulu forces.

To deny the Boers access to the sea, the British annexed the seaport city of Natal in 1844. The Boers then journeyed to the north and founded the republics of the Transvaal and the Orange Free State, which Britain recognized as independent states in the 1850s.

The discovery of diamonds in 1867 and gold in 1886 in the two republics attracted many English-speaking immigrants. British and Afrikaner businessmen cooperated in Cape Colony, but the discovery of gold only strained relations between Britain and the Transvaal. The Transvaal refused to enter into any political or economic union with Britain's colonies.

In 1895 the Cape Colony's prime minister, Cecil Rhodes, supported the Jameson Raid, an attempt to overthrow the Transvaal's president, Paul Kruger, and install an English-speaking government. The raid turned the political conflict into an ethnic conflict between Afrikaners and Englishmen. In 1899 the dispute erupted into the Boer, or South African, War, which the British won.

By 1902 Britain had conquered the Afrikaner republics, but granted them self-government in 1906. On May 31, 1910 the British colonies of Cape Colony and Natal were united with the former republics to form an independent Union of South Africa. At that time reserves of land were marked off for occupation by the Bantu-speaking peoples.

The Union. During World War I South Africa fought with Britain against Germany. Led by two Afrikaners, Jan Christiaan Smuts and Louis Botha, South African forces captured the German colony of South West Africa. In 1919 Smuts became South Africa's first prime minister.

After World War I a steady price for gold and cheap labor enabled the country to industrialize. Taxes, drought, and overcrowding on government-created reserves had driven many young Negro Africans off the land in search of jobs. Racial segregation was extended into industry, and labor agitation became a punishable crime.

In the 1920s the National Party, formed by conservative Afrikaners, came to power. The party extended racial segregation beyond the industrial color bar. Apartheid legislation came to include residential segregation, prohibitions against individual ownership of land by Negro Africans, restriction of movement, segregated churches, separate and unequal educational facilities, and denial of the vote to Negro Africans.

In 1952 the African National Congress, an African association formed in 1912 to protest racial discrimination, organized boycotts and demonstrations to protest the racial laws. The government retaliated by jailing some 10,000 participants and by enacting a law declaring government critics "subversive."

In 1960 South African police fired into a crowd of nonwhites demonstrating against racial policies in Sharpeville, some 30 miles south of Johannesburg. World opinion rallied against South Africa, but the government turned a deaf ear. In 1961 Albert Luthuli, a Zulu chief, received the Nobel Peace Prize for advocating peaceful methods for resolving South Africa's racial problems.

The Republic. On May 31, 1961 South Africa withdrew from the British Commonwealth and became a republic. In 1962 South Africa withdrew its delegation to the United Nations when the General Assembly voted economic sanctions against South Africa because of its racial policies. But heavy British and U.S. investments in South Africa blocked the effective application of sanctions.

In 1963 South Africa created the Transkei, an all-African Bantustan, or homeland, with a government separate from, but not independent of, the republic. Chief Kaizer Mantanzima became chief minister of the Transkei.

On Sept. 6, 1966 a white South African assassinated Prime Minister Hendrik Verwoerd. He was succeeded by Balthasar Vorster, as firm a supporter of apartheid as his predecessor had been.

In October 1966 the UN General Assembly voted to end South Africa's mandate to govern South West Africa because it had failed to fulfill its obligations. Vorster declared the resolution illegal and announced South Africa's intention to continue administering South West Africa.

Renewed protests against South Africa's administration of South West Africa came in 1968, when a number of South West African nationalists were tried and given long prison terms by South African courts.

—Hibberd V. B. Kline, Jr.;
Gary A. Weissman

SOUTH YEMEN

Official name: People's Republic of South Yemen
Area: (1967 est.) 112,000 square miles
Population: (1967 est.) 1,000,000
Capital: Medina as-Shaab
Language: Arabic
Religion: Islam
Currency unit: Dinar

The People's Republic of South Yemen is an Arab state in the southwestern Arabian Peninsula. It was created in 1967 from the former British colony of Aden and the protectorates of South Arabia, a group of 20 sheikhdoms and sultanates, most of which had been united in the British-protected Federation of South Arabia between 1959 and 1967.

South Yemen is bordered on the north and west by Yemen and the Rub al Khali desert of Saudi Arabia, on the east by the sultanate of Muscat and Oman, and on the south by the Gulf of Aden and the Indian Ocean. Socotra, an island in the Indian Ocean off the northeast coast of the Somali Republic, is part of South Yemen, as are Kamaran, an island off the coast of Yemen in the southern Red Sea, and Perim, an island in the Bab al Mandab strait.

The status of the Kuria Muria Islands, off the southern coast of Muscat and Oman, is disputed. Britain wants the islands to go to Muscat and Oman, and South Yemen claims them for itself.

THE LAND AND PEOPLE. Rugged mountains rise in western South Yemen, but most of the region is a high rolling desert plateau on which almost no rain falls.

The country's population, composed almost entirely of Muslim Arabs, is concentrated along the coast, especially in Aden, the largest city.

ECONOMY. Herding and farming are the principal occupations of South Yemen's people. Cotton, grains, and fruits are raised, and sheep and goats are grazed on the fringes of the desert. There is some fishing along the coast. Soap and cigarette manufacturing, oilseed production, and salt refining are important.

The port city of Aden is the principal commercial center for the lower Arabian Peninsula. It has a large oil refinery and oil storage facilities, and is a major Arabian port for oil exporting

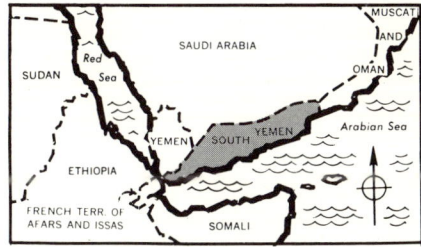

VAST GRAIN FIELDS of the Soviet Ukraine are part of the European-West Siberian Plain.

and ship refueling. Income from this transit trade is vital to the economy of South Yemen. Trade in South Yemen's own goods is small.

GOVERNMENT. A provisional government, composed of South Yemen's National Liberation Front, controls the affairs of the republic, which is divided for administrative purposes into six governorates.

HISTORY. For centuries, the former sheikhdoms that now make up South Yemen were controlled by Egyptians, Turks, and Yemenis before being ruled by independent sultans. The port of Aden has been an important and prosperous trading center since ancient times.

Ottoman Turks captured the port in 1538, when Aden's importance was already in decline, due to the establishment of trade routes around the Cape of Good Hope. In 1839 the British East India Company seized the port for use as a coaling station for ships traveling between Bombay and Suez. With the opening of the Suez Canal in 1869, Aden once again became a major port.

During the 1800s the British, eager to keep peace in the area, signed agreements promising to protect the neighboring sheikhdoms.

In 1959 six of the protected sheikhdoms established a federation, which by 1965 included 16 sheikhdoms and Aden. Yemen's independence was in part achieved by the efforts of Arab nationalist groups that were active in the area in the 1960s. In 1964 Britain promised independence to the federation by 1968, but as the independence date approached violence in the region increased and Britain was reluctant to withdraw.

Yemen intensified warfare along the border, hoping to gain control of the territory, and two nationalist groups—the National Liberation Front (NFL) and the Front for the Liberation of Occupied South Yemen—engaged in anti-British terrorism and competed for control of the protectorate. The NFL won out over its rival, and in November 1967 Britain agreed to grant independence to South Yemen and withdraw its troops.

NFL chief Qahtan al-Shaabi became president of South Yemen and established a provisional government composed of other NFL leaders. The military held power in the new government, which began to seek foreign technical and economic aid to make possible the development of the new nation.

—Charles Issawi; Alexander Melamid

SOVIET UNION

Official name: Union of Soviet Socialist Republics
Area: 8,649,534 square miles
Population: (1966 est.) 233,105,000
Capital: Moscow (Pop., 1965 est., urban area, 6,423,000)
Language: Russian
Religion: Orthodox Christianity, Islam
Currency unit: Ruble
National holiday: Anniversary of the revolution, November 7

The Union of Soviet Socialist Republics, the world's largest sovereign state, is bounded on the north by the Arctic Ocean; on the east by the Pacific Ocean; on the south by North Korea, the Mongolian People's Republic, China, Afghanistan, Iran, the Caspian Sea, Turkey, and the Black Sea; and on the west by Romania, Hungary, Czechoslovakia, Poland, the Baltic Sea, Finland, and Norway.

The country is sometimes referred to by its initials, U.S.S.R., but more often by a short form, the Soviet Union. Before the seizure of power by communists in 1917, the country was called Russia. The term Russia now properly applies only to one part of the Soviet Union, the Russian Soviet Federated Socialist Republic (R.S.F.S.R.).

THE LAND

The Soviet Union covers one-sixth of the land surface of the earth and extends over two continents, occupying much of eastern Europe and all of northern Asia. A natural boundary between the European and Asian parts of the country is formed by the Ural Mountains, the Ural River, and the Caspian Sea.

PHYSICAL REGIONS. The Soviet Union may be divided into five major land regions: the European-West Siberian Plain, the Central Siberian Plateau, Eastern Siberia, the Soviet Far East, and Soviet Central Asia.

European–West Siberian Plain. The dominant physical feature of the Soviet Union is the great plain that extends from the European border into Siberia, broken only by the Ural Mountains. The great majority of the Soviet People live within the confines of this plain.

The European part of the plain is far from uniform, and consists of rolling plains, low hills, wide river valleys, and coastal lowlands. The Siberian part is a nearly level plain,

COUNTRIES OF THE WORLD

stretching unbroken for some 1,200 miles east from the Urals to the Yenisey River and nearly the same distance northward to the shores of the Arctic Ocean.

Central Siberian Plateau. East of the Yenisey lies the Central Siberian Plateau, which extends to the Lena River. Varying in elevation from 600 to 3,000 feet, the plateau is covered almost entirely by forest. It is sparsely settled, and its few inhabitants are mostly miners, hunters, and trappers.

Eastern Siberia. Beyond the Lena, stretching eastward to the Pacific Ocean and the Bering Strait, is Eastern Siberia. Vast mountain chains, comparable in length to the Appalachians, divide this area into subregions, most of which are drained by rivers that flow into the Arctic Ocean. The mountains and valleys of Eastern Siberia are the most remote, least inhabited, and the least known part of the Soviet Union.

Soviet Far East. The Soviet Far East, separated from the Central Siberian Plateau and Eastern Siberia by the Stanovoy and Yablonovvy Mountains, is the Soviet Union's link with China, Japan, and the Pacific Ocean. The Amur River, which drains into the Pacific Ocean north of Japan, is the region's major waterway. Its valley and that of its tributary, the Ussuri, are the most heavily settled areas of the region.

Soviet Central Asia. East of the Caspian Sea and south of Siberia is Soviet Central Asia. In the north it consists of a plateau; in the center and south, lowlands. The few rivers that cross it either drain into salty, brackish lakes such as Lake Aral and Lake Balkhash, or disappear into desert sands.

MOUNTAIN SYSTEMS. The mountains of the Soviet Union vary greatly in size, elevation, and characteristic features. The Ural Mountains are for the most part a low, worn-down range. They are among the most highly mineralized parts of the earth, and one of the principal centers of Soviet mining and manufacturing.

Most of the uplands of the European parts of the Soviet Union are not really mountains. The sole exception is a small segment of the Carpathians, near the western border, which became part of the Soviet Union after World War II.

Caucasus. In the southwest the Caucasus Mountains, a major physical feature of the Soviet Union, run some 700 miles from the Black Sea to the Caspian Sea. They form the traditional boundary between European Russia and the countries of the Near East. Early in the 1800s, the Russian Empire extended its rule south of the Caucasus and conquered what is now known as the Trans-Caucasus, or Transcaucasia.

The northern part of Transcaucasia is composed of two lowlands: that of the Rion River in the west, which drains into the Black Sea; and that of the Kura and Araks rivers in the east, which drains into the Caspian. The southernmost part of Transcaucasia consists of dry, desert mountains, and is generally known as the Little Caucasus.

Eastern Ranges. From the eastern shores of the Caspian Sea to eastern Siberia the borders of the Soviet Union are dominated by a series of mountain systems. Farthest west are the Kopet Dagh Mountains and the foothills of the Hindu Kush chain, which separate the Soviet Union from Iran and Afghanistan. Beyond the valley of the Amu River, which flows into Lake Aral, lie the Pamir Plateau and the Alai Mountains.

The mountains north of the Pamir and Alai form the boundary between the Soviet Union and China. The principal components of this complex range are the Tien Shan, Ala Tau, Tarbagatay, Altai, and Sayan mountains. The Sayan Mountains lie in southern Siberia and overlook the deepest lake in the world, Lake Baykal.

VEGETATION ZONES. The combined result of the influences of surface features, climate, and soils on the land of the Soviet Union is several different vegetation zones, which extend in a general east-west direction across Soviet territory.

Tundra. In the far north, along the shores of the Arctic Ocean, on the Arctic islands, and inland for a distance varying from 100 to 400 miles is the tundra zone. This is an arctic desert, where low year-round temperatures inhibit the growth and variety of vegetation.

During the short growing season, which seldom exceeds three months, the tundra is covered with moss, lichens, scattered clumps of wild flowers, and, along the southern, warmer edge of the zone, small, bushy plants and dwarf trees. During the greater part of the year, however, the tundra is an empty, storm-swept place, covered with snow and ice.

Taiga. South of the tundra and stretching across the entire width of the Soviet Union is the northern forest zone, or taiga. The taiga is composed mostly of coniferous evergreen trees—pine, fir, and larch—interspersed with clumps of birches.

Mixed Forest. South of the taiga, in the European part of the Soviet Union, is a triangle-shaped mixed-forest zone with its points located near the cities of Leningrad in the northwest, Kiev in the southwest, and Perm, in the Urals. Oak, beech, birch, pine, and fir trees predominate in this region, but there are sizable natural clearings along the rivers.

Much of the original mixed forest has long since been cut, and substantial areas are under the plough. Moscow, Leningrad, and Kiev, the three largest Soviet cities, are located within this zone, as are some of the leading Soviet industrial areas and the bulk of the population.

Steppe. South of the mixed forest is the grassland zone, or steppe. This area is covered with black earth, one of the most fertile soils known to man. Virtually all of the steppe in the European part of the Soviet Union and in western Siberia is now under cultivation.

Along the southern edge of the steppe rainfall gradually becomes more scarce and the soils have less organic content. This transition zone south of the steppe is known as the dry steppe or "semidesert." In this zone irrigation is essential for the successful growing of crops; otherwise only grazing can be carried on.

Desert. The southernmost of the great vegetation zones is the desert region of Soviet Central Asia. Annual rainfall there is usually only 3 to 8 inches, but a long growing season, over six months, the longest in the Soviet Union, can guarantee rich harvests of certain crops, such as cotton, fruit, and vegetables, if water for irrigation is available.

Farms and settlements cling closely to rivers, irrigation canals, or artesian wells. The adjacent mountains provide good grazing during the spring, summer, and early fall.

Subtropical. The one exception to the great vegetation zones that cross the Soviet Union is a small area, lying along the westernmost flanks of the Great Caucasus overlooking the Black Sea, which the Soviets call the "subtropical zone." There a narrow coastal strip and the adjacent low hillsides sheltered by the Caucasus range are favored by mild winters and usually heavy rainfall.

CLIMATE. The greater part of Soviet territory is too distant from the sea, or faces too cold a sea, to enjoy the moderating effect that large bodies of water have on climate. With the exception of a few coastal areas on the Black Sea and on the Caspian, the greatest part of the Soviet Union has a continental climate, characterized by extremes of temperature and rainfall.

Winter temperatures throughout most of the Soviet Union are well below freezing, but it is coldest in the northeast. Siberia, the coldest part of the country, has average January temperatures of −20°F, and northeastern Siberia has January averages that run as low as −50° to −60°F.

Summers, on the other hand, are likely to be warm, except in the far north. Some of the highest summer temperatures on earth have been recorded in Soviet Central Asia.

Rainfall ranges from an annual average of 70 to 80 inches in the western Caucasus to less than 8 inches in Soviet Central Asia.

One important consequence of climatic extremes is the soils characteristic of the Soviet Union. Over 40 percent of the area of the Soviet Union is covered by permafrost, or permanently frozen soil which varies in depth from one foot to several hundred feet and thaws only a few inches during the summer months. Agriculture, as well as road and railroad building, can be carried out only with extreme difficulty and at great expense on this permanently frozen ground.

THE PEOPLE

ETHNIC GROUPS. The Soviet Union is a multinational state, and the 1959 census listed 108 separate groups. Nearly three-fourths of the population of the Soviet Union is part of the East Slavic language group, however.

Slavs. The Slavic group has three major subdivisions—Russian, Ukrainian, and Belorussian (White Russian). The Russians, who number about 114 million according to the 1959 census, are the largest Slavic subgroup, as well as the country's largest national group. They are represented in every region of the Soviet Union, and Russian is the official language of the Soviet Union.

The Ukrainians (37.3 million) are the second largest subgroup and second in size among all national groups. They inhabit the southern European part of the Soviet Union, and have a separate historical and cultural heritage. The third group, the Belorussians (7 million), live north of the Ukrainians.

Western Borders. Along the shores of the Baltic are the Estonians, Latvians, and Lithuanians, often referred to as the Baltic peoples. The Lithuanians (2.3 million) and the Latvians (1.4 million) speak languages of the Indo-European group. The Estonians (969,

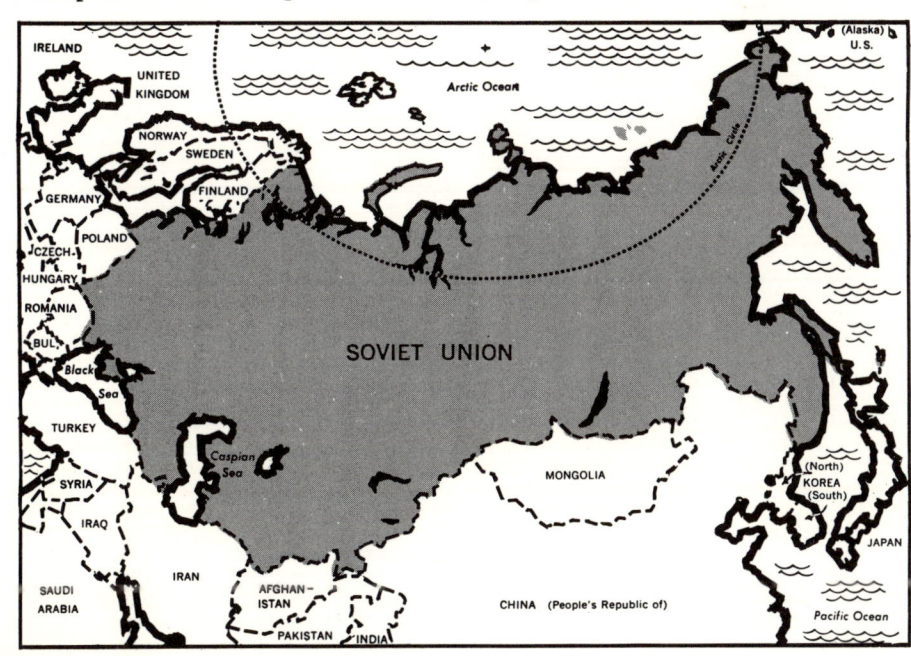

000), who live farthest north of the three Baltic peoples, speak a language of the Finno-Ugric group, which is closely related to Finnish.

Along the southwestern boundary of the Soviet Union live the Moldavians (2.2 million), who are closely related to the Romanians and speak Romanian. In the Middle Volga Valley there are the Chuvash (1.5 million), who speak a Turkic language, and the Mordovians (1.3 million), who speak a Finno-Ugric language; as well as the Tatars (5 million), who speak Asian languages, and Bashkirs (989,000), who speak a Turkic language.

Caucasus and Central Asia. The peoples of the Caucasus are the most diverse within the Soviet Union. The three major groups in this area are the Georgians (2.7 million), Armenians (2.8 million), and Azerbaijanis (2.9 million). There are also about 25 other minority groups, ranging in size from 268,000 to less than 4,000 people.

The peoples of Soviet Central Asia are, for the most part, Turkic and fall into four major groups. The Uzbeks (6 million) live in the central part of the region; the Kazakhs (3.6 million) are concentrated in the north; and the Turkmenians (1 million) live in the mountains and valleys of the east. The Tajiks (1.4 million), who speak a language related to Persian, live near the border with Afghanistan.

Eastern Region. Siberia has a small but diverse native population. Except for the Yakuts, a Turkic-speaking people of the Lena valley in eastern Siberia, who number about 230,000, none of the surviving native groups of Siberia has a population of over 25,000, and some number less than 1,000.

Koreans are found in the Soviet Far East, and Buryats, related to the Mongols of neighboring Mongolia, live in southern Siberia.

Jews. In the Soviet Union, Jews are listed as a separate national group, and the census of 1959 listed 2.3 million Soviet citizens as Jews, a decrease of nearly one-half since the previous census in 1939. The decrease was largely a result of the persecution of Jews in German-occupied parts of the Soviet Union in World War II.

DISTRIBUTION. Owing to climate and geography, the distribution of population is very uneven in the Soviet Union. The majority of the people live within the European part of the country, but there has been a marked increase in the population east of the Urals and the Caspian Sea. Between 1939 and 1959, for example, Western Siberia increased its population by 34 percent and Soviet Central Asia by 30 percent.

There has also been a substantial migration from the countryside to the cities. Still, about 50 percent of the people live in nonurban areas, a much larger proportion than is found in most of Western Europe and North America.

According to 1966 estimates, the Soviet Union had 187 cities with populations of over 100,000 and 28 cities of over 500,000. Eight cities—Moscow, Leningrad, Kiev, Tashkent, Gorky, Baku, Novosibirsk, and Kharkov—had more than one million inhabitants.

ECONOMY

In the 50 years following the Russian Revolution, the Soviet Union made significant economic progress, changing from an agricultural to an industrial nation with a gross output second only to that of the United States. Soviet gains, however, were made by concentrating on heavy industry at the expense of consumer goods, services, and agriculture.

In the first half of the 1960s, economic growth began to lag. In 1965 the government initiated a reform program designed to make the economy less rigid and more efficient. Industrial management was decentralized, and emphasis was shifted from output to profits. Economic problems remained, however. Agricultural production is often insufficient for domestic needs, there is an acute housing shortage, and consumer goods remain in short supply.

NATURAL RESOURCES. The Soviet Union is extremely rich in natural resources. Most metals and minerals are produced in such quantities that imports from abroad are of minor importance.

There are large deposits of iron ore, copper, lead, zinc, nickel, chrome, manganese, bauxite, and mercury. The Soviet Union produces substantial quantities of gold, and following the discovery of a large deposit of diamonds in Siberia the country became one of the world's leading diamond producers.

Fuels. The Soviet Union also has abundant fuel resources. Coal is the major fuel used in Soviet transportation, homes, and factories, and in 1967 coal production amounted to 595 million metric tons. The Donets basin, in the southern European part of the Soviet Union, is first in coal production and has the largest reserves.

The Kuznetsk basin of southern Siberia is second in production, eastern Siberia is third, and the Karaganda area of Soviet Central Asia is fourth. Other important coal deposits are in the Urals and in the Moscow area.

The oil fields of the eastern Caucasus, near the city of Baku on the Caspian, have been working for more than 75 years and until the mid-1950s were the leading producers in the Soviet Union. A major shift in oil production occurred during World War II, and after 1954 the oil fields between the Ural Mountains and the middle Volga River became first in output. It is now estimated that the Volga-Ural fields represent four-fifths of known Soviet oil reserves.

Other major oil fields are found along the northern edge of the Caucasus, along the Soviet-Polish boundary, in Soviet Central Asia, and in the Soviet Far East. Pipelines not only connect the Volga-Ural fields with the major industrial areas in the European and Siberian parts of the Soviet Union, but with Poland, East Germany, Czechoslovakia, and Hungary. In 1967 crude oil production reached 288 million metric tons.

Natural gas deposits for the most part overlie existing oil fields. The most important gas field, however, is located in the southern part of Soviet Central Asia. It is now being tapped to pipe natural gas to the great industrial centers.

Hydroelectric power is a relatively unimportant energy source in the Soviet Union, for most of the available sites for hydroelectric development are far removed from major cities and industrial areas. The most spectacular hydroelectric project is on the Volga River, where five dams have transformed the Volga into a series of enormous reservoirs. In the mid-1960s larger projects were under construction in Siberia on the Yenisey River and its tributary, the Angara.

AGRICULTURE. Use of arable land in the Soviet Union is severely limited by cold in the north and drought in the south. As a result, fully tillable farmland is confined to an area known as the Fertile Triangle, with its corners in Leningrad on the Baltic Sea, Odessa on the Black Sea, and the lowland of Western Siberia.

Soviet cropland equals the combined sown areas of the United States and Canada. The northerly location of the country (the bulk of the Fertile Triangle lies north of the U.S.-Canadian boundary), however, results in a shorter growing season, and the distances separating Soviet cropland from warm seas are reflected in limited and undependable rainfall.

These severe handicaps are responsible for the low yields that have characterized Soviet agriculture. They have not been compensated for by the extension of cropland into areas of marginal rainfall, nor by attempts to develop varieties of plants that could mature quickly in areas farther north, where growing seasons are very short.

Collectivization. To these environmental difficulties the Soviet system added man-made ones. The fact that virtually all cultivable land is under either collective or state farms has deprived the Soviet farmer of the incentive present when men work on land they own. The reluctance of the Soviet government to offer farm workers sufficient rewards for their labor, and the policy of directing investments into industry while ignoring the needs of agriculture, have added further difficulties.

In the 1960s, about 40 percent of the active population of the Soviet Union was engaged in agriculture, as opposed to less than 10 percent in the United States. But yields, productivity, and farm income are much lower in the Soviet Union, and the output of foods has risen only very slowly over the past 40 years.

An interesting characteristic of Soviet farming is the significance of the "private sector" in the production of certain essential foods. Although farmland is owned by collective and state farms, farm workers are entitled to small plots of land, usually about half an acre in size but never more than one acre. The produce of these plots is either consumed by the worker's family or, more frequently, sold directly to consumers, without state control.

More than half the meat, nearly half the milk, and four-fifths of the eggs produced in the Soviet Union come from these tiny plots. Despite strong government efforts to shift production

HEAVY INDUSTRY, symbolized by these Volgograd smokestacks, is vital to the Soviet economy.

to the collective and state farms, the "private sector" continues to play a vital role in Soviet food production.

Products. Grains, the leading crop of Soviet farms, include wheat, rye, and barley. The Soviet Union grows virtually all the cotton it needs, exports considerable amounts of flax, and produces part of the hemp its industry consumes. Sugar beets and oilseeds—sunflower, rapeseed, and castor beans—are among the leading industrial crops.

Soviet livestock suffered severe losses during the drive for collectivization (1929–1933), when nearly half the cattle and two-thirds of the hogs in the country were destroyed by farmers unwilling to turn over their animals to collective ownership.

The livestock levels of 1929 were not regained until 1956, and further growth, with the exception of hogs, has been very slow. The output of meat, milk, eggs, and other dairy products remains well below that of the United States and Western Europe.

INDUSTRY. Iron and steel production is a general indicator of industrial strength, and since 1945 the Soviet Union has ranked next to the United States as the world's largest producer of pig iron and steel. In 1967 the Soviet Union produced more than 102 million metric tons of crude steel and almost 75 million metric tons of pig iron.

Two regions, the Ukraine and the Urals, account for more than four fifths of the iron and more than three-fourths of the steel produced. The Ukraine has iron ore, good coking coal, limestone, and ferroalloys available within a small area, and until the 1950s it led in ferrous metallurgy.

The vast iron deposits of the Urals have caused the region to surpass the Ukraine although coking coal must be imported from other parts of the Soviet Union. During the mid-1960s a third major center of iron and steel production was being built in Siberia, where coal and iron are both locally available.

Major Centers. Before the Revolution of 1917, Russian industry was concentrated in the European part of the country. St. Petersburg (renamed Leningrad in 1924) and Moscow were among the leading centers of light industry. Heavy industry was concentrated in the Ukraine.

The temporary loss of much of Russia's industrial capacity during World War I and the civil war that followed led to efforts to decentralize industry and develop new centers further removed from the vulnerable western borders of the Soviet Union. One of the tasks of planning the Soviet economy after 1927 was the establishment of new industrial areas far away from the former manufacturing centers.

Four major regions dominate Soviet industry. The Central Industrial Region, in the Moscow area, contains the country's most valuable industries. This region produces electrical equipment, ball bearings, engines, and automobiles, as well as a number of consumer goods including textiles, shoes, clothing, processed foods, and household articles.

The Ukraine is noted for iron and steel, heavy machinery, and chemicals. It is a less concentrated area than the Central Industrial Region, and consists of four distinct subregions: the Dnepr valley, the Donets basin, the shores of the Sea of Azov, and the area surrounding the city of Kharkov.

The Ural industrial region owes its present large-scale development to Soviet planning, although small-scale industry has been in operation there for over 100 years. In addition to iron and steel, the Urals are important for the production of petroleum and its byproducts, heavy machinery, and chemicals.

The fourth major industrial center, also largely a creation of the Soviet government, is spread out across the edges of the Siberian lowland and adjacent river valleys near the Soviet-Chinese border. Large resources of coal and a variety of metals have given rise to substantial metallurgical, chemical, and machine industries in the area.

Smaller Centers. In accordance with its policy of industrial decentralization, the Soviet government has developed other, smaller industrial centers to lessen the dependence of its farflung territories on the major industrial areas and thereby reduce the burden on its transportation system. Some of the more important smaller industrial centers are located in Transcaucasia, Soviet Central Asia, and the Soviet Far East.

In each of these centers an attempt was made to provide for the needs of the surrounding area. Thus steel pipes are made in Transcaucasia, cotton machinery in Central Asia, and ships in the Far East. Each center also manufactures a variety of consumer goods.

TRADE. In 1966 the Soviet Union's exports earned $8,841 million and its imports cost $7,913 million. Major exports include petroleum, coal, timber, iron ore, industrial equipment, and iron and steel. Principal imports are ships, wheat, sugar, clothing, metal ores, and industrial machinery.

The Soviet Union carries on most of its trade with East Germany, Czechoslovakia, Poland, Bulgaria, Hungary, Romania, Cuba, and Britain.

GOVERNMENT

The Communist Party of the Soviet Union (CPSU) dominates political life. The presidium, formerly the politburo, or political bureau, of the party's central committee determines national policy, and the party's first secretary is the most powerful figure in the government.

Formally, the highest authority in the Soviet Union is the national legislature, the Supreme Soviet. It has two houses, the Soviet of the Union, elected on the basis of population, and the Soviet of Nationalities, elected on the basis of territorial units. The two houses have equal powers and the members of both are directly elected to four-year terms.

The Supreme Soviet elects a presidium to act as the supreme state authority between its relatively short sessions. The chairman of the presidium serves as head of state. The Supreme Soviet also appoints a council of ministers, or cabinet, which is the highest executive and administrative organ of the government.

The Soviet Union is a member of the United Nations and the Warsaw Pact, a military alliance of East European communist countries.

HISTORY

Archeological evidence indicates that various societies existed in European Russia before there were written records. The earliest Slavic inhabitants probably arrived there from an unknown point of origin several hundred years before the birth of Christ.

Slowly their language, as well as some of their political organization and social customs, became dominant. Their settlements tended to concentrate in the south, near the Black Sea, and along the river systems that stretch inland from the Baltic and Black seas.

The river routes made it possible for groups of Scandinavian, or "Varangian," warriors and traders to move through the same regions. From this composite of Slavs, Scandinavians, and remnants of earlier populations the oldest Russian state emerged during the 800s AD.

KIEVAN RUSSIA. The oldest Slavic state, known as Kiev Rus', was a confederation of Slavic-dominated principalities. Its two most important cities, Kiev and Novgorod, were located along the major river trade routes, and the Kievan principalities contained a mixture of merchants, peasants, and warrior-politicians.

The sources of Kievan power and wealth, and of Kiev's social and political structure, were agrarian as well as commercial. This duality made for complex patterns of political administration, which included a hereditary prince and his warrior-administrator retinue, or *druzhina*; an elected city council, or *veche*, which often acted as a check on the prince and reflected the interests of wealthy merchants; and village assemblies in the agrarian areas.

In the 900s Orthodox Christianity was introduced into Kievan Russia from the Byzantine Empire. Like other cultural importations from Byzantium and the Balkan Peninsula, eastern Christianity made a deep and lasting impression on Russia.

The most severe problems of Kievan society were political and military. Much of the princely administrative system was gradually rendered ineffective by strife among claimants to the princely thrones within the confederation. The final blow came from without, however. Mongols swept into Europe from the east in the 1200s, and in 1240 Kiev fell to them.

RISE OF MOSCOW. The era which succeeded that of Kiev Rus' is often called the Appanage Period because of the subdivision of the country into a large number of tiny principalities, or appanages. In the 1300s and 1400s, however, certain appanage princes were able to reverse the process of frequent subdivision of their principalities and increase their holdings by purchase, marriage, or conquest.

Among the most aggressive and skillful of the appanage princes were those who ruled Moscow, or Muscovy. The first of these was Ivan I (r.1325–1340). By the time of Ivan's death Moscow had secured important advantages over its neighbors. Ivan I granted administrative posts to the boyars, or great nobles, loyal to him, and he encouraged the growth of agriculture, which was the basis of the region's economy.

Ivan III (r.1462–1505). Under Prince Ivan III, called "the Great," the ambitions of Moscow and of its ruling house began to be fulfilled. Moscow succeeded in establishing its sovereign authority over important independent principalities in central European Russia, as well as over "frontier" territories to the east and north.

The most important challenge to Muscovite expansion was the flourishing commercial principality of Novgorod. Nevertheless, the principality fell easily under Muscovite pressure. After Novgorod's defeat in 1478, the incorporation into Muscovy of other independent but minor principalities presented no difficulty.

By the early 1500s Muscovy had grown to many times its original size and this increase in area was more than matched by an increase in power and prestige. Muscovite expansion tended to resolve problems of Mongol domination. With larger territories under their command the princes of Moscow were better able to resist Mongol demands and began to strive to throw off Mongol control.

As Moscow grew strong, the Mongol political system became weakened by internal division and dissension. After the 1400s Mongol settlements to the south and east of the expanding boundaries of Moscow were more a source of irritation, as a source of armed raids, than a threat to Muscovite independence.

Muscovite expansion to the north and west brought the state into conflict with the Baltic countries of Europe, especially Poland, Lithuania, and Sweden. Moreover, by the early 1500s serious internal problems beset the Muscovite state.

To ensure continued support from their boyar warriors and administrators, the Muscovite princes often rewarded them with special privileges and large grants of land. As a result, the power of the boyars increased and some members of this Muscovite aristocracy began to challenge the authority of the sovereign prince himself.

Muscovite Russia. Ivan IV (r.1533–1584), wishing to continue the expansionist policies of his predecessors and determined to preserve and increase sovereign authority, met these problems aggressively.

Ivan IV, sometimes called "the Terrible," was one of the most brutal and bloody figures in Russian history. Taking for himself the titles of *tsar* (caesar) and autocrat, he proceeded to attempt to acquire dominions befitting a tsar, or emperor, and to wield the absolute political power of an autocrat.

During the first years of Ivan IV's reign, the young tsar undertook reforms generally regarded as enlightened and necessary. Muscovy was a patchwork of formerly independent principalities and separate local units of varying independence, and the Muscovite state was badly in need of administrative reorganization and legal reform.

Among Ivan's measures were a codification of laws (*Sudebnik* of 1550) and a reorganization of local administration. In 1549 Ivan ordered the convocation of the first national assembly, or *Zemski Sobor*.

During the 1550s Ivan also became deeply involved in wars of territorial expansion. At first Muscovite military power was concentrated against a fragment of the old Mongol empire, the Khanate of Kazan on the middle Volga River. This campaign, however, invited conflicts with other khanates at Astrakhan and in the Crimea.

A much more serious campaign began in 1557 at the opposite corner of the Muscovite state against the inhabitants of the eastern Baltic region. Although weak, they blocked Russian access to the Baltic Sea and northern Europe. This conflict gradually expanded until Ivan IV's armies were involved in an exhausting war with the large and powerful states of Poland and Sweden.

Centralization. At the same time the tsar's policies of expansion and domestic reform ran into mounting opposition, particularly from the boyars, who felt themselves threatened by administrative reforms and who bore the burden of the military campaigns. This political struggle came to a crisis in the early 1560s, when Ivan IV renounced the throne and retired to a monastery. Ivan returned only after the boyars and the church agreed to meet certain of his demands.

The victorious tsar then organized the central territories of Muscovy as a separate administrative unit subservient to his will. Using hand-picked men, called *oprichniks*, Ivan began to punish "evildoers" as he saw fit. It soon became clear that he intended to classify as an "evildoer" anyone who stood in his way or objected to his policies of expansion and creating a centralized state.

A virtual reign of terror was unleashed against the boyars, and Muscovy was plunged into near civil war. Crushing most opposition, Ivan IV became far more powerful than any previous Muscovite prince.

Theodore I (r.1584–1598), Ivan IV's successor, was too weak to master the legacy of power and antagonism bequeathed him by his father, and real authority began to fall into the hands of court favorites. When Theodore died, the ancient Muscovite dynasty died with him.

Time of Troubles. The church, boyars, petty nobility, and merchants then had to establish and support a new ruler and a new dynasty, or else find a way of administering Russian society without the autocracy. During the years immediately following the death of Theodore, both alternatives were tried, without success.

The failure of these efforts, each occurring amidst a background of increasing domestic strife, foreign wars and, finally, Polish invasion, is known as the Time of Troubles (1598-1613). Poland was eventually defeated, and peasant uprisings and other social disorders were suppressed. The Time of Troubles finally ended in 1613 with the accession to the throne of the new Romanov dynasty.

ROMANOVS. Physically exhausted and verging on economic ruin, Russian society only slowly regained the international independence and domestic order that had characterized it in the early days of Ivan IV. The first Romanovs were unable to claim the prestige and authority of the earlier rulers of Moscow.

Nevertheless, Tsar Michael Romanov (r.1613–1645) and his successor, Alexis (r.1645–1676), managed to reassert and extend centralized autocratic authority, and to restore some measure of prosperity. They also recovered possessions, such as Smolensk and Novgorod, which had been lost to Poland and Sweden.

Serfdom. Change was not accomplished without sacrifices, however, and by the 1600s the institution of serfdom had become central to the functioning of the state. Exploitation of the large areas of land granted by the tsars to their royal servitors since the early days of Muscovite expansion was feasible only through the use of serf labor.

A community of interest between the warrior landowners and the tsar known as the *pomiestie* system developed. The noble landowner became responsible not only for providing soldiers and military leadership during time of war, but also for administering the land under his control.

Gradually the landowner became the immediate representative of authority over the peasant who worked the land. To insure social stability and to placate an increasingly demanding nobility, the state made it legally more difficult for the peasant to escape bondage to land and lord.

Renewed Expansion. By the mid-1600s Russia had largely regained the territory it had lost during the Time of Troubles. It had also renewed the policy of relentless expansion, which brought it into conflict with the Ottoman Empire in the south and with Poland and Sweden in the west.

Some government leaders, including, perhaps, Tsar Alexis himself, recognized that to continue this process of expansion Russia had to be able to draw on all its resources and to make use of Western organization and technology. It was Peter the Great, however, who initiated an era of rapid modernization and reform.

Peter the Great (r.1689–1725). Peter's reign inaugurated the Imperial period of Russian history. One of Peter's major goals was to modernize Russia as quickly as possible. He made the church subordinate to the state, reorganized the central government and provincial administration, and introduced a new military and civil service based on merit. Peter also required the nobility to serve the state, undertook tax and financial reforms, and developed trade and industry.

Following the acquisition of the eastern Baltic coastlands from Sweden in 1703, Peter built a new capital, St. Petersburg, on the Gulf of Finland. He called it Russia's "window to the West."

In carrying out his reforms, Peter continued the process of concentrating state power in royal hands. In addition, Peter fought the Poles and the Turks and became deeply involved in European diplomacy. By the end of his reign, in 1725, it was clear that Russia had become a major power in Europe, and that old Muscovy had been shaken to its foundations and transformed into the Russian Empire.

Early Empire. Certain of Peter's reforms were more permanent than others. For example, the apparatus of government administration he established remained largely intact under the tsars of the 1700s. Under the unremitting pressure of the nobility, however, the requirements of noble service and of merit competition were abandoned.

The nobles were given greater and finally absolute authority over their serfs, while owing fewer and fewer

ANCIENT SAMARKAND, in Soviet Central Asia, came under Russian rule in the 1800s.

obligations to the state. Finally, in 1762, the nobility was freed entirely from compulsory state service, although it still remained a ruling class because of its control over the peasantry and the tsar's dependence on it for political support.

The emergence of the nobility from the service position it had occupied under Peter was partly due to the weakness or indifference of his successors. Lax leadership allowed groups such as the Guards' Regiments in St. Petersburg, which were composed exclusively of nobles, to gain power. During the reign of the powerful, brilliant Catherine II, "the Great," (r. 1762–1796) the nobles suffered no loss of power. Catherine, who had come to the throne through a coup d'etat, needed their political backing and administrative talents. On the other hand, public office and thus public power came to be held by a group of individuals drawn from an increasingly smaller professionalized reservoir of nobles and civil servants.

The bureaucracy continued to be dominated by the nobility, but many nobles settled into a life of apathy and indolence on their estates. As a result, in the 1800s men of various classes, or *raznochintsi*, began to fill the lower ranks of the administration, and the direct authority and influence of the nobility was gradually reduced.

Imperial Expansion. In the mid-1700s Russia's former great enemies to the west and south, Poland and Turkey, became increasingly impotent because of growing Russian power and their own internal weaknesses. By the end of Catherine the Great's reign in 1796, Russian control of the Ukraine had been consolidated, and areas north of the Black Sea that had been protectorates of the Ottoman Empire had been added to the Russian state.

All of Siberia to the Pacific Ocean and more and more of Central Asia had also been incorporated into the Russian Empire, which had become by far the largest land state in the world. Most important, however, Russian expansion brought with it direct and constant contact with the great European powers—France, Britain, Austria, and Prussia.

Contact with the powers resulted in Russian involvement in major European wars of the 1700s and Russian participation between 1772 and 1795 in the partitions of Poland. Thus, the Russian Empire found it difficult to escape involvement in the wars of the French Revolution and the Napoleonic wars (1789–1815).

Alexander I (r.1801–1825). In 1812, despite efforts by Alexander I to hold Russia aloof from the Napoleonic struggle in the west, Napoleon invaded Russia. After heroic resistance and great suffering, the Russian armies forced the French to retreat, and Russia joined Austria and Prussia in a coalition which helped defeat Napoleon in 1813–1814.

As a result of these events Russia rose to new heights of European importance. The conclusion of the Napoleonic wars also left the Russian tsar in control of additional territories bordering the empire, including Finland and Bessarabia.

Before his accession to the throne, and during the first years of his reign, Alexander discussed the possibility of undertaking extensive reforms, including the easing or abolition of serfdom and the drawing up of a constitution for the empire. In spite of the fact that Alexander surrounded himself with individuals favorable to his ideas, the projects themselves were never effectively realized.

When real reform failed to materialize, a protest movement was formed by educated Russians. By the mid-1800s demands for radical social and economic reform had grown into a chorus of opposition to the government.

Nicholas I (r.1825–1855). Unfortunately, Alexander's successor, Nicholas I, was naturally conservative and did not favor reform. Furthermore, his accession to the throne was immediately followed by the Decembrist Revolt, an attempted seizure of the government by a group of liberal and reformed-minded officers and nobles. The rising made Nicholas determined to dominate not only the actions, but the thoughts, of his subjects.

The government attempted to protect society from "radical" political and social influences, and it viewed most proposals for change with great suspicion. This policy was disastrous for Russia. It not only allowed severe problems to go unsolved, but it stifled Russia intellectually, technologically, and economically at a time when Europe was being transformed by the profound changes resulting from the industrial and the French revolutions.

The foreign policies of Nicholas I were easily as conservative as his domestic ones. Nevertheless, he was drawn into a major conflict with Britain, France, and the Ottoman Empire in the Crimean War (1853–1856). Russia was defeated in the conflict, and the defeat of Russian armies, on Russian soil, by countries supplying their troops by sea over many thousands of miles was a disaster.

Reform. On Nicholas' death in 1855 the new tsar, Alexander II (r.1855–1881), realized, as did everyone else, that the time for talking of reforms had passed and the time for action had come. Critics of the regime considered the continued existence of serfdom the central problem, and in 1861 the serfs were freed. The first reform had been undertaken.

Other reforms encouraged economic growth and social change, which were seen as essential to Russia's survival in the modern European world. They included reforms in state finance, in local government, in the judicial system, and in military administration. But the inertia of a tradition-bound society, combined with the conservatism of the landed nobility and the government bureaucracy, prevented rapid social change.

As a result, liberal critics were not stilled by Alexander's reforms, and they became increasingly frustrated and isolated from society as a whole. After the 1860s their dissatisfaction was manifested by the formation of groups dedicated to overthrowing the autocracy. In 1881 one of these groups assassinated Alexander II, hoping thereby to touch off a revolution.

Alexander III (r.1881–1894). Although Alexander III succeeded in crushing his father's assassins, the revolutionary movement continued to grow. It grew not only inside Russia, but also among the many Russian émigrés in Western Europe.

Alexander III determined to meet the problems of Russian society with force and more thorough bureaucratic control. But even Konstantin Pobedonostsev, the extremely reactionary adviser of Alexander, could not prevent industrialization and urbanization and the social changes that accompanied them.

Consequently, in the 1880s government policy became ambivalent. The ministry of finance promoted rapid change, while the ministry of the interior remained extremely conservative. At the same time Russia's position in international affairs was delicate, and in contrast to its most powerful European neighbors, Russia became politically and militarily weaker.

Nicholas II (r.1894–1917). The stage was set for a social and political crisis of unprecedented dimensions when the able and determined Alexander III was succeeded by the weak and indecisive Nicholas II. Nicholas pursued the same domestic policies as his predecessor, and continued his conservatism and repression. But the policies evoked only greater protest and unrest, spurred by an agricultural crisis. It was a disaster in foreign affairs, however, that touched off Russia's first modern revolution.

War and Revolution (1904–1905). Conflicting interests of Russia and Japan in East Asia led to war between Russia and a recently strengthened and Westernized Japan. The conflict broke out in February 1904, and the Russians experienced a series of humiliating defeats on land and sea. In September 1905, through the mediation of U.S. Pres. Theodore Roosevelt, a peace settlement was reached at Portsmouth, New Hampshire.

The domestic repercussions of this war were serious. In addition to the burdensome and unimaginative rule of Nicholas II, basic changes taking place in the social and economic structure of Russia produced a revolutionary spirit. By 1902–1903 the whole country was in ferment. The disastrous war with Japan reinforced and encouraged widespread dissatisfaction, and during 1904 a broadly based revolutionary movement emerged.

A series of peaceful meetings, protests, and discussions erupted into violence in January 1905, when Imperial troops opened fire on a crowd of unarmed workers trying to present a petition of grievances to the tsar. This incident, known as "Bloody Sunday," fanned the fires of revolution. The Revolution of 1905, as it is known, spread widely in the cities and countryside, and even to some units of the armed forces.

The tsar offered minor concessions, but they failed to stem the tide. By the autumn of 1905 peasant riots and seizure of their landlords' estates, together with a general strike, virtually paralyzed the government. With the situation out of control, Nicholas II called in Count Sergei Witte.

Witte pointed out the two alternatives facing the tsar—military dictatorship or extensive reform. Reluctantly Nicholas chose reform and issued the October Manifesto, which promised basic civil liberties and the convocation of a national assembly, the Duma.

The Duma (1906–1917). The Duma did not have full parliamentary powers, and its members were chosen by indirect and unequal suffrage. Moreover, in theory and to a considerable extent in practice, the tsar retained complete sovereignty over the country.

Despite their restricted nature, the first two Dumas elected proved to be so critical of the government that the tsar dissolved them. In 1906 Nicholas dismissed Count Witte as prime minister and appointed Peter A. Stolypin, who promptly revised the electoral laws to weight the franchise even more heavily in favor of the propertied classes.

As a result, the third Duma, elected in 1907, and the fourth Duma, chosen in 1912, were able to last out their normal terms of five years in a state of uneasy truce with the government. Duma deputies on the right supported the tsar and his policies, and liberal leaders and parties of the center tried to work within the Duma.

The liberals and moderates worked to achieve necessary reform and to extend gradually the Duma's authority and influence so that it might become a representative parliament like those of the Western democracies. The few deputies of the extreme left, primarily Social Democrats (Marxists), continued to oppose the government wholeheartedly.

In 1907 the continued restlessness of the peasantry, caused by land hunger and general economic hardship, led Prime Minister Stolypin to introduce agrarian reforms. He sought to break up the traditional peasant commune, under which land was owned collectively, and to encourage individual peasant proprietors.

It was hoped that if the peasants became property owners they would have a stake in the existing social order and develop a less revolutionary attitude. The transfer of land belonging to the state and to the nobles into peasant hands was also stepped up. World War I interrupted these reforms before their full impact could be measured.

World War I. In 1914 the Austrian Archduke Francis Ferdinand was assassinated at Sarajevo, in present-day Yugoslavia, by Bosnian terrorists. Serbia, faced with a sweeping ultimatum from Austria-Hungary, turned to Russia for help. The Russians decided to back Serbia, although many Russian leaders realized that Russia was ill-prepared for war and might not be able to withstand the strain on its resources.

Russia's leader hoped the war would be short and victorious, and that they would receive substantial territorial gains in the Balkans. These hopes were to be bitterly disappointed, and the war soon proved disastrous for the Russians as German and Austro-Hungarian armies battered Russia's western areas.

Losses in men and equipment were high, mismanagement of supplies and of the general war effort was common, and morale sagged badly, both at the front and at home. By 1916 the economy as a whole had begun to collapse, and there were severe food and fuel shortages in the cities.

The situation was complicated by a general disintegration in leadership at the upper level. Gregory Rasputin, a charlatan "holy man," had acquired considerable influence over the Empress Alexandra as a result of his success on several occasions in preventing her only son, the heir to the throne, from dying of hemophilia.

In 1915 Nicholas II decided to go to the front to take personal command of the armies. Rasputin, through his hold on Alexandra, began to have a strong influence on the appointment of ministers and the formation of government policy. Although Rasputin was murdered in 1916 by a group of patriotic noblemen, the weakness, inefficiency, and political ineptitude of the government persisted.

REVOLUTION. The situation became critical in March 1917. Quite unexpectedly food riots, coupled with strikes, lockouts, and general labor unrest, led to a mass demonstration in the capital, St. Petersburg (Petrograd), against which the government proved powerless. Within one week the tsar had been toppled from the throne.

With the collapse of the government there was no legally constituted authority, but two centers of power sprang up. One was the Provisional Government, a temporary committee formed by members of the Duma to rule until elections could be held for a constituent assembly. The other was the Petrograd Soviet (Council) of Workers' and Soldiers' Deputies, the revival of an institution which had existed briefly during the Revolution of 1905.

Provisional Government and Soviet. The Soviet was more representative of the Russian people than the Provisional Government. The Soviet fell at first under the domination of doctrinaire socialists, primarily Mensheviks (moderate Marxists) and Social Revolutionaries (agrarian socialists). At that time the extreme wing of the Marxists in Russia, the Bolsheviks, constituted only a tiny minority of the Soviet.

A compromise between the Soviet and the Provisional Government was reached, and the Soviet agreed to let the Provisional Government run the basic governmental system, provided civil liberties and other democratic guarantees were maintained. The Soviet retained control over certain services, such as communications, and exerted a strong influence in the army. The resulting "dual power" system provided a rather shaky government for a society wracked by revolution and war.

Moreover, there were a number of basic social and economic issues on which the Provisional Government and the Soviet disagreed. The leaders of the Provisional Government wanted to continue the war until victory could be achieved. The leaders of the Soviet, however, wanted a rapid end to the war and opposed annexations of territory by the victors.

For the masses of the Russian people the key issues were the ending of the war, the distribution of land, and better living conditions. The general population wanted immediate peace and instant reform. V. I. Lenin, leader of the Bolshevik, or extremist, faction of the Russian Marxists, stepped into this breach.

Bolsheviks. Taking advantage of the basic desires as well as the growing radicalism of the masses, Lenin propounded the slogan, "Peace, Land, and Bread," and saw that the Soviet might be the means by which his Bolshevik party could seize power. As a result, after an abortive popular uprising in the summer of 1917, Lenin began to lay plans to overthrow the Provisional Government, which had become a coalition of liberals and moderate socialists.

Overcoming the opposition of some of his own comrades in the party, Lenin, with the brilliant assistance of Lev Trotsky, seized power in Petrograd on Oct. 25–26, 1917, and shortly thereafter in most of Russia. This "October Revolution," which became the November Revolution when the Russian calendar was changed, easily overthrew the existing moderate regime and instituted sweeping changes in Russia.

SOVIET UNION. After the Bolshevik seizure of power, Lenin turned to the tasks of consolidating the authority of his government and meeting the basic demands of the people. He called for peace and nationalized all land, although permitting the peasants to use the acreage they had seized during the revolution. Lenin also decreed the separation of church and state, and nationalized major industries and banks.

Lenin also promulgated a new, "socialist," constitution for the Russian Soviet Federated Socalist Republic (R.S.F.S.R.). He encouraged the formation of separate but closely allied socialist republics under Bolshevik control in non-Russian areas of the former tsarist empire, and between 1922 and 1924 these were joined to the R.S.F.S.R. to form the Union of Soviet Socialist Republics (U.S.S.R.).

Dictatorship. Lenin suppressed opposition parties and ended freedom of expression. He also dissolved the Constituent Assembly, which he had allowed to be elected in November 1917, when it convened with the Bolsheviks in a minority, and established the Cheka, the forerunner of the secret police, to ferret out and punish "counter-revolutionaries."

Despite considerable opposition not only within the Bolshevik party but throughout the country, Lenin finally forced through his policy of obtaining peace for Russia. On Mar. 3, 1918 the war with Germany and Austria-Hungary was ended by the Treaty of Brest-Litovsk.

Under the terms of the treaty of Brest-Litovsk Russia suffered heavy territorial and economic losses. The treaty outraged many patriotic Russians and contributed to the outbreak of civil war between Bolshevik supporters (Reds) and those opposed to the new Soviet government (Whites). The treaty also helped lead to intervention in Russia by U.S. and Allied troops.

The Western Powers, furious at what they considered Russia's betrayal of the common cause against German militarism, and desperately anxious to reestablish an eastern front against Germany, sent small forces to northern Russia and Siberia and money, supplies, and advisers to various anti-Bolshevik forces.

After the end of World War I, in November 1918, the Allies continued a half-hearted intervention in the hope of overthrowing the Bolshevik regime. But by the end of 1920 the Soviet government had succeeded in defeating its internal and external foes, although the country was exhausted, near starvation, and demoralized.

Ruthlessly putting down peasant protests and disorders, as well as a serious popular uprising at the city and naval base of Kronstadt, Lenin made it clear that the Bolsheviks would not tolerate opposition from the people. In addition, at the Tenth Party Congress in 1921, Lenin crushed dissent within the party itself, making it clear that the leadership would not tolerate opposition from the rank and file. Thus the foundation was laid for the Communist party's dictatorship over Russia.

NEP. Lenin began reconstruction of the devastated country by launching the New Economic Policy, or NEP, under which some of the controls and centralization that had characterized the previous period of wartime communism were abandoned.

Considered a temporary expedient from the start, the NEP did not solve the problem of how to increase Russia's productive forces and build an economy firm enough to support the socialist society envisaged by the com-

PORTRAIT OF V. I. LENIN, who led the 1917 Bolshevik Revolution, overlooks modern Moscow.

munist leaders. By 1927, however, the economy had been restored to its 1913 level and Soviet leaders were faced with the problem of establishing new goals.

This situation was complicated by a power struggle within the Communist party following Lenin's death in 1924. Joseph Stalin, the general secretary of the party, emerged victorious, first defeating Lev Trotsky and his "Left" supporters, and then the so-called Right opposition. Stalin established one-man rule over both the party and the country.

Stalinism. After expelling Trotsky from the party's politburo, Stalin adopted Trotsky's domestic policy, which called for rapid and extensive industrialization. To achieve this, the First Five-Year Plan was begun in 1928, and completed ahead of schedule in 1932. But to obtain the labor and capital for industrialization, Stalin found it necessary to control the peasants. This he accomplished by forcing them onto state-owned collective farms.

Massive peasant resistance bordered on civil war, and an estimated 5 to 10 million peasants were killed, died of starvation, or were exiled to Siberia and Central Asia. But by 1933 Stalin had won out. He also directed the energies of the Russian people toward the goal of industrialization.

Stalin established complete party control over every aspect of private and public life and instituted a rigid totalitarian regime, known as "Stalinism." At the cost not only of lives but of an almost total loss of freedom, Soviet society thus achieved remarkable industrial growth during the decade of the 1930s.

Fearing that critics of his program were springing up within the party, Stalin began a "great purge" in 1936, starting with former party colleagues and rivals. The elimination of alleged "traitors to the party" soon spread to all levels of the party and to people in all walks of Soviet life.

No one was immune from the purge, and many thousands were arrested, imprisoned, exiled to slave labor camps, or executed. The blood bath finally ended in 1938, but by then terror had become a major ingredient of Soviet daily life under the Stalinist regime.

Foreign Policy. During the 1920s Soviet foreign policy had been directed toward gaining recognition and support for the new Soviet state and preventing the possibility of Western intervention in Russia, such as had occurred during the revolution. Soviet leaders also founded and directed an organization of Communist parties throughout the world, the Third, or Communist, International (Comintern, 1919–1943).

The Comintern was designed to coordinate and assist the development of the proletarian revolution in other countries, but it had little success. During the 1930s the Comintern deemphasized its promotion of revolution and urged Communist parties in Europe to cooperate with socialist and moderate parties in antifascist coalitions known as "popular fronts" or "united fronts."

In foreign policy the Soviet Union proposed disarmament and the formation of alliances against Adolf Hitler's Nazi Germany and Benito Mussolini's Fascist Italy. But Stalin finally became disillusioned with the "appeasement" policies of France and England and embarked on a bold and dangerous gamble in power politics.

In August 1939, ignoring communist ideology, which decried fascism, and the anguished protests of millions of communists and Soviet sympathizers around the world, Stalin signed a nonaggression pact with Hitler. In so doing he bought time and some territory in Eastern Europe, but he also permitted Hitler to conquer Poland and France, which meant that by June 1941 Hitler was able to launch a major offensive against the Soviet Union.

World War II. After sweeping initial successes, facilitated by Stalin's unwillingness to believe that Hitler would attack and by inadequate Soviet preparations, the Nazi armies were checked before Moscow and Leningrad (formerly Petrograd) in the late fall of 1941. The Soviet Union's allies, Britain and the United States, furnished considerable aid to the Soviet Union, and all three nations subscribed to general war aims set forth in the Atlantic Charter.

The Soviet armies continued to bear the brunt of the fighting, and Stalin pressed the United States and Britain to open a "second front" in Europe. Despite the considerable successes of the Germans in 1942, the Soviet forces remained intact and inflicted a major defeat on the Nazi armies in the last months of 1942 at the battle of Stalingrad, the present-day city of Volgagrad.

From that time on Soviet troops began to push the Germans back, a process assisted by the British-U.S. landing in France in June 1944. Attacked on two fronts, the Germans surrendered in May 1945. The Soviet Union attacked Japan on Aug. 8, 1945 and completely occupied Manchuria after token Japanese resistance.

Cold War. After victory the Soviet Union faced two major problems: reconstruction and its relationship with its Western allies. Despite attempts in a series of wartime conferences to work out cooperative arrangements for the postwar period, friction soon arose between the Western powers and the Soviet Union, marking the beginning of the "cold war."

The chief issues were Germany and Eastern Europe. The Soviet Union, which had agreed to joint four-power occupation of Germany, began to extract unilateral reparations to assist its own reconstruction effort. As a result, Germany soon became divided into a pro-Allied West Germany and a Soviet-dominated East Germany.

In Eastern Europe the Soviet Union, whose armies had liberated much of the area from German domination, exerted pressure to insure the emergence of pro-Soviet governments despite Soviet promises at the Yalta Conference—held by representatives of Britain, the United States, and the Soviet Union in February 1945—that free elections would be held in those countries.

LOOK MAGAZINE

MOSCOW, viewed from the Kremlin, reflects the Russian past and the Soviet present.

Between 1946 and 1948 one country after another in Eastern Europe came under Soviet domination over the protests of the Western nations, who were powerless, short of starting a new war, to reverse this trend. Hostility between the West and the Soviet Union was carried into the United Nations.

Stalin clearly intended to extend Soviet domination as far west into Europe as possible, assuming that by doing so he not only ensured the security of the Soviet Union, but aided the spread of "socialist" revolutions in the world. The opportunity for Soviet expansion in Western Europe arose through the disorder left by the war and the large Communist parties that existed in France and Italy.

The United States instituted the Marshall Plan, a massive aid program that permitted Western Europe to recover political and economic stability and avert the threat of communist engulfment. It also launched programs of military aid to West European nations, as well as to Greece and Turkey. The Western powers thus embarked on a policy of "containment," to limit Soviet expansion and support anticommunist governments.

Iron Curtain. At home Stalin launched a renewed program of industrialization and totalitarianism. The mild freedom of thought and activity that had been permitted during the war was ended, and strict adherence to anti-Western and nationalistic dogma was demanded in all areas of Soviet life.

To prevent Soviet and East European peoples from comparing themselves with the West and to keep out Western influences, Stalin drew an "iron curtain" between Western and Eastern Europe, cutting off all contacts and normal interchange. At the same time he forced the Soviet people to make even greater sacrifices to rebuild the country and further advance the process of industrialization.

Post-Stalin Era. When Stalin died in 1953 there was a change in Soviet foreign and domestic policy. At home the new leaders were anxious to eliminate the worst abuses of Stalinism without undermining their own control. After a brief power struggle, Nikita S. Khrushchev emerged as the strongest figure, and soon began a daring experiment in "de-Stalinization."

Blaming the evils of the Soviet system on Stalin personally, Khrushchev attempted to reduce substantially the use of terror and to increase material incentives to achieve higher economic performance. To do this meant encouraging initiative, providing a higher standard of living, and permitting a slightly wider range for intellectual and artistic creativity.

Khrushchev was deposed in 1964, largely because of the personal and arbitrary nature of his rule, but his successors, Leonid Brezhnev and Aleksei Kosygin, followed the same basic policies. To a considerable degree these have been successful. The first Soviet space vehicle (*Sputnik*) was launched in 1957, followed by other pioneering Soviet efforts in space. Housing and living conditions improved, and Soviet artists and intellectuals were given somewhat less restricted opportunities for creative work.

Problems, of course, remained. The economy continued to be sluggish, partly because of the difficulties involved in central planning for such a huge, complex, industrialized society. Agricultural productivity remained low, and the commitment to communism of many citizens, particularly young people, was formalistic or nonexistent.

Peaceful Coexistence. In foreign policy, the Soviet leaders accepted the realities of the nuclear age and espoused a policy of "peaceful coexistence." Realizing that the Soviet Union and the United States each had the nuclear capability to destroy one another, they decided that the contest between "capitalism" and "communism" must take place on nonmilitary grounds.

The new approach to the East-West struggle led to serious problems for the Soviet Union within the communist camp. Relaxation of Stalinist controls had ended direct Soviet power over the communist governments it had established in Eastern Europe. Many of those governments chose to act independently of the Soviet Union, and by 1968 Romania had become the prime example of open opposition to Soviet policies.

A more critical divison arose between the Soviet Union and China, where a communist regime had won power in 1949 with little Soviet aid. The Chinese communist leaders sought to continue and intensify the worldwide struggle between East and West. The Chinese moved to replace the Soviet Union as leader of the world communist movement, and pursued a policy of denouncing Soviet "revisionism" and "appeasement."

—George Kish; Don Karl Rowney; John M. Thompson

SPAIN

Official name: The Spanish State
Area: 194,885 square miles
Population: (1967 est.) 32,140,000
Capital: Madrid (Pop., 1964 est., 2,558,583)
Language: Spanish
Religion: Roman Catholicism
Currency unit: Peseta
National holiday: Spanish labor day, July 18

Spain occupies the bulk of the Iberian Peninsula in southwestern Europe. It is bounded on the north by the Bay of Biscay and France, on the east and southeast by the Mediterranean Sea, on the south by the Strait of Gibraltar, and on the west by Portugal and the Atlantic Ocean.

The Canary Islands, which lie in the Atlantic about 800 miles off the southwest coast, and the Balearic Islands, in the Mediterranean just off the east coast, are also part of Spain.

THE LAND. Most of Spain consists of a high tableland, the Meseta, which has an average elevation of more than 2,500 feet above sea level. Most of the Meseta is flat, but it has many hilly and mountainous areas.

The principal mountain ranges of the Meseta are the Sierra de Gata, the Sierra de Gredos, and the Sierra de Guadarrama, to the west and north of Madrid; the Sierra Morena in the south-central area; and the Cantabrian Mountains in the north.

Northeastern Spain is dominated by the rugged Pyrenees, which run along the border with France, isolating the Iberian Peninsula from the rest of Europe.

There is a relatively narrow coastal plain in the east, along the Mediterranean, which widens substantially only in the lower Ebro River valley. This plain is broken in many places by mountains that extend to the sea. In southwestern Andalusia, along the Atlantic shore, the coastal plain is fairly wide.

Spain's major rivers are the Ebro, the Duero, the Tagus, the Guadiana, and the Guadalquivir. The Guadalquivir is the only river navigable for any significant distance.

Climate. The climate of Spain is varied. The southern and eastern coasts have a Mediterranean climate, with long, hot, dry summers and short, cool, moderately rainy winters.

The interior has a continental climate, with very hot summers and cold winters. It is generally quite dry. Galicia and the northern coast have a maritime climate, by far the rainiest in Spain. The higher elevations experience cooler summers and much colder winters.

THE PEOPLE. The Spanish people tend to reflect strong regional differences due to the country's historical development and to the mountainous terrain, which helps isolate one part of the country from another.

The official language is Castilian Spanish, which is generally understood throughout the country. Numerous regional dialects are spoken, however, including Galician in the northwest and Andalusian in the south. Catalan, spoken in the northeast, and Basque, spoken in the mountains of the north, differ greatly from Castilian.

The state religion is Roman Catholicism, and more than 99 percent of the population is at least nominally Roman Catholic. There are small minorities of Jews, Muslims, and Protestants.

Spain has one of the highest birth rates and lowest death rates in Europe, but substantial emigration has kept the average annual increase in population low. From 1958 to 1966 the annual rate of increase was only 0.8 percent, slightly under the average for Western Europe. The population density in 1966 was about 165 persons per square mile, lower than in most European countries.

Spain's principal city is the capital, Madrid, located almost at the geographic center of the country. Spain's second largest city is the Mediterranean port of Barcelona. Other major cities are Valencia, Seville, Zaragoza, and Bilbao.

ECONOMY. The Spanish economy is one of the least developed in Western Europe. Nonetheless, substantial improvement has taken place since 1959, when the government instituted a vigorous economic program, which included devaluation of the peseta, liberalization of trade restrictions, and promotion of foreign investment.

Foreign investment greatly increased following the relaxation of government restrictions. In addition, there has been a phenomenal rise in income from tourism, which reached more than $1,000 million in 1965, and a large gain in remittances from Spaniards working in many booming, but labor-short, Western Europe countries.

In 1964 the government initiated a four-year economic and social development plan to raise the gross national product by 6 percent. This plan was successful, and in 1968 a second plan, emphasizing agricultural development, went into effect.

Natural Resources. Spain's mineral resources compare favorably with those of the rest of southern Europe, but fuels, including high-grade coal, petroleum, and natural gas, are in short supply.

Spain has large deposits of mercury and in 1965 led in world production with 3,100 metric tons. Spain has long been a major producer and exporter of iron ore, and lead, zinc, tungsten, and copper are also mined.

Agriculture. Spain is traditionally an agricultural nation, and about 35 percent of the labor force is engaged in farming. As a result of the country's varied climate, Spanish agriculture is quite diversified.

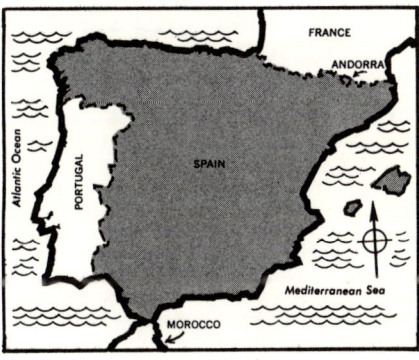

The Mediterranean coast specializes in olives, grapes, and almonds. Valencia and areas further south produce oranges in abundance. Rice is raised in a number of irrigated coastal areas. Wheat and barley are grown in the Meseta, which also provides pasturage for Merino sheep and goats. Galicia and Asturias produce corn, potatoes, and apples. Cattle are also raised in these regions.

Cork is gathered from cork oaks, which are planted throughout the country in hilly areas unsuited to the raising of other crops. Spain generally leads the world in cork production.

Industry. Spanish industry has been growing steadily and in 1964 it contributed 30 percent to the gross domestic product. But it is still largely undeveloped and is unable to meet domestic requirements.

Of the few industrial areas, the port of Barcelona, in the northeast, is by far the most important and most diversified. Its chief industries include textiles, chemicals, iron and steel, metal working, vehicle production and assembly, and printing and publishing.

The Bilbao-Santander district in the north and Avilés and Oviedo further west have developed sizable iron and steel industries. Ship building, zinc smelting, and chemical production are important in the coastal part of this area. Murcia and Cartagena in the southeast form Spain's only other true industrial district, although some manufacturing takes place in nearly all of the larger cities.

Trade. In 1967 Spain's imports cost $3,462 million and its exports earned $1,384 million. The country's principal exports are oranges, nuts, fresh and dried fish, vegetables, wine, textiles, olive oil, and cork. The chief imports include machinery, foodstuffs, chemicals, manufactured goods, and petroleum. Spain's major trading partners are the United States, West Germany, France, and Britain.

GOVERNMENT. Although Spain officially became a monarchy in 1947, no king sits on the throne. In actual fact Spain is a dictatorship led by Gen. Francisco Franco, who is head of state and chief of government as well as commander in chief of the armed forces.

An Organic Law approved by popular referendum in December 1966 allows General Franco to lighten his load if he so wishes by appointing a prime minister as chief of government from a list of three nominees selected by the Council of the Realm. In addition to the Council of the Realm, which is an advisory body, there is a cabinet, or Council of Ministers, that meets with Franco to determine state policy.

The legislative branch of government consists of a parliament, the Cortes. By the Organic Law of 1966, 104 members of the Cortes—two from each of Spain's 52 provinces—may be directly elected by heads of households and married women. The remaining members are government officials and representatives of municipal councils, trade unions, and various professional and social organizations.

Once the master of a vast empire, Spain now holds only a few sparsely populated areas along the west coast of Africa, including the overseas provinces of Ifni, the Spanish Sahara, and Fernando Póo and Río Muni, which form Equatorial Guinea. In Morocco, the tiny enclaves of the Peñón de Alhucemas, Ceuta, Chafarinas, Melilla, and the Peñón de Vélez are under Spanish sovereignty.

Spain is a member of the United Nations.

HISTORY. Spain was peopled in prehistoric times by primitive Basques and Iberians. In about 900 BC Celts began entering the peninsula from the north.

The Phoenicians began founding trading colonies on the southeastern coast in about 800 BC, and the Greeks followed suit from about 500 BC. The Phoenician city of Carthage, in North Africa, acquired control over southern Spain during the 200s BC. In 202 BC Rome defeated Carthage in the Second Punic War and subsequently undertook the conquest of Spain. By the beginning of the first century AD, Roman control over the peninsula was complete.

Under Roman rule classical civilization entered Spain, which soon became one of the most Romanized provinces of the empire. Spain made significant contributions to Latin literature and produced one of Rome's greatest emperors, Trajan. Spain was also one of the first parts of the empire to accept Christianity.

In 409 AD Spain was overrun by the Vandals, who were in turn driven out by the Visigoths. In 419 the Visigoths established a kingdom that included Spain and southern France. They contributed little to Spain culturally, and put up little resistance when Arab and Berber Muslims from North Africa invaded the country in 711. The Muslims, or Moors as they were called, ruled most of Spain from Córdoba, which became the center of a brilliant civilization.

Reconquest. A small Christian nucleus survived the Muslim invasions in the Asturian Mountains, which in 722 became the kingdom of Asturias. The establishment of this kingdom marked the beginning of the Reconquest, the 800 year struggle of the Christians to rid Iberia of the Muslims.

In addition to Asturias, which evolved into the kingdom of León in the 1000s, there arose the Christian kingdoms of Aragon and Navarre, the county of Catalonia, and the county—later the kingdom—of Castile. Each of these medieval Christian states had its own body of law and feudal customs. Each also had a *côrtes*, or representative assembly.

For 300 years these kingdoms waged unsuccessful wars with the Caliphate of Córdoba, the ruling power of Muslim Spain. In the 1000s civil war among the Muslims shattered the unity of the caliphate. Its disintegration aided the Reconquest, and by 1300 the Christians had reduced the Muslim hold to a narrow strip in southern Spain known as the kingdom of Granada.

Aragon and Catalonia had merged in the 1100s, and Castile and León had done the same in the 1200s. But Portugal separated from Castile in 1143 and became an independent kingdom. Further unification of Christian Spain

VEJER DE LA FRONTERA, in Cadiz, Spain, is an old city with narrow winding streets.

was brought about by the marriage in 1469 of Ferdinand of Aragon (r. 1479–1516) and Queen Isabella of Castile (r. 1474–1504).

In 1478 they supported the Inquisition, whose ecclesiastical courts sought out the thousands of converted Jews and Muslims living in Spain, whose allegiance to Roman Catholicism was doubted.

In 1492 Ferdinand and Isabella conquered Granada, the last Muslim stronghold, and to completely unify the country they expelled the remaining Jews and Muslims. In the same year Christopher Columbus discovered the New World and claimed it for Spain, thus opening up vast new territories for colonization.

The Hapsburgs. Joanna, the daughter of Ferdinand and Isabella, married Philip of Hapsburg, the heir to the Holy Roman Empire and to much of northern Europe. Their son, Charles I of Spain (r. 1516–1556), became the Holy Roman Emperor Charles V in 1519.

Charles encouraged Spanish colonial expansion, and during his reign Spain gained control of most of Middle America and northwestern South America. In his role as emperor, however, he embroiled Spain in a series of wars against France. A devout Roman Catholic, he made an unsuccessful attempt to defeat Lutheranism in Germany and engaged in a long struggle against the Muslims of North Africa.

Philip II. Charles' son, Philip II (r. 1556–1598), did not succeed to the Holy Roman Empire, but he did inherit Spain, the New World possessions, Franche-Comté, Milan, Naples, and the Netherlands. As staunch a Roman Catholic as his father, Philip's foreign policy was often largely the result of his religious feelings.

Philip was determined to suppress Protestantism among his subjects in the Netherlands, but his attempts failed and the Netherlands declared their independence from Spain in 1581. His greatest failure, however, was his attempt to conquer England, which was not only Protestant but also Spain's rival for control of the seas.

In 1588 Philip launched the Spanish Armada against the English. The Armada was largely destroyed, and its destruction marked the beginning of the end of Spanish sea power. Philip's only notable success in foreign affairs was the acquisition of Portugal in 1580.

Decline and Renewal. Spain declined rapidly in the 1600s, partially as a result of mediocre and indolent kings, who left governing to inferior ministers. The country grew poorer, government revenue proved insufficient despite heavy gold imports from Spain's American colonies, and the population declined. The Dutch and English crippled Spanish trade on the seas, and Portugal regained its independence in 1640.

The nation was at its weakest when Charles II (r. 1665–1700) died without heirs and the throne passed to Philip V (r. 1700–1746) of the French Bourbon line. Under the Bourbons, Spain underwent a revival in the 1700s. Trade and industry grew, the population increased, colonial administration improved, and the Spanish army and navy regained some of their former strength. These gains, however, were swept away during the Napoleonic era.

Spain in the 1800s. In 1807 Napoleon I of France seized the Spanish throne for his brother Joseph, and the Spanish monarch, Ferdinand VII, was forced to abdicate. The Spanish carried on guerrilla warfare against the French, and in 1813, aided by the British, they finally drove Napoleon's troops from the peninsula.

In 1814 Ferdinand VII was restored to the throne, but Spain had been seriously weakened. The mainland American colonies, which had proclaimed their independence during Ferdinand's reign, were completely lost by 1825, and a family quarrel among Spanish Bourbons over the throne led to a fierce civil war, the Carlist struggle, that raged from 1834 to 1839.

The reign of Isabella II, who had come to the throne in 1833 as an infant, was marked by political unrest and internal disorder. In addition, she was personally unpopular and in 1868 was forced to abdicate.

After an experiment with an imported Italian monarch, Amadeo I (r. 1871–1873), a republic was established in 1873. The following year, however, Isabella's son, Alfonso XII (r. 1875–1885), came of age and was recalled to the throne.

Alfonso XII died in 1885 and was succeeded by Alfonso XIII (r. 1885–1931), who was born after his father's death. In 1898 Spain fought a disastrous war with the United States, the Spanish-American War. It lost Cuba, Puerto Rico, the Philippines, and Guam, reducing Spain's colonial empire to a few minor holdings in Africa.

Instability. Spain was neutral in World War I, but the wartime demand for goods led to an expansion of Spanish industry. In the postwar period, when the demand for goods and munitions ceased, Spain suffered labor problems and political instability. The country was also burdened with the financial and miltiary problem of putting down uprisings in Spanish Morocco, where a Spanish zone had been established in the early 1900s.

In 1921 a military disaster in Morocco seriously threatened the monarchy. The political situation grew steadily worse, and in 1923 Gen. Miguel Primo de Rivera seized power with the king's consent and established a dictatorship. Primo de Rivera resigned in 1930, and the republicans took advantage of the overwhelming majority they had won in parliamentary elections in 1931 to proclaim a republic.

The Second Spanish Republic, which attempted liberal reforms, was unpopular with the Roman Catholic Church and the aristocracy. General dissatisfaction with the republic increased as the world economic depression of the 1930s began to affect Spain.

The army, the monarchists, the landowning aristocracy, and the church were united in their opposition to the republic. The republic was supported, on the other hand, by the socialists, communists, republicans, and various liberal groups.

Civil War. Following a republican victory in elections held in 1936, violence broke out and the army, led by Gen. José Sanjurjo, rose against the government. General Sanjurjo was killed in an airplane crash, and Gen. Francisco Franco assumed leadership of the rebels.

Soon after the outbreak of the hostilities foreign nations began to intervene. The Loyalists, as the supporters of the government were called, were aided by sympathizers in the United States and other countries as well as by the Soviet Union. Franco, however, received large-scale aid from Nazi Germany and Fascist Italy, and by 1939 the Loyalists were defeated.

Franco set up a dictatorship and governed with the title "El Caudillo," or "the leader," aided by the Falangists, the Spanish equivalent of the Italian Fascists.

Contemporary Spain. Although openly favorable to the Axis powers in World War II, Franco remained neutral. In 1947 Franco promulgated the Law of Succession, which restored the monarchy by providing for the election of a king by a Regency Council after his death.

In 1953, during the Cold War, the United States changed its previously unfavorable attitude toward Franco's government and obtained military bases in Spain in return for $226 million in financial aid. In 1955 Spain became a member of the United Nations.

During the mid-1960s Franco's government began to show signs of political liberalization, and in 1966 a new constitution was adopted. The new constitution provided for the appointment of a prime minister and the direct election of two members of parliament from each province. A greater measure of freedom of religion was granted non-Roman Catholics, and less stringent censorship regulations and labor restrictions were decreed.

In December 1967 Spain's claim to the British colony of Gibraltar, an issue that had severely strained relations between the two countries during the mid-1960s, came before the UN General Assembly. The assembly called for talks between Britain and Spain to arrange for the decolonization of the area.

—Charles E. Nowell

SUDAN

Official name: Republic of Sudan
Area: 967,499 square miles
Population: (1967 est.) 14,355,000
Capital: Khartoum (Pop., 1964 est., 173,500)
Language: Arabic, African languages
Religion: Islam, Christianity, traditional religions
Currency unit: Pound
National holiday: Independence day, January 1

Sudan, a republic in northern Africa, is bordered on the north by the United Arab Republic (Egypt); on the east by the Red Sea and Ethiopia; on the south by Kenya, Uganda, and the Congo (Kinshasa); and on the west by the Central African Republic, Chad, and Libya. Between 1899 and 1953 Sudan was ruled jointly by Britain and Egypt as a condominium. From 1954 to 1956, Sudan was self-governing, and on Jan. 1, 1956 it became independent.

THE LAND. Sudan, the largest country in Africa, has a varied landscape. Most of northern Sudan is occupied by the desert region of the Sahara. The Nile River flows north through central Sudan, creating a fertile region. The river's two main branches, the Blue Nile and the White Nile, meet at Khartoum, and then the great, single river flows northward into the United Arab Republic.

In west-central Sudan the Marra mountains reach elevations above 10,000 feet. East of the Marra Mountains is the Kordofan Plateau. In central Sudan the Nuba Mountains reach elevations of over 4,300 feet. South of Khartoum, in east-central Sudan, there are tropical savanna lands.

In the south there are tropical rain forests, and in the extreme southern part of the country the White Nile

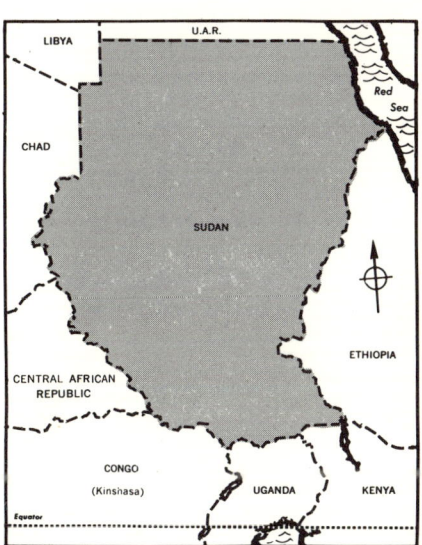

SUDAN'S PEOPLE include many different ethnic groups, among them the Dogon.

overflows to create a swampy region called the *Sudd*. The Atbara River, a tributary of the Nile, flows through eastern Sudan.

Rainfall averages only about four inches a year in east-central Sudan, and the Red Sea coast is arid and hot. It is relatively rainy in the western mountain region, and the south has a hot and humid tropical climate.

THE PEOPLE. There are two distinct groups of people in Sudan: Muslims in the northern provinces of Kassala, Khartoum, Blue Nile, Kordofan, Darfur, and Northern; and Negro tribes in the southern provinces of Upper Nile, Bahr el Ghazal, and Equatoria.

Most of the Muslims, who make up the majority of Sudan's population, are Arabic-speaking. They are divided into great tribal groups including the Jaaliin, Shaiqiyya, and Kababish. The more important non-Arabic-speaking peoples in northern Sudan are the Beja, who live near the Red Sea; the Nubians, along the Nile from Dongola to the Egyptian border; the Negroid Nuba, in southern Kordofan; and the Negroid Fur in Darfur.

Most of the southern tribes are pagan or Christian. They make up about one third of the population. The major tribes include the Dinka, Shilluk, Nuer, and Azande.

ECONOMY. The economy of Sudan is based on agriculture. The main food crops are millet, sesame seeds, peanuts, castor beans, and dates. The major cash crop is cotton, and in 1965 an estimated 163,000 metric tons of cotton were produced. Much of Sudan's cotton is grown in the Gezira, a flat region, ideal for irrigation, between the Blue and White Nile South of Khartoum.

Gum arabic is produced for export, and camels and sheep are raised in many parts of the country.

Sudan's poorly developed industry is concerned primarily with processing agricultural products. Although Sudan has deposits of chrome ore, which it began to export in the mid-1960s, mining is generally underdeveloped. A ten-year development program was begun in 1960 to improve transportation facilities and build irrigation systems and dams.

In 1966 imports cost $217 million and exports earned $205 million. The major imports are petroleum products, textiles, machinery, and foodstuffs. The major exports are cotton, sesame seed, and gum arabic. Most trade is conducted with Britain, West Germany, and Italy.

GOVERNMENT. In 1956 a transitional constitution was adopted. The constitution was reinstated in 1965, after a period of military rule that began in 1958. The constitution vests executive power in a five member Supreme Council of State, headed by a president.

Legislative power is held by a Constituent Assembly whose members are popularly elected. The assembly elects a prime minister, who appoints a cabinet. Cabinet members are responsible to the legislature.

Sudan is a member of the United Nations, the Organization of African Unity, and the Arab League.

HISTORY. Sudan's history has always been closely linked with Egypt. In about 3000 B.C. the pharaohs of ancient Egypt sent expeditions into Sudan to raid for slaves, and by about 2000 BC Egypt had extended its rule into Sudan. The region of present-day Sudan came to be called Kush. The power of Egypt began to decline after about 2000 BC.

A Nubian from Napata, in north-central Sudan, proclaimed himself king of Kush in 750 BC. He gained control of Egypt and established a Sudanese dynasty, which lasted until 661 BC, when the Assyrians conquered Egypt. After that time, Egyptian civilization in Sudan declined.

The kingdom of Kush reestablished itself as an independent state and survived until about 350 AD, at which time it was destroyed by the kingdom of Axum, in northern Ethiopia. After that, Negro peoples from the south began to migrate into northern Sudan. Beginning in the 500s the peoples of Northern Sudan became Christians, and two Christian dynasties, Maqurra and Alwa, were established.

In the late 1200s the Mamluks, a Muslim dynasty in Egypt, destroyed Maqurra. Arabs began migrating into northern Sudan, and many of the people were converted to Islam. Alwa survived until the early 1500s, at which time a Negro tribe called the Funj established the powerful Muslim state of Sennar. Until its decline some 300 years later, the Funj dynasty provided much of Sudan with unity and security.

Egyptian conquest of Sudan began in 1820, and Sennar was overrun by Egyptian armies. At the junction of the White and Blue Niles, Egypt created a military and administrative center, Khartoum, which became the capital of Egyptian Sudan. Egyptian rule lasted until 1885. In that year a Sudanese, Muhammad Ahmad al-Mahdi, captured Khartoum after a four year religious and political struggle against Egyptian rule.

Condominium. Sudan remained under the control of Muhammad Ahmad's successor until an Anglo-Egyptian force conquered Sudan in 1896–1898. Sudan became a condominium ruled jointly by Britain and Egypt in 1899, but in fact Britain controlled Sudan. The period of British rule was considered by many a model of good colonial administration, achieving security and economic development.

Although nationalist movements emerged in the 1920s, they became important only during World War II. The nationalist movement was strongly marked by rivalry between two major Muslim religious brotherhoods, the Khatmiya and the Ansar. The Khatmiya, led by Sayyid Ali al-Mirghani, favored union with Egypt. The Ansar, led by Sayyid Abd al-Rahman al-Mahdi, a posthumous son of Muhammad Ahmad al-Mahdi, took a more pro-British stand and favored complete independence.

In 1953 Egypt and Britain signed an agreement granting Sudan self-government, and soon all sides were able to agree on complete independence for Sudan. A parliament was established in January 1954, and the National Unionist Party (NUP), which represented a more secular policy than the brotherhoods, formed the first cabinet. On Jan. 1, 1956 Sudan became an independent republic.

Independence. The Umma Party, mainly the Ansor, and the People's Democratic Party, largely the Khatmiya, formed a coalition, and in July 1956 the National Unionist Party was forced from power. Political instability followed, and in 1958 parliamentary government was ended by a bloodless coup led by Lt. Gen. Ibrahim Abboud. In 1964 demonstrations against the military forced Abboud's resignation and a return to civilian rule.

Elections held in 1965 gave the NUP and the Umma Party a majority in the assembly. The two formed a coalition government with Muhammad Ahmad Mahjoub as prime minister. The three southern provinces did not vote in the elections. They had gone into rebellion against the Muslim-Arab north in 1963.

Early in 1968 the Constituent Assembly was dissolved, and a draft constitution abandoned. New elections were called for April, and prospects brightened for the participation of the Southern provinces.

—L. Carl Brown;
Hibberd V. B. Kline, Jr.

SWAZILAND

Official name: Swaziland
Area: 6,704 square miles
Population: (1966 est.) 375,000
Capital: Mbabane (Pop., 1962 est., urban area, 8,390)
Language: Swazi, English
Religion: Traditional religions, Christianity
Currency unit: South African rand

Swaziland, a country in southeastern Africa, is bordered on the north, south, and west by the Republic of South Africa, and on the east by Mozambique. Britain granted Swaziland internal self-government in 1967 and agreed to full independence effective Sept. 6, 1968.

THE LAND. Swaziland has three well-defined veld, or grassland, regions—the highveld, middleveld, and lowveld.

COUNTRIES OF THE WORLD

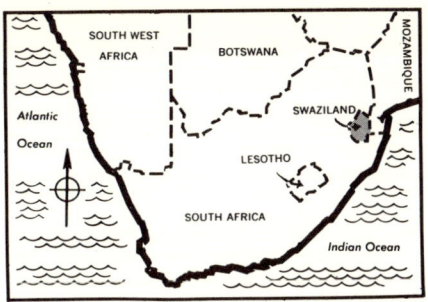

The highveld, in western Swaziland, is mountainous and has an average elevation of 3,500 feet. To the east is the middleveld, with an average elevation of 2,000 feet. The lowveld, in eastern Swaziland, has average elevations of 1,000 feet. The Lebombo, a plateau region, is in the extreme eastern part of the country.

The Great Escarpment, a geological feature of southern Africa that rises some 6,000 feet above the plain, runs through Swaziland.

The highveld is humid and receives between 40 and 90 inches of rain each year. The climate in the middleveld and Lebombo plateau is subtropical and drier, receiving between 30 and 45 inches of rain each year. The lowveld receives between 20 and 30 inches of rain each year.

THE PEOPLE. Most of the people of Swaziland belong to the Bantu-speaking Swazi tribe. The Swazi have traditionally been a pastoral people. There is also a small number of Bantu-speaking Zulu people in southern Swaziland.

About 2.5 percent of the people are of European origin, mainly Afrikaans-speaking in southern Swaziland and English or Afrikaans-speaking in the north. There is a small community of people of mixed European and African descent.

There are only two large cities in Swaziland—Mbabane, the capital, and Manzini, formerly known as Bremersdorp, the country's commercial center.

ECONOMY. Swaziland's economy is based on agriculture. The country has rich mineral and forest resources and fertile soils. In recent years the Swazi have become successful farmers. The basic food crops are corn and sorghum. The chief cash crops are cotton and tobacco. Sugar cane, citrus, rice, and other fruits and vegetables are grown in irrigated areas.

Cattle are raised in most parts of the country. The Swazi have traditionally valued the cattle as a symbol of social status and only in recent years have cattle acquired economic importance. Forestry, mainly in the highveld, is of growing importance to the economy.

Swaziland's mineral resources include large deposits of iron ore and asbestos. There are also deposits of coal, gold, tin, barytes, and pyrophyllite. Iron ore mined at Ngwenya, in western Swaziland, is carried by rail to the port of Lourenço Marques, in Mozambique, for export. There is little manufacturing apart from the processing of minerals and agricultural products.

Swaziland's main imports are textiles, machinery, and petroleum products. The leading exports are iron ore, asbestos, and sugar. Most trade is conducted with South Africa, Britain, and Japan.

Swaziland has close economic ties with South Africa, and many Swazis find work in South Africa. Customs duties for Swaziland are collected by South Africa, and Swaziland receives a fixed percentage of South Africa's customs revenue each year. Swaziland also uses South African currency.

GOVERNMENT. Swaziland has a parliamentary system of government. The king, or Ngwenyama, of Swaziland is head of state. Actual executive power is held by a prime minister and cabinet responsible to the legislature.

Legislative power is held by a parliament made up of a 30-member House of Assembly and a 12-member Senate. Twenty-four of the House members are popularly elected, and six are appointed by the king. Six members of the Senate are elected by the House of Assembly, and six are appointed by the king.

HISTORY. In the mid-1700s a group of tribal peoples in southern Africa, the Ngoni, broke away from the main body of Bantu-speaking peoples. They came into conflict with another group of Bantu-speaking people, the Zulu, and by the early 1800s the Zulu had forced them northward into present-day Swaziland.

A Ngoni chief, Sobhuza, founded the Swazi nation by fusing several Ngoni clans with some Sotho-speaking people they had conquered. Sobhuza's son Mswati, from whom the Swazi derive their name, extended Swazi power and prestige among neighboring Bantu-speaking peoples.

European Influence. Europeans began to settle in the area in the 1800s, and the Swazi ruler granted them many land concessions. Both the British colony of Natal, in present-day South Africa, and the Afrikaner, or Boer, Republic of the Transvaal, also in present-day South Africa, claimed Swaziland. In 1890 a compromise was reached, and a provisional government was established composed of representatives of the Swazi, the British, and the Transvaal Afrikaners.

To appease the Afrikaners, the British ceded administration of Swaziland to the Transvaal in 1894, despite Swazi protests. In the Boer, or South African, War (1899–1902) the British conquered the Transvaal, and assumed control of Swaziland. In 1907 the British High Commissioner for South Africa took over the administration of Swaziland.

The rise of nationalism in the 1940s and 1950s threatened the Swazi aristocracy and the white community, both of whom feared the loss of power and privilege. In 1960 these groups jointly requested Britain to grant a constitution that would in effect preserve the status quo. A British-sponsored constitution promulgated in 1964 did not satisfy traditionalists, nationalists, or the white minority.

Independence. Traditionalist forces, led by the Swazi paramount chief Sobhuza II, formed the Imbokodvo Party, which won a majority of seats in the legislative council in Swaziland's first elections in 1964. In April 1967, Britain granted Swaziland internal self-government, and promised independence not later than 1969.

The Imbokodvo won elections held in April 1967, and Sobhuza II became king of Swaziland. Prince Makhosini Diamini, his cousin, became prime minister. In July 1967 the king asked Britain to speed independence, and Britain agreed to grant full independence effective Sept. 6, 1968.

—Hibberd V. B. Kline, Jr.;
Gary A. Weissman

SWEDEN

Official name: Kingdom of Sweden
Area: 173,666 square miles
Population: (1967 est.) 7,869,000
Capital: Stockholm (Pop., 1965 est., urban area, 1,179,340)
Language: Swedish
Religion: Lutheranism
Currency unit: Krona
National holiday: Birthday of the king

Sweden, a kingdom in northern Europe, occupies the eastern half of the Scandinavian peninsula. It is bordered on the north by Norway and Finland; on the east by Finland, the Gulf of Bothnia and the Baltic Sea; on the south by the Baltic Sea; and on the west by the Kattegat and the Skagerrak, arms of the North Sea, and Norway. Gotland and Öland islands in the Baltic are part of Sweden.

THE LAND. Sweden may be divided into two geographic regions—the Norrland, the northern two thirds of the country, and the south. Part of the Norrland lies north of the Arctic Circle. In western Norrland the Kjölen Mountains, the backbone of the Scandinavian peninsula, rise to nearly 7,000 feet. The Northern Plateau occupies the center, and in the east there is a relatively narrow coastal plain. The main rivers of the region drain eastward into the Gulf of Bothnia.

The southern third of Sweden includes the broad, level Central Lowland and the Skåne, a flat plain in the extreme south. These two regions are separated by a rough upland zone, the Småland plateau, which has many rivers and includes Sweden's largest lakes, Vänern and Vättern.

Each region has a distinct climate. The Norrland is subarctic, with long, cold winters and short, cool summers. The severity of the climate increases to the north and in the higher elevations. Southern Sweden has much milder winters and slightly warmer, although still cool, summers. The country as a whole is rather dry, receiving only about 20 inches of rainfall a year, most of it concentrated in the south.

THE PEOPLE. The Swedish people are ethnically and culturally homogeneous. Swedish is the universal language, and the dominant religion is Lutheranism. There are small minorities of Lapps and Finns in the north.

Although Sweden is one of Europe's largest countries in area, its population density—44 persons per square mile in 1965—is one of Europe's lowest. With one of the lowest rates of increase in the world, 0.6 percent a year between 1958 and 1965, the population is growing very slowly. Although fairly large numbers of im-

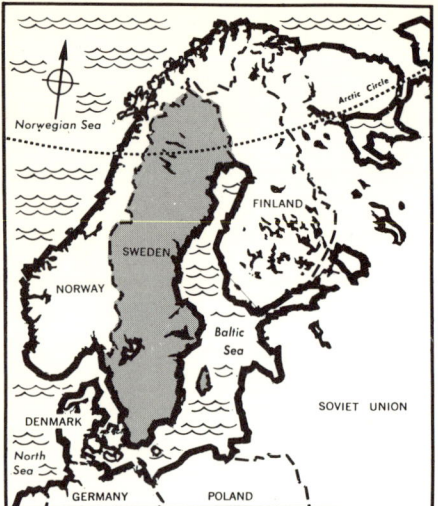

migrants from the Baltic states arrived in Sweden after World War II, the net gains from migration are negligible.

Most Swedes live in the southern third of the country, especially in the central lowland and the Skåne. The Småland plateau and the Baltic Coast are rather thinly populated, and the northern interior is sparsely settled. Sweden's major cities include Stockholm, the capital, on the southeast coast; Göteborg, on the southwest coast; and Malmö, at the southern tip of Sweden.

ECONOMY. Sweden has a highly industrialized economy based upon rich natural resources. All of Norrland and much of the south are heavily forested, and the dense timber stands make Sweden's forestry output one of Europe's largest. Sweden's many swift rivers and streams are harnessed for electricity, and electrical production increased steadily during the 1950s and 1960s, reaching a total of 50,640 million kilowatt hours in 1966.

Sweden's most important mineral resources are its exceptionally large deposits of high quality iron ore. There are also modest reserves of lead, zinc, manganese, tungsten, sulfur, copper, gold, silver, and uranium.

Agriculture. Due to poor climate, poor soil, and rough topography, only about 7 percent of the land can be cultivated, most of it in the south, and agriculture employs only about 14 percent of the labor force. Nevertheless, efficient farming techniques produce high yields per acre.

Dairying is the main agricultural activity, and dairy products account for about half of farm revenue. Oats, wheat, rye, barley, and potatoes are the main crops. Commercial fishing prospers and provides important export products.

Manufacturing and Shipping. Manufacturing is the most important part of the Swedish economy. Industry, which expanded greatly after World War I, is modern and diverse. Although there is some iron and steel production, metal working, and shipbuilding, emphasis has been placed on producing electrical machinery, vehicles, furniture, scientific instruments, paper, porcelain, and glass.

Merchant shipping makes an important contribution to the economy. Sweden's merchant fleet in 1966 totalled 4.4 million gross registered tons. The earnings of the fleet help to offset Sweden's unfavorable balance of trade.

Trade. In 1967 imports cost more than $4,700 million and exports earned over $4,500 million. The leading imports are machinery and transportation equipment, petroleum products, iron and steel products, and foodstuffs. The major exports are machinery, lumber and wood pulp, iron and steel, paper and cardboard, sawed timber, and ships. Most Swedish trade is with West Germany, Britain, the United States, Denmark, Norway, and the Netherlands.

GOVERNMENT. Sweden is a constitutional monarchy, with a king as head of state. Actual executive power is exercised by a prime minister and cabinet responsible to the legislature, the *Riksdag*.

The *Riksdag* consists of two houses with equal powers. One eighth of the Upper Chamber is elected indirectly each year and the entire Lower Chamber is elected directly to a normal term of four years. Under a planned constitutional reform, the *Riksdag* is to become a unicameral body by 1971.

Sweden is a member of the United Nations and the Nordic Council, an association of Scandinavian states.

HISTORY. In about 1000 BC Germanic peoples related to modern-day Swedes appeared in the land. The settlers remained divided into numerous small bands and kingdoms until about 600 AD, when two large tribal groups became dominant—the Goths, on the shores of Lake Vättern, and the Svear, around Lake Mälaren, near Stockholm.

As other Scandinavian Vikings, or adventurers, sailed westward between 800 and 1050, Sweden's Vikings thrust eastward along European river systems. In the 1100s they established colonies on the eastern shore of the Baltic and governed territory between the Baltic and the Black Sea.

Although the kingdoms of Gothia and Svealand were united in the early 800s, competition for power continued between the Goths and the Svear. Nevertheless, by the end of the 1100s a unified Swedish state had emerged in which Svear, or Swedish, influence tended to prevail.

Christianity spread to Sweden in the 800s, and by 1000 the Church was a powerful influence. During the 1100s Christianity was an important part of the culture the Swedes carried to the Finnish peoples of the territories they conquered.

The 1200s and early 1300s were turbulent, as a newly formed land-owning aristocracy challenged the political and economic dominance of a powerful middle class of townsmen and merchants. Contacts with the German merchants of the Hanseatic League introduced strong German influence into Sweden in the 1300s, and in 1363, a member of the German family of Mecklenburg took the Swedish throne.

Kalmar Union. When opposition to the king arose, the nobility in 1388 called on Margaret, Queen of Denmark and Norway, to intervene. She became Queen of Sweden, and laid the basis for the Kalmar Union (1397–1483), which united the three kingdoms. The union was dominated by Denmark, and throughout the 1400s Sweden remained a restless partner.

Both the peasants and the nobility rebelled against the Danish rulers in the 1400s and Sweden gradually regained its autonomy. In 1520 Denmark, trying to reassert its supremacy, invaded Sweden and killed Swedish nationalist leaders. This sparked a nationalist revolt led by Gustavus Vasa, a young nobleman.

Vasa Kings. Sweden succeeded in breaking away from the Kalmar Union, and in 1523 Gustavus became the first king of the House of Vasa. He had the strong support of the merchants and townsmen, and one of his first acts was to end the German Hanseatic League's monopoly of trade in the Baltic area. During his rule, too, the Reformation came to Sweden, and by the mid-1500s Lutheranism was the dominant religion.

Under generally able kings of the house of Vasa, Sweden developed a prosperous economy, and a position of prestige and power in the world. In 1630 the intervention of King Gustavus II Adolphus on the side of Protestantism in the religious-political conflict of the Thirty Years' War was decisive in making Protestantism dominant in northern Europe and in bringing the fighting to an end.

Sweden spent most of the rest of the 1600s and the early 1700s in wars of conquest against Poland, Russia, and Denmark. Sweden's greatest soldier-king, Charles XII, died in 1718, and Russia soon won from Sweden most of the territory conquered from Poland and Denmark in the preceding century.

The country returned briefly to constitutional government, but absolutism was restored in 1772 under Gustavus III, who feared that Sweden would come totally under the control of Prussia. At first he ruled as an "enlightened despot," introducing progressive and liberal measures, but in the 1780s his rule grew more repressive.

Gustavus invaded Russian Finland in an unsuccessful attempt to regain dominance in the Baltic. However, he succeeded in making Sweden dominant in Scandinavia by defeating the Danes and briefly uniting Denmark and Sweden before his assassination in 1792.

Turmoil followed the death of Gustavus. His successor, Gustavus IV, lost Sweden's Finnish provinces in still another war with Russia in 1808, and he was forced by the dissatisfied nobility to abdicate in 1809 in favor of Charles XIII. In 1809 a new constitution was adopted giving great power to the aristocracy.

Reforms and Growth. In 1812 Sweden joined the coalition against Napoleonic France, and the end of the Napoleonic era brought major territorial changes. In 1814 Sweden acquired control of Norway from Denmark and the two states were joined in a personal union under the Swedish king. A change of dynasty also came about. In 1818 Jean Baptiste Bernadotte, on of Napoleon's marshals, who had been

SWEDISH CASTLE, dating from the 100s.

chosen crown prince in 1810 in an effort to prevent Napoleon from conquering the country by force, succeeded to the throne as Charles XIV John.

Bernadotte's tendency toward arbitrary rule stimulated liberal reform movements. Under his successor, Oscar I, the Liberals made some headway toward universal education and the limitation of royal power. Under Oscar's successor, Charles XV, they achieved electoral reforms and finally, in 1864, a Liberal constitution establishing parliamentary government.

During the later 1800s Sweden underwent rapid industrialization, especially after 1872, when Oscar II came to the throne and initiated programs that made Sweden a commercial and industrial state. The social upheaval that accompanied rapid industrialization resulted in progressive social welfare and suffrage legislation, the growth of trade unionism, and the development of the cooperative movement.

Prosperity and political reform affected Norway, too, and by the 1890s Norwegian nationalism was a major force. In 1905, in a dispute over consular service, Norway proclaimed its independence, which Sweden accepted late in the year.

Modern Sweden. Political and social progress continued in the 1900s. Under Gustavus V, who came to the throne in 1907, universal suffrage and a system of proportional representation were introduced. In 1914 Sweden's Socialist Party won about one-third of the seats in the lower house of the parliament, and the pace of social legislation accelerated.

Sweden managed to stay neutral in World War I and suffered little from it. During the 1920s and 1930s under continuing Socialist direction, prosperity continued. Sweden successfully combatted the world economic depression of the 1930s by heavily involving the government in the economy and introducing unemployment insurance legislation.

When Adolf Hitler's Nazi party came to power in Germany in the 1930s, Sweden armed itself but maintained its neutrality. Its neutrality was severely tested in 1939, when Finland was invaded by the Soviet Union, and later in 1940, during World War II, when Denmark and Norway were attacked and occupied by German forces. Sweden was forced to make some concessions to Germany, but it also gave asylum to refugees.

After the war Sweden's economy continued to expand and its standard of living rose to one of the highest levels in Europe. Prosperity and a successful combination of socialism and individualism combined to produce a stable society that was at the same time dynamic and liberal.

Sweden participated actively in the international organizations of the postwar world and used its historic position of neutrality to work for international peace. Swedish troops served with UN peacekeeping forces throughout the world, and a Swede, Dag Hammarskjöld, served as Secretary General of the UN from 1953 until 1961, when he was killed while on a peacekeeping mission to the Congo (Kinshasa).

SWITZERLAND

Official name: Swiss Confederation
Population: (1966 est.) 5,999,000
Area: 15,941 square miles
Capital: Bern (Pop., 1965 est. urban area, 247,300)
Language: French, German, Italian, Romansh
Religion: Protestantism, Roman Catholicism
Currency unit: Franc
National holiday: Anniversary of the founding of the Swiss Confederation, August 1

Switzerland, a small, landlocked country in western Europe, is bounded on the north by West Germany, on the east by Austria and Liechtenstein, on the south by Italy, and on the west by France.

The Swiss have achieved a remarkable internal cohesiveness in spite of a rugged physical environment, a long history of decentralized government, and considerable cultural and linguistic diversity.

THE LAND. Switzerland has three major physical regions: the Jura Mountains in the northwest, the central Swiss Plateau, and the Alps, which cover the southern three-fifths of the country.

Switzerland has many lakes, of which Lake Geneva is the largest. The principal rivers are the Rhine and the Rhône, which have their headwaters high in the Swiss Alps only a few miles from one another.

Switzerland's climate is humid, with mild to cool summers and mostly cold winters. Winters increase in severity with altitude, and the more rugged parts of the Alps are very cold and snowy. In the south and along Lake Geneva the climate is much milder.

THE PEOPLE. The Swiss are descended from several different ethnic groups. Rhaetic and Celtic tribes who lived in Switzerland in Roman times were overwhelmed by the Germanic Alemanni and Burgundians in the 400s. Roman culture and the Latin language remained strongest in the south. These ethnic differences have remained and are expressed linguistically.

Switzerland has four official languages—French, German, Italian, and Romansh—and most Swiss have at least a working knowledge of more than one language. According to the 1960 census, German is the principal language of 69.3 percent of the population, French of 18.9 percent, and Italian of 9.5 percent. About 60,000 Swiss concentrated in the southeastern canton of Graubünden speak Romansh, a language derived from Latin.

Slightly more than half of the population is Protestant, and slightly less than half is Roman Catholic. Protestants predominate in the cities and Roman Catholics in the rural areas.

The annual natural rate of population growth between 1958 and 1965 was about 1.9 percent, almost exactly the European average. But substantial immigration gave Switzerland a net annual population growth rate of 2.1 percent, the highest in Western Europe. The highest population density is found on the Swiss Plateau, in an east-west band from Zurich to Geneva, and in the Rhine corridor.

Switzerland in 1966 had six cities with urban area populations of more than 100,000. These included Zurich, 651,600; Basel, 345,300; Geneva, 285,200; Bern, 247,300; Lausanne, 202,100; and Lucerne, 140,400.

ECONOMY. Switzerland has few natural resources, and agriculture is limited by the rugged terrain. But the Swiss have developed a prosperous economy based on the manufacture of high quality, low bulk goods that involve a high degree of skilled workmanship, such as watches and clocks. These goods enjoy an excellent reputation and have a steady market abroad.

The economy has also been aided by the country's political stability and policy of strict neutrality, which have made it a great international banking and insurance center. Switzerland also derives large revenues from international transit traffic, mainly between West Germany and Italy, and from tourism.

Natural Resources. Switzerland has no important mineral deposits other than salt and stone. But the country's rivers provide an excellent source of hydroelectric power, which the Swiss have developed to compensate for the lack of fuels. In 1965 Switzerland had an installed hydroelectric capacity of 8.1 million kilowatts.

Agriculture. Agriculture employs about 11 percent of the labor force. It is efficient but production does not meet domestic requirements.

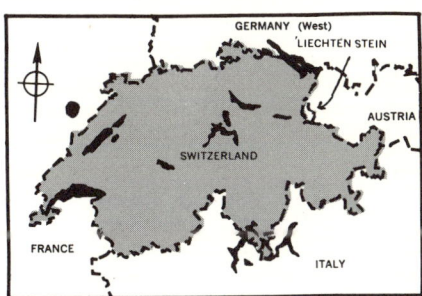

AROSA, SWITZERLAND. The historic church of Arosa is more than 500 years old.

The raising of livestock, particularly dairy cattle, is the most important agricultural activity. The major crops are wheat and potatoes, which are grown in the central plateau.

Industry. Swiss industry must import a large part of its raw materials and most of its products are exported. The most important industries produce textiles, chemicals, dyestuffs, inks, pharmaceuticals, clocks and watches, and precision machinery. Printing is also important.

Trade. In 1967 Swiss exports earned $3,502 million and imports cost $4,118 million. The country's chief exports are watches and clocks, medicines and pharmaceuticals, chemicals, dyestuffs, textiles, and machinery. Major imports include foodstuffs, machinery, iron and steel, motor vehicles, raw fibers, and petroleum.

Switzerland conducts the bulk of its trade with West Germany, France, Italy, the United States, and Britain.

GOVERNMENT. Switzerland is a federal republic of 22 cantons, which are roughly equivalent to provinces or states. The executive branch of government consists of the Federal Council, composed of seven ministers who head various administrative departments.

The head of state is the president, who is elected to a one-year term from among the members of the Federal Council by the legislature. The president has comparatively little power and cannot serve consecutive terms.

Legislative power is vested in the Coucil of States and the National Council. The Council of States has 44 members, two from each canton, and their terms of membership and means of election are determined by each canton. The National Council has 200 members directly elected to four-year terms. Women have the right to vote in only four cantons, where they may participate in local elections.

Neutral Switzerland is not a member of the United Nations, but it does cooperate with a number of UN agencies, many of which have their headquarters in Geneva.

The principality of Liechtenstein, on the Austrian-Swiss border, is closely associated with Switzerland. It has been united with Switzerland in a customs union since 1924. The tiny country uses Swiss currency and the Swiss postal administration, and its transportation system is integrated into Switzerland's. The Swiss also represent Liechtenstein abroad.

HISTORY. The earliest recorded inhabitants of present-day Switzerland were a number of Celtic tribes, among them the Helvetii, who had at an earlier time probably subjected the Rhaeti, who also lived in the area. In the first century BC these tribes were defeated by the Romans under Julius Caesar, and Switzerland became Roman territory.

During the 400s AD, when Roman power began to decline, the area was conquered by the Alamanni, the Burgundians, and Franks. By the early 800s Switzerland had become part of Charlemagne's empire, although it was divided under Charlemagne's successors.

Independence. During the 1200s the area around Lake Lucerne came under the rule of the Swabian Hapsburg family. In 1921 the Swiss communities, or cantons, of Schwyz, Uri, and Unterwalden entered into a defensive league, or confederation, against the Hapsburgs, whose rule was oppressive. The Hapsburgs were decisively defeated in 1315 at the battle of Morgarten, and the cantons gained their independence.

By 1513 the confederation had expanded to include 13 cantons, and Switzerland became an important military power. Swiss expansionism, however, was permanently checked by Francis I of France, who won a crushing victory over the Swiss at Marignano in 1515.

In the 1500s the Reformation, led by Ulrich Zwingli in Zurich and John Calvin in Geneva, provoked civil war between Roman Catholic and Protestant cantons and seriously weakened the league. Switzerland remained neutral throughout the Thirty Years War, but was able to gain international recognition of its independence and neutrality in 1648 at the Peace of Westphalia, which ended the conflict.

For 100 years following the Peace of Westphalia, Switzerland was in a decline, which came to an end in the mid-1700s with the growth of industry and an intellectual renaissance. In 1798, during the French Revolutionary Wars, the confederation was replaced by the French-sponsored Helvetic Republic, which had a strong central government and abolished the sovereignty of the cantons.

Neutrality. In 1815 the Congress of Vienna, which redrew the map of Europe after Napoleon's defeat, reaffirmed Switzerland's independence and perpetual neutrality. It also drew up a federal plan for the cantons that granted them a large degree of individual autonomy. In 1848 a new constitution was adopted which strengthened the central government. It was revised in 1874 to strengthen central authority even further.

In the 1800s and 1900s Switzerland's neutrality led many international organizations to choose the country as the site of their headquarters. The country stayed neutral, although heavily armed, throughout both world wars.

Contemporary Switzerland. In 1946, to maintain is neutrality, Switzerland decided not to join the United Nations, although it participates in the work of some of the organizations specialized agencies. Many international conferences are held in Switzerland, and the Atomic Test-Ban Treaty of 1963 was agreed upon at Geneva.

Postwar prosperity, especially in the 1950s and 1960s, led to an influx of foreign workers into labor-short Switzerland. By the mid-1960s the number of foreign workers exceeded 14 percent of the total population.

Reaction against the presence of so many foreign workers, strongest in the financial and industrial center of Zurich, led the Swiss government in 1967 to announce a referendum to determine whether or not to limit constitutionally the number of foreign workers to a smaller percentage of the total population.

—Sergio Barzanti

SYRIA

Official name: Syrian Arab Republic
Area: 71,498 square miles
Population: (1966 est.) 5,400,000
Capital: Damascus (Pop., 1964 est., 562,907)
Language: Arabic
Religion: Islam
Currency unit: Pound
National holiday: Independence day, April 17

The Syrian Arab Republic, a Middle Eastern state, is bounded by Turkey on the north, Iraq on the east, Jordan on the south, and Lebanon, Israel, and the Mediterranean Sea on the west. The present country of Syria was created after World War I out of a larger, historical region which included present-day Jordan, Lebanon, and Israel.

THE LAND. A narrow, fertile plain follows Syria's Mediterranean coast. To its east the rugged Alawite and the Anti-Lebanon mountains rise to over 9,000 feet on the northwestern border.

The Orontes River waters a fertile valley east of the mountains, and in northern and northeastern Syria are the rolling plains and rich valley of the Euphrates River. In central Syria, arid, rolling hills give way to the barren Syrian Desert, which occupies the southeastern corner of the country.

Syria's coastal climate is mild and rather moist, with about 30 inches of rainfall each year along the coast. Central and eastern Syria are quite dry, with extremely hot summers and cold winters.

THE PEOPLE. Most Syrians are Muslim Arabs, but the population also includes Kurds, Druze, and Armenians. Population is densest in the temperate, fertile western part of the country. Damascus, the capital and largest city, lies in the southwest near the Lebanese border.

ECONOMY. The Syrian economy is based on agriculture. The country has few natural resources other than the fertile soil of its coastal areas and river valleys. Asphalt and gypsum are mined, and oil deposits do exist, but by the mid-1960s oil production was only in the early stages.

Agriculture. Farming is the occupation of most Syrians, and agriculture contributed over one-third of the gross domestic product in the mid-1960s. About one-third of the country's land is cultivated, and one-third is suitable for pasturage. Most farmland is in the west and north, and much of it requires irrigation. A land redistribution program in the 1950s and 1960s created many small farms from large estates.

The leading farm crops are cotton, wheat, and barley. Corn and other grains, dates, olives, sugar beets, and tobacco are also raised, and wool and silk are important commodities. Large herds of goats and sheep are grazed on the central plains.

Industry. The processing of agricultural products is Syria's most important industry. Textiles, leather products, dried fruits, and wines are the leading manufactures. Gypsum and asphalt are processed. Many industrial, commercial, and financial enterprises were nationalized in the 1960s.

Trade. International trade is important in the Syrian economy, and the country's chief port, Latakia, is a major Middle Eastern commercial center. Syria collects fees and taxes on oil from Iraq carried to the Mediterranean by pipeline across Syria. In 1967 exports earned $155 million and imports cost $264 million. Cotton, grains, and other farm products are the chief exports, and machinery, industrial raw materials, clothing, and other consumer items are imported.

Most trading activity is controlled by the government. Lebanon, France, the Soviet Union, the United States, and West Germany are Syria's leading trading partners.

GOVERNMENT. Syria has a republican form of government that is dominated by the military. Traditionally there is an appointed president, who serves as head of state, and a prime minister, who functions as chief executive.

Syria is a member of the United Nations and the Arab League.

HISTORY. The modern nation of Syria has roots in the ancient region of Syria, which was the site of some of the world's earliest civilizations. Syria was the center of the prosperous trade routes used by the great nations of the ancient world.

Located between the Tigris-Euphrates Valley and the Nile Valley, it was often the object of rivalry between the powerful nations that grew up in both valleys. Trade and war between the civilizations to the north and south of Syria brought many different peoples and cultures to the area.

Between 2000 BC and 333 BC, the Akkadians, the Sumerians, the Amorites, the Hittites, the Egyptians, the Assyrians, and the Persians succes-

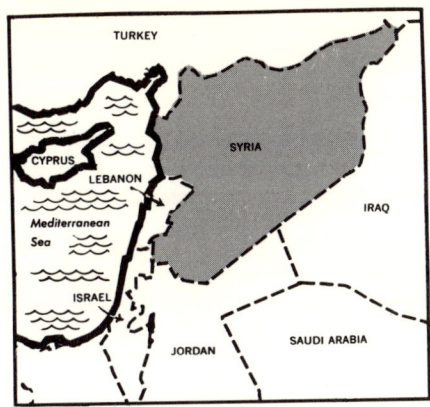

sively occupied the Syrian region. During that time three groups, the Hebrews, the Aramaeans, and the Canaanites, made permanent settlements in the land.

In 333 BC Alexander the Great conquered Syria from the Persian empire. After his death, Syria went to one of his generals, Seleucus, who founded the Seleucid dynasty that ruled Syria (including modern Israel, Lebanon, and Jordan) until the Romans conquered the region in 64 BC.

Syria was one of the first Roman provinces to accept Christianity, in the first century AD, and Syria's language, Aramaic, was the language of the early Christians, most of whom lived within what was then western Syria.

In the 630s Muslim Arab armies conquered the region. Islam replaced Christianity, Arabic replaced Aramaic, and Syria became an Arab country. The city of Damascus became the center of a great Arab empire and Syria's prosperity increased.

As the Arab empire weakened, however, Syria entered a decline. Ruled by outsiders, it suffered neglect. The Christian crusades against the Muslim Middle East in the 1000s, 1100s, and 1200s did great damage to Syria and its economy, and the invasions of Mongols and Tatars from the north and east in the 1200s and 1300s left Syria weak and impoverished.

Ottoman Rule. In 1516 the Ottoman Turks conquered Syria and made it part of their empire. Under the Ottoman Turks Syria remained peaceful, but neglect and poor government caused the economy and cultural life to decline further, especially in the 1700s, when the disintegration of the empire brought anarchy to Syria.

The opening of the Suez Canal in 1869 also hurt the country by taking away much of the trade between the Mediterranean and the Indian Ocean that had previously passed through Syria. Some economic improvements were made in the later 1800s, but the country remained largely undeveloped.

Nationalism. In the late 1800s Syria began to feel the impact of the spirit of nationalism that had been growing in Europe. Syria became a center for an Arab cultural revival and for Arab nationalism, and Syrians demanded self-government.

When the Ottoman Empire entered World War I on the side of Germany, Syria cooperated with the Allies. In return, Britain supported Syrian Arab nationalism and aided a 1916 Arab uprising against the Ottoman government.

At the end of the war in 1918 French troops tried to occupy the country, but Faysal ibn-Husayn, a leader of the nationalist rebellion, proclaimed Syria's sovereignty. A Syrian National Congress was called, and in 1920 Faysal was proclaimed king. France, which had received a League of Nations mandate over Syria, deposed Faysal later in 1920 and set up its own government.

Syrian discontent with French rule led in 1925 to a two-year rebellion, which the French put down harshly. Discontent grew. In 1930 the French proposed a constitution that would have made the country a republic but would not have granted complete independence. The Syrians rejected it.

Independence. In World War II the Vichy French government of Syria was driven out in 1941 by British and Free French forces. Syria was formally declared an independent republic, although British and French troops did not withdraw until after the war, in 1946.

In 1943 Shukri al-Kuwatly was elected the first president of the republic, and in 1945 Syria entered the United Nations and joined other Arab states in forming the Arab League.

Turmoil marked the first two decades of the republic, and the military became the dominant factor in political life. In 1949 an army officer, Husni al-Zaim, ousted the civilian government. More coups followed, and from 1949 to 1954 the government was dominated by Col. Adib Shishakly, who ruled behind the official presidency of Hashim al-Atasi. In 1954 Shishakly was forced into exile, and the next year Kuwatly again became president.

In 1958 Syria merged with Egypt to form the United Arab Republic (U.A.R.), with Egypt's Gamal Abdel Nasser as president. In 1961 the Cairo government imposed an unpopular socialist program on the Syrian part of the U.A.R., and Syria withdrew from the union.

Contemporary Syria. Political instability increased. In March 1963 a military coup overthrew the government and a new cabinet was appointed. The new cabinet was dominated by Baathists, members of the pan-Arab Baath party, which advocated a strongly socialist and pan-Arab program. In 1966 a new military coup brought Nureddin al-Atassi to power.

Syria's frequent changes of government in the 1950s and 1960s hampered the country's economic development, and also affected its foreign relations. Most of the Baathist governments tended to be anti-Western. Syria's only consistent foreign policy, however, one shared with its Arab neighbors, was hostility toward the state of Israel.

In June 1967 Arab-Israeli warfare broke out anew, and Syrian forces were beaten by Israeli troops. Israel occupied the southwestern tip of Syria, along the Israeli border, including the heights overlooking the Sea of Galilee.
—Charles Issawi; Alexander Melamid

TANZANIA

Official name: United Republic of Tanzania
Area: 362,820 square miles
Population: (1966 est.) 11,833,000
Capital: Dar es Salaam (Pop., 1965 est., 190,200)
Language: Swahili, Arabic, English
Religion: Traditional religions, Islam, Christianity
Currency unit: Shilling
National holiday: Union day, April 26

Tanzania, a republic in eastern Africa, was formed in 1964 by the merger of the mainland nation of Tanganyika and the offshore island nation of Zanzibar. Britain had granted independence to Tanganyika in 1961 and to Zanzibar in 1963.

Mainland Tanzania is bordered on the north by Uganda and Kenya; on the east by the Indian Ocean; on the south by Mozambique, Malawi, and Zambia; and on the west by the Congo (Kinshasa), Burundi, and Rwanda. The Indian Ocean islands of Zanzibar and Pemba, the former republic of Zanzibar, lie some 20 miles east of the mainland.

THE LAND. Tanganyika is by far the larger part of the republic, with an area of some 361,800 square miles. Zanzibar, which includes Zanzibar and Pemba islands, has an area of 1,020 square miles.

Tanganyika is occupied mainly by a plateau with an elevation of between 2,000 and 4,000 feet above sea level. Much of the plateau surface is semi-arid. There are mountain masses in the northeast and southwest.

The highest point, located near the border with Kenya, is Mt. Kilimanjaro, which reaches an elevation of about 19,340 feet. There is an extensive lowland in the north, which is partly occupied by Lake Victoria. A narrow plain extends along most of the coast.

The coastal plain is hot and humid, and the plateau is hot and drier. The Rufiji River flows through central Tanganyika.

Zanzibar and Pemba are low-lying coral islands with many inlets. There are mangrove swamps on the islands. The islands' temperatures are high from December to March and lower between June and October. Heavy rains fall in April and May, and there are light rains in November and December.

THE PEOPLE. Over 96 percent of Tanzania's population lives on the mainland, and the country's largest cities, Dar es Salaam and Mwanza, are in Tanganyika. Tanganyika's people include members of some 120 tribes, most of which are Bantu-speaking. The largest tribe is the Sukuma. There are also groups of Arabs, Europeans, and people of Indian and Pakistani origin.

Zanzibar and Pemba also have many different peoples, including Shirazis, descendants of ancient Persians, Africans from the mainland, Arabs, Asians, and people from the Comoro Islands.

ECONOMY. The economy of Tanzania is based on agriculture. The basic food crops are rice, corn, and sorghum.

CATTLE SALE held in northern Tanzania.

In Tanganyika, cotton, coffee, and sisal, a fiber used in rope, are the most important commercial crops. Tanganyika is one of the most significant producers of sisal in the world, and in 1964, production totaled 241,600 metric tons.

Sisal and coffee are generally grown on mountain slopes, and cotton is produced mainly in the lowlands near Lake Victoria. Most of the plantations are owned by Europeans, but Africans also grow coffee on small plots. Cattle are raised in most parts of the mainland.

Large quantities of cloves are grown on plantations in Zanzibar and Pemba. Coconuts are also an important commercial crop. Fishing is significant in the islands' economy.

Industry in Tanzania consists mainly of food processing. Mineral resources are considerable on the mainland, but they are widely distributed and transportation costs are high. Diamonds are mined, and there are also deposits of lead, gold, and iron ore.

In 1964 Tanzania instituted a Five Year Plan for Economic and Social Development to expand industry and develop land for agriculture. In 1967

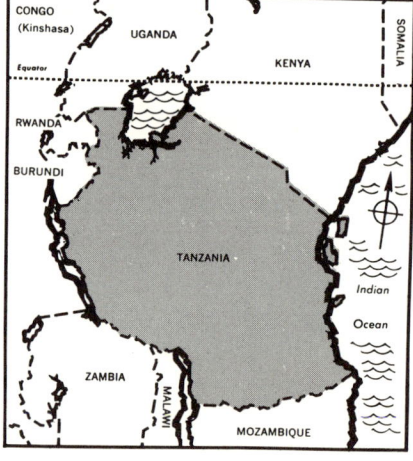

the government nationalized banks and much of the country's industry.

In 1966 imports cost $178 million and exports earned $235 million. The major imports are petroleum products, textiles, and machinery. The major exports are sisal, coffee, cotton, and cloves. Most trade is conducted with Britain, Hong Kong, West Germany, Japan, and India.

GOVERNMENT. Tanzania has a presidential system of government. Executive power is vested in a president, who is popularly elected to a five-year term. The president is assisted by two vice presidents. The First Vice President is responsible for the administration of Zanzibar, and the Second Vice President assists in the administration of Tanganyika.

Legislative power is held by a 204-member National Assembly, with 107 members popularly elected and 77 appointed by the president. There are also three commissioners from districts in Zanzibar, and 17 commissioners from districts in Tanganyika.

Tanzania is a member of the United Nations, the Organization of African Unity (OAU), and the Commonwealth of Nations.

HISTORY. The 1964 union of Tanganyika and Zanzibar merged the histories of two separate regions in eastern Africa.

Zanzibar. Arabs began colonizing Zanzibar in the 700s. Portuguese arrived in the late 1500s and brought the area under Portuguese rule. Arabs from Oman broke Portugal's control of the islands in about 1700, and established a sultanate. The Arabs developed a prosperous slave market and they encouraged clove plantations.

In the 1800s Britain gained control of the islands and ended the slave trade. In 1890 Britain formally established a protectorate over Zanzibar. The sultan remained as nominal ruler, however, and until 1956 the islands were ruled primarily by Arabs under British supervision.

Two political parties were formed in the 1950s—the Zanzibar Nationalist Party (ZNP), representing the Arabs, and the Afro-Shirazi Party (ASP), representing mainly the African population and some Shirazi. In 1957 the ASP split, and the Zanzibar and Pemba Peoples' Party (ZPPP) was formed.

On June 24, 1963, Zanzibar became self-governing, and elections were held in July. Although the African-dominated ASP won the largest number of the votes, the government was controlled by a coalition of the ZNP and ZPPP.

Zanzibar received its independence on Dec. 9, 1963, and Sheikh Muhammad Shamte became prime minister of the coalition government. The opposition, consisting largely of Africans, staged a bloody coup against Arab rule on Jan. 12, 1964. The Sultan was overthrown and a republic proclaimed. Sheikh Adeid Amani Karume, leader of the ASP, became president.

Tanganyika. In the 700s Arabs also established settlements in the coastal region of Tanganyika. The Portuguese settled in the region in the late 1400s. The Arabs developed a prosperous slave trade in the interior, which flourished until the 1800s, when it was checked by Christian missionaries led by David Livingstone.

Germany began colonizing the area in 1884, and in 1890 the region became part of German East Africa. After World War I Tanganyika became a British mandate under the League of Nations, and in 1946 it became a UN trust territory. Nationalism grew in the 1950s, and in 1954 Julius Nyerere formed a nationalist political party, the Tanganyika African National Union (TANU). TANU candidates were victorious in the first elections for a legislative council held in 1958.

In 1959 Britain took steps to establish internal self-government for Tanganyika, and Neyerere was named Chief Minister. In May 1961 Tanganyika became autonomous and Nyerere became prime minister. Tanganyika became an independent member of the Commonwealth of Nations on Dec. 9, 1961, and a republic one year later with Nyerere as president.

United Republic. A union of Tanganyika and Zanzibar was announced on Apr. 26, 1964, and the two countries took the name Tanzania. Nyerere became the first president of the new nation and Karume became First Vice President.

In 1967 Nyerere announced the government's intention of placing the country's means of production under the control of the workers and farmers, and many businesses were nationalized.

—Hibberd V. B. Kline, Jr.; Vera L. Zolberg

THAILAND

Official name: Kingdom of Thailand
Area: 198,450 square miles
Population: (1967 est.) 32,680,000
Capital: Bangkok (Pop., 1963 est., urban area, 1,608,305)
Language: Thai
Religion: Buddhism
Currency unit: Baht
National holiday: King's birthday

Thailand, called Siam until 1939, is a kingdom in Southeast Asia. It is bounded on the north by Burma and Laos, on the east by Laos and Cambodia, on the south by the Gulf of Siam and Malaysia, and on the west by the Andaman Sea and Burma.

THE LAND. Thailand has several distinct land regions. The north-south trending Bilauktaung mountain range follows the border with Burma. It extends southward across the Kra Isthmus into peninsular Thailand, forming the backbone of the Malay Peninsula.

In northwestern Thailand, a deeply dissected upland area with an elevation of 600 to 3,000 feet above sea level, lies between the Salween and the Mekong river basins. This rugged region forms an obstacle to communications. It contains the major tributaries of the Mae Nam Chao Phraya, the principal river system of the country.

The basin of the Chao Phraya, which contains the fertile Bangkok Plain, is the core region of Thailand. The basin has an inverted U-shaped outline, with the Dawna and the Bilauktaung mountain ranges on the west, the uplands of the hilly Shan Plateau on the north, and the Phetchabun Mountains on the east.

The Phetchabun Mountains form the western margin of the Khorat Plateau, a rolling basin with elevations generally below 700 feet. Rising in the Khorat Plateau is the Mun River, the chief Thai tributary of the Mekong River. The Dang Raek scarp establishes the southern boundary of the Khorat Plateau, and between this scarp and the Cardamon Mountains on the Gulf of Siam coast, a narrow lowland connects the Tonle Sap basin of Cambodia with the delta of the Chao Phraya.

Climate. Thailand lies within the monsoon area of Southeast Asia, but due to the "rain shadow" effect of the surrounding mountains, annual precipitation is limited in the lowlands.

Much of the delta receives less than 60 inches of rain a year and some areas close to the base of the mountains receive less than 40 inches. Moreover, there is considerable variability in rainfall from year to year. The peninsular portion of the country is wetter, and receives rain during both the southwest and northeast monsoons. The dry season is short and yearly variations small.

Thailand is in the tropical zone, and temperatures are generally above 50°F in the lowlands, although it is slightly cooler at higher elevations. The coolest months are December and January, and the hottest period is February through May.

THE PEOPLE. Almost all of Thailand's people are Thai, related to the people of Laos and eastern Burma. They speak Thai, and most are Buddhists. The largest minority group is Chinese.

Compared with most Southeast Asian countries, Thailand, with a population density of about 175 people per square mile in 1967, is rather thinly settled. Its population is growing at a rapid rate, however, averaging 3 percent a year between 1958 and 1965.

Population is concentrated in the river valleys, especially that of the Chao Phraya. Bangkok (Krung Thep), the capital and largest city, is located near the mouth of the Chao Phraya.

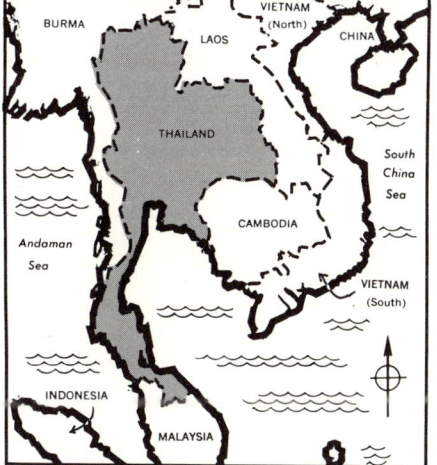

ECONOMY. Thailand is a relatively prosperous country. Agriculture is the basis of economic life, but industry increased in the 1950s and 1960s based largely on exploitation of Thailand's rich natural resources.

One of Thailand's most valuable resources is timber. More than half of the country is covered by forests. Tropical evergreen rainforests in the mountains contain a great variety of hardwoods and dense monsoon forests contain teak, of which Thailand is one of the world's leading producers. There is an abundance of fish in the waters off Thailand's long coast and in its rivers.

The country also has a rich variety of minerals. Tin is the most important, and in 1966 Thailand was the world's third greatest producer of tin, with over 17,000 metric tons. Other minerals include tungsten, manganese, and gold, and there are precious and semiprecious gems.

Thailand has a considerable waterpower potential, but it lacks well developed supplies of fuel, although there are deposits of lignite, bituminous coal, and petroleum. Wood and charcoal from the forests remained the chief fuels in the mid-1960s.

Agriculture. One of Thailand's richest resources is its soil. Agriculture contributed one-third of the gross domestic product in 1965 and occupied the majority of the work force. Most Thai farms are small and individually owned. In the rich Bangkok rice region, however, farms are larger, and there are a number of estates cultivated by tenant farmers.

Rice is central to Thai prosperity, and in the mid-1960s about 90 percent of the cultivated land was planted in rice. Three-fourths of Thailand's rice area is in the Bangkok plain, where terrain, soil, and moisture are most suitable for paddy rice. Thai rice is of excellent quality, and its price is controlled by the government to make it highly competitive in the world's rice market.

Other agricultural activities include rubber production, both on large estates and on small holdings. Some short-staple cotton is produced on the peninsula in the northern sections of the central plain. Other crops include tobacco, sugarcane, corn, cassava, peanuts, soybeans, coconuts, sesame, castor beans, silk, and peppers.

Industry. Forestry, mining, and related operations are the country's leading nonagricultural activities, and industry is limited. In 1965 it contributed only 15 percent of the gross domestic product. Aside from the processing of natural resources and agricultural products, there is little manufacturing.

The leading industrial establishments include rubber factories, sawmills, textile mills, and cement, glass, and plywood factories. In the early 1960s the country's first large tin-smelting plant began operations.

Government efforts to stimulate industrialization in the 1950s and 1960s received financial and technical aid from abroad, especially from the United States. The development of hydroelectric power resources, which began in the early 1960s with the construction of several huge dams, was expected to spur industrialization.

Trade. Thailand's international trade depends primarily on the country's farms, forests, and mines. In 1966 exports earned $694 million and imports cost $1,166 million. Rice, rubber, tin, and teak are the major exports. Fuels and manufactured goods are the major imports.

The major markets for Thai rice are Malaysia, Indonesia, and Hong Kong. Much of the rubber and tin are exported to Malaysia and Singapore for processing and re-export. Thai imports come chiefly from Japan, the United States, and Britain.

GOVERNMENT. Thailand is a constitutional monarchy with a king as head of state. An appointed prime minister and a cabinet hold executive power. The parliament, which exercised legislative power, was dissolved in 1958, and the constitution was revoked by the ruling military-supported government.

A constituent assembly was appointed in 1959 to draft a new constitution. But in the 1960s the government operated under an interim constitution, which placed great power in the office of prime minister.

Thailand is a member of the United Nations and the Southeast Asia Treaty Organization (SEATO).

HISTORY. The Thai have a long history, and people speaking closely related dialects of the Thai language have been living throughout the hilly region of southern China and northern Southeast Asia since nearly the beginning of recorded history. Modern Thailand has its origins in a state created by small warbands of Thai-speaking people who moved down into the lowlands of the Chao Phraya Valley in the 1200s.

In the late 1200s, under their first important kingdom, Sukhot'ai, the Thai conquered most of the area of present-day Thailand from Mon and Khmer peoples. They accepted the Theravada Buddhism of their Mon subjects, and they adopted the political system of the Khmer rulers whom they displaced.

Between the 1300s and the 1700s, the Thai ruled from a capital located at Ayut'ia, about 75 miles north of modern Bangkok. The Thai state, like others in Southeast Asia at that time, had no real boundaries. The king ruled his palace-city and its surrounding area directly.

The king exercised some control over most of the Chao Phraya plain through semiautonomous noble-officials. If the king was powerful, he exacted tribute from more distant vassals in Malaya, Cambodia, Laos, and northern Thailand. Wars were common and were generally fought to enforce claims to tribute or to capture new subjects rather than to acquire territory.

Chakri Dynasty. In the 1500s the Burmans overran the kingdom and sacked Ayut'ia. The Thai recovered, only to suffer another crushing defeat by Burma in 1767. A powerful Thai revival led to the founding of a strong, new dynasty, the Chakri, in 1782. The Chakri kings established their capital at the port city of Bangkok, and it was from there that Thailand—called Siam by Westerners—faced the might of European imperialism in the 1800s.

A WOMAN SPINS silk into thread, which will then be woven into Thailand's famous silk.

The Chakri kings, unlike their Burman, Vietnamese, and Chinese counterparts, were actively interested in commerce and aware of what was happening in the world outside. In 1855 King Mongkut willingly signed a treaty with the British opening Siam to international trade, and he took the first steps to modernize and westernize the monarchy.

Mongkut's son, Chulalongkorn, ruled from 1868 to 1910. He carefully steered the country toward modernization while avoiding the dangers presented by European imperialists and Siamese reactionaries.

Slowly but steadily Chulalongkorn abolished slavery, replaced the traditional forced labor with money taxes, drawn in part from rapidly rising exports of rice and teak, and reorganized the administration with the help of European advisors. He was obliged to yield control of large vassal areas to the British and French, but at the same time he greatly extended the area effectively ruled by Bangkok.

During Chulalongkorn's reign old Siam was transformed into new Thailand, a recognizably modern nation-state. It was the only country in Southeast Asia not to fall under colonial rule, thanks in part to its position as a buffer state between the British colonial territory in Burma and India and the French colonies in Indochina.

In the early 1900s Siam's prosperity grew as demands for its rubber, tin, and timber increased. The country's progressive social, economic, and educational policies enabled all classes of Thais to share in its prosperity.

Constitutional Monarchy. Chulalongkorn's successors were less able men, and the changes he inaugurated had created a new class of Western-educated administrators and army officers who were increasingly restive under the rule of the absolute monarchy. In 1932 a small group of civilians and officers seized power in a bloodless coup.

The Chakris were reduced to the status of constitutional monarchs. The king was apparently ready to yield what he considered archaic absolute powers, and his willingness contributed to the stability of the constitutional system despite frequent changes of administration.

Following Chulalongkorn's "survival diplomacy," the Thais joined Japan as a passive ally during World War II to avoid invasion and occupation. When Japan's defeat became inevitable, Thailand quietly let it be known that it supported the Allies. After 1945 Thailand was actively pro-Western and in 1954 was a founding member of SEATO, although it also attempted to maintain informal, friendly contacts with Communist China.

Contemporary Thailand. In the decades after the war Thailand concentrated on industrializing and modernizing its economy and on protecting itself from the military conflicts that raged in Southeast Asia. Several coups d'etat did not weaken political stability, and although the governments were more autocratic than democratic they were not oppressive.

The threat of rebellion by Communist-supported guerrillas in the late 1950s led in 1958 to a suspension of the parliament and the constitution. There was a tightening of executive control, and, in the rebellious areas, an increase in military strength and an expansion of social and economic programs.

Thailand permitted U.S. planes participating in the Vietnamese War to use airstrips in Thailand, and in 1967 the Thai announced plans to send combat troops to aid South Vietnamese and U.S. forces in the war.

—M. G. Inaba

TOGO

Official name: Republic of Togo
Area: 21,620 square miles
Population: (1967 est.) 1,724,000
Capital: Lomé (Pop., 1962 est., urban area, 90,000)
Language: French, African languages
Religion: Traditional religions, Christianity
Currency unit: Franc CFA (African Financial Community)
National holiday: Independence day, April 27

Togo, a republic in western Africa, is bordered on the north by Upper Volta; on the east by Dahomey; on the south by the Gulf of Guinea, an arm of the Atlantic Ocean; and on the west by Ghana.

After World War I Togo was divided by Britain and France into separate League of Nations mandates, and after 1946 they were administered as separate UN trust territories. In 1957 the British territory became part of Ghana, and in 1960 the French territory received its independence.

THE LAND. Grasslands occupy most of Togo. There is a sandy coast, behind which are lagoons. Inland from the lagoons is the Terre de Barre, a low, clay plain which rises to a sandy plateau. The Togo Atakora mountains

COUNTRIES OF THE WORLD

cross the center of the country. The Mono and Ogou rivers flow through Togo. The climate is hot and humid.

THE PEOPLE. There are many different ethnic groups in Togo. The largest groups are the Ewe and the Adja-Watyi in the south and the Kabrai-Losso in the north. Lomé, the capital, is Togo's largest city.

ECONOMY. The economy of Togo is based on agriculture. Yams, rice, corn, millet, and sorghum, grown mainly in the interior, are the main food crops. Cacao and coffee are the leading commercial crops. Palm products, such as copra and palm oil, are important, and the peoples near the coast and the lagoons prepare copra and coconut oil. Palm oil, cacao, and coffee are produced in the Terre de Barre region.

Togo has rich phosphate deposits, and in 1965, 974,000 metric tons of phosphate were produced. There is little industry. In 1966 the government instituted a Five-Year Development Plan to promote the growth of agriculture and industry.

In 1966 imports cost $47 million and exports earned $36 million. The main imports are machinery, foodstuffs, textiles, and petroleum products. The major exports are phosphate, coffee, and cacao. Most trade is conducted with France, West Germany, and Japan.

GOVERNMENT. Until January 1967 Togo had a presidential system of government. Executive power was vested in a president, who was popularly elected to a five-year term. Legislative power was held by a 52-member National Assembly, also popularly elected every five years. The legislature was dissolved in 1967 and a new government was established, composed of eight civilians and four military men, headed by a president.

Togo is a member of the United Nations and the Organization of African Unity (OAU).

HISTORY. Between about the 1200s and the 1800s many African tribal kingdoms established their rule over the area of present-day Togo. In the 1400s Portugal developed trade relations with the Ewe. By the mid-1890s Germany had established a protectorate over Togo. After World War I the German protectorate was divided into separate British and French mandates under the League of Nations. In 1946 the mandates became UN trust territories.

Britain administered its trust territory along with the Gold Coast colony. In 1956 British Togoland voted to join the Gold Coast, which became the independent nation of Ghana in 1957.

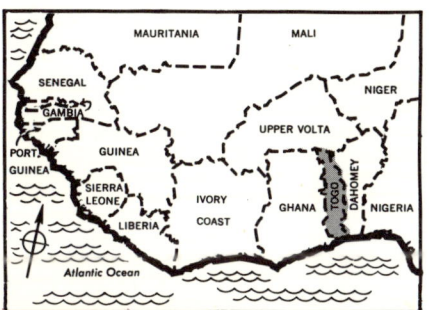

After World War II France established a locally elected territorial assembly in French Togoland. In 1956 French Togoland obtained internal self-government from France, and Nicolas Grunitzky, of the Togolese Progressive Party, became the country's first prime minister. Grunitzky's party lost elections held in 1958, and his brother-in-law, Sylvanus Olympio, leader of the Committee for Togolese Unity party, became prime minister.

Independence. On April 27, 1960 Togo became independent, and Olympio became president. On Jan. 13, 1963 Olympio was assassinated, and in May, Grunitzky was elected president. Grunitzky was ousted in January 1967 after a bloodless coup led by Lt. Col. Etienne Eyadema.

Eyadema suspended the constitution, dissolved the National Assembly, and formed a Committee of National Reconciliation. In April 1967 Eyadema assumed the position of president.

—Hibberd V. B. Kline, Jr.;
Vera L. Zolberg

TRINIDAD AND TOBAGO

Official name: Trinidad and Tobago
Area: 1,980 square miles
Population: (1966 est.) 995,000
Capital: Port-of-Spain (Pop., 1960 est., 93,954)
Language: English
Religion: Roman Catholicism, other Christian, Hinduism, Islam
Currency unit: Dollar
National holiday: Independence day, August 31

Trinidad and Tobago, an independent island country in the West Indies, lies off the eastern coast of South America between the Caribbean Sea and the Atlantic Ocean. Venezuela, on the South American mainland, is only 7 miles from Trinidad.

The country consists of two islands, Trinidad, the second largest island in the West Indies, 1,864 square miles in area, and Tobago, some 20 miles northeast of Trinidad, 116 square miles in area. Some tiny islets lie off the coast.

THE LAND. Trinidad is crossed by three mountain ranges—the Central, Southern, and Northern ranges. The mountains rise to a peak of more than 3,000 feet and are separated by lowlands. Tropical forests cover about one-half of Trinidad. There are many small streams, and the east-central coast is swampy.

Tobago's terrain is rugged. A central core of volcanic hills rises over 1,800 feet and drops sharply to the sea in the northeast. Except for some isolated coastal plains, flat land is limited to the southwestern tip of Tobago.

The climate of the islands is tropical with temperatures averaging 77°F throughout the year. Rainfall ranges from about 120 inches a year on Tobago and in northern Trinidad to about 50 inches a year in southwestern Trinidad.

THE PEOPLE. Most of Trinidad and Tobago's people are of African descent. About one-third of the population is of East Indian origin and 14

percent is mulatto, of mixed European and African origins. There are also people of Chinese, European, and Near Eastern background.

English is the official language, but a dialect combining English with French, Spanish, and other tongues is widely spoken.

About 90 percent of the country's population lives on Trinidad. The population grew at the rapid rate of 3.1 percent between 1958 and 1965.

ECONOMY. Trinidad and Tobago has a moderately prosperous economy based on international trade, tourism, and on the exploitation of its rich natural resources, especially petroleum and asphalt.

Agriculture. Arable land is limited in Trinidad and Tobago, but agriculture employs about one-fifth of the labor force and provides important exports.

Sugarcane is the most important commercial crop and is grown in western Trinidad. Cocoa, second in importance, is raised mainly on Tobago and in the wetter regions of Trinidad. Coffee, citrus fruits, and bananas are also raised for export, and limited quantities of fruits and vegetables are grown for local consumption.

Industry. Industry is of prime importance in the economy, and the processing of petroleum is the leading industrial activity. The major oil producing areas are in Trinidad's Southern Range and off its western coast.

The processing of asphalt extracted from Pitch Lake at La Brea, one of the world's largest sources of natural asphalt, is also important, as is the quarrying of building stone. Other significant manufactures are rum, cement, chemicals, paper products, and metal goods.

Trade. In 1967 exports earned $438 million and imports cost $403 million. The principal imports are crude petroleum, foodstuffs, machinery, transportation equipment, and iron and steel. Petroleum products, sugar, fruit, and cocoa are the main exports.

The country's main trading partners are Britain and the United States. Tourism is important, and in the mid-1960s it was one of the country's major sources of income.

GOVERNMENT. Trinidad and Tobago has a parliamentary system of government. The head of state is the British monarch, who is represented by a governor-general. Actual executive powers are wielded by a prime minister and cabinet responsible to the legislature, which consists of an appointed Senate and a popularly elected House of Representatives.

TRINIDAD SURF breaks on a sandy beach.

Trinidad and Tobago is a member of the United Nations, the Commonwealth of Nations, and the Organization of American States (OAS).

HISTORY. Both Trinidad and Tobago were visited by Christopher Columbus on his third voyage to the New World in 1498. Trinidad was at that time inhabited by Arawak Indians. Tobago was uninhabited when Dutch settlers arrived in 1632.

Trinidad was settled by Spain, which made it a colony in about 1550. The island was subject to constant raids by French, Dutch, and British privateers, and the Spanish maintained their control only with difficulty. Cocoa crop failures in the early 1700s led to the abandonment of most settlements on the island.

The colony revived after 1783, when the Spanish government invited Roman Catholics from other countries to settle in Trinidad. Many Frenchmen moved to the island, bringing with them sugarcane, cotton, coffee, and new types of cocoa. Plantation agriculture prospered, based on the labor of slaves imported from Africa.

British Rule. In 1798 Britain captured Trinidad and its control was recognized in 1802 by the Treaty of Amiens. The treaty gave Tobago to France, but the French ceded the island to Britain in 1814. The sugar and cocoa industries prospered and were expanded under British colonial rule.

In the 1830s the slaves were freed, and a critical labor shortage in the second half of the 1800s led to contract workers being brought from India. Oil was discovered in the early 1900s and soon played a key role in the economy.

The islands had been made a single colony in 1889, and they began to move toward independence in 1925, when popular representatives were first elected to the governing council. Popular participation in government gradually increased. In 1958 the colony entered the Federation of the West Indies, which united a number of Britain's West Indian and Caribbean colonies, but it withdrew in 1961 when Jamaica left the federation.

Independence. In 1962, a year after complete internal self-government had been granted, Trinidad and Tobago became an independent country. The new nation concentrated on improving its economy by encouraging foreign investment and by diversifying its activities.

Trinidad and Tobago was admitted to the Organization of American States in 1967. It thus became the second English-speaking member state in the organization.

—George W. Carey; Jerome Fischman

TRUCIAL OMAN

Official name: Trucial States
Area: 32,300 square miles
Population: (1966 est.) 130,000
Language: Arabic
Religion: Islam
Currency unit: Qatar/Dubai dinar, Bahrain dinar

The Trucial Oman, often referred to as the Trucial Coast, is an association of seven independent sheikhdoms on the southern coast of the Persian Gulf. The Trucial Oman is bordered on the north by Qatar, on the east by Muscat and Oman, on the south by Muscat and Oman and Saudi Arabia, and on the west by Saudi Arabia.

Abu Dhabi, Dubai, Sharjah, Ajman, Umm al Qaiwain, Ras al Khaimah, and Fujairah make up the association, whose name derives from a series of truces signed with Britain in the 1800s.

THE LAND AND PEOPLE. Flat, hot, and dry except for the humid coast, the region is mainly barren desert dotted with a few oases. Rainfall averages only three inches a year.

The native population of the Trucial Oman is entirely Arab and Muslim. Dubai, capital of Dubai state, is the major port and the principal city.

ECONOMY. Nomadic grazing of livestock, pearl diving, fishing, trading, and date-farming, were once the only means of livelihood in the states. They became of secondary importance after 1958, when the production of oil became the mainstay of the economy. The principal oil fields lie within the sheikhdom of Abu-Dhabi, which gains the greatest income from them in the form of royalty fees and taxes collected from foreign oil companies for exploitation rights.

Of the seven sheikhdoms, Abu Dhabi has the most prosperous trade because of its oil exports. Dubai, however, with its good port, has long done a brisk transshipment trade and is the chief commercial center for the region. It has also recently struck oil.

The states export hides, dates, pearls, and fish products and import machinery, foodstuffs, and manufactured items. Most trade is with neighboring countries and with Britain, Japan, and India.

GOVERNMENT. Each sheikhdom is governed by an absolute ruler, a sheikh. Britain is responsible for defense and foreign affairs of the states.

HISTORY. For centuries the sheikhs of the region now known as the Trucial Oman battled for control of the territory. In the 1500s, when Portugal controlled the Persian Gulf, the sheikhs turned to piracy and the slave trade. By the 1700s their ships ranged over the entire Persian Gulf and into the Arabian Sea. They waged undeclared war against the British East India Company, the principal trader in the area.

At the beginning of the 1800s the company and Britain suppressed the piracy, and in 1820 they signed a treaty of peace with the sheikhdoms. By later agreements the sheikhs promised to abandon slaving and piracy, turned control of their foreign affairs and defense over to Britain, and granted the British exclusive trading privileges.

Until the 1950s the sheikhdoms experienced little internal or external strife. The discovery of oil in the 1950s, however, and the wealth and influx of foreigners that oil production brought to the states disrupted the traditional society. In the 1960s programs were initiated to use oil revenues for health care, education, and technological improvements.

In the 1950s and 1960s border disputes with neighboring states were frequent. In 1967, when Aden and the South Arabian sheikhdoms became independent as South Yemen, there were discussions of incorporating the Trucial sheikhdoms into the new state.

—Charles Issawi; Alexander Melamid

TUNISIA

Official name: Republic of Tunisia
Area: 63,379 square miles
Population: (1966 est.) 4,460,000
Capital: Tunis (Pop., 1964 est., urban area, 662,000)
Language: Arabic
Religion: Islam
Currency unit: Dinar
National holiday: Independence day, June 1

Tunisia, a republic in northern Africa, is bounded on the north and east by the Mediterranean Sea, on the south by Libya, and on the west by Algeria. Tunisia received its independence from France in 1956.

THE LAND. Tunisia has four contrasting geographical regions—the Sahel, or plains, along the east coast; a steppe region inland from the coast; the Atlas mountain system in the north; and a low-lying desert region, part of the Sahara, in the south.

The Sahel is occupied by low rolling hills. Paralleling the eastern coast, but further inland, is the flatter steppe region. The Tell Atlas in the far north

COUNTRIES OF THE WORLD

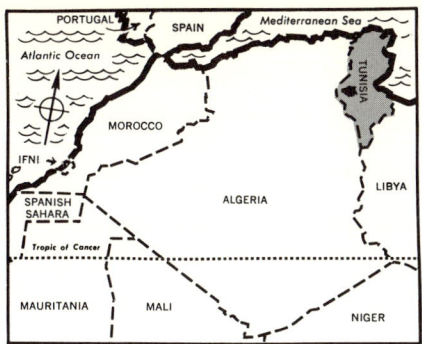

is separated from the Saharan Atlas, or High Tell, by the Medjerda River valley. The Tell Atlas extends to the coast in Cape Blanc, and the Saharan Atlas extends to the coast in Cape Bon.

South of the mountains is the Shott el Jerid, a salt lake close to sea level, which receives some streams from the mountains. In the southwest, along the boundary with Algeria, lies part of the Great Eastern Erg, a major sand area of the Sahara.

In the northern part of the country winters are mild and rainy and summers are hot and dry. South of the Shott el Jerid the climate is hot and dry with less than 4 inches of rain a year.

THE PEOPLE. Most of Tunisia's people are Muslim, and are descended from indigenous Berber-speaking peoples and later Arab immigrants. There are small communities of Jews and Europeans, mainly French, Italian, and Maltese. There are nomadic Berber tribes in the desert region.

Tunis, the capital, is the country's largest city and principal port. Bizerte, Sfax, Sousse, and Gabès are also important seaports. Qairouan is an historic Muslim holy city.

ECONOMY. The economy of Tunisia is based on agriculture. The main crops are wheat, barley, and olives. Tunisia is one of the world's largest producers of olive oil, and in 1965 about 105,000 metric tons of olive oil were produced. Figs and citrus fruits are also grown, as are wine grapes. Nomads raise sheep, goats, cattle, and camels.

Tunisia has rich phosphate and iron ore deposits, and in 1965 produced more than 3 million metric tons of phosphate rock and 609,000 metric tons of iron ore. There are also deposits of lead and silver. Industry has developed since the time of independence in 1956. Most factories process the country's agricultural and mineral products.

In 1966 imports cost $249 million and exports earned $140 million. The major imports are lumber, petroleum, textiles, iron and steel, and machinery. The major exports are fruits, phosphates, iron ore, and olive oil. Most trade is conducted with France, Indonesia, the United States, and Italy.

GOVERNMENT. Tunisia has a presidential system of government. Executive power is vested in a president, who is popularly elected to a five-year term. Legislative power is held by the National Assembly, which is also popularly elected every five years.

Tunisia is a member of the United Nations, the Arab League, and the Organization of African Unity.

HISTORY. In 814 BC the Phoenicians founded the city of Carthage, near the site of present-day Tunis. In 146 BC Rome destroyed Carthage and Tunisia came under Roman domination. Roman rule ended in the 400s AD with invasions by the Vandals. In the 500s the region came under Byzantine rule.

A decisive break in Tunisian history occurred with the arrival of Muslim Arabs in the mid-600s. Although the native Berber-speaking peoples were the most Romanized and Christianized people of northwestern Africa, Tunisia became part of the Arab-Muslim world.

Tunisia shared the fortunes of the dynasties that arose in northern Africa and Spain. In the early 800s the Aghlabids gained control of Tunisia. The Fatimids controlled much of Tunisia in the 900s, and in the 1100s a Morocco-based dynasty, the Almohad, gained control of the region. In 1228 the Almohads were succeeded by the Hafsids, who controlled Tunisia until the early 1500s, when the Ottoman Turks began a series of invasions.

By 1574 Tunisia had become part of the Ottoman Empire, but it was soon able to achieve a considerable measure of self-rule. In 1705 an Ottoman Turkish ruler of Tunisia, owing allegiance to the sultan, established the Husayn Dynasty, which lasted until the monarchy was abolished in 1957.

The Tunisian government attempted internal reforms and westernization early in the 1800s. But Tunisia soon fell victim to foreign indebtedness and increasing European interference. In 1881, after a brief military campaign, France established a protectorate over Tunisia.

French Control. Although large numbers of French and other Europeans settled in the country, native institutions were left largely intact. Tunisians learned technical skills from the French and benefited from the country's economic growth without being overwhelmed in the process.

Nationalism developed rapidly after World War I, and the Tunisian struggle for independence came to be personified by Habib Bourguiba, who organized the nationalist Neo-Destour party in 1934. The Neo-Destour itself grew out of an earlier, more traditional party, the Destour, or Constitution.

After a long period of intermittent negotiations and armed struggle, France agreed to grant Tunisia internal self-government in 1954. On Mar. 20, 1956 France granted Tunisia complete independence, and in 1957 Tunisia became a republic with Bourguiba as president.

Independence. Tunisia, since its independence, has made impressive domestic reforms in education and economic development. Diplomatically, the period from 1956 until neighboring Algeria won its independence from France in 1962 placed Tunisia in the delicate position of attempting to maintain necessary relations with France while supporting the Algerian independence movement.

Fighting erupted in Tunisia between the French and the Tunisian supporters of the Algerians, and in 1958 France bombed the Tunisian border city of Sakiet-Sidi-Youssef. In 1961 Tunisia demanded the removal of troops France had maintained in Bizerte after independence.

The Tunisian demand for the withdrawal of the troops further strained French-Tunisian relations. In 1963, after months of fighting, France withdrew its troops. In 1964 Tunisia nationalized French holdings in Tunisia, and France ended its technical and economic assistance.

In 1965 relations between Tunisia and the United Arab Republic (U.A.R.) became strained when Bourguiba suggested a reconciliation between the Arab states and Israel, and in 1966 diplomatic relations were broken off with the U.A.R. In 1967 diplomatic relations were resumed after Tunisia pledged its full support to the Arab states in renewed warfare with Israel.

—L. Carl Brown; Hibberd V. B. Kline, Jr.

TURKEY

Official name: Republic of Turkey
Area: 301,382 square miles
Population: (1967 est.) 33,823,000
Capital: Ankara (Pop., 1965 est., urban area, 902,218)
Language: Turkish
Religion: Islam
Currency unit: Lira
National holiday: Republic Day, October 29

Turkey is a republic located both in Asia and Europe. Most of the country lies in Asia Minor, or Anatolia. The small European portion, called Thrace, is on the Balkan peninsula. The republic was formed in 1923 from the Turkish region which for centuries had been the core of the Ottoman Empire.

Turkey is bordered on the north by Bulgaria, the Black Sea, and the Soviet Union; on the east by Iran; on the south by Iraq, Syria, and the Mediterranean Sea; and on the west by the Aegean Sea and Greece.

THE LAND. Thrace consists of rolling plains bounded by uplands in the north and a mountainous coastline in the south. It is separated from Anatolia by a small sea—the Sea of Marmara—and two straits—the Bosporus in the east and the Dardanelles in the west.

In Asian Turkey the Pontic Mountains rising over 11,000 feet, follow the shores of the Black Sea. The Taurus mountain range on the southern coast rises to a peak of over 11,500 feet above the Mediterranean. Narrow, fertile plains separate both ranges from the sea.

Between the mountain ranges is the Anatolian Plateau, with an average elevation of 3,000 feet. Toward the west the plain breaks into a series of fertile river valleys separated by low ridges. In the east the plateau merges with the Pontic and Taurus mountains in the rugged highland of Armenia, where Mt. Ararat, Turkey's highest point, rises to 16,946 feet. Turkey's largest lakes—Van, in the east and Tuzi, in the west—are salt-water lakes.

Many rivers flow from Turkey's highlands towards the long coastline. The longest is the Kizil, which rises

Turkey

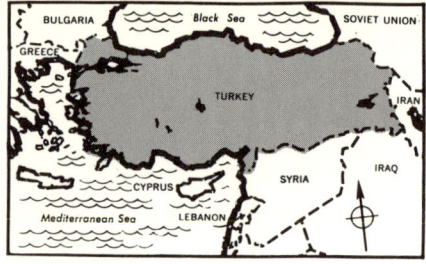

in the eastern highlands and flows west and north to empty into the Black Sea. Other important rivers are the Firat, or Euphrates, which rises in Turkey and flows south, the Seyhan in central Anatolia, and the Sakarya in the northwest.

Climate. Thrace and coastal Anatolia have a mild, moist climate. Temperatures range from 40° to 80°F, and rainfall averages 20 to 40 inches annually. Most rain falls in the winter.

In the dry Anatolian Plateau only 10 to 20 inches of rain falls a year, and temperatures are hotter in summer and colder in winter than on the coasts. The inland mountains have a colder climate and are often snow-covered.

THE PEOPLE. Most Turks are Turkish —related to peoples of Central Asia. They speak Turkish. Over 98 percent of the population is Muslim. The largest minority group is the Kurds, a seminomadic people who inhabit the eastern highlands. There are also small Greek and Armenian minorities.

Most Turks live in small towns encircling the Anatolian Plateau. The interior of the plateau is quite sparsely settled. The densest population is in northwestern Anatolia and eastern Thrace, where Istanbul, the country's largest city is located. The capital, Ankara, is in central Anatolia.

ECONOMY. Throughout history the area which is now Turkey has been famous for its agricultural and mineral products. Turkey's economy is still based heavily on agriculture, but industrialization began in the 1950s.

Turkey's wide variety of known minerals include rich deposits of coal and chrome and fairly large reserves of oil, zinc, copper, iron, and lead. Turkey also has abundant waterpower resources, which were under development in the 1960s.

Agriculture. Farming and herding were the occupations of over two-thirds of the people in the mid-1960s, and in 1965 agriculture contributed 36 percent of the gross domestic product. Some one-third of the land area is cultivated, and over one-third is used for pasture. Sheep, goats, cattle, and other livestock are grazed on the Anatolian plain and in the eastern highlands.

Cereals, especially wheat, are the major farm crops. Cotton and sugar beets are also important, and legumes, citrus and other fruits, and nuts are raised. Tobacco is the most important commercial crop. Most farms are small, and agricultural methods are generally outmoded and inefficient.

Evergreen forests cover some 13 percent of the country's area, and forestry is important. There is some fishing off the coasts.

Industry. Although Turkey's industry expanded greatly in the 1950s and early 1960s, by 1965 it contributed only 18 percent of the gross domestic product and consisted primarily of the processing of agricultural products. Textile weaving is the leading industry. Refined sugar, flour, paper, tobacco products, dried fruits, oils, canned foods, cement, and iron and steel and chrome products are among Turkey's leading manufactured products.

Trade. Turkey has a generally unfavorable balance of trade. In 1967 exports earned $522 million and imports cost $691 million. The chief exports are agricultural products, especially grain, tobacco, cotton, and sugar. Metal ores are also exported. Machinery and motor vehicles, fuels, manufactured consumer goods, and industrial raw materials are the main imports.

Most Turkish trade is carried on with the United States, Britain, West Germany, Italy, Belgium, and Czechoslovakia.

GOVERNMENT. Turkey is a republic. A 1961 constitution vested legislative power in the Grand National Assembly, a popularly elected legislature of two houses. The assembly elects a president from among its members to a 7-year term as head of state. A prime minister appointed by the president and responsible to the assembly is chief executive.

Turkey is a member of the United Nations, the North Atlantic Treaty Organization (NATO), and the Central Treaty Organization (CENTO).

HISTORY. Although the Turks did not appear there until the Middle Ages, the region called Turkey has been inhabited since ancient times. The history of the land extends back nearly 4,000 years to the civilization of the Hittites.

After conquests by Persians, Greeks, and Romans, Turkey became in the 200s AD the core of the eastern half of the Roman Empire. In 330 AD Byzantium (later called Constantinople, the modern Istanbul) became the capital of the Byzantine Empire, the successor to the Roman empire.

In the 900s the first Turks, the Seljuks, migrated into Asia Minor from Central Asia. In the 1000s they conquered territory in Anatolia, adopted Islam, and established a kingdom ruled from central Turkey. The Byzantine emperors, with the aid of Christian Crusaders, successfully defended Western Anatolia and the rest of the empire from the Seljuks, who were overwhelmed by the Mongols in the 1200s.

Ottomans. A second group of Turks renewed the attack on the Byzantine empire in the late 1200s. These were the Ottomans named after their leader, Osman. The Ottomans, after 200 years, succeeded in conquering the empire. In 1453 they captured the capital, Constantinople.

From Constantinople the Ottomans ruled a mighty empire which, at its height under Sulayman the Magnificent, who ruled from 1520 to 1566, was probably the most powerful in the world. It stretched from Austria in the north to the Indian Ocean in the south, and from Persia (Iran) in the east to Algeria in the west.

The Ottoman Empire in the 1500s was not only the largest and the most powerful state in the world, but the most efficiently governed as well. Its society was ordered along a feudalistic pattern, and its leaders combined political power with religious influence. The Ottoman Empire had an administrative bureaucracy, a court system, taxation methods, and an army and navy that were excellent even by modern standards.

Decline. The 300 years following Suleiman's reign, however, witnessed an almost uninterrupted decline. A disastrous defeat by the armies of the Holy Roman Empire in 1571 ended Ottoman world military supremacy and put the once-conquering Turkish armies on the defensive. Governmental administration collapsed under weak sultans and bureaucratic corruption, and military discipline crumbled.

Local authorities gradually assumed power, and by the 1800s many provinces were independent in fact, if not in name. In addition, France, Britain, Austria, and Russia conquered parts of the empire, and the Balkan provinces rebelled, leaving Turkey only Thrace of its once considerable European possessions. The Ottoman Em-

TURKISH INFORMATION SERVICE
DOLMABAHÇE SQUARE on the Bosphorus in Istanbul, showing the Mosque with its minarets.

pire in the 1800s had become the "Sick Man of Europe."

Toward the end of the 1800s progress was made in reforming the government and restoring order. The era also saw the beginning of a cultural and literary revival. In 1876 Sultan Abd-al-Hamid II took the throne and a liberal constitution was proclaimed.

The Sultan soon ended the reform efforts, however. He revoked the constitution, abused his subjects, especially the minority nationalities, and took Turkey into wars that resulted in disastrous losses.

Young Turks. In the discontent caused by his failures and abuses, a revolutionary party was formed, the Committee of Union and Progress, or the "Young Turks." The party hoped to restore Turkish power by Westernizing the country and by expanding Turkish territory.

In 1908, with the support of the army, the young Turks forced Abd-al-Hamid to grant a new constitution and parliamentary government. In 1909 he was deposed and replaced by his brother.

Soon, however, the Young Turks divided into factions. Moreover, in trying to regain lost territories they lost still more. As each of their projects failed, their government grew more despotic. By 1913 a military wing of the party assumed power by a coup-d'etat.

Under this government Turkey entered World War I on the side of Germany and suffered terrible losses. When the war ended in 1918, the country was occupied by troops from many Allied countries and was threatened with partition among the Allied states. All that remained of the Ottoman Empire was Anatolia and Thrace, and the Young Turk government fled into exile.

In 1920 a nationalist party organized an unofficial Turkish government under Mustafa Kemal to drive out the Allied occupation forces. Kemal, with the support of the majority of Turks, organized an army and by 1923 had forced the Allies to leave and to recognize Turkey's sovereignty over Asia Minor and eastern Thrace in the Treaty of Lausanne.

The Republic. In October 1923 Turkey was proclaimed a republic, with an elected legislature and with Kemal as president. The political and religious authority of the old sultanate and the caliphate were abolished.

Kemal, who was later given the surname "Atatürk," or "father of the Turks," radically reformed Turkish government, economy, and society, turning its medieval Islamic social and political structure into that of a modern, Western-style nation. At Atatürk's death in 1938 his prime minister, Ismet Inönü, became the president and continued the Westernization program.

Turkey did not participate in World War II, but it favored the Allies. After the war it pursued a pro-Western policy, joining the North Atlantic Treaty Organization. Turkey was aided in its fight against expanding Communist influence by U.S. economic aid under the Truman Doctrine and Marshall Plan.

In 1950 the Democratic Party took power from Inönü's Republican People's Party government. The Democratic government faced rising discontent at home. Economic expansion and modernization had proceeded rapidly, and in 1950 severe inflation threatened the economy. The government responded with unpopular financial restrictions. Unrest was met with repression, which the people, especially Turkey's new educated class, resented.

Contemporary Turkey. In 1960 a military group seized power and placed Gen. Cemal Gürsel at the head of a provisional government. In 1961 a new constitution was written, establishing a second republic.

Inönü became prime minister, and Gürsel remained as president. The government instituted reforms and initiated ambitious economic development programs, which were designed to develop natural resources, modernize agriculture, and expand industry at a moderate pace.

Inönü's government fell in 1965. The Justice party won elections held in 1965, and Süleyman Demiral became prime minister. The legislature elected Gen. Cevdet Sunay president in 1966 when President Gürsel became ill.

In 1967 Turkey threatened war with Greece over the status of the Turkish minority on the island-nation of Cyprus. The crisis was one in a series that had arisen between the two states since 1963, when fighting erupted on Cyprus between Greek and Turkish Cypriots. UN emissaries and a U.S. negotiator prevented open fighting and arranged a temporary settlement of the dispute.

—Charles Issawi; Alexander Melamid

UGANDA

Official name: Republic of Uganda
Area: 91,134 square miles
Population: (1966 est.) 7,934,000
Capital: Kampala (Pop., 1959 est., urban area, 123,300)
Language: English, Luganda and other African languages
Religion: Christianity, Islam, traditional religions
Currency unit: Shilling
National holiday: Independence day, October 9

Uganda, a republic in eastern Africa, is bounded on the north by Sudan, on the east by Kenya, on the south by Tanzania and Rwanda, and on the west by the Congo (Kinshasa). Uganda received its independence from Britain in 1962.

THE LAND. Most of Uganda is occupied by a plateau with elevations between 3,000 and 6,000 feet above sea level. The Ruwenzori Mountains run along the western border, reaching an elevation of more than 16,760 feet in the Margherita Peak. In the east Mount Elgon reaches an elevation of almost 14,180 feet.

Lake Victoria is at the southeastern corner of Uganda. Lakes Edward and Albert are in western Uganda, and Lake Kyoga is in central Uganda. The Albert Nile and the Victoria Nile are among the many rivers flowing through Uganda.

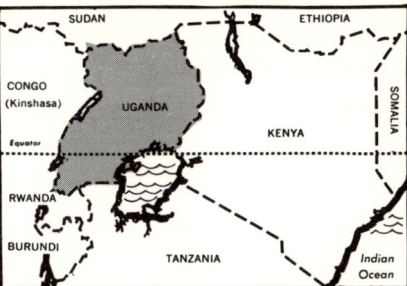

Uganda has a tropical climate. In the northeast rainfall averages about 20 inches a year, but in the southwest and west it averages between 50 and 60 inches a year.

THE PEOPLE. There are many tribal groups in Uganda, most of which are Bantu-speaking. The largest Bantu-speaking tribe is the Baganda. Other large groups include the Iteso, the Banyankole, and the Basoga. There are also peoples of Nilotic and Nilo-Hamitic stock, and small communities of Asians and Europeans.

Uganda's largest cities include Kampala, the capital; Entebbe; and Jinja. All three are near Lake Victoria.

ECONOMY. Uganda's economy is based on agriculture. The basic food crops are corn, beans, and cassava, and the main cash crops are cotton and coffee. Tobacco, sugarcane, and tea are also grown. Cattle are raised in many parts of the country, and fish from Uganda's lakes are important to the economy.

Uganda has rich copper deposits, and in 1965, 17,200 metric tons of copper were produced. There are also deposits of apatite, beryl, and bismuth, although production of these minerals is limited.

Most industry is engaged in the processing of Uganda's mineral and agricultural products. The Owen Falls hydroelectric plant, near Lake Victoria, supplies most of the country's electricity, and industry is concentrated in the Owen Falls region. The government instituted a five-year development plan in 1962, and at its completion in 1966 a new five-year plan began.

In 1966 imports cost $119 million and exports earned $188 million. The major imports are textiles, petroleum products, iron and steel, and machinery. The main exports are coffee, cotton, and copper. Most trade is conducted with Britain, the United States, Belgium, and Luxembourg. Uganda has close economic ties with Kenya and Tanzania.

GOVERNMENT. In 1967 a new constitution was promulgated in Uganda. Legislative powers are vested in a National Assembly, which is popularly elected every five years. Executive power is vested in a president, who is elected by the legislature to a five-year term.

Uganda is a member of the United Nations, the Organization of African Unity (OAU), and the Commonwealth of Nations.

HISTORY. Between the 1400s and 1600s various peoples established kingdoms in present-day Uganda. In the 1600s the Buganda kingdom became powerful and conquered many of the existing states.

James Augustus Grant and John Hanning Speke explored the source of the Nile in 1862 and established trade relations between Britain and Mutesa I, the *kabaka*, or king, of Buganda. Protestant and Roman Catholic missionaries followed, as well as Muslims, who were in contact with neighboring regions. In the 1880s, Mutesa's successor, Mwanga, attempted to stop the spread of Christianity in the area, and many Christians were killed in a widespread persecution.

British Rule. In 1888 the Imperial British East Africa Company concluded a treaty with Buganda, and the kingdom came under company administration. The company withdrew from Uganda because of economic difficulties, and in 1894 Britain established a protectorate over the region. By 1896 the protectorate included all of present-day Uganda.

In 1900 the Buganda regent signed the Uganda Agreement with Britain, which established administrative arrangements that endured until Uganda achieved self-government in 1962. The kabaka, or king, with his *lukiko*, or assembly, was recognized as the ruler of Uganda as long as he cooperated with Britain. Four regions were marked out—the Eastern, Western, Northern, and Buganda regions. The Buganda region occupied south-central Uganda.

Britain established a legislative council following World War I, and African members were appointed to the council after World War II. In 1953 Buganda demanded independence from the rest of Uganda because of fears of being forced into federation with the British protectorate of Kenya and Tanganyika, and thereby coming under the control of Kenya's white-settler community. In the same year, Kabaka Edward Mutesa II was exiled after refusing to nominate Buganda members to the legislative council.

In March 1961 elections were held for representatives to the legislative council and a majority of seats was won by the largely Roman Catholic, Democratic Party (DP). Buganda boycotted the election. In September 1961 a constitutional conference was held in London, and an agreement was reached granting Uganda self-government in March 1962. Differences between Buganda and the legislative council were settled, and Buganda stopped threatening to secede.

Independence. In 1961 Milton Obote of the Uganda People's Congress (UPC) formed an alliance with the Kabaka Yekka, a Buganda party which supported the kabaka. In April 1962 elections were held for a new parliament established by the 1961 London conference.

A coalition government composed of the UPC and the Kabaka Yekka came to power with Obote as prime minister. On Oct. 9, 1962 Uganda became independent, with Obote as prime minister and the king of Buganda, Edward Mutesa II, as president.

In 1966 Obote took full control of the government, suspended the constitution, and ousted President Mutesa. Obote assumed the position of president. Fighting broke out in Buganda, protesting Obote's seizure of the government, but the rising was quickly suppressed and the kabaka fled the country. A new constitution was promulgated in 1967.

—Hibberd V. B. Kline, Jr.;
Vera L. Zolberg

UNITED ARAB REPUBLIC (EGYPT)

Official name: United Arab Republic
Area: 386,100 square miles
Population: (1966 est.) 30,147,000
Capital: Cairo (Pop., 1962 est., 3,518,200)
Language: Arabic
Religion: Islam
Currency unit: Pound
National holiday: National day, July 23

The United Arab Republic (U.A.R.) is an independent country in northern Africa formerly known as Egypt. In 1958 Egypt and Syria joined to form the U.A.R. Syria withdrew from the Union in 1961, but Egypt continued to use the name United Arab Republic. The country is a major center of Arab culture and a leading force in the movement for unity in the Arab world.

The United Arab Republic is bordered on the north by the Mediterranean Sea; on the east by Israel and the Red Sea; on the south by Sudan; and on the west by Libya. In 1967, during the Arab-Israeli war, Israel occupied the Gaza Strip and almost all of the Sinai region of the United Arab Republic.

THE LAND. The United Arab Republic consists of two main regions, which are divided by the Suez Canal. East of the canal is the Sinai Peninsula, a rugged desert country with only a few oases. The region west of the canal is occupied mainly by desert.

The Nile River flows northward through the western region. The fertile valley formed by the river is between 2 and 10 miles wide. In the north the valley widens into a delta through which the Nile reaches the Mediterranean Sea. The desert begins at the edge of the valley. The flow of the Nile is regulated by several dams to provide a maximum of water for irrigation.

The Western Desert, west of the Nile, contains a few oases, including El Faiyum in the northern part of the country. The Qattara Depression, Africa's lowest point, is in the north. The Eastern Desert, east of the Nile, is rugged and contains no important oases.

Summers in the U.A.R. are very hot and dry, and winters are warm and dry. A little winter rain falls in the area of Alexandria, in the north.

THE PEOPLE. The population of the U.A.R. is concentrated in the Nile valley and its delta. The country has a high rate of population growth, and between 1958 and 1965 the population grew at a rate of 2.6 percent a year.

Most Egyptians are descended from Hamitic-speaking peoples who inhabited the Nile valley in ancient times with some mixture of Arab stock from the time of the Muslim conquest in the 600s. Over 90 percent of the people are Muslim, and the Egyptians speak Arabic. Most of the remaining people are Copts, Egyptian Christians. Nomadic herdsmen, or Bedouin, roam the desert regions in search of food and water for their livestock.

Cairo, the capital, lies at the junction of the Nile valley and delta. Alexandria, the main port, had a population of over 1.5 million in the mid-1960s. Other large cities are Port Said, Tanta, and Aswan.

ECONOMY. The economy of the United Arab Republic depends on agriculture. In recent years industry, which is under government control, has been expanded.

Agriculture. Between 1945 and 1964 agriculture was the occupation of 57 percent of the labor force. In ancient times, barley and wheat were the main crops. With improvements in irrigation techniques, sugar and cotton have largely replaced them as the major crops. In 1965 over 4 million metric tons of sugar and 504,000 metric tons of cotton were produced. Rice and corn are also grown.

The Nile River irrigates about 7 million acres of land. The Aswan Dam on the Nile River provides water for irrigation as well as hydroelectric power.

Manufacturing and Mining. The main industries process the cotton grown in the country. Modern textile and chemical plants have been established in many towns, especially in and near Tanta, near the Mediterranean Sea. Armament industries have also been founded. Tourism provides additional income. The United Arab Republic received revenues from the operation of the Suez Canal. In 1967, as a result of the Arab-Israeli war, all shipping through the canal was stopped.

Petroleum is produced in the Sinai Peninsula and on the western shore of the Red Sea. In 1966, 6.2 million metric tons of petroleum were produced, but production was insufficient for domestic needs. Iron ore is mined in the southern part of the country, and is converted into steel in a plant near Cairo. Some copper is also mined.

Trade. In 1967 imports cost over $754 million and exports earned $567 million. The main imports are cereals, petroleum, and machinery. The major exports are cotton and textiles. Most trade is conducted with

COUNTRIES OF THE WORLD

the Soviet Union, West Germany, and Czechoslovakia. The United Arab Republic has received large-scale economic assistance from the Soviet Union, the United States, and other countries.

GOVERNMENT. The United Arab Republic has a presidential system of government. The president is nominated by the legislature and approved by popular vote. He is elected to a six-year term. The president appoints a cabinet, headed by a prime minister, which is responsible to the legislature.

Legislative power is vested in a National Assembly, with 350 popularly-elected members and 10 additional members appointed by the president. Members serve five-year terms. The United Arab Republic is a one-party state, the Arab Socialist Union being the only recognized party in the country.

The United Arab Republic is a member of the United Nations, the Arab League, and the Organization of African Unity (OAU).

HISTORY. Civilization has existed in Egypt for over 7,000 years. Successive Egyptian dynasties ruled until foreign invaders overran the country. The first of these invasions occurred in 945 BC, when a Libyan prince, Sheshonk, seized control of Egypt. Libyans ruled Egypt until the late 700s BC, when an Ethiopian dynasty took power. In about 670 BC Assyrians established control over the country, only to be conquered by Persians in 525 BC.

In 332 BC Alexander the Great of Macedonia conquered Egypt and brought the country into his empire. At Alexander's death in 323 BC, one of his generals, Ptolemy, took control of Egypt and founded the Ptolemaic dynasty. Egyptian culture and politics became infused with the Greek tradition, or Hellenized. Egypt prospered under the Ptolemies—academies were built and trade was encouraged.

In 30 BC Egypt, weakened by internal conflicts, fell to the powerful forces of Rome. During the Roman occupation, probably in about the 300s AD, Christianity spread to Egypt, and the Coptic Church, the church of the Christian Egyptians, was established.

Islam. Egypt remained under Roman authority until 639 AD. In that year, Arab-speaking Muslims conquered Egypt. Since that time, Egypt has been closely identified with the Islamic world. The Muslims converted most of the Egyptian people, and Egypt became a major part of early Muslim empires.

In 969 a Muslim dynasty, the Fatimid, established its control over Egypt and made Cairo its capital. In the 1100s Christian Crusaders threatened the Muslim empire. Saladin, a Syrian officer, came to the aid of the Muslim rulers, repulsed the Christian troops, and in 1169 founded the Ayyubid dynasty.

In 1250 the slave guards of the Ayyubids, the Mamluks, seized control of the country and ruled it until 1517. In that year the Ottoman Turks defeated the Mamluks and absorbed Egypt into the Ottoman Empire. But the Ottoman Turks maintained only loose control over Egypt, and they left the Mamluks most of their former political power.

MERCHANTS display wares on a Cairo street.

European Influence. In 1798 Napoleon I of France invaded Egypt, but French rule was short-lived. In 1801 British and Ottoman forces expelled the French. In 1805 an Albanian Muslim soldier, Muhammad Ali, seized power and established a dynasty that lasted until 1952. Although Muhammad Ali and his successors did much to Westernize Egypt, their attempts were only partially successful.

In 1869 the Suez Canal was opened. The canal, built by the French Suez Canal Company, which obtained operations rights for 99 years, shortened the routes between Europe and the East, and increased Britain's interest in Egypt.

In 1876 Egypt, near bankruptcy from enormous expenditures from efforts to westernize the country, was forced to accept French and English financial advisors. In 1882, after a brief Egyptian nationalist uprising led by Ahmad Arabi, British troops occupied Egypt. Between 1883 and 1907 Sir Evelyn Baring (Lord Cromer) exercised chief responsibility for Egypt, and did much to develop the country economically.

In 1914 Britain declared a protectorate over Egypt. Egyptians resented British rule and called for independence. In 1922 Britain gave Egypt limited independence, but continued to control defense, foreign policy, and other important matters. On Aug. 26, 1936 Britain and Egypt signed a treaty whereby Britain withdrew its troops from all regions except the Suez Canal zone.

In the same year, 1936, King Faruq succeeded to the throne. In 1945 Egypt and six other Arab nations formed the Arab League to promote unity among member nations. In 1948 Egypt and the other Arab nations fought an unsuccessful war against the newly created state of Israel. Israel drove the invaders out, and the United Nations negotiated separate armistice agreements between the Arab states and Israel, but no final peace treaty was signed. Egypt obtained control of the Gaza Strip,

United Arab Republic 193

ON THE NILE, a camel turns a waterwheel.

a small area on the Mediterranean Sea once part of Palestine.

Republic. After the Arab-Israeli clash Egypt, troubled with the causes for failure in the war, a corrupt regime, and social unrest, fell into political turmoil. In 1952 an army group called the Free Officers seized control of the government and forced the king to abdicate.

Gen. Muhammad Najib (Naguib) became prime minister. In June 1953 Egypt became a republic, and Najib became president. In 1954 Lt. Col. Gamal Abdel Nasser, a leader of the military revolt, ousted Najib and assumed the position of president.

In 1956 the United States withdrew offers of a loan for the building of a high dam at Aswan. Because of the withdrawal of the loan offer, Nasser nationalized the Suez Canal and announced his intention to use canal revenues to build the dam. Nasser also accepted large-scale Soviet aid for the project. A dispute over free access to the canal arose after nationalization, and a new conflict erupted. British, French, and Israeli forces attacked in October 1955, and after a brief but intensive struggle, both sides accepted a UN cease-fire.

U.A.R. On Feb. 1, 1958 Egypt, in an effort to build Arab unity, joined with Syria to form the United Arab Republic. The following month, the U.A.R. joined with the Kingdom of Yemen to form the United Arab States. In September 1961 Syria withdrew from the U.A.R., and three months later Egypt ended its tie with Yemen. In 1962 the United Arab Republic supported republican forces in Yemen fighting against Yemeni royalist forces.

In 1967 The United Arab Republic blockaded the Gulf of Aqaba, cutting off Israel's outlet to the Red Sea. On June 5 fighting erupted between the Arab states and Israel, and the Israeli army again defeated the Arab forces. Israel opened the Gulf of Aqaba, occupied the Sinai Peninsula and the Gaza Strip, and seized control of the east bank of the Suez Canal. The United Nations again arranged a ceasefire, but a permanent solution to the conflict was not achieved.

—L. Carl Brown; Alexander Melamid

UNITED KINGDOM

Official name: United Kingdom of Great Britain and Northern Ireland
Area: 94,220 square miles
Population: (1967 est.) 55,068,000
Capital: London (Pop., 1965 est., urban area, 7,948,300)
Language: English
Religion: Anglicanism, Protestantism, Roman Catholicism
Currency unit: Pound
National holiday: Queen's birthday

The United Kingdom of Great Britain and Northern Ireland, usually referred to as Great Britain or Britain, lies on the British Isles, off the northwest coast of continental Europe.

The major island, Great Britain, includes England, in the south and east, Wales, in the west, and Scotland, in the north. It is separated from France on the south by the English Channel and the strait of Dover, and from northern Europe on the east by the North Sea. The Norwegian Sea, an arm of the North Atlantic Ocean, lies to the north.

Great Britain is separated from the other large island of the group, Ireland, by St. George's Channel, the Irish Sea, and the North Channel. Northern Ireland, part of the United Kingdom, shares the island with the independent Republic of Ireland.

Most of the islands near Great Britain, including the Hebrides, Shetland, and Orkney groups off Scotland and the Isle of Wight off England, are British. The Channel Islands in the English Channel and the Isle of Man in the Irish Sea are British dependencies.

THE LAND. A complex geological structure gives the British Isles a varied topography despite their limited size. On Great Britain a moderately high highland region arches northward from the Cambrian Mountains in southwestern Wales and the Cotswold hills in western England. It extends through the Pennine Mountains in north-central England and the Cheviot Hills, the Southern Uplands, and the Grampian Mountains of Scotland to the Scottish Highlands, where the island's and the nation's highest peak, Ben Nevis, rises to 4,406 feet.

Most of England is occupied by low plains. In central England the Midlands occupy the basins of the Mersey and the Trent rivers between the Cotswold to the south and the Pennines to the north. In the south and east the lowlands are called the Downs and Fens. The Central Lowland, in Scotland between the Southern Upland and the Highlands, is the only major lowland outside of England.

Narrow plains skirt the deeply indented coasts of Wales, northern England, and southern Scotland, but the highlands of northern Scotland drop sharply into the sea. The northern and western sections of Northern Ireland are rolling uplands, levelling off in the south and east.

The most important of Britain's rivers are the Thames and the Severn in England and the Tweed and the Clyde in Scotland. Most British lakes are in the "Lake District" of northwestern England and in the Scottish highlands, which are also marked by long, narrow fjord-like inlets. Britain's largest lake, Lough Neagh, lies in the center of Northern Ireland.

Climate. Britain has a temperate maritime climate. The cold temperatures usual for the islands' northerly location are moderated by the warm Gulf Stream flowing just west of the islands, and by warm winds off the Atlantic Ocean. As a result, winters are generally mild and summers cool, with few temperature extremes. Average temperatures for the country as a whole are about 40°F in winter and 60°F in summer.

Rainfall is moderate to heavy, ranging from 20 inches a year in the southeast to 120 inches on the west coast, and averages about 40 inches a year for the country as a whole. Cloudiness is the rule, with southeastern England having the most sunshine, about 6 hours a day in summer.

THE PEOPLE. Britain is one of the world's most densely settled countries, with a density of 582 persons per square mile in 1966. The bulk of the country's population lives in England and Wales, which had a density of 824 persons per square mile in 1966. Settlement is sparser towards the north and west.

Britain is also a highly urbanized nation, and most Britons live in cities or suburbs. In 1967 there were six cities with urban areas of over 1 million people. The metropolitan area of London, the capital, has the largest population, with more than 8 million people in 1967.

Between 1958 and 1966 the population grew at the slow rate of 0.7 percent a year, and the country limits immigration.

Britain's population is quite homogeneous. Most Britons are descendants of Celtic, Scandinavian, French, and Germanic peoples who had settled in the islands by the 1000s.

English is the universal language, although the Celtic languages of Welsh and Gaelic are spoken in the north and west. The Church of England (Anglican) is the established church and the dominant religion, but other Protestant denominations and Roman Catholicism are also important.

The few ethnic minority groups of any significance are made up of immigrants from member nations of the British Commonwealth of Nations. Most prominent are people from the West Indies and from India and Pakistan.

ECONOMY. The British economy, once the most stable and prosperous in the world, faced serious difficulties in the mid-1900s. Its earlier prosperity was based on commerce, made possible by its strategic maritime location, and upon mineral resources which provided an excellent base for the early development of industry.

Britain's natural resources include abundant fields of excellent coal and rich iron ore deposits, mostly in the Pennines, as well as quantities of limestone, gravel, chalk, and fine clays. There are also small deposits of zinc, tin, and lead, and bauxite is mined in northern Ireland. With the depletion over the years of the coal and iron ore deposits, and lacking petroleum, natural gas, and water-power resources, Britain was at a disadvantage by the mid-1900s.

Agriculture. The soils of Britain's lowlands and river valleys, especially in eastern England and northern Ireland, are quite fertile, but limited in quantity. The highlands are generally unsuitable for farming, but they provide excellent grazing land.

In the mid-1960s about 30 percent of Britain's land area was used for farming. In 1965, however, agriculture contributed only some 3 percent of the gross domestic product and occupied a very small proportion of the labor force.

A great variety of crops are raised. Wheat and barley are important, and fruits, vegetables, and other grains are also raised. Dairy farming prospers, particularly in Wales, Northern Ireland, the Scottish lowlands, and western England. Large herds of sheep are grazed in the Highlands and the Midlands, and pigs, poultry and beef cattle are important throughout the country.

Fishing contributed less than 1 percent of the gross domestic product in the mid-1960s, but it provides an important item in the British diet and is vital to the economies of Scotland and the northern islands.

Industry. Britain is a highly industrialized nation, and in 1965 manufacturing contributed 36 percent of the gross domestic product, one of the highest percentages in the world. British industry, originally based upon its coal, its iron, and its wool, was forced to shift in the mid-1900s to keep pace with modern technology and to meet the varied demands of modern markets. Heavy industry remained central to British industry, however.

Iron and steel working, metal finishing, chemical production, shipbuilding, and the manufacture of machinery, machine tools, and vehicles are the most important activities. Textiles, both wool and the newer synthetics, are an important element in British industry.

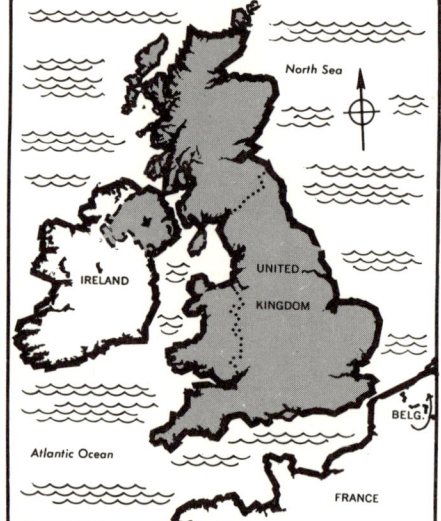

COUNTRIES OF THE WORLD

United Kingdom

GREAT BRITAIN'S HOUSES OF PARLIAMENT lie on the banks of the Thames River in London.

The centers of British heavy industry are in the Midlands, in southern Wales, in the Scottish lowlands, and, to a lesser extent, in coastal northern Ireland and on the northern English coast. Greater London is the center of British light industry, including paper making, printing, food processing, and the production of finished consumer foods. It is also the commercial and financial center of the country.

The British government plays an active role in the economy, stimulating and regulating agriculture and industry and providing broad social services for the British people. The government owns and operates in whole or in part the country's rail and air transport systems, its coal and steel industries, and its radio, television, and telecommunications networks.

The government exercises controls over wages and prices in most areas of the economy, but in the 1950s and 1960s it was unable to control a series of recessions and inflationary booms. Late in 1967 the government was forced to devalue the pound from $2.80 to $2.40.

Trade. International trade is vital to Britain's economy, and Britain for many years was the world's first-ranking trading nation. In the 1950s an increasingly poor balance of trade developed. Once trade imbalances had been made up by "invisible items," including foreign investment and shipping, but by the 1950s income from invisible items had declined greatly.

In 1967 Britain's exports earned $17,248 million and its imports cost $13,847 million. Foodstuffs constitute the largest single import classification, and fuels, industrial raw materials, and finished and semi-finished consumer goods are also imported. Machinery, vehicles, and scientific instruments are the leading exports, and textiles, chemicals, metals, and other manufactured goods are also important.

The United States, Canada, Australia, West Germany, France, the Netherlands, and the Scandinavian countries are Britain's major trading partners. As a leading member of the Commonwealth of Nations, Britain has many special trade arrangements with other Commonwealth nations.

GOVERNMENT. Britain is a constitutional monarchy with a parliamentary system of government. The British queen is head of state. Actual executive power is wielded by a prime minister and cabinet responsible to the legislature, the Parliament. Parliament has two houses—a popularly elected lower house, the House of Commons, and the less powerful, hereditary and appointive upper house, the House of Lords.

Britain does not have a single written constitution; rather, its government is based upon a series of documents, judicial decisions, and traditions that have the force of law. These define the civil rights of British citizens and outline the powers of the organs of government.

Commonwealth and Empire. Britain is the central member of the Commonwealth of Nations, a group of nations all of which were once colonies of Britain and all of which recognize the British monarch as the symbolic head of the Commonwealth. The Commonwealth nations hold frequent meetings to discuss mutual problems, and member nations provide financial, technical, and often military aid to one another.

By 1968 Britain's once vast colonial empire had shrunk greatly. During the two decades following World War II, most of Britain's African and Asian colonial territories won their independence, as did many colonial areas in the western hemisphere. Moreover, Britain began withdrawing from the Middle East, where it had established many protectorates, particularly in the Persian Gulf area.

Britain still held a considerable number of territories, however, although most were internally self-governing. In Europe, the empire included the Channel Islands, the Isle of Man, and Gibraltar. In Asia and the Pacific, Hong Kong, the Indian Ocean Territories, Fiji, the Gilbert and Ellice Islands, and other small areas remained British. In the western hemisphere, Britain retained Bermuda, British Honduras, and a number of West Indian Islands.

International Relations. Britain is a member of the United Nations, the North Atlantic Treaty Organization (NATO), the European Free Trade Association (EFTA), the Central Treaty Organization (CENTO), and the Southeast Asia Treaty Organization (SEATO).

Britain also has special treaty relations with a number of countries, such as the Trucial Oman, under which Britain is responsible for the defense and foreign relations of those countries.

HISTORY. The British Isles have been inhabited since prehistoric times. In about 600 BC Celtic peoples from the mainland of Europe began to settle on the island. They were divided into two groups: Gaels and Britons. The Gaels arrived first and settled in the north and west. The Britons occupied the south and east.

The Roman emperor Julius Caesar invaded the British Isles in 55 BC and found Gaels and Britons living in informal communities whose economies were based on agriculture, metalworking, and trading. But the Romans did not seriously attempt to conquer the Celts until 43 AD, when the emperor Claudius led a military expedition to the islands and occupied present-day England.

The Romans established settlements, founded cities, built roads and forts, and eventually extended Roman civil and military administration up to the present-day Scottish border. There the emperor Hadrian had a wall built in the 120s.

Many Celtic tribes remained outside of Roman control in present-day Ireland, Wales, and Scotland, and they, along with such non-Celtic peoples as the Picts in Scotland, were a constant threat to the Romans. Present-day England, however, inhabited by Britons, was Roman, and from the 40s AD to the 300s its history is part of the history of the Roman empire.

As England shared in Rome's greatness, it shared in its decline. After more than 100 years of attempted invasions from the north, in 367 the Picts and the Scots breached Hadrian's wall. Within the next 50 years Rome withdrew its troops from Britain to defend the empire in other areas. With the departure of the Roman troops, the cities, laws, prosperity, and culture that had been associated with Roman rule degenerated and in many cases disappeared.

The departure of the Romans left Britain subject to foreign invasions. From about 450 to 600 successive waves of invaders from northern Germany—Jutes, Angles, and Saxons—conquered the Celts or forced them to retreat to the western areas of the island, into Cornwall and Wales.

The various tribes of Anglo-Saxon invaders eventually created a number of kingdoms in the various parts of the island each had settled. The most important kingdoms were Northumbria, in the northeast; Mercia, in the Midlands; and Wessex, stretching from London westward to the Severn River. The other kingdoms included East Anglia, Essex, Kent, and Sussex in the south and east.

In the 600s all the Anglo-Saxon kingdoms were converted to Christianity through the influence of a missionary from Rome, Augustine, who baptized Ethelbert, king of Kent, and in 601 became the first archbishop of Canterbury. With the conversion of the Anglo-Saxons, English Christianity changed from the variety preserved by the Celts into the form of Rome.

Monastic life flourished in England and produced notable figures like the Venerable Bede (673–735), a monk at Jarrow, who wrote a history of the English people. Through the work of the monasteries, the Germanic Anglo-Saxon tongue became a written language, English. Church structure developed early, and religious leaders often exerted great influence, especially in Mercia and Wessex.

Rivalries among the kingdoms prevented any real unity for many centuries. Mercia, under Offa II (r. 757–796), and Wessex, led by Egbert of Wessex (r.802–839), underwent marked political development and extended their boundaries westward. By the early 800s a unique English social and political structure had taken shape, and the once warlike, semi-nomadic Anglo-Saxons had become a settled, agricultural people, enjoying peace and stability. Protected only by an army of untrained farmers, however, they were prey to more warlike peoples.

A people the Anglo-Saxons called "Danes," the inhabitants of present-day Denmark, Sweden, and Norway, began raiding the east coast of Britain in 787. In the 850s the Danes began a systematic conquest of the island, and by 870 all of the Anglo-Saxon kingdoms except Wessex had surrendered.

Wessex, led by King Alfred the Great (r.871–899), successfully resisted, and in 878 Alfred made a treaty with the Danes that divided England along a line running from London northwest to the Irish Sea. The area northeast of the line remained in Danish hands and was called the "Danelaw." The area southwest of the line was an enlarged kingdom of Wessex.

Alfred created in Wessex a strong political and cultural unit, and in 955 his grandson was able to conquer the Danelaw. Alfred's descendants ceased to be kings merely of Wessex and became the first kings of all England.

Unity did not bring security, however, and in about 980 the Danes renewed their raids. The reign of Ethelred the Redeless, or Unready, from 978 to 1016, was troubled by Danish invasions. In an attempt to buy off the Danes, Ethelred resorted to direct taxation of his subjects by instituting the Danegeld. The tribute paid from the Danegeld did not satisfy the Danes, and by 1017 they had defeated the English in battle.

Ethelred and his son both died in 1016 and the Witan, responsible for choosing a new king, was forced to name the Danish king, Canute, king of England (r.1017–1035). Canute ruled England, Denmark, and Norway, and established an orderly system of government in each. His two sons lacked his ability, however, and in 1042 the Witan chose one of Alfred's descendants, Edward "the Confessor," as king (r.1042–1066).

During Edward's reign, two groups competed for power. One was led by Godwin, the earl of Wessex, and his son Harold, whose family controlled not only Wessex but other earldoms as well. Their rivals were Normans, the descendants of a group of marauding Northmen, who in 910 had settled opposite England's south coast on the French peninsula that came to be called Normandy. They had built a strong, well organized duchy by the 1000s. The Norman faction was led by William, duke of Normandy.

Edward the Confessor favored the Normans, and he was said to have promised the English throne to William. It was also claimed that Harold himself had sworn to support William's succession to the throne. But when Edward died in 1066 the Witan chose Harold as king (r. January–October, 1066).

Norman Conquest. William of Normandy immediately made plans to take by force the throne that he claimed was rightfully his. In his efforts he had the valuable support of the pope and the aid of Harold's brother, Tostig, and of Harold Hardrada, the king of Norway, whose army united with Tostig against Harold.

Harold was forced to go to the north to meet the Norwegian threat, and at the Battle of Stamford Bridge in September 1066 Harold was victorious and both Hardrada and Tostig lost their lives.

Immediately following this victory, however, William of Normandy landed on the south coast of England. Harold rushed his army southward

BRITISH TRAVEL ASSOCIATION
DOVER CASTLE in Kent is built around what is believed to be Britain's oldest building.

and attacked the invaders at Hastings on October 14. By the end of the day, Harold was dead and William, "the Conqueror," triumphant.

He pressed on with his army to London, where the Witan submitted and recognized him as king. For several years William had to suppress English revolts against the Normans, but he had acquired the crown of England, perhaps by right, as he asserted, but certainly by conquest.

The Norman conquest of England did not involve a replacement of all things English with all things Norman. William retained the Anglo-Saxon divisions of the kingdom and the offices and practices associated with them. The Danegeld, the English courts and laws, their army, and, for a time, the Witan, remained as well.

William. Gradually, William replaced England's informal democracy with more rigid institutions. The Witan became the *curia regis,* or king's court, a council of lay and clerical nobles who advised and assisted the king.

Feudalism also was introduced into England as a result of the Norman conquest, when the lands and offices of dispossessed, rebel Anglo-Saxons were granted to loyal Normans in return for their accepting military and other duties. The oaths by which William bound these tenants to him were the legal framework for a feudal structure of government that had in it elements of both Anglo-Saxon and Norman custom, yet was itself unique.

By 1085 William's rule over England was firm. His Norman followers held lands throughout the kingdom and acknowledged him as their feudal overlord; his castles were built at strategic points to protect the land from internal and external violence. The thoroughness and efficiency of William's rule is illustrated by the "Domesday" survey of 1086, in which the king's officials compiled a complete report, chiefly for tax purposes, of property ownership throughout England.

In religious matters, William worked to make the church in England conform to the standards of the papacy while preventing papal influence in England from becoming superior to his own.

Most importantly, William's conquest of England bound the island, through Normandy, to Latin Christendom and turned it away from those ties it had had with Scandinavian lands, peoples, and customs.

Henry I (r.1100–1135). When William died in 1087 he left the kingdom of England to his second son, William Rufus (William II, r.1087–1100), who lacked his father's wisdom and ruled oppressively. Another of the Conqueror's sons, Henry I, who followed William II to the throne, showed something of his father's skill and energy in government.

Because some disputed his right to the throne, Henry's first acts as king were bids for popular favor. One of the most significant was his issuance of a charter promising to remedy many grievances the people had held against his predecessor. By this limiting of the king's own powers, his charter provided a precedent for later demands upon royal prerogatives.

Henry also made legal and administrative reforms. He developed further the *curia regis,* and began the practice of sending itinerant justices of the king's court throughout the land. The creation of these circuit courts added royal justice to the decrees of local and clerical courts.

Henry II (r.1154–1189). Many of the gains in the direction of an ordered royal government were lost when dynastic disputes followed Henry I's death in 1135. The king left no direct male heir, and the nobles' rivalry for power brought near anarchy between 1135 and 1154. In 1154 Henry I's grandson, Henry of Anjou, gained the throne as Henry II.

Through inheritance and marriage, Henry controlled nearly all of southwestern France and was thus lord of not only England, but of continental territories far larger than those directly controlled by the actual king of France. Ireland, too, came at least nominally under the English king's authority when in 1154 Pope Adrian IV allowed Henry to extend his kingdom there.

Henry II strengthened the position of the monarchy, which had been weakened during the dynastic struggle. He reestablished royal preeminence by using powers that his predecessors had only rarely or poorly exercised and in making their application regular and normal. By defining royal rights, he strengthened the position of the king over the barons, and he employed his additional powers in continually making improvements in the machinery of government.

Henry II also carried forward the legal reforms of Henry I. He strengthened the powers of the *curia regis,* he regularized the procedure by which the itinerant justices acted, and he extended the use of the sworn testimony of "jurors" to help in arresting criminals. It is largely due to Henry II that English common law, not Roman law, and trial by jury, not trial by inquisition, became the English legal tradition.

To have his courts and his law prevail over the private courts of feudal barons and over the independent courts of the church, Henry issued the Constitutions of Clarendon in 1164 and other royal edicts to make royal law common to the whole land and superior to law of other courts. By weakening church courts, however, these reforms brought Henry into conflict with his archbishop of Canterbury, Thomas Becket.

Four of Henry's knights murdered Becket in 1170, and Becket was immediately regarded as a martyred saint. Henry was forced to make a public act of penance and to accept the church's view of the role of church courts.

Richard I (r.1189–1199). Henry was succeeded by his son Richard. Richard I, "the Lionhearted", was great in legend, but of little importance in fact as far as England was concerned. Throughout almost all of his reign he was engaged in the Third Crusade, which kept him out of the country.

The absence of a king did not cause the degeneration of royal power, largely as a result of Henry II's reforms and the work of Hubert Walter, Archbishop of Canterbury.

By the 1100s English society was well settled into its particular pattern of feudalism. Differing from continental feudalism, the English manorial system led more to internal peace than to internal conflict, for, with armed castles required to be licensed by the king and thus few in number, the noblemen of England were more gentlemen landowners than warriors. Feudal duties to higher lords, including the king, were fulfilled more often through the courts of law than on the battlefield.

Serfs, bound to the land of their lord's manor, kept the agricultural economy running. Each manor-town was largely self-sufficient, and its land was rich enough to support its inhabitants without a need for trade.

At the end of the 1100s, the towns began to grow in size and significance, and the free townsmen began to gain importance. Both towns and townsmen were encouraged in their rise by Hubert Walter. He granted town charters which gave an extraordinary degree of self-government to the towns.

John (r.1199–1216). John, upon the death of his brother, came to the throne full of ambition and talent. He wanted to press forward the claims of the crown against both the church and the nobility, but his efforts failed, largely because he both inherited and created many formidable enemies.

During John's reign England lost its continental Angevin possessions, including Normandy, to France. Moreover, John's attempts to control the nomination of the archbishop of Canterbury failed, and in 1213 he had to humble himself before the pope and acknowledge that England was a papal fief.

In his attempt to extend royal power at the expense of the barons, especially in the dispensing of justice and the levying of taxes, John was brought to heel by a revolt of the barons. In 1215, at Runnymede, the discontented nobles forced him to grant a long and detailed charter, which came to be known as the Great Charter, or *Magna Carta.*

The charter was not a comprehensive grant of liberties to all of John's subjects. It dealt very specifically with certain complaints that the influential classes in England raised with the policies of Henry II and John. Most of its clauses were meant to apply only to barons, clergymen, wealthy townsmen, or freemen. Few were of general application or referred to the majority of Englishmen, the serfs.

The charter's most significant aspect, the requirement that the king must act according to laws or customs that he could not set aside at will, was modeled on the charter granted by Henry I. John's charter's significance lay in the fact that the king's subjects demanded the grant as their right. The nobles' demand for control over the king was a first step away from absolutism. The significance of the charter increased in later years as it came to be regarded as protecting the rights of all Englishmen.

Henry III (1216–1272). The nobility increased its control over the monarchy during the reign of Henry III, who came to the throne as a child in 1216. Later, Henry, a pious man and a patron of the arts, to the disgust of many of his English subjects, filled his court with foreigners and dismissed Englishmen who had served him well. As a result, many of the English nobility and clergy banded together against him.

In 1258 Henry was forced to accept an agreement, the Provisions of Oxford, which established a permanent committee of barons to control the king's government. By 1264, however, this settlement had broken down, and the quarrel between Henry and his nobles degenerated into civil war in which the barons, led by Simon de Montfort, Henry's brother-in-law, defeated Henry.

To gain broad support for their government, the baronial council of government, organized and dominated by de Montfort, called for a "Model Parliament" in 1265. The Model Parliament was to be attended by two knights elected from each shire and, for the first time, two representatives from each city and borough.

Under such a strong threat to their power, however, the king and the more conservative barons rallied, and late in 1265 the king's forces led by his son and heir, Prince Edward, defeated the barons in battle and killed Montfort. The baronial rebellion and experiment with government ended. All charters granted were annulled.

Edward I (r.1272–1307). Edward became king while in the Holy Land on a crusade. On his return in 1274, he determined to bring order to the kingdom by extending the power of the crown. Moreover, Edward saw that the gathering of a parliament bringing together the greater clergy, the nobility, and representatives of the towns could serve his purposes in extending royal authority.

For Edward, the gathering of the higher clergy, the nobility, and the representatives of counties and boroughs in parliament was an enlarged *curia regis*, or council of advisors. Through it he could discover the outstanding abuses that existed in the kingdom, and at the same time, it could effectively announce royal policy and influence public opinion. Moreover, Parliament could be most useful in opening to the king new sources of revenue beyond the limited and inadequate income that the crown derived from its traditional source, fixed feudal dues.

Edward needed new sources of money and support because of his ambitious foreign and domestic policies. While he was making inroads in the power of the barons and the church in England, he was at war with France on the continent to defend one of his French territories. Even more aggressive and costly were wars he waged in Wales and Scotland.

Wales had for centuries been a troublesome and occasionally threatening land on the western frontier of the English kingdom. In the early 1200s Wales had been united under Llewelyn the Great (r. 1194–1240) and

ROYAL GUARDSMAN, one of the Queen's personal escorts, stands duty at Whitehall.

started to take advantage of the rifts existing among English political factions.

In the late 1200s Edward I decided that the peace of England required the conquest of Wales, and by 1284 he had conquered the kingdom. Although Welsh laws, customs, and language survived, independent Wales ceased to exist, and Edward's castles dominated the land. In 1301 Edward proclaimed his son and heir the "Prince of Wales."

Edward had less success in Scotland, the kingdom to the north. Scotland, like Wales, had had a troubled domestic history, and for centuries had been a threat to England. After the death in 1286 of its king, Alexander III, Scotland found itself without a ruler and prey to the evils arising from a disputed succession to the throne. Edward I was called in to choose a king, and in 1292 he declared John Baliol king of Scotland. Taking advantage of his position, Edward then made extensive demands on the Scots.

To resist the king's aggression, the Scots made a military alliance with the king of France. John Baliol, William Wallace, and Robert Bruce led Scotland in wars against English domination, which continued for over 30 years and did not end until 1328, when King Edward III recognized Bruce's title to the Scottish crown.

Edward II (r.1307–1327). Although Edward had strengthened the position of the monarchy, his failures in other fields left it open to attack on other fronts. Thus, although he left his son Edward II the benefits of advancements in the laws and institutions of the realm, he also left a drained treasury, an exhausting war in Scotland, and a host of enemies at home and abroad. Edward II was not the man to take advantage of the benefits or overcome the difficulties or take full advantage of the benefits of his position.

In Edward II's reign, the barons sought with some success to supervise royal policy through a commission known as the Lord's Ordainers. When, in 1327, Edward, surrounded by plots and conspiracy, was deposed and murdered, it was Parliament that named his successor, proclaiming his 15-year-old son King Edward III.

Edward III (r.1327–1377). The young king came to the throne during a turbulent period in England's social and political development. During the 1200s and early 1300s English cultural and economic life had quickened most dramatically, and the speed of the resulting social change was increased by a long series of wars and a major epidemic during the 1300s.

English cities and towns, which had grown into thriving centers of trade, had developed a particularly active commerce in cloth with the Low Countries—Belgium, the Netherlands, and Luxembourg.

In part to insure the continuation of this commerce and to foil the attempts of the French king to interrupt it, Edward III in 1337 began a conflict with the French that lasted so long it earned the name, the Hundred Years' War. The French alliance with the Scots in their war against England also encouraged Edward III to go to war against France. He used the pretext that, as a descendant of Philip II of France, he had a valid claim to the crown of France.

Britain enjoyed early victories, and the Treaty of Brétigny in 1360 brought the first phase of the long war to an end. By it, England received the port of Calais, protection for its cloth trade, title to a large section of southwestern France, and promise of ransom for the heir to the French throne, whom the English had captured.

France had been ravaged by the war, and England also suffered, both from financial exhaustion and from the violent onset in 1348 of the plague known as the Black Death. The plague killed perhaps one-third of the English population.

By causing a manpower shortage that broke the traditional bonds of the serf to the land and the manor, the Black Death hastened the process of social change. Feudalism began to disintegrate and the position of the towns and of a newly formed middle class was strengthened. Aided by the collapse of feudal loyalties and by the new spirit of nationalism inspired by the wars with France, the English monarchy in the late 1300s was able to centralize its power at the expense of the local lords and clergy.

The new social order not only increased the power of the monarchy and its local representatives, the justices of the peace; it also enhanced the status of the representatives of the expanding middle class in Parliament, and it was during the mid-1300s that the practice developed of having Parliament divide into two groups, one body of nobles and higher clergy and one of knights of the shire and townsmen.

Between 1339 and 1349 the knights and burgesses began to be designated as the "Commons," because they had by custom established a common meeting place, a common clerk, and had begun electing a common speaker to speak for them before the king.

The continuing wars with France also strengthened Parliament, as the growth of parliamentary power depended primarily on the control of taxation, and Edward III was continually in need of funds to wage the war. He asked Parliament to take on the burden of levying taxes, and Parliament consented to grant the funds in return for the king's remedying grievances or giving additional privileges sought by Commons.

By the end of Edward's reign, Parliament's power was great. Not only had the nobles succeeded in increasing their control over finance, but they had also secured an important role in formulating legislation, and had even exerted occasional pressures to control executive policy.

Richard II (r.1377–1399). Edward was succeeded in 1377 by his grandson, Richard, still a minor. As Richard II, he came to a troubled throne. In the wars with France, the English had suffered many defeats and, by 1375 had been driven from all but a few coastal points on the continent.

In England, the burdens of war and taxation added to the discontent the lower classes felt in the era's rapid social changes and economic instability and led in 1381 to a briefly successful "Peasants' Revolt."

Richard responded to foreign failures and domestic unrest by arbitrary, absolute rule which made many enemies who rallied behind Richard's cousin, Henry of Lancaster, in 1399 and forced Richard to abdicate.

Henry IV (r.1399–1413). Parliament's proclamation of Henry of Lancaster as King Henry IV marked a great step in Parliament's growth. Henry reigned as a frankly constitutional monarch. By putting down several attempted rebellions and invasions, Henry passed on to his son Henry V a kingdom more secure than the one he had taken, and it looked as though stability had returned to England.

Henry V (r.1413–1422). Henry V was able to pursue the long war with France with remarkable success. By his victories and by his marriage to the daughter of the king of France, Henry became heir to the French throne in 1420. But two years later, he unexpectedly died, and left only an infant son, Henry VI. Both France and England were ruled by regents, and under these circumstances, both kingdoms deteriorated.

Henry VI (r.1422–1461). France recovered first. It improved its military position, and between 1429 and 1431 the tide of battle turned against the English. The French heir won his claim to the French throne against the young English king's, and bit by bit the French won back the English Continental territories.

England's reverses on the Continent had repercussions at home. Unfavorable terms accepted after England's losses caused the House of Commons to raise treason charges against the king's ministers. A brief rebellion by landed gentry followed and weakened Henry VI's shaky hold on the throne. In 1455 the weakness of the monarchy caused rivalries among contenders for the throne to erupt into civil war.

Henry VI's Lancastrian followers opposed the supporters of other descendants of Edward III, who were led by Richard of York, Henry's cousin. The conflicts that arose between the two houses were known collectively as the War of the Roses, because the traditional badge worn by Lancastrians was the red rose, and the Yorkists' badge was the white rose.

Bloody civil war between the houses dragged on for 30 years with the leaders of each faction claiming the right by inheritance to be king, but an end seemed to be in sight in 1461. Richard of York had been killed the year before, but his son, Edward, defeated the Lancastrians in 1461.

York. Edward of York was proclaimed king as Edward IV (r. 1461–1483). His reign and that of his brother, Richard III (1483–1485), were marked by continuing warfare and violence. Many powerful groups in England, including Yorkists, turned to Henry Tudor, earl of Richmond. Henry had only a remote claim to the throne as a Lancastrian, but he had resided safely in France during the dynastic wars. Henry invaded England in 1485 and defeated Richard III's army. As a result of Richard's death in the battle, Henry gained the crown as Henry VII.

Henry VII (r.1485–1509). Henry had come to the throne through military victory and parliamentary consent; hereditary right had played little part. He sought to make his throne secure for himself and his descendants and to bring peace and order back to England. To achieve both ends, in 1486 he united the formerly warring houses by marrying Elizabeth of York, the eldest daughter of Edward IV, and founded the Tudor dynasty.

Under the Tudors, England entered one of its greatest eras. Under Henry's guidance, the first royal navy was built, and the Cabots explored the coasts of North America, preparing the way for English colonies there.

Henry VIII (r.1509–1547). Henry VII's son, Henry VIII (r.1509–1547), had the ambition and talent to make the most of the powerful Tudor position his father had established. In the early part of his reign Henry VIII led England into participation in the diplomatic and military affairs of Europe. From 1515 to 1529, Thomas Wolsey, lord chancellor, was his brilliant adviser and agent in foreign affairs.

But Wolsey ultimately failed the king in the matter that after 1527 became Henry's chief concern—his desire to divorce his wife, Catherine of Aragon, who had failed to bear him a male heir. At the outset, Henry attempted to obtain a divorce through the papal courts at Rome, but this attempt failed in 1529.

Henry resented the church for reasons other than its refusal to grant him a divorce. That an outsider, like the pope, should exercise independent power within the realm of England was unpleasant to Henry. His predecessors had tried for centuries to limit church authority. Henry VII had come close to subordinating the nobility to the monarchy, but the church remained, with its courts, laws, taxes, and massive properties. Henry's divorce would provide the occasion for a sweeping reform of the relations between the monarchy and the church.

By 1533 Henry had an English court declare his marriage to Catherine invalid, and he had married Anne Boleyn. In 1534 Henry passed an Act of Supremacy, making himself and his successors head of the church in England, and declared all appeals to Rome illegal.

Although at the time that Henry defied the church, the Protestant Reformation was sweeping Europe, the

BRITISH TRAVEL ASSOCIATION
BUCKLAND-IN-THE-MOOR. A thatched cottage in the Dart Valley near southern Dartmoor.

impetus for England's "reformation" was more political than religious. The Anglican Church differed little from Roman Catholicism, except that Henry, not the pope, was its head.

Henry's marriage to Anne Boleyn did not serve his dynastic purposes. In 1533 she bore him a daughter, Elizabeth, but no son. In 1536 he had Anne executed, and he married Jane Seymour, who died in 1537 while giving birth to a son, Edward. Two other wives preceded Henry's sixth, Catherine Parr, who survived him.

Edward VI (r.1547–1553). Henry's actions had made religion a vital issue in English politics, and its importance increased after Henry's death. Henry was succeeded by his 10-year-old son, Edward VI, whose policies were determined by the Duke of Somerset and the Duke of Northumberland, both of whom worked to make the English church more Protestant.

Mary (r.1553–1558). After Edward VI's death, however, the crown passed to Mary, the devoutly Roman Catholic daughter of Henry VIII and Catherine of Aragon. Mary tried unsuccessfully to restore Roman Catholicism in England. She married Philip II of Spain, heir to the Holy Roman Empire, but their marriage was unpopular because of English fears of intervention and domination by Roman Catholic Spain.

Mary's persecution of Protestants earned her the name "Bloody Mary," although in her insistence on a single national religion she was in company with every other European ruler in the 1500s. Her death brought her half-sister, Elizabeth, to the throne.

Elizabeth (r.1558–1603). Elizabeth combined the Tudor qualities of determination and practicality most happily. She saw the importance of bringing order and peace to the realm, and with the help of talented advisors she found means and developed policies to do so with remarkable success.

In the area of religion, Elizabeth moved cautiously, not making a decision until Parliament did. By the Act of Supremacy (1559) and Uniformity (1563), passed by Parliament, she achieved a broad religious settlement that was moderate enough to satisfy the great majority of her subjects.

Elizabeth increased royal power by gaining widespread popular support through insuring the welfare of the people. Elizabeth initiated a program of national regulation of economic and social affairs unprecedented in Europe. Currency was stabilized, and industry was stimulated by grants of patents and monopolies. The "poor laws" provided relief for the disabled and the indigent, and the Statute of Apprentices regulated the hours and conditions of labor. Laws against religious dissent were enforced only when it threatened the peace of the realm.

The economic vitality of the kingdom found expression in the formation, near the end of Elizabeth's reign, of a number of trading companies—the most famous of which was the East India Company—that established commercial relations and trading outposts in many parts of the world.

Elizabeth also used the English institutions of government to her, and England's, benefit. Under the Tudors the privy council, consisting of the monarch's personal advisors, usually led Parliament, which passed into law many of the measures initiated by the council. The centralizing of these institutions, together with the elimination of older ones associated with feudalism or Roman Catholicism, made the English machinery of government more efficient.

Elizabeth's government brought England international prestige, as well. By successfully facing a series of crises brought on by the Spanish king and other Roman Catholic leaders determined to restore Roman Catholicism in England, Elizabeth gained new respect for her country.

Moreover, in Elizabeth's reign English sailors broke the Spanish monopoly of trade with the New World and established England as a leading maritime nation. They plundered Spanish galleons, raided Spanish colonial outposts, and seized Spanish treasure. These exploits increased Englishmen's national pride and their awareness of the importance of the sea to England's world position.

England's maritime supremacy led Philip II of Spain to build a great Armada in 1586 to destroy the English fleet and to make possible the conquest of England. Faced with this great crisis, the English navy defeated the Spanish Armada in 1588, and thus opened the way for the further expansion of trade and, eventually, for the building of an empire.

James I (r.1603–1625). Elizabeth had never married, and upon her death in 1603, the crown passed to James VI of Scotland, son of her cousin, Mary of Scotland. James became the first of the Stuart kings, as James I of England. Although the crowns of England and Scotland were united in one person, the kingdoms remained separate.

Religion was one of the first issues confronting James. Dissatisfaction with the vagueness and breadth of Elizabeth's church settlement had increased in the late 1500s, and many hoped that further changes could be made in the law to eliminate vestiges of Roman Catholicism in the Church of England. The term "Puritan" came to be applied to those who were thus dissatisfied.

These Puritans turned first to Parliament for church reform, but with little effect. James, himself an Anglican, was unwilling to commit himself on the issue and gave the Puritans little more than permission to make a new translation of the Bible. The king's stubbornness was one cause for the departure of some Puritans to America, where they established a colony—the second English colony in the New World. "Jamestown," a settlement of James' followers in Virginia, had been the first.

Roman Catholics, too, were unhappy over James' refusal to revoke the Elizabethan anti-Roman Catholic laws. In 1605 they formed a conspiracy called the "Gunpowder Plot," designed to blow up Parliament. When the plot was exposed, it inspired strong anti-Roman Catholic feeling in the general public, and resulted in further restrictions on Roman Catholics.

James was also unsuccessful in dealing with Parliament, and during his reign the conflicts between king and commons over religion, foreign policy, and economic affairs grew increasingly sharp. The central issue of James' reign was the extent of royal authority.

James held to the "divine right" theory of kingship—royal authority came from God and the king was above the law. James' ineptitude in handling the institutions of government caused the Commons to become equally rigid in asserting the rights of subjects and in fixing constitutional limits upon the arbitrary use of royal power.

Unable to deal with Parliament, James ruled without it almost continuously from 1611 to 1621. Parliament's hostility toward James impelled it to develop powerful procedures and strong leaders capable of initiating and carrying through policies. The conflicts between the king and the Commons grew still sharper during the reign of James' son, Charles I.

Charles I (r.1625–1649). Charles' economic and governmental policies hardened and enlarged opposition to the king. Charles, after dissolving two Parliaments which opposed his arbitrary rule, was forced by Parliament in 1628 to grant the Petition of Right, a document which declared illegal certain royal taxes, such as forced loans, and practices, such as arbitrary imprisonment. Charles had had to reconvene Parliament and grant its demands because he needed Parliamentary approval to finance English involvement in the Thirty Years' War, a European religious and political conflict which had begun in 1618.

When Parliament continued to refuse funds, Charles ruled without it between 1628 and 1640, resorting to makeshift methods of taxation and dictatorial behavior, which alienated the populace. In 1640, when the additional expense of a war with Scotland forced Charles to reconvene Parliament, the members were ready to challenge the king.

They passed measure after measure eliminating institutions that Charles had used to maintain his absolute rule. Two of his advisors were executed. In 1641 the House of Commons formulated a program called the "Grand Remonstrance," that would have created a limited parliamentary monarchy in England and would have modified the episcopal organization of the church.

In 1642, a few months after the Commons had passed the Remonstrance, Charles accused the Parliamentary leaders of treason and tried personally to arrest them. Unsuccessful, he left London, and it was clear that more than votes would be needed to settle the conflict between king and Parliament.

EDINBURGH, SCOTLAND, with Ed Castle *(left)* and the Sir Walter Scott Memorial *(right).*

In 1642 civil war began between the royalists, called "Cavaliers," who supported the king, and the Parliamentarians, called "Roundheads." The Cavaliers were generally Anglican nobles or gentry; the Roundheads were mostly Puritan burghers and townsmen who wanted to abolish the episcopacy.

Led by Oliver Cromwell, the Puritans and their allies, the Scots, won many important early victories, and in 1646 Charles surrendered to the Scots, who handed him over to the Parliamentarians in 1647. The victors, however, then quarreled among themselves as to what forms of government should replace the old form.

Charles took advantage of these disagreements and made an alliance with his former opponents, the Scots. A second civil war broke out in 1648, and again Cromwell and the Parliamentarians were victorious. They decided that, to achieve any permanent victory, they must execute Charles.

Commonwealth. Charles I was tried and beheaded early in 1649. The monarchy and the House of Lords were abolished and England was declared to be a commonwealth. An executive council led by Cromwell ran the government, and Cromwell discovered how difficult it was to rule with Parliament.

Between 1649 and 1653 under the Commonwealth, and then between 1653 and 1658 under a similar government called the Protectorate, Cromwell had as much difficulty with Parliament as Charles had had, and several times he found it necessary to dismiss Parliament.

Cromwell's revolutionary government made little progress with constitutional experiments it had planned. One of the few benefits of the commonwealth was the needed support it gave to Puritan colonists in America. In Scotland and Ireland, however, its excessive zeal only alienated the populations and made future union more difficult.

Charles II (r. 1660–1685). After Cromwell's death in 1658 the Protectorate was too weak to survive, and in 1660 Charles I's son took the throne as Charles II. Religion continued to be the central issue, and in the 1670s Parliament passed a series of laws directed against Catholic and Protestant dissenters.

Much of the parliamentary debate centered on a bill that would have excluded Charles' brother, James, from the throne because he was a Roman Catholic. During this debate the labels "Whig" and "Tory" came into use, and the attitudes associated with them developed.

Whig designated one favoring religious toleration and the exclusion of James, that is, asserting Parliamentary control over the succession. Tory designated one favoring an intolerant and exclusive Anglican church policy and the hereditary right of kingship, even if it should involve bringing a Roman Catholic to the throne.

James II (r. 1685–1688). The issue of religion and royal succession arose again in the 1680s and led to the firm establishment of a constitutionally limited monarchy in England.

James II followed his brother to the throne in 1685, and most Englishmen were willing to be loyal to him, accepting his declaration that he would defend the Anglican church and keep his own Roman Catholic loyalties a purely private matter. By 1688, however, James' actions, such as giving Roman Catholics high positions in his council and in the army and his harshness toward Anglican opponents, had caused many men to contemplate acting against him.

The birth of a son to James' wife in June 1688 brought this discontent to a head, for in the absence of a son, the throne would have gone to James' daughter, Mary. Mary, a staunch Protestant, was married to William of Orange, head of the Dutch state and leader of the Protestant forces in Europe against Roman Catholic Louis XIV of France. Thus Mary's succession and the future of Protestantism in England seemed doubtful.

In June 1688 a small group of both Whigs and Tories invited William of Orange to invade England, and William and an army landed in England in November 1688. Finding little support in England against this challenge, James II fled to France.

William of Orange (r. 1689–1702). A specially convened Parliament declared the throne vacant and offered it to William and Mary, with William acting as king. In making its offer, Parliament made it clear that it and the law were above the king's will.

In accepting a Declaration of Rights along with the crown, the new sovereigns accepted constitutional limitations upon their royal authority, which were written into the Bill of Rights. The absolutist theory of "divine right" was dead. The king ruled by grace of legally constituted popular representatives who could remove his authority as well as grant it.

The events of the "Glorious Revolution" were confirmed in a number of statutes. By them, the king could not suspend acts of Parliament, and was required to convene Parliament annually. In addition, Roman Catholics were excluded from the throne, but limited toleration was granted to Protestant dissenters.

As king, William had to deal with unrest in Scotland and Ireland. Scotland, though still officially ruled by the English king, was more loyal to the deposed James II than to England, and William only barely managed to maintain his position there. Roman Catholic Ireland, still smarting from harsh treatment under Cromwell, was more rebellious, and the Protestant king responded with severity.

As soon as the political situation in England was stabilized, William brought England into the League of Augsburg, an alliance that united both Protestant and Roman Catholic Europe against the territorial aggression of Louis XIV of France. War began in 1689 and continued with brief interludes of peace until 1713.

Anne (r. 1702–1714). Despite strong allies and Parliament's vigorous support of the war, England and its allies did not begin to win until William's successor, Mary's sister Anne, appointed John Churchill, first duke of Marlborough, as commander of the armed forces. His brilliant victories resulted in the defeat of Louis XIV's policies and led to the Treaty of Utrecht in 1713.

The terms of the treaty laid the groundwork for the expansion of England's empire. By the treaty,

England received as colonies Gibraltar and Minorca in the Mediterranean and the Hudson Bay Region and Newfoundland in Canada. In addition Britain gained trading rights with Spanish colonies and a monopoly of the slave trade in Europe for the next 30 years.

At the head of this embryonic empire was the newly formed "United Kingdom." Scotland and England had been formally joined in 1707 into "Great Britain." All of the British Isles were under the control of the British monarch, although Ireland's membership in the union was in little more than name. The Irish still resisted British rule that was no more than a military occupation.

None of Queen Anne's children outlived her, and upon her death the Parliamentary rules concerning the succession operated, thus excluding from the throne the Roman Catholic Stuarts.

House of Hanover. The next in line was the head of the German state of Hanover, a descendant of James I. He ascended the throne of England as George I (r.1714–1727). Because George I and his son, George II (r. 1727–1760), spoke poor English, had little knowledge of British politics, and were more interested in the affairs of their German state, Britain's development into a nation governed by ministers advanced rapidly during their reigns.

Cabinet government had gradually developed from the monarchs' custom of using members of the privy council as their active agents in Parliament. Because it was expedient to have a united cabinet, supported by the majority in the House of Commons, the kings found it necessary to consider Parliament's desires when choosing a cabinet. The Georges were often absent from cabinet meetings, allowing the ministers great autonomy, and this custom hardened into a precedent.

Both Georges employed the political genius of their advisor, Sir Robert Walpole, in making the difficult machinery of government work. Walpole was the first man in British history to warrant the designation of prime minister. Walpole's policies gave England political stability, and his reforms of fiscal and commercial regulations stimulated internal industry, shipping, and foreign trade. Moreover, he had refused to let England become involved in European conflicts.

In 1739, however, the House of Commons forced Walpole to declare war on Spain to protect British mercantile interests from Spain's interference with British ships. The "War of Jenkins' Ear," as it was called, went badly for England at first, and Walpole, opposed to the war, resigned in 1742.

As the conflict continued, England gradually became involved in a general European struggle known as the War of the Austrian Succession (1740–1748). The war had imperial and commercial overtones, as Europe's overseas colonies and international trading privileges were at stake.

Hostilities stopped in 1748, only to resume in 1756, as the Seven Years' War, which was more directly between England and France, the leading European powers. An important part of the conflict stemmed from colonial and commercial rivalries in North America and in India.

Britain's victory in the war, directed by the war minister William Pitt, made England the most powerful nation in Europe and the foremost colonial and commercial power in the world. By the Peace of Paris of 1763 England received most French possessions in North America east of the Mississippi and increased trading power in India.

George III (r.1760–1820). George II's successor, George III, played a stronger personal role in politics than had his predecessors. But neither his ministers nor the policies he and they pursued were particularly successful. An important failure was the loss of the prosperous American colonies.

George III's attempts to strengthen the ties between England and the colonies and extend his own influence through repressive legislation ended in 1775 with the outbreak of the American War of Independence. Britain recognized the independence of the colonies in 1782, and signed the Treaty of Paris in 1783, formally ending the United States' colonial status.

George's policies were more successful after 1783, when he named Pitt's son, William Pitt "the Younger," as prime minister. Pitt's genius for finance led to fruitful economic reforms, and he did much to eliminate governmental corruption. Above all, he organized a massive war effort against the government established in France after the French Revolution of 1789, and later against the French empire under Napoleon in the early 1800s.

The war machine that Pitt created contributed to the final defeat of Napoleon in 1815 and Pitt's diplomacy helped lay the international foundations for peace, which prevailed in Europe for the next 100 years.

In 1800, to strengthen England's strategic position, Pitt brought about the incorporation of Ireland into the "United Kingdom" as an equal partner. The union was doomed from the first, for Pitt had promised some religious freedom for Irish Roman Catholics, but the king forbade him to keep the promise, and in 1801 the union was repealed.

Ireland was not the only discontented part of the United Kingdom. All Britons were restless as the pace of social change accelerated. During the 1700s and 1800s agricultural production in England increased as the result of improved techniques, fertilizers, and land management. Increased agricultural output was needed to support the population that had grown enormously in George III's reign and continued to grow rapidly after 1820.

New farm methods reduced the number of laborers needed to produce the extra food, however, and an increasing portion of the enlarged population moved from the farms into the cities. What in 1750 had been a predominantly rural society was 100 years later an increasingly urban society in which half the population lived in towns.

MINISTRY OF PUBLIC BUILDINGS AND WORKS
THE HOUSE OF LORDS. The throne is reserved for the Queen at each opening session.

Simultaneously with this urbanization, rapid technological innovation and invention caused an "industrial revolution." The significance of this so-called revolution, actually a complex and protracted evolution, lay in the chain reaction of events that it set off in economic, political, social, and cultural life.

These developments, together with the difficult shift from war to peace in 1815, led to considerable social unrest. Fearing a revolution similar to that in France in 1789, political leaders introduced legislation that made criticism of the government dangerous and radical agitation impossible.

Moreover, the people were unsure of the strength of the government, for after 1811 George III was completely insane. His son served as prince regent until George III's death in 1820, when he became king George IV.

George IV (r. 1820–1830). By that time, however, Parliament, not the king, actually ruled. It formulated policy that merely required the king's approval, which was seldom withheld. The Tory, or conservative, faction, in power for nearly 30 years at the beginning of the 1800s, was responsible for many of the restrictive laws passed at that time. Some fairly liberal Tories, however, felt that public protests of injustice had validity and responded by passing legislation reforming labor, criminal, and religious toleration laws.

The Tories refused to reform electoral laws, however, which, written centuries before the radical population shifts and class changes forced by the Industrial Revolution, deprived many citizens of representation. The Tories lost the 1830 election on this issue of election reform, and the new Whig, or liberal, majority in the House of Commons gave priority to the issue, and began a gradual reform of the electoral system.

Victoria (r. 1837–1901). Reform was achieved in other areas, as well. For the remainder of the 1800s both Whig and Tory cabinets under Queen Victoria passed masses of legislation that radically changed the structure of English society.

Slavery in the colonies was abolished in 1833. Factory acts limited working hours and set standards for conditions and wages, while other laws regulated trade unions. Poor laws established national relief programs. As the century drew to a close, Parliament overhauled the judiciary and the educational systems and established a public health system.

During Victoria's reign, especially in the 1850s and 1860s, many Englishmen felt that their constitution and their society, adjusted by these legislative changes, had reached a perfect balance that insured peace at home and abroad and guaranteed continued prosperity. England seemed to be at a peak of power and progress, and the interruption of European peace during the Crimean War (1854–1856) into which England blundered did little to shake the prevailing optimism.

BRITISH INFORMATION SERVICE

NUMBER 10 DOWNING STREET, the official residence of the prime minister of Britain.

Industry and trade had made Britain the world's most prosperous state. It became the leading political power after the 1850s, when it acquired colonies all over the world. Benjamin Disraeli, who became prime minister in 1868, was the guiding light of English imperialism.

In 1875, to enlarge the empire, he acquired on his own a controlling interest in the Suez Canal Company and turned it over to England. By the end of the century Britain had colonies or commercial interests in the Far East, the Middle East, and Africa, in addition to its older colonies in North America and the Caribbean.

But Britain's imperial role brought the country into conflicts with other colonial powers. All the major European countries were establishing colonies in Africa and Asia, and Britain sought to compete. It became involved in a series of crises and conflicts over colonial territories, from the Afghan and Zulu wars of the late 1870s through the South African, or Boer War of 1899–1902.

By the end of the 1800s the optimism and confidence that had marked the mid-1800s had waned considerably in Britain. In addition to conflicts abroad, industry at home ceased to enjoy the unquestioned superiority it had once held over other nations, and agriculture began to suffer from foreign competition.

Edward VII (1901–1910). In the early years of the 1900s, during the reign of Queen Victoria's son, Edward VII, two Liberal governments passed radical social welfare legislation, including old age pensions and national unemployment and medical insurance.

In 1909 the Liberals in the House of Commons introduced a radical "people's budget" designed to put the burden of taxes on the rich. By refusing to pass the bill, the House of Lords lost its dominant position in the government.

George V (1910–1936). In 1910, the year that George V came to the throne, the House of Commons passed a law limiting the power of the Lords over the Commons on all issues.

Ireland remained a problem. In 1912 the introduction of a series of bills that would have provided home rule for Ireland led to a crisis between the government and the people of Protestant Ulster, who declared their intention to resist home rule. A showdown was prevented only by the outbreak of war in Europe in 1914.

A series of international crises involving the great powers after 1900 had encouraged Britain to make alliances with France (1904) and Russia (1907) to counteract the Triple Alliance of Germany, Austria-Hungary, and Italy. A dispute between Austria-Hungary and Serbia in the summer of 1914 led to the outbreak of World War I. Britain declared war on Germany on August 4, 1914.

The war was costly for England and resulted in a staggering loss of men before it ended in November 1918. The war also severely damaged the British economy and drained industrial resources. As a result, Britain lost its preeminent world economic position to newly industrialized nations that had suffered less during the war, notably the United States.

British international political power declined as well, as the nation's colonial empire began to disintegrate. At a conference in 1926, Britain and its domains agreed to form an association in which no member should have subordinate status—the British Commonwealth of Nations. The era of British imperial power was drawing to a close. The Commonwealth agreement was formalized in 1931 by the Statute of Westminster.

The United Kingdom itself lost one of its members when Ireland rebelled in 1920. In 1922 it became the Irish Free State, and only Ulster, in the north, remained British.

Britain's main problems in the 1900s were economic. Neither the coalition Liberal-Conservative governments, nor the first governments of the newly formed socialistic Labor Party, nor the Conservative governments in power between 1918 and 1931, succeeded in improving England's poor economic situation.

The economy never fully recovered after World War I, and unemployment spread. As Britain lost colonies and fell behind in manufacturing, its trade also declined. The worldwide economic depression of the 1930s worsened Britain's situation.

George VI (1936–1952). In 1936 Edward VIII came to the throne and abdicated in less than a year. He was succeeded by his brother George VI. A national coalition government of Conservatives, Liberals, and Laborites, formed in 1931, held power throughout the 1930s.

The government's attempts to cope with the depression extended Britain's broad social welfare programs and introduced great control by the government over industry and trade. Little progress was made, however, and the depression's cure was left largely to time.

Inactivity marked the coalition's foreign policy. Britain had entered the "collective security" agreements of the League of Nations and the Locarno Pact in the 1920s, but, in a policy of appeasement, failed to stand by these agreements when confronted by the aggressive foreign policies of Fascist Italy and Nazi Germany.

The policy of appeasement reached its peak in 1938 when Prime Minister Neville Chamberlain consented to Nazi occupation of the Sudeten German region of Czechoslovakia in meetings with Adolf Hitler at Munich. In March 1939 Hitler repudiated the Munich agreements by annexing the remainder of Czechoslovakia.

World War II. Realizing the failure of Chamberlain's appeasement policy, the British and French governments reaffirmed their guarantee of the independence of Poland. By the end of the summer, however, Hitler invaded Poland, and on Sept. 3, 1939 Britain and France declared war on Germany.

Within nine months Holland, Belgium, and France had fallen, and Britain stood virtually alone against the Germans. In May 1940 Winston Churchill succeeded Chamberlain as prime minister, and, at the head of a coalition government, provided vigorous leadership in the resistance to German air attacks in 1940 and 1941.

Churchill led Britain into alliances with the Soviet Union and the United States which brought about the defeat of Italy in 1943 and of Germany in 1945. After the war Britain took on a large measure of responsibilty in the making of the peace and in the subsequent formation of the United Nations. In July 1945 a general election replaced Churchill with a Labor government led by Clement Attlee.

Contemporary Britain. Labor took advantage of its first clear majority over all other parties and carried through a sweeping program of economic reform before it fell in 1951. It greatly expanded programs of national insurance; it created the National Health Service, which provided low cost medical care; and it nationalized the Bank of England, the coal industry, and the railroads, among others.

The great cost of World War II to Britain had worsened its already critical economic situation. The national debt had tripled during the war, and the domestic economy was drastically dislocated. It was essential that Britain regain its all-important overseas markets and increase trade by 50 percent above prewar levels to get the country back on a sound economic basis.

In 1949 the pound sterling was devalued, to stimulate exports and industry. Rationing of food, fuel, and other consumer goods imposed during the war continued into the 1950s.

The economy remained the central problem of Conservative governments that held power from 1951 through 1963 under Churchill, Anthony Eden, Harold MacMillan, and Alec Douglas-Home. The difficulty in the early 1950s lay in expanding the domestic economy without incurring greater balance-of-payments deficits by too heavy reliance on foreign nations.

George VI died in 1952, and his daughter, Elizabeth, came to the throne as Elizabeth II. In the late 1950s inflation became a problem, and the government was forced to reimpose many unpopular economic restrictions. Losses in local elections followed, and in 1964, the Conservative government gave way to a Labor cabinet led by Harold Wilson.

Labor's efforts to restore economic balance met with little early success. Wilson's government imposed tight controls on wages and prices, reduced private spending abroad, reduced overseas defense commitments, nationalized the steel industry, and accelerated the pace of granting independence to remaining British dependencies in Asia, Africa, and the Caribbean.

A major problem for Britain and the Commonwealth arose in 1965, when the southern African colony of Rhodesia declared itself independent after refusing to yield to British demands that it grant popular representation to its black African citizens as a condition for independence.

To improve its international status as well as its economy, Britain made several attempts in the 1960s to join the European Economic Community, the Common Market, formed in 1957. Due largely to the opposition of Pres. Charles de Gaulle of France, it was refused admission.

In November 1967, after a series of monetary crises, Britain again devalued its currency, forcing a monetary reshuffling in many countries of the world. The devaluation was followed by new austerity measures at home. It was hoped that the move would stimulate the domestic economy and help create an era of stability and prosperity. The immediate result, however, was the defeat of Labor candidates in a series of by-elections held in 1968. —Dudley W. R. Bahlman

UNITED STATES

Official name: United States of America
Area: 3,615,211 square miles
Population: (1967 est.) 199,118,000
Capital: Washington (Pop., 1965, urban area, 2,413,000)
Language: English
Religion: Protestantism, Roman Catholicism, Judaism
Currency unit: Dollar
National holiday: Independence day, July 4

The United States of America occupies the central portion of the North American continent and the continent's northwest corner, as well as a small archipelago in the mid-Pacific Ocean. Of the country's 50 states, 48 are conterminous, that is, they share the central portion of the continent. The remaining continental state, Alaska, is separated from the conterminous United States by Canada. The Pacific islands of Hawaii, some 2,000 miles off the west coast, form the 50th state.

The conterminous United States is bordered on the north by Canada, on the east by the Atlantic Ocean, on the south by the Gulf of Mexico and Mexico, and on the west by the Pacific Ocean.

Alaska is bordered on the north by the Arctic Ocean; on the east by Canada; on the south by the Gulf of Alaska; and on the west by the Bering Sea, the Bearing Strait—which separates Alaska from the Soviet Union—and the Chukchi Sea. The island state of Hawaii is surrounded by the Pacific Ocean.

THE LAND. The United States is the world's fourth largest nation in area and contains a great variety of landscapes and climates. Its three segments—the conterminous states, Alaska, and Hawaii—are topographically distinct.

The conterminous United States extends some 3,000 miles from east to west and 1,500 miles from north to south and contains five major regions.

Regions. In the east, the Atlantic and Gulf coastal region consists mainly of a wide, fertile plain. The northeastern shoreline is rocky.

Between 100 and 200 miles inland the plain rises into a region of rolling hills, called the Piedmont, the foothills of the Appalachian Mountains. The Appalachians extend from just north of the southern coast across the northern border and contain rounded, forested mountains generally below 4,000 feet in elevation.

West of the mountains, across the Appalachian Plateau, is a vast interior plains region which includes the prairies of the Central Lowlands and the high plains of the continent's Great Plains. The prairies are generally flat and range from 1,000 to 1,500 feet in elevation. The land slopes toward the center into the valley of the Mississippi River. In the north it slopes toward the basin of the Great Lakes, and in the south it rises slightly in the Ozark hills.

To the west, the plains rise gradually in elevation into the high plains, which reach elevations of nearly 5,000 feet in the foothills of the Rocky Mountains. This rugged mountain range stretches the entire length of the continent, with elevations reaching over 14,000 feet. Along its ridge lies the Continental Divide, the watershed dividing westward and eastward flowing rivers.

West of the Rockies is a series of ranges, plateaus, and basins. There, the Great Basin contains the country's deserts—the Mojave in the southwest and the Great Salt Lake and Black Rock deserts to the north.

Within the basin is Death Valley, 280 feet below sea level, and the lowest point on the continent. The high, steep Sierra Nevada and Cascade ranges form the western boundary of this rugged region.

A narrow, fertile valley separates these mountains from those of the Coastal Range, which runs the length of the west coast and in places drops sharply into the Pacific Ocean.

Lakes and Rivers. Of the country's many lakes, the five huge freshwater Great Lakes in the north-central region, the Great Salt Lake in the west, Lake Pontchartrain and Lake Okeechobee in the south, and Iliamna Lake in Alaska are the largest.

COUNTRIES OF THE WORLD

The conterminous United States has many mighty rivers. In the east the Hudson, the Delaware, the Potomac, and the Savannah are among the many that flow into the Atlantic Ocean.

In the center, the 2,470-mile long Mississippi, with its many branches, including the Tennessee, the Ohio, the Missouri, and the Arkansas, drains the entire plains region. The Rio Grande flows southeast from the Rockies and forms part of the country's southern border.

In the west the Colorado, the Snake, and the Columbia are the most important rivers that flow westward from the mountains.

Coastlines. The western coastline of the conterminous United States is generally straight, but there are several inlets that provide good harbors, notably at San Francisco, in California, and in northwestern Washington.

The Atlantic and Gulf coasts are lower and deeply indented. In the south the shore tends to be silted or swampy, and the extreme north is rocky. The major inlets include the Delaware and Chesapeake bays in the east and Tampa and Mobile bays in the south.

The coastline of Alaska is deeply indented and fringed with islands. The islands of the Aleutian Archipelago stretch westward from the mainland. Lowlands lie along most of the coast, and include a tundra region above the Arctic Circle.

The barren, rugged Alaskan Range follows the state's southern border. Mt. McKinley, the highest point in North America, rises 20,320 feet in the Alaskan Range. The Brooks Range rises to about 8,000 feet in the north. The long Yukon River flows through an interior basin.

Hawaii consists of several large islands and many islets and reefs. The islands are volcanic in origin and consist generally of a mountainous core ringed by narrow coastal lowlands.

Climate. Although all but the Arctic northern third of Alaska lies within the temperate zone, the U.S. climate varies quite sharply from region to region. The north tends to be colder than the south, and the interior and the east coast are subject to greater extremes in climate than the rest of the country.

The Atlantic coast generally receives adequate rainfall, and has hot to mild summers and mild to cold winters. The central plains region is quite dry and has very cold winters and very hot summers.

The western mountains are damp with generally moderate temperatures, but the higher regions are colder and the deserts south and west of the Rockies are hot and dry. The west coast has moderate rainfall, mild winters and warm to hot summers.

Alaska's climate ranges from mild and damp on the southern coast to warm summers and cold winters in the interior, and to the arctic climate of the north. Hawaii's climate is mild, with moderate rainfall and little seasonal variation in temperature.

THE PEOPLE. With more than 200 million people in 1968, the United States has the fourth largest population in the world. Between 1960 and 1966 the population grew at the rate of 1.4 percent a year. Population density was about 55 persons per square mile in the mid-1960s, although the mountains and arid regions in the interior are rather sparsely settled.

Distribution. The east coast, particularly the Middle Atlantic region, is the most densely populated part of the United States. It contains eight of the country's largest cities, including New York, the largest city in the country, with some 12 million people living in its urban area in the mid-1960s.

Major cities in other regions include Los Angeles, California, on the west coast; Chicago, Illinois, in the interior; Denver, Colorado, in the western mountains; and Dallas, Texas, in the southwest.

The country underwent rapid urbanization in the mid-1900s, and in 1960 nearly 70 percent of the population was classified as urban.

SANTA FE RAILWAY
SIERRA NEVADA PEAKS, capped by snow, are seen in Yosemite National Park in California.

Origins. The United States is a land of immigrants, and Americans, as the people of the United States call themselves, represent a variety of ethnic backgrounds. The overwhelming majority of the people are of European descent, but there are also large groups from other parts of the world.

By the mid-1900s most ethnic differences had become all but unidentifiable, but some groups remained separate from the dominant culture. These include large numbers of American Indians; people of Chinese and Japanese origin; Negroes, who comprise about one-tenth of the total population; and Spanish-speaking people of Mexican and Caribbean origin.

Language and Religion. English is the dominant language, although first-generation immigrants often continue to speak their native tongues. Most of the world's religions are represented in the United States.

The many Protestant sects have the most adherents. Roman Catholics are second in number, and Jews third. There are also Orthodox Christians and Muslims, and Latter Day Saints, members of an indigenous religious community popularly known as Mormons.

ECONOMY. The United States is the richest of the world's major nations, and its people enjoy a high standard of living. The prosperity of the United States is based primarily on industry. The country's size and economic and political unity have been basic to its economic growth, derived from the exploitation of abundant natural resources, including rich soils and a large variety of minerals.

The United States is a leading world producers of aluminum, copper, iron ore, uranium, sulfur, phosphates, potash, and molybdenum. Its energy resources include petroleum, natural gas, and coal, and much of its waterpower potential is exploited, especially on the Columbia, Colorado, and Tennessee rivers.

Agriculture. The relative importance of agriculture in the U.S. economy decreased steadily in the 1900s as the value of manufactures rose. The number of farms and the number of persons employed in agriculture dropped sharply. In 1965 agriculture contributed only 4 percent of the gross domestic product and employed only about 7 percent of the labor force.

Nevertheless, the country is one of the world's most important agricultural producers, and the output of farm

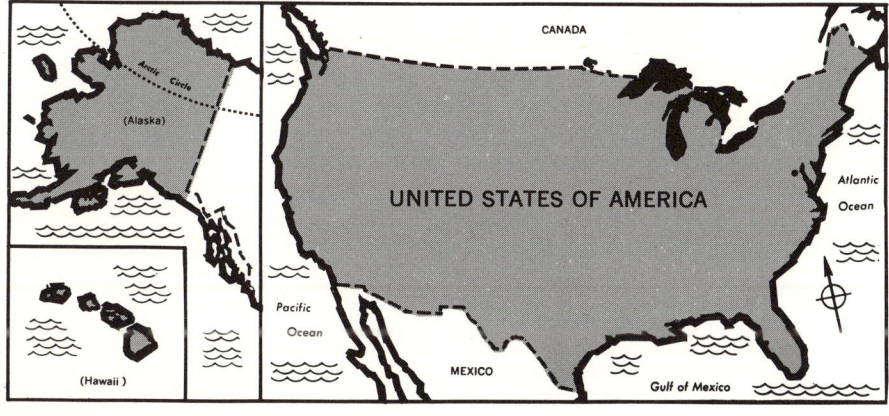

products increased greatly between the 1940s and 1960s. Improvements in agricultural technology have enabled the country to produce sufficient food for domestic needs and large surpluses for export.

The United States is the world's leading grower of corn and oats and one of the world's leading producers of wheat and other grains. In the mid-1960s the country also led the world in the production of tobacco and cotton. Other major crops are sugarcane and sugar beets; oranges, apples, grapes, peaches, and other fruits; and potatoes, beans, cabbage, lettuce, and other vegetables.

Livestock, especially cattle, hogs, and poultry, are raised in large numbers, and dairying is an important activity.

Crops vary from region to region. East coast farms concentrate on raising fruits and vegetables and poultry. Cotton, sugarcane, and tobacco are raised mostly in the south. The central plains contain vast grain-growing areas, and in the north-central region dairy cattle are raised and fruits and vegetables are grown.

In the more arid regions of the west and southwest, cattle-raising is a major activity, and large-scale irrigation systems make it possible to produce large quantities of vegetables. Fruits and vegetables are raised in the moister valleys of the far west.

Forestry and Fishing. About one-third of the country is forested with a variety of hard and soft woods, and forestry and the production of wood and paper products are important activities.

Fishing thrives in inland lakes and rivers and along the coasts, especially in the Gulf of Mexico and off the northwestern coast.

Industry. The leading factor in the country's economy is industry, and in 1965 manufacturing contributed about one-third of the gross domestic product. Metal processing, especially iron and steel making, and the production of machinery and transportation equipment from those metals are basic industries.

Chemicals, petroleum products, lumber and wood products, building materials, fine instruments, textiles, foodstuffs, furniture, clothing, and household appliances are also major industrial products. The construction and transportation and communications industries are also important in the economy, contributing 5 and 6 percent respectively to the 1965 gross domestic product.

Trade. The United States is the world's most prosperous trading nation. In 1967 its exports earned over $31,000 million and its imports cost almost $27,000 million.

Machinery and vehicles, foodstuffs, industrial raw materials, chemicals, and manufactured consumer goods are the leading exports. Raw materials, foodstuffs, machinery and vehicles, fuels, and clothing are among the larger imports.

The United States trades with most of the world's countries, but its major trading partners are Canada, Britain, and the western European countries. In addition to trade, U.S. businesses and industries have extensive investments abroad, especially in Western Europe, Latin America, and the Middle East.

The United States has military bases and commitments throughout the world, and the government gives financial and technical aid to the developing nations. These programs require heavy expenditures and in the mid-1960s created problems in the balance of payments, despite the country's favorable trade balance.

GOVERNMENT. The United States is a federal republic. The chief executive and head of state is the president, who is popularly elected to a four-year term of office.

Legislative power is exercised by a popularly elected Congress, which consists of two houses—the Senate and the House of Representatives. The Senate has 100 members, two from each state, elected to six-year terms. Members of the House of Representatives, elected from each state on a population basis, serve two-year terms.

Each of the 50 states has a governor and a legislature elected according to its state constitution.

U.S. overseas territories include the Commonwealth of Puerto Rico, the Virgin Islands, and a number of small islands in the Caribbean; Guam, American Samoa, and other islands in the Pacific; and the Canal Zone, which cuts through the Isthmus of Panama in Central America.

The United States is a member of the United Nations, the Organization of American States (OAS), the North Atlantic Treaty Organization (NATO), and the Southeast Asia Treaty Organization (SEATO).

—Sara D. Gilbert

UPPER VOLTA

Official name: Republic of Upper Volta
Area: 105,870 square miles
Population: (1967 est.) 5,054,000
Capital: Ouagadougou (Pop., 1961 est., 59,100)
Language: French, African languages
Religion: Traditional religions, Islam, Christianity
Currency unit: Franc CFA (African Financial Community)
National holiday: Republic day, December 11

Upper Volta, a republic in western Africa, is bounded on the north and west by Mali, on the east by Niger, and on the south by Dahomey, Togo, Ghana, and the Ivory Coast. Upper Volta received its independence from France in 1960.

THE LAND. Most of Upper Volta is occupied by sandy plains. In the east, along the border with Niger, is a region of swamps. The Volta Noire, or Black Volta, the Volta Rouge, or Red Volta, and the Volta Blanche, or White Volta, flow through the country. The climate in most of Upper Volta is hot and dry.

THE PEOPLE. There are many different tribal groups in Upper Volta. Almost half of the population are of the Mossi tribe. Other large tribal groups include the Bobo, the Gurunsi, the Samo, and the Marka. There is a small French population.

The largest cities are Ouagadougou, the capital, and Bobo Dioulasso.

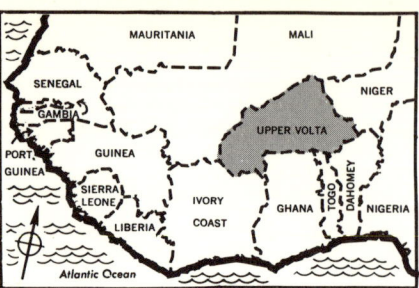

ECONOMY. The economy of Upper Volta is based on agriculture. The basic food crops are millet and sorghum. Peanuts and cotton are also grown. Cattle, sheep, and goats are raised in most parts of the country.

Industry is poorly developed. There are deposits of manganese, bauxite, and gold, but mining is basically undeveloped. Many of the people work outside the country, mostly in Ghana and the Ivory Coast. A railroad connects Ouagadougou with the Ivory Coast port of Abidjan.

In 1964 imports cost $40 million and exports earned $11 million. The main imports are foodstuffs, textiles, and machinery. The major exports are live animals, and hides and skins. Most trade is conducted with Ghana, the Ivory Coast, and France. Upper Volta is a member of an economic union with Dahomey, the Ivory Coast, Niger, and Togo.

GOVERNMENT. Until 1966 Upper Volta had a presidential system of government. Executive power was vested in a president, popularly elected to a five-year term. Legislative power rested with a National Assembly, which was also popularly elected every five years.

In January 1966 the government was overthrown, and a provisional government made up of a Council of Ministers and a consultative committee was established.

Upper Volta is a member of the United Nations and the Organization of African Unity (OAU).

History. In about 1000 AD the Mossi people migrated into Upper Volta and established two principal kingdoms—Ouagadougou and Yatenga. The kingdoms competed with the Dagomba and Mamprussi peoples to the south for primacy in the area. In about 1300 the Mossi came into conflict with the warriors of the ancient empires of Mali and Songhai.

In the 1400s and 1500s Mossi armies raided areas beyond Timbuktu, in present-day Mali. They later raided areas in what is now Dahomey and Nigeria. The Mossi successfully guarded the northern approach routes to Upper Volta until the 1800s, when the French began to conquer the area.

French Rule. France gained control over most the region in 1896, and in 1904 the area became part of the colony of Upper Senegal and Niger. In 1919 a separate colony of Upper Volta was created. In 1932 Upper Volta was divided among Niger, the Ivory Coast, and French Sudan (present-day Mali), but the territory was reestablished as a single unit in 1947.

During the 1950s politics in Upper Volta largely reflected African, rather than exclusively national, considera-

COUNTRIES OF THE WORLD

tions. At that time a local branch of the African Democratic Rally (RDA), an African regional organization with headquarters in the Ivory Coast, had many followers in Upper Volta. In the late 1950s, however, the Upper Volta branch of the RDA began to take up national issues and joined with a smaller reform group to form the Voltaic Democratic Union (VDU).

Independence. In August 1960 Upper Volta became an independent country, and Maurice Yaméogo, leader of the VDU, became president. In January 1966 Lt. Col. Sangoulé Lamizana ousted Yaméogo, suspended the constitution, and established a provisional government.

—Hibberd V. B. Kline, Jr.;
Robert I. Rotberg

URUGUAY

Official name: Oriental Republic of Uruguay
Area: 72,173 square miles
Population: (1967 est.) 2,783,000
Capital: Montevideo (Pop., 1963, 1,158,632)
Language: Spanish
Religion: Roman Catholicism
Currency unit: Peso
National holiday: Independence day, August 25

MONTEVIDEO, URUGUAY. Shoppers examine fresh produce in one of the open air markets.

Uruguay, a small republic on the east coast of South America, is bounded on the north and east by Brazil, on the south by the Atlantic Ocean, and on the west by Argentina.

THE LAND. Most of Uruguay consists of low, gently rolling plains. There are two long ranges of hills known as *cuchillas*, or "knives"—the Cuchilla de Haedo in the west and the Cuchilla Grande in the east. The eastern coast is edged by tidal lakes, lagoons, and sand dunes. The southern coast is characterized by wide, sandy beaches.

The climate of Uruguay is subtropical. The summers are warm and winter temperatures are generally above freezing. Rainfall is fairly evenly distributed throughout the year and averages about 35 inches.

THE PEOPLE. The people of Uruguay are mostly of Italian and Spanish descent. The native Churrúa Indians were almost completely driven out during the Spanish colonial period, and today less than 10 percent of the population can be classified as Indian or mestizo. Spanish is the official language and Roman Catholicism the principal religion.

Uruguay's population increased at an annual rate of 1.4 percent between 1958 and 1965, one of the lowest rates in Latin America. Uruguay has no sparsely populated areas but approximately 45 percent of the people live in the capital, Montevideo.

THE ECONOMY. Uruguay has almost no natural resources other than its fertile land, and the economy is based on agriculture. About 70 percent of the country's land is devoted to the raising of cattle and sheep, and almost 90 percent of exports consist of wool, hides, meat, and various meat products.

About 11 percent of the total land area is under cultivation. Wheat is the principal crop but rice, oats, corn, and barley are grown in large quantities. Sunflower seeds and linseed are also major crops.

Uruguay's industry is largely undeveloped, and consists for the most part of meat packing, food processing, and the manufacture of a few domestic consumer goods. Manufactured products include textiles, glass, rubber, paper, cement, ceramics, beverages, and tobacco.

Trade. In 1967 Uruguay's exports earned $150 million and imports cost $169 million. Principal exports are wool, meat, and hides. Major imports include motor vehicles and parts, machinery, chemicals and pharmaceuticals, raw cotton, and paper.

Uruguay's exports go primarily to the United States, Britain, the Netherlands, West Germany, Italy, and Spain. Most imports come from the United States, West Germany, Britain, Brazil, and Venezuela.

GOVERNMENT. Uruguay is a republic. The chief executive and head of state is the president, who is directly elected to a five-year term. Legislative power is vested in the General Assembly, which consists of the 31-member Senate and the 99-member Chamber of Deputies. Senators and deputies are directly elected on the basis of proportional representation to five-year terms.

Uruguay is a member of the United Nations and the Organization of American States (OAS).

HISTORY. Uruguay was discovered by the Spanish navigator Juan Díaz de Solís in 1516 and further explored in 1520 by the Portuguese captain, Ferdinand Magellan. It was not colo-

nized until 1680, however, when Portugal built a fort at Colonia. During the 1700s the area's location between Brazil and what is now Argentina made it a bone of contention between the Portuguese and Spanish empires.

Spain had a better legal title to Uruguay than Portugal, however. Furthermore, Uruguay was too close to the Spanish military and administrative center of Buenos Aires for Spain to allow it to remain in hostile hands. In 1776 Spain incorporated Uruguay into the newly formed Viceroyalty of Río de la Plata, and in 1777 seized control of the Portuguese settlement at Colonia.

In 1810 Argentina began its struggle for independence from Spain, and in 1811 Uruguay followed suit under the leadership of José Gervasio Artigas. Artigas favored the formation of a loose confederation with Argentina, but Argentina was unwilling to accept this solution.

A complex struggle soon developed among the forces of Artigas, Argentina, and Spain, as well as Portugal, which took advantage of the general confusion to revive its earlier claim to the country. The Portuguese were successful, and when Brazil gained its independence in 1822 Uruguay became a Brazilian province.

Independence. In 1825 a new group of Uruguayan revolutionists rose up against Brazil and declared Uruguay annexed to Argentina. The result was a war between Argentina and Brazil which ended in a military stalemate. In 1828 British mediation brought about a peace treaty, which provided for Uruguay's independence.

Independence did not mark the end of foreign intervention in Uruguayan affairs. Uruguay soon developed two political parties, the Blancos and the Colorados, and Argentina, Brazil, and Paraguay frequently intervened in the struggles for power between the two parties. In 1865 a five-year war broke out, in which Uruguay was allied with Argentina and Brazil against Paraguay.

During the last two decades of the 1800s, Uruguay began to achieve a degree of stability. Educational facilities were expanded, agricultural production increased, and large-scale immigration took place.

Batlle Era. It was not until the early 1900s, however, under the Colorado leader José Batlle y Ordóñez, that Uruguay made major social and economic progress. Batlle twice served as president (1903–1907, 1911–1915) and exerted a strong influence over the country until his death in 1929.

Batlle helped make Uruguay a model of democratic government and encouraged such social and economic reforms as workers' accident compensation, and a minimum wage. He also initiated government enterprises in banking, meat-packing, and other areas.

Contemporary Uruguay. Some democratic procedures were suspended during the world economic depression of the 1930s under the administration of Gabriel Terra (1931–1938), but constitutional procedures were reinstated later in the 1930s. In 1942 Uuruguay broke diplomatic relations with the Axis powers and in February 1945 declared war on them. Later that year Uruguay became a charter member of the United Nations.

In 1951 Uruguay adopted a new constitution, which replaced the president with a nine-member executive council. In the late 1950s the country began to suffer from serious economic difficulties caused in part by a decline in foreign trade and the heavy financial burden of extensive social welfare programs.

The executive council proved unable to provide the leadership necessary to deal effectively with these and other problems, and in November 1966 a new constitution reinstating the presidential system was approved in a referendum.

Oscar Gestido was elected president in November 1966. Gestido initiated an austerity program and he took strong fiscal measures, which slowly began to improve the country's economic situation. Gestido died suddenly in December 1967 and was succeeded by the vice president, Jorge Pacheco Areco.

—David Bushnell; Kempton E. Webb

VATICAN CITY

Official name: State of the Vatican City
Area: 109 acres
Population: (1964 est.) 1,000
Language: Italian, Latin
Religion: Roman Catholicism
Currency unit: Lira
National holiday: Celebration of the coronation of the Holy Father

The Vatican City, located in Rome, Italy, is the world's smallest sovereign state. It is the seat of the central administration of the Roman Catholic Church and the residence of the supreme pontiff, or pope. The term "the Vatican" is frequently used to refer to both the central administration of the church and the government of the Vatican City.

Vatican City lies on the west bank of the Tiber River. It includes St. Peter's Basilica, St. Peter's Square, the Vatican palaces, Belvedere Park, and the Vatican Gardens.

The Vatican also exercises extraterritorial sovereignty over a dozen buildings and some territory in or near Rome, including the basilicas of St. Mary Major, St. John Lateran, and St. Paul without the Walls; the pope's summer residence at Castel Gandolfo; and the Vatican radio station at Santa Maria di Galeria.

The Vatican population consists of clergy of all nations, the Vatican guard, and a number of lay personnel in the service of the Vatican.

GOVERNMENT. The Vatican is ruled by the pope, who has absolute power. He delegates much of the actual administration of the Vatican to the Pontifical Commission for the State of the Vatican City. The commission has five members and is headed by a governor.

The Vatican's diplomatic relations with foreign countries are carried on by the Secretariat of State, and the Vatican maintains diplomatic relations with about 60 countries. The pope is pledged to neutrality in political disputes between governments except when his mediation is requested by both sides. The Vatican also has a permanent observer at the United Nations.

HISTORY. The traditional seat of the papacy has always been Rome. Throughout the Middle Ages the popes controlled not only the city of Rome but large territories in central Italy, the Papal States. The popes lost most of the territory that formed the Papal States during the Italian struggle for unification in the 1850s and 1860s.

In 1849 a Roman Republic was declared, and France, intervening on behalf of the pope, sent troops to Rome. The Kingdom of Italy was formed in 1861, and in 1870, when French troops were withdrawn on the outbreak of the Franco-Prussian War, Rome was added to the new kingdom.

In 1871 the Italian government passed the Law of Guarantees granting the papacy full sovereignty over Vatican City and an annual income from the Italian treasury. The pope refused the offer. But the 1929 Lateran Treaties restored relations between the papacy and the Italian government.

AIR FRANCE
VATICAN CITY LANDMARK is St. Peter's Basilica, with a dome designed by Michelangelo.

The treaties recognized the sovereignty of the papacy within Vatican City, regulated the status of the church in Italy, and arranged for an indemnity to be paid to the papacy as compensation for the loss of the Papal States. In 1947 the terms of the Lateran Treaties were incorporated into the constitution of the Italian Republic.

—Sergio Barzanti

VENEZUELA

Official name: Republic of Venezuela
Area: 352,144 square miles
Population: (1967 est.) 9,352,000
Capital: Caracas (Pop., 1965 est., urban area, 1,674,728)
Language: Spanish
Religion: Roman Catholicism
Currency unit: Bolívar
National holiday: Independence day, July 5

Venezuela, a republic on the northern coast of South America, is bounded on the north by the Caribbean Sea, on the east by Guyana, on the south by Brazil and Colombia, and on the west by Colombia. Seventy-two small offshore islands are also part of Venezuela. The largest of these is Margarita Island, which is famous for its pearl fisheries.

THE LAND. Venezuela has four major geographic regions—the northern highlands, the Maracaibo lowlands, the Orinoco *llanos*, or plains, and the Guiana highlands. The northern highlands, part of the Andes mountain system, extend from the Colombian border in the southwest to the Paria peninsula in the northeastern part of the country.

The mountainous highland area has five subdivisions: the Sierra de Perijá in the extreme west; the Sierra Nevada de Mérida in the southwest; the Segovia highlands, which run eastward from the Sierra Nevada de Mérida along the coast; the central highlands, which run parallel to the coast; and the northeastern highlands in the Araya and Paria peninsulas.

Although the northern highlands cover only about 12 percent of Venezuela's land area, they contain three-fifths of the population and constitute the economic, political, and cultural core of the country.

The Maracaibo lowlands lie to the northwest of the northern highlands. In the center of this area is Lake Maracaibo, which has an area of 6,300 square miles and is the largest lake in South America.

The Orinoco *llanos* extend from the northern highlands south to the Orinoco River. This region is a rolling savanna, or grassland, dotted with a few scattered trees and bushes, and crossed by the numerous streams that feed the Orinoco. These streams swell enormously during the rainy season, and large areas in the *llanos* are flooded for almost half the year.

The Guiana highlands lie to the south of the Orinoco and cover roughly half of the country's territory. This area is a high, jungle-covered tableland with elevations ranging between 3,000 and 6,000 feet above sea level. It is not easily accessible and parts of the area have not been thoroughly explored.

The country's major river is the Orinoco, which rises in the south and flows northeast for about 1,500 miles before emptying into the Atlantic Ocean. The Orinoco and its many tributaries provide Venezuela with excellent water transportation routes.

Climate. Venezuela lies entirely within the tropics, but its climate varies widely according to altitude. The lowlands are hot and humid, and Maracaibo has an annual average temperature of 86°F, the highest registered in South America. The capital, Caracas, in the central highlands at an altitude of about 3,000 feet, has an annual average temperature of 71°F. Temperatures become cooler as the elevation increases.

Venezuela has a wet summer season from May to November and a dry winter season from December through April. Rainfall is generally heavier at higher altitudes. It ranges from about 17 inches a year at Maracaibo on the coast to over 70 inches at Mérida in the northern highlands.

THE PEOPLE. About 70 percent of Venezuela's population is mestizo, of mixed Indian and European descent. Pure-blooded Indians are few in number and live in the more remote parts of the Guiana highlands, the Orinoco delta, and the western Maracaibo lowlands. Europeans constitute about 20 percent of the population and are mainly concentrated in the larger cities. Negroes and mulattos, who make up about 7 percent of the population, live largely along the coast.

Spanish is the official language and Roman Catholicism the predominant religion.

In 1968 an estimated 74 percent of Venezuela's population was urban. Major cities include Caracas, Maracaibo, Barquisimeto, and Valencia.

ECONOMY. The Venezuelan economy depends heavily on petroleum, which in 1966 contributed about 20 percent to the gross national product and accounted for over 90 percent of exports. In recent years, however, the government has made an attempt to diversify the economy by expanding industry and strengthening agriculture through agrarian reform measures.

Natural Resources. Venezuela's most important natural resource is its petroleum deposits, most of which are located in the Maracaibo lowlands. In 1965 Venezuela produced 182.4 million metric tons of petroleum, making it the third largest producer in the world.

The country also has extremely valuable iron ore deposits at El Pao and Cerro Bolívar in the Guiana highlands. Iron ore ranks as the second largest export. In 1965 production amounted to 10.8 million metric tons. Gold, diamonds, natural gas, asbestos, bauxite, sulfur, copper, gypsum, limestone, and salt are also mined.

Agriculture. Agriculture employed about 32 percent of the labor force in 1964, and agricultural production increased 34 percent between 1960 and 1966. The major crops are sugarcane, corn, bananas, and rice. Coffee and cacao are important commercial crops. Beans, sesame, cotton, casava, sisal, potatoes, and tobacco are also raised in large quantities.

Cattle are raised in the Orinoco *llanos*, but are generally of poor quality. The government has been working to improve the breed and to better grazing conditions. In 1966 Venezuela had more than 6.5 million head of cattle.

Industry. Venezuelan industry has expanded rapidly since World War II. Major industries include cotton and wool textiles, leather goods, cement, petrochemicals, and automobile assembly. Other important industries are food processing, meat packing, construction materials, fats and oils, tires, automobile parts, soap, matches, and liquor.

During the mid-1960s plans were underway for the development of a major industrial center at Santo Tomé de Guayana in the Orinoco delta. Although formerly sparsely populated, this area has great potential value because of its access to nearby iron ore deposits and abundant hydroelectric power resources.

Trade. In 1966 Venezuela's exports earned $2,713 million and imports cost $1,188 million. Major exports include petroleum, iron ore, coffee,

and cocoa. Principal imports are industrial raw materials, machinery, transportation equipment, construction materials, foodstuffs, and a variety of consumer goods.

Venezuela exports primarily to the United States, the Netherlands Antilles, Canada, and Britain. Imports come mainly from the United States, West Germany, Canada, Britain, Japan, and Italy.

GOVERNMENT. Venezuela is a republic. The head of state and chief executive is the president, who is popularly elected to a five-year term. Legislative power is vested in the Congress, which consists of the Senate and the Chamber of Deputies.

Two senators are elected from each of Venezuela's 20 states and from its Federal District, Caracas. Additional senators are appointed to represent minorities. There is one seat in the Chamber of Deputies for every 50,000 inhabitants. Both senators and deputies are elected to five-year terms.

Venezuela is a member of the United Nations and the Organization of American States (OAS).

HISTORY. Venezuela was discovered in 1498 by Christopher Columbus on his third voyage to the New World. The first permanent settlement was made by Spain about 1520 at Cumaná, on the Caribbean coast. In 1528 Charles I of Spain (Charles V of the Holy Roman Empire) granted a contract to settle Venezuela to the Welser mercantile firm of Augsburg, Germany. The Welsers were ruthless administrators, and in 1556 the contract was cancelled.

In 1526 the original colony of Venezuela was placed under the jurisdiction of the Audiencia of Santo Domingo. Later it was included in the Viceroyalty of New Granada (Colombia). In 1777 Venezuela became the Captaincy-General of the United Provinces of Venezuela, and in 1786 the Audiencia of Caracas was created. In the last half of the 1700s Venezuela became prosperous from plantation agriculture and a flourishing cattle industry.

Struggle for Independence. In 1806 a Venezuelan patriot, Francisco de Miranda, and a group of volunteers attempted to free the country from Spain. But most Venezuelans remained loyal to Spain, and the attempt failed. In 1808 Napoleon Bonaparte of France deposed Spain's King Ferdinand VII and placed his brother Joseph Bonaparte on the throne. In 1810 a successful revolt took place at Caracas, which deposed the Spanish captain-general of Venezuela and installed a junta, or ruling council.

In 1811 Venezuela declared its independence from Spain, but for several years control passed back and forth between Venezuelan patriots and forces loyal to Spain. Leadership of the struggle for independence passed to Simón Bolívar.

In 1819 Bolívar defeated the Spanish at the battle of Boyacá in what is now Colombia. He subsequently formed the Republic of Gran Colombia, which included present-day Venezuela, Colombia, Panama, and Ecuador. In 1821 Bolívar virtually

CREOLE PETROLEUM CORP.
VENEZUELA'S OIL INDUSTRY, one of the world's largest, centers around Lake Maracaibo.

completed the struggle for independence with a decisive victory at the battle of Carabobo.

Independence. In 1830, under the leadership of Gen. José Antonio Paéz, Venezuela seceded from the republic of Gran Colombia. Páez, an outstanding military leader during the struggle for independence, governed Venezuela from 1830 to 1846. He gave the country stability without resorting to oppression, but those who benefited most were mainly the members of a small elite of the educated and well-to-do.

During the 1850s and 1860s the government was often dictatorial, and the political scene was marked by confusion and instability. Nonetheless, a few constructive measures were undertaken, including the abolition of slavery in 1854.

In 1870 Antonio Guzmán Blanco seized power and ruled the country for 18 years. During his dictatorship there was relative peace, and although corrupt and autocratic, Guzmán Blanco did much to extend public education and to stimulate economic development. In 1889 he lost control, and the country entered a new period of turmoil.

During 1895–1896 Venezuela engaged in a dispute with Britain over its border with British Guiana, the present-day nation of Guyana. In 1902–1903 the country was blockaded by Britain, Germany, and Italy as the result of financial claims of their citizens against the Venezuelan government. The United States intervened to promote a settlement.

In 1909 domestic peace returned following the seizure of the presidency by Juan Vicente Gómez, who ruled the country with a heavy hand for 26 years. Gómez encouraged the rapid growth of the petroleum industry through liberal concessions to British and U.S. companies, but he used the oil revenues for personal gain, military expenses, and showy public works rather than for education, public welfare, or development.

Reform and Reaction. Gómez died in 1935 and his immediate successors gradually dismantled the apparatus of dictatorship and devoted attention to social and labor legislation. Nevertheless, many Venezuelans were dissatisfied with the pace of change. In 1945 a popular rising brought the leftist Acción Democrática party, led by Rómulo Betancourt, to power.

The new regime's most notable achievement was an agreement with the oil companies which stipulated that half their profits were to go to the Venezuelan government, which hoped to use this income for a far-reaching program of social betterment. Presidential elections were held in 1947 and Rómulo Gallegos, the Acción Democrática candidate, was elected.

In 1948 the government was overthrown by the army, which set up a military junta. In 1952, after an interlude of confusion, Marcos Pérez Jiménez was made provisional president. He soon established a new military dictatorship that was in many ways a repetition of the Gómez regime.

Public opposition to the dictatorship was strong, and in 1958 Pérez Jiménez was forced to resign. A brief provisional government restored political liberty, increased the government's share of oil industry profits, and in December 1958 held free elections. The elections returned the Acción Democrática to power with Rómulo Betancourt as president.

Betancourt launched an aggressive program of agrarian reform, agricultural and industrial development, and educational expansion. He was bitterly opposed by supporters of Pérez Jiménez and harassed by communist terrorist activities, but he managed to finish his term of office. In 1963 Raúl Leoni, the Acción Democrática candidate, was elected president. He continued the reform and development policies begun under Betancourt.

—David Bushnell;
Kempton E. Webb

COUNTRIES OF THE WORLD

VIETNAM

NORTH VIETNAM
Official name: Democratic People's Republic of Vietnam
Area: 61,294 square miles
Populaion: (1967 est.) 20,100,000
Capital: Hanoi (Pop., 1960 est., urban area, 643,600)
Language: Vietnamese
Religion: Buddhism, Roman Catholicism
Currency unit: Dong

SOUTH VIETNAM
Official name: Republic of Vietnam
Area: 65,949 square miles
Population: (1967 est.) 16,973,000
Capital: Saigon (Pop., 1964 est., 1,370,600)
Language: Vietnamese
Religion: Buddhism, Roman Catholicism
Currency unit: Piastre
National holiday: Anniversary of the revolution, November 1

Vietnam is a divided country on the east coast of the Indochinese peninsula in Southeast Asia. The Peoples' Democratic Republic of Vietnam, or North Vietnam, a communist-dominated state, lies north of a demarcation line set in 1954 at the 17th parallel and the Republic of Vietnam, or South Vietnam, lies to the south.

North Vietnam is bounded on the north by Communist China; on the east by the Gulf of Tonkin, an arm of the South China Sea; on the south by the Republic of Vietnam; and on the west by Laos. South Vietnam is bounded on the north by North Vietnam, on the east by the South China Sea, on the south by the South China Sea and the Gulf of Siam, and on the west by Cambodia and Laos.

A union of three small kingdoms in eastern Indochina—Tonkin in the north, Annam in the center, and Cochin China in the south—Vietnam was a French colony until 1945. After proclaiming its independence in 1945, Vietnam was torn by warfare.

Until 1953 France and the Viet Minh, a communist-led nationalist movement, fought for control of the country. After the French defeat in 1954 Vietnam was divided.

In the south, communist-led uprisings and infiltration from the north continued, however, and the United States aided the South Vietnamese government in its efforts to defeat the insurgents. Fighting intensified until by the mid-1960s a full-scale air, ground, and sea war was being waged in Vietnam.

THE LAND. North and South Vietnam share a narrow, S-shaped strip of territory, which consists of two river deltas—the Red and the Mekong—and a connecting mountain range—the Annam Cordillera. The 1954 division gave the two Vietnams almost equal areas.

Lying entirely within the tropics, all the lowlands of Vietnam have warm, moist, frost-free weather. The total amount of rainfall and the maximum period of rainfall depend upon exposure to the northeast and southwest monsoons.

From mid-September to March, the northeast monsoons bring cool weather to the Red delta area, rain to the entire east coast, and sunny skies to the Mekong delta. From June to September, the southwest monsoons bring high humidity and rain to all Vietnam. From July to November the country is subjected to irregular and sometimes damaging typhoons.

North Vietnam. The core of North Vietnam is the Red River delta, in the east. It is the compound delta of the Red, the Black, and other lesser rivers, most of which originate in adjacent China and Laos. The delta has many levels because of the uneven sedimentation in each of the component rivers.

The Red River surmounts the delta on a raised bed and has several distributaries, which branch out about 70 miles inland. The delta is the only major lowland in North Vietnam, but there are a few smaller, isolated delta lowlands along the coastal fringe.

Mountains and highlands trending northwest to southeast dominate the landscape throughout the western two-thirds of the country. In central Tonkin rocky, deeply incised mountains rise steeply to more than 10,000 feet.

Lower ranges include the Thai Hills in the western corner of the country, the hilly North Vietnamese Midlands north of the delta, and a deeply dissected high plateau south of the Red River. Further south, along the western border, the northern edge of the Annam Cordillera attains elevations of 8,000 feet in places and drops sharply to the sea.

North Vietnam's climate is tropical monsoon, with temperatures averaging between 60° and 80°F. Between September and April the weather is cool and rather dry. In the monsoon season, from June to September, temperatures are high, rain is heavy, and typhoons are a threat.

South Vietnam. South of the 17th parallel, the Annam Cordillera and its foothills form a central massif known as the Southern Mountain Plateau. It occupies some two-thirds of South Vietnam's area and leaves room for only a few small, enclosed coastal plains. The south's only major lowland lies in the poorly drained, swampy delta of the Mekong River at the southern tip of the country.

The climate of South Vietnam is warm and humid, with temperatures ranging from about 60°F to about 90°F in Saigon. During the monsoon season, from June to September, about 80 inches of rain fall in the south, and typhoons are a danger. From September through to April, the weather is drier and cooler, except along the central coast, where rainfall is heavy throughout the year.

THE PEOPLE. Almost all of the people of both North and South Vietnam are Vietnamese, descended from Mongol and Indonesian peoples. They speak Vietnamese. The major religions are Roman Catholicism and Buddhism.

The largest minority group consists of *Montagnards*, the aboriginal people of the country, of Malay-Indonesian or Mon stock, who lead semi-nomadic lives in the mountains. There are also minorities of Chinese, Cham, Indian, and Malay peoples.

North Vietnam. In North Vietnam the population is concentrated in the Red River delta. In 1965 the density for the country as a whole was about 312 persons per square mile. The highlands are only sparsely settled. All the north's major towns and its only large cities—Hanoi, the capital, and Haiphong, the major port—are located in the delta.

South Vietnam. In South Vietnam the overall population density was about 244 persons per square mile in 1965. The most densely settled area is in the Mekong delta region, especially around Saigon, the capital and largest city. The coastal fringe is thinly settled, and the hills have a very sparse population.

After 1954 the south's population was swollen by an influx of refugees, especially Roman Catholics from the north. The influx created housing and employment problems.

ECONOMY. The economies of both North and South Vietnam were in a state of disarray in the 1950s and 1960s due to war in the country. In normal times, the economies of both are agricultural, with rice production the leading activity.

North Vietnam. In the north, the major rice-growing area is located in the Red River delta, where the population density averages over 1,200 persons per square mile. The north cannot produce sufficient rice to feed its people despite the high productivity of the Red River delta region. Sugarcane, corn, and cotton are also important crops, and tea, coffee, tobacco, castor oil seeds, and silk are produced. Most agriculture is collectivized.

The mountains of the north are heavily forested and contain some minerals. Coal, tin, and tungsten are mined. Some industries were developed in the 1950s, chiefly in Hanoi and Haiphong. They included shipbuilding and iron and steel working.

No trade statistics are available for North Vietnam, but it is assumed that most of the country's foreign trade consists of importing necessary supplies and war materials from Communist China and the Soviet Union.

South Vietnam. Before the war, South Vietnam had an economy based almost wholly on agriculture. Rice was grown in the Mekong delta, and other crops included sweet potatoes, peanuts, tea, and corn. There was also some rubber raised on delta

UNITED NATIONS
VIETNAMESE SCENE, unmarred by years of war, is the tranquil Gulf of Nhatrang.

plantations, but the plantations became inoperative as the intensity of the war increased in the late 1950s and the 1960s.

The country has little industry. Saigon is the chief commercial and transportation center.

With exports almost nonexistent, South Vietnam had a trade deficit exceeding $300 million in 1965, and the gap was widening between exports and imports. The economy was almost entirely dependent on U.S. aid.

GOVERNMENT. North Vietnam's government is democratic in form but controlled in fact by the Lao Dong, or Workers, Party of Vietnam, the North Vietnamese communist party. The constitution adopted in 1960 vests supreme governmental authority in the popularly elected National Assembly, which chooses a standing committee to act for it between its short sessions.

The assembly also elects a president as head of state. The president appoints the prime minister and other cabinet members.

The Worker's Party nominates all candidates for the National Assembly, and government leaders are usually top officers of the party. The political bureau, or politburo, of the party's central committee determines national policy.

By a constitution adopted in 1967 South Vietnam is a republic. Executive power is wielded by a popularly-elected president as chief of state and a prime minister appointed by the president. Legislative power is exercised by a popularly elected assembly of two houses. Because of the war and several political upheavals in the 1960s, power is concentrated in the military.

HISTORY. Vietnam has been inhabited for many centuries, but little is known of its early history. It is thought to have been settled by people moving northward and westward from elsewhere in Indochina and from the neighboring islands, and by people moving southward from China.

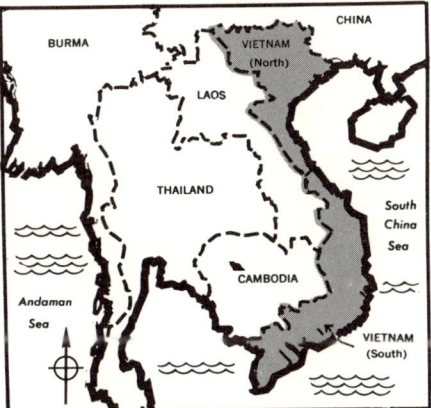

By about 500 BC a kingdom had been established by these Viet peoples, as they called themselves. It extended from present-day North Vietnam across the modern southern Chinese province of Kwangtung. In the 200s BC the Viet began to feel the cultural influence of China, and their kingdom was conquered by generals of the disintegrating Ch'in dynasty of China.

Chinese Rule. These Chinese ruled until 111 BC, when armies of China's Han dynasty, the successor to the Ch'in, conquered Vietnam and annexed it to China. It remained Chinese for about 1,000 years.

During this period, despite rule by Chinese, incorporation into the Chinese economy, and the imposition of Chinese language, customs, and religion, the Vietnamese retained much of their own culture. Several rebellions were attempted against the Chinese, but they were crushed.

The T'ang dynasty came to power in China in 618, and one of its first steps was to make its border areas secure by imposing stricter controls over the non-Chinese population and tying them closer to China. When Vietnam had come under the complete control of China's central government, it was called the "Pacified South," or *An-Nam*.

The T'ang government, unpopular because of its success in subduing the Viet, was even more disliked in the late 700s, when it was unable to prevent the Indochinese kingdom of Champa, south and west of Annam, from conquering large pieces of Vietnamese territory. Vietnamese resentment increased in the late 800s when T'ai peoples from the northwest invaded Tonkin and conquered Hanoi, the capital and central city.

Independence. In 907 the T'ang dynasty collapsed, and in the chaos the Vietnamese successfully rebelled. In 939 a rebel leader, Ngo Quyen, founded a Vietnamese dynasty that by 940 had regained control of all the territory from the 17th parallel to the southern Chinese province of Yünnan. China never recognized Annam's independence, and the country remained under nominal Chinese control.

The early Vietnamese rulers had little success in strengthening the power of the throne over the country's many petty chieftains and separate tribes, and between 939 and 1009 the ruling dynasty changed three times. The first strong dynasty was the Li, which ruled between 1009 and 1225.

During the Li era, the Vietnamese launched a successful drive to regain territory from the Chams of Champa. In 1471, after the Chams had been severely weakened by civil war, the Vietnamese were able to conquer the entire Champa kingdom and extend their Annamese empire across Cochin and into present-day Cambodia. Annam had become a great power in Southeast Asia, but its era of unity, power, prestige, and peace, was short.

Dissension. The 1500s were years of political upheaval that in 1620 erupted into civil war between two powerful families—the Trinh in the north, or Tonkin, and the Nguyen in the

LOOK MAGAZINE
VIETNAMESE WORKERS unloading rice.

south, or Annam. Each supported and controlled rival dynasties.

Civil war continued with a few peaceful interludes for almost 200 years. The country was in fact split into two kingdoms, with neither side able to gain a foothold on the territory of the other.

While the Vietnamese were fighting each other during the 1700s, Europeans began establishing colonies in Southeast Asia. Missionaries, explorers, and merchants arrived in Vietnam from Britain, France, Holland, Portugal, and Spain. Despite their internal warfare, the Vietnamese successfully prevented any of the foreigners from establishing colonies. But Roman Catholic missionaries, most of whom were French, were successful in converting and influencing many people.

Unification. One of the missionaries, Pigneau de Behaine, had become a close advisor of Nguyen Anh, the emperor of Annam. Through him in 1787 the emperor first requested French aid in conquering all of Vietnam. French volunteer sailors and soldiers helped reorganize and train the Annamese army. They helped Nguyen Anh put down a rebellion in Annam and then assisted him in a successful attack upon Tonkin.

By 1802 the Annamese had conquered all of Tonkin, and in 1802 Nguyen Anh proclaimed himself Emperor Gia-Long of all Vietnam, which included much of present-day Cambodia as well. Gia-Long restored peace to his newly unified country. He practiced toleration of all religions and permitted friendly Westerners to live in the country. His death in 1820, however, brought to the throne Minh-Mang, who was anti-Western and anti-Christian.

France tried to open Vietnam to trade by offering to negotiate commercial and diplomatic treaties with Minh-Mang. He rejected all offers and in 1826 broke off formal relations with France. He also refused to tolerate Christianity in the kingdom. In the 1830s he ordered the persecution of Christians, and some Western missionaries were killed.

Minh-Mang's successor, Thieu-Tri, practiced even harsher persecution of the missionaries and merchants, most of whom were French. By the 1840s France held a strong position in Southeast Asia, and it was no longer willing to have its citizens undergo such treatment. France began to press Thieu-Tri to change his policies, but the persecution of Christians—Vietnamese as well as Europeans—increased. It worsened under Thieu-Tri's successor, Tu-Duc.

In 1851, when a French missionary was put to death, French ships bombarded Vietnamese coastal forts. In 1856 another French missionary was killed, and in 1857 a Spanish bishop was executed. Vietnam refused to apologize or grant restitution. In response, France joined Spain in attacking Vietnam in 1858.

French Conquest. France's emperor, Napoleon III, had been looking for a means of getting Vietnamese territory, and this seemed a good opportunity. In 1859 French forces occupied Saigon, in the south. By 1861 France controlled Cochin China and most of the Mekong delta. In 1862 Tu-Duc signed a treaty ceding the southern region to France, and France used the area as a base for French expansion into the rest of Indochina.

Meanwhile, Annam and Tonkin were in chaos. Tu-Duc had lost control of his kingdom, which was in rebellion and which both France and China were trying to seize. Tu-Duc placed Vietnam under Chinese protection in the 1870s, but in the 1880s French armies conquered Tonkin. In 1884 the Treaty of Hué placed all Vietnam under French protection by giving France the right to maintain troops in the country.

China protested that Vietnam was part of the Chinese empire and that no treaty signed without Chinese approval was valid. France responded by sending more troops into Vietnam. The Chinese also sent troops, but China was not actually prepared to fight France. By 1887 France had established its control over the region and united Cambodia, Cochin China, Annam, and Tonkin into the colony of French Indochina.

By the 1890s the French colonial government had put down the many rebellions raging throughout the country and had established itself as master of the area. The French established rubber, tea, and coffee plantations and opened forestry operations.

Rebellions were frequent. In the 1920s France granted the Vietnamese a partially elected council to advise the colonial governor-general. Vietnamese representation was not effective, however, and in 1930–1931 more violent rebellions occurred. They were put down quite harshly. Opposition to French rule grew and Vietnamese nationalist groups were organized.

World War II. In 1940, after the outbreak of World War II, Japan invaded and occupied Vietnam, and took control of the colony from the Vichy-French regime. The Japanese permitted Vietnamese leaders to participate more fully in the government than the French had allowed, and although the Japanese exploited the country economically, they gave the people greater freedom than the French had.

During the war, a communist-led movement had gained power in Vietnam. The Viet Minh, as it was called, led by Ho Chi Minh, was the first anti-Japanese guerrilla force in Vietnam. In March 1945, near the end of the war, Japan declared Vietnam independent.

In August 1945 Ho's forces seized Hanoi and demanded the abdication of the emperor, Bao Dai. In September Ho proclaimed the independence of the "Democratic Republic of Vietnam." A struggle for power followed between the Viet Minh, non-communist Vietnamese, and French forces, which had returned to Vietnam in October.

Division. In December 1946 full-scale war broke out between French soldiers and Viet Minh forces. The people tended to support the Viet Minh. Communist countries aided the rebels, especially after 1949 when a communist regime came to power in China. The United States became involved in the struggle in 1950, when the United States declared support of Vietnamese independence, under Bao Dai.

Finally, in 1954, at the battle of Dien Bien Phu, the French suffered a shattering defeat and decided to withdraw. The 1954 Geneva Conference, which arranged for a ceasefire, provisionally divided Vietnam into northern and southern sectors at the 17th parallel. The unification of Vietnam was to be achieved by general elections to be held in July 1956 in both sectors under international supervision. In the north, the "Democratic Republic of Vietnam" was led by its president, Ho Chi Minh, and was dominated by the Communist party.

In the south, Ngo Dinh Diem, a Roman Catholic who was prime minister under Emperor Bao Dai, took over the government when Bao Dai left the country in 1954. As the result of a referendum held in 1955, a republic was established in South Vietnam, with Diem as president.

Diem's government proved unable to solve South Vietnam's problems. Political power was concentrated in Diem's family, and his brother, Ngo Dinh Nhu organized a secret police force to enforce Diem's policies. Hostility toward the increasingly repressive regime aided the organization of Communist-supported rebels, the Vietcong, who opened guerrilla activity in the late 1950s. In December 1960 the communists created the National Liberation Front of South Vietnam.

Vietnam War. The United States, committed to supporting the Diem regime, sent military and political advisors to train the South Vietnamese army and assist the government. Little headway was made against either the insurgents or the country's pressing social and economic problems, due in part to widespread corruption in the government. The elections for a constituent assembly required by the 1954 Geneva agreements were not held.

Resentment against the government increased, especially among Buddhist leaders, who believed the government discriminated against Buddhists. Anti-government riots, led by the Buddhists, broke out in Saigon and Hué, and several Buddhist monks and nuns burned themselves to death in protest. Finally, in November 1963, a military group seized power. During the coup, Diem and his brother were killed.

After 1963 the war intensified as the United States poured more and more men, arms, and equipment into the country. U.S. forces expanded their role in the war from training and advising to actual combat in the early 1960s. Also assisting the South Vietnamese army were Australian, Filipino, Korean, New Zealand, and Thai forces. Air raids began carrying the war to the north in 1965.

Between 1963 and 1965 several military groups seized power in the south. In 1966, under U.S. pressure, an election was held in the south to choose a constituent assembly. A constitution was drafted, and in 1967 a president and a parliament were elected. Nguyen Van Thieu, leader of the ruling military junta, became president.

No end to the war was in sight, despite growing world pressure for a negotiated settlement. The governments of North Vietnam and South Vietnam, the National Liberation Front, and the United States were unable to find common ground on which to begin negotiations.

—Thomas E. Ennis; George Inaba

WESTERN SAMOA

Official name: The Independent State of Western Samoa
Area: 1,097 square miles
Population: (1967 est.) 135,000
Capital: Apia (Pop., 1961, urban area, 21,700)
Language: Samoan, English
Religion: Protestantism, Roman Catholicism
Currency unit: Tala

Western Samoa, an island republic in the South Pacific Ocean, lies some 1,600 miles northeast of New Zealand. A former German protectorate, Western Samoa was administered by New Zealand as a League of Nations mandate from 1920 to 1946, and as a UN trust territory from 1946 to 1962. In 1962 Western Samoa received its independence.

THE LAND. Western Samoa is made up of two large islands, Savai'i (660 square miles) and Upolu (430 square miles), and several small islands, including Manono and Apolima. The islands are volcanic in origin and are almost entirely surrounded by coral reefs. Mountains form the core of the two major islands, reaching an elevation of 3,608 feet in Upolu and 6,094 feet in Savai'i.

Western Samoa has a tropical climate. Temperatures average about 80°F, and yearly rainfall is 112 inches.

THE PEOPLE. Most of the people of Western Samoa are of Polynesian stock, and most are Christian. About 70 percent of the people live on Upolu, and about 28 percent live on Savai'i. Apia, on Upolu, is the largest city and the commercial center of the islands.

Western Samoa has a rapidly growing population, with a rate of increase of almost 3 percent a year between 1958 and 1965.

ECONOMY. The economy of Western Samoa is based on agriculture. The basic food crops are taro, yams, breadfruit, and papaya. Fish are also important in the diet of the people, and poultry and pigs are raised. Cocoa, coconuts, and bananas are grown for export. The islands have few mineral resources, and there is little industry.

In 1965 imports cost about $9 million and exports earned about $6 million. The major imports are food, wood, textiles, and machinery. The major exports are bananas, cocoa, and copra. Most trade is conducted with New Zealand, the Netherlands, Australia, and Britain.

GOVERNMENT. The constitution of Western Samoa provides for a head of state, known as *O le Ao o le Malo*, elected by the legislature for a five-year term. Executive power is exercised by a cabinet, headed by a prime minister responsible to the legislature.

Legislative powers are held by the Legislative Assembly. In the assembly, 45 members are elected by the chiefs of clans, and two members are popularly elected to a three-year term. New Zealand represents Western Samoa in foreign affairs.

HISTORY. Western Samoa was discovered in 1722 by a Dutchman, Jacob Roggeveen. The islands were later visited by other explorers, but European penetration did not begin until 1830, initiated by British missionaries. British, U.S., and German traders came to the islands in the following years.

Foreign Interests. The British were interested in the islands as a place for missionary work, trade, and the development of plantations. U.S. interest centered on trade and the control of the exceptional harbor at Pago Pago, in present-day American Samoa. The Germans came first to trade and then developed the largest plantation interests.

New Zealand also held an interest in the political fate of the islands, but the Samoans were able politicians and were bent upon retaining their independence.

The last three decades of the 1800s saw periodic clashes arising from efforts of the three great powers to "settle" the Samoan question. Much of the time they assumed that Samoa would be independent, but with one of the powers exercising a dominant political influence in the islands. The United States, firmly in control of Pago Pago, was most consistently concerned with Samoan independence. Germany and Britain favored an agreement to leave a single power in control.

By an international agreement in 1900, the islands were divided. Germany gained control of present-day Western Samoa, and granted Britain territories elsewhere in the Pacific. The United States annexed Eastern

Samoa. From 1900 to World War I Western Samoa was a German colony.

New Zealanders occupied the islands early in the war, and in 1920 began to administer the islands as a League of Nations mandate. In 1946 Western Samoa became a UN trust territory under New Zealand administration. The Samoans had continuously sought independence, and in 1959 Western Samoa became self-governing.

Independence. In 1961 a plebiscite was held under UN supervision, and the people voted overwhelmingly for independence. On Jan. 1, 1962 Western Samoa became the first independent Polynesian state of modern times, but close ties were maintained with New Zealand. Fiame Mata'afa Faumuina Mulinu'u II, the first prime minister, retained his position in elections held in 1964 and 1967.

YEMEN

Official name: Yemen Arab Republic
Area: 75,000 square miles
Population: (1965 est.) 5,000,000
Capital: Sana (Pop., 1956 est., 60,000)
Language: Arabic
Religion: Islam
Currency unit: Riyal
National holiday: Proclamation of the republic, September 26

The Yemen Arab Republic lies in the southwestern corner of the Arabian peninsula on the coast of the Red Sea. It is bordered on the north and east by Saudi Arabia, on the south by South Yemen, and on the west by the Red Sea. The eastern boundary is undefined.

THE LAND. East of a narrow coastal plain, rugged mountains rise to over 12,000 feet, towering above a high central plateau. The eastern border is also mountainous, and desert land lies at the northern border.

In the desert and along the coastal plain less than 10 inches of rain fall a year and temperatures rise to over 130°F. A more temperate climate prevails in the mountains and the central plateau, where an average of 12 inches of rain fall a year and average temperatures range from 60°F to 80°F.

THE PEOPLE. The Yemeni are Arab Muslims of the Sunni and the Shi'i sects. Population is concentrated on the coast and on the central plateau, where the capital, Sana, is located.

ECONOMY. Yemen's economy is based on agriculture. There are no known important mineral resources.

Farming, the chief occupation, prospers on carefully terraced mountainsides and in irrigated fields in the central plateau. Qat, a mild narcotic shrub, cotton, and coffee are the most important crops. Yemeni farmers also raise grains, citrus fruits, vegetables, and tobacco. Herders graze sheep, goats, camels, and horses in the more barren regions.

The tanning of hides and the working of leather are important crafts, and Yemen manufactures some soap and glass, but it has no large-scale industries. Yemen receives financial and technical aid from such countries as the Soviet Union, Communist China, and the United States.

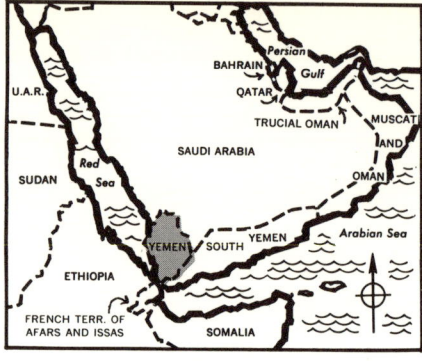

Trade is traditionally important in the economy, and the port facilities at Al Hudaydah were modernized in 1961. Civil war in the mid-1960s disrupted almost all commercial activity, however, and the country became dependent on foreign aid for nearly all necessities. Traditional exports include coffee, qat, cotton, hides, salt, and fruit.

GOVERNMENT. Yemen's government is republican in form, with actual power concentrated in the military. A president is chief executive and he appoints a prime minister and cabinet responsible to him.

Yemen is a member of the United Nations and the Arab League.

HISTORY. During the first 1,000 years before our era, several states, of which the best known was the Sabean, or Sheban, developed in Yemen. A high degree of economic prosperity earned the country the name of *Arabia Felix* among the Greeks and Romans.

Yemen's prosperity was based on an elaborate system of irrigation and the export of frankincense, precious jewels, and spices. Yemen also controlled a large part of the trade between India and the Mediterranean.

In the first centuries of the Christian era prosperity declined as the India-Mediterranean trade moved along new routes, and the irrigation works broke down. The cultural level also fell.

Early in the 500s Christian Ethiopians crossed the Red Sea and conquered the country. Later in the 500s Persian invaders conquered Yemen.

Yemen was converted to Islam in the 600s and formed part of the Islamic empires ruled successively from Medina, Damascus, and Baghdad. During the 500s and 600s Yemen's prosperity and culture deteriorated further. A revival came under the Zaydi imams, a family of political-religious leaders. In the 800s they founded a dynasty that ruled Yemen until 1962.

In the 1500s and 1600s Portugal and the Ottoman Turks competed for control of Yemen, but their invading forces were driven off. During the next 200 years the country suffered a cultural and economic relapse caused by its isolation and the diversion of trade routes around Africa.

In 1872 the Ottoman Turks succeeded in making Yemen part of their empire, but Yemeni resistance continued in the highlands until World War I. The Ottomans were forced to withdraw in 1918, at the end of World War I, leaving Yemen independent under the Zaydi ruler, the Imam Yahya.

The imam closed the country to outsiders, and although Yemen joined the Arab League in 1945 and the United Nations in 1947, it had almost no contact with the rest of the world. In 1948 Yahya was killed during an attempted revolution, and his son, Ahmad, succeeded him.

Ahmad gradually allowed foreign diplomats into Yemen. In 1958 Yemen and the United Arab Republic (U.A.R.) formed a federation, the United Arab States. By early 1962 the union had been abolished, however.

In September 1962 Ahmad died, and a week later the government of his son Imam Muhammad al-Badr, was overthrown by Yemeni army officers led by Abdullah al-Sallal.

The rebels declared Yemen a republic, with Sallal as president, and a constitution was drafted. After the revolution, civil war raged between the royalist forces of the deposed imam and republican army troops. The war involved the rest of the Middle East. The U.A.R. sent arms and troops to aid the republicans, and Jordan and Saudi Arabia provided the royalists with arms and money.

On November 5, 1967, a republican military coup ousted President al-Sallal, and Abdul Rahman al-Iryani became provisional president. At the end of November the U.A.R. pulled its troops out of Yemen after reaching an agreement with Saudi Arabia. The Egyptian withdrawal, however, was accompanied by a Soviet announcement that its aid to the Yemen Republic would continue. Saudi Arabian assistance to Yemeni royalists also continued.

—Charles Issawi; Alexander Melamid

YUGOSLAVIA

Official name: Socialist Federal Republic of Yugoslavia
Area: 98,766 square miles
Population: (1967 est.) 19,958,000
Capital: Belgrade (Pop., 1961 est., 585,200)
Language: Serbo-Croatian, Slovenian, Macedonian
Religion: Orthodox Christianity, Roman Catholicism, Islam
Currency unit: Dinar
National holiday: Proclamation of the republic, November 29

Yugoslavia, a nation at the western edge of the Balkan peninsula in southeastern Europe, is bounded on the north by Austria and Hungary, on the east by Romania and Bulgaria, on the south by Greece and Albania, and on the west by the Adriatic Sea and Italy.

The country is a federal union of six republics: Slovenia in the northwest; Croatia in the north; Serbia in the east; Bosnia-Herzegovina in the center; Macedonia in the southeast; and Montenegro in the south. There are also two autonomous provinces, Vojvodina in the north, and Kosovo-Metohija in the south.

THE LAND. Yugoslavia has three major geographic regions: the coastal plain, the mountains, and the interior lowlands.

Coastal Plain. Traditionally called Dalmatia, the coastal plain is a narrow band of territory extending along the Adriatic Sea. The coastline is irregular and lined with many offshore islands.

Mountains. Mountains cover about two-thirds of Yugoslavia. In the extreme northwest, along the border with Austria and Italy, are the Julian Alps, which contain the country's highest peak, the Triglav, 9,393 feet.

To the southeast of the Julian Alps are the Dinaric Alps, which run parallel to the coast southward to the Albanian border. The Dinaric Alps rise sharply from the shores of the Adriatic and, except in the far northwest, present a serious barrier to travel inland. The central portion of this range consists largely of a dry limestone plateau. Water quickly disappears underground and the surface is pockmarked with many large and small depressions.

Further inland the Dinaric Alps are less rugged and are composed of more resistant rock. Water is retained in valleys, and rivers are formed. The rivers of this inner region—the Kupa, the Vrbas, the Bosna, and the Drina—flow north into the Sava, a tributary of the Danube River.

Interior Lowlands. The Sava River valley forms the center of the Slovenian-Croatian hills. These hills grade eastward into the plains of northern Yugoslavia, where the Danube and its tributaries form a wide lowland, the Vojvodina. This area has rich soil and is Yugoslavia's chief food-producing region.

South of the Vojvodina in Serbia is the valley of the Morava River, the country's second major agricultural region. To the south, the Vardar valley separates Serbia from Macedonia, the southernmost region of the country. Much of Macedonia's land is eroded and not fit for cultivation, but agriculture is carried on wherever the soil is deep enough.

Climate. Yugoslavia has a varied climate. The Adriatic coast has a mild climate with cool, rainy winters and hot, dry summers. The northwest and the Dinaric Alps have warm summers and cold winters. The northeast has a continental climate with seasonal extremes of heat and cold.

THE PEOPLE. Yugoslavia is a multinational state. The great majority of its people, however, are of the group known as South Slavs. According to the 1961 census they consisted of 7.8 million Serbs, 4.3 million Croatians, 1.6 million Slovenes, 1 million Macedonians, and 500,000 Montenegrins. The largest minorities were Albanians (915,000), Hungarians (500,000), and Turks (183,000).

There is as much religious as ethnic diversity among Yugoslavs. About 41 percent of the population is Orthodox Christian, 32 percent is Roman Catholic, 12 percent is Muslim, and 1 percent is Protestant.

The majority of the population speaks Serbo-Croatian, a South Slavic language written in the Cyrillic alphabet by the Serbs and in the Latin alphabet by the Croatians. The Slovenes and Macedonians speak South Slavic languages of their own.

The country's principal city is the capital, Belgrade. Other large cities include Zagreb, the capital of Croatia and an important industrial center; Skopje, the capital of Macedonia; Sarajevo, the capital of Bosnia-Herzegovina and a major commercial center; and Ljubljana, the capital of Slovenia and a transportation center.

ECONOMY. Before World War II the Yugoslav economy was based on agriculture and mining. During the postwar period, however, the role played by industry increased greatly under the direction of the Yugoslav Communist party, which had come to power during the war.

Economic growth in the 1950s and early 1960s was rapid, and the gross domestic product more than doubled between 1953 and 1965. But the economy has been troubled by an unfavorable balance of payments caused by the necessity of importing large quantities of foodstuffs and industrial raw materials.

Natural Resources. Yugoslavia is well endowed with minerals and has important deposits of copper, zinc, lead, iron ore, bauxite, mercury, and chromite as well as some magnesite, asbestos, and pyrites. In 1965 copper production was 62,600 metric tons and zinc production 67,000 metric tons.

Yugoslavia's most important energy resource is petroleum. Production in 1965 amounted to more than 2 million metric tons. Coal reserves are mostly low-grade, but Yugoslavia's rivers have a high hydroelectric power potential.

In the mid-1960s hydroelectric plants existed on most of the major rivers or were under construction. In the 1960s plans went into effect for the construction of a huge hydroelectric project on the Danube. In 1965 Yugoslavia had an installed electric capacity of 3.7 million kilowatts (kw), of which hydroelectric plants represented 2.3 million kw.

Agriculture. After a brief and not very successful experiment with collectivization in the immediate postwar period, Yugoslavia returned to a system of private landownership. Collective farms do exist, particularly in the north, but about 80 percent of the country's arable land is privately owned.

Private holdings tend to be small, averaging less than 25 acres, and thus are not well suited to modern farming methods. This fact, coupled with recurrent droughts, has kept agricultural production low, and during the mid-1960s foodstuffs had to be imported.

YUGOSLAVIA'S DALMATIAN COAST

Cereal grains, particularly corn and wheat, are planted on most of the land. Other major crops include potatoes, sugar beets, and hemp. Feed crops are gaining in importance. Tobacco, which is raised in Macedonia, is a leading export crop. Wine grapes are grown on the Adriatic coast and fruit is raised in Croatia and Serbia.

The raising of livestock and poultry is important, and meat is one of Yugoslavia's most valuable exports.

Industry. Yugoslav industry was largely underdeveloped before World War II, but it expanded rapidly during the 1950s and early 1960s. By 1965 industry contributed 38 percent to the gross domestic product.

Growth has been greatest in heavy industry, and major increases have been made in the production of iron, steel, and chemicals. Other industries produce ships, machinery, textiles, foodstuffs, construction materials, leather, paper, rubber, tobacco, and beverages.

Yugoslavia has a thriving handicraft industry, and textiles, leather, wood, and metal goods are made in many parts of the country.

Trade. In 1967 Yugoslavia's exports earned $1,252 million and imports cost $1,707 million. Major exports are live animals, machinery and transportation equipment, minerals, chemicals, beverages and tobacco, and textiles. Principal imports are cereal grains, industrial raw materials, chemicals, coal, manufactured goods, and machinery and transportation equipment. Yugoslavia's major trading partners include the Soviet Union, Italy, East and West Germany, the United States,

by the country's Communist party, however, which is officially called the League of Communists of Yugoslavia (LCY). Key government posts are filled by league members and the league's central committee determines government policy.

Under a constitution adopted in 1963, the head of state and chief executive is a president, who is elected by majority vote of the federal legislature to a four-year term. He may not serve more than two consecutive terms, but this restriction does not apply to Pres. Josip Broz Tito.

Legislative power is vested in the Federal Assembly, which consists of five chambers: the Federal Chamber, the Economic Chamber, the Chamber of Education and Culture, the Chamber of Social Welfare and Public Health, and the Organizational-Political Chamber. Each chamber has 120 members, who serve four-year terms. The Federal Chamber consists of an additional 70 members who represent Yugoslavia's six republics and two autonomous provinces. They make up a Chamber of Nationalities.

Members of the Federal Chamber are directly elected by popular vote but members of the other chambers are indirectly elected by various social, economic, and professional groups.

The executive organ of the Federal Assembly is the Federal Executive Council, whose chief function is to carry out the Assembly's policies. It is headed by a president, who is a member of the Federal Assembly, nominated by the president of the republic, and elected by the Federal Assembly.

Yugoslavia is a member of the United Nations.

HISTORY. In the 500s the South Slavs, or "Yugo Slavs," migrated into the Balkan peninsula from territories to the east. During the Middle Ages the histories of the various tribes that composed the South Slavs began to diverge.

The Slovenes in the northwest became part of the Frankish empire in the 700s and were under German rule until 1918. The Croatians in the north had an independent kingdom until they came under Hungarian domination in 1102.

The Serbs in the east were part of the Byzantine empire until the 1100s, when they established a kingdom which reached its height in the 1300s under Stephen Dushan. It remained independent until 1389, when it was absorbed by the Ottoman Empire. By 1500 not only Serbia, but also Macedonia, Bosnia, Herzegovina, and Montenegro had fallen to the Ottoman Turks. After the Ottoman defeat of Hungary in 1520, most of Slovenia and Croatia were added to the Ottoman Empire.

Independence and Unity. During the 1800s, with the decline of the Ottoman Empire, the South Slavs began to agitate for independence. In 1878 the Treaty of Berlin, which settled the Russo-Turkish War of 1877–1878, guaranteed the independence of Serbia and Montenegro.

These two small states, influenced by the doctrine of Pan-Slavism, or Slavic unity, enlisted the support of Russia, the most powerful Slavic state, in the struggle for complete South Slav independence and unity.

In October 1908 Austria announced the annexation of Bosnia and Herzegovina, two Slav provinces that Serbia had hoped to bring under Serbian authority. To resist the encroachments of the Ottoman and Austrian empires, a Balkan League was organized in the spring of 1912. Balkan Wars broke out in 1912 and 1913, and Serbia conquered much of Macedonia from Turkey.

In 1914 World War I was precipitated by the assassination at Sarajevo, the capital of Bosnia, of Franz Ferdinand, heir to the Austro-Hungarian throne, by a Bosnian nationalist. The defeat of Austria-Hungary and of Ottoman Turkey in the war and the sympathy of the Allies, particularly of the United States, helped the South Slavs to gain full independence.

In November 1918 Montenegro declared itself united with Serbia, and on December 1, 1918, the Kingdom of the Serbs, Croats, and Slovenes was proclaimed. King Peter of Serbia became king under the regency of Prince Alexander. In January 1921 a new constitution providing for a centralized government was proclaimed. In August, King Peter died and was succeeded by Alexander.

Internal Dissension. Success in bringing all Yugoslavs into the new kingdom was soon overshadowed by the enormous problems facing the new state. The Yugoslavs had been ruled for hundreds of years by empires with varying cultures, and they not only had different traditions but different religions. The Yugoslavs who had been under Austria-Hungary were Roman Catholic, whereas those ruled by the Turks were either Orthodox Christian or Muslim.

National and religious diversity presented a serious difficulty, particularly because the 1921 constitution reflected the centralistic wishes of the Serbs, who dominated the new state. The kingdom of Serbia was the nucleus of Yugoslavia, whose army and bureaucracy were generally dominated by Serbia. This, combined with Serbian insensitiveness to the feelings of the other groups, especially the Croatians, led to animosity and friction.

In 1929 King Alexander established a dictatorship, and changed the name of the country to Yugoslavia. Alexander was assassinated by a Macedonian revolutionary associated with Croatian extremists while on a visit to France in 1934. The 11-year-old Peter II became king under the regency of his cousin, Prince Paul, who continued the dictatorship until August 26, 1939, when Yugoslavia returned to democratic government. A federal system was to be established, and Croatians were to enjoy full cultural and economic freedom. But a week later Yugoslavia found itself engulfed in World War II.

After 1934 the Yugoslav government had drifted steadily into a pro-German position. On Mar. 25, 1941 Prince Paul endorsed the Tri-Partite Pact of Germany, Japan, and Italy. Two days later Prince Paul was overthrown by a military coup led by pro-Allied Serbs, and the young Peter was declared king.

World War II. Following the coup, on April 6, Germany invaded Yugoslavia. King Peter fled the country and set up a government in exile in London. Pro-German puppet states were established in Croatia and Serbia, and the rest of the country was divided among Germany, Italy, Hungary, Italian-ruled Albania, and Bulgaria.

Yugoslavia became one of the bloodiest battlefields of the war. Between 1941 and 1945, 1.7 million Yugoslavs, or more than 10 percent of the population, lost their lives. This toll was caused not only by guerrilla fighting against the occupying armies, but also by a bitter civil war that developed between the resistance forces themselves.

Early in the war Col. Draža Mihajlović, a Serbian army officer, organized patriot guerrilla bands known as the Chetniks. The initial Chetnik fighting brought brutal German reprisals, and Mihajlović decided to proceed with caution. The government-in-exile in London promoted him to general and made him commander in chief of the resistance forces.

After German armies invaded the Soviet Union in June 1941, the Partisans were organized by the head of Yugoslavia's Communist party, Josip Broz, who was generally known as Tito.

In 1943 the Allies, who had recognized the Chetniks as the official Yugoslav resistance movement, concluded that Tito's group was doing most of the actual fighting, and threw their support to the Partisans. With the help of the Allies, Tito and the Partisans gained control of Yugoslavia.

Communist Control. Elections were held in November 1945, but they were controlled by the communists and resulted in the election of a constituent assembly composed mostly of communists or pro-Tito elements. On Nov. 29, 1945 the assembly proclaimed the Federal People's Republic of Yugoslavia. In 1946 General Mihajlović was sentenced to death and executed on charges of collaboration with the Germans.

During the immediate postwar period Yugoslavia was a firm supporter of the Soviet Union. In 1948, however, Premier Joseph Stalin of the Soviet Union, who had been disturbed by Tito's independence in foreign and domestic policy, broke with Yugoslavia. The other communist-controlled states of Eastern Europe followed the lead of the Soviet Union and severed all political and economic ties with Yugoslavia.

Following its break with the other communist countries, Yugoslav leaders began to reevaluate their economic policies. Central controls were somewhat relaxed, and in the early 1950s workers' councils were established in industrial plants to give workers greater responsibility. Municipal and district producers' councils were also formed to give workers an even larger role in decision making. Collectivized agriculture was abandoned in favor of private ownership, and the federal constitution was revised in 1953 to provide for less control by the central government.

After 1948 Yugoslav foreign policy also underwent a change. Inasmuch as the communist countries had broken economic as well as political ties with Yugoslavia, the country was forced to direct its foreign trade to the West and to neutral countries. Yugoslavia began to receive economic and military assistance from the United States and formed political, cultural, and economic ties with the countries of Western Europe.

Western economic aid, technical advice, and cultural exchanges helped keep Yugoslavia independent of the Soviet Union. At the same time Tito steered a middle course in international affairs, supporting the Soviet Union whenever it relaxed its hostility toward Yugoslavia.

Soviet-Yugoslav relations improved after the death of Joseph Stalin in 1953, and remained good until Soviet suppression of the Hungarian Revolution in 1956. In the 1960s, however, Soviet-Yugoslav relations were again strengthened.

—Robert F. Byrnes; George Kish

ZAMBIA

Official name: Republic of Zambia
Area: 290,586 square miles
Population: (1967 est.) 3,947,000
Capital: Lusaka (Pop., 1965 est., urban area, 138,300)
Language: English, African languages
Religion: Traditional religions, Christianity
Currency unit: Kwacha
National holiday: Independence day, October 24

Zambia, a republic in southern Africa, is bordered on the north by the Congo (Kinshasa) and Tanzania; on the east by Malawi; on the south by Mozambique, Rhodesia, Botswana, and South West Africa; and on the west by Angola.

In 1953 Britain joined Zambia, formerly known as Northern Rhodesia, with Southern Rhodesia and present-day Malawi, the former Nyasaland, to form the Federation of Rhodesia and Nyasaland. In 1963 the federation was dissolved, and in 1964 Britain granted Zambia its independence.

THE LAND. Most of Zambia is occupied by a high plain, with elevations between 3,000 and 4,000 feet above sea level. In the east are the Muchinga Mountains, with a peak of over 6,000 feet. The Abercorn Highlands are in the far north of the country.

The Zambezi River flows along the border with Rhodesia, and the Luangwa and Kafue rivers, tributaries of the Zambezi, flow through Zambia. Along the Zambezi River is Victoria Falls, where the river plunges more than 300 feet into a deep canyon. Kariba Lake, formed by the Kariba Dam on the Zambezi River, is one of the largest man-made lakes in the world, covering about 2,000 square miles.

In the northeast is the Chambeshi River, which flows into a swampy region near Lake Bangweulu. Lakes Mweru and Tanganyika lie along the northern border.

Zambia has a subtropical climate. The country receives between 25 and 30 inches of rain a year.

THE PEOPLE. Most of the people in Zambia are Bantu-speaking Africans. About 2 percent of the population is European. Most Europeans live in the north-central part of the country. There are also some Asians and people of mixed origins.

ECONOMY. The Zambian economy depends heavily on copper mining. Although some 70 percent of the population is engaged in farming, in 1965 agriculture contributed only 10 percent of the gross domestic product, and mining contributed over 5 percent. The basic food crops are corn, cassava, and millet. Tobacco, peanuts, and cotton are also grown.

Zambia is one of world's largest producers of copper, and in 1967 617,000 metric tons of copper were produced. Most copper is mined in the "Copper Belt," in north-central Zambia. The Kariba Dam provides most of the hydroelectric power for smelting and refining the copper. Zinc, lead, and cobalt are also mined. In 1967 a four-year development plan was instituted to develop industry and agriculture.

In 1966 imports cost $345 million and exports earned $691 million. The main imports are textiles, petroleum products, iron and steel, and machinery. The major exports are copper, zinc, and tobacco. Most trade is conducted with Britain, West Germany, Rhodesia, and Japan.

In 1965, when the white minority government of Rhodesia declared Rhodesia's independence from Britain, the UN Security Council requested that member nations impose economic sanctions against Rhodesia. Since that time, Zambia has made efforts to reduce its dependence on Rhodesian products.

GOVERNMENT. Zambia has a presidential system of government. Executive power is vested in a president, who is popularly elected to a five-year term. The president appoints a vice-president. Legislative power rests with the 75-member National Assembly. Assembly members are popularly elected to five-year terms.

Zambia is a member of the United Nations, the Commonwealth of Nations, and Organization of African Unity (OAU).

HISTORY. Little is known of the early history of Zambia. In the early 1800s, Mulambwa, chief of one Bantu-speaking tribe, the Lozi, built a powerful state in Barotseland, in the northwestern part of the country.

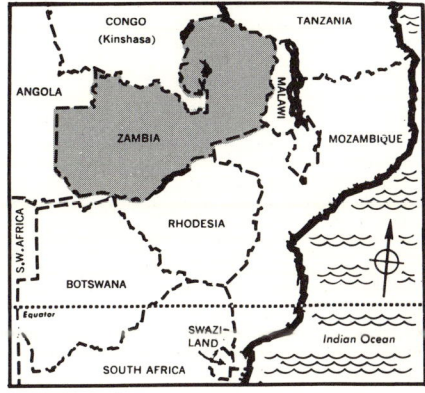

RHODESIA NATIONAL TOURIST BOARD

ZAMBIA'S KARIBA LAKE, fed by the Zambezi River, is part of a modern resort area.

In the 1830s the Lozi state crumbled before the Kololo, a military band composed of different Bantu-speaking clans. In the 1860s, however, the Lozi reestablished their dominance in Barotseland. By the late 1800s, under the Lozi ruler Lewanika, Lozi authority in the region was acknowledged by neighboring peoples.

In the mid-1800s Europeans began to settle in present-day Zambia, and in 1890 Cecil Rhodes' British South Africa Company obtained a monopoly over rights from Lewanika. In 1891 Rhodes divided the region north of the Zambezi River into three protectorates—Nyasaland, Northeastern Rhodesia, and Northwestern Rhodesia (which included Barotseland). In 1911 the company joined Northeastern and Northwestern Rhodesia to form Northern Rhodesia.

Control of the region by the British South Africa Company ended in 1923, and the British government took over the administration of Northern Rhodesia. Southern Rhodesia, however, became self-governing, and white-settler governments came to power there. Thus when representatives of the Southern Rhodesian government and the white settlers of Northern Rhodesia, at a meeting in Victoria Falls in 1936, decided to work for the union of the two countries, the Africans of Northern Rhodesia were outraged. Nonetheless, in 1953 Britain established the Federation of Rhodesia and Nyasaland.

Opposition from African nationalists in Northern Rhodesia and Nyasaland led Britain to dissolve the federation in December 1963. In parliamentary elections held in Rhodesia in January 1964, the United National Independence Party led by Kenneth Kaunda won a majority of the seats. On Oct. 24, 1964, Britain granted Northern Rhodesia its independence, and the country adopted the name Zambia. Kaunda became the first president.

—Hibberd V. B. Kline, Jr.; Gary A. Weissman

COLONIES AND DEPENDENCIES

ANGOLA

Status: Overseas province of Portugal
Area: 481,351 square miles
Population: (1966 est.) 5,225,000
Capital: Luanda (Pop., 1960, urban area, 224,540)

Angola, on the southwestern coast of Africa, consists of two sections, Angola proper and Cabinda. Angola proper is bounded on the north by the Congo (Kinshasa), on the east by the Congo (Kinshasa) and Zambia, on the south by South West Africa, and on the west by the Atlantic Ocean.

The smaller Cabinda region, about 2,800 square miles in area, is an enclave separated from Angola proper by the Congo (Kinshasa). It is bounded on the north by the Congo (Brazzaville) and on the west by the Atlantic Ocean.

THE LAND. Most of Angola lies on a deeply dissected plateau with an average elevation of 4,000 feet. A narrow coastal plain skirts the plateau on the west, and in the east a higher plateau rises to 7,000 feet. Low-lying Cabinda is covered by dense tropical jungle.

Much of the interior of Angola is heavily forested. Some portions of the east are swampy, and the Moçâmedes Desert lies in the southwest. Many rivers rush from the plateau toward the borders.

Angola's climate is varied. Cabinda and the coastal and northern regions are tropical, with high heat and humidity. The south and southeast are generally drier. The lower areas are hot, and the higher regions cool.

THE PEOPLE. The overwhelming majority of the people are Bantu-speaking Africans of many tribal groups, including the Bakongo, Kimbundu, Ovimbundu, and Chokwe. About 4 percent of the population is European, and there is a small group of mixed African and European origin.

The official language is Portuguese, but a number of African languages are spoken. The illiteracy rate is extremely high among both Africans and Europeans. Roman Catholicism is the predominant religion, but many Africans are members of Protestant groups, and many follow traditional religions.

ECONOMY. Angola is a rich land. There are diamonds, oil, copper, manganese, iron, gold, and other minerals, and the hydroelectric potential is considerable. Farming is the chief economic activity of most of the people, however.

The basic food crops are manioc, corn, rice, and vegetables. Coffee, cotton, sisal, and sugarcane are the major cash crops and are raised on plantations. The country's forests yield palm products and timber, and there is fishing off the coasts.

Mining is Angola's major industrial activity. An oil refinery was opened in the 1960s. Among the many smaller industries are food processing and the manufacture of building materials. Large-scale industry awaits the development of the country's hydroelectric capacity, which was begun in the 1960s.

Angola's trade is prosperous and growing. In 1966 imports cost $209 million, and exports earned $221 million. Coffee, gold, iron ore, fish products, corn, sisal, and oil are the chief exports. Machinery and vehicles, textiles, drugs, and manufactured goods are imported. Most trade is with Britain, the United States, West Germany, and Portugal.

GOVERNMENT. Angola is officially a province of Portugal. The administration is headed by an appointed governor-general, who wields both executive and legislative powers. He is responsible to the Overseas Ministry in metropolitan Portugal.

An elected Legislative Council and an elected Economic and Social Council advise the governor-general and have limited authority in local matters. Angola elects representatives to the Portuguese National Assembly, in Lisbon.

HISTORY. Angola was part of the large, advanced Bantu-speaking kingdom of the Congo when it was visited in 1482 by the Portuguese explorer Diogo Cão. Friendly relations were established, and Portugal sent missionaries, traders, and settlers to the territory in the 1500s. Although portions of the territory later came under direct Portuguese administration when the Congo kingdom began to disintegrate, Portugal did little to develop or exploit the region's resources.

During the 1600s the Portuguese defeated Dutch attempts to win control of Angola, and in the 1700s and 1800s Angola was a major source of slaves for Portugal's Brazil colony. In 1878 slaving was prohibited and replaced by a system of contract labor. Under the contract system, men over 18 who were employed fewer than six months a year could be forced to work. In practice, women and young children were frequently drafted to meet labor needs.

Portugal's title to Angola was affirmed and the colony's boundaries set in 1885 and 1886. Colonial development was largely in private hands until the 1930s, when the government encouraged Portuguese to settle there.

The government initiated full exploitation of the area's resources and imposed centralized control by breaking the power of local chiefs. Portugal's official policy was to incorporate Angola into the culture, society, and economy of European Portugal.

Nationalism. Although some political participation was permitted Angolans after 1951, when Angola was declared an overseas province, the government failed to meet the education, health, and welfare needs of the majority of the people, and concentrated on exploiting the land. This neglect spurred the growth of a nationalist movement, and in 1961 an insurrection broke out in Cabinda and northern Angola.

Portugal moved to suppress the revolt by military force, but guerrilla warfare continued in the north and

ANGOLA. Fort São Miguel (left) is located in Luanda, the capital. Illiteracy is high and many Angolan children still do not attend school.

SECRETARIADO NACIONAL DA INFORMACAO

LOOK MAGAZINE

COLONIES AND DEPENDENCIES

nationalist leaders established a government-in-exile and demanded independence.

Portugal's administration in Angola came under criticism in the United Nations, and self-determination for Angola's people has been urged. No grounds for discussion of the problem could be agreed upon that satisfied Portugal and Angolan nationalist leaders, however.

In the 1960s the Portuguese government initiated programs to broaden the economy by developing industry and to improve the education and social condition of the Angolans while keeping the territory part of Portugal. Rich oil finds in 1966 held out the prospect of greater funds for Angolan development, but guerrilla warfare continued.

—Hibberd V. B. Kline, Jr.; John E. Oliver; Vera L. Zolberg

ANTIGUA

Status: State in association with Britain.
Area: 170 square miles
Population: (1966 est.) 60,000
Capital: St. John City (Pop., 1960, 21,595)

Antigua, one of the Leeward Islands of the Lesser Antilles chain, between the Caribbean Sea and the Atlantic Ocean, lies northeast of the island of Montserrat. The territory includes two smaller nearby islands, Barbuda and Redonda.

THE LAND AND PEOPLE. The island's terrain is rolling to hilly, and the climate is warm. About 45 inches of rain falls each year. Most of the people are of mixed European and African descent, and they speak English.

ECONOMY. Antigua's economy is based on the raising of sugarcane and cotton. Fruits, corn, and vegetables are grown for domestic consumption. Droughts are frequent.

Efforts were underway in the mid-1960s to expand industry beyond the processing of sugar and cotton, and an oil refinery was built in 1966. Tourism became of increasing importance to the economy in the 1960s.

Trade is limited. Imports of necessities, supplied largely by Britain and the United States, far outweigh exports of cotton and sugar, which go mainly to Britain.

GOVERNMENT. Antigua is self-governing. An appointed governor is the nominal chief executive. Actual executive powers are wielded by an executive council responsible to a small elected assembly.

HISTORY. Antigua was discovered by Christopher Columbus in 1493. It was first colonized by the British in 1632, with competition from French and Dutch settlers. Plantations were established, and slaves were imported from West Africa to work them in the 1700s. The slaves were freed in 1838.

In 1871 Antigua was included in the colony of the federated Leeward Islands. This federation was replaced in 1958 by the Federation of the West Indies, an internally self-governing British dependency disbanded in 1962. In 1967 Antigua became self-governing and with St. Christopher (St. Kitts), Nevis, and Anguilla formed the West Indies Associated States.

BERMUDA. Tourists enjoy the scenery while riding in an open carriage.

BAHAMAS

Status: British colony
Area: 4,403 square miles
Population: (1967 est.) 144,000
Capital: Nassau (Pop., 1964, 80,907)

The Bahamas form an archipelago in the Atlantic Ocean off the southeastern tip of Florida.

THE LAND AND PEOPLE. The 22 islands and 650 islets of the archipelago have low, rocky, flat, or rolling terrain and are ringed with coral reefs. The climate is warm throughout the year. About 50 inches of rain falls each year. Three-quarters of the people are Negro, and the rest are of European or mixed descent. The people are English speaking.

ECONOMY. Tourism is the prime factor in the economy, but agriculture is also significant on most of the islands. Bananas, citrus fruits, and vegetables are grown. Forestry and salt production are important and, with food processing, constitute the only industrial activities.

In the 1960s government programs sought to persuade businesses to make their headquarters on the islands. The poor balance of trade caused by the need to import necessities is partially offset by the expenditures of tourists.

GOVERNMENT. The Bahamas have internal self-government under a prime minister and cabinet responsible to a popularly elected legislative assembly. An appointed administrator represents Britain.

HISTORY. The Bahamas were discovered in 1492 by Christopher Columbus, but the first settlements were made by the English in the 1600s. Plantations were established, and Negro slaves were imported. The islands became a British colony in 1783 and retained that status until 1964, when self-government was granted. In 1967 the islands' first Negro prime minister took office and began to move the colony toward greater independence from Britain.

—George Carey; Jerome Fischman

BERMUDA

Status: British crown colony
Area: 20 square miles
Population: (1967 est.) 50,000
Capital: Hamilton (Pop., 1965, 3,000)

Bermuda, an archipelago of 20 islands and numerous islets in the Atlantic Ocean, lies some 600 miles east of the United States.

THE LAND AND PEOPLE. The coral-rimmed islands of Bermuda are rather flat and heavily forested. The climate is warm and humid throughout the year. Most of the people are of mixed African and European descent. There are groups of Europeans and a large number of U.S. military personnel.

ECONOMY. Bermuda's economy is based on tourism. U.S. military bases also contribute to the islands' income. Some fruits and vegetables are raised, and there is some fishing, but most foodstuffs must be imported. Pharmaceuticals and perfume essences are among the islands' few manufactures.

Favorable taxation policies encourage many foreign-owned corporations to make Bermuda their headquarters. Most of the islands' trade is with the United States and Canada, which supply foodstuffs, clothing, and other necessities.

GOVERNMENT. An appointed governor administers the colony with the advice of an executive council. The legislature, which consists of one popularly elected house and one appointed house, has considerable control over local affairs.

HISTORY. Bermuda was discovered in 1503 by a Spaniard, Juan de Bermudez, but no settlement was made until after British colonists were shipwrecked there in 1609. Under a royal charter, colonization increased through the 1600s. Plantations were opened, and Africans were brought as slaves to work them. They soon constituted the bulk of the population.

In the 1900s the islands became a popular resort for the wealthy. An aristocratic form of government with suffrage limited to property owners continued until 1963, when universal adult suffrage was introduced. In the mid-1960s pressure grew for increased independence from Britain.

BRITISH ANTARCTIC TERRITORY

Status: British colony
Area: 2,040 square miles (excluding Graham Land)
Population: No permanent population

The British Antarctic Territory consists of the South Orkney and the South Shetland islands, in the south Atlantic Ocean off the southern tip of South America, Graham Land, on the Antarctic peninsula, and Coatsland and Caird coast, along the Antarctic's Weddell coast.

The islands are rocky and barren, and the mainland is ice-covered and barren. The climate is cold and dry. There are no permanent inhabitants. Sealing and whaling are the colony's chief economic activities. The colony is the site of scientific research stations. It is administered by the governor of the nearby Falkland Islands colony.

The islands and Graham Land were discovered in the 1820s by British explorers and sealers. The other mainland territory was charted in the early 1900s by British explorers. The British Antarctic territory was part of the Falkland Island colony until 1962, when the two were separated.

BRITISH HONDURAS

Status: British colony
Area: 361 square miles
Population: (1967 est.) 113,000
Capital: Belize (Pop., 1964, urban area, 45,572)

British Honduras lies on the eastern coast of Central America. It is bounded on the north by Mexico, on the east by the Caribbean Sea, on the south by the Gulf of Honduras and Guatemala, and on the west by Guatemala.

THE LAND AND PEOPLE. British Honduras has a varied landscape. The northern and coastal lowlands are swampy, and the Maya Mountain range dominates the south. Much of the land is covered by dense jungle. The climate is tropical, with high heat and humidity throughout the year.

Negroes, Maya and Carib Indians, and people of mixed origins form the bulk of the population. There are also small groups of East Indian and European origins. English is the official language, but Spanish, Maya, and Carib are spoken.

ECONOMY. Farming and forestry are the main economic activities. Sugarcane, citrus fruits, bananas, rice, coconuts, cacao, vegetables, and nuts are grown commercially, and livestock is raised. The forests yield pine, mahogany, cedar, and rosewood. There are sawmills, sugar refineries, distilleries, and other plants for the processing of farm products. Boatbuilding and handicrafts are also important in the economy.

British Honduras has a poor balance of trade. In 1965, for example, exports earned $12 million and imports cost $24 million. Sugar and sugar products, citrus fruits, and lumber are the main exports. Manufactured goods, machinery, foodstuffs, and fuels are imported. The United States, Britain, and the islands of the West Indies are the principal trading partners.

GOVERNMENT. British Honduras' government is headed by an appointed governor, whose powers are limited by a popularly elected legislative assembly.

HISTORY. British Honduras was a site of early Mayan civilization. It was crossed by the Spanish conqueror, Hernan Cortes, in the 1500s and was first settled by British privateers in the early 1700s. In the late 1700s British colonists settled the interior and established plantations using slave labor, and in 1789 Honduras became a British colony.

The colony was governed from Jamaica until the 1880s, when a separate administration was established. During the 1900s the government concentrated on developing the economy of the colony. Popular participation in government was broadened with the goal of eventual independence, and in 1964 full internal self-government was achieved.

—George Carey; Jerome Fischman

BRITISH INDIAN OCEAN TERRITORY

Status: British colony
Area: 30 square miles.
Population: (1966 est.) 2,000

The British Indian Ocean Territory consists of scattered islands in the Indian Ocean lying from 500 to 2,000 miles off the eastern coast of Africa. The colony was formed in 1965 from former dependencies of Seychelles and Mauritius. It consists of the Chagos Archipelago, the Farquhar group, Desroches Island, and the Aldabra islands.

The colony's chief importance is its strategic location, and there is a military base at Diego Garcia, in the Chagos group.

THE LAND AND PEOPLE. Most of the islands are very small. They are volcanic in origin and are mountainous and forested. They have a tropical monsoon climate.

The population is of varied origins, and includes Africans, Indians, Chinese, Europeans, and people of mixed background. French, English, and a variety of other languages are spoken in the territory.

ECONOMY. The colony's economy is based primarily on fishing and agriculture. Coconuts, cinnamon, and vanilla are the main agricultural products. Coffee and some fruits and vegetables are raised and sugarcane is grown in the Chagos group. The only industries are coconut processing and fish salting. The colony imports food, clothing, and consumer goods, and exports fish, coconuts, and spices. Most trade is with Britain and neighboring islands.

GOVERNMENT. The colony is administered by an appointed commissioner, who is also governor of Britain's Seychelles colony.

HISTORY. The islands of the territory were uninhabited and visited only by Malay and Arab sailors until the 1500s, when the Portuguese landed on the western islands of the Farquhar, Desroches, and Aldabra islands. The islands, important in the spice trade, were controlled at various times by Portugal, the Netherlands, and France. In the early 1800s they became British possessions.

The islands were part of the Crown Colony of Mauritius until 1903, when those near the Seychelles were made part of that colony. In 1965 the British government bought the Chagos group from Mauritius and created the territory. In 1967 Britain and the United States agreed to use the islands jointly for military bases.

BRITISH SOLOMON ISLANDS

Status: British protectorate
Area: 11,500 square miles
Population: (1966 est.) 141,000
Capital: Honiara (Pop., 1956 est., 6,700)

The British Solomon Islands, a dozen large islands and many islets, extend for over 900 miles in the South Pacific Ocean, some 300 miles east of New Guinea.

THE LAND AND PEOPLE. The islands are mountainous, rugged, and rimmed by coral reefs. The climate is warm and rainfall is heavy.

Melanesian, Polynesian, and Micronesian people make up the bulk of the population, and there is a small group of Europeans. English is the official language, but pidgin English is more widely spoken.

ECONOMY. The islands' forests have a rich, but untapped, potential and there are deposits of gold, which are only partially exploited. Most of the people live by subsistence farming and fishing. Coconuts are the chief commercial crop. There is little manufacturing.

Coconut products and timber are the chief exports, and manufactured goods are imported. Britain, Japan, and Australia are the islands' major trading partners.

GOVERNMENT. The Solomon Islands are administered by Britain's Western Pacific High Commission. The high commissioner has the assistance of the Solomon Islands executive council, which is responsible to the partially elected Solomon Islands legislative assembly. Local government officials are popularly elected.

HISTORY. Little is known of the islands before their discovery by the Spanish in 1567. They were soon lost to Europeans again, and were authoritatively relocated by the French only in 1792. They served Europeans as a source of copra and labor until the 1890s, when the British established a protectorate. In the 1900s British settlers established plantations, Christian missions, and trading posts.

The islands, especially Guadalcanal in the southwest, were the scene of fierce fighting between Japanese and

COLONIES AND DEPENDENCIES

Allied troops in World War II. In the decades after the war Britain concentrated on raising the islanders' standard of living and expanding the economy by developing natural resources.

BRITISH VIRGIN ISLANDS

Status: British colony
Area: 59 square miles
Population: (1966 est.) 9,000
Capital: Road Town (Pop., 1960, 891)

The British Virgin Islands lie at the northern end of the Leeward Islands group of the Lesser Antilles, between the Caribbean Sea and the Atlantic Ocean. The group includes three large and several smaller islands and some 30 islets.

THE LAND AND PEOPLE. The islands are generally low-lying, with interior hills. The climate is warm throughout the year and rather dry. The population is almost entirely of African descent and speaks English.

ECONOMY. Fishing, cattle raising, and farming are the major economic activities. The few light industries include a distillery and boatyards. Tourism makes a substantial contribution to the economy, and remittances of islanders who work in the United States and nearby U.S. Virgin Islands help to offset a poor trade balance.

Cattle, fish, and farm products are the only exports, and most necessities are imported. The United States is the islands' chief trading partner.

GOVERNMENT. The British Virgin Islands are administered by an appointed governor with the advice of an executive council and a partly elected legislative council.

HISTORY. The islands were discovered in 1493 by Christopher Columbus. They served primarily as a base for pirates until the early 1700s, when English planters settled on the larger islands. Slaves imported to work the plantations soon became the islands' principal inhabitants.

The islands became a colony in 1774 and were governed as part of the Territory of the Leeward Islands until 1956, when they became a dependency of the Leeward Islands colony. In the 1960s the British Virgin Islands became a separate colony. In the 1950s and early 1960s migration to Britain was heavy, and the British government concentrated on improving social and economic conditions in the islands.

BRUNEI

Status: British-protected state
Area: 2,225 square miles
Population: (1966 est.) 104,000
Capital: Brunei Municipal (Pop., 1960, 9,702)

Brunei, a sultanate on the island of Borneo, is bordered on the north by the South China Sea and on the east, south, and west by the East Malaysian state of Sarawak.

The western and coastal regions of Brunei are swampy, and there is a rugged, hilly region in the east. The climate is tropical, with high heat and humidity throughout the year. Malays and Chinese form the bulk of the population, and there are several smaller groups of Borneo native peoples. Islam is the official religion and Malay the official language.

Brunei has rich oil deposits, and oil production and refining constitute the major economic activity. Rubber and rice are grown, and forest products are produced. Brunei's chief export is oil, and its main imports are foodstuffs, raw materials, and machinery.

Brunei's government is headed by a sultan, who rules with the assistance of a council and a British commissioner, and with the advice of an elected legislative assembly. Britain is responsible for Brunei's foreign affairs and defense.

Once the center of a powerful island empire, Brunei signed a treaty of protection with Britain in 1888 as a defense against piracy. Oil was discovered in 1929, and Brunei's importance increased. In 1959 the sultan issued a constitution that introduced limited democracy.

In 1963, when the federation of Malaysia was formed, Brunei was the only British Malay dependency in the area not to join. In 1967 Sultan Omar Ali Saifuddin abdicated after 17 years on the throne, and was succeeded by his son, Pengiran Muda Mahkota Hassanal Bolkiah.

BRUNEI. The modern section of the capital city is dominated by the great mosque built in 1958.

CAPE VERDE ISLANDS

Status: Overseas province of Portugal
Area: 1,557 square miles
Population: (1965 est.) 232,000
Capital: Praia (Pop., 1960, urban area, 13,142)

The Cape Verde Islands lie in the Atlantic Ocean some 275 miles west of Senegal, on the African mainland. There are 10 islands and several islets in the group.

THE LAND AND PEOPLE. The islands are volcanic in origin and are mountainous, rocky, and barren. The climate is extremely hot and dry. The majority of the islands' population is of mixed African and Portuguese descent. About one-third is African, and a very small proportion is European. Portuguese is the official language, but a creole dialect of Portuguese and other languages is widely spoken. Roman Catholicism is the predominant religion.

ECONOMY. The islands have no exploitable mineral resources, and their soil is generally too dry and poor to support vegetation. Bananas, coffee, nuts, oil seeds, and corn are raised, and some salt is produced. Fish are abundant off the coasts and some livestock is grazed. The islands have several good ports, and the refueling of ships is the main economic activity.

Trade is limited. In 1965 imports cost $8 million and exports earned $11 million. Coffee, fish, banana, and nuts are exported, and foodstuffs, textiles, and building materials are imported. Most trade is with mainland Portugal.

GOVERNMENT. The Cape Verde Islands are administered as a province of Portugal and elect representatives to the Portuguese National Assembly. Local government is in the hands of an appointed governor-general, who is advised by a small, partly elected legislative council.

HISTORY. The Cape Verde Islands were uninhabited when they were discovered in 1456 by the Portuguese. The Portuguese began to settle the islands in the late 1400s and early 1500s, and African slaves began to be imported. In 1587 a governor was appointed for the colony, and in the 1600s and 1700s settlers from Spain, Italy, and Britain joined the Portuguese on the islands. The colony thrived on plantation agriculture and trading.

In 1951 the colony was made an overseas province of Portugal, and in 1961 the islanders received full Portuguese citizenship.

CAYMAN ISLANDS

Status: British colony
Area: 100 square miles
Population: (1966 est.) 9,000
Capital: Georgetown (Pop., 1960, 2,573)

The Cayman Islands—Grand Cayman, Little Cayman, and Cayman Brac—lie in the Caribbean Sea some 100 miles northwest of Jamaica and about 100 miles south of Cuba.

CHANNEL ISLANDS. This view of the Isle of Jersey shows St. Orgueil Castle.

Low, rocky, and coral-rimmed, the islands have densely-forested interiors. The climate is tropical, with high heat and humidity throughout the year. The population includes people of European, African, and mixed origins.

Coconuts and sisal are the only significant crops, and seafaring, boatbuilding, ropemaking, and tourism are the major sources of income.

The islands are governed by an appointed administrator, a partially elected legislative assembly, and an executive council chosen by the assembly.

Discovered by Christopher Columbus in 1503, the islands were uninhabited until the 1700s, when British from Jamaica settled them. They were governed as part of Jamaica until Jamaica became independent in 1962, when the Caymans were placed under a separate administration.

CHANNEL ISLANDS

Status: Dependency of the British crown
Area: 75 square miles
Population: (1966 est.) 115,000
Capital: Jersey—St. Helier; Guernsey—St. Peter Port

The Channel Islands lie in the English Channel 10 to 35 miles off the western coast of France. They include Jersey, Guernsey, and six small dependencies of Guernsey—Alderney, Brechou, Little Sark, Great Sark, Herm, Jethou, and Lihou.

THE LAND AND PEOPLE. The Channel Islands consist mainly of rolling plains. Their climate is rather damp and mild, with an average temperature in the 60°s F.

The population is of French and British origin. French is the official language in Jersey, and English is the official language in Guernsey.

ECONOMY. The islands have excellent farm and pasture land, and agriculture and dairying are the main economic activities. Jersey cattle are raised on Jersey, and Guernsey cattle on Guernsey and its dependencies. Jersey farmers grow flowers, potatoes, tomatoes, and other vegetables, and Guernsey farms produce fruits, tomatoes, and flowers. There is some stone quarrying on the islands.

Tourism is a major source of income. Almost all trade is with Britain. The islands export farm products and import fuels, foodstuffs, and machinery.

GOVERNMENT. Each island is administered by an appointed bailiff responsible to a popularly elected assembly. An appointed governor represents the British crown.

HISTORY. The Channel Islands were part of the French duchy of Normandy during the Middle Ages. After the Norman conquest of England in 1066, the islands were ruled with England and Normandy. England gradually lost all of mainland Normandy, and by the 1500s the Channel Islands remained the British crown's sole Norman possessions.

In 1940, during World War II, the islands were occupied by German forces. The Germans deported many of the islanders and built extensive fortifications. The islands were liberated in 1945.

CHRISTMAS ISLAND

Status: Territory of Australia
Area: 52 square miles
Population: (1960 est.) 3,000

Christmas Island lies in the Indian Ocean some 200 miles south of the Indonesian island of Java. It is hilly, rocky, and rather barren. The climate is warm and dry. The island's small population is mostly of Chinese and Malayan origins.

Phosphate rock is the island's only important resource, and the extraction of phosphate is the only economic activity.

The island is under the direct authority of the Australian government, which appoints a representative to administer local affairs.

Christmas Island was uninhabited when it was discovered in the 1600s by British sailors. In 1888 Britain formally annexed it and governed the island through the Colony of the Straits Settlements between 1889 and 1900, when it was incorporated into Singapore.

Phosphate extraction was begun in the early 1900s, using Chinese and Malay labor. In 1948 Australia and New Zealand bought out the private company that had mined the phosphate and agreed to joint operation of the phosphate work. In 1958 Britain transferred sovereignty over the island to Australia.

COCOS ISLANDS

Status: Territory of Australia
Area: 5.4 square miles
Population: (1966 est.) 1,000

The Cocos, or Keeling, Islands, in the Indian Ocean some 500 miles southwest of the Indonesian island of Java, consist of 27 small coral islands forming two atolls. The islands are low-lying and rather flat, with a warm climate and moderate rainfall. About two-thirds of the population is of Malayan descent, and about one-third is European.

The cultivation of coconuts is the mainstay of the islands' economy, and the production of copra and coconut oil is the islands' only industry.

The islands are administered by an appointed representative of the Australian government.

Discovered in 1609 by Capt. William Keeling of the British East India Company, the islands remained uninhabited until 1826, when British and Malay settlements were established. Britain annexed the islands in 1857.

The Cocos Islands were governed through the colony of Ceylon between 1878 and 1882, when responsibility for them was placed with the Colony of the Straits Settlements. They were incorporated into the colony of Singapore in 1903 and were made an Australian territory in 1955.

COMORO ISLANDS

Status: Overseas territory of France
Area: 838 square miles
Population: (1965 est.) 220,000
Capital: Moroni (Pop., 1966, urban area, 11,515)

The Comoro Islands lie in the Mozambique Channel between the eastern coast of Africa and the island of Madagascar. The territory consists of four main islands—Mayotte, the southernmost, is 144 square miles, Anjouan is 164 square miles, Mohéli is 112 square miles, and Grande Comore, the northernmost, is 443 square miles.

THE LAND AND PEOPLE. The islands are of volcanic origin and consist of mountainous or deeply dissected plateau cores ringed by very narrow coastal plains. Coral reefs surround the islands. The climate is tropical.

Most of the people of the Comoro Islands are a mixture of Arab and African stocks, but there are Arabs, Indians, and Europeans. The language is Malagasy, which is spoken on Madagascar, and Islam is the predominant religion.

ECONOMY. The islands have almost no mineral resources, but their soil is very rich, and agriculture is the mainstay of the economy. Rice, corn, vegetables, and fruits are raised for local consumption. The chief commercial crops are vanilla, spices, coffee, sisal, and coconuts. Industry is limited to the processing of the agricultural products of the islands.

The Comoras trade mainly with France, Madagascar (the Malagasy Republic), and the United States. They export copra, vanilla, and spices. Imports consist primarily of foodstuffs, textiles, and metals.

GOVERNMENT. Executive power in the territory is wielded by an appointed high commissioner and by an appointed government council, which is responsible to a popularly elected territorial assembly. The islanders also elect two representatives to the French National Assembly.

HISTORY. The Comoro Islands have been known since ancient times and were conquered by Arabs in the 600s. In the 1500s they were visited by the

COLONIES AND DEPENDENCIES

Portuguese, French, and Dutch, and the French established a settlement. In the 1800s the Arab kingdoms on the islands were attacked by Malagasy armies from Madagascar, and years of warfare followed. By the 1900s the rulers of the islands had ceded authority to France.

The French expanded agricultural production by opening plantations. In 1912 the islands were joined with Madagascar into a single French colony. In 1946 their status was changed to that of an overseas territory, and they were granted internal autonomy. In the 1960s a nationalist organization demanding complete independence caused unrest in the islands. The majority of the people were thought to favor no more than loose ties with France, which was responsible for economic and social improvements on the islands.

COOK ISLANDS

Status: Self-governing country in free association with New Zealand
Area: 90 square miles
Population: (1966 est.) 19,000

The Cook Islands, in the South Pacific Ocean some 2,000 miles northeast of New Zealand, consist of the Northern Group of seven islands and the Southern Group of eight islands. The Northern Group consists of low-lying, barren, coral atolls; the islands of the Southern Group are higher and fertile. The climate is hot and dry, and the islands are subject to hurricanes.

Population is concentrated on the Southern Group. Most Cook Islanders are Maori Polynesians, and there is a small group of Europeans.

Agriculture is the mainstay of the economy, with citrus fruits, bananas, pineapples, tomatoes, and coconuts the main commercial crops.

The islands have internal self-government under a prime minister responsible to an elected legislative assembly. New Zealand manages foreign affairs and defense.

The islands were discovered in 1773 by a Briton, James Cook. Britain made the islands a protectorate in 1888 and attached them to New Zealand in 1901.

British and New Zealander colonists established plantations on the islands, which were governed as a New Zealand territory until 1965, when they were granted internal self-government.

DOMINICA

Status: State in association with Britain
Area: 290 square miles
Population: (1966 est.) 68,000
Capital: Roseau (Pop., 1960, 10,417)

Dominica is one of the Windward Islands of the Lesser Antilles, lying between the Caribbean Sea and the Atlantic Ocean. It has a rugged, mountainous terrain. The climate is hot throughout the year, and rainfall is heavy.

Dominica's population is of mixed African, European, and Carib Indian descent. The people speak English and a Creole dialect.

The economy is agricultural. Bananas, limes and other citrus fruits, cacao, vanilla, and coconuts are the chief crops. The only industries process farm products and manufacture straw goods. Exports of bananas, copra, and lime juice are outweighed by imports of foodstuffs, machinery, and other necessities, and most of the limited trade is with Britain, the United States, and the other islands of the West Indies.

The island has internal self-government, with a council of ministers responsible to an elected assembly. An appointed administrator represents Britain.

The island was inhabited by Indians when discovered by Chistopher Columbus in the 1490s. Between the 1600s and the 1800s it was settled by colonists from several European countries. They developed plantations worked by imported African slave labor. In 1814 the island became British, and it was governed as part of the Leeward Islands until 1940, when it became a separate colony. In 1967 Dominica gained self-government as a state in association with Britain, and it joined the West Indies Associated States.

EQUATORIAL GUINEA

Status: (1966) Self-governing territory of Spain.
Area: 10,830 square miles
Population: (1966 est.) 272,000
Capital: Santa Isabel (Pop., 1960, 37,237)

Equatorial Guinea, formerly known as Spanish Guinea, consists of two provinces—Río Muni and Fernando Póo. Río Muni, on the west African mainland and adjacent islands, is bounded on the north by Cameroon, on the east and south by Gabon, and on the west by the Gulf of Guinea, an arm of the Atlantic Ocean. Fernando Póo occupies two islands and several islets in the Gulf of Guinea. Fernando Póo, the larger island, is about 20 miles northwest of Río Muni; Annobón, the smaller, is some 370 miles southwest of the mainland province.

THE LAND. In Río Muni, a coastal plain gives way some 12 miles inland to a higher, rolling plateau, which rises in the east to a hilly region. Fernando Póo consists of two volcanoes separated by a narrow valley. Its coastline is steep except in the southwest, where there is an excellent harbor at San Carlos. Annobón is also volcanic in origin, and has a rugged terrain.

The climate of the territory is tropical, with high heat and humidity throughout the year.

THE PEOPLE. Most of the people of Fernando Póo are descended from the islands' native people, the Bubes. There are also Europeans and other Africans. Most of Río Muni's population is part of the Fang people. There are people of other African tribal groups and a small number of Europeans. Río Muni's population is nearly triple Fernando Póo's.

Catholicism is the predominant religion, although there are some Protestants, Muslims, and people who have held to traditional religions. Spanish is the official language, but a number of African languages are spoken.

ECONOMY. Equatorial Guinea's economy is chiefly agricultural, and its mineral resources remained largely unexplored and unexploited in the mid-1960s. The main products are cacao, grown in Fernando Póo, and coffee, timber, and forest products from Río Muni. There is little manufacturing.

Most of Equatorial Guinea's products are exported to Spain, which furnishes needed imports, although West Germany, Britain, and the United States purchase some items.

GOVERNMENT. Equatorial Guinea became self-governing in 1963. Executive power is vested in an Executive Council, which is chosen by a popularly elected legislature. The Spanish government is represented by a commissioner general and retains final authority in most matters.

HISTORY. Little is known of the history of the region before it was visited by Europeans. The islands of Fernando Póo and the nearby mainland were discovered in the 1470s by the Portuguese, and they remained Portuguese until 1778, when they were ceded to Spain. Possession of the mainland was disputed until 1900, when the Treaty of Paris granted Río Muni to Spain. Spanish settlers established plantations using African laborers.

In the 1950s and 1960s Spain's goal was the improvement of the welfare of the people, the expansion of the economy, and the incorporation of the territory into the Spanish nation.

After the granting of internal self-government in 1963, however, various political groups developed, some favoring independence or incorporation into Cameroon, same favoring separation of Fernando Póo and Río Muni, and some favoring the maintenance of the system introduced in 1963. In 1967 Spain and Equatorial Guinea convened a constitutional conference to plan the territory's future.
—Hibberd V. B. Kline, Jr.;
Vera L. Zolberg

FAEROE ISLANDS

Status: Self-governing national community within the Danish kingdom
Area: 540 square miles
Population: (1966 est.) 37,000
Capital: Thorshavn (Pop., 1964, 7,447)

The Faeroe Islands, in the North Atlantic Ocean midway between Norway and Iceland, lie some 250 miles north of Scotland. They consist of 17 islands separated by narrow channels.

THE LAND AND PEOPLE. The islands are generally low-lying and grass-covered, with interior hills and many lakes. The climate is mild and damp. The people are descended from early Scandinavian settlers, and speak Faeroese, a dialect of Old Norse, although Danish is also spoken.

ECONOMY. Fishing and whaling are the major economic activities of the islands. Sheepherding is the most important agricultural occupation. The processing of fish and wood-working are the islands' main industries. Fish constitute the bulk of the islands' exports, which are shipped largely to Britain, Italy, and Brazil. Necessities are imported from Denmark and Britain.

GOVERNMENT. The Faeroe Islands have internal self-government under a popularly elected assembly, which chooses an administrative council. The islands also send representatives to the Danish legislature.

HISTORY. The Faeroe Islands were settled in the 900s AD by Viking navigators from Norway, and they became part of the kingdom of Norway. In 1390, the islands came under Danish control.

During World War II Denmark was occupied by German forces, and the Faeroes were occupied by Britain. A nationalist movement developed, and after the war the Faeroes demanded independence. In 1948 they were granted autonomy within the Danish kingdom and were permitted to use their own currency and flag. In the 1950s and the 1960s the islands concentrated on improving their economy by modernizing the fishing fleet and expanding fish processing facilities.

FALKLAND ISLANDS

Status: British crown colony
Area: 4,618 square miles
Population: (1966 est.) 2,000
Capital: Stanley (Pop., 1962, 1,074)

The Falkland Islands lie in the South Atlantic Ocean off the southeastern coast of Argentina. They consist of East Falkland and West Falkland, which are separated by the Falkland Strait, and many smaller islands.

The islands are hilly and grass-covered, and their climate is cool and rainy. Almost all of the population is of British origin. Sheep raising is the chief economic activity, and sealing and whaling are important. The colony's only industries process sheep, seal, and whale carcasses and hides for export to Britain.

The colony is administered by an appointed governor and a small elected council. Its two dependencies, South Georgia and South Sandwich islands to its east, house whaling, sealing, and meteorological stations.

A British explorer first sighted the islands in 1592. In the 1760s France settled East Falkland and later ceded it to Spain. Britain occupied West Falkland. All the settlements soon were abandoned, and in the 1820s Argentina colonized the islands. In the 1830s Britain occupied both islands, but Argentina continued to claim them.

FIJI ISLANDS

Status: British colony
Area: 7,015 square miles
Population: (1967 est.) 490,000
Capital: Suva (Pop., 1965 est., 60,000)

The Fiji Islands, consisting of two large islands, Viti Levu and Vanua Levu, many islets, and numerous atolls, lie in the South Pacific Ocean about 1,000 miles north of New Zealand.

THE LAND AND PEOPLE. The islands are coral-rimmed and consist primarily of densely forested volcanic mountains deeply etched by rapid rivers. The climate is tropical, with high year-round heat and humidity.

Nearly three-quarters of the people live on Viti Levu. The population is divided between Fijians, a Melanesian people, and people of East Indian origin. There are small groups of Europeans and Chinese. English is the official language.

ECONOMY. The islands have good forest resources, some gold deposits, and rich farmland in river deltas. Agriculture is the mainstay of the economy, with fruits, sugarcane, coconuts, cacao, and rice the chief commercial crops.

Forestry, gold mining, and the processing of agricultural products are the chief industries. There is some boat building and repair.

Agricultural products are the main exports, and manufactured goods, fuels, and equipment are imported. Britain, Australia, and Japan are the islands' major trading partners.

GOVERNMENT. The islands are internally self-governing under an executive council that is responsible to a partially elected legislature, in which the Fijian and Indian groups are represented proportionately. An appointed governor represents the British crown.

HISTORY. Little is known of the islands before they were discovered in the 1600s by the Dutch. They were virtually ignored by Europeans until the 1700s, when traders came in search of sandalwood, coconut products, and other exotic goods. The traders were followed by Christian missionaries, who converted many of the islanders.

Tribal warfare raged on the islands in the mid-1800s, and in 1874 the tribal chiefs ceded power to Britain. Plantations were established in the late 1800s, and East Indian laborers were imported to work them. The islands' economy prospered on farming and forestry. The East Indians soon grew to be a majority of the population, and disputes between the Indians and Melanesians continued into the mid-1900s. In 1966 a constitution came into effect that divided representation between them in an effort to settle the ethnic conflict.

FRENCH GUIANA

Status: Overseas department of France
Area: 35,135 square miles
Population: (1966 est.) 37,000
Capital: Cayenne (Pop., 1961, urban area, 18,235)

French Guiana, on the northeastern coast of South America, is bordered on the north by the Atlantic Ocean, on the east and south by Brazil, and on the west by Surinam (Dutch Guiana).

THE LAND. A narrow, low, swampy plain, the Terres Basses ("the Lowlands") skirts the coast. The interior, the Terres Hautes ("the Uplands"), is an eroded granite plateau. Dense rain forest almost completely covers the country, and many rivers flow from the interior. The climate is tropical, with high temperatures throughout the year and abundant rainfall.

THE PEOPLE. Most of the population is of mixed African and European descent, but groups of Negroes and American Indians inhabit the interior. About half the population lives in Cayenne, the capital and major port.

ECONOMY. Guiana is rich in bauxite, and there are deposits of gold, manganese, nickel, copper, and molybdenum. The forests contain valuable wood. Farmland is limited, but cassava, corn, breadfruit, and sugarcane are grown, and cattle, goats, hogs, and poultry are raised. Efforts to expand and diversify agriculture were underway in the 1960s. River and offshore fishing is profitable. Mining and logging are the major industries. There are paper mills, sawmills, and food processing plants. Other industries were being started in the mid-1960s, as exploitation began of the country's excellent hydroelectric potential. There are numerous scientific research stations in the country, including an international space research installation. French Guiana's exports consist largely of minerals and lumber. Exports are far outweighed by imports, mostly foodstuffs and manufactures. Most trade is with France.

GOVERNMENT. Guiana is administered by an appointed prefect with the advice of a popularly elected assembly. The department elects representatives to the French National Assembly.

HISTORY. Guiana has been inhabited for many hundreds of years by American Indians. Christopher Columbus sighted the Guiana coast in 1498, and rumors of fabulous treasures in the interior attracted adventurers from all parts of Europe in the 1500s. In the early 1600s Frenchmen established a settlement at present-day Cayenne and gained trading rights to a large part of the interior.

French possession was reaffirmed in 1814, when the boundaries of Guiana were set. In 1848 full French citizenship and universal suffrage were granted to the inhabitants. In the mid-1800s France established prison colonies in Guiana. The most notorious was on Devil's Island, a small island off the coast. In 1945 the prison colonies were abolished, and in 1946 Guiana was made an overseas department of France.

During the 1950s and 1960s Guiana concentrated on expanding its economy and improving the standard of living of its people.

—David Bushnell

FRENCH POLYNESIA

Status: Overseas territory of France
Area: 1,544 square miles
Population: (1966 est.) 90,000
Capital: Papeete, Tahiti (Pop., 1960 est., 16,000)

French Polynesia, in the South Pacific Ocean, consists of 130 islands divided into 5 archipelagos.

THE LAND. The Society, Marquesas, Gambier, and Austral groups are of volcanic origin and consist of rugged, mountainous cores encircled by narrow coastal plains and ringed by coral reefs. The Tuamotu Archipelago and Clipperton Island, attached to the Austral group, are low-lying, barren, coral atolls. The climate is hot, humid, and windy throughout the year.

THE PEOPLE. Most of the islanders are Maori Polynesians. There are some Asians and a few Europeans. Population is concentrated in the Society Islands, especially on Tahiti, near the center of the territory.

ECONOMY. Agriculture and the mining of phosphates are the main economic activities of the islands. The phosphates are found on the Tuamotu atoll. The soil of the islands is very rich, and coconuts, vanilla, coffee, tropical fruits, and vegetables are raised. There is some fishing, and mother-of-pearl shells are collected.

The processing of phosphates, coconuts, and foodstuffs are the main industries. The islands' limited trade consists of the export of phosphates, copra, and vanilla to France, New Zealand, and Japan, and the import of manufactured goods, foodstuffs, and fuels from France and the United States.

GOVERNMENT. The islands are administered by an appointed governor and by a government council chosen by a popularly elected legislature. The islanders elect representatives to the French National Assembly.

HISTORY. The scattered islands of French Polynesia have been inhabited for many centuries by Polynesian peoples. They were discovered by Europeans during the 1500s, 1600s, and 1700s. European traders and missionaries came to the islands, and in the early 1800s the islands placed themselves under French protection. By 1880 all the islands of the group had become French colonies.

French settlers expanded agriculture and took responsibility for the health and education of the islanders. In 1946 Polynesia was made an overseas territory of France, and in 1958 the islanders voted to retain their territorial status.

FRENCH SOUTHERN AND ANTARCTIC TERRITORIES

Status: Overseas territory of France
Area: 2,918 square miles
Population: No permanent population

The French Southern and Antarctic Territories consist of the Crozet and Kerguelen archipelagos, Ile Amsterdam, and Ile St. Paul, all in the Indian Ocean, and Terre Adélie, a region on the Indian Ocean coast of Antarctica.

The territory is barren and frigid. The only inhabitants are members of the French scientific research teams, and St. Paul is totally uninhabited. The territories are under the authority of an appointed administrator and council which sits in Paris.

St. Paul was discovered by Portuguese seamen and Amsterdam by Ferdinand Magellan in the 1500s. Frenchmen discovered the Crozet and Kerguelen archipelagos in the 1700s, and a Frenchman, Dumont D'Urville, explored Terre Adélie in the 1840s.

TAHITI, the largest and most famous of French Polynesia's more than 100 islands.

The territories remained uninhabited through the mid-1900s, although France opened research stations in Terre Adélie in 1947 and on Amsterdam in 1950.

FRENCH TERRITORY OF THE AFARS AND THE ISSAS

Status: Overseas territory of France
Area: 8,494 square miles
Population: (1961 est.) 81,200
Capital: Djibouti (Pop., 1963 est., urban area, 43,200)

The French Territory of the Afars and the Issas, formerly French Somaliland, is bordered on the north by Ethiopia and the Red Sea; on the east by the Bab al Mandab strait, the Gulf of Tadjoura, an inlet of the Gulf of Aden, and the Somali Republic; and on the south and west by Ethiopia.

THE LAND. Most of the territory is desert. The interior is a low, rolling desert basin. North of the Gulf of Tadjoura, the Mabla and Gouda mountains rise to a peak of just under 6,000 feet. Their slopes hold the territory's only forests. The coastline is low and flat except along the southern shore of the Tadjoura gulf, which is steep. The climate is hot and dry.

THE PEOPLE. The original inhabitants of the region are Issa Somalis and the Hamitic Afar people. There are now large minorities of Arabs and Europeans. Almost all the people are Muslim, and they speak French, Afar, Arabic, and Somali. Most of the Issas and Afars are semi-nomadic, and the only cities are along the coast.

ECONOMY. The territory's strategic location at the mouth of the Red Sea insures its economic importance. Its only known mineral resource is salt, which remained largely unexploited in the mid-1960s. Herding, especially of goats, is the chief activity of the people. Some farming is possible with irrigation near the coast, and vegetables, melons, and dates are the main crops. Shipbuilding and construction are the only industries.

Trade is the mainstay of the economy. A modern port at Djibouti, the capital, is an important refueling, storage, and distribution point for Red Sea and Indian Ocean commerce. Most of the country's own small trade consists of the importing of necessities from France.

GOVERNMENT. Territorial administration is under the direction of the Head of the Territory, appointed by the French government. He is assisted by a government council chosen by a popularly elected territorial assembly, which has authority over local matters. The territory elects two representatives to the French National Assembly.

HISTORY. The region has been inhabited for many years by the semi-nomadic Issas and Afars. In 1862 Afar chiefs ceded power to the French government, and by 1869, several French trading settlements and ports that had been established on the coast were prosperous.

Treaties signed in the 1880s with the Afars and the Issas extended French authority, and in 1896 the territory became known as the colony of French Somaliland. Djibouti rapidly became an important port and refueling station, and in the early 1900s a railroad was built between it and the capital of Ethiopia.

In 1946 the colony was made an overseas territory, and in 1956 it was granted internal self-government. In the 1950s and 1960s France initiated programs to improve education and welfare in the territory and to broaden its economy. In 1967, acting on a request by the territorial assembly, the French National Assembly changed the name French Somaliland to the more accurate French Territory of the Afars and the Issas. In a 1967 referendum the people voted to remain under French control. The Issas, however, generally favored independence whereas the Afars opposed it. Ethiopia and the Somali Republic challenged the fairness of the vote, and rioting broke out after the election.

—Hibberd V. B. Kline, Jr.;
Vera L. Zolberg

GIBRALTAR

Status: British crown colony
Area: 2.3 square miles
Population: (1966 est.) 25,000
Capital: Gibraltar (Pop., 1964 est., 24,836)

Gibraltar, occupying a small peninsula on the southern coast of Spain, is bordered on the north by Spain, on the east by the Alboran Sea, an arm of the Mediterranean, and on the south and west by the Strait of Gibraltar.

THE LAND AND PEOPLE. The flat sandy terrain of the northern part of Gibraltar gives way in the south to the 1,400 foot Rock of Gibraltar, which overlooks the sea. The limestone rock is filled with caves, and shrubs grow on its surface. Gibraltar's climate is warm and rather dry.

Most of the population is of Italian, Portuguese, Maltese, and Spanish origins. There is a large group of British government and military personnel and many non-resident Spanish workers who commute to the colony daily. English is the official language, and Spanish is widely spoken.

ECONOMY. Gibraltar has no natural resources and no useable farmland, and the colony depends heavily on tourism, transit trade, and its excellent harbor and drydock facilities. A British naval base contributes heavily to the economy.

GOVERNMENT. The colony is administered by an appointed governor, who is also the commander of the military base. He is assisted by a partially elected executive council and a partially elected legislative council.

HISTORY. Because of its strategic location and fortress-like defenses, Gibraltar has been important since ancient times. It was occupied by Carthaginians, Romans, and Visigoths before being captured in 711 by Muslim forces under the general Tariq, for whom the rock was named Jabal Tariq (Tariq's Mountain), or Gibraltar.

Spain conquered the rock in 1462 and held it until 1704, when a joint Dutch-British force captured it. By the Treaty of Utrecht in 1713 Britain gained title of Gibraltar, which it made into a fortress and naval base.

In the 1960s Spain intensified efforts to regain possession of the rock, but in a 1967 referendum Gibraltar's residents voted to remain a British colony rather than join Spain.

GILBERT AND ELLICE ISLANDS

Status: British colony
Area: 342 square miles
Population: (1967 est.) 56,000
Capital: Tarawa (Pop., 1965, 7,911)

The Gilbert and Ellice Islands colony consists of 35 islands scattered across more than 2 million square miles of the South Pacific Ocean. It includes the 16 Gilbert, nine Ellice, three Line, and six Phoenix islands, and Ocean Island. Two additional Phoenix islands, Canton and Enderbury, and five other Line islands are under separate administrations.

THE LAND AND PEOPLE. All but one of the islands are low-lying, coral atolls. The exception, Ocean Island, is of volcanic origin with a rather rugged, mountainous terrain. The islands' climate is hot and humid year-round, with rainfall ranging from 40 to 120 inches annually.

The people of the Gilbert Islands are Micronesian; Ellice islanders are Polynesian. The Phoenix Islands are uninhabited, and the Line group and Ocean Island are peopled by Gilbert and Ellice islanders, Chinese, and Europeans. Population is concentrated on Ocean Island and in the Gilberts.

ECONOMY. Ocean Island has rich deposits of lime phosphate, and phosphate mining is the primary source of income. Coconuts grow on the other islands, and copra production is important.

GOVERNMENT. The colony is governed by an appointed commissioner with the aid of appointed islanders, who administer the affairs of each island.

HISTORY. Many of the islands have been inhabited for centuries by Polynesian and Micronesian peoples. The first Europeans to sight them may have been Spanish sailors in the 1500s, but it is certain that most were discovered in the late 1700s and early 1800s by British seamen.

Britain proclaimed the Gilbert and Ellice islands a protectorate in 1888, and added Ocean Island in 1900. At the request of the islanders, they annexed them as a colony in 1916. The other islands were added to the colony between 1916 and 1938. British settlers established copra plantations, and the British government has used the islands as cable stations, ports, and radar stations.

The Gilbert Islands were the scene of heavy fighting in World War II. After the war, efforts were made to expand the economy of the islands, extend self-government, and relieve population pressure on the crowded islands.

GREENLAND

Status: Province of Denmark
Area: 840,003 square miles
Population (1966 est.) 41,000
Capital: Godthab (Pop., 1960, 3,179)

Greenland, the world's largest island, lies off the northwestern coast of North America. It is bounded on the north by the Arctic Ocean, on the east by the Greenland Sea, on the south by the Atlantic Ocean, and on the west by Davis Strait and Baffin Bay.

THE LAND. Greenland consists of a high interior plateau rimmed with mountains. The coastline is irregular and deeply indented. Most of the island lies north of the Arctic Circle and is covered with thick ice. Vegetation is limited to the southern coastlines. The climate is quite cold and dry throughout the year. The southwestern coast has the most moderate climate.

THE PEOPLE. The island is very thinly populated, and most of the people live on the southwestern coast. Native Greenlanders, who form the bulk of the population, are Eskimo or of Eskimo-Danish descent. There is also a large group of Danish settlers, scientists, and administrators. Greenlandic, an Eskimo dialect, is the official language, but Danish is also widely spoken on the island.

ECONOMY. The island's mineral resources are largely unexplored, but Greenland is the world's leading source of cryolite, used in glassmaking and aluminum processing, and it has deposits of lead, zinc, uranium, molybdenum, and coal. Fishing and sealing are the main occupations of the people. Sheep herding is important, and there is some farming. Mining and fish processing are the only important industries. The island is also the site of military bases and scientific research stations.

The island's trade balance is poor, with exports earning $13 million in 1965 and imports costing $34 million. Cryolite, fur, and fish products are exported, and foodstuffs, textiles, machinery, and fuels are imported. Most trade is with Denmark.

GOVERNMENT. Greenland is a province of Denmark and is administered by an appointed commissioner and a popularly elected national council. Greenlanders send two representatives to the Danish parliament.

HISTORY. Inhabited for many hundreds of years by Eskimos, Greenland was settled in the 900s AD by Scandinavians under Eric the Red. In 1261 the Greenlanders yielded their independence to the Norwegian crown. European settlements slowly died out, and by the 1500s had completely disappeared. In the 1700s a new colonization was undertaken, principally by Danes, and by the Treaty of Kiel in 1814 the island formally became a Danish colony.

It remained relatively undeveloped until World War II, when Denmark was occupied by German forces. Greenland remained free and was used by Allied forces for important military bases. After the war, Denmark expanded health, welfare, and educational programs for the islanders and began to develop the economy. In 1951 the United States and Denmark agreed to jointly defend the island, and U.S. and NATO military bases and observation posts were established there. In 1953 Greenland became a province of Denmark. Military operations and meteorological research expanded rapidly during the 1960s.
—Sergio Barzanti

GRENADA

Status: State in association with Britain
Area: 133 square miles
Population: (1966 est.) 97,000
Capital: St. George's (Pop., 1960, 7,303)

Grenada is one of the Windward Islands of the Lesser Antilles, which lie between the Caribbean Sea and the Atlantic Ocean. It has a mountainous terrain. The climate is hot throughout the year and rainfall is heavy. The population is of mixed African, European, and Carib Indian origin.

Grenada's economy is based on agriculture. Cocoa, nutmegs, mace, and bananas are the chief crops. Processing these products constitutes the only industry. There is limited trade with Britain and the United States, which supply the island with textiles, flour, and equipment.

Grenada has internal self-government under a council of ministers responsible to an elected legislative assembly. An appointed administrator represents Britain.

The island was inhabited by Indians when discovered by Christopher Columbus in the 1490s. Colonists from several European countries settled in Grenada in the 1600s and 1700s. They established plantations worked by slaves brought from Africa. In 1814 the island became British.

Grenada was governed as a unit with the other Windward Island colonies until 1967, when it gained self-government as a state in association with Britain.

COLONIES AND DEPENDENCIES

GUADELOUPE

Status: Overseas department of France
Area: 686 square miles
Population: (1967 est.) 320,000
Capital: Pointe-à-Pitre (Pop., 1954, urban area, 26,160)

Guadeloupe is one of the Windward Islands of the Lesser Antilles, which lie between the Caribbean Sea and the Atlantic Ocean.

Guadeloupe consists of two adjacent islands, Basse-Terre and Grande-Terre, and four smaller islands to the east.

Basse-Terre is mountainous, with rugged terrain and a steep shoreline. Grande-Terre is low and rocky with a deeply indented coast. The climate is warm and humid throughout the year. Annual rainfall ranges from less than 40 inches on the easternmost island to nearly 400 inches on Basse-Terre's highest elevations. The population, mostly of mixed African and European origin, is growing rapidly.

The economy is based on agriculture. Sugarcane and bananas are the main commercial crops. Sugar refining and distilling are the only important industries. Most of the islands' limited trade is with France and nearby French islands.

The department is administered by an appointed prefect with the assistance of a popularly elected assembly. Guadeloupe is represented in the French National Assembly.

Guadeloupe was discovered by Christopher Columbus in 1493 and first settled in 1635 by Frenchmen. In 1674 France annexed the islands and developed plantation agriculture, employing slaves imported from Africa. Slavery was abolished in the early 1800s and universal suffrage introduced in 1848. In 1946 Guadeloupe was made an overseas department of France.

HONG KONG

Status: British crown colony
Area: 398 square miles
Population: (1966 est.) 3,732,000
Capital: Victoria (Pop., 1961, urban area, 674,962)

Hong Kong is situated on the South China Coast 80 miles southeast of the Chinese city of Canton. It is bordered on the north by China, on the east and south by the South China Sea, and on the west by China's Pearl River. The colony includes the island of Hong Kong and Stonecutters Island, and on the Chinese mainland, Kowloon and the New Territories. Victoria Channel separates the two most important parts of the colony, Kowloon and the capital and port city of Victoria on tiny Hong Kong island.

THE LAND AND PEOPLE. The colony consists almost entirely of urban areas and hilly or swampy wasteland. It has a monsoon subtropical climate, with long, hot, and humid summers. Three-fourths of the annual rainfall of 85 inches falls between June and August, when the southwest monsoons prevail. Winters are temperate and very dry.

Chinese comprise 99 percent of Hong Kong's population. There are small Malay and British groups. Most of the Chinese are from adjacent areas of south China, and many settled in the colony after the 1949 Communist takeover of the Chinese mainland. The colony is densely populated—over 9,300 people per square mile in 1966—and population pressure is accentuated by the fact that so much of the land is hilly and unusable for food production or habitation.

ECONOMY. Commerce, finance, and industry are the bases of the colony's economy. There is virtually no agriculture, although reclamation projects were begun in the 1960s to increase farmland. The original basis for the economy of the colony was its port and entrepot function. It has the best harbor facilities between Shanghai and Singapore, and it serves as a distribution point for most of Southeast Asia.

With government encouragement, entrepreneurs who fled China in 1949 used their technical skill and capital to make manufacturing an important part of the economy. Textile weaving is the major industry. Shipbuilding and iron and steel working are important, and many small industries developed, so that by the beginning of the 1960s about 40 percent of the goods shipped from Hong Kong were manufactured there.

Although the colony has a rather poor balance of trade, with exports earning $1,527 million in 1967 and imports costing $1,818 million, the deficit is made up by earnings from tourism and shipping. Chief exports are manufactured goods and textiles. Foodstuffs, raw materials, and equipment are imported. Hong Kong's principal trading partners are the countries of Southeast Asia, China, Britain, the United States, and Japan.

GOVERNMENT. An appointed governor and executive council administer the colony. They are assisted by an appointed legislative council including members of the colony's ethnic and interest groups.

HISTORY. Hong Kong was a part of China until the rocky island was ceded to Britain "in perpetuity" in 1842. It rapidly grew in importance as the best port for Western trade with China. In 1860 the colony was extended to include Kowloon and Stonecutters Island, and in 1898 the New Territories were leased from China for 99 years. The Chinese revolution of the 1920s and the Sino-Japanese war of the 1930s increased Hong Kong's importance as a safe and stable port for Asian trade.

In 1941, during World War II, the colony fell to Japanese forces after a stiff resistance, but Britain reoccupied it in 1945. Long an outpost of British colonial conservatism, the character of the colony changed after the Chinese Communists took power on the mainland in 1949 and many thousands of Chinese fled to the colony. Although this immigration greatly increased the prosperity of Hong Kong, the nearness of the Communist regime posed a constant threat to the colony.

In the mid-1960s China's Communist government increased its pressure on Britain by inciting riots and terrorism in the colony.

—Thomas E. Ennis; George Inaba

IFNI

Status: Overseas territory of Spain
Area: 579 square miles
Population: (1964 est.) 52,000
Capital: Sidi-Ifni (Pop., 1960, 12,751)

Ifni, a Spanish enclave in the northwestern coast of Africa, is bounded on the north, east and south by Morocco and on the west by the Atlantic Ocean.

THE LAND AND PEOPLE. Ifni is arid and mountainous. The climate is dry, with moderate temperatures. The population consists almost entirely of Berber-speaking Muslims.

PAN AMERICAN
HONG KONG, on the south China coast, has one of the finest natural harbors in the world.

ECONOMY. Ifni is a poor country. The people subsist on farming and herding. Barley, corn, wheat, and some fruits are grown, and goats, sheep, cows, and camels are raised. Industry is limited to handcrafting such items as carpets, furniture, and jewelry. Ifni's limited trade consists of importing necessities from Spain.

GOVERNMENT. Ifni's administration is in the hands of an appointed governor-general responsible to the government of Spain.

HISTORY. Ifni has been inhabited for many centuries by semi-nomadic Berber-speaking peoples. It was a part of Morocco until 1860, when Morocco ceded the territory to Spain after a Spanish military victory over Morocco.

In 1912 international treaties reaffirmed Spain's possession of Ifni, but Spain did not occupy the enclave until 1934. Spain then established schools and hospitals, built roads, and initiated agricultural improvement projects in the province.

Morocco, after it became independent in 1956, claimed sovereignty over Ifni, and in the 1950s and 1960s Ifni was attacked several times by Moroccan forces. In 1966 the UN General Assembly formally requested Spain to cede Ifni to Morocco, but no action was taken.
—L. Carl Brown;
Hibberd V. B. Kline, Jr.

ISLE OF MAN

Status: Dependency of the British crown
Area: 227 square miles
Population: (1966 est.) 50,000
Capital: Douglas (Pop., 1961, 18,821)

The Isle of Man is a large, rugged island in the Irish Sea between England and Northern Ireland.

THE LAND AND PEOPLE. The Isle of Man consists of a mountainous core that rises to a peak of 2,034 feet, rimmed on the north and east by a narrow coastal plain. In the west, it drops sharply to the sea. The climate is rather warm and dry due to the warm Gulf Stream flowing around it.

The people are of English and Scandinavian origin, with a strong Celtic strain. Manx, a Celtic language, was traditionally the language of Man, but its use declined in the mid-1900s as English became dominant.

ECONOMY. Agriculture is the mainstay of the economy, with oats, wheat, and barley the chief crops. Livestock, especially sheep, are herded. Stone quarrying is the main industry, and wool is woven. Tourism is of some importance. The island's limited trade is entirely with the other British Isles.

GOVERNMENT. The Isle of Man has an ancient traditional form of democracy, and is almost completely independent of the British government. Executive power is wielded by the Court of Tynwald, which consists of a governor appointed to represent the crown; the island's bishop; its "First Deemster," or chief judge; the attorney general; two appointees; and five members elected by the House of Keys, the legislature. The House is popularly elected.

HISTORY. The Isle of Man was settled by Celts in the first centuries AD and remained independent until it was conquered by the Danes in the 800s. In 1266 Denmark ceded it to Scotland, and in 1399 the British crown gained possession.

By the 1400s it had developed its own culture, different from that of the other British Isles, and its people continued in their traditional ways of life. Periodic demands were made in the 1800s and 1900s for independence, but no serious negotiations were undertaken.

MACAO

Status: Overseas province of Portugal
Area: 6 square miles
Population: (1965 est.) 280,000
Capital: Macao (Pop., 1960, 161,252)

Macao, on the Macao peninsula of eastern China, is bounded on the north and west by China, on the east by the mouth of China's Pearl River, and on the south by the mouth of the Hsi River. The province consists of the city of Macao and the islands of Taipa and Colôane in the Pearl River.

The province is hilly. Macao is almost completely urban, but the islands are densely forested. The climate is rather hot and humid. With the exception of a small group of Portuguese and others, the population is Chinese.

Macao's excellent harbor and its many light industries that specialize in finishing Chinese goods are the backbone of the economy. Although there is some fishing, there is almost no agriculture and most food must be imported. Most of the province's exports originate in China. Tourism adds to the earnings derived from trade.

Macao is administered by an appointed governor and is represented in the Portuguese National Assembly.

Portugal made its first settlement on Macao in the 1550s, with Chinese permission. Although China revoked its permission when Portugal began treating Macao as a possession, the Portuguese refused to leave and the dispute continued into the 1800s. In 1833 Portugal made Macao an overseas province. In 1849 it convinced China to make Macao a free port, and in 1887 China ceded Macao to Portugal without defining the boundaries.

Macao prospered in the early 1900s. After the Commuist regime gained power in China in 1949, the province's fortune declined somewhat as trade with China decreased and as refugees from China flooded the tiny enclave. By the mid-1960s Portugal held little but formal power in Macao. After Chinese-incited rioting in 1967, provincial leaders yielded to China's demands for control over the province and agreed to ban activities of anti-Communist Chinese groups.

MARTINIQUE

Status: Overseas department of France
Area: 425 square miles
Population: (1967 est.) 330,000
Capital: Port-de-France (Pop., 1954, urban area, 60,648)

Martinique is one of the islands of the Lesser Antilles, which lie between the Caribbean Sea and the Atlantic Ocean. It is of volcanic origin, with a generally hilly to mountainous terrain. The climate is warm and humid throughout the year. Annual rainfall ranges from less than 40 inches on the southern coast to nearly 200 inches on the mountains. The population is of mixed African, European, and Carib Indian descent.

Agriculture, especially the cultivation of bananas, sugarcane, and pineapples, is the mainstay of the economy. The processing of agricultural products constitutes the islands' main industry, and agricultural products make up the bulk of exports. Most trade is with France.

Martinique is administered by an appointed prefect with the assistance of a popularly elected legislative council. The island is represented in the French National Assembly.

Martinique was discovered by Christopher Columbus in 1502. It was first settled in 1635 by Frenchmen, and was annexed by France in 1674. Plantations were established, and Africans were brought to the island as slaves. Slavery was abolished in the 1800s and universal suffrage introduced in 1848. In 1946 the island was made an overseas department of France.

BRITISH TRAVEL ASSOCIATION
ISLE OF MAN. The famous lighthouse is at Douglas, the capital city and chief port.

MONTSERRAT

Status: British colony
Area: 38 square miles
Population: (1966 est.) 14,000
Capital: Plymouth (Pop., 1960, 1,911)

Montserrat is one of the Leeward Islands of the Lesser Antilles, which lie between the Caribbean Sea and the Atlantic Ocean. Montserrat is situated between the islands of Nevis and Guadeloupe.

The island consists of a rocky, forested, mountainous spine flanked on the east and west by coastal lowlands. The climate is warm throughout the year, and rainfall is abundant. Most of the population is of mixed African and European origin.

Cotton is the mainstay of the economy. Some sugarcane is raised for rum, and fruits and vegetables are grown. Cotton ginning and rum making are the only important industries, although there is some tourism. The trade balance is poor with imports of necessities outweighing exports of cotton and sugar. Most trade is with Britain and the United States.

The colony is administered by an appointed governor with the advice of a partly-elected legislative council.

The island was discovered by Columbus in 1493 and settled by Irish colonists in 1632. It formally became a British colony in 1783 and was governed as a unit with other British West Indian territories until 1962, when it received its own administration.

MOZAMBIQUE

Status: Overseas province of Portugal
Area: 302,328 square miles
Population: (1966 est.) 7,040,000
Capital: Lourenço Marques (Pop., 1960, 177,929)

Mozambique, on the eastern coast of Africa, is bounded on the north by Tanzania, on the east by the Mozambique Channel and the Indian Ocean, on the south by Swaziland and South Africa, and on the west by Rhodesia, Zambia, and Mali.

THE LAND. Most of the long, irregularly shaped land consists of a flat or rolling plateau, ranging from 800 to 2,000 feet in elevation. In the east a narrow lowland skirts a coast, and in the west a zone of high plateaus and mountains reaches a peak of nearly 8,000 feet. The most important of the country's many rivers are the Zambezi, which crosses central Mozambique, and the Limpopo, in the south.

The climate is hot and humid along the coast, especially in the north. Temperatures are moderate in the interior, which is also drier.

THE PEOPLE. About 98 percent of Mozambique's population is African. Europeans comprise about 1.5 percent, and the remainder is of Chinese, Indian and Pakistani, and mixed background. Most of the Africans belong to a variety of Bantu-speaking tribes.

Portuguese is the official language, but many African languages are more commonly spoken. Most of the people follow traditional religions, but there are large numbers of Muslims and Roman Catholics.

ECONOMY. Mozambique is a very poor land, with a primarily agricultural economy. Its mineral resources have not been fully exploited, although some coal, bismuth, bauxite, and other minerals are mined. The forests that cover some 90 percent of the land remained uncut, and Mozambique's vast hydroelectric power potential was virtually unexploited in the mid-1960s.

Farming is especially productive in the river valleys and in the north, where sugarcane, cotton, corn, copra, tea, sisal, manioc, fruits, and vegetables are raised, mostly on large, European-owned commercial plantations. Cashew nuts grow wild and are picked for sale. Restrictions imposed by the government on food crops until 1961 severely damaged Mozambique's traditional agriculture, but recovery had begun by the mid-1960s.

Industry is limited to the processing of agricultural products, the milling of cotton textiles, and the manufacture of such items as rope, soap, cement, and leather goods. An important contribution to the economy is made by money earned by Mozambique laborers hired to work in the mines of neighboring Rhodesia and South Africa.

Mozambique has a very poor balance of trade. In 1966 imports cost $208 million and exports earned only $112 million. Nuts, cotton, sisal, sugar, and copra are among the leading exports, and machinery, vehicles, fuels, and industrial raw materials are among the imports. The bulk of the country's overseas trade is with metropolitan Portugal.

GOVERNMENT. Mozambique is constitutionally a province of Portugal. Its government is administered by a governor-general appointed by the Portuguese cabinet, and he is advised by an economic and social council representing various interest groups, such as business and labor. Limited legislative power is vested in a small elected legislative council, and Mozambique elects members to the Portuguese National Assembly. Tribal leaders unofficially retain considerable local authority.

HISTORY. Mozambique has been inhabited for many centuries by Bantu-speaking peoples. Between the 900s and 1300s sophisticated city states, such as Sofala, developed on the basis of iron and gold exports to Asia and the Arab world. When the Portuguese, the first Europeans to reach the region, arrived in the early 1500s, Arab trading colonies had been established along the coast. In the 1530s the Portuguese sacked the coastal trading cities and broke the trade network established with Africa and India. The Portuguese established a monopoly over sea trade and explored the interior.

Unsuccessful in their search for gold and silver, the Portuguese turned to the slave trade for revenue. The slave trade had been carried on before the arrival of the Europeans, but the Portuguese expanded it, and it soon became the colony's most profitable enterprise.

Soldier-settlers, called *prazeros*, established petty chieftainships in the interior. They seized African villages, which they converted into peasant colonies and ruled independently of Portuguese authority. Slavery was legally abolished in 1878, but the labor situation scarcely changed. *Prazeros* kept their slaves, but referred to them as "contractual laborers." Local officials cooperated with the *prazeros* by declaring unemployed Africans vagrants and thus eligible to be forced into contracts requiring them to work for the Europeans.

In the 1930s Portugal tightened its control over its colonies. The government took over the exploitation of the colonies' resources.

In 1951 Mozambique's status was changed to that of an overseas province, and in 1961 Portugal granted its African inhabitants full Portuguese citizenship, with an announced goal of integrating all the country's overseas provinces into Portuguese national life. Although some reforms were initiated in 1961 to improve the welfare and education of the Africans, little progress was made. Forced labor continued in many places, and African political rights were limited. Poverty, illiteracy, and disease remained common.

In the 1960s, the United Nations and many countries, and some groups within Mozambique increased pressure on Portugal to improve conditions in the colony and to grant Mozambique self-determination. In the 1960s, with support from other African states, a Mozambique nationalist liberation organization developed and in 1964 began a rebellion against Portugal. Guerrilla warfare, concentrated in the north, continued through the 1960s despite an increase in Portuguese military strength in Mozambique.

—Hibberd V. B. Kline, Jr.;
Robert I. Rotberg

NETHERLANDS ANTILLES

Status: Autonomous part of the kingdom of the Netherlands
Area: 371 square miles
Population: (1967 est.) 212,000
Capital: Willemstad, Curaçao (Pop., 1966, 343,700)

The Netherlands Antilles consists of six islands in the Caribbean Sea. The islands of Arbua, Bonaire, and Curaçao lie off the northwest coast of Venezuela, on the South American mainland. They are part of the Leeward Islands. Saba, St. Eustacious, and St. Maarten, which is shared with France, are in the Windwards, some 200 miles east of Puerto Rico.

THE LAND. The larger islands, in the Leeward group, are generally flat, except for a mountainous region on northern Bonaire, and arid or semiarid. The small Windward Islands are mountainous, rather moist, and densely forested. Temperatures on all the islands average in the 80°s F. throughout the year.

THE PEOPLE. The people of the Netherlands Antilles are of varied origins. Negroes and people of mixed background predominate on Curaçao and Bonaire. The population of Aruba is of Carib Indian and European descent, and the Windward Islands are populated primarily by Europeans and Negroes.

Roman Catholicism is the predominant religion on the Leeward Islands; Protestantism on the Windward Islands. Dutch is the official language, but Papiamento, a dialect combining Dutch, Spanish, and African and Indian tongues, is spoken.

ECONOMY. The islands have no important mineral deposits, and the larger islands have poor soils. Fruits, sugarcane, and some vegetables are raised on the eastern islands, and there is fishing off the coasts.

The mainstays of the economy, however, are the income derived from tourism and the operation of two large oil refineries on Curaçao and Aruba that process crude oil shipped from Venezuela. These refineries are the only important industries, although the government is attempting to attract other businesses to the islands. In 1966 exports earned $592 million and imports cost $616 million. Oil is exported to Western Europe and North America, and foodstuffs, machinery, textiles, and other necessities are imported, mostly from the Netherlands and Caribbean nations.

GOVERNMENT. The Netherlands Antilles is administered by an appointed governor and council, whose powers are limited by a popularly elected legislature. Each island has authority over local matters and the administration is headed by an appointed lieutenant governor.

HISTORY. The islands of the Netherlands Antilles were discovered in the late 1400s and early 1500s by Spanish navigators. They were successively occupied and claimed by Spain, Portugal, Britain, and the Netherlands. They were formally ceded to the Dutch in 1815 by the Treaty of Paris.

From the first, Curaçao was the most important island, and in the 1700s and 1800s it was a center for the Caribbean slave trade. The island declined in importance when slaving was abolished in the 1860s, but its status rose again after 1916, when the Royal Dutch Shell Company built a refinery there.

In 1954 the islands' status was changed from that of a colony to that of a self-governing region within the kingdom of the Netherlands. In the 1950s and 1960s economic expansion became the main concern of the islands' government.

NEW CALEDONIA

Status: French overseas territory
Area: 7,336 square miles
Population: (1966 est.) 93,000
Capital: Nouméa (Pop., 1960 est., 30,000)

New Caledonia is an island in the South Pacific Ocean about 1,115 miles east of Australia. The nearby Loyalty Islands, the Isle of Pines, and the Huan and Chesterfield archipelagos are dependencies of New Caledonia.

THE LAND AND PEOPLE. New Caledonia has an area of 6,530 square miles and consists of rather high, rugged, forested mountain cores. There are fertile valleys and a plains area in the west. The island is encircled by coral reefs. The Isle of Pines and the three Loyalty Islands are coral and filled with caverns. Huan and Chesterfield are low-lying atolls. The climate is mild throughout the year.

The population is divided almost evenly between the Australo-Melanesian aboriginal people of New Caledonia and people of European origin. There are also groups of temporary workers from Asian lands.

ECONOMY. New Caledonia is rich in minerals, especially nickel, chrome, iron, and manganese, and mining is the chief source of income. There are also abundant, well developed hydroelectric power resources.

The territory of New Caledonia also has rich farmlands. Coffee and coconuts are the chief commercial crops, and rice, fruits, and vegetables are grown for local food needs. There are also large numbers of cattle, pigs, and other livestock. Metal processing is the chief industry, and the processing of agricultural products is also important. The island's trade is profitable, based on the export of nickel and other metals.

GOVERNMENT. The territory is administered by an appointed high commissioner and a government council. There is a popularly elected territorial assembly, and the islands are represented in the French National Assembly.

HISTORY. New Caledonia has been inhabited by Melanesian peoples for many centuries. In 1768 a French navigator was the first European to visit New Caledonia, which was named in 1774 by an English sailor. Between the 1790s and 1820s the French explored the islands, and in 1844 France claimed them. In 1853 they became a French colony. Mines and plantations were opened in the late 1800s and early 1900s. In 1946 the colony was made an overseas territory of France, and in 1958 the islands' assembly voted to retain territorial status.

NEW GUINEA

Status: UN trust territory under Australian administration
Area: 92,159 square miles
Population: (1966 est.) 1,582,000

The trust territory of New Guinea consists of the northeastern quarter of the Southwest Pacific island of New Guinea, the islands of the nearby Bismarck Archipelago, Bougainville and Buka islands, and some 600 smaller nearby islands. The islands lie just north of Australia.

The mainland territory is bordered on the north by the Bismarck Sea, on the east by the Solomon Sea, on the south by the Territory of Papua, and on the west by the Indonesian region of West Irian.

THE LAND AND PEOPLE. The surface of northeastern New Guinea rises sharply from a swampy interior lowland to peaks of over 14,500 feet. Some of the mountains are active volcanoes. Many of the islands are encircled by coral reefs.

The climate of New Guinea is hot throughout the year and humid at lower elevations. Rainfall ranges from 45 inches to 245 inches a year.

AUSTRALIAN NEWS AND INFORMATION BUREAU
NEW GUINEA. Outrigger canoes under sail.

Indigenous Melanesian peoples form a majority of the territory's population, and there are groups of Australians, Europeans, and Asians. The population is concentrated in northeastern New Guinea and on the larger islands of New Britain and New Ireland.

ECONOMY. Although there are petroleum deposits in the territory, agriculture is the mainstay of the economy. Most farms are owned by the New Guineans and islanders. Copra, rubber, coffee, and cocoa are the chief commercial crops. Sisal, spices, hemp, tobacco, sugarcane, tobacco, and other crops are also raised for export.

Food production is insufficient for local needs. Industry is limited to the processing of agricultural products.

GOVERNMENT. Australia administers the trust territory as a unit with the Australian territory of Papua, in southeastern New Guinea. An appointed commissioner manages the territory with the assistance of local commissioners and with the advice of a partially elected legislative assembly.

HISTORY. New Guinea and the adjacent islands have long been inhabited by Melanesians. Spanish and Dutch sailors visited them in the 1600s, but no European settlement was made until 1828, when the Dutch occupied western New Guinea.

After a German company began trading in eastern New Guinea, Queensland, Australia, annexed the territory in 1882 without British approval. In 1884 Britain established a protectorate over southeastern New Guinea and Germany established a protectorate over North East New Guinea.

In 1914, at the beginning of World War I, Australian troops occupied German New Guinea. In 1921, after Germany had been defeated in the war, the League of Nations gave Australia a mandate over the German territory. In 1945, after World War II, the territory was made a UN trusteeship under Australian administration.

In the 1950s and 1960s Australia initiated projects to develop the territory's natural resources and improve agriculture. Popular participation in government was expanded, and in 1964 an elected assembly was introduced.

COLONIES AND DEPENDENCIES   Portuguese Guinea   231

NEW HEBRIDES
Status: Condominium of Britain and France
Area: 5,700 square miles
Population: (1966 est.) 70,000
Capital: Vila (Pop., 1962 est., 3,700)

The New Hebrides, a chain of approximately 80 islands, extends across the southwestern Pacific for some 400 miles.

THE LAND AND PEOPLE. The islands are of volcanic origin and have rugged, mountainous interiors rimmed by low coastal plains. The climate is hot and humid throughout the year. Most of the islanders are Melanesian, and there are people of British and French origin.

ECONOMY. The economy is agricultural, with coconut palms and coffee the chief commercial crops. Yams, bananas, and manioc are grown for local consumption. Large herds of cattle are raised, and there is considerable fishing. Industry is limited to the processing of farm products, hides, and fish.

GOVERNMENT. The islands are governed jointly by Britain and France through the French governor of New Caledonia and the British governor of Fiji, each of whom is represented in the islands by a commissioner.

HISTORY. The New Hebrides have been inhabited for many centuries by Melanesian peoples. European planters and traders began visiting the islands after their discovery in 1606 by the Spanish.

By the mid-1800s British and French settlers outnumbered other Europeans, and in 1887 the two nations formed a joint commission to protect their mutual interests. In 1906 the condominium was established. In the mid-1900s projects were undertaken to modernize and expand the islands' economy and to improve the health and welfare of the islanders.

NIUE
Status: Territory of New Zealand
Area: 100 square miles
Population: (1967 est.) 5,000

Niue, an island of the Cook Archipelago in the South Pacific Ocean, is so far from the other islands of the group that it is administered separately.

Niue is a low-lying, rather barren, coral island with a hot, dry climate. Hurricanes are frequent. The population is overwhelmingly Polynesian, but there are a few Europeans and New Zealanders.

Coconuts, sweet potatoes, and bananas are the major crops, and industry is limited to the processing of agricultural products.

The island is administered by an appointed commissioner with the advice of an appointed council of islanders.

Niue was inhabited by Polynesian peoples when it was discovered in the 1770s by the British. With the other Cook Islands, it became a British protectorate in 1888 and was made part of New Zealand in 1901. The island received its own administration in 1903.

NORFOLK ISLAND
Status: Territory of Australia
Area: 14 square miles
Population: (1966 est.) 1,000

Norfolk Island lies in the South Pacific Ocean about 600 miles east of Australia. It is hilly and covered with lush vegetation. The climate is mild throughout the year. Most of the people are of British descent.

Norfolk has fertile soil and valuable forests. Citrus fruits, vegetables, bananas, and beans are raised commercially, and forestry is of increasing importance. Tourism is a major source of income.

The island is governed by an appointed administrator with the assistance of an appointed council of islanders.

Norfolk Island was discovered in 1774, and in the late 1700s and early 1800s it served as a British penal colony. In 1856 descendants of mutineers from the British ship *Bounty* migrated to Norfolk from Pitcairn island.

Norfolk was administered as part of the colony of New South Wales, in Australia, until 1913, when it was placed under the authority of the Australian Minister of Territories. The island's economy expanded in the mid-1900s with the encouragement of tourism and the development of Norfolk's natural resources.

PAPUA
Status: Territory of Australia
Area: 86,099 square miles
Population: (1966 est.) 601,000
Capital: Port Moresby (Pop., 1965 est., 42,000)

The Papua Territory consists of the southeastern quarter of the South Pacific island of New Guinea, or Papua proper, and the Trobriand, Woodlark, D'Entrecasteaux, and Louisiade archipelagos lying off the east coast of New Guinea.

Papua proper is bordered on the north by the Territory of New Guinea and the Solomon Sea, on the east and south by the Coral Sea, and on the west by the Indonesian region of West Irian.

THE LAND AND PEOPLE. The interior and eastern tip of Papua proper are extremely mountainous, but there are lowlands in the south and west. There are many rivers. The islands are also mountainous, and coral reefs ring Papua and most of the islands.

Indigenous Melanesian peoples form the bulk of the population. There are also Europeans and Asians.

ECONOMY. The economy of the territory is based on agriculture, and coconuts, cacao, coffee, and rubber are the chief commercial crops. There is also commercial forestry and fishing. Most industries process the territory's agricultural products, but light manufacturing was developing in the 1960s.

GOVERNMENT. Papua forms an administrative unit with the territory of New Guinea and is governed by an appointed commissioner with the advice of a partially elected assembly and elected local councils.

HISTORY. New Guinea and the adjacent islands were inhabited by Melanesian peoples when they were first visited by the Spanish and Dutch in the 1600s. No settlement was made until 1828, when the Dutch occupied the western half of New Guinea. In 1882, after a German company had begun trading in eastern New Guinea, Queensland, Australia occupied Papua without British approval, but in 1884 Britain made southeastern New Guinea a protectorate, as British New Guinea. Australia was given sovereignty over the area in 1905.

New Guinea was occupied by Japanese forces in the 1940s, during World War II. After the war, economic development projects were begun. Forestry and fishing were developed, and new industries were started. Popular participation in government also increased, and in 1964 a representative assembly was introduced.

PITCAIRN ISLAND
Status: British colony
Area: 1.9 square miles
Population: (1966) 92

Pitcairn, a small, isolated island in the southeastern Pacific, is of volcanic origin and mountainous. The climate is warm throughout the year. The people are of mixed British and Polynesian origin.

Subsistence agriculture and fishing are the main economic activities. Fruit and handcrafts are sold to passing ships.

The governor of Fiji has authority over the island, but actual administration is in the hands of a small island council.

Discovered in 1767 by a French explorer, the island remained uninhabited until 1790, when mutineers from the British ship *Bounty* settled there with a few Tahitian men and women. In 1856, when over-crowding became a problem, the islanders were moved to Norfolk Island, but in the 1860s some of them returned to Pitcairn. Three tiny uninhabited adjacent islands were annexed in 1902.

In 1959 responsibility for the island was shifted from the Western Pacific High Commissioner to the governor of Fiji. In the 1960s emigration outpaced natural growth, and the population began to decrease.

PORTUGUESE GUINEA
Status: Overseas province of Portugal
Area: 13,948 square miles
Population: (1966 est.) 529,000
Capital: Bissau (Pop., 1950, urban area, 18,309)

Portuguese Guinea lies on the western coast of Africa. It is bounded on the north by Senegal, on the east and south by Guinea, and on the west by the Atlantic Ocean.

THE LAND. Portuguese Guinea consists of a mainland, with a deeply indented coast, and a number of offshore islands, including those of the Bijagos archipelago. Most of the province consists of low coastal plain, much of which is swampy. In the east is a higher, drier savannah region.

There are many rivers and streams, and the Cacheu, Mansoa, Geba, and Crubal rivers have large deltas. The climate is characterized by high temperatures and extreme humidity.

THE PEOPLE. Most of the population is African, and there are small groups of Portuguese and mulattoes, people of mixed African and European origin. The Africans are members of many tribal groups, including the Balante, Mandyako, and Malinke.

Many languages are spoken, including Portuguese and African languages, but a Creole patois is the most commonly understood tongue. Roman Catholicism, Islam, and traditional religions are all represented.

ECONOMY. Portuguese Guinea is an agricultural land, and the standard of living is very low. The country's forests are exploited for their timber. The main commercial crops are palm kernels and peanuts raised on European-owned plantations. Basic food crops include rice, millet, coconuts, manioc, beans, and bananas. There is little industry.

Almost all of the province's limited trade is with Portugal. Peanuts and palm kernels are the chief exports, and machinery and consumer goods are imported.

GOVERNMENT. Constitutionally a province of Portugal, Portuguese Guinea is administered by a governor-general appointed by the Portuguese national government.

A cabinet assists the governor in his executive functions, and a small, partly elected legislative council advises him as well. Tribal chieftains unofficially exercise authority in the localities.

HISTORY. Portuguese sailors were the first Europeans to visit present-day Portuguese Guinea, in 1446, and Portugal established trading posts and ports at the mouth of the rivers and on the Bijagos islands. In the late 1400s the region was made a dependency of the nearby Portuguese colony of Cape Verde Islands. From the late 1500s through the mid-1800s the colony prospered from the slave trade.

Portugal occupied only coastal portions of the territory, and sent very few permanent settlers. In the 1800s Portuguese claims to the region were disputed by Britain and France. In the late 1800s agreement was reached on the division of west-central Africa among the European powers, and Portuguese control of the area was formally recognized.

Portuguese attempts to control the interior led to rebellions among the Africans, angered by Portugal's participation in the slave trade. The rebellions were put down by 1915, and Portuguese settlers expanded their plantations in the colony. In the 1930s colonial administration was centralized.

In 1951 the colony was made an overseas province. Portugal did little to develop the economy and virtually ignored the education, health, and general welfare needs of the African population. Forced labor, under the "contract labor" system, remained the rule. In 1961 Portugal did, however, formally grant full Portuguese citizenship to African Guineans.

With encouragment from neighboring African states, a national liberation movement developed in the early 1960s and in 1961 began a rebellion for independence. By the mid-1960s the rebel leaders claimed control over most of the country and its people, and the Portuguese armed forces had been unable to quell the uprising.

In 1968 Portugal's president, Americo Rodrigues Thomas, visited Portuguese Guinea to reaffirm Portuguese sovereignty in the face of the widespread rebellion.

—Hibberd V. B. Kline, Jr.;
Robert I. Rotberg

PORTUGUESE TIMOR

Status: Overseas province of Portugal
Area: 146 square miles
Population: (1966 est.) 560,000
Capital: Dili (Pop., 1960, 52,158)

Portuguese Timor consists of the eastern half of the Southeast Asian island of Timor in the Malay Archipelago, several smaller islands, and an enclave, Ocussi-Ambeno, on the Savu Sea coast of the western half of Timor island, surrounded by Indonesian Timor.

Portuguese Timor proper is bounded on the north by the Ambai Strait, on the east by the Wetar Strait, on the south by the Timor Sea, and on the west by Indonesian Timor.

THE LAND AND PEOPLE. A central spine of mountains in Timor proper is flanked by coastal plains. The climate in the coastal areas is hot and humid. The climate in the mountains is moderate and rainfall is heavy most of the year.

The bulk of the varied population is native to the island and similar to Indonesian and Melanesian peoples. There are also Chinese, Arabs, Africans, Europeans, and people of mixed origins.

ECONOMY. Despite the availability of rich forest and agricultural resources, the main economic activity is subsistence farming. Coffee, copra, and rubber grown for exports are shipped to Portugal. Manufactured items are imported from Japan and Hong Kong.

GOVERNMENT. An appointed governor administers the province. Representatives are elected to the Portuguese National Assembly.

HISTORY. Timor was inhabited for many centuries by island peoples before Portugal established its first settlement there in the 1500s. The Dutch disputed the Portuguese presence on Timor, and a boundary dividing the island between the two countries was not established until 1850. Disputes continued into the 1900s, however.

In the 1940s, during World War II, Timor was occupied by Japan, but Portugal regained control in 1945. In the 1960s Portugal introduced economic and social development projects.

RÉUNION

Status: Department of France
Area: 969 square miles
Population: (1967 est.) 418,000
Capital: Saint-Denis (Pop., 1961, 65,614)

Réunion is a mountainous tropical island in the Indian ocean, east of Madagascar and southwest of Mauritius. Its population is of Indian, French, Chinese, Southeast Asian, and African origins. The island is densely populated, and the rate of population growth is extremely high.

The island's economy is based on the cultivation and processing of sugarcane and making perfume essences. Most foodstuffs must be imported. Trade is mainly with France.

Government is in the hands of an appointed prefect and a popularly elected council. The island sends representatives to the French National Assembly.

Réunion was uninhabited when it was discovered in 1528 by the Portuguese. The first settlers were Frenchmen who arrived in the early 1600s, and in the late 1600s France claimed it as Bourbon Island. Immigration increased rapidly from France, Africa, and Asia, and the island's plantations prospered. Its name was changed to Réunion in 1793. In 1946 it became a department of France.

FRENCH EMBASSY PRESS & INFORMATION DIV.

RÉUNION'S CAPITAL, Saint-Denis, lies on the north coast of the French Indian Ocean island.

ST. HELENA

Status: British colony
Area: 121 square miles
Population: (1965 est.) 5,815
Capital: Jamestown (Pop., 1958 est., 1,600)

St. Helena and its two dependencies, Ascension and Tristan de Cunha, are islands in the Atlantic Ocean off the west coast of Africa. Ascension, the northernmost of the three, lies about 1,000 miles off the coast of Angola. St. Helena is about 600 miles to the southeast, and the Tristan de Cunha group lies approximately 1,000 miles southwest of St. Helena.

All the islands are mountainous. St. Helena is inhabited by descendents of Portuguese, British, and Dutch settlers. Its economy is agricultural, with flax the main crop. Rope-making is the island's only industry. Most trade is with Britain and South Africa.

St. Helena's two dependencies are only sparsely inhabited. Ascension is important as a cable station and satellite and missile tracking station. Of the four islands of the Tristan De Cunha group, only Tristan de Cunha is inhabited. Its people are descendants of early British settlers. Catching, canning, and freezing crayfish is the basis of the island's economy.

An appointed governor, aided by a partially elected council, administers the islands from St. Helena.

HISTORY. St. Helena was uninhabited when discovered by the Portuguese in 1502. The British and the Dutch both claimed it until 1673, when the British gained possession of it. St. Helena was the site of the French emperor Napoleon I's exile between 1815 and 1821.

Ascension was discovered by the Portuguese in 1501, but it remained uninhabited until a British garrison was placed on the island in 1816 to guard Napoleon on St. Helena. During the 1800s it was an important port on the sea route around Africa. During World War II it was the site of a vital airbase.

Tristan de Cunha was also first settled by soldiers of a British garrison established in 1816. Its inhabitants thrived on the crayfish industry until 1961, when a volcano on the island erupted and devastated the community. After temporary relocation in Britain, the islanders returned in 1963 and rebuilt their homes and factories.

ST. KITTS-NEVIS-ANGUILLA

Status: State in association with Britain
Area: 3,435 square miles
Population: (1966 est.) 58,000
Capital: Basse-Terre (Pop., 1960, 15,726)

St. Kitts-Nevis-Anguilla, three islands in the Leeward Islands of the Lesser Antilles, lie between the Caribbean Sea and the Atlantic Ocean. St. Kitts (St. Christopher) and Nevis are adjacent. Anguilla lies some 50 miles to their north, beyond several French and Dutch islands.

THE LAND AND PEOPLE. St. Kitts and Nevis have mountainous, rugged interiors rimmed by lowlands or bluffs. Coral-rimmed Anguilla is generally flat and low-lying. The climate is warm throughout the year, and about 55 inches of rain falls each year. The people are mostly of mixed African and European descent.

THE ECONOMY. The cultivation of sugarcane and cotton is the mainstay of the economy. Plantation agriculture predominates on St. Kitts, but small farms are the rule on the other islands. Sugar refining and cotton processing are the only important industries. Tourism was of increasing importance in the 1960s.

The islands' limited trade consists of exporting sugar, molasses, and cotton and importing foodstuffs and other necessities. Britain and the United States are the islands' major trading partners.

GOVERNMENT. The islands are self-governing, with an appointed governor as nominal chief executive. Actual powers are wielded by an executive council responsible to a small, popularly elected legislative assembly.

HISTORY. The islands were discovered in 1493 by Christopher Columbus. In 1623 St. Kitts was the site of the first British settlement in the West Indies, and Nevis was settled in 1628. St. Kitts was shared with France until 1783, when the three islands became British possessions. In 1871 the islands were made part of the federated Leeward Islands colony, which in 1958 joined the Federation of the West Indies.

The federation was dissolved in 1962, and in 1967 St. Kitts-Nevis-Anguilla became a single self-governing state in association with Britain. Anguilla proclaimed its independence in 1967 but was prevented from breaking away.

ST. LUCIA

Status: State in association with Britain
Area: 238 square miles
Population: (1966 est.) 5,000
Capital: Castries (Pop., 1960, 4,353)

St. Lucia is one of the Windward Islands of the Lesser Antilles chain, which lies between the Caribbean Sea and the Atlantic Ocean. It has a rugged, mountainous terrain. The climate is hot throughout the year, and rainfall is abundant. The population is of mixed African, European, and Indian origin.

Agriculture is the mainstay of the economy, and bananas, copra, cocoa, and spices are the chief commercial crops. Processing these crops constitutes the islands' industry. The bulk of exports go to Britain, the United States, and nearby islands. Imports are fertilizer, fuels, machinery, and other manufactured goods.

St. Lucia has internal self-government under a council of ministers responsible to an elected assembly. An administrator represents Britain.

St. Lucia was inhabited by Indians when it was discovered by Europeans in the late 1400s. It was settled in the 1600s by colonists from several European countries. They established plantations worked by slaves brought from Africa in the 1700s. St. Lucia became a British colony in 1814 and gained self-government in 1967.

ST. PIERRE AND MIQUELON

Status: Overseas territory of France
Area: 93 square miles
Population: (1966 est.) 6,000
Capital: St. Pierre

St. Pierre and Miquelon consists of three islands and several islets in the Atlantic Ocean off the southern coast of Newfoundland, Canada.

The islands' terrain is generally rocky and hilly, with many swamps and peat bogs. The climate is cold and damp. The islands are peopled by the descendants of early French settlers.

Fishing is the mainstay of the economy, and cod is the most important catch. Fish processing is the main industry. Fish and fish products constitute the bulk of exports, and most necessities must be imported. The islands trade mainly with France, the United States, and Canada.

An appointed administrator governs the territory with the assistance of a popularly elected council. The islands send representatives to the French National Assembly.

The islands were probably first discovered in the 1000s, but the first permanent settlement was made by Frenchmen in 1604. In 1713 the islands were ceded to Britain, and the small group of settlers was deported. France regained possession in 1783, and the colony grew slowly. In 1946 the islands were made an overseas territory, and in a referendum in 1958 the inhabitants voted to retain that status.

ST. VINCENT

Status: State in association with Britain
Area: 150 square miles
Population: (1966 est.) 90,000
Capital: Kingstown (Pop., 1960, 2,339)

St. Vincent is one of the Windward Islands of the Lesser Antilles, which lie between the Caribbean Sea and the Atlantic Ocean. It consists of a heavily forested spine of mountains flanked by coastal plains. The climate is hot throughout the year and rainfall is abundant. The people are of mixed African, European, and Indian origin.

The economy is based on agriculture. Bananas, arrowroot, copra, cotton, fruits, spices, and yams are the chief crops. Processing of these crops is the main industrial activity, but development of harbor and fishing facilities was undertaken in the 1960s. Exports of farm products are outweighed by imports of foodstuffs, raw materials, and machinery.

St. Vincent has internal self government under a council of ministers responsible to an elected assembly. An appointed administrator represents Britain.

Inhabited by Indians when discovered by Christopher Columbus in the 1490s, St. Vincent was settled in the 1600s by Europeans from several countries. They established plantations worked by slaves brought from Africa. The island became a British colony in 1814 and was governed with the other Windward Islands until 1967, when it gained self-government.

SÃO TOMÉ AND PRINCIPE

Status: Overseas province of Portugal
Area: 372 square miles
Population: (1964 est.) 59,000
Capital: São Tomé (Pop., 1960, 5,714)

The islands of São Tomé and Principe and their offshore islets lie some 124 miles off western Africa in the Gulf of Guinea, an arm of the Atlantic Ocean.

THE LAND AND PEOPLE. The islands are volcanic in origin and consist of a hilly, forested interior ringed by a wide, flat, coastal plain. The climate is extremely hot. The humidity is high, and rainfall is heavy.

São Tomé, the southern island, has nearly 15 times as many inhabitants as the slightly smaller Principe. Most of the permanent population is descended from Portuguese and African settlers, but in the mid-1900s temporary workers from other Portuguese provinces in Africa outnumbered the native population. Portuguese is the major language, and Roman Catholicism the religion of most of the people.

ECONOMY. The island province has a rather prosperous economy based primarily on the cultivation of cacao. Copra, coffee, and palm trees are also important commercial crops. Industry is limited to the processing of agricultural products.

The standard of living of the islanders is quite high in comparison with the low levels of most of Portuguese Africa. Because of poor working conditions on the plantations, however, labor must be imported.

The province's trade is balanced. In 1965, for example, exports earned $5 million and imports cost $5 million. Cacao, palm and coconut products, and coffee are exported. Food, textiles, and other necessities are imported. The Netherlands, the United States, Britain, and Portugal are the main markets, and imports come largely from Portugal and Portuguese provinces in Africa.

GOVERNMENT. An appointed governor administers the province, which sends representatives to the Portuguese National Assembly.

HISTORY. The islands were discovered by the Portuguese in the 1470s and in 1522 were made a Portuguese colony. Emigrants from Portugal and people from western Africa settled the islands, and cocoa plantations prospered.

In 1951 the colony was incorporated into the Portuguese nation as an overseas province. In 1966 Portugal arrested and imprisoned a group of island nationalists for anti-government activities.

SEYCHELLES

Status: British crown colony
Area: 156 square miles
Population: (1965 est.) 48,000
Capital: Port Victoria, Mahé (Pop., 1960, urban area, 10,504)

The Seychelles Archipelago consists of about 90 islands and islets in the Indian Ocean, some 1,000 miles east of Africa. The largest is Mahé. Others include Silhouette, Praslin, La Digue, and Curieuse.

THE LAND. Most of the smaller islands are coral, barren, and uninhabitable. The large ones consist of a mountainous, forested interior ringed by a low, flat coastal plain. The climate is warm, with heavy rainfall.

THE PEOPLE. Population is clustered on Mahé and the other large islands. Most of the people are descendants of early French and African settlers. There are also people of British, Chinese, and Indian origin. The rate of population growth is rapid, about 3 percent a year between 1958 and 1966.

English and a Creole dialect are spoken. Roman Catholicism is the predominant religion.

ECONOMY. The islands are poor. Although large plantations produce coconuts, palms, and spices, most of the islanders subsist by farming small plots and fishing. Projects were undertaken in the 1960s to diversify agriculture and to expand fishing into a commercial activity.

The colony's industries process coconuts, palm kernels, and spices. A U.S. satellite tracking station established on the islands in the early 1960s contributes to the economy.

Exports of copra and other coconut products and spices are far outweighed by imports of foodstuffs, clothing, and other necessities. Most of the limited trade is with Indian Ocean coastal nations.

GOVERNMENT. An appointed governor administers the colony with the advice of a partly elected legislative council.

HISTORY. The Seychelles were uninhabited when discovered by the Portuguese in the early 1500s. They were not settled until the mid-1700s, when the French established communities on the islands and claimed them for France.

Britain received the islands in 1814 by the Treaty of Paris and administered them with the Mauritius colony until 1888, when the two were separated. In 1903 Seychelles became a crown colony.

In the mid-1900s popular participation in government was gradually increased. Political parties developed in the 1960s and concerned themselves mainly with improving the islands' economy.

SOUTH WEST AFRICA

Status: Territory administered by South Africa
Area: 318,259 square miles
Population: (1966 est.) 584,000
Capital: Windhoek (Pop., 1960, 36,051)

South West Africa is a large territory in southwestern Africa bounded on the north by Angola and Zambia, on the east by Zambia, Botswana, and South Africa, on the south by South Africa, and on the west by the Atlantic Ocean.

The status of South West Africa is disputed, for although the League of Nations mandated it to South Africa in 1920, The United Nations did not reaffirm the mandate and the United Nations does not recognize the authority that South Africa exercises over South West Africa.

THE LAND. A strip of low desert borders the Atlantic coast. The interior is a rugged, arid region of plains interspersed with mountains ranging from 3,000 to 6,500 feet in elevation. In the eastern third of the territory is the sand and limestone Kalahari Desert.

The climate is warm and very dry. There is little rainfall except for occasional, extremely heavy downpours in the central region.

THE PEOPLE. The vast majority of the population is African, belonging to a variety of tribal groups. There is a white minority and a small group of people of mixed origin. The Negro Africans speak a variety of African languages, and the whites speak English, German, and Afrikaans. Protestantism and traditional religions predominate.

The country is very sparsely populated, with only 2.6 persons per square mile in 1965. Most of the white population lives in the south, and Negro Africans are concentrated in the north.

ECONOMY. The territory's most valuable resource is diamonds. Other minerals that are mined include copper, lead, manganese, and zinc. Most of the people live by grazing goats, cattle, and sheep—especially the valuable karakul breed. Fishing is important on the coast.

Mining is the major industry, and the processing of fish, karakul skins, and meat is also important. Diamonds and other minerals and fish are exported, and foodstuffs and other necessities are imported through South Africa.

GOVERNMENT. An administrator appointed by South Africa directs the government with the advice of a legislative assembly elected by suffrage limited to whites. The white voters of the territory also send representatives to South Africa's national legislature.

The Apartheid, or segregation, laws of South Africa extend to South West Africa and restrict nonwhite South West Africans from significant participation in the control of the territory's government, economy, or social life.

HISTORY. South West Africa has been inhabited for many centuries. Its earliest known inhabitants were Khoisan peoples, the Bushmen, Bergdama, and Nama (Hottentot) peoples. In the 1500s they were joined by Bantu-speaking peoples—the agricultural Ovambo and the pastoral Herero groups.

Europeans first came to South West Africa in the 1700s. In 1884 Germany, which had established a port and trading colonies in the area, proclaimed it a German protectorate. In the early 1900s the Germans put down a series of uprisings by killing some 100,000 of the Africans.

In 1915, during World War I, South African troops conquered South West Africa. After Germany's defeat in the war, the League of Nations made South West Africa a mandate under the administration of South Africa. After the United Nations was formed in 1945 it reviewed the status of all mandated territories, but South Africa

COLONIES AND DEPENDENCIES

did not recognize UN authority and did not submit South West Africa for review.

In the 1950s and 1960s South Africa gradually incorporated South West Africa's administration into that of its own, and the territory became a part of South Africa in all but name.

A case brought before the international Court of Justice in 1962 by Ethiopia and Liberia charging a violation of South Africa's mandate was ruled invalid in 1966 because the plaintiff nations had no legal standing in the matter.

In 1966 the United Nations, which had officially terminated the mandate and had repeatedly censured South Africa for its handling of the territory, established a committee to study the problem of the territory's native population and to recommend a means by which it could achieve self-determination.

In 1967 South Africa placed on trial several African nationalists for terrorist activities in South West Africa. The trial was protested as invalid, but the terrorists were convicted in 1968.

—Hibberd V. B. Kline, Jr.;
Gary Weissmann

SPANISH SAHARA

**Status: Overseas province of Spain
Area: 102,702 square miles
Population: (1964 est.) 48,000
Capital: El Aiún (Pop., 1961 est., 5,500)**

Spanish Sahara lies on the northwestern coast of Africa. It is bounded on the north by Morocco, on the east by Algeria and Mauritania, on the south by Mauritania, and on the west by the Atlantic Ocean.

THE LAND AND PEOPLE. The province is almost entirely desert or semidesert, and the climate is hot and dry. The people include Spanish, Arab, Berber, and some Negro groups.

Spanish Sahara is sparsely populated, with fewer than 1 person per square mile in 1966. The population is concentrated near the coast, although nomads roam parts of the interior.

ECONOMY. Spanish Sahara is rich in phosphates, which were first mined in the 1960s, and there are oil, iron, and other mineral deposits which remained unexploited. But in the mid-1960s fishing was the mainstay of the economy. Goats, sheep, and camels are raised, but there is almost no farming.

The chief industry is fish processing, and dried fish and other fish products are the major exports. Phosphates are also exported. Most trade is with Spain.

GOVERNMENT. Spanish Sahara is administered as a province of Spain by an appointed governor-general.

HISTORY. The region has been inhabited for many centuries. Spain established a port at Tarfaya on the coast in 1884 and in 1886 claimed a large region of the interior as a protectorate. Spanish claims were disputed by France.

In 1912 Spanish territory was defined in treaties which also divided Morocco into French and Spanish protectorates. In addition to the Spanish Sahara, it included southern Morocco and the enclave of Ifni, which was the capital of the entire region, called Spanish West Africa.

Morocco became independent in 1956, and the capital was moved to El Aiún, on the coast. In 1958 Spain ceded Tarfaya to Morocco.

Morocco and Mauritania both claim Spanish Sahara, and in 1966 the United Nations requested Spain, Morocco, and Mauritania to arrange for a referendum to permit the people of the territory to decide their future. No action was taken. In 1966 Spain established a commission to begin the social and economic development of the province.

—L. Carl Brown;
Hibberd V. B. Kline, Jr.

SURINAM

**Status: Autonomous part of the Kingdom of the Netherlands
Area: 16,533 square miles
Population: (1966 est.) 350,000
Capital: Paramaribo (Pop., 1964, 110,876)**

Surinam, or Dutch Guiana, is situated on the northeastern coast of South America. It is bordered on the north by the Atlantic Ocean, on the east by French Guiana, on the south by Brazil, and on the west by Guyana.

THE LAND AND PEOPLE. Surinam has a flat, narrow, fertile coastal plain and a hilly, forested interior, from which flow many rivers. The climate is warm and damp.

The population is of varied origins, but most of the people are of Indian, Indonesian, African, and mixed origins. There are some American Indians (Amerindians), Chinese, and Europeans. The population is growing at an extremely rapid rate, 4.4 percent a year between 1958 and 1965.

Dutch and Sranantongo, a local language, are the chief languages. Religious life is as diverse as the people, and there are Hindus, Muslims, Protestants, and Roman Catholics.

ECONOMY. Surinam has rich deposits of bauxite, from which aluminum is made, and excellent timber resources. Farming is important, and rice, sugar, cacao, fruits, and coffee are raised. Mining and forestry are the only important industries.

Exploitation of the country's hydroelectric resources was begun in the mid-1960s to prepare the way for the development of other industries, made necessary to keep pace with the rapid growth of population.

Surinam's balance of trade is poor. In 1965, for example, imports cost $95 million, and exports earned $58 million. Bauxite, timber, and fruits are exported, and foodstuffs, raw materials, textiles, and consumer goods are imported. The United States, the Netherlands, and Canada are Surinam's chief trading partners.

GOVERNMENT. Surinam is internally self-governing. The queen of the Netherlands appoints a governor, who functions as head of state. Executive power is exercised by a council of ministers, headed by a minister president, equivalent to a prime minister. The council is responsible to a popularly elected legislature, the Staten.

HISTORY. Surinam was first visited in the 1500s by Spaniards in search of gold. They abandoned the territory, and in the 1600s and 1700s it changed hands among Britain, the Netherlands, and France.

In 1815 the area was ceded to the Netherlands by the Treaty of Paris. The Dutch established plantations and began extensive mining and timber operations in the late 1800s and early 1900s, when they brought Indian and Indonesian laborers to Surinam.

During the 1900s Surinam gained an increasing measure of popular government, and in 1954 it became a self governing part of the Kingdom of the Netherlands. Surinam faced severe economic and social problems because of its rapid rate of population growth and the variety of ethnic groups comprising its population. In the 1950s and 1960s the government concentrated on expanding industry and improving agriculture.

SVALBARD AND JAN MAYEN ISLANDS

**Status: Territory under Norwegian sovereignty
Area: 24,101 square miles
Population: (1965 est.) 3,000**

The Svalbard Archipelago and Jan Mayen Island lie well above the Arctic Circle.

THE LAND AND PEOPLE. Jan Mayen, some 300 miles north of Iceland in the Greenland Sea, is rocky, mountainous, and barren. Tundra predominates on the eight islands and many islets of the Svalbard Archipelago. The climate is very cold and rather dry.

The Svalbard islands are sparsely populated by Norwegian and Soviet workers who mine the islands' rich coal deposits. Jan Mayen has no permanent population and serves only as the site of a Norwegian weather station.

NORWEGIAN EMBASSY INFORMATION SERVICE
SVALBARD. Coal mining is the key activity.

GOVERNMENT. The Svalbard islands are governed by an administrator appointed by the Swedish government, and the Soviet Union has jurisdiction over the mining areas. The manager of the Jan Mayen meteorological station has police power over that island.

HISTORY. Jan Mayen was discovered in the early 1600s by Henry Hudson and was rediscovered in 1611 by a Dutch whaler, Jan May. It was visited only by sealers and whalers until 1921, when Norway established a weather station on the island. In 1929 Norway gained sovereignty.

The Svalbard group was discovered by Norwegians in the 1100s and rediscovered in the 1500s by the Dutch. In the 1600s whale-hunting attracted sailors from the Netherlands, Britain, and Norway, and all three claimed the islands. The dispute ended in the 1700s when whaling declined. Russian and Norwegian fur trappers hunted on the islands through the 1800s.

Coal was discovered in the early 1900s, and possession of the islands was again disputed. A 1920 treaty gave sovereignty to Norway, and Norway ceded some mineral rights to the Soviet Union. In 1925 the islands were incorporated into the Norwegian state. In the 1960s French, Norwegian, Soviet, and U.S. prospectors began searching for oil.

TOKELAU ISLANDS

Status: Territory of New Zealand
Area: 3.8 square miles
Population: (1966 est.) 2,000

The Tokelau Islands lie in the South Pacific Ocean north of Western Samoa. They consist of three coral atolls—Atafu, Nukunono, and Fakaofo. The climate is hot and very wet, and hurricanes are frequent. The people are Polynesian.

Subsistence farming, fishing, and the production of copra are the only economic activities. The islands are under the authority of an appointed official with headquarters on Western Samoa. Local administration is by appointed islanders.

The Tokelau Islands were visited by the French in the 1760s, and in the 1800s Britain made them part of its Gilbert and Ellice Islands colony. New Zealand was given authority over the Tokelau Islands in 1925, and they were incorporated into New Zealand in 1949.

TONGA

Status: British protectorate
Area: 270 square miles
Population: (1966 est.) 77,000
Capital: Nuku'alofa (Pop., 1965, 9,202)

The Tonga, or Friendly, Islands lie in the South Pacific Ocean about 400 miles east of Fiji. They include about 150 small islands which form three major groups—Tongatapu, the largest, in the south; Ha'apai; and Vava'u, in the north.

THE LAND AND PEOPLE. Some of the Tonga Islands are volcanic in origin and have a mountainous, rugged terrain. Others are coral formations and are flat and low. Coral reefs ring most of the islands of the group. The climate is mild throughout the year and rainfall is moderate.

Tongans, a Polynesian people, make up about 99 percent of the population, and there are small groups of Europeans and other islanders. Tonga, a Polynesian language, and English are spoken, and most of the people are Protestant.

ECONOMY. The Tongan economy is based on agriculture. Coconuts, bananas, melons, and pineapples are the main commercial crops, and taros, yams, fruits, and corn are grown for local consumption. Pigs and cattle are raised, and there is some fishing.

With no mineral resources other than a small quantity of building stone, and no important fuel resources, the islands' only industry is copra production. Tonga exports copra and fruit and imports foodstuffs, fuels, and machinery. New Zealand, Japan, and Britain are its major trading partners.

GOVERNMENT. Tonga is a constitutional monarchy with a hereditary king as chief of state. An administrative council assists the king and is responsible to a popularly elected legislative assembly.

Tonga is under the protection of Britain, which is responsible for foreign affairs and defense. Britain is represented in the islands by a commissioner.

HISTORY. Traditional Tongan history extends back to the 900s, at the least, when it is said the first Tongan ruling dynasty was founded. Europeans reached the islands in the 1600s, and in the late 1700s European ships began to visit Tonga. In the 1820s European Christian missionaries arrived on the islands, and by the mid-1800s most of the islanders were Christian.

The islands, governed by petty chieftains, were not united into a single kingdom until 1845, when the king of Ha'apai won the thrones of Vava'u and Tongatapu as well. The king granted a democratic constitution in 1875. In 1900 Tonga and Britain signed a treaty of friendship, and the islands became a British protectorate.

Under a new treaty ratified in 1959 Tonga received greater local autonomy, and in 1965 Britain further relaxed its authority over Tongan affairs. In December 1965 King Taufa'ahau Tupou IV took the throne, after the death of his mother, Queen Charlotte.

TURKS AND CAICOS ISLANDS

Status: British colony
Area: 166 square miles
Population: (1966 est.) 6,000
Capital: Grand Turk (Pop., 1960, 2,339)

The Turks and Caicos Islands, numerous small islands of the Bahama Archipelago, lie in the Atlantic Ocean about 100 miles north of the island of Hispaniola.

Low, rocky, and generally barren, the islands have a hot, dry climate broken by frequent hurricanes. Only about six of the islands are permanently inhabited. The population is mainly of African origin with some people of European and mixed background.

Salt is the islands' only important resource, and salt-raking is the only industry. Crayfish, conch, and other fish are caught, and there is little agriculture. The United States maintains a guided missile base and a tracking station on Grand Turk island. Trade is limited to the export of salt and fish and the import of foodstuffs, clothing, and other necessities.

Administration is in the hands of an appointed governor and an executive council responsible to an elected legislative assembly.

Discovered by Spain in the 1500s, the islands remained uninhabited until the 1600s, when Bermudians opened the salt-raking industry. France and Spain tried unsuccessfully to occupy the islands in the 1700s and 1800s, and in 1873 the islands were incorporated into the British colony of Jamaica. When Jamaica became independent in 1962, the islands were made a separate colony.

WALLIS AND FUTUNA ISLANDS

Status: Overseas territory of France
Area: 77 square miles
Population: (1966 est.) 8,000
Capital: Mata Utu

The Wallis and Futuna islands lie in the South Pacific Ocean about 800 miles north of New Zealand. They consist of 21 islands in the Wallis Archipelago and two islands in the Futuna group.

The islands of both groups are volcanic in origin, mountainous, densely forested, and ringed by coral reefs. The climate is hot and very wet. Most of the people are Polynesians, but there are a few Europeans.

The economy of the islands is based on agriculture, and coconuts are the chief commercial crop. Yams, bananas, taros, and melons are grown for local consumption. Pigs and chickens are raised, and there is some fishing. Copra production is the only industry.

The islands are governed by an appointed administrator with the advice of a partially elected executive council and a popularly elected assembly. The islands are represented in the French National Assembly.

The islands were first settled by people from the Tonga Islands. The Futuna group was discovered in the 1600s by the Dutch, and the Wallis group in the 1700s by the British. French Roman Catholics opened missions on the islands in the 1800s, and in the 1880s France made the islands a protectorate, at the islanders' request.

The islands served as an Allied base during World War II. In 1959 the islanders voted in a referendum to change their status from that of a protectorate to that of a territory. The islands officially became an overseas territory in 1961.

NATURAL FEATURES

ABERDARE, a mountain range of southeastern Africa, in western Kenya. It has an average elevation of 10,000 feet and peaks of 13,000 feet.

ACONCAGUA, a South American mountain in the Andes chain situated on the Chile-Argentina border. Aconcagua is the highest mountain in the western hemisphere, rising to an altitude of 22,834 feet above sea level.

ADEN, GULF OF, an arm of the Indian Ocean, bounded on the north by Arabia and on the south by Africa's Somali coast. The gulf is 550 miles long and connects with the Red Sea to the west through the Mandeb Strait.

ADRIATIC SEA, an arm of the Mediterranean Sea lying between Italy on the southwest and Yugoslavia and Albania on the northeast. The Adriatic is about 500 miles long and 100 miles wide. To the south, the Strait of Otranto links it with the Ionian Sea.

AEGEAN SEA, an arm of the Mediterranean Sea between Greece and Turkey. The Aegean is about 400 miles long and 200 miles wide, and flows into the Sea of Crete in the south. It contains a great many dry, rocky islands, including those in the Cyclades, Sporades, and Dodecanese groups.

AFRICA, the second largest of the world's continents, with an area of more than 11.6 million square miles. It had a 1965 population of 310 million. Africa is separated from Europe, to the north, by the Mediterranean Sea and from Asia, to the east, by the Red Sea and the Gulf of Aden. The Atlantic Ocean lies to its west and the Indian Ocean to its east.

Moderately high mountains rim the coasts of the continent. The northern and southern interiors are mostly desert or semi-desert. The central portion is hilly and covered by dense tropical vegetation. Central Africa is threaded by rivers and contains several large lakes.

AGUSAN, a river on the Philippine island of Mindanao. The river valley, about 150 miles long, has a moderate, tropcal climate and rich soils that produce fruits, corn, hemp, and tobacco.

AHAGGAR, a mountainous plateau in northern Africa, in the Sahara region of southern Algeria. It is a barren volcanic rock mass with peaks rising to 10,000 feet.

AÏR, or Azbine, a mountainous region of Africa, in the southern Sahara in the Republic of Niger. It reaches a peak of over 6,000 feet. Its valleys are fertile and produce fruits and grains.

ÅLAND, a group of more than 300 small islands at the southern end of the Gulf of Bothnia off the southwestern coast of Finland. Most of the islands, which belong to Finland, are uninhabited.

ALBERT, a lake in east-central Africa, on the border between the Congo (Kinshasa) and Uganda. The lake is 100 miles long and 25 miles wide, and lies at an altitude of about 2,000 feet. The Semliki River enters it in the southwest, and the Victoria Nile enters in the northeast. The Albert Nile flows from the northern end of the lake.

ALIA, a mountain range of Soviet Central Asia, extending westwards from the Tien Shan through Khirgizia, and into Tadzhikistan. The average elevation is about 16,000 feet, and its peak is over 19,000 feet.

ALPS, an extensive and complex mountain system in central Europe, extending from southeastern France east through southwestern Austria, and south into western Yugoslavia. Mountains of a crystalline formation in the center of the range are flanked on the north and south by limestone. High, rugged, and dotted with glaciers, the range is narrow in the west and widens toward the east.

A variety of regional names are applied to the Alps. Some of the more important sections are the Maritime Alps, in France; the Dolomites and Pennines, in northern Italy; the Dinaric Alps, in Yugoslavia; and the Leopontines, in Switzerland.

Alpine pastures support dairy industries, and the valleys produce grains, wine grapes, and vegetables. Some of Europe's major rivers flow from the Alps, including the Rhine, the Rhône, and the Po, and Alpine water power is a valuable resource for European industry.

ALTAI, a mountain range in western Mongolia and northwestern China. Its highest peaks rise above 15,000 feet. The Irtysh and the Ob rivers of Central Asia rise in the Altai.

ANDES HIGHWAY twisting through the South American chain near La Paz, Bolivia.

ALTIPLANO, in Spanish a high flat area or plain, usually used to refer to a high South American plateau in Peru and Bolivia. The plateau ranges from 12,000 to 15,000 feet above sea level and has a gently rolling surface. The eastern edge, or montaña zone, is deeply cut by rivers. Its climate is cool and dry. The Altiplano was the heartland of the American Indian empire of the Incas which flourished in the 1300s and 1400s.

AMAZON, a South American river, the largest river in the world in terms of volume and catchment area. It extends 3,900 miles across Brazil and Peru, and its tributaries form a basin of some 2.7 million square miles in central South America. Its basin includes the floodplain, or *varzea*, which is fertile after rains between November and May, and the unflooded areas, or *terra firme*, which have sterile soils.

AMU, or Jahun, a river of south-central Asia that rises in the Pamir mountains. It flows 1,500 miles through the Hindu Kush, along the northern border of Afghanistan, and into the Soviet Union, where it empties into the Aral Sea.

AMUR, a river of northeastern Asia marking part of the boundary between China and the Soviet Union. It is formed by the Argun and the Shilka rivers. The Amur flows eastward for about 1,800 miles and then turns northeastward before emptying into the Tatar Strait. The Ussuri and the Sungari are its major tributaries.

ANATOLIA, or Asia Minor, a peninsula of western Asia, lying west of an indefinite line between the Gulf of Alexandretta (Iskenderun) and the Black Sea. It is bounded on the west by the Aegean Sea and on the south by the Mediterranean. It is part of Turkey.

ANDAMAN, a sea to the east of the Bay of Bengal, an arm of the Indian Ocean. It is bounded on the west by the Andaman and Nicobar islands and on the east by the Malay Peninsula.

ANDES, a massive mountain system of western South America. The Andes stretch for more than 4,000 miles in a great crescent from northeastern Venezuela westward and then southward to the southernmost tip of the continent. Elevations range generally from 10,000 to 20,000 feet, but there are several peaks over 20,000 feet.

The system consists largely of ranges that merge and separate in a wide variety of structures that are folded, faulted, and, in parts, made up of volcanic elements.

In places, the Andes are separated from the Pacific coast by coastal ranges. Their foothills to the east across the altiplano, or high plain, include the Occidental, Central, and Oriental ranges. Further east, the piedmont includes the lower hills of the montaña that are part of the yungas, or the slope into the interior lowlands.

ANGARA, a river in southeastern Siberia, in the eastern Soviet Union. It flows for some 1,100 miles from Lake Baykal north-northwest and then west, and joins the Yenisey River near the city of Yeniseysk.

ANGEL FALLS, the highest waterfall in the world, located in southeastern Venezuela on a tributary of the Caroni River. Actually a series of falls, it drops a total of 3,212 feet, and its highest fall is 2,650 feet.

ANNAM CORDILLERA, a mountain range of Southeast Asia. It extends northwest to southeast along the central portion of the border between Laos and Vietnam. The peaks are between 5,000 and 9,000 feet high.

ANTARCTICA, the continent surrounding the South Pole, about 5.5 million square miles in area. It is washed by the Atlantic, Pacific, and Indian oceans. From a mountainous interior, it slopes toward the coast. Antarctica is ice-covered, and very cold and dry.

ANTILLES, a large archipelago between North and South America lying partly in the Caribbean Sea and partly in the Atlantic Ocean. The Greater Antilles, at the northwestern end of the curving chain, includes the large islands of Cuba, Jamaica, Hispaniola, and Puerto Rico.

The Lesser Antilles, the southern and eastern portions of the archipelago, includes the many small islands off the coast of Venezuela in the south and the islands of the Windward and Leeward groups in the east. Many of the Antilles are volcanic in origin, and most are mountainous.

APENNINES, a mountain range that forms the backbone of peninsular Italy. The Apennines extend in a long arch from the Ligurian Alps in northwestern Italy to Calabria in the south. Elevations range from 6,000 feet to just under 10,000 feet. Pastures and forests cover the upper slopes, and fruits and grains are grown in the valleys.

AQABA, GULF OF, an extension of the Red Sea lying between the Sinai Peninsula and the Arabian Peninsula. The gulf is 100 miles long and from 5 to 17 miles wide.

ARABIA, a large peninsula in southwestern Asia, separated from the bulk of the continent in the northeast by the Persian Gulf and the Gulf of Oman. High mountains along the western and southern boundaries are separated from the Red Sea on the west and the Gulf of Aden on the south by narrow coastal plains. The central Arabian Plateau slopes gently eastward into the Persian Gulf basin.

Most of the land is desert or semidesert with few perennial rivers, and the climate is generally hot and dry. In its oases dates, grains, indigo, and cotton are grown, and the peninsula has rich petroleum deposits.

ARABIAN SEA, an arm of the Indian Ocean lying between the Indian subcontinent and the Arabian Peninsula.

NEW ZEALAND INFORMATION SERVICE

ANTARCTICA is the icy home of these emperor penguins guarding their young.

ARAFURA SEA, a sea between Australia and southeastern Indonesia, with an area of about 280,000 square miles.

ARAKAN, a mountain range in western Burma with a peak of over 10,000 feet, but with elevations averaging about 6,000 feet. The coastal plain to its west, along the Bay of Bengal, is known as the Arakan Coast.

ARAL SEA, a lake in Soviet west-central Asia in the Kazakh and Uzbek republics. It lies in a desert region 175 miles east of the Caspian Sea. Some 240 miles long and 175 miles wide, the slightly saline Aral Sea is fed by two large rivers, the Amu and the Syr, but it has no outlet.

ARARAT, a mountain in eastern Turkey near the border with Iran. Of volcanic origin, Ararat consists of two peaks, Great Ararat, about 17,000 feet, and Little Ararat, about 13,000 feet. Great Ararat is the legendary landing place of Noah's Ark.

ARAVALLI, a mountain range in northwestern India, extending about 350 miles in southern and central Rajasthan state. The range has an average elevation of 2,000 feet and peaks of over 5,000 feet.

ARCTIC OCEAN, a large body of water surrounding the North Pole, north of the Arctic Circle. It has an area of more than 5 million square miles. The many arms of the Arctic Ocean include the Barents Sea and the Norwegian Sea north of Europe; the Laptev Sea and the East Siberian Sea above the Soviet Union; the Beaufort Sea northwest of Canada; and the Greenland Sea near Greenland.

ARDENNES, a forested plateau in northern France, southeastern Belgium, and northwestern Luxembourg, south and east of a bend in the Meuse River.

ARGONNE, a forested plateau in northeastern France, south of the Ardennes and west of the Meuse River.

ARNO, a river in Italy that rises in the Apennines in central Italy, passes through Florence, and flows about 150 miles west to empty into the Ligurian Sea near Pisa. It is navigable but subject to sudden flooding.

ASAMA, an active volcano in Japan, on Honshu Island, about 100 miles northwest of Tokyo. It is one of Japan's largest volcanoes, rising more than 8,300 feet.

ASIA, the largest of the continents, with an area of 17 million square miles and a population of about 2 billion in the mid-1960s. It lies west of the Pacific, north of the Indian Ocean, south of the Arctic Ocean, and east of a line that generally follows the Ural Mountains, the Caspian Sea, the Dardanells, the west coast of Anatolia, and the Red Sea.

The Himalayas and their foothills form the east-west backbone of the continent. Lowlands and plateaus lie north and south of the Himalayan mountain system.

ATACAMA, a desert region of South America that extends for about 600 miles southward from the southernmost point of Peru through Atacama Province in Chile. It lies between the Pacific coastal range on the west and the Andean piedmont on the east. The desert proper, with an elevation of about 2,000 feet, is a series of dry salt basins rich in nitrates, and is so dry that in some places rainfall has never been recorded.

ATBARA, a river in northeastern Africa. It rises in northern Ethiopia and flows northward for about 500 miles to enter the Nile at Atbara, in Sudan.

ATHABASCA, a lake of west-central Canada, lying in northeastern Alberta and northwestern Saskatchewan provinces at the edge of the Canadian Shield. It has an area of nearly 3,000 square miles. The Athabasca River flows into it in the southwest, and the Great Slave River flows out of it in the northwest.

ATLANTIC, one of the world's major oceans, with an area of about 32 million square miles. The Atlantic separates Europe and Africa from North and South America. The North Atlantic Ocean lies between North America and Europe; the South Atlantic Ocean lies between South America and Africa.

ATLAS MOUNTAINS, a 1,500-mile-long mountain system of North Africa, extending from the southwest coast of Morocco westward to Cape Bon on the northeast coast of Tunisia. The Atlas system includes the Anti-Atlas in the southwest; the Grand, or High, Atlas in central Morocco; and the Saharan Atlas stretching across northern Algeria. The Grand Atlas includes Toubkal, 13,661 feet, the highest peak in the Atlas system.

AWASH, a river of northeastern Africa. It rises in central Ethiopia and follows a twisting course for about 500 miles through the Great Rift Valley and

NATURAL FEATURES

into the western Somali Republic, where it disappears into the arid Danakil Depression.

AZORES, a group of small volcanic islands belonging to Portugal and lying in the Atlantic Ocean about 750 miles west of mainland Portugal.

BAFFIN BAY, an inlet of the Arctic Ocean located between Canada's Arctic archipelago and Greenland. The bay is deep and dotted with icebergs brought down from the Arctic Ocean by the Labrador Current.

BAJA CALIFORNIA, a long, narrow peninsula in western Mexico south of California. The Pacific Ocean is to its west, and the Gulf of California to the east separates it from the rest of Mexico. Mountain ridges occupy the eastern and central portions of the peninsula. Most of the land is desert or arid plains.

BALATON, a lake in western Hungary located between the Danube and the Drava rivers. It has an outlet to the Danube. About 250 square miles in area, it is the largest lake in Central Europe.

BALEARIC ISLANDS, a group of five large islands and 12 islets in the Mediterranean Sea belonging to Spain. Mallorca is the largest, and Minorca, Cabrera, Ibiza, and Formentera are the other large islands of the group. Mountain scenery and the islands' warm, dry, climate foster a thriving tourist industry.

BALKAN MOUNTAINS, a range of mountains in Bulgaria with elevations under 8,000 feet. They extend from the Iron Gate on the Danube River to the Black Sea.

BALKAN PENINSULA, Western Europe's southeastern coast, washed by the Adriatic and Ionian seas on the west, the Mediterranean on the south, and the Aegean and the Black seas on the east. The Balkan states, the countries on or adjacent to the peninsula, are Albania, Bulgaria, Greece, Romania, and Yugoslavia. The European portion of Turkey is also part of the Balkans.

The peninsula is mountainous and contains the southern Carpathian Mountains, the Dinaric Alps, and the Balkan, Rhodope, and Pindus ranges.

BALKHASH, a salt lake in the southeastern part of the Soviet Union's Kazakh republic. It lies between the Kazakh Hills on the north and the Sary-Ishikotrau Desert on the south at an altitude of about 1,110 feet. Lake Balkhash is 375 miles long and from 15 to 55 miles wide, and has an average depth of 20 feet. There is no outlet.

BALTIC SEA, an arm of the North Atlantic Ocean separating the Scandinavian Peninsula and Finland from the rest of continental Europe. It flows into the North Sea to the west through the Kattegat and Skagerrak straits.

The Baltic is a vital link with the open ocean for the nations surrounding it, although most of it is icebound for part of the winter. The Baltic has two large branches—the Gulf of Bothnia in the north and the Gulf of Finland in the east.

BANDA SEA, in Southeast Asia, lies northwest of the Arafura Sea and east of the Flores Sea. The Banda Sea is surrounded by Indonesian islands and is dotted with islands, including the Banda group.

BANGWEULU, a lake in north Zambia in south-central Africa. About 60 miles long and 25 miles wide, the lake is shallow and surrounded by extensive swamps, and it appears to be drying up.

BARENTS SEA, a shallow arm of the Arctic Ocean north of Norway and the Soviet Union. It lies between Novaya Zemlya and Spitzbergen.

BAYKAL, a large lake in Soviet Central Asia, just north of Mongolia. It is the deepest lake in the world, with a maximum depth of 5,315 feet. It lies about 1,500 feet above sea level and measures nearly 400 miles in length and 50 miles in width. More than 300 rivers, including the Selenge, feed Lake Baykal, but the Angara River is its only outlet.

BEAUFORT SEA, a part of the Arctic Ocean. It lies northeast of Alaska, northwest of Canada, and west of Banks Island.

BENGAL, BAY OF, an arm of the Indian Ocean between India and Burma.

BERING SEA, the northernmost portion of the Pacific Ocean. It is bounded by Siberia on the west and northwest, by Alaska on the east and northeast, and by the Aleutian Islands on the south.

The Siberian Anadyr and the Alaskan Yukon and Kuskokwim rivers flow into the sea, which is connected with the Chukchi Sea and the Arctic Ocean to the north through the Bering Strait. Whaling, fishing, and seal-hunting are major activities.

BHIMA, an Indian river in the northern Deccan. It rises in the Western Ghats near Bombay and flows southeast for about 400 miles to join the Kistna River.

BIÉ, a plateau in central Angola, in West Africa, with an average elevation of 6,000 feet. The outstanding physical characteristic of Angola, it is also one of the main watersheds of the continent, separating the headwaters of the Congo River drainage system in the north from the Zambezi River system in the south.

BIHOR, a mountain massif of Transylvania, in west-central Romania. It is a dissected plateau with an average elevation of 5,000 feet but rising above 6,000 feet in places. It is forested and contains mineral deposits.

BILAUKTAUNG, a mountain range of Southeast Asia running north-south along the central portion of the Thailand-Burma border. Elevations range between 2,000 and 5,000 feet.

BISCAY, BAY OF, an inlet of the Atlantic Ocean, bounded by France on the north and east and by Spain on the south.

BIWA, a Japanese lake on Honshu Island just northeast of Kyoto. About 480 square miles in area, it is the largest lake in Japan. The lake is drained by the Yodo River.

BLACK FOREST, a mountainous region in southwestern Germany. The mountains reach a peak of nearly 5,000 feet and are thickly forested. They contain the sources of the Danube and Neckar rivers.

BLACK SEA, a large inland sea in eastern Europe lying north of Asian Turkey, west and south of the Soviet Union, and east of Romania, Bulgaria, and European Turkey. About 170,000 square miles in area, it receives the Danube, the Dnester, the Dnepr, and other major rivers. The Sea of Azov, a small arm of the Black Sea, lies to the north. The Bosporus, the Sea of Marmara, and the Dardanelles link the Black Sea with the Aegean.

BOHEMIAN FOREST, a mountainous region in southeastern Germany and western Czechoslovakia. It has a peak of over 4,700 feet and is densely forested.

BORNEO, or Kalimantan, an island in Southeast Asia lying between the South China Sea on the north and west, the Java Sea on the south, and the Makassar Strait, Celebes Sea, and Sulu Sea on the east. It straddles the equator. The island, about 290,000 square miles in area, is the third largest in the world.

Rugged mountains rising above 13,000 feet occupy most of Borneo. It is rich in oil and other minerals and is heavily forested. Indonesia, Malaysia, and Brunei share the island.

BOSPORUS, a strait between European and Asian Turkey. It joins the Sea of Marmara with the Black Sea.

BOTHNIA, GULF OF, the northern arm of the Baltic Sea. It lies between Sweden on the west and Finland on the east.

BRAHMAPUTRA, or Tsangpo, or Jumna, a river on the Indian subcontinent that rises in the Kailas Mountains of southwestern Tibet. As the Tsangpo, it flows through Tibet for about 700 miles before turning sharply southward to flow for 1,100 miles to the Bay of Bengal. Its southern course is navigable for 800 miles and it waters a vast valley.

BRITISH ISLES, an island group of western Europe lying between the Atlantic Ocean and the North Sea. It includes the two large islands of Britain and Ireland and many smaller adjacent islands.

CAGAYAN, a river on the Philippine island of Luzon. It rises in the eastern mountains and flows north for about 250 miles into the Babuyan Channel, an arm of the Philippine

Sea. The 50-mile-wide Cagayan Valley is the island's richest forest and farming region.

CAMEROON MOUNTAIN, in west-central Africa near the Atlantic coast of Cameroon. It is of volcanic origin and is over 13,300 feet high.

CAMPECHE BAY, a broad inlet of the Gulf of Mexico on Mexico's curving southeastern coast. The Yucatan Peninsula is to the east.

CANARY ISLANDS, an archipelago in the Atlantic Ocean, off the northwestern coast of Africa, belonging to Spain. The seven islands and three islets of the archipelago are of volcanic origin, and are rocky and mountainous. They have a warm, dry climate.

CANTABRIAN MOUNTAINS, or Cordillera Cantabrica, a mountain range in northern Spain. The mountains lie parallel to the Bay of Biscay coast. Elevations range between 5,000 and 8,000 feet.

CAPE AGULHAS, the southernmost point of Africa. It is some 100 miles east of the Cape of Good Hope, in the Republic of South Africa.

CAPE BLANC, the northernmost point of Africa. It projects into the Mediterranean Sea from the north coast of Tunisia.

CAPE BON, a headland in North Africa at the northeastern tip of Tunisia. It is a part of the Atlas mountain system. Cape Bon projects into the Strait of Sicily, in the Mediterranean Sea.

CAPE COMORIN, the southern tip of the Indian subcontinent. It projects into the Laccadive Sea, an arm of the Indian Ocean.

CAPE GARDAFUI, the tip of the eastern horn of Africa, located in Somalia. The cape forms an impressive headland almost 1,000 feet high.

CAPE HORN, the southernmost point of South America, part of the Wollaston Island group south of Tierra del Fuego. It is a rock rising to an altitude of 1,390 feet above sea level.

CAPE OF GOOD HOPE, a point of land near the southern tip of Africa, on the southwest coast of the Republic of South Africa.

CAPE YORK PENINSULA, the northernmost point of Australia, east of the Gulf of Carpentaria and west of the Great Barrier Reef in the Coral Sea. It ends in Cape York, in Torres Strait.

CARIBBEAN SEA, a body of water between North and South America at the western edge of the Atlantic Ocean. On the north and east it is ringed by the islands of the Greater and Lesser Antilles. The Caribbean Sea is over 1 million square miles in area and has an average depth of more than 8,000 feet.

CAROLINE ISLANDS, an archipelago in the western Pacific Ocean lying east of the Philippines. The archipelago consists of nearly 1,000 small islands and coral reefs. The chief island of the group is Caroline Island, and the archipelago includes the Palau Islands, also called the Western Carolines.

CARPATHIANS, a mountain system of central and eastern Europe extending more than 1,000 miles through Czechoslovakia, Hungary, Poland, Romania, and the Soviet Union. Although a continuation of the Alps, the Carpathians are more rounded and lower than the Alps; the highest peak is less than 9,000 feet.

The Carpathians are usually divided into four groups—the Western, Central, and Eastern Carpathians, and the Transylvanian Alps. They are rich in minerals and contain the sources of many rivers, including the Vistula and the Dnestr.

CARPENTARIA, GULF OF, an inlet of the Arafura Sea in northern Australia. It lies between Arnhemland, on the west, and Cape York Peninsula on the east.

CASPIAN SEA, a large lake located between the Soviet Union and Iran, at the border of Europe and Asia. The world's largest saltwater lake, it is 759 miles long and from 140 to 300 miles wide. There are no outlets, but the Ural, Volga, Kuma, Terek, and Atrek rivers flow into the Caspian.

The Soviet Union uses the Caspian as an inland water route and as a source of fish, including salmon, herring, sturgeon, and carp.

CAUCASUS MOUNTAINS, an extensive mountain range in the Soviet Union, forming part of the boundary between Europe and Asia. The Caucasus lie between the Sea of Azov and the Black Sea on the west and the Caspian Sea on the east.

The Greater Caucasus, in the north, is about 750 miles long and has average elevations of between 10,000 and 12,000 feet with peaks over 18,000 feet. Volcanic in origin, this chain has hot springs and occasional earthquakes.

The lower Surami Range to the south is the link between the Greater Caucasus and the Lesser Caucasus, a mountain system formed in Asia Minor by the northern ranges of the Armenian Highland.

CEVENNES, a mountain range in southeastern France with an average elevation of 3,000 feet. The mountains contain the sources of many French rivers, including the Loire and the Ardèche.

CHAD, a lake in north-central Africa, located at the junction of the boundaries of Chad, Niger, and Nigeria. Lake Chad contains fresh water and is fed by the Chari, Logone, and Komadugu rivers.

CH'ANGPAI, a Chinese mountain range in southern Manchuria. It extends along the China-Korea border and has a peak of over 9,000 feet.

CHAO PHRAYA, the principal river of Thailand, formed from the Ping, the Yom, and the Nan, which rise in the northern mountains and then merge at Nakhon Sawan. The river's total length is about 750 miles from the mountains to its mouth on the Gulf of Siam.

CHARI, or Shari, a river rising in the Central African Republic and flowing northwest for about 1,400 miles to Lake Chad, where it forms an extensive delta.

CHEJU, a mountainous island off the southern coast of Korea, in the Korea Strait.

CHERSKI, a mountain range in northeastern Siberia, in the eastern Soviet Union. The range is about 600 miles long and has a peak above 10,000 feet.

CHIH-LI, or Po Hai, a gulf on the eastern coast of China. It is an arm of the Yellow Sea, and is partially enclosed by the Liaotung and Shantung peninsulas.

CHU, or Pearl, a river on the east China coast, one channel in the Si River delta. The important Chinese city of Canton is situated on its banks, and the British island colony of Hong Kong lies in its broad estuary.

CLYDE, a river in Scotland, flowing from South Lanarkshire in the Southern Uplands through the Scottish Lowland, past Glasgow, and into the Firth of Clyde. Its valley, Clydeside, is one of Britain's leading industrial districts.

COLORADO, a river 550 miles long in southeastern South America. It rises in the Andes near the Chilean border and flows southeast across south-central Agentina to the Atlantic Ocean.

COMO, a lake in northern Italy, about 20 miles north of Milan, in Lombardy. There are many resorts around the lake, and Como is the largest town on its shores.

CONGO, a river in central Africa. With its tributaries, it is one of the world's longest rivers, about 2,900 miles, and it drains a basin about 1.6 million square miles in area. The Lualaba, its main headstream, rises on the Katanga Plateau in the Congo (Kinshasa) and flows northward to join the Luapula and Lukuga rivers.

Before turning to the west at Kisaugani (Stanleyville), where it becomes the Congo proper, the river crosses the 60-mile stretch of the Stanley Falls. About 350 miles from its mouth, it widens to form Stanley Pool, where Brazzaville and Kinshasa (Léopoldville) are located, the end of the inland navigation route. The Congo then falls some 850 feet over Livingstone Falls, which lead into the river's estuary.

CONSTANCE, or Boden, a lake bordering Germany, Austria, and Switzerland. It is fed largely by the Upper Rhine.

NATURAL FEATURES OF THE WORLD

UNITED ARAB REPUBLIC TOURIST OFFICE

THE NILE, the world's longest river, flows for more than 4,000 miles through northeastern Africa to the Mediterranean Sea.

FPG

MT. EVEREST, the world's highest mountain, rises more than 29,000 feet in the Himalayas.

VENEZUELA MINISTRY OF DEVELOPMENT

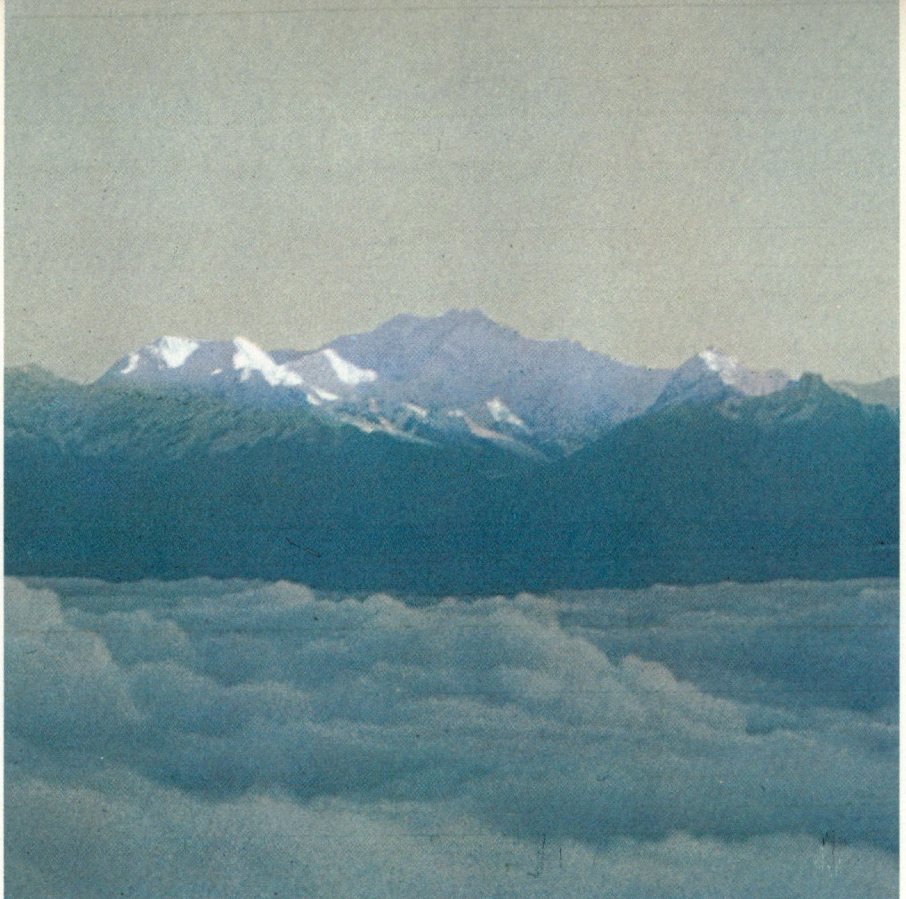

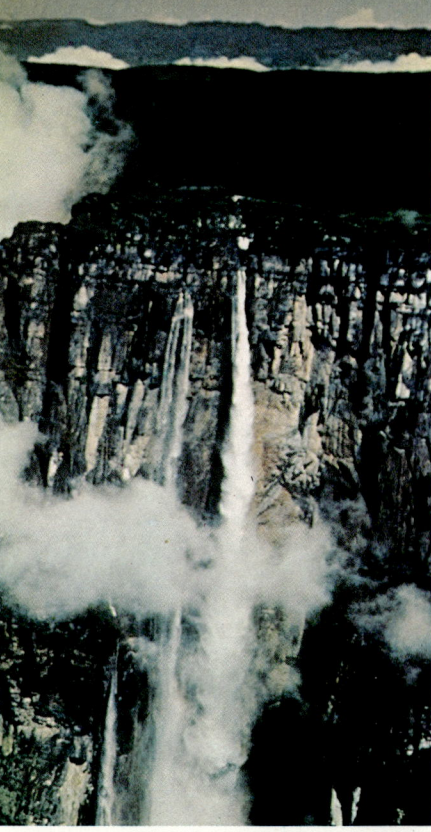

ANGEL FALLS, the world's highest waterfall, in Venezuela, has a drop of more than 3,200 ft.

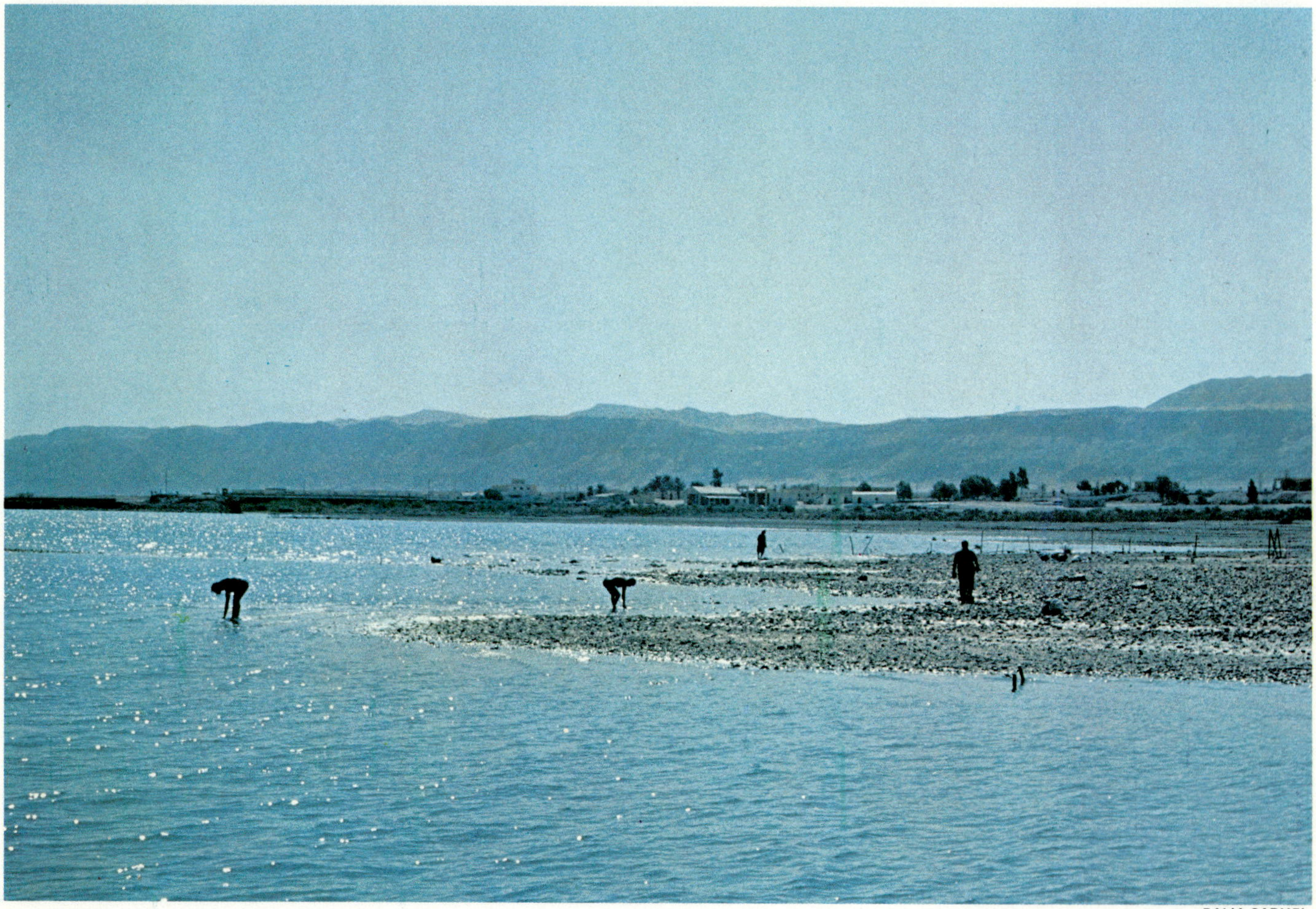

DALIA CARMEL

DEAD SEA, almost 1,300 feet below sea level, is the world's lowest land point. It lies on the border of Israel and Jordan.

CORAL SEA, a western arm of the South Pacific Ocean lying between Australia, New Guinea, and the Melanesian islands. It is dotted with small islands and coral atolls.

COROMANDEL, the southeastern coast of India extending from the eastern end of Palk Strait, separating India and Ceylon, north to the mouth of the Krishna River. The important city of Madras lies at about the center of the coast, which lacks good natural harbors.

CRIMEA, a peninsula in the southern part of the Ukrainian republic, in the southwestern Soviet Union. It extends 120 miles into the Black Sea and measures about 200 miles from west to east. The narrow Perekop Isthmus connects it with the mainland.

The Crimea can be divided into four distinct geographical regions: the level and dry northern steppe; the Crimean Mountains on the southern coast, with peaks above 5,000 feet; the subtropical Black Sea coast at the foot of the steep Crimean Mountains; and the arid, mineral-rich Kerch Peninsula.

CRYSTAL, a West African mountain massif lying inland from the coastal plain of Gabon. Elevations are generally under 5,000 feet.

CUNENE, a river of southwestern Africa that rises in central Angola. It flows south and then west for 700 miles and has many rapids and cataracts. The Cunene forms part of the boundary between Angola and South West Africa.

CUQUENÁN, or Kukenan, a waterfall in eastern Venezuela on a tributary of the Arabopó River. Dropping some 2,000 feet, it is one of the world's highest waterfalls.

DANUBE, a major river of central and southeastern Europe. It rises in the Black Forest of southwestern Germany and flows for some 1,750 miles through or along the borders of eight countries before emptying into the Black Sea in northeastern Romania. Its major tributaries include the Drava, the Sava, and the Prut.

DARDANELLES, a strait separating parts of European and Asian Turkey. It links the Aegean Sea and the Sea of Marmara.

DEAD SEA, a salt lake, about 450 square miles in area, on the Israel-Jordan border at the southern end of the Jordan River. Lying 1,296 feet below sea level, its shores and surface are at the lowest known point of land on earth. It is saltier than sea water and contains many other minerals as well.

DHAULAGIRI, a Himalayan peak in Nepal with an elevation of 26,810 feet. It is the fifth highest mountain in the world.

DIU, an island in the Gulf of Cambay off India's west coast. A former Portuguese enclave, it was occupied by India in 1961.

DNEPR, a major river of the western Soviet Union. It rises near Smolensk and flows southwest and south for over 1,400 miles, emptying into the Black Sea. Its tributaries include the Sozh, Desna, and Berezina rivers.

The entire course of the Dnepr is navigable, and it is an important source of hydroelectric power. Connected by canals to the Dvina, Niemen, and Vistula rivers, it forms part of a continuous waterway from the Black Sea to the Baltic Sea.

DOGGER BANK, a submerged sand bank beneath the North Sea, about 60 miles east of Britain. It is an important fishing zone.

DON, a major river of the western Soviet Union. It rises in the Central Russian Upland, southwest of Moscow. It flows southeastward until it nears Volgograd (Stalingrad), and then flows southwest and west for a total of over 1,200 miles before emptying into the Sea of Azov.

Tributaries of the Don include the Donets, Medveditsa, Sal, and Manych rivers. Seagoing ships can travel as far as Rostov, the principal port, near the mouth of the river, and the entire course is navigable by smaller vessels.

DONEGAL BAY, an inlet of the Atlantic Ocean on the northwest coast of Ireland at the mouth of the Eask River.

DOURO, a river that rises in north central Spain. It flows west for nearly 500 miles, emptying into the Atlantic Ocean at Porto, Portugal.

DRAKE PASSAGE, a channel separating the southern tip of South America from Antarctica, joining the Pacific and the Atlantic oceans.

DRAKENSBERG, a mountain range of southern Africa extending some 700 miles southwest to northeast in the Republic of South Africa. Elevations reach 10,000 feet.

DRAVA, or Drau, a river of eastern Europe, about 450 miles long, that rises in southern Austria. It flows east through Yugoslavia to the border with Hungary, and then turns southeast to join the Danube River in northeastern Yugoslavia.

DRINA, a river of central Yugoslavia, formed by the confluence of the Tava and Piva rivers. Flowing generally northward for about 200 miles, it joins the Sava River about 50 miles west of Belgrade.

DVINA, two rivers in Europe. The Western, or Southern, Dvina rises in the western Soviet Union and flows about 650 miles to the Gulf of Riga, on the Baltic. The Northern Dvina is formed by the confluence of the Vychegda and Sukhona rivers in the northern part of the Soviet Union's Russian republic. It flows generally northwest for over 540 miles to its outlet into the Gulf of Dvina, at Archangelsk.

EAST CHINA SEA, an arm of the western Pacific Ocean off the east coast of China. It lies between the Yellow Sea on the west and the Ryukyu Islands on the east.

EAST INDIES, a general term for the Malay Peninsula, the Malay Archipelago, Indochina, India, and Indonesia.

EAST SIBERIAN SEA, a part of the Arctic Ocean. It lies north of eastern Siberia, in the Soviet Union, east of the New Siberian Islands, and west of Wrangel Island.

EBRO, a river of northeastern Spain that rises in the Cantabrian Mountains and flows eastward for about 500 miles to the Mediterranean Sea at Cape Tortosa. It is partly navigable and an important source of water for irrigation.

EDWARD, a lake in East Africa, in the western part of the Great Rift Valley, located on the Uganda-Congo (Kinshasa) border. It lies southwest of Lake George and is about 800 square miles in area.

ELBA, an Italian island in the Tyrrhenian Sea between Corsica and the Italian mainland. It is mountainous and rich in minerals.

ELBE, or Labe, a river in central Europe. Over 700 miles long, it rises on the Poland-Czechoslovakia border in the Erg Gebirge range and flows north-northwest through Czechoslovakia and Germany, forming part of the boundary between East and West Germany.

Near Hamburg, numerous channels of the Elbe unite to form a 60-mile estuary that empties into the North Sea near Cuxhaven. The Elbe is partly navigable and is linked with the Rhine and Oder rivers by several canals.

ELBRUS, a mountain peak in the Caucasus, in the northern part of the Soviet Union's Georgian republic. It has an elevation of 18,481 feet and is the highest peak in Europe.

ELBURZ, a mountain range in northern Iran separating the Caspian Sea from the Iranian Plateau. A 650-mile-long crescent-shaped chain, it consists of several steep, parallel ranges whose summits often reach above 13,000 feet. Mt. Demayend, nearly 19,000 feet, is the highest peak.

ENGLISH CHANNEL, a body of water between Britain and France that joins the Atlantic Ocean and the North Sea. It is less than 20 miles wide at its narrowest point, the Strait of Dover, between Dover, in Britain, and Calais, in France.

ETHIOPIAN HIGHLANDS, an extensive upland region of eastern Africa, lying mainly in Ethiopia. It rises sharply from surrounding lowlands and has an average elevation of between 10,000 and 13,000 feet.

The region is divided into two parts by the Great Rift Valley. To the northwest the region is broken by very deep, steep-sided valleys through which flow many rivers, including the Blue Nile. To the southeast of the Rift Valley, the highlands are flatter and less rugged.

EUPHRATES, a river in southwest Asia that rises in eastern Turkey. It flows southeast for over 1,700 miles through Syria and Iraq to the Persian Gulf. The river is formed by two headstreams, the Kara and the Murat, and about 120 miles from the Persian Gulf, the Euphrates joins the Tigris River to form the Shatt al-Arab.

Syria and Iraq depend on the Euphrates for water for irrigation, and ancient peoples built a complex system of canals that allowed the Tigris and Euphrates plain to support great civilizations.

EUROPE, a continent with an area of about 4 million square miles and a population of some 620 million people in the mid-1960s. It is bounded on the north by the Arctic Ocean, on the east by the Ural Mountains, on the south by the Mediterranean Sea, and on the west by the Atlantic Ocean.

The continent is customarily divided into Western Europe—those nations from Germany and Austria westward—and Eastern Europe—the lands from Poland and Czechoslovakia eastward.

EYRE, a lake in south-central Australia, some 200 miles north of the Eyre Peninsula. It is the largest lake in Australia. Eyre is a salt lake in an arid region. Its size varies with the season, but its normal area is about 2,700 square miles.

FINLAND, GULF OF, a shallow eastern arm of the Baltic Sea, about 260 miles long and varying in width from 40 to 85 miles. It is bordered by Finland on the north and the Soviet Union's Estonian republic on the south. The gulf receives the waters of lakes Ladoga and Onega as well as other streams.

FOUTA DJALLON, a mountainous region with a peak of about 5,000 feet, forming the western edge of the Guinea Highlands in Guinea, West Africa.

FRANZ JOSEF LAND, a group of some 85 islands in the Arctic Ocean, east of Spitzbergen and north of Novaya Zemlya. The islands are part of the Soviet Union. They include Aleksandra Land, George Land, and Graham Bell Island. The northernmost land in the Eastern Hemisphere, the islands are almost completely covered by glaciers.

FRISIAN ISLANDS, a series of low barrier beaches that jut into the North Sea. They belong to the Netherlands, West Germany, and Denmark.

FUJI, a Japanese volcanic peak on central Honshu Island. The single peak rises nearly 12,400 feet from the surrounding plain. It last erupted in the 1600s and is now considered dead.

FUNDY, BAY OF, an inlet of the Atlantic Ocean between Nova Scotia and New Brunswick, Canada. It is about 180 miles long and from 30 to 50 miles wide. It divides into Chignecto Bay and Minas Channel. At the narrow entrance to Chignecto Bay tides sometimes vary more than 50 feet.

GALILEE, SEA OF, or Lake Tiberias, a freshwater lake in northeastern Israel at the border with Syria. It is more than 680 feet below sea level and is fed and drained by the Jordan River.

GAMBIA, a river in West Africa, about 450 miles long, that rises in Guinea. It flows northwest through Senegal and then west to the Atlantic Ocean through the country of Gambia.

GANGES, a river of northern India that rises in the Himalayas and flows south and east for more than 1,550 miles to the Bay of Bengal, off the coast of East Pakistan. It is heavily used for transportation, and provides power for industries and water for irrigation. The Gangetic Plain is a plateau formed by the river in northern India. The Ganges is a sacred river for Hindus.

The major southern tributaries of the Ganges are the Son and the Jumna. The major northern tributaries are the Gumti, the Kusi, the Gogra, and the Gandak. The Ganges is joined by the Brahmaputra (Jumna) River about 100 miles from its mouth to form the Padma. The delta is the largest in the world.

At its mouth, the river breaks into several major channels: the Meghna, the Tetulia, the Madhumata, the Baleswar, and the Hooghly (Bhagirathi). There are swampy jungles, called Sundarbans, along the coast.

GARDA, a lake in northern Italy, about 300 square miles in area. Its mild climate and majestic scenery make it an important tourist center.

GARONNE, a river in Western Europe that rises in the Spanish Pyrenees and flows northwest through France for 400 miles. The Garonne flows through Toulouse and past Bordeaux to join the Dordogne and form the Gironde River before emptying into the Bay of Biscay.

GASPÉ, a peninsula of eastern Canada, between the St. Lawrence River on the west, the Gaspé Passage on the north, and the Gulf of St. Lawrence on the east. The Notre Dame Mountains in the interior are ringed by a low and often rocky coastal plain.

GENEVA, or Leman, a crescent-shaped lake on the border of France and Switzerland.

GERSOPPA, a waterfall in southwestern India, on the Sharivari River. With a drop of 830 feet, it is the highest known waterfall in Asia. The falls are used to provide hydroelectric power for the region.

GHATS, two mountain ranges on India's southern coasts. The Eastern Ghats run parallel to the Bay of Bengal for about 500 miles south from the Mahanadi River and have an average elevation of 1,800 feet. The Western Ghats run parallel to the Arabian

TURIZM VE TANITMA BAKANLIĞI

EUPHRATES RIVER carved this gorge in its upper course near Malatya, eastern Turkey.

Sea and have an average elevation of 4,000 feet. Both ranges are heavily forested.

GIBSON DESERT, an arid area in western Australia. It has a rolling, sandy surface.

GOBI, a desert region in southern Mongolia and north-central China, about 500,000 square miles in area. It lies in a depression of the Mongolian Plateau ringed with mountains and steppes. The Gobi is covered by scrub grass that is suitable in some areas for grazing.

GODAVARI, a river in central India that rises in the Western Ghats and flows eastward for 900 miles to the Bay of Bengal. It is navigable in the east and is vital for irrigation in the region. Hindus consider it a sacred river.

GODWIN AUSTIN, or K2, a mountain in the Karakorum Range in northeastern Pakistan. The second highest mountain in the world, it has an elevation of 28,250 feet.

GOTLAND, an island in the Baltic Sea about 55 miles off the southeastern coast of Sweden. Gotland is a province of Sweden. Sheepherding and fishing are the main economic activities.

GRAN CHACO, a lowland region of south-central South America, divided among Argentina, Bolivia, and Paraguay. Much of the region is arid, but there are swampy areas and the climate is quite hot. It is barren and sparsely populated.

GRAND BANKS, a submerged plateau in the Atlantic Ocean southeast of Newfoundland, about 300 miles long, 200 miles wide, and from 120 to 600 feet deep. Most of the area is crossed by the cold Labrador Current, but the warm Gulf Stream passes along the eastern part. The mixing of the two currents makes the Grand Banks rich in marine life and a major cod-fishing region.

GREAT AUSTRALIAN BIGHT, a wide, cresent-shaped bay of the Indian Ocean on the south coast of Australia.

GREAT BARRIER REEF, a coral reef off the coast of northeastern Australia and southeastern New Guinea at the edge of the continental shelf. It protects the coastline, and forms a channel that contains many small coral islets.

GREAT BEAR, a lake in northwestern Canada, drained by the Great Bear River, a tributary of the Mackenzie. It is Canada's largest lake, with an area of 12,275 square miles.

GREAT DIVIDING RANGE, a mountain chain bordering the eastern coast of Australia. The mountains are generally below 5,000 feet, but Mt. Kosciusko, in the south, rises more than 7,300 feet. Among the foothills of the range are the Australian Alps, the Snowy Mountains, and the New England, Calliope, Drummond, Connors, Clark, and Gregory ranges.

GREAT RIFT VALLEY, a depression in southwestern Asia and northeastern Africa, formed by a downfaulting of the earth's crust. The depression consists of two rifts—the Main, or Eastern Rift, and the Western Rift.

The Main Rift extends for roughly 4,000 miles from southern Turkey, in southwestern Asia, to Mozambique, in southeastern Africa. The Western Rift extends 1,100 miles from southern Sudan to Malawi, where it joins the Main Rift. The rift valleys vary in width from 30 miles in the south to 250 miles toward the north.

The floor of the depression lies below sea level in the northernmost area, but rises to over 6,000 feet in Kenya. Many lakes and seas are located in the valleys outlined by the Great Rift.

GREAT SANDY DESERT, an arid region in northwestern Australia between the King Leopold Ranges on the northeast and the Hamersley Ranges on the southwest. It contains salt marshes and some scrub vegetation.

GREAT SLAVE, a lake in west-central Canada, over 10,500 square miles in area. It is fed by the Great Slave and Hay rivers and drained by the Mackenzie River.

GREAT VICTORIA DESERT, an arid region in southwestern Australia, north of the Nullarbar Plain. It has a sandy surface broken by salt marshes.

GREENLAND, the largest island in the world, 840,000 square miles in area. A dependency and former colony of Denmark, it lies northeast of North America and is washed by the North Atlantic and Arctic oceans and by the Greenland Sea. About three-quarters of its area lies above the Arctic Circle, and almost seven-eighths of Greenland is covered by ice.

GREENLAND SEA, a part of the Arctic Ocean east of Greenland, west of the Barents Sea, and north of the Norwegian Sea, of which it is generally considered an extension.

GUADALQUIVIR, a river in southwestern Spain that flows for over 350 miles, passing Córdoba and Seville, to enter the Atlantic Ocean in the Gulf of Cádiz.

GUAYAQUIL, GULF OF, an inlet of the Pacific Ocean in Ecuador, in northwestern South America. It is dotted with islands and has several good harbors.

GUIANA HIGHLANDS, an area of northeastern South America, extending from central Venezuela across northern Brazil and through southern Guyana and Surinam to French Guiana. It is the central portion of Guiana—a region bounded by the Orinoco, Negro, and Amazon rivers and the Atlantic Ocean.

GUINEA, GULF OF, a great inlet of the Atlantic Ocean in West Africa. Generally accepted as extending from Senegal to Angola, it includes the bights of Benin and Biafra. The adjacent mainland is known as the Guinea Coast.

HAINAN, a large Chinese island lying about 15 miles south of the mainland. The island is mountainous, thickly forested, and rich in minerals.

HARI, a river that rises in the mountains of central Afghanistan and flows for about 650 miles, ending in the Kara Kum desert. The Hari flows west through the Herat Valley and then north along the Iranian border into the Soviet Union.

HEBRIDES, a group of British islands lying in the Atlantic Ocean off the northwestern coast of Scotland. The islands have an area of about 2,900 square miles and are divided into the Inner Hebrides and the Outer Hebrides, separated by a strait, the Little Minch.

HELMAND, a river in southwestern Afghanistan that rises in the central mountains and flows west for about 650 miles, emptying into Lake Helmand on the border with Iran. The Helmand river is being developed for navigation, irrigation, and power production.

HIGHLANDS OF SCOTLAND, or the Northern Highlands, a mountainous region in the north of Scotland. Most of the highlands are part of a hilly, rocky plateau, but there are some high ranges. The hills are broken by valleys, and there are many lochs, or lakes. Sheepherding is the main economic activity.

HIMALAYAS, a mountain system in southeastern Asia containing the world's highest peaks. The range extends for about 1,600 miles from Kashmir in the west to Assam in the east. It forms an arc separating the subcontinent of India from the rest of Asia.

The system may be divided into three sections—the Greater Himalayas in the north, the Lesser Himalayas in the center, and the Outer Himalayas in the south. The Greater Himalayas contain Mt. Everest, 29,028 feet, the highest peak in the world.

The Himalayas contain the sources of several of Asia's important rivers, including the Ganges, the Tsangpo-Brahmaputra system, and the Sutlej.

HINDU KUSH, a mountain range in northeastern Afghanistan that extends for about 500 miles along the border with West Pakistan as far as Kashmir. The mountains form a barrier between the Soviet Union and Afghanistan, Pakistan, and Kashmir. The highest peak is Tirich Mir, more than 25,000 feet above sea level. The Hindu Kush is also a watershed between the Amu and Indus river systems.

HISPANIOLA, a large island of the Greater Antilles between the Caribbean Sea and the Atlantic Ocean. Its two mountain ranges are separated by a deep valley and ringed by narrow coastal plains. The climate is tropical and the vegetation is lush. Hispaniola is shared by Haiti and the Dominican Republic.

HONDURAS, GULF OF, an outlet of the Caribbean Sea touching British Honduras, Guatemala, and Honduras. It is dotted with coral islands and atolls.

HUDSON BAY, an inland sea in east-central Canada at the center of the Canadian Shield lowland. Over 475,000 square miles in area, it receives the Churchill, Nelson, Nottaway, and other rivers. Its major arms are the Fox Basin in the north and St. James Bay in the south. It joins the Labrador Sea, an arm of the North Atlantic, through Hudson Strait.

HWANG, or Yellow, river, the second longest river of China. The Hwang rises in the Kunlun Mountains of northwestern China and flows in a generally easterly direction for 2,700 miles, emptying into the Gulf of Chihli. Its tributaries include the Fen, Huai, and Wei rivers. The Hwang is navigable for most of its course. The river has been the cause of numerous floods.

IBERIA, a peninsula in the southwestern corner of Europe, between the Mediterranean Sea and the Atlantic Ocean, occupied by Spain and Portugal. It is ringed with mountains, with the Pyrenees and the Cantabrian Mountains on the north, the Sierra da Estrella on the west, and the Cordillera Penibética on the southeast.

NATURAL FEATURES

PAN AMERICAN AIRWAYS
IGUASSÚ FALLS, a series of cataracts along part of the Brazil-Argentina border.

The interior is also mountainous, with the Sierra Morena and Sierra de Guadarrama the most important chains. The major rivers crossing the peninsula are the Duero, the Tejo (Tagus), the Guadiana, the Ebro, and the Guadalquivir.

IGUASSÚ FALLS, a great waterfall on the Brazil-Argentina border. It is on the Iguassú River, 14 miles upstream from its confluence with the Upper Paraná River. Iguassú Falls, a 2.5-mile-wide series of cataracts, has a vertical drop of about 215 feet.

IJSSEL MEER, formerly the Zuider Zee, an inlet of the North Sea within the Netherlands. Flooding joined the former lake to the sea, but diking and draining in the 1950s and the 1960s separated the two again to reclaim over 500,000 acres for farmland.

ILI, a river in northwestern Sinkiang province, in western China. It rises in the Tien Shan range and flows west for 800 miles through a fertile valley to Lake Balkhash, in the Soviet Union.

INDIAN OCEAN, the third largest body of water in the world, more than 28 million square miles in area. It is bounded by Africa on the west, Asia on the north, Australia and the Australasian Islands on the east, and Antarctica on the south. The meridian of longitude at 20° East separates the Indian and Atlantic oceans.

The Indian Ocean's greatest depth is over 24,000 feet, in the Java Trench, but the average depth is 13,000 feet, exceeding that of the Atlantic. Several large rivers feed the ocean, including the Indus, Ganges, Irrawaddy, and, through the Persian Gulf, the Tigris-Euphrates of Asia, and the Zambezi and Limpopo of Africa. The Arabian Sea and the Bay of Bengal are its two major arms.

INDOCHINA, a general name for the peninsula of Southeast Asia occupied by Vietnam, Laos, Cambodia, Thailand, Burma, and the mainland portion of Malaysia. French Indochina was a French colony that included present-day Cambodia, Laos, and Vietnam.

INDUS, one of the major rivers of South Asia. Rising on the northern slopes of the Kailas range of southwestern Tibet, it flows northwest into Kashmir, then southwest through central Pakistan to the Arabian Sea—a total of more than 1,800 miles. Its major tributaries include the Chenab, the Sutlej, the Jhelum, and the Ravi. The Indus has a wide delta known as "the Mouths of the Indus," flowing into the Arabian Sea.

INLAND SEA, a shallow inlet of the Pacific Ocean between the Japanese islands of Honshu, on the north, and Shikoku and Kyushu, on the south. It is separated from the open sea by the Kii Strait on the southeast, the Bungo Strait on the south, and the Shimonoseki Strait on the west.

INN, a European river that is a major tributary of the Danube. It rises in Switzerland and flows 320 miles through northwestern Austria and southeastern Germany to join the Danube at Passau.

IONIAN SEA, a portion of the Mediterranean Sea between Italy and Greece, connected to the Adriatic Sea through the Strait of Otranto. It contains many rocky islets and islands, including Corfu, Paxos, Leukas, and Ithaca.

IRISH SEA, an arm of the Atlantic Ocean between the western coast of England and the eastern coast of Ireland. It is connected with the Atlantic Ocean through North Channel on the north and St. George's Channel on the south.

IRON GATE, a two-mile-long gorge cut by the Danube River through the southwestern Transylvanian Alps on the border of Romania and Yugoslavia.

IRRAWADDY, a major river of Burma that rises in Tibet and flows for more than 1,300 miles to empty into the Gulf of Martaban of the Bay of Bengal near Rangoon. The delta of the Irrawaddy is about 150 miles long. The river's chief tributaries are the Nmai and the Chindwin.

IRTYSH, a major river of northeastern Asia. It is over 2,200 miles long and a major tributary of the Ob River. Rising in the northern part of China's Sinkiang province, the river flows westward and is known as the Kara Irtysh until it enters Lake Zaysan in the Soviet Union's Kazakh republic. It then travels north and northwest through the Altai Mountains and the western Kulunda Steppe into the Russian republic, meeting the Ob at Khanty-Mansiysk.

ISLANDS. Greenland, 840,000 square miles in area, is the world's largest island. Lying partly in the Arctic Ocean and partly in the Atlantic, it is adjacent to the fifth largest island, Baffin, 183,810 square miles, which lies north of Hudson Bay.

The world's second and third largest islands lie at the western edge of the Pacific. New Guinea, 317,000 square miles, is separated from Australia, to its south, by the Arafura Sea and the Coral Sea. To its west is Borneo, 287,400 square miles, washed by the South China, Sulu, Celebes, and Java seas.

Madagascar, 229,812 square miles, is the world's fourth largest island. It lies in the Indian Ocean and is separated from East Africa by the Mozambique Channel.

JAPAN, SEA OF, an arm of the western Pacific Ocean between Japan and the East Asian mainland. About 400,000 square miles in area, it is linked with the East China Sea on the south through the Korea Strait, between the Japanese island of Kyushu and Korea, and with the Sea of Okhotsk on the north through the Tatar Strait and La Perouse Strait.

JORDAN, a river in the Middle East that rises in four headstreams in the anti-Lebanon Mountains of Syria. It flows south for some 200 miles in Israel and Jordan through the Sea of Galilee and into the Dead Sea. The Yarmuk River is the principal tributary of the Jordan, whose course lies in the Great Rift Valley.

JOS, a plateau region in West Africa, in the center of the Northern Region of Nigeria. Rising steeply from the valley of the Benoué River, the plateau has an average elevation of 4,000 feet, with a maximum height of nearly 6,000 feet near the town of Jos. The plateau contains important mineral deposits.

JUNGFRAU, a mountain in the Bernese Alps, in southwestern Switzerland. Rising over 13,600 feet, it is one of Europe's highest mountains.

JURA, a mountain range along the French-Swiss border north of Geneva. It is a spur of the western Alps, and has a peak of over 5,500 feet.

JUTLAND, or Jylland, a peninsula in northern Europe extending north from Germany. It lies between the North Sea on the west and the Baltic on the east and is separated from Scandinavia by the Skagerrak.

Jutland is low-lying, with a flat to rolling surface and an irregular coastline. Part of it is occupied by the Danish mainland and part by the West German state of Schleswig-Holstein.

KAILAS, a mountain range of southwestern Tibet with a peak of more than 23,000 feet. The Range is the source of the Indus, Sutlej, and Brahmaputra rivers.

KALAHARI, a desert of southern Africa. It extends southward from Lake Ngami through central Botswana into northern South Africa as far as the Orange River, and westward from eastern Botswana into South West Africa.

KAMCHATKA, a peninsula in northeastern Siberia, in the Soviet Union. It is 750 miles long and from 80 to 300 miles wide, and divides the Bering Sea and the Pacific Ocean on the east from the Sea of Okhotsk on the west. Two tall, volcanic mountain ranges run the length of the peninsula and enclose a central valley, which is drained by the Kamchatka River.

KANCHENJUNGA, a mountain in the Himalayas on the Nepal-Sikkim border. With one of its three peaks rising to 28,165 feet, it is the third highest mountain in the world.

KARAKORAM, a mountain range lying along the northern borders of West Pakistan and Kashmir. It extends eastward into China's Tibet region and along the southern border of Sinkiang. It lies between the Hindu Kush and the Kunlun Mountains.

The Karakoram range includes many peaks above 22,000 feet. The Karakoram Pass, the chief route between Kashmir, in northern India, and China, lies at an elevation of nearly 18,300 feet.

KARIBA, a man-made lake, 165 miles long, in southeastern Africa. It was formed by the Kariba Dam on the Zambezi River, between Zambia and Rhodesia.

KARROO, a tableland region in South Africa, west and northwest of the Drakensberg Mountains. It is divided into three parts: the North Karroo, a desert area south of the Orange River; the Great, or Central, Karroo, a dry area between the North Karroo and the Swartberg; and the Little, or Southern, Karroo, in places a fertile area, south of the Swartberg along the southern coast of South Africa.

KARUN, a 450-mile-long river in western Asia. It rises west of Isfahan, in Iran, and has cut large gorges through the Zagros Mountains. It flows south and west, joining the Shatt-al-Srab near the north end of Abadan Island in the Persian Gulf.

KASAI, a 1,200-mile-long African river, rising in northeastern Angola. It flows east and north to form part of the Angola-Congo (Kinshasa) boundary, and then northwest to the Congo River near Brazzaville. It is the main southern tributary of the Congo River.

KATHIAWAR, a peninsula on India's western coast, northwest of the Gulf of Cambay and southeast of the Gulf of Kutch.

KATTEGAT, a strait between Sweden on the east and the Danish Jutland Peninsula on the west. It connects the Baltic Sea to the Skagerrak and the North Sea.

KENYA HIGHLANDS, a mountainous region of East Africa, running west to southwest in Kenya. The mountains are largely of volcanic origin, and include Mt. Kenya, over 17,000 feet, the second-highest mountain in Africa. The region is cut by the Great Rift Valley.

KERULEN, a river of northeastern Mongolia. It flows about 800 miles across the Mongolian Plateau and empties into Lake Hulun.

KHASI HILLS, uplands of west-central Assam, in northeastern India, east of the Brahmaputra River. The highest elevation in the Khasi Hills is over 6,400 feet.

KHINGAN, a mountain system of northeastern China. The system forms an inverted V, with the fertile Manchurian Plain lying between the two flanks.

The western flank is the Greater Khingan Range, which runs northeast to southwest through north-central Inner Mongolia and averages 3,000 to 5,000 feet. The eastern flank is the Lesser Khingan Range, which runs northwest to southeast near the northeastern border of Heilungkiang and the Soviet Union. The highest peak is over 3,500 feet.

KILIMANJARO, the highest mountain in Africa, located in East Africa on the border of Kenya and Tanzania. Kibo, the site of relatively recent volcanic activity, is the highest peak at 19,340 feet. It is covered by glaciers. Mawenzi, the other major peak, is 17,500 feet and has no glaciers.

KING LEOPOLD RANGES, a mountain system in northwestern Australia. It lies at the southwestern edge of the Kimberley Plateau and has elevations generally below 3,000 feet.

KISTNA, or Krishna, an Indian river that rises in the Western Ghats and flows eastward for about 800 miles to the Bay of Bengal.

KIVU, an African lake lying on the border of the Congo (Kinshasa) and Rwanda, in the western portion of the Great Rift Valley. It is about 1,000 square miles in area.

KJÖLEN, a Scandinavian mountain range extending along the border between northeastern Norway and northwestern Sweden. The highest peak is Kebnekaise, 6,965 feet.

KLONDIKE, a region south of the Ogilvie Mountains in the Yukon Territory of northwestern Canada. Gold was found there in 1896.

KOKO, or Tsinghai, a large lake in northeastern Tsinghai Province, in northern China. It lies south of the Nan Shan range and north of the eastern end of the Kunlun Mountains.

KOLYMA, a mountain range in the eastern Soviet Union, in northeastern Siberia. The mountains contain rich deposits of gold, mined in the Kolyma Gold Fields. The range has a peak of nearly 7,300 feet and is the source of the 1,500-mile-long Kolyma River.

KOREA BAY, the northeastern arm of the Yellow Sea, in East Asia. It lies between the Korean Peninsula, on the northeast, and China's Liaotung Peninsula, on the northwest.

KRA, ISTHMUS OF, the narrow section of the Malay Peninsula, occupied by Burma and Thailand. The Gulf of Siam is to the east and the Andaman Sea is to the west.

KRIMML, a waterfall on the Krimml River in west-central Austria. It is the highest waterfall in Europe, with a total drop of 1,250 feet.

KUNLUN MOUNTAINS, a range on the northern edge of Tibet, just south of the Takla Makan and the Astin Tagh ranges. The highest peak, Ulugh Maz Tagh, is over 25,000 feet. The Kunlun range contains the sources of the Yellow, the Yangtze, and the Mekong rivers.

KURIL ISLANDS, an archipelago of 32 islands in northeastern Asia, belonging to the Soviet Union. They extend northeast-southwest for some 730 miles between the Japanese island of Hokkaido and the Soviet Kamchatka Peninsula. The islands separate the Sea of Okhotsk from the Pacific Ocean and are separated from the Kamchatka Peninsula by the Kuril Strait.

KUTCH, GULF OF, or Cutch, an inlet of the Arabian Sea north of India's Kathiawar Peninsula and south of the Rann of Kutch, a salt marsh in west-central India.

KYOGA, a 1,000-square-mile lake in East Africa, in south-central Uganda. The Victoria Nile flows through the lake.

LACCADIVE SEA, an arm of the Arabian Sea between the southwestern coast of India and the Laccadive, Minicoy, Amindivi, and Maldive islands.

LADOGA, the largest lake in Europe, covering some 7,000 square miles. It lies 40 miles northeast of Leningrad, in the northwestern Soviet Union. Once divided between Finland and Russia, it is now wholly within the Soviet Union, about 20 miles southeast of the border with Finland.

LAGOA DOS PATOS, a tidal lagoon on the southeastern coast of Brazil. This "Lake of the Ducks" is about 30 miles wide and 150 miles long. It is linked with the Atlantic Ocean by a narrow, shallow opening at Rio Grande. The lagoon is separated from the ocean by an offshore sand bar, from 5 to 20 miles wide.

LAKE DISTRICT, a hilly region of northwestern England, in eastern Lancashire. A portion of Lombardy, in north-central Italy, is sometimes called the "Italian Lake District."

LAKES. The largest lake in the world is the 143,550-square-mile saltwater Caspian Sea, on the border of the Soviet Union and Iran. Second in size is North America's Lake Superior, 31,800 square miles, which is the world's largest freshwater lake.

Lake Victoria, in eastern Africa, ranks third, with an area of 26,828 square miles. The saltwater Aral Sea, in southwestern Soviet Asia, is the world's fourth largest lake, with an area of 25,300 square miles. Lake Huron, 23,000 square miles, in North America, ranks fifth.

The world's deepest lake is Lake Baykal, in the western Soviet Union, which has a depth of 5,315 feet. The largest lake wholly within Europe is Lake Ladoga, about 7,000 square miles in area, in the northwestern Soviet Union. Latin America's largest lake is Lake Nicaragua, 2,972 square miles, in central Nicaragua. In Australia, the largest is the saltwater Lake Eyre, whose area varies with the seasons and averages 3,700 square miles.

LAPLAND, an area of about 150,000 square miles within the Arctic Circle. It extends across northern Norway, Sweden, and Finland and into the Kola Peninsula of the northwestern Soviet Union.

Lapland is mountainous in the west and is largely forest or tundra further east. It is sparsely populated by about 35,000 Lapps, a nomadic people who subsist by fishing and reindeer herding.

LAPTEV SEA, a part of the Arctic Ocean along the northern coast of Siberia, in the Soviet Union. It lies between the Taymyr Peninsula and the New Siberian Islands. Vil'katskiy Strait links it with the Kara Sea on the west and Laptev Strait connects it with the East Siberian Sea on the east.

LAURENTIAN HIGHLANDS, a low, rounded mountain range in the southeastern part of Canada's Quebec Province. The highlands lie between the northern coast of the St. Lawrence river and the southern edge of the Canadian Shield. The highest point in the range is Mt. Tremblant, 3,130 feet.

LEBANON MOUNTAINS, a 100-mile-long range, extending almost the length of Lebanon parallel to the Mediterranean coast. The highest mountains are to the north. They include Qurnat as Sawda, 10,130 feet, the highest peak. East of northern Lebanon are the Anti-Lebanon Mountains, running along the Lebanese-Syrian border.

LENA, the longest river in the Soviet Union, 2,650 miles. It rises near Lake Baykal, in Siberia, and flows north and northeast to Yakutsk. There it turns and flows northwest and then north into the Laptev Sea. The Vitim, Alden, Olekema, and Vilyuy rivers are its major tributaries.

LEOPOLD II, an African lake in the western part of the Congo (Kinshasa), lying in the lowest part of the interior Congo depression. The lake varies in area from about 900 square miles in the dry season to about 3,200 square miles in the wet season.

LIAO, a 700-mile-long river of Eastern Asia, in southern Manchuria. It rises in the Greater Khingan Mountains and flows northeast and then southwest to the Gulf of Chihli (Po Hai), an arm of the Yellow Sea.

LIGURIAN SEA, an arm of the western Mediterranean between northern Corsica and the Italian Riveria. The inner portion of the Ligurian Sea is called the Gulf of Genoa.

LIMPOPO, a 1,000-mile-long river of southeastern Africa. It rises in the Witwatersrand area of South Africa and flows northwest to the Botswana border. It continues northeast along the Botswana border, turns east at the Rhodesian border, and then flows southeast through Mozambique to the Indian Ocean. Its major tributary is the Olifants River, which joins the Limpopo in Mozambique.

LIONS, GULF OF, a bay of the Mediterranean Sea on the southern coast of France. It extends from the eastern side of the Rhône delta to the coast of Spain.

LIPARI ISLANDS, a group of small volcanic islands in the southeastern Tyrrhenian Sea, off the northeastern tip of Sicily.

LITANI, a river of southern Lebanon. About 95 miles long, it rises near Baalbek and flows southwest along the eastern side of the Lebanon Mountains, turning west to empty into the Mediterranean north of Tyre.

LLANOS, a low-lying plains region of South America, in eastern Colombia and the Orinoco basin of central Venezuela.

LOFOTEN ISLANDS, a Norwegian island group in the Norwegian Sea, off the northwestern coast of the mainland.

LOGONE, an African river that rises in the highlands of the Central African Republic and flows north to Lake Chad. It meets the Chari river at Fort Lamy, and forms part of the boundary between northeastern Cameroon and Chad.

LOIRE, the longest river of France. It rises in the Cévennes Mountains in the southeast, flows northwest and west for about 625 miles, and empties into the Bay of Biscay through a wide estuary at St. Nazaire.

LOLLAND, or Laaland, one of the three main islands of Denmark. It lies southwest of Zealand, or Sjaelland, and just north of the German coast. With Falster Island it forms a Danish county.

LUANGWA, a 400-mile-long river of southeastern Africa. It rises in the Muchinga Mountains of northeastern Zambia and flows southwest to join the Zambezi River on the western border of Mozambique.

LUCERNE, a roughly cross-shaped lake in central Switzerland, bounded by the cantons of Lucerne, Unterwalden, Uri, and Schwyz.

MACDONNELL RANGES, a highland in central Australia with elevations reaching 5,000 feet. It is generally arid and barren.

MACKENZIE, a major North American river that flows for 1,200 miles through northwestern Canada, just east of the Mackenzie Mountains. The Mackenzie proper originates in Great Slave Lake, but the lake's major feeder stream, the Great Slave River, which is formed from the Peace and Athabasca rivers, is generally considered part of the Mackenzie. The entire Mackenzie system flows for some 2,500 miles before emptying into the Beaufort Sea, an arm of the Arctic Ocean.

MACDONNELL RANGES of central Australia.

MADAGASCAR, one of the largest islands in the world, lying in the Indian Ocean some 250 miles across the Mozambique Channel from Africa's southeast coast. It consists of a mountainous core ringed with coastal lowlands and swamps. It has an area of about 230,000 square miles, and is occupied by the Malagasy Republic.

MADEIRA, an archipelago with two large islands and several islets in the Atlantic Ocean, some 350 miles east of North Africa. The islands belong to Portugal. They are mountainous and noted for their fine scenery and mild climate. Sugarcane is grown and wine is produced.

MADEIRA, a river in central South America formed from the union on the Bolivia-Brazil border of the Beni and the Mamore rivers, which rise in Bolivia. The Madeira flows for over 1,500 miles north and east to join the Amazon east of Manaus.

MAGDALENA, a South American river that flows northward for some 1,000 miles through Colombia. It lies between the massive Cordillera Central, to the west, and the Cordillera Oriental, to the east. It is joined near its mouth by the Cauca.

MAGGIORE, a lake, about 80 square miles in area, in the Alpine region of northern Italy and southern Switzerland. Its mild climate and scenic beauty attract many tourists.

MAIN, a river in central Germany that rises in Bavaria and flows westward for some 300 miles through Wurzburg and Frankfurt to the Rhine, at Mainz.

NATURAL FEATURES

MAKALU, a mountain in the Himalayas on the border between Nepal and the Tibet region of China. It is the fourth highest mountain in the world, with an elevation of 27,824 feet.

MAKARIKARI, a large salt basin in arid northeastern Botswana, in south-central Africa. Although usually dry, it may receive the overflow of water from Lake Ngami during the wet season. There are brine deposits of commerical importance in the north.

MALABAR COAST, India's southwestern coast, lying between the Western Ghats and the Arabian Sea.

MALAY ARCHIPELAGO, the world's largest island group, extending east from the Malay Peninsula. The archipelago is bounded on the north by the South China Sea, on the east by the Pacific Ocean, and on the south and west by the Indian Ocean. It includes the islands of the Philippines, Indonesia, and the Federation of Malaysia, which are separated by many straits and small seas.

MALAY PENINSULA, a projection of mainland Southeast Asia between the Andaman Sea, on the west, and the Gulf of Siam, an arm of the South China Sea, on the east. It is occupied by Burma, Thailand, and West Malaysia. The peninsula is heavily forested and hilly and is rich in minerals.

MANAGUA, a lake in Central America, the northernmost of Nicaragua's two major lakes.

MANILA BAY, an inlet of the South China Sea on the southwestern coast of Luzon Island, in the Philippines. It is one of the best natural harbors in eastern Asia.

MANNAR, GULF OF, an inlet of the Indian Ocean between Ceylon and southern India. It is connected to the Bay of Bengal by Palk Strait.

MARACAIBO, a brackish lagoon, 130 miles long and 75 miles wide, in northwestern Venezuela. It is a major South American petroleum-producing area. Petroleum was discovered there in the early 1900s and many oil wells are located around the eastern shore and in the middle of the lake.

MARAJÓ, a large South American is-island, located at the eastern end of the Amazon River and forming a part of the Amazon delta. It is about 150 miles long and 100 miles wide. The western half is covered mostly with tropical rainforest, and the eastern half is grassland, which is flooded during the rainy season. Beef cattle are grazed, and rubber, timber, and medicinal plants are extracted.

MARIAS ISLANDS, an archipelago of four small mountainous islands in the Pacific Ocean off Mexico's eastern coast.

MARITSA, a river of eastern Europe that rises in the Rhodope mountains of western Bulgaria. It flows eastward and then south for about 300 miles along the boundary of Greece and Turkey and empties into the Aegean Sea.

MARMARA, an inland sea, some 175 miles long and up to 50 miles wide, separating European Turkey from Asian Turkey. It is linked with the Aegean Sea by the Dardanelles and with the Black Sea by the Bosporus. The city of Istanbul is located on its northeastern shore.

MARNE, a river that rises in eastern France and flows north and west for about 325 miles through a rich agricultural region. It empties into the Seine at Charenton.

MARRA, an African mountain range in western Sudan that rises to a peak of more than 10,000 feet, at Mt. Marra.

MASAI STEPPE, an African plateau region of volcanic origin, in southwestern Kenya near the Zambian border. A dry pasture area, it is used by seminomadic peoples for cattle grazing.

MASSIF CENTRAL, a high mountainous plateau occupying all of southwestern France. It contains the headwaters of many important rivers.

MEDITERRANEAN, the largest inland sea in the world, 2,400 miles long and up to 1,000 miles wide. It separates the continents of Europe to the north, Asia to the east, and Africa to the south. The Mediterranean is linked with the Atlantic Ocean by the Strait of Gibraltar and with the Red Sea by the Suez Canal.

The irregularly-shaped sea is divided into two deep basins by the Italian Peninsula, the island of Sicily, and a submarine ridge joining Sicily and Tunisia. There are islands in each basin. The western basin, connected to the Black Sea by the Bosporus and Dardanelles, has two northern extensions—the Adriatic and Aegean seas.

Among the several rivers feeding the Mediterranean are the Rhône, Po, and Nile. The climate of the Mediterranean Basin consists of hot, dry summers and warm, wet winters.

MEKONG, a major river of eastern Asia rising in the Himalayas, in eastern Tibet. It follows a twisting, generally southeasterly course for 2,600 miles before emptying into the South China Sea through a wide delta at the southern tip of Indochina.

The Mekong's major tributaries include the Mun, the Hou, the Khong, the Srepok, and the Chinit. The Tonle Sap, a large lake in west central Cambodia, serves as a reservoir for the Mekong's flood waters.

The river marks parts of the Burma-China, Burma-Laos, and Thailand-Laos borders. It is navigable to north-central Laos and has a fertile valley and delta.

MENDERES, the name of three rivers of Asia Minor, the most notable being the Büyük Meander. This river, rising in western Turkey and flowing southwest and west into the Aegean Sea, is about 250 miles long. Its wandering course has given us the term, meander.

MEUSE, a river that rises in northeastern France and flows into Belgium, where it is joined by the Sambre at Namur. The Sambre-Meuse valley is underlain by rich coal deposits and is Belgium's most important industrial district. In the Netherlands, the Meuse becomes the Maas. It turns west near Nijmegen, and enters the North Sea south of Dordrecht.

MORAVA, a 260-mile-long river in Yugoslavia. It rises north of Skopje and flows northward to join the Danube near Smederevo.

MOSELLE, a major river of France and Germany. Rising in the French Vosges Mountains, it flows north through the Lorraine industrial district of northeastern France, enters Germany, and joins the Rhine River at Koblenz.

MOSKVA, a river of the Moscow region of the Soviet Union. Rising in the Smolensk-Moscow Upland, west of the city of Moscow, it flows for some 300 miles to join the river Oka after passing through the city. Navigable below Moscow, it is connected to the Volga River by canal.

MOSQUITO COAST, the eastern, Caribbean, coast of Nicaragua and Honduras, in Central America. It is named for the indigenous Mosquito Indians.

MOULOUYA, a North African river. It rises in the Atlas Mountains in Morocco and flows northeastward for some 300 miles to the Mediterranean Sea.

MOUNTAINS. Mt. Everest, 29,028 feet, and the world's next four highest mountains—Godwin Austin, Kanchinjunga, Makalu, and Dhaulagiri, each more than 26,000 feet in elevation—all lie in the Himalayas, in Southern Asia. The highest peaks on each of the other continents are much lower.

South America's highest peak, Aconcagua, rises 22,834 feet. North America's Mt. McKinley is 20,320 feet. Kilimanjaro, in Africa, rises 19,340 feet, and El'brus, in Europe, is 18,481 feet. The Antarctic's highest known point, the Vinson Massif, is about 16,860 feet in elevation. Australia's highest mountain, Kosciusko, rises only 7,316 feet.

MT. COMMUNISM, a mountain in the Pamir range in the southeastern part of the Soviet Union's Tadzhik republic. Formerly called Garmo Peak, and later Stalin Peak, it is the highest mountain in the Soviet Union, rising more than 24,500 feet.

MT. EVEREST, the world's highest mountain. It rises 29,028 feet in the Himalayas on the border between Nepal and Tibet in south-central Asia.

MURRAY-DARLING, Australia's principal river system. The Murray rises near Mt. Kosciusko, in southeastern Australia and flows westward to its mouth at Encounter Bay, off the Indian Ocean on the south Australian coast.

The Darling, among whose headstreams are the Barwon and Macquarie rivers, flows westward and southward from northern New South Wales to

Wentwork, where it joins the Murray. The Murray-Darling watercourse, 2,310 miles long, is used extensively for irrigation.

MWERU, a lake in central Africa on the border between the Congo (Kinshasa) and Zambia, and some 100 miles west of the southern tip of Lake Tanganyika.

NAN, a mountain range in north-central China at the northern end of the Tibetan Plateau. Its peaks range from 18,000 to over 20,000 feet above sea level. The range is cut by deep valleys.

NEGEV, a semi-desert region in southern Israel. The Negev contains copper, potash, phosphate, and oil deposits. Limited agriculture is carried on with water brought by pipeline from the north.

NEVA, a river in the western Soviet Union that flows from Lake Ladoga westward into the Gulf of Finland. Although only 45 miles long, the Neva is an important part of the North Russian canal system, which allows large ships to reach Leningrad.

NEW GUINEA, the world's second largest island, lying in the southwest Pacific Ocean, north of Australia. The island, with an area of 317,000 square miles, has a mountainous interior and swampy coastlands. New Guinea has extensive mangrove and sandalwood forests and contains deposits of gold, oil, cobalt, and nickel.

Politically New Guinea is divided into three parts—West Irian, a part of Indonesia; the Trust Territory of New Guinea, a UN trust administered by Australia; and the Territory of Papua, an Australian territory.

NICARAGUA, the largest lake in Central America, with an area of 3,060 square miles. It is located in southwestern Nicaragua.

NIGER, a major river in West Africa, rising in southeastern Guinea and flowing northeast into Mali and then southeast into the Republic of Niger and Nigeria. The river flows for some 2,600 miles and empties into the Gulf of Guinea. About 80 miles from its mouth, the Niger forms an extensive delta.

NILE, the longest river in Africa and in the world. Its course can be traced from the Kagera River headwaters in northern Tanzania to the Mediterranean Sea, a distance of 4,145 miles.

The Nile is formed by the joining of the White Nile and the Blue Nile at Khartoum, in Sudan. The White Nile flows north from Tanzania into Uganda and Sudan, where it is joined by its major tributaries, the Ghazal and the Sobat, before joining the Blue Nile. The Nile proper continues north through the United Arab Republic (Egypt) and forms an extensive delta north of Cairo.

NIMBA, a range of mountains in West Africa, in northern Liberia and southern Guinea. The Nimba Mountains contain rich iron ore deposits.

NORTH AMERICA, a continent in the northern half of the western hemisphere, with an area of more than 9.4 million square miles and a population of over 300 million in the mid-1960s.

North America extends from islands north of the Arctic Circle to the Isthmus of Panama, near the equator. It is bounded on the west by the Pacific Ocean, on the east by the Atlantic Ocean, and it includes the West Indies islands in the Caribbean Sea. High mountains dominate the western part of the continent, vast plains cover most of its central portion, and lower mountains and coastal plains mark the eastern coast.

NORTH CHANNEL, a strait between the Irish Sea and North Atlantic Ocean. It separates Scotland from Northern Ireland.

NORTH SEA, an arm of the North Atlantic Ocean, separating Britain from the northwestern European mainland.

NORWEGIAN SEA, a body of water off the western coast of Norway between the North Atlantic and the Arctic oceans.

NOVAYA ZEMLYA, an archipelago in the Arctic Ocean between the Barents Sea on the west and the Kara Sea on the east. It is composed of two large islands, separated by Matochkin Shar Strait, and several small islands. The archipelago is part of the Soviet Union.

NUBIAN DESERT, a desert area in northeastern Sudan, lying between the Nile River and the Red Sea.

NYASA, the third largest lake in Africa, located on the border of Tanzania, Malawi, and Mozambique. The lake has a surface area of over 11,000 square miles and a mountainous shoreline. Its only outlet is the Shire River, a tributary of the Zambezi River.

OB, a river in the Soviet Union, over 2,000 miles long. The Ob rises in the Altai Mountains of western Siberia. It flows northwest to join the Irtysh River and then north into the Gulf of Ob, an inlet of the Kara Sea.

ODER, a river in central Europe, over 500 miles long. It rises in Silesia, flows north through western Poland, is joined by the Neisse River, and continues north to the Baltic Sea. The Oder forms a major part of the border between East Germany and Poland.

OKAVANGO, a river of southwestern Africa, some 1,000 miles long. The Okavango rises in central Angola and flows generally southeast, forming part of the border between South West Africa and Angola. It empties into Okavango Basin, a marsh in northern Botswana.

OKHOTSK, SEA OF, a western arm of the North Pacific Ocean off the eastern coast of the Siberian region of the Soviet Union. It is bounded on the east by the Kamchatka Peninsula and the Kuril Islands, and on the southwest by Sakhalin and Hokkaido islands. It joins the Sea of Japan, to the southwest, through the Tatar and the Soya, or La Perouse, straits.

OLYMPUS, or Olimbus, a mountain range in Greece, near the coast of Thessaly. Mt. Olympus, 9,550 feet, the highest point in the range and in Greece, was thought in ancient times to be the home of the gods.

OMAN, GULF OF, an arm of the Arabian Sea between Arabia and Iran. It is linked with the Persian Gulf by the Strait of Hormuz.

ONEGA, the second largest lake in Europe, lying in the northwestern Soviet Union. Onega has a surface area of over 3,500 square miles. Its outlet is the Svir River, which flows into Lake Ladoga, Europe's largest lake.

ORANGE, a river of southern Africa, rising in northeastern Basutoland and flowing 1,300 miles in a generally westward direction to the Atlantic Ocean. The river forms part of the boundary between South West Africa and South Africa.

ORDOS, a desert region of Inner Mongolia. It lies within the great bend of the Hwang Ho (Yellow River).

ORE, or Erz, a mountain range in eastern Germany and northwestern Czechoslovakia with a peak of just over 4,000 feet.

ORIENT, a general term for Asia and especially eastern Asia. The region known as the Orient, or East, is divided into three sections—the Near East, including the countries at the eastern end of the Mediterranean Sea, northeastern Africa, and the Arabian peninsula; the Middle East, including the southern Asian countries from Iraq to Burma, and sometimes including the Near East; and the Far East, including China, Korea, Japan, the Malay Peninsula, and the Malay archipelago.

ORINOCO, a river of South America that flows for about 1,500 miles from the Parima Mountains of Venezuela west and then north along the Venezuela-Colombia border, and then northeast to the Atlantic Ocean. The Orinoco forms a wide delta in northeastern Venezuela.

ORKNEY ISLANDS, a Scottish archipelago, lying off the northeastern coast of Scotland and separated from it by Pentland Firth. The largest island is Pomona, locally known as the Mainland. South of Pomona lies a treacherous bay, the Scapa Flow.

ORONTES, a 246-mile-long river in western Syria. It rises in northeastern Lebanon and flows north to the Turkish border, where it turns and flows west to the Mediterranean Sea.

PACIFIC OCEAN, the largest of the oceans, almost 64 million square miles in area. It lies between the American continents, Australia, the Malay Archi-

NATURAL FEATURES

pelago, and Asia, and extends from the Arctic Circle to the Antarctic Region. Between the Arctic and the equator it is known as the North Pacific; from the equator to the Antarctic it is called the South Pacific.

PAMIR, a mountain range in the southern Soviet Union, lying along the borders of Pakistan, Kashmir, and China, north of the Hindu Kush and Karakorum ranges. Peaks in the Pamirs rise over 25,000 feet above sea level.

PAMPAS, grassy treeless plains of South America. They extend some 1,000 miles through east-central Argentina from the lower Paraná River south to the Colorado River.

PANAMA, ISTHMUS OF, a narrow neck of land in southern Central America separating the Caribbean Sea from the Gulf of Panama, an arm of the Pacific Ocean. It is occupied by Panama and by the Panama Canal Zone, the U.S.-controlled site of a canal across the isthmus.

PARAGUAY, a river of South America, rising in southwestern Brazil and flowing generally south for some 1,500 miles. The Paraguay forms parts of the boundaries between Brazil and Bolivia, Brazil and Paraguay, and Paraguay and Argentina before it empties into the Paraná River in the southwestern corner of Paraguay.

PARANÁ, the second longest river in South America. Formed by the junction of the Grande and Paranaíba rivers in south-central Brazil, it flows generally southwest for some 2,500 miles.
The river forms part of the boundary between Brazil and Paraguay and all of the boundary between Paraguay and Argentina. It joins the Paraguay River in the southwestern corner of Paraguay, and flows south through Argentina to the Río de la Plata.

PARIA, GULF OF, an arm of the Atlantic Ocean lying between the northeast coast of Venezuela and the west coast of Trinidad. The Paria peninsula of Venezuela is on the north.

PAROPAMISUS, a mountain range of western Asia, in northwest Afghanistan near the western end of the Hindu Kush.

PATAGONIA, a barren tableland of southern South America lying between the Andes and the Atlantic Ocean. It extends south of the Negro River to the Strait of Magellan.

PAULO AFONSO FALLS, a series of three waterfalls in eastern Brazil, with a height of over 270 feet. They form the principal cataract along the São Francisco River.

PELOPONNESOS, a peninsula and province of southern Greece, connected with the mainland by the narrow Isthmus of Corinth. The Peloponnesos is the site of ancient Corinth and Sparta.

PENNER, two rivers in south-central India, both of which rise in the hills of Mysore state. The Northern Penner flows east for about 350 miles, emptying into the Bay of Bengal near Nellore. The Southern Penner flows southeast for about 245 miles into the Bay of Bengal near Cuddalore.

PERSIAN GULF, a shallow extension of the Arabian Sea, bounded by the Trucial Coast, Qatar, Saudi Arabia, Kuwait, Iraq, and Iran. It is some 550 miles long and is connected with the Gulf of Oman to the southeast. The Persian Gulf is important for pearl fishing and petroleum.

PESCADORES, or P'enghu, a group of Chinese islands lying in the Formosa Strait between the China mainland and Taiwan.

PINDUS, a mountain range in southeastern Europe that begins in central Albania and extends generally southeast through central Greece.

PLATA, RÍO DE LA, an estuary in the southeast coast of South America. It forms part of the border between Uruguay and Argentina, stretching some 250 miles from the Atlantic Ocean to the mouths of the Paraná and Uruguay rivers.

POYANG, a lake in southeastern China, the second largest in the country. It lies in Kiangsi province in the basin of the Yangtze River, which feeds it.

PRUT, a river of eastern Europe that rises in the Carpathian Mountains of the southwestern Soviet Union and flows generally southeast for some 520 miles. The Prut forms part of the border between the Soviet Union and Romania and joins the Danube about 75 miles from the Black Sea.

PYRENEES, a European mountain range extending some 270 miles along the entire Spanish-French border, from the Bay of Biscay to the south coast of the Gulf of Lions. The highest peak is Pico de Aneto, 11,168 feet.

QATTARA DEPRESSION, a low area of northern Africa, in the northwestern United Arab Republic (Egypt). Its lowest point is 436 feet below sea level.

RED, or Hong, a principal river of North Vietnam. It rises in Yünnan, in China, as the Yüan and flows about 500 miles southeast into the Gulf of Tonkin, an arm of the South China Sea. Its chief tributaries are the Da (Black), the Gam, and the Lo rivers. The lower valley forms the economic, political, and cultural center of North Vietnam.

RED RIVER OF THE NORTH, a river of North America. It rises in the northeastern corner of South Dakota and flows north into Canada some 350 miles to the south end of Lake Winnipeg.

RED SEA, an inland sea between northeastern Africa and the Arabian Peninsula, part of the Great Rift Valley system. It is about 1,450 miles long

THE PYRENEES form a mountain barrier on the boundary between France and Spain.

and less than 250 miles wide, and its greatest depth is more than 7,250 feet.
Two arms of the Red Sea, the Gulf of Aqaba and the Gulf of Suez, lie to the north. The sea is connected to the Mediterranean by the Suez Canal and to the Gulf of Aden through the strait of Bab el Mandeb. An ancient trade route, it assumed new importance with the opening of the Suez Canal in 1869.

RHINE, a west European river that rises in the Swiss Alps and flows north and west, forming parts of the boundaries of Liechtenstein, Switzerland, France, and Germany. In Germany it crosses a rich, densely populated, and highly industrialized region before turning west into the Netherlands, where it divides into two branches, the Nederrijn and the Waal, which empty into the North Sea near Rotterdam.
The Rhine is over 800 miles long, and its major tributaries include the Neckar, Main, Ruhr, Lippe, and Moselle rivers. It is navigable for most of its course, and is connected by canal with other major European river systems.

RHÔNE, a west European river that flows some 500 miles through Switzerland and France. It rises in the Swiss Alps, passes through Lake Geneva and crosses into France. Joined at Lyon by the Saône River, it turns south and empties into the Mediterranean Sea west of Marseilles. Its large delta around Marseilles, called the Camargue, is the center of French rice-growing and processing.

RIVERS. The world's longest river is Africa's 4,145-mile-long Nile. Second in length, but greater in volume, is the Amazon, which flows for 3,900 miles in South America. The Mississippi-Missouri-Red Rock river system is the third largest, extending for a total of 3,860 miles in North America.
The Ob-Irtysh waterway, in western Asia, is 3,460 miles long and ranks fourth. The Yangtze, flowing for 3,400 miles in eastern Asia, is the world's fifth longest river. Europe's

longest river is the Volga, which follows a curving course for 2,290 miles in east-central Europe. The Murray-Darling waterway, 2,310 miles, is Australia's longest river. The Antarctic continent has no rivers.

RIVIERA, a Mediterranean seacoast in southern France and northwestern Italy. Its blue water and white beaches have made it one of the world's most popular resort areas.

ROSS SEA, an arm of the Pacific Ocean extending into Antarctica between Victoria Land and Marie Byrd Land. McMurdo Sound is an inlet of Ross Sea in the coast of Victoria Land.

RUB AL KHALI, or Empty Quarter, a desert region, with an area of some 300,000 square miles, in the southern half of the Arabian Peninsula. It contains no known vegetation or sources of water and is uninhabited.

RUDOLF, an African lake in northwestern Kenya in the Great Rift Valley. It has an area of about 2,400 square miles, and is fed by the Omo River.

RUFIJI, an African river that rises in the plateau of south-central Tanzania. It flows northeast and east to empty into the Indian Ocean through a wide delta.

RUWENZORI, an African mountain massif between lakes Albert and Edward on the Uganda-Congo border. The highest nonvolcanic peak in Africa, its highest part, Mt. Stanley, consists of two summits—Mt. Margherita and Mt. Alexandria—both over 16,700 feet. The Ruwenzori is generally accepted as being the "Mountains of the Moon" of the ancient geographers.

SABARMATI, a river of western India that rises in the Aravalli Mountains. It flows southward through a rich agricultural region for about 200 miles to the Gulf of Cambay.

SAHARA, a desert region of North Africa extending about 3,000 miles from west to east and 1,000 miles from north to south. It is the world's largest desert, and its relief is extremely varied.

The Sahara includes high, deeply dissected plateaus, such as the Tibesti, Ahaggar, and Aïr, the summits of which may attain 10,000 feet, and depressions, such as the Bodélé, or Chad, which are less than 500 feet above sea level. The landscape includes both sandy desert, or erg, and stony desert, or reg.

Rainfall averages less than 10 inches a year, and the only permanent rivers are the Nile and Niger. Inhabited largely by nomadic peoples, the desert has rich mineral deposits.

SAKHALIN, an island about 550 miles long and 30 miles wide, located in the Sea of Okhotsk, an arm of the Pacific Ocean. It lies off the eastern coast of the Siberian region of the Soviet Union, of which it is a part. Sakhalin is separated from the mainland by the Tatar Strait and from the Japanese island of Hokkaido by the Soya, or La Perouse, Strait. Two parallel mountain ranges on the island are divided by a central valley through which the Tym and Poronai rivers flow.

SALWEEN, a major Asian river that rises in the Thanglha Mountains of Tibet. It flows east and south for about 1,750 miles through China and Burma to empty into the Gulf of Martaban, an arm of the Andaman Sea.

SANAGHA, a river of southwestern Africa that rises in Cameroon and flows southeast to join the Congo river below its confluence with the Ubangi River.

SÃO FRANCISCO, a South American river that flows northward from the highlands of east-central Brazil to the arid northeast, and then eastward to the Atlantic Ocean. It is partially navigable, but broken by rapids.

SATPURA, a mountain range in west-central India, between the Narbada and the Tapti rivers, with an average elevation of about 3,000 feet. The mountains are forested and contain manganese and copper.

SAVA, a river of northern Yugoslavia that rises in the Karawanken Alps on the Italian-Yugoslav border. It flows eastward for some 450 miles to join the Danube at Belgrade. The Drina, the Boma, and the Verbas rivers are its main tributaries.

SAYAN, a mountain range of the Soviet Union that lies to the east of the Altai, in the southern part of the Irkutsk region. It has a peak of over 11,000 feet. The lower slopes of the mountains are forested and contain important deposits of iron ore, gold, silver, mercury, and graphite.

SCANDINAVIA, a peninsula of northwestern Europe washed by the Arctic Ocean on the north, the Norwegian Sea on the west, the North Sea, Skagerrak and Kattegat straits on the south, and the Baltic Sea and Gulf of Bothnia on the southeast. Western Scandinavia is mountainous; lowlands occupy the east. Much of it lies above the Arctic Circle, and the climate is cold. It is shared by Norway, Sweden, and Finland.

SCHELDE, a Belgian river that rises in northern France. It flows north and west for some 250 miles to empty into the North Sea through a broad estuary near the port of Antwerp.

SCILLY ISLANDS, a group of about 140 British islands in the Atlantic Ocean off the Land's End cape in southwestern Britain. Once a pirates' haven, today they are important for vegetable and flower growing.

SEINE, a river of northern France that rises in the highlands northwest of Dijon. It flows through Troyes and Paris and empties into the English Channel through a broad estuary.

SEISTAN, a marshy area of western Asia south of the Plateau of Iran. It is on the Iran-Afghanistan border and includes Lake Helmand.

SELENGE, an Asian river that rises in northwestern Mongolia and flows northeast for about 750 miles into the Soviet Union's Lake Baykal. Its principal tributary is the 300-mile-long Orkhon, which joins it near Mongolia's northern border.

SÉNÉGAL, a river of western Africa, formed by the joining of the Bafing and Bakoy rivers in western Mali. It flows in a generally northwest direction, forming the boundary between Mauritania and Senegal, and empties into the Atlantic Ocean. Including the Bafing, the Sénégal River is over 1,000 miles long.

SEVERNAYA ZEMLYA, or Northern Land, a group of Arctic islands lying to the north of Cape Chelyuskin on the Taimyr Peninsula of the Soviet Union. The group consists of three main islands, and many smaller ones, and covers an area of over 13,000 square miles. They divide the Laptev Sea from the Kara Sea and are separated from the mainland by Vilkitski Strait.

SEVERN, a river of southeastern Britain that rises in east-central Wales, flows northeast into England, then east and south into the Bristol Channel through a broad estuary.

SHANNON, a river in Ireland that rises in the north and flows southward for 250 miles. It drains the north-central, central, and southwestern parts of the island, and enters the Atlantic Ocean through a long and deep estuary.

SHETLAND ISLANDS, a British archipelago in the Atlantic Ocean northeast of the Orkney Islands. The Shetlands have an area of about 550 square miles. Livestock herding and fishing are the principal occupations.

SI, a river about 1,000 miles long in southern China. Formed by the Hungshui and the Yu, it enters the South China Sea near Canton.

SIAM, GULF OF, an arm of the South China Sea on the southeast coast of Thailand. It lies between the Malay peninsula on the southwest and Cambodia and Vietnam on the northeast.

SICILY, the largest island of the Mediterranean. A part of Italy, it is separated from the southwestern tip of the mainland by the narrow Strait of Messina. Most of Sicily is mountainous and rugged, and the climate is dry and mild. The island produces olives and has deposits of sulfur, petroleum, and natural gas.

SIDRA, GULF OF, an inlet of the Mediterranean Sea on the coast of northern Libya.

SIERRA MADRE, three high mountain ranges that dominate the landscape of Mexico. The Sierra Madre Oriental runs from north to south in central

NATURAL FEATURES

Mexico. The Sierra Madre Occidental lies in the west, and the Sierra Madre del Sur is in the southwest.

All three ranges have peaks between 12,000 and 15,000 feet, and they converge in south-central Mexico. The lower slopes are densely forested, and the mountains are rich in minerals.

SINAI, a triangular peninsula that forms the easternmost portion of the United Arab Republic (Egypt). It extends southward from a 150-mile-long Mediterranean coast for over 200 miles to the northern tip of the Red Sea. Two extensions of the Red Sea—the Gulf of Suez and the Gulf of Aqaba—form the western and eastern boundaries of the peninsula.

This dry, barren land, inhabited by nomads, is considered a part of Asia rather than Africa. The extensive central plateau of El-Tih rises to the south and culminates in Mt. Katherina, over 8,000 feet high. Nearby is Musa Mountain, thought by many to be the Mount Sinai of the Old Testament. Sinai is a source of crude oil, iron, and manganese. The peninsula was occupied by Israeli forces in 1967.

SITTANG, a river of east-central Burma. It rises in the central mountains and flows southward for about 350 miles to the Gulf of Martaban.

SIWALIK, a mountain range of north-central India, in the foothills of the Himalayas. The average elevation is 2,500 feet. It is an important source of forest products and contains some copper.

SKAGERRAK, a strait between Norway and Denmark, about 150 miles long and 80 miles wide. It leads into the North Sea in the southwest and the Kattegat in the northeast, and forms an important link in the North Sea-Baltic waterway.

SOBAEK, a mountain range in Korea extending from the east-central coast to the southwestern tip of the peninsula.

SOCOTRA, an island in the Indian Ocean about 120 miles east of Africa's Cape Guardafui and 220 miles south of the coast of Arabia. About 1,380 square miles in area, it consists largely of a barren plateau with mountains rising to 4,500 feet.

SOMME, a river that rises in north-central France and flows westward for 150 miles to the English Channel.

SOUTH AMERICA, a continent in the southern half of the western hemisphere, with an area of nearly 7 million square miles and a 1967 population of about 175 million. It is bordered on the north by the Caribbean Sea, on the east by the Atlantic Ocean, on the south by the Drake Passage, which separates it from Antarctica, and on the west by the Pacific Ocean.

High mountains of the Andes system tower over a narrow coastal plain in the west. The interior consists of lowlands that are densely forested in the north and swampy or arid in the south. Highlands dominate the east.

SOUTH CHINA SEA, a body of water between southeastern China and Indochina on the west, and the Philippine and Indonesian islands on the east and south. About 1.3 million square miles in area, it is the world's largest sea.

SUDETES, a mountain system in east-central Europe extending about 200 miles along the German-Czechoslovakian and the Polish-Czechoslovakian borders. Elevations are less than 5,300 feet.

SULAIMAN, a mountain range in central West Pakistan between the Indus valley and northeastern Baluchistan. It has a peak over 11,000 feet, and its most important passes are the Bolan and the Gumal, both of which lie at about 6,000 feet.

SUNGARI, the chief river of Manchuria, in northeastern China. It rises near Korea and flows north and west for 800 miles to join the Amur on the China-Soviet Union border. The Nonni is its most important tributary.

SUTHERLAND, a waterfall in southwestern New Zealand. The fifth highest in the world, it falls 1,904 feet.

SYR, an Asian river extending 1,500 miles from headwaters in the Tien Mountains to the Aral Sea of the Soviet Union. In its upper course, the river flows through deep gorges and is called Naryn. The river is navigable for 850 miles in its lower course and, flowing through an arid and semi-arid area, is used extensively for irrigation.

TAEBAEK, a mountain range in Korea running parallel to the eastern coast of the peninsula.

TAGUS, or Tejo, a major river of the Iberian Peninsula that rises in Spain's eastern mountains, flows west across Spain, and forms a small section of the border with Portugal before turning southwest to enter the Atlantic through a broad estuary at Lisbon. Nearly 600 miles long, it is the longest river on the Iberian peninsula.

TAKLA MAKAN, a desert region near the western border of China, north of Tibet and the Himalayas. It lies in the basin of the Tarim River.

TANA, an East African river that rises near Mt. Kenya in south-central Kenya. It flows in a great arc for some 500 miles to the Indian Ocean at Formosa Bay.

TANGANYIKA, an African lake on the border of Tanganyika and the Congo (Kinshasa). Long and narrow, it has an area of over 12,500 square miles, and its depth of some 4,700 feet makes it one of the world's deepest lakes.

TAPA, a mountain range of west-central China, with peaks to about 9,500 feet. The Yangtze River cuts spectacular gorges through the mountains.

TARANTO, GULF OF, an inlet of the Mediterranean Sea on the southeastern coast of Italy.

TASMANIA, an island off the southeastern coast of Australia, lying between the Indian Ocean and the Tasman Sea. Tasmania, about 180 miles by 190 miles, is geologically a continuation of the Australian continent. A high central plateau is surrounded by forested mountains in the west and agricultural lands in the north and southeast.

TEHUANTEPEC, GULF OF, an inlet of the Pacific Ocean on the coast of the Isthmus of Tehuantepec, in southwestern Mexico. Its irregular coastline is backed by steep mountains.

THAMES, a river about 200 miles long in southern Britain. It rises in Gloucestershire, flows east into the densely settled fertile English Lowlands, through London, and empties into the North Sea.

THANGLHA, a mountain range in the Tibet region of China. It lies north of the Himalayas and south of the Kunlun Mountains.

IRISH TOURIST BOARD

IRELAND'S SHANNON RIVER, some 250 miles long, flows past St. John's Castle in Limerick.

THAR, a desert on the Indian subcontinent between the Aravalli Mountains and the Indus River.

TIBER, a river of central Italy, about 250 miles long. It rises in the central Apennines, flows south through Umbria and northern Latium, turns southwest through Rome, and enters the Tyrrhenian Sea at Ostia.

TIBESTI, a high mountain range in the central Sahara of northern Africa. Situated in northern Chad and in Libya, the massif is approximately 250 miles in diameter. Its rugged peaks, of volcanic origin, reach their highest point in Koussi Volcano, over 11,000 feet.

TIERRA DEL FUEGO, a group of islands at the southern tip of South America. They lie south of the Strait of Magellan and extend to Cape Horn, a headland on the southernmost island. They are divided between Chile and Argentina.

TIGRIS, a river of southwestern Asia that rises in two headstreams in the Taurus Mountains of eastern Turkey. After forming a small part of the Turkish-Syrian border, the river flows southeastward through Iraq for over 1,100 miles until it joins the Euphrates River at Qurna, to form the combined river of Shatt al-Arab. The Tigris has several tributaries, including the Great Zab, the Little Zab, and the Diyala.

TIMOR, an island of the lesser Sunda group lying across the Timor Sea from northeastern Australia. It consists of a mountainous core rimmed with lowlands. Timor is divided between Portugal and Indonesia.

TISZA, a river of eastern Europe that rises in the Carpathian Mountains in the Soviet Union's Ukrainian republic. It flows west and south for about 850 miles on a tortuous, meandering course to join the Danube River about 30 miles north of Belgrade, in Yugoslavia.

TITICACA, a lake in South America on the border of Peru and Bolivia. It lies more than 12,500 feet above sea level in the altiplano of the central Andes. Lake Titicaca is about 110 miles long, 35 miles wide, and 700 feet deep.

TONLE SAP, a lake in Southeast Asia, in west central Cambodia. Literally "Great Lake," its area varies between 1,000 and 9,500 square miles according to the season.

TORRES STRAIT, a channel between northeastern Australia and southeastern New Guinea. It links the Arafura Sea to the west with the Coral Sea to the east.

TROODOS, or Olympus, a mountain range of west-central Cyprus. It contains deposits of copper pyrites, chrome ore, and asbestos. The highest point is Mt. Troodos, over 6,400 feet.

TSINLING, a mountain range of central China, running from east to west between the Han and the Wei rivers.

THE VAAL RIVER OF SOUTH AFRICA flows through the Transvaal into the Cape Province.

The mountains rise to about 11,000 feet and are the traditional dividing line between north and south China.

TUGELA, a series of waterfalls in eastern South Africa on the Tugela River. The world's second highest waterfalls, they drop a total of 3,110 feet.

TUMEN, a 220-mile-long Asian river that rises in northeastern Korea and forms part of the border of China and Korea. It flows generally northeast, turning sharply southeast at the tip of Korea to flow into the Sea of Japan.

TUNGTING, a large, shallow lake in southeastern China. Fed by the Yuan, Lin, and Tzu rivers, it also serves as a reservoir for the Yangtze River during the high water season. Its area varies with the season from 2,000 square miles to 4,000 square miles. The basin is a rich agricultural region.

TUZ, a salt lake of western Asia, in central Turkey. It lies at an altitude of 3,100 feet and at times is dry.

TYRRHENIAN SEA, an arm of the Mediterranean Sea. It lies between Italy on the east, Corsica and Sardinia on the west, and Sicily on the south.

UBANGI, a river of central Africa, formed in the northern Congo (Kinshasa) by the joining of the Bomi and Uele rivers. It flows generally southwest for about 700 miles to the Congo River. The Ubangi forms part of the boundaries between the Congo (Kinshasa) and the Central African Republic, and the Congo (Kinshasa) and the Congo (Brazzaville).

UNGAVA, a bay on the northern coast of Quebec, Canada, between the Ungava Peninsula, on the west, and Labrador, on the east.

URAL, a river in the west-central Soviet Union. It rises in the southern Ural Mountains and flows southwest, and south again, emptying into the Caspian Sea. The river is about 1,500 miles long.

URAL MOUNTAINS, a mountain system in the Soviet Union that extends from the Arctic Ocean to the Ural River, forming the geographic boundary between Europe and Asia. The Urals can be divided into three sections—the Northern Urals, which contain the highest peaks; the Central Urals, which are gently rounded and are crossed by rail lines; and the Southern Urals, which are formed by a series of parallel ridges.

URUGUAY, a 980-mile-long river of southeastern South America. It rises in the Serra do Mar of southern Brazil and flows west, southwest, and then south into the Río de la Plata.

VAAL, a river in South Africa. It rises in the Transvaal and flows generally west for about 700 miles before joining the Orange River in northern Cape Province.

VAN, a large salt lake of western Asia, in eastern Turkey near the border of Iran. It has an area of some 1,425 square miles and lies at an altitude of 5,260 feet.

VANCOUVER, a Canadian island lying off the southwestern coast of British Columbia. It is separated from the Canadian mainland by the Strait of Georgia and Queen Charlotte Sound. The Juan de Fuca Strait separates Vancouver from Washington in the United States.

VÄNERN, a Scandinavian lake in southwestern Sweden. It has an area of 2,141 square miles.

VÄTTERN, a Scandinavian lake in southern Sweden, east of Lake Vänern. It has an area of 733 square miles and is connected to the Baltic through the Göta Canal.

VENEZUELA, GULF OF, an inlet of the Caribbean Sea on the north coast of South America. It lies between the Paraguana Peninsula of Venezuela, on the east and the Guajira Peninsula of Colombia, on the west, and extends south as Lake Maracaibo.

VERKHOYANSK, a mountain range of the eastern Soviet Union, in northeastern Siberia, east of the Lena River valley and west of the Cherskiy range. The mountains have a peak of nearly 8,000 feet and contain deposits of zinc, lead, coal, and other minerals.

NATURAL FEATURES

VESUVIUS, an active volcano in Italy, lying on the eastern shore of the Bay of Naples. Vesuvius is about 4,000 feet above sea level, but its exact height varies with each eruption.

VICTORIA, a lake in east-central Africa, the world's second largest lake. Lake Victoria is bounded by Uganda on the northwest and north, Kenya on the east, and Tanzania on the southeast, south, and southwest. The lake, which is about 250 miles long and 200 miles wide, is the major source of the Nile River.

VICTORIA FALLS, a waterfall in southern Africa on the Zambezi River between Zambia and Rhodesia. The falls are about 350 feet high.

VINDHYA, a mountain range in central India that runs from southwest to northeast and separates the Ganges basin from the Deccan Plateau. The highest peaks are about 5,000 feet. The Narbada River flows along the southern foot of the range.

VINSON MASSIF, the highest Antarctic peak, 16,864 feet above sea level. It is in the Ellsworth Mountains near the Filchner Ice Shelf at the head of the Weddell Sea.

VISTULA, or Wista, a river in Poland, over 650 miles long. The Vistula rises in the southwest, near the border with Czechoslovakia, and flows northeast in an arc as far as Warsaw. At Warsaw it turns west and then flows north into the Baltic Sea.

VOLGA, the longest river of the Soviet Union and of Europe, 2,290 miles. It rises in the Kalinin Region of the northwestern Soviet Union and follows a winding course to the Caspian Sea. The Volga flows first east and southeast to Kazan and then generally south to Astrakhan, where it forms an extensive delta.

Under the Greater Volga Scheme, dams have been built on the river for flood control, irrigation, and the generation of power. A comprehensive series of canals joins the Volga to the Baltic and Black Sea river systems.

VOLTA, a river of western Africa, some 900 miles long. The Volta, which empties into the Gulf of Guinea, is formed by the joining of the Black Volta and the White Volta in central Ghana.

The Black Volta rises in southwestern Upper Volta and flows northeast and then south, forming parts of the Ghana-Upper Volta and Ghana-Ivory Coast borders. The White Volta rises in central Upper Volta and flows generally south.

WATERFALLS. Two of the world's highest waterfalls, measured by their total drop, are in Venezuela, in South America. The world's highest fall, 3,212-foot Angel Falls, and the fourth highest, 2,000-foot Cuqenán, are in southeastern Venezuela.

Tugela, in South Africa, 3,110 feet, is the second highest waterfall, and the 2,425-foot Yosemite waterfall in North America is the world's third highest. The fifth highest waterfall is Sutherland, in New Zealand, which drops 1,904 feet.

Europe's highest waterfall, 1,250 feet, is the Krimml in Austria. Asia's highest known fall is only 830 feet high—the Gersoppa Falls on the Shanan River in southwestern India.

WEDDELL SEA, an arm of the South Atlantic Ocean extending into Antarctica between the Antarctic Peninsula, and Princess Martha Coast in Coats Land.

WESER, a West German river, formed by the confluence of the Fulda and Werra rivers in central Germany. It flows generally north for nearly 300 miles across the North German Plain and empties into the North Sea at Bremerhaven.

WEST INDIES, a group of islands in the western hemisphere, lying between southeastern North America and northern South America, and enclosing the Caribbean Sea. The group is divided into the Greater Antilles (Cuba, Hispaniola, Jamaica, and Puerto Rico), the Lesser Antilles (the Virgin, Leeward, and Windward islands, including Trinidad, Tobago, and Barbados), and the Bahama Islands.

WIGHT, a British island and county in the English Channel off the southern coast of Britain. It is a resort center.

WINNIPEG, a lake in south-central Canada, north of Winnipeg, Manitoba. It is nearly 9,400 square miles in area and is fed by the Winnipeg and Red Rivers from the south. It is drained to the north by the Nelson River.

WITWATERSRAND, a region in eastern South Africa that consists of a 150-mile-long ridge where several industrial cities, including Johannesburg, Germiston, and Krugersdorp, are located. It has the most productive gold field in the world, and also yields manganese and coal.

WORLD. The world has an area of 196,940,000 square miles. Slightly less than 30 percent of that is land and slightly more than 70 percent is water. The land area is divided into seven continents—Asia, the largest; Africa; North America; South America; Europe; Australia; and Antarctica, the smallest. The world's largest island, Greenland, lies partly in the Arctic Ocean and partly in the North Atlantic Ocean.

More than 90 percent of the world's water area is made up of four oceans—the Pacific, the largest; the Atlantic; the Indian; and the Arctic. There are also smaller bodies of intercontinental water, or seas. The largest are the South China Sea and the Caribbean Sea. The largest inland body of water is the Caspian Sea, lying partly in Europe and partly in Asia.

The lowest and highest points on the earth's land surface are both in Asia. The lowest point, 1,296 feet below sea level, is on the shores of the Dead Sea, in western Asia. The highest point, 29,028 feet, is at the top of Mt. Everest, the highest mountain, in south-central Asia.

The world's longest river, the Nile, flows for 4,145 miles in northern Africa. The river with the greatest volume is the Amazon, in South America. The highest waterfall in the world is also in South America—Angel Falls, with a total drop of 3,212 feet.

YALU, a river that rises in northeastern Korea and forms the western part of the Korea-China border. It flows for 300 miles, emptying into Korea Bay.

YANA, a river in Siberia, in the northeastern Soviet Union. Three main headstreams rise in the Verkhoyansk Mountains, and the river flows northward for about 750 miles to the Laptev Sea.

YANGTZE, one of the principal rivers of China and of the world. It rises in Tibet and follows a twisting course for 3,400 miles before it empties into the East China Sea. The portion east of its rugged gorges—about one-sixth of its length—is navigable by ocean vessels.

The tributaries of the Yangtze include the Kialing, the Yalung, the Chinsha, the Wu, and the Han. It flows through rich farmland, and over one-tenth of the world's population lives in its basin.

YELLOW SEA, a shallow arm of the Pacific Ocean between the Chinese mainland and the Korean peninsula.

YENISEY, a major river of the Soviet Union located in central Russia. It is formed from two rivers, the Greater Yenisey, rising in the Sayan Mountains of Mongolia, and the Lesser Yenisey, rising in the Siberian highlands. They meet at Kyzyl to form the Yenisey proper.

Major tributaries of the Yenisey include the Lower Tunguska, Stony Tunguska, Angara, and Abakan rivers. The Yenisey empties into the Yenisey Gulf of the Kara Sea.

YUCATAN, a large peninsula off Mexico's southeastern coast. It lies between Campeche Bay and the Caribbean Sea and is separated from Cuba, to the northeast, by the Yucatan Channel. The terrain is low and barren and consists largely of swamps and semi-desert.

ZAGROS, a mountain range in southwestern Iran that forms the western and southern borders of the Iranian plateau. The range is about 1,000 miles long and rises to a height of 15,000 feet.

ZAMBEZI, a river in southern Africa that rises in eastern Angola. It flows southeast, then northeast, and turns southeast again over the Cohorabasa Rapids in Mozambique before entering the Mozambique Channel. The Zambezi follows the boundary between Zambia and Rhodesia, and forms the Victoria Falls near Livingston, in Zambia. Its tributaries include the Kabompo, Cuando, Kafue, and Luangwa rivers.

CITIES OF THE WORLD

ABADAN, in southwestern Iran, situated on the northern end of Abadan Island, at the head of the Persian Gulf. Pipelines link the city with oil fields to the north, and Abadan is a major oil refining and shipping center of the Middle East. Pop., 1963 est., 302,200.

ABIDJAN, in West Africa, the capital of the Ivory Coast. The city is located on the Ebrie Lagoon, which is connected to the Gulf of Guinea by the Vridi Canal. Abidjan has modern port facilities and is the terminus of a highway network and a railroad from Ouagadougou, in neighboring Upper Volta. Pop., 1963 est., 250,800.

ACAJUTLA, a seaport on the Pacific coast of El Salvador, located about 50 miles southwest of San Salvador. The city is connected by railroad and highway to all parts of the country. New harbor facilities were constructed between 1956 and 1961, making Acajutla one of the most modern ports in Central America. The city also has oil refineries and a large fertilizer plant. Pop., 1965 est., 15,000.

ACCRA, on the northwestern coast of Africa, the capital of Ghana. The city lies on the Gulf of Guinea and is a seaport. Accra has an international airport and is linked by railroad to the cacao-growing districts of Ghana's interior. The University of Ghana is in Accra. Pop., 1966 est., urban area, 600,200.

ADANA, in southern Turkey, on the Seyhan River about 30 miles inland from the Mediterranean Sea. The city is the commercial and industrial center of the surrounding Cilician Plain. The manufacture of cotton textiles is the chief industry. Pop., 1965, 290,515.

ADDIS ABABA, in northern Africa, the capital and largest city of Ethiopia. It is situated in a hilly region in the central part of the country. Addis Ababa is the country's chief commercial, industrial, and educational center. Its industries produce cement, cigarettes, metal and leather goods, and soap. Ethiopia's first university, Haile Selassie I University, was founded at Addis Ababa in 1961. Pop., 1965 est., 560,000.

ADELAIDE, the capital of South Australia, located on the Torrens River about seven miles inland from the Gulf of St. Vincent. The city has knitting mills, food processing plants, and automobile works. It is the seat of the University of Adelaide. Pop., 1966, urban area, 726,930.

ADEN, in South Yemen, located on southern Arabia's Aden Peninsula, which extends into the Gulf of Aden. Situated along the important shipping lane between the Mediterranean Sea and the Indian Ocean, Aden is a leading port. Light industries produce textiles, cigarettes, soap, and metal utensils. Pop., 1964 est., urban area, 225,000.

AGANA, the capital of Guam, an island territory of the United States in the West Pacific Ocean. Agana is located on the island's west coast, on Agana Bay, about eight miles northeast of Apra Harbor. Pop., 1960, urban area, 1,642.

AGRA, in northern India, on the Jumna River in Uttar Pradesh State. One of the oldest cities in India, Agra is famous as the site of the Taj Mahal, the Red Fort, and other historic monuments. It is an important agricultural trading center and is well known for gold and silver inlay work. Pop., 1966 est., urban area, 579,600.

AHMADABAD, in northwestern India, on the Sabarmati River. It is the capital of Gujarat State. Ahmadabad is a major commercial and industrial center noted for the manufacture of cotton textiles. Metal-working is an important handicraft. Pop., 1966 est., urban area, 1,381,300.

AHMADNAGAR, in west central India, in Maharashtra State, 65 miles northeast of Poona. It is a district capital and an important market town. Pop., 1966, 126,353.

AHVAZ, in southwestern Iran, the capital of Khuzistan Province. Ahvaz is the commercial and transportation center of an oil producing area. It is connected by rail to ports on the Persian Gulf. Pipelines that carry oil to refineries at Abadan also pass through the city. Pop., 1963 est., 155,100.

AIÚN, the capital of the province of Spanish Sahara in Spanish West Africa. It is located on the El Hamra River, about 35 miles from the Atlantic Ocean. Aiún's economy is based on coastal fishing and nomadic grazing in the desert. Pop., 1961 est., 5,500.

AJMER, in northwestern India, in Rajasthan State, 84 miles southwest of Jaipur. Ajmer is an important trade center, especially for salt, and has a thriving cotton textile industry. It is noted for its historic monuments and its educational institutions, including Mayo Rajkumar College, which was founded in 1875. Pop., 1966, 249,699.

AKITA, the capital of Japan's Akita Prefecture, at the mouth of the Omono River near the northwest coast of Honshu. The chief industries include oil refining and the manufacture of textiles. Bronze, silver, and gold ornamental articles are also produced. Pop., 1965, 216,607.

AKYAB, the capital of the Arakan Division of Burma, located at the mouth of the Kaladan River on the Bay of Bengal. Akyab is one of Burma's chief seaports and exports much of the rice grown in the surrounding area. Pop., 1953, 42,329.

ALBERTVILLE, in the Congo (Kinshasa), located in Katanga Province on the western shore of Lake Tanganyika. It is a port and is connected by rail to Kabalo and the Congo River transport system. There is steamer service between Albertville and Kigoma, Tanganyika, on the eastern shore of the lake. Pop., 1958 est., 29,500.

ALEPPO, in northwestern Syria, an important trading center that is connected by rail with major cities in Turkey and Iraq. There is some light manufacturing, and local factories produce soap, carpets, textiles, and vegetable oils. Pop., 1965 est., 599,700.

ALEXANDRIA, situated west of the Rosetta mouth of the Nile River on the Mediterranean Sea, the principal seaport and second largest city of the United Arab Republic (Egypt). The city has an eastern and a western harbor, but the western harbor is deeper and handles most maritime traffic. Raw cotton is the main export.

UNITED NATIONS
ABIDJAN, the capital of the Ivory Coast, is one of West Africa's most modern cities.

CITIES OF THE WORLD

Alexandria was founded by Alexander the Great in 332 BC and became an important port and intellectual center. It was famous for its lighthouse, which was one of the seven wonders of the ancient world; its library; and its school of medicine. Pop., 1966, 1,800,951.

AL FAYYUM, in the United Arab Republic (Egypt), west of the Nile River and about 70 miles southwest of Cairo. It is a provincial capital and a commercial center. Pop., 1963 est., 121,100.

ALGIERS, the capital of Algeria, the major Mediterranean port on the northwest coast of Africa. The city's port facilities handle such exports as wool, fruit and vegetables, and wine, most of which are sent to France. Local industries produce cement, metal products, shoes, and perfume. Tourism is also important. Pop., 1966, 943,142.

ALIGARH, in Uttar Pradesh State in north central India, on the upper Ganges plain. Aligarh is an important trade center for the agricultural produce of the surrounding area, including grain and sugarcane. Its chief industries are butter production and cotton processing. The city is also the seat of Aligarh Muslim University. Pop., 1966, 208,167.

ALLAHABAD, in Uttar Pradesh State in northern India, at the confluence of the Ganges and Jumna rivers. The city is a shipping and trade center for local agricultural produce, especially sugarcane and cotton. Allahabad is also a holy city for Hindus. It was built in 1583 by the Mughal emperor Akbar the Great and has many historic monuments. Pop., 1966 est., urban area, 483,200.

ALLEPPEY, a seaport on the west coast of India, in Kerala State. The city is a center for the manufacture of coir, or coconut fiber, products. Coir, copra, coconuts, pepper, ginger, and cardamoms are the port's major exports. Pop., 1966 est., 150,700.

ALMA ATA, in Soviet Central Asia, the capital of the Kazakh Soviet Socialist Republic of the Soviet Union. Founded in 1855 as a military post, the city developed as a trading and transportation center. Alma Ata is the hub of a large fruit-growing area. The principal industries include fruit and vegetable canning and textile manufacture. Pop., 1966 est., 634,000.

AMBALA, in northern India, the capital of Punjab State. The city is a railroad junction and trade center for the surrounding area. Pop., 1966 est., urban area, 197,600.

AMMAN, the capital of Jordan, in the northwestern part of the country about 25 miles northeast of the Dead Sea. Amman is Jordan's chief industrial and commercial center and the hub of a rail and highway network. Industries include food processing and the manufacture of textiles, leather goods, cement, and tiles. Pop., 1966 est., 330,000.

AMSTERDAM'S CANALS accommodate houseboats and the barges that carry commercial traffic.

AMOY, a seaport in southeastern China, located on a small island off the coast of Fukien Province. The city has an excellent harbor and was a major Chinese port until 1949, when it was blockaded by Nationalist Chinese forces based on nearby Quemoy Island. Pop., 1953, 224,300.

AMRAVATI, in central India, the capital of the Berar Division and Amravati District of Maharashtra State. The city is a cotton trading center and has cotton gins and oilseed mills. Pop., 1966 est., 156,600.

AMRITSAR, in northeastern India, the capital of Amritsar District in Punjab State. The city is an important commercial and manufacturing center. The principal industry is textiles. Amritsar is the site of the Golden Temple, the major shrine of the Sikh religion. Pop., 1966 est., urban area, 432,000.

AMSTERDAM, the capital and largest city of the Netherlands, located in the province of North Holland. The city lies at the junction of the Amstel and IJ rivers near the IJsselmeer (formerly the Zuider Zee) and is connected by canal with the North Sea and the Rhine River.

Amsterdam is the commercial and industrial center of the Netherlands and one of its busiest ports. The most important manufactures include iron and steel, machinery, chemicals, paper, printed matter, and beer. Amsterdam also is a center of the diamond-cutting industry. Pop., 1965 est., 864,900.

ANKARA, the capital and second largest city of Turkey, located on the central Anatolian plateau on the Ankara River. The city is almost completely modern and is an important commercial and industrial center.

Ankara markets and processes agricultural products of the surrounding region and is famous for the production of Angora goat wool, or mohair. Other manufactures include beer, cement, textiles, leather goods, and tile. Pop., 1965, urban area, 902,216.

ANNABA, a port on the northeast coast of Algeria, near the border with Tunisia, about 260 miles east of Algiers. Annaba was formerly called Bône. Manufactures include tobacco and olive oil. Exports include phosphates and iron ore. Pop., 1966, urban area, 168,790.

ANSHAN, located in the Chinese province of Liaoning in southern Manchuria. The city, which lies near large coal and iron ore deposits, is China's largest producer of iron and steel. Pop., 1957 est., 805,000.

ANTUNG, a seaport on the northeast coast of China, situated at the mouth of the Yalu River in Liaoning Province. The chief export is timber, which is floated down the Yalu from the interior. Antung's industries include soybean processing and the manufacture of silk and synthetic fibers, matches, and paper pulp. Pop., 1953 est., 360,000.

ANTWERP, the second largest city in Belgium and the country's chief port. It is located on the Schelde River about 50 miles inland from the North Sea. Antwerp has one of the world's largest harbors and is among the busiest ports in Europe.

Antwerp's major industries include shipbuilding, metallurgy, brewing, distilling, lacemaking, sugar refining, and diamond cutting. The city has many historic buildings and art treasures. Pop., 1965 est., urban area, 657,500.

APARRI, a seaport in the Philippines, located in Cagayan Province on the northern end of Luzon Island, at the mouth of the Cagayan River. The city lies at the head of the fertile Cagayan valley and exports its agricultural produce, including tobacco, corn, and rice. Fishing and lumbering are also important. Pop., 1960, urban area, 33,500.

APIA, the capital, largest city, and chief port of Western Samoa, in the northwest South Pacific Ocean. Apia is located on the north coast of the island of Upolu, the largest and southernmost of the Marianas Archipelago. Apia is a commercial center. Chief exports are copra, bananas, and cocoa. Pop., 1961, urban area, 21,699.

AQABA, in southwestern Jordan, situated at the southern end of the great valley Wadi el'Araba on the Gulf of Aqaba. Known in ancient times as Elath, it commanded the caravan trade route from Egypt to Arabia. Jordan's only seaport, Aqaba began to be developed in 1952, when new harbor facilities were installed. Pop., 1965 est., 10,560.

ARAD, in western Romania, the capital of Arad District. The city is situated on the Mures River at the junction of the Hungarian lowland and the Transylvanian highlands. Arad is a commercial and industrial center that manufactures transport equipment, furniture, leather goods, machinery, and flour. Pop., 1965 est., urban area, 125,800.

ARKHANGEL'SK, a seaport on the northeastern coast of the Soviet Union, at the mouth of the Dvina River on the Gulf of Dvina, an inlet of the White Sea. Due to its northern location, Arkhangel'sk is blocked by ice for six months of the year, although it is kept open longer by ice-breakers. The port has numerous sawmills, and timber is its chief export. Railroads connect the city with Moscow and Leningrad. Pop., 1966 est., 308,000.

ASAHIGAWA, located on Hokkaido Island, Japan. It lies on the Ishikari River in the central part of the island in the midst of an important rice-growing region. Asahigawa is a major railroad junction and served as the headquarters of the Japanese army during World War II. Pop., 1965, 245,246.

ASHKHABAD, in the southwestern Soviet Union, the capital of the Turkmen Soviet Socialist Republic. Located near the Iranian border in the Akhal-Tekinsk Oasis, the city is a major commercial center on the Trans-Caspian Railroad. Ashkhabad is joined by oil pipeline to Krasnovodsk on the Caspian Sea. Pop., 1966 est., 230,000.

ASMARA, the capital of Eritrea, a province of Ethiopia, in East Africa. The city is the trade center of an agricultural region that produces fruit, vegetables, coffee, and oilseeds. Asmara is a modern city that has numerous attractive public and private buildings. It is connected by rail to the port of Massawa, 40 miles to the northeast on the Red Sea, and by highway to other Ethiopian cities. Pop., 1964 est., 131,800.

ASUNCIÓN, the capital of Paraguay, a port on the Paraguay River about 630 miles north of Buenos Aires. It is the country's political, economic, and cultural center. It is connected to Buenos Aires by air and rail and to other American capitals by air.

Paraguay has no seacoast and Asunción's river port handles most of the country's trade. Asunción has few industries and they consist for the most part of food processing and the manufacture of consumer goods. Pop., 1962, 306,160.

ASWAN, the capital of Aswan province, United Arab Republic (Egypt), located on the east bank of the Nile River about 550 miles south of Cairo. The city is the site of Aswan and Aswan High dams and the southern terminus of the U.A.R.'s main railroad. Aswan's dry, mild climate makes it a popular tourist resort during the winter months. Pop., 1967 est., 30,000.

ASYUT, the largest city in Upper Egypt, the capital of Asyut Province, the United Arab Republic. Occupying the site of ancient Lycopolis, Asyut lies on the left bank of the Nile River about 235 miles south of Cairo. The city is well known for its handicrafts, especially pottery, carved ivory, and wood inlay work. Pop., 1963 est., 137,000.

ATHENS, the capital and largest city of Greece, located on the Attic plain about five miles inland from its port of Piraeus on the Saronic Gulf. Named after the classical Greek goddess of wisdom, Athens was an important city in ancient Greece. The flat-topped hill of the Acropolis, which overlooks the city, contains the ruins of some of the most beautiful buildings of ancient Greece.

Modern Athens is the center of Greece's political, cultural, and economic life. It is also the manufacturing center of the country. The products of its wide variety of industries include ships, flour, alcoholic beverages, and textiles. Athens is one of the busiest ports on the Mediterranean Sea and lies on major railway and airline routes. Pop., 1961, urban area, 1,852,709.

AUCKLAND, the largest city and chief port of New Zealand, located on North Island between the harbors of Waitemata and Manukau. The major exports of the port are dairy products, hides, wool, timber, and gold. Auckland is New Zealand's largest industrial center, and it produces ships, refined sugar, chemicals, shoes, ammunition, and processed foods. It is the site of the University of Auckland and the Auckland War Memorial Museum, noted for its Maori collection. Pop., 1966, urban area, 547,915.

AYUTHIA, in northern Thailand, located on an island in the lower Chao Phraya River about 40 miles north of Bangkok. The city serves as the trade center for the forest and agricultural products of the surrounding area, notably rice and teak. Ayuthia was the capital of the country from 1350 to 1767 and has many ruins of historic interest. Pop., 1960, 32,368.

AZ ZAHRAN, or Dhahran, a city of east-central Saudi Arabia, situated about five miles west of the Persian Gulf. It is an international air center, developed in the late 1930s as the headquarters of an oil company. The city, which has a plant for the removal of hydrogen sulfide from oil, is linked by pipeline to Saudi Arabian oil fields. Pop., 1961 est., 12,500.

BAALBEK, in eastern Lebanon, located in the Bika valley, about 35 miles north of Damascus. Known in ancient times as Heliopolis, the city is on the old route from Beirut to Homs that has been followed by modern roads and railroads. Baalbek is noted for its Hellenistic and Roman ruins. The city is visited by many tourists.

BACOLOD, the capital of Negros Occidental Province, the Philippines, located on the northwest coast of Negros Island. The city lies in the center of the most important sugar-producing region of the Philippines and its economy is based on the processing and exporting of this commodity. Bacolod is also the site of the University of Negros Occidental. Pop., 1965 est., 142,000.

BAGHDAD, the capital and largest city of Iraq, located on the banks of the Tigris River, in the east central part of the country. The city is the intellectual, commercial, and indus-

ASUNCIÓN, capital and chief port of Paraguay, is on the east bank of the Paraguay River.

BANGKOK, the capital of Thailand, is an important transportation and administrative center.

trial center of Iraq. The chief industry is oil refining, but factories manufacture a variety of products, including shoes, clothing, and cement.

Baghdad was founded in 762 AD by Caliph al-Mansur. It was the capital of the Islamic world and a brilliant cultural center until 1258, when it was destroyed by the Mongols. Pop., 1965, 1,745,328.

BAKU, the capital of the Azerbaizhan Soviet Socialist Republic in the southwestern Soviet Union, situated on the western shore of the Caspian Sea. Located in the center of an extensive oilfield, it has large oil refineries and distribution pipelines. The city also has a variety of industries that produce ships, flour, tobacco, chemicals, tires, machinery, and shoes. Baku is one of the Soviet Union's largest cities and a major port. Pop., 1966 est., urban area, 1,164,000.

BAMAKO, the capital of Mali Republic in western Africa, situated on the Niger River, in the southwestern part of the country. It serves as the trade center for the surrounding area and exports peanuts, cotton, and tobacco. Bamako is connected to Dakar in Senegal by rail and has an international airport. Pop., 1965 est., urban area, 165,000.

BANARAS, in India, one of the most sacred Hindu holy cities, located on the banks of the Ganges River in southeastern Uttar Pradesh state. Hindu pilgrims from all over India come to wash away their sins in the waters of the Ganges at Banaras, which is reputedly the oldest city in India.

A cultural center, the city is the seat of Banaras Hindu University and Banaras Sanskrit College. Banaras' numerous handicraft industries produce brocades, saris, shawls, gold and silver jewelry, and brassware. Pop., 1966 est., urban area, 561,400.

BANDUNG, the capital of West Java Province, Indonesia, located on the island of Java, about 75 miles southeast of Djakarta. The city is an important resort because of its cool climate. It is the site of many medical and educational institutions, including the Pasteur Institute and Padjajaran University. Bandung industries produce textiles, rubber goods, chemicals, quinine, and machinery. Nearby Malabar radio station is one of the most powerful in the world. Pop., 1961, 972,566.

BANGALORE, the captial of Mysore State in southeastern India, located on the Deccan Plateau, about 180 miles west of Madras. The city serves as a trade center for the surrounding agricultural area and is an important railroad junction. Bangalore has modern factories, including a large aircraft assembly plant, as well as numerous handicraft industries. It is also an educational center and the site of the Indian Institute of Science. Pop., 1966 est., 124,200.

BANGKOK, the largest city and capital of Thailand, located on the Chao Pharaya River about 20 miles inland from its mouth on the Gulf of Siam. The city is Thailand's major port and handles almost all the country's foreign trade. Bangkok is an important rail center and has one of the most modern airports in Southeast Asia.

Bangkok is the headquarters of the Southeast Asia Treaty Organization (SEATO), and many Far Eastern divisions of UN specialized agencies are located in the city. Pop., 1963 est., 1,608,300.

BANGUI, the capital of the Central African Republic, located on the Ubangi River near the western border. The city is the country's major port and handles almost all foreign trade. Bangui is linked by road with Chad and Cameroon and has an international airport. Local industry consists for the most part of food processing and the manufacture of a few consumer goods. Pop., 1964, urban area, 126,602.

BARCELONA, on the northeast coast of Spain, the capital of Catalonia Province and the second largest city in the country. Barcelona is Spain's leading manufacturing center and its largest port. The major industries produce textiles, chemicals, machinery, precision instruments, paper, and printed matter. Barcelona is connected by rail with other Spanish cities. Pop., 1965 est., 1,696,800.

BAREILLY, in north-central India, located in Uttar Pradesh state on the Ramganga River, about 130 miles east of Delhi. The city is an important railroad junction and serves as a trade center for the sugarcane, corn, rice, wheat, and barley grown in the surrounding area. Pop., 1966 est., urban area, 307,400.

BARODA, in western India, one of the leading cities of Gujarat State. It is situated on the Viswamitra River, about 245 miles north of Bombay. Baroda is a transportation center and serves as the market for the surrounding agricultural region. Its most important industries produce dyes, textiles, chemicals, rubber goods, and machinery. The city is the seat of Baroda University. Pop., 1966 est., 339,800.

BASEL, in northern Switzerland, situated on the Rhine River near the French and German borders. It is the second largest city in Switzerland and a major port handling a large portion of the landlocked country's foreign trade. Basel is also an important railroad junction and travel center. The chief local industries produce dyes, chemicals, silk ribbons, gloves, paper, and beer. Pop., 1966 est., 212,200.

BASRA, in northern Iraq, a port on the Shatt-al-Arab, about 60 miles inland from the Persian Gulf. The city handles most of the trade of Iraq, and exports include dates, wool, hides, and oil. Basra is connected by oil pipeline to Fao on the Persian Gulf and by rail to Bagdad. Pop., 1965, 313,327.

BASSEIN, the leading port of Burma, located on the Bassein River, which flows from the Irawaddy River to the Bay of Bengal. It lies in a major rice-growing region, and rice is its chief export. Pop., 1953, 77,900.

BASSE-TERRE, the captial of St. Kitts Island and the St. Kitts-Nevis territory in the Leeward Island colony, British West Indies. The city lies on the southwest coast. Pop., 1960 est., 15,700.

BATA, on the west coast of Africa, is the capital of Río Muni, an overseas province of Spain. The city lies on the Gulf of Guinea about 125 miles north of the equator. The major export of Bata is timber, which is floated down rivers from the interior. Pop., 1960, 27,024.

BATHURST, the capital of Gambia, on the west coast of Africa, located on St. Mary's Island at the mouth of the Gambia River. The city's major industry is the processing of peanuts, which are Gambia's chief export. Bathurst is linked with other parts of the country by road and has an international airport. Pop., 1965 est., 29,800.

BATUMI, in the southwestern Soviet Union, the capital of the Adzhar Autonomous Soviet Socialist Republic, which is within the Georgian S.S.R. The city lies on the east coast of the Black Sea near the Turkish border. It is connected by rail and oil pipeline to Baku and Tiflis. Oil refining is the major industry and oil is the chief export. Pop., 1966 est., 98,000.

BEERSHEBA, in central Israel, located about 50 miles southwest of Jerusalem, at the northern edge of the Negev Desert. Founded in Biblical times, Beersheba is being developed as the administrative and industrial center of the Negev District. It is linked by rail to Tel Aviv and by road to Elath on the Red Sea. Beersheba is the site of the Negev Institute for Arid Research. Pop., 1965, 65,200.

BEIRA, a seaport on the southeastern coast of Mozambique, Africa, located at the mouth of the Pungwe River. The port is one of the busiest on the east coast of Africa and has railroad connections with Zambia, Malawi, and Rhodesia. Major exports include grain, cotton, sugar, and tobacco. Pop., 1960, 40,000.

BEIRUT, the capital of Lebanon, located on the eastern shore of the Mediterranean Sea, about 75 miles west of Damascus, Syria. Long an important center for east-west trade, Beirut is a busy port and transportation center. It lies on the Cairo-Istanbul-Bagdad railway, is the hub of a good road network, and has an international airport. Beirut is also a banking and educational center. It is the site of several universities, including the American University of Beirut. Pop., 1964 est., 700,000.

BELÉM, the capital of Pará State, Brazil, located on the Pará River, about 90 miles inland from the Atlantic Ocean. The city lies at the mouth of the Amazon River system and is a transshipment point for Amazon River traffic. It is linked by highway with the capital of Brasilia. Belém's industries produce ships, soap, beer, cement, and forest products. Pop., 1966 est., 471,000.

BELGRADE, the capital of Yugoslavia, located on the Danube River, about 50 miles from the Romanian border. The city is an active port and a transportation and industrial center. Belgrade industries produce automobiles, farm machinery, airplanes, electrical equipment, paper, textiles, and processed foods. It is the seat of the University of Belgrade and has many museums. Pop., 1961, 585,234.

BELFAST, the capital of Northern Ireland, located on the east coast, at the mouth of the Lagan River. The city is Northern Ireland's leading port and manufacturing center. Belfast industries produce linen and other textiles, ships, aircraft, processed foods, tobacco, and whiskey. Many educational institutions are located in Belfast, including Queen's University. Pop., 1965 est., 406,800.

BELIZE, the capital, largest city, and chief port of British Honduras. It is located at the mouth of the Belize River, on the Caribbean Sea, in northeastern Central America. Belize is a trading center and exports chicle, lumber, coconuts, and bananas. Pop., 1964 est., urban area, 45,600.

BELO HORIZONTE, in southeastern Brazil, the capital of Minas Gerais State. The first planned city in South America. It was inaugurated in 1897. Belo Horizonte processes the iron ore, manganese, gold, and precious stones mined in the state. Other industries include food processing, meat packing, and the manufacture of textiles. The city has several universities and is the educational center of Minas Gerais. Pop., 1966 est., 929,000.

BENGAZI, one of Libya's two capitals and the capital of Cyrenaica Province, situated on the shore of the Gulf of Sidra on the Mediterranean Sea. The city is a transportation and tourist center and serves as a market for the agricultural produce of the Jebel-el-Akhdar region. Local industries include brewing, food processing, and the manufacture of bricks and cement. Pop., 1964, 137,294.

BERGEN, the second largest city in Norway, lying at the head of By Fiord on the Atlantic coast. The city is an important trade center for fish and has flour mills, distilleries, iron foundries, textile mills, and paper, glass, and furniture factories. Norway's largest and most important city in the 1800s, Bergen is now a major cultural center. It is the site of the University of Bergen. Pop., 1965 est., 117,300.

BERLIN, in East Germany, located on the Spree River, about 165 miles southeast of Hamburg. Berlin was the capital of Germany until the end of World War II, when it was divided into four zones and occupied by the United States, France, Britain, and the Soviet Union.

In 1949 the U.S., British, and French zones became West Berlin and the Soviet zone became East Berlin. East Berlin is the capital of East Germany and West Berlin has close ties with West Germany. Although partition caused its importance to decline, Berlin is a financial, commercial, and manufacturing center. Pop., West Berlin, 1966 est., 2,190,600; East Berlin, 1965 est., 1,073,600.

BERN, the capital of Switzerland and of Bern canton, located in the west-central part of the country, on the Aare River. The city has some light industry and is a cultural, educational, banking, and commercial center. The older sections contain some excellent examples of medieval architecture. Pop., 1966 est., 165,900.

BETHLEHEM, in western Jordan, located about five miles southwest of Jerusalem. Bethlehem was the birthplace of Jesus and is mentioned often in the Bible. The Church of the Nativity, built by Emperor Constantine in 330 AD, occupies the reputed site of the stable where Jesus was born. The major business is the sale of souvenirs to tourists and pilgrims. Pop., 1961, 22,453.

BHAVNAGAR, in northwestern India, located in Gujarat State, on the Gulf of Cambay. The city is the most important seaport on the Kathiawar Peninsula. Industries include the manufacture of silk and cotton textiles, metal goods, and bricks and tile. Pop., 1966 est., 192,000.

BHOPAL, in central India, the capital of Madhya Pradesh State. The city is a major commercial and transportation center. After Hyderabad, Bhopal is the most important Muslim city in India. Pop., 1966 est., urban area, 287,300.

BHUBANESWAR, in northeastern India, the capital of Orissa State. The city serves as a trade center for rice produced in the surrounding agricultural

BERLIN is divided into East Berlin and the larger and more prosperous enclave of West Berlin.

region. Bhubaneswar is well known as the site of a large group of Hindu temples built between 700 and 1100 AD. Pop., 1961, 38,211.

BIALYSTOK, the capital of Bialystok Province, Poland, about 100 miles northeast of Warsaw. Bialystok is an important railroad junction and textile manufacturing center. Pop., 1965 est., 137,800.

BIKANER, in northwestern India, located about 250 miles west of New Delhi. Bikaner is an important trade center and is famous for the manufacture of wool rugs and carpets. It is the site of Anup Sanskrit Library, which contains one of the world's major collections of Sanskrit manuscripts. Pop., 1966 est., 168,500.

BIRMINGHAM, in south-central England, located in Warwickshire with suburbs extending into parts of Staffordshire and Worcestershire. The second largest city in England, Birmingham is one of the world's leading industrial centers. The city specializes in the manufacture of motor vehicles and electrical products and is a major center of the hardware industry. The production of iron, steel, and nonferrous metals is also important. Pop., 1965 est., urban area, 2,392,600.

BISSAU, on the west coast of Africa, the capital and chief port of Portuguese Guinea. The major exports are peanuts and copra. The city is linked by rivers to communities in the interior and has an airport. Pop., 1965 est., 25,000.

BIZERTE, in northern Tunisia, a port on the Mediterranean Sea. It has an inner harbor that is connected to an outer one by canal. The city is strongly fortified and has naval and air bases. Exports include grapes, olives, iron, lead, and zinc. Bizerte has large oil refineries. Pop., 1956, 44,721.

BLOEMFONTEIN, the capital of Orange Free State Province in the Republic of South Africa, located in the central part of the country. The city is primarily a market center for the agricultural produce of the surrounding area. It is also a transportation hub and the educational center of the Orange Free State. The highest court in South Africa is located at Bloemfontein. Pop., 1960, urban area, 145,273.

BOBO-DIOULASSO, in southwestern Upper Volta, West Africa. The second largest city in Upper Volta, Bobo-Dioulasso serves as a trade center for local agricultural products. It has an airport and is on the railroad that runs from Ouagadougou, the capital, to Abidjan, Ivory Coast. Pop., 1960 est., 45,000.

BOGOTÁ, the capital of Colombia, located in the central part of the country. The city is the political, economic, and cultural center of Colombia. Light industries produce a variety of consumer goods for domestic consumption. Bogotá is the seat of the National

BRASILIA, inaugurated as the capital of Brazil in 1960, is a model of modern urban design.

University and has a number of other educational institutions. Pop., 1964, 1,697,311.

BOLOGNA, in north-central Italy, at the foot of the Apennine Mountains, about 50 miles north of Florence. Bologna is the capital of the political region of Emilia-Romagna. The city is an industrial, commercial, and educational center. Manufactures include machinery, chemicals, paper, glass, and plastics. Bologna is also a tourist center and an important agricultural market. Pop., 1965 est., urban area, 481,527.

BOMBAY, the largest city in India and the capital of Maharashtra State, located on the west coast of the subcontinent. The city is a major commercial, financial, and industrial center. As a port Bombay ranks second only to Calcutta. Its major industries produce cotton textiles, chemicals, drugs, refined oil, processed foods, and motion pictures. Bombay has many educational institutions, including the University of Bombay. Pop., 1966 est., 4,784,000.

BONN, the capital of West Germany, situated on the Rhine River, about 20 miles northeast of Cologne. Long an educational and cultural center, the city is noted for its architecture, its museums, and its university. After it became the West German capital in 1949 Bonn expanded rapidly. The city's industries produce electrical equipment, chemicals, pharmaceuticals, and precision instruments. Pop., 1965 est., 141,700.

BORDEAUX, in southwestern France, located on the Garonne River. The city is an important seaport and a leading commercial and cultural center. Its principal industries are oil refining, shipbuilding, and food processing. It produces and exports wines, liqueurs, pharmaceuticals, and dyes. The history of Bordeaux dates back to Roman times, and in old sections there are Roman ruins and medieval buildings. Pop., 1962, urban area, 462,171.

BRAILA, in southeastern Romania, located in Walachia, on the Danube River. The city is an important trade center for grain. Its industries produce paper, flour, cement, paint, furniture, and hardware. Pop., 1965 est., urban area, 127,000.

BRASILIA, the capital of Brazil, located in the interior of the country, about 600 miles northwest of Rio de Janeiro. Brasilia is a planned city which was built in the late 1950s and inaugurated as the capital in April 1960. It was designed by Lúcio Costa and Oscar Niemeyer. The city is linked by highway to Belo Horizonte and Belém and has an airport. Pop., 1965 est., 200,000.

BRATISLAVA, the capital of Slovakia Province, Czechoslovakia, on the Danube River, near the borders with Hungary and Austria. The city is a railroad junction and a major river port. Oil pipelines connect Bratislava with the Ukraine and oil refining is an important industry. The city also produces chemicals, machinery, and cloth. Pop., 1965 est., 268,500.

BRAZZAVILLE, the capital and largest city of the Congo (Brazzaville), on the Congo River directly opposite Kinshasa (formerly Léopoldville). Brazzaville is an important river port and the country's commercial and educational center. Major industries include food processing and the manufacture of furniture, cigarettes, soap, and bricks. Pop., 1962, 136,200.

BREMEN, the capital of the West German state of Bremen, located on the Weser River, about 40 miles inland from the North Sea. The city is one of West Germany's largest ports and handles much of its foreign trade.

CITIES OF THE WORLD

EGYPTIAN STATE TOURIST ADMINISTRATION
CAIRO, the capital of the United Arab Republic, is an old city with many new sections.

Shipbuilding is the major industry, but oil refining and the manufacture of textiles are also important. Pop., 1965 est., 592,400.

BRIDGETOWN, the capital, largest city, and chief port of Barbados, an island nation in the West Indies. The city is located on the southwest coast of the island, on Carlisle Bay. Bridgetown is a railroad terminus and the financial, commercial, and tourist center of Barbados. Exports include sugar, molasses, and rum. Pop., 1960, 11,452.

BRISBANE, the capital and principal port of Queensland, Australia, on the Brisbane River, 14 miles from Moreton Bay. The city is an important industrial center, manufacturing steel, automobiles, munitions, and electrical appliances. Exports include wool, meat, hides, sugar, and dairy products. Brisbane is the seat of the University of Queensland. Pop., 1966, urban area, 719,140.

BRISTOL, a port on the west coast of Britain, located at the junction of the Avon and Frome rivers, near the Bristol Channel. The city is one of Britain's most important ports. The leading industry is shipbuilding, but automobile and aircraft assembly, food processing, and printing are also important. Bristol is an ancient city and has many historic buildings. It is the seat of several fine secondary schools and of Bristol University. Pop., 1965 est., 430,000.

BROKEN HILL, in central Zambia, southern Africa, about 70 miles north of Lusaka, the capital. Broken Hill is located in an important mining center that produces lead, zinc, and vanadium. It is the site of the discovery of the fossil skull of prehistoric Rhodesian Man. Pop., 1963 est., 44,600.

BRUNEI, capital of Brunei, a sultanate under British protection on the northwest coast of Borneo. The city is located on Brunei Bay, an inlet of the South China Sea. It exports rubber, petroleum, and wood. Pop., 1960, 9,702.

BRNO, or Brünn (German), in south central Czechoslovakia, located about 115 miles southeast of Prague. Brno is the second largest city in Czechoslovakia and an important industrial center. Its chief manufactures include iron and steel, textiles, machinery, chemicals, and automobiles. Pop., 1965 est., 328,500.

BRUSSELS, the capital and largest city of Belgium, located near the center of the country, on the Senne River. Brussels is an important administrative, financial, and cultural center. It is the headquarters of both the European Economic Community and the European Atomic Energy Commission and is often the site of international conferences. The city manufactures chemicals, furniture, clothing, and soap. Brussels is famous for its lace and carpets. Pop., 1965 est., urban area, 1,695,900.

BUCHAREST, the capital and largest city of Romania, located in central Walachia, on the Dimbovita River. The city is the country's commercial, industrial, and cultural center. Its industries produce machinery, munitions, aircraft, textiles, clothing, chemicals, and processed foods. Bucharest is known for its parks, churches, and many cultural and educational institutions. Pop., 1965 est., urban area, 1,382,200.

BUDAPEST, the capital and largest city of Hungary, on the Danube River in the north-central part of the country. Hungary's largest industrial center, Budapest produces iron and steel, textiles, furniture, shoes, drugs, machinery, refined oil, and processed foods. The city is also the cultural and educational center of Hungary and has several museums and libraries. It is the seat of the University of Budapest. Pop., 1965 est., 1,944,000.

BUENOS AIRES, the capital of Argentina and the largest city in Latin America, located on the Rio de la Plata, about 170 miles inland from the Atlantic Ocean. The city is the financial, commercial, and industrial center of Argentina. The chief industries are meat packing, tanning, flour milling, and the manufactures of textiles and chemicals. Buenos Aires has one of the world's largest and busiest ports and is an important rail and air center. The city has many libraries, museums, and theaters. It is the seat of the University of Buenos Aires, one of the leading universities of Latin America. Pop., 1960 est., urban area, 7,000,000.

BUJUMBURA, the capital of Burundi, in east-central Africa, located at the northern end of Lake Tanganyika. The city, which was formerly called Usumbura, is an important lake port and trade center for agricultural produce from the surrounding region. Pop., 1965 est., 71,000.

BULAWAYO, the second largest city in Rhodesia and the capital of Rhodesia's Bulawayo Province, in Matabeleland. The city is an important railroad junction and commercial and industrial center. Bulawayo manufactures iron and steel, soap, clothing, and processed foods. It is the site of the National Museum of Rhodesia, a mining school, and a meteorological station. Pop., 1965 est., 226,000.

BURGAS, a seaport in eastern Bulgaria, located on the Gulf of Burgas, an inlet of the Black Sea. The city's major exports are grain and tobacco. Industries produce ships, metalware, machinery, cotton textiles, and processed foods. Burgas is a popular summer resort. Pop., 1965 est., 105,700.

CAIRO, the capital of the United Arab Republic (Egypt) and the largest city in Africa, at the head of the Nile Delta. It is an important transportation, commercial, and industrial center. Manufactures include iron and steel, textiles, and chemicals. Al-Ahzar University, founded in 970 AD, is the world's oldest and largest center of Islamic scholarship. The ancient pyramids are nearby. Pop., 1966, 4,196,998.

CALCUTTA, the largest city in India, on the east bank of the Hooghly River, a tributary of the Ganges, about 80 miles north of the Bay of Bengal. It is the capital of West Bengal State. Calcutta is one of the world's busiest ports. Exports include jute products, animal hides, and tea; manufactured articles are imported. From 1833 to 1912, Calcutta was the capital of British India. Pop., 1966 est., urban area, 4,703,400.

CALGARY, in southern Alberta, Canada, at the junction of the Bow and Elbow rivers, in the foothills of the Rocky Mountains. Calgary is the center of Alberta's cattle and oil industries. Manufactures include iron and steel products and cement. Pop., 1965 est., urban area, 323,000.

CAMBRIDGE, in eastern England, on the Cam River, about 50 miles north of London. It is the home of Cambridge University and contains many medieval and Renaissance churches. Pop., 1966 est., 99,800.

CITIES OF THE WORLD

CANBERRA, the capital of Australia, in the Australian Capital Territory, in the southeastern corner of New South Wales. A model city, Canberra was founded in 1913 and became the seat of government in 1927. The Australian National University is located there. Pop., 1966, urban area, 95,913.

CANTERBURY, in southeastern England, on the Stour River, about 55 miles southeast of London. The cathedral of Canterbury is the seat of the Church of England's ranking prelate, the Archbishop of Canterbury. The city has many other churches and buildings of historic interest. Pop., 1966 est., 32,800.

CANTON, in southern China, on the Pearl River, about 80 miles from the South China Sea. It is the capital of Kwangtung Province and an important commercial and industrial center. A major river port, Canton was first visited by Europeans in the 1500s and until 1842 was the only Chinese port open to foreign trade. Pop., 1957 est., 1,840,000.

CAPE TOWN, the legislative capital of the Republic of South Africa and the capital of Cape Province. Cape Town is located on the southwestern shore of Table Bay, near the southern tip of Africa. It is an important manufacturing center and port. Exports include gold and other minerals. Pop., 1960, urban area, 807,211.

CARACAS, the capital and largest city of Venezuela, in a mountain basin more than 3,000 feet above sea level. It is linked by superhighway with nearby La Guaira, its port on the Caribbean. Earnings from the nation's oil industry have financed extensive development. The Central University occupies a modern campus covering 307 acres in the city. Caracas is the birthplace of Simón Bolívar, South American patriot. Pop., 1966 est., urban area, 1,764,300.

CARDIFF, the capital and largest city of Wales, on the Taff River, near Bristol Channel in western Britain. Cardiff is the cultural and educational center of Wales. Its major industries include coal mining and processing, iron and steel manufacture, and ship repairing. Pop., 1965 est., 260,200.

CASABLANCA, the largest city in Morocco, on the Atlantic coast of North Africa. One of the world's largest artificial ports, Casablanca handles most of Morocco's passenger traffic and foreign trade. Phosphates are the city's chief export. Industries include textile, cement, and glass manufacture. Pop., 1965 est., 1,085,000.

CASTRIES, the capital, largest city, and chief port of St. Lucia, one of the Windward Islands of the British West Indies. Castries is located on the northwest coast of the island and has a fine, landlocked harbor. Chief exports are bananas, cocoa, copra, and coconut oil. Castries is also the tourist center of the island of St. Lucia. Pop., 1960, 4,353.

CAWNPORE, on the Ganges River in northern India. It is a district capital, railroad junction, and the most important industrial center in the state of Uttar Pradesh. Cawnpore processes grain, wool, cotton, and leather and manufactures textiles and machinery. Pop., 1966 est., urban area, 1,112,800.

CAYENNE, the capital of French Guiana, on the northeast coast of South America. It lies on an island near the mouth of the Cayenne River and is French Guiana's largest city and principal port. Nearby Devil's Island was the site of a French penal colony from 1851 to 1945. Exports include tropical woods, sugar, coffee, spices, and gold. Its most famous product is Cayenne pepper. Pop., 1961, 18,615.

ČESKÉ BUDĚJOVICE, in western Czechoslovakia, on the Vltava River, about 75 miles south of Prague. It is also known by its German name, Budweis. České Budějovice has manufacturing plants, lumber and paper mills, and breweries. Pop., 1962 est., 65,900.

CEUTA, a Spanish enclave on the coast of Morocco, administered by Spain as part of the Province of Cádiz. It is located on a low, narrow peninsula and guards the eastern entrance to the Strait of Gibraltar. Ceuta has extensive harbor facilities. Pop., 1966 est., 81,700.

CHAMPERICO, on the Pacific coast of southwestern Guatemala. It is a railroad terminus and port. Exports include coffee, lumber, and sugar. Pop., 1950, 982.

CHANDIGARH, in northern India, near the Ghaggar River, at the foot of the Himalayas. It is a Union Territory and the joint capital of Punjab and Haryana states. Chandigarh was designed by the Swiss architect, Le Corbusier. Construction was begun in 1950 and the city was inaugurated as the capital of Punjab state on Oct. 7, 1953. It is a model of modern city planning. Pop., 1961, 119,881.

CHANGCHUN, in northeastern China, on the west bank of the Itung River, about 175 miles northeast of Mukden. It is the capital of Kirin Province in Manchuria. An important industrial center, Changchun's manufactures include motor vehicles, locomotives, and machinery. Pop., 1957 est., 975,000.

CHANGSHA, in south-central China, on the east bank of the Hsiang River, 45 miles south of Tungting Lake. It is the capital of Hunan Province. Changsha is an important marketing and transportation center. Pop., 1957 est., 703,000.

CHANKIANG, a port in southeastern China, on the east side of the Luichow Peninsula, about 270 miles west of Hong Kong. A former French treaty port, it was restored to China in 1946. Pop., 1953, 166,000.

CHARLOTTE AMALIE, the capital, largest city, and chief port of the Virgin Islands of the United States. The city is located on the south-central coast of St. Thomas Island, about 40 miles east of Puerto Rico. It was formerly called St. Thomas. The city is the chief commercial and tourist center of the Virgin Islands. Pop., 1960, 12,880.

CHENGTEH, in northeastern China, on the Luan River in Hopeh Province, about 110 miles northeast of Peking. It is also called Jehol. The city is enclosed by walls and was once the summer residence of the Ch'ing (Manchu) emperors of China. It is an important commercial center. Pop., 1953, 92,900.

CHENGTU, in west-central China, on the Min River, a branch of the Yangtze, about 170 miles northwest of Chungking. It is the capital of Szechwan Province and one of China's oldest cities. Once a capital of imperial China, Chengtu is an agricultural and commercial center. Pop., 1957 est., 1,107,000.

CARACAS, Venezuela's capital, is a city of modern highways and high-rise apartment houses.

COLOGNE, in West Germany, is a cathedral city situated on both banks of the Rhine River.

CHIANG MAI, the largest city in northern Thailand and the capital of Chiang Mai Province. It is located on the upper course of the Ping River, about 80 miles east of the Burma border. Chiang Mai is a railroad terminus and commercial center. Pop., 1960, 65,736.

CHIBA, on Honshu Island, Japan, on the eastern shore of Tokyo Bay. It is the capital of Chiba prefecture and a manufacturing center. Pop., 1965, urban area, 332,118.

CHINCHOW, in northeastern China, at the head of the Gulf of Chihli, about 130 miles southwest of Mukden. It is a railroad junction and an industrial center. Pop., 1953, 352,200.

CHINNAMPO, on the west coast of North Korea, at the mouth of the Taedong River. It is about 25 miles southwest of the capital, Pyongyang. Chinnampo is an industrial center and Pyongyang's port. The city's exports include iron and coal. Pop., 1955, 82,162.

CHITTAGONG, in East Pakistan, near the mouth of the Karnaphuli River. It is a district capital and the chief port of East Pakistan. Exports include rice, tea, cotton, jute, and hides. Pop., 1961, 364,205.

CHONGJIN, on the northeastern coast of North Korea, about 140 miles southwest of the Soviet city of Vladivostok. It is an industrial center and port. Exports include iron and textiles. Pop., 1944, 184,301.

CHRISTCHURCH, in New Zealand, near the east coast of South Island. Its port is Lyttelton. Christchurch is New Zealand's largest city and South Island's commercial and industrial center. It is the chief market for grain, dairy products, timber, and coal from the nearby Canterbury Plains. The city has fertilizer plants, tanneries, woolen mills, meat-freezing plants, and iron foundries. Pop., 1966, urban area, 246,773.

COCHIN, on India's Malabar coast, about 120 mile west of Madurai in Kerala state. A major naval station, port, and railroad terminus, Cochin serves much of India's southwest coast. Pop., 1961 est., urban area, 300,000.

COIMBATORE, in southern India, on the Noyil River, about 280 miles southwest of Madras. Important products are cotton yarn and cloth, hides, and coffee. Pop., 1966 est., 333,500.

COLOGNE, or Köln, in western West Germany, on both banks of the Rhine River in the state of North Rhine-Westphalia. The Rhineland's most important industrial center, Cologne manufactures motor vehicles, railroad cars, diesel engines, machinery, and textiles. It is a busy river port and has extensive shipyards. It is also a leading cultural and educational center. Cologne Cathedral is the city's most famous landmark. Pop., 1965 est., 854,500.

COLOMB BÉCHAR, in western Algeria, about 300 miles southwest of Oran, near the border with Morocco. It is a railroad terminus and a coal mining center. Pop., 1954, urban area, 43,250.

COLOMBO, the capital, largest city, and chief port of Ceylon. It is located at the mouth of the Kelani River on the island's southwestern coast. Colombo exports most of Ceylon's tea, coconut products, cotton, and rubber. It was settled in 1517 by the Portuguese and named in honor of Christopher Columbus. Pop., 1963, 510,947.

COMODORO RIVADAVIA, in southern Argentina, on the Gulf of San Jorge (Atlantic Ocean), about 900 miles southwest of Buenos Aires. It is Argentina's chief petroleum refining center and oil port. Pop., 1960, 35,966.

CONAKRY, the capital of Guinea in West Africa. It is located on the small island of Tombo and is joined to the mainland by a bridge. Conakry is Guinea's largest city, chief port, and commercial and industrial center. Its deepwater harbor is one of West Africa's finest. Exports include bauxite and iron ore. Pop., 1964 est., urban area, 175,000.

CONCEPCIÓN, in south-central Chile, on the banks of the Bío Bío River. Concepción is one of Chile's largest cities and an industrial center. Its port, Talcuhuano, lies nearby to the northwest. Concepción, which was founded in the mid-1500s, has been struck by several destructive earthquakes. Pop., 1965 est., 174,200.

COPÁN, in western Honduras, on the Copán River, near the border with Guatemala. It is a tourist center for the nearby ruins of the Mayan city of Copán. Pop., 1950, 977.

COPENHAGEN, or København, the capital and largest city of Denmark, lying on Zealand and Amager islands. An important industrial center, the city produces ships, machinery, and chemicals. It has an excellent natural harbor and is a major European port. The city's Kastrup Airport is the busiest in northern Europe. Copenhagen's Tivoli Gardens, founded in 1843, is a famous amusement center. The city is the seat of Copenhagen University. Pop., 1965, urban area, 1,377,608.

CÓRDOBA, or Cordova, a city of south-central Spain, situated on the Guadalquivir River at the foot of the Sierra Morena. The city is an industrial, commercial, and tourist center. The manufacture of leather goods, traditionally Córdoba's most important industry, has been surpassed by textile mills, distilleries, and heavy industries. The city also serves as the market center for an area that produces wheat and corn.

Once a center of Arab power, Córdoba shows strong Muslim influence in its architecture. Notable are the Cathedral of Córdoba, formerly a mosque, and the Alcázar, or citadel. Pop., 1965 est., 214,300.

CORINTO, on the Pacific coast of Nicaragua, at the southeastern end of Aserradores Island. It is joined to the mainland by a bridge. Corinto is Nicaragua's main port of entry. Exports include coffee, sugar, timber, and hides. Pop., 1950, 4,765.

COTONOU, on the Atlantic coast of Dahomey, in West Africa, on a thin strip of land between the Gulf of Guinea and Lake Nakoué. It is Dahomey's largest city, chief commercial center, and main port, with a modern, deepwater harbor. Exports include palm kernels and palm oil. Pop., 1964, 109,328.

CURITIBA, in southern Brazil, on a plateau near the Iguaçu River, about 65 miles west of Paranaguá, its port on the Atlantic Ocean. Curitiba is the capital of the state of Paraná and an important transportation, trade, and industrial center. The city's products include timber, coffee, bananas, and sugar. Pop., 1966 est., 582,000.

CITIES OF THE WORLD

CUZCO, in southern Peru, about 350 miles southeast of Lima. It lies at an altitude of about 11,000 feet above sea level in the Andes. Cuzco, the capital of the Inca Empire, was captured by the Spanish in 1533. The city's Inca ruins and Spanish colonial buildings attract many tourists. Cuzco is also a commercial center. Pop., 1961, 79,857.

CUTTACK, in northeastern India, on the south bank of the Mahanadi River. It is about 60 miles inland from the Bay of Bengal and 220 miles southwest of Calcutta. Cuttack is a district capital in the state of Orissa. It manufactures ice, cigarettes, and shoes. Pop., 1966 est., 160,700.

CZESTOCHOWA, in south-central Poland, on the left bank of the Warta River, about 125 miles southwest of Warsaw. It is a railroad junction and a major industrial center, producing iron, steel, and textiles. Czestochowa is an important religious center. Pop., 1965 est., 175,200.

DACCA, the capital of East Pakistan, lies between the Meghna and Ganges rivers. The city is a trade and processing center for the surrounding agricultural area, and is noted for the production of gold and silver jewelry, carved shells, and jute. It is the seat of the University of Dacca. Pop., 1961, 556,712.

DAKAR, the capital and chief seaport of Senegal, located on the Cape Verde Peninsula on Africa's west coast. The city, which has a strategic location and an excellent harbor is a transportation center with important air, rail, and shipping facilities.
Dakar's diversified industries produce canned fish, refined sugar, chocolate, vinegar, rope, and textiles. The city is the seat of the University of Dakar, the Pasteur Institute, and the Institut Français d'Afrique Noire. Pop., 1961 est., urban area, 374,700.

DAMASCUS, or Dimashaq, the capital and largest city of Syria, situated in the southwestern part of the country on the Barada River. The city is an oasis that has been continuously inhabited since biblical times. Modern Damascus is a major Middle Eastern administrative, communications, commercial, and industrial center. Its products include cement, glass, textiles, and sugar.
Damascus was a noted market place on the caravan route as early as the 600s AD. The city retains its citadel, bazaars, Roman gates, and historic churches. Damascus is the seat of the Syrian University and Damascus College. Pop., 1965 est., 599,700.

DAR ES SALAAM, the capital of Tanzania, is a major seaport of East Africa. Its harbor is on a bay, linked by a narrow channel to the Indian Ocean. The city is an administrative, transportation, and economic center. Among its exports are coffee, copra, peanuts, gold, diamonds, and tin. Dar es Salaam's industries produce furniture, pharmaceuticals, and processed foods. Pop., est. 1965, 190,200.

DAVAO, a port in the Philippines, is situated in the southeastern part of Mindanao Island at the mouth of the Davao River. The city's major industries process the abaca (Manila hemp) grown in the surrounding area. Pop., 1965 est., 269,300.

DEBRECEN, a marketing center in eastern Hungary, situated on the East Hungarian Plain. It lies in an agricultural region that grows grain and raises livestock. Debrecen's major industries produce processed foods and agricultural machinery. Pop., 1965 est., 147,000.

DEHRA DUN, a commercial and administrative center of northern India, situated in the Himalayan foothills, about 150 miles northeast of Delhi. Dehra Dun is a trade center for the surrounding agricultural area and a popular resort. A military institute and college of forestry are located in the city. Pop., 1966 est., urban area, 162,800.

DELHI. See *New Delhi.*

DILI, the capital of Portuguese Timor, situated on northeastern Timor, an island at the eastern end of the Indonesian chain. Dili lies in an area that trades in coffee, cocoa, hides, and shells. Pop., 1960, 52,158.

DJIBOUTI, the capital of the French Territory of the Afars and Issas (French Somaliland), an East African port, located on the Gulf of Tadjoura. Djibouti is the terminal of a railway from Addis Ababa, Ethiopia, and its exports are mainly Ethiopian products. These include coffee, hides, and skins, and oilseeds. Pop., 1963 est., urban area, 43,200.

DNEPRODZERZHINSK, an industrial city of the western Soviet Union, situated on the Dnieper River. Nearby iron and coal deposits and electric power from the river, combine to make the city a major iron and steel center. Pop., 1966 est., 219,000.

DNEPROPETROVSK, an administrative, commercial, and railroad center of the western Soviet Union, located on the Dnieper River near the head of the rapids. The city is an important manufacturer of steel and metal products. It is also a trade center for the surrounding wheat growing area. Pop., 1966 est., 790,000.

DOHA, the capital and chief port of Qatar, located on the east side of the Qatar Peninsula on the Persian Gulf. Since the discovery of oil in Qatar in the 1940s, Doha has become an important commercial center, with oil as its chief export. Pop., 1963 est., 45,000.

DOUALA, the main seaport of Cameroon, situated on the west coast of Africa on the Gulf of Guinea. Douala serves as a port for aluminum refined at nearby Edea and for agricultural products raised in the interior. Pop., 1965 est., urban area, 200,000.

DOUGLAS, the capital of the Isle of Man, an island in the Irish Sea. Douglas is a seaport and resort town with some commerce and industry. Pop., 1961, 18,821.

DRESDEN, an East German industrial city situated on the Elbe River. Its manufactures include chemicals, machinery, optical instruments, and glass. It is also an important river port. The city's buildings include some excellent examples of Baroque architecture. Pop., 1965 est., 504,900.

DUBLIN, the capital, largest city, and chief port of the Republic of Ireland, located on Ireland's east coast at the mouth of the Liffey River.
Dublin is a major transportation, commercial, and administrative center. Its industries include brewing and distilling, flour milling, and textile weaving. The city is Ireland's cultural and educational center, containing a large university, a cathedral, and many museums and libraries. Pop., 1966, urban area, 125,790.

LOOK MAGAZINE

DUBLIN, Ireland's capital and chief seaport, has retained much of its traditional character.

FLORENCE, with the city's famous Ponte Vecchio, or Old Bridge, spanning the Arno River.

DURBAN, a major seaport and tourist resort on the east coast of South Africa. The city, which lies on Natal Bay in the Indian Ocean, has a subtropical climate and excellent beaches. Its chief exports are coal, manganese, and other minerals. Durban's industries produce machinery, furniture, textiles, glass, paper, and processed foods. Pop., 1960, urban area, 681,492.

DURRËS, Albania's chief seaport, situated on the Adriatic Sea, about 20 miles west of Tiranë, to which it is joined by rail. Its products include flour, cigarettes, clothing, and soap. An ancient settlement, known as Epidamnus, was founded on the site of Durrës by Greeks from Corcyra (Corfu) and Corinth in the 600s BC. Pop., 1960, 39,946.

DUSHANBE, in the south-central Soviet Union, the capital of the Tadzhik Soviet Socialist Republic. The city is an important market area for the surrounding agricultural district and a growing industrial center. Pop., 1966 est., 323,000.

DÜSSELDORF, the capital of the West German state of North Rhine-Westphalia, situated on the Rhine north of Cologne. One of the largest and most industrialized cities of the Rhineland, Düsseldorf manufactures iron and steel, chemicals, textiles, and glass. The city has a large harbor and an excellent railway system. Pop., 1965, 700,080.

EAST LONDON, in southeastern Cape Province, South Africa. It is located at the mouth of the Buffalo River on the Indian Ocean, about 540 miles east of Capetown. East London is an important industrial, agricultural, and fishing center. Exports include wool and citrus fruit. Pop., 1960, urban area, 116,056.

EDEA, in western Cameroon, West Africa. The city is on the Sanaga River, about 40 miles southeast of Douala. An aluminum smelter was completed at Edea in 1956.

EDINBURGH, the capital of Scotland and the seat of Midlothian county. It is located on the south shore of the Firth of Forth (North Sea) in southeastern Scotland. Edinburgh is primarily a residential and administrative city. It is noted for its cultural and educational activities and historic buildings. The chief industry is printing. Breweries and distilleries are also important. Pop., 1965 est., 476,400.

EDMONTON, the capital and largest city of Alberta, Canada. The North Saskatchewan River flows through the city, which is in the south-central part of the province. Edmonton lies in a region of coal mines and gas and oil wells. It is the headquarters of Canada's oil industry and the transportation center of the Canadian Northwest. Pop., 1965 est., urban area, 385,000.

ELATH, port city at the southern tip of Israel, at the head of the Gulf of Aqaba. It was founded in 1948 and is connected to northern ports by an oil pipeline and a road. Pop., 1965 est., 9,700.

ELBASAN, in east-central Albania, on the Shkumbi River, about 20 miles southeast of Tiranë, the capital. Elbasan is a market center for olives, tobacco, and fruit. Manufactures include textiles and leather. Pop., 1960, 29,787.

EL FASHER, in western Sudan, about 500 miles southwest of Khartoum, the capital. El Fasher is a market center situated on an ancient caravan route. Pop., 1956, 26,161.

ENTEBBE, in Uganda, East Africa, on a peninsula on the north shore of Lake Victoria, about 20 miles southwest of Kampala, the capital. Entebbe was the capital of Uganda until 1960. It is a commercial center. Pop., 1959, 10,941.

ENUGU, capital of the former Eastern Region of Nigeria in West Africa. It is located in a coal mining region about 50 miles east of the Niger River. Enuga was proclaimed the capital of the break-away state of Biafra in 1967, when the Eastern Region attempted to secede from Nigeria. Pop., 1963, 138,457.

ERZURUM, in northeastern Turkey, about 450 miles east of Ankara. It lies in the mountains of Turkish Armenia and is the capital of Erzurum Province. The city is an important military, commercial, and rail center. Pop., 1965, 106,301.

ESSEN, in western West Germany, located between the Ruhr and Lippe rivers in the state of North Rhine-Westphalia. An industrial city in a region of coal and iron fields, Essen manufactures steel, locomotives, and machinery. Other products include textiles, glass, and chemicals. Essen is also an important railroad junction. Pop., 1965 est., 726,800.

ESZTERGOM, in northern Hungary, about 25 miles northwest of Budapest. It is located on the Danube River and is a river port and railroad terminus. Manufactures include woolen textiles, machinery, and lumber. Pop., 1963 est., 24,700.

FAMAGUSTA, in the eastern Mediterranean Sea, on the east coast of Cyprus, about 40 miles east of Nicosia. It is a district capital and port. Pop., 1967 est., 39,000.

FÈS, in northern Morocco, North Africa, about 150 miles northeast of Casablanca. Fès is an historic city and a major Muslim religious center. It is also an important commercial city. Pop., 1965 est., 235,000.

FLORENCE, in central Italy, on the bank of the Arno River, in the western Apennines. It is the capital of Tuscany and a center of commerce and light industry. One of the world's foremost art centers, Florence attracts many tourists. Handicrafts include textiles, pottery, jewelry, and leather goods. A flood in 1966 damaged many art treasures and buildings. Pop., 1965 est., urban area, 454,900.

FOOCHOW, a port on the southeast coast of China, near the mouth of the Min River, at the northern end of Formosa Strait. It is the capital of Fukien Province. Foochow is a port and an industrial center. Manufactures include chemicals and textiles. Pop., 1957 est., 616,000.

FORTALEZA, on the northeast coast of Brazil, about 270 miles northwest of Natal. Fortaleza is the capital of the state of Ceará and an educational center. The city manufactures textiles and processes agricultural products. Coffee, sugar, and cotton are shipped from is port. Pop., 1966 est., 486,000.

FORT-DE-FRANCE, the capital and largest city of Martinique, French West Indies. Located on the Bay of Fort-de-France, on the southwest coast of the island, the city has a large, landlocked harbor. Exports include sugar, rum, and bananas. Pop., 1954, urban area, 60,648.

CITIES OF THE WORLD

FORT-LAMY, the capital of Chad, in north-central Africa, about 70 miles south of Lake Chad. It is the largest city and chief transportation, industrial, and commercial center of Chad. Pop., 1964 est., urban area, 99,000.

FRANKFURT AM MAIN, in central West Germany, on the north bank of the Main River, about 100 miles southeast of Cologne. A leading industrial city, Frankfurt manufactures machinery, electrical equipment, and chemicals. The city is a commercial and financial center and its location makes it the transportation hub of West Germany. Frankfurt is also an educational and cultural center. Pop., 1965 est., 690,900.

FREDERICTON, the capital of New Brunswick, Canada. It lies on the Saint John River, about 85 miles from the Bay of Fundy. Fredericton is situated in a hunting and fishing region. Manufactures include lumber products, textiles, and leather goods. Pop., 1966, 22,460.

FREETOWN, the capital and chief port of Sierra Leone in West Africa. It is located on the estuary of the Sierra Leone River and has an excellent natural harbor. Freetown is the transportation and commercial center of Sierra Leone. Exports include minerals and palm kernels and oil. Pop., 1966 est., 148,000.

FRUNZE, capital of the Kirghiz republic in the Central Asia region of the Soviet Union. Frunze is about 300 miles northeast of Tashkent. Manufactures include machinery and textiles. Pop., 1966 est., 380,000.

FUKUOKA, on the northwest coast of Kyushu Island, Japan. The island's largest city, Fukuoka is a port and an industrial center. Manufactures include paper, textiles, and machinery. Pop., 1965, urban area, 749,808.

FUKUSHIMA, on the island of Honshu, Japan, about 160 miles north of Tokyo. Fukushima is a railroad junction and a leading commercial center. Pop., 1965, urban area, 173,678.

GABERONES, the capital of Botswana, situated in south-central Africa in an arid cattle-grazing region. Water is provided by a dam on a nearby branch of the Limpopo River. Pop., 1965 est., 4,200.

GANGTOK, the capital of Sikkim, situated about 30 miles northeast of Darjeeling, India. The city is a commercial center on the trade route between India and Tibet. Pop., 1961, 6,848.

GDAŃSK, formerly Danzig, a Polish seaport situated on the Baltic Sea, on the delta of the Wisła (Vistula) River. Gdańsk, which was settled by the 900s, was a port city in the Hanseatic League in the late 1300s. Later it became part of Poland, and in the late 1700s it became part of Prussia. Following World War I, it became the Free City of Danzig, under the League of Nations. Early in World War II the Germans captured Danzig, holding it until 1945. Following the war, the city was returned to Poland.

The port of Gdańsk handles coal, lumber, and grain. Products of the city's varied industries include ships, processed foods, and chemicals. Pop., 1965 est., 319,400.

GDYNIA, a port and naval base in Poland, lying on the Baltic Sea. Before 1924 Gdynia was a small fishing village. It was developed as a port to compete with the Free City of Danzig (Gdańsk). Gdynia's modern facilities ship coal, coke, lumber, chemicals, and food products. Pop., 1965 est., 165,000.

GENEVA, or Genève, the capital of Geneva canton in southwestern Switzerland, located on the Rhône River at the southern end of Lake Geneva. The city serves as the headquarters for a number of international organizations. Its industries include tourism and the manufacture of clocks, jewelry, precision tools, surgical and optical equipment, leather goods, and textiles.

Geneva is an ancient city that became important during the Reformation. It is an intellectual and cultural center with many schools, museums, libraries, and old buildings. Pop., 1966 est., 174,500.

GENOA, or Genova, a port in northwestern Italy on the Gulf of Genoa in the Mediterranean Sea. It is the capital of the province of Genoa and the region of Liguria. Genoa's exports include foodstuffs, marble, and silk. Among the many products of the city's industries are steel, metal goods, and cement. Pop., 1965 est., 845,400.

GEORGETOWN, capital and chief city of the British Cayman Islands, located on Grand Cayman Island, about 200 miles northwest of Jamaica. Pop., 1960, 2,573.

GEORGETOWN, the capital, largest city, and chief port of Guyana, on the northeastern coast of South America.

GENEVA, a center of international business, lies on the shores of scenic Lake Geneva.

Georgetown is located at the mouth of the Demerara River, on the Atlantic Ocean. It is a railroad terminus and Guyana's communications and transportation center. Chief exports are sugar, bauxite, and rice. Pop., 1960, urban area, 148,391.

GERMISTON, a city in South Africa situated about 10 miles east of Johannesburg. Germiston is an important gold-refining center with excellent air and rail facilities. Pop., 1960, urban area, 214,393.

GIFU, a Japanese city in central Honshu, lying on the Nagara River. It is the capital of Gifu prefecture and an educational and manufacturing center. Its products include paper goods and textiles. Pop., 1965, 358,190.

GLASGOW, a port and industrial city of west-central Scotland, lying on the Clyde River. Glasgow is the largest city in Scotland, and the third largest in the British Isles. Its principal industries are shipping and shipbuilding, followed by the production of chemicals, bricks, glass, and textiles. Pop., 1965 est., 1,013,000.

GORKI, formerly Nizhni-Novgorod, a river port in the Soviet Union, the capital of Gorki Oblast. The city lies at the confluence of the Volga and Oka rivers, about 250 miles east of Moscow. Its port handles foodstuffs, building materials, and manufactured goods. Gorki's industries produce automobiles, aircraft, and refrigeration equipment. Pop., 1966 est., 1,100,000.

GÖTEBORG, or Gothenburg, the capital of the Swedish province of Göteborg och Bohus, in southwestern Sweden on an estuary of the Göta River. The city, which has access to the North Sea, is Sweden's most important seaport and the center of an excellent canal and rail system. Shipping and shipbuilding are the leading industries, followed by the manufacture of machinery, automobiles, and electrical equipment. Pop., 1966 est., urban area, 615,900.

GRANADA, the capital of the province of Granada, situated in southern Spain on the Genil River. The city is the commercial and industrial center for the region. Its chief industries are food processing, brewing and distilling, chemical production, and leather and metal handcrafting. Granada is the site of the Alhambra, an ancient Muslim fortress and palace, and other Muslim and Renaissance buildings. Pop., 1965 est., 158,000.

GRENOBLE, a commercial and industrial center of southeastern France, and the capital of Isère Province. The city lies on the Isère River, near the Grande Chartreuse range of the Alps. In 1968 the winter Olympics were held in Grenoble. The city is famous for the manufacture of gloves. Other products include cement, paper, and chemicals. Grenoble is the seat of the University of Grenoble. Pop., 1962, urban area, 233,243.

GROZNY, a city in the Soviet Union, the capital of the Chechen-Ingush Autonomous Soviet Republic. Grozny lies in the Caucaucus on a tributary of the Terek River. The city is an important producer of petroleum and a manufacturer of mining machinery and chemicals. Pop., 1966 est., 319,000.

GUADALAJARA, the second largest city in Mexico and capital of the state of Jalisco, located about 380 miles northwest of Mexico City. Guadalajara is the commercial center for a rich agricultural and mining region and is an important rail and highway hub. Its industries produce flour, textiles, leather goods, pottery, and glassware. Pop., 1966 est., 1,105,900.

GUATEMALA CITY, the capital and largest city of Guatemala, in Central America. It is located in the central highlands, at an altitude of about 5,000 feet, about 75 miles from the Pacific Ocean. It is the commercial, cultural, educational, financial, and political center of the country. Manufactures include textiles, soap, cement, and furniture. Guatemala City is a transportation, communications, and tourist center. Pop., 1964 est., 577,100.

THE HAGUE, or 's Gravenhage, the seat of the Netherlands' legislature and royal residence, and the capital of the province of South Holland. The Hague lies near the country's west coast. It is the site of many international conferences and the headquarters of several international organizations. The Hague is mainly a residential city. Pop., 1965 est., 596,700.

HAIFA, Israel's major port and an important industrial center. The city is situated in northern Israel, at the foot of Mt. Carmel, on the Bay of Acre in the Mediterranean Sea. Among its many industries are flour and textile mills, foundries, cement works, and an oil refinery. The Haifa Institute of Technology is in the city. Pop., 1965 est., 596,700.

HAIPHONG, the chief port of North Vietnam, situated on the Gulf of Tonkin about 60 miles east of Hanoi. The harbor must be constantly dredged to prevent silt deposits. There are auto, rail, and canal routes from Haiphong to the interior. The city has several heavy industries, including shipbuilding. In the mid-1960s, during the Vietnamese War, Haiphong harbor was subject to U.S. bombing raids. Pop., 1960, urban area, 369,-248.

HAKODATE, a Japanese seaport on the southwestern coast of Hokaido. It has a railroad and a ferry terminus, in addition to its shipping facilities. The city lies in an important dairying region. Pop., 1965, 243,418.

HALIFAX, a seaport in southeastern Canada, the capital of Nova Scotia, located on the Atlantic Coast. The port is ice-free throughout the year, making Halifax an important winter terminal for trans-Atlantic shipping. The city is a rail, fishing, and commercial center. Its industries include shipbuilding, food processing, and the manufacture of clothing and furniture. Pop. 1961, urban area, 369,248.

HAMBURG, the capital of the West German state of Hamburg, situated at the confluence of the Elbe, Alster, and Bille rivers, near the North Sea. Hamburg is Germany's largest seaport and an important industrial center. Shipping and shipbuilding are the city's major industries, followed by the manufacture of machinery, textiles, and beer. Hamburg also has important food processing industries. Pop., 1965 est., 1,857,000.

HAMILTON, capital and chief port of the Bermuda islands in the western Atlantic Ocean, about 600 miles east of North Carolina. The city lies in the center of a popular resort area. Pop., 1965 est., 3,000.

HANGCHOW, a port in east-central China, the capital of Chekiang province. It lies at the southern end of the Grand Canal, on Hangchow Bay in the East China Sea. The city, which was founded in about 2200 BC, is now highly industrialized. It is famous for the production of silk and tea. Pop., 1957 est., 784,000.

HANNOVER, in northern West Germany, on the Leine River, about 80 miles south of Hamburg. Hannover is the capital of the state of Lower Saxony. The city is a railroad junction and an industrial and commercial center. Manufactures include machinery, chemicals, textiles, tobacco, and glass. Hannover is an important educational and cultural center. Pop., 1965 est., 559,000.

HANOI, the capital of North Vietnam, situated on the Red River delta. Until 1946, Hanoi was the capital of French Indochina. The city, which lies in the middle of a rich agricultural region, is an important commercial and industrial center. Pop 1960, urban area, 643,576.

HARBIN, the capital of the Chinese province of Heilungkiang, situated in the northeast on the Sungari River. Harbin, which is located near the center of Manchuria, is an important commercial and transportation center for a large part of the region. Pop., 1957 est., 1,552,000.

HAVANA, capital and chief commercial city of Cuba, located on the island's northwestern coast. Havana is Cuba's major port and exports the island's chief commercial crops, sugar and tobacco. Cigars, cigarettes, consumer goods, and heavy machinery are manufactured in the city.

Havana is also Cuba's cultural center and has universities, libraries, and museums. Until Fidel Castro came to power in Cuba in 1959, Havana was a popular resort. Pop., 1965 est., urban area, 1,543,900.

HELSINKI, the capital and largest city of Finland. It is situated on the southern coast, on the Gulf of Finland. Helsinki is a major seaport and the country's chief trading center.

Shipbuilding is Helsinki's leading industry. The production of textiles, foodstuffs, paper and wood products, and ceramics is also important. Helsinki is an educational center with a university and several colleges. Pop., 1965 est., urban area, 652,000.

GERMAN INFORMATION CENTER
HAMBURG, in West Germany, has an architectural mixture of modern and historic buildings.

CITIES OF THE WORLD

HIMEJI, an industrial center of Japan, situated on the southeastern coast of Honshu, on the Inland Sea. The city's industries produce iron and steel, textiles, and matches. Pop., 1965, 367,807.

HIROSHIMA, a Japanese seaport, the capital of Hiroshima Prefecture, lying on the Inland Sea. The city is an important industrial, commercial, and cultural center for the surrounding farming and fishing area. Hiroshima was the target of an atom bomb attack near the end of World War II. The city, which was almost completely destroyed, has been largely rebuilt. Pop., 1965, 504,245.

HOMS, a city in western Syria, lying on the Orontes River. Homs is the marketing center for the surrounding fruit-producing area, and an important road and rail junction. Pop., 1965 est., 189,900.

HONIARA, capital of the British Solomon Islands, located on the northern coast of Guadalcanal, east of New Guinea. Pop., 1964 est., 4,300.

HOWRAH, an industrial city in northeastern India, situated on the Hooghly River, opposite Calcutta. The city's rail, docking, and warehousing facilities also serve Calcutta. Howrah's industries produce rope and twine, textiles, and iron and steel. Pop., 1966 est., 554,700.

HUBLI, a city in southwestern India, situated about 300 miles southeast of Bombay. Hubli is a rail junction, commercial center, and military base. Milling and ginning cotton and the production of textiles are its most important industries. Pop., 1966 est., 193,600.

HUE, a South Vietnamese port on the Hue River, near the South China Sea. The city was once the capital of the Vietnamese empire in Indochina, and of the French colonial state of Annam. In 1968 Hue became a major battleground of the Vietnamese War. Pop., 1964 est., 103,600.

HYDERABAD, in south-central India, the capital of Andhra Pradesh, situated on the Musi River. Until 1956, Hyderabad was a separate state. The city is noted for the production of pottery, paper, textiles, and rugs. Pop., 1966 est., urban area, 1,316,000.

IASI, in northeastern Romania, on the Bahluiu River. The city is a commercial center and railroad junction. The most important industry is the manufacture of textiles. Iasi has several historic churches and cultural and educational institutions. Pop., 1965 est., 159,600.

IBADAN, the largest city in Nigeria and the capital of the former Western Province, in the southwest part of the country. The city lies in a rich agricultural region that produces cacao, cotton, yams, and corn, and its industries process these products. Ibadan is connected by rail to Lagos on the Gulf of Guinea and has an airport. Pop., 1963, 627,379.

PAN AMERICAN AIRWAYS
ISFAHAN, IRAN, a city famous for its magnificent mosques with their colored tile domes.

ICHANG, a walled port on the Yangtze River in Hupeh Province, China. The city lies at the head of the Yangtze Gorges region and is the transshipment point for river boats coming upstream from Shanghai and Hangchow. Pop., 1948 est., 81,000.

ILOILO, a port on the southeast coast of Panay Island, the Phillipines. The city is the capital of Iloilo Province and a leading port and commercial center. The chief export is sugar. Iloilo is also an important educational center and is the site of Central Phillipines University and the University of San Augustin. Pop., 1965 est., 180,900.

IMPHAL, the capital of the Union Territory of Manipur in northeastern India. The city is situated on the Imphal Plain, about 400 miles northeast of Calcutta. Imphal is a transportation center and serves as a market for the rice, sugarcane, fruit, mustard, and tobacco grown in the surrounding region. Pop., 1961, 67,717.

INDORE, in northwestern India, located in Madhya Pradesh State, about 320 miles northeast of Bombay. The city serves as a market for the surrounding agricultural region and has a number of cotton mills. Pop., 1966 est., 439,800.

IRKUTSK, capital of the Irkutsk Region in Soviet Asia. The city is located on the Angara River, about 45 miles from the southwest shore of Lake Baikal. Irkutsk is one of the major cities of Eastern Siberia and a main station on the Trans-Siberian Railway It lies in the midst of a gold-mining area and is a commercial, industrial, and educational center. Pop., 1966 est., 409,000.

ISFAHAN, the major city of central Iran, about 200 miles south of Tehran, located on the Zaindah River. The city is famous for its magnificent architecture, particularly its mosques, which are decorated with brilliantly colored tile. Most of the city's finest buildings were constructed during the reign of Shah Abbas the Great (r. 1586–1628). Isfahan is the center of the Iranian textile industry and is known for its metalwork. Pop., 1963 est., 339,900.

ISKENDERUN, a seaport in southern Turkey, on the southeastern shore of the Gulf of Iskenderun, an inlet of the Mediterranean Sea. The city is Turkey's major port on the Mediterranean and a market for the crops and livestock raised in the surrounding agricultural area. Pop., 1965, 69,300.

ISLAMABAD, the capital of Pakistan, situated on the Potwar Plateau in West Pakistan, about eight miles northeast of Rawalpindi. Still under construction, the city is scheduled for completion in 1976. The interim capital is Rawalpindi but the legislature meets in Dacca, East Pakistan.

ISTANBUL, the largest city in Turkey, located on the banks of the Bosporus at its entrance to the Sea of Marmara. One of the Mediterranean's busiest ports, Istanbul is Turkey's principal transportation, commercial, and industrial center. Its manufactures include processed foods, tobacco, leather goods, cement, glass, and soap.

The city was the capital of the Byzantine and Ottoman empires and has many historic buildings. The most famous of these is Hagia Sophia, a fourth century church that is now a museum, whose dome dominates the city. In 1968 plans were announced for building a bridge across the Bosphorus, joining Europe and Asia. Pop., 1965, urban area, 1,750,642.

IZMIR, a seaport in western Turkey, located at the southern end of the Gulf of Izmir on the Aegean Sea. Formerly called Smyrna, the city is Turkey's second largest port and a major transportation center. Izmir's industries concentrate on processing the agricultural products shipped from its port. Pop., 1965, urban area, 417,411.

JABALPUR, in central India, near the Narbada River, about 150 miles northeast of Nagpur. Jabalpur is an important manufacturing and commer-

JAIPUR

cial center. It is located on the Bombay-Calcutta railroad line. Pop., 1966 est., urban area, 425,700.

JAIPUR, in northern India, about 140 miles west of Agra. Jaipur is the capital of the state of Rajasthan. The city is a commercial center. Manufactures include textiles and jewelry. Pop., 1966 est., 463,300.

JAMESTOWN, the capital and port of St. Helena, a British colonial island in the South Atlantic Ocean. The island is located about 1,200 miles west of Africa and 1,800 miles east of Brazil. Its chief export is flax.

JAMSHEDPUR, in northeastern India, about 140 miles west of Calcutta. Jamshedpur is an important industrial city in the state of Bihar. The steel center of India, Jamshedpur also manufactures metal products and machinery. It is situated on the Bombay-Calcutta railroad line. Pop., 1966 est., 386,600.

JERUSALEM, one of the great religious centers of the world and the capital of Israel. Jerusalem is located in the Judean Hills of central Palestine, about 35 miles from the Mediterranean Sea and about 15 miles west of the north end of the Dead Sea. The Old City of Jerusalem, occupied by Jordan in 1948, contains most of the holy places, while the New City is the religious, economic, and administrative center of Israel. During the brief Arab-Israeli war of June 1967, Israeli troops captured the Old City. Pop., 1965 est., 191,700.

JESSELTON, a port in Malaysia, on the northwest coast of the island of Borneo. It is the capital of the state of Sabah. Pop., 1960, 21,719.

JINJA, in East Africa, on the north shore of Lake Victoria in Uganda. The city is an important copper smelting center. Pop., 1959, 29,741.

JODHPUR, in western India, about 300 miles southwest of Delhi. Jodhpur is a walled city in the state of Rajasthan. It is a railroad junction and trade center for locally produced grain. Pop., 1966 est., 248,200.

JOHANNESBURG, the largest city in the Republic of South Africa, in southern Transvaal Province, about 30 miles southwest of Pretoria. Johannesburg is situated on a plateau more than 5,700 feet above sea level. It is the industrial and commercial center of South Africa. Gold mining is the chief industry. Pop., 1960, urban area, 1,152,525.

JOLO, a port in the Philippines, on the northwest coast of Jolo Island in the Sulu Archipelago, about 600 miles south of Manila. Jolo is the capital of Sulu Province. Exports include coconuts and hemp. Pop., 1960, 33,259.

JOS, in the former Northern Region of Nigeria, West Africa. It is about 150 miles south of Kano and is a tin-mining center. Pop., 1963, 90,402.

JERUSALEM, a major world religious center, is sacred to Christians, Jews, and Muslims.

JUDDAH, in Saudi Arabia, a port on the Red Sea about 45 miles west of Mecca. Juddah is a walled city and the chief port for pilgrims to Mecca. Pop., 1965 est., 194,000.

JULLUNDUR, in northern India, south of the Himalayan foothills and about 80 miles east of Lahore. Jullundur is a district capital in the state of Punjab. The city processes agricultural products and is an important railroad junction. Pop., 1966 est., urban area, 298,700.

KABUL, the capital of Afghanistan, situated on the Kabul River about 50 miles from the Pakistani border. The city is a commercial center, and its industries produce wool cloth, leather, furniture, and glass. It is the seat of Kabul University and other educational institutions. Pop., 1965, urban area, 438,854.

KADUNA, the capital of the former Northern Region of Nigeria. It is situated in north-central Nigeria on the Kaduna River. It is a transportation and distribution center for the surrounding agricultural area. Kaduna's main industry is the production of textiles. Pop., 1963, 149,910.

KAGOSHIMA, a Japanese port, situated on southern Kyushu on Kagoshima Bay. The city is the capital of Kagoshima Prefecture. It is noted for the production of fine pottery known as Satsuma ware. Its other products include textiles, glass, wood, and bamboo goods. Pop., 1965. 328,446.

KAIFENG, the capital of Honan Province in east-central China, situated in the Hwang Ho valley. The city was the capital of China from the 900s to the 1100s AD. It is now a commercial center that produces silk and flour. Pop., 1953, 299,100.

KALGAN, or Changkiakow, a communications center of northern China, about 100 miles northwest of Peking. Originally a caravan terminus, the city is now a rail and highway hub. Pop., 1953, 229,300.

KALININ, a river port in the western Soviet Union, situated on the Volga River about 100 miles northwest of Moscow. The city is the capital of the Kalinin Region. Kalinin, formerly known as Tver, was founded in the 1200s. It is a commercial and industrial center that manufactures iron and steel products, transportation equipment, and textiles. Pop., 1966 est., 311,000.

KALININGRAD, formerly Königsberg, a port in the western Soviet Union, situated on the Pregel River and connected with the Bay of Danzig (Gdańsk) by canal. An industrial and commercial center, its manufactures include machinery, transportation equipment, iron and steel products, chemicals, and cement.

Kaliningrad, which was founded in the 1200s, was once part of East Prussia. Following World War II it became part of the Soviet Union under the agreement reached at the 1945 Potsdam Conference. Pop., 1966 est., 261,000.

KAMAKURA, a Japanese resort and historic city, situated on Honshu Island on Sagami Bay. The city was a capital of Japan from the late 1100s to the early 1300s. Kamakura is widely known for its large statue of Buddha. Pop., 1965, 118,329.

KAMPALA, the capital of Uganda and the province of Buganda, situated in east-central Africa, near the equator. The city is a trade and transportation center for the surrounding region, which produces coffee, tea, sugarcane, cotton, tobacco, and livestock. The city also has small industries. It is the seat of the University of East Africa. Pop. 1959, urban area, 123,332.

KANDAHAR, the capital of Kandahar Province in southeastern Afghanistan. The city is a trading center for fruit and tobacco grown in the surrounding agricultural area. It is also noted for the production of silk and felt.

Kandahar is an ancient walled city, reputedly founded by Alexander the Great. In the 1700s it was made the capital of Afghanistan by Ahmad Shah, whose imposing tomb is one of the city's most impressive sights. Pop., 1966 est., 121,200.

KANDY, the capital of Ceylon's Central Province, situated on the Mahaweli River among the mountains and lakes of the central highlands. The capital of the former Kingdom of Kandy, the city contains many temples, mosques, palaces, and crypts. Pop., 1963 est., 67,800.

KANO, in northern Nigeria, the capital of Kano Province. The city, with its international airport and railroad, is the major marketing center for agricultural products of the region. It is also Nigeria's leading manufacturing center. Its products include soap, metalware, leather goods, and peanut and cotton oils. Pop., 1963, 295,432.

KARACHI, the largest city and most important port of Pakistan, situated in West Pakistan on the Arabian Sea and the delta of the Indus River. The city has excellent air, rail, and shipping facilities. Its industries produce textiles, chemicals, transportation equipment, cigarettes, and cement. Printing is also an important industry in Karachi, as is movie-making. Pop., 1961, 1,912,598.

KARAGANDA, a city in the southwest-central Soviet Union, situated near the Nura River in the Kazakh Hills. The city lies in the center of the important Karaganda coal basin, and mining is its main industry. The city's manufactures include iron and steel, cement, and mining equipment. Pop., 1966 est., 489,000.

KATAMANDU, the capital of Nepal in South Asia, situated in the Valley of Nepal in the foothills of the Himalaya. The city, located on an ancient trade route, is a marketing center for rice, fruit, vegetables, and livestock raised in the area. Katmandu has some small industries and is the seat of several educational institutions. Pop., 1961, 122,507.

KATOWICE, or Kattowitz, the capital of the Polish province of Katowice, situated about 40 miles west of Kraków. The city is an important coal-mining center with iron and steel industries. Pop., 1965 est., 286,300.

KAUNAS, a river port in the western Soviet Union in the Lithuanian Soviet Socialist Republic, situated at the confluence of the Neman and Vilia rivers. In the 1920s and 1930s Kaunas served as the capital of Lithuania. The city is an important trade and communications center. It handles agricultural produce, livestock, and textiles, and its industries produce metal goods. Pop., 1966 est., 804,000.

KAZAN, in the eastern European Soviet Union, the capital of the Tatar Autonomous Soviet Socialist Republic. The city lies on a tributary of the Volga River and is one of the most important commercial and industrial centers of the mid-Volga area. Its industries produce soap, chemicals, textiles, leather goods, and metal products.

Kazan, which was founded in 1437 near the site of an older settlement, has suffered from invasions and revolutions. Its old buildings include a kremlin (walled fortress), cathedral, mosques, and a monastery. The city is the seat of Kazan University. Pop., 1966 est., 804,000.

KHABAROVSK, a city in the eastern Soviet Union. The city lies on the Amur River. Once an agricultural and fur trading center, Khabarovsk is now a transportation center on the Trans-Siberian Railroad and an industrial city with oil refineries. Pop., 1966 est., 420,000.

KHARKOV, a city in the southwestern Soviet Union. The city, which lies on a tributary of the Donets River, near the Donbas coal and iron region, is an industrial center and a rail and air junction. Its manufactures include mining, transportation, and electrical equipment. Kharkov is the seat of the Institute of People's Education. Pop., 1966 est., 1,092,000.

KHARTOUM, the capital of Sudan, in northern Africa, situated near the junction of the White Nile and the Blue Nile. Khartoum is the communication, commercial, financial, and educational center of Sudan. It contains modern stores and boulevards, as well as a bazaar and several mosques and churches. Pop., 1964 est., 173,500.

KIEV, a city in the western Soviet Union, the capital of the Ukranian Soviet Socialist Republic. It is situated on the Dnepr River about 450 miles southwest of Moscow. Kiev is a commercial, industrial, and transportation center. Its industries produce electric motors, agricultural machines, radio and telephone equipment, and cables.

Kiev was the capital of a Russian principality in the 800s, and the first seat of the Russian Orthodox Church. It is an educational and cultural center, with museums and a national library. Pop., 1966 est., 1,367,000.

KIGALI, the capital of Rwanda, situated about 135 miles south of the equator in central Africa. It lies in a poor agricultural area, where coffee is the leading cash crop. Pop., 1959 est., urban area, 4,200.

KIMBERLEY, a city in central South Africa, one of the major diamond centers of the world. Founded after the discovery of diamonds in 1870, the city's main industries are mining, cutting, and polishing diamonds. Pop., 1960, urban area, 79,031.

KINGSTON, the capital and chief port of Jamaica, located on the southeastern coast of the island in the western Caribbean Sea. It exports Jamaica's rum, sugar, molasses, bananas, bauxite, and alumina. Pop., 1960, urban area, 376,520.

KINGSTOWN, capital and seaport of St. Vincent island, one of the British Windward Islands, located on the southern coast, in the eastern Caribbean Sea. Pop., 1960, 4,308.

KINSHASA, formerly Léopoldville, the capital and largest city of the Republic of the Congo, situated in west-central Africa on the Congo River. Kinshasa is the cultural, administrative, financial, commercial, and transportation center of the country. Its industries manufacture chemicals, textiles, processed foods, ships, and metal products. It is the seat of Lovanium University. Pop., 1966 est., 507,900.

KIRIN, or Chilin, a city in the Manchurian region of eastern China, on the Sungari River. The city is a trade center for tobacco and lumber, and there is an important chemical industry. Pop., 1957 est., 568,000.

KIRKUK, an oil center in northeastern Iraq. Before the discovery of oil in the 1920s, the city was a market for sheep raised in the surrounding area. Kirkuk is connected by oil pipeline with Baniyas, Syria, and Tripoli, Lebanon. Pop., 1965, urban area, 176,148.

UNITED NATIONS
KATMANDU'S SINGHA DARBAR, a 1,500 room palace, now the seat of the Nepal government.

KISANGANI, formerly Stanleyville, a city in the northeastern Congo (Kinshasa), situated on the Congo River near Stanley Falls. A river port and a rail and air transportation center, it serves as a market for local cotton, rice, and fish. It has textile, pharmaceutical, and printing industries. Pop., 1966, 149,887.

KISHINEV, in the southwestern Soviet Union, the capital of the Moldavian Soviet Socialist Republic and the former capital of Bessarabia. Kishinev lies on a tributary of the Dnestr River. It is a commercial center for the surrounding agricultural area. Pop., 1966 est., 289,000.

KLAIPEDA, or Memel, a seaport of the western Soviet Union, situated on the Baltic Sea at the mouth of the Niemen River. The city, which was founded in the 1200s, has been held by Sweden, Russia, Prussia, and Germany. It is a commercial and manufacturing center. Klaipeda's exports include wood and wood products, iron products, and chemicals. Pop., 1966 est., 125,000.

KOCHI, a Japanese seaport on Shikoku Island. Fishing and shipping are important industries, and the city manufactures textiles, chemicals, and paper products. Pop., 1965, 217,889.

KOKURA, a Japanese seaport on Kyushu Island. It is a transportation, commercial, and industrial center that produces machinery and heavy cotton cloth. Pop., 1960, 286,476.

KOLHAPUR, a city in west-central India, about 180 miles southeast of Bombay. Kolhapur is a trade, education, and motion picture center. The Mahalaxmi Temple in Kolhapur is a famous religious sanctuary. Pop., 1966 est., 214,400.

KOMSOMOLSK, a city in the eastern Soviet Union, situated on the Amur River. It was established in 1932 on the site of a small village by volunteers of the Young Communist League (Komsomol). The city is an industrial center with good rail connections. Its industries include steelworks, shipyards, and oil refineries. Pop., 1966 est., 207,000.

KOŠICE, a city in southeastern Czechoslovakia, situated on the Hernad River near the Hungarian border. It is a market center with industries that produce wine, woolens, and tobacco. At various times in its history, Košice has been part of Hungary. Pop., 1965 est., 102,000.

KOZHIKODE, formerly Calicut, a port of India, lying on the southwestern coast. It is a trade center for coconut palms grown in the region. Other exports include rubber, lumber, and spices. Pop., 1966 est., urban area, 296,500.

KRAKÓW, or Cracow, a city in southern Poland on the Vistula (Wista) River. It is a rail and commercial center that manufactures machinery, construction materials, chemicals, paper, and clothing. The city is also a cultural and educational center with medieval buildings, a Gothic cathedral, a castle, and a university. Pop., 1965 est., 516,600.

KRASNOVODSK in the southern Soviet Union, a seaport on the Caspian Sea. The city is an important gateway to central Asia, to which it is linked by rail. Its imports include oil, grain and timber, and its exports include cotton and fruit. Pop., 1956 est., 38,000.

KUALA LUMPUR, the capital of Malaysia, situated on the western part of the Malay Peninsula, about 200 miles northwest of Singapore. It is a transportation center with industries based on rubber and tin production. Pop., 1957, 316,230.

KUCHING, the capital of Sarawak, situated on the northwestern coast of Borneo. The city is a port with steamer service to Singapore. Pop., 1960, 50,579.

KUMAMOTO, a city in Japan on Kyushu Island, situated on the Shira River. It is a tourist resort, with a feudal castle, and an educational center. Pop., 1965, 407,052.

KUMASI, a city of central Ghana, the former seat of the Ashanti tribal chiefs. It is a commercial center with good transportation facilities. Cacao, wood products, and bauxite are shipped from Kumasi. Pop., 1965, 230,500.

KUNMING, a city in southwestern China, situated about 380 miles southwest of Chungking. Kunming is a distribution center for, and the capital of, Yünnan Province. Its principal exports are tin and copper goods and spices and herbs. The city is also a tourist resort. Pop., 1957 est., 880,000.

KURUME, a Japanese city on Kyushu Island, about 50 miles northeast of Nagasaki. The city is a distribution center for the surrounding agricultural area, and is noted for its cotton textiles. Pop., 1965, 158,974.

THE UNITED NATIONS
LAHORE, in West Pakistan, is a city of mosques and minarets, Mughal forts, and royal tombs.

KUWAIT CITY, or Al Kuwait, the capital of Kuwait and a port, located at the northwestern end of the Persian Gulf. The city's main export is oil, but pearls, horses, and woollens are also important. Pop., 1965, 99,609.

KUYBYSHEV, formerly Samara, a city in the central European Soviet Union, situated at the confluence of the Volga and Samara rivers. The city is a distribution and trade center for grains, and its industries produce machinery, transportation equipment, and electrical goods. Pop., 1966 est., 969,000.

KWEIYANG, a transportation center of southwestern China, located on the route between Kunming and Chungking. Kweiyang is both an agricultural and an industrial city, whose products include grains, tobacco, and tea. Textiles, chemicals, and lacquerware are also produced in Kweiyang. Pop., 1957 est., 504,000.

KYOTO, the former capital of Japan, situated on west-central Honshu Island. Kyoto is a cultural and artistic center, known for its handicraft industries. There are many temples and shrines in the city, and parts of the old imperial palace are preserved. Kyoto's industries produce chemicals and electrical goods. Pop., 1965, 1,365,007.

LADYSMITH, in Natal Province, Republic of South Africa, about 200 miles northwest of Durban. The city is a railroad junction and a shipping center for the livestock raised in the surrounding area. It is the site of a famous siege of the British by Transvaal troops during the Boer War. Pop., 1960, 23,000.

LAGOS, the capital and major port of Nigeria, located on the mainland and on islands in Lagos Lagoon, off the Gulf of Guinea. Its modern harbor handles much trade, including exports of rubber, cacao, peanuts, and hardwood. Lagos is connected by road and rail to other Nigerian cities and is served by an international airport. Pop., 1963, 665,246.

LAHORE, capital of the province of West Pakistan in Pakistan, located in the Punjab about 270 miles northwest of New Delhi, India. The second largest city in Pakistan, Lahore is an important railroad junction and industrial center. It also serves as the market for the agricultural produce raised in the surrounding area. Lahore has many cultural and educational institutions and is the site of Punjab University. Pop., 1961, 1,296,477.

LAMBARÉNÉ, in Gabon, West Africa, located in the western part of the country on the Ogooué River. The city serves as a trade center for the surrounding agricultural area. It is the site of a hospital and medical center founded in 1913 by Dr. Albert Schweitzer.

LANCHOW, capital of Kansu Province in northwestern China, located on the Hwang Ho, near the Great Wall. The city lies on the medieval caravan route known as the Silk Road and because of its position near the border was known as the Gateway to China. Modern Lanchow is an important industrial center that produces machinery, refined petroleum, and chemicals. It is also a major railroad junction. Pop., 1957 est., 699,000.

LA PAZ, the chief capital and largest city of Bolivia, in west-central South America. Situated at an altitude of more than 11,000 feet on the high plateau of western Bolivia, La Paz is the highest capital and major city in the world. It is the industrial, commercial, political, and cultural center of Bolivia, although Sucre is the legal capital. Manufactures include textiles, cement, glass, and furniture. Pop., 1965 est., 360,300.

LASHIO, in northeastern Burma, on the Shan Plateau, about 130 miles northeast of Mandalay. The city is a trade center and the northeastern terminus of the railroad from Mandalay. Lashio was formerly an important point on the old Burma Road. Pop., 1956, 5,869.

LATAKIA, seaport in western Syria and capital of Latakia Province, located on the Mediterranean Sea about 110 miles north of Beirut. An ancient city, Latakia reached a height of prosperity during the Crusades and then declined until the 1700s, when it became the center of an important tobacco-raising district. The port's main exports are tobacco, silk, and sponges. Pop., 1963 est., 75,400.

LEEDS, in north-central England, on the Aire River, about 165 miles northwest of London. Leeds is an industrial city located near coal and iron mines. It is the center of England's wool industry. Manufactures include textiles and clothing, iron and steel, machinery, chemicals, and leather goods. The city is an important cultural and educational center. Pop., 1965 est., urban area, 1,726,200.

LE HAVRE, an important seaport on the northern coast of France at the mouth of the Seine River on the English Channel. Le Havre handles imports and exports for Paris and northwestern France, trading primarily with North America and northern Europe. The city's industries include shipbuilding and the manufacture of machinery, electrical equipment, and chemical products. Le Havre also has an important oil-refinery. Pop., 1962, urban area, 222,565.

LEIPZIG, an East German city on the Pleisse River at its junction with the Elster and the Parthe. It is a major commercial and industrial center, manufacturing vehicles and machinery, chemicals, steel, and textiles. It lies at the junction of many rail, road, and river transportation routes, and it is an important river port. Leipzig has many colleges and museums and is a leading German cultural center. Pop., 1965 est., 594,700.

LENINGRAD, the second largest city in the Soviet Union, located at the mouth of the Neva River on the Gulf of Finland, an inlet of the Baltic Sea. The city was known as St. Petersburg until 1914 and as Petrograd until 1924. Leningrad is a major industrial center. Its industries produce electrical equipment, precision tools, machinery, chemicals, textiles, and paper. It is also an important shipbuilding center. The city has many cultural and educational institutions, including the Hermitage art museum and the University of Leningrad.

Leningrad was founded in 1703 by Peter the Great. It was the capital of Russia from 1713 until 1918 and was the place where the Russian Revolution began in 1917. Pop., 1965 est., urban area, 3,665,000.

LIBREVILLE, capital of Gabon in West Africa, located 30 miles north of the equator on the Atlantic Ocean. It is Gabon's largest city and a major port. Hardwoods are Libreville's leading exports. Pop., 1964, 45,909.

LIÈGE, capital of Liège Province, Belgium, in the eastern part of the country, on the Meuse River. Surrounded by a coal-mining region, Liège is an important industrial center. Its chief manufactures are steel, firearms, crystal, and glass. Liège has a number of historic buildings, a notable art museum, and a university. Pop., 1965 est., urban area, 452,700.

LIEPAYA, seaport and second largest city in Latvia, located on an isthmus between Lake Liepaya and the Baltic Sea. The city is a naval base and industrial center. Its chief manufactures are steel, chemicals, machinery, ships, and processed foods. Pop., 1966 est., 84,000.

LIKASI, the former Jadotville, in Katanga Province, southeastern Congo (Kinshasa), West Africa. The city is located about 60 miles northwest of Lubumbashi and is an important copper smelting center. Pop., 1966 est., 102,200.

LIMA, capital and largest city of Peru, on the Rimac River, about 8 miles inland from the Pacific Ocean and its port, Callao. The city is the political and cultural center of Peru. Founded in 1535 by Francisco Pizzaro, Lima retains many buildings from its colonial past and is one of the most picturesque capitals of South America. It is connected by rail and road to Callao and other cities in Peru. Pop., 1961, urban area, 1,436,231.

LIMASSOL, a seaport on the south coast of Cyprus, located on Akrotiri Bay. The city exports the wine, barley, and livestock of the surrounding area and minerals from the interior. Local industries produce alcoholic beverages, perfumes, and cigarettes. Pop., 1960, 43,593.

LISBON, the capital and largest city of Portugal, located at the mouth of the Tagus River on the Atlantic Ocean. It is Portugal's leading port and exports the country's fish, olive oil, and wine. Lisbon contains most of the country's industry and produces ships, refined oil, textiles, chemicals, processed foods, and tile. The city has

BRANIFF AIRWAYS
LA PAZ, in western Bolivia, is the world's highest capital, over 11,000 feet above sea level.

LOMÉ, the capital of Togo, is a commercial center and seaport with busy outdoor markets.

many beautiful churches and a number of interesting Muslim and Renaissance buildings. Pop., 1965 est., 822,000.

LIVERPOOL, the second largest seaport in Britain, situated on the Mersey River, near the Irish Sea. The city's economy is based on shipping and warehouse storage, especially of cotton, wool, tobacco, and grain. Liverpool is a rail center and is connected with Manchester and its industrial region by the deep-water Manchester Ship Canal. Its industries produce flour, refined sugar, candy, soap, and glass. Pop., 1965 est., urban area, 1,381,100.

LJUBLJANA, the capital of Slovenia, Yugoslavia, located on the Sava River. The city lies in a rich agricultural region for which it serves as a trade center. It is also an important railroad junction. Ljubljana's industries produce textiles, machinery, and paper. Pop., 1961, 134,169.

LOBITO, the principal port of Angola, in southwestern Africa, located on the Atlantic Ocean about 24 miles north of Benguela. The city is the terminus of a railroad from the Katanga copper mines in the Congo and copper is one of its major exports. Lobito also exports Angola's sisal, cotton, corn, and iron ore. It is linked by air to other cities in Africa and Europe. Pop., 1960, 50,164.

LÓDŹ, the second largest city of Poland, about 75 miles southwest of Warsaw, in the central part of the country. It is an important industrial center and produces textiles, machinery, electrical equipment, paper, and processed foods. Pop., 1965 est., 742,900.

LOMÉ, in West Africa, the capital and major seaport of Togo, located on the Gulf of Guinea. The city is the chief commercial and industrial center of the country. Its port exports phosphate, cacao, coffee, copra, timber, and palm oil. Lomé is connected by rail with the cities of the interior. Pop., 1966 est., 86,400.

LONDON, the capital of Britain and one of the world's largest cities, located on the Thames River about 40 miles from the North Sea. London is Britain's major port and commercial center. Its industries produce mostly finished consumer goods, including clothing, metal and electrical goods, chemicals, processed foods, plastics, and cigarettes. London is also a major center for banking, insurance, publishing, and printing.

A city since Roman times, London has many points of historical interest and its fine educational institutions, libraries, and museums make it an important cultural and intellectual center. London is joined to other parts of Britain and the world by an excellent network of land, sea, and air transportation. Pop., 1965 est., urban area, 7,948,300.

LOURENÇO MARQUES, the capital and largest city of Mozambique, Africa, located on an inlet of the Indian Ocean, near the country's southern border. Rail connections with Transvaal and Natal, South Africa, and a modern harbor make the city a leading port and an outlet for South African products. Major exports are coal, cotton, hardwoods, meat, and hides. Pop., 1960, urban area, 177,929.

LUANDA, seaport on the west central coast of Africa, capital of Angola. The city is Angola's major industrial center and produces soap, tobacco, and wood veneer. There is also a large oil refinery. Luanda's chief exports are coffee, sugar, cotton, fish, and diamonds. It is linked to Malange and Casengo in the interior by rail and is served by an airport. Pop., 1960, urban area, 224,540.

LUANG PRABANG, in Laos, situated on the Mekong River, about 130 miles north of the capital of Vientiane. Located at the last navigable point on the river, the city serves as a trade center for the rice, teakwood, and other forest products of the surrounding area. Pop., 1962 est., 25,000.

LUBLIN, in eastern Poland, on the Bystryzca River, about 105 miles southwest of Warsaw. The city is a railroad junction and a trade center for the grain, potatoes, flax, and hemp raised in the surrounding area. Lublin's industries produce agricultural machinery, aircraft, trucks, and textiles. Pop., 1965 est., 202,900.

LUBUMBASHI, formerly Elisabethville, in Katanga, the Congo (Kinshasa), located near the border with Zambia. The city is a transportation and industrial center. Katanga is rich in copper, which is smelted in Lubumbashi. Other industries include printing, brewing, and the manufacture of textiles, flour, and vegetable oil. Pop., 1966 est., 507,900.

LUCKNOW, the capital of Uttar Pradesh state, India, located on the Gumti River, about 270 miles southeast of Delhi. The city is an important railroad junction and industrial center. It also serves as a market for the grain, sugarcane, mangoes, and oilseeds produced in the surrounding area. Lucknow handicraft industries produce metal goods, pottery, and embroidered muslins. Pop., 1966 est., urban area. 740,400.

LUSAKA, the capital of Zambia, in south-central Africa, located in the south-central part of the country. The city lies in an agricultural region near a mining district that produces copper, gold, and bismuth. Lusaka is the hub of an extensive road and rail network that links it to the Congo, Rhodesia, and Malawi. Pop., 1965 est., 138,000.

LUXEMBOURG, capital of Luxembourg, located in the south-central part of the country. The city is an important financial center and the headquarters of the European Coal and Steel Community. Luxembourg's industries produce iron and steel, textiles, leather goods, machinery, and processed foods. Pop., 1965 est., 78,700.

LVOV, formerly Lwów, in the Ukrainian Soviet Socialist Republic of the Soviet Union, near the Polish border. Formerly part of Poland, the city has a long history and was once one of the great trade centers of medieval Europe. It is now an important railroad junction and commercial center. Its major industries produce textiles, machinery, and refined oil. Pop., 1966 est., 502,000.

LYON, the third largest city in France, situated at the confluence of the Saône and Rhône rivers, in the southeastern part of the country. Lyon is second only to Paris as a commercial and industrial center.

The leading industry of Lyon is the manufacture of silk textiles, but the city also produces chemicals, drugs, dyes, and electrical machinery. A stock exchange and international banks make it a financial center, and yearly international trade fairs are held in the city. Over 2,000 years old, Lyon has many points of historical interest. Pop., 1962, urban area, 885,944.

MADRAS, a port on the southeastern coast of India, about 640 miles southeast of Bombay. Madras is the capital of Madras State and one of India's largest cities. It is a transportation and commercial center. Exports include cotton, coffee, tea, rice, and tobacco. Pop., 1966 est., 1,896,100.

MADRID, the capital and largest city of Spain. The city is located in the region of New Castile, at the geographical center of the Iberian Peninsula. Madrid is situated on a plateau, at an altitude of about 2,150 feet above sea level. It is Spain's leading administrative, financial, and cultural center. It is also among the nation's chief educational and tourist centers. Manufactures include machinery, leather goods, and paper. Pop., 1965 est., urban area, 2,599,300.

MADURA, in southern India, on the Vaigai River, about 265 miles southwest of Madras. Madura is a district capital in the state of Madras and an important industrial and commercial center. The chief manufacture is textiles. Exports include rice and tobacco. Pop., 1966 est., 458,400.

MAGNITOGORSK, in the Ural Mountains of the Soviet Union, on the left bank of the Ural River, about 800 miles east of Moscow. Magnitogorsk is a leading Soviet steel center. Mining machinery is also manufactured. Pop., 1966 est., 352,000.

MAIDUGURI, in West Africa, in the northeastern part of the former Northern Region of Nigeria. It is about 315 miles east of Kano. Maiduguri is a transportation center. Pop., 1963, 139,965.

MAKASAR, a port in Southeast Asia, on the island of Celebes in Indonesia. It is one of Indonesia's largest cities and the capital of the province of South Sulawesi. Exports include coffee, copra, rice, and spices. Pop., 1961, 384,159.

MALACCA, a Southeast Asian port, capital of the state of Malacca in Malaysia. The city is located on the southwest coast of the Malay Peninsula, about 125 miles northwest of Singapore. Exports include rubber and tin. Pop., 1957, 69,848.

MALE, the capital of the Indian Ocean nation of Maldive Islands, situated on Male atoll. The town processes and exports local fish and coconuts. Pop., 1965, 11,202.

MANAGUA, capital and largest city of Nicaragua, situated in the west on the southern shore of Lake Managua. It lies on the main rail and road transportation routes and is the economic and cultural center of the country. It has food-processing plants, textile mills, pharmaceutical factories, and other industries. The city has been severely damaged by earthquakes several times. Pop., 1965 est., 262,000.

MANAMA, the capital and principal town of the sheikhdom of Bahrain, situated on the northern coast of Bahrain Island, on the Persian Gulf. Refining and exporting the sheikhdom's petroleum are the port city's main industries, and there is some boatbuilding and fishing. Pop., 1959, urban area, 61,726.

MANCHESTER, in northwestern England, on the Irwell River in Lancashire, about 30 miles northeast of Liverpool. Manchester, Britain's leading manufacturing center, is among the world's chief producers of cotton goods. Other products include aircraft, motor vehicles, machinery, chemicals, and rubber goods. Manchester is a railroad junction and an ocean port, linked to the Irish Sea by the deepwater Manchester Ship Canal. Pop., 1965 est., urban area, 2,457,300.

MANDALAY, in Southeast Asia, on the left bank of the Irrawaddy River in central Burma, about 350 miles north of Rangoon, the capital. Mandalay is an important religious and cultural center. The leading industry is silk weaving. Pop., 1958 est., 195,300.

MANGALORE, a port on the southwest coast of India, at the mouth of the Netravati River, about 190 miles west of Bangalore. Mangalore is a district capital in the state of Mysore. The city is a railroad terminus and shipping center. Exports include coffee, pepper, and tea. Pop., 1966 est., 198,600.

MANILA, the largest city, chief port, and administrative center of the Philippines. It lies on Luzon Island on Manila Bay. The city is a transportation, manufacturing, and educational center. Its products include coconut oil, sugar, rice, textiles, and transportation equipment. Pop., 1965 est., 1,356,00.

MARRAKECH, in west-central Morocco, on the western slopes of the Grand Atlas Mountains in North Africa. Marrakech is one of the largest cities of Morocco and a major Muslim religious center. Manufactures include wool, flour, carpets and leather goods. Pop., 1965 est., 255,000.

MARSEILLE, in southeastern France, the greatest port on the Mediterranean Sea. It is located on the Gulf of Lions, about 25 miles east of the mouth of the Rhône River. It is the capital of the department of Bouches-du-Rhône and a leading European industrial center. Manufactures include motor vehicles, machinery, sugar, textiles, and olive oil. Pop., 1962, urban area, 807,499.

MASERU, the capital of Lesotho, in southern Africa. The city is located near the western border with South Africa, at an altitude of more than 5,000 feet above sea level. Maseru is the nation's transportation center. Exports include wool, mohair, and hides. Workers for South African mines are recruited in Maseru. Pop., 1966, urban area, 18,000.

MASHHAD, in northeastern Iran, near the border with the Soviet Union, about 440 miles east of Tehran, the capital. Mashhad is an important holy city and a leading commercial and transportation center. Manufactures include cotton, wool, and leather. Pop., 1963 est., 312,200.

MATADI, in the extreme western Congo (Kinshasa), near the mouth of the Congo River, at the border with Angola. Matadi is the chief port of the Congo and exports agricultural and forest products. Pop., 1958 est., 59,000.

MATHURA, in northern India, on the right bank of the Jumna River, about 30 miles northwest of Agra. Mathura is an important religious and cultural center. Manufactures include cotton and paper. Pop., 1966 est., urban area, 135,700.

MBABANE, the capital and chief town of Swaziland, in southeastern Africa. Mbabane is located about 95 miles southwest of Lourenço Marques, the

THE UNITED NATIONS
RUSH HOUR IN MANILA, the administrative center and chief port of the Philippines.

MECCA, in Saudia Arabia, is Islam's holiest shrine and a city of modern parks and avenues.

capital of Portuguese Mozambique, with which it is linked by rail. Exports from Mbabane include iron ore and asbestos. Pop., 1962 est., urban area, 8,400.

MECCA, the chief holy city of the Muslim world. It is located in a valley in west-central Saudi Arabia, about 45 miles east of Juddah, its port on the Red Sea. Mecca is the birthplace of Muhammad and contains the Kaaba, chief shrine of Islam, which is visited by many thousands of pilgrims each year. The city is also the capital of the province of Hejaz and a commercial center. Pop., 1965 est., 185,000.

MEDELLÍN, in Colombia, in a mountain valley at an altitude of about 5,000 feet above sea level, about 150 miles northwest of Bogotá. Medellín is the capital of the department of Antioquia and the second largest city of Colombia. Medellín is an educational center and the nation's chief industrial city. It manufactures steel, textiles, chemicals, sugar, and paper. Pop., 1964, 772,887.

MEDINA, in northwestern Saudi Arabia, about 100 miles from the Red Sea coast. It is second only to Mecca as a Muslim holy city. The Great Mosque in Medina contains the tomb of Muhammad and is annually visited by many thousands of pilgrims. The city is located in a fertile oasis and is a market center for agricultural products. Pop., 1963 est., 72,000.

MEERUT, in northern India, on a branch of the Ganges River, about 35 miles northeast of Delhi. It is a district capital in the state of Uttar Pradesh and a trade and transportation center. Manufactures include steel, chemicals, sugar, and soap. Pop., 1966 est., urban area, 311,100.

MELBOURNE, the capital, largest city, and chief port of Victoria, Australia. Melbourne is located at the mouth of the Yarra River on Port Phillip Bay, in southeastern Australia. The city is an important railroad terminus and one of Australia's leading commercial centers. Manufactures include aircraft, motor vehicles, textiles, and processed foods. Pop., 1966, urban area, 2,228,511.

MELILLA, a Spanish enclave on the north coast of Morocco, administered by Spain as part of the province of Málaga. The city is situated about 30 miles west of the border with Algeria. Melilla is an important fishing port. It exports iron ore and lead. Pop., 1966 est., 77,900.

MEXICO CITY, the capital of Mexico, located in the southern part of the Central Plateau. Mexico City is one of the oldest cities in North America. In 1325 the Aztecs built their capital, Tenochtitlán, on the site. Today one of the largest cities in the Western Hemisphere, Mexico City is a major cultural, commercial, and industrial center. Its fine buildings and sites of historical interest, beautiful location, and pleasant climate attract many tourists. Pop., 1966 est., 3,287,300.

MILAN, in northern Italy, located between the foothills of the Alps and the Po River, near the border with Switzerland. Milan is the second largest city in Italy and the nation's leading industrial and commercial center. Manufactures include aircraft, motor vehicles, heavy machinery, chemicals, and textiles. Pop., 1965 est., urban area, 1,669,500.

MINSK, in the far western Soviet Union, the capital of the Byelorussian Soviet Socialist Republic. The city is located on a branch of the Berezina River, about 470 miles southwest of Moscow and about 150 miles east of the border with Poland. Minsk is Byelorussia's leading industrial, cultural, and transportation center. Manufactures include trucks, tractors, and radios. Pop., 1966 est., 739,000.

MISKOLC, in northeastern Hungary, on the Sajó River, about 85 miles northeast of Budapest. Miskolc is an important industrial city and trade center. Manufactures include iron and steel, motor vehicles, textiles, and lumber. Pop., 1965 est., 169,000.

MOGADISCIO, the capital and chief port of Somalia, in eastern Africa. It is located on the Indian Ocean, about 700 miles southeast of Addis Ababa, the capital of Ethiopia. Mogadiscio exports bananas and hides. Pop., 1966 est., 170,000.

MOKPO, a port in southwestern South Korea, on the Yellow Sea, about 190 miles south of Seoul. Mokpo's industries include fishing and food processing. Pop., 1965, est., 157,400.

MOMBASA, the chief port of Kenya, off the coast of eastern Africa. Mombasa is located on a small island in the Indian Ocean and is linked to the mainland by a causeway, a bridge, and ferries. The city exports coffee, cotton, tea, sugar, and other agricultural products. Pop., 1962, urban area, 179,575.

MONROVIA, the capital, largest city, and chief port of Liberia in West Africa. Monrovia is located on Cape Montserrado, near the mouth of the Saint Paul River, on the Atlantic Ocean. The city is the commercial, educational, and cultural center of Liberia. Exports include rubber, iron ore, gold, and coffee. The city was named for U. S. Pres. James Monroe. Pop., 1962, 80,992.

MONTE CARLO, a commune in the principality of Monaco. It is located on the French Riviera, nine miles from Nice, France. Monte Carlo is a famous resort. Pop., 1965, 9,038.

MONTEVIDEO, the capital, largest city, and chief port of Uruguay. It is located on the north shore of the Rio de la Plata, about 135 miles southeast of Buenos Aires, Argentina. Montevideo is the industrial, commercial, and cultural center of Uruguay. The city's leading industry is meat packing. Chief exports are wool, meat, and hides. Pop., 1963, 1,158,632.

MONTREAL, the largest city in Canada. It is located on the island of Montreal, at the confluence of the Ottawa and St. Lawrence rivers, in southern Quebec. Montreal is situated at the entrance to the St. Lawrence Seaway. Although the city is about 1,000 miles from the Atlantic Ocean, it is one of the world's largest inland ports. It is Canada's industrial, financial, and transportation center. Manufactures include aircraft, iron and steel, oil, chemicals, electrical equipment, processed foods, and clothing. Pop., 1966, urban area, 2,436,817.

MORADABAD, in northern India, on the right bank of the Ramganga River, about 90 miles east of Delhi. Moradabad is a district capital in the state of Uttar Pradesh and an important trade and transportation center. Pop., 1966 est., urban area, 207,800.

MORONI, the capital of the Comoro Islands, a French possession at the north entrance to the Mozambique Channel. Moroni is located on the east coast of Grande Comore Island. The town is the chief port. Pop., 1966 est., urban area, 11,500.

MOSCOW, the capital and largest city of the Soviet Union. It is located on both banks of the Moscow River, about 400 miles southeast of Leningrad. Moscow is the Soviet Union's industrial, political, and transportation center. Manufactures include motor vehicles, machinery, electrical equipment, chemicals, textiles, and steel.

Moscow is the headquarters of the Communist Party of the Soviet Union and the administrative and cultural center of the nation. Landmarks include the Kremlin, Red Square, and St. Basil's Cathedral. Pop., 1966 est., urban area, 6,463,000.

MOSHI, in eastern Africa, on the southern slope of Mt. Kilimanjaro in northeastern Tanzania. Moshi is a trading center in an agricultural region. Pop., 1957, 13,726.

MOSUL, in Iraq, on the west bank of the Tigris River, about 220 miles northwest of Bagdad, the capital. Mosul is situated in an oil producing region and is Iraq's oil center. The ruins of ancient Nineveh are nearby. Pop., 1965, urban area, 315,157.

MOULMEIN, a port in Southeast Asia, situated at the mouth of the Salween River in lower Burma, on the Gulf of Martaban. Moulmein is a district capital and commercial center. Exports include tea and rice. Pop., 1958 est., 108,000.

MUNICH, or München, capital of the state of Bavaria and the third largest city in West Germany. Munich is situated on the Isar River, about 25 miles north of the Bavarian Alps in southeastern West Germany. The city is an important industrial, commercial, and transportation center.

In addition to beer, for which the city is famous, Munich manufactures vehicles, machinery, chemicals, and textiles. The city is also a major cultural, educational, and tourist center. Pop., 1965 est., 1,210,500.

MURMANSK, the Soviet Union's chief port on the Arctic Ocean. The city is located on the Kola Peninsula in the far north, on the east bank of the Tuloma River, about 35 miles from the Barents Sea. It is the largest city north of the Arctic Ocean and the only large Soviet ice-free port.

Murmansk is a naval and fishing center and is linked by railroad to Leningrad, which is about 625 miles to the south. Exports include fish, lumber, and minerals. Pop., 1966 est., 279,000.

MURORAN, in northern Japan, situated on the southwest coast of Hokkaido Island, at the entrance to Uchiura Bay. Muroran is a naval base and an iron and steel center. Coal is the chief export. Pop., 1965, urban area, 161,252.

MUSCAT, capital of Muscat and Oman, a country in the southeastern part of the Arabian Peninsula. The city is located on Muscat Bay, an arm of the Gulf of Oman, at the entrance to the Persian Gulf. Pop., 1960 est., urban area, 6,200.

UNITED NATIONS
MOSCOW CITIZENS shop in GUM, the largest department store in the Soviet Union's capital.

NACALA, a seaport of northern Mozambique in southeastern Africa. Its deep natural harbor was improved during a six-year plan ending in 1958. The port's subsequent growth reflects development of the hinterland for agriculture and utilization of local deposits of graphite, copper, and chrome ores. It is the coastal terminus of a rail line to Lake Nyasa.

NAGASAKI, a seaport on the northwest coast of Kyushu Island, Japan. Opened to foreign trade in 1568, it has had the longest contact with the Western world of any Japanese city. A large steel rolling mill and nearby coal fields have made it an important shipbuilding center and coaling station. Almost half of the city was destroyed on Aug. 9, 1945 by the second U. S. atomic bomb used in warfare. Pop., 1965, 405,479.

NAGOYA, the third largest city of Japan, located on the south coast of Honshu Island at the head of Ise Bay. A major port, industrial and rail center, the city produces pottery and porcelain, textiles, machine tools, automobiles, and chemicals. It is the site of Nagoya University. Pop., 1965, 1,935,430.

NAGPUR, a city in Maharashtra state, India, 420 miles northeast of Bombay. An important rail center, the city also has many cotton and woolen mills and an important hand-weaving industry. The city is the site of Nagpur University. Pop., 1966 est., urban area, 799,700.

NAHA, a seaport and the capital of the U.S.-controlled Ryukyu Islands, located on the southeast coast of Okinawa Island. The city was the capital of the Okinawa Prefecture of Japan until the island was captured by the United States in 1945. Its manufactures include lacquerware and textiles. Pop., 1965 est., 226,000.

NAIROBI, the capital and largest city of Kenya, in east Africa. It is the focus of several rail lines which carry coffee, cotton, tea, and sisal from parts of Kenya and Uganda to the Indian Ocean port of Mombasa. Principal industries include meat packing, flour milling, and the manufacture of furniture, soap, chemicals, foodstuffs, and paper products. Pop., 1962, urban area, 314,760.

NANCHANG, the capital of Kiangsi Province, China. It is on the Kan River, southwest of Poyang Lake. Located at the junction of two rail lines, the city is the commercial center of a rich agricultural area. Its industries include cotton milling, food processing, and the manufacture of machine tools, farm implements, paper, and matches. Pop., 1957 est., 508,000.

NANKING, the capital of Kiangsu Province, China. It is on the Yangtze River, which seagoing vessels can navigate to the city. Rail lines connect it to Peking and Shanghai. Traditional industries include the manufacture of silk and cotton cloth and a firm, durable cotton fabric called Nankeen. Since communist rule began in 1949, heavy industrial and chemical plants have been established.

An important cultural and educational center, Nanking is the site of scientific research institutes and several institutions of higher learning, including Nanking University. It was the capital of China during the Nationalist period, which ended in 1949. Pop., 1957 est., 1,419,000.

NAPLES, or Napoli, a major seaport in Italy on the Bay of Naples, off the Tyrrhenian Sea. It is 10 miles northwest of Mount Vesuvius. The third largest city in Italy, it is an industrial center and important for the manufacture of ships, engines, textiles, glass, gloves, wine, and machinery.

Naples was founded several hundred years before the birth of Christ. Many relics from the ruins of Pompeii are in the National Museum. Naples has medieval and Renaissance buildings, as well as a university, libraries, and museums. Pop., 1965 est., 1,228,100.

NARA, a Japanese city, within 50 miles of Kyoto and Osaka. It was the first capital of Japan, from 710 to 784. During the Nara Period, Japanese culture began to develop independently of the earlier Chinese domination. The city is the site of the Nara National Museum. Pop., 1965, 160,641.

NAZARETH, an ancient town of northern Israel, southwest of the Sea of Galilee (Lake Tiberias). Although the site of the boyhood of Jesus, it was not recognized as significant until about 600 AD. Tourism is the major source of income. Pop., 1965 est., 29,100.

NDOLA, a town of western Zambia, in south-central Africa. Located in the copperbelt, it is a mining and refining center. The city is linked by rail to the capital, Lusaka, to the south. Pop., 1965 est., urban area, 100,000.

NEICHIANG, a city in Szechwan Province, China. It is on a rail line between Chungking and Chengtu. Neichiang is a commercial center. Pop., 1953, 190,200.

NEW DELHI, the capital of India, situated in the north-central part of the country on the Jumna River. New Delhi lies adjacent to Delhi, or Old Delhi. Together the cities form a trade, transportation, and industrial center. Manufactures include textiles, clothing, metal products, chemicals, and handicrafts of gold, silver, ivory, and wood. Old Delhi is the seat of the University of Delhi.

The site of Old and New Delhi has been inhabited since about 400 BC. The present city of New Delhi was designed and constructed as an administrative center. The seat of government was transferred from Calcutta to Delhi in 1912 and to New Delhi in 1931. Pop., 1966 est., New Delhi, 314,400; Delhi, 2,440,500.

NIAMEY, the capital of the Republic of Niger in West Africa. An inland port on the Niger River, it is a market center for the agricultural products of the region. Pop., 1962 est., 40,172.

NICE, an ancient city in southern France on the Mediterranean Sea near the Italian border. The Maritime Alps lie to the north, and the city's beautiful location and climate make it a world-renowned resort. The tourist trade is the city's chief industry but also important are the manufacture of perfume oils, soap, clothing, and the preparation of olive oil. Flowers and olive trees are cultivated, and there is an important trade in cut flowers. Pop., 1962, urban area, 310,063.

NICOSIA, the capital of Cyprus, an island in the eastern Mediterranean Sea near Turkey. It is a commercial center of the Messaori Plain, which produces wheat, wine, olive oil, almonds, citrus fruits, and livestock. Textiles, leather, machine tools, and cigarettes are manufactured in the city. Pop., 1964 est., urban area, 103,000.

NINGPO, or Ninghsien, a seaport of China, south of Hangchow Bay in the East China Sea. An important fishing center, the city manufactures furniture, lace, and straw products and exports cotton, drugs, tea, and fish. Pop., 1953, 237,500.

FRENCH GOVERNMENT TOURIST OFFICE
NICE, a resort city, lies on the curving Mediterranean seacoast of the French Riviera.

NIS, a city of eastern Yugoslavia, on the Morava River, some 120 miles southeast of Belgrade. A commercial center, the city has rail connections with the major cities of the country. Its manufactures include furniture, liquor, cigarettes, leather, and textiles. Pop., 1961, 81,073.

NOUAKCHOTT, capital of the Islamic Republic of Mauritania, in West Africa. Lying four miles from the Atlantic Ocean, it is a market center with limited port facilities. Pop., 1965 est., 15,000.

NOUMÉA, seaport and capital of New Caledonia, an overseas territory of the French Community, in the Southwest Pacific Ocean. An attractive city with a pleasant climate, Noméa attracts many tourists. It is the site of the French Research Institute of Oceania and headquarters of the six-nation South Pacific Commission. The principal industry is nickel smelting. Pop., 1963, 34,990.

NOVI SAD, a city in northeastern Yugoslavia, on the Danube River about 45 miles northwest of Belgrade. An important Danube port and rail center, it is the market for agricultural products of the region, and manufactures machinery, pottery, textiles, and chemicals. The city is the chief Serbian religious and cultural center. Pop., 1961, 102,469.

NOVOSIBIRSK, capital of the Novosibirsk Oblast, U.S.S.R. It is some 1700 miles east of Moscow. The largest city in Siberia, it is on the Ob River, at the point where it is crossed by the Trans-Siberian Railroad. It has long been an agricultural center.

With iron and coal sources nearby, the city's industrial capacity was increased when many industrial plants were moved there from threatened areas of western Russia in World War II. It manufactures steel, automobiles, machinery, ships, textiles, plastics, and foodstuffs. It is also a cultural center with a branch of the Academy of Sciences, a university, and ballet, opera, and dramatic theaters. Pop., 1966 est., 1,049,00.

NUKU'ALOFA, seaport and capital of Tonga, a British protectorate in the Southwest Pacific. It is located on the north coast of Tongatabu Island. Pop., 1956, 9,202.

NURNBERG, or Nuremberg, in southern West Germany, on the Pegnitz River, about 90 miles northwest of Munich. Nurnberg is an industrial and transportation center. Manufactures include machines, chemicals, textiles, electrical equipment, and beer. It is a center of German culture and history. Pop., 1965 est., 472,000.

ODESSA, a city in the southwestern Soviet Union, situated on the Black Sea near the mouth of the Dnestr River. The city is one of the major seaports of the Soviet Union. Its excellent harbor handles a variety of exports, including grain, wood, wool, and foodstuffs. Imports include coal, cotton, and tea. Odessa manufactures such products as machinery, clothing, housewares, and processed foods. Pop., 1966 est., 753,000.

OKAYAMA, a Japanese port, situated on Honshu Island on the Inland Sea. The city is a rail center. Fishing and the manufacture of cotton textiles, chemicals, and porcelain are important industries. Pop., 1965, 291,825.

OMUTA, a Japanese port, situated on Kyushu Island on Shimabara Bay. The city's industries, which produce coke, steel, zinc, and fertilizers, use coal from the nearby Miike deposits. Pop., 1965, 193,875.

ONITSHA, a Nigerian city in the former Eastern Region, situated on the Niger River, about 130 miles from its mouth. Onitsha is an industrial city, lying in the middle of a coal and oil producing region. Pop., 1963, 163,032.

ORADEA, or Oradea Mare, a city of northwestern Romania, situated on the Koros River near the Hungarian border. Oradea is a communications and trading center for an area that produces wine, grain, fruit, and livestock. Pop., 1965 est., urban area, 124,100.

ORAN, a port of northwestern Algeria, situated on the Mediterranean Sea. The city, originally a small market town, was founded by the Moors and has been held by the Spanish, Turks, and French. In 1791 it was destroyed by an earthquake. Oran is a commercial center. The city exports minerals and agricultural products. Pop., 1966, urban area, 328,257.

OSAKA, a Japanese port, situated on the southwestern coast of Honshu Island. Osaka is one of the most important industrial and commercial centers of Japan. Its industries produce a wide variety of goods, including cotton textiles, automobiles, and chemicals. Osaka is also an educational center. Pop., 1965, 3,156,222.

OSHOGBO, a Nigerian city in the former Western Region. The city, which lies on a railroad, is a trading center in a region that produces lead and zinc, cocoa, and tobacco. Pop., 1963, 208,966.

OSLO, the capital of Norway, lying at the northern end of Oslo Fjord, near the Skaggerak straits. The largest city in Norway, Oslo is also the country's principal port and its adminstrative, commercial, and industrial center. Industrial activities include shipbuilding and the manufacture of textiles, paper products, and chemicals. The city has many historic sites and cultural institutions, and is the seat of the University of Oslo. Pop., 1965 est., 483,200.

OSTRAVA, formerly Moravska Ostrava, a city in north-central Czechoslovakia, situated on the Ostravice River near its confluence with the Oder River. Ostrava is strategically located at the Moravian Gate. The city is the center of an important coal-mining region, and its industries produce iron and steel, and iron and steel products. Pop., 1965 est., 262,100.

OTARU, a Japanese port, situated on the west coast of Hokkaido Island. The city's protected harbor and large piers are used in the shipping and storing of coal from the nearby Ishikari fields. Pop., 1965, 196,771.

OTTAWA, the capital of Canada, situated in southeastern Ontario Province on the Ottawa River, about 100 miles west of Montreal. The city is primarily an administrative center, but there are some industries. The manufacture of wood, pulp, and paper products is most important. Hydroelectric power is supplied by Chaudière Falls on the Ottawa River. Pop., 1965 est., urban area, 482,000.

OUAGADOUGOU, the capital and leading city of Upper Volta in West Africa. It is connected by rail with Abidjan, an Atlantic port in the Ivory Coast. Ouagadougou is the trade center for the surrounding agricultural region. Its main exports are peanuts, cotton, and animal hides. Pop., 1961, 59,126.

OUJDA, a city in northeastern Morocco, situated near the Algerian border. It is a rail and commercial center for the nearby mining and agricultural regions. It exports lead and zinc, grains, citrus fruits, and wool and hides. Pop., 1965 est., 130,000.

OXFORD, a city in central England, situated on the Thames River. Oxford is the seat of Oxford University, which was founded in the 1100s. The city was the meeting place of some of the earliest English parliaments. Oxford's industries include the production of automobiles and printing and publishing. Pop., 1965 est., 109,300.

PADANG, an Indonesian port, situated on the west coast of the island of Sumatra. The city is an export center for coal, rice, tobacco, tea, palm oil, and rubber. Padang is noted for the manufacture of textiles. Pop., 1961, 143,699.

PAGO PAGO, the capital of American Samoa, situated on Tutuila Island in the South Pacific Ocean. The city is a seaport and air transportation center, with an important fishing industry. Pop., 1960, 1,251.

PALEMBANG, a river port of Indonesia, situated in southeastern Sumatra on the Moesi River. It is the most important trade center and the largest city of Sumatra. Palembang, which has important oil refineries, exports oil and petroleum products, rubber, coffee, spices, and coal. Pop., 1961, 474,971.

PALERMO, an Italian port, the capital of the province of Palermo and the region of Sicily, situated on the northern coast of Sicily. The city has shipyards and warehouses, and its industries produce wine, chemicals, textiles, and steel. Palermo, which is thought to be over 2,500 years old, has many historical and architectural monuments. Pop., 1965 est., 628,100.

PANAMA CITY, the capital of Panama, situated at the Pacific end of the Panama Canal. The city is a transportation and commercial center with an important tourist industry. Its manufactures include food products and clothing. Panama City is the seat of two universities. Pop., 1966 est., 343,700.

PANJIM, a port of west-central India, the capital of the former Portuguese territory of Goa. The port handles fish, rice, and other agricultural products. Pop., 1950, 31,950.

PAPEETE, the capital of French Polynesia, a seaport situated on Tahiti Island in the east-central Pacific Ocean. The city exports mother-of-pearl, copra, sugar, and rum. Pop., 1962, urban area, 27,786.

PARAMARIBO, the capital of Surinam, a Netherlands territory situated in northeastern South America. The city is a port that has good rail and road connections with the interior. Its exports include bauxite, gold, sugar, and rice. Pop., 1964, 110,867.

PARIS, the capital of France and of the Seine department, situated in east-central France on the Seine River. The city is the administrative and commercial center of France, and one of the cultural and intellectual centers of the world. Its collections of art and architecture are outstanding, and its excellent educational facilities attract students from all over the world.

Among the best known points of interest in Paris are the Louvre, Notre Dame Cathedral, the Opera, and the Eiffel Tower. Paris is also an industrial city that produces machinery, electronic equipment, and a variety of luxury consumer goods. Pop., 1962, urban area, 7,369,387.

PATNA, a city in northeastern India, the capital of Bihar state, situated on the Ganges River. It was formerly known as Pataliputra. It is a transportation and trade center for a rich agricultural region that produces grains, oilseeds, and sugarcane. The city is considered sacred by the Sikhs, and is the seat of two universities.

Patna is an ancient city. It served as the capital of the Magadha kingdom in about 500 BC and remained important until about 300 AD. The city was restored in about 1500 AD under the Mughal emperors. Pop., 1966 est., 406,500.

ITALIAN STATE TOURIST OFFICE
CATHEDRAL OF PALERMO, on the Italian island of Sicily, was built in the 1100s and 1200s.

POINTE-A-PITRE, capital of Guadeloupe, is a seaport at the mouth of the Salee River.

PÉCS, or Fünfkirchen, a city in southern Hungary, situated on the slopes of the Mecsek Hills. The city, which lies in a coal mining area, is a rail and industrial center that transports coal to other industrial regions. Its industries produce textiles, clothing, and leather goods. Pécs is the seat of the University of Poszony. Pop., 1965 est., 135,000.

PEKING, or Peiping, the capital of Communist China, situated in northeastern China at the northern end of the Grand Canal. The city is an air and rail center, with links throughout China and connections with the Soviet Union and Korea. Its major industries produce steel, transportation equipment, agricultural machinery, and textiles. Peking serves as a trade center for the grain, fruit, and cotton raised in the surrounding area.

Peking is an ancient walled city, probably founded earlier than 1000 BC. It is composed of the Inner City in the north, the Outer City in the south, and recently annexed suburban areas. Pop., 1957 est., 4,010,000.

PERM, formerly Molotov, a city in the west-central Soviet Union, lying on the Kama River west of the Ural Mountains. Perm is an important industrial, commercial, and cultural center, as well as a river port and rail junction. Its manufactures include lumber products, steel, and agricultural machinery. Pop., 1966 est., 785,000.

PERTH, the capital of the Australian state of Western Australia, situated on an estuary of the Swan River, about 10 miles from its mouth. The city is the commercial, financial, and cultural center of the state. Its manufactures include cement, textiles, automobiles, furniture, fertilizer, and munitions. Pop., 1966, urban area, 499,494.

PESHAWAR, a city in West Pakistan, strategically situated near the entrance to the Khyber Pass. The city serves as a gateway to Afghanistan and central Asia. Peshawar, a road and rail junction, is the trade center for a region that produces grain, oilseed, cotton, and sugarcane. Pop., 1961, 218,691.

PHNOM PENH, the capital of Cambodia, situated at the junction of the Tonle Sap and Mekong rivers about 130 miles northwest of Saigon. Phnom Penh is a rail center and a river port. It has an important fishing industry and produces handicrafts of silver, leather, and wood. The city also has a soft-drink factory. Pop., 1962, urban area, 403,500.

PIETERMARITZBURG, a city in east-central South Africa, the capital of Natal Province. It is an administrative and commercial center, serving an area that produces grain, citrus fruits, and wattle. Pietermaritzburg is a rail junction and an industrial city with tanneries and shoe, furniture, and carpet factories. Pop., 1960, urban area, 128,589.

PIRAEUS, a port in southeastern Greece, situated on the Saronic Gulf of the Aegean Sea. Piraeus, which serves as the port for Athens, is Greece's leading port and industrial city. Its manufactures include chemicals, fertilizers, soap, drugs, flour, machinery, and jute. Pop., 1961, 183,957.

PLOIEŞTI, a city in south-central Romania. Ploieşti, with its extensive pipelines, refineries, and storage tanks, is the center of Romania's petroleum industry. The city's manufactures include petroleum products, glass, paper, rubber, furniture, hardware, and textiles. Pop., 1965 est., 177,300.

PLOVDIV, a city in south-central Bulgaria on the Maritsa River. It lies in a fertile lowland and serves as a market center for livestock, tobacco, grain, and grapes and wine. Plovdiv's manufactures include textiles, soap, furniture, flour, and sugar. Pop., 1965 est., 220,600.

PLYMOUTH, the capital of Montserrat, one of the British Leeward Islands in the eastern Caribbean Sea. The city exports some of the agricultural products of the island. Pop., 1960, 1,911.

PLZEŇ, or Pilsen, a city in western Czechoslovakia about 50 miles southwest of Prague. Nearby coal and iron ore deposits supply the city's enormous metallurgical works. Plzeň is famous for the production of beer. Its other manufactures include machinery, hardware, chemicals, paper, and clothing. Pop., 1965 est., 140,200.

POINTE-A-PITRE, the capital and chief city of Guadeloupe, in the West Indies. The city is a seaport that exports food products, especially sugar, rum, cacoa, coffee, and bananas. Pop., 1954, urban area, 26,160.

POONA, a city in west-central India, situated about 80 miles southeast of Bombay. The city is an educational and commercial center, with rice, sugar, and cotton mills; distilleries; and metal works. Poona is the summer residence of the governor of Bombay. Pop., 1966 est., urban area, 810,500.

PORT-AU-PRINCE, the capital and chief port of Haiti, situated on the west coast of Hispaniola, on the Caribbean Sea. The chief exports of Port-au-Prince are coffee, bananas, rum, sugar, and sisal. Pop., 1960 est., 240,000.

PORT ELIZABETH, a port in South Africa, situated on the country's southeastern coast, on the Indian Ocean. Port Elizabeth is a transportation center with a well-equipped harbor and several rail and air lines. Its principal exports are hides and fruit. Fishing, food processing, and the production of textiles, glass, soap, chemicals, furniture, and machinery are the main industries. Pop., 1960, urban area, 290,693.

PORT HARCOURT, a port in southeastern Nigeria, situated near the mouth of the Bonny River. It is an industrial city with important petroleum refineries. The city's exports include coal and palm oil. Pop., 1963, 179,563.

PORT LOUIS, the capital and chief port of Mauritius, an island in the Indian Ocean about 500 miles east of Madagascar. Sugar, the main crop and export of Mauritius, is shipped from Port Louis. Pop., 1965 est., urban area, 129,700.

PORT MORESBY, the capital of the Australian territory of Papua, in the South Pacific Ocean. Port Moresby lies on the southeastern coast of Papua Island. It is a commercial center that exports copra, rubber, and wood products. Pop., 1966, urban area, 42,133.

PORTO, or Oporto, the second largest city of Portugal, situated on the Atlantic coast at the mouth of the Douro River. Porto is known for the export of port wine. Its industries produce beverages, textiles, clothing, and pottery. Pop., 1965 est., 319,300.

CITIES OF THE WORLD

PORTO–NOVO, the capital of Dahomey, situated on the southern coast of western Africa, on the Gulf of Guinea. Porto-Novo is a seaport that exports palm products and cotton. Pop., 1964, 69,500.

PORT SAID, a port of the United Arab Republic, situated at the northern end of the Suez Canal. It lies on a narrow strip of land between the Mediterranean Sea and Lake Manzala. Port Said is primarily a fueling stop for ships passing through the canal, although there is some industry. Pop., 1966, 282,876.

PORT SUDAN, a port of northeastern Sudan, situated on the Red Sea. The city has rail connections with most of Sudan's cities. Its main exports include cotton and cotton seed and gum arabic. Pop., 1963 est., 56,000.

PORT VICTORIA, capital of the Seychelles, a British Crown Colony occupying an archipelago in the Indian Ocean. The city lies on Mahe Island. Its port is the base for a fishing fleet and exports the islands' cinnamon, vanilla, and coconut products. Pop., 1960, urban area, 10,504.

POTSDAM, an East German city on the Havel River adjacent to Berlin. It has pharmaceutical, precision instrument, and textile industries, and it is the site of several historically important buildings and monuments. Pop., 1965 est., 110,100.

POZNAN, a city in west-central Poland, situated on the Warta River. Poznan is an important railway junction with industries that produce transportation equipment, agricultural machinery, and furniture. Pop., 1965 est., 436,000.

PRAGUE, or Praha, the capital of Czechoslovakia, situated in the west-central part of the country on the Vltava (Moldau) River. The city is the seat of the central Bohemian regional government, as well as an educational center and a transportation hub. Its manufactures include hydraulic and electrical equipment, chemicals, and textiles. Prague has many historic monuments representing Romanesque, Gothic, Italian Renaissance, and Baroque styles. Pop., 1965 est., 1,023,000.

PRAIA, the capital of the Cape Verde Islands, which lie in the Atlantic Ocean, about 500 miles west of Africa. Praia, situated on São Tiago Island, is a seaport that exports citrus fruits, sugarcane, coffee, and castor beans. Fishing is an important industry. Pop., 1960, urban area, 13,142.

PRETORIA, the administrative capital of South Africa and the capital of Transvaal Province, situated on the Apies River about 40 miles northeast of Johannesburg. Pretoria, a transportation, industrial, and political center, is also the seat of two universities. Its manufactures include steel, chemicals, ceramics, glassware, processed foods, and tobacco. Pop., 1960, urban area, 422,590.

IN PRAGUE, the Neo-Renaissance National Theatre viewed from the Vltava (Moldau) River.

PUERTO BARRIOS, a port in eastern Guatemala, situated on the Caribbean Sea. Its exports include bananas and other fruits, chicle, and wood. Pop., 1964, 22,242.

PYONGYANG, the capital of North Korea, situated on the Taedong River in the western part of the country. The city lies in a productive agricultural area and is close to important coal mines. Pop., 1960 est., 653,100.

QUEBEC, capital of Quebec Province, Canada, situated near the southeastern corner of the province on the St. Lawrence River. Part of the city, Upper Town, lies on a high bluff called Cape Diamond, and Lower Town is built around the waterfront. The capital of the French colony in Canada in the 1600s and 1700s, Quebec remains the cultural and political center of French Canada.

The city has an excellent harbor and port facilities accessible to ocean-going vessels, and it serves as a distribution point for much of eastern Canada. Its industries include paper milling, shipbuilding, tanning, brewing, and tobacco processing. Pop., 1965 est., urban area, 392,000.

QUE QUE, a recently developed industrial town of Rhodesia, located about 100 miles southwest of Salisbury. It lies on an extensive deposit of iron ore, of which production for export began in 1962. The ore is also utilized for local iron and steel manufacturing. Pop., 1963 est., 17,700.

QUETTA, a city in West Pakistan, the capital of the Quetta division in the Baluchistan region. It controls access to the important Bolan Pass over the Sulaiman Mountains and is a center for trade with Iran and Afghanistan. Fruit is grown and chromite is mined in the surrounding area. Pop., 1961, 106,633.

QUEZON CITY, the official capital of the Philippine Islands, situated on Luzon Island, 10 miles northeast of Manila. Quezon City is primarily a residential area and the site of the national university, however, and most government offices are located in Manila. Pop., 1965 est., 482,400.

QUITO, the capital and second largest city of Ecuador, located on a 9,350-foot plateau in the Andes at a point near the equator. An important city in the empire of the Inca Indians, it still has a large Indian population. Quito is primarily an administrative center, and its industry is limited to textile milling. Pop., 1965 est., 401,800.

RABAT, the capital of Morocco, situated on the south bank of the Bou Regneg, near its mouth on the Atlantic Ocean. Local handicraft industries produce leather goods, baskets, tapestries, and embroidered cloth. The city is the site of Mohammed V University. Pop., 1965 est., 355,000.

RAMPUR, in northern India, located in Uttar Pradesh state on the Kosi River, about 115 miles east of Delhi. The city is the capital of Rampur District and a commercial center. Rampur is known for its library, which houses a collection of rare Oriental manuscripts. It is also the site of an Arabic college. Pop., 1966 est., 136,000.

RANCHI, in northeastern India, a district capital in Bihar State. It is a commercial and administrative center. A radium institute, two mental hospitals, and several colleges are located in the city. Pop., 1966 est., urban area, 158,100.

RANGOON, the capital of Burma, on the Rangoon River, 21 miles from the Bay of Bengal. It is Burma's largest city and chief port. Rice and teakwood are the major exports. Local industries produce silk and cotton textiles and pottery. There are also shipyards and sawmills. The city is modern in appearance and has many cultural and educational institutions, including the University of Rangoon. The skyline is dominated by the 368-

foot-high Shwe Dagon Pagoda, which is covered with gold leaf and reputedly over 2,000 years old. Pop., 1957 est., 821,800.

RAWALPINDI, in western Pakistan, situated on the Potwar plateau, near the Himalayan foothills. The city is an industrial center and has an oil refinery, a steel mill, a locomotive works, and chemical plants. In 1949 Rawalpindi was made the interim federal capital pending the completion of a new capital at Islamabad, eight miles away. Pop., 1961, 340,175.

RECIFE, capital of Pernambuco State, Brazil, located at the mouths of the Capibaribe and Beberibe rivers on the Atlantic Ocean. It is the third largest city in Brazil. The city's economy is based on processing and exporting the agricultural products of the interior, including coffee, cotton, sugar, and hides. A rail and road network links Recife with other parts of Brazil. The city has two universities and many fine churches, some of which date from the colonial period. Pop., 1966 est., 1,010,000.

REGINA, the capital of Saskatchewan Province, in west-central Canada, located about 100 miles north of the U.S. border. The city has excellent railway connections and is the distribution center for a large area. Industries include automobile assembly, oil refining, printing, woodworking, bookbinding, meat packing, and the manufacture of dry batteries. Pop., 1965 est., 126,000.

REYKJAVÍK, the capital of Iceland, located on the southwestern coast of the country. It is the country's leading seaport and only major city. Reykjavík has a large fishing industry, busy shipyards, and publishing houses. It is the site of the University of Reykjavík. Pop., 1965 est., 89,400.

REZA'IYEH, also known as Urmia, capital of the administrative province of western Azerbaijan in northwestern Iran, located on the west bank of Lake Urmia. It is situated in a fruit and tobacco growing area. Pop., 1956 est., 67,605.

RIGA. the capital and largest city of the Latvian Soviet Socialist Republic of the Soviet Union. The city lies on the Dvina River, about eight miles inland from the Gulf of Riga on the Baltic Sea. It is a major Baltic port and Latvia's leading industrial and cultural center. Local industries produce machinery, chemicals, textiles, wood products, cameras, and construction materials. Pop., 1966, 668,000.

RIO DE JANEIRO, the second largest city in Brazil, located on Guanabara Bay, on the Atlantic Ocean. It served as the capital of the country from 1763 to 1960. Rio de Janeiro is Brazil's cultural center and a major port, ranking second only to São Paulo. There are three universities and several museums. Local industries produce domestic consumer goods, including shoes, clothing, furniture, drugs, and processed foods. Pop., 1966 est., 3,909,000.

RIYADH, the capital of Saudi Arabia, located in the east-central part of the country on the Nejd Plateau. An ancient oasis settlement, Riyadh serves as a trade center for the dates, vegetables, and grain produced in the surrounding area. After the city became the capital in 1953, it was greatly modernized. Riyadh is connected by rail to Ad Dammam on the Persian Gulf. Pop., 1965 est., 225,000.

ROAD TOWN, capital of the British Virgin Islands, located on Tortola Island. It is situated in the central part of the island on the Caribbean coast. Pop., 1960, 891.

ROME, the capital of Italy, located in the west-central part of the country, on the Tiber River, 17 miles inland from the Tyrrhenian Sea. Rome has been a major center of civilization for over 2,000 years. It was the capital of the Roman Empire and retained its importance during the Middle Ages as the seat of the papacy. In the 1500s and 1600s Rome became the center of the Italian Renaissance, and many magnificent palaces and churches, decorated with beautiful sculpture and paintings, were built.

Modern Rome is an important commercial, financial, and transportation center. Its industries include leathercrafting, metalworking, distilling, food processing, printing, and publishing. The city attracts many tourists and is an international center for the arts. Pop., 1965 est., 2,484,000.

ROSEAU, the capital and largest city of Dominica in the Windward Islands group of the Lesser Antilles. The city is located in the southwestern part of the island on the Caribbean Sea. Primarily a port, Roseau exports the island's limes, lime juice, bananas, and copra. Pop., 1960, 10,417.

ROTTERDAM, the second largest city in the Netherlands, on the New Maas River, an outlet of the Rhine River, near the North Sea. The centers of Pernis, Botlek, and Europoort to the west are also part of the port. With easy access to both the North Sea and Rhine River, Rotterdam is one of the busiest ports in Europe. Shipping and shipbuilding are Rotterdam's leading industries, but chemicals, sugar, furniture, refined petroleum, lumber, and processed foods are also produced. Pop., 1965 est., 731,315.

RUSE, the largest city in northern Bulgaria, located on the Danube River, about 40 miles south of Bucharest. The city is Bulgaria's largest port on the Danube and an important transportation center. Ruse's major industries produce textiles, leather, processed foods, refined petroleum, and agricultural implements. Pop., 1965 est., 128,000.

SAGA, the capital of the Japanese prefecture of Saga, on northwestern Kyushu island. It is a distribution point for coal mined and rice grown in the surrounding area, and it has textile and ceramics industries. Pop., 1965, 134,575.

SAIGON, the capital of South Vietnam, situated on the Saigon River near the country's southeastern coast. It is the commercial and political center of the country, and with its industrial suburb, Cholon, it is South Vietnam's major port and industrial complex. The leading industries include shipbuilding, distilling, and food processing. Pop., 1965 est., 1,485,300.

SAINT-DENIS, the capital and chief town of Réunion, an Overseas Department of France, on Réunion Island in the Indian Ocean, some 400 miles east of Madagascar. The town's industries process local sugar, distill rum, and produce perfume essences. Pop., 1961, 65,614.

ST. GEORGE'S, the capital and principal town of Grenada, a British-associated island state in the Caribbean Sea. The town, on the island's southwestern coast, has a deep natural harbor and exports locally grown cocoa, bananas, and spices. Pop., 1960, 7,303.

PAN AMERICAN
ST. GEORGE'S, a seaport, trading center, and the capital of Grenada, British West Indies.

SANTIAGO, Chile, lies in a valley between the Andes Mountains and the Pacific coastal range.

ST. JOHN CITY, the capital of Antigua, a British-associated island state in the Caribbean Sea. It is a port that exports sugar cane and cotton and imports petroleum to be refined on the island. Pop., 1960, 21,595.

SAINT JOHN'S, the capital of Newfoundland province, Canada, located on the southeastern coast of Newfoundland Island. It is a seaport with an excellent harbor that is the center of a large fishing fleet. Fish processing and fish-oil refining are the main industries, and margarine, soap, paints, and fishing and marine equipment are manufactured. Pop., 1966, urban area, 101,161.

SAINT–LOUIS, a coastal town in northern Senegal, in West Africa, situated on an island at the mouth of the Sénégal River. The site of the first permanent French settlement in Africa, it served as the capital of French West Africa in the 1800s and was the capital of Senegal until 1968. It exports hides and peanuts from the surrounding area and is connected by rail with Dakar. Pop., 1961 est., 48,800.

SAKAI, a Japanese industrial center on Honshu Island, located on Osaka Bay. Textile, chemical, and electronics manufacturing are its major industries. Pop., 1965, 466,412.

SALEM, a city in southeastern India, in Madras state, located in the Cauvery River basin. Iron and manganese are mined in the surrounding area, and the city has mineral-processing and textile-milling industries. It is on a rail route and is a regional trade center. Pop., 1966 est., 274,100.

SALISBURY, the capital of Rhodesia, located in the northeastern part of the country. Surrounded by a rich gold-mining region, it is a transportation and commercial center for southeastern Africa. Tobacco processing is its major industry. Pop., 1965 est., urban area, 325,000.

SALVADOR, a port and industrial city on the eastern coast of Brazil. It processes and exports sugar, cotton, cacao, and tobacco grown in the surrounding region, and it manufactures textiles and cigars. It is the oldest city in Brazil and for 200 years was the capital of the Portuguese colony there. Pop., 1966 est., 832,000.

SALZBURG, a resort city in Austria, situated on the Salzach River at the foot of the Alps. The city is a noted music center, and its manufactures include musical instruments. Salzburg is also a rail junction between Munich and Vienna. Pop., 1965 est., 115,700.

SAMARKAND, an ancient city of Soviet Asia, located in the Central Uzbekh Soviet Socialist Republic, on the slopes of the Alai mountains. Samarkand is one of the oldest cities in the world, and it still prospers on commerce and light industry, especially the weaving of cotton and silk textiles. Pop., 1966 est., 240,000.

SAN'A, the capital of Yemen, located in a high mountain valley in southwestern Arabia. It lies in the center of a rich irrigated agricultural region that produces fruits and coffee, and it is the cultural and commercial center for the area. Pop., 1965 est., 60,000.

SAN JOSÉ, the capital and largest city of Costa Rica, situated on the Rio Grande near the center of the country. It is on international air and rail routes and is the commercial center for a coffee-growing region. It produces furniture and textiles. Pop., 1965 est., urban area, 339,100.

SAN SALVADOR, the capital and largest city of El Salvador, situated in the mountains in the west-central portion of the country. It is a commercial center for locally grown coffee, sugar, tobacco, and rubber. The city is subject to severe earthquakes and has frequently been badly damaged. Pop., 1963 est., 281,100.

SANTA ISABEL, the capital of Equatorial Guinea, a Spanish overseas province, located on the island of Fernando Póo off the western coast of Africa. It is a seaport that exports cacao and coffee raised on local plantations. Pop., 1960, 37,237.

SANTIAGO, the capital of Chile, situated in a high valley near the center of the country. In addition to being the political, cultural, and commercial heart of Chile, it manufactures iron and steel, chemicals, textiles, paper, and other products. Pop., 1965 est., urban area, 2,248,400.

SANTO DOMINGO, the capital and largest city of the Dominican Republic. Its refineries and distilleries process locally grown sugar. The city has textile mills and is the chief port of the country. Founded in 1492, it has been continuously inhabited longer than any other city in the western hemisphere. Pop., 1966 est., 560,600.

SANTO TOMÉ DE GUAYANA, a city in northeastern Venezuela at the junction of the Caroni and Orinoco rivers. The city is a planned grouping of four small neighboring towns. Its industries are concerned with processing and shipping iron ore mined in the region. Pop., 1965 est., 75,000.

SÃO PAULO, capital of São Paulo state in southeastern Brazil. It is the commercial and industrial center of Brazil, with oil refineries, chemical plants, and factories manufacturing heavy machinery, vehicles, pharmaceuticals, electrical devices, and textiles. Pop., 1966 est., 4,098,000.

SÃO TOME, capital and port city of the Portuguese overseas province of São Tome and Principe. It lies on the island of São Tome in the Gulf of Guinea some 125 miles off Africa's west coast. It processes and exports cacao, coffee, and coconuts raised on the island. Pop., 1960, 5,714.

SAPELE, an industrial town in the former Western Region of Nigeria, on the Benins River. It is the site of a large lumber mill and plywood plant which process local timber. The city also processes locally grown rubber. Pop., 1963, 61,007.

SAPPORO, the capital of the Japanese island of Hokkaido, located in the southwestern portion of the island. It is a cultural center, and it has food, hemp, and rubber processing industries. Pop., 1965, 794,908.

SARAJEVO, the capital of the Yugoslavian constituent republic of Bosnia and Herzegovina. Sarajevo is an industrial and commercial center that manufactures textiles, electrical equipment, metal goods, and carpets, and serves as the shipping point for locally mined minerals. It is a Muslim cultural center. Pop., 1961, 143,117.

SARATOV, the capital of the Saratov Region in the southeastern Soviet Union, situated on the Volga River. It is a major river port, shipping local minerals and farm products. Industries include an oil refinery, shipyard, and plants producing precision instruments, chemicals, and machinery. Pop., 1966 est., 699,000.

SATU-MARE, a city of northwestern Romania, situated on the Somesul River. The market center for an agricultural region, it also has industries manufacturing mining and farming equipment, machinery, and textiles. Pop., 1963 est., 63,700.

SEKONDI-TAKORADI, coastal towns of southern Ghana joined into a single municipality in the 1940s. Fishing is important, and fish-processing plants and sawmills are the main industries. The towns' ports ship cacao, timber, and minerals. Pop., 1966 est., urban area, 181,000.

SENDAI, the capital of Miyagi prefecture, Japan, on northern Honshu Island. It is an industrial city, manufacturing silk textiles, machinery, chemicals, and metal products. It lies on the Sendai Plain, a rich agricultural region. Pop., 1965, 480,925.

SEOUL, the capital of the Republic of Korea (South Korea), situated near the Han River in the northwestern corner of the country. The cultural and economic center of South Korea, it is the site of several colleges, and its industries include flour mills, rail yards, and textile mills. It is on international air routes and is connected by rail with its port, Inchon. Pop., 1966 est., 3,800,000.

SEVASTOPOL, a Black Sea port on the Crimean peninsula in the southern Ukraine region of the Soviet Union. It is the site of an important naval base, and its industries include shipbuilding and food processing. Pop., 1966 est., 200,000.

SEVILLA, or Seville, a city of southwestern Spain, situated on the Guadalquivir River. Sevilla is a river port that handles iron, lead, and food products. It is also a transportation, marketing, and industrial center. Its manufactures include munitions, machine tools, and pottery.

Sevilla, which was founded by the Phoenicians and has been held by Romans, Vandals, Visigoths, and Moors, is noted for its architecture and art treasures. Pop., 1965 est., 474,100.

SFAX, a Mediterranean seaport on the eastern coast of Tunisia. The site of ancient Phoenician and Roman trading colonies, today it processes and exports olives and dates raised in the region and phosphates mined nearby. Pop., 1956, 65,645.

SHANGHAI, a port city on the eastern coast of China, near the mouth of the Yangtze River. It is the largest city in China and is a major East Asian industrial and commercial center. It manufactures machinery, ships, aircraft, weapons, textiles, iron and steel, books, and other products. It lost its former importance in foreign trade after the Communist takeover in 1949. Pop., 1957 est., 6,900,000.

UNITED NATIONS
SEOUL, capital of South Korea, is a busy commercial city with a rapidly growing population.

SHILLONG, the capital of Assam state, in northeastern India. Situated high in the Khasi Hills, it has a mild climate and is a popular vacation and health resort. Pop., 1966 est., urban area, 125,800.

SHIMONOSEKI, a seaport at the southwestern tip of Japan's Honshu island, situated on the Shimonoseki Strait at the western end of the Inland Sea. In addition to its port facilities, it has shipyards and chemical, metal-working, and engineering industries. Pop., 1965, 254,376.

SHIRAZ, capital of Fars Province, in southwestern Iran. It is a commercial center for fruits, silk, and tobacco grown in the surrounding region, and it produces wine, carpets, and silk textiles. Founded in the 600s, it served as the country's capital several times before the 1900s, and it became a center for Persian culture and learning. Pop., 1963, 229,761.

SHIZUOKA, capital of Shizuoka prefecture on Japan's Honshu island, situated on Suruga Bay. It is a commercial center for an orange- and tea-growing region, and its industries produce lacquerware, paper, and textiles. Pop., 1965, 367,705.

SHKODER, a town in northwestern Albania, near the southern end of Lake Scutari. It is the commercial center for a rich agricultural region and has food-processing industries. An ancient fortified city, it was colonized by the Romans in the 100s AD, and was conquered and reconquered by many nations until the 1900s. Pop., 1960, 43,234.

SHOLAPUR, a south-central Indian city in Maharashtra state. Situated in a cotton-growing region, it has important textile mills. Pop., 1966 est., 3,695,800.

SIBIU, a city in the Transylvanian region of central Romania. It is a commercial center for the surrounding agricultural region. Sibiu's industries produce chemicals, textiles, and farm machinery. The former capital of Transylvania, it remains an important cultural center. Pop., 1965, urban area, 104,434.

SIDI-IFNI, the capital of Ifni, a small Spanish overseas territory on the northwest coast of Africa. It is a port with limited trade and a small fishing industry. Pop., 1960, 12,751.

SINING, capital of Tsinghai province in western China, situated on the Sining River. Located on a main route to Tibet, it is a trading center for timber, wool, and hides. Pop., 1957 est., 300,000.

SKOPJE, capital of the Macedonian region of southeastern Yugoslavia, situated on the Vardar River. It is a trade center for minerals mined in the region. Much of the town was demolished in a severe earthquake in 1963, but it was later rebuilt. Pop., 1961, 165,529.

SOFIA, the capital and largest city of Bulgaria, situated in the western foothills of the Balkan Mountains. It is the economic center of the country, with industries producing machinery, electrical equipment, textiles, and processed foods. Sofia is the home of the country's main educational institutions. It lies on the site of the ancient Roman city of Sardica. Pop., 1965 est., 793,300.

SOOCHOW, a port city in eastern China, on the Grand Canal in Kiangsu province. Soochow manufactures textiles and produces many handcrafted items. Threaded by canals, it is known as the Venice of China. Pop., 1957 est., 633,000.

SOPRON, an ancient town in western Hungary near the border with Austria. Sopron has a long history as a cultural center and produces wines and textiles. Pop., 1963 est., 43,400.

SOUSSE, a Mediterranean port on the east coast of Tunisia. Situated on the site of an ancient Carthaginian city that was occupied by the Romans, today the city serves primarily as a shipping point for local minerals and farm products. Pop., 1965, 48,185.

SPLIT, an ancient seaport on the Adriatic coast of the Dalmatian region of Yugoslavia. In addition to its harbor facilities, it has shipyards and chemical, cement, and metal processing plants. It lies on major transportation routes and is a commercial and tourist center. The city was founded by the Roman emperor Diocletian and contains ancient ruins and historic monuments. Pop., 1961, 99,462.

SPRINGS, a town in the Transvaal region of South Africa. It is the commercial center for a region where coal, gold, and uranium are mined. Pop., 1960, urban area, 141,943.

SRINIGAR, capital of the state of Kashmir in northwestern India. It is situated on the Jhelum River in the Vale of Kashmir. Srinigar produces silk and woolen textiles, carpets, and wood and metal handcrafts. It is also a major resort. Pop., 1961, urban area, 295,084.

STANLEY, capital and chief city of the Falkland Islands, a British crown colony in the South Atlantic Ocean. It is located on the northeast coast of East Falkland Island. Possessing a good harbor, Stanley handles almost all the colony's trade. Pop., 1962, 1,074.

STOCKHOLM, the capital and largest city of Sweden. It is situated in the southeast, on Malaren Lake near the Baltic Sea. The city is Sweden's chief port and its industries include shipyards, food-processing plants, chemical and machinery factories, and paper and textile mills. It is an important commercial and financial center, and its many schools, museums, libraries and theaters give it great cultural importance as well. Pop., 1966 est., urban area, 1,247,300.

STUTTGART, in southern West Germany, on the Neckar River, about 95 miles south of Frankfurt. Stuttgart is the capital of the state of Baden-Württemberg. Manufactures include motor vehicles, textiles, chemicals, and machinery. It is an educational and cultural center with a flourishing publishing industry. Pop. 1965 est., 632,800.

SUBOTICA, an ancient town in northeastern Yugoslavia. It is a market center for the surrounding grain-growing region. The city's manufactures include chemicals, textiles, machinery, and processed food. Pop., 1961, 74,832.

SUCRE, the official capital of Bolivia, situated in a high Andean valley in the south-central part of the country. Although Sucre is the site of the national university and many government buildings, La Paz is the working capital. Sucre is important mainly as a commercial center for an agricultural and mining region. Pop., 1965 est., 58,400.

SUDBURY, a city of southeastern Ontario, Canada. It is in the center of a region where rich nickel deposits as well as copper, lead, zinc, and silver are mined. Metal-processing is the city's main industry. Other important manufactures include machinery, bricks, and lumber. Pop., 1961, urban area, 110,694.

SUEZ, or El Suweis, a seaport of the United Arab Republic (Egypt) situated at the southern end of the Suez Canal, at the head of the Gulf of Suez. The port is a refueling station and a center for petroleum trade. The city has a large oil refinery and chemical fertilizer plants. Pop., 1966, 264,025.

SUKARNAPURA, capital of the Indonesian province of West Irian (the western half of the island of New Guinea) north of Australia. Located on the northern coast, the city has an excellent harbor. A university is also located in the city. Pop., 1961 est., 14,500.

SURABAJA, a seaport on the eastern coast of the Indonesian island of Java. It exports rubber, oil, sugar, spices, tobacco, and other local goods, and Surabaja has shipyards, oil refineries, textile mills, rubber processing plants, and chemical factories. Pop., 1961, 1,007,945.

SURAT, a small city in Gujarat state in western India, situated on the Gulf of Cambay. A center of early European colonial and commercial activity in India, today the city is a small port with some light industries producing paper and textiles. Pop., 1966 est., 348,300.

SUVA, the capital of the British South Pacific colony of Fiji, situated on Viti Levu Island. It is a port of call on international shipping routes, and it processes and exports island products including fruits, sugar, coconuts, cacao, and timber. Pop., 1966 est., 54,900.

SVERDLOVSK, the capital of the Sverdlovsk region of the Soviet Union, situated just east of the Ural Mountains. It is the center of a region rich in copper, gold, and iron. The city's major industries include metal processing and the manufacture of heavy machinery and precision instruments. Pop., 1966 est., 940,000.

SWATOW, a seaport in Kwangtung province in southeastern China. It exports citrus fruits, tea, and tobacco grown in the surrounding region. Pop., 1953, 280,400.

SYDNEY, the capital of New South Wales, on the southeastern coast of Australia. It is the country's largest city and chief industrial and commercial center. Industrial facilities include metal-processing plants, textile mills, automobile and chemical factories, and a sugar refinery. It has a deep natural harbor and an excellent port that ships such products as coal, timber, grain, and wool. Sydney is the site of several colleges and of the national art and history museums. Pop., 1966, 2,444,735.

SYDNEY, an industrial city of Nova Scotia, Canada, on the eastern coast of Cape Breton Island. Coal mining is Sydney's main industry, and it also has steel mills, shipyards, chemical factories and metal-working plants. Pop., 1966, 32,767.

SZCZECIN, the capital of Szczecin department in northwestern Poland, situated at the mouth of the Oder River. It is a leading Baltic port and has shipyards, iron founderies, and other industrial facilities. Founded in the Middle Ages, it has been administered by several European nations, including Sweden, Prussia, France, and Germany. Pop., 1965 est., 310,000.

SZEGED, a city in southeastern Hungary, on the Tisza River. It is a river port and an important commercial center. Industries include boat building, textile milling, and tobacco processing. Pop., 1965 est., 115,000.

TABRIZ, a city in northwestern Iran, situated near the border with the Soviet Union. It is an ancient city that has repeatedly suffered damage from earthquakes. Tabriz is a com-

BRITISH EUROPEAN AIRWAYS
STOCKHOLM is often called the "Venice of the North" because of its many waterways.

mercial center for an area that produces rice, tobacco, and fruits. Its manufactures include rugs, leather goods, and cotton thread. Pop., 1963 est., 387,800.

TAEGU, a city of South Korea, situated in the south-central part of the Korean peninsula. Taegu is a rail and commercial center where silk is manufactured. Pop., 1965 est., 811,400.

TAIPEI, the capital of Nationalist China, situated at the northern end of Taiwan (Formosa). The city is a commercial and industrial center with good transportation facilities. Its manufactures include processed foods, chemicals, and metal products. Taipei is the seat of the National Taiwan University. Pop., 1965 est., 1,135,500.

TAIYÜAN, a city of east-central China, situated on the Fen River, about 250 miles southwest of Peking. Taiyüan is an industrial and rail center, lying near important coal fields. Its industries produce iron and steel, agricultural equipment, and chemicals. The city also has machine shops and oil refineries. Pop., 1957 est., 1,020,000.

TAKAMATSU, a Japanese port situated on the northeastern coast of Shikoku Island. The city is a rail center and the main port in the trade between Shikoku and Honshu islands. Pop., 1965, 243,444.

TALLINN, the capital of the Estonian Soviet Socialist Republic, in the northwestern Soviet Union. It is a leading port, situated on the southern coast of the Gulf of Finland, opposite Helsinki. Tallinn is a commercial and industrial center that manufactures textiles, glass, paper, furniture, and mining equipment. Pop., 1966 est., 335,000.

TANANARIVE, the capital of the Malagasy Republic, situated on the east-central part of Madagascar Island. The city is an administrative and commercial center, connected by rail to the port of Tamatave. Pop., 1965 est., 321,700.

TANGIER, a port of northern Morocco, strategically situated on the Atlantic coast, just west of the Strait of Gibraltar. The city is a transportation center that exports cork, hides, and food products. Tourism and the production of leather goods, pottery, and rugs are important industries. Pop., 1965 est., 110,000.

TANJORE, or Thanjavor, a city in southeastern India. It is an agricultural, commercial, and rail center in an area that grows rice, tobacco, and sugarcane. Tanjore's industries produce jewelry, carpets, and embroidered handicrafts. Pop., 1966 est., 116,700.

TANTA, a city in the northern United Arab Republic (Egypt), about 50 miles north of Cairo. Tanta is an important transportation and manufacturing center. Its products include cotton goods, sugar, and soap. Pop., 1963 est., 215,400.

TARAWA, capital of the Gilbert and Ellice Islands, a British colony in the central Pacific Ocean. It is located on an atoll eight square miles in area and is the colony's major port of entry and commercial center. Exports include copra, phosphates, and pearl shell. During World War II Tarawa was occupied by the Japanese. It was captured by the United States in November 1943. Pop., 1966 est., 8,700.

TASHKENT, a city in the southwest-central Soviet Union, the capital of the Uzbek Soviet Socialist Republic. Tashkent, an oasis settlement, lies on a small tributary of the Syr Darya. The city has good rail facilities and is an industrial and commercial center. Textiles, leather goods, metal products, and farm machinery are manufactured, and cotton and grain are traded. Tashkent is also the focus of cultural and educational activities in central Soviet Asia. Pop., 1966 est., 1,127,000.

TBILSI, or Tiflis, a city in the southwestern Soviet Union, capital of the Georgian Soviet Socialist Republic. The city, which lies on the Kura River, is a resort with thermal springs. It is also an agricultural and economic center. Tbilsi's industries produce textiles and clothing, wood products, and industrial equipment. Pop., 1966 est., 823,000.

TEHRAN, or Teheran, the capital of Iran, situated in the north, about 70 miles from the Caspian Sea. The city is the cultural, industrial and transportation center of Iran. Manufactures include cotton, glass, metal products, construction materials, and automobile parts. Pop., 1963 est., 2,317,100.

TEL AVIV, a port in Israel, situated on the Mediterranean Sea. The city, which includes the ancient port of Jaffa, is the industrial and commercial center of Israel. Its industries include woodworking, textile milling, food processing, and the manufacture of chemicals and tobacco products. Tel Aviv supports several theaters, an orchestra, and a university. Pop., 1965 est., 392,100.

THESSALONÍKI, or Salonika, a seaport in northeastern Greece, situated on the Gulf of Thessaloníki. It is an important trading center and an industrial city that manufactures cotton, silk, and wool textiles; leather goods; and carpets. Pop., 1961, urban area, 378,444.

THORSHAVN, the capital and chief city of the Faroe Islands of Denmark. It is located on Stömö Island, the largest of the Faroes, about 190 miles northwest of the Shetland Islands. The chief industry is fishing and the primary export is fish. Pop., 1960, 7,447.

TIENTSIN, or Tienching, a port of northeastern China, situated at the junction of the Pei River and the Grand Canal, about 80 miles southeast of Peking. Tientsin is a commercial center that handles much of the import-export trade of the surrounding region. It is also the seat of several institutions of higher education. Pop., 1957 est., 3,220,000.

TIMIŞOARA, a city in western Romania, situated on the Béga Canal, near the Hungarian border. The city is a communications and rail center with an extensive grain and lumber trade. Pop., 1965 est., urban area, 170,800.

TIRANË, or Tirana, the capital of Albania. Tiranë is served by Durrës, an Adriatic seaport some 20 miles to the west. The city is a commercial and industrial center in an agricultural region noted for the production of olives. Tiranë's manufactures include building materials, metal products, and textiles. Tiranë is the seat of a university, a science institute, and several museums. Pop., 1964 est., 157,000.

UNITED NATIONS
TEHRAN, capital of Iran, is one of the largest and most modern cities of the Middle East.

CITIES OF THE WORLD

TOKYO at night is ablaze with one of the world's greatest concentrations of neon signs.
CONSULATE GENERAL OF JAPAN N.Y.

TIRUCHIRAPPALLI, formerly Trichinopoly, a city in southeastern India, situated on the Cauvery River about 200 miles southwest of Madras. The city is a trade and transportation center in a region that produces rice, millet, sugar, cotton, and oilseed. Manufactures include textiles and cement. Pop., 1966 est., 266,400.

TOKYO, the capital of Japan and one of the largest cities in the world, situated on Honshu Island, on Tokyo Bay. The city is the administrative, economic, and industrial center of Japan. Its manufactures include automobiles, airplane parts, electrical equipment, machine tools, and chemicals.

It is served by an excellent port, national and private railroads, an international airport, an extensive highway system, and a rapid transit system. Tokyo is also Japan's cultural, educational, and religious center. It is the seat of Tokyo University and has many museums, theaters, and religious shrines. Pop., 1965, urban area, 10,869,800.

TORONTO, the capital of Ontario in south east-central Canada, on Lake Ontario. Toronto is the second largest city in Canada and one of the busiest of the Great Lakes ports. It is a financial, commercial, and industrial center with railroad shops and metalworks. Meat-packing, printing and publishing, and shipbuilding are important industries. Pop., 1965 est., urban area, 2,066,000.

TOULOUSE, a city in southern France on the Garonne River. Industries include food and beverage processing, flour milling, textile and shoe manufacturing and airplane production. Toulouse is also a market for the agricultural products of the surrounding region. The University of Toulouse dates from the 1200s. Pop., 1962, urban area, 329,044.

TOURS, in the Loire Valley of France, about 130 miles southwest of Paris. The city's manufactures include textile products, chemicals, leather goods, pottery, and printed matter. Tours is the commercial center for the surrounding agricultural region, handling products such as wine, grain, and dried fruit. Tours was the capital of a Roman province in France and the site of a decisive battle in 732 AD, when the Franks defeated an invading Arab army. Pop., 1962, urban area, 151,359.

TOYAMA, a Japanese port situated on Honshu Island, on the Sea of Japan. The city is an industrial and market center in a rice-growing region. Manufactures include textiles and drugs. Pop., 1965, 239,810.

TRIESTE, a port in northeastern Italy, situated on the Adriatic Sea, near the border with Yugoslavia. Trieste serves as a port for Czechoslovakia, Austria, Hungary, Yugoslavia, and Italy. Following World War II the city was made part of a free territory, but in the 1950s it was returned to Italy. The main industry is shipbuilding. Pop., 1965 est., 280,500.

TRIPOLI, a port in Lebanon, situated on the Mediterranean Sea, about 40 miles northeast of Beirut. The city has rail connections with Beirut and Syria, and is the terminus of an oil pipeline from Iraq. The principal industries are oil refining, sponge fishing, and the manufacture of soap. Pop., 1964 est., 127,600.

TRIPOLI, with Bengasi the capital of Libya, situated in northwestern Libya on the Mediterranean Sea. The city is a transportation and trading center for an agricultural region. Its industries produce armaments, tobacco products, and salt. Pop., 1964, 213,506.

TRIVANDRUM, a port in southwestern India, situated on the Indian Ocean. The city is a religious and educational center. It lies near a forest area that produces teak, bamboo, and ebony. Pop., 1966 est., urban area, 358,000.

TSINAN, or Chinan, a city of eastern China, the capital of Shantung Province. The city is a railroad junction and an industrial center. Its most important manufactures are silk and cotton textiles. Pop., 1957 est., 862,000.

TSINGTAO, a port in northeastern China, situated on the Yellow Sea at the southern end of the Shantung Peninsula. The port is one of the largest in China. Tsingtao's manufactures include textiles and processed foods. Pop., 1957 est., 1,121,000.

TSITSIHAR, or Chichihar, a city of northeastern China, situated on the Nonni River, about 175 miles northwest of Harbin. The city is a rail junction and river port, with trade in grain and other agricultural products. Pop., 1957 est., 668,000.

TUNIS, the capital of Tunisia, situated in the northeastern part of the country between the Lake of Tunis and the Sedjoumi salt flat. Tunis is connected to the Mediterranean Sea by a channel. The city is the major commercial, industrial, and transportation center of the country. Its products include processed foods, soap, chemicals, and perfume. Pop., 1964 est., urban area, 662,000.

TURIN, or Torino, the capital of the Italian province of Torino, situated on the Po River in northwestern Italy. Turin, with Milan and Genoa, forms the industrial triangle of northern Italy. The principal manufactures include iron and steel, machinery, tools, automobiles, and textiles. The city is the seat of the University of Turin, founded in the 1400s. Pop., 1965 est., 1,111,700.

UFA, capital of the Bashkir Soviet Socialist Republic of the Soviet Union, in the southern Ural Mountains, at the confluence of the Belaya and Ufa rivers. The city has important oil, chemical, metallurgical, coal, and steel industries. A state university and a branch of the Academy of Sciences are also located there. Pop., 1966 est., 683,000.

UJJAIN, a city in Madhya Pradesh state, India. The city has important flour milling and textile industries. Vikram University, with about 30,000 students, is located there. Ujjain is one of the seven sacred Hindu cities and an important pilgrimage center. Pop., 1966 est., 151,800.

ULAN BATOR, capital of the Mongolian People's Republic, located on the Tuula River. It is connected by the Trans-Mongolian railroad and by air service with the Soviet Union and China. Ulan Bator contains a state university and the major Buddhist monastery in the country. The city's industries produce woolen textiles, leather goods, and processed sheep and goat skins. Pop., 1962 est., 195,300.

ULAN–UDE, in the Soviet Union, capital of the Buryat Autonomous Soviet Socialist Republic, at the confluence of the Uda and Selenge rivers near Lake Baykal. Manufactures include building materials, leather goods, and textiles. Coal is mined nearby. The city is a junction for a railroad line connecting the Trans-Siberian railroad with the frontier between the Soviet Union and Mongolia. Pop., 1966 est., 220,000.

UMTALI, in east central Rhodesia, on the Mozambique border. It is the eastern gateway to Rhodesia on the railway connecting the port of Beira, Mozambique, with Salisbury, the capital of Rhodesia. A large oil refinery is located nearby. Pop., 1963 est., 39,600.

VADUZ, capital of the European principality of Liechtenstein, situated on the banks of the Rhine River. As the country's chief city, it is primarily an administrative center. Tourism is important. Pop., 1961 est., 3,514.

VALENCIA, capital of Valencia province in eastern Spain, situated on the Turia River near the Mediterranean. It is Spain's third largest city and an important commercial and industrial city. It manufactures chemicals, textiles, and furniture and processes grains, fruits, tobacco, and vegetables grown nearby. Pop., 1965 est., 501,800.

VALLETTA, the capital and largest city of the Republic of Malta, situated on the northeastern coast of Malta island. Valletta has two deep natural harbors. Shipbuilding and ship repair are the main industries. Pop., 1965 est., 25,000.

VANCOUVER, a port city in southwestern British Columbia, Canada, situated opposite Vancouver Island on the Strait of Georgia, an arm of the Pacific Ocean. It is Canada's third largest city and the leading Canadian Pacific port, shipping grain, fish, lumber, and metals. Industrial facilities include shipyards, lumber mills, metal works, and food-processing plants. Pop., 1965 est., urban area, 850,000.

VARNA, a Black Sea port of northeastern Bulgaria. It exports grains, dairy products, and cattle. Industrial facilities include shipyards, textile mills, and metal-processing plants. Pop., 1965 est., 177,400.

VENICE, the capital of the province of Venezia, in northeastern Italy. Occupying more than 100 islets in a lagoon off the Adriatic Sea, the city is built on a foundation of sunken piles and is connected with the mainland by bridges. Transportation within the city is by boat along numerous canals.

Venice is noted for its outstanding architecture in a variety of styles, and it has long been an artistic center for Italy and the world. The city's chief source of income is tourism; its few light industries produce glass, jewelry, textiles, furniture, and handicrafts. Pop., 1965 est., 362,000.

VENTSPILS, a Baltic port at the mouth of the Venta River on the west coast of Latvia in the Soviet Union. It exports timber and agricultural products. Pop., 1959 est., 27,400.

VEREENIGING, an industrial city located on the Vaal River in southern Transvaal, Republic of South Africa. The city is situated in an important coal-mining region and produces iron, steel, and machinery. In 1902 British and Boer representatives met in Vereeniging to discuss terms for ending the Boer War. Pop., 1960, 78,835.

VICTORIA, capital of the province of British Columbia, Canada, situated at the southern tip of Vancouver island, just off the mainland. Victoria is a major port that ships lumber, pulp, cement, fish, and fruit. It also serves as a base for a large deep-sea fishing fleet. Industrial facilities include lumber and paper mills, fish canneries, and plants that turn out furniture, machinery, and building supplies. Pop., 1961, urban area, 154,152.

VIENNA, or Wien, the capital of Austria, located in the northeastern part of the country on the Danube River. Vienna is Austria's major commercial and industrial city, producing chemicals, textiles, machinery, and food products. As capital of the Austrian Empire, Vienna was for centuries a European cultural center. With its state university, technical schools, and music, drama, and fine arts academies, Vienna is still an important intellectual center. Pop., 1965 est., 1,640,100.

VIENTIANE, in Southeast Asia, the administrative capital of Laos, on the Mekong River near the border with Thailand. The city is a commercial center, dealing in textiles and wood products. River and air service connects Vientiane and other Laotian cities, and there is also air service to Saigon, in South Vietnam. Pop., 1962 est., urban area, 162,300.

VILA, a port and the capital of the New Hebrides, a group of islands located about 1,000 miles east of Australia and administered by Britain and France. Vila is situated on the south coast of Efate Island. Exports include coffee, copra, and wool. Pop., 1948 est., 800.

VILNIUS, capital of the constituent republic of Lithuania in the Soviet Union, on the Neris River. An important commercial city since the 1300s, Vilnius has been fought over by many nations, including Poland and the Soviet Union. It is an important railway junction and produces textiles and leather goods. Pop., 1966 est., 305,000.

VLADIVOSTOK, a port on the Sea of Japan, in southeastern Siberia in the Soviet Union. It is the most important Soviet port on the Pacific Ocean and is kept open in the winter by icebreakers. The city is the terminus of the Moscow-Vladivostok airline. Fishing fleets are based in Vladivostok, and the city's industries include fish canning, shipbuilding, and mineral refining. The city is also a Soviet naval base. Pop., 1966 est., 379,000.

VLONË, a seaport on the southwestern coast of Albania. Inhabited since antiquity because of its fine harbor, Vlonë exports petroleum and agricultural products. Pop., 1960, 41,285.

VOLGOGRAD, from 1925 to 1961 called Stalingrad, an industrial city on the Volga River in the southwestern Soviet Union, about 280 miles northwest of the Caspian Sea. The city's industries produce agricultural machinery, ships, aluminum, chemicals, refined oil, and food products. Volgograd is an important river port and railway center. The Battle of Stalingrad in 1942 saw Russian troops decisively defeat German armies. Pop., 1966 est., 720,000.

VOLTA REDONDA, an industrial city on the Paraíba River in southeastern Brazil, about 70 miles northwest of Rio de Janeiro. Latin America's leading iron and steel manufacturing center, Volta Redonda was built in 1947 along the railroad and highways linking Rio de Janeiro and São Paulo. Located near raw materials, markets, transportation facilities, and labor supplies, the city's industrial plants produce rails, plates, and structural steel. Pop., 1960 est., urban area, 135,000.

IN VENICE, the main thoroughfare is the Grand Canal, and many people travel by gondola.

MARKET IN YAOUNDE, the capital of Cameroon, displays colorful fabric used for clothing.

WAKAYAMA, port in Japan, on the south coast of Honshu Island. The city lies near the mouth of the Kino River, about 35 miles southwest of Osaka. Wakayama is a prefectural capital and the southernmost part of Osaka's industrial region. Textiles are a major manufacture. Pop., 1965, urban area, 328,657.

WARSAW, the capital and largest city of Poland. It is located on both banks of the Vistula River, in the east-central part of the country, about 30 miles east of Berlin. Warsaw is the commercial, political, educational, and cultural center of Poland. Manufactures include machinery, chemicals, textiles and clothing, and food products. Warsaw is a river port and the communications and transportation center of Poland. Pop., 1965 est., 1,249,100.

WELLINGTON, the capital of New Zealand. It is located at the southwestern tip of North Island, overlooking Cook Strait. Wellington has a large harbor and is one of New Zealand's busiest ports. It is a railroad terminus and an industrial center, manufacturing automobiles, chemicals, and textiles. Pop., 1966, 167,844.

WIESBADEN, in central West Germany, at the southern foot of the Taunus Mountains, about 20 miles west of Frankfurt. Wiesbaden is the capital of the state of Hesse and an important tourist resort. Industries include printing and publishing and boatbuilding. Pop., 1965 est., 261,100.

WILLEMSTAD, the capital, largest city, and chief port of the Netherlands Antilles. It is located on the southwest coast of the island of Curaçao. Willemstad has a fine harbor and is a world center of oil refining. Pop., 1960, urban area, 94,133.

WINDHOEK, the capital of the territory of South West Africa. It is located on a plateau at an altitude of about 5,400 feet, some 250 miles east of Walvis Bay. Windhoek is a commercial and distributing center and is linked by railroad to South Africa. Pop., 1960, 36,051.

WINNIPEG, the capital and chief city of Manitoba, Canada. It is located at the junction of the Assiniboine and Red rivers in central Canada, about 65 miles north of the border with the United States. Winnipeg is the railroad and grain market center of Canada. It is also a financial, commercial, and industrial center. Manufactures include motor vehicles, meat products, and clothing. Pop., 1965 est., urban area, 490,000.

WONSAN, a port on the east coast of North Korea. It is a commercial and transportation center with a fine natural harbor. Fishing is a major industry and exports include fish, rice, and soybeans. Pop., 1944, 112,952.

WROCLAW, in southern Poland, on both banks of the Oder River, about 190 miles southwest of Warsaw. Wroclaw, formerly called Breslau, is a river port and railroad junction. Manufactures include machinery, chemicals, textiles, and food. The city is a cultural center. Pop., 1965, est., 471,300.

WUHAN, in east-central China, at the confluence of the Han and Yangtze rivers. It consists of three cities, Hankow, Hanyang, and Wuchang, and is the capital of Hupeh Province. Wuhan is an industrial, administrative, and transportation center. Manufactures include iron and steel, and textiles. Pop., 1957 est., 2,146,000.

YAMAGATA, in Japan, on the Mogami River, in the north-central part of Honshu Island, about 180 miles north of Tokyo. Yamagata is a commercial and resort center situated in an agricultural region. Pop., 1965, urban area, 193,737.

YAOUNDE, the capital of Cameroon in West Africa. It is located in the west-central part of the country, about 130 miles east of Douala, its port on the Atlantic Ocean. Yaounde is Cameroon's commercial and educational center. It is also a transportation center and market for the region. Pop., 1965 est., 101,000.

YEREVAN, in the southwestern Soviet Union, near the border with Turkey, at the foot of Mount Ararat. Yerevan is the capital of the Armenian Soviet Socialist Republic. The city is an industrial, commercial, and cultural center. Manufactures include machinery, chemicals, textiles, clothing, and furniture. Pop., 1966 est., 643,000.

ZAGREB, in northern Yugoslavia, near the Sava River, about 230 miles northwest of Belgrade. Zagreb is the second largest city in Yugoslavia and the nation's commercial and financial center. Is is the capital and cultural and educational center of Croatia. Manufactures include machinery, textiles, and paper. Pop., 1961, 430,802.

ZAMBOANGA, a port in the southern Philippines, at the southwestern tip of Mindanao Island, about 550 miles south of Manila. Zamboanga is a commercial and tourist center located in a fertile agricultural region. Pop., 1965 est., urban area, 158,000.

ZANZIBAR, the capital and chief port of the island of Zanzibar, in Tanzania, off the southeastern coast of Africa. The city is located on the west coast of the island, about 45 miles north of Dar es Salaam, the capital of Tanzania. Exports include cloves, citrus fruit, and copra. Pop., 1958, 57,923.

ZAPOROZHYE, in the far western Soviet Union, on the Dnepr River in the Ukrainian Soviet Socialist Republic. Zaporozhye is a river port, railroad junction, and industrial center. Manufactures include iron and steel, aluminum, machinery, and chemicals. Pop., 1966 est., 571,000.

ZARIA, in the former Northern Region of Nigeria, in West Africa. It is a rail junction and market center in an agricultural region producing cotton and tobacco. Pop., 1963, 166,170.

ZHDANOV, in the southwestern Soviet Union, on the northern shore of the Sea of Azov in the Ukraine. Zhdanov is a port, railroad terminus, and steel center. Exports include iron and steel, machinery, chemicals, coal, and grain. Pop., 1966 est., 373,000.

ZOMBA, the capital of Malawi, about 70 miles south of Lake Nyasa, in southeastern Africa. Zomba is a transportation and market center in an agricultural region producing cotton and tobacco. Pop., 1966, 19,000.

ZURICH, in Switzerland, at the mouth of the Limmat River, on the northern shore of Lake Zurich. It is the capital of the canton of Zurich and the largest city in Switzerland. The city is the industrial, commercial, and financial center of the country. Manufactures include machinery, textiles, radios, and paper. The city is also a leading cultural, educational, and tourist center. Pop., 1966 est., urban area, 435,000.

BIBLIOGRAPHY

GENERAL

LANGER, WILLIAM L. *An Encyclopedia of World History* (rev.). Houghton Mifflin Co., 1957.

PALMER, R. R. (ed.). *Atlas of World History.* Rand McNally & Co., 1957.

STEINBERG, S. H. (ed.). *The Statesman's Year-Book.* St. Martin's Press (annual).

UNITED NATIONS, *Demographic Yearbook* (annual).

UNITED NATIONS, *Statistical Yearbook* (annual).

AFRICA

BARBOUR, NEVILL (ed.). *A Survey of North West Africa.* Oxford University Press, 1959.

FAGE, J. D. *An Atlas of African History.* Edwin Arnold Ltd., 1966.

JUNOD, VIOLAINE I., and IDRIAN N. RESNICK (eds.). *The Handbook of Africa.* New York University Press, 1963.

KITCHEN, HELEN (ed.). *A Handbook of African Affairs.* Frederick A. Praeger, 1964.

MARSH, Z. A. and G. KINGSNORTH. *An Introduction to the History of East Africa* (2nd ed.). Cambridge University Press, 1961.

MOORE, CLARK D., and ANN DUNBAR (eds.). *Africa Yesterday and Today.* Bantam Books, 1968.

OLIVER, ROLAND and J. D. FAGE. *A Short History of Africa.* New York University Press, 1963.

ROTBERG, ROBERT I. *A Political History of Tropical Africa.* Harcourt, Brace, & World, Inc. 1965.

WALKER, ERIC A. *A History of Southern Africa.* Longmans, Green & Co., 1965.

WARD, W. E. F. *A History of Africa* (2 vols.). George Allen & Unwin Ltd., 1966.

ASIA

BOSWORTH, C. E. *The Islamic Dynasties.* Aldine Publishing Co., 1967.

BROCKELMANN, CARL. *History of the Islamic Peoples.* Routledge & Kegan Paul Ltd., 1950.

DURDIN, TILLMANN. *Southeast Asia.* Atheneum, 1966.

FAIRBANK, JOHN K., EDWIN O. REISCHAUER, and ALBERT M. CRAIG. *East Asia—The Modern Transformation.* Houghton Mifflin Co., 1965.

FAIRBANK, JOHN K., and EDWIN O. REISCHAUER. *East Asia—The Great Tradition.* Houghton Mifflin Co., 1958.

GOODRICH, L. CARRINGTON. *A Short History of the Chinese People* (3d ed.). Harper & Row, 1963.

HALL, D. G. E. *A History of South-East Asia* (2nd ed.). St. Martin's Press, 1964.

HAY, RUPERT. *Persian Gulf States.* Middle East Institute, 1959.

HERRMANN, ALBERT. *An Historical Atlas of China.* Aldine Publishing Co., 1966.

JANOWSKY, OSCAR I. *Foundations of Israel.* D. Van Nostrand Co., Inc., 1959.

LENCZOWSKI, GEORGE. *The Middle East in World Affairs* (3rd ed.). Cornell University Press, 1962.

LEWIS, BERNARD. *The Arabs in History.* Hillary House, 1966.

MORELAND, W. H., and ATUL CHANDRA CHATTERJEE. *A Short History of India.* Longmans, Green & Co., 1947.

ONORATO, MICHAEL P. *Historical Atlas of the Far East in Modern Times.* Denoyer-Geppert, 1967.

SHARABI, H. B. *Governments and Politics of the Middle East in the Twentieth Century.* D. Van Nostrand Co., Inc., 1962.

SPEAR, PERCIVAL. *A History of India* (vol. 2). Penguin Books, Inc., 1965.

THAPAR, ROMILA. *A History of India* (vol. 1). Penguin Books, Inc., 1965.

WINT, GUY (ed.). *Asia—A Handbook.* Frederick A. Praeger, 1967.

AUSTRALIA AND OCEANIA

ALLEN, JACK, and A. E. HOWLAND. *Pacific Islands and Antarctica.* Prentice-Hall, Inc., 1965.

ORD, I. G. *Atlas of the South-West Pacific.* Tri-Ocean Books, 1967.

SHAW, A. G. L. *Short History of Australia.* Frederick A. Praeger, 1967.

STAMP. L. DUDLEY. *Australia and New Zealand* (9th ed.). John Wiley & Sons, Inc., 1965.

GRATTEN, C. HARTLEY. *The Southwest Pacific to 1900.* University of Michigan Press, 1963.

EUROPE

ADAMS, ARTHUR, and others. *Atlas of Russian and East European History.* Frederick A. Praeger, 1966.

ATKINSON, WILLIAM C. *A History of Spain and Portugal.* Penguin Books, Inc., 1960.

BAYERSCHMIDT, CARL F., and E. J. FRIIS (eds.). *Scandinavian Studies.* University of Washington Press, 1965.

CHARQUES, RICHARD D. *A Short History of Russia.* E. P. Dutton & Co., 1958.

CHEW, ALLEN F. *An Atlas of Russian History.* Yale University Press, 1967.

COBBAN, ALFRED. *History of Modern France.* (rev. ed., 3 vol.). Penguin Books, 1961-1963.

DANIELS, ROBERT V. *Russia.* Prentice-Hall, Inc., 1964.

DILL, MARSHALL, JR. *Germany—A Modern History.* University of Michigan Press, 1961.

DMYTRYSHYN, BASIL. *The U.S.S.R.: A Concise History.* Charles Scribner's Sons, 1965.

DUNLOP, JOHN K. *Short History of Germany.* Dufour Editions, 1966.

EYCK, F. GUNTHER. *The Benelux Countries.* D. Van Nostrand Co., 1959.

GOTTMANN, JEAN. *A Geography of Europe* (3rd ed.). Holt, Rinehart, & Winston, Inc., 1954.

GRINDROD, MURIEL. *Italy.* Oxford University Press, 1964.

HOFFMAN, GEORGE W. and others. *Geography of Europe* (2nd ed.). Ronald Press Co., 1963.

HOLBORN, HAJO. *History of Modern Germany.* (3 vols.). Alfred A. Knopf, Inc., 1958-1968.

LIVERMORE, HAROLD. *A History of Spain.* Grove Press, Inc., 1960.

LIVERMORE, HAROLD. *A New History of Portugal.* Cambridge University Press, 1966.

LOPEZ, ROBERT. *The Birth of Europe.* M. Evans & Co., 1967.

PALMER, R. R., and JOEL COLTON. *A History of the Modern World* (3rd ed.). Alfred A. Knopf, Inc., 1966.

PETERS, D. J. *Short History of France.* Pergamon Press, 1967.

RIASANOVSKY, NICHOLAS V. *History of Russia.* Oxford University Press, 1963.

SHABAD, THEODORE. *Geography of the U.S.S.R.* Columbia University Press, 1963.

STAVRIANOS, LEFTEN S. *Balkans Since 1453.* Holt, Rinehart, & Winston, Inc., 1958.

TREVELYAN, G. M. *History of England* (3 vols.). Doubleday-Anchor, 1952.

TREVELYAN, JANET P. *Short History of the Italian People From the Barbarian Invasion to the Present Day.* Pitman Publishing Corp., 1956.

WOLFF, ROBERT L. *The Balkans in Our Time.* W. W. Norton & Co., 1967.

WUORINEN, JOHN H. *Scandinavia.* Prentice-Hall, Inc., 1965.

NORTH AMERICA

CREIGHTON, DONALD G. *Story of Canada.* Houghton Mifflin Co., 1960.

McHENRY, J. P. *Short History of Mexico.* Doubleday & Co., 1962.

McINNIS, EDGAR. *Canada, A Political and Social History.* Holt, Rinehart & Winston, Inc., 1959.

MORTON, W. L. *The Kingdom of Canada.* Bobbs-Merrill Co., 1963.

PARKES, HENRY B. *History of Mexico* (rev.). Houghton Mifflin Co., 1960.

RODRIGUEZ, MARIO. *Central America.* Prentice-Hall, Inc., 1965.

WEST, ROBERT C., and J. P. AUGELLI. *Middle America: Its Lands and Peoples.* Prentice-Hall, 1966.

WILGUS, CURTIS A. (ed.). *Caribbean: The Central American Area.* University of Florida Press, 1968.

SOUTH AMERICA

BELLO, JOSÉ MARIA. *A History of Modern Brazil.* Stanford University Press, 1966.

FAGG, JOHN EDWIN. *Latin America—A General History.* Macmillan Co., 1968.

HERRING, HUBERT. *A History of Latin America.* Alfred A. Knopf, Inc., 1961.

LEVENE, RICARDO. *A History of Argentina.* Russell & Russell, 1963.

MORÓN, GUILLERMO. *History of Venezuela.* Roy Publishers.

ROBINSON, HARRY. *Latin America—A Geographical Survey.* Frederick A. Praeger, 1967.

PARALLELS OF LATITUDE

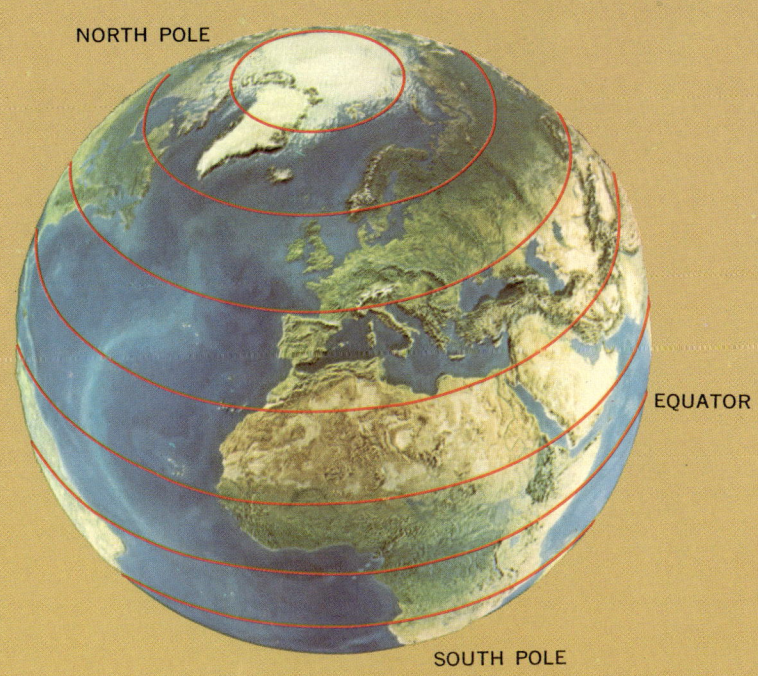

MERIDIANS OF LONGITUDE

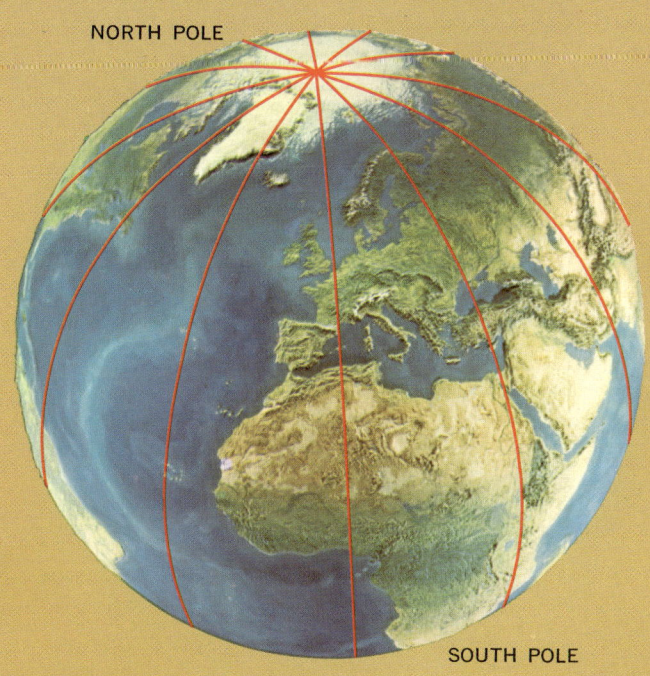

LATITUDE AND LONGITUDE

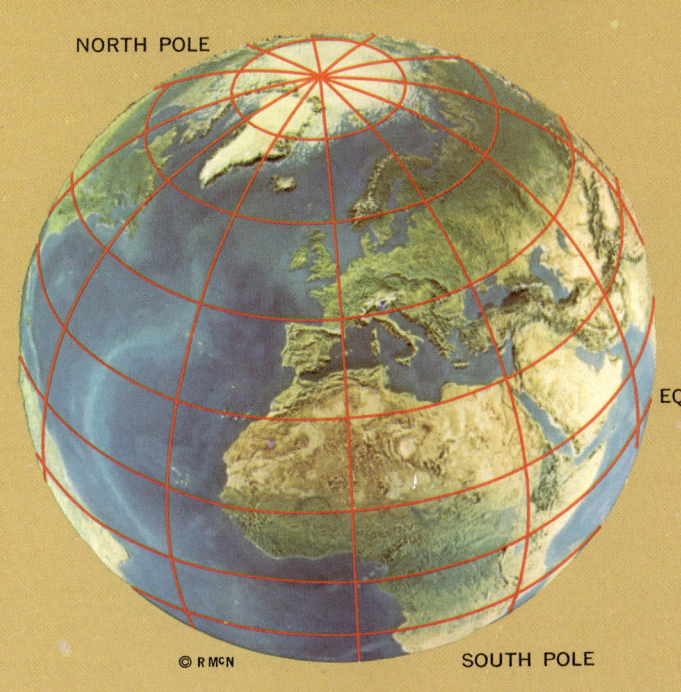

The indexing system used on these maps is based upon the conventional pattern of parallels and meridians used to indicate latitude and longitude. Place names in the index are followed by a key letter and number. The key letter is placed between corresponding degree numbers of latitude in the vertical borders of the map and the key number is placed between corresponding degree numbers of longitude in the horizontal borders of the map. The intersection of the parallels and meridians thus identified forms a confining "box" in which the given place appears.

MAP PROJECTIONS

A map projection is merely an orderly system of parallels and meridians on which a flat map can be drawn. There are hundreds of projections, but no one represents the earth's spherical surface without some distortion. The distortion is relatively small for most practical purposes when a small part of the sphere is projected. For larger areas, a sacrifice of some property is necessary.

Most projections are designed to preserve on the flat map some particular property of the sphere. By varying the systematic arrangement or spacing of the latitude and longitude lines, a projection may be made either equal-area or conformal. Although most projections are derived from mathematical formulas, some are easier to visualize if thought of as projected upon a plane, or upon a cone or cylinder which is then unrolled into a plane surface. Thus, many projections are classified as plane (azimuthal), conic, or cylindrical.

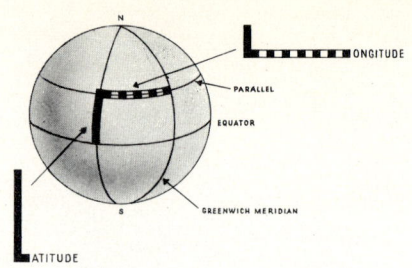

SIMPLE CONIC PROJECTIONS

A perspective projection on a tangent cone with the origin point at the center of the globe. At the parallel of tangency, all elements of the map are true angles, distances, shapes, areas. Away from the tangent parallel, distances increase rapidly, giving bad distortion of shapes and areas.

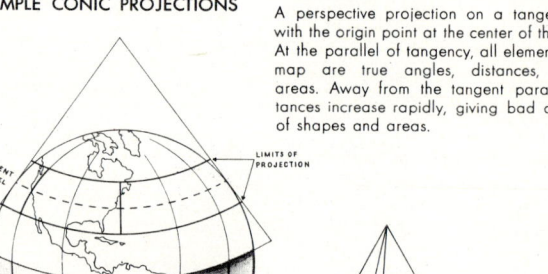

EARTH PROJECTED UPON A TANGENT CONE   CONE CUT FROM BASE TO APEX

MODIFIED CONIC PROJECTION

EARTH PROJECTED UPON AN INTERSECTING CONE

This modification of the conic has two standard parallels, or lines of intersection. It is not an equal-area projection, the space being reduced in size between the standard parallels and progressively enlarged beyond the standard parallels. Careful selection of the standard parallels provides however, good representation for areas of limited latitudinal extent.

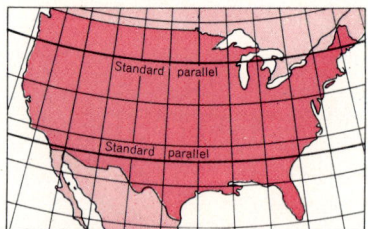

CONIC PROJECTION WITH TWO STANDARD PARALLELS

BONNE PROJECTION

An equal-area modification of the conic principle. Distances are true along all parallels and the central meridian; but away from it, increasing obliqueness of intersections and longitudinal distances, with their attendant distortion of shapes, limits the satisfactory area.

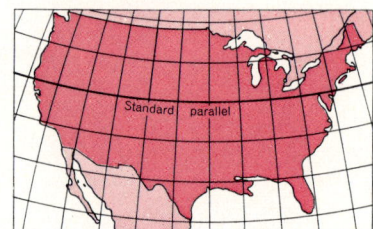

CONE DEVELOPED INTO A PLANE SURFACE

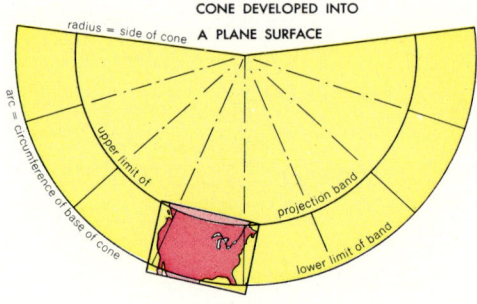

EARTH CONSIDERED AS FORMED BY BASES OF CONES   DEVELOPMENT OF THE CONICAL BASES   POLYCONIC PROJECTION

POLYCONIC PROJECTION

This variation is not equal-area. Parallels are nonconcentric circles truly divided. Distances along the straight central meridian are also true, but along the curving meridians are increasingly exaggerated. Representation is good near the central meridian, but away from it there is marked distortion.

TYPICAL PLANE PROJECTIONS

ATLAS 3

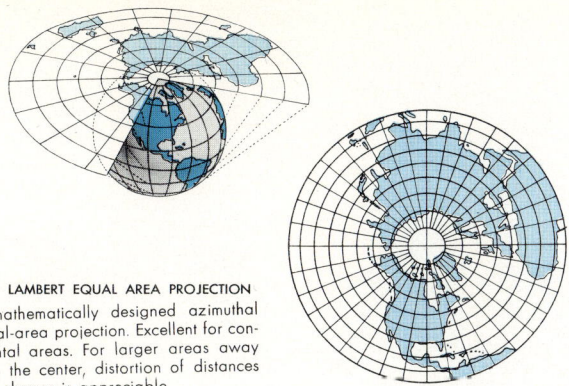

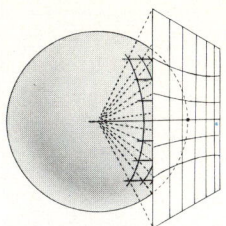

LAMBERT EQUAL AREA PROJECTION

A mathematically designed azimuthal equal-area projection. Excellent for continental areas. For larger areas away from the center, distortion of distances and shapes is appreciable.

GNOMONIC PROJECTION

A geometric or perspective projection on a tangent plane with the origin point at the center of the globe. Shapes and distances rapidly become increasingly distorted away from the center of the projection. Important in navigation, because all straight lines are great circles.

CYLINDRICAL PROJECTIONS

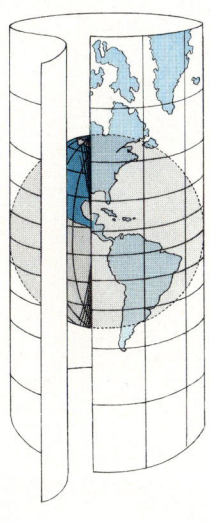

EARTH PROJECTED UPON A CYLINDER

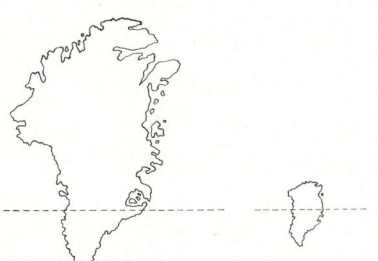

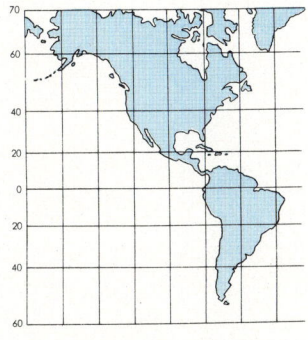

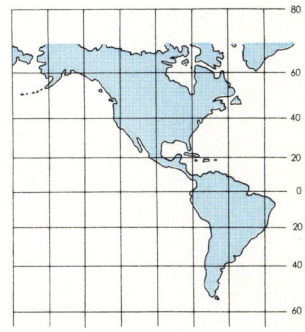

PERSPECTIVE PROJECTION

A perspective projection on a tangent cylinder. Because of rapidly increasing distortion away from the line of tangency and the lack of any special advantage, it is rarely used.

Note the increasing distortion of Greenland (above left) compared to an equal area projection (above right).

MERCATOR CONFORMAL PROJECTION

Mercator's modification increases the longitudinal distances in the same proportion as latitudinal distances are increased. Thus, at any point shapes are true, but areas become increasingly exaggerated. Of value in navigation, because a line connecting any two points gives the true direction between them.

MILLER PROJECTION

This recent modification is neither conformal nor equal-area. Whereas shapes are less accurate than on the Mercator, the exaggeration of areas has been reduced somewhat.

EQUAL AREA PROJECTIONS OF THE WORLD

The earth's surface peeled like the skin from an orange.

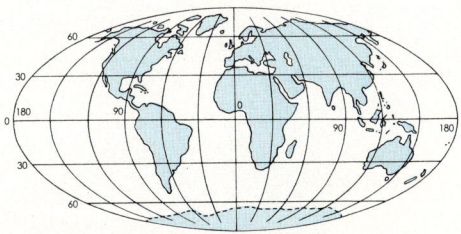

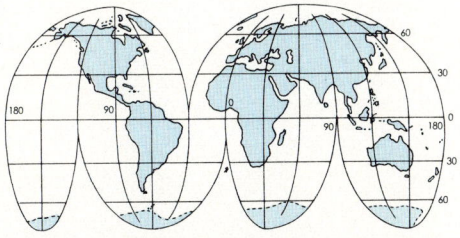

MOLLWEIDE'S HOMOLOGRAPHIC PROJECTION

GOODE'S INTERRUPTED HOMOLOGRAPHIC PROJECTION

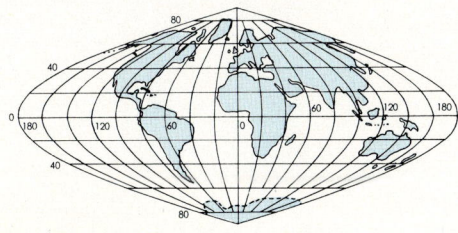

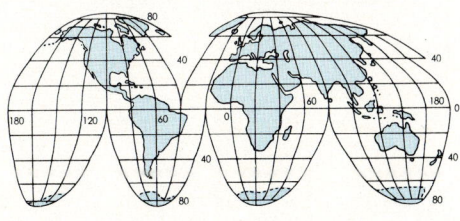

SINUSOIDAL PROJECTION

GOODE'S INTERRUPTED HOMOLOSINE PROJECTION

Although each of these projections is equal-area, differences in the spacing and arrangement of latitude and longitude lines result in differences in the distribution and relative degree of the shape and distance distortion within each grid. On the homolographic, there is no uniformity in scale. It is different on each parallel and each meridian. On the sinusoidal, only distances along all latitudes and the central meridian are true. The homolosine combines the homolographic, for areas poleward of 40°, with the sinusoidal. The principle of interruption permits each continent in turn the advantage of being in the center of the projection, resulting in better shapes.

ATLAS 4   POLAR MAP OF THE WORLD

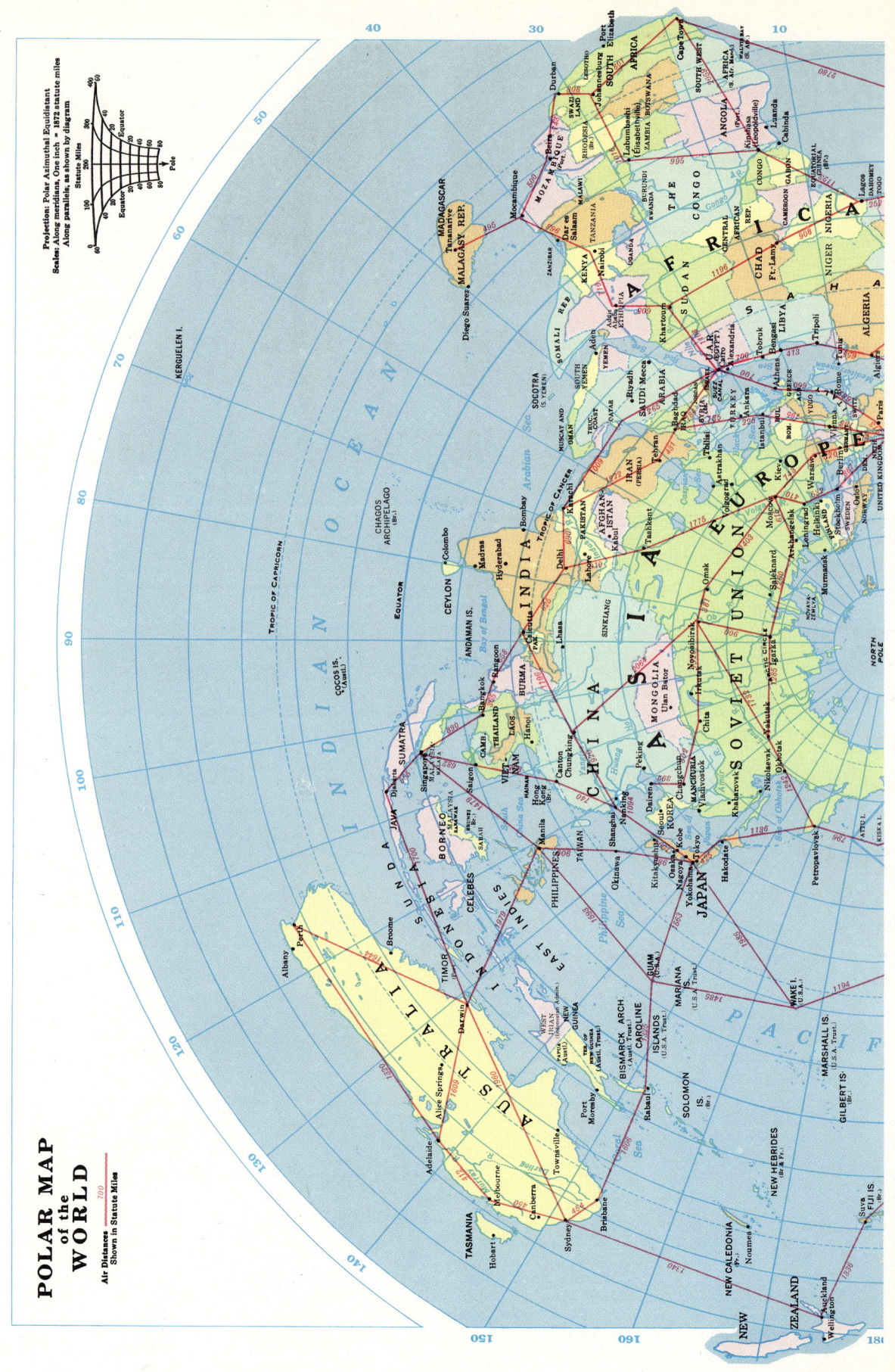

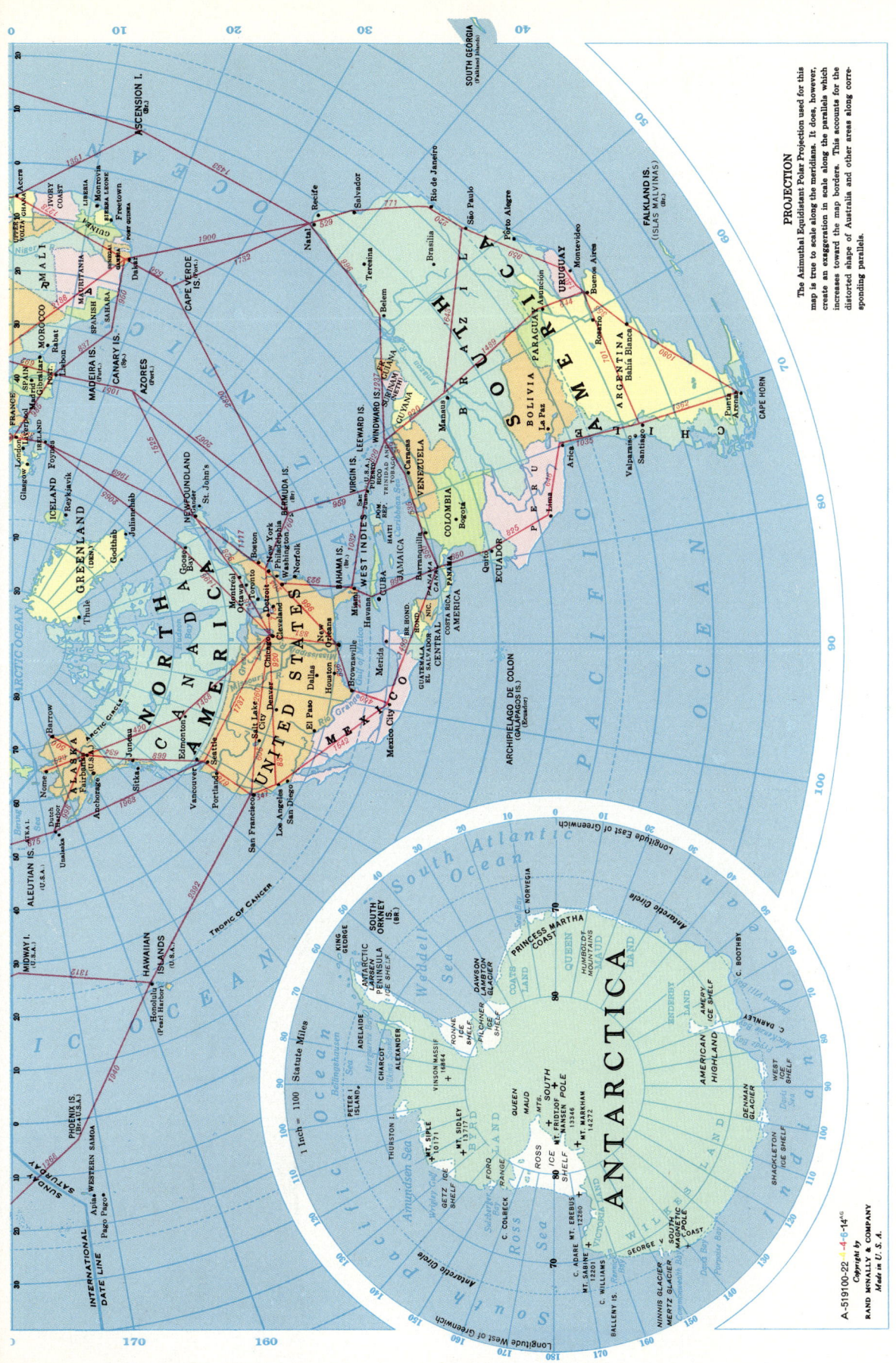

ATLAS 5

ATLAS 6 THE WORLD

THE WORLD

Afars & Issas	F23
Afghanistan	D 1
Albania	D22
Algeria	D21
Andorra	*D21
Angola	G21
Argentina	I16
Australia	H 5
Austria	C22
Azores	D19
Bahama Islands	E15
Barbados	F17
Belgium	C21
Bermuda	D16
Bhutan	E 3
Bolivia	H16
Botswana	H22
Brazil	G17
British Honduras	E15
Brunei	*F 4
Bulgaria	D22
Burma	E 3
Burundi	G23
Cambodia	F 3
Cameroon	F21
Canada	C13
Canary Islands	E19
Cape Verde Islands	E19
Central African Republic	F22
Ceylon	F 2
Chad	E22
Chile	I16
China	D 4
Colombia	F19
Congo (Brazzaville)	G22
Congo, (The Democratic Republic of the Congo)	G22
Costa Rica	F15
Cuba	E15
Cyprus	*D23
Czechoslovakia	C21
Dahomey	*F21
Denmark	C21
Dominican Republic	E16
Ecuador	G15
Egypt, see U.A.R.	
El Salvador	F15
Equatorial Guinea	F21
Ethiopia	F23
Faeroe Islands	B20
Falkland Islands	J17
Finland	B22
Formosa, see Taiwan	
France	C21
French Guiana	F17
Gabon	G21
Gambia	F19
Germany	C21
Ghana	F20
Greece	D22
Greenland	A17
Guadeloupe	E16
Guatemala	F14
Guinea	F20
Haiti	E16
Honduras	F15
Hong Kong	*E 4
Hungary	C22
Iceland	B19
Ifni	*E20
India	E 2
Indonesia	G 4
Iran	D24
Iraq	D23
Ireland	C20
Israel	D23
Italy	D21
Ivory Coast	*F20
Jamaica	E15
Japan	D 6
Jordan	D23
Kenya	F23
Korea	D 5
Kuwait	E24
Laos	E 3
Lebanon	D23

ATLAS 7

Lesotho	H22
Liberia	F20
Libya	E22
Liechtenstein	*C21
Luxembourg	*C21
Macao	*E 4
Malagasy Republic	H24
Malawi	G23
Malaysia	F 4
Mali	E20
Martinique	F16
Mauritania	E19
Mauritius	H24
Mexico	E14
Mongolia	C 3
Morocco	D20
Mozambique	H23
Muscat & Oman	E24
Nauru	G 8
Nepal	E 2
Netherlands	C21
New Caledonia	H 8
New Hebrides	H 8
New Zealand	I 8
Nicaragua	F15
Niger	E21
Nigeria	F21
Norway	B21
Pakistan	E 1, E 3
Panama	F15
Papua	G 6
Paraguay	H17
Peru	G15
Philippines	F 5
Poland	C22
Portugal	D20
Portuguese Guinea	F19
Puerto Rico	E16
Qatar	*E24
Rhodesia	H22
Romania	C22
Rwanda	G22
San Marino	*D21
Saudi Arabia	E23
Senegal	*E19
Sierra Leone	F20
Singapore	F 3
Somali Republic	F24
South Africa	H22
South Yemen	E24
South West Africa	H22
Soviet Union	B 3
Spain	D20
Spanish Sahara	E20
Sudan	F22
Surinam	F17
Swaziland	H23
Sweden	B22
Switzerland	C21
Syria	D23
Taiwan (Formosa)	E 5
Tanzania	G23
Thailand	E 3
Togo	*F21
Trinidad & Tobago	F17
Trucial Coast	*E24
Tunisia	D21
Turkey	D23
Uganda	F23
United Arab Republic (Egypt)	E22
United Kingdom	C20
United States	D14
Upper Volta	*E20
Uruguay	I17
Vatican City	*D21
Venezuela	F16
Vietnam	E 4
Virgin Islands	E16
Western Samoa	G 9
West Indies	E16
West Irian	G 6
Yemen	E23
Yugoslavia	D22
Zambia	G22

* Not shown on map. Index key denotes approximate location.

ATLAS 8 WESTERN EUROPE

WESTERN EUROPE

✪ Capitals

Amsterdam, Neth	E 9
Belgrade, Yugo	G12
Berlin, Ger., E	E10
Bern, Switz	F 9
Bonn, Ger., W	E 9
Brussels, Bel	E 8
Bucharest, Rom	G13
Budapest, Hung	F11
Copenhagen, Den	D10
Dublin, Ire	E 6
Helsinki, Fin	C12
London, Eng	E 7
Oslo, Nor	D10
Paris, Fr	F 8
Prague, Czech	E10
Reykjavík, Ice	C 3
Sofia, Bulg	G12
Stockholm, Swe	D11
The Hague, Neth	E 8
Vienna, Aus	F11
Warsaw, Pol	E12

Physical Features

Adriatic, sea	G11
Aegean, sea	H13
Alps, mts	F 9
Apennines, mts	G10
Balearic, is	H 8
Balkan, mts	G12
Baltic, sea	D11
Barents, sea	A13
Biscay, bay	G 7
Black, sea	G14
Blanc, mtn	F 9
Bosporus, strait	G13
Bothnia, gulf	C12
Brenner, pass	F10
Cantabrian, mts	G 6
Carpathians, mts	F12
Channel, is	F 7
Cheviot, hills	E 7
Clear, cape	E 6
Corsica, isl	G 9
Crete, isl	H12
Crete, sea	H12
Cyclades, is	H12
Danube, riv	G13
Dardanelles, strait	G13
Denmark, strait	B 3
Dinaric Alps, mts	G11
Dnepr, riv	F14
Dnestr, riv	F13
Douro, riv	G 6
Drin, riv	G12
Drina, riv	G11
Ebro, riv	G 7
Elba, isl	G10
Elbe, riv	E10
English, chan	E 7
Etna, mtn	H10
Faeroe, is	C 6
Faxafloi, bay	C 3
Finland, gulf	C13
Firth of Forth, chan	D 7
Galdhöppigen, mtn	C 9
Gibraltar, strait	H 6
Gotland, isl	D11
Grampians, mts	D 7
Guadalquivir, riv	H 6
Guadarrama, mts	G 7
Guadiana, riv	H 6
Hardangerfjord, fjord	D 8
Hardangervidda, plat	C 9
Hebrides, is	D 6
Inari, lake	B13
Ionian, sea	H11
Irish, sea	E 6
Jan Mayen, isl	A 6
Karkinitskiy, bay	F14
Kattegat, chan	D10
Kemijoki, riv	B13
Kola, pen	B15
Ladoga, lake	C14

ATLAS 9

Lågen, riv............D 9
Land's End, cape......E 6
Ligurian, sea.........G 9
Lions, gulf...........G 8
Lofoten, is...........B10
Loire, riv............F 8
Mälaren, lake.........D11
Mallorca, isl.........H 8
Malta, isl............H10
Maritime Alps, mts....G 9
Maritsa, riv..........G13
Marmara, sea..........G13
Marne, riv............F 8
Massif Central, mts...F 8
Matapan, cape.........H12
Mediterranean, sea....H10
Menderes, riv.........H13
Menorca, isl..........H 8
Morava, riv...........G12
Moray, firth..........D 7
Morena, mts...........H 6
Mulhacén, mtn.........H 7
Muonio, riv...........B12
Muresul, riv..........F12
Normandy, hills.......F 7
North, cape...........A13
North, sea............D 8
Northern Dvina, riv...C16
Norwegian, sea........B 7
Oder, riv.............E11
Olympus, mtn..........G12
Onega, lake...........C15
Onega, riv............C15
Orkney, is............D 7
Otteraen, riv.........D 9
Palos, cape...........H 7
Passero, cape.........H11
Peipus, lake..........D13
Pindus, mts...........H12
Po, riv...............G10
Pripyat, riv..........E13
Pskov, lake...........D13
Pyrenees, mts.........G 8
Rhine, riv............E 9
Rhône, riv............G 8
Riga, gulf............D12
Rybinsk, res..........D15
St. George's, chan....E 6
St. Vincent, cape.....H 6
Saone, riv............F 8
Sardinia, isl.........G 9
Scutari, lake.........G11
Seine, riv............F 8
Shetland, is..........C 7
Shipka, pass..........G13
Sicily, isl...........H10
Skagerrak, chan.......D 9
Somme, riv............E 8
Spartivento, cape.....H 9
Spartivento, cape.....H11
Sporades
 (Dodecanese), is.....H13
Squillace, gulf.......H11
Storavan, lake........B11
Tajo, riv.............H 6
Tanaelv, riv..........B13
Taranto, gulf.........G11
Tevere, riv...........G10
The Minch, strait.....D 6
The Naze, cape........D 9
Tornetrask, lake......B12
Transylvanian Alps, mts.F12
Tyrrhenian, sea.......H10
Umeälven, riv.........C11
Vänern, lake..........D10
Vardar, riv...........G12
Vattern, lake.........D10
Vesterålen, is........B10
Vestfjorden, fjord....B10
Vesuvius, mtn.........G10
Vienne, riv...........F 8
Vistula, riv..........E11
Warta, riv............E11
Weser, riv............E 9
Western Dvina, riv....D14
White, sea............B15
Wrath, cape...........D 6

Conic Projection
SCALE 1:16,000,000   1 Inch = 252 Statute Miles

ATLAS 10 — BRITISH ISLES

UNITED KINGDOM
ENGLAND
Principal Cities

Pop.—Thousands

Pop.	City	Ref.
144	Birkenhead	D 5
1,116	Birmingham	D 6
105	Blackburn	D 5
151	Blackpool	D 5
160	Bolton	D 5
151	Bournemouth	E 6
297	Bradford	D 6
163	Brighton	E 6
434	Bristol	E 5
80	Burnley	D 5
96	Cambridge	D 7
314	Coventry	D 6
17	Cowes	E 6
84	Darlington	C 6
132	Derby	D 6
87	Doncaster	D 6
110	Enfield	k12
103	Gateshead	C 6
97	Grimsby	D 6
96	Halifax	D 6
132	Huddersfield	D 6
301	Hull (Kingston-upon-Hull)	D 6
119	Ipswich	D 7
514	Leeds	D 6
270	Leicester	D 6
740	Liverpool	D 5
7,973	London	E 6, k12
136	Luton	E 6
655	Manchester	D 5
158	Middlesbrough	C 6
263	Newcastle-on-Tyne	C 6
105	Northampton	D 6
120	Norwich	D 7
315	Nottingham	D 6
114	Oldham	D 5
107	Oxford	D 6
210	Plymouth	E 4
94	Poole	E 5
225	Portsmouth	E 6
112	Preston	D 5
122	Reading	E 6
86	Rochdale	D 5
153	Salford	D 5
495	Sheffield	D 6
84	Slough	E 6, k11
207	Southampton	E 6
166	Southend-on-Sea	E 7
109	South Shields	C 6
143	Stockport	D 5
266	Stoke-on-Trent	D 5
191	Sunderland	C 6
96	Swindon	D 6
103	Wallasey	D 5
121	Walsall	D 5
98	West Bromwich	D 6
150	Wolverhampton	D 5
67	Worcester	D 5
80	Worthing	E 6
104	York	D 6

WALES
Principal Cities

Pop.—Thousands

Pop.	City	Ref.
39	Aberdare	E 5
10	Aberystwyth	D 4
15	Bangor	D 4
9	Caernarvon	D 4
261	Cardiff	E 5
13	Carmarthen	E 4
8	Denbigh	D 5
10	Holyhead	D 4
17	Llandudno	D 5
59	Merthyr Tydfil	E 5
13	Milford Haven	E 4
31	Neath	E 5
14	Pembroke	E 4
100	Rhondda	E 5
21	Rhyl	D 5
170	Swansea	E 4
36	Wrexham	D 5

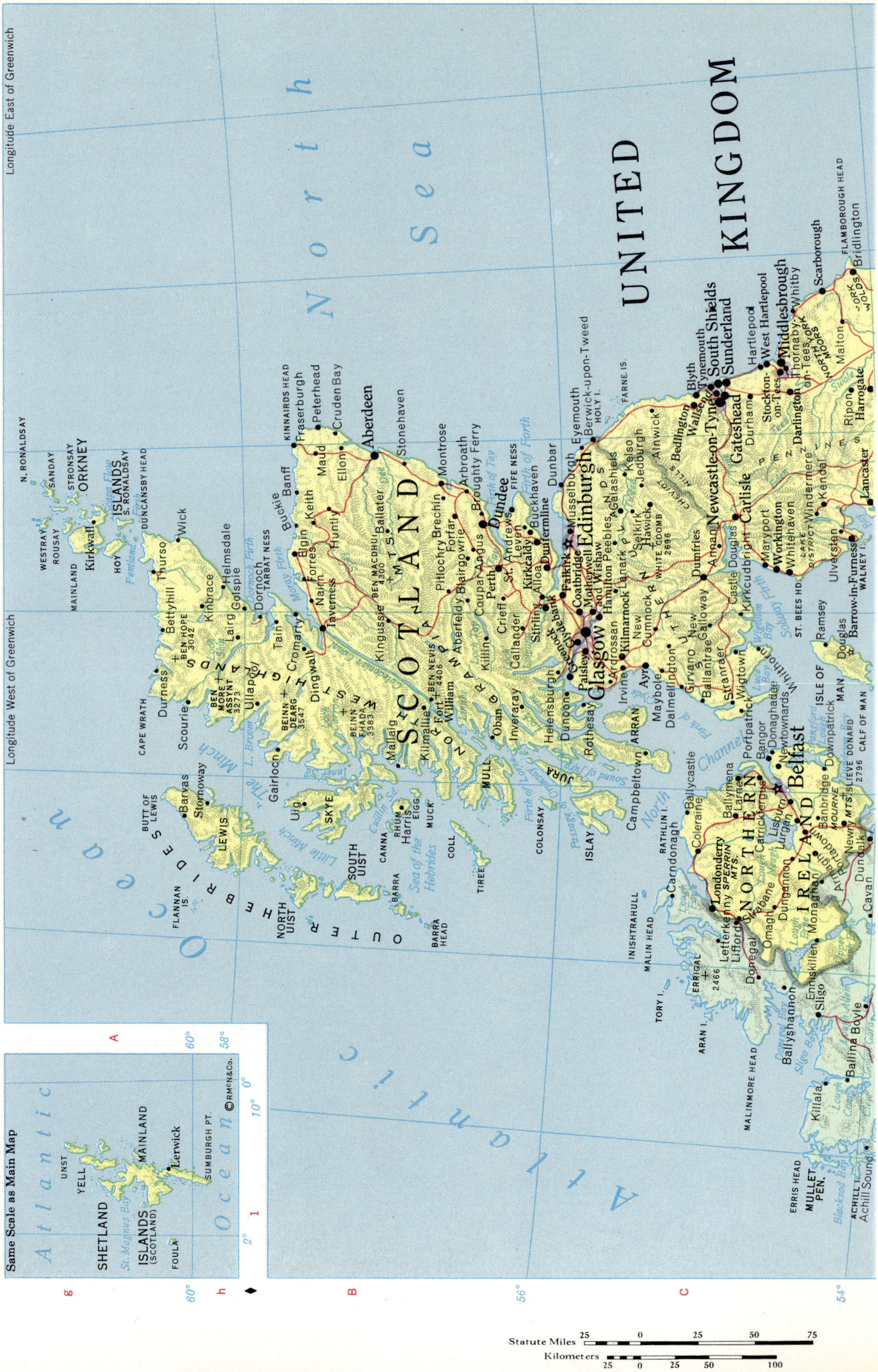

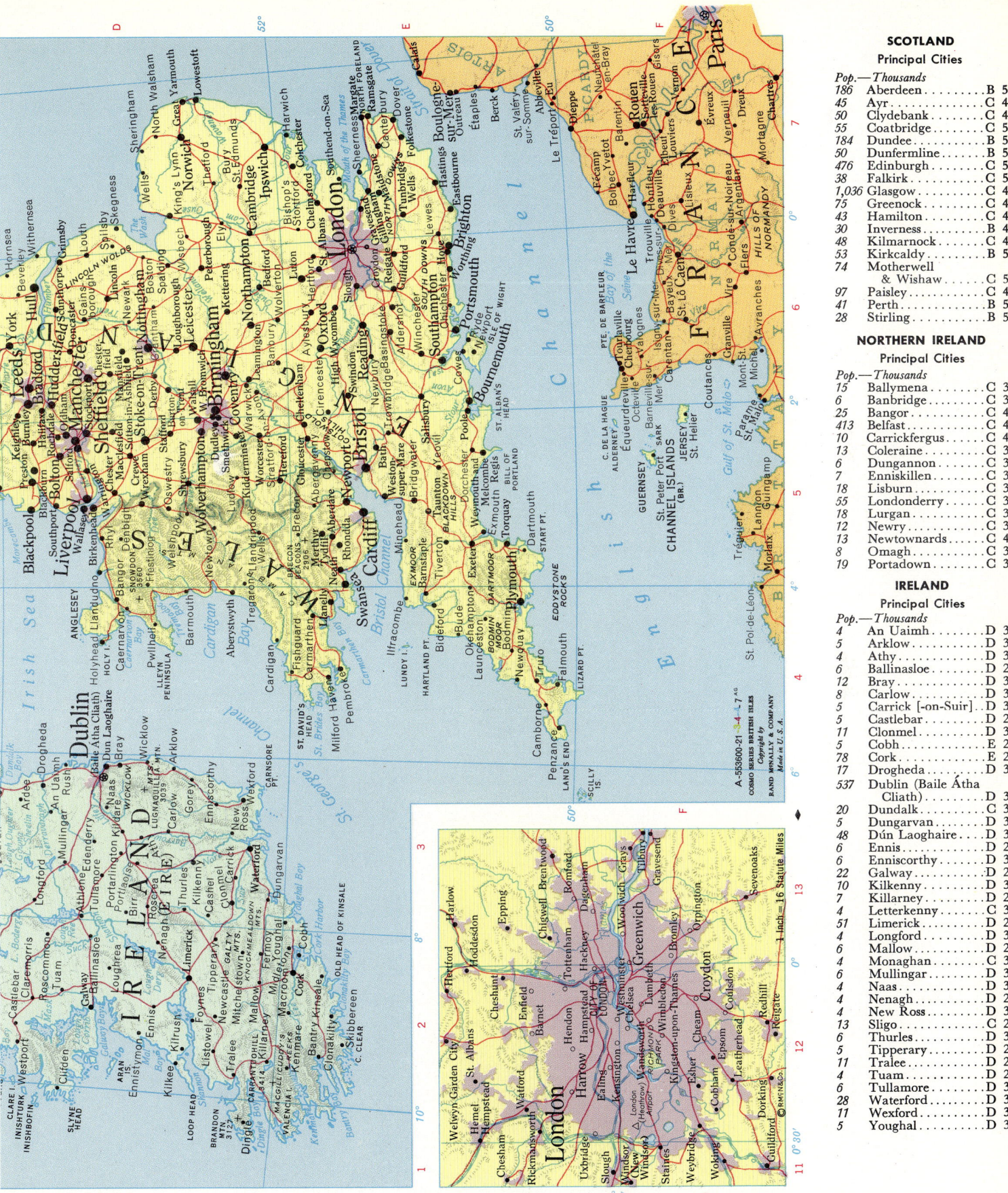

ATLAS 11

SCOTLAND
Principal Cities

Pop.—Thousands		
186	Aberdeen	B 5
45	Ayr	C 4
50	Clydebank	C 4
55	Coatbridge	C 5
184	Dundee	B 5
50	Dunfermline	B 5
476	Edinburgh	C 5
38	Falkirk	C 5
1,036	Glasgow	C 4
75	Greenock	C 4
43	Hamilton	C 4
30	Inverness	B 4
48	Kilmarnock	C 4
53	Kirkcaldy	B 5
74	Motherwell & Wishaw	C 5
97	Paisley	C 4
41	Perth	B 5
28	Stirling	B 5

NORTHERN IRELAND
Principal Cities

Pop.—Thousands		
15	Ballymena	C 3
6	Banbridge	C 3
25	Bangor	C 4
413	Belfast	C 4
10	Carrickfergus	C 4
13	Coleraine	C 3
6	Dungannon	C 3
7	Enniskillen	C 3
18	Lisburn	C 3
55	Londonderry	C 3
18	Lurgan	C 3
12	Newry	C 3
13	Newtownards	C 4
8	Omagh	C 3
19	Portadown	C 3

IRELAND
Principal Cities

Pop.—Thousands		
4	An Uaimh	D 3
5	Arklow	D 3
4	Athy	D 3
6	Ballinasloe	D 2
12	Bray	D 3
8	Carlow	D 3
5	Carrick [-on-Suir]	D 3
5	Castlebar	D 2
11	Clonmel	D 3
5	Cobh	E 2
78	Cork	E 2
17	Drogheda	D 3
537	Dublin (Baile Átha Cliath)	D 3
20	Dundalk	C 3
5	Dungarvan	D 3
48	Dún Laoghaire	D 3
6	Ennis	D 2
6	Enniscorthy	D 3
22	Galway	D 2
10	Kilkenny	D 3
7	Killarney	D 2
4	Letterkenny	C 3
51	Limerick	D 2
4	Longford	D 3
6	Mallow	D 2
6	Monaghan	C 3
6	Mullingar	D 3
4	Naas	D 3
4	Nenagh	D 2
4	New Ross	D 3
13	Sligo	C 2
6	Thurles	D 3
4	Tipperary	D 2
11	Tralee	D 2
4	Tuam	D 2
6	Tullamore	D 3
28	Waterford	D 3
11	Wexford	D 3
5	Youghal	D 3

Conic Projection
SCALE 1:4,000,000   1 Inch = 63 Statute Miles

ATLAS 12

WESTERN MEDITERRANEAN

WESTERN MEDITERRANEAN

⊕ **Capitals**

Andorra, And	C 7
Lisbon, Port	E 2
Madrid, Sp	D 5
Rome, It	D13

Physical Features

Adige, riv	B12
Adour, riv	C 6
Adriatic, sea	B13
Alboran, isl	G 5
Alps, mts	B11
Amaro, mtn	C14
Aneto, mtn	C 7
Apennines, mts	C13
Arno, riv	C12
Asinara, isl	D11
Atlas Saharien, mts	H 6
Baïse, riv	C 7
Balearic, is	E 8
Belle, isl	A 5
Biscay, bay	B 5
Blanc, cape	F11
Blanc, mtn	B10
Bon, cape	F12
Bonifacio, strait	D11
Bosna, riv	B16
Bougaroun, cape	F10
Brač, isl	C15
Cantabrian, mts	C 3
Caprara, pt	D11
Capri, isl	D14
Carbonara, cape	E11
Carvoeiro, cape	E 2
Cévennes, mts	C 8
Cher, riv	A 8
Chergul, salt lake	G 7
Cinto, mtn	C11
Columbretes, isl	E 7
Corno, mtn	C13
Corse, cape	C11
Corsica, isl	C11
Côtes du Nivernais, hills	A 8
Danube, riv	B16
D'Hyères, is	C10
Dinaric Alps, mts	B15
Djerba, isl	H12
Djerid, salt lake	H11
D'Oléron, isl	B 6
Dordogne, riv	B 7
Douro, riv	D 2
Drava, riv	B15
Dugi Otok, isl	C14
Durance, riv	C 9
D'Yeu, isl	A 5
Ebro, riv	D 6
Écrins, mtn	B10
Egadi, is	F13
Elba, isl	C12
Espichel, cape	E 2
Etna, mtn	F14
Ferrat, cape	G 6
Finisterre, cape	C 2
Formentera, isl	E 7
Gabès, gulf	G12
Garonne, riv	C 7
Gata, cape	F 6
Genoa, gulf	C11
Gibraltar, strait	G 3
Giglio, isl	C12
Grand Atlas, mts	I 3
Grand Erg Oriental, sand dunes	H10
Gredos, mtn	D 4
Grossglockner, mtn	A13
Guadalquivir, riv	F 4
Guadarrama, mts	D 5
Guadiana, riv	E 4
Hammamet, gulf	F12
Hauts, plat	H 6
Hodna, salt lake	G 9

ATLAS 14 — NORTHERN EUROPE

NORWAY
Principal Cities
Pop.—Thousands

Pop.	City	Ref
19	Ålesund	F 2
11	Arendal	H 3
5	Askim	p29
116	Bergen	G 1
13	Bodø	D 6
31	Drammen	H 4, p28
14	Fredrikstad	H 4, p28
8	Gjøvik	G 4
10	Halden	H 4
14	Hamar	G 4
27	Haugesund	H 1
14	Horten	H 4, p28
10	Kongsberg	H 3, p27
5	Kragerø	H 3
17	Kristiansund	F 2
11	Larvik	H 4, p28
6	Lillehammer	G 4
11	Lilleström	H 4, p29
21	Moss	H 4, p28
13	Narvik	C 7
8	Notodden	H 3
5	Odda	G 2
477	Oslo	H 4, p28
11	Porsgrunn	p27
6	Rjukan	H 3
7	Sandefjord	p28
13	Sarpsborg	p29
16	Skien	H 3, p27
53	Stavanger	H 1
12	Tönsberg	H 4, p28
12	Tromsö	C 8
59	Trondheim	F 4

SWEDEN
Principal Cities
Pop.—Thousands

Pop.	City	Ref
18	Alingsås	I 5
13	Angelholm	I 5
16	Arvika	H 5
14	Boden	E 9
67	Borås	I 5
27	Borlänge	G 6
13	Enköping	H 7, t35
59	Eskilstuna	H 7, t34
16	Fagersta	G 6
14	Falköping	H 5
19	Falun	G 6
15	Finspång	u33
6	Gällivare	D 9
55	Gävle	G 7
405	Göteborg	I 4
39	Halmstad	I 5
77	Hälsingborg	I 5
17	Härnösand	F 8
14	Hässleholm	I 5
14	Huskvarna	I 6
51	Jönköping	I 6
36	Karlskoga	H 6
33	Karlskrona	I 6
43	Karlstad	H 5
19	Katrineholm	H 7, u34
19	Kiruna	D 9
18	Köping	H 6, t33
26	Kristianstad	I 6
29	Landskrona	J 5
29	Lidingö	H 8, t36
17	Lidköping	H 5
65	Linköping	H 6
12	Ludvika	G 6
31	Luleå	E10
40	Lund	J 5
229	Malmö	J 5
27	Mölndal	I 5
27	Motala	H 6
18	Nässjö	I 6
2	Njurunda	F 7
91	Norrköping	H 7, u34
24	Nyköping	H 7, u34
75	Örebro	H 6, t33
13	Oskarshamn	I 7

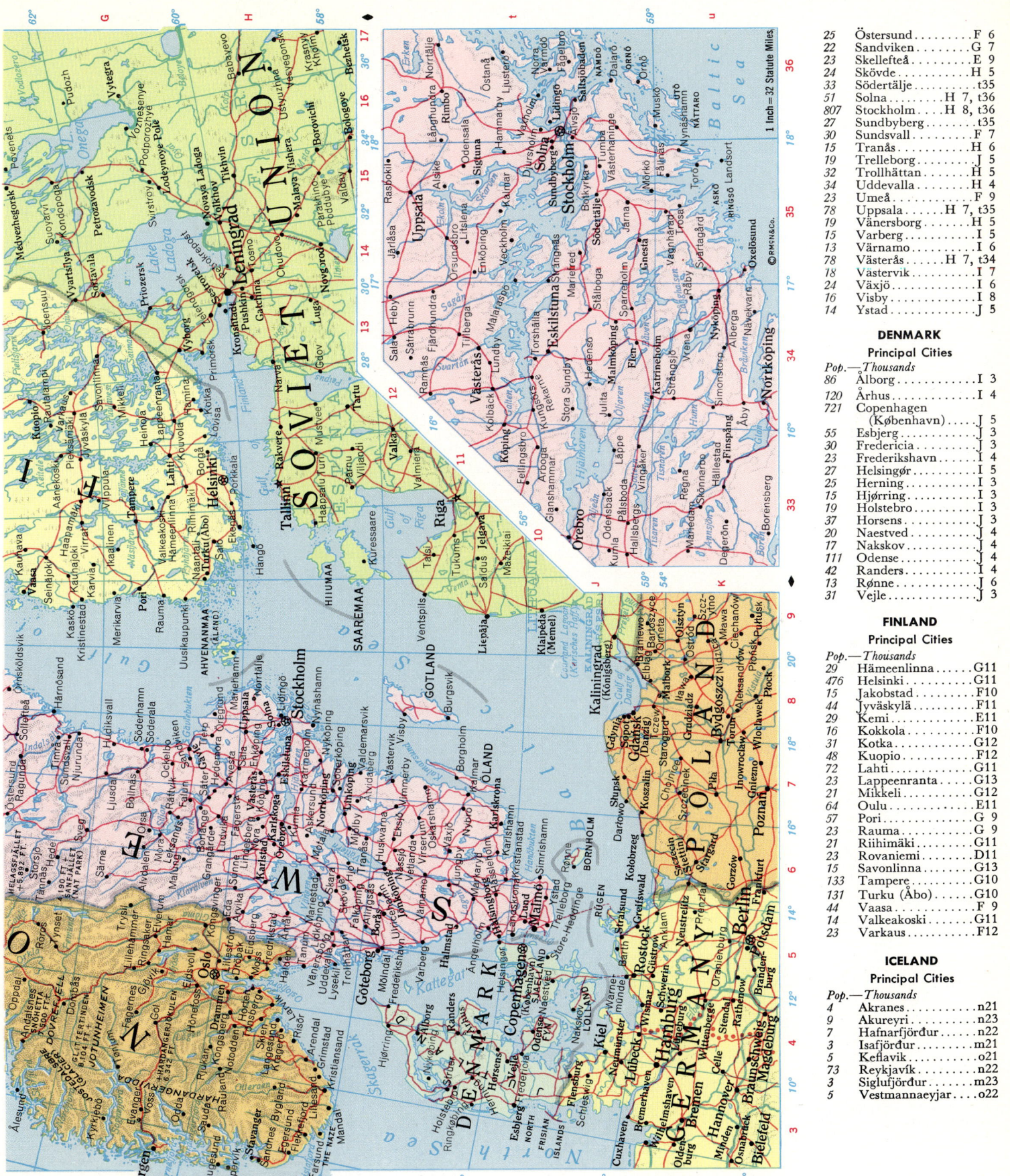

ATLAS 16 — GERMANY, AUSTRIA AND SWITZERLAND

GERMANY†
Principal Cities
Pop.—Thousands

Pop.	City	Grid
178	Aachen	C 3
211	Augsburg	D 5
1,072	Berlin, East	†B 6
2,197	Berlin, West	B 6
170	Bielefeld	B 4
356	Bochum	C 3
141	Bonn	C 3
90	Brandenburg [an der Havel]	†B 6
235	Braunschweig	B 5
596	Bremen	B 4
146	Bremerhaven (Wesermünde)	B 4
139	Darmstadt	D 4
96	Dessau	†C 6
657	Dortmund	C 3
504	Dresden	†C 6
487	Duisburg	C 3
698	Düsseldorf	C 3
190	Erfurt	†C 5
725	Essen	C 3
97	Flensburg	A 4
683	Frankfurt [am Main]	C 4
154	Freiburg [im Breisgau]	D 3
96	Fürth	D 5
371	Gelsenkirchen	C 3
107	Gera	†C 6
89	Görlitz	†C 7
203	Hagen [in Westfalen]	C 3
274	Halle [an der Saale]	†C 6
1,854	Hamburg	B 5
553	Hannover	B 4
125	Heidelberg	D 4
99	Hildesheim	B 4
84	Jena	†C 5
86	Kaiserslautern	D 3
294	Karl-Marx-Stadt (Chemnitz)	†C 6
253	Karlsruhe	D 3
215	Kassel	C 4
270	Kiel	A 5
102	Koblenz	C 3
857	Köln (Cologne)	C 3
222	Krefeld	C 3
595	Leipzig	†C 6
240	Lübeck	B 5
176	Ludwigshafen [am Rhein]	D 4
265	Magdeburg	†B 6
144	Mainz	D 4
328	Mannheim	D 4
154	Mönchengladbach	C 3
191	Mülheim [an der Ruhr]	C 3
1,215	München (Munich)	D 5
196	Münster [in Westfalen]	C 3
472	Nürnberg (Nüremberg)	D 5
259	Oberhausen	C 3
117	Offenbach [am Main]	C 4
129	Oldenburg	B 4
143	Osnabrück	B 4
81	Plauen	†C 6
110	Potsdam	†B 6
128	Recklinghausen	C 3
125	Regensburg	D 5
134	Remscheid	C 3
179	Rostock	†A 6
134	Saarbrücken	D 3
117	Salzgitter	B 5
91	Schwerin	†B 5
175	Solingen	C 3
629	Stuttgart	D 4
86	Trier	D 3
93	Ulm	D 4
64	Weimar	†C 5
260	Wiesbaden	D 4
101	Wilhelmshaven	B 4
422	Wuppertal	C 3
122	Würzburg	D 4
129	Zwickau	†C 6

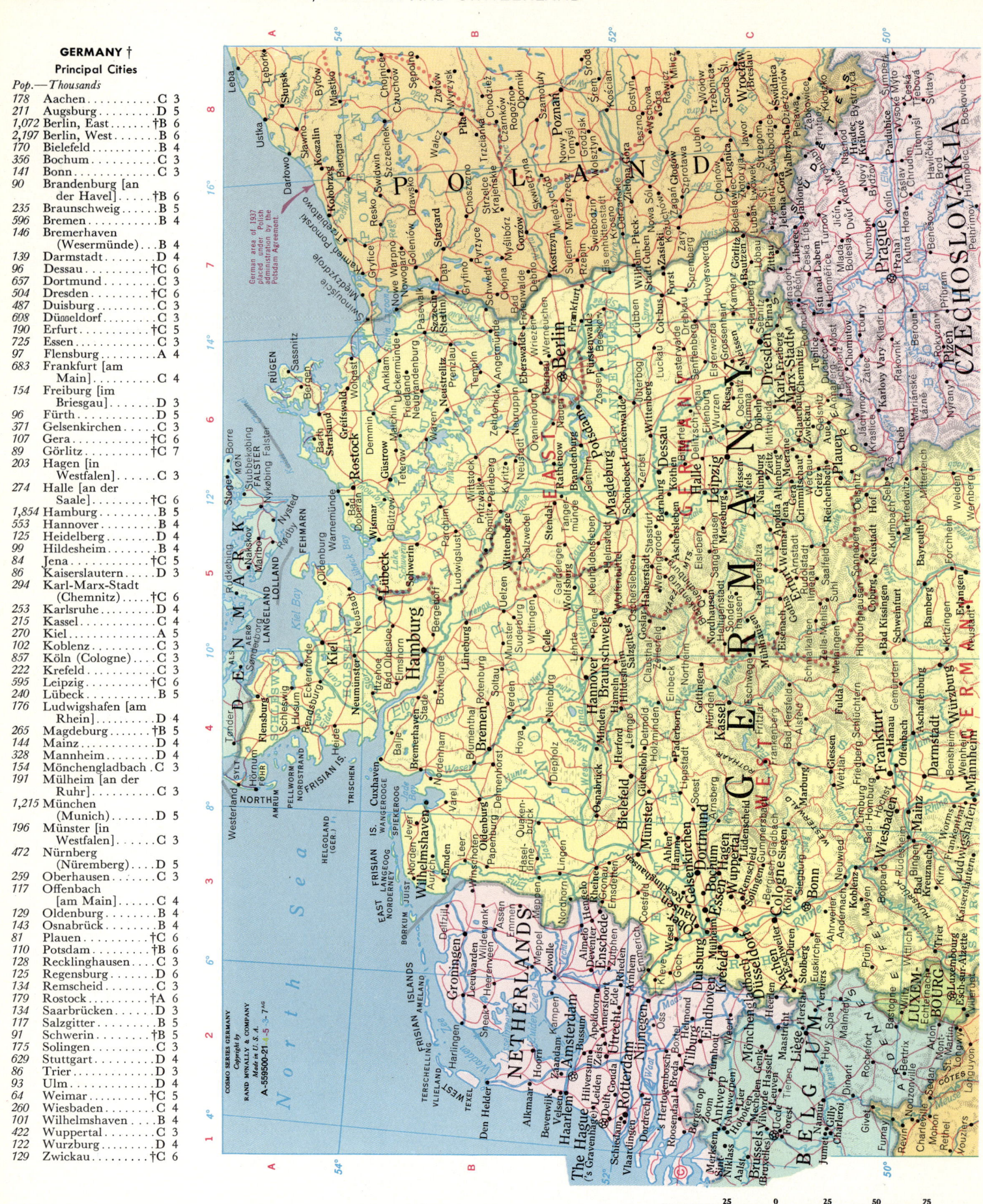

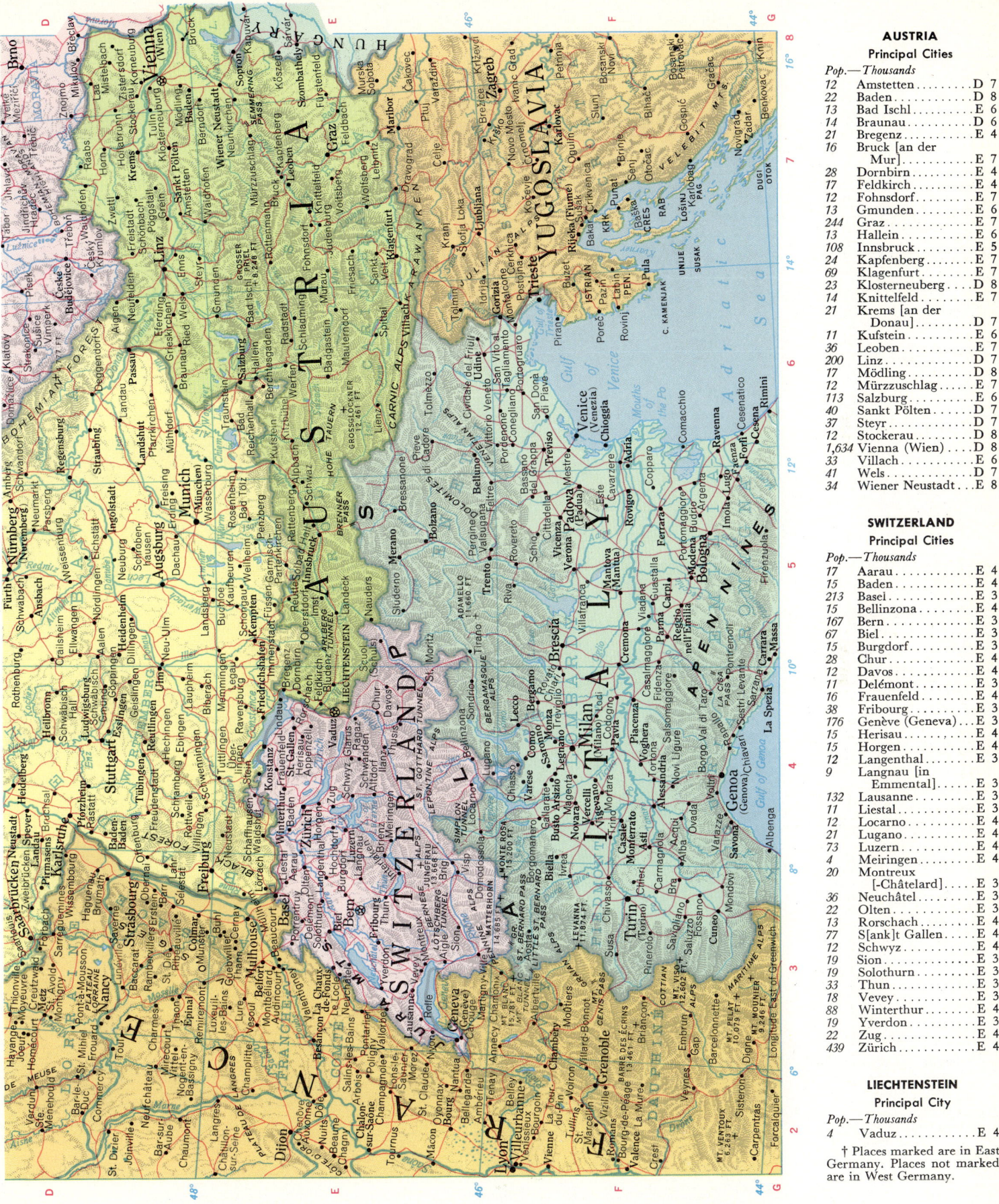

ATLAS 17

AUSTRIA
Principal Cities
Pop.—Thousands

Pop	City	Ref
12	Amstetten	D 7
22	Baden	D 8
13	Bad Ischl	E 6
14	Braunau	D 6
21	Bregenz	E 4
16	Bruck [an der Mur]	E 7
28	Dornbirn	E 4
17	Feldkirch	E 4
12	Fohnsdorf	E 7
13	Gmunden	E 6
244	Graz	E 7
13	Hallein	E 6
108	Innsbruck	E 5
24	Kapfenberg	E 7
69	Klagenfurt	E 7
23	Klosterneuburg	D 8
14	Knittelfeld	E 7
21	Krems [an der Donau]	D 7
11	Kufstein	E 6
36	Leoben	E 7
200	Linz	D 7
17	Mödling	D 8
12	Mürzzuschlag	E 7
113	Salzburg	E 6
40	Sankt Pölten	D 7
37	Steyr	D 7
12	Stockerau	D 8
1,634	Vienna (Wien)	D 8
33	Villach	E 6
41	Wels	D 7
34	Wiener Neustadt	E 8

SWITZERLAND
Principal Cities
Pop.—Thousands

Pop	City	Ref
17	Aarau	E 4
15	Baden	E 4
213	Basel	E 3
15	Bellinzona	E 4
167	Bern	E 3
67	Biel	E 3
15	Burgdorf	E 3
28	Chur	E 4
12	Davos	E 4
11	Delémont	E 3
16	Frauenfeld	E 4
38	Fribourg	E 3
176	Genève (Geneva)	E 3
15	Herisau	E 4
15	Horgen	E 4
12	Langenthal	E 3
9	Langnau [in Emmental]	E 3
132	Lausanne	E 3
11	Liestal	E 3
12	Locarno	E 4
21	Lugano	E 4
73	Luzern	E 4
4	Meiringen	E 4
20	Montreux [-Châtelard]	E 3
36	Neuchâtel	E 3
22	Olten	E 3
13	Rorschach	E 4
77	S[ank]t Gallen	E 4
12	Schwyz	E 4
19	Sion	E 3
19	Solothurn	E 3
33	Thun	E 3
18	Vevey	E 3
88	Winterthur	E 4
19	Yverdon	E 3
22	Zug	E 4
439	Zürich	E 4

LIECHTENSTEIN
Principal City
Pop.—Thousands

Pop	City	Ref
4	Vaduz	E 4

† Places marked are in East Germany. Places not marked are in West Germany.

ATLAS 18 — YUGOSLAVIA, ROMANIA, HUNGARY, AND BULGARIA

ALBANIA
Principal Cities

Pop.—Thousands

Pop.	City	Grid
30	Elbasan	E 5
40	Korcë	E 5
43	Shkodër	D 4
153	Tiranë	E 4

BULGARIA
Principal Cities

Pop.—Thousands

Pop.	City	Grid
25	Asenovgrad	E 7
22	Blagoevgrad (Gorna Dzhumaya)	D 6
73	Burgas	D 8
15	Chirpan	D 7
34	Dimitrovgrad	D 7
38	Gabrovo	D 7
31	Kazanlŭk	D 7
39	Khaskovo	E 7
21	Kŭrdzhali	F 7
25	Kyustendil	D 6
23	Lom	D 6
18	Lovech	D 7
15	Nova Zagora	D 8
39	Pazardzhik	D 7
60	Pernik	D 6
16	Petrich	E 6
58	Pleven	D 7
185	Plovdiv	D 7
18	Razgrad	D 8
110	Ruse	D 7
17	Samokov	D 6
42	Shumen	D 8
20	Silistra	C 8
46	Sliven	D 8
695	Sofia (Sofiya)	D 6
25	Stanke Dimitrov (Dupnitsa)	D 6
55	Stara Zagora	D 7
18	Svishtov	D 7
43	Tolbukhin (Dobrich)	D 8
25	Tŭrnovo	D 7
145	Varna (Stalin)	D 8
24	Vidin	C 6
27	Vratsa	D 6
42	Yambol	D 8

HUNGARY
Principal Cities

Pop.—Thousands

Pop.	City	Grid
30	Baja	B 4
43	Békéscsaba	B 5
1,900	Budapest	B 4
30	Cegléd	B 4
140	Debrecen	B 5
31	Dunaujváros	B 4
39	Eger	B 5
25	Esztergom	B 4
29	Gyöngyös	B 4
75	Györ (Raab)	B 3
23	Hajdúböszörmény	B 5
40	Hódmezővásárhely	B 5
47	Kaposvár	B 3
49	Kecskemét	B 4
23	Kiskunfélegyháza	B 5
30	Makó	B 5
160	Miskolc	A 5
34	Nagykanizsa	B 3
42	Nyíregyháza	B 5
27	Orosháza	B 5
34	Ózd	A 5
25	Pápa	B 3
127	Pécs	B 4
32	Salgótarján	A 4
43	Sopron	B 3
107	Szeged	B 5
61	Székesfehérvár	B 4
25	Szentes	B 5
51	Szolnok	B 5
58	Szombathely	B 3
57	Tatabánya	B 4
25	Vác	B 4
25	Veszprém	B 3

ATLAS 19

ROMANIA
Principal Cities
Pop.—Thousands

Pop.	City	Ref.
114	Arad	B 5
63	Bacău	B 8
43	Baia-Mare	B 6
35	Bîrlad	B 8
21	Bistriţa	B 7
31	Botoşani	B 8
113	Brăila	C 8
130	Braşov (Oraşul-Stalin)	C 7
1,229	Bucharest (Bucureşti)	C 8
52	Buzău	C 8
28	Călăraşi	C 8
163	Cluj	B 6
115	Constanţa	C 9
112	Craiova	C 6
30	Focşani	C 8
107	Galaţi (Galacz)	C 9
34	Giurgiu	D 7
51	Hunedoara	C 6
125	Iaşi	B 8
32	Lugoj	C 5
31	Lupeni	C 6
38	Mediaş	B 7
117	Oradea	B 5
28	Petroşeni	C 6
46	Piteşti	C 7
128	Ploieşti	C 8
46	Reşiţa	C 5
33	Roman	B 8
61	Satu-Mare	B 6
98	Sibiu	C 7
25	Sighet	B 6
23	Suceava	B 8
26	Tecuci	C 8
148	Timişoara	C 5
27	Tîrgovişte	C 7
29	Tulcea	C 9
38	Turda	B 6
35	Turnu-Severin	C 6

YUGOSLAVIA
Principal Cities
Pop.—Thousands

Pop.	City	Ref.
50	Banja Luka	C 3
25	Bečej	C 5
585	Belgrade (Beograd)	C 5
49	Bitola (Bitolj)	E 5
16	Celje	B 2
40	Karlovac	C 2
34	Kikinda	C 5
52	Kragujevac	D 5
31	Kumanovo	D 5
34	Leskovac	D 5
134	Ljubljana	B 2
82	Maribor	B 2
35	Mostar	D 3
81	Niš	D 5
102	Novi Sad	C 4
72	Osijek	C 4
41	Pančevo	C 5
28	Peć	D 5
19	Pirot	D 5
37	Prilep	E 5
39	Priština	D 5
28	Prizren	D 5
37	Pula (Pola)	C 1
100	Rijeka (Fiume)	C 2
30	Šabac	C 4
143	Sarajevo	D 4
25	Senta	C 5
166	Skopje (Skoplje)	D 5
38	Sombor	C 4
99	Split	D 3
75	Subotica	B 4
38	Tetovo	D 5
38	Tuzla	C 4
32	Vršac	C 5
431	Zagreb	C 2
33	Zenica	C 3
49	Zrenjanin (Petrovgrad)	C 5

ATLAS 20   WESTERN SOVIET UNION

WESTERN SOVIET UNION
Principal Cities

Pop.—Thousands

Pop.	City	Ref
32	Akhtyrka	F10
66	Artemovsk	G12, q21
64	Balashikha	D11
68	Balashov	F14
18	Balta	H 7
64	Baranovichi	E 5
72	Bataysk	H12
92	Belgorod	F11
73	Beltsy	H 6
57	Berdichev	G 7
108	Bobruysk	E 7
29	Borislav	G 4
57	Borisoglebsk	F13
65	Borisov	D 7
44	Borovichi	B 9
82	Brest	E 4
249	Bryansk	E10
142	Cheboksary	C16
124	Cherepovets	B11
103	Cherkassy	G 9
113	Chernigov	F 8
152	Chernovtsy	G 5
74	Daugavpils (Dvinsk)	D 6
207	Dneprodzerzhinsk	G10
738	Dnepropetrovsk	G10
774	Donetsk	H11, q20
180	Dzerzhinsk	C14
105	Elektrostal	n18
106	Engels	F16
37	Gatchina	B 8
199	Gomel	E 8
1,042	Gorki (Gorkiy)	C15
309	Gorlovka	G12, q21
88	Grodno	E 4
59	Gus-Khrustalnyy	D13
368	Ivanovo	C13
192	Kadiyevka	G12, q21
292	Kalinin	C10
238	Kaliningrad (Königsberg)	D 3
157	Kaluga	D11
40	Kamenets-Podolskiy	G 6
62	Kamensk-Shakhtinskiy	G13
65	Kamyshin	F15
247	Kaunas	D 4
107	Kerch	I11
1,006	Kharkov	G11
192	Kherson	H 9
51	Khimki	n17
72	Khmelnitskiy	G 6
1,248	Kiev	F 8
91	Kineshma	C14
142	Kirovograd	G 9
254	Kishinev	H 7
105	Klaipėda (Memel)	D 3
60	Klin	C11
42	Klintsy	E 9
125	Kolomna	D12, n18
110	Kommunarsk	G12, q21
56	Konotop	F 9
94	Konstantinovka	q20
193	Kostroma	C13
105	Kovrov	C13
126	Kramatorsk	G11, q20
368	Krasnodar	I12
98	Krasnyy Luch	q21
40	Krasnyy Sulin	H13
100	Kremenchug	G 9
448	Krivoy Rog	H 9
40	Kronshtadt	B 7
59	Kropotkin	I13
233	Kursk	F11
64	Kuznetsk	E16
3,180	Leningrad	B 8
77	Liepāja	C 3
205	Lipetsk	E12
314	Lugansk	G12, q22
69	Lutsk	F 5
469	Lvov	G 5
100	Lyubertsy	n17
381	Makeyevka	G11, q20
104	Melitopol	H10
85	Michurinsk	E13
644	Minsk	E 6

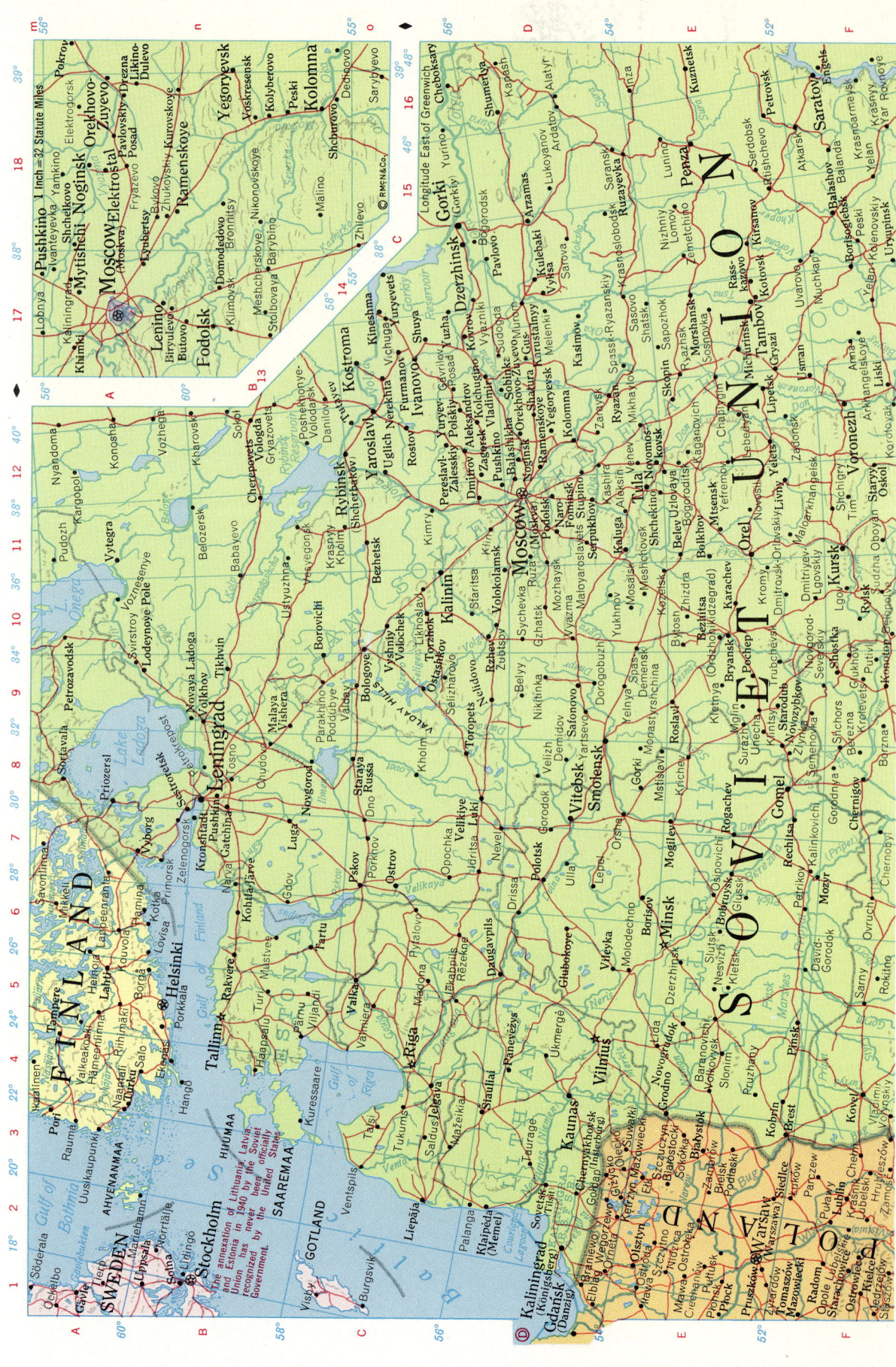

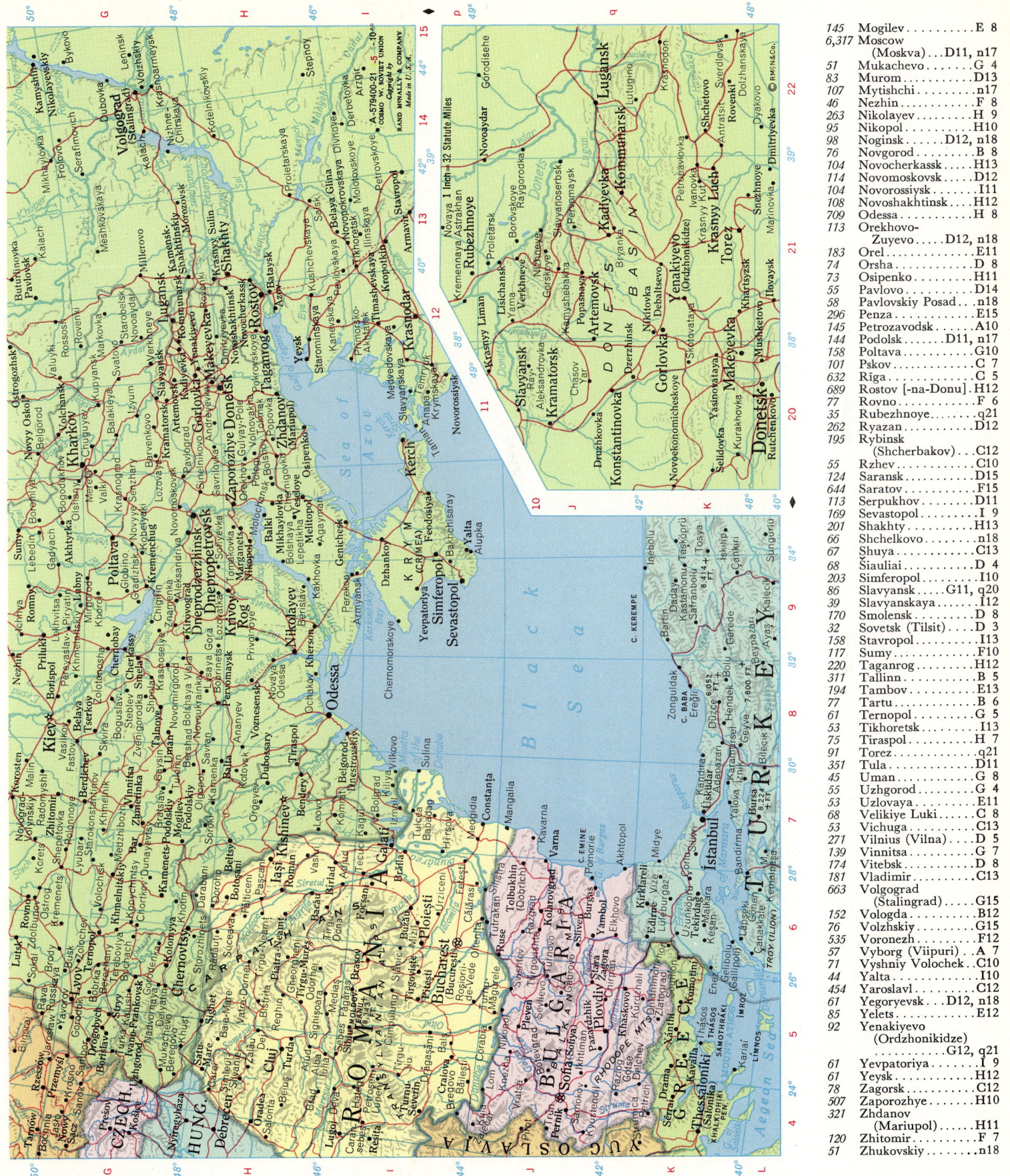

ATLAS 22 FRANCE

FRANCE
Principal Cities
Pop.—Thousands

Pop	City	Ref
68	Aix-èn-Provence	F 6
41	Alès	E 6
105	Amiens	C 5
115	Angers	D 3
48	Angoulême	E 4
82	Argenteuil	C 5, g10
82	Asnières	C5, g10
71	Aubervilliers	g10
48	Aulnay-sous-Bois	g11
73	Avignon	F 6
48	Belfort	D 7
96	Besançon	D 7
250	Bordeaux	E 3
107	Boulogne-Billancourt	C 5, g 9
49	Boulogne [-sur-Mer]	B 4
61	Bourges	D 5
136	Brest	C 1
40	Brive [-la-Gaillarde]	E 4
91	Caen	C 3
70	Calais	B 4
58	Cannes	F 7
41	Carcassonne	F 5
42	Châlons-sur-Marne	C 6
44	Chalon-sur-Saône	D 6
58	Champigny-sur-Marne	g11
45	Châteauroux	D 4
37	Cherbourg	C 3
48	Clamart	g10
128	Clermont-Ferrand	E 5
56	Clichy	g10
52	Colmar	C 7
77	Colombes	g10
59	Courbevoie	g10
136	Dijon	D 6
48	Douai	B 5
66	Drancy	g10
37	Fontenay [-sous-Bois]	g10
157	Grenoble	E 6
52	Issy	g10
53	Ivry-sur-Seine	g10
67	La Rochelle	D 3
184	Le Havre	C 4
132	Le Mans	C 4
43	Lens	B 5
62	Levallois Perret	g10
193	Lille	B 5
118	Limoges	E 4
61	Lorient	D 2
529	Lyon	E 6
51	Maisons-Alfort	g10
778	Marseille	F 6
103	Metz	C 7
55	Montluçon	D 5
119	Montpellier	F 5
92	Montreuil [-sous-Bois]	C5, g10
45	Montrouge	g10
109	Mulhouse	D 7
129	Nancy	C 7
83	Nanterre	g 9
240	Nantes	D 3
73	Neuilly-sur-Seine	g11
293	Nice	F 7
100	Nîmes	F 6
84	Orléans	D 4
46	Pantin	g10
2,790	Paris	C 5, g10
60	Pau	F 3
39	Périgueux	E 4
83	Perpignan	F 5
62	Poitiers	D 4
40	Puteaux	g 9
134	Reims	C 6
152	Rennes	C 3
52	Roanne	D 6
113	Roubaix	B 5
121	Rouen	C 4
43	St. Brieuc	C 2
94	St. Denis	C 5, g10
201	St. Étienne	E 6

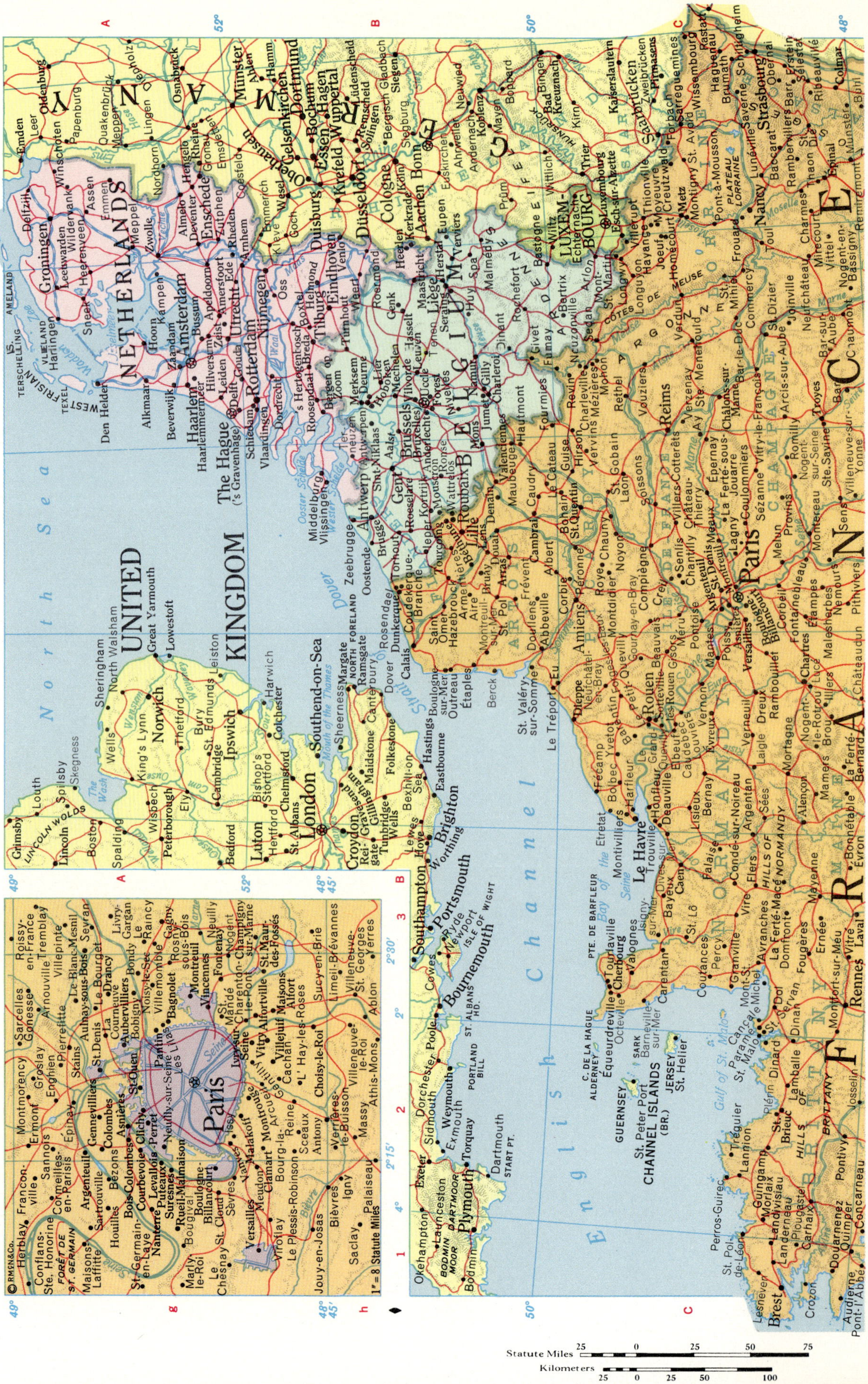

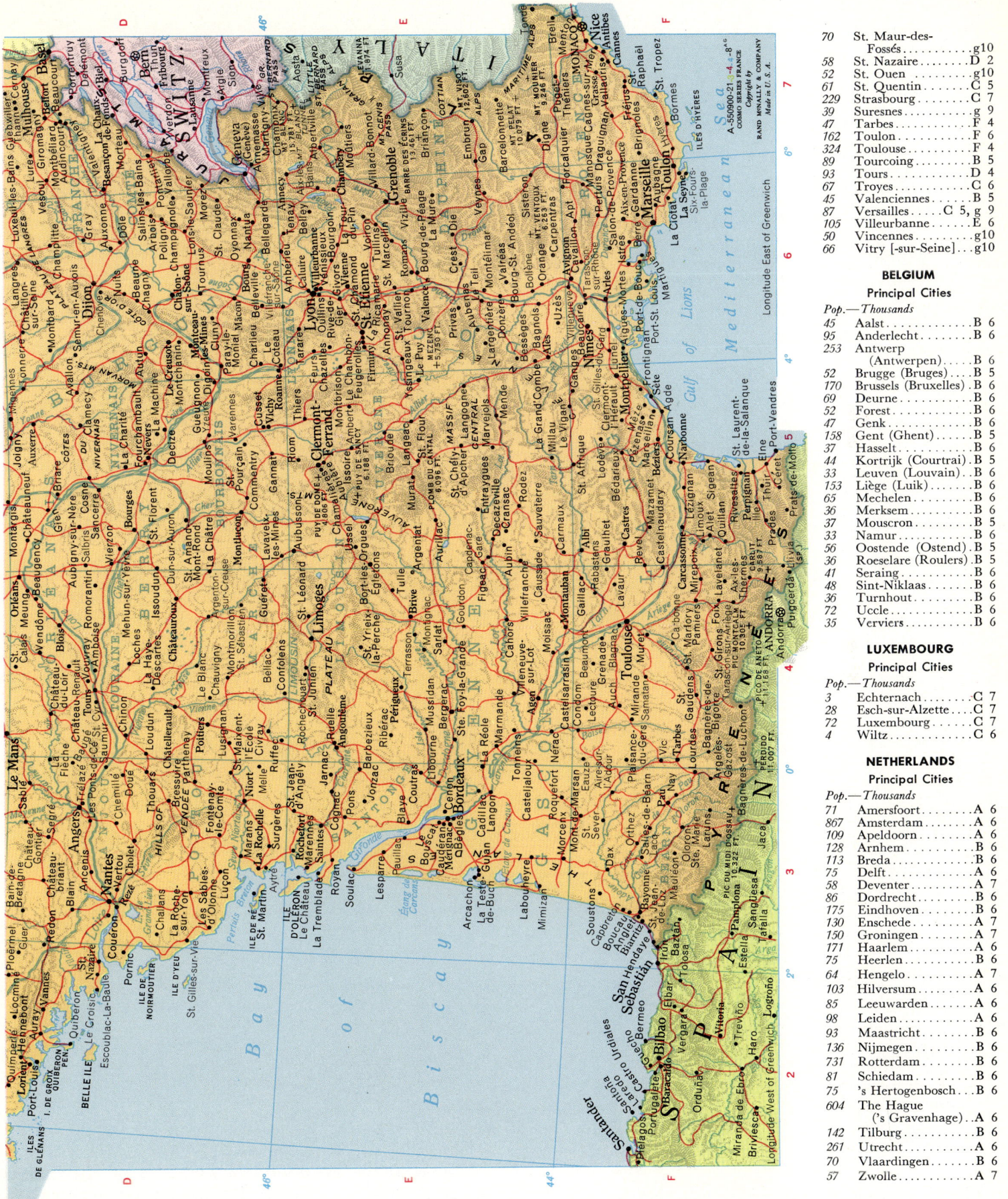

ATLAS 23

Pop.	City	Grid
70	St. Maur-des-Fossés	g10
58	St. Nazaire	D 2
52	St. Ouen	g10
61	St. Quentin	C 5
229	Strasbourg	C 7
39	Suresnes	g 9
47	Tarbes	F 3
162	Toulon	F 6
324	Toulouse	F 4
89	Tourcoing	B 5
93	Tours	D 4
67	Troyes	C 6
45	Valenciennes	B 5
87	Versailles	C 5, g 9
105	Villeurbanne	E 6
50	Vincennes	g10
66	Vitry [-sur-Seine]	g10

BELGIUM
Principal Cities
Pop.—Thousands

45	Aalst	B 6
95	Anderlecht	B 6
253	Antwerp (Antwerpen)	B 6
52	Brugge (Bruges)	B 5
170	Brussels (Bruxelles)	B 6
69	Deurne	B 6
52	Forest	B 6
47	Genk	B 6
158	Gent (Ghent)	B 5
37	Hasselt	B 6
44	Kortrijk (Courtrai)	B 5
33	Leuven (Louvain)	B 6
153	Liège (Luik)	B 6
65	Mechelen	B 6
37	Merksem	B 6
37	Mouscron	B 5
33	Namur	B 6
56	Oostende (Ostend)	B 5
36	Roeselare (Roulers)	B 5
41	Seraing	B 6
48	Sint-Niklaas	B 6
36	Turnhout	B 6
72	Uccle	B 6
35	Verviers	B 6

LUXEMBOURG
Principal Cities
Pop.—Thousands

3	Echternach	C 7
28	Esch-sur-Alzette	C 7
72	Luxembourg	C 7
4	Wiltz	C 6

NETHERLANDS
Principal Cities
Pop.—Thousands

71	Amersfoort	A 6
867	Amsterdam	A 6
109	Apeldoorn	A 6
128	Arnhem	B 6
113	Breda	B 6
75	Delft	A 6
58	Deventer	A 7
86	Dordrecht	B 6
175	Eindhoven	B 6
130	Enschede	A 7
150	Groningen	A 7
171	Haarlem	A 6
75	Heerlen	B 6
64	Hengelo	A 7
103	Hilversum	A 6
85	Leeuwarden	A 6
98	Leiden	A 6
93	Maastricht	B 6
136	Nijmegen	B 6
731	Rotterdam	B 6
81	Schiedam	B 6
75	's Hertogenbosch	B 6
604	The Hague ('s Gravenhage)	A 6
142	Tilburg	B 6
261	Utrecht	A 6
70	Vlaardingen	B 6
57	Zwolle	A 7

Conic Projection
SCALE 1:4,000,000   1 Inch = 63 Statute Miles

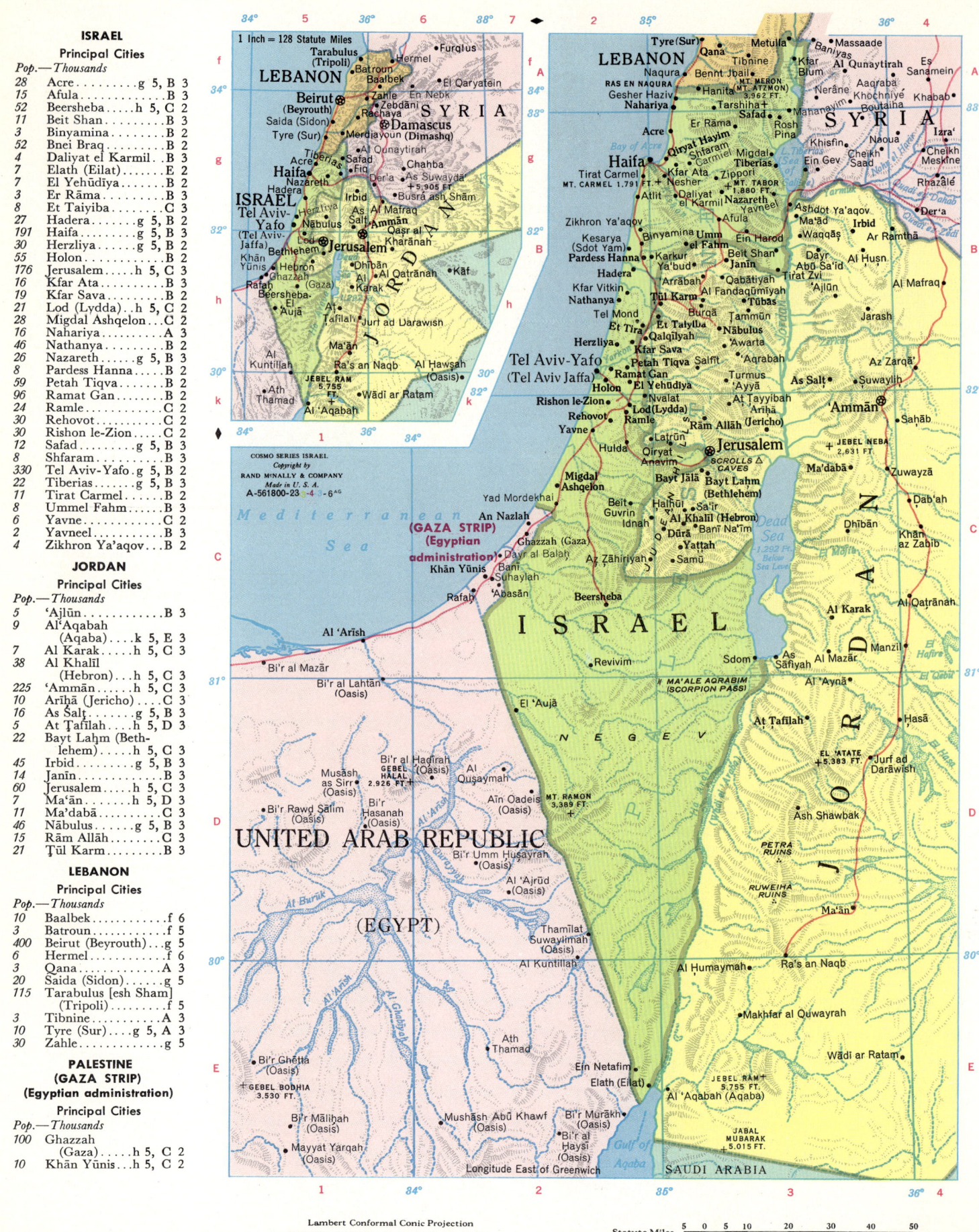

ARABIAN PENINSULA — ATLAS 25

BAHRAIN
Principal Cities
Pop.—Thousands
27 Al Muḩarraq......D 5
56 Manama..........D 5

IRAQ
Principal Cities
Pop.—Thousands
126 Al Kadhimain.....C 3
74 An Najaf..........C 3
35 As Sulaymānīyah..B 4
356 Baghdad..........C 3
165 Basra............C 4
46 Hilla.............C 3
34 Irbīl.............B 3
45 Karbalā..........C 3
121 Kirkuk...........B 3
180 Mosul...........B 3

KUWAIT
Principal City
Pop.—Thousands
97 Kuwait..........D 4

MUSCAT & OMAN
Principal Cities
Pop.—Thousands
14 Maṭraḩ..........E 6
6 Muscat..........E 6

QATAR
Principal City
Pop.—Thousands
35 Doha............D 5

SAUDI ARABIA
Principal Cities
Pop.—Thousands
85 Al Hufūf.........D 4
60 Al Madīnah
  (Medina).......E 2
50 Buraydah........D 3
148 Juddah (Jidda)...E 2
159 Mecca (Makkah)..E 2
169 Riyadh (Ar Riyāḑ).E 4
50 'Unayzah........D 3

SOUTH YEMEN
Principal Cities
Pop.—Thousands
99 Aden............G 4
25 Al Mukallā......G 4
   Madīnat ash Sha'b.G 4

SYRIA
Principal Cities
Pop.—Thousands
425 Aleppo (Halab)...B 2
530 Damascus
  (Dimashq).......C 2
97 Hamāh...........B 2
137 Homs............C 2

TRUCIAL COAST
Principal Cities
Pop.—Thousands
55 Dubayy..........D 6

YEMEN
Principal Cities
Pop.—Thousands
40 Al Ḩudaydah
  (Hodeida).......G 3
25 Ibb.............G 3
25 Ṣa'dah..........F 3
89 Ṣan'ā'..........F 3

Lambert Conformal Conic Projection
SCALE 1:18,500,000 1 Inch = 290 Statute Miles

ATLAS 26 ASIA

ASIA
⊕ Capitals †

Baghdad, Iraq	F 7
Bangkok, Thai.	H13
Brunei, Bru.	I14
Colombo, Cey.	I10
Dacca, Pak.	G12
Hanoi, Viet., N.	G13
Islamabad, Pak.	F10
Kuala Lumpur, Mala.	I13
Macao, Macao	G14
Madīnat ash Sha'b, S. Yem.	H 7
New Delhi, India	G10
Peking, China	F14
Phnom Penh, Camb.	H13
P'yŏngyang, Kor., N.	F15
Quezon City, Phil.	H15
Rangoon, Bur.	H12
Saigon, Viet., S.	H13
Seoul, Kor., S.	F15
Singapore, Singapore	I13
Taipei, Taiwan	G15
Tōkyō, Jap.	F16
Ulan Bator, Mong.	E13
Victoria, Hong Kong	G14
Vientiane, Laos	H13

† For capital cities of Indonesia, Portuguese Timor, Singapore and West Irian see map of Southeastern Asia; for Nepal and Sikkim see map of South Central Asia.

Physical Features

Aden, gulf	H 7
Aldan, riv.	D16
Altai, mts.	E11
Altyn Tagh, mts.	F11
Amu Darya, riv.	E 9
Amur, riv.	D16
Anadyr, range	C20
Andaman, is.	H12
Angara, riv.	D13
Arabian, sea	H 9
Arafura, sea	J16
Aral, sea	E 8
Balkhash, lake	E10
Banda, sea	J15
Baykal, lake	D13
Bengal, bay	H11
Black, sea	E 6
Bonin (Ogasawara), is.	G17
Borneo, isl.	I14
Buru, isl.	J15
Caspian, sea	E 8
Celebes, isl.	I15
Celebes, sea	I15
Ceram, isl.	J15
Ceylon, isl.	I11
Chelyuskin, cape	B14
Cherskiy, mts.	C16
Comorin, cape	I10
Cyprus, isl.	F 6
Deccan, plat.	H10
Demavend, mtn.	F 8
Dzhugdzhur, mts.	D16
East China, sea	F15
Eastern Ghats, mts.	H10
East Siberian, sea	B19
Elburz, mts.	F 7
Euphrates, riv.	F 7
Everest, mtn.	G11
Formosa, strait	G14
Franz Josef Land, is.	A 9
Ganges, riv.	G10
Gobi, des.	E13
Godavari, riv.	H10
Grand, canal	F14
Greater Khingan, mts.	E14
Gydan, mts.	C18
Hainan, isl.	H14
Himalaya, mts.	F10
Hindu Kush, mts.	F 9
Hokkaidō, isl.	E17
Honshū, isl.	F17
Hwang Ho, riv.	F14
Indian, des.	G10
Indus, riv.	G 9
Iran, plat.	F 8
Irrawaddy, riv.	H12
Irtysh, riv.	D10

ATLAS 27

Issyk-Kul, lake	E10
Japan, sea	E16
Kamchatka, pen	D18
Karakoram, range	F10
Khatanga, riv	B13
Koko, lake	F12
Kolyma, riv	C18
Korea, strait	F15
Kunlun, mts	F11
Kuril, is	E18
Kuril, strait	D18
Kutch, gulf	G 9
Kyūshū, isl	F16
Laccadive, is	H10
Laptev, sea	B15
Lena, riv	C15
Leyte, isl	H15
Long, strait	B20
Lopatka, cape	D18
Luzon, isl	H15
Macassar, strait	I14
Malacca, strait	I13
Malay, pen	I13
Mannar, gulf	I10
Martaban, gulf	H12
Mindanao, isl	I15
Mindoro, isl	H14
Molucca, is	J15
Molucca, sea	I15
Mongolia, plat	E13
Mui Bai Bung, pt	I13
Narbada, riv	G10
Negrais, cape	H12
Negros, isl	H15
Nicobar, is	I12
Nizhnyaya Tunguska, riv	C12
Novosibirskiye (New Siberian), is	B16
Ob, bay	C10
Ob, riv	D11
Okhotsk, sea	D17
Olenek, riv	C14
Oman, gulf	G 8
Palawan, isl	H14
Pamir, mts	F10
Panay, isl	H15
Persian, gulf	G 8
Philippine, sea	H15
Pidurutalagal, mtn	I11
Red, sea	G 6
Rub al Khali, des	G 8
Ryūkyū, is	G15
Sakhalin, isl	D17
Salween, riv	H12
Sayan, mts	D12
Selenge, riv	E13
Severnaya Zemlya, is	A12
Shikoku, isl	F16
Siam, gulf	H13
Sikhote-Alin, mts	E16
South China, sea	H14
Sōya, strait	E17
Sulu, arch	I15
Sulu, sea	I14
Sumatra, isl	I12
Syr Darya, riv	E 9
Taiwan (Formosa), isl	G15
Takla Makan, des	F11
Talaud, is	I15
Tarim Darya, riv	E11
Tatar, strait	D17
Taymyr, pen	B12
Tibet, plat	F11
Tien Shan, mts	E10
Tigris, riv	F 7
Tobol, riv	D 9
Tsinling Shan, mts	F13
Ural, mts	D 8
Ust-Urt, plat	E 8
Vilyuy, riv	C14
Vitim, riv	D14
Western Ghats, mts	H10
West Siberian, lowland	D10
Wrangel, isl	B21
Yablonovy, mts	D14
Yamal, pen	B10
Yana, riv	C16
Yangtze, riv	G13
Yellow, sea	F15
Yenisey, riv	C11
Zaysan, lake	E11

Lambert Azimuthal Equal Area Projection
SCALE 1:42,000,000   1 Inch = 663 Statute Miles

ATLAS 30   SOUTHEASTERN ASIA

BRUNEI
Principal Cities
Pop.—Thousands
10	Brunei	E 4
18	Seria	E 4

CAMBODIA
Principal Cities
Pop.—Thousands
39	Battambang	C 2
28	Kompong Cham	C 3
13	Kompong Chhnang	C 2
12	Kratie	C 3
404	Phnom Penh	C 2
15	Pursat	C 2
11	Svay Rieng	C 3

INDONESIA
Principal Cities
Pop.—Thousands
55	Amboina	F 7
89	Balikpapan	F 5
213	Bandjermasin	F 4
966	Bandung	G 3
25	Banjuwangi	G 4
17	Bengkulu	F 2
147	Bogor	G 3
2,922	Djakarta (Batavia)	G 3
109	Djambi	F 2
71	Gorontalo	E 6
309	Jogjakarta	G 3
34	Kutaradja	k 11
92	Magelang	G 4
368	Makasar	G 5
332	Malang	G 4
128	Manado	E 6
466	Medan	E 1, m 11
144	Padang	F 2
69	Pakanbaru	E 2
459	Palembang	F 2
25	Pamekasan	G 4
59	Pangkalpinang	F 3
63	Parepare	F 5
63	Pasuruan	G 4
100	Pekalongan	G 3
147	Pontianak	F 3
68	Probolinggo	G 4
68	Samarinda	F 5
12	Sambas	E 3
12	Sawahlunto	F 2
487	Semarang	G 4
37	Sibolga	E 1, m 11
79	Sukabumi	G 3
990	Surabaja	G 4
363	Surakarta	G 4
16	Tandjungpandan	F 3
25	Tebingtinggi	E 1, m 11
132	Telukbetung	G 3
28	Tjilatjap	G 3
153	Tjirebon	G 3

LAOS
Principal Cities
Pop.—Thousands
	Luang Prabang	B 2
8	Pakse	B 3
10	Thakhek	B 2
162	Vientiane	B 2

MALAYSIA
Principal Cities
Pop.—Thousands
53	Alor Star	D 2
43	Butterworth	D 2
126	Ipoh	E 2
22	Jesselton	D 5
75	Johore Bahru	E 2
76	Klang	E 2
38	Kota Bharu	D 2
316	Kuala Lumpur	E 2
51	Kuching	E 4
70	Malacca	E 2
13	Miri	E 4
235	Penang	E 2
29	Sandakan	D 5
52	Seremban	E 2
30	Sibu	E 4

ATLAS 31

Pop. (Thousands)		
48	Taiping	E 2
37	Telok Anson	E 2

PHILIPPINES
Principal Cities
Pop.—Thousands

58	Angeles	o13
89	Bacolod	C 6
50	Baguio	B 6, n13
34	Batangas	C 6, p13
34	Butuan	D 7
38	Cabanatuan	o13
35	Cagayan de Oro	D 6
146	Caloocan	o13
19	Catbalogan	C 6
55	Cavite	o13
251	Cebu	C 6
28	Cotabato	D 6
34	Dagupan	n13
93	Davao	D 7
24	Dumaguete	D 6
151	Iloilo	C 6
33	Jolo	D 6
25	Laoag	B 6
36	Legaspi	C 6
41	Lucena	C 6, p13
1,139	Manila	C 6, o13
18	Masbate	C 6
56	Naga	C 6
18	Ozamiz	D 6
133	Pasay	C 6
62	Pasig	o13
398	Quezon City	C 6, o13
30	Roxas	C 6
33	San Fernando	o13
30	San Pablo	o13
16	Surigao	D 7
36	Tacloban	C 6
42	Tarlac	B 6, o13
24	Tuguegarao	B 6
52	Zamboanga	D 6

PORTUGUESE TIMOR
Principal City
Pop.—Thousands

52	Dili	G 7

SINGAPORE
Principal City
Pop.—Thousands

925	Singapore	E 2

THAILAND
Principal Cities
Pop.—Thousands

32	Ayutthaya	C 2
1,300	Bangkok (Krung Thep)	C 2
66	Chiang Mai	B 1
36	Hat Yai (Bon Hat Yai)	D 2
36	Lampang	B 1
35	Nakhon Sawan	B 2
31	Songkhla	D 2
18	Yala	D 2

VIETNAM, NORTH
Principal Cities
Pop.—Thousands

182	Haiphong	A 3
415	Hanoi	A 3
86	Nam Dinh	A 3
31	Thanh Hoa	B 3

VIETNAM, SOUTH
Principal Cities
Pop.—Thousands

111	Da Nang	B 3
69	Gia Dinh	C 3
106	Hue	B 3
55	Phan Thiet	C 3
1,251	Saigon	C 3

WEST IRIAN
Principal Cities
Pop.—Thousands

8	Sorong	F 8
15	Sukarnapura	F 10

ATLAS 32 — EASTERN CHINA

CHINA
Principal Cities
Pop.—Thousands

Pop	City	Ref
224	Amoy	G 8
805	Anshan	C 9
360	Antung	C 9
1,840	Canton	G 7
297	Changchow	E 8
975	Changchun (Hsinking)	C10
703	Changsha	F 7
166	Chankiang	G 7
766	Chengchow	E 7
1,107	Chengtu	E 5
352	Chinchow	C 9
208	Chinkiang	E 8
1,800	Chungking	F 6
950	Dairen (Talien)	D 9
616	Foochow	F 8
985	Fushun	C 9
189	Fusin	C 9
784	Hangchow	E 9
1,814	Harbin	B10
235	Hengyang	F 7
304	Hofei	E 8
314	Huhehot (Kweisui)	C 7
178	Ipin	F 5
299	Kaifeng	E 7
229	Kalgan (Changkiakow)	C 7
146	Kiamusze	B11
568	Kirin (Chilin)	C10
160	Kochiu	G 5
880	Kunming	F 5
145	Kweilin	F 7
504	Kweiyang	F 6
699	Lanchow	D 5
171	Loyang	E 7
159	Luichow	G 6
2,411	Mukden (Shenyang)	C 9
151	Mutankiang	C10
508	Nanchang	F 8
165	Nanchung	E 6
1,419	Nanking	E 8
264	Nanning	G 6
190	Neichiang	F 5
238	Ningpo (Ninghsien)	F 9
265	Paoting (Tsingyüan)	D 8
400	Paotow	C 7
3,500	Peking (Peiping)	D 8
253	Pengpu	E 8
449	Penki	C 9
6,900	Shanghai	E 9
1,310	Sian (Hsian)	E 6
184	Siangtan	F 7
171	Sinsiang	D 7
663	Soochow	E 9
676	Süchow	E 8
280	Swatow	G 8
1,020	Taiyüan	D 7
229	Tatung	D 7
2,850	Tientsin	D 8
862	Tsinan (Chinan)	D 8
1,121	Tsingtao	D 9
668	Tsitsihar	B 9
291	Tzekung	F 5
275	Urumchi	C 2
149	Weifang	D 8
45	Weihai	D 9
202	Wenchow	F 9
2,146	Wuhan	E 7
242	Wuhu	E 8
613	Wusih	E 9

MONGOLIA
Principal Cities
Pop.—Thousands

Pop	City	Ref
11	Choibalsan	B 7
5	Jibhalanta (Uliassutai)	B 4
5	Öndör Haan (Chechenhan)	B 7
195	Ulan Bator (Urga)	B 6

ATLAS 33

TAIWAN (FORMOSA)
Principal Cities

Pop.—Thousands
201	Chilung (Keelung)	F 9
114	Hsinchu	G 9
410	Kaohsiung	G 9
232	T'aichung	G 9
288	T'ainan	G 9
1,027	Taipei	G 9

JAPAN
Principal Cities

Pop.—Thousands
224	Aomori	C13
245	Asahigawa	C13
332	Chiba	D13
170	Fukui	D12
750	Fukuoka	E11
272	Fuse	E12
358	Gifu	D12
197	Hakodate	C13
393	Hamamatsu	E12
504	Hiroshima	E11
328	Kagoshima	E11
336	Kanazawa	D12
855	Kawasaki	D12
1,042	Kitakyūshū	E11
1,217	Kōbe	E11
218	Kōchi	E11
407	Kumamoto	E11
225	Kure	E11
159	Kurume	E11
174	Kushiro	C13
1,365	Kyōto	D12
283	Matsuyama	E11
173	Nagano	D12
405	Nagasaki	E10
1,935	Nagoya	D12
356	Niigata	D12
292	Okayama	E11
3,156	Ōsaka	E12
197	Otaru	C13
795	Sapporo	C13
247	Sasebo	E10
481	Sendai	D13
254	Shimonoseki	E11
368	Shizuoka	E12
243	Takamatsu	E11
193	Tokushima	E12
8,893	Tōkyō	D12
240	Toyama	D12
266	Utsunomiya	D12
329	Wakayama	E12
219	Yokkaichi	E12
1,789	Yokohama	D12
317	Yokosuka	D12

KOREA †
Principal Cities

Pop.—Thousands
52	Andong	D10
184	Chŏngjin (Seishin)	†C10
175	Chŏnju	D10
144	Hungnam	†D10
486	Inchŏn	D10
100	Kaesŏng (Kaijō)	†D10
42	Kangnŭng	D10
68	Kimchaek (Sŏngjin)	†C10
100	Kunsan	D10
300	Kwangju	D10
48	Kyŏngju (Keishū)	D10
159	Masan	D10
157	Mokpo	D10
34	Najin (Rashin)	†C11
1,420	Pusan (Fusan)	D10
653	P'yŏngyang (Heijō)	†D10
3,471	Seoul (Sŏul)	D10
118	Sinŭiju	†D 9
811	Taegu (Taikyū)	D10
113	Wŏnsan (Gensan)	†D10

† Places marked are in North Korea. Places not marked are in South Korea.

ATLAS 34　　AFRICA

AFRICA
⊛ Capitals

Abidjan, I.C.	F 5
Accra, Ghana	F 5
Addis Ababa, Eth.	F 9
Aiún, Sp. Sah.	D 4
Bamako, Mali	E 5
Bangui, Cen. Afr. Rep.	F 7
Bata, Equat. Gui.	F 6
Bathurst, Gam.	E 4
Bissau, Port. Gui.	E 4
Brazzaville, Congo	G 7
Bujumbura, Burundi	G 8
Cape Town, S. Afr.	J 7
Conakry, Guinea	F 4
Dakar, Sen.	E 4
Dar es Salaam, Tan.	G 9
Djibouti, Afaras & Issas	E10
Fort-Lamy, Chad	E 7
Freetown, S.L.	F 4
Gaberones, Botswana	I 8
Kampala, Ug.	F 9
Khartoum, Sud.	E 9
Kigali, Rwanda	G 9
Kinshasa, Congo, The	G 7
Lagos, Nig.	F 6
Libreville, Gabon	F 6
Lomé, Togo	F 6
Lourenço Marques, Moz.	I 9
Luanda, Ang.	G 7
Lusaka, Zambia	H 8
Maseru, Lesotho	I 8
Mbabane, Swaz.	I 9
Mogadiscio, Som.	F10
Monrovia, Lib.	F 4
Nairobi, Ken.	G 9
Niamey, Niger	E 6
Nouakchott, Maur.	E 4
Ouagadougou, Upper Volta	E 5
Porto-Novo, Dah.	F 6
Pretoria, S. Afr.	I 8
Santa Isabel, Equat. Gui.	F 6
Salisbury, Rhodesia	H 8
Tananarive, Malag.	H10
Windhoek, S. W. Afr.	I 7
Yaoundé, Cam.	F 7
Zomba, Malawi	H 9

Physical Features

Aden, gulf	E10
Agulhas, cape	J 7
Ahaggar, mts.	D 6
Albert, lake	F 9
Ascension, isl.	G 4
Aswān High, dam	D 9
Atlas, mts.	C 5
Azores, is.	C 3
Batu, mtn.	F 9
Bíjagós (Bissagos), is.	E 4
Blanc, cape	D 4
Blue Nile, riv.	E 9
Bodélé, depression	E 7
Brandberg, mtn.	I 7
Cape Verde, is.	E 3
Chad, lake	E 7
Chari, riv.	E 7
Chech, sand dunes	D 5

Chiamboni, cape	G10
Congo, riv.	G 7
Cuando, riv.	H 8
Cuanza, riv.	G 7
Cunene, riv.	H 7
Delgado, cape	H10
Drakensberg, mts.	J 8
Eyasi, lake	G 9
Fernando Póo, isl.	F 6
Frio, cape	H 7
Gibraltar, strait	C 5
Giuba, riv.	F10
Good Hope, cape	J 7
Guardafui, cape	E11
Guinea, gulf	F 6
Iguidi, sand dunes	D 5
Jilf al Kabīr, plat.	D 8
Kalahari, des.	I 8
Kasai, riv.	G 8
Kenya, mtn.	F 9
Kilimanjaro, mtn.	G 9
Kordofan, plat.	E 9
Kwango, riv.	G 7
Kyoga, lake	F 9
Léopold II, lake	G 7
Libyan, des.	D 8
Limpopo, riv.	I 9
Madagascar, isl.	H10
Madeira, is.	C 4
Maromokotro, mtn.	H10
Marrah, mtn.	E 8
Mediterranean, sea	C 7
Mozambique, chan.	H10
Mweru, lake	G 8
Namib, des.	I 7
Niger, riv.	E 6
Nile, riv.	D 9
Nyasa, lake	H 9
Okovango, riv.	H 7
Orange, riv.	I 7
Ouarane, sand dunes	D 4
Palmas, cape	F 5
Pemba, isl.	G10
Qattara, depression	D 8
Red, sea	D 9
Ruaha, riv.	G 9
Rudolf, lake	F 9
Rufiji, riv.	G 9
Sahara, des.	D 5
Ste. Marie, cape	I10
St. Helena, isl.	G 5
St. Lucia, cape	I 9
Sankuru, riv.	G 8
Sénégal, riv.	E 4
Shabalē, riv.	F10
Sidra, gulf	C 7
Socotra, isl.	E11
Stefanie, lake	F 9
Sudd, swamp	F 8
Suez, canal	C 8
Tana, lake	E 9
Tanezrouft, des.	D 6
Tanganyika, lake	G 8
Tibesti, plat.	D 7
Ubangi, riv.	F 7
Verde, cape	E 4
Victoria, falls	H 8
Victoria, lake	G 9
Volta, lake	F 5
White Nile, riv.	F 9
Zambezi, riv.	H 8

ATLAS 35

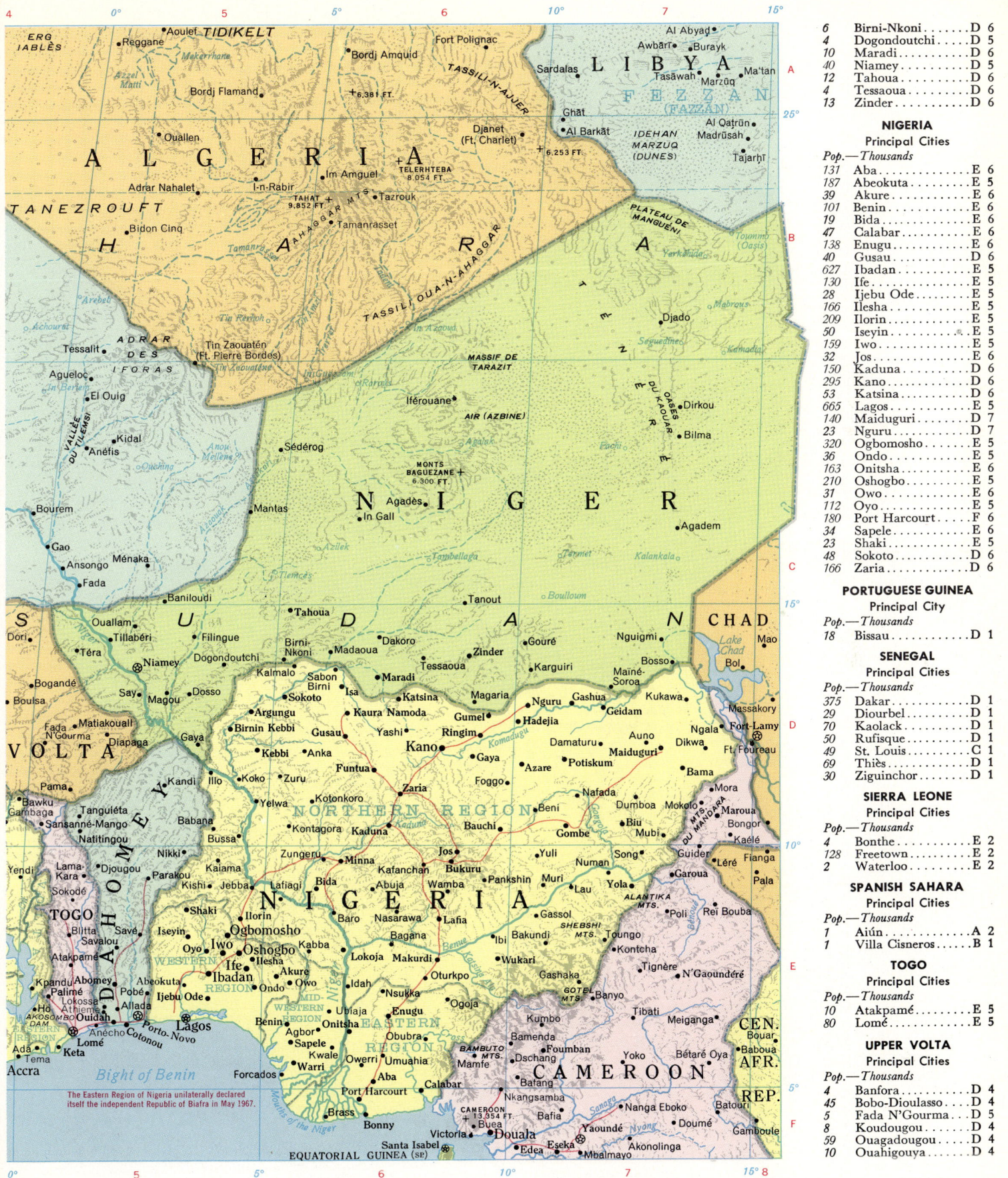

ATLAS 37

Pop. (Thousands)	City	Grid
6	Birni-Nkoni	D 6
4	Dogondoutchi	D 5
10	Maradi	D 6
40	Niamey	D 5
12	Tahoua	D 6
4	Tessaoua	D 6
13	Zinder	D 6

NIGERIA
Principal Cities
Pop.—Thousands

Pop.	City	Grid
131	Aba	E 6
187	Abeokuta	E 5
39	Akure	E 6
101	Benin	E 6
19	Bida	E 6
47	Calabar	E 6
138	Enugu	E 6
40	Gusau	D 6
627	Ibadan	E 5
130	Ife	E 5
28	Ijebu Ode	E 5
166	Ilesha	E 5
209	Ilorin	E 5
50	Iseyin	E 5
159	Iwo	E 5
32	Jos	E 6
150	Kaduna	D 6
295	Kano	D 6
53	Katsina	D 6
665	Lagos	E 5
140	Maiduguri	D 7
23	Nguru	D 7
320	Ogbomosho	E 5
36	Ondo	E 5
163	Onitsha	E 6
210	Oshogbo	E 5
31	Owo	E 6
112	Oyo	E 5
180	Port Harcourt	F 6
34	Sapele	E 5
23	Shaki	E 5
48	Sokoto	D 6
166	Zaria	D 6

PORTUGUESE GUINEA
Principal City
Pop.—Thousands

Pop.	City	Grid
18	Bissau	D 1

SENEGAL
Principal Cities
Pop.—Thousands

Pop.	City	Grid
375	Dakar	D 1
29	Diourbel	D 1
70	Kaolack	D 1
50	Rufisque	D 1
49	St. Louis	C 1
69	Thiès	D 1
30	Ziguinchor	D 1

SIERRA LEONE
Principal Cities
Pop.—Thousands

Pop.	City	Grid
4	Bonthe	E 2
128	Freetown	E 2
2	Waterloo	E 2

SPANISH SAHARA
Principal Cities
Pop.—Thousands

Pop.	City	Grid
1	Aiún	A 2
1	Villa Cisneros	B 1

TOGO
Principal Cities
Pop.—Thousands

Pop.	City	Grid
10	Atakpamé	E 5
80	Lomé	E 5

UPPER VOLTA
Principal Cities
Pop.—Thousands

Pop.	City	Grid
4	Banfora	D 4
45	Bobo-Dioulasso	D 4
5	Fada N'Gourma	D 5
8	Koudougou	D 4
59	Ouagadougou	D 4
10	Ouahigouya	D 4

ATLAS 38 CENTRAL AFRICA

ANGOLA
Principal Cities
Pop.—Thousands

Pop.	City	Grid
23	Benguela	D 1
5	Caconda	D 2
9	Caxito	C 1
5	Gabela	D 1
50	Lobito	D 1
225	Luanda	C 1
13	Malange	C 2
7	Moçâmedes	E 1
39	Nova Lisboa	D 2
14	Sá da Bandeira	D 1
4	São Salvador	C 1
12	Silva Porto	D 2
4	Vila Luso	D 2
4	Vila Robert Williams	D 2
5	Vila Teixeira da Silva	D 2

BURUNDI
Principal Cities
Pop.—Thousands

Pop.	City	Grid
50	Bujumbura	B 4
3	Kitega	B 5

CONGO (BRAZZAVILLE)
Principal Cities
Pop.—Thousands

Pop.	City	Grid
	Abala	B 2
134	Brazzaville	B 2
13	Dolisie	B 1
	Ewo	B 1
	Makoua	A 2
	Pangala	B 1
80	Pointe Noire	B 1
	Zanaga	B 1

CONGO, THE (DEMOCRATIC REPUBLIC OF THE CONGO)
Principal Cities
Pop.—Thousands

Pop.	City	Grid
4	Aba	A 5
12	Aketi	A 3
30	Albertville	C 4
41	Bakwanga	C 3
5	Bandundu	B 2
32	Boma	C 1
34	Bukavu	B 4
5	Bunia	A 5
11	Buta	A 3
10	Isiro	A 4
75	Jadotville	D 4
32	Kamina	C 4
11	Kikwit	C 2
14	Kindu [-Port Empain]	B 4
403	Kinshasa (Léopoldville)	B 2
15	Kipushi	D 4
127	Kisangani (Stanleyville)	A 4
48	Kolwezi	D 4
8	Lubudi	C 4
115	Luluabourg	C 3
184	Lubumbashi (Élizabethville)	D 4
10	Lusambo	B 3
20	Manono	C 4
59	Matadi	C 1
38	Mbandaka	A 2
4	Port-Francqui	B 3
12	Sakania	D 4
11	Shinkolobwe	D 4
12	Thysville	C 1
6	Tshikapa	C 3
13	Yangambi	A 3

KENYA
Principal Cities
Pop.—Thousands

Pop.	City	Grid
20	Eldoret	A 6
8	Kericho	B 6
24	Kisumu	B 5
9	Kitale	A 5
180	Mombasa	B 6
267	Nairobi	B 6
38	Nakuru	B 6

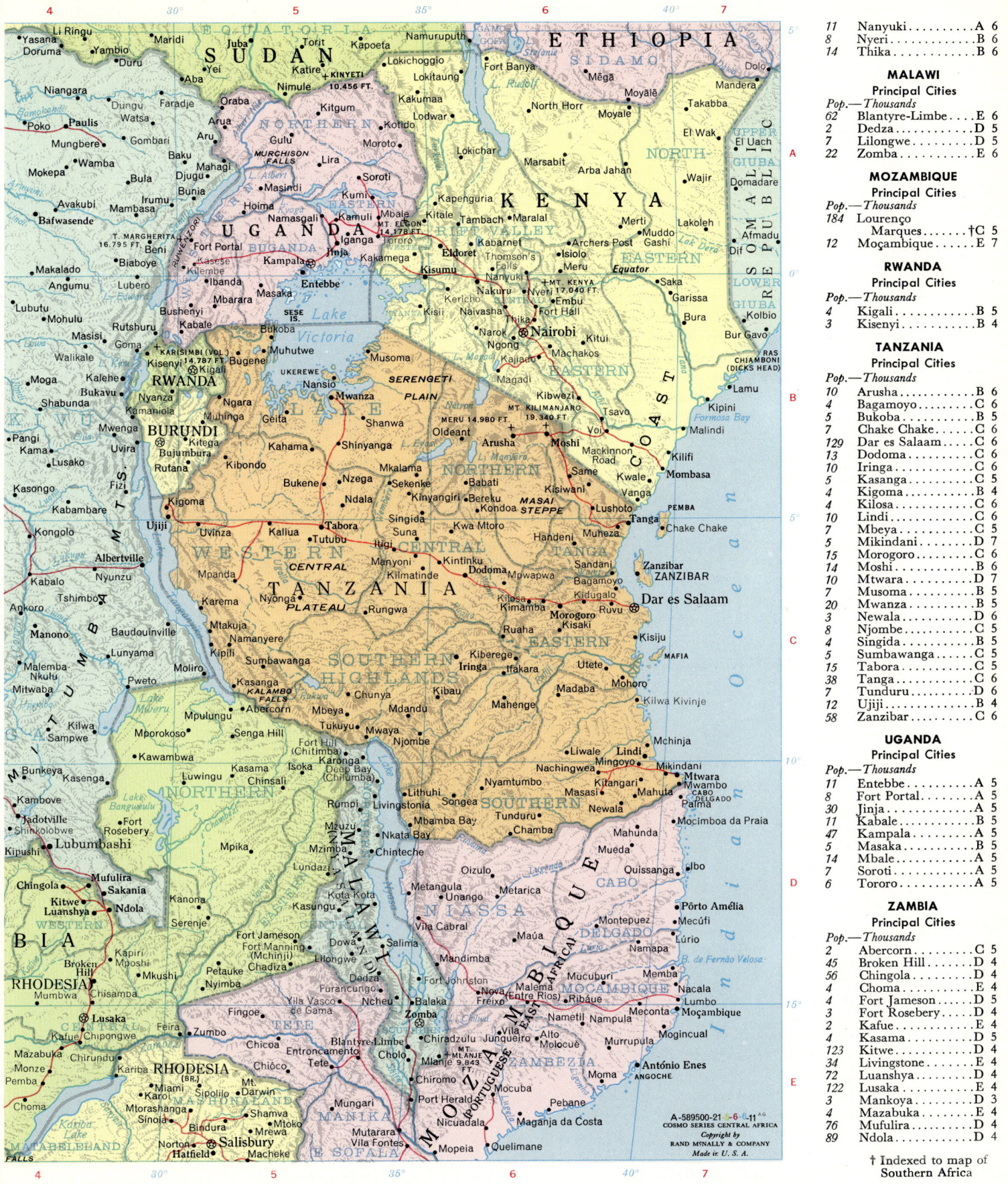

ATLAS 40   SOUTHERN AFRICA

BOTSWANA
Principal Cities
Pop.—Thousands

10	Francistown	B 4
10	Gaberones	B 4
34	Kanye	B 4
18	Mochudi	B 4
30	Molepolole	B 4
34	Serowe	B 4

LESOTHO
Principal City
Pop.—Thousands

9	Maseru	C 4

MALAGASY REPUBLIC
Principal Cities
Pop.—Thousands

5	Ambalavao	h 9
12	Ambositra	h 9
12	Antalaha	f 10
23	Antsirabe	g 9
3	Belo	g 8
3	Betroka	h 9
30	Diégo-Suarez (Antsirane)	f 9
10	Farafangana	h 9
36	Fianarantsoa	h 9
11	Fort-Dauphin	h 9
7	Hellville	f 9
3	Maevatanana	g 9
4	Mahanoro	g 9
3	Maintirano	g 8
34	Majunga	g 9
12	Manakara	h 9
3	Mananara	h 9
16	Mananjary	h 9
5	Maroantsetra	g 9
14	Marovoay	g 9
6	Moramanga	g 9
11	Morondava	h 8
4	Port Bergé	g 9
40	Tamatave	g 9
270	Tananarive	g 9
34	Tuléar	h 8

RHODESIA
Principal Cities
Pop.—Thousands

214	Bulawayo	B 4
32	Gwelo	A 4
18	Que Que	A 4
220	Salisbury	A 5
40	Umtali	A 5
20	Wankie	A 4

SOUTH AFRICA
Principal Cities
Pop.—Thousands

11	Aliwal North	D 4
11	Barberton	C 5
16	Beaufort West	D 3
24	Bethlehem	C 4
113	Bloemfontein	C 4
78	Brakpan	C 4
5	Bredasdorp	D 3
7	Burgersdorp	D 4
5	Calvinia	D 2
508	Cape Town	D 2
4	Carnarvon	D 3
4	Carolina	C 5
6	Christiana	C 4
5	Colesberg	D 4
19	Cradock	D 4
14	De Aar	D 3
4	Dordrecht	D 4
4	Douglas	C 3
11	Dundee	C 5
560	Durban	C 5
114	East London	D 4
7	Empangeni	C 5
17	Ermelo	C 5
9	Estcourt	C 4
8	Ficksburg	C 4
10	Fort Beaufort	D 4
15	George	D 3

ATLAS 42 AUSTRALIA

AUSTRALIA
⊛ Capital
Canberra............G 8

Physical Features
Arafura, sea...........B 5
Banks, isl............B 7
Blue Mud, bay.........B 6
Cape York, pen........B 7
Carpentaria, gulf.....B 6
Coral, sea............C 9
D'Entrecasteaux, is...k13
D'Entrecasteaux, pt...F 2
Encounter, bay........G 6
Eyre, pen.............F 6
Flinders, range.......F 6
Gairdner, lake........F 6
Geographe, chan.......D 1
Gibson, des...........D 3
Hamersley, range......D 2
Jacquinot, bay........k13
Joseph Bonaparte, gulf.B 4
King Leopold, ranges..C 4
Macdonnell, ranges....D 5
Neales, riv...........E 6
Nullarbor, plain......F 4
Owen Stanley, range...k12
Papua, gulf...........k11
Port Phillip, bay.....G 7
Princess Charlotte, bay.B 7
Sir Edward Pellew Group,
  is..................C 6
Spencer, gulf.........F 6
Swain, reefs..........D 9
Tasman, sea...........G 9
Thursday, isl.........B 7
Timor, sea............B 4
Torrens, lake.........F 6
Torres, strait........A 7
Van Diemen, gulf......B 5
Wellesley, isl........C 6

Principal Cities
Pop.—Thousands
20 Adelaide..........F 6
12 Albany............F 2
25 Albury............G 8
6   Alice Springs.....D 5
8   Ararat............G 7, n14
14 Armidale..........F 9
7   Bairnsdale........G 8, n15
42 Ballarat..........G 7, n14
2   Barcaldine........D 8
17 Bathurst..........F 8
4   Bega..............G 8, n15
31 Bendigo...........G 7
2   Blackall..........D 8
1   Bombala...........G 8, n15
6   Boulder...........F 3
3   Bourke............F 8
5   Bowen.............C 8
1   Brewarrina........E 8
644 Brisbane..........E 9
30 Broken Hill.......F 7
1   Broome............C 3
15 Bunbury...........F 2
24 Bundaberg.........D 9
15 Burnie............o15
3   Busselton.........F 2
26 Cairns............C 8
86 Canberra..........G 8
2   Carnarvon.........D 1
35 Cessnock..........F 9
5   Charleville.......E 8
8   Charters Towers...D 8
2   Clermont..........D 8
2   Cloncurry.........D 7
8   Collie............F 2
3   Condobolin........F 8
3   Coolgardie........F 3
9   Cooma.............G 8
3   Coonamble.........F 8
2   Cunnamulla........E 8
8   Dalby.............E 9
16 Darwin............B 5
6   Deniliquin........G 7
1   Derby.............C 3
14 Devonport.........o15
1   Dirranbandi.......E 8
15 Dubbo.............F 8
7   Echuca............G 7

ATLAS 43

2	Emerald	D 8
7	Forbes	F 8
24	Fremantle	F 2
19	Geelong	G 7, n14
13	Geraldton	E 1
8	Gladstone	D 9
1	Gladstone	F 6
6	Glen Innes	E 9
21	Goulburn	F 8
16	Grafton	E 9
8	Griffith	F 8
12	Gympie	E 9
10	Hamilton	G 7, n14
3	Hay	F 7
53	Hobart	o15
10	Horsham	G 7
2	Hughenden	D 7
5	Ingham	C 8
7	Innisfail	C 8
9	Inverell	E 9
53	Ipswich	E 9
9	Kalgoorlie	F 3
3	Katanning	F 2
8	Kempsey	F 9
4	Kerang	G 7
1	Kingscote	G 6
37	Launceston	o15
19	Lismore	E 9
14	Lithgow	F 9
4	Longreach	D 7
18	Mackay	D 8
28	Maitland	F 9
20	Maryborough	E 9
7	Maryborough	G 7
76	Melbourne	G 7, n14
1	Mildura	F 7
1	Miles	E 9
1	Moonta	F 6
7	Moree	E 8
17	Mount Gambier	G 7
13	Mount Isa	D 6
4	Mount Morgan	D 9
6	Mungindi	E 8
6	Muswellbrook	F 9
4	Naracoorte	G 7
6	Narrabri	F 8
5	Narrandera	F 8
5	Narrogin	F 2
145	Newcastle	F 9
6	New Norfolk	o15
2	Norseman	F 3
8	Northam	F 2
1	Northampton	E 1
3	Nyngan	F 8
20	Orange	F 8
2	Ouyen	F 7
96	Perth	F 2
3	Peterborough	F 6
40	Port Adelaide	F 6
10	Port Augusta	F 6
7	Portland	G 7
8	Port Lincoln	F 6
7	Port Macquarie	F 9
14	Port Pirie	F 6
5	Queenstown	o15
6	Renmark	F 7
45	Rockhampton	D 9
6	Roma	E 8
3	St. George	E 8
3	Smithton	o15
39	Southport	E 9
7	Swan Hill	G 7
167	Sydney	F 9
2	Tailem Bend	G 6
21	Tamworth	F 9
3	Tenterfield	E 9
54	Toowoomba	E 9
56	Townsville	C 8
3	Tully	C 8
6	Ulverstone	o15
24	Wagga Wagga	G 8
2	Walgett	E 8
2	Wallaroo	F 6
18	Warrnambool	G 7, n14
10	Warwick	E 9
1	Wentworth	F 7
19	Whyalla	F 6
2	Winton	D 7
151	Wollongong	F 9
4	Wonthaggi	G 8, n15
5	Woomera	F 6
2	York	F 2

Lambert Azimuthal Equal Area Projection
SCALE 1:16,000,000   1 Inch = 252 Statute Miles

ATLAS 44   SOUTH AMERICA

SOUTH AMERICA

⊛ Capitals †

Asunción, Par.	F 5
Belize, Br. Hond.	B 2
Bogotá, Col.	C 3
Brasília, Braz.	E 6
Buenos Aires, Arg.	G 5
Caracas, Ven.	B 4
Cayenne, Fr. Gu.	C 5
Georgetown, Guy.	C 5
Guatemala, Guat.	B 1
Havana, Cuba	A 2
Kingston, Jam.	B 3
La Paz, Bol.	E 4
Lima, Peru	E 3
Managua, Nic.	B 2
Montevideo, Ur.	G 5
Nassau, Ba. Is.	A 3
Panamá, Pan.	C 3
Paramaribo, Sur.	C 5
Port-au-Prince, Hai.	B 3
Port-of-Spain, Trin.	B 4
Quito, Ec.	D 3
San José, C.R.	C 2
San Juan, P.R.	B 4
San Salvador, Sal.	B 2
Santiago, Chile	G 3
Santo Domingo, Dom. Rep	B 4
Sucre, Bol.	E 4
Tegucigalpa, Hond.	B 2

† For capital city of Mexico see map of Mexico.

Physical Features

Aconcagua, mtn.	G 4
Amazonas (Amazon), riv.	D 5
Andes, mts.	D 3, H 3
Andros, isl.	A 3
Angamos, pt.	F 3
Araguaia, riv.	D 6
Atrato, riv.	C 3
Bascuñán, cape	F 3
Bermejo, riv.	F 5
Branco, riv.	C 4
Brazilian, highlands	E 5
Caquetá, riv.	D 3
Caribbean, sea.	B 3
Caroní, riv.	C 4
Catoche, cape.	A 2
Cauca, riv.	C 3
Chico, riv.	H 4
Chiloé, isl.	H 3
Chimborazo, vol.	D 3
Chonos, arch.	H 3
Chubut, riv.	H 4
Colón (Galápagos), arch.	C 1
Colorado, riv.	G 4
Corrientes, cape.	C 3
Corumiquara, pt.	D 7
Cuba, isl.	A 2
Curaçao, isl.	B 4
Cuyuni, riv.	C 5
Desengaño, cape.	H 4
Devils, isl.	C 5
Dos Bahías, cape.	H 4
Essequibo, riv.	C 5
Falkland (Islas Malvinas), is.	I 4
Fernando de Noronha, isl.	D 7
Fitz Roy, mtn.	H 3
Frio, cape.	F 6
Gallinas, pt.	B 3
Gracias a Dios, cape.	B 2
Gran Chaco, plain.	F 4
Greater Antilles, is.	B 3
Guaporé, riv.	E 4
Guaviare, riv.	C 3
Guayaquil, gulf.	D 2
Honduras, gulf.	B 2
Horn, cape.	I 4
Huascarán, mtn.	D 3
Icá, riv.	D 4
Isabela, isl.	D 1
Isle of Pines, isl.	A 2
Jamaica, isl.	B 3
Japurá, riv.	D 4
Jari, riv.	D 5
Javari, riv.	D 3
Jequitinhonha, riv.	E 6

Juan Fernández, is	G	3
Juruá, riv	D	4
Lavapie, pt	G	3
Lesser Antilles, is	B	2
Limay, riv	G	4
Loa, riv	F	4
Llanos, plains	C	4
Llullaillaco, vol	F	4
Madeira, riv	D	4
Madre de Dios, riv	E	4
Magdalena, riv	C	3
Magellan, strait	I	4
Mamoré, riv	E	4
Maracá, isl	C	5
Maracaibo, lake	C	3
Marajó, isl	D	6
Marañón, riv	D	4
Margarita, isl	B	2
Mato, pt	D	7
Mato Grosso, plat	E	5
Meta, riv	C	3
Mexico, gulf	A	2
Mirim, lake	G	5
Misti, vol	E	3
Mogotes, pt	G	5
Monsarás, pt	E	7
Mosquitos, gulf	C	2
Mutá, pt	E	7
Napo, riv	D	3
Negro, riv	D	4
Negro, riv	G	4
Negra, pt	D	2
Nicaragua, lake	B	2
Oiapoque, riv	D	5
Orange, cape	C	5
Orinoco, riv	C	3
Pakaraima, mts	C	4
Pampa de las Salinas, salt flats	G	4
Panama, gulf	C	3
Pará, riv	D	6
Paraguay, riv	F	5
Paraíba, riv	F	6
Paraná, riv	G	4
Paranapanema, riv	F	5
Parecis, mts	E	5
Parnaíba, riv	D	6
Patos, lake	G	5
Pilcomayo, riv	F	4
Plata, riv	G	5
Poopó, lake	E	4
Puerto Rico, isl	B	2
Purus, riv	D	4
Putumayo, riv	D	3
Robinson Crusoe, isl	G	3
Rocas, is	D	7
Rosa, pt	H	4
Salado, riv	F	4
Salinas Grandes, salt flats	F	4
San Ambrosio, isl	F	3
San Antonio, cape	G	5
San Felix, isl	F	2
San Francisco, cape	G	5
San Jorge, gulf	H	4
San Matías, gulf	H	4
San Valentín, mtn	H	3
São Francisco, riv	E	6
São Roque, cape	D	7
São Tomé, cape	F	6
Taitao, pen	H	3
Tapajós, riv	D	5
Taquari, riv	F	5
Tetas, pt	F	3
Tierra del Fuego, isl	I	4
Tietê, riv	F	5
Titicaca, lake	E	4
Tocantins, riv	D	6
Tres Puntas, cape	H	4
Trombetas, riv	D	5
Uaupés, riv	D	4
Ucayali, riv	D	3
Uruguay, riv	G	5
Uyuni, salt lake	F	4
Valdés, pen	H	4
Venezuela, gulf	B	3
Vírgenes, cape	I	4
Wellington, isl	H	3
Xingú, riv	D	5
Yerupaja, mtn	E	3
Yucatán, chan	A	2
Zumbi, pt	D	6

ATLAS 46

CENTRAL AND SOUTHERN ARGENTINA AND CHILE

SOUTHERN ARGENTINA
Principal Cities

Pop.—Thousands

Pop.	City	Ref
6	Adolfo Alsina	B 4
12	Alta Gracia	A 4
8	Arrecifes	g 6
275	Avellaneda	A 5, g 7
9	Ayacucho	B 5
29	Azul	B 5
136	Bahía Blanca	B 4
15	Balcarce	B 5
10	Baradero	f 7
16	Bell Ville	A 4
2	Bernasconi	B 4
14	Bolívar	B 5
16	Bragado	B 4, g 6
2,967	Buenos Aires	A 5, g 7
6	Cañuelas	B 5, g 7
8	Carlos Casares	B 4
5	Carmen de Patagones	C 4
11	Casilda	A 4
13	Chacabuco	A 4, g 6
9	Chascomús	B 5
23	Chivilcoy	A 4, g 6
8	Colón	A 5
26	Comodoro Rivadavia	D 3
31	Concepción del Uruguay	A 5
64	Concordia	A 5
580	Córdoba	A 4
4	Coronel Brandsen	B 5, g 7
7	Coronel Dorrego	B 4
13	Coronel Pringles	B 4
11	Coronel Suárez	B 4
16	Cruz del Eje	A 4
14	Deán Funes	A 4
14	Dolores	B 5
6	Esquel	C 2
5	General Acha	B 4
4	General Belgrano	B 5
7	General Madariaga	B 5
11	General Pico	B 4
8	General Viamonte	B 4
5	Gonzáles Chaves	B 5
24	Gualeguay	A 5
37	Gualeguaychú	A 5
4	Henderson	B 4
8	Juárez	B 5
36	Junín	A 4
5	Justo Daract	A 3
9	Laboulaye	A 4
15	La Paz	A 5
295	La Plata	A 5, g 8
9	Las Flores	B 5
13	Lincoln	A 4
8	Lobería	B 5
8	Lobos	B 5, g 7
19	Luján	g 7
5	Maipú	B 5
10	Marcos Juárez	A 4
203	Mar del Plata	B 5
109	Mendoza	A 3
17	Mercedes	A 5, g 7
26	Mercedes	A 3
11	Monte Caseros	A 5
18	Necochea	B 5
7	Neuquén	B 3
12	Nogoyá	A 5
14	Nueve de Julio	B 4
24	Olavarría	B 4
110	Paraná	A 4
14	Pehuajo	B 4
32	Pergamino	A 4
5	Quequén	B 5
24	Rafaela	A 4
5	Rauch	B 5
70	Río Cuarto	A 4
6	Río Gallegos	E 3
11	Río Tercero	A 4
7	Rojas	A 4
595	Rosario	A 4
11	Rosario Tala	A 5
11	Rufino	A 4
8	Saladillo	B 5
4	San Antonio Oeste	C 4

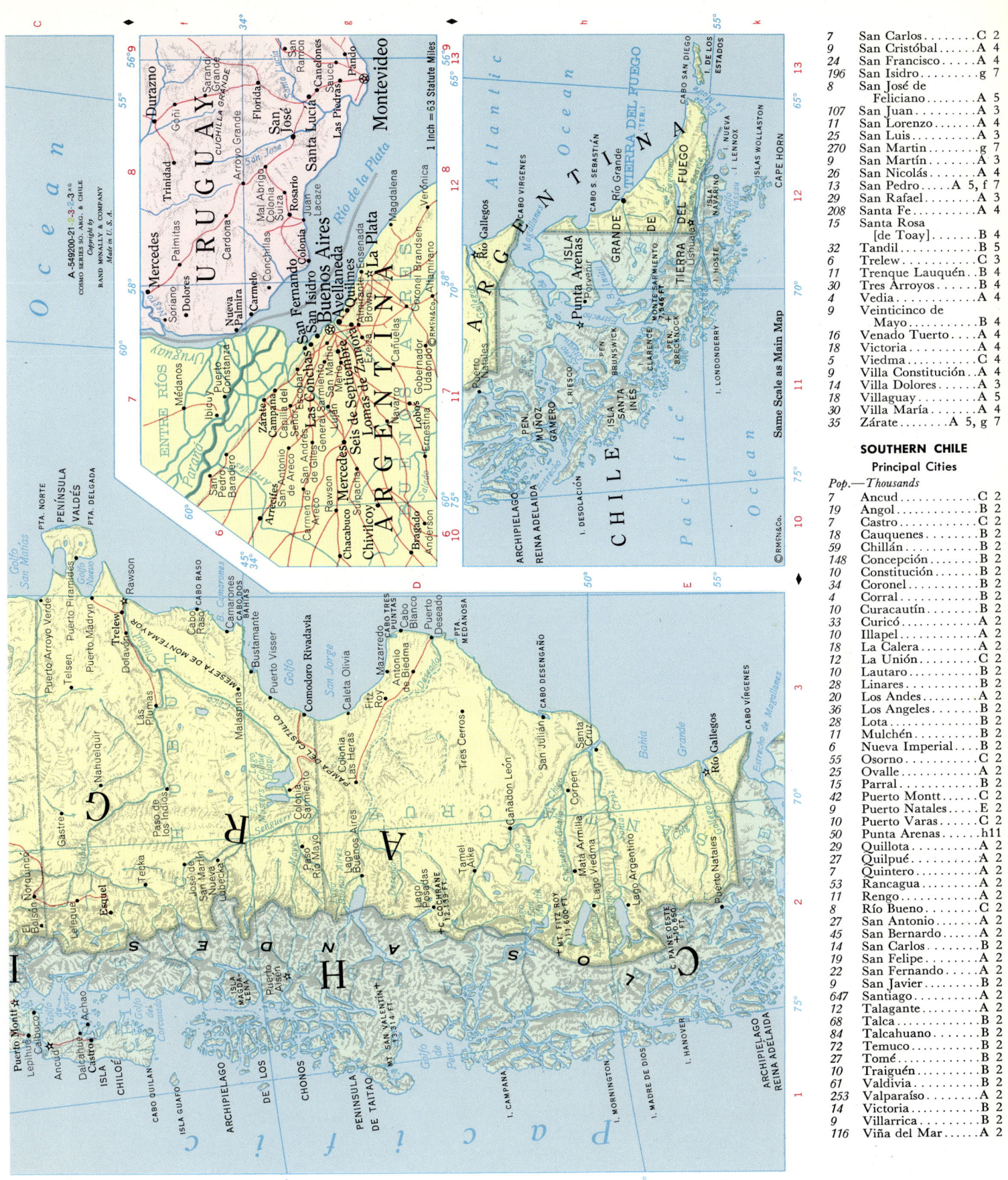

ATLAS 48   BRAZIL

BRAZIL
Principal Cities
Pop.—Thousands

Pop	City	Ref
38	Alagoinhas	E 5
34	Alegrete	p11
49	Anápolis	F 3
113	Aracaju	E 5
54	Araçatuba	G 2
36	Araguari	F 3
58	Araraquara	G 3
24	Araras	G 3
24	Araxá	F 3
30	Assis	G 2
20	Avaré	G 3
48	Bagé	q12
42	Barbacena	G 4
29	Barra do Piraí	G 4
47	Barra Mansa	G 4
40	Barretos	G 3
85	Bauru	G 3
18	Bebedouro	G 3
360	Belém (Pará)	C 3
643	Belo Horizonte	F 4
47	Blumenau	H 3, p13
34	Botucatú	G 3
27	Bragança Paulista	G 3
150	Brasília	F 3
16	Brusque	H 3, p13
39	Cachoeira do Sul	q12
39	Cachoeiro do Itapemirim	G 4
116	Campina Grande	D 5
180	Campinas	G 3
64	Campo Grande	G 2
91	Campos	G 4
22	Caratinga	F 4
18	Caràzinho	p12
64	Caruaru	D 5
21	Cataguases	G 4
37	Catanduva	G 3
19	Caxias	C 4
61	Caxias do Sul	p12
29	Conselheiro Lafaiete	G 4
37	Corumbá	F 1
28	Crato	D 5
33	Cruz Alta	p12
27	Cruzeiro	G 4
43	Cuiabá	F 1
345	Curitiba	H 3
22	Curvelo	F 4
42	Divinópolis	G 4
15	Dom Pedrito	q12
25	Erechim	H 2, p12
16	Estância	E 5
62	Feira de Santana	E 5
74	Florianópolis	H 3, p13
19	Formiga	G 3
355	Fortaleza	C 5
47	Franca	G 3
34	Garanhuns	D 5
18	Garça	G 3
19	Goiana	D 6
133	Goiânia	F 3
70	Governador Valadares	F 4
38	Guaratinguetá	G 3
46	Ilhéus	E 5
54	Itabuna	E 5
39	Itajaí	H 3, p13
31	Itajubá	G 3
29	Itapetininga	G 3
23	Itu	G 3
34	Jaboatão	D 6
20	Jaboticabal	G 3
31	Jaú	G 3
40	Jequié	E 4
136	João Pessoa (Paraíba)	D 6
44	Joinville	H 3, p13
21	Juàzeiro	D 4
53	Juàzeiro do Norte	D 5
125	Juiz de Fora	G 4
80	Jundiaí	G 3
35	Lajes	H 2, p12
24	Lavras	G 3
45	Limeira	G 3
21	Limoeiro	D 5
32	Lins	G 3
38	Livramento	q11
74	Londrina	G 2

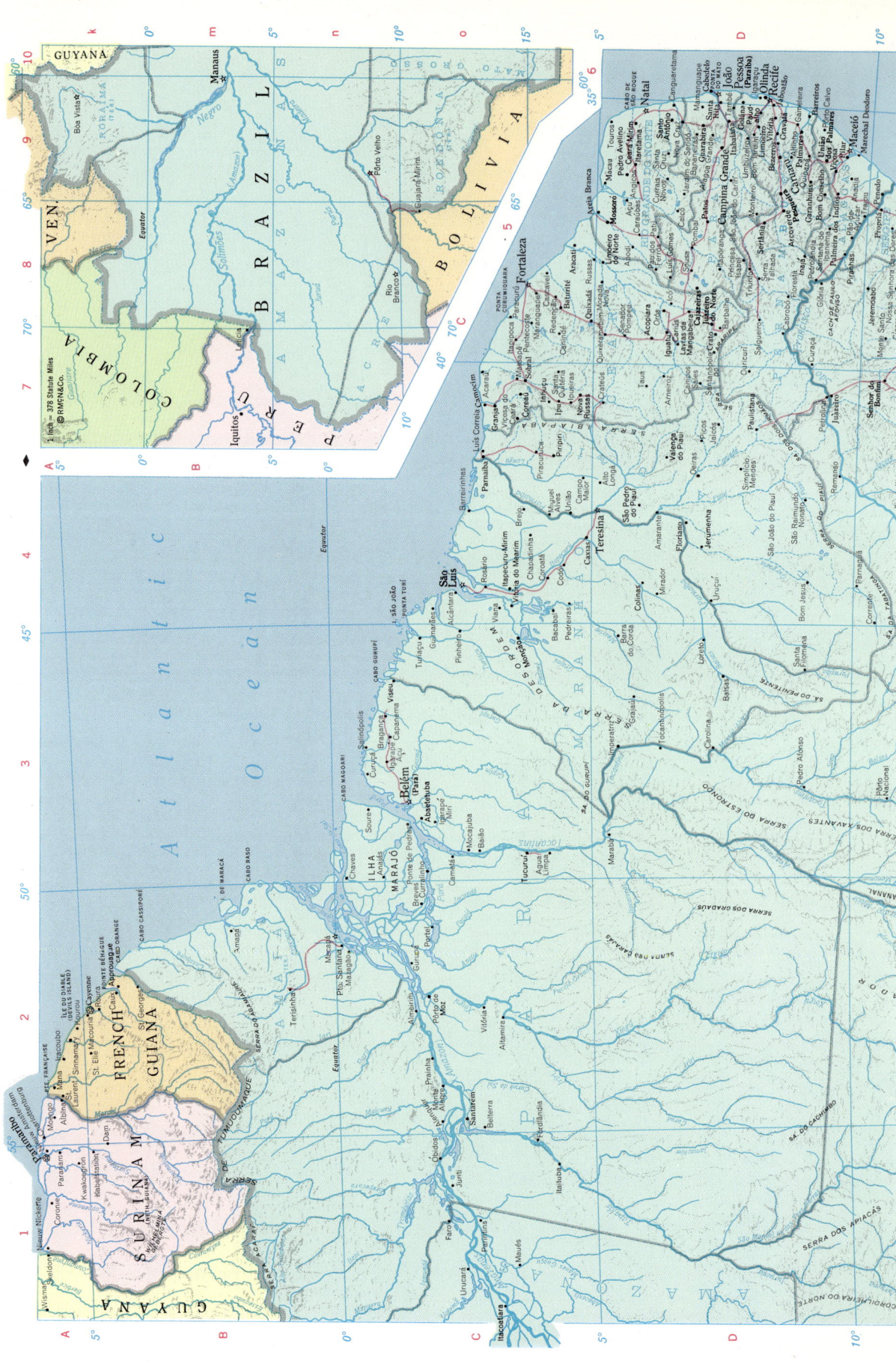

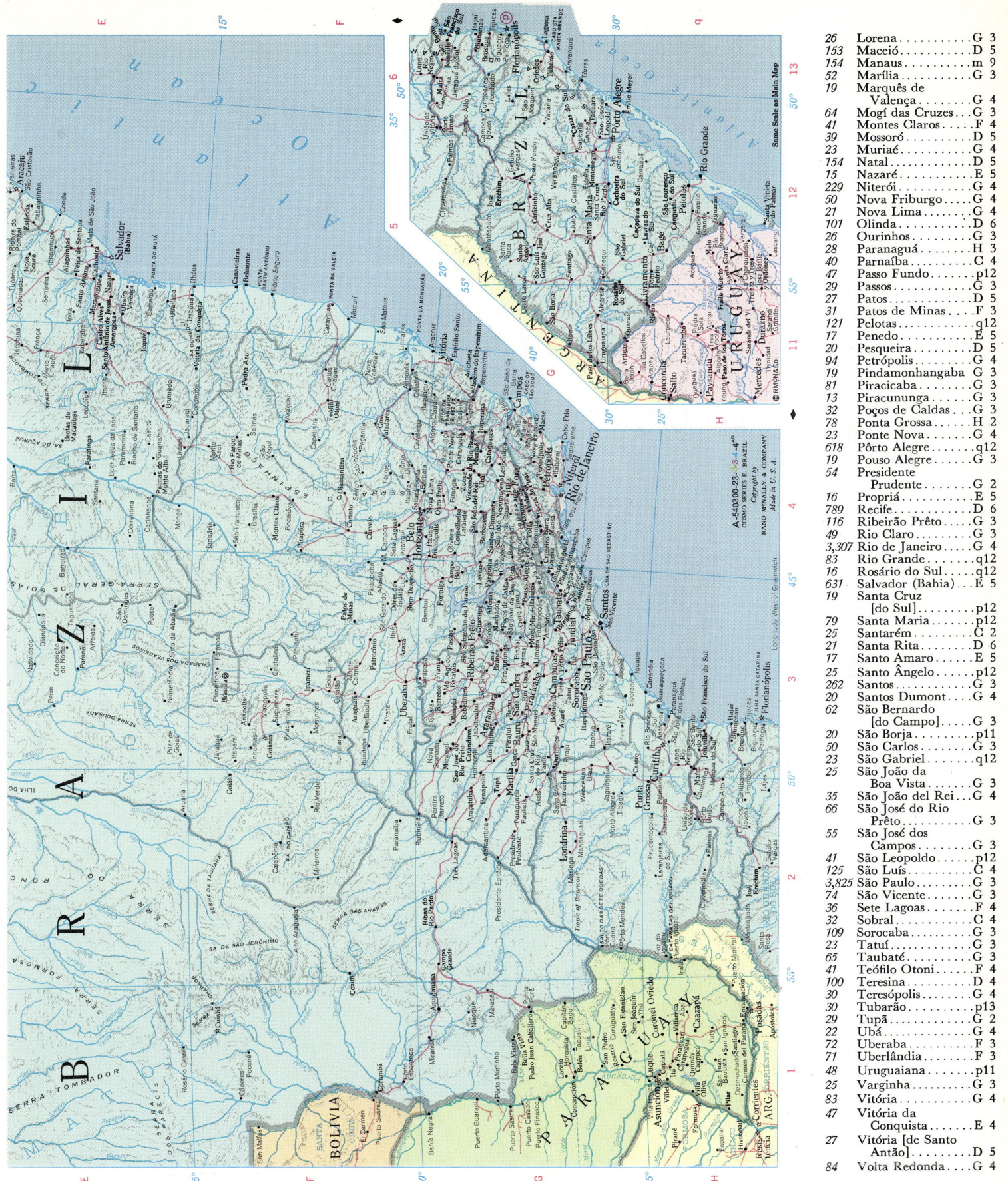

ATLAS 49

26	Lorena	G 3
153	Maceió	D 5
154	Manaus	m 9
52	Marília	G 3
19	Marquês de Valença	G 4
64	Mogí das Cruzes	G 3
41	Montes Claros	F 4
39	Mossoró	D 5
23	Muriaé	G 4
154	Natal	D 5
15	Nazaré	E 5
229	Niterói	G 4
50	Nova Friburgo	G 4
21	Nova Lima	G 4
101	Olinda	D 6
26	Ourinhos	G 3
28	Paranaguá	H 3
40	Parnaíba	C 4
47	Passo Fundo	p12
29	Passos	G 3
27	Patos	D 5
31	Patos de Minas	F 3
121	Pelotas	q12
17	Penedo	E 5
20	Pesqueira	D 5
94	Petrópolis	G 4
19	Pindamonhangaba	G 3
81	Piracicaba	G 3
13	Piracununga	G 3
32	Poços de Caldas	G 3
78	Ponta Grossa	H 2
23	Ponte Nova	G 4
618	Pôrto Alegre	q12
19	Pouso Alegre	G 3
54	Presidente Prudente	G 2
16	Propriá	E 5
789	Recife	D 6
116	Ribeirão Prêto	G 3
49	Rio Claro	G 3
3,307	Rio de Janeiro	G 4
83	Rio Grande	q12
16	Rosário do Sul	q12
631	Salvador (Bahia)	E 5
19	Santa Cruz [do Sul]	p12
79	Santa Maria	p12
25	Santarém	C 2
21	Santa Rita	D 6
17	Santo Amaro	E 5
25	Santo Ângelo	p12
262	Santos	G 3
20	Santos Dumont	G 4
62	São Bernardo [do Campo]	G 3
20	São Borja	p11
50	São Carlos	G 3
23	São Gabriel	q12
25	São João da Boa Vista	G 3
35	São João del Rei	G 4
66	São José do Rio Prêto	G 3
55	São José dos Campos	G 3
41	São Leopoldo	p12
125	São Luís	C 4
3,825	São Paulo	G 3
74	São Vicente	G 3
36	Sete Lagoas	F 4
32	Sobral	C 4
109	Sorocaba	G 3
23	Tatuí	G 3
65	Taubaté	G 3
41	Teófilo Otoni	F 4
100	Teresina	D 4
30	Teresópolis	G 4
30	Tubarão	p13
29	Tupã	G 2
22	Ubá	G 4
72	Uberaba	F 3
71	Uberlândia	F 3
48	Uruguaiana	p11
25	Varginha	G 3
83	Vitória	G 4
47	Vitória da Conquista	E 4
27	Vitória [de Santo Antão]	D 5
84	Volta Redonda	G 4

Oblique Conic Conformal Projection
SCALE 1:12,000,000 1 Inch = 189 Statute Miles

ATLAS 50 — ECUADOR AND PERU

ECUADOR
Principal Cities
Pop.—Thousands

Pop.	City	Grid
7	Alausí	B 2
53	Ambato	B 2
8	Azogues	B 2
16	Babahoyo	B 2
9	Bahía de Caráquez	B 1
7	Balzar	B 2
4	Baños	B 2
5	Calceta	B 1
5	Cañar	B 2
5	Cariamanga	B 2
4	Catacocha	B 2
8	Cayambe	A 2
3	Celica	B 2
13	Chone	B 1
60	Cuenca	B 2
7	Daule	A 2
33	Esmeraldas	A 2
2	Girón	B 2
3	Gualaceo	B 2
10	Guaranda	B 2
511	Guayaquil	B 2
26	Ibarra	A 2
13	Jipijapa	B 1
15	Latacunga	B 2
27	Loja	B 2
5	Macará	B 2
4	Machachi	B 2
29	Machala	B 2
34	Manta	B 1
5	Montecristi	B 1
9	Otavalo	A 2
13	Pasaje	B 2
3	Píllaro	B 2
32	Portoviejo	B 1
3	Pujilí	B 2
355	Quito	B 2
42	Riobamba	B 2
4	Rocafuerte	B 1
3	Salcedo	B 2
5	Salinas	B 1
7	San Gabriel	A 2
4	Santa Ana	B 1
4	Santa Elena	B 1
9	Santa Rosa	B 2
1	Sigsig	B 2
16	Tulcán	A 2
6	Vinces	B 2
3	Yaguachi	B 2
9	Zaruma	B 2

PERU
Principal Cities
Pop.—Thousands

Pop.	City	Grid
9	Abancay	D 3
2	Acobamba	D 3
2	Acomayo	D 3
2	Andahuaylas	D 3
2	Andamarca	D 3
2	Anta	D 3
2	Antabamba	D 3
157	Arequipa	E 3
4	Ascope	C 2
2	Ayabaca	B 2
24	Ayacucho	D 3
8	Ayaviri	D 3
5	Azángaro	D 3
3	Cabana	C 2
11	Cajabamba	C 2
23	Cajamarca	C 2
3	Cajatambo	D 2
3	Calca	D 3
161	Callao	D 2
5	Camaná	E 3
7	Cañete	D 2
3	Caraz	C 2
3	Carhuaz	C 2
5	Casma	C 2
9	Castilla	C 1
9	Catacaos	C 1
6	Celendín	C 2
6	Cerro de Pasco	D 2
7	Chachapoyas	C 2
3	Chalhuanca	D 3
3	Chancay	D 2
8	Chepén	C 2
87	Chiclayo	C 2

ATLAS 51

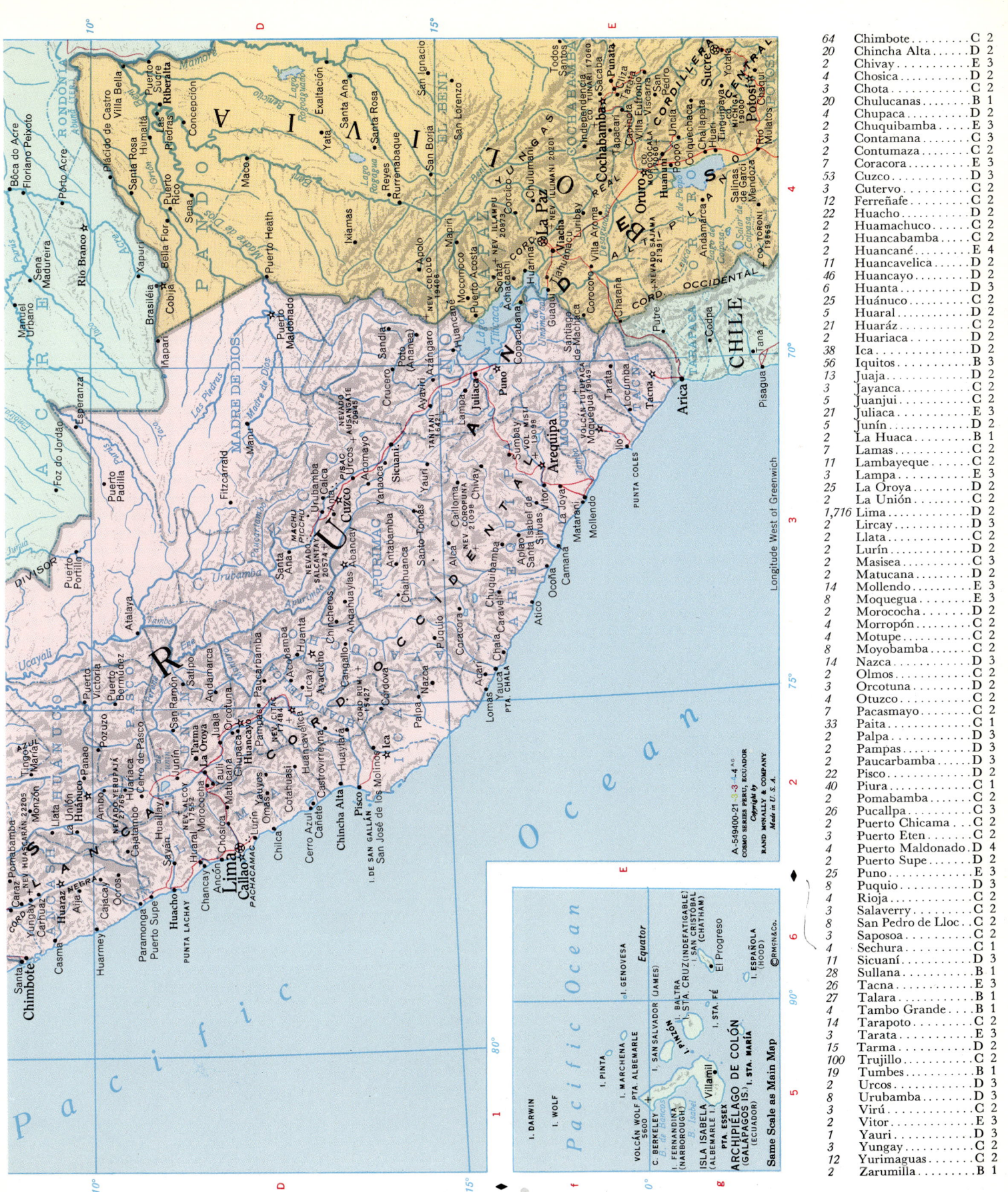

64	Chimbote	C	2
20	Chincha Alta	D	2
2	Chivay	E	3
4	Chosica	D	2
3	Chota	C	2
20	Chulucanas	B	1
4	Chupaca	D	2
2	Chuquibamba	E	3
3	Contamana	C	3
2	Contumaza	C	2
7	Coracora	E	3
53	Cuzco	D	3
3	Cutervo	C	2
12	Ferreñafe	C	2
22	Huacho	D	2
2	Huamachuco	C	2
2	Huancabamba	C	2
2	Huancané	E	4
11	Huancavelica	D	2
46	Huancayo	D	2
6	Huanta	D	3
25	Huánuco	D	2
5	Huaral	D	2
21	Huaráz	C	2
2	Huariaca	D	2
38	Ica	D	2
56	Iquitos	B	3
13	Juaja	D	2
3	Jayanca	C	2
5	Juanjui	C	2
21	Juliaca	E	3
5	Junín	D	2
2	La Huaca	B	1
7	Lamas	C	2
11	Lambayeque	C	2
3	Lampa	E	3
25	La Oroya	D	2
2	La Unión	D	2
1,716	Lima	D	2
2	Lircay	D	3
2	Llata	D	2
2	Lurín	D	2
2	Masisea	C	3
2	Matucana	D	2
14	Mollendo	E	3
8	Moquegua	E	3
4	Morococha	D	2
2	Morropón	C	2
2	Motupe	C	2
8	Moyobamba	C	2
14	Nazca	D	3
2	Olmos	C	2
2	Orcotuna	D	2
4	Otuzco	C	2
7	Pacasmayo	C	2
33	Paita	C	1
2	Palpa	D	3
2	Pampas	D	3
2	Paucarbamba	D	3
22	Pisco	D	2
40	Piura	C	1
2	Pomabamba	C	2
26	Pucallpa	C	3
2	Puerto Chicama	C	2
2	Puerto Eten	C	2
4	Puerto Maldonado	D	4
2	Puerto Supe	C	2
25	Puno	E	3
8	Puquio	D	3
4	Rioja	C	2
8	Salaverry	C	2
8	San Pedro de Lloc	C	2
3	Saposoa	C	2
4	Sechura	C	1
11	Sicuaní	D	3
28	Sullana	B	1
26	Tacna	E	3
27	Talara	B	1
4	Tambo Grande	B	1
14	Tarapoto	C	2
3	Tarata	E	3
15	Tarma	D	2
100	Trujillo	C	2
19	Tumbes	B	1
2	Urcos	D	3
8	Urubamba	D	3
3	Virú	C	2
2	Vitor	E	3
1	Yauri	D	3
3	Yungay	C	2
12	Yurimaguas	C	2
2	Zarumilla	B	1

Oblique Conic Conformal Projection
SCALE 1:8,000,000   1 Inch = 126 Statute Miles

ATLAS 52 — COLOMBIA AND VENEZUELA

COLOMBIA
Principal Cities
Pop.—Thousands

Pop.	City	Grid
8	Aguadas	B 2
8	Anserma	B 2
12	Arjona	A 2
78	Armenia	C 2
10	Armero	C 3
25	Barrancabermeja	B 2
498	Barranquilla	A 3
28	Bello	B 2
1,697	Bogotá	C 3
230	Bucaramanga	B 3
57	Buenaventura	C 2
48	Buga	C 2
11	Caicedonia	C 2
16	Calarcá	C 2
638	Cali	C 2
242	Cartagena	A 2
49	Cartago	C 2
12	Chaparral	C 2
10	Chiquinquirá	B 3
24	Ciénaga	A 3
130	Cúcuta	B 3
8	Duitama	B 3
10	El Banco	B 3
10	El Carmen de Bolívar	B 2
9	Espinal	C 3
13	Facatativá	C 3
49	Girardot	C 3
16	Honda	B 3
90	Ibagué	C 2
12	Ipiales	C 2
15	La Dorada	B 3
12	Líbano	C 3
17	Magangué	B 2
222	Manizales	B 2
773	Medellín	B 2
9	Mompós	B 2
39	Montería	B 2
66	Neiva	C 2
15	Ocaña	B 3
83	Palmira	C 2
16	Pamplona	B 3
68	Pasto	C 2
121	Pereira	C 2
55	Popayán	C 2
9	Puerto Berrío	B 3
9	Puerto Tejada	C 2
43	Quibdó	B 2
14	Sabanalarga	A 3
10	San Gil	B 3
48	Santa Marta	A 3
17	Sevilla	C 2
22	Sincelejo	B 2
12	Socorro	B 3
14	Sogamoso	B 3
20	Soledad	A 3
11	Sonsón	B 2
29	Tuluá	C 2
13	Tumaco	C 2
69	Tunja	B 3
10	Turbaco	A 2
9	Valledupar	A 3
30	Villavicencio	C 3
10	Yarumal	B 2
13	Zipaquirá	B 3

NETHERLANDS ANTILLES
Principal City
Pop.—Thousands

44	Willemstad	A 4

PANAMA
Principal Cities
Pop.—Thousands

9	Chitré	B 1
60	Colon	B 2
23	David	B 1
319	Panamá	B 2

TRINIDAD & TOBAGO
Principal Cities
Pop.—Thousands

94	Port-of-Spain	A 5
40	San Fernando	A 5

VENEZUELA
Principal Cities

Pop.—Thousands

Pop.	City	Key
32	Acarigua	B 4
14	Altagracia	A 3
14	Altagracia de Orituco	B 4
27	Anaco	*B 5
35	Antímano	*A 4
11	Araure	*B 4
41	Barcelona	A 5
26	Barinas	B 3
197	Barquisimeto	A 4
42	Baruta	*A 4
10	Boconó	*B 3
93	Cabimas	A 3
14	Cagua	*A 4
15	Calabozo	B 4
14	Cantaura	B 5
787	Caracas	A 4
19	Caripito	A 5
22	Carora	A 3
38	Carúpano	A 5
62	Chacao	*A 4
10	Chivacoa	*A 4
56	Ciudad Bolívar	B 5
45	Coro	A 3
72	Cumaná	A 5
97	El Recreo	*A 4
42	El Tigre	B 5
15	El Tocuyo	B 4
106	El Valle	*A 4
9	El Viga	B 3
10	Encontrados	B 3
11	Guacara	*A 4
17	Guanare	B 4
14	Guarenas	*A 4
11	Guatire	*A 4
11	Güiria	A 5
20	La Guaira	A 4
68	Lagunillas	*A 3
62	La Vega	*A 4
23	La Victoria	A 4
44	Los Dos Caminos	*A 4
35	Los Teques	A 4
14	Machiques	A 3
73	Maiquetía	A 4
433	Maracaibo	A 3
134	Maracay	A 4
53	Maturín	B 5
13	Mene Grande	*B 3
40	Merida	B 3
14	Ocumare del Tuy	A 4
11	Palo Negro	*A 4
75	Petare	*A 4
21	Porlamar	A 5
51	Puerto Cabello	A 4
55	Puerto la Cruz	A 5
16	Punta Cardón	*A 3
42	Punto Fijo	A 3
10	Rosario	*A 3
12	Rubio	*B 3
15	San Antonio del Táchira	*B 3
12	San Carlos	B 4
14	San Carlos del Zulia	B 3
96	San Cristóbal	B 3
28	San Felipe	A 4
32	San Felix	*B 5
22	San Fernando de Apure	B 4
26	San Juan de los Morros	B 4
12	Santa Rita	A 3
75	Santo Tomé de Guayana	B 5
19	Trujillo	B 3
10	Tucupita	B 5
12	Upata	B 5
161	Valencia	A 4
45	Valera	B 3
24	Valle de la Pascua	B 4
20	Villa de Cura	A 4
10	Zaraza	B 4

* Not shown on map. Index key denotes approximate location.

ATLAS 54 — MEXICO

EL SALVADOR
Principal Cities
Pop.—Thousands

13	Ahuachapán	E 7
11	La Unión	E 7
40	San Miguel	E 7
256	San Salvador	E 7
73	Santa Ana	E 7
15	San Vicente	E 7
24	Sonsonate	E 7

GUATEMALA
Principal Cities
Pop.—Thousands

11	Antigua Guatemala	E 6
9	Chiquimula	E 7
7	Comalapa	E 6
3	Gualán	D 7
573	Guatemala	E 6
7	Jalapa	E 6
5	Jutiapa	E 7
11	Mazatenango	E 6
15	Puerto Barrios	D 7
28	Quezaltenango	E 6
9	Retalhuleu	E 6
3	San José	E 6
8	Zacapa	E 7

HONDURAS
Principal Cities
Pop.—Thousands

4	Catacamas	E 7
11	Choluteca	E 7
8	Comayagua	E 7
6	Danlí	E 7
25	La Ceiba	D 7
17	Puerto Cortés	D 7
59	San Pedro Sula	D 7
134	Tegucigalpa	E 7

MEXICO
Principal Cities
Pop.—Thousands

26	Acámbaro	C 4, m13
49	Acapulco [de Juárez]	D 5
127	Aguascalientes	C 4, m12
20	Apatzingán [de la Constitución]	n12
31	Atlixco	n14
64	Azcapotzalco	h 9, n14
44	Campeche	D 6
59	Celaya	m13
150	Chihuahua	B 3
20	Ciudad Acuña	B 4
23	Ciudad Mante	C 5
24	Ciudad de Valles	C 5, n14
31	Ciudad Guzmán	D 4, n12
262	Ciudad Juárez	A 3
68	Ciudad Obregón	B 3
51	Ciudad Victoria	C 5
37	Coatzacoalcos (Puerto Mexico)	D 6
44	Colima	D 4, n12
47	Córdoba	n15
55	Coyoacán	h 9, n14
37	Cuernavaca	D 5, n14
85	Culiacán	C 3
97	Durango	C 4
43	Ensenada	A 1
36	Fresnillo	C 4
61	Gómez Palacio	B 4
737	Guadalajara	C 4, m12
28	Guanajuato	C 4, m13
35	Guaymas	B 2
103	Gustavo A. Madero	h 9
96	Hermosillo	B 2
41	Hidalgo del Parral	B 3
27	Iguala	D 5, n14

ATLAS 55

Pop.	City	Ref.
84	Irapuato	C 4, m13
66	Jalapa Enríquez	D 5, n15
24	Lagos de Moreno	C 4, m13
24	La Paz	C 2
24	La Piedad	m12
210	León [de los Aldamas]	C 4, m13
38	Los Mochis	B 3
92	Matamoros	C 5
76	Mazatlán	C 3
171	Mérida	C 7
175	Mexicali	A 1
2,832	Mexico City	D 5, h 9, n14
35	Minatitlán	D 6
43	Monclova	B 4
597	Monterrey	B 4
101	Morelia	D 4, n13
31	Navojoa	B 3
38	Nogales	A 2
34	Nueva Rosita	B 4
93	Nuevo Laredo	B 5
72	Oaxaca	D 5
25	Ocotlán	C 4, m12
70	Orizaba	D 5, n15
65	Pachuca [de Soto]	C 5, m14
43	Piedras Negras	B 4
20	Poza Rica de Hidalgo	m15
289	Puebla [de Zaragoza]	D 5, n14
68	Querétaro	C 4, m13
74	Reynosa (Reinosal)	B 5
26	Sahuayo [de Díaz]	m12
33	Salamanca	m13
99	Saltillo	B 4
29	San Luis Río Colorado	A 2
160	San Luis Potosí	C 4, k13
123	Tampico	C 5, k15
42	Tapachula	E 6
32	Tehuacán	D 5, n15
54	Tepic	C 4, m11
152	Tijuana	A 1
38	Tlaquepaque (San Pedro Tlaquepaque)	m12
77	Toluca [de Lerdo]	D 5, n14
180	Torreón	B 4
27	Tulancingo	C 5, m14
41	Tuxtla Gutiérrez	D 6
46	Uruapan	D 4, n13
145	Veracruz [Llave]	D 5, n15
52	Villahermosa	D 6
31	Villa Obregón	h 9
32	Zacatecas	C 4
34	Zamora de Hidalgo	C 4, m12
24	Zitácuaro	n13

NICARAGUA
Principal Cities

Pop.—Thousands

Pop.	City	Ref.
9	Bluefields	E 8
9	Corinto	E 7
10	Diriamba	E 7
3	El Sauce	E 7
13	Estelí	E 7
29	Granada	E 7
8	Jinotega	E 7
9	Jinotepe	E 7
44	León	E 7
235	Managua	E 7
23	Masaya	E 7
15	Matagalpa	E 7
4	Ocotal	E 7
6	Puerto Cabezas	E 8
8	Rivas	E 7
2	San Juan del Sur	E 7
4	Somota	E 7

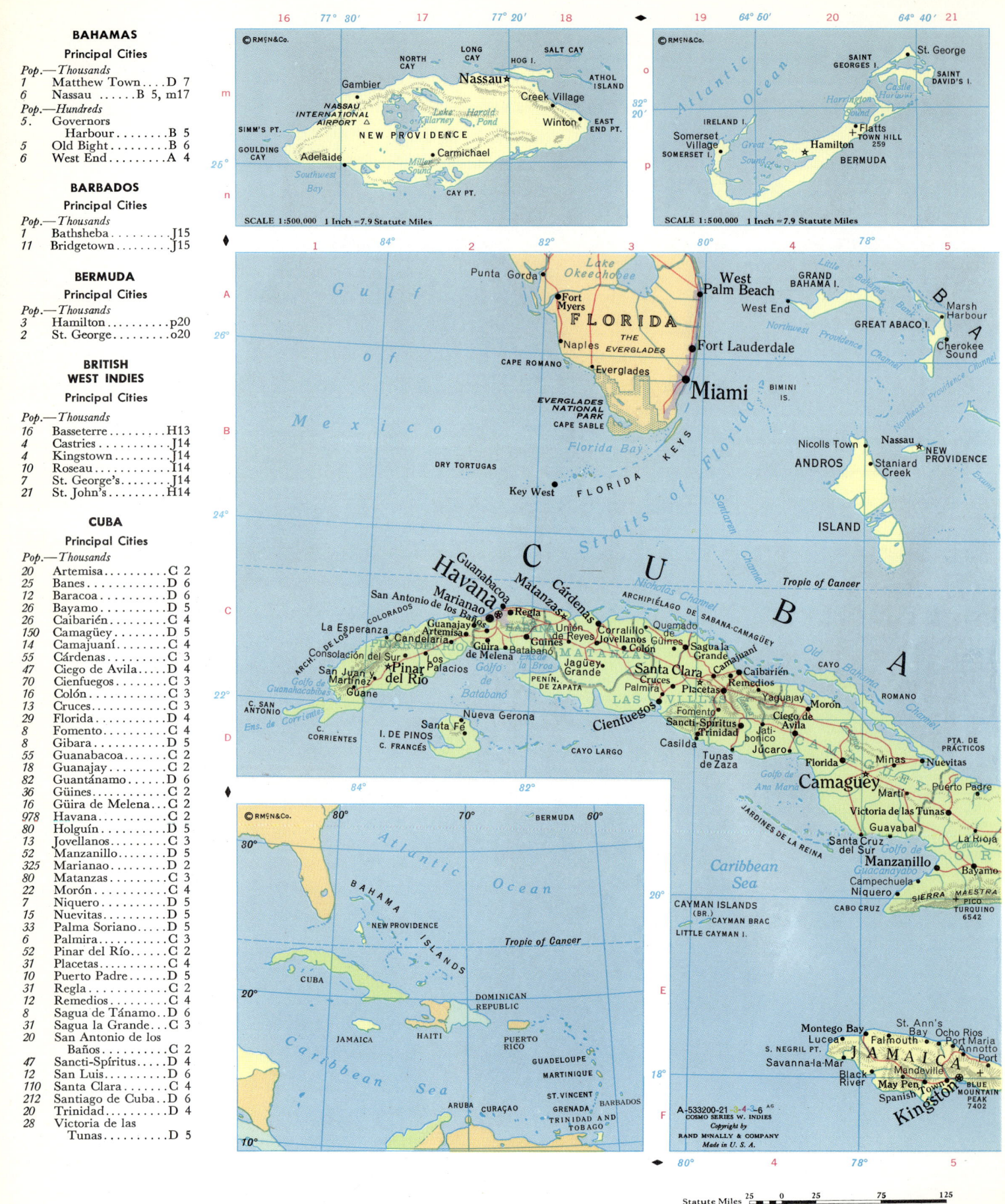

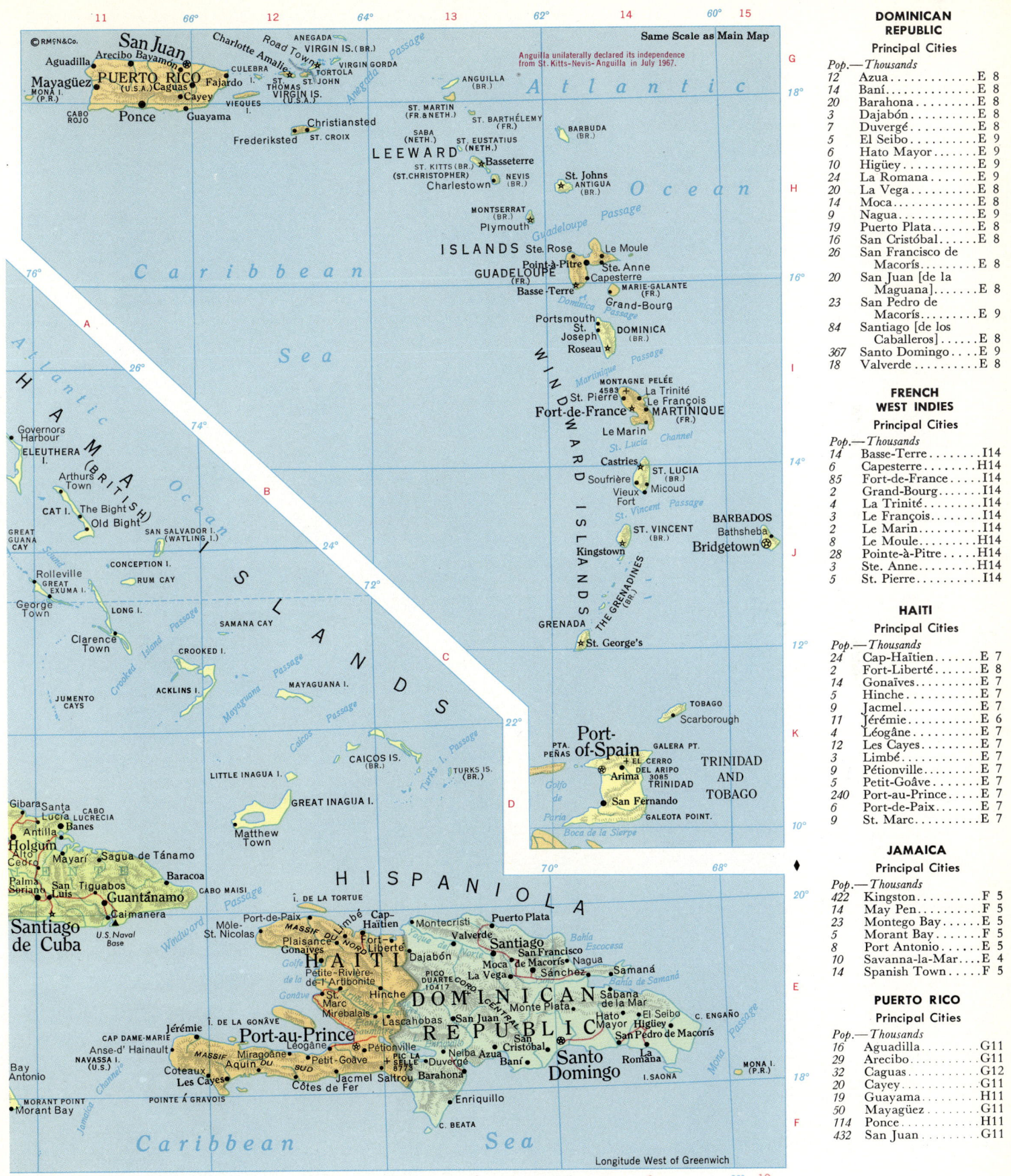

ATLAS 58   CANADA

CANADA
Physical Features

Albanel, lake	F19
Albany, riv	F16
Amadjuak, lake	C19
Amundsen, gulf	B 8
Arctic, ocean	k27
Aston, cape	B20
Athabasca, lake	E12
Athabasca, riv	E11
Atlantic, ocean	I20
Attawapiskat, riv	F16
Baffin, bay	n35, B19
Baffin, isl	n34, B19
Banks, isl	B 9
Barrow, strait	n31, B14
Beaufort, sea	B 4
Belle Isle, strait	F22
Black, lake	E12
Bonavista, bay	G23
Boothia, gulf	B15
Boothia, pen	B14
Breton, cape	G21
Brodeur, pen	B16
Bylot, isl	n35, B18
Caniapiscau	E20
Chidley, cape	D21
Churchill, riv	E14
Coast, mts	E 7
Cree, lake	E12
Cree, riv	E12
Cumberland, sound	C20
Davis, strait	B21
Dease, strait	C12
Devon, isl	m32, A15
Dolphin and Union, strait	C10
Dubawnt, lake	D13
Eau-Claire, lake	E18
Ellesmere, isl	k33, A16
Erie, lake	H17
Feuilles, riv	E19
Fort George, riv	F18
Foxe, pen	C18
Foxe, basin	C17
Foxe, channel	C17
Franklin, mts	C 8
Fundy, bay	H20
Garry, lake	C13
Goodhope, mtn	F 9
Great Bear, lake	C 9
Great Slave, lake	D11
Grizzly Bear, mts	C 9
Hamilton, inlet	F22
Hay, riv	E10
Hayes, riv	E15
Hazen, strait	m28, A11
Hecate, strait	F 7
Henrietta Maria, cape	E17
Home, bay	C20
Hopes Advance, cape	D20
Horn, mts	D10
Hudson, bay	D16
Hudson, strait	D19
Hunt, mtn	D 8
Huron, lake	G17
Island, lake	F15
James, bay	F17
James Ross, strait	B14
Keele, peak	D 7
Kellett, cape	B 8
Lake of the Woods, lake	G15
Lancaster, sound	n33, B16
Larch, riv	E19
Liard, riv	E 8
Liverpool, bay	B 7
Logan, mts	D 5
Mackenzie, bay	C 6
Mackenzie, mts	C 7
Mackenzie, riv	C 7
Maclean, strait	m29, A12
Manitoba, lake	F14
Manitoulin, isl	G17
McClintock, channel	B13
Melville, isl	m29, A10
Melville, lake	F21
Mercy, cape	C21
Michikamau, lake	F21
Minto, lake	E18
Mistassini, lake	F18
Nass, riv	E 8

ATLAS 60 — WESTERN UNITED STATES

WESTERN UNITED STATES
Principal Cities

Pop.—Thousands

Pop	City	Grid
23	Aberdeen, S. Dak.	A 8
90	Abilene, Tex.	D 8
22	Alamogordo, N. Mex.	D 6
201	Albuquerque, N. Mex.	C 6
138	Amarillo, Tex.	C 7
44	Anchorage, Alsk.	F 4
14	Arkansas City, Kans.	C 8
12	Artesia, N. Mex.	D 7
187	Austin, Tex.	D 8
57	Bakersfield, Calif.	C 4
28	Bartlesville, Okla.	C 8
35	Bellingham, Wash.	A 3
111	Berkeley, Calif.	C 3
31	Big Spring, Tex.	D 7
53	Billings, Mont.	A 6
31	Bismarck, N. Dak.	A 7
72	Boise, Idaho	B 4
38	Boulder, Colo.	C 6
29	Bremerton, Wash.	A 3
12	Brigham City, Utah	B 5
48	Brownsville, Tex.	E 8
28	Butte, Mont.	A 5
26	Carlsbad, N. Mex.	D 7
5	Carson City, Nev.	C 4
39	Casper, Wyo.	B 6
44	Cheyenne, Wyo.	B 7
24	Clovis, N. Mex.	D 7
14	Coeur d'Alene, Idaho	A 4
17	Coffeyville, Kans.	C 8
70	Colorado Springs, Colo.	C 7
168	Corpus Christi, Tex.	E 8
21	Corvallis, Oreg.	B 3
56	Council Bluffs, Iowa	B 8
680	Dallas, Tex.	D 7
494	Denver, Colo.	C 7
277	El Paso, Tex.	D 6
18	Emporia, Kans.	C 8
39	Enid, Okla.	C 8
51	Eugene, Oreg.	B 3
40	Everett, Wash.	A 3
13	Fairbanks, Alsk.	E 4
50	Fargo, N. Dak.	A 8
24	Farmington, N. Mex.	C 6
14	Fergus Falls, Minn.	A 8
25	Flagstaff, Ariz.	C 5
25	Fort Collins, Colo.	B 6
356	Fort Worth, Tex.	D 8
20	Fremont, Nebr.	B 8
134	Fresno, Calif.	C 4
123	Glendale, Calif.	D 4
38	Grand Forks, N. Dak.	A 8
26	Grand Island, Nebr.	B 8
19	Grand Junction, Colo.	C 6
55	Great Falls, Mont.	A 5
26	Greeley, Colo.	B 7
41	Harlingen, Tex.	E 8
21	Hastings, Nebr.	B 8
20	Helena, Mont.	A 5
26	Hilo, Haw. Is.	F 7
26	Hobbs, N. Mex.	D 7
294	Honolulu, Haw. Is.	F 6, F 7
938	Houston, Tex.	E 8
14	Huron, S. Dak.	B 8
38	Hutchinson, Kans.	C 8
36	Idaho Falls, Idaho	B 5
7	Juneau, Alsk.	F 5
28	Kailua, Haw. Is.	F 6
14	Kearney, Nebr.	B 8
6	Ketchikan, Alsk.	F 5
17	Klamath Falls, Oreg.	B 3
18	Laramie, Wyo.	B 6
61	Laredo, Tex.	E 8
29	Las Cruces, N. Mex.	D 6

ATLAS 61

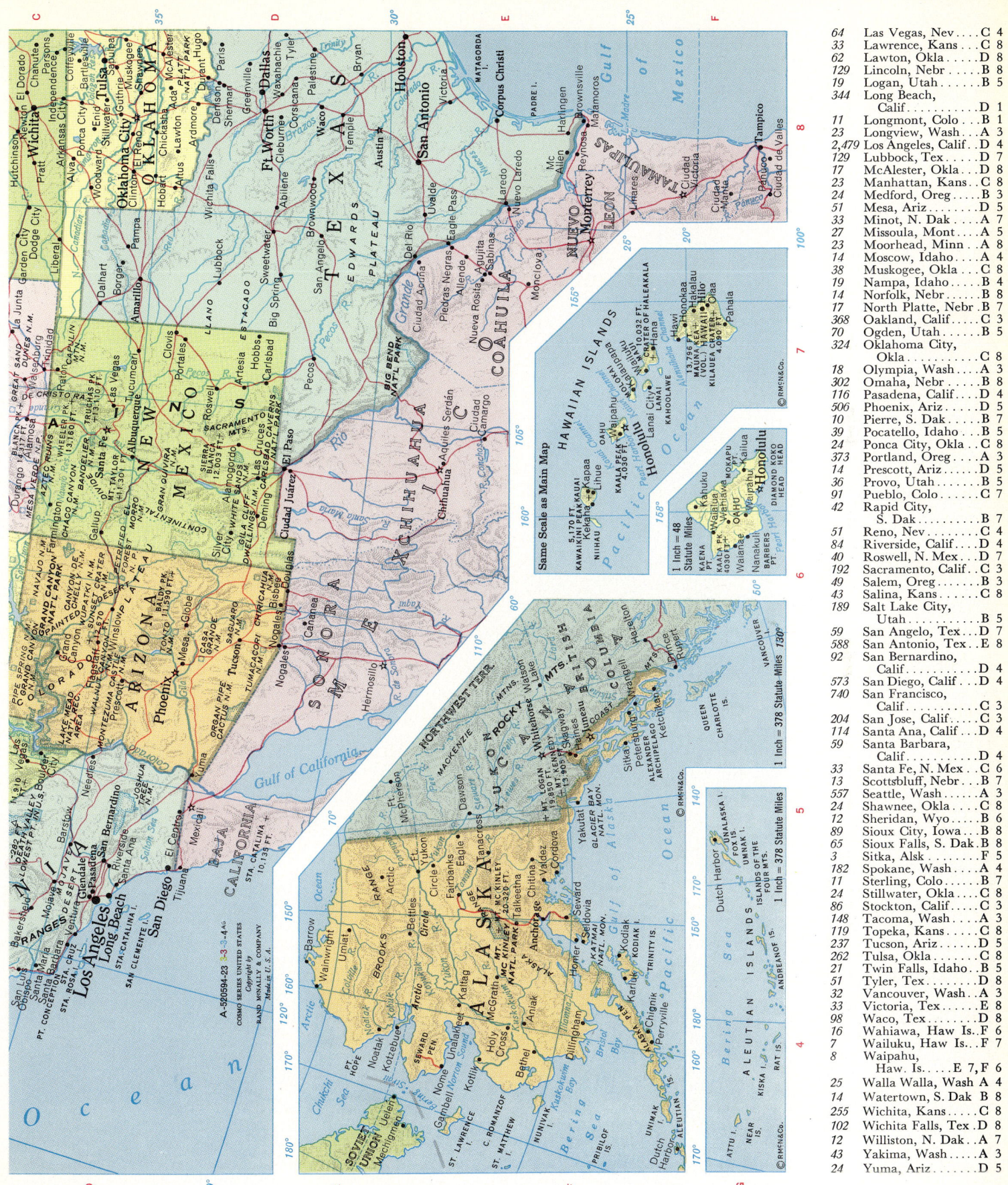

64	Las Vegas, Nev	C 4
33	Lawrence, Kans	C 8
62	Lawton, Okla	D 8
129	Lincoln, Nebr	B 8
19	Logan, Utah	B 5
344	Long Beach, Calif	D 4
11	Longmont, Colo	D 1
23	Longview, Wash	A 3
2,479	Los Angeles, Calif	D 4
129	Lubbock, Tex	D 7
17	McAlester, Okla	D 8
23	Manhattan, Kans	C 8
24	Medford, Oreg	B 3
51	Mesa, Ariz	D 5
33	Minot, N. Dak	A 7
27	Missoula, Mont	A 5
23	Moorhead, Minn	A 8
14	Moscow, Idaho	A 4
38	Muskogee, Okla	C 8
19	Nampa, Idaho	B 4
14	Norfolk, Nebr	B 8
17	North Platte, Nebr	B 7
368	Oakland, Calif	C 3
70	Ogden, Utah	B 5
324	Oklahoma City, Okla	C 8
18	Olympia, Wash	A 3
302	Omaha, Nebr	B 8
116	Pasadena, Calif	D 4
506	Phoenix, Ariz	D 5
10	Pierre, S. Dak	B 7
39	Pocatello, Idaho	B 5
24	Ponca City, Okla	C 8
373	Portland, Oreg	A 3
14	Prescott, Ariz	D 5
36	Provo, Utah	B 5
91	Pueblo, Colo	C 7
42	Rapid City, S. Dak	B 7
51	Reno, Nev	C 4
84	Riverside, Calif	D 4
40	Roswell, N. Mex	D 7
192	Sacramento, Calif	C 3
49	Salem, Oreg	B 3
43	Salina, Kans	C 8
189	Salt Lake City, Utah	B 5
59	San Angelo, Tex	D 7
588	San Antonio, Tex	E 8
92	San Bernardino, Calif	D 4
573	San Diego, Calif	D 4
740	San Francisco, Calif	C 3
204	San Jose, Calif	C 3
114	Santa Ana, Calif	D 4
59	Santa Barbara, Calif	D 4
33	Santa Fe, N. Mex	C 6
13	Scottsbluff, Nebr	B 7
557	Seattle, Wash	A 3
24	Shawnee, Okla	C 8
12	Sheridan, Wyo	B 6
89	Sioux City, Iowa	B 8
65	Sioux Falls, S. Dak	B 8
3	Sitka, Alsk	F 5
182	Spokane, Wash	A 4
11	Sterling, Colo	B 7
24	Stillwater, Okla	C 8
86	Stockton, Calif	C 3
148	Tacoma, Wash	A 3
119	Topeka, Kans	C 8
237	Tucson, Ariz	D 5
262	Tulsa, Okla	C 8
21	Twin Falls, Idaho	B 5
51	Tyler, Tex	D 8
32	Vancouver, Wash	A 3
33	Victoria, Tex	E 8
98	Waco, Tex	D 8
16	Wahiawa, Haw Is	F 6
7	Wailuku, Haw Is	F 7
8	Waipahu, Haw. Is	E 7, F 6
25	Walla Walla, Wash	A 4
14	Watertown, S. Dak	B 8
255	Wichita, Kans	C 8
102	Wichita Falls, Tex	D 8
12	Williston, N. Dak	A 7
43	Yakima, Wash	A 3
24	Yuma, Ariz	D 5

Lambert Conformal Conic Projection
SCALE 1:12,000,000   1 Inch = 189 Statute Miles

ATLAS 62

EASTERN UNITED STATES

EASTERN UNITED STATES
Principal Cities

Pop.—Thousands

Pop.	City	Ref.
290	Akron, Ohio	C 3
56	Albany, Ga.	E 3
130	Albany, N.Y.	C 5
40	Alexandria, La.	E 1
91	Alexandria, Va.	D 4
108	Allentown, Pa.	C 4
69	Altoona, Pa.	C 4
41	Anderson, S.C.	E 3
23	Annapolis, Md.	D 4
60	Asheville, N.C.	D 3
41	Athens, Ga.	E 3
487	Atlanta, Ga.	E 3
60	Atlantic City, N.J.	D 5
71	Augusta, Ga.	E 3
22	Augusta, Maine	C 6
939	Baltimore, Md.	D 4
39	Bangor, Maine	C 6
152	Baton Rouge, La.	E 1
119	Beaumont, Tex.	E 1
19	Biddeford, Maine	C 5
44	Biloxi, Miss.	E 2
69	Binghamton, N.Y.	C 4
341	Birmingham, Ala.	E 2
697	Boston, Mass.	C 5
157	Bridgeport, Conn.	C 5
533	Buffalo, N.Y.	C 4
114	Canton, Ohio	C 3
104	Cedar Rapids, Iowa	C 1
76	Charleston, S.C.	E 4
86	Charleston, W. Va.	D 3
202	Charlotte, N.C.	D 3
130	Chattanooga, Tenn.	D 2
64	Chester, Pa.	D 4
3,550	Chicago, Ill.	C 2
503	Cincinnati, Ohio	D 3
812	Cleveland, Ohio	C 3
97	Columbia, S.C.	E 3
117	Columbus, Ga.	E 3
471	Columbus, Ohio	D 3
29	Concord, N.H.	C 5
60	Covington, Ky.	D 3
89	Davenport, Iowa	C 1
262	Dayton, Ohio	D 3
78	Decatur, Ill.	D 2
207	Des Moines, Iowa	C 1
1,670	Detroit, Mich.	C 3
7	Dover, Del.	D 4
57	Dubuque, Iowa	C 1
107	Duluth, Minn.	B 2
78	Durham, N.C.	D 4
82	East St. Louis, Ill.	D 1
138	Erie, Pa.	C 4
79	Evansville, Ill.	C 2
142	Evansville, Ind.	D 2
100	Fall River, Mass.	C 5
197	Flint, Mich.	C 3
84	Fort Lauderdale, Fla.	F 3
64	Fort Smith, Ark.	D 1
162	Fort Wayne, Ind.	C 2
18	Frankfort, Ky.	D 3
67	Galveston, Tex.	E 1
178	Gary, Ind.	C 2
177	Grand Rapids, Mich.	C 2
63	Green Bay, Wis.	C 2
120	Greensboro, N.C.	D 4
42	Greenville, Miss.	E 1
66	Greenville, S.C.	E 3
80	Harrisburg, Pa.	C 4
162	Hartford, Conn.	C 5
62	High Point, N.C.	D 4
84	Huntington, W. Va.	D 3
124	Huntsville, Ala.	E 2
476	Indianapolis, Ind.	D 2
144	Jackson, Miss.	E 1
34	Jackson, Tenn.	D 2
201	Jacksonville, Fla.	E 3
28	Jefferson City, Mo.	D 1
276	Jersey City, N.J.	C 5
31	Johnson City, Tenn.	D 3
82	Kalamazoo, Mich.	C 2
122	Kansas City, Kans.	D 1
476	Kansas City, Mo.	D 1

ATLAS 63

68	Kenosha, Wis	C 2
112	Knoxville, Tenn	D 3
50	Lafayette, La	E 1
63	Lake Charles, La	E 1
108	Lansing, Mich	C 3
71	Lawrence, Mass	C 5
63	Lexington, Ky	D 3
129	Little Rock, Ark	E 1
389	Louisville, Ky	D 2
92	Lowell, Mass	C 5
94	Lynn, Mass	C 5
70	Macon, Ga	E 3
158	Madison, Wis	C 2
88	Manchester, N.H.	C 5
498	Memphis, Tenn	D 2
49	Meridian, Miss	E 2
292	Miami, Fla	F 3
741	Milwaukee, Wis	C 2
483	Minneapolis, Minn	C 1
203	Mobile, Ala	E 2
52	Monroe, La	E 1
134	Montgomery, Ala	E 2
9	Montpelier, Vt	C 5
171	Nashville, Tenn	D 2
405	Newark, N.J.	C 5
102	New Bedford, Mass	C 5
152	New Haven, Conn	C 5
628	New Orleans, La	F 1
114	Newport News, Va	D 4
7,782	New York, N.Y.	C 5
102	Niagara Falls, N.Y.	C 4
305	Norfolk, Va	D 4
88	Orlando, Fla	F 3
34	Ottumwa, Iowa	C 1
42	Owensboro, Ky	D 2
34	Paducah, Ky	D 2
45	Parkersburg, W. Va	D 3
144	Paterson, N.J.	C 5
103	Peoria, Ill	C 2
2,003	Philadelphia, Pa	C 5
44	Pine Bluff, Ark	E 1
604	Pittsburgh, Pa	C 4
82	Pontiac, Mich	C 3
67	Port Arthur, Tex	F 1
73	Portland, Maine	C 5
27	Portsmouth, N.H.	C 5
115	Portsmouth, Va	D 4
187	Providence, R.I.	C 5
89	Racine, Wis	C 2
94	Raleigh, N.C.	D 4
98	Reading, Pa	C 4
220	Richmond, Va	D 4
97	Roanoke, Va	D 4
306	Rochester, N.Y.	C 4
132	Rockford, Ill	C 2
18	Rutland, Vt	C 5
98	Saginaw, Mich	C 3
80	St. Joseph, Mo	D 1
750	St. Louis, Mo	D 1
313	St. Paul, Minn	B 1
181	St. Petersburg, Fla	F 3
149	Savannah, Ga	E 6
82	Schenectady, N.Y.	C 5
111	Scranton, Pa	C 4
164	Shreveport, La	E 1
132	South Bend, Ind	C 2
44	Spartanburg, S.C.	E 3
83	Springfield, Ill	D 2
174	Springfield, Mass	C 5
96	Springfield, Mo	D 1
83	Springfield, Ohio	D 3
216	Syracuse, N.Y.	C 5
58	Tallahassee, Fla	E 3
275	Tampa, Fla	F 3
73	Terre Haute, Ind	D 2
318	Toledo, Ohio	C 3
114	Trenton, N.J.	C 5
63	Tuscaloosa, Ala	E 2
100	Utica, N.Y.	C 4
764	Washington, D.C.	D 4
107	Waterbury, Conn	C 5
72	Waterloo, Iowa	C 1
53	Wheeling, W. Va	C 3
64	Wilkes-Barre, Pa	C 4
96	Wilmington, Del	D 4
111	Winston-Salem, N.C.	D 3
187	Worcester, Mass	C 5
202	Yonkers, N.Y.	C 5
167	Youngstown, Ohio	C 3

Lambert Conformal Conic Projection
SCALE 1:12,000,000   1 Inch = 189 Statute Miles

ATLAS 64 — North America

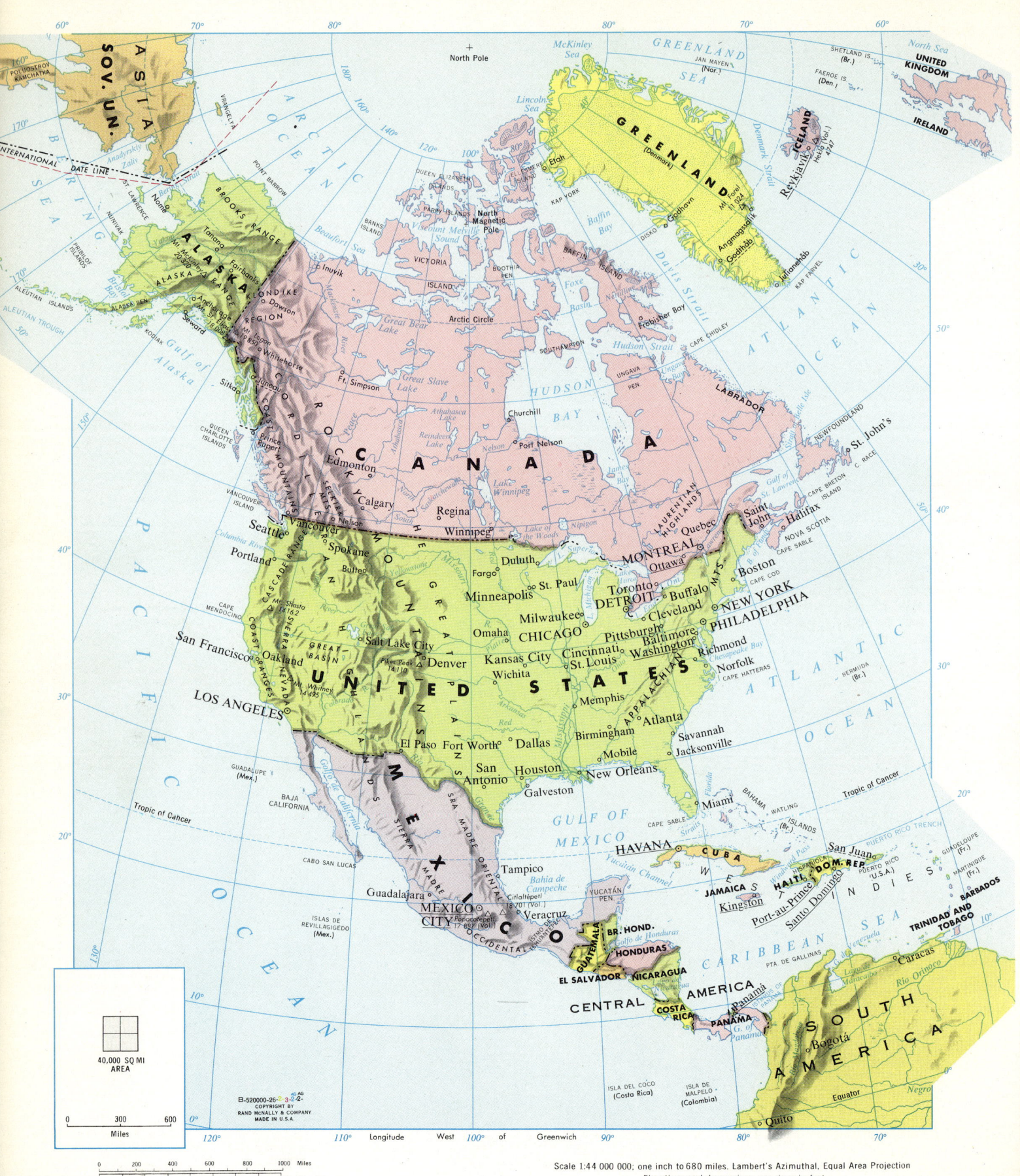

INDEX

A

Aare River 260c
Abadan, Iran 260a
Abbas the Great, Shah (Persia) 269c
Abboud, Ibrahim 278a
Abd-al-Aziz Al Saud 259b
Abd-al-Hamid II, Sultan (Turkey) 191a
Abd-al-Kader *see* Abd-al-Qadir
Abd-al-Krim 134b
Abd-al-Qadir 4a
Abd-al-Wahhab, Muhammad ibn *see* Muhammad ibn Abd-al-Wahhab
Abd-ar-Rahman, King (Afghanistan) 2a
Abdullah al-Sallal 214c
Aberdare Mountains 237a
Abidjan, Ivory Coast 109a, 260a
Abomey 57a
Aborigines, Australian *see* Australian aborigines
Abu Dhabi 188b
 see also Trucial Oman
Abyssinia *see* Ethiopia
Acadia 30c
Academy of Sciences (Soviet Union) 278b, 287c
Acajutla, El Salvador 256a
Acapulco, Mexico 150a
Acción Democrática party (Venezuela) 210b
Accra, Ghana 79c–80a, 256a
Achimeta, Ghana
 Institute of public administration *il* 80
Achmed Zogu *see* Zog I, King (Albania)
Aconcagua (mountain) 5b, 37b, 237a
Acre, Bay of 268b
Acropolis (Athens)
 il 81
Act of Supremacy (England) 199c, 200a
Action Group (Nigeria) 141c
Adamawa Mountains 141a
Adams, Grantley 13c
Adana, Turkey 256a
Addis Ababa, Ethiopia 61c, 62a, 256a–256b
Adelaide, Australia 9a, 256b
Adelaide, University of 256b
Aden, South Yemen 165c, 256b
 map *Atlas*-25
Aden, Gulf of 237a
Adenauer, Konrad 79c
Adige River 106a
Adjas 56c
Adja-Watyi 187a
Adolphe of Nassau, Grand Duke 123c
Adoula, Cyrille 51b
Adouma 71b
Adrian IV, Pope 197b
Adrianople, Treaty of 82b
Adriatic Sea 237a
Adua, Battle of 62b
Aegean Sea 237a
Afars 225b
Afghan Wars 203b
Afghani (currency unit) 1a
Afghanistan 1a–2a, 101b
 agriculture 1b
 area 1a
 capital 1a
 climate 1a
 currency unit 1a
 economy 1b
 flag *il* ii
 foreign interference 1c–2a
 geography 1a
 government 1b
 history 1c–2a
 Iran and 101a–101b
 language 1a
 map 1, *Atlas*-28
 national holiday 1a
 official name 1a
 people of 1a
 population 1a
 religion 1a, 1c
—Cities 1a–1b
 Herat 1b

Kabul 1a, 1b, 270b
Kandahar 1b, 270c
Afonso I, King (Portugal) *see* Afonso Henriques, King (Portugal)
Afonso II, King (Portugal) 153c
Afonso Henriques, King (Portugal) 153c
Africa 237a
 map *Atlas*-34
African Democratic Rally (RDA)
 Upper Volta 207a
African National Congress (South Africa) 165b
Afrikaners 164b
 Botswana 17c
 Lesotho 120b
Afro-Shirazi Party (ASP) (Tanzania) 184c
Agalega Islands 128c
Agana, Guam 256b
Agincourt, Battle of 67a
Agni 109a
Agra, India 256b
Agram, Yugoslavia *see* Zagreb, Yugoslavia
Agriculture *see under individual countries, such as* Afghanistan, agriculture
Aguinaldo, Emilio 150b
Aguirre Cedra, Pedro 38c
Aguiyi-Ironsi, Johnson 142a
Agulhas, Cape *see* Cape Agulhas
Agusan River 237a
Ahaggar (mountains) 3c, 137a
Ahidjo, Ahmadou 26b
Ahmad, Imam (Yemen) 214c
Ahmad al-Mahdi, Muhammad *see* Muhammad Ahmad al-Mahdi
Ahmad Shah Durrani, King (Afghanistan) 1c, 271a
Ahmad ibn Said, Sultan (Muscat and Oman) 135c
Ahmadabad, India 94a, 256b
al Ahmadi, Kuwait 117c
Ahmadnagar, India 256c
Ahmed bey Zogolli *see* Zog I, King (Albania)
Ahmedabad, India *see* Ahmahabad, India
Ahomadegbé, Justin 57c
Ahvaz, Iran 256c
Ahvenanmaa Islands *see* Aland Islands
al-Ahzar University 262c
Ainu 112a
Air Mountains 140b, 140c, 237a
Aire River 273b
Akhal-Tekinsk Oasis 258a
Akita, Japan 256c
Akosombo, Ghana 79c
Akrotiri Bay 273c
Akyab, Burma 256c
al- *(for Arabic names beginning with al, see under the second part of the name)*
Ala Mountains 40a
Ala Tau Mountains 167a
Alai Mountains 167a, 283b
Aland Islands 62c, 63c, 237a
Alashan Desert 39c, 40a
Ala-ud-din Khalji 96b
Alaungpaya 23b
Albania 2–3
 agriculture 2b
 area 2a
 capital 2a
 climate 2b
 communism 2b, 3b
 currency unit 2a
 economy 2b
 flag *il* ii
 geography 2a
 government 2b
 history 2c–3b
 language 2a
 map 2, *Atlas*-18
 national holiday 2a
 official name 2a
 people of 2b
 population 2a
 religion 2a, 2b
—Cities
 Durrës 266a
 Elbasan 266b
 Shkodër 284b
 Tiranë 2a, 286c
 Vlonë 288c
Albanian Democratic Front 2c

Albert, Lake 50c, 191b, 264b
Albert Nile (river) 191b, 237b
Alberta (province), Canada 262c, 266b
Albertville, Congo (Kinshasa) 256c
Alcazar 264c
Aldabra Islands 220b, 220c
Alderney Island 222a
Aleksandra Land *see* Franz Josef Land
Alemanni 181b, 182b
Aleppo, Syria 256c
Alessandri, Arturo 38b, 38c
Alexander, King (Greece) 83a
Alexander III, King (Macedonia) *see* Alexander the Great
Alexander I, Tsar (Russia) 63b, 171c
Alexander II, Tsar (Russia) 172a
Alexander III, Tsar (Russia) 172a
Alexander III, King (Scotland) 198b
Alexander, King (Serbia) *see* Alexander, King (Yugoslavia)
Alexander, King (Yugoslavia) 216b
Alexander the Great
 Afghanistan 1c, 270c
 Alexandria 193a, 257b
 Egypt 193a, 257b
 India 95c
 Iran 101a
 Kandahar 270c
 Syria 183b
Alexander John I, Prince (Romania) *see* Cuza, Alexander
Alexandretta, Gulf of 237c
Alexandria, United Arab Republic (Egypt) 192c, 256c–257a
Alfonso XIII, King (Spain) 177a
Alfred the Great, King (Wessex) 196b
Algeria 3b–4b
 agriculture 3c–4a
 area 3b
 capital 3b
 currency unit 3b
 economy 3c–4a
 flag *il* ii
 French occupation 4a
 geography 3b
 government 4a
 history 4a
 independence struggle 4b
 language 3b
 map 3, *Atlas*-9, 12–13
 national holiday 3b
 official name 3b
 people of 3c
 population 3b
 religion 3b, 4a
—Cities
 Algiers 3b, 3c, 257a
 Annaba (Bône) 257c
 Colomb Bechar 264b
 Oran 279a
Algiers, Algeria 3b, 3c, 257a
Alhambra 268a
Ali al-Sanusi, Muhammad bin *see* Muhammad bin Ali al-Sanusi
Ali Khan, Liaqat 97c, 145c
Alia Mountains 237b
Alid dynasty 134a
Aligarh, India 257a
Allahabad, India 257a
Alleppey, India 257a
Alliance for Progress 51c
Alma Ata, Soviet Union 257a
Alps 237b
 Austria 10b
 France 64a, 64b
 Germany 73b
 Italy 106a
 Liechtenstein 122b
 Romania 155c
 Switzerland 181b
 Yugoslavia 215a
Alsace 64a, 65b, 69c, 70b, 77b, 77c
Alster River 268b
Altai Mountains 39c, 132b, 167a, 237b
Althing 92b, 92c
Altiplano 237c
Aluminum
 Cameroon 26a
 Jamaica 109c
 Japan 111c
 Surinam 235b
 U.S. 205c
Alvarado, Pedro de 84c
Alvarez, Juan 131a
Amadeo I, King (Spain) 177a

Amager Island 264c
Amanullah, King (Afghanistan) 2a
Amazon River 16a, 18a, 48b, 237c
Ambala, India 257a
American Colonization Society 121a–121b
American Popular Revolutionary Alliance (APRA) (Peru) 149b
American Samoa
 Pago Pago 279b
American University of Beirut 260a
Amerindians *see* Indians, American
Amhara (people) 62a
Amiens, Treaty of 188a
Amman, Jordan 113c, 257a
Amo Chu River 15b
Amoy, China 257b
Amravati, India 257b
Amritsar, India 257b
Amsterdam, Netherlands 136c, 137a, 257b
Amu Darya (river) *see* Amu River
Amu River 1a, 167a, 237c
Amur River 132b, 166c, 237c, 271c
An Lu-shan 43b
Anadyr River 239b
Anatolia (peninsula) 237c
Andaman Sea 237c
Andean Indians 148b
Andes Mountains 5b, 37b, 48a, 59b, 148a, 148b, 148c, 237c, 281c
Andhra Pradesh (state), India 269a
Andorra 4b–4c
 agriculture 4c
 area 4b
 capital 4b
 currency unit 4b
 economy 4c
 flag *il* ii
 geography 4b
 government 4c
 history 4c
 language 4b
 map 4, *Atlas*-23
 official name 4b
 people of 4c
 population 4b
 religion 4b, 4c
Andorra la Vella, Andorra 4b
Angara River 238a, 269b
Angel Falls 238a, *il* 242
Angkor, Cambodia 25a
Angles (people) 196a
Anglican Church *see* Church of England
Anglo-Afghan War (1839–1842) 2a
Anglo-Afghan War (1878–1879) 2a
Anglo-Saxons 196a
Angola 50a, 153c, 218–219
 agriculture 218a
 area 218a
 capital 218a
 economy 218b
 geography 218a
 government 218b
 history 218c–219a
 map *Atlas*-38
 people of 218a–218b
 population 218a
 religion 218b
 status 218a
—Cities
 Lobito 274a
 Luanda 218a, 274b
Anguilla Island 233
Anjouan Island 222c
Ankara, Turkey 189c, 257b
Ankara River 257b
Ankrah, J. A. 80c
Annaba, Algeria 257c
Annam 118c
Annam Cordillera (mountains) 118a, 210a, 211a, 238a
Anne, Queen (England) 201c–202a
Annobón Island 223b
 see also Equatorial Guinea
Antarctica 274a
Anti-Atlas Mountains *see* Atlas Mountains
Anti-Comintern Pact 113b
Anticosti Island 238a
Anti-Fascist Peoples Freedom League (AFPFL) (Burma) 23c, 24a
Antigua 219a
 area 219a

355

Antigua

Antigua (cont.)
  capital 219a
  population 219a
  St. John City 283a
  status 219a
Antigua, Guatemala 84c
  Cathedral of San José il 85
Antilles Archipelago 238a
Antioquia department, Colombia 276a
Anti-Semitism 78a, 78b
Antoinette, Marie see Marie Antoinette
Antonescu, Ion 157c
Antung, China 257c
Antwerp, Belgium 14a, 14b, 257c
Anup Sanksrit Library 261a
Aparri, Philippines 257c
Apennines (mountains) 106a, 238a, 261b
Apia, Western Samoa 213b, 257c–258a
Apies River 281a
Apithy, Sourou-Migan 57a
Aponte, José 53b
Appalachian Mountains 204c
Aqaba, Jordan 258a
Aqaba, Gulf of 105c, 113c, 193c, 238a, 266b
al-Arab, Shatt 244a
Arab League 118a, 120a
  flag il iv
Arabi, Ahmad 193b
Arabian Peninsula 134c, 238a
Arabian Sea 238a
Arab-Israeli War (1948-1949)
  Egypt 193b–193c
  Israel 104a, 105c
  Jordan 114a
Arab-Israeli War (1967)
  Israel 104a, 105c
  Jerusalem 270a
  Jordan 114b
  Sinai Peninsula 253a
  Syria 183c
  United Arab Republic (Egypt) 192b, 193c
Arad, Romania 258a
Arafura Sea 238a
Arakan Coast 238b
Arakan Mountains 238b
Araks River 166c
Aral, Lake see Aral Sea
Aral Sea 166c, 167a, 238b
  map Atlas-26
Ararat, Mount 189c, 238b, 289c
Araucanian Indians 37b, 38a
Aravalli Mountains 238b
Arawak Indians
  Barbados 13b
  Cuba 53b
  Haiti 88a
  Jamaica 110b
  Trinidad and Tobago 188a
Arc, Joan of see Joan of Arc
Arc de Triomphe (Paris) il 69
Arctic Ocean 238b
Ardennes (plateau) 64a, 238b
Arellano, Oswaldo López 89b
Arequipa, Peru 148b
Argentina 5–7, 147c, 148a
  agriculture 5c
  area 5a
  capital 5a
  currency unit 5a
  economy 5c–6b
  flag il ii
  geography 5a
  government 6a
  Indians 6a
  industry 6a
  language 6a
  map 6, Atlas-45–47
  national holiday 6a
  official name 6a
  people of 6b
  population 6a
  religion 6a
  trade 6a–7a
  —Cities 5b–5c
    Buenos Aires 5a, 5b, 262b–262c
    Comodoro Rivadavia 264b
    Cordoba 5b
    Mar del Plata 5b
    Rosario 5b
    Tucumán 5c
  —History 7a–8a
    Church-state relations 6b, 6c
    European exploration 6a
    federalism 6b
    independence 6a
    Peron era 6c–7a
    Spanish rule 6a
    War of the Triple Alliance 6b
    war with Bolivia 6b
    war with Brazil 207c
    war with Paraguay 147c
    World War I 6c
    World War II 6c
Argonne Plateau 238b
Argun (river) 237c
Arif, Abdel Rahman 102b
Arif, Abdel Salaam 102b
Arkansas River 205a
Arkhangel'sk, Soviet Union 258a
Armas, Carlos Castillo see Castillo Armas, Carlos
Armenian Highlands 240b
Armenian Soviet Socialist Republic 289c
Armenians 168a
Arnhem Land (Australia) 240b
Arno River 106a, 106b, 106c, 238c, 266c
Arnold, Benedict 31a
Arosa, Switzerland il 182
Arosemena Gómez, Otto 60c
Arosemena Monroy, Carlos Julio 60c
Árpád, Prince (Hungary) 90b
Arquello, Leonardo 140b
Arrashia Lake 120c
Artibonite River 87c
Artigas, José Gervasio 207c
Aruba Island 229a
Aryana
  Afghanistan 1c
Aryans
  Afghanistan 1c
  Ceylon 36a
  India 95b
Asahigawa, Japan 258a
Asama Volcano 238c
Ascension Island 233a
Aserradores Island 264c
Ashanti 80b, 80c, 272c
  Ivory Coast 109b
Ashford Castle il 103b
Ashkhabad, Soviet Union 258a
Ashoka, King (India) see Asoka, King (India)
Asia 238c
  map Atlas-26–27
Asia Minor 237c
Asir Mountains 158c
Asmara, Ethiopia 62a–62b, 258a
Asoka, King (India) 95c
Assam state, India 284c
Assiniboine River 289b
Astin Tagh (mountain) 39c
Asturian Mountains 176b
Asunción, Paraguay 147a, 147b, 258b
Aswan, United Arab Republic (Egypt) 192c, 258a
Aswan Dam 192c, 193c, 258a
Asyut, United Arab Republic (Egypt) 258b
Atacama Desert 37b, 238c
al-Atasi, Hashim 183c
Atatürk see Kemal, Mustafa
Atbara River 178a, 238c
Athabasca (lake) 238c
Athabasca (river) 238c
Athens, Greece 80c–81a, 258b
  Acropolis il 81
Atitlan, Lake il 85
Atlantic Ocean 238c
Atlas (maps) 291–354
Atlas Mountains 3b, 133b–133c, 238c
Atomic Test-Ban Treaty (1963) 182c
Attlee, Clement 204a
Aubame, Jean-Hilaire 72a
Auckland, New Zealand 138b, 138c, 258b–258c
Auckland, University of 258c
Auckland War Memorial Museum 258c
Augrabies Falls 164a
Augsburg, League of 201c
Augsburg, Peace of 76a–76b
Augustín I, Emperor (Mexico) see Iturbide, Augustín de
Augustine (missionary) 196a
Aurangzeb, Emperor (India) 96c
Aurelian, Emperor (Rome) 156b
Austral Islands 224c–225a
Australia 7a–10a
  agriculture 8a
  animal life 7c–8a
  area 7a
  capital 7a
  climate 7c
  Country Party 9a
  currency unit 7a
  economy 8a
  Eucumbene Dam il 7
  flag il ii
  geography 7a–8a
  Labor Party 9b
  language 7a
  map Atlas-42–43
  mining 8b
  national holiday 7a
  official name 7a
  people of 8a
  plant life 7c
  population 7a
  religion 7a
  trade 8b
  transportation 8b
  —Cities 8a
    Adelaide 256b
    Brisbane 262b
    Broadmeadows 8a
    Canberra 7a, 263a
    Geelong 8a
    Melbourne 8a, 276a
    Perth 280a
    Sydney 8a, 285c
  —History 8c–10a
    Colonial
      Christmas Island 222c
      Cocos Islands 222b–222c
      Nauru 235b
      New Guinea 230b–230c
      Norfolk Island 231b
      Papua 231b–231c
    convict system 8c, 9a
    World War I 9b–9c
    World War II 10a
  —Natural features 7b
    Cape York Peninsula 240a
    Carpentaria, Gulf of 240b
    Eyre, Lake 244a
    Gibson Desert 244c
    Great Australian Bight 245a
    Great Barrier Reef 245a
    Great Dividing Range 245a
    Great Sandy Desert 245a
    Great Victoria Desert 245a
    King Leopold Ranges 247b
    Macdonnell Ranges 248b
    Murray-Darling river system 249c–250a
    Tasmania 253c
Australian Aborigines 8a, 8c
Australian Alps 7b
Australian Capital Territory 7a, 263a
Australian Colonies Government Act 9a
Australian National University 263a
Austria 10b–12b
  agriculture 11a
  Alps il 10
  Anschluss (union with Germany) 12a–12b
  area 10b
  capital 10b
  Christian Socialist Party 11c–12b
  climate 10c
  currency unit 10b
  Dual Monarchy of Austria-Hungary 11b, 91a
  economy 10c–11a
  flag il ii
  geography 10b–10c
  government 11a
  history 11a–12b
  in Hungary 90c–91a
  industry 10c–11a
  language 10b
  map 10, Atlas-17
  national holiday 10b
  official name 10b
  people of 10c
  population 10b
  religion 10c
  Social Democratic Party 11c–12b
  World War I 11b–11c, 77c, 91a
  World War II 12b, 70c, 78c
  in Yugoslavia 216b
  —Cities
    Salzburg 283b
    Vienna 10b, 10c, 288b
Austria-Hungary 11b–11c, 91a
Austrian Alps il 10
Austrian State Treaty 12b
Austrian Succession, War of 202b
Austro-Prussian War see Seven Weeks' War
Avars 156b
Avignon, France 66c
Avilés, Spain 176a
Awash River 62a, 238c–239a
Awolowo, Obafemi 141c
Axum, Kingdom of 178a
Avacucho, Peru 16c
Ayacucho, Battle of 149a
Aymara Indians
  Bolivia 16b
  Peru 148b
Ayuthia, Thailand 186a, 258c
Ayyubid dynasty 193a
Azana, Emperor (Ethiopia) 62b
Azande 178a
Azbine Mountains see Aïr Mountains
Azerbaijan 282a
Azerbaijanis 168a
Azikiwe, Nnamdi 141c–142a
Azios 56c
Azores (islands) 153a, 239a
Azov, Sea of 239c
Aztecs 129c, 130b–130c
Azurdía, Enrique Peralta 85b

B

Baalbek, Lebanon 258c
Baath Party (Syria) 183c
Bab el Mandeb see Mandeb Strait
Babur 1c, 96b
Babuyan Channel 239c
Babylonia 104c
Bacolod, Philippines 258c
Bacongo
  Angola 218a, 218c
  Congo (Brazzaville) 50a
  Congo (Kinshasa) 50a
Bactria
  Afghanistan 1c
Baden-Württemberg 285a
Badoglio, Pietro 108c
Báez, Buenaventura 59a
Baffin Bay 239a
Baffin Island 26c
Baganda 191c
Bagdad, Iraq 101c, 102a, 258c–259a
Baghdad, Iraq see Bagdad, Iraq
Baghmati River 135c
Bagirmi (sultanate) 37a
Bahamas 219b
  area 219b
  capital 219b
  map Atlas-56
  population 219b
  status 219b
Bahliuiu River 269a
Bahrain 12c–13a
  agriculture 12c
  area 12c
  capital 12c
  climate 12c
  currency unit 12c
  economy 12c
  flag il ii
  geography 12c
  government 12c
  history 13a
  language 12c
  Manama 12c
  map 12, Atlas-25
  official name 12c
  people of 12c

INDEX

population 12c
religion 12c
Bahrain Island 275b
Baht 185a
Baikal, Lake see Baykal, Lake
Baja California 239a
Bakongo see Bacongo
Bakony Mountains 89c
Baku, Soviet Union 168a, 259a
Balaguer, Joaquín 59b, 88b
Balali 50a
Balante 232a
Balaton, Lake 89c, 239a
Balboa (currency unit) 146a
Balboa, Vasco Núñez de 146b
Baldwin, Robert 31c–32a
Balearic Islands 175b, 239a
Baleswar (river) 244b
Balewa, Abubakar Tafawa 142a
Balfour, Arthur 105b
Balfour Declaration 105b
Bali 98c
Balkan Mountains 21a, 239a, 284c
Balkan Peninsula 284a
  see also Albania; Bulgaria; Greece; Turkey; Yugoslavia
Balkan Wars
  Albania 3a
  Bulgaria 22a
  Greece 83a
  Yugoslavia 216b
Balkhash, Lake 166c, 239a
Balmaceda, José Manuel 38b
Balsas Valley 129c
Baltic peoples 167c
Baltic Sea 150c, 151a, 152a, 239a–239b, 267a, 267b
Baluhya 132b
Bamako, Mali 126c–127a, 259a
Bamangwato 17b
Bambara 126c
Bamileke 25c
Bamina, Joseph 24b
Banaras, India il 94, 259a
Banaras Hindu University 259a
Banaras Sanskrit College 259a
Banat 157c
Banda (people) 35b
Banda, Hastings 125a
Banda Sea 239b
Bandama River 109a
Bandaranaike, S. W. R. D. 36b
Bandung, Indonesia 98c, 259a
Bangalore, India 94a, 259a
Bangka Island 99a
Bangkok, Thailand 185a, 185b, 186b, 259b
Bangui, Central African Republic 35a, 259b
Bangweulu, Lake 217a, 239b
Bankole-Bright, H. C. 161a
Bantus
  Angola 218a, 218c
  Cameroon 26a
  Botswana 16b
  Congo (Kinshasa) 50c
  Gabon 71b
  history 26a, 124c, 165a
    Monomotapa 155b
    Zimbabwe 155b
  Lesotho 120b
  Malawi 124b
  Mozambique 229a, 229c
  Rhodesia 155a
  Somali Republic 163a, 163b
  South Africa 164b
  South West Africa 234c
  Swaziland 179a
  Tanzania 184a
  Uganda 191a
  Zambia 217c
Banyankole 191c
Bao-Dai, Emperor (Vietnam) 213a
Bara 123c
Barada River 265a
Barakzay tribe 2a
Barbados 13a–13c
  agriculture 13a, 13b
  area 13a
  Bridgetown 13a, 262a
  capital 13a
  climate 13a
  currency unit 13a
  economy 13a–13b
  flag il ii
  geography 13a
  government 13b
  history 13b–13c
  language 13a
  map Atlas-57
  national holiday 13a
  official name 13a
  people of 13a
  population 13a

religion 13a
slavery 13b–13c
World War I 13c
Barbados Labor Party (BLP) 13c
Barbary States 122b
Barcelona, Spain 175c, 176a, 259b–259c
Bareilly, India 259c
Barents Sea 239b
Baribas 56b
Baring, Evelyn 193b
Baroda, India 259c
Barrios, Justo Rufino 85a, 89b
Barrow, Errol 13c
Basel, Switzerland 181c, 259c
Bashkir Soviet Socialist Republic 287c
Bashkirs 168a
Basle, Switzerland see Basel, Switzerland
Basoga 191c
Basques 175b, 176b
Basra, Iraq 102a, 259c
Bassein, Burma 259c
Basse-Terre, St. Kitts-Nevis-Anguilla 233a, 259c
Basse-Terre Island 227a
Bastidas, Rodrigo de 146b
Basuto (people) 120b
Basutoland 120a, 120c
  see also Lesotho
Basutoland African Congress 120c
Bata, Spanish Guinea 259c
Bataan Peninsula 150b
Batavian Republic 137b
Batéké 50a
Bathurst, Gambia 72a, 259c–260a
Batista, Fulgencio 53c
Batlle y Ordóñez, José 208a
Battles see under the latter part of the name, such as Agincourt, Battle of
Batumi, Soviet Union 260a
Baule 109a
Baunsgaard, Hilmar 58b
Bauxite
  France 64b
  French Guiana 224c
  Ghana 80a
  Guinea 86a
  Guyana 86c
  Haiti 87c
  Hungary 90a
  Indonesia 99b
  Jamaica 109a
  Mozambique 229b
  Nepal 135c
  Nicaragua 139c
  Soviet Union 168b
  Surinam 235b
  United Kingdom 194c
  Upper Volta 206c
  Venezuela 209b
  Yugoslavia 215c
Bavaria, Germany il 73
Bay Islands (Islas de la Bahía) 88c, 89b
Baykal, Lake 132b, 167a, 239b, 269b
Bayrut, Lebanon see Beirut, Lebanon
Beaufort Sea 239b
Beberibe River 282a
Bechuanaland see Botswana
Bechuanaland Democratic Party 17c
Becket, Saint Thomas à 197b
Bede 196a
Beersheba, Israel 260a
Béga Canal 286c
Behaine, Pigneau de 212b
Beira, Mozambique 260a
Beirut, Lebanon 119b, 260a
Beja 178a
Belalcázar, Sebastian de 60b
Belaúnde Terry, Fernando 149b
Balaya River 287c
Belém, Brazil 260a–260b
Belfast, Ireland 260b
Belgian Congo 15a
  see also Congo (Kinshasa)
Belgium 14a–15b
  agriculture 14b
  area 14a
  capital 14a
  currency unit 14a
  economy 14b
  flag il ii
  geography 14a
  government 14b
  language 14a
  map 14, Atlas-22
  national holiday 14a
  official name 14a
  people of 14a

population 14a
religion 14a, 14c
—Cities 14a
  Antwerp 14a, 14b, 257c
  Brussels 14a, 14b, 262b
  Charleroi 14a
  Ghent 14a, 14b
  Liège 14a, 273c
  Louvain 14a
—History 14c–15b
  African empire 15a
    Burundi 24b
    Congo 51a
    Rwanda 157c
  World War I 15a
  World War II 15a, 78c, 204a
Belgrade, Yugoslavia 214c, 215b, 260b
Belgrade, University of 260a
Belitung (Billiton) Island 99a
Belize, British Honduras 220a, 260b
Belize River 260b
Bello, Ahmadu 141c
Belo Horizonte, Brazil 18b, 260b
Ben Bella, Ahmed 4b
Benavides, Oscar 149b
Benelux Customs Union 14a, 123a, 136c
Beneš, Eduard 56a
Bengal, Bay of 93c, 239c, 262c, 265a
Bengazi, Libya 122a, 260b–260c
Benghazi, Libya see Bengazi, Libya
Beni River 16a
Benins River 283c
Berbers
  Algeria 3c, 4a
  Ifni 227c, 228a
  Libya 121c
  Mauritania 128b
  Morocco 133c, 134a
  Spain 176b
  Tunisia 189a, 189b
  see also Tuareg
Berbice River 86c
Berezina River 243b
Bergdama 234c
Bergen, Norway 142b, 260c
Bergen, University of 260c
Bering Sea 239b
Bering Strait 239b
Berlin, Germany 73a, 73c, 74c, 260c
Berlin, Treaty of (1878) 22a, 157a, 216a
Berlin blockade 79a
Berlin Conference on African Affairs (1884) 50a–51a
Berlin wall 79b
Bermuda 219–220
  area 219c
  capital 219c
  economy 219c
  geography 219c
  government 219c
  Hamilton 268c
  history 219c–220a
  map Atlas-56
  people of 219c
  population 219c
  slavery 219c
  status 219c
Bermudez, Juan de 219c
Bern, Switzerland 181b, 181c, 260c
Bern (canton), Switzerland 260c
Bernadotte, Jean Baptiste 180c–181a
Berne, Switzerland see Bern, Switzerland
Bessarabia 157a, 272a
Bétancourt, Romulo 59b, 210b
Bethlehem, Jordan 260c
Betsiboka River 123c
Betsileo 123c
Betsimisaraka 123c
Beyrouth, Lebanon see Beirut, Lebanon
Bhadgeon, Nepal 135c
Bhagirathi River see Hooghly River
Bhavnagar, India 260c
Bhils 94c
Bhima River 239b
Bhopal, India 260c
Bhotias 15b
  Sikkim 161b
Bhubaneswar, India 260c–261a
Bhutan 15b–15c
  agriculture 15b
  area 15b
  capital 15b
  climate 15b
  communism 15c

currency unit 15b
economy 15b–15c
flag il ii
geography 15b
government 15c
history 15c
language 15b
map 15, Atlas-29
official name 15b
people of 15b
population 15b
religion 15b
Thimbu 15b
Biafra 142a
Bialystok, Poland 261a
Bié Plateau 239b
Biha, Léopold 24b
Bihar State, India 95c, 270a, 279c, 281c
Bihor Mountains 155c, 239b
Bijagos Archipelago 231c
Bika Valley 258c
Bikaner, India 261a
Bilauktaung Mountains 185b, 239b
Bilbao, Spain 175c, 176a
Bille River 268c
Bío-Bío River 37b, 264c
Birmingham, England 261a
Biscay, Bay of 239c
Bismarck, Otto von 69c, 77a, 77b
Bismarck Archipelago 230b
Bissau, Portuguese Guinea 231c, 261a
Biwa, Lake 239c
Bizerte, Tunisia 189a, 261a
Black Forest (mountains) 73b, 239c
Black River 211a
Black Sea 152a, 239c
Black Volta River 79c
Blanc, Louis 69b
Blanc, Cape see Cape Blanc
Blancos Party (Uruguay) 207c
Blantyre, Malawi 124b
Bligh, William 8c
Bloemfontein, South Africa 261a
Blue Mountains 7b, 13c
Bluetooth, Harold 58a
Blum, Léon 70c
Bobo 206b
Bobo Dioulasso, Upper Volta 206b, 261a
Boden, Lake see Constance, Lake
Boer War 203b, 288a
Boers see Afrikaners
Boganda, Barthelemy 35b
Bogotá, Colombia 48a, 48b–48c, 261a–261b
Bohemia 55b–56a
Bohemian Forest 54c, 239c
Bohul, Philippines 149c
Bokassa, Jean Bedel 35b
Bolan Pass 281b
Bolívar (currency unit) 208c
Bolívar, Simón 16c, 49a, 60b, 149a, 209c–210a, 263a
Bolivia 6b, 16–17, 148a
  agriculture 16b
  area 16a
  capital 16a
  currency unit 16a
  economy 16b–16c
  geography 16a
  government 16c
  language 16a
  map 16, Atlas-51
  mining 16a
  national holiday 16a
  official name 16a
  people of 16a–16b
  population 16a
  religion 16a
—Cities 16b
  Cochabamba 16b
  La Paz 16b, 273a
  Oruru 16b
  Potosí 16b
  Santa Cruz 16b
  Sucre 16a, 16b, 285c
  Tarija 16b
—History 16c–17a
  Spanish rule 16c
  war with Chile 38b
  war with Paraguay 148a
  World War I 17a
Bologna, Italy 261b
Bolshevik Revolution 70b, 173a–173b
Bombay, India 94a, 261b
Bombay, University of 261b
Bomi Hills, 121a
Bon, Cape see Cape Bon
Bonaire Island 229a

Bonaparte, Charles Louis Napoleon
  see Napoleon III
Bonaparte, François Charles Joseph
  see Napoleon II
Bonaparte, Joseph 209c
Bonaparte, Louis Napoleon see Napoleon III, Emperor (France)
Bonaparte, Napoleon see Napoleon I, Emperor (France)
Bône, Algeria see Annaba, Algeria
Bongo, Bernard-Albert 72a
Boniface VIII, Pope 66c
Bonin Islands 17b
Bonn, Germany 73a, 261b
Bonny River 280c
Bordeaux, France 64b–65b, 261b
Borden, Robert 33c–34a
Borgia family 158b
Boris, Emperor (Bulgaria) 21c
Borneo 99a, 239c, 270a, 272b
Bornholm Island 57a
Bornu 37a
Boru, Brian see Brian Boru, King (Ireland)
Börzsöny Mountains 89c
Bosch, Juan 59b
Bosna River 215a
Bosnia 77c
Bosnia and Herzegovina 283c
Bosporus (strait) 189c, 239c, 269c
Botany Bay 8c
Botha, Louis 165b
Bothnia, Gulf of 239c
Botlek 282b
Botswana 17
  agriculture 17b
  area 17b
  capital 17b
  cattle 17b
  climate 17b
  currency unit 17b
  economy 17b–17c
  flag il ii
  Gaberones 17b, 267a
  geography 17b
  government 17c
  history 17c
  language 17b
  map 17, Atlas-40
  national holiday 17b
  official name 17b
  people of 17b
  population 17b
  religion 17b
Bou Regneg (river) 281c
Bouches-du-Rhône (department), France 275c
Bougainville Island 230b
Bourbon Island 232c
Bourbon kings
  France 67c–68c, 69a
  Spain 177a
Bourguiba, Habib 189b, 189c
Bow River 262c
Boxer Rebellion 45c
Boyne, Battle of 103c
Bragança dynasty 154a
Brahmaputra River 15b, 93a–93b, 144a, 239c
Braila, Romania 261c
Brandt, Willy 79a
Brasilia, Brazil 18a, 18c, 261c
Brasov, Romania 156a
Bratislava, Czechoslovakia 55a, 261c
Brazil 6b, 18–20
  agriculture 18a, 19a
  area 18a
  capital 18a
  currency unit 18a
  economy 18c–19b
  flag il ii
  geography 18a–18b
  government 19b
  Indians 18c, 19c
  language 18a
  map 18, Atlas-48
  national holiday 18a
  official name 18a
  people of 18b–18c
  population 18a
  religion 18a, 20a
  slavery 18c, 19c, 20a
  transportation 19a
—Cities 18c
  Belem 260a
  Belo Horizonte 260b
  Brasilia 18a, 18c, 261c
  Curitiba 264c
  Fortaleza 266c
  Recife 282a
  Rio de Janeiro 18c, 282a
  Salvador 283b
  São Paulo 18c, 283c
  Volta Redonda 288c
—History 19b–20c
  Colonial era 19c–20a
  Empire 20a–20b
  Republic 20b
  Tordisillas, Treaty of 19b
  Vargas era 20b–20c
  war with Argentina 207c
  war with Paraguay 147c
  World War II 20b
Brazza, Pierre Savorgnan de 50a
Brazzaville, Congo (Brazzaville) 35b, 49c, 50a, 261c
Brechou Island 222a
Bremen, Germany 261c–262a
Bremersdorp, Swaziland 179a
Brest-Litovsk, Treaty of 173c
Brezhnev, Leonid 175a
Brian Boru, King (Ireland) 103a
Bridgetown, Barbados 13a, 262a
Brisbane, Australia 262a
Brisbane River 262a
Bristol, England 262a
Bristol Channel 262a, 263a
Bristol University 262a
British Antarctic Territory 220
  area 220a
  population 220a
  status 220a
British Cameroons see Cameroon
British Central Africa Protectorate 124c
British Columbia, Canada il 28, 288a, 288b
British East African Company 120c
British Honduras 220
  agriculture 220a
  area 220a
  Belize 260b
  capital 220a
  economy 220a–220b
  geography 220a
  government 220b
  history 220b
  people of 220a
  population 220a
  status 220a
British Indian Ocean Territory 220
  area 220b
  population 220b
  status 220b
British Isles 239c
  see also Ireland; United Kingdom
British Solomon Islands 220–221
  agriculture 220c
  area 220c
  capital 220c
  economy 220c
  geography 220c
  government 220c
  history 220c–221a
  Honiara 269c
  people of 220c
  population 220c
  status 220c
  World War II 220c–221a
British South Africa Company 124c, 155c, 217c
British Virgin Islands 221
  area 221a
  capital 221a
  population 221a
  Road Town 282b
  slavery 221a
  status 221a
Britons 195c
Brittany, France il 67
Brno, Czechoslovakia 55a, 262b
Broken Hill, Zambia 262a
Brooke, James 125c
Brown, George 32a
Broz, Josip see Tito, Josip Broz
Bruce, Robert see Robert I, King (Scotland)
Bruges, Belgium 14c
Brunei 221
  area 221a
  Brunei Municipal 262a
  capital 221a
  population 221a
  status 221a
Brunei Bay 262a
Brunei Municipal, Brunei 221a, 262a
Brünn, Czechoslovakia see Brno, Czechoslovakia
Brussels, Belgium 14a, 14b, 262b
Bryan-Chamorro Treaty 140b
Bubes 223b
Buchanan, Liberia 121a
Bucharest, Romania 155c, 156a, 262b
Bucharest, Peace of (1812) 156c
Bucharest, Treaty of 83a
Budapest, Hungary 89b, 90a, 262b
Budapest, University of 262c
Buddhism
  Afghanistan 1c
  Bhutan 15b
  Burma 22, il 23
  Cambodia 26c
  Ceylon 35c, 36a
  China 41a, 43b
  India 95c, 96c
  Indonesia 99a, 99b–99c
  Japan 110c, 112a–112b
  Korea 115c, 116b
  Laos 118a, 118c
  Malaysia 125c
  Mongolia 133b, 133c
  Nepal 135c, 136a
  Sikkim 161c
  Thailand 185b, 186a
  Vietnam 211b, 213b
Buenos Aires, Argentina 5a, 6a, 147c, 262b–262c
  Plaza del Mayo il 5
Buenos Aires, University of 262c
Buganda (kingdom) 191c–192a
Buganda Province, Uganda 270c
Bujumbura, Burundi 24a, 262c
Buka Island 230b
Bükk Mountains 89c
Bukovina 157a
Bulawayo, Rhodesia 262c
Bulgaria 21–22, 83a
  agriculture 22b, 23b
  Albania and 2c
  area 21a
  capital 21a
  communism 21b–21c, 22a–22b
  currency unit 21a
  economy 21a–21b
  flag il ii
  geography 21a
  government 21b–21c
  history 21a–22b
  language 21a
  map 21, Atlas-18
  national holiday 21a
  official name 21a
  people of 21a
  population 21a
  religion 21a, 21c
  Soviet Union and 22a–22b
  World War I 22a, 77c
  World War II 22a
—Cities 21a
  Burgas 21a, 282c
  Plovdiv 21a, 280b
  Ruse 21a, 282c
  Sofia 21a, 284c
  Varna 21a, 288a
Bungo Strait 110c
Burebistas 156b
Burgas, Bulgaria 21a, 262b
Burgas, Gulf of 262c
Burghers (people) 35c
Burgundians 75a
  Switzerland 181b, 182b
Burma 22–24, 22c
  agriculture 23a
  area 22b
  capital 22b
  climate 22b
  currency unit 22b
  economy 23a
  geography 22b–22c
  government 23a–24a
  language 22b
  map 22, Atlas-29
  national holiday 22b
  official name 22b
  people of 22c
  population 22b
  religion 22b
  World War II 23c
—Cities
  Akyab 256c
  Bassein 259c
  Lashio 273a
  Mandalay 22c, 275b
  Moulmein 277a
  Rangoon 22b, 281c
Burmans 22c, 23a–23b
  Thailand 186a
Burnham, Forbes 87a–87b
Burundi 24
  agriculture 24b
  area 24a
  Bujumbura (Usumbura) 24a, 262c
  capital 24a
  climate 24a
  currency unit 24a
  economy 24b
  flag il ii
  geography 24a
  government 24b
  history 24b
  language 24a
  map 24, Atlas-38
  national holiday 24a
  official name 24a
  people of 24b
  population 24a
  religion 24a
  World War I 24b
Buryat Autonomous Soviet Socialist Republic 287c
Buryat Mongols 168a
Bushmen 155b, 234c
Bustamante, Alexander 110b
By Fiord 260c
Byelorussian Soviet Socialist Republic 276b
Bystrzyca River 274c
Byzantine Empire 81b–81c, 190b–190c
  Albania 2c
  Algeria 4a
  Bulgaria 21c
  Cyprus 54b
  Istanbul (Constantinople) 269c
  Italy 107a
  Kievan Russia and 170a
  Malta 127c
  Palestine 105a
  Serbia 216a
  Tunisia 189b

C

Caamaño Deñó, Francisco 59b
Cabot, John 29c, 199c
Cabot, Sebastian 147b
Cabral, Donald Reid 59b
Cabral, Pedro Alvares 19c
Cabrera, Manuel Estrada 85a
Cabrera see Balearic Islands
Cacao
  Brazil 19a
  Cameroon 26a
  Colombia 48c
  Dominica 223b
  Dominican Republic 58c
  Ecuador 60a
  Equatorial Guinea 223c
  Fiji Islands 224b
  Ghana 80a
  Grenada 226a
  Haiti 87c
  Indonesia 99a
  Ivory Coast 109a
  New Guinea 230c
  Nicaragua 139c
  Nigeria 141c
  Panama 146b
  Papua 231b
  Peru 148c
  St. Lucia 233b
  Sao Tomé and Principe 234a
  Sierra Leone 160c
  Surinam 235b
  Togo 187a
  Trinidad and Tobago 187c
  Venezuela 209b
  Western Samoa 213c

INDEX

Cáceres, Ramón 59a
Cacheu River 232a
Cadiz, Spain il 176
Cadiz Province, Spain 263b
Caesar, Julius 14c, 66a, 137a, 182b
　invasion of Britain 195c
Cagayan River 239c–240a
Caicos Islands 236
Cairo, United Arab Republic (Egypt) 192b, 192c, 262c
Calais, France 67a, 67b
　Hundred Years' War 198c
Calcutta, India 94a, 262c
Calgary, Canada 262c
Calicut, India *see* Kozhikode, India
Callao, Peru 148b
Calles, Plutarco Elías 131c
Calvin, John 182b
Cam River 262c
Camacho, Manuel Avila 131c
Camaguey, Cuba 52c
Cambay, Gulf of 243a, 260c
Cambodia 24–25
　agriculture 24c
　area 24b
　capital 24b
　currency unit 24b
　economy 24c
　climate 24c
　flag *il ii*
　geography 24b–24c
　government 24c–25a
　history 25a–25b
　language 24b
　map 25, *Atlas*-30
　national holiday 24b
　official name 24b
　people of 24c
　population 24b
　Phnom Penh 24c, 280b
　religion 24b
　World War II 25b
Cambrian Mountains 194a
Cambridge, England 262c
Cambridge University 262c
Cameroon 25–26, 141c–142a
　agriculture 26a
　area 25c
　capital 25c
　climate 25c
　currency unit 25c
　economy 26a
　flag *il ii*
　geography 25c
　government 26a
　history 26a–26b
　language 25c
　map 26, *Atlas*-35
　national holiday 25c
　official name 25c
　people of 25c
　population 25c
　religion 25c
　—Cities 25c
　　Douala 25c, 265c
　　Edea 266a
　　Yaoundé 25c, 289b
Cameroon Mountain 240a
Cameroun *see* Cameroon
Campeche Bay 240a
Canada 26–35
　agriculture 26c, 28a–28b, 30b
　area 26b
　capital 26b
　climate 27a–27b
　currency unit 26b
　economy 28a–28c
　Eskimos 27b
　Expo '67 34c
　flag *il ii, il* 27, 34c
　geography 25b, 25c–26b
　government 28c–35a
　Indians 27b, 29c, 30a, 30c
　language 26b
　map 27, *Atlas*-58–59
　national holiday 26b
　official name 26b
　people of 27b–28a
　population 26b
　provinces 26c
　religion 26b, 27c, 30a, 31a, 33a
　U.S., relations with 31b, 32a, 32b, 32c, 33c, 34b, 34c, 35a
　—Cities 28a
　　Calgary 262c
　　Edmonton 266b
　　Fredericton 267c
　　Halifax 268b
　　Montreal 276c
　　Ottawa 279b
　　Quebec 281b
　　Regina 282a
　　Saint John's 283a
　　Sudbury 285b
　　Sydney 285c
　　Toronto 287a
　　Vancouver 288a
　　Victoria 288b
　　Winnipeg 289b
　—History 29a–35a
　　American Revolution 31a
　　assimilation policy 30c–31a
　　British North America Act (1867) 32b
　　British rule 30c–32a
　　Centennial 34c–35a
　　Commonwealth of Nations 34
　　Confederation 32a–32b
　　Dominion 32b–33c
　　European exploration 29b–29c
　　French rule 29c–30c
　　fur trade 29c, 30a–30b, 31b
　　Korean War 34b
　　Louis XIV 30a
　　New France 29c–30c
　　responsible government 32a
　　Riel rebellions 32c, 33a
　　Treaty of Paris (1783) 31a
　　Treaty of Washington (1871) 32c
　　World War I 33c
　　World War II 34b, 79a
Canadian National Railroad 28c
Canadian Pacific Railways 28c, 32c
Canary Islands 140a, 175b
Canberra, Australia 7a, 263c
Canellopoulos, Panayotis 83c
Cantabrian Mountains 240a
Canterbury, England 263c
Canterbury Plains 264c
Canton, China 44b, 44c–45a, 263c
Canute, King (England) 58a, 196b
Cão, Diogo 218c
Cape Agulhas 164a, 240a
Cape Blanc 240a
Cape Bon 240a
Cape Breton Island 26c, 285c
Cape Colony 120c
Cape Comorin 240a
Cape Diamond (Quebec, Canada) 281b
Cape Gardafui 240a
Cape of Good Hope 164a, 240a
Cape Horn 240a
Cape Montserrado 276c
Cape Province, South Africa 263a
Cape Range 164a
Cape Tortosa 243c
Cape Town, South Africa *il* 163, 164b, 263a
Cape Verde Islands 153c, 154a, 221, 232a
　area 221b
　capital 221b
　population 221b
　Praia 281a
　status 221b
Cape Verde Peninsula 265a
Cape York Peninsula 240a
Capet, Hugh *see* Hugh Capet
Capetians 66b–66c
Capibaribe River 282a
Capraia Island 105c
Capri Island 105c
Caracas, Venezuela 208c, 263c
Carbonari 107c
Cardamon Mountains 185b
Cardiff, Wales 263a
Cargados Carajos Islands 128c
Carías Andino, Tiburcio 89b
Carib Indians
　Aruba 229c
　British Honduras 220a
　Cuba 53b
　Dominica 223a
　Grenada 226c
　Martinique 228c
Caribbean Sea 240a
Carleton, Guy 31a
Carlos (Spanish kings) *see* Charles
Carlos de Bourbon, Don *see* Charles III, King (Spain)
Carlos I, King (Portugal) 154a
Carmel (mountain) 268b
Carol I, King (Romania) 156c, 157a
Carol II, King (Romania) 157a
Caroline Islands 240b
Carolingians 66a–66b
Caroni River 283c
Carpathian Mountains 54c, 154c, 166c, 240b
Carpentaria, Gulf of 7b, 240a
Carranza, Venustiano 131b–131c
Carrera, Rafael 85a, 89b
Carrillo, Braulio 52a
Cartagena, Colombia 48c, 49a
Cartagena, Spain 80c
Cartago, Costa Rica 52c
Cartier, Jacques 29c

Casablanca, Morocco 133c, 263a
Casamance River 159c
Cascade Mountains 204c
Casimir the Great 152a
Caspian Sea 240b
Castaneda, Jorge Ubico 85a
Castello Branco, Humberto 20c
Castilla, Ramón 149a
Castillo Armas, Carlos 85b
Castries, St. Lucia 233b, 263a
Castriota, George *see* Kastrioti, Gjergj
Castro, Fidel *il* 53, 53c
Castro Ruz, Raúl 53c
Castro, Salvador Castañeda 61b–61c
Catalans 175b
Cateau-Cambrésis, Treaty of 107c
Catherine, Queen (England) *see* Catherine of Aragon
Catherine of Aragon 199c, 200a
Catherine the Great *see* Catherine II, Empress (Russia)
Catherine de Médicis 67b
Catherine II, Empress (Russia) 68b, 171b
Catholic Popular Republican Movement (MRP) (France) 71a
Cattle
　Argentina 5c
　Australia 8a, 9b
　Botswana 17b
　British Virgin Islands 221a
　Chad 36c
　Channel Islands 222a
　Colombia 48c
　Denmark 57b
　Ifni 228a
　India 94b
　Italy 106c
　Ivory Coast 109a
　Mauritania 128c
　Mongolia 132c
　New Caledonia 230b
　New Zealand 138b
　Nicaragua 139c
　Niger 140c
　Paraguay 147b
　Rhodesia 155a
　Rwanda 157c
　South Africa 164b–164c
　South West Africa 234c
　Soviet Union 169a
　Spain 176a
　Swaziland 179a
　Switzerland 182a
　Tanzania 184a
　Tunisia 189a
　Turkey 190a
　Uganda 191c
　United States 206a
　Upper Volta 206c
　Uruguay 207a
Cauca River 48a–48b
Caucasus Mountains 166c, 240b, 268a
Cauvery River 93c, 283a, 287a
Cavour, Camillo Benso di 107c
Cawnpore, India 263b
Cayenne, French Guiana 224b, 263b
Cayenne River 263b
Cayman Islands 221–222
　area 221c
　capital 221c
　Georgetown 267c
　population 221c
　status 221c
Ceará State, Brazil 266c
Ceausescu, Nicholai 157a
Cebu, Philippines 149c, 150a
Cedars of Lebanon 119c
Cedi 79c
Celebes Island, Indonesia 99a, 275a
Celts
　Britain 194b, 195c, 196a
　France 65c
　Ireland 103a
　Isle of Man 228a, 228b
　Netherlands 137a
　Switzerland 181b
Central African Republic 35
　agriculture 35b
　area 35a
　Bangui 259b
　capital 35a
　currency unit 35a
　economy 35b
　flag *il ii*
　geography 35a–35b
　government 35b
　history 35b
　language 35a
　map 35, *Atlas*-35
　national holiday 35a
　official name 35a
　people of 35b

population 35a
religion 35a
Central American Andes 88c, 139b
Central American Common Market 51c, 52b, 84b, 85c, 89b
Central American Cordillera 84a
Central Asia (region) Soviet Union 267a
Central Cordillera (Philippines) 149c
Central Philippines Univeristy 269b
Central Plateau, Mexico 276b
Central Province, Ceylon 271a
Central Siberian Plateau 166c
Central University (Caracas) 263a
Ceram 99
Cerro de Punta (mountains) 114a
České Budějovice, Czechoslovakia 263c
Céspedes, Carlos Manuel de 53b
Cess River 120c
Ceuta 263b
Cevennes Mountains 240b
Ceylon 126b–126c, 131–132
　agriculture 35c
　area 35c
　capital 35c
　climate 35c
　currency unit 35c
　economy 35c–36a
　flag *il ii*
　geography 35c
　government 36a
　history 36a–36c
　language 35c
　national holiday 35c
　official name 35c
　people of 35c
　population 35c
　religion 35c
　—Cities
　　Colombo 264b
　　Kandy 271a
Chaco War 148c
Chad 35b, 36–37
　agriculture 36c
　area 36c
　capital 36c
　climate 36c
　currency unit 36c
　economy 36c
　flag *il ii*
　Fort-Lamy 267a
　geography 36c
　government 36c–37a
　history 37a
　language 36c
　map 37, *Atlas*-34–35
　national holiday 36c
　official name 36c
　people of 36c
　population 36c
　religion 36c, 37a
　World War II 37a
Chad, Lake 36c, 44b, 240b
Chad Progressive Party 37a
Chagos Archipelago 220b, 220c
Chaine des Cardamones 24c
Chaine des Matheux (mountains) 87b
Chaka 165a
Chakri dynasty 186a–186b
Cham 24c, 25a, 211a
Chamberlain, Neville 204a
Chambeshi River 217c
Champerico, Guatemala 263b
Champlain, Samuel de 29c
Chandigarh, India 263b
Chandragupta Maurya 95b–95c
Changchun, China 263c
Changkiakow, China 270b
Changkiang, China 263c
Changos 37b
Changsha, China 263c
Channel Islands 194a, 195c, 222
　area 222a
　capital 222a
　population 222a
　status 222a
Ch'anpai Mountains 240b
Chao Phraya River 240c
Chari (river) 240c
Charlemagne 4c, 11a, 14c, 66a, 75a, 107a, 137a, 182b
Charleroi, Belgium 14a
Charles (German kings) *see* Charles (Holy Roman emperors)
Charles I, King (England) 210a
　reign 200c–201a
Charles II, King (England) 103b
　reign 201b

Charles II, King (France) see Charles the Fat
Charles VI, King (France) 67a
Charles VII, King (France) 67a–67b, 107b
Charles IX, King (France) 67b
Charles X, King (France) 69a–69b
Charles I, Emperor (Holy Roman Empire) see Charlemagne
Charles IV, Emperor (Holy Roman Empire) 55b, 123b
Charles V, Emperor (Holy Roman Empire) 14c, 67b, 76a, 137b, 176c, 209a, 209c
Charles XIV, King (Norway) see Charles XIV, King (Sweden)
Charles XV, King (Norway) see Charles XV, King (Sweden)
Charles I, King (Spain) 209c
  see also Charles V, Emperor (Holy Roman Empire)
Charles II, King (Spain) 177a
Charles XII, King (Sweden) 180c
Charles XIII, King (Sweden) 180c
Charles XIV, King (Sweden) 181a
Charles XV, King (Sweden) 181a
Charles of Anjou 186c
Charles the Bald, King (France) 66b, 66c
Charles Edward, Prince (England) see Stuart, Charles Edward
Charles the Fat, King (France) 66b
Charles the Great see Charlemagne
Charles Martel 66a
Charles the Well-Beloved see Charles VI, King (France)
Charles the Wise see Charles V, King (France)
Charlotte, Grand Duchess (Luxembourg) 123c
Charlotte, Queen (Tonga) 236b
Charlotte Amalie, Virgin Islands 263c
Charter of Barbados 13b
Chatham Island 137c
Chaudière Falls 279b
Chechen-Ingush Autonomous Soviet Republic 268a
Cheju Island 240c
Chekiang Province, China 268c
Chengteh, China 263c
Chera Kingdom 95c
Cherski Mountains 240c
Chesterfield Archipelago 230a, 230b
Cheviot Hills 194c
Chiang Kai-shek 46b, 46c–47a, 47b, 47c, 133b
Chiang Kuo 47c
Chiang Mai, Thailand 264a
Chiba, Japan 264a
Chicago, Illinois 205b
Chignecto Bay see Fundy, Bay of
Chihli, Gulf of 40b, 240c, 264a
Chile 16c, 37–38, 149a–149b
  agriculture 37c
  area 37b
  capital 37b
  climate 37b
  currency unit 37b
  economy 37b–38a
  flag il ii
  geography 37b
  government 38a
  history 38a–38c
  Indians 37b, 38a
  language 37b
  map 37, Atlas-44–47
  minerals 37b–37c
  national holiday 37b
  official name 37b
  people of 37b
  population 37b
  religion 37b
  World War I 38b
  World War II 38c
  —Cities 37b
    Concepción 37b, 264c
    Puerto Montt 37b
    Punta Arenas 37b
    Valparaíso 37b
    Santiago 37b, 283c
    Talchuhano 37b, 264c
Chilin, China 271c
Chin (people) 22c
Ch'in dynasty 37a, 42c–43a
Ch'in Ling Mountains 40a
China 15c, 39–47
  agriculture 39, 40a, 41a–41b
  area 39b
  climate 40b–40c
  economy 41a–41c
  government 41c–42a
  Great Wall 42c, 43b

map 40, Atlas-32–33
natural resources 41b
people of 41a
philosophers 42b–42c
religion 41a
—Cities
  Amoy 257b
  Anshan 257c
  Antung 257c
  Canton 263a
  Changchun 263c
  Changsha 263c
  Chankiang 263c
  Chengteh (Jehol) 263c
  Chengtu 263c
  Chinchow 264a
  Foochow 266c
  Hangchow 268c
  Harbin 268c
  Ichang 269b
  Kaifeng 270b
  Kalgan (Changkiakow) 270b
  Kirin (Chilin) 271c
  Kunming 272b
  Kweiyang 272c
  Lanchow 273a
  Nanchang 277c
  Nanking 277c
  Neichiang 278a
  Ningpo (Ninghsien) 278a
  Peking (Peiping) 278a
  Shanghai 284a
  Sining 284c
  Soochow 284c
  Swatow 285c
  Taipei 286a
  Taiyüan 286a
  Tientsin (Tienching) 286c
  Tsinan (Chinan) 287b
  Tsingtao 286c
  Tsitsihar (Chichihar) 287c
  Wuhan (Hangkow, Hanyang, Wuchang) 289b
—Geography 39b–40c
  lowlands 40a–40b
  regions 39c
  rivers 40b
  uplands 39c–40a
—History 42a–47c
  Boxer Rebellion 45c
  Ch'ing dynasty 42c–43a, 44a–44b, 44c, 45a, 46b
  Chou dynasty 42a–42b
  communism 46c–47b
  Han dynasty 43a
  Hsia dynasty 42a
  influence on Japan 112a–112b
  Manchus see Ch'ing dynasty
  Ming dynasty 43a–44a
  missionaries 44a, 44b, 44c, 45a
  Mongolia and 133a, 133b
  rebellions 44c
  Shang dynasty 42a
  Sui dynasty 43b
  Sung dynasty 43c
  Taiping Rebellion 44c
  T'ang dynasty 43b–43c
  in Vietnam 212a, 212b
  Western influence 44b–44c
  World War I 46a
  World War II 46c
  Yin dynasty 42a
  Yüan dynasty 43c
China, Communist 15c, 175a
  agriculture il 39, 40a–40b
  area 39a
  capital 39a
  Cuba and 53a
  currency unit 39a
  economy 41a–41c
  flag il ii
  geography 39b–40c
  government 41c–42a
  history 42a–47b
  India and 98a
  industry 41b
  language 39a
  official name 39a
  people of 41a
  population 39a
  recognized by France 71a
  trade 41c
China, Nationalist 39
  area 39a
  capital 39a
  currency unit 39a
  economy 41c
  flag il ii
  geography 40c–41a
  government 42c
  history 47b–47c
  language 39a
  national holiday 39a
  official name 39a
  people of 41a
  population 41a
  see also Nationalist Party (China)
China Democratic Party 47c
Chinchow, China 264a
Chinese
  in Brunei 221b

in Hong Kong 227b
in Indonesia 100b
in Macao 228c
in Malaysia 125b, 126a
in Mauritius 128c
in Mongolia 133b–133c
in Nauru 135a
in Philippines 149c
in Singapore 162b
in Vietnam 211a
see also China, people of
Ch'ing dynasty 44a–44b, 44c, 45a, 46b, 116b, 133a, 263c
Chinnampo, North Korea 264a
Chios 80c
Chiriquí Volcano 146a
Chittagong, Pakistan 264a
Chittagong Hills 93c
Chokwe 218a
Chola kingdom 95c, 96a
Chola Range 161b
Cholon, South Vietnam 282c
Chomo-lungma see Everest (mountain)
Ch'ondogyo 116c
Ch'ongch'on River 115b–115c
Chongjin, North Korea 264a
Chosen see Korea
Chou dynasty 42a
Christchurch, New Zealand 138b, 138c, 264a
Christian IV, King (Denmark) 143a
Christian X, King (Denmark) 58b
Christian Democratic Party (Chile) 38c
Christian Democratic Party (Italy) 108c
Christian Democratic Party (San Marino) 158b
Christian Democratic Party (West Germany) 79a
Christian Frederick, King (Norway) 143a
Christian Socialist Party (Austria) 11c–12b
Christmas Island 222b
  area 222b
  population 222b
  status 222b
Christophe, Henri 88b
Chrome
  New Caledonia 230b
  Turkey 190a
  Soviet Union 168b
Chromite
  Cuba 52c
  Pakistan 144b
  Philippines 150a
  Yugoslavia 215b
Chu River 240c
Chu Yüan-chang 43c
Chuang 41a
Chukchi Sea 239b
Chulalongkorn, King (Thailand) 186b
Chungyang Mountains 40c, 41c
Church of England 200a
Churchill, John 201c
Churchill, Winston 204a
  World War II 204a
Chúrrua Indians 207a
Chuvash 168a
Cicilian Plain 256a
Cimbri 58a
Cintra, Pedro da 160c
Civil War, English see United Kingdom—History
Civil War, Spanish see Spanish Civil War
Clarendon, Constitutions of 197b
Claudius, Emperor (Rome) 195c
Clement V, Pope 66c
Clermont-Ferrand, France 65b
Clovis I, King 66a
Cluj, Romania 155c
Clutha River 137c
Clyde River 240c, 267c
Coal
  Australia 8b
  Brazil 19a
  Canada 28a
  China 41b
  France 64c, 64c
  Germany 74a
  Greenland 226b
  Hungary 90a
  Jan Mayen Island 236a
  Japan 111a
  Korea 115c
  Laos 118b
  Mongolia 132c
  Mozambique 229b
  Nepal 135c

Pakistan 144b
Poland 151a–151b
Portugal 153b
South Africa 164c
Soviet Union 168b, 169a
Spain 175c
Svalbard Archipelago 236a
Swaziland 179a
Turkey 190a
United Kingdom 194c
U.S. 205c
Yugoslavia 215b
Cobalt
  Congo (Kinshasa) 50c
  Cuba 52c
  Germany 74b
  Morocco 133c
Cochabamba, Bolivia 16a, 16b
Cochin, India 264a
Coconuts
  British Indian Ocean Territory 220b
  British Solomon Islands 220c
  Cayman Islands 222a
  Ceylon 35c, 36a
  Cocoas Islands 222c
  Comoro Islands 222c
  Cook Islands 223a
  Dominica 223b
  Fiji Islands 224b
  French Polynesia 225a
  Gilbert and Ellice Islands 226a
  Maldive Islands 126b
  Muscat and Oman 134c
  New Caledonia 230b
  New Hebrides 231a
  Niue 231b
  Panama 146b
  Papua 231b
  Philippines 149c
  Portuguese Guinea 232a
  Seychelles 234b
  Singapore 162b
  Tanzania 184b
  Thailand 185c
  Tonga 236b
  Wallis and Futuna Islands 236c
  Western Samoa 213c
Cocos Islands 222b–222c
  area 222b
  population 222b
  status 222b
Code Napoléon 69a
Coffee
  Angola 218c
  Brazil 18c, 19a, 19b, 20b
  British Indian Ocean Territory 220b
  Burundi 24b
  Cameroon 26a
  Cape Verde Islands 221c
  Central African Republic 35b
  Colombia 48c, 49c
  Comoro Islands 222c
  Cuba 52c
  Dominican Republic 58c
  Ecuador 60a
  Equatorial Guinea 223c
  Ethiopia 62c
  French Polynesia 225a
  Guatemala 84b
  Guinea 86a
  Haiti 87c
  Honduras 88c
  India 94b
  Indonesia 99a
  Ivory Coast 109c
  Jamaica 110a
  Kenya 114b
  Liberia 121a
  Madagascar 124a
  New Caledonia 230b
  New Guinea 230c
  New Hebrides 231a
  Nicaragua 139c
  Panama 146b
  Papua 231b
  Paraguay 147b
  Peru 148c
  Portuguese Timor 232b
  Rwanda 157c
  Sao Tomé and Principe 234a
  Sierra Leone 160c
  Surinam 235b
  Tanzania 184b
  Togo 187a
  Trinidad and Tobago 187c
  Uganda 191c
  Venezuela 209b
  Vietnam 211b
  Yemen 214a
Coimbatore, India 264b
Colbert, Jean Baptiste 30a, 68a
Cold War
  France 71a
  Norway 143c–144a
  Soviet Union 174b–174c
  Spain 177b
Coloane Island 228b

INDEX

Cologne, Germany 264b
Colomb Béchar, Algeria 264b
Colombia 48–49, 50c
  agriculture 48c
  area 48a
  capital 48a
  climate 48b
  currency unit 48a
  economy 48c
  flag *il ii*
  geography 48a–48b
  government 48c
  history 48c–49c
  Indians 48b
  language 48a
  map 49, Atlas-52–53
  national holiday 48a
  Negroes 52b
  official name 48a
  people of 48b–48c
  population 48a
  religion 48a–48b
  —Cities 48b–48c
    Bogotá 48b, 261a
    Barranquilla 48c
    Cali 48c
    Cartagena 48c
    Medellín 48c, 276a
Colombo, Ceylon 35c, 264b
Colón (currency unit)
  Costa Rica 51b
  El Salvador 60c
Colón, Panama 146a, 146c
Colorado River (United States) 205a
Colorado River (South America) 240c
Colorados Party (Uruguay) 207c
Columbia River 27a, 205a
Columbus, Bartholomew 58c
Columbus, Christopher 51c, 53b, 59a, 88a, 89a, 110a, 140a, 146b, 148c, 176c, 209c, 224c, 228c
  islands discovered by 219a, 219b, 221a, 222a, 223b, 224c, 226c, 227a, 228c, 229a, 233b, 233c
COMECON *see* Council for Mutual Economic Cooperation (COMECON)
Common law
  origins 197b
Common Market 15a, 204b
Commonwealth of Nations 8c, 26b, 28c, 195c
Communism
  Albania 2b, 3b
  Bulgaria 21b–21c, 22a–22b
  China 41c–42a
  Cuba 52b, 53a–54a
  Czechoslovakia 55a, 56a–56b
  Finland 63b
  France 70c
  Germany, East 74c
  Greece 83b
  Hungary 90a–90b, 91a, 91b–91c
  Indonesia 100b
  Italy 108c
  Ivory Coast 109b
  Korea, North 116a, 117a, 117b
  Laos 119a
  Mongolia 132c, 133b
  Poland 150a, 151b, 151c, 152a
  Romania 155a, 156a, 156b, 157a–157b
  San Marino 157b
  Thailand 186a
  Vietnam 213a
  Yugoslavia 215b, 215c–216a, 216c–217a
  see also China, Communist; Soviet Union
Communism (mountain) 249c
Communist China *see* China, Communist
Communist Party of Cuba 53a–53b
Communist Party of the Soviet Union (CPSU) 169c
Como, Lake 240c
Comodoro Rivadavia, Argentina 264b
Comoé River 109a
Comorin, Cape *see* Cape Comorin
Comoro Islands 222–223
  area 222c
  capital 222c
  Moroni 276c
  population 222c
  status 222c
Company of New France 30a
Company of One Hundred Associates 30a
Conakry, Guinea 85c, 86a, 86b, 264b–264c
Concepción, Chile 37b, 37c, 264c
Concepción, Paraguay 147b
Conception Island *see* Grenada
Concordat of 1929 108c
Confederation of the Rhine 76c

Confucianism 42b–42c, 43a, 43b, 45b
Confucius 42b–42c
Congo (Brazzaville) 35b, 49c–50b
  agriculture 50a
  area 49c
  Brazzaville 261c
  capital 49c
  climate 49c
  currency unit 49c
  economy 50a
  flag *il ii*
  geography 49c
  government 50a
  history 50a–50b
  language 49c
  map 50, Atlas-38
  national holiday 49c
  official name 49c
  people of 50a
  population 49c
  religion 49c
  slavery 50a
  World War II 50b
Congo (Kinshasa) 50–51
  agriculture 50c
  area 50b
  capital 50b
  currency unit 50b
  economy 50b–51a
  flag *il ii*
  geography 50b–50c
  government 51a
  history 51a–51b
  language 50b
  map 50, Atlas-38–39
  national holiday 50b
  official name 50b
  people of 50b
  population 50b
  religion 50b, 51a
  —Cities 50c
    Albertville 256c
    Kinshasa (Leopoldville) 271c
    Kisangani (Stanleyville) 272a
    Likasi 273c
    Lubumbashi 274c
    Matadi 275c
Congo River 49c, 50c, 240c, 271c, 272a, 275c
Congress of Vienna (1815) 14c, 69a, 76c, 107c, 128b, 137b, 152a, 182b
Conselheiro, Antônio 20b
Conservative Party (Britain) 203c–204b
Conservative Party (Canada) 32a, 32c, 33b, 33c, 34b, 34c
Constance, Lake 240c
Constantine I, King (Greece) 83a
Constantine II, King (Greece) 83b–83c
Constantinople 81b, 81c; *see also* Istanbul, Turkey
Convention People's Party (CPP) (Ghana) 80b, 80c
Cook, James 8c, 138c, 223a
Cook Islands 223, 231a
  area 223a
  population 223a
  status 223a
Cook (mountain) 137c
Cook Strait 137c, 289a
Cooperative Commonwealth Federation 34b
Copán, Honduras 264c
Copán River 264c
Copenhagen, Denmark 57a, 264c
Copenhagen University 264c
Copper
  Angola 218b
  Australia 8b
  Chile 37c
  Congo (Kinshasa) 50c
  Cuba 52c
  Cyprus 54a
  French Guiana 224c
  Germany 74b
  Korea, North 115c
  Korea, South 115c
  Laos 118b
  Mauritania 128b
  Mexico 130a
  Mongolia 132c
  Nepal 135c
  Nicaragua 139c
  Peru 148b
  Philippines 150a
  Poland 151b
  Portugal 153b
  South West Africa 234c
  Soviet Union 168b
  Spain 175c
  Sweden 180a
  Turkey 190a
  Uganda 191c
  United Arab Republic (Egypt) 192c
  United States 205c
  Venezuela 209b

Copra
  Cocos Islands 222c
  Gilbert and Ellice Islands 226a
  Indonesia 99a
  Mozambique 229b
  New Guinea 230c
  Portuguese Timor 232b
  St. Lucia 233b
  St. Vincent 233c
  Sao Tomé and Principe 234a
  Tokelau Islands 236a
  Wallis and Futuna Islands 236c
Coptic Church *il* 62, 193a
Coral Sea 243a
Cordillera Cantabrica *see* Cantabrian Mountains
Cordillera Central (mountains, Colombia) 48a, 51b, 58c
Cordillera Central (mountains, Costa Rica) 51b
Cordillera Central (mountains, Dominican Republic) 58c
Cordillera de Guanacaste (mountains, Costa Rica) 51b
Cordillera Occidental (mountains, Colombia) 48a, 59c
Cordillera Occidental (mountains, Ecuador) 59c
Cordillera Oriental (mountains, Colombia) 48a, 59c
Cordillera Oriental (mountains, Ecuador) 59c
Cordillera Septentrional (mountains, Dominican Republic) 58c
Cordillera de Talamanca (mountains, Costa Rica) 51b
Córdoba (currency unit) 139b
Cordoba, Argentina 5b
Cordoba, Spain 264c
Cordoba, Cathedral of 264c
Corinto, Nicaragua 264c
Cork
  Portugal 153b
  Spain 176a
Corn
  Albania 2b
  Argentina 5c
  Bulgaria 21b
  Cape Verde Islands 221c
  Comoro Islands 222c
  French Guiana 224c
  Greece 81a
  Hungary 90a
  Ifni 228a
  India 94b
  Italy 106b–106c
  Mali 127a
  Mauritania 127b
  Mexico 130a
  Mozambique 229b
  Pakistan 144b
  Panama 146b
  Paraguay 147b
  Peru 148b
  Philippines 149c
  Rhodesia 155a
  Romania 156a
  Rwanda 157c
  Sikkim 161c
  South Africa 164b–164c
  Spain 176a
  Swaziland 179a
  Syria 183a
  Tanzania 184a
  Thailand 185c
  Togo 187a
  Uganda 191c
  United Arab Republic (Egypt) 192c
  United States 206a
  Uruguay 207c
  Venezuela 209b
  Vietnam 211b
  Yugoslavia 215b
  Zambia 217b
Coromandel Coast 243a
Coronado, Juan Vásquez de 52a
Corregidor Island 150b
Cortés, Hernán 130c, 220b
Cortines, Adolfo Ruiz 131c
Costa, Lúcio 261c
Costa Rica 51–52
  agriculture 51c
  area 51b
  capital 51b
  climate 51b
  currency unit 51b
  economy 51c
  flag *il ii*
  geography 51b
  government 51c
  history 51c–52a
  language 51b
  map 51, Atlas-44
  national holiday 51b
  official name 51b

  people of 51c
  population 51b
  religion 51b
  San José 283b
Costa e Silva, Artur da 20c
Costello, John A. 103c
Cotapaxi (volcano) 59c
Côte d'Azur *see* Riviera
Cotonou, Dahomey 56c, 57a, 264c
Cotton
  Albania 2b
  Angola 218b
  Antigua 219a
  Brazil 19a
  Cameroon 26a
  Central African Republic 35b
  Chad 36c
  Colombia 48c
  Guatemala 84b
  Honduras 88c
  India 94b, 94c
  Iraq 101c
  Malawi 124c
  Mali 127a
  Montserrat 129a
  Mozambique 129b
  Nicaragua 139c
  Niger 140c
  Nigeria 141b
  Pakistan 144b
  Paraguay 147b
  Peru 148c
  St. Vincent 233c
  South Yemen 165c
  Soviet Union 169a
  Sudan 178a
  Swaziland 179a
  Syria 183a
  Tanzania 184b
  Thailand 185c
  Turkey 190a
  United Arab Republic (Egypt) 192c
  Uganda 191c
  United States 206a
  Upper Volta 206c
  Venezuela 209b
  Vietnam 211b
  Yemen 214c
  Zambia 217b
Council of Europe 142c
Council for Mutual Economic Cooperation (COMECON) 74a
Counter-Reformation 30a
Country Party (Australia) 9c, 10a
Courantyne River 86c
CPP *see* Convention People's Party (CPP) (Ghana)
CPSU *see* Communist Party of the Soviet Union (CPSU)
Cracow, Poland *see* Krakow, Poland
Creoles 130c–131a, 160b
Crete 80c, 82c–83a
Crimea (peninsula) 243a, 284a
Crimean Mountains 243a
Crimean War (1853–1856) 156c, 172a, 203a
Croatia 216a, 216c
Croatians 215a, 216a
Cromwell, Oliver 103b, 201b
  Commonwealth government 201a–201b
Crozet Archipelago 225a
Crubal River 232a
Crusades 2c, 105a, 183b, 197b
Cruzeiro 18a
Crystal Mountains 71b, 243a
Cserhát Mountains 89c
Cuba 52–54
  agriculture 52c
  area 52b
  capital 52b
  communism 52b, 53a–54a
  Communist China and 53a
  currency unit 52b
  economy 52c–53a
  flag *il ii*
  geography 52b
  government 53a–53b
  history 53b–54a
  Indians 53b
  language 52b
  map Atlas-56–57
  national holiday 52b
  official name 52b
  people of 52c
  population 52b
  religion 52b
  slavery 53b
  Soviet Union and 53a, 54a
  U.S. and 52b, 52c, 53a, 53b–54a
  —Cities 52c
    Camaguez 52c
    Havana 52b, 52c, 268c
    Santiago 52c

Cunen River 243a
Cuquenán Waterfall 243a
Curaçao 229a, 289a
Curitiba, Brazil 264c
Curleuse Island 234a
Currency unit *see under the name of individual countries, such as Ghana, currency unit*
Curzon Line 152b
Cusco, Peru
  see Cuzco, Peru
Cuttack, India 265c
Cuza, Alexander 156c
Cuzco, Peru 148c, 265a
Cyclades Islands 81a
  Mykonos *il* 82
Cyprus 54, 191b
  agriculture 54a
  area 54a
  capital 54a
  currency unit 54a
  economy 54a
  flag *il ii*
  geography 54a
  government 54b
  history 54b
  language 54a
  national holiday 54a
  official name 54a
  people of 54a
  population 54a
  religion 54a
  World War I 54b
  —Cities
    Famagusta 266c
    Limassol 273c
    Nicosia 278a
Cyrenaica, Libya 121b, 122a, 260b
Czechoslovakia 11c, 54–56
  agriculture 55a
  area 54c
  capital 54c
  climate 54c
  communism 55a, 56a–56b
  currency unit 54c
  economy 55a
  flag *il iii*
  geography 54c
  government 55a–55b
  Hapsburg rule 55b–56a
  history 55b–56b
  industry 55a
  language 54c
  map 54, *Atlas*-9
  national holiday 54c
  official name 54c
  people of 54c–55a
  population 54c
  religion 54c, 55b, 55c
  Soviet Union 56a–56b
  Sudeten Germans 204a
  trade 55a
  World War I 55c
  World War II 56a, 70c, 78c
  —Cities
    Bratislava 261c
    Brno (Brünn) 262b
    České Budějovice 263b
    Košice 272a
    Plzeň (Pilsen) 280c
    Ostrava (Moravska Ostrava) 279a
    Prague (Praha) 281a
Czestochowa, Poland 265a

D

Dacca, Pakistan 265a
Dacca, University of 265a
Dacians 156b
Dacko, David 35b
Dagomba 206c
Dahomey 56–57
  agriculture 56c
  area 56b
  capital 56b
  climate 56b
  currency unit 56b
  economy 56c
  flag *il iii*
  geography 56b
  government 56b
  history 57a
  language 56b
  map 56, *Atlas*-37
  national holiday 56b
  official name 56b
  people of 56b–56c
  population 56b
  religion 56b
  slavery 57a
  —Cities 56c
    Cotonou 264c
    Porto-Novo 281a
Daigo II, Emperor (Japan) 112b
Dairy products
  Denmark 57b
  Ireland 103a
  San Marino 158a
  Soviet Union 169a
  Sweden 180a
  Switzerland 182a
  United Kingdom 194c
  United States 206a
Dakar, Senegal 159a, 265a
Dakar, University of 265a
Dalai Lama 15c
Dallas, Texas 205b
Dalmatia 215a
Dalmatian Islands 108b
Damascus, Syria 182c, 183b, 265a
Damascus College 265a
Dams 192c, 217a, 217b
Danakil Depression 239a
Danquah, J. B. 80b
Danube River 10b, 10c, 21a, 54c, 73b, 89b, 89c, 155c, 215a, 243a
Danzig 78c, 152b
  see also Gdańsk, Poland
Danzig, Bay of 270c
Danzig, Free City of 267c
Dar es Salaam, Tanzania 184a, 265a
Dardanelles 189c, 243a
Darjeeling, India 136a
Darling Downs 7b
Darling River *see* Murray-Darling Rivers
Dasht-i-Kavir (desert) 100c
Dasht-i-Lut (desert) 100c
Dasht-i-Margo (desert) 1a
Dates
  French Territory of the Afars and the Issas 225b
  Iraq 101c
  Libya 122a
  Mauritania 128a
  Muscat and Oman 134c
  Saudi Arabia 159a
  Sudan 178a
  Syria 183a
  Trucial Oman 188b
Davao, Philippines 265b
Davao River 265b
Dávila, Gil González 140a
De Gasperi, Alcide 108c
De Gaulle, Charles 4b, 34c, 71a, 204b
  Andorra visit 4c
  World War II 70c–71a
De Valera, Eamon 103c
Dead Sea 104b, 243a
Deakin, Alfred 9b
Death Valley 204c
Debrecen, Hungary 90a, 265b
Dehra Dun, India 265b
Delaware River 205a
Delhi, India 265b, 278a
  see also New Delhi, India
Delhi, University of 278a
Demayend (mountain) 243c
Demerara River 86c, 267c
Democratic Labor Party (Barbados) 13c
Democratic Party (Turkey) 191b
Democratic Party (Uganda) 192a
Denmark 57–58
  agriculture 57b
  area 57a
  capital 57a
  in British Isles 196a
  climate 57b
  Copenhagen (København) 264c
  currency unit 57a
  economy 57b–57c
  in Faeroe Islands 223c–224a
  flag *il iii*
  geography 57b
  government 57c
  in Greenland 226b–226c
  history 58a–58b
  in Iceland 92b
  language 57a
  map 57, *Atlas*-15
  national holiday 57a
  Norway and 142c–143a
  official name 57a
  people of 57b
  population 57a
  religion 57a, 58a
  World War I 58
  World War II 58b, 78c
D'Enrecasteaux Archipelago 231b
Denver, Colorado 205b
Depression of 1837
  Canada 31b–31c
Depression of 1930s
  Australia 9c–10a
  Barbados 13c
  Brazil 20b
  Canada 34a
  Czechoslovakia 56c
  New Zealand 139a
  Norway 143c
  Panama 146c
  Sweden 181a
Deserts
  Afghanistan 1a
  Algeria 3a–3b
  Angola 218a
  Botswana 17b
  Chile 37b
  China 39c–40a, 40b, 40c
  Ethiopia 62a
  Iran 100c
  Israel 104a, 104b
  Jordan 113c
  Kuwait 117c
  Libya 121b, 121c
  Mali 126c
  Mauritania 128a
  Mongolia 132b
  Pakistan 144b
  Saudi Arabia 158c
  South West Africa 234c
  South Yemen 165c
  Soviet Union 167c
  Sudan 177c
  Syria 182c
  Tunisia 188c
  United Arab Republic (Egypt) 192b–192c
  United States 204c
  Yemen 214a
Desna River 243b
Desroches Island 220b, 220c
Dessalines, Jean Jacques 88b
Destour Party (Tunisia) 189b
Deutsche Mark 73a
Devils Island 224c, 263b
Dhahran, Saudi Arabia 258c
Dhaulagiri Peak 243a
Dia, Mamadou 160b
Diamonds
  Angola 218b
  Brazil 19a
  Central African Republic 35b
  Congo (Kinshasa) 50c
  Ghana 80a
  Ivory Coast 109a
  Lesotho 120b
  Liberia 121a
  Sierra Leone 160c
  South Africa 164c
  South West Africa 234c
  Soviet Union 168c
  Tanzania 184b
  Venezuela 209b
Dias, Bartholomeu 154a, 165a
Díaz, Adolfo 140b
Díaz, Julio Lozano 89b
Díaz, Porfirio 131b
Díaz de Solís, Juan 6a, 207b
Díaz Ordaz, Gustavo 131c–132a
Diefenbaker, John 34c
Diem, Ngo Dinh 213a, 213b
Dien Bien Phu, Battle of 213a
Dili, Portuguese Timor 232b, 265b
Dimashq, Syria
  see Damascus, Syria
Dimitrov, Georghi 22b
Dinar
  Algeria 3b
  Bahrain 12c
  Iraq 101c
  Jordan 113c
  Kuwait 117b
  Qatar 154b
  South Yemen 165c
  Yugoslavia 214a
Dinaric Alps 215a, 237b
Din-i-Ilahi 96c
Dinka 178a
Dirham 133b
Diu (island) 243a
Djibouti, French Territory of the Afars and the Issas 225b, 225c, 265b
Dnepr River 243b, 265b, 265c, 271c, 289c
Dneprodzerzhinsk, Soviet Union 265c
Dnepropetrovsk, Soviet Union 265c
Dnestr River 272a, 278c
Dobruja
  ceded to Bulgaria 157a
Dodecanese Islands 81a, 108b
Dogger Bank 243b
Doha, Qatar 154b, 265c
Dollar
  Australia 7a
  Barbados 13a
  Canada 26b
  East Caribbean 13a
  Ethiopia 61c
  Guyana 86b
  Malaysia 125a
  New Zealand 137c
  Singapore 162a
  Taiwan 39a
  Trinidad and Tobago 187b
  United States 204b
Dollfuss, Engelbert 12a
Dolomites (mountains) 237b
Dolores, Mexico 130c
Dom João, Prince Regent (Portugal)
  in Brazil 19c–20a
Domesday survey of 1086 197a
Dominica 223a–223b
  area 223a
  capital 223a
  population 223a
  Roseau 282b
  status 223a
Dominican Republic 58–59, 88b
  agriculture 58c
  area 58c
  capital 58c
  climate 58c
  currency unit 58c
  economy 58c–59a
  geography 58c
  flag *il iii*
  government 59a
  history 59a–59b
  language 58c
  map 59, *Atlas*-57
  national holiday 58c
  official name 58c
  people of 58c
  population 58c
  religion 58c
  Santo Domingo 283c
Dominican Revolutionary Party 59b
Don River 243b
Donbas (region), Soviet Union 271c
Donegal Bay 243b
Donets River 271b, 243b
Dong 210c
Dost Muhammad (ruler, Afghanistan) 1c–2a
Douro River 153a, 153b, 175b, 243b
Dover Castle *il* 196
Dover, Strait of 243c
Douala, Cameroon 25c, 265c
Douglas, Isle of Man 228a, 265c
Douglas-Home, Alec 204a
Drachma 80c
Drake Passage 243b
Drakensberg (mountains) 243b
Drau River 89c, 243b
Drava River *see* Drau River
Dravidians 94a, 95b
Dresden, Germany 74a, 265c
Dreyfus, Alfred 70a
Dreyfus Affair 70a
Drina River 215a, 243b
Drogheda, Ireland 103b
Druze 182c

Dubai 188b
see also Trucial Oman
Dublin, Ireland 102b, 102c, 103b, 103c, 265c
Duero River see Douro River
Duisberg, Germany il 75
Dunedin, New Zealand 138c

Durban, South Africa 164b, 266a
Durrani, Ahmad see Ahmad Shah Durrani
Durrës, Albania 266a
D'Urville, Dumont 225a
Dushan, Stephen 216a
Dushanbe, Soviet Union 266a

Düsseldorf, Germany 266a
Dutch East India Company see East India Company (Dutch)
Dutch Guiana 237c
see also Surinam
Dutch New Guinea see Netherlands New Guinea

Dutch War (1672–1678) 68a
Dutra, Enrico Gaspar 20c
Duvalier, François 88a, 88b
Dvina River 243b
Dvina, Gulf of 243b
Dyerma 240c

E

Eask River 243b
East Africa, University of (Uganda) 270c
East Anglia, Kingdom of 196a
East Berlin 260c
East Caribbean dollar
  Barbados 13a
East China Sea 243b–243c
East Falkland Island 285a
East Germany see Germany, East
East Hungarian Plain 265b
East India Company (British) 15c, 44b, 200a–200b
East India Company (Dutch) 36b, 99c, 165a
East Indians see Indians (India)
East Indies 243c
East London, South Africa 266a
East Prussia 73a
East Siberian Sea 243c
Eastern Ghats 93b
Eastern Roman Empire see Byzantine Empire
Eastern Samoa see American Samoa
Ebrie Lagoon 256a
Ebro River 243c
Ecuador 49a, 59–60, 146c
  agriculture 59c–60b
  area 59c
  capital 59c
  currency unit 59c
  economy 60a–60b
  flag il iii
  geography 59c–60a
  government 60b
  history 60b–60c
  Indians 60a, 60b
  language 59c
  map 60, Atlas-50
  national holiday 59c
  Negroes 60a
  official name 59c
  people of 60a
  population 59c
  religion 59c, 60b
  San Francisco Cathedral il 59
  —Cities 60a
    Guyaquil 60a
    Quito 59c, 60a, 281c
Edea, Cameroon 266a
Eden, Anthony 204a

Edict of Nantes 67c, 68a
Edinburgh, Scotland il 201, 266b
Edmonton, Canada 266b
Edward I, King (England)
  reign 198a–198b
Edward II, King (England)
  reign 198b–198c
Edward III, King (England) 198b, 199b
  reign 198c–199a
Edward IV, King (England) 199b
Edward VI, King (England) 200a
Edward VII, King (England)
  reign 203b–203c
Edward VIII, King (England)
  abdication 203c
  see also Windsor, Duke of
Edward the Confessor, King (England) 196b–196c
Edward, Lake 50c, 191b, 243c
Efate Island 288b
Egbert of Wessex 196a
Egypt see United Arab Republic
Eiffel Tower il 64, 279c
Einaudi, Luigi 108c
Eindhoven, Netherlands 136c, 137a
Ekaterinburg, Soviet Union see Sverdlovsk, Soviet Union
El Aaiún, Spanish Sahara 235a
El Fasher, Sudan 266c
El Hamad see Syrian Desert
El Hamra River 256c
El Salvador 60–61, 84b, 89b
  agriculture 61a–62b
  area 60c
  capital 60c
  climate 61a
  currency unit 60c
  economy 61a–61b
  flag il iii
  geography 60c–61a
  government 61b
  history 61b–61c
  Indians 61a
  language 60c
  map 61, Atlas-54
  national holiday 60c
  official name 60c
  people of 61a
  population 60c
  religion 60c
  —Cities
    Acajutla 256a
    San Salvador 60c, 283b
Elath, Israel 266b
Elba Island 105c, 243c
Elbasan, Albania 266b

Elbe River 54c, 243c, 268b
Elbow River 262c
Ebro River 175b
Elbrus Mountain 243c
Elburz Mountains 100c, 243c
Eleanor of Aquitaine 66c
Elgon (mountain) 191a
Elisabethville
  see Lubumbashi, Congo (Kinshasa)
Elizabeth I, Queen (England) 103b
  reign 200a–200b
  birth of 200a
Elizabeth II, Queen (England) 204b
Elizabeth of York 199b
Ellesmere Island 26c
Ellice Islands see Gilbert and Ellice Islands
Emilia-Romagna (region), Italy 261b
Empty Quarter (desert) see Rub al Khali
Ems River 73b
English Channel 194a, 243c, 273b
Enisei River see Yenisey River
Enlightenment 68b
Enriquillo, Lake 58c
Entebbe, Uganda 191c, 266b
Entente Cordiale 70a, 77c
Enugu, Nigeria 266b–266c
Epidamnus
  Durrës, Albania 266a
Epirus 2c
Equatorial Guinea 223
  area 223b
  capital 223b
  population 223b
  status 223b
  Santa Isabel 283c
Eric the Red 226a
Erie Canal 31b
Eritrea 62c, 108b
Erz Mountains 54c, 250c
Erzurum, Turkey 266c
Eschira 71b
Escudo
  Chile 37b
  Portugal 153a
Eskimos
  Canada 27b
  Greenland 226c
Essen, Germany 266c
Essequibo River 86c
Essex, Kingdom of 196a

Este family 107b
Estigarribia, José Félix 148a
Estonian Soviet Socialist Republic 286a
Estonians 167c
Estrada Cabrera, Manuel 85a
Estrada Palma, Tomás 53c
Esztergom, Hungary 266c
Ethelbert, King 196a
Ethelred II, King (England) 196b
Ethiopia 61–62
  agriculture 62a, 62b
  area 61c
  capital 61c
  currency unit 61c
  economy 61c
  flag il iii
  geography 61c–62a
  government 62b
  history 62b–62c
  Italian invasion 108c
  language 61c
  map 61, Atlas-34–35
  national holiday 61c
  official name 61c
  people of 61a
  population 61c
  religion 61c, 62a, 62b
  —Cities
    Addis Ababa 256a–256b
    Asmara 258a
    Massawa 258b
Ethiopian Highlands 243c–244a
Etruscans 107a
Eucumbene Dam il 7
Euphrates River 101c, 182c, 190a, 244a
Europe 244a
  map Atlas-8, Atlas-14
European Atomic Energy Commission 262b
European Coal and Steel Community 15a, 64b, 123c
European Economic Community 15a, 64b, 262b
  see also Common Market
European Monetary Agreement (1950) 15a
European Secret Army Organization (OAS) 4b
Europoort 282b
Everest, Mt. 135b, 249c
Ewe (people) 187a
Eyadema, Etienne 187b
Eyre, Lake 7b, 244a
Eyre Peninsula 244a

F

Faeroe Islands 223–224
  area 223c
  capital 223c
  population 223c
  status 223c
  Thorshavn 286c
Faidherbe, Louis Léon César 160a
Fairhair, Harold (Harald Haarfager), King (Norway) 142c, 143a
Faisal I, King (Iraq) 102a, 102b
Faisal II, King (Iraq) 102b
Faisal, King (Saudi Arabia) 159b–159c
Falkland Islands 224
  area 224a
  capital 224a

population 224a
Stanley 285c
status 224a
Famagusta, Cyprus 266c
Fang
  Equatorial Guinea 223b
  Gabon 71b, 72a
Fa-Ngum, King (Laos) 118b–118c
Fanti 79c, 80a
Faridabad, India il 95a
Farnese, Alessandro see Paul III, Pope
Farquhar Islands 220b, 220c
Farrell, Edelmiro 6c
Fars Province 284b
Fascism
  Italy 108b–108c
Fatimid dynasty 189b, 193a
Faysal, King (Syria) 183c
Al Fayyum, United Arab Republic 257a

Federalist party (Argentina) 6a–6b
Federation of French Equatorial Africa 26b, 35b, 37a
Federation of French West Africa 57a
Federation of the West Indies 13c, 14b, 219a
Fen River 286a
Ferdinand, Prince (Bulgaria) 22a
Ferdinand I, King (Castile and León) 153c
Ferdinand II, King (Spain) 176c
Ferdinand VII, King (Spain) 6a, 38a, 49a, 89a, 130c, 131a, 133c, 134a, 177a, 209c
Fernando Póo Island 223b, 283c
Ferrara, Francisco 89a
Ferrara, Italy 107b
Ferry, Jules 70a
Fès, Morocco 266c

Feudalism
  China 42a
  France 66b
  Germany 75b
  Hungary 90b–90c
  United Kingdom 197a, 197c, 198c
Fezzan (desert) 121c, 122a, 122b
Figueres, José 52a
Fiji Islands 195c, 224a–224b
  area 224a
  capital 224a
  economy 224b
  government 224b
  people of 224b
  population 224a
  status 224a
  Suva 285c
Filali dynasty 134a
Finland 62–63
  agriculture 63a
  Aland islands 237a

area 62c
capital 62c
climate 62c
communism 63b
currency unit 62c
economy 63a
flag il iii
geography 62c
government 63a–63b
history 63b–63c
language 62c
national holiday 62c
official name 62c
people of 62c–63a
population 62c
religion 62c, 63a, 63b
Russia and 171c
Sweden and 180b, 180c
World War II 63c
—Cities 62c
  Helsinki 62c, 268c
  Tampere 62c
  Turku 62c
Finland, Gulf of 244a, 268c, 273b, 286a
Finlay, Carlos 53c
Firat River 190a
Firenze, Italy *see* Florence, Italy
Firestone Rubber Company 121a, 121b
Fischer von Erlach, Johann Bernhard
  Schoenbrunn castle *il* 11
Fishing
  Angola 218b
  Bermuda 219c
  British Indian Ocean Territory 220b
  British Solomon Islands 220c
  British Virgin Islands 221a
  Canada 28b, 29b, 31b
  Faeroe Islands 223c
  France 64c, *il* 67
  French Polynesia 225a
  Gabon *il* 71
  Greenland 226b
  Greece *il* 83
  Iceland 92b, 93a
  Iran 100c
  Ivory Coast 109a
  Japan 111b
  Korea, South 115c
  Labrador 28b
  Macao 228c
  Maldive Islands 126b
  Netherlands Antilles 230a
  Newfoundland 28b
  Norway 142b
  Papua 231b
  Peru 148b
  Philippines 149c–150a
  Pitcairn Island 231c
  Portugal 153b
  Qatar 154b
  St. Pierre and Miquelon 233c
  Senegal 160a
  Seychelles 234b
  Sierra Leone 160c
  South Yemen 165c
  Spain 176a
  Spanish Sahara 235a
  Sweden 180a
  Tanzania 184b
  Tokelau Islands 236a
  Trucial Oman 188b
  United Kingdom 194c
  U.S. 206a
  Western Samoa 213b
Fjords 242a
Flags
  Nations of the world *il* ii–iv
Flemmings 14a
FLN *see* National Liberation Front (Algeria)
Florence, Italy 106b–106c, 107b, 266c
Flores, Juan José 60b
Fock, Jenö 91c
Foix, counts of
  Andorra 4c
Fons 56b
  see also Abomey
Foochow, China 266c

Forests and forestry
  Angola 218b
  Austria 11a
  Bahamas 219b
  British Honduras 220a
  British Solomon Islands 220c
  Brunei 221b
  Canada 28b
  Equatorial Guinea 223c
  Fiji Islands 224b
  Finland 63a
  Gabon 71c
  Guatemala 84b
  Honduras 89a
  Ivory Coast 109a
  Japan 111b–111c
  Korea, North 115c
  Laos 118b
  Lebanon 119c
  Mozambique 229b
  Nicaragua 139c
  Nigeria 141b
  Norfolk Island 231b
  Norway 142b
  Papua 231b
  Paraguay 147a–147b
  Peru 148b
  Philippines 150a
  Portugal 153b
  Portuguese Guinea 232a
  Portuguese Timor 232b
  Surinam 235b
  Swaziland 179a
  Sweden 180a
  Thailand 185c
  Turkey 190a
  U.S. 206a
Forint 89b
Formentera
  see Balearic Islands
Formosa Strait 266c
Fort Garry, Canada 32c
Fort Gourand, Mauritania 128a, 128b
Fortaleza, Brazil 266c
Fort-de-France, Martinque 266c
Forth, Firth of 266b
Fort-Lamy, Chad 36c, 267a
Fouta Djallon (mountains) 85c, 244a
Fragoso Carmona, António Oscar de 154b
Franc
  Belgium 14a
  Burundi 24a
  France 64a
  Guinea 85c
  Luxembourg 123a
  Mali 126c
  Rwanda 157b
  Switzerland 181b
Franc CFA (African Financial Community)
  Cameroon 25c
  Central African Republic 35a
  Chad 36c
  Congo (Brazzaville) 49c
  Dahomey 56b
  Gabon 71b
  Ivory Coast 109a
  Madagascar 123c
  Mauritania 128a
  Niger 140b
  Senegal 159c
  Togo 186c
  Upper Volta 206b
France 64–71
  agriculture 64c–65a
  area 64a
  capital 64a
  climate 64a, 64c
  communism 70c
  constitution 65c
  currency unit 64a
  economy 64b–65c
  flag *il* iii
  geography 64a
  government 65b–66a
  industry 65a–65b
  language 64a
  map 64, *Atlas*-22–23
  national holiday 64a
  natural resources 64b–64c
  nuclear power 71a

  official name 64a
  people of 64a–64b
  population 64a
  religion 64a, 66a, 67b–67c
  trade 65b–65c
  transportation 65b
—Cities 64b
  Bordeaux 261b
  Grenoble 268a
  Le Havre 273c
  Lyon 274c
  Marseille 275c
  Nice 278a
  Paris 279c
  Toulouse 287a
  Tours 287b
—History
  Andorra and 4c
  Bourbons 67c
  Capetians 66b–66c
  Carolingians 66a–66b
  Cold War 71a
  colonial
    Algeria 4a
    Cambodia 25a–25b
    Canada 29a, 29c–30c
    Central African Republic 35b
    Chad 37a
    China 45a, 45c
    Comoro Islands 222c–223a
    Congo (Brazzaville) 50a–50b
    Dahomey 57c
    Egypt 193b
    French Guiana 224b–224c
    French Polynesia 224c–225a
    French Southern and Antarctic Territories 225a–225b
    French Territory of the Afars and the Issas 224b–225c
    Gabon 71c–72a
    Guadeloupe 227a
    Guinea 86a–86b
    Guyana 87a
    Haiti 88a
    Ivory Coast 109b
    Laos 118c–119a
    Lebanon 120a
    Madagascar 124a–124b
    Mali 127c
    Martinique 228c
    Mauritania 128b–128c
    Mauritius 129c
    Morocco 134b
    New Caledonia 230a–230b
    New Hebrides 231a
    Niger 141a
    Réunion 232c
    Senegal 160a–160b
    Tunisia 189b–189c
    Upper Volta 206a–207a
    Vietnam 212c–213a
    Wallis and Futuna Islands 236c
  the Directory 68c–69a
  Fifth Republic 65c, 71b
  First Republic 68c
  Fourth Republic 71a
  Hundred Years' War 198c
  the Merovingians 66a
  Napoleonic Era 69a
  recognizes Communist China 71a
  Second Empire 69b–69c
  Second Republic 69b
  Seven Years' War 202b
  Third Republic 69b–70a
  the Valois kings 66c–67b
  World War II 70a–71a, 78c, 204a
  occupation of Germany 79a
  occupied by Germany 70c–71a
Francia, José Gaspar Rodríguez de 147c
Francis I, Emperor (Austria) 76c
Francis I, King (France) 29c, 67b, 182b
Francis II, King (France) 67b
Francis I, King (Hungary) *see* Francis II, Emperor (Holy Roman Empire)
Francis II, Emperor (Holy Roman Empire) 11b
Francis Joseph I, Emperor (Austria) 77a

Francis Xavier, Saint 112c
Franco, Francisco 108c, 176a, 177b
Franco-Prussian War 69c
Franks
  France 66a
  Germany 75a
  Italy 107a–107b
  Netherlands 137a
  Switzerland 182b
Franz Ferdinand, Archduke (Austria-Hungary) 216b
Franz Josef I, Emperor (Austria) *see* Francis Joseph I, Emperor (Austria)
Franz Josef Land 244a
Fraser River 27a
Frederick II, King (Prussia) 76c
Frederick the Great *see* Frederick II, King (Prussia)
Frederick of Prussia 68b
Frederick William IV, King (Prussia) 77a
Fredericton, Canada 267a
Free French *see* French Committee of National Liberation
Freetown, Sierra Leone 160b, 161a, 267a
Frei Montalva, Eduardo 38c
French Committee of National Liberation (Free French) 70c
French East India Company 129a
French Equatorial Africa 71c
French Guiana 224
  Cayenne 263c
French Indochina 268c
  see also Cambodia; Laos; Vietnam
French Polynesia 224–225
  Papeete 279c
French Research Institute of Oceania 278b
French Revolution 68b–68c, 202c
French Somaliland *see* French Territory of the Afars and the Issas
French Southern and Antarctic Territories 225a–225b
French Territory of the Afars and the Issas 225b–225c
  Djibouti 265c
French Union 72c
French West Africa 86b
Friendly Islands *see* Tonga
Frisian Islands 136c, 244a
Frondizi, Arturo 7a
Frunze, Soviet Union 267a
Fuegians 37b
Fuentes, Miguel Ydígoras 85b
Fujairah 188c
  see also Trucial Oman
Fuji (volcano) 110b, 244a
Fujiwara family 112b
Fukien Massif (mountains) 40a
Fukien Province, China 266c
Fukuoka, Japan 267a
Fukushima, Japan 267a
Fula *see* Fulani
Fulani
  Cameroon 25c, 26a
  Gambia 72a
  Guinea 86a
  Mali 126c
  Niger 140c
  Nigeria 141b, 141c
  Senegal 159c
Fumicello River 158a
Funan, Kingdom of 25a
Fundy, Bay of 244a–244b, 267a
Funj 178b
Fur (people) 178a
Fur trade
  Canada 28b, 29b, 31b
  Finland 63a
Futuna Island *see* Wallis and Futuna Islands

G

Ga 79c
Gaberones, Botswana 17b, 267a
Gabès, Tunisia 189a
Gabon 35b, 71b–72a
  area 71b
  capital 71b
  currency unit 71b
  economy 71c

  fishing *il* 71
  flag *il* iii
  geography 71b
  government 71c
  history 71c–72a
  Lambaréné 273a

  language 71b
  Libreville 273c
  map 71, *Atlas*-35
  national holiday 71b
  official name 71b
  people of 71b–71c

INDEX

population 71b
religion 71b, 72a
slavery 71c
Gabonese Democratic Bloc (BDG) 72a
Gabonese Social and Democratic Union (UDSG) 71a
Gadsden Purchase 131a
Gaels 195c
Gaitán, Jorge E. 49b
Galapagos Islands 49c
Galilee, Sea of 105b, 244b, 278a
Galla (people)
  Ethiopia 62a, 62b
  Somali Republic 163b
Gallegos, Rómulo 210b
Gálvez, Juan Marval 89b
Gambia 72a–72c
  agriculture 72a–72b
  area 72a
  Bathurst 259c
  capital 72a
  currency unit 72a
  economy 72a–72b
  flag *il iii*
  geography 72a
  government 72b
  history 72b–72c
  language 72a
  map 72, *Atlas*-36
  national holiday 72a
  official name 72a
  people of 72a
  population 72a
  religion 72a
  slavery 72c
Gambia River 72a–72c, 127a, 159c, 244b
Gambier Islands 224c–225a
Gan Island 126c
Gandak River 135c
Gandhi, Indira 98b
Gandhi, Mohandas K. 97b, 97c, 145b
Ganges River 93b, *il* 94, 144a, 244b, 276a, 279c
Gangetic Plain 244b
Gangtok, Sikkim 161b, 267a
García, Alejo 147b
García, Carlos 150c
García Iñiguez, Calixto 53b
García Moreno, Gabriel 60b
García-Godoy, Héctor 59b
Garda, Lake 244b
Gardafui, Cape *see* Cape Gardafui
Garmo Peak 249c
Garonne River 64a, 244b, 261b, 287a
Gaspé Peninsula 244b
Gaul 66a
Gaza Strip 104a, 192b, 193b–193c
Gdańsk, Poland 151a, 267a–267b
Gdynia, Poland 151a, 267b
Geba River 232a
Geneva, Switzerland 181c, 182c, 267b
Geneva, Lake 181b, 244b, 267b
Geneva Canton, Switzerland 267b
Geneva Conference (1954) 213a
Gengis Khan 1c, 96b, 132c, 133a
Genil River 268a
Genoa, Italy 106c, 267b
Genoa, Gulf of 267b
Genoa Province, Italy 267b
Genoa, Republic of 107b
George I, King (England) 202a–202b
George II, King (England) 202a–202b
George III, King (England)
  American Revolution 202c
  insanity 203a
  reign of 202c–203a
George IV, King (England)
  reign of 203a
George V, King (England)
  reign of 203c
George VI, King (England)
  reign of 203a–204b
George I, King (Greece) 82c
George Land
  see Franz Josef Land
Georgetown, Cayman Islands 221c, 267b
Georgetown, Guyana 86b, 267b–267c
Georgetown, Malaysia 125b
Georghiu-Dej, Gheorghe 157a
Georgia, Strait of 288a
Georgian Soviet Socialist Republic 286b
Georgians 168a
German East Africa 185a

Germany 73–79
  agriculture 74a, 74b
  climate 73b
  division of 79a–79b
  economy 74a–74c
  geography 73b
  government 74c–75a
  industry *il* 74
  map 73, *Atlas*-16-17
  people of 73c–74a
  religion 73a, 73c, 75a, 76a–76b, 77b
  unification 77a–77b
  —Cities 73c–74a
    Berlin 260c
    Bonn 261b
    Bremen 261c
    Cologne (Köln) 264b
    Dresden 265b
    Düsseldorf 266a
    Essen 266c
    Frankfurt am Main 267a
    Hamburg 268b
    Hannover 268c
    Leipzig 273b
    Munich (München) 277a
    Nürnberg (Nuremberg) 277c
    Potsdam 281a
    Stuttgart 285a
    Wiesbaden 289a
  —History 75a–79b
    Allied occupation of 79a
    Austria's union with 12a–12b
    Czechoslovakia occupied by 56a
    Denmark occupied by 58b
    France occupied by 70c–71a
    Frankish Kingdom 75a
    the Hapsburgs 75c–76a
    Iceland occupied by 92c
    Jews 73c, 78a, 78b
    Kiaochow Bay seized by 45b
    Nazi Era 78a–78c
    nonaggression pact with Soviet Union 78c
    Reformation 76a–76b
    in Romania 157a
    in Rwanda 157c
    Saxons 75a–75c
    Weimer Republic 77c–78a
    World War I 11b–11c, 15a, 77c, 203c
    World War II 15a, 70c–71a, 78c, 79a
Germany, East
  area 73a
  capital 73a
  communism 74c
  currency unit 73a
  economy 74b–74c
  flag *il iii*
  government 74c–75a
  language 73a
  map 73, *Atlas*-16-17
  official name 73a
  population 73a
  religion 73a
  Soviet Union and 79b
Germany, West
  area 73a
  capital 73a
  currency unit 73a
  economy 74a–74b
  flag *il iii*
  government 74c
  language 73a
  map 73, *Atlas*-16-17
  official name 73a
  population 73a
  religion 73a
Germiston, South Africa 267c
Gersoppa Waterfall 244b
Gestido, Oscar 208a
Ghaggar River 263b
Ghana 79c–80b
  agriculture 80a
  area 79c
  capital 79c
  currency unit 79c
  economy 80a
  flag *il iii*
  geography 79c
  government 80a
  history 80a–80b
  language 79c
  map 80, *Atlas*-36-37
  national holiday 79c
  official name 79c
  people of 79c–80a
  population 79c
  religion 79c
  slavery 80b
  —Cities 80a
    Accra 256a
    Kumasi 272b
    Sekondi-Takoradi 284a
    Tema 80a
Ghats (mountains) 244b–244c
Ghazi, King (Iraq) 102a–102b
Ghaznavids 96b
Ghegs 2b
Ghent, Belgium 14a, 14b

Gia-Long, Emperor (Vietnam) 212b
Gibraltar 177c, 195c, 225c–226a
Gibraltar, Strait of 263b
Gibson Desert 244c
Gifu, Japan 267c
Giglio Island 105c
Gilbert and Ellice Islands 226a–226b
  area 226a
  capital 226a
  population 226a
  status 226a
  Tarawa 286b
Giovine Italia 107c
Girondist party (France) 68c
Giuba River 163a
Glasgow, Scotland 267c
Glorious Revolution 103b–103c
Goa 279c
Gobi Desert 40a, 244c
Godavari River 93c, 244c
Godthab, Greenland 267c
Godwin, Earl of Wessex 196c
Godwin Austin (mountain) 244c
Goetzen, Graf von 157c
Gogra River 244b
Gola (people) 121a
Gold
  Angola 218b
  Australia 8b, 9a
  Brazil 19b, 19c
  British Solomon Islands 220c
  Congo (Kinshasa) 50c
  Fiji Islands 224b
  Ghana 80a
  Laos 118c
  Liberia 121a
  Mexico 130a
  Mongolia 132c
  New Zealand 138c
  Nicaragua 139c
  Panama 146a
  Philippines 150a
  Rhodesia 155a
  Romania 156a
  South Africa 164b, 164c
  Soviet Union 168b
  Swaziland 179a
  Sweden 180a
  Tanzania 184b
  Thailand 185c
  Upper Volta 206c
  Venezuela 209b
Gold Coast *see* Ghana
Gold Coast Colony 2164b
  see also Ghana
Golden Temple (Sikh) 257b
Gómez, José 53c
Gómez, Juan Vicente 210a–210b
Gómez, Máximo 53b
Gomulka, Wladyslaw 152c
Gondwanaland 7a
Good Hope, Cape of *see* Cape of Good Hope
Gorée Island 160a
Gorky, Soviet Union 168a, 267c
Gorton, John 10a
Göta River 267c
Göteborg, Sweden 267c–268a
Göteborg och Bohus Province, Sweden 267c
Gothenburg, Sweden *see* Göteborg, Sweden
Gothia, Kingdom of 180b
Goths 75a
  Sweden 84b
Gotland Island 244c
Gottwald, Klement 56a
Gouda Mountains 225b
Goulart, João 20c
Gourde (currency unit) 87b
Gowon, Yakubu 142a
Gozo Island 127b
Graham Bell Island
  see Franz Josef Land
Grampian Mountains 194a
Gran Chaco 244c–245a
Gran Colombia 49a, 60b
Granada, Nicaragua 139c, 140a
Granada, Spain 268a
Granada Province, Spain 268a
Granados, Federico Tinoco 52a
Grand Atlas (mountains)
  see Atlas (mountains)
Grand Banks Plateau 245a
Grand Canal (China) 268c, 280a, 284c, 286c
Grand Cayman Island 267b
Grand Duchy of Warsaw 152a
Grand Lama *see* Dalai Lama
Grand Turk, Turks and Caicos Islands 236b

Grande Chartreuse Range 268a
Grande Comore Island 222c, 276c
Grande-Terre Island 227a
Grant, James Augustus 192a
Grant, John Peter 110a
Grant, Ulysses S. 59a
Graphite
  Korea, South 115c
  Madagascar 124a
  Mexico 130a
Grau San Martín, Ramón 149c
's Gravenhage, Netherlands 268b
Great Australian Bight 245a
Great Barrier Reef 7b, 245a
Great Bear Lake 245a
Great Britain *see* United Kingdom
Great Charter *see* Magna Carta
Great Dividing Range 245a
Great Indian Desert *see* Thar Desert
Great Interregnum 75c
Great Lakes 26c, 28c, 204c
Great Mosque
  Muhammad's tomb 277a
Great Rebellion (England) *see* United Kingdom—History
Great Rift Valley 61c–62a, 124b, 245a
Great Salt Lake 204c
Great Sandy Desert *see* Rub al Khali (desert)
Great Sark Island 222a
Great Sea *see* Mediterranean Sea
Great Slave Lake 245a
Great Victoria Desert 245a
Great Wall of China *il* 42, 273a
Greater Antilles (islands) 87b, 238a
Greater Khingan Mountains 40a
Greater Sundas Islands 98c
Greece 80c–83c
  agriculture 81a–81b
  Albania and 3a
  ancient 81b–81c
  area 80c
  Balkan Wars 83c
  capital 80c
  climate 81a
  communism 83b
  currency unit 80c
  Cyprus controversy 54b
  economy 81a–81b
  flag *il iii*
  geography 80c–81a
  government 81b
  history 81b–83c
  language 80c
  map 81, *Atlas*-9
  national holiday 80c
  official name 80c
  people of 81a
  population 80c
  religion 80c, 81b, 83c
  Turkey and 81c–83c
  World War I 83a
  World War II 83a–83b
  —Cities
    Athens 258b
    Piraeus 280b
    Thessaloníki (Salonika) 286c
Greece, Ancient 81b
  Albania 2c
  Cyprus 54b
  Italy 107a
  Spain 176b
Greenland 57a, 57c, 58a, 58b, 92c, 143a, 226b–226c, 245b
  area 226b
  capital 226b
  population 226b
  status 226b
Greenland Sea 245b
Gregory II, Pope 107a
Gregory X, Pope 75c
Grenada 226
  area 226c
  capital 226c
  population 226c
  St. George's 282c
  status 226c
Grenoble, France 65b, 268a
Grenoble, University of 268a
Grévy, Jules 69c
Grimaldi family 132a–132b
Groningen, Netherlands 137a
Grozny, Soviet Union 268a
Grunitzky, Nicolas 187b
Guadalajara, Mexico 129b, 130a, 268a
Guadalcanal Island 220c, 269a
Guadalquivir River 175b, 245b, 264c, 284a
Guadalupe Hidalgo, Treaty of (1848) 131a

Guadeloupe 227a
  area 227a
  capital 227a
  Pointe-à-Pitre 280c
  population 228a
  slavery 228a
  status 228a
Guadiana River 175b, 253a
Guam 256b
Guanabara Bay 282a
Guantanamo Bay 52b–53c
Guaraní Indians 147a
  Argentina 5b
Guaraní (currency unit) 147a
Guardia, Calderón 52a, 52b
Guardia, Tomás 52a
Guatemala 52a, 84a–85c, 89b
  agriculture 84a–84b
  area 84a
  capital 84a
  climate 84a
  currency unit 84a
  economy 84a–84c
  flag *il iii*
  geography 84a
  government 84a
  history 84c–85c
  Indians 84a, 84c, 85a
  industry 84b
  language 84a
  national holiday 84a
  official name 84a
  people of 84a
  population 84a
  religion 84a
  —Cities
    Champerico 263b
    Guatemala City 268a
    Puerto Barrios 281b
Guatemala City, Guatemala 84a, 84c, 268a
Guayaquil, Ecuador 60a, 60b
Guayas River 60a
Guernsey Island 222a
Guerrero Gutiérrez, Lorenzo 140b
Guevara, Ernesto "Ché" 20c, 54a
Guiana, British *see* Guyana
Guiana, Dutch *see* Surinam
Guiana, French *see* French Guiana
Guiana Highlands 245b
Guided Democracy 99b, 100b
Guilder 136c
Guinea 85c–86b
  agriculture 86a
  area 86b
  capital 85c
  climate 85c–86a
  Conakry 264b
  currency unit 85c
  economy 86a
  flag *il iii*
  geography 85c–86a
  government 86a
  history 86a–86b
  language 85c
  map 86, *Atlas*-36–37
  national holiday 85c
  official name 85c
  people of 86a
  population 85c
  religion 85c, 86a
Guinea, Gulf of 264c, 265c, 272c, 274a, 283c
Guinea, Portuguese *see* Portuguese Guinea
Guinea, Spanish *see* Spanish Guinea
Gujarat State, India 260c
Gumti River 244b, 274c
Guptas 95c–96a
Gürsel, Cemal 191b
Gurunsi 206b
Gustavus II, King (Sweden) 180c
Gustavus IV, King (Sweden) 180c
Gustavus V, King (Sweden) 181a
Guyana 86b–87b
  agriculture 86b, 86c
  area 86b
  capital 86b
  climate 86c
  currency unit 86b
  economy 86c–87a
  flag *il iii*
  geography 86b–86c
  Georgetown 267b
  government 87a
  history 87a–87b
  language 86b
  map 86, *Atlas*-44
  national holiday 86b
  official name 86b
  people of 86c
  population 86b
  religion 86b, 86c
  slavery 86c, 87a
Guzmán, Jacobo Arbenz 85b
Guzmán Blanco, Antonio 210a

H

Haakon IV, King (Norway) 143a
Haakon VII, King (Norway) 143b, 143c
Ha'apai Islands 236a
Haarlem, Netherlands 136c
Habana, Cuba *see* Havana, Cuba
Hadrian, Emperor (Rome) 195c
Hafsids 139b
Hagia Sophia 269c
Hague, The, Netherlands 136c, 268b
Haifa, Israel 104b, 268b
Haifa Institute of Technology 268b
Haile Selassie, Emperor (Ethiopia) 158c
Haile Selassie I University 256b
Hainan Island 39b, 40c, 245b
Haiphong, North Vietnam 211b, 268b
Haiti 87b–88b
  agriculture 87c, 88a
  area 87b
  capital 87b
  climate 87c
  currency unit 87b
  in Dominican Republic 59a
  economy 87c–88a
  flag *il iii*
  geography 87b–87c
  government 88a
  history 88a–88b
  Indians 88a
  language 87b
  map 87, *Atlas*-57
  Mardi gras *il* 87
  national holiday 87b
  official name 87b
  people of 87b
  population 87b
  Port-au-Prince 280c
  religion 87b, 88b
  slavery 88a
Hakodate, Japan 268b
Halifax, Canada 268b
Hamburg. Germany 73c, 268b–268c
Hamilton, Bermuda 219c, 268c
Hammarskjöld, Dag 181b
Han (people) *see* China, people of
Han dynasty 43a, 212a
Han River 19b–19c, 289b
Hangchow, China 268c
Hangchow Bay 268c, 278a
Hangkow *see* Wuhan
Hanno 72b
Hannover, Germany 268c
Hanoi, North Vietnam 210a, 211b, 213a, 268c
Hanover family 202a–203a
Hanseatic League 267a
Hanyang *see* Wuhan
Hapsburg family 11a–11b, 14c, 67b, 55b–56c, 67c, 123b
Germany 75c–76a
Spain 176c
Switzerland and 182b
Haraldsson, Olaf, King (Norway) 143a
Harbin, China 268c
Hari River 245b
Hari Singh, Maharaja 97c, 98a
Harold Hardrada, King (Norway) 196c
Harold II, King (England) 196c
Harper, Liberia 121a
Harsha 96a
Haryana State, India 263b
Hasan II, King (Morocco) 134b
Hashemite dynasty 114a
Hassan, Sayyid Muhammad Abdulla 163c
Hausa
  Niger 140c
  Nigeria 141b, 141c
Havana, Cuba 52b, 52c, 150b, 268c
Havel River 281b
Hawaii 205a
Haya de la Torre, Victor Raúl 149b
Hay-Herrán Treaty 146c
Hazara 1a
Hebrew University *il* 105
Hebrides Islands 194a, 245b
Heilungkiang Province, China 268c
Hejaz (province), Saudi Arabia 276a
Hejaz Mountains 158c
Hellespont *see* Dardanelles
Helmand River 1a, 245b
Helsinki, Finland 62c, 268c
Helvetii 182b
Henriques, Afonso *see* Afonso Henriques, King (Portugal)
Henry, kings (Germany) *see* Henry, emperors (Holy Roman Empire)
Henry, Prince (Portugal) *see* Henry the Navigator
Henry I, King (England)
  judicial reforms 197b
  reign 197a–197b
Henry II, King (England) 66b–66c, 67b, 103a, 197c
  legal reforms 197b
  reign 197b
Henry III, King (England)
  reign 198a
Henry IV, King (England)
  reign 199a
Henry V, King (England) 67a
  reign 199a
Henry VI, King (England)
  reign 199a–199b
Henry VII, King (England) 29b, 103b
  reign 199b–199c
Henry VIII, King (England) 103b
  reign 199c–200a
Henry III, King (France) 67b, 75b
Henry IV, King (France) 29c, 67b–67c
Henry III, Emperor (Holy Roman Empire) 75b
Henry of Burgundy 153c
Henry the Fowler 75b
Henry of Luxembourg, Count 123b
Henry of Navarre *see* Henry IV, King (France)
Henry the Navigator 153c
Herat, Afghanistan 1b
Herero 234c
Herm Island 222a
Hermitage (Leningrad) 273c
Hernad River 272a
Heruli 107a
Hesse (state), Germany 289a
Hetairia Philiké 81c
Heureaux, Ulises 59a
Hidalgo y Costilla, Miguel 130c
Hideyoshi 112b
High Atlas (mountains) *see* Atlas Mountains
Highlands of Scotland 245b–245c
Himalayas (mountains) 15b, 93a–93b, 161b, 245c
Himeji, Japan 269a
Hindu Kush (mountains) 167a, 245c
  Afghanistan 1a
Hirohito, Emperor (Japan) 113b
Hiroshima, Japan 113b, 268a
Hispaniola 87b, 88a, 245c, 280c
  see also Dominican Republic; Haiti
Hitler, Adolf 12a, 12b, 56a, 70b, 70c, 78a–79a, 91b, 108c, 152b, 174b, 181b, 204a
Ho Chi Minh 213a
Hohenzollern family 76b–76c
Hojo family 112b
Hokkaido Island 110b, 110c, 268b, 279a, 283c
Holland *see* Netherlands
Holland, Sydney 139b
Holstein 77a
Holt, Harold 10a
Holy Roman Empire 10b, 11a–11b, 14c, 107b, 137a–137b, 190c
  birth of 66a
Holyoake, Keith 139b
Home Rule League (Ireland) 103c
Homs, Syria 269a
Honan Province, China 270b
Honduras 88c–89b
  agriculture 88c–89a
  area 88c
  capital 88c
  climate 88c
  Copán 264c
  currency unit 88c
  economy 88c–89a
  flag *il iii*
  geography 88c
  government 89a
  history 89a–89b
  independence 89a–89b
  Indians 88, 89a
  language 88c
  map 88, *Atlas*-55
  national holiday 88c
  official name 88c
  people of 88c
  population 88c
  religion 88c
Honduras, Gulf of 245c
Hong Kong 44c, 195c, 227
  area 227a
  capital 227a
  climate 227a
  economy 227b
  geography 227a–227b
  government 227b–227c
  history 227c
  people of 227a–227b
  population 227a
  status 227a
Hong River 251b
Honiara, British Solomon Islands 220c, 269a
Honshu Island 264a, 267a, 267c, 269a, 270c, 272c, 277b, 278c, 279a, 283c, 284b, 287b, 287c, 289a, 289b
Hooghly River 224b, 262c, 269a
Hoover, Herbert 88b
Hopeh Province, China 263c
Horn, Cape *see* Cape Horn
Horthy, Miklós 91a
Hottentots 165a, 235c
Houphouët-Boigny, Felix 109b
Hova 123c, 124a
Howrah, India 269a
Hoxha, Enver 3b
Hoysalas 96a
Hsi River 40a
Hsia dynasty 42a
Hsiang River 263c
Hsüntzu 42b, 42c
Huan Archipelago 230b
Huang River 40b
Hubli, India 269a
Al Hudaydah, Yemen 214b
Hudson, Henry 236a
Hudson Bay 26c, 27b, 30c, 245c
Hudson River 205a
Hudson's Bay Company 32c
Hué, South Vietnam 269a
Hué, Treaty of 212c
Hué River 269a
Huerta, Victoriano 131b
Hugh Capet, King (France) 66b
Hughes, William Morris 9c
Hukbalahap 150b, 150c
Humayun 96b
Humbert II, King (Italy) 108c
Humboldt Current 148a
Hume, Allan Octavian 97a
Hunan Province, China 263c
Hundred Years' War 67a, 103a, 198c
Hunedoara, Romania 156a
Hungarian Socialist Workers Party 186a–186b

INDEX

Hungary 11c, 55b–56a, 89b–91c
  agriculture 90a
  area 89b
  Austrian rule 90c–91a
  capital 89b
  climate 89c
  communism 90a–90b, 91a–91c
  constitution 90b
  currency unit 89b
  dual monarchy 91a
  economy 90a
  flag *il* iii
  geography 89b–89c
  government 90a–90b
  history 90b–91c
  industry 90a
  language 89b
  map 89, *Atlas*-18–19
  national holiday 89b
  natural resources 90a
  official name 89b
  Ottoman Era 90c
  people of 89c–90a
  population 89b
  religion 89b, 90c
  revolution of 1956, 91c
  trade 90a
  World War I 91a
  World War II 91b
  —Cities 89c–90a
    Budapest 262b
    Debrecen 265b
    Esztergom 266c
    Miskolc 266b
    Pécs 280a
    Sopron 284c
    Szeged 285c
Huns
  Germany 75a
  Hungary 90b
  India 96a
  Italy 107a
  Romania 156b
  White Huns 1c
Hunyadi, János 90c
Hunter Mountains 7b
Hupeh Province, China 269b, 289b
Hus, John 55b
Husain, Zakir 98b
Hussein, King (Jordan) 114a, 114b
Hussein, Sharif 159b
Hussein, Abdullah ibn, Emír (Jordan) 132a
Hussein, Haja Muhammad 163b
Hutu
  Burundi 24b
  Rwanda 156b, 156c
Hwang Ho 39c, 40b, 245c, 270b, 273a
Hyderabad, India 269a
Hydroelectric power
  Austria 11a
  Cameroon 26a
  Canada 28a
  El Salvador 61a
  Guinea 86a
  Iceland 92b
  Japan 111b, 111c
  Liechtenstein 122c
  Nepal 135c
  New Caledonia 230b
  Nigeria 141b
  Pakistan 144c
  Portugal 153b
  Soviet Union 168c
  Thailand 185c–186a
  Uganda 191c
  U.S. 205c
  Yugoslavia 215b
  Zambia 217b

I

Iași, Romania 156a, 269a
Ibadan, Nigeria 141b, 269a
Ibañez, Cárlos 38c
Iberian Peninsula 245c–246a
Iberians 176b
Ibiza *see* Balearic Islands
Ibo 141b
Iceland 58a, 58b, 92a–93a, 143a
  area 92a
  capital 92a
  climate 92a
  currency unit 92a
  economy 92a
  flag *il* iii
  geography 92a
  government 92b
  history 92b–93a
  independence 92c
  industry 92b
  language 92a
  map *Atlas*-14
  national holiday 92a
  official name 92a
  people of 92a
  population 92a
  religion 92a, 92c
  Reykjavík 282a
  World War II 92c
Ichang, China 269b
Idris 122b, 134a
Ieyasu, Tokugawa 112b
Ifni 227–228
  area 227c
  capital 227c
  population 227c
  Sidi-Ifni 284c
  status 227c
Iguassú Falls 246a
Iguassu River 264c
IJ River 257b
IJssel Meer Inlet 245a
Ile Amsterdam 225a
Ile de France *see* Mauritius
Ile St. Paul 225a
Ili River 246a
Iliamna Lake 204c
Illia, Arturo 7a
Illyrians 2c
Iloilo, Philippines 269b
Iloilo Province, Philippines 269b
Imbokodvo Party (Swaziland) 179b–179c
Imperial War Conference (1917) 33c–34a
Imphal Plain 269b
Imstel River 257b
Inca Empire *see* Incas
Incas
  Argentina 6a
  Bolivia 16c
  Chile 38c
  Ecuador 60b, 281c
  Peru 148c, 265a
India 15c, 36c, 93a–97b
  agriculture 94a
  area 93a
  capital 93a
  climate 93c–94a
  currency unit 93a
  economy 94a–94c
  flag *il* iii
  geography 93a–94a
  government 94c–95a
  industry 94c
  language 93a
  map 93, *Atlas*-28–29
  national holiday 93a
  natural resources 94b
  official name 93a
  people of 94a
  population 93a
  religion 93a, 94a, 95b, 96a–96b, 97b
  temples 96a–96b, 96c
  trade 94c
  —Cities 94a
    Agra 256b
    Ahmadabad 256b
    Ahmadnagar 256c
    Ajmer 256c
    Aligarh 257a
    Allahabad 257a
    Alleppey 257a
    Ambala 257a
    Amratavi 257b
    Amritsar 257b
    Banaras 259a
    Bangalore 259b
    Bareilly 259c
    Baroda 259c
    Bhavnagar 260c
    Bhopal 260b
    Bhubaneswar 260b
    Bikaner 261a
    Bombay 261b
    Calcutta 262c
    Cawnpore 263b
    Chandigarh 263b
    Cochin 264b
    Coimbatore 264b
    Cuttack 265a
    Darjeeling 267a
    Dehra Dun 265b
    Howrah 269a
    Hubli 269b
    Hyderabad 269a
    Imphal 269b
    Indore 269b
    Jabalpur 269c
    Jaipur 270a
    Jamshedpur 270a
    Jodhpur 270a
    Jullundur 270b
    Kolhapur 272a
    Kozhikode 272a
    Lucknow 274c
    Madras 275a
    Madura 275a
    Mangalore 275b
    Mathura 275c
    Meerut 276a
    Moradabad 276c
    Nagpur 277b
    New Delhi 278a
    Panjim 279c
    Patna 279c
    Poona 280c
    Rampur 281c
    Ranchi 281c
    Salem 283a
    Shillong 284b
    Sholapur 284b
    Srinigar 285b
    Surat 285c
    Tanjore (Thanjavor) 286a
    Tiruchirappalli (Trichinopoly) 287a
    Trivandrum 287b
    Ujjain 287c
  —History 95a–98b
    Communist China and 98a
    first empires (600 BC–AD 300) 95b–95c
    Guptas 95c–96a
    independence 97c–98a
    Muslim dominance (1200–1700) 96b–97c
    Pakistan and 93a, 97c–98a, 144c, 145c
    Rajputs 96a, 96c
    rise of nationalism 97a–97c
    Sikkim and 161c
    Western dominance 96c–97a
    World War II 97b–97c
Indian Desert *see* Thar Desert
Indian Institute of Science 259b
Indian National Congress 145a, 145b
Indian Ocean 123c, 246a
Indians *see* Indians (America); Indians (India)
Indians (America)
  Argentina 6a
  Aruba 229c
  Bolivia 16a–16b, 16c
  Brazil 18c, 19c
  British Honduras 220a, 220b
  Canada 27b, 29c, 30a, 30c
  Chile 37b, 38a
  Colombia 48b
  Cuba 53b
  Dominica 223a
  Ecuador 60a, 60b
  El Salvador 61a
  French Guiana 224c
  Grenada 229c
  Guatemala 84a, 84c, 85a
  Guyana 86c
  Haiti 88b
  Honduras 88c, 89a
  Jamaica 110a
  Martinique 228c
  Mexico 129c, 130b–130c
  Netherlands Antilles 229c
  Nicaragua 139b–139c
  Panama 146a, 146c
  Paraguay 147a, 147c
  Peru 148b, 148c, 149a
  St. Lucia 233b
  Surinam 235b
  Trinidad and Tobago 188a
  U.S. 205c
  Uruguay 207a
  —Peoples, tribes
    Araucanian 133b, 134a
    Arawak 13a, 53b, 88a, 110a, 188a
    Aymara 16b, 148b
    Aztec 129c, 130b, 130c
    Carib 53b, 220a, 226c, 228c, 223a, 229c
    Changos 37b
    Churrúa 207a
    Fuegian 37b
    Guaraní 5b, 147a, 147c
    Inca 16c, 38a, 52c, 60b
    Iroquois 29c
    Maya 84a, 84c, 130b, 220a, 220b
    Mosquito 139b–139c
    Quechua 16a, 148b
    Toltec 130b
Indians (India)
  Guyana 86c, 87a
  Kuwait 117c
  Malaysia 125b, 126b
  Mauritius 128c, 129a
  Singapore 162b
  Trinidad and Tobago 187b, 188a
  see also India, people of
Indochina 45a, 246a
Indonesia 98b–100b
  agriculture 99a, *il* 99
  area 98b
  capital 98b
  climate 98c
  communism 100b
  currency unit 98b
  economy 98c–99a
  flag *il* iii
  geography 98c
  government 99a–99b
  history 99b–100b
  independence 100a–100b
  language 98b
  map 98, *Atlas*-30–31
  national holiday 98b
  official name 98b
  people of 98c
  population 98b
  religion 98b, 98c, 99c
  World War II 100a
  —Cities 98c
    Bandung 259a
    Makasar 275a
    Padang 279b
    Palembang 279b
    Sukarnapura 285b
    Surabaja 285b
Indore, India 269b
Indus River 93a, 93b, 97c, 144a, 144b, 245b, 271a
Industrial Reconstruction Institute 106c
Industrial Revolution 203a
Inland Sea 245b, 269a, 278c, 284b
Inn River 73b, 245b
Inner City *see* Peking
Inönü, Ismet 191a
Inquisition
  Netherlands 137b
  Portugal 154a
  Spain 176c
Institut Français d'Afrique Noire 265a
Institute of People's Education (Kharkov, Soviet Union) 271b
Integrated Revolutionary Organizations (ORI) (Cuba) 53a
Inter-American Conferences *see* Pan-American Conferences
Internal Macedonian Revolutionary Organization (IMRO) 22a
Invincible Armada 200b
Ionian Sea 245b
Ipoh, Malaysia 125b
Iran 13a, 100c–101c
  agriculture 100c–101a
  area 100c
  capital 100c
  climate 100c
  currency unit 100c
  economy 100c–101a
  flag *il* iii
  geography 100c
  government 101a
  industry 100c–101a
  language 100c
  map 100, *Atlas*-26
  national holiday 100c
  official name 100c
  people of 100c
  population 100c
  religion 100c
  World War II 101b
  —Cities
    Abadan 256a
    Ahvaz 256c
    Isfahan 269b
    Mashhad 275c
    Reza'iyeh (Urmia) 282a
    Shiraz 282b
    Tabriz 283c
    Tehran (Teheran) 284b

Iraq 101c–102b, 117c–118a
  agriculture 101c–102a
  area 101c
  capital 101c
  climate 101c
  currency unit 101c
  economy 101c–102a
  flag *il iii*
  geography 101c
  government 102a
  history 102a–102b
  independence 102a–102b
  language 101c
  map 101, *Atlas*-25
  national holiday 101c
  official name 101c
  people of 101c
  population 101c
  religion 101c
  World War II 102b
  —Cities
    Bagdad 258c
    Basra 259c
    Kirkuk 271c
    Mosul 277a
Ireland 102b–103c, 194a, 195c
  agriculture 102c–103a
  area 102b
  capital 102b
  climate 102c
  currency unit 102b
  Dublin 265c
  economy 102c–103a
  emigration 102c, 103c
  flag *il iii*
  geography 102c
  government 103
  history 103a–103c
  independence 103c, 203c
  industry 195a
  language 102b
  map 102, *Atlas*-10–11
  national holiday 102b
  official name 102b
  people of 102c
  population 102b
  religion 102b, 102c, 103a
Irigoyen, Hipólito 102c
Irish Free State *see* Ireland
Irish Republican Army (IRA) 103c
Irish Sea 246b, 265c
Irkutsk, Soviet Union 269b
Iron Gate Gorge 245b
Iron
  Angola 218b
  Australia 8b
  Austria 10a
  Belgium 14b
  Brazil 19a
  Chile 37c
  China 41b
  Cuba 52c
  Cyprus 54a
  France 64b
  Gabon 71c
  Germany 74b
  India 94c
  Korea, North 115c
  Korea, South 115c
  Laos 118b
  Lebanon 119b
  Liberia 121a
  Luxembourg 123a–123b
  Mauritania 128b
  Mongolia 132c
  Morocco 133c
  Nepal 135c

  New Caledonia 230b
  Nicaragua 139c
  Pakistan 144b
  Peru 148b
  Philippines 150a
  Poland 151b
  Portugal 153b
  Romania 156a
  Sierra Leone 160c
  Somali Republic 163a
  South Africa 164c
  Soviet Union 168b, 169a
  Spain 175c
  Spanish Sahara 235a
  Swaziland 179a
  Sweden 180a
  Turkey 190a
  United Arab Republic (Egypt) 192c
  United Kingdom 194c
  U.S. 205c
  Venezuela 209b
  Yugoslavia 215b
Ironwood 23a
Iroquois Indians 29c
Irrawaddy River 22c, 245b, 275b
Irtysh River 245b
Irwell River 275b
Isabella I, Queen (Spain) 176c
Isabella II, Queen (Spain) 177a
Isar River 277a
Ischia Island 105c
Ise Bay 110c, 277b
Isère River 268a
Isfahan, Iran 101a–101b, 269b–269c
Ishikari River 110c, 258a
Iskenderun, Turkey 269c
Iskenderun, Gulf of 269c
Islam
  Afghanistan 1c
  Albania 2b, 3a
  Algeria 3c, 4a
  Bahrain 12c
  Brunei 221b
  Bulgaria 21a, 21c
  Cameroon 25c, 26a
  Chad 37a
  China 44c
  Comoro Islands 223c
  Congo (Kinshasa) 50c
  Cyprus 54a, 54b
  Dahomey 56b
  Ethiopia 62a, 62b
  French Territory of the Afars and the Issas 225b
  Gabon 71b
  Gambia 72a
  Ghana 79c
  Greece 81c
  Guinea 86a
  Guyana 86c
  Ifni 227c
  India 94a, 96b–96c, 97b–98a
  Indonesia 99a, 99c, 100a
  Iran 100c, 101a
  Iraq 101c, 102a
  Israel 104b, 105a
  Ivory Coast 109b
  Jordan 113c
  Kenya 114c
  Kuwait 117b
  Lebanon 119b, 119c
  Libya 121c, 122b
  Malaysia 125b, 125c
  Maldive Islands 126b

  Mali 126c, 127b
  Mauritania 128a, 128b
  Mauritius 128c
  Morocco 133c, 134a
  Muscat and Oman 134b
  Niger 140c
  Nigeria 141b, 141c
  Pakistan 144a, 144b, 144c–145b
  Qatar 154b
  Saudi Arabia 158c, 159a
  Somali Republic 163b
  South Yemen 165c
  Spain 176b
  Spanish Sahara 234a
  Sudan 178a, 178b
  Syria 182c, 183b
  Tanzania 184a, 184c
  Trucial Oman 188b
  Tunisia 189a, 189b
  Turkey 190a
  United Arab Republic (Egypt) 192c, 193a
  Yemen 214a, 214b
  Yugoslavia 215a
Islamabad, Pakistan 144a, 269c
Islands 246b–246c
Isle of Man 194a, 195c, 228a–228b
  area 228a
  capital 228a
  Douglas 265c
  population 228a
  status 228a
Israel 104a–105c
  agriculture 104b
  area 104a
  capital 104a
  climate 104b
  currency unit 104a
  economy 104b–104c
  flag *il iii*
  geography 104a–104b
  government 104b
  Hebrew University *il* 105
  history 104b–105c
  language 104a
  map 104, *Atlas*-24
  national holiday 104a
  official name 104a
  people of 104b
  population 104a
  religion 104a, 104b, 104c
  trade 104c
  United Arab Republic (Egypt) and 102b, 104a, 104b, 105c
  —Cities 104b
    Beersheba 260a
    Elath 266b
    Haifa 268b
    Jerusalem 270a
    Nazareth 270a
    Tel Aviv 286b
Issa, Abdullah 163b
Issa Somalis 225b
Istanbul, Turkey 190a, 190b, 269c
Isthmus of Panama 146c
Italian East Africa 62c
Italian Somaliland 62c, 108b
  see also Somali Republic
Italy 105–108
  agriculture 106b–106c
  Albania 3a–3b
  area 105c
  capital 105c
  city-states 107b
  climate 108a

  communism 108c
  currency unit 105c
  economy 106b–106c
  fascism 108b–108c
  flag *il iii*
  foreign domination 107b–107c
  geography 106a
  government 106c–107a
  history 107a–108c
  industry 106c
  language 105c
  Libya and 122b
  map 106, *Atlas*-13
  national holiday 105c
  natural resources 106b
  official name 105c
  people of 106a
  population 105c
  religion 105c, 106a, 108c
  Renaissance 107b
  risorgimento 107c
  trade 106c
  World War I 77c, 108b, 203c
  World War II 108c
  —Cities 106a
    Bologna 261b
    Florence 266c
    Genoa 267b
    Milan 276b
    Naples 277c
    Palermo 279c
    Rome 282b
    Trieste 287b
    Turin 287c
    Venice 288a
Italy, Kingdom of 108a
Iteso 191c
Itung River 263c
Iturbide, Augustín de 52a, 61b, 84c–85a, 89a, 131a
Ivan I, Prince (Muscovy) 170a
Ivan III, Prince (Muscovy) 170a–170b
Ivan IV, Tsar (Russia) 170b–170c
Ivan the Terrible, *see* Ivan IV, Tsar (Russia)
Ivory Coast 109a–109b
  Abidjan 256a
  agriculture 109a
  area 109a
  capital 109a
  climate 109a
  communism 109b
  currency unit 109a
  economy 109a–109b
  flag *il iii*
  geography 109a
  government 109b
  history 109b
  independence 109b
  language 109a
  map 109, *Atlas*-36
  national holiday 109a
  official name 109a
  people of 109a
  population 109a
  religion 109a
Ivory Coast Democratic Party (PDCI) 109b
Izalco, El Salvador *il* 61
Izmir, Turkey 269c
Izmir, Gulf of 269c
Iztaccíhuatl (mountain) 129c

J

Jaaliin 178a
Jabalpur, India 269c–270a
Jacobin party (France) 68c
Jacques I, Emperor (Haiti) 88b
Jadotville *see* Likasi, Congo (Kinshasa)
Jadwiga, Queen (Hungary) 152a
Jaffa, Israel 104b
Jagan, Cheddi 87a, 87b
Jagello, Ladislas 152a
Jahan, Shah (India) 96c
Jahangir 96c
Jahun River *see* Amu River
Jaipur, India 270a
Jalisco, Mexico 129b
Jalisco State, Mexico 268a

Jamaica 13c, 109c–110b
  agriculture 109c–110a
  area 109c
  capital 109c
  climate 109c
  currency unit 109c
  economy 109c
  flag *il iii*
  geography 109c
  government 110
  history 110a–110b
  independence 110b
  Indians 110a
  Kingston 271c
  language 109c
  map *Atlas*-56–57
  national holiday 109c
  official name 109c
  people of 109c
  population 109c
  religion 109c
  slavery 110a
  World War II 110b
Jamaica Labor Party 110b

James I, King (England) 103b, 103c
  divine right theory 200c
  reign 200b–200c
James II, King (England) 103b
  reign 201b–201c
Jamestown, St. Helena 233a, 270a
Jamestown, Virginia 200b
Jamshedpur, India 270a
Jan Mayen Island 142a, 235–236
Jansz, Willem 8c
Japan 110b–113b
  agriculture 111b
  area 110b
  capital 110b
  climate 110c
  currency unit 110b
  economy 111a–112a
  fishing 111b
  flag *il iii*
  forestry 111b–111c
  geography 110b–110c
  government 112a

  industry 111c
  language 110b
  map 110, *Atlas*-33
  national holiday 110b
  natural resources 111a–111b
  official name 110b
  people of 110c–111a
  population 110b
  religion 110b, 110c–111a, 112a, 112c
  trade 111c–112a
  —Cities 111a
    Akita 256c
    Asahigawa 258a
    Chiba 264a
    Fukuoka 267a
    Fukushima 267a
    Gifu 267c
    Hakodate 268b
    Himeji 269a
    Hiroshima 269a
    Kagoshima 270b
    Kamakura 270c
    Kochi 272a

Kokura 272a
Kumamoto 272b
Kurume 272b
Kyoto 272c
Muroran 277a
Nagasaki 277b
Nagoya 277b
Nara 277c
Okayama 278c
Omuta 278c
Osaka 279a
Otaru 279a
Saga 282c
Sakai 283a
Sapporo 283c
Sendai 284a
Shimonoseki 284b
Shizuoka 284b
Takamatsu 286a
Tokyo 287b
Toyama 287b
Wakayama 289a
Yamagata 289b
—History 112a–113b
  in Cambodia 25b
  China, war with 46c
  Chinese influence 112a–112b
  in Indonesia 100a
  Kamakura era 112b
  in Korea 45a, 116c–117a
  in Laos 119a
  in Malaysia 126a
  Manchuria invasion 46b–46c
  Meiji Restoration 112c–113a
  Mongolia and 133a, 133b
  in Nauru 135b
  in the Philippines 150b
  in Singapore 162c
  in Taiwan 45a
  Tokugawa era 112b–112c
  in Vietnam 212c–213a
  World War I 113a
  World War II 100a, 113b
Japan, Sea of 110c, 246c, 287b
Japan Socialist Party (JSP) 113b
Java, Indonesia 98c, 99a, 99b, 99c, 285b
Jawara, Dawda 72c
Jaxartes River *see* Syr River
Jean, Grand Duke (Luxembourg) 123c
Jeanne d' Arc *see* Joan of Arc
Jebel-el-Akhdar 260c
Jehol *see* Chengteh
Jelenia Góra, Poland 151c
Jena, Battle of 76c
Jenkins' Ear, War of 202b
Jersey Islands 222a
Jerusalem (city) 104a, 104c, 105a–105b, 270a
Jesselton, Malaysia 270a
Jesuits 247a
Jethou Island 222a
Jews 104a–105c
  culture 104c
  diaspora 105a
  Germany 73c, 78a, 78b
  Soviet Union 168a
  Spain 176c
  Zionism 105a–105b
Jhelum River 144c, 285a
Jiménez, Mario Echandi 52b
Jiménez de Quesada, Gonzalo 49a
Jinja, Uganda 270a
Jinnah, Muhammad Ali 145b, 145c
Joan of Arc 67a
Jodhpur, India 270a
Johannesburg, South Africa 164b, 270a
John, King (England) 197c
John II, King (Portugal) 154a
John XII, Pope 107b
John of Avís, King (Portugal) 153c
John Baliol, King (Scotland) 198b
John of Bragança, King (Portugal) 154a
Joliet, Louis 30b
Jolo, Philippines 270a
Jonathon, Leabua 120c
Joppa, Israel *see* Jaffa, Israel
Jordan 105c, 113c–114b
  agriculture 113c
  Arab-Israeli conflict 114b
  area 113c
  capital 113c
  climate 113c
  currency unit 113c
  economy 113c
  flag *il iii*
  geography 113c
  government 114a
  history 114a–114b
  language 113c
  map 114, *Atlas*-24
  national holiday 113c
  official name 113c
  people of 113c
  population 113c
  religion 113c
  World War II 114a
—Cities
  Amman 257c
  Aqaba 258a
  Bethlehem 260c
Jordan River 104a, 113a, 114a, 246c
Jos, Nigeria 270a
Jos Plateau 246c
Juárez, Benito 131a, 131b
Judaean Hills 104b, 270a
Juddah, Saudi Arabia 270b
Juliana, Queen (Netherlands) 137c
Jullundur, India 270b
Jumna River 239c, 275c, 278a
  see also Brahmaputra River
Jungfrau (mountain) 246c
Jura Mountains 64a, 181b, 246c
Justice Party (Turkey) 191b
Justicialismo 6c
Jutes 196a
Jutland Peninsula 246c
Juxon-Smith, Andrew 161b
Jylland Peninsula 246c

K

K2 (mountain) *see* Godwin Austin
Kaaba 276a
Kababish 178a
Kabaka Yekka Party (Buganda) 192a
Kabul, Afghanistan 1a, 270b
Kabul Kingdom 96b
Kabul River 1a, 270b
Kabul University 270b
Kachin (people) 22c
Kadár, Janos 91c
KADU *see* Kenya African Democratic Union (KADU)
Kaduna, Nigeria 270b
Kaduna River 270b
Kaédi, Mauritania 128a
Kafue River 217a
Kagera River 157b
Kagoshima, Japan 270b
Kagoshima Bay 270b
Kagoshima Prefecture, Japan 270b
Kaifeng, China 270b
Kailas Mountains 246c
Kaladan River 256c
Kalahari Desert 17b, 234c, 246c
Kalgan, China 270b
Kalimantan Island 98c
  see also Borneo
Kalinin, Soviet Union 270c
Kaliningrad, Soviet Union 270c
Kállai, Gyula 91c
Kalmar Castle (Sweden) 181a
Kalmar Union 143a, 180b–180c
Kama River 280c
Kamakura, Japan 270c
Kamakura Era 112b
Kamba 114b
Kamchatka, Sea of *see* Bering Sea
Kamchatka Peninsula 246c–247a
Kamerun *see* Cameroon
Kamikaze 112b
Kampala, Uganda 191c, 192b, 270c
Kan River 277c
Kanchenjunga Mountain 247a
Kanchipuram, India 96a
Kandahar, Afghanistan 1b, 270c–271a
Kandy, Ceylon 271a
Kandy, Kingdom of 36b, 126c, 271a
Kanem Empire 37c
K'ang Yu-wei 45b
Kanishka, King (India) 95c
Kankan, Guinea 86b
Kano, Nigeria 141b, 271a
Kanpur, India 94a
Kansu Province, 273a
KANU *see* Kenya African National Union (KANU)
Kaolack, Senegal 159c
Kapodistrias, Ioannes 82b
Kara River 244a
Karachi, Pakistan 144b, 271a
Karaganda, Soviet Union 271a
Karaganda coal basin 271a
Kariba, Lake 155a, 217a, 247a
Kariba Dam 217b
Karkoram Mountains 247a
Karl (kings) *see* Charles
Karnali River 135c
Karnaphuli River 264a
Karume, Adeid Amani 184c, 185a
Kasai River 50c, 247a
Kasavubu, Joseph 51a, 51b
Kashmir 93c, 97c, 98a, 98b, 144a, 145c, 285a
Kastrioti, Gjergj 3a
Katanga Plateau 240c
Katanga Province, Congo (Kinshasa) 273c, 274c
Kathiawar Peninsula 247a, 260c
Katmandu, Nepal 235b, 235c, 271a
Katmandu Valley 135c, 136a
Katowice, Poland 151b, 271b
Kattegat Strait 247a
Kattowitz, Poland *see* Katowice, Poland
Kaunas, Soviet Union 271b
Kaunda, Kenneth 217c
Kayibanda, Grégoire 158a
Kazakh Hills 271a
Kazakhs 168a
Kazan, Soviet Union 271b
Kazan University 271b
Keeling, William 222c
Keeling Islands 222
Keita, Modibo 127b
Kelani River 264b
Kelly, Grace 132c
Kemal, Mustafa 191a
Kennedy, John F. 54a
Kent, Kingdom of 196a
Kenya 114b–115b
  agriculture 114b
  economy 114b–114c
  flag *il iii*
  geography 114b
  government 114c
  history 114c–115a
  independence 115b
  map 114, *Atlas*-39
  Mombasa 276c
  Nairobi 277b
  nationalism 115a
  people of 114c
  religion 114b
  slavery 114b
Kenya (mountain) 114b
Kenya African Democratic Union (KADU) 115a
Kenya African National Union (KANU) 115a
Kenya Highlands 247a
Kenyatta, Jomo 115a
Kerala State, India 264b
Kerch Peninsula 243a
Kerguelen Archipelago 225a
Kerulen River 132c, 247a
Kha 118a, 118b
Khabarovsk, Soviet Union 271b
Khalifa dynasty 13a
Khalji, Ala-ud-din *see* Ala-ud-din Khalji
Khalkha Mongols 132c
Khama, Seretse 17c
Kharkov, Soviet Union 168a, 169b, 271b
Khartoum, Sudan 117c, 118b, 271c
Khasi Hills 93c, 247b, 284b
Khasis 94c
Khayr-ad-Din 4a
Khingan Mountains 40a, 247b
Khmer 24c, 25a, 186a
Khrushchev, Nikita 79b, 175a
Khyber Pass 144b, 280a
Kiangsi Province, China 277c
Kiangsu Province, China 277c, 284c
Kiaochow Bay 45b
Kiel, Treaty of 226c
Kiesinger, Kurt 79a
Kiev, Soviet Union 168a, 170a, 271c
Kigali, Rwanda 156b, 271c
Kii Strait 110c
Kikuyu 114b, 115a
Kilimanjaro (mountain) 184a, 247b, 277a
Kimba, Evariste 51b
Kimberley, South Africa 164c, 271c
Kimbundu 218a
King, Charles D. B. 121b
King, (William Lyon) Mackenzie 34a, 34b
King Leopold Ranges 247b
Kingston, Jamaica 109c, 271c
Kingstown, St. Vincent 233a, 271c
Kino River 289a
Kinshasa, Congo (Kinshasa) 50a, 271c
Kip 118a
Kirdi 25c
Kirin, China 271c
Kirin Province, China 263c
Kirkuk, Iraq 102a, 271c
Kisangani, Congo (Kinshasa) 50c, 272a
Kishinev, Soviet Union 272a
Kissi 121c
Kistna River 247b
Kitakyushu, Japan 111a
Kivu, Lake 50c, 157b, 247b
Kizil River 189c–190a
Kjölen Mountains 179c, 247b
Klaipeda, Soviet Union 272a
Klaus, Josef 12b
Klondike 247b
KMT *see* Kuomintang (KMT)
Kobe, Japan 111a
Köbenhaven, Denmark *see* Copenhagen, Denmark
Kochi, Japan 272a
Koguryo (kingdom) 116a
Koh-i-Baba (mountains) 1a
Koirala, B. P. 136b
Kokura, Japan 272a
Kola Peninsula 277c
Kolhapur, India 272a
Köln, Germany *see* Cologne, Germany
Kololo 217c
Kolyma Mountains 247b
Komsomolsk, Soviet Union 272a
Kong, Ivory Coast 109b
Königsberg, Soviet Union 270c
Kopet Dagh Mountains 167a
Korea 43c, 45a, 115b–117b
  agriculture 115c, 116c
  climate 115c
  economy 115c–116a
  geography 115b–115c
  government 116a
  history 116a–117b
  independence 45b
  Japanese control 45a
  map 115, *Atlas*-33
  people of 115c
  religion 115b, 115c, 116b
  Yi dynasty 116b
  see also Korea, North and Korea, South
Korea, North
  agriculture 115c
  climate 115c
  communism 116a, 117a, 117b
  economy 115c
  flag *il iii*
  map 115, *Atlas*-33
  religion 115b
—Cities 264a
  Chinnampo 264a
  Chongjin 264a

Korea, South
  Pyongyang 281b
  Wonsan 289b
Korea, South
  agriculture 115c, 116c
  climate 115c
  economy 115c–116a
  flag *il* iii
  map 115, *Atlas*-33
  religion 115b
  —Cities 276c
    Mokpo 276c
    Seoul 284a
    Taegu 286a
Korea Bay 247b
Korean Peninsula 286a
Korean War 47a, 113b, 117a
Korean Workers Party 116a
Koreans
  Japan 110c
  Soviet Union 168a
Koros River 278c
Koruna 54c
Koryo dynasty 116b
Kosala Kingdom 95b
Kosciusko (mountain) 7b
Kosi River 135c, 281c
Košice, Czechoslovakia 272a
Kosovo (region), Yugoslavia 3b
Kosovo-Metohija (region), Yugoslavia

Albanians in 3b
Kosygin, Aleksei 98b, 175a
Kouilou River 49c
Kozhikode, India 272a
Kra, Isthmus of 185a, 247b
Krag, Jens Otto 58b
Kraków, Poland 151a, 272a–272b
Kraków, University of 152a
Krasnovodsk, Soviet Union 272b
Kremlin 277a
Krimml Waterfall 247c
Krishna River 93c, 249b
Króna 92a, 179c
Krone
  Denmark 57a
  Norway 142a
Kronstadt, Soviet Union 173c
Kru
  Ivory Coast 109a
  Liberia 121a
Kruger, Paul 165a
Kuala Lumpur, Malaysia 125a, 125b, 272b
Kubitschek, Juscelino 20c
Kublai Khan 16b, 37a, 43c
Kuching, Sarawak 272b
Kukenan Waterfall *see* Cuquenán Waterfall

Kumasi, Ghana 80a, 272b
Kunamoto, Japan 272b
Kunlun Mountains 39c, 43a, 247c
Kunming, China 272b
Kuomintang (KMT) (party, China) 46a, 46c, 47c
  see also Nationalist Party (China)
Kupa River 215a
Kura River 166c, 286b
Kurds
  Iran 100c
  Iraq 101c, 102b
  Syria 182c
Kuria Muria Islands 165c
Kuril Islands 247c
Kurume, Japan 272b
Kush, Kingdom of 178c
Kushan dynasty 1c
Kushans 95c
Kusi River 245b
Kuskokwim River 239b
Kutch, Gulf of 247c
Kuwait 117b–118a
  agriculture 117c
  area 117b
  capital 117b
  currency unit 117b
  economy 117c
  flag *il* iii

  geography 117c
  government 117c
  history 117c–118a
  independence 117c
  Kuwait City 272c
  language 117b
  map 117, *Atlas*-25
  national holiday 117b
  official name 117c
  people of 117c
  population 117b
  religion 117b
Kuwait City, Kuwait 272c
Kuwait Fund for Arab Economic Development 118a
al-Kuwatly, Shukri 183c
Kuybyshev, Soviet Union 272c
Kwacha 217c
Kwangchow Bay 45c
Kwangtung Province, China 263a, 285c
Kweiyang, China 272c
Kyat 22b
Kyoga (lake) 191b, 247c
Kyoto, Japan 111a, 112a, 112b, 272c
Kyrenia Mountains 54a
Kyushu Island 110b, 110c, 267a, 270b, 272a, 272b, 277b, 277c, 282c

L

La Brea, Trinidad 187c
La Digue Island 234a
La Paz, Bolivia 16b, 21c, 273a
La Salle, Robert Cavelier, Sieur de 30b
Laaland Island 248b
Labe River *see* Elbe River
Labor Party (Australia) 9b, 10a
Labor Party (Britain) 203c, 204a, 204b
Labor Party (New Zealand) 139a
Labrador
  fishing 28b
Laccadive Sea 247c
Lackland, John *see* John, King (England)
Ladislas, King (Hungary) 90b
Ladoga (lake) 247c
Ladrone Islands
  see Marianas Islands
Ladysmith, South Africa 272c
Lafontaine, Louis H. 32a
Lagan River 260b
Lagoa dos Patos 247c
Lagos, Nigeria 149a, 149b, 149c, 272c
Lagos Lagoon 272c
Lahore, Pakistan 244b, 273b
Lajos, kings (Hungary) *see* Louis, kings (Hungary)
Lake District 247c
Lakes 247c–248a
Lamartine, Alphonse de 69b
Lambaréné, Gabon 273a
Lambton, John George 32a
Lamizana, Sangoulé 207b
Lan Chang 118b–118c
Lancashire, England 275b
Lanchow, China 273a
Lao Tzu 42b
Laos 118a–119b
  agriculture 118a
  area 118a
  capital 118a
  climate 118a
  communism 119a
  currency unit 118a
  economy 118a–118b
  flag *il* iii
  geography 118a
  government 118a
  history 118b–119a
  independence 119a
  language 118a
  map 118, *Atlas*-30
  national holiday 118a
  official name 118a
  people of 118a

  population 118a
  religion 118a, 118c
  —Cities 118a
    Luang Prabang 274b
    Vientiane 288b
    World War II 119a
Lapland 62c, 248a
Lapps
  Finland 63a
  Sweden 179c
Laptev Sea 247a
Lashio, Burma 273a
Latakia, Syria 183a, 273a
Lateran Treaties 208b–208c
Latvia *see* Latvian Soviet Socialist Republic
Latvian Soviet Socialist Republic 282a, 288a
Latvians 167c
Laurentian Highlands 248a
Laurier, Wilfrid 33b–33c
Lausanne, Switzerland 181c
Lausanne, Treaty of 191a
Le Corbusier 263b
Le Havre, France 65b, 77b
Lead
  Australia 8b
  Greenland 226b
  Korea, North 115c
  Liberia 121a
  Mexico 130a
  Peru 148b
  Poland 151b
  Portugal 153b
  South West Africa 234c
  Soviet Union 168b
  Spain 175c
  Sweden 180a
  Tanzania 184b
  Turkey 190a
  United Kingdom 194c
  Yugoslavia 215b
League of Communists of Yugoslavia (LCY) 215c
League of Nations 11c, 12a, 34a, 62c, 78a, 152b, 204a
Lebanon 119b–120a
  agriculture 119b
  area 119b
  capital 119b
  climate 119b
  currency unit 119b
  economy 119b–119c
  emigration 119b
  flag *il* iii
  geography 119b
  government 119b
  history 119c–120a
  independence 120a
  industry 119b
  language 119b
  map 119, *Atlas*-24–25
  national holiday 119b
  official name 119b
  Ottoman Era 119c–120a
  people of 119b

  population 119b
  religion 119b, 119c
  trade 119b, 120a
  —Cities 119b
    Baalbek 258b
    Beirut 260a
    Sidon 119b
    Tripoli 287b
Lebanon Mountains 119b
Leeds, England 273b
Leeward Islands 219a, 221a, 223b, 229c
Legazpe, Miguel López de 150a
Leguía y Salcedo, Augusto B. 149b
Leine River 268c
Leipzig, Germany 74a, 273b
Lek 2a
Leman (lake) *see* Geneva, Lake
Lemass, Sean 103c
Lempira 88c, 89a
Lemus, José Mariá 61c
Lena River 248a
Lenin, Nikolay *see* Lenin, V.I.
Lenin, V. I. 173b–174a
Leningrad, Soviet Union 168a, 169b, 174b, 273b–273c
Leningrad, University of 273c
Leo III, Pope 107b
León, Nicaragua 139c, 140a
Leone 160b
Leoni, Raúl 210b
Leopold I, King (Belgium) 14c, 15a
Leopold II, King (Belgium) 15a, 51a
Leopold III, King (Belgium) 15a
Leopold II, Lake 248a
Léopoldville, Congo (Kinshasa) *see* Kinshasa, Congo (Kinshasa)
Leopontines (mountains) 237b
Lepchas 161b, 161c
Lerdo de Tejada, Sebastián 131b
Lesbos 80c
Lesotho 120a–120c
  agriculture 120b
  area 120a
  capital 120a
  currency unit 120a
  economy 120b
  flag *il* iii
  geography 120a
  government 120b
  history 120b–120c
  industry 120b
  language 120
  map 120, *Atlas*-40–41
  Maseru 275c
  national holiday 120a
  nationalism 120c
  official name 120a
  people of 120b
  population 120a
  religion 120a, 120b
Lesser Antilles 238a

Lesser Khingan Mountains 40a
Lesser Sundas Islands 98c
Leu 155c
Lev (currency unit) 21a
Lewanika 217c
Leyte (island) 149c, 150a, 150b
Li dynasty 212a
Li Tzu-ch'eng 44a
Li Yüan 43b
Li Yüan-hung 46b
Liang Ch'i-ch'ao 46a
Liao River 40a, 248a
Liaotung, Gulf of 40a
Libau, Latvia *see* Liepaya, Soviet Union
Liberal Democratic Party (LDP) (Japan) 113b
Liberal Party (Austria) 10a
Liberal Party (Britain) 203a, 203b, 203c
Liberal Party (Canada) 30a, 30c, 31b, 32a, 32b, 32c
Liberal Party (New Zealand) 139a
Liberator, The *see* Bolívar, Simón
Liberia 120c–121b
  agriculture 121a
  area 120c
  capital 120c
  currency unit 120c
  economy 121a
  flag *il* iii
  geography 120c
  government 121a
  history 121a–121b
  independence 121b
  language 120c
  map 121, *Atlas*-36
  Monrovia 276c
  national holiday 120c
  official name 120c
  people of 121a
  population 120c
  religion 120c
  World War II 121b
Libreville, Gabon 71b–71c, 273c
Libya 108b, 121b–122b
  agriculture 122a
  area 121b
  capital 121b
  currency unit 121b
  economy 122a
  flag *il* iii
  geography 121b–121c
  government 122a
  history 122a–122b
  independence 122b
  industry 122a
  language 121b
  map 121, *Atlas*-34
  national holiday 121b
  official name 121b
  people of 121c–122a
  population 121b

religion 121b, 122b
World War II 122b
—Cities 121a
  Bengazi 268b
  Tripoli 287b
Lie, Trygve 143c
Liechtenstein 122b–123a
  agriculture 122c
  area 122b
  capital 122b
  currency unit 122b
  economy 122c
  flag il iii
  geography 122b–122c
  government 122c
  history 122c–123a
  language 122b
  map 122, Atlas-17
  national holiday 122b
  official name 122b
  people of 122c
  population 122b
  religion 122b
  Switzerland and 182a
  Vaduz 288a
Liechtenstein family 122c
Liège, Belgium 14a, 273c
Liepaya, Soviet Union 273c
Liepaya, Lake 273c
Lietuva see Lithuanian Soviet Socialist Republic
Liffey River 265c
Liguria (region) Italy 267b
Ligurian Sea 248a
Lihou Island 222c
Likasi, Congo (Kinshasa) 273c
Lille, France 65a
Lilongwe, Malawi 28b
Lima, Peru 148a, 148b, 149c, 273c
Limassol, Cyprus 273c
Limburg, Netherlands 136c, 137a
Limmat River 289c
Limpopo River 17b, 154c, 164a, 229a
Lion Mountain 160c
Lions, Gulf of 248c, 275c
Lipari Islands 105c, 248b
Lippe River 266c
Lira
  Italy 105c
  Turkey 189c
Lisbon, Portugal 153a, 153b, 153c
Litani River 119b, 248b

Lithuania
  see Lithuanian Soviet Socialist Republic
Lithuanian Soviet Socialist Republic 271b, 288b, 288c
Lithuanians 167c
Little Entente 70b, 91b
Little Sark Island 222a
Liu Pang 43a
Liuchow Peninsula 263c
Liverpool, England 274a
Liverpool Range 7b
Livingstone, David 124c, 185a
Livingstone Falls 240c
Ljubljana, Yugoslavia 215b, 274a
Llanos (plains) 248b
Llewelyn the Great, Prince (Wales) 198b
Loango Kingdom 71c
Lobito, Angola 274a
Lobo, Ahmadu see Ahmadu Lobo
Locarno Pact 70b, 204a
Łódź, Poland 151a, 151c, 274a
Lofa River 120c
Lofoten Islands 248b
Logone River 248b
Loire River 64a, 248b
Loire Valley 287a
Lolang Kingdom 116a
Lolland Island 57a, 248b
Loma Mountains 160b
Lombards
  Italy 107a
  Monaco 132a
  Romania 156b
Lomé, Togo 186c, 187a, 274a–274b
London, England 194a, 195a, 274b
London, Treaty of (1915) 108b
London Protocol (March 1829) 82b
Longwy, France 65a
López, Alfonso 49b
López, Carlos Antonio 147c
López, Francisco Solano 147c
López, Narciso 53c
López Mateos, Adolfo 131c
Lorraine 64b, 65a–65b, 67, 68b, 69c, 70b, 77b, 77c
Los Angeles, California 205b
Lot, Sea of see Dead Sea

Lothair I, Emperor (Holy Roman Empire) 66b
Lough Neagh (lake) 194b
Louis, Saint, King (France) see Louis IX, King (France)
Louis VI, King (France) 66b, 66c
Louis VII, King (France) 66b–66c
Louis IX. King (France) 66c
Louis XI, King (France) 67a
Louis XIII, King (France) 67c
Louis XIV, King (France) 27b, 29c, 30a, 67c–68a, 137b, 201c
Louis XV, King (France) 68b
Louis XVI, King (France) 68b–68c
Louis XVIII, King (France) 69a
Louis I, King (Hungary) 152a
Louis I, King (Portugal) 154a
Louis the German, King (Germany) 66b, 75a
Louis Napoleon see Napoleon III, Emperor (France)
Louis Philippe, King (France) 69b
Louis the Pious, Emperor (Carolingian Empire) 66a–66b
Louisiade Archipelago 231b
Lourenço Marques, Mozambique 179a, 229a, 274b
Louvanium University see Lovanium University
Louvois, Marquis de 68a
Louvre (Paris) 279c
Lovanium University 51a, 271c
L'Overture, Toussaint see Toussaint L'Overture
Low Countries see Belgium; Luxembourg; Netherlands
Lower California see Baja California
Lower Saxony (state) West Germany 268c
Lower Town see Quebec, Canada
Loyalty Islands 230a
Lozi 217b
Lualaba River 240c
Luan River 263c
Luanda, Angola 218a, 274b
Luang Prabang, Laos 118a, 118c, 274b–274c

Luangwa River 217a, 248b
Lublin, Poland 274c
Lubumbashi, Congo (Kinshasa) 50c, 274c
Lucca, Republic of 107b
Lucerne, Switzerland 181c
Lucerne, Lake 182b, 248c
Lucknow, India 274c
Lukuga River 240c
Lulua 50c
Lumumba, Patrice 51a–51b
Luo 114b
Lusaka, Zambia 117a, 274c
Luther, Martin 76a
Luthuli, Albert 165b
Luxembourg 14a, 14b, 15b, 123a–123c, 274c
  agriculture 123a
  area 123a
  capital 123a
  climate 123a
  currency unit 123a
  economy 123a–123b
  flag il iii
  geography 123a
  government 123b
  history 123b–123c
  language 123a
  Luxembourg (city) 274c
  map 123, Atlas-22
  national holiday 123a
  official name 123a
  people of 123a
  population 123a
  religion 123a
  World War I 123c
  World War II 123c
Luxembourg (city), Luxembourg 123a, 274c
Luya Mountains 40a
Luzon (island) 149c, 150a, 150c, 275b, 281b
Lvov, Soviet Union 274c
Lwów, Soviet Union see Lvov, Soviet Union
Lyautey, Louis 134c
Lynch, Jack 103c
Lyon, France 64b, 65b, 274c–275a, 275c

M

Ma Chu River 15b
Maas River see Meuse River
Mabla Mountains 225b
Macao 45a, 153c, 228b, 228c
  area 228b
  capital 228b
  Macao (city) 228b
  population 228b
  status 228b
Macapagal, Diosdado 150c
MacArthur, Douglas 47a, 113b
Macdonald, John A. 32c, 33a, 33b
MacDonnell Mountains see Macdonnell Ranges
MacDonnell Ranges 7b, 248b
Macedonia, Ancient 81b
  see also Alexander the Great
Macedonians 215a
Maceo, Antonio 53b
Machado, Gerardo 53c
Mackenzie, Alexander 32c
Mackenzie, William Lyon 31c
Mackenzie River 248b–248c
MacMillan, Harold 204a
MacMurrough, Dermot, King (Ireland) 103a
Macquarie, Lachlan 8c
Madagascar (Malagasy Republic) 123c–124b
  agriculture 124a
  area 123c
  capital 123c
  currency unit 123c
  economy 124a
  flag il iii
  geography 123c

government 124a
history 124a–124b
independence 124b
language 123c
map Atlas-41
national holiday 123c
official name 123c
people of 123c–124a
population 123c
religion 123c
Tannarive 286a
Madagascar Island 248c
Madeira Archipelago 248c
Madeira Islands 153a, 154a
Madeira River 248c
Madeira wine 153b
Madero, Francisco 131b
Madhya Pradesh (state), India 260c, 269b, 287c
Madras, India 94a, 275a
Madras State, India 283a
Madrid, Spain 175b, 175c, 275a
Madrid, Treaty of 110a
Madura, India 175a
Mae Nam Chao Phraya River 185b
Maga, Hubert 57a
Magadha Kingdom 95b, 279c
Magdalena River 48a–48b, 248c
Magellan, Ferdinand 150a, 207b, 225a
Maggiore, Lake 248c
Magna Carta 197c
Magnitogorsk, Soviet Union 275a
Magnus VI, King (Norway) 143a
Magsaysay, Ramón 150c
Magyars 89b, 90b
  Moravia 55b
  Romania 156b
  Slovakia 55b
Mahalaxmi Temple 272a
Mahanadi River 265a

Maharashtra State, India 261b, 277b, 284b
Mahaweli River 271a
al-Mahdi see Muhammad Ahmad al-Mahdi
Mahé Island 234a, 281a
Mahendra, King (Nepal) 136b
Mahjoub, Ahmad Muhammed 178c
Mahomet see Muhammad
Maiduguri, Nigeria 275a
Main River 73b, 248c, 267a
Maine (ship) 150b
Majapahit Kingdom 99c, 125c
Makabulas, Francisco 150b
Makalu Mountain 249a
Makarikari Basin 249a
Makarios, Archbishop 54b
Makasar, Indonesia 275a
Malabar Coast 249a, 264c
Malacca, Malaysia 275a
Malacca, Strait of 125a, 125b
Malacca State, Malaysia 275a
Málaga (province), Spain 276b
Malagasy Republic see Madagascar
Malären, Lake 180b, 285a
Malaria
  Liberia 121b
  Mauritius 128c
Malawi 124b–125a
  agriculture 124b–124c
  area 124b
  capital 124b
  climate 124b
  currency unit 124b
  economy 124b–124c
  flag il iii
  geography 124b
  government 124c
  history 124c–125a
  independence 125a
  language 124b
  map 124, Atlas-39

national holiday 124b
nationalism 125a
official name 124b
people of 124c
population 124b
religion 124b, 124c
Zomba 289c
Malawi (people) 124c
Malawi, Lake 124b, 124c
Malawi Congress Party 125a
Malay Archipelago 249a
Malay Peninsula 272b
  see also Malaysia
Malaya 100b
  see also Malaysia
Malaya, Federation of 126a
  see also Malaysia
Malaysia 100b, 125–126
  agriculture 125b
  area 125a
  capital 125a
  climate 125b
  currency unit 125a
  economy 125b–125c
  flag il iii
  geography 125a–125b
  government 125c
  history 125c–126b
  independence 126a–126b
  language 125a
  map 125, Atlas-30
  national holiday 125a
  official name 125a
  people of 125b
  population 125a
  religion 125a, 125c
  World War II 126a
—Cities 125b
  Georgetown 125b
  Ipoh 125b
  Jesselton 270a
  Kuala Lumpur 272b
  Kuching 272b
  Malacca 275a

Maldive Islands 126
  area 126b
  capital 126b
  currency unit 126b
  economy 126b
  flag *il iii*
  geography 126b
  government 126b
  history 126b–126c
  language 126b
  Male 275a
  map *Atlas-28*
  official name 126b
  people of 126b
  population 126b
  religion 126b
  World War II 126c
Male, Maldive Islands 126b, 275a
Mali 86b, 126–127
  agriculture 127a
  area 126c
  Bamako 259a
  capital 126c
  currency unit 126c
  economy 127a
  flag *il iii*
  geography 126c
  government 127a
  history 127a–127b
  language 126c
  map 127, *Atlas-36–37*
  national holiday 126c
  official name 126c
  people of 126c–127a
  population 126c
  religion 126c, 127b
Mali Federation 160b
Malinke
  Guinea 86a
  Mali 126c
Malla dynasty 136a
Mallorca *see* Balearic Islands
Malta 127–128
  agriculture 127c
  area 127b
  capital 127b
  climate 127b
  currency unit 127b
  economy 127c
  emigration 127c
  flag *il iii*
  geography 127b
  government 127c
  history 127c–128a
  independence 128a
  language 127b
  map *Atlas-13*
  national holiday 127b
  official name 127b
  people of 127b
  population 127b
  religion 127b, 128a
  Valletta 288a
  World War II 127a
Mamallapuram, India 96a
Mamprussi 206c
Man, Isle of *see* Isle of Man
Managua, Nicaragua 139b, 139c, 140a, 275a
Managua, Lake 139b, 139c, 249a, 275a
al-Manama, Bahrain 12c, 275a
Manas River 15b
Manchester, England 275b
Manchester Ship Canal 274a
Manchu dynasty *see* Ch'ing dynasty
Manchukuo 46c
Manchuria (region), China 39c, 43c, 113a, 113b, 268c, 271c
  Japanese invasion (1931) 46b–46c
  see also China
Manchurian Plain 40a
Manchus 41a
  see also Ch'ing dynasty; China, History
Mandalay, Burma 22c, 275b
Mandeb (strait) (Bab al-Mandeb) 165c, 237a, 251a
Mandingo
  Gambia 72a
  Liberia 121a
  Mali 126a, 126c
  Portuguese Guinea 232a
  Senegal 159c
Mandjia-Baya 35b
Mandyako 232a
Mangalore, India 275b
Manganese
  Angola 218b
  Brazil 19a
  Cuba 52c
  French Guiana 224c
  Gabon 71c
  Ghana 80a, 86c
  Ivory Coast 109a
  Laos 118b

Morocco 133c
New Caledonia 230b
Nicaragua 139c
Panama 146a
Romania 156a
South West Africa 234c
Soviet Union 168b
Sweden 180a
Thailand 185c
Upper Volta 206c
Mangla Dam 144c
Mangoky River 123c
Mania River 123c
Manila, Philippines 149c, 150b, 275b
Manila Bay 149c, 150b, 249a, 275b
Manipur (Union Territory), India 269b
Manitoba, Canada 289b
Manley, Norman 110b
Manner, Gulf of 249a
Manono Island 213b
Mansfield, William 160c
Mansoa River 232a
Mantanzima, Kaizer 165b
Manuel I, King (Portugal) 154b
Manuel II, King (Portugal) 154a
Manukau, New Zealand 258b
Manych River 243b
Manzini, Swaziland 179a
Mao Tse-tung 46b, 46c, 47a
Maori 138a, 138c–139a
  Cook Islands 223a
  French Polynesia 225a
Maps *Atlas-4–64*
  projections *Atlas-2–3*
  see also under the names of individual countries, such as France, map
Mar del Plata, Argentina 5b
Maracaibo, Lake 209a, 249a
Marajo Island 249a
Marathas 96c
Maravi *see* Malawi (people)
Marcos, Ferdinand 150c
Margai, Albert 161b
Margai, Milton 161a
Margaret, Queen (Denmark) 143a, 180b, 180c
Margaret, Queen (Denmark and Norway) *see* Margaret, Queen (Denmark)
Margaret, Queen (Sweden) *see* Margaret, Queen (Denmark)
Margaret of Valois 67b
Marianas Islands 115c, 249a
Marie Antoinette, Queen (France) 68c
Marinid dynasty 134a
Marinus 158b
Maritime Alps 237a, 278a
Maritsa River 21a, 249a–249b, 280b
Mark
  Germany, East 73a
  Germany, West 73a
Marka 206b
Markka 62c
Marmara, Sea of 249b, 269c
Marne River 249b
Maronites 119c
Maroons 110a
Marquesa Islands 224c–225a
Marquette, Jacques 30b
Marra Mountains 177c, 249b
Marrakech, Morocco 128c, 133c, 134a, 275b–275c
Marseille, France 64b, 65b, 275c
Marshall, George C. 46c
Marshall Plan 56b, 58b, 71a, 174c, 191a
Martaban, Gulf of 277a
Martel, Charles *see* Charles Martel
Martínez, Maximiliano Hernández 61b
Martinique 228
  area 228c
  capital 228c
  Fort-de-France 266c
  population 228c
  status 228c
Marxists 172c, 173a–173b
Mary (Queen of Scots) 200b
Mary I, Queen (England) 103b
  persecution of Protestants 200a
  reign of 200a
Mary II, Queen (England) 201c
Mary of Burgundy 137a
Mary Stuart *see* Mary (Queen of Scots)
Mary Tudor *see* Mary I, Queen (England)
Masai 114c

Masai Steppe 249b
Masaryk, Tomáš 55c, 56a
Maseru, Lesotho 120a, 275c
Mashhad, Iran 275c
Mashona *see* Shona
Massacre of St. Bartholomew's Day 67f
Massamba-Debat, Alphonse 50b
Massif Central (mountains) 249b
Massif de la Hotte (mountains) 87b
Massif du Nord (mountains) 87b
Massif de la Salle (mountains) 87b
Matabele 120b, 155a, 155b
Matabeleland 155b
Matadi, Congo (Kinshasa) 275c
Mata-Utu, Wallis and Futuna Islands 236c
Mathura, India 275c
Mátra Mountains 89c
Matrah, Muscat and Oman 134c
Matsu 47c
Matthews Ridge, Guyana 86c
Matthias, King (Hungary) 90c
Mau Mau 115a
Maurice, Prince (Netherlands) 129a
Mauritania 128, 235b
  agriculture 128a
  area 128a
  capital 128a
  climate 128a
  currency unit 128a
  economy 128a–128b
  flag *il iii*
  geography 128a
  government 128b
  history 128b–128c
  language 128a
  map 128, *Atlas-36*
  national holiday 128a
  Nouakchott 278a
  official name 128a
  people of 128a
  population 128a
  religion 128a, 128b
Mauritius 128–129
  agriculture 129a
  area 128c
  capital 128c
  climate 128c
  currency unit 128c
  economy 129a
  flag *il iii*
  geography 128c
  government 129a
  history 129a–129b
  independence 129b
  language 128c
  official name 128c
  people of 128c
  population 128c
  Port Louis 280c
  religion 128c
Mauritius Island 128c
Maurya empire 129b–129c
Maximilian, Emperor (Mexico) 131b
Maximilian I, Emperor (Holy Roman Empire) 137a
Maya Mountains 220a
Mayas
  British Honduras 220a, 220b
  Guatemala 84a, 84b
  Mexico 130b
Mayo Rajkumar College 256c
Mayombé Mountains 71b
Mayon (mountain) 149c
Mayotte Islands 223c
Mazarin, Cardinal 67c
Mazatlán, Mexico 130a
Mazzini, Giuseppe 107c
M'Ba, Leon 72a
Mbabane, Swaziland 178c, 275c–276a
M'Baka 35b
M'Bochi 50a
McKinley, William 150b
McKinley (mountain) 205a
Meander River *see* Menderes River
Mecca, Saudi Arabia 186a
Mecsek Hills 280a
Medellín, Colombia 276a
Medici, Caterina de' *see* Catherine de Médicis
Medici family 107b
Medina, Saudi Arabia 276a
Medina as-Shaab, South Yemen 165a
Mediterranean Sea 249b
Medjerda River 189a
Medveditsa River 243b
Meerut, India 276a

Meghna River 244b, 265a
Meighen, Arthur 35a
Meiji Restoration 112c–113a
Mekong River 24b, 24c, 118a, 185a, 210c, 211a, 249b, 274b, 280b, 288b
Melbourne, Australia 8a, 9a, 276a–276b
Melilla, Morocco 276b
Melita 127c
Memel, Soviet Union *see* Klaipeda, Soviet Union
Mencius 42b
Mende 160b
Menderes River 249b
Mendoza, Pedro de 6a
Mercia, Kingdom of 196a
Mercier, Honoré 33a
Mercury
  Italy 106b
  Mexico 130a
  Nicaragua 139c
  Soviet Union 168b
  Spain 175c
  Yugoslavia 215b
Merina *see* Hova
Merovingians 66c
Mersey River 194a, 274a
MESAN *see* Movement for the Social Evolution of Black Africa
Mesopotamia 102a
Messaori Plain 278a
Metaxas, Ioannes 83a
Metternich, Prince Klemens von 11b, 76c, 77a
Meuse River 14a, 249c, 273c
Mexico 129–132
  agriculture 130a
  area 129b
  capital 129b
  climate 129c
  currency unit 129b
  economy 130a
  flag *il iii*
  geography 129b–129c
  government 130b
  history 130b–132a
  independence 131b
  Indians 130b–130c
  industry 130a
  language 129b
  map 129, *Atlas-54–55*
  national holiday 129b
  natural resources 130a
  in Nicaragua 140a
  official name 129b
  people of 129c–130a
  population 129b
  religion 129b
  trade 130a
  war with U.S. 131a
  World War II 131c
  —Cities 130a
    Ciudad Juárez 130a
    Guadalajara 268a
    Mazatlán 130a
    Mexico City 276b
    Monterrey 130a
    Puebla 130a
    Tampico 130a
    Veracruz 130a
Mexico, University of 130b–130c
Mexico City, Mexico 129b, 130a, 130b, 130c, 276b
Miao 118a
Michael the Brave, Prince (Walachia) 156b
Micombero, Michel 24b
Midlothian County, Scotland 266b
Mieszko, Prince (Poland) 152a
Mihajlović, Draža 216c
Milan, Italy 106a, 106c, 107b, 276b
Min River 263c, 266c
Minas Channel *see* Fundy, Bay of
Minas Gerais, Brazil 260b
Mindanao Island, Philippines 149c, 150a, 265b, 289c
Ming dynasty 43c–44a
Minh-Mang, Emperor (Vietnam) 212b–212c
Minorca *see* Balearic Islands
Minsk, Soviet Union 276b
Miranda, Francisco de 209c
Miskolc, Hungary 90a, 276b
Missionaries
  British Isles 196a
  China 44a, 44b, 44c, 45a
  Congo 51a
  Fiji Islands 224b
  Korea 117c
  Lebanon 119a–120a
  Malawi 124c

Malaysia 125c
New Zealand 138c
Paraguay 147c
Tanzania 185a
Tonga 236b
Uganda 192a
Vietnam 212b, 212c
Western Samoa 213c
Mississippi River 205a
Missouri River 205a
Mitre, Bartolomé 6b
Miyagi prefecture 284a
Mlanje (mountain) 124b
MNR see National Revolutionary Movement (MNR) (Bolivia)
Moa River 160b
Mobutu, Joseph 51b
Moçambes Desert 218a
Moesi River 279b
Mogadiscio, Somali Republic 162c, 163a, 276b–276c
Mogadishu, Somali Republic see Mogadiscio, Somali Republic
Mogami River 289b
Mohammed V University (Rabat) 281c
Mohammadans see Islam
Mohéli Island 222c
Mokpo, South Korea 276c
Moldavia 156b, 156c
Moldavian Soviet Socialist Republic 272a
Moldavians 168a
Molopo River 17b
Moluccas Islands 98c
Molybdenum
  French Guiana 224c
  Greenland 226b
  U.S. 205c
Mombasa, Kenya 114b, 276c
Mon
  Burma 23a, 23b
  Thailand 186a
  Vietnam 211a
Monaco 132
  area 132a
  capital 132a
  currency unit 132a
  economy 132a
  flag il iii
  geography 132a
  government 132a
  history 132a–132b
  language 132a
  map 132, Atlas-23
  Monte Carlo 276c
  national holiday 132a
  official name 132a
  people of 132a
  population 132a
  religion 132a
Money see under the names of individual countries, such as India, currency unit; and under currency units, such as Dinar
Mongkut, King (Siam) 186b
Mongolia 39c, 43c, 132–133
  agriculture 132c
  area 132b
  capital 132b
  climate 132b
  communism 132c, 133b
  currency unit 132b
  economy 132c
  flag il iii

  geography 132b–132c
  government 132c
  history 132c–133b
  language 132b
  map 133, Atlas-32-33
  national holiday 132b
  official name 132b
  people of 132b
  population 132b
  religion 132b, 132c, 133a
  Ulan Bator 287c
  World War II 133b
Mongolian People's Revolutionary Party 132c
Mongols 132b
  Afghanistan 1c
  Burma 23b
  India 96b
  Iran 101a
  Iraq 102a
  Soviet Union 168a, 170a
  Syria 183b
Monomotapa empire 155b
Monrovia, Liberia 120c–121b, 276c
Monsoons 22c
  Hong Kong 227a
  India 93c
  Laos 118a
Montagnes Noires (mountains) 87b
Montagnes du Trou d'Eau (mountains) 87b
Montagu-Chelmsford Reforms 97b
Montcalm, Louis 30c
Monte Carlo, Monaco 276c
Montenegrins 215a
Montenegro, Julio César Méndez 85c
Montenegro
  Albania and 3a
Monterrey, Mexico 130a
Montes, Ismael 17a
Montevideo, Uruguay 207a, 276c
Montezuma 130c
Montfort, Simon de 198a
Montgomery, Richard 31a
Montreal, Canada 27b, 29c, 30a, 31a, 276c
Mont-Saint-Michel il 68
Montserrat 229
  area 229a
  capital 229a
  Plymouth 280c
  population 229a
  status 229a
Moors
  Mauritania 128a
  Spain 176b
Mopti, Mali 127a
Moradabad, India 276c
Moraes Barros, Prudente José de 20b
Morales, Ramón Villeda 89b
Morava River 21a, 54c, 215a, 249c, 278b
Moravia 54c, 55b–56a, 81c
Moravian Gate 151a, 279a
Moravians (people) 55b
Morazan, Francisco 52a
Mordovians 168a
Morelos, José María 131a
Morínigo, Higinio 148a
Morley-Minto Reforms 97b
Morocco 77c, 133–134

  agriculture 133c
  area 133b
  capital 133b
  currency unit 133b
  economy 133c
  flag il iii
  geography 133b–133c
  government 133c
  history 133c–134a
  independence 134a
  language 133b
  map 134, Atlas-34
  national holiday 133b
  nationalism 134b
  official name 133b
  people of 133c
  population 133b
  religion 133b, 134a
  World War II 134b
  —Cities 133c
  Casablanca 263a
  Fès 266c
  Marrakech 275b
  Oujda 279b
  Rabat 281c
  Tangier 286b
Moroni, Comoro Islands 222c, 276c
Moscow, Soviet Union 166b, 168a, 169a–169b, 170a–170c, 174b, 277a
Moscow River see Moskva River
Moselle River 73b, 249c
Moshesh 120b, 120c
Moshi, Tanzania 277a
Moshi-Dagomba 79c
Moshoeshoe II, King (Lesotho) 120c
Moskva River 249c, 277a
Mosquito Coast 249c
Mosquito Indians 139b–139c
Mossadegh, Muhammad 101b
Mossi 206b, 206c
Mosul, Iraq 102a, 277a
Moulmein, Burma 277a
Moulouya River 133c, 249c
Mountbatten, Louis 97c
Movement for the Social Evolution of Black Africa (MESAN) 35b
Mowat, Oliver 33a
Mozambique 153c, 229
  agriculture 229b
  area 229a
  capital 229a
  climate 229a
  economy 229b
  geography 229a
  government 229b
  history 228b–229c
  people of 229a
  population 229a
  religion 229a
  slavery 229c
  status 229a
  —Cities
  Beira 260a
  Lourenço Marques 274b
  Nacala 277b
Mozambique Channel 276c
MRP see Catholic Popular Republican Movement (MRP) (France)
Mswati 179b
Muang Swa, Laos 118c
Muchinga Mountains 217a
Mufti of Jerusalem 105b
Mughal Empire 279c
  Afghanistan 1c

Muhammad, Ahmad al-Mahdi 178b, 178c
Muhammad al-Badr, Imam (Yemen) 214c
Muhammad Ali 193b
Muhammad Ali Jinnah 97b, 97c
Muhammad bin Ali al-Sanusi 122b
Muhammad bin Yusuf (Muhammad V) 134b
Muhammad, Dost see Dost Muhammad
Muhammad Hatta 100a
Muhammad Ibn Abd al-Wahhab 159a
Muhammad ibn Saud 159a–159b
Muhammad Nadir, Shah (Afghanistan) 2a
Muhammad Nadir, Shah (Iran) 96c, 101a–101b
Muhammad Riza 101b–101c
Muiscas 48b
Mulambwa 217b
Mulhouse, France 65b
Mulinu'u II, Fiame Mata'afa Faumuina 214a
Munich, Germany 73c, 74a, 277a
  Oktoberfest il 74
Murat River 244a
Murcia, Spain 176a
Mures River 155c, 258a
Murillo, Pedro Domingo 16c
Murmansk, Soviet Union 277a
Muroran, Japan 277a
Murray-Darling rivers 249c
Musa, King (Mali) 127a, 127b
Muscat and Oman 134–135, 277a
  agriculture 134b
  area 134b
  capital 134b
  climate 134c
  currency unit 134b
  economy 134c
  flag il iii
  geography 134c
  government 134c
  history 134c–135a
  language 134b
  map 134, Atlas-25
  Muscat (city) 277a
  official name 134b
  people of 134c
  population 134b
  religion 134b
Muscat Bay 277a
Muscovy see Soviet Union, History
Musgrave Mountains 7b
Musi River 269a
Muslim League 97b, 97c
Muslims see Islam
Mussolini, Benito 12a, 12b, 62b, 70c, 78c, 91b, 108b, 108c, 150b, 174b
Mutesa II, Kabaka (King) (Uganda) 192a, 192b
Mwambutsa IV, Mwami (King) Burundi 24b
Mwanga, King (Uganda) 192a
Mweru, Lake 50c, 217a, 250a
Mykonos, Greece il 82
Mysore State, India 275b

N

Nacala, Mozambique 277b
Nadir Shah see Muhammad Nadir
Nagara River 267c
Nagas 94a
Nagasaki, Japan 112c, 113b, 277b
Nagots 56b
Nagoya, Japan 110c, 111a, 277b
Nagoya University 277b
Nagpur, India 277b
Nagpur University 277b
Nagy, Imre 91c
Naha, Ryukyu Islands 277b
Nairobi, Kenya 114b, 277b–277c

Najib, Muhammad 193c
Nakoué, Lake 264c
Nama see Hottentots
Namgyal, Maharajah Gyalsay Palden Thondup 161c
Nan Mountains 250a
Nan River 240c
Nan Ling Mountains 40a
Nan Shan (mountains) 39c
Nanchang, China 277c
Nancy, France 65a
Nanda dynasty 95b
Nanking, China 277c
Nanking, Treaty of (1842) 44c
Nanking University 277c
Nantes, France 65b
Naples, Italy 106a, 107a, 107c, 277c
Naples, Kingdom of 107b

Napoleon, Louis 69b
Napoleon I, Emperor (France) 14c, 38a, 68c–69a, 75c, 107c, 127c, 130c, 137b, 152a, 180c, 181a, 181b, 193b, 202c, 209c
  St. Helena 233a
  seizes Spanish throne 177a
Napoleon III, Emperor (France) 69b–69c, 106a, 131b, 212c
Napoli, Italy see Naples, Italy
Nara, Japan 112a, 277c–278a
Nara National Museum 278a
Nara Period 277c
Narbada River 269c
Narbada-Tapi River 93c
Narcotics 44b, 44c
Nash, Walter 139b
Nassau, Bahamas 219b
Nasser, Gamal Abdel 159b, 159c, 183c, 193c

Natal Bay 266a
Natal Province, South Africa 272c
National Council of Nigeria and Cameroons (NCNC) 141c
National Health Service (Great Britain) 204a
National holiday see under the name of individual countries, such as Argentina, national holiday
National Hydrocarbons Agency 106c
National Indonesian Party 100a
National Liberation Front (FLN) (Algeria) 4b
National Party (New Zealand) 139b
National Party (South Africa) 165b

National Power Authority 106c
National Revolutionary Movement (MNR) (Bolivia) 17a
National Revolutionary Party (PNR) (Mexico) 131c
National Rwanda Union 157c
National Socialism see Nazi Party
National Socialist German Workers' Party see Nazi Party
National Taiwan University 286a
National Union and Progress Party (UPRONA) (Burundi) 24b
National Unionist Party (Sudan) 178c
National University (Bogotá) 261a
Nationalist Party (Australia) 9c–10a
Nationalist Party (China) 42a, 46a
  see also Kuomintang (KMT)
NATO see North Atlantic Treaty Organization
Natong River 115b–115c
Nauru 135
  area 135a
  capital 135a
  climate 135a
  economy 135a–135b
  flag *il* iii
  geography 135a
  government 135b
  history 135b
  language 135a
  map *Atlas*-6
  official name 135a
  people of 135a
  population 135a
  religion 135a
Navarino, Greece 82a
Navarre, Spain
  Andorra and 4c
Nazareth, Israel 278a
Nazi Party (National Socialist German Workers' Party) 12a, 78a–79a, 91b
NCNC see National Council of Nigeria and Cameroons
Ndebele see Matabele
Ndola, Zambia 278a
Neckar River 285a
Negev Desert 104a, 250a
Negros Island, Philippines 149c
Negros Occidental, University of 258c
Nehru, Jawaharlal, 97b, 97c, 98a
Neichiang, China 278a
Neisse River 73a, 150c
Nejd Plateau 282b
Nelson, New Zealand 138c
Neman River 271b
Nenni, Pietro 108c
Neo–Destour Party (Tunisia) 189b
Nepal 135–136
  agriculture 135c
  area 135b
  capital 135b
  climate 135c
  currency unit 135b
  economy 135c–136a
  flag *il* iii
  geography 135b–135c
  government 136a
  history 136a–136b
  Katmandu 271a
  language 135b
  map 136, *Atlas*-29
  national holiday 135b
  official name 135b
  people of 135c
  population 135b
  Rana rule 136b
  religion 135b, 135c, 136a
Nepal, Valley of 271a
Nepalese
  Sikkim 161b, 161c
Nepalis 135c
  Bhutan 15b
Neris River 288b
Netherlands 14a, 136–137
  agriculture 136c
  area 136c
  capital 136c
  currency unit 136c
  economy 136c–137a
  flag *il* iii
  geography 136c
  government 137a
  independence 137a
  industry 136c–137a
  language 136c
  map 137, *Atlas*-22
  national holiday 136c
  official name 136c
  people of 136c
  population 136c
  religion 136c, 137b
—Cities 136c
  Amsterdam 257b
  Eindhoven 136c
  Haarlem 136c
  The Hague ('s Gravenhage) 268b
  Rotterdam 282b
  Utrecht 136c
—History 137a–137c
  Belgium and 14c
  in Guyana 87b
  in Indonesia 99c–100a
  Luxembourg and 123b
  in Netherlands Antilles 229c–230a
  in Surinam 235b–235c
  World War I 137b
  World War II 78c, 137b–137c, 204a
Netherlands Antilles 137a, 137c, 229–230
  agriculture 230a
  area 229c
  capital 229c
  climate 229c
  economy 230a
  geography 229c
  government 230a
  history 230a
  Indians 229c
  map *Atlas*-53
  people of 229c–230a
  population 229c
  religion 230a
  slavery 230a
  status 229c
  Willemstad 289a
Netherlands Guiana see Surinam
Netherlands New Guinea (West Irian) 137c
Netravati River 275b
Neuilly, Treaty of 22a
Neva River 273b
New Brunswick, Canada 267a
New Caledonia 230
  area 230a
  capital 230a
  Nouméa 278b
  population 230a
  status 230a
New Castile (region), Spain 275a
New Delhi, India 93a, 278a
New France 29a, 29c–30c
New Granada, Viceroyalty of 49a, 49b, 60b, 146b, 149a, 209c
New Guinea 98c, 230
  agriculture 230c
  area 230b
  climate 230b
  economy 230c
  geography 230b–230c
  government 230c
  history 230c
  people of 230b–230c
  population 230b
  status 230b
  World War I 230c
New Guinea Island 250a
  Papua 231b, 231c
New Hebrides, 231
  area 231a
  capital 231a
  population 231a
  status 231a
  Vila 288b
New Maas River 282b
New South Wales, Australia 263a, 285c
New Spain 130c
New Zealand 137–139
  agriculture 138a–138b
  area 137c
  capital 137c
  climate 138a
  in Cook Islands 223a
  currency unit 137c
  economy 138a–138b
  flag *il* iv
  geography 137c–138a
  government 138b–138c
  history 138c–139b
  language 137c
  national holiday 137c
  in Nauru 135c
  in Niue 231a
  official name 137c
  people of 138a
  population 137c
  religion 137c
  in Tokelau Islands 236a
  trade 138b
  World War I 139a
  World War II 139b
—Cities
  Auckland 258b
  Christchurch 264a
  Lyttleton 264a
  Wellington 289a
Newfoundland, Canada 29b, 30c, 32b
Newfoundland Island 283a
Ngendandumwe, Pierre 24b
Ngoni 179b
Nguru, Nigeria 141b
Nguyen Anh see Gia-Long, Emperor (Vietnam)
Ngwenya, Swaziland 179a
Nhu, Ngo Dinh 213a, 213b
Niamey, Niger 140b, 140c, 278a
Nicaragua 89b, 139–140, 146c
  agriculture 139c
  area 139b
  capital 139b
  climate 139b
  currency unit 139b
  economy 139c
  flag *il* iv
  geography 139b
  government 139c–140a
  history 140a–140b
  Indians 139b–139c
  industry 139c
  language 139b
  map 139, *Atlas*-55
  national holiday 139b
  official name 139b
  people of 139b–139c
  population 139b
  religion 139b
  trade 139c
  World War II 140b
—Cities 139c
  Corinto 264c
  Granada 139c
  León 139c
  Managua 275a
Nicaragua, Lake 139b, 139c, 250a
Nice, France 64b, 278a
Nicholas I, Tsar (Russia) 117c–118a
Nicholas II, Tsar (Russia) 118b–119a
Nickel
  Cuba 52c
  French Guiana 224c
  New Caledonia 230b
  Soviet Union 168b
Nicosia, Cyprus 54a, 278a
Niemen River 243b, 272a
Niemeyer, Oscar 261c
Niger 140–141
  agriculture 140c
  area 140b
  capital 140b
  climate 140b–140c
  currency unit 140b
  economy 140c
  flag *il* iv
  geography 140b–140c
  government 140c
  history 140c–141a
  language 140b
  map 140, *Atlas*-37
  national holiday 140b
  Niamey 278a
  official name 140b
  people of 140c
  population 140b
  religion 140b, 140c
Niger Progressive Party 141a
Niger River 85c, 126c, 127a, 140b, 140c, 141a, 250a, 266b, 278a, 278c
Nigeria 17b, 141–142
  agriculture 141b
  area 141a
  capital 141a
  currency unit 141a
  economy 141b
  flag *il* iv
  geography 141a
  government 141b–141c
  history 141c–142a
  independence 141c–142a
  industry 141b
  language 141a
  map 141, *Atlas*-37
  national holiday 141a
  official name 141a
  people of 141a–141b
  population 141a
  religion 141a
  slavery 141c
—Cities 141b
  Enugu 266b
  Ibadan 269a
  Jos 270a
  Kaduna 270b
  Kano 271a
  Lagos 272c
  Maiduguri 275a
  Ogbomosho 141b
  Onitsha 278c
  Oshogbo 279a
  Port Harcourt 280c
  Sapele 283c
  Zaria 289c
Nile River 177c, 192b, 192c, 193c, 250a
Nimba Mountains 120c, 121a, 250a
Nineveh 277a
Ninghsien, China 278a
Ningpo, China 278a
Nis, Yugoslavia 278b
Niue, 231
  area 231a
  population 231a
  status 231a
Nizhni-Novgorod, Soviet Union see Gorki, Soviet Union
Nkrumah, Kwame 80b–80c, 86b
Noah's Ark
  Ararat (mountain) 238b
Nobunaga, Oda 112b
Nombre de Dios, Panama 146b
Nonni River 287c
Nordic Council 142c
Norfolk Island 231
  area 231b
  population 231b
  status 231b
Normandy, Duke of see William II, King (England)
Normandy, France *il* 231
Normans
  Albania 2c
  Britain 196c–197a
  Italy 107c
North America 250b
North America Act (1867) 32b
North Atlantic Ocean see Atlantic Ocean
North Atlantic Treaty Organization (NATO) 34b, 142c, 143c
  flag *il* iv
North Borneo see Sabah
North Channel 194a, 250b
North German Confederation 77b
North Island, New Zealand 137c, 138a–138b, 258b, 289a
North Korea see Korea, North
North Rhine-Westphalia, West Germany 264b, 266a, 266c
North Saskatchewan River 266b
North Sea 250b
North Vietnam see Vietnam, North
Northern Dvina (river) see Dvina (rivers)
Northern Highlands (Scotland) 245b–245c
Northern Region, Nigeria 270a, 270b
Northern Rhodesia see Zambia
Northumbria, Kingdom of 196a
Northwest Territories, Canada 30c, 33a
Norway 142–144
  agriculture 142b
  area 142a
  capital 142a
  climate 142a
  currency unit 142a
  Danish rule 58a
  Denmark and 142c–143a
  economy 142b–142c
  fjords 142a
  flag *il* iv
  geography 142a
  government 142c
  history 142c–144a
  in Iceland 92c
  independence 143b–143c
  language 142a
  manufacturing 142b
  map 142, *Atlas*-14–15
  national holiday 142a
  official name 142a
  people of 142a
  population 142a
  raids on the British Isles 196a
  religion 142a, 142b, 143a
  in Svalbard and Jan Mayen Islands 235c–236a
  Sweden and 143a–143b
  trade 142b–142c
  Vikings 142c, 224a
  World War I 143b
  World War II 78c, 143c
—Cities 142b
  Bergen 260c
  Oslo 278c
  Trondheim 142b
Norwegian Sea 250b
Noteć River 150c
Notre Dame Cathedral 279c
Nouakchott, Mauritania 128a, 278b
Nouméa, New Caledonia 230a, 278b
Nova Scotia, Canada 30c, 31a–31b, 32a, 32c, 268b, 285c
Novaya Zemlya Archipelago 250b

INDEX

November Revolution (Russia) 173b–173c
Novgorod, Soviet Union 170a
Novi Sad, Yugoslavia 278b
Novosibirsk, Soviet Union 168a, 278b
Novosibirsk Oblast, Soviet Union 278b
Nowa Huta, Poland 151b
Novil River 262b
Ntare V, Mwami (king) (Burundi) 24b
Nu, U 23c, 24a
Nuba 178a
Nuba Mountains 177c
Nubian Desert 250b
Nubians 178a
Nuclear power
  France 71a
  Japan 111c
  Soviet Union 175a
Nuer 178a
Nuku'alofa, Tonga 236a, 278a
Núñez, Rafael 49b
Nura River 271a
Nuremberg, Germany see Nürnberg, Germany
Nürnberg, Germany 278c
  war crimes trials *il* 78
Nyanja 124b
Nyasa, Lake 124b, 250b
Nyasaland 124c–125a, 155b
  see also Malawi
Nyasaland African Congress (1944) 125a
Nyerere, Julius 185a

O

OAS *see* European Secret Army Organization
OAS *see* Organization of American States
Oaxaca, Mexico 129b, 129c
Ob River 250b, 278b
Obregón, Alvaro 131c
Oder River 54c, 73a, 73b, 150c, 151a, 151c, 250b, 285c, 289b
Odessa, Soviet Union 278c
Odoacer 107a
O'Donnell, Hugh 103b
Offa II, King (Mercia) 196a
Ogbomosho, Nigeria 141b
Ogooué River 71b, 273a
Ogotai 37a
O'Higgins, Bernardo 38a
Oil
  Angola 218b
  Bahrain 12c, 13a
  Brunei 221b
  Canada 28a
  China 41b
  Colombia 48c
  Germany 74b
  Indonesia 99a
  Iran 100a, 101a, 101b
  Iraq 101c, 102a
  Israel 104b
  Jan Mayen Island 236a
  Kuwait 117b, 117c
  Libya 122a
  Mauritania 128b
  Mongolia 132c
  Muscat and Oman 134c
  Netherlands Antilles 230a
  New Guinea 230c
  Nigeria 141b
  Pakistan 144b
  Qatar 154b–154c
  Romania 156a
  Saudi Arabia 158a, 158c–159a
  South Yemen 165c–166a
  Soviet Union 168b
  Spain 175c
  Spanish Sahara 235a
  Svalbard Archipelago 236a
  Syria 183a
  Trinidad and Tobago 187c
  Turkey 190a
  United Arab Republic 192c
  U.S. 205c
  Venezuela 210a–210b, *il* 211
Oil Rivers Protectorate 141c
Oka River 267c
Okande 71b
Okavango River 17b, 250b
Okayama, Japan 278c
Okeechobee, Lake 204b
Okhotsk, Sea of 250b–250c
Okinawa Island 277b
Oktoberfest (Munich) *il* 74
Olaf II, King (Norway and Denmark) 143a
Olaf V, King (Norway) 144a
Olives
  Greece 81a
  Italy 106c
  Lebanon 119b
  Portugal 153b
  Spain 176a
  Syria 183a
  Tunisia 189c
Oltul River 155c
Olympio, Sylvanus 187b
Olympus Mountains 54a, 250c 254a
Oman *see* Muscat and Oman
Oman, Gulf of 134c, 250c, 277a
Omo River 62a
Omono River 256c
Omuta, Japan 278c
Onega, Lake 250c
O'Neill, Hugh 103b
Onganía, Juan 7a
Onitsha, Nigeria 278c
Ontario, Lake 31b, 287a
Ontario Province, Canada 287a
Opium 44c
Opium War 44c
Oporto, Portugal *see* Porto, Portugal
Oradea, Romania 278c
Oradea Mare, Romania *see* Oradea, Romania
Oran, Algeria 279a
Orange, William of *see* William III, King (England)
Orange Free State, South Africa 120b, 261a
Orange River 120a, 164a, 250c
Orbegoso, Luis José 149a
Ordos Desert 40a, 40b
Oregon Treaty (1846) 31c, 32c
Oreti River 137c
Organization of American States (OAS) 54a, 59b
  flag *il* iv
Orient 250c
Orinoco River 48b, 209a, 250c, 283c
Orissa State, India 260c, 265a
Orkhon River 132b
Orkney Islands 194a, 250c
Orlich, Francisco 52b
Orontes River 182c, 250c, 269a
Orozco, Pascual 131b
Ortuño, René Barrientos 17a
Oruro, Bolivia 16b
Osaka, Japan 110c, 279a
Osaka Bay 283c
Oscar I, King (Sweden) 181a
Oscar II, King (Sweden) 181a
Oshogbo, Nigeria 279a
Oslo, Norway 142a, 142b, 279a
Oslo, University of 279a
Oslo Fjord 279a
Osman, Aden Abdullah 163b
Osorio, Oscar 61c
Ostrava, Czechoslovakia 279a
Ostravice River 279a
Ostrogoths 107a
Otaru, Japan 279a
Oti River 79c
Otranto, Strait of 237a
Ottawa, Canada 26a, *il* 33, 279b
Ottawa River 276c, 279b
Otto, King (Greece) 82b, 82c
Otto I, Emperor (Holy Roman Empire)
  Germany 75b
  Italy 107f
Ottoman Empire 190c–191a
  Albania 3a
  Algeria 4a
  Bosnia and Herzegovina 216a
  Bulgaria 21c–22a
  Cyprus 54b
  Egypt 193a–193b
  Greece 81c–82b
  Hungary 90c
  Iraq 102a
  Jordan 114a
  Kuwait 117c
  Lebanon 119c–120a
  Libya 122a–122b
  Macedonia 216a
  Montenegro 216a
  Muscat and Oman 134c
  Palestine and 105b
  Qatar 154c
  Romania 156b–156c
  Russia, war with 22a, 82a–82b
  Saudi Arabia 159a–159b
  Serbia 216a
  South Yemen 166a
  Syria 183b
  Tunisia 189b
  World War I 77c, 191a
  Yemen 214b
  Young Turk Movement 191a
  Yugoslavia 216a–216b
Ou River 118a
Ouagadougou, Upper Volta 206a, 279b
Oujda, Morocco 279b
Outer Mongolia *see* Mongolia
Ovambo 234c
Oviedo, Spain 176a
Ovimbundu 218a
Owen Falls 191c
Oxford, England 279b
Oxford, Provisions of 198a
Oxford University 279b
Oxus River *see* Amu River

P

Pacassi, Nicolas
  Schoenbrunn Castle *il* 11
Pacheco Areco, Jorge 208a
Pacific Ocean 250c–251a
Padang, Indonesia 279b
Padjajaran University 259b
Padma 244b
Paekche Kingdom 116a, 116b
Paéz, José Antonio 210a
Pagan, Burma 23b
Pago Pago, Samoa 279b
Pago Pago, Tahiti 213c
Pahang River 125b
Pakistan 97c, 144–145
  agriculture 144b–144c
  area 144a
  capital 144a
  climate 144a
  currency unit 144a
  economy 144b–144c
  flag *il* iv
  geography 144a–144b
  government 144c
  history 144c–145c
  India and 93a, 97c–98a, 144c, 145c
  industry 144b
  language 144a
  manufacturing 144c
  map 145, *Atlas*-28–29
  national holiday 144a
  official name 144a
  people of 144b
  population 144a
  religion 144a, 144b, 144c
  trade 144c
  —Cities
    Chittagong 264a
    Dacca 265a
    Islamabad 269c
    Karachi 271a
    Lahore 273a
    Peshawar 280a
    Quetta 281b
    Rawalpindi 282a
Pakistan Industrial Development Corporation 144c
Palau Islands 240b
Palembang, Indonesia 279b–279c
Palermo, Italy 279c
Palestine 104c–105c, 270a
  see also Israel
  see also Jordan
Palk Strait 243a
Pallavas 96a
Pamir Mountains 251a
Pampa 251a
  Argentina 5a
Panama 146a–146c
  area 146a
  agriculture 146b
  capital 146a
  climate 146a
  currency unit 146a
  economy 146a–146b
  flag *il* iv
  geography 146a
  government 146a
  history 146b–146c
  independence 146c
  Indians 146a, 146c
  language 146a
  map 146, *Atlas*-52
  national holiday 146a
  official name 146a
  people of 146a
  population 146a
  religion 146a
  trade 146b
  World War II 146c
  —Cities
    Colón 146b
    Nombre de Dios 146b
    Panama City 146b, 279c
    Portobelo 146b
Panamá, Panama *see* Panama City, Panama
Panama, Isthmus of 251a
Panama Canal 13c, 146a, 146c
Panama Canal Zone 146a, 146b, 146c
Panama City, Panama 146a, 146b, 279c
Panay Island, Philippines 149c, 150a, 269b
Panchayat 136a
Pandyas 95c, 96a
Panjim, India 279c
Pannonia 90b
Pan-Slav Congress 77a
PAP *see* Popular Action Party (PAP) (Peru)
Papal States 107b, 107c
Papandreou, Andreas 83c
Papandreou, George 83b, 83c
Papeete, Tahiti 224c, 279c

Papua 231
  area 231b
  capital 231b
  population 231b
  status 231b
Pará River 260a
Para State, Brazil 260a
Paraguay 6b, 17a, 20a, 147–148
  agriculture 147b
  area 147a
  Asuncion 258b
  Bolivia, war with 148a
  capital 147a
  climate 147a
  currency unit 147a
  economy 147a–147b
  flag *il* iv
  geography 147a
  government 147b
  history 147b–148a
  independence 147c
  Indians 147a, 147c
  industry 147b
  language 147a
  map 147, *Atlas*-45
  national holiday 247a
  official name 147a
  people of 147a
  population 147a
  religion 147a
  trade 147b
  war of the Triple Alliance 147c
Paraguay River 147a, 147b, 251a
Paraíba River 288c
Paramaribo. Surinam 235b, 279c
Paraná, Brazil 264c
Paraná Plateau 147a
Paraná River 5a, 147a, 147b, 251a
Pardo, Manuel 149a
Paria, Gulf of 251c
Paris, France 64a, 64b, 279c
  Arc de Triomphe *il* 69
  Eiffel Tower *il* 64
  industrial district 65a
Paris, Convention of (1858) 156c
Paris, Peace of (1763) *see* Treaty of Paris (1763)
Paris, Treaty of (1763) 30c, 202c
Paris, Treaty of (1783) 31a, 202c
Paris, Treaty of (1814) 129a, 234b
Paris, Treaty of (1898) 150b
Park, Chung Hee 117b
PARMEHUTU *see* Party of the Hutu Emancipation Movement (Rwanda)
Parnell, Charles Stewart 103c
Paropamisus Mountains 251a
Parr, Catherine 200a
Parthians 101a
Party of the Hutu Emancipation Movement (Rwanda) 157c, 158a
Pashto language 1a
Pashtuns 1a
Pasteur Institute (Bandung) 259b
Pasteur Institute (Dakar) 265c
Patagonia 251a
Patagonian Indians 5b
Pataliputra, India 95b, 95c, 279c
Patan, Nepal 135c
Pathans *see* Pashtuns
Pathet Lao 119a
Patna, India 95c, 279c
Patrick, Saint 103a
Paul, Prince (Yugoslavia) 216b
Paul I, King (Greece) 83b
Paul III, Pope 158b
Paulo Afonso Falls 251a
Paz Estenssoro, Victor 17a
Peanuts
  Chad 36c
  Gambia 72a–72b
  Guinea 86a
  Indonesia 99a
  Libya 122a
  Mali 127a
  Niger 140c
  Nigeria 141b
  Portuguese Guinea 232a
  Senegal 160a
  Sudan 178a
  Thailand 185c
  Upper Volta 206c
  Vietnam 211b
  Zambia 217b
Pearl Harbor
  Japanese attack 113b
Pearl River 44b, 228b, 240c, 263b
Pearls
  Bahrain 12c
  Qatar 154b
  Trucial Oman 188b
Pearson, Lester 34b, 34c
Peasants' Revolt (England) 199a

Pécs, Hungary 90a, 280a
Pedro I, Emperor (Brazil) 20a
Pedro II, Emperor (Brazil) 20a–20b
Pegnitz River 278c
Pei River 286c
Peiping, China *see* Peking, China
Peking, China 39a, 39b, 43c, 44a, 45a, 280a
Peking man 42a
Peloponnesos, Greece 81a, 251a
Penang Island 125b
Penang, Malaysia 125c
P'enghu Islands 251b
Pengiran Muda Mahkota Hassanal Bolkiah 221b
Penguins *il* 274a
Penner (rivers) 251a
Pennine Mountains 194a
People's Democratic Party (Sudan) 178c
People's Liberation Army (Laos) 119a
People's National Congress (PNC) (Guyana) 87a
People's National Party (Jamaica) 110b
People's Party (Austria) 12b
People's Progressive Party (PPP) (Guyana) 87a, 87b
Peoples' Socialist Community (Cambodia) 25b
Pepin III, King 107a
Pepin the Short, King 66a
Peralta Azurdía, Enrique 85b
Pereira de Souza, Washington Luís 20c
Perekop Isthmus 243a
Pérez Jiménez, Marcos 210b
Perm, Soviet Union 280a
Pernambuco State, Brazil 282a
Pernis, Netherlands 282b
Perón, Juan D. 6c–7a
Perry, Matthew C. 112c
Persian Empire 101a–101b
  Afghanistan 1c
Persian Gulf 134b, 134c, 251b, 275b
Persian Gulf Indian rupee 134c
Perth, Australia 9a, 280a
Peru 16c–16a, 38a, 60b, 60c, 148–149
  agriculture 148b, 148c
  area 148a
  capital 148a
  climate 148a
  currency unit 148a
  economy 148b–148c
  flag *il* iv
  geography 148a–148b
  government 148c
  history 148c–149b
  independence 149a–149b
  Indians 148b, 148c, 149a
  industry 148c
  language 148c
  map 148, *Atlas*-50–51
  national holiday 148a
  official name 148a
  people of 148b
  population 148a
  religion 148a, 148b
  slavery 149a
  trade 148c
  war with Chile 38b
—Cities 148b
  Arequipa 148b
  Callao 148b
  Cuzco 265a
  Lima 273c
  Trujillo 148b
Pescadores Islands 39b, 251b
Peseta 175b
Peshawar, Pakistan 280a–280b
Peso
  Argentina 5a
  Bolivia 16a
  Colombia 48a
  Cuba 52b
  Dominican Republic 58c
  Mexico 129b
  Philippines 149b
  Uruguay 207a
Pétain, Henri-Philippe 70c
Peter, King (Serbia) 175b
Peter, King (Yugoslavia) 216b
Peter I, Tsar (Russia) 171a–171b
Peter II, King (Yugoslavia) 216b, 216c
Peter V, King (Portugal) 154a
Pétion, Alexandre 88b
Petrograd *see* Leningrad, Soviet Union
Petroleum *see* Oil
Peuhls *see* Peuls

Peuls
  Dahomey 56c
  Senegal 159c
Phanariots 156b–156c
Phetchabun Mountains 185b
Philip II, King (France) 66c, 198c
Philip IV, King (France) 66c
Philip VI, King (France) 66c, 67b
Philip II, King (Spain) 14c, 123b, 137b, 154a, 176c–177a, 200a, 200b
Philip V, King (Spain) 68b, 177a
Philip Augustus *see* Philip II, King (France)
Philip the Good of Burgundy 123b
Philippines 126b, 149–150
  agriculture 149c
  area 149b
  capital 149b
  climate 149c
  currency unit 149b
  economy 149c–150a
  flag *il* iv
  geography 149c
  government 150a
  history 150a–150c
  independence 150c
  language 149b
  map *Atlas*-30–31
  national holiday 149b
  official name 149b
  people of 149c
  population 149b
  religion 149b, 150a
  World War II 150b
—Cities
  Aparri 257c
  Bacolod 258c
  Davao 265b
  Iloilo 269b
  Jolo 270a
  Manila 275b
  Quezon City 281b
  Zamboanga 289c
Philippine Sea 239c–240a
Phillip, Arthur 8c
Phnom Penh, Cambodia 24b, 280b
Phosphate
  Christmas Island 222b
  French Polynesia 225a
  Gilbert and Ellice Islands 226a
  Jordan 17c
  Morocco 133c
  Nauru 135a, 135b
  Senegal 160a
  Spanish Sahara 235a
  Togo 187a
  Tunisia 189a
  United States 205c
Piast dynasty 151c–152a
Piastre 210c
Picts 196a
Pieck, Wilhelm 79b
Pietermaritzburg, South Africa 280b
Pilsen, Czechoslovakia *see* Plzeň, Czechoslovakia
Pilsudski, Józef 152b
Pindus Mountains 80c, 251b
Pines, Isle of 230a
Ping River 240a, 264a
Piraeus, Greece 280b
Pirin Mountains 21a
Pitcairn Island 231
  area 231c
  population 231c
  status 231c
Pitch Lake 187c
Pitt, William (the elder) 202c
Pitt, William (the younger) 202c
Piva (river) 243b
Pizarro, Francisco 60b, 146b, 148c, 149a
Pizarro, Gonzalo 16c
Pizarro, Hernando 16c
Plata, Río de la 251b
Platt Amendment 53c
Pleisse River 273b
Ploiești, Romania 156a, 280b
Plovdiv, Bulgaria 21a, 280b
Plymouth, Montserrat 229a, 280c
Plzeň, Czechoslovakia 55a
PNC *see* People's National Congress (PNC) (Guyana)
PNR *see* National Revolutionary Party (Mexico)
Po Hai (gulf) *see* Chih-li, Gulf of
Po River 106a, 287c
Po Valley 106b–106c
Pobedonostsev, Konstantin 172a
Pointe Noire, Congo 50a
Pointe-à-Pitre, Guadaloupe 227a, 280c

Poland 11c, 79a, 150–152
  agriculture 151a, 151b
  area 150c
  capital 150c
  climate 151a
  communism 150a, 151b, 151c, 152c
  currency unit 150c
  economy 151a–151c
  flag *il* iv
  geography 150c–151a
  government 151c
  history 151c–152c
  independence 152b
  industry 152b–152c
  language 150c
  map 151, *Atlas*-8–9
  national holiday 150c
  natural resources 151a–151b
  official name 150c
  partitions 152a
  people of 151a
  population 150c
  religion 150c, 151a, 152a, 152c
  trade 151c
  World War I 152b
  World War II 70c, 78c, 151a, 152b–152c, 204a
—Cities 151a
  Bialystok 261c
  Częstochowa 265a
  Gdańsk (Danzig) 267a
  Gdynia 267b
  Katowice 271b
  Kraków (Cracow) 272a
  Łódź 274a
  Lublin 274c
  Poznan 281a
  Szczecin 285c
  Warsaw 289a
  Wroclaw (Breslau) 289b
Polar Regions *see* Antarctica; Arctic Ocean
Polish Committee of National Liberation 152c
Polish Corridor 152b
Polish National Committee 152b
Polish United Worker's Party 151c
Polo, Marco 43c
Pombal, Marquis of 154a
Ponce, Federico 85a
Ponce Enríquez, Camilo 60c
Poniatowski, Stanislas 152a
Pontchartrain, Lake 204c
Pontic Mountains 189c
Poona, India 280c
Popocatépetl (mountain) 129b–129c
Popular Action Party (PAP) (Peru) 149b
Port Elizabeth, South Africa 164b, 280c
Port Etienne, Mauritania 128a, 128b
Port Gentil, Gabon 71c
Port Harcourt, Nigeria 141b, 280c
Port Louis, Mauritius 128c, 280c
Port Moresby, Papua 231b, 280c
Port Phillip Bay 276a
Port Said, United Arab Republic (Egypt) 192c, 281a
Port Sudan, Sudan 281a
Port Victoria, Seychelles 234a, 281a
Port wine 153b
Portales, Diego 38a
Port-au-Prince, Haiti 87b, 87c, 280c
Port-de-France, Martinique 228c
Porto, Portugal 153b, 280c
Portobelo, Panama 146b
Port-of-Spain, Trinidad and Tobago 187b
Porto-Novo, Dahomey 56b, 56c, 281a
Portugal 153–154
  agriculture 153b
  area 153a
  capital 153a
  climate 153a
  currency unit 153a
  economy 153b
  flag *il* iv
  geography 153a
  government 153b–154a
  industry 153b
  language 153a
  map 153, *Atlas*-12
  national holiday 153a
  natural resources 153b
  official name 153a
  people of 153a–153b
  population 153a
  religion 153a
  trade 153b

INDEX   Riga   377

—Cities 153b
  Lisbon 273c
  Porto (Oporto) 280c
—History 153c–154b
  Avís dynasty 153c
  Azores 239a
  Bragança dynasty 154a
  colonial
    Angola 218a–219a
    Brazil 19b–20b
    Cape Verde Islands 221b–221c
    Ethiopia 62b
    Indonesia 99c
    Macao 45a, 228b–228c
    Mozambique 229a–229c
    Muscat and Oman 134c–135a
    Nigeria 141c
    Portuguese Guinea 231c–232b
    Portuguese Timor 232b–232c
    Principe 234b
    São Tomé 234a
    Uruguay 207c
  independence 176b–177a
  World War I 154b
  World War II 154b
Portuguese Guinea 153c, 231–232
  agriculture 232a
  area 231c
  Bissau 261a
  capital 231c
  economy 232a
  geography 231c–232a
  government 232a
  history 232a–232b
  map Atlas-36
  people of 232a
  population 231c
  slavery 232a
  status 231c
Portuguese India see Diu
Portuguese Timor 232
  area 232b
  capital 232b
  Dili 265b
  population 232b
  status 232b
Portuguese West Africa see Angola
Poszony, University of 280c
Potomac River 205a
Potosí, Bolivia 16b
Potsdam, Germany 79a, 281a
Potsdam Agreement 150c, 151a
Potwar Plateau 269c, 282a
Pound (currency unit)
  Cyprus 54c
  Gambia 72a
  Ireland 102b
  Israel 104a
  Jamaica 109c
  Lebanon 119b
  Libya 121b
  Malawi 124b
  Malta 127b
  Nigeria 141a
  Rhodesia 154c
  Sudan 177c
  Syria 182c
  United Arab Republic (Egypt) 192b
  United Kingdom 194a
Poyang (lake) 251b, 277c
Poznań, Poland 151c, 152c, 281a
PPP see People's Progressive Party (PPP) (Guyana)
Prague (Praha), Czechoslovakia 54c, 55a, 281a
Praha, Czechoslovakia see Prague, Czechoslovakia
Praia, Cape Verde Islands 221b, 281a
Praslin Island 234a
Pregel River 270c
Prempeh I, King (Ashanti) 80b
Pretoria, South Africa 163c, 164b, 281a
Primo de Rivera, Miguel 177b
Prince Edward Island, Canada 26c, 32b, 32c
Principe see São Tomé and Principe
Prithvi, Narayan 136a
Progressive Party (Togo) 187b
Progressive People's Party (Gambia) 72c
Prussia 11b, 69c, 76b–76c, 77a–77b, 91a
Prut River 155c, 251b
Ptolemy I (Ptolemy Soter), King (Egypt) 193a
Ptolemy Soter, King (Egypt) see Ptolemy I, King (Egypt)
Puebla, Mexico 130a
Puebla, Battle of 131b
Puerto Barrios, Guatemala 281b
Puerto Montt, Chile 37b
Pungwe River 260a
Punjab (region), Pakistan 273c
Punjab State, India 263b, 270a
Punjab University 273c
Punta Arenas, Chile 37b
Pusan, South Korea 115c
Pygmies
  Cameroon 25c
  Congo (Kinshasa) 50c
  see also Twa
Pyongyang, North Korea 115b, 115c, 281b
Pyrenees Mountains 175b, 251b
Pyrrhus, King (Epirus) 2c
Pyu 23a

Q

Qahtan al-Shaabi 166a
Qairouan, Tunisia 189a
Qajar dynasty 101b
Qaramanli dynasty 122b
Qasim, Abdel Karim 102b
Qat 214a
Qatar 154
  area 154b
  capital 154b
  climate 154b
  currency unit 154b
  Doha 265c
  economy 154b–154c
  flag il iv
  geography 154b
  government 154c
  history 154c
  language 154c
  map Atlas-25
  official name 154b
  oil 154b–154c
  people of 154b
  population 154b
  religion 154b
Qatar Peninsula 265c
Qattara Depression 251b
Que Que, Rhodesia 281b
Quebec, Canada 29c, 31a, 281a
Quebec Act of 1774 31a
Quechua 16a, 148b
  see also Incas
Queen's University (Belfast) 260b
Queensland, Australia 230c, 231c
Quemoy 47c
Quetta, Pakistan 281b
Quetzal (currency unit) 84a
Quezon, Manuel 150b
Quezon City, Philippines 149b, 281b–281c
Quisling, Vidkun 143c
Quito, Ecuador 59c, 60a, 281c
Quito, Kingdom of 60b
Quyen, Ngo 212a

R

Rabat, Morocco 133b, 133c, 281c
Rabeh 37a
Radhakrishnan, Sarvepalli 98b
Radical Party (Argentina) 6c–7a
Radical Socialist Party (France) 70b–70c
Raffles, Stamford 162c
Rahman al-Iryani, Abdul 214c
Rainier III, Prince (Monaco) 132b
Rajang River 125b
Rajasthan State, India 270a
Rajputs 96a, 96b, 96c
Rakosi, Mátyás 91b
Raleigh, Walter 87a
Ramganga River 259c
Ramgoolam, Seewoosagur 129b
Ramírez, Pedro 6c
Rampur, India 281c
Rampur District, India 281c
Ranchi, India 281c
Rand (currency unit) 162c
Rangitaiki River 137c
Rangoon, Burma 22b, 22c, 281c–282a
Rangoon, University of 281c
Rangoon River 281c
Ras al Khaimah 188b
  see also Trucial Oman
Ras Taffari 62b
Rasputin, Gregory 172c–173a
Ravenna, Italy 107c
Rawalpindi, Pakistan 144a, 282a
Recife, Brazil 282a
Reciprocity Agreement (1911) 33c
Reciprocity Treaty (1854) 31c, 32b
Red Fort (Agra) 256b
Red Guards 41b, 47a
Red (Hong) River (Vietnam) 210c, 211a, 251b, 268c
Red River of the North 251b, 289b
Red Sea 251b–251c, 281a
Red Square (Moscow) 277a
Reformation
  Britain 199c–200a
  France 67b
  Germany 76b–76c
  Sweden 180c
  Switzerland 182c
Regina, Canada 282a
Registan (desert) 1a
Religion see under the names of individual countries, such as Panama, religion
Republican Peoples Party (Turkey) 191b
Restrepo, Carlos Lleras 49c
Réunion 232c
  area 232c
  capital 232c
  population 232c
  Saint-Denis 282c
  status 232c
Reval, Estonia see Tallinn, Soviet Union
Revolutionary Party (Guatemala) 85c
Reykjavik, Iceland 92a, 282a
Reza'iyeh, Iran 282a
Rhaeti 181b, 182b
Rhee, Syngman 117a, 117b
Rhine River 64a, 73b, 122b–122c, 181b, 251c
Rhineland 264b, 266a
Rhodes (island) 80c
Rhodes, Cecil 124c, 155b, 165a, 217c
Rhodesia 154–155
  agriculture 155a
  area 154c
  capital 154c
  climate 155a
  currency unit 154c
  economy 155a
  flag il iv
  geography 154c–155a
  government 155a–155b
  history 155b
  independence 204b
  language 154c
  map 155, Atlas-40–41
  official name 154c
  people of 155a
  population 154c
  religion 154c
—Cities
  Bulawayo 262c
  Que Que 281b
  Salisbury 283a
  Umtali 288a
Rhodesia and Nyasaland, Federation of 155b
  see also Malawi; Rhodesia; Zambia
Rhodope Mountains 21a
Rhône River 64a, 65b, 181b, 251c, 267c, 274c
Rial 100c
Rice
  British Honduras 220a
  Brunei 221b
  Burma 23a
  China 41b
  Comoro Islands 222c
  Fiji Islands 224b
  Guyana 86b, 86c
  India 94b
  Indonesia 99a
  Iraq 101c
  Italy 106b–106c
  Japan 111b
  Korea, South 115c
  Laos 118b
  Liberia 121a
  Madagascar 124a
  Malawi 124c
  Malaysia 125b
  Mali 127a
  Mauritania 128a
  Mexico 130a
  New Caledonia 230b
  Niger 140c
  Pakistan 144b
  Panama 146b
  Paraguay 147b
  Peru 148c
  Philippines 149c
  Portugal 153b
  Portuguese Guinea 232a
  Senegal 160a
  Sierra Leone 160c
  Spain 176a
  Surinam 235b
  Swaziland 179a
  Taiwan 41c
  Tanzania 184a
  Thailand 185c
  Togo 187a
  United Arab Republic (Egypt) 192c
  Uruguay 207a
  Venezuela 209b
  Vietnam 211b
Richard, Duke of York 199b
Richard I, King (England) 197b–197c
Richard II, King (England) 199a
Richard III, King (England) 199b
Richelieu, Cardinal 30a, 67c
Riel 24b
Riel, Louis 32c, 33a
Rif Atlas (mountains) 133b–133c, 134b
Riga, Soviet Union 152b, 282a
Riga, Gulf of 243b, 282a

Rila Mountains 21a
Rimac River 273c
Rio de Janeiro, Brazil 18a–18c, il 19, 282a
Rio de Janeiro Protocol (1942) 60c
Río de la Plata 251b
Rio Grande (river) 132a, 205a
Río Muni see Equatorial Guinea
Río Ulúa (river) 88c
Rion River 166c
Rivera, Julio Adalberto 70c
Rivers 251c–252a
    see also under names of individual rivers, such as Mississippi
Riviera 252a
Riyadh, Saudi Arabia 258b, 282b
Riyal 214c
Riza, Muhammad, Shah (Iran) 101b, 101c
Riza Pahlavi, Shah (Iran) 101b
Rizal, José 150a–150b
Road Town, British Virgin Islands 221a, 282b
Robert I, King (Scotland) 198b
Robespierre, Maximilien de 68c
Rocky Mountains 27a, 27c, 204c
Rodrigues Island 128c
Roggeveen, Jacob 213c
Rojas Pinilla, Gustavo 49b–49c
Rokel River 160b
Roman Catholic Church
    Vatican City 208a–208c
Roman Empire see Rome, Ancient
Roman law 197b
Roman y Reyes, Victor Manuel 140b
Romania 155–157
    agriculture 156a, 157a
    area 155c
    capital 155c
    communism 155a, 156a, 156b, 157a–157b
    currency unit 155c
    economy 156a–156b
    flag il iv
    geography 155c
    government 156b
    history 156b–157b
    independence 156c–157a
    industry 156a
    language 155c
    map 156, Atlas-18–19
    national holiday 155c
    natural resources 156a
    official name 155c
    people of 155c–156a
    Phanariot rule 156b–156c
    population 155c
    religion 155c
    trade 156a–156b
    World War I 157a
    World War II 157a
    —Cities 155c–156a
    Arad 258a
    Braila 261c
    Bucharest 262b
    Cluj 155c–156a
    Iasi 269a
    Oradea (Oradea Mare) 278c
    Ploieşti 280b
    Satu-Mare 284a
    Sibiu 284b
    Timişoara 286c
Romanov family 170c–173a
Rome, Italy 105c, 106a, 107a, 208a, 282b
Rome, Ancient 107a
    Albania 2c
    Algeria 4a
    Andorra 122c
    Britain 195c–196a
    Bulgaria 21c
    Egypt 193a
    France 66a
    Germany 75a
    Greece 81b
    Malta 127c
    Morocco 134a
    Netherlands 137a
    Palestine 105a
    Romania 156b
    Spain 176b
    Switzerland 182b
    Syria 183b
    Tunisia 189b
Romulus Augustus, Emperor (Rome) 107a
Roosevelt, Franklin 88b, 150b
Roosevelt, Theodore 59a, 146c, 172b
Rosario, Argentina 5b
Rosas, Juan Manuel de 6b
Roseau, Dominica 223a
Roseau, Windward Islands 282b
Roses, War of the 199b
Ross Sea 252a
Rotterdam, Netherlands 136c, 137a, 282b, 282c
Roubaix, France 65a
Roxas, Manuel 150c
Royal Dutch Shell Company 230a
Royal Niger Company 141c
Ruanda-Urundi 24b, 157c
    see also Burundi; Rwanda
Ruapehu (mountain) 137c
Rub al Khali (desert) 245a, 252a
Rubber
    Brunei 221b
    Ceylon 35c, 36a
    Congo (Kinshasa) 51a
    Indonesia 99a
    Liberia 121a
    Malaysia 125b, 126a
    New Guinea 230c
    Nigeria 141b
    Papua 231b
    Singapore 162b
    synthetic 111c
    Thailand 185c
    Vietnam 211b
Ruble 166b
Rudolf of Hapsburg, Emperor (Holy Roman Empire) 75c
Rudolf, Lake 114b, 252a
Rufiji River 184a, 252a
Ruhr River 266c
Runnymede, England 197c
Rupee
    Ceylon 35c
    India 93a
    Maldive Islands 126b
    Mauritius 128c
    Nepal 135b
    Pakistan 144a
Rupiah 98b
Ruse, Bulgaria 21a, 282c
Russia
    Afghanistan and 1c–2a
    China, treaty with (1896) 45b
    Duma 172b–172c
    history 169c–173b
    in Iran 101b
    Japan, war with 172b
    in Korea 117a
    Mongolia and 133a, 133b
    in Poland 152a–152b
    religion 170a
    revolutions (1917) 173a–173b
    in Romania 156b–157a
    serfdom 170a–171a
    Turkey, war with (1877) 22a, 82a–82b
    World War I 70b, 73b, 76c–77a, 77c
    see also Union of Soviet Socialist Republics (after 1917)
Russo-Japanese War (1904–1905) 113a
Russo-Turkish War (1828–1829) 156c
Russo-Turkish War (1877–1878) 82c, 156c–157a
Ruwenzori (mountain) 50c
Ruwenzori Mountains 191b, 252a
Rwanda 24b, 157–158
    agriculture 157c
    area 157b
    capital 157b
    currency unit 157b
    economy 157c
    flag il iv
    geography 157b
    government 157c
    history 157c–158a
    Kigali 271c
    language 157b
    map 157, Atlas-39
    national holiday 157b
    official name 157b
    people of 157b–157c
    population 157b
    religion 157b
Ryukyu Islands 113b

S

Saba Island 229c
Sabah 100b, 270a
Sabarmati River 252a, 256b
Sabeans 62b
Sa'dis 134a
Sadozay tribe 1c
Safavid dynasty 1c
Saga, Japan 282c
Sagami Bay 110c, 270c
Sagauli, Treaty of 136b
Sahara (desert) 3c, 86a, 121c, 122a, 126c, 177b, 252a
Saharan Atlas (mountains) 3b
Saifuddin, Sultan Omar Ali 221b
Saigon, South Vietnam 210a, 211b, 282c
Saigon River 282c
St. Basil's Cathedral (Moscow) 277a
Saint Christopher (island) see Saint Kitts–Nevis–Anguilla
Saint-Denis, Réunion Island 232c, 282c
St. Dominique 88a
St. Etienne, France 65b
St. Eustacious Island 229c
St. George's, Grenada 226c, 282c
St. George's Channel 194c
St. Germain, Treaty of 11c, 56a
St. Helena Island 233a
    area 233a
    capital 233a
    Jamestown 270a
    population 233a
    status 233a
St. Helier, Jersey Island 222a
St. John, New Brunswick (Canada) il 29
St. John, Lake 26c
St. John City, Antigua 219a, 283a
St. John River 120c, 267a
Saint John's, Newfoundland 283a
St. Kitts-Nevis-Anguilla 233a–233b
    area 233a
    Basse Terre 259c
    capital 233a
    population 233a
    status 233a
St. Laurent, Louis 34b
St. Lawrence, Gulf of 26c
St. Lawrence River 29c, 31b, 276c, 281b
St. Lawrence Seaway 34b, 276c
St. Lawrence Valley 26c, 29c
Saint-Louis, Senegal 159c, 160a, 283a
St. Lucia 233b
    area 233b
    capital 233b
    Castries 263a
    Indians 233b
    population 233b
    status 233b
St. Maarten Island 229c
St. Mary's Island (Gambia) 72a, 259c
St. Paul River 120c
St. Peter Port, Guernsey Island 222a
St. Peter's Basilica il 208
St. Petersburg, Russia 169a, 171a, 171b, 173b
    see also Leningrad, Soviet Union
St. Pierre, St. Pierre and Miquelon 233c
St. Pierre and Miquelon 233c
    area 233c
    capital 233c
    population 233c
    status 233c
St. Thomas Island, U.S. Virgin Islands 263c
St. Vincent 233c
    area 233c
    capital 233c
    Kingstown 271c
    population 233c
    status 233c
St. Vincent, Gulf of 256b
Sajó River 276b
Sakai, Japan 283a
Sakalava 123c
Sakarya River 190a
Sakas see Scythians
Sakhalin Island 252a–252b
Sakiet-Sidi-Youssef, Tunisia 189c
Sal River 243b
Saladin 193a
Salazar, António de Oliveira 153b, 154b
Salem, India 283a
Salisbury, Rhodesia 154c, 283a
Salonika, Greece see Thessaloníki, Greece
Saloum River 159c
Salvador, Brazil 19c, 283b
Salween River 22c, 185a, 252b, 277m
Salzach River 283b
Salzburg, Austria 283a
Sam Sene T'ai, King (Laos) 118c
Samara, Soviet Union 272c
Samarkand, Soviet Union il 171, 283b
Sambre River 14a
Samo 206b
Samoa see American Samoa; Western Samoa
Samori ibn Ture 86a, 86b
Samos 80c
Samudragupta 95c
Samurai 112c
San Augustin, University of (Iloilo) 269b
San Blas Islands 146c
San Cristóbal Island see Chatham Island
San Jacinto, Battle of 131a
San Jorge, Gulf of 264b
San José, Costa Rica 51b, 51c, 283b
San Marino 158
    agriculture 158a
    area 158a
    capital 158a
    climate 158a
    communism 158b
    currency unit 158a
    economy 158a
    flag il iv
    geography 158a
    government 158b
    history 158b
    language 158a
    map 158, Atlas-13
    national holiday 158a
    official name 158a
    people of 158a
    population 158a
    religion 158a
    World War I 158b
    World War II 158b
San Marino, San Marino 158a
San Marino River 158a
San Martin (mountain) 129b
San Martin, José de 38a, 149a
San Salvador, El Salvador 60c, 283b
San'a, Yemen 214a, 283b
Sanagha River 252b, 266c
Sánchez Cerro, Luis 149b
Sanchez Hernández, Fidel 61c
Sancho I, King (Portugal) 153c
Sancho II, King (Portugal) 153c
Sandwich Islands see Hawaii
Sangay (volcano) 59c
Sangha 50a
Sangha River 49c
Sanjurjo, José 177b
Santa Anna, Antonio López de 131a
Santa Cruz, Andrés 16c
Santa Cruz, Bolivia 16b
Santa Isabel, Equatorial Guinea 223a, 283c

INDEX

Santa Marta, Colombia 49a
Santals 94a
Santana, Pedro 59a
Santander, Francisco de Paula 49a
Santander, Spain 176a
Santiago, Chile 37b, 37c, 283c
Santiago, Cuba 52c
Santo Domingo, Dominican Republic 58c, 283c
Santo Domingo (island) see Hispaniola
Santo Domingo (republic) see Dominican Republic
Santo Tomé de Guayana, Venezuela 209b, 283c
São Francisco River 252b
São Paulo, Brazil 18b, 18c, 283c
São Tiago Island 281a
São Tomé and Principe 153c, 234a
  area 234a
  capital 234a
  government 234a
  history 234a
  people of 234a
  population 234a
  religion 234a
  São Tomé (city) 234a, 283c
  status 234a
São Tomé, São Tomé and Principe 234a, 283c
Saône River 65b, 274c
Sapele, Nigeria 283c
Sapporo, Japan 283c
Sara (people) 36c
Sarajevo, Yugoslavia 215b, 216b, 283c
Sarakolle 126c
Saratov, Soviet Union 283c–284a
Sarawak 100b, 125c, 272b
Sardinia 105c, 132b
Sardinia, Kingdom of 107c, 108a
Sarmiento, Domingo F. 6a
Saronic Gulf 258b
Sary-Ishikotrau Desert 239a
Saskatchewan Province, Canada 282c
Sassandra River 109a
Sato, Eisaku 113b
Satpura Mountains 252b
Satsuma ware (pottery) 270b
Satu-Mare, Romania 284a
al-Saud, Abd al-Aziz see Abd al-Azis Al Saud
Saud, Muhammad ibn see Muhammad ibn Saud
Saudi Arabia 13a, 117c, 158–159
  agriculture 159a
  area 158b
  capital 158b
  climate 158c
  currency unit 158b
  economy 158c–159a
  flag il iv
  geography 158c
  government 159a
  history 159a
  language 158b
  map 158, Atlas-25
  national holiday 158b
  official name 158b
  oil 158a, 158c–159a
  people of 158c
  population 158b
  religion 158b, 159a
  —Cities
    Az Zahran (Dhahran) 258c
    Juddah 270b
    Mecca 276a
    Medina 276a
    Riyadh 282b
Sauer River 123a
Sava River 215a, 252b, 274a, 289c
Savai'i Island 213b
Savannah River 205a
Saxons
  Britain 196a
  Germany 75a
Sayan Mountains 167a, 252b
Sayyid Abd al-Rahman al Mahdi 178c
Sayyid Ahmad Khan 145a
Sayyid Ali al-Mirghani 178c
Scandinavia see Denmark; Norway; Sweden
Scandinavia (peninsula) 252b
Schelde River 14a, 252b, 257c
Schick Gutiérrez, René 140b
Schleswig (duchy) 77a
Schoenbrunn Castle il 11
Scilly Islands 252b
Scotland 194a, 195c, 196a
  industry 195a
  map Atlas-10
  see also United Kingdom

Scots 196a
Scutari, Lake 284b
Scythians 95c
Seas see under the names of individual seas, such as Galilee, Sea of
SEATO see Southeast Asia Treaty Organization
Seddon, Richard 139a
Sedjoumi salt flat 287c
Ségou, Mali 127a
Seine River 64a, 252b, 273b
Seistan 1a, 252c
Seizal, Portugal 153b
Sekondi-Takoradi, Ghana 284a
Selenge River 132b, 252c, 287c
Seleucid Empire 183b
  Afghanistan 1c
Seleucus 183b
Seljuk Turks 101a, 105a
Semliki River 237b
Sendai, Japan 284a
Sendai Plain 284a
Senegal 72c, 159–160
  agriculture 160a
  area 159c
  capital 159c
  climate 159c
  currency unit 159c
  Dakar 265a
  economy 160a
  flag il iv
  geography 159c
  government 160a
  history 160a–160b
  independence 160b
  language 159c
  map 159, Atlas-36
  national holiday 159c
  official name 159c
  people of 159c
  population 159c
  religion 159c
  Saint-Louis 283a
Sénégal River 85c, 126c, 127a, 128a, 159c, 252c, 283a
Senegalese Progressive Union 160b
Seng River 118a
Senghor, Léopold 160b
Senufo 109a
Seoul, South Korea 115b, 115c, 284a
Serbia 77c, 83a, 216b, 216c
  Albania and 2c, 3a
  World War I 203c
  see also Yugoslavia
Serbs 215a, 216a
Serer 159c
Sevastopol, Soviet Union 284a
Seven Weeks' War 77b
Seven Years' War (1756–1763) 68b, 202b
Severn River 194a, 196a, 252c
Severnaya Zemlya Islands 252c
Sevilla, Spain 175c, 284a
Seville, Spain see Sevilla, Spain
Sèvres, Treaty of 83a
Seychelles 234a–234b
  area 234a
  economy 234b
  capital 234b
  government 234b
  history 234b
  land 234b
  people 234b
  population 234a
  Port Victoria 281a
  status 234a
Seyhan River 190a
Seymour, Jane 200a
Seyss-Inquart, Arthur 12b
Sfax, Tunisia 189a, 284a
Sforza family 107b
Shabali River 163c
Shah dynasty 136a
Shah Jahan see Jahan, Shah (India)
Shaiqiyya 178a
Shan (people) 22c, 23b
Shan Plateau 273a
Shanghai, China 39b, 284a
Shannon River 252c
Shantung Peninsula 287c
Shantung Province, China 287c
Shari River 35a, 239c
  see also Chari River
Sharjah Ajman 188b
  see also Trucial Oman
Sharpeville, South Africa 165b
Sharqi Mountains 119b
Shashi River 154c
Shastri, Lal Bahadur 98b
Shatt al-Arab see al-Arab, Shatt

Sheba, Queen of 62b
Sheep
  Afghanistan 1b
  Albania 2b
  Argentina 5c
  Australia 8c
  Faeroe Islands 223c
  Falkland Islands 224a
  Greece 81a
  Greenland 226b
  Ifni 228a
  Iraq 101c–102a
  Isle of Man 228b
  Lebanon 119b
  Libya 122a
  Mauritania 128a
  Mongolia 132c
  Nepal 135c
  New Zealand 138a–138b
  Niger 140c
  Pakistan 144b
  Poland 151b
  Rhodesia 155a
  Romania 156a
  Saudi Arabia 159a
  Somali Republic 163a
  South West Africa 234c
  South Yemen 165c
  Spanish Sahara 235a
  Tunisia 189a
  Turkey 190a
  United Kingdom 194c
  Upper Volta 206c
  Uruguay 207a
  Yemen 214a
Sher Shah 96b, 96c
Shermarke, Abdi Rashid 163b
Sherpas 135c
Sheshonk, Prince (Egypt) 193a
Shetland Islands 194c, 252c
Shikoku Island 110b, 272a, 286a
Shilka River 237c
Shilling
  Austria 10b
  Kenya 114b
  Somali Republic 162c
  Tanzania 184a
  Uganda 191b
Shillong, India 284b
Shilluk 178a
Shimabara Bay 278c
Shimonoseki, Japan 284b
Shimonoseki, Treaty of 45c
Shimonoseki Strait 110c, 284b
Shinano River 110c
Shiraz, Iran 284b
Shirazis 184a
Shire River 124b, 124c, 272b
Shishakly, Adib 183c
Shizuoka, Japan 284b
Shkodër, Albania 284b
Sholapur, India 284b
Shona 155a, 155b
Shwe Dagon Pagoda 282a
Si River 252c
Siam see Thailand
Siam, Gulf of 252c
Siberia 44a, 166c, 168b, 169a, 171b
Sibiu, Romania 284b–284c
Sicily 105c, 252c 279c
Sidi-Ifni, African 191 227c, 284c
Sidon, Lebanon 119b
Sidra, Gulf of 121b, 122a, 252c, 260b
Siegfried I, Count (Luxembourg) 123b
Sierra de Bahoruco (Dominican Republic) 58c
Sierra de Gata (Spain) 175b
Sierra de Gaudarrama (Spain) 175b
Sierra de Gredos (Spain) 175b
Sierra Leone 72c, 160–161
  agriculture 160c
  area 160b
  capital 160b
  climate 160b
  currency unit 160b
  economy 160c
  flag il iv
  Freetown 267a
  geography 160b
  government 160c
  history 160c–161b
  independence 161a–161b
  map 160, Atlas-36
  national holiday 160b
  official name 160b
  people of 160b
  population 160b
  religion 160b
  slavery 160c
Sierra Leone Company 161b
Sierra Leone People's Party 161a, 161b
Sierra Leone River 267a

Slavery   379

Sierra Madre (Mexico) 252c–253a
Sierra Madre (Philippines) 149c
Sierra Madre Occidental (Mexico) 129b
Sierra Madre Oriental (Mexico) 129b
Sierra Madre del Sur (Mexico) 129c
Sierra Maestra (Cuba) 52b–52c
Sierra Morena (Spain) 175b, 264c
Sierra de Neiba (Dominican Republic) 58c
Sierra Nevada (United States) 204c
Sierra Nevada de Mérida (Venezuela) 208c
Sierra de los Organos (Cuba) 52c
Sierra de Perijá (Venezuela) 208c
Sierra de Zacatecas (Mexico) 129b
Sigismund Augustus, King (Poland) 152a
Sihanouk, Norodom, Prince (Cambodia) 25a, 25b
Sikkim 161–162
  agriculture 161c
  area 161b
  capital 161b
  climate 161b
  currency unit 161b
  economy 161c
  flag il iv
  Gangtok 267a
  geography 161b
  government 161c
  history 161c–162a
  language 161b
  map 161, Atlas-29
  official name 161b
  people of 161b–161c
  population 161b
  religion 161b
Silesia 76c
Silhouette Island 234a
Silla Kingdom 116a, 116b
Silva Quadros, Jânio da 20c
Silver
  Honduras 89a
  Mexico 130a
  Nicaragua 139c
  Panama 146a
  Peru 149a
  Romania 156a
  Sweden 180a
Sinai Peninsula 104a, 192b, 192c, 193c, 253a
Singapore 100b, 162a, 162b–162c
  agriculture 162a
  area 162a
  capital 162a
  climate 162a
  currency unit 162a
  economy 162a–162b
  flag il iv
  geography 162a
  government 162b
  history 162b–162c
  independence 162c
  industry 162b
  language 162a
  map 162, Atlas-30
  national holiday 162a
  official name 162a
  people of 162a
  population 162a
  religion 162a
  trade 162b
  World War II 162c
Sinhalese (people) 35c, 36a
Sining, China 284c
Sining River 284c
Sinn Féin 103c
Sino-Japanese War (1894–1895) 45a, 113b
Sino-Japanese War (1937–1945) 17b, 46c
Siret River 155c
Sisal
  Cayman Islands 222a
  Comoro Islands 222c
  Kenya 114b
  Mozambique 229b
  Tanzania 184a
  Venezuela 209b
Sittang River 22c, 253a
Siwalik Mountains 253a
Sjaelland Island 57a, 264c
Sjkumbi River 266b
Skagerrak Strait 253a
Skanderbeg see Kastrioti, Gjergj
Skopje, Yugoslavia 215b, 284c
Slavery
  Antigua 219a
  Bahamas 219b

Barbados 219b–219c
Bermuda 219c
Brazil 18c, 19c, 20a
British Virgin Islands 221a
Congo (Brazzaville) 50a
Cuba 53b
Dahomey 57a
Gabon 71c
Gambia 72c
Ghana 80b
Guadeloupe 227a
Guyana 86c, 87a
Haiti 88a
Jamaica 110a
Kenya 114c
Martinique 228c
Mozambique 229c
Netherlands Antilles 230a
Nigeria 141c
Peru 149a
Portuguese Guinea 232a
Sierra Leone 160c
Tanzania 184c–185a
Trinidad and Tobago 188c
United Kingdom 202a, 203a
Slavs
  Albania 2c
  Bulgaria 21c
  Czechoslovakia 55b
  Hungary 90b, 90c, 91a
  Poland 151c
  Romania 156b
  Soviet Union 167c, 169c
  Yugoslavia 215a, 216a
Slovakia 55b–56a
Slovenes 215a, 216a
Smith, Ian 155b
Smuts, Jan Christiaan 33c–34a, 165b
Smyrna, Turkey *see* Izmir, Turkey
Snake River 205a
Sobaek Mountains 253a
Sobhuza II, King (Swaziland) 179b, 179c
Socarrás, Carlos Prío 53c
Social Credit Party (Canada) 34b
Social Democratic Party (Austria) 11c–12b
Social Democratic Party (Iceland) 93a
Social Democratic Party (Madagascar) 124b
Social Democratic Party (West Germany) 79a
Socialist Party (France) 70a, 70b, 71a
Socialist Party (Italy) 108c
Socialist Party (Sweden) 181a
Socialist Unity Party (Germany) 74c
Society for the Abolition of Slavery 160c
Society of Friends (Greek patriotic organization) 81c
Society Islands 224c–225a
Soekarno *see* Sukarno
Sofia, Bulgaria 21a, 284c
Soglo, Christophe 57a
Sol 148a
Solís, Juan Díaz de *see* Díaz de Solís, Juan
Somali (people) 163a
  Issas 225b
Somali Republic 62c, 162–163
  agriculture 163a
  area 162c
  capital 162c
  currency unit 162c
  economy 163a
  flag *il* iv
  geography 163a
  government 163a–163b
  history 163b–163c
  independence 163b–163c
  language 162c
  map 163, *Atlas*-35
  Mogadiscio 276c
  national holiday 162c
  official name 162c
  people of 163a
  population 162c
  protectorates 163b
  religion 162c
Somali Youth League (SYL) 163b
Somalia *see* Somali Republic
Somaliland *see* Somali Republic
Somaliland, British *see* Somali Republic
Somaliland, French *see* French Territory of the Afars and Issas
Somaliland, Italian *see* Somali Republic
Somes River 155c
Somesul River 284a

Somme River 253a
Somoza, Anastasio 79a, 140b
Somoza Debayle, Anastasio 140b
Somoza Debayle, Luis 140b
Son River 244b
Songhai empire 140c
Songhai kings 127b
Soochow, China 284c
Soong Ch'ing-ling 46b
Sopron, Hungary 284c
Sotho 120b
  South Africa 164b
  Swaziland 179b
Soto, Bernardo 52a
Soudan colony 127b
Sousse, Tunisia 189a, 284a–285a
South Africa 163–165
  agriculture 164b
  area 163c
  capital 163c
  climate 164a–164b
  currency unit 163c
  economy 164b–164c
  flag *il* iv
  geography 164a–164b
  government 164c
  history 165a–165c
  language 163c
  map 164, *Atlas*-40–41
  national holiday 163c
  official name 163c
  people of 164b
  population 163c
  religion 163c
  in South West Africa 234b–235a
  trade 164c
  World War I 165b
  —Cities 164b
    Bloemfontein 261a
    Cape Town 263a
    Durban 266a
    East London 266a
    Germiston 267c
    Johannesburg 270a
    Kimberley 271c
    Ladysmith 272c
    Pietermaritzburg 280b
    Port Elizabeth 280c
    Pretoria 281a
    Springs 285a
    Vereeniging 288a
South African War (1899–1902) 165a, 179b, 203b, 288a
South America 253a–253b
  map *Atlas*-44–45
  see also under names of individual countries, such as Brazil
South China Sea 253b
South Holland Province, Netherlands 268b
South Island, New Zealand 137c, *il* 138, 264a
South Korea *see* Korea, South
South Orkney Island 220a
South Pacific Commission 278b
South Shetland Island 220a
South Sulawesi Province, Indonesia 275a
South Vietnam *see* Vietnam, South
South West Africa 234–235
  area 234b
  capital 234b
  climate 234c
  economy 234c
  geography 234c
  government 234c
  history 234c–235a
  people of 234c
  population 234b
  status 234b
  Windhoek 289a
  World War I 234c
South Yemen 165–166
  Aden 256b
  agriculture 165c
  area 165c
  capital 165c
  currency unit 165c
  economy 165c–166a
  flag *il* iv
  geography 165c
  government 166a
  history 166a
  language 165c
  map 165, *Atlas*-25
  official name 165c
  people of 165c
  population 165c
  religion 165c
Southeast Asia Treaty Organization (SEATO)
  flag *il* iv
Southern Alps (New Zealand) 137c
Southern Dvina (river) *see* Dvina rivers

Souvanna Phouma 119a
Soviet Union 12b, 166–175
  agriculture 168c–169a
  area 166b
  capital 166b
  climate 167c
  currency unit 166b
  economy 168b–169c
  flag *il* iv
  geography 166b–167c
  government 169c
  history 173a–175a
  industry 169a–169c
  language 166b
  map 167, *Atlas*-20–21
  mountains 166c–167c
  national holiday 166b
  natural resources 168b–168c
  nuclear power 175a
  official name 166b
  people of 167c–168a
  population 166b
  religion 166b
  space program 175a
  trade 169c
  vegetation zones 167a–167c
  —Cities
    Alma Ata 257a
    Arkhangel'sk 258a
    Ashkhabad 258a
    Baku 259a
    Batumi 260a
    Dneprodzerzhinsk 265b
    Dnepropetrovsk 265c
    Dushanbe 266a
    Frunze 267a
    Gorki (Nizhni-Novgorod) 267c
    Grozny 268a
    Irkutsk 269b
    Kalinin (Tver) 270c
    Kaliningrad 270c
    Karaganda 271a
    Kaunas 271b
    Kazan 271b
    Khabarovsk 271b
    Kharkov 271b
    Kiev 271c
    Kishinev 272a
    Klaipeda (Memel) 272a
    Komsomolsk 272a
    Krasnovodsk 272b
    Kuybyshev (Samara) 272c
    Leningrad 273b
    Liepaya 273c
    Lvov 274c
    Magnitogorsk 275a
    Minsk 276b
    Moscow 277a
    Murmansk 277a
    Novosibirsk 278b
    Odessa 278c
    Perm 280a
    Riga 282a
    Samarkand 283b
    Saratov 283c
    Sevastopol 284a
    Sverdlovsk 285c
    Tallinn 286a
    Tashkent 286b
    Tbilsi (Tiflis) 286b
    Ufa 287b
    Ulan-Ude 287c
    Ventspils 288a
    Vilnius 288b
    Vladivostok 288c
    Volgograd (Stalingrad) 288c
    Yerevan 289c
    Zaporozhye 289c
    Zhdanov 289c
  —Foreign Affairs
    Bulgaria 22a–22b
    China 47a
    Cuba 53a, 54a
    Czechoslovakia 56a–56b
    Germany, East 79b
    Hungary 91b–91c
    Poland 152b, 152c
    Romania 157a–157b
    U.S. 174a–175a
  —History
    Cold War 174b–174c
    communism 169c
    in Finland 63b–63c
    Iron Curtain 174a–175a
    nonaggression pact with Germany 78c
    World War II 70c, 78c, 79a, 174b, 204a
      occupation of Germany 79a
    see also Russia
Sozh River 243b
Spain 175–177
  agriculture 175c–176a
  area 175b
  Balearic Islands 239a
  Canary Islands 240a
  capital 175b
  climate 175b
  currency unit 175b
  economy 175c–176a
  flag *il* iv

  geography 175b
  government 176a–176b
  industry 176a
  language 175b
  map 175, *Atlas*-12
  national holiday 175b
  natural resources 175c
  official name 175b
  people of 175b–175c
  population 175b
  religion 175b, 176c–177a, 177b
  —Cities 175c
    Barcelona 259b
    Ceuta 263b
    Cordoba (Cordova) 264c
    Granada 268a
    Madrid 275a
    Sevilla (Seville) 284a
    Valencia 288a
  —History 176b–177c
    Civil War 177b
    Cold War 177b
    colonial
      Bolivia 16c
      Chile 38a
      Colombia 49a
      Cuba 53b
      El Salvador 61b
      Equatorial Guinea 223b–223c
      Gibraltar 226a
      Guatemala 84c
      Haiti 88a
      Ifni 227c–228a
      Mexico 130b–130c
      Morocco 134b
      Nicaragua 140a
      Panama 146c
      Paraguay 147c
      Peru 149a
      Philippines 150a–150b
      Spanish Sahara 235a–235b
      Uruguay 207c
      Venezuela 209c
    Muslims 176b–176c
    World War I 177a
    World War II 177b
Spalato, Yugoslavia *see* Split, Yugoslavia
Spanish-American War 177a
Spanish Sahara 235a–235b
  Aiún 256c
  area 235a
  capital 235a
  economy 235a
  government 235a
  history 235a–235b
  land 235a
  map *Atlas*-34
  people 235a
  population 235a
  status 235a
Speke, John Hanning 192a
Spice Islands *see* Moluccas Islands
Spices
  Ceylon 35c, 36b
  Comoro Islands 222b
  Grenada 226c
  India 94b
  Indonesia 99a, 99c
  St. Lucia 233b
  St. Vincent 233c
  Seychelles 234b
  Sierra Leone 160c
  Tanzania 184b
Spitsbergen Island 142a
Split, Yugoslavia 285a
Sporades 81a
Spree River 260c
Springs, South Africa 285a
Sri Lanka Freedom Party (SLFP) (Ceylon) 36b
Srinigar, India 285a
Srivijaya Kingdom 99b–99c, 125c
Stalin, Joseph 3b, 91c, 174a–175a, 216c, 217a
Stalin Peak 249c
Stalingrad, Soviet Union *see* Volgograd, Soviet Union
Stalingrad, Battle of 288c
Stamboliski, Aleksandr 22a
Stamford Bridge, Battle of 196c
Stanley, Henry 51a
Stanley, Falkland Islands 224a, 285a
Stanley Falls 240c, 272c
Stanley Pool 240c
Stanleyville, Congo (Kinshasa) *see* Kisangani, Congo (Kinshasa)
Stanovoy Mountains 166c
Stein, Heinrich 76b
Stephen, King (Hungary) 90b
Stephen II, Pope 107a
Steppes 167b
Stevens, Siaka 161b

Stewart Island 137c
Stockholm, Sweden 179c, 285a
Stolypin, Peter A. 172b–172c
Stōmō Island 286c
Stonecutters Island 227c
Stour River 263a
Strait
 see under latter part of name, such as Malacca, Strait of
Strasbourg, France 65b
Stuart family 200b–202a
Stuttgart, Germany 285a–285b
Subotica, Yugoslavia 285b
Sucre (currency unit) 59c
Sucre, Antonio José de 16c, 60b
Sucre, Bolivia 16a, 285b
Sudan 177–178
 agriculture 178a
 area 177c
 capital 177c
 climate 178a
 currency unit 177c
 economy 178a–178b
 flag il iv
 geography 177c–178a
 government 178b
 history 178b–178c
 independence 178a
 language 177c
 map 177, Atlas-34–35
 national holiday 177c
 official name 177c
 people of 177c–178a
 population 177c
 religion 177c, 178b, 178c
 World War II 178c
 —Cities
  El Fasher 266b
  Khartoum 271c
  Port Sudan 281a
Sudbury, Canada 285c
Sudeten Mountains see Sudetes
Sudetes (mountains) 54c, 150c, 253b
Suez, United Arab Republic (Egypt) 285b
Suez, Gulf of 285b
Suez Canal 105c, 126a, 183b 192b, 192c, 281a
 crisis of 1957–1958 34c
 nationalized 193c
 opening of 193b
Suez Canal Company 203b
Sugar
 Antigua 219a
 Barbados 13a, 13c
 Brazil 18c, 19b, 19c
 British Honduras 220a
 Colombia 48c
 Cuba 52c, 53c, 53b
 Dominican Republic 58c
 Fiji Islands 224b
 French Guiana 224c
 Guadeloupe 227a
 Guyana 86b, 86c, 87a
 Haiti 87a
 India 94b
 Indonesia 99a

Ireland 103a
Jamaica 109a, 110a
Madagascar 124a
Martinique 228c
Mauritius 229a
Montserrat 229a
Mozambique 229b
Netherlands Antilles 230a
Nicaragua 139c
Pakistan 144b
Panama 146b
Paraguay 147b
Peru 148c
Réunion 232c
Rhodesia 155a
St. Kitts–Nevis–Anguilla 233b
Surinam 235b
Swaziland 179a
Syria 183a
Taiwan 41c
Thailand 185c
Trinidad and Tobago 187c
Turkey 190a
Uganda 191c
United Arab Republic (Egypt) 192c
U.S. 206a
Venezuela 209b
Vietnam 211b
Yugoslavia 215b
Suharto 100b
Sui dynasty 43b
Sukarnapura, Indonesia 285b
Sukarno 100a–100b, 126a
Sukhona River 243b
Sukhot'ai Kingdom 186a
Sukuma 184a
Sulaiman Mountains 253b, 281b
Sulawesi Island 98c, 100b
Sulu Archipelago 270a
Sulu Province, Philippines 270a
Sumanguru 127a
Sumatra 98c, 99a, 100a–100b, 279b
Sunay, Cevdet 191b
Sundarban 244b
Sundiata 127a
Sung dynasty 43c
Sungari River 40a, 253b, 268c 271c
Superior, Lake 26c
Surabaja, Java 285b–285c
Surami Mountains 240b
Surat, India 285c
Surinam (Dutch Guiana) 137a, 235b–235c
 area 235b
 capital 235b
 economy 235b
 geography 235b–235c
 government 235b–235c
 history 235c
 map Atlas-48
 Paramaribo 279c
 people of 235b
 population 235b
 status 235b
Suruga Bay 110c, 284b
Sussex, Kingdom of 196a
Susu 127a

Sutherland Waterfall 253b
Suva, Fiji Islands 224a, 285c
Suvadiva 126c
Svalbard and Jan Mayen Islands 235c–236a
 area 235c
 geography 235c
 government 236a
 history 236a
 people of 235c
 population 235c
 status 235c
Svealand, Kingdom of 180b
Svear 180c
Sverdlovsk, Soviet Union 285c
Sverdrup, Johan 143b
Swan River 280a
Swatow, China 285c
Swazi 179a
Swaziland 178–179
 agriculture 179a
 area 178c
 capital 178c
 climate 179b
 currency unit 178c
 economy 179a–179b
 flag il iv
 geography 178c–179a
 government 179b
 history 179b–179c
 independence 179b–179c
 language 178c
 map 179, Atlas-41
 Mbabane 175c
 official name 178c
 people of 179a
 population 178c
 religion 178c
Sweden 63b, 179–181
 agriculture 180a
 area 178c
 capital 179c
 currency unit 179c
 economy 180a–180b
 flag il iv
 geography 179c
 government 180b
 language 178c
 map 180, Atlas-14–15
 merchant shipping 180b
 national holiday 179c
 official name 179c
 people of 179c–180a
 population 178c
 religion 179c, 180b, 180c
 trade 180b
 —History 180b–181b
  British Isles, raids on 196a
  Danish crown 58a
  Kalmar Union 180b–180c
  Norway and 142c–143a
  Vasa Kings 180c
  Vikings 180b
  World War I 181a
  World War II 181b
 —Cities 180a
  Göteborg 267c
  Malmö 180a
  Stockholm 285a

Switzerland 181–182
 agriculture 181c–182a
 area 181b
 capital 181b
 climate 181b
 currency unit 181b
 economy 181c–182a
 flag il iv
 geography 181b
 government 182a
 history 182b–182c
 independence 182b
 industry 182a
 language 181b
 Liechtenstein and 122c–123a
 map 181, Atlas-17
 national holiday 181b
 natural resources 181c
 neutrality 182b–182c
 official name 181b
 people of 181b–181c
 population 181b
 religion 181b, 181c, 182b
 trade 182a
 —Cities 181c
  Basel 259c
  Bern 260c
  Geneva 267c
  Zürich 289c
Sydney, Australia 8a, 8c, il 9, 285c
Sydney, Nova Scotia 285c
SYL see Somali Youth League
Syr River 253c
Syria 102b, 114a, 182–183
 agriculture 183a
 area 182c
 capital 182c
 climate 182c
 currency unit 182c
 economy 183a
 flag il iv
 geography 182c
 government 183a
 history 183a–183c
 independence 183c
 industry 183a
 language 182c
 map 183, Atlas-25
 national holiday 182c
 official name 182c
 Ottoman Turks in 183b
 people of 182c–183a
 population 182c
 religion 182c, 183b
 trade 183a
 World War II 183c
 —Cities
  Aleppo 256c
  Damascus (Dimashaq) 260a, 265a
  Homs 269a
  Latakia 273b
Syrian Desert 182c
Syrian University 265a
Szczecin, Poland 151c, 285c
Szechwan Province, China 263c, 278a
Szeged, Hungary 90a, 285c

T

Table Bay 263a
Tabriz, Iran 285c–286a
Tadjoura, Gulf of 265b
Tadzhik Soviet Socialist Republic 266a
Taebaek Mountains 115b, 253b
Taedong River 264a, 281b
Taegu, South Korea 286a
Taff River 263c
Taft, William Howard 89b, 150b
Taft Commission 150b
Tagus River 153a, 153b–153c, 175b, 273c
Tahiti il 225, 279c
Tai (people) 118a, 118b
Taiga 167a
Taipa Island 228b
Taipei, Taiwan 39a, 286a
Taiping Rebellion 44c
Taiwan 44a
 Japanese invasion 45a

 World War II 47b
 see also China, Nationalist
Taiyüan, China 286a
Taj Mahal 256b
Tajiks 1a, 168a
Tajumulco (mountain) 84a
Takamatsu, Japan 286a
Takkaze River 62a
Takla Makan Desert 39c, 253c
Takoradi, Ghana 80a
Tala 213b
Talcahuano, Chile 37b, il 38
Tallinn, Soviet Union 286a
Talon, Jean 30a, 30b
Tamerlane 1c, 96b, 133a
Tamils (people)
 Ceylon 35c, 36a 36c
Tampere, Finland 62c
Tampico, Mexico 130a
Tana, Lake 62b
Tana River 253c
Tananarive, Madagascar (Malagasy Republic) 123c, 124a, 286a
T'ang dynasty 43b–43c, 212a
Tanganyika see Tanzania

Tanganyika, Lake 50c, 217a, 253c, 270c
Tanganyika African National Union (TANU) 185a
Tangier, Morocco 133b, 133c, 134b, 286a
Tanjore, India 286a
Tanta, United Arab Republic (Egypt) 192c, 286a
TANU see Tanganyika African National Union
Tanzania 184–185
 area 184a
 capital 184a
 climate 184a
 currency unit 184a
 economy 184a–184c
 flag il iv
 geography 184a
 government 184a
 history 184c–185a
 language 184a
 map 184, Atlas-39
 national holiday 184a
 official name 184a
 people of 184a
 population 184a
 religion 184a
 slavery 184c–185a

 —Cities
  Dar es Salaam 265a
  Moshi 277a
  Zanzibar 289c
Taoism 43b
Tapa Mountains 253c
Tarabulus see Tripoli, Lebanon
Taranto, Gulf of 253c
Tarawa, Gilbert and Ellice Islands 226a, 286b
Tarbagatap Mountains 167a
Tarija, Bolivia 16a, 16b
Tariq 226a
Taruc, Luis 150b
Tashkent, Soviet Union 168a, 286b
Tashkent Agreement 98b
Tasman, Abel 8c, 138c
Tasmania 7a, 8a, 8c, 253c
Tatar Autonomous Soviet Socialist Republic 271b
Tatars 168a
Taufa'ahau Tupou IV, King (Tonga) 236b
Taunus Mountains 289a
Taurus Mountains 189c

Tbilsi (Tiflis), Soviet Union 286b
Tea
  Ceylon 35c, 36a, 36b
  China 41b
  India 94b
  Indonesia 99a
  Kenya 114b
  Malawi 124c
  Mauritius 129a
  Mozambique 229b
  Pakistan 144b
  Uganda 191c
  Vietnam 211b
Teguicigalpa, Honduras 88c, 89a
Teheran, Iran 100c, 286b
Tehuantepec, Gulf of 252c
Tejo River 252b–252c
Tel Aviv, Israel 104b, 286b–286c
Tell Atlas (mountains) 3b, 188c–189a
Tema, Ghana 80a
Temne 160b
Ten Years' War (1868–1878) 53b
Tennessee River 205a
Tenochtitlán, Mexico 130b, 130c, 276b
Terek River 268a
Terra, Gabriel 208a
Tetulia River 244b
Teutons
  Denmark 58a
  Germany 75a
Texas 131a
Texcoco, Lake 130b
Thai (people) 185b
  Cambodia 25a
  see also Tai
Thailand 23a, 25b, 118b–118c, 185–186
  agriculture 185c
  area 185a
  Cambodia and 25b
  capital 185a
  climate 185b
  communism 186c
  currency unit 185a
  economy 185c–186a
  flag il iv
  geography 185a–185b
  government 186a
  history 186a–186c
  industry 185c–186a
  language 185a
  map 185, Atlas-30
  national holiday 185a
  official name 185a
  people of 185b
  population 185a
  religion 185a, 185b, 186a
  trade 186a
  World War II 186c
  —Cities
  Ayuthia 258c
  Bangkok 259b
  Chiang Mai 264a
Thames River 194a, 253c, 274b, 279b
Thanglha Ri (mountains) 39c, 253c
Thanjavor, India 286a
Thar Desert 254a
Theodore I, Tsar (Russia) 170c
Theodoric, King (Ostrogoth) 107a
Thessaloníki, Greece 286c
Thessaloníki, Gulf of 286c
Thessaly, Greece il 82
Thiers, Adolphe 69c
Thiès, Senegal 159c
Thieu, Nguyen Van 213b
Thieu-Tri, Emperor (Vietnam) 212c
Thimbu, Bhutan 15a
Thionville, France 65c
Third Crusade 197b
38th parallel (Korea) 115c, 117a
Thomas, Rodrigues 232b
Thorshavn, Faeroe Islands 223c, 286c
Thuku, Harry 115a
Thuringians 75a
Tibasti Massif 36c
Tiber River 106a, 254a, 282b
Tiberias, Lake see Galilee, Sea of
Tibesti Mountains 254a
Tibet 15c, 23a, 39a, 39c, 44a, 98a
  climate 40c
  Nepalese invasions of 136a
  see also China
Tien Shan (mountains) 39c, 167a
Tienching, China 286c
Tientsin, China 286c
Tientsin treaties 45a
Tierra Del Fuego Islands 254a
Tiflis, Soviet Union see Tbilsi, Soviet Union

Tigre 62a
Tigris River 101c, 254a, 277a
Tilak, Bal Gangadhar 97b
Timișoara, Romania 156a, 286c
Timor Island 254a
Tin
  Bolivia 16b, 17a
  Indonesia 99a
  Malaysia 125b
  Portugal 153c
  Swaziland 179a
  Thailand 185c
  United Kingdom 194c
Tiradentes conspiracy 19c
Tirana, Albania see Tiranë, Albania
Tiranë, Albania 2a, 286c
Tiruchirappalli, India 287a
Tista River 161b
Tisza River 89c, 90a, 254a
Titicaca, Lake 16a, 254a
Tito, Josip Broz 216a, 216c
Tobacco
  Albania 2b
  Andorra 4c
  Bulgaria 21b
  Colombia 48c
  Cuba 52c
  Dominican Republic 58c
  Greece 81a
  India 94b
  Indonesia 99a
  Iraq 101c
  Lebanon 119b
  Malawi 124c
  Nicaragua 139c
  Niger 140c
  Pakistan 144b
  Paraguay 147b
  Peru 146c
  Portugal 153c
  Rhodesia 155a
  Singapore 162b
  Swaziland 179a
  Syria 183a
  Thailand 185c
  Turkey 190a
  Uganda 191c
  United States 206a
  Venezuela 204b
  Vietnam 211b
  Yemen 214a
  Yugoslavia 215b
  Zambia 217b
Tobago see Trinidad and Tobago
Togliatti, Palmiro 108c
Togo 186–187
  agriculture 187a
  area 186c
  capital 186c
  climate 187a
  currency unit 186c
  economy 187a
  flag il iv
  geography 186c–187a
  government 187a
  history 187a–187b
  independence 187b
  language 186c
  Lomé 274a
  map 187, Atlas-37
  national holiday 186c
  official name 186c
  people of 187a
  population 186c
  religion 186c
Togo Atakora (mountains) 79c, 186c–187a
Tokelau Islands 236
  area 236a
  population 236a
  status 236a
Tokugawa Era 112b–112c
Tokyo, Japan 110b, 110c, 111a, 287a
Tokyo Bay 110c, 264a
Tokyo University 287a
Toltec Indians 130b
Tombalbaye, François 37a
Tombo Island 86a, 264b
Tombouctou (Timbuktu), Mali 127a
Tone, Wolfe 103c
Tone River 110c
Tonga 236
  area 236a
  capital 236a
  Nuku'alofa 278a
  population 236a
  status 236a
Tongatapu Island 236a, 278c
Tonghak movement 116c
Tonkin, Gulf of 268b
Tonle Sap (lake) 24c, 254a, 280b
Tordesillas, Treaty of 19b, 19c
Torino, Italy 287c

Toronto, Canada 124a, 287a
Torres, Luis Vaez de 8c
Torres Strait 254a
Tortola Island 282b
Tortosa, Cape see Cape Tortosa
Tosks 2b
Tostig, Earl (Northumbria) 196c
Toubkal (mountain) 238c
Toulouse, France 64b, 65b, 287a
Tourcoing, France 65a
Touré, Sékou 86b
Tourism
  Andorra 4c
  Antigua 219a
  Bahamas 219b
  Bermuda 219c
  British Virgin Islands 219a
  Bulgaria 21a
  Canada 28c
  Cayman Islands 222a
  Channel Islands 222a
  Colombia 48c
  Cyprus 54a
  Denmark 57c
  Gibraltar 226a
  Ireland 103a
  Isle of Man 228b
  Italy 106b
  Jamaica 109a
  Lebanon 119c
  Liechtenstein 122c
  Monaco 132a
  Netherlands Antilles 230a
  Norfolk Island 231b
  St. Kitts–Nevis–Anguilla 233b
  San Marino 158a
  Spain 175c
  Trinidad and Tobago 187c
  United Arab Republic (Egypt) 192c
Tours, France 287a–287b
Toussaint L'Overture 88a
Toyama, Japan 287b
Trajan, Emperor (Rome) 156b, 176b
Trans-Canada Highway 28c
Transjordan 114a
  see also Jordan
Transvaal Province, South Africa 270a, 281a, 288a, 285a
Transylvania 90c, 156a, 157a, 284c
Transylvanian Alps 155c
  see also Carpathians (mountains)
Trejos Fernández, José Joaquin 52b
Trent River 194a
Trianon, Treaty of 91a
Tribhuvana, King (Nepal) 136b
Trichinopoly, India 287b
Trieste, Italy 108b, 287b
Trinidad and Tobago 13c, 187–188
  agriculture 187c
  area 187b
  capital 187b
  climate 187b
  currency unit 187b
  economy 187c
  flag il iv
  geography 187b
  government 187c–188a
  history 188a–188b
  independence 188b
  Indians 188a
  industry 188b
  language 187b
  map 187, Atlas-53
  national holiday 187c
  official name 187b
  people of 187b–187c
  population 187b
  religion 187b
  slavery 188a
  trade 187b
Triple Mountains 52c
Triple Alliance (1882) 108b
Triple Entente 77c
Tripoli, Lebanon 119b, 287b
Tripoli, Libya 121b, 122a, 287b
Tripolitania, Libya 121b, 122a
Tristan de Cunha Island 233a
Trisuli River 135c
Trivandrum, India 287b
Trobriand Archipelago 231b
Trondheim, Norway 142b
Troodos Mountains 254a
Trotsky, Lev (Leon) 173b, 174a
Trucial Coast see Trucial Oman
Trucial Oman 188
  area 188b
  climate 188b
  currency unit 188b
  economy 188b–188c
  flag il iv
  geography 188b

  government 188c
  history 188c
  language 188b
  map 188, Atlas-25
  official name 188b
  people of 188b
  population 188b
  religion 188b
Trucial States see Trucial Oman
Trujillo, Peru 148b
Trujillo Molina, Rafael Leonidas 59b
Truman Doctrine
  Greece 83b
  Turkey 191a
Tryggvesson, Olaf, King (Norway) 143a
Tsangpo River 239c
  see also Brahmaputra (river)
Tshombe, Moise 51b
Tsinan, China 287b
Tsinghai, Lake 247b
Tsinghai province, China 284c
Tsingtao, China 287c
Tsinling Mountains 254a–254b
Tsiranana, Philibert 124b
Tsitsihar, China 287c
Tswana-speaking people 113c
Tuamotu Archipelago 225a
Tuareg
  Mali 126c
  Mauritania 128a
  Niger 140c
Tubman, William V. S. 121b
Tucumán, Argentina 5c
Tudors 199b–200b
Tu-Duc, Emperor (Vietnam) 212c
Tugela Waterfalls 254b
Tughluq dynasty 96b
Tugrik 132b
Tukulor 159c
Tuloma River 277a
Tumen River 115b–115c, 254b
Tundra 167a
T'ung-meng hui 45c
Tungsten
  Korea, North 115c
  Korea, South 115c
  Nicaragua 139c
  Spain 175c
  Sweden 180a
  Thailand 185c
Tungting, Lake 254b, 263c
Tunis, Tunisia 188c, 189a, 287c
Tunis, Lake of 287c
Tunisia 108b, 188–189
  agriculture 189a
  area 188c
  capital 188c
  climate 189a
  currency unit 188c
  economy 189a
  flag il iv
  geography 188c–189a
  government 189a
  history 189b–189c
  independence 189b–189c
  language 188c
  map 189, Atlas-34
  national holiday 188c
  official name 188c
  people of 189a
  population 188c
  religion 188c
  —Cities 189a
  Bizerte 261a
  Gabès 189a
  Quairouan 189a
  Sfax 284a
  Sousse 284c
  Tunis 287c
Tunku Abdul Rahman 126b
Tupac Amaru 149a
Turia River 288a
Turin, Italy 106c, 287c
Turin, University of 287c
Turkey 189–191
  agriculture 190a
  area 189c
  capital 189c
  climate 190a
  currency unit 189c
  Cyprus controversy 54b
  economy 190a–190b
  flag il iv
  geography 189c–190a
  government 190b
  Greece and 81c–83c
  history 190b–191b
  language 189c
  map 190, Atlas-26
  national holiday 189c
  official name 189c

INDEX

Uruguay 383

people of 190a
population 189c
religion 189c
World War II 191a
see also Ottoman Empire
—Cities
Adana 256a
Ankara 257b
Erzurum 266c
Iskenderun 269c
Istanbul 269c

Izmir (Smyrna) 269c
Turkish Armenia 269c
Turkish Islands 83a
Turkmenians 168a
Turkomans 1a
Turks and Caicos Islands 236
area 236b
capital 236b
population 236b
status 236b

Turku, Finland 62c
Tuscany, Italy 266c
Tusi
Burundi 24b
Rwanda 157b, 157c
Tutuila Island 279b
Tuula River 287c
Tuz, Lake 254c
Tver, Soviet Union see Kalinin, Soviet Union

Twa 157b
Tweed River 194a
Two Sicilies, Kingdom of the 107b
Tydings-McDuffie Act 150b
Tyrone Wars 103b
Tyrrhenian Sea 254b
Tz'u-hsi, Dowager Empress (China) 45b

U

U.A.R. see United Arab Republic (Egypt)
Ubangi River 35a, 49c, 50a, 50c, 254b, 259b
Ubangi-Shari 35b
see also Central African Republic
Uchiura Bay 277a
Uda River 287c
Ufa, Soviet Union 287c
Ufa River 287c
Uganda 191–192
agriculture 191c
area 191b
capital 191b
climate 191c
currency unit 191b
economy 191c
flag il iv
geography 191b–191c
government 191c
history 191c–192b
language 191b
map 191, Atlas–39
national holiday 191b
official name 191b
people of 191c
population 191c
religion 191b, 192a
—Cities
Entebbe 266b
Jinja 270a
Kampala 270c
Uganda Agreement (1900) 192a
Uganda People's Congress (UPC) 192a
Uighurs 41a
Ujjain, India 95c, 287c
Ukraine see Ukrainian Soviet Socialist Republic
Ukrainian Soviet Socialist Republic 271c, 274c
Ulan Bator, Mongolia 132b, 132c, 287c
Ulan-Ude, Soviet Union 287c
Ulate, Otilio 52a
Ulbricht, Walter 79b
Umar, al-hajj 127b
Umm al Qaiwain 188b
see also Trucial Oman
Umma Party (Sudan) 178c
Umtali, Rhodesia 288a
Unam sanctam (papal bull) 66c
Ungava Bay 254c
Union Act (1840) 32a
Union of South Africa see South Africa
Union of Soviet Socialist Republics see Soviet Union
see also Russia (before 1917)
Union of Utrecht 14c, 137b
Unitarios (Argentina) 6b
United Africa Company 141c
United Arab Republic (Egypt) 102b, 120a, 192–193
agriculture 192c
area 192b
capital 192b
climate 192c
currency unit 192b
economy 192c–193a
flag il iv
geography 192b–192c
government 193a
history 193a–193c
Israel and 102b, 104a, 104b, 105b, 105c, 192b, 192c, 193a
language 192b
manufacturing 192c
map 192, Atlas–34

national holiday 192b
official name 192b
people of 192c
population 192b
religion 192b
Sudan and 178b–178c
—Cities 192c
Alexandria 256c
Aswan 258a
Asyut (Lycopolis) 258b
Cairo 262c
Al Fayyum 257a
Port Said 281a
Suez 285b
Tanta 286a
United Australia Party 10a
United Fruit Company 85a, 85b, 89b
United Gold Coast Convention (UGCC) 80b
United Kingdom 194–204
area 194a
capital 194a
climate 194b
currency unit 194a
empire 195c, 203b
flag il iv
geography 194a–194b
government 195b–195c
language 194b
map 194, Atlas–10–11
maritime power 200b
National Health Service 204a
national holiday 194a
official name 194a
people of 194b–194c
population 194a
religion 194a, 194b–194c, 196a
slavery 202a, 203a
Zionism 105b
—Cities
Belfast 260b
Bristol 262a
Cambridge 262c
Canterbury 263a
Cardiff 263c
Edinburgh 266b
Glasgow 267c
Leeds 273b
Liverpool 274a
London 274b
Manchester 275b
Oxford 279b
—Economy 194c–195b, 204a–204b
agriculture 194c, 202c
balance-of-payments deficits 204b
industry 194c–195a, 203b, 204b
manufacturing 194c
nationalizes steel industry 204b
sterling devaluation 204a, 204b
trade 195a–195b, 203b
—History 195c–204b
Act of Supremacy 199c, 200a
Afghanistan and 197c–198a
Black Death 198c
China and 44b–45a, 45c
Civil War 200c–201a
Colonial 200b, 201c–202a, 203b
Antigua 219a
Australia 8c–9a
Bahamas 219b
Bermuda 219c–220a
Botswana 17c
British Antarctic Territory 220a
British Honduras 220a–220b
British Indian Ocean Territory 220a–220b
British Solomon Islands 220c–221a
British Virgin Islands 221a
Brunei 221a–221b
Burma 23b–23c
Caicos Islands 236b–236c
Canada 28c–29a, 29b, 30c–32b, 34c
Cayman Islands 221c–222a
Channel Islands 221a–221b

Commonwealth of Nations 203c
Cyprus 54b
Dominica 223a–223b
Egypt 193b
Ellice Islands 226a–226b
Falkland Islands 224a
Fiji Islands 224a–224b
Ghana 80b–80c
Gibraltar 225c–226a
Gilbert Islands 226a–226b
Guyana 87a–87b
Hong Kong 227a–227c
India 93b, 97a–98a
Ireland 103a–103c, 201c, 202a, 203a
Isle of Man 228a–228b
Jamaica 109c, 110a–110b
Kenya 114c–115a
Lesotho 120c
Malaysia 125c–126a
Maldive Islands 126a
Malta 127c–128a
Mauritius 129a–129b
Montserrat 229a
Muscat and Oman 135a
Nauru 135b
New Hebrides 231a
New Zealand 138a–138b
Nigeria 141c
Pakistan 145a–145c
Pitcairn Island 231c
Qatar 154c
Rhodesia 155a–155b, 204b
St. Helena 233a
St. Kitts–Nevis–Anguilla 233a–233b
St. Lucia 233b
St. Vincent 233c
Seychelles 234a–234b
Sierra Leone 161a
Sikkim 161c
Singapore 162c
South Africa 165a
South Yemen 166b
Sudan 178c
Tobago 188a–188b
Tonga 236a–236b
Turks and Caicos Islands 236b–236c
Uganda 192a
Zambia 217c
Commonwealth 201a–201b
curia regis 197a, 197b, 198a
Declaration of Rights 201c
Domesday survey 197a
feudalism 197a, 197c
Hundred Years' War 198c
Iceland and 93a
Iran and 101b
Kuwait and 117c–118a
Norman conquest 196c–197a
papal fief 197c
Peasants' Revolt 199a
Reformation 199c–200a
Revolution of 1688, 201c
Seven Years' War 202b
War of the Roses 199b
World War I 70b, 203c
World War II 78c, 79a, 204a
occupation of Germany 79a
United National Independence Party (Zambia) 217c
United National Party (UNP) (Ceylon) 36b–36c
United Nations 34b
in Cyprus 54b
in Indian-Pakistani conflict 93b, 98a
in Israeli-Arab conflicts 105c
United Party of the Cuban Socialist Revolution (PURSC) 53a
United Provinces of Central America 52a, 61b, 85a, 89a, 140a
United States of America 204–206
agriculture 205c–206a
area 204b
Canada and 31b, 32a, 32b, 32c, 33c, 34c, 35b, 35c, 36a
capital 204b

climate 205a–205b
Cuba and 52b, 52c, 53a, 53b–54a
currency unit 204b
in Dominican Republic 59a–59b
economy 205c–206b
fishing 206a
flag il iv
forests 206a
geography 204c–205b
Germany, occupation of 79a
government 206b
in Haiti 88b
Iceland and 92c
Indians 205c
industry 206a
in Korea 117a, 117b
language 204b
in Lebanon 120a
map 205, Atlas–60–61, 62–63
Mexico, war with 131a
national holiday 204b
in Nicaragua 140a–140b
official name 204b
Open Door policy 45c
in Panama 146c
people of 205b–205c
in the Philippines 150b
population 204b
religion 204b, 205c
Soviet Union and 173b–174a
Suez Canal crisis 34b
territories of 206b
trade 206a–206b
in Vietnam 213a–213b
World War I 70b, 77c
World War II 78c, 79a, 204a
Unity Party (Togo) 187b
UNP see United National Party (Ceylon)
UPC see Uganda People's Congress
Upolu Island 213c
Upper Volta 206–207
agriculture 206c
area 206b
Bobo-Dioulasso 261a
capital 206b
currency unit 206b
economy 206c
flag il iv
geography 206b
government 206c
history 206c–207a
independence 207a
language 206b
map 206, Atlas–36–37
national holiday 206b
official name 206b
Ouagadougou 279b
people of 206b
population 206b
religion 206b
UPRONA see National Union and Progress Party (UPRONA) (Burundi)
Ural Mountains 154b–154c, 166b, 166c, 275a, 285c, 287c
Ural River 254b, 275a
Uranium
Germany 74b
Greenland 226b
Romania 156a
Sweden 180a
U.S. 205c
Urgel, Spain 4c
Urmia, Iran 282a
Urmia, Lake 282a
Urquiza, Justo José de 6b
Uruguay 6b, 207–208
agriculture 207a
area 207a
capital 207a
climate 207a
currency unit 207a
economy 207a–207b
flag il iv
geography 207a
government 207b

384   Uruguay River

history 207b–208a
independence 207c
language 207a
map 207, *Atlas*-45
Montevideo 276c
national holiday 207a
official name 207a
people of 207a
population 207a
religion 207a
World War II 208a
Uruguay River 5a, 254c
U.S.S.R. *see* Soviet Union
Ussuri River 166c, 237c
Usuman dan Fodio 140c–141a
Utrecht, Netherlands 136c, 137c
Utrecht, Treaty of 30c, 201c
Uttar Pradesh (state) India 256b, 263b, 274c, 276a, 276c
Uzbek Soviet Socialist Republic 286b
Uzbeks 168a
   Afghanistan 1a

V

Vaal River 164a, 254c, 288a
Vaduz, Liechtenstein 122a, 122b, 122c, 288a
Vai tribe 121a
Vaigai River 275a
Valdivia, Pedro de 38a
Valencia, Spain 175c, 288a
Valenciennes, France 65a
Valera River 4c
Valletta, Malta 127b, 288a
Valois kings 66c–67b
Valparaíso, Chile 37b, 37c
Van, Lake 254c
Vancouver, Canada 26c, 254c, 288a, 288b
Vandals
   Algeria 4a
   Germany 75a
   Morocco 134c
   Spain 176b
   Tunisia 189a
Vanderbilt, Cornelius 140a
Vänern, Lake 179c, 254c
Vanua Levi Island 224a
Varangians 169c–170a
Vardar River 284c
Vargas, Getulio 20b–20c
Varna, Bulgaria 21a, 288a
Vasa, Gustavus 180c
Vasa kings 180c
Vásquez, Horacio 59b
Vatican *see* Vatican City
Vatican City 208
   area 208a
   currency unit 208a
   flag *il iv*
   government 208b
   history 208b–208c
   language 208a
   national holiday 208a
   official name 208a
   population 208a
   religion 208a
Vättern, Lake 179c, 180b, 254c
Vauban, Marquis de 68a
Vava'u Islands 236a
Veddas (people) 36a
Velasco Ibarra, José María 60c
Velázquez, Diego 53b
Venetian Republic *see* Venice, Republic of
Venezuela 49a, 50c, 208–210
   agriculture 209b
   area 208c
   capital 208c
   climate 209a
   currency unit 208c
   economy 209a–209c
   flag *il iv*
   geography 208c–209a
   government 209c
   history 209c–210a
   independence 209c–210a
   industry 209b
   language 208c
   map 209, *Atlas*-52–53
   national holiday 208c
   natural resources 209b
   official name 208c
   people of 209a
   population 208c
   religion 208c, 209a
   trade 209b–209c
  —Cities 209a
   Barquisimeto 209a
   Caracas 263a
   Maracaibo 209a
   Santo Tomé de Guayana 283c
   Valencia 209a
Venezuela, Gulf of 254c
Venice, Italy 107b, 288a
Venice, Republic of 107b
Venizelos, Eleutherios 82c, 279a
Venta River 288a
Ventspils, Soviet Union 288a
Verdun, Treaty of 66b, 75a
Vereeniging, South Africa 288a
Verkhoyansk Mountains 254c
Versailles, Treaty of 34a, 46b, 92c, 152b
Versailles Palace 68a
Vértes Mountains 89c
Verwoerd, Hendrik 165b
Vesuvius, Mount 255a, 277c
Viceroyalty of Peru 149a
Viceroyalty of Rio de la Plata 6a, 147c, 149a
Victor Emanuel, King (Italy) 108a
Victor Emanuel III, King (Italy) 108b
Victoria, Queen (England) 203a–203b
Victoria (state), Australia 276a
Victoria, Canada 288b
Victoria, Hong Kong 227a
Victoria, Lake 114b, 184a, 191a, 191c, 255a, 266b, 279c
Victoria Falls 217a, 255a
Victoria Nile River 191b, 237b
Vienna, Austria 10b, 288b
Vienna, Treaty of 132b
Vienna Award 157a
Vientiane, Laos 118a, 118c, 288b
Viet (people) 212a
Viet Minh 210c, 213a
Vietnam 210–213
   agriculture 211b–211c
   communism 214a
   economy 210b–211c
   geography 210c–211a
   government 211c
   history 211c–213b
   people of 211a–211b
   religion 210a, 211a, 212b, 213b
   17th parallel 213a
   World War II 212c–213b
   see also Vietnam, North; Vietnam South
  —Cities
   Haiphong 268b
   Hanoi 268c
   Hue 269a
   Saigon 282c
Vietnam, North
   agriculture 211b
   area 210c
   capital 210c
   climate 211a
   currency unit 210c
   economy 211b
   flag *il iv*
   geography 211a
   government 211b
   language 210c
   official name 210c
   people of 211b
   population 210c
   religion 210c
Vietnam, South
   agriculture 211b–211c
   area 210c
   capital 210c
   climate 211a
   currency unit 210c
   economy 211b–211c
   flag *il iv*
   geography 211a
   government 211c
   language 210c
   national holiday 210c
   official name 210c
   people of 211b
   population 210c
   religion 210c
Vietnam War 10a, 25b, 186c, 213a–213b, 268b
Vikings 29b, 142c
   Denmark 58a
   Greenland 226b
   Iceland 92b, 92c
   Ireland 103a
   Norway 224a
   Soviet Union 169c–170a
   Sweden 180b
Vikram University 287c
Vila, New Hebrides 231a, 288b
Vili 50a
Vilia River 271b
Villa, Francisco 131b, 131c
Villazón, Eleodoro 17a
Vilna, Lithuania *see* Vilnius, Soviet Union
Vilnius, Soviet Union 152b, 288b–288c
Vindhya Mountains 255a
Vindhya-Satpura Mountains 93b
Vinson Massif 255a
Virgin Islands (U.S.) 263c
   see also British Virgin Islands
Virunga Mountains 157b
Visconti family 107b
Visigoths
   Italy 107b
   Romania 156b
   Spain 176b
Vistula (Wista) River 150c, 151a, 151c, 255a, 267a, 272a, 289a
Visurgis River *see* Weser River
Viswamitra River 259c
Viti Islands *see* Fiji Islands
Viti Levu Island 224a, 285c
Vladivostok, Soviet Union 288c
Vlonë, Albania 288c
Vltava (Moldau) River 281a
Vogel, Julius 139a
Volcanoes
   Ecuador 59c
   Hawaii 205a
   Iceland 92a
   Japan 110b–110c
   Madagascar 123c
   Mauritius 128c
   Mexico 129b–129c
   New Zealand 137c
   Nicaragua 139b
   Niger 140b
   Panama 146a
   Philippines 149c
Volga River 168c, 255a, 267c, 270c, 272c, 283c, 288c
Volgograd, Soviet Union *il* 169, 174b, 288c
Volta Redonda, Brazil 288c–289a
Volta River 79c, 255a
Voltaic Democratic Union (VDU) (Upper Volta) 207a
Vorster, Balthasar 165b
Vosges Mountains 64a
Vrbas River 215a
Vridi Canal 256a
Vychegda River 243b

W

Wadai Empire 37a
Wadi al Araba 113c, 258a
Wahhabis 159a–159b
Waikato River 137c
Waitaki River 137c
Waitangi, Treaty of 138c
Waitemata, New Zealand 258b
Wakayama, Japan 289a
Walachia 81c, 156b, 156c, 261c, 262b
Walbrzych, Poland 151c
Wales 194a, 195a
   See also United Kingdom
Walker, William 140a
Wallace, William 198b
Wallace-Johnson, I. T. A. 161a
Wallis and Futuna Islands 236
   area 236c
   capital 236c
   population 236c
   status 236c
Wallonia 15b
Walloons 14a
Walpole, Robert 202b
Walter, Hubert 197c
Wang Mang 43a
Wanganui, New Zealand 138b
Wanganui River 137c
Wangchuk, Ugyen 15c
War of the Austrian Succession 107b
War of Devolution 68a
War of 1812 31b
War of the League of Augsburg 68a
War of the Pacific 16c, 38b, 149a–149b
War of the Polish Succession 68b, 107b
War of Restoration 59a
War of the Roses 103a–103b
War of the Spanish Succession 68a–68b, 107b, 137b
War of the Triple Alliance 6b, 147c
Warsaw, Poland 150c, 151a, 151c, 289a
Warsaw Pact 75a, 151c
Warta River 150c, 265a
Washington, D.C. 204b
Washington, Treaty of (1871) 32c
Washington Conference (1922) 113a
Waterfalls 255a–255b
Waterloo, Belgium 69b
Watusi *see* Tusi
Webster-Ashburton Treaty 31c
Weddell Sea 255a
Weimar Republic 77c–78a
Welland Ship Canal 31b
Wellington, New Zealand 137c, 138c, 289a
Weser River 73b, 255b
Wessex, Kingdom of 196a, 196b
Wessin y Wessin, Elías 59b
West Bengal State, India 262c
West Berlin, Germany *see* Berlin, Germany

INDEX

West Germany *see* Germany, West
West Indies 255b
West Indies Associated States 219a
West Irian 98c, 100b, 285b
West Pakistan Province, Pakistan 269c, 271a, 273a
  see also Pakistan
Western Carolines (islands) *see* Palau Islands
Western Desert 192b
Western Dvina River *see* Dvina rivers
Western Ghats 93b, 93c
Western Islands *see* Hebrides Islands
Western Samoa 213–214
  agriculture 213c
  Apia 257c
  area 213b
  capital 213b
  climate 213b
  currency unit 213b
  economy 213c
  flag *il* iv
  geography 213b
  government 213c
  history 213c–214a
  independence 214a
  language 213b
  map *Atlas*-6
  official name 213b
  people of 213b–213c
  population 213b
  religion 213b
Western Togoland 80b
Westphalia, Peace of 67c, 76b, 137b, 182b
Weyler, Valeriano 53b
Wheat
  Albania 2b
  Algeria 3c
  Argentina 5c
  Australia 8a
  Bulgaria 21b
  Canada 28a, 28c
  China 41b
  France 64c
  Ifni 228a
  India 94b
  Iran 100c
  Iraq 101c
  Ireland 103a
  Isle of Man 228a
  Italy 106b–106c
  Japan 111b
  Jordan 113c
  Mexico 130a
  Morocco 133c
  Niger 140c
  Pakistan 144b
  Poland 151b
  Romania 156a
  San Marino 158a
  Soviet Union 169a
  Spain 176a

Sweden 180a
Switzerland 182a
Syria 183a
Tunisia 189a
Turkey 190a
United Arab Republic (Egypt) 192c
United Kingdom 194c
U.S. 206a
Uruguay 207a
Yugoslavia 215b
White Huns 1c
White Volta River 79c
Wien, Austria *see* Vienna, Austria
Wiesbaden, Germany 289a
Wight, Isle of 194a, 255b
Wilhelmina, Queen (Netherlands) 137c
Willemstad, Curaçao 229c, 289a
William, Duke (Normandy) *see* William I, King (England)
William I, King (England)
  conquest of England 196c–197a
  reign 197a
William II, King (England) 197a
William III, King (England) 137b
  reign 201c
William II, Emperor (Germany) 77b–77c
William I, King (Netherlands) 14c, 123b
  see also William III, King (England)
William of Wied, King (Albania) 3a
Wilson, Harold 204b
Wilson, Woodrow 59a–59b, 88b, 152b
Wiman Chosen 116a
Win, Ne 24a
Windhoek, South Africa 234b, 289a–289b
Windward Islands 229c, 233b, 238a, 263a
Wine
  Algeria 4a
  France 64c
  Greece 81b
  Italy 106c
  Portugal 153b
  Morocco 133c
  Tunisia 189a
  Yugoslavia 215c
Winnipeg, Canada 289b
Winnipeg, Lake 255b
Wista River *see* Vistula River
Witte, Count Sergei 172b
Witwatersrand 255b
Wolfe, James 30c
Wolof
  Gambia 72a
  Senegal 159c
Wolsey, Archbishop Thomas 199c

Won
  Korea, North 115b
  Korea, South 115b
Wonsan, North Korea 289b
Woodlark Archipelago 231b
Workers Party (North Vietnam) 211c
World 255b–255c
  geophysical globe *il* i
  map *Atlas*-6–7
World War I 77c
  Barbados 13c
  Burundi 24b
  New Guinea 230c, 231c
  San Marino 158b
  South West Africa 234c
  —Countries involved
  Australia 9b–9c, 10a
  Austria 11b–11c, 91a
  Austria-Hungary 77c
  Belgium 15a
  Bolivia 17a
  Bulgaria 77c
  Canada 33c
  Chile 38b
  China 46a
  Cyprus 54b
  Czechoslovakia 55c
  Denmark 58b
  France 70a–70b
  Germany 11b–11c, 15a, 70b
  Greece 83a
  Hungary 91a
  Italy 77c, 108b
  Japan 113a
  Jordan 114a
  Luxembourg 123c
  Netherlands 137b
  New Zealand 139a
  Norway 143c
  Poland 152b
  Portugal 154b
  Romania 157a
  Russia 70b, 77c, 169b, 172c–173a
  South Africa 165b
  Spain 177a
  Sweden 181a
  Syria 183b
  Turkey 77c, 191a
  United Kingdom 70b, 203c
  United States 70b, 77c
  Yugoslavia 216b
World War II 78c–79a, 191a, 220c–221a
  War crimes trials (Germany) *il* 78
  —Countries involved
  Argentina 6c
  Austria 12b, 70c, 78c
  Belgium 15a, 78c
  Brazil 20b
  Bulgaria 22a
  Burma 23c
  Cambodia 25b
  Canada 34b, 79a
  Chad 37a
  Channel Islands 213b
  Chile 38c

China 46c
Congo (Brazzaville) 50b
Czechoslovakia 57c, 70c, 78c
Denmark 58b, 78c
Faeroe Islands 224a
Finland 63c
France 70c–71a, 78c
Germany 15a, 70c–71a
Gilbert Islands 226b
Greece 83–83b
Greenland 226c
Hong Kong 227c
Hungary 91b
Iceland 92c
India 97b–97c
Indonesia 100a
Iran 101c
Iraq 102b
Italy 108c
Jamaica 110b
Japan 100a, 113b
Laos 119a
Liberia 121b
Libya 122b
Luxembourg 123c
Malaysia 126a
Maldive Islands 126c
Malta 128a
Mexico 131c
Mongolia 133b
Morocco 134b
Nauru 135b
Netherlands 78c, 137b–137c
New Guinea 231c
New Zealand 139b
Nicaragua 140b
Norway 78c, 143c
Panama 146c
Philippines 150b
Poland 70c, 78c, 151a, 152b–152c, 204a
Portugal 154b
Portuguese Timor 232c
Romania 157a
St. Helena 233a
Singapore 162c
Soviet Union 70c, 78c, 79a, 174a, 204a
Spain 177b
Sudan 178c
Sweden 181b
Syria 183c
Thailand 186c
United Kingdom 78c, 79a, 204a
United States 78c, 79a, 204a
Uruguay 208a
Vietnam 212c–213a
Wallis and Futuna Islands 236c
Yugoslavia 216c
Wroclaw, Poland 151c, 289b
Wu, King 42a
Wu Ti 43a
Wuchang, China *see* Wuhan, China
Wuhan, China 289b
Wut'ai Mountains 40a
Wyszynski, Cardinal Stefan 152c

X

Xhosa 164b

Y

Yablonovvy Mountains 166c
Yadavas 96a
Yahya, Imam (Yemen) 214c
Yakuts 168a
Yalta Conference 174b
Yalu River 115b, 115c, 255c
Yamagata, Japan 289b
Yamato clan 112a
Yaméogo, Maurice 207a
Yana River 255c

Yangtze Gorges 269b
Yangtze River 39c, 40a, 40b, 255c, 269b, 277c, 284a, 289b
Yao 124b
Yaoundé, Cameroon 25c, 289b–289c
Yarra River 276a
Ydígoras Fuentes, Miguel 108b
Yedo (Yeddo) *see* Tokyo
Yellow fever 53b
Yellow River 39c, 42a, 245c
  see also Hwang Ho
Yellow Sea 255c, 276c
Yemen 193c, 214
  agriculture 214a
  area 214a

capital 214a
climate 214a
currency unit 214a
economy 214a–214b
flag *il* iv
geography 214a
government 214b
history 214b–214c
language 214a
map 214, *Atlas*-25
national holiday 214a
official name 214a
people of 214a
population 214a
religion 214a, 214b
San'a 214a, 283b
Yen (currency unit) 110b

Yenisey River 166c, 255c,
Yerevan, Soviet Union 289c
Yerovi Indaburu, Clemente 60c
Yi (people) 41a
Yi dynasty 116b
Yin dynasty 42a
Yin Shan (mountains) 40a
Yokohama, Japan 110c, 112c
Yom River 240c
Yoritomo 112b
York, Cape *see* Cape York
Yoruba 141b, 141c
Youlou, Fulbert 50b

Young Communist League (Komsomol) 272a
Ypsilanti, Alexander 81c–82a
Yuan (currency unit) 39a
Yüan dynasty 43c, 133a
Yüan Shih-K'ai 46a–46b
Yucatán Peninsula 129c, 255c
Yueh-chi 1c
Yugoslavia 11c, 83b, 214–217
  agriculture 215b–215c
  area 214c
  capital 214c
  climate 215c
  communism 215b, 215c–216a, 216c–217a
  currency unit 214c
  economy 215b–215c
  flag *il* iv
  geography 214c–215a
  government 215c–216a
  history 216a–217a
  industry 215c
  language 214c
  map 214, *Atlas*-18–19
  national holiday 214c
  natural resources 215b
  official name 214c
  people of 215a–215b
  population 214c
  religion 214c, 216b
  trade 215c
  World War I 216b
  World War II 216c
  —Cities 215b
    Belgrade 260b
    Ljubljana 274a
    Nis 278b
    Novi Sad 278b
    Sarajevo 283c
    Skopje 284c
    Split 285a
    Subotica 285b
    Zagreb 289c
Yukon River 239b
Yung-lo 43c
Yünnan Province, China 272b

Z

Zagreb, Yugoslavia 215b, 289c
Zagros Mountains 100c, 101c, 255c
az-Zahran, Saudi Arabia 258c
Zaindah River 269b
Zaire 51b
Zambales Mountains 149c
Zambezi River 154c–155a, 217a, 229a, 255c
Zambia 217
  agriculture 217b
  area 217a
  capital 217a
  climate 217c
  currency unit 217a
  economy 217b
  flag *il* iv
  geography 217a
  government 217b
  history 217b–217c
  language 217a
  map 217, *Atlas*-38–39
  national holiday 217a
  official name 217a
  people of 217b
  population 217a
  religion 217a
  —Cities
    Broken Hill 262a
    Lusaka 274c
    Ndola 278a
Zamboanga, Philippines 289c
Zamora, Treaty of 153c
Zande 35b
Zanzibar *see* Tanzania
Zanzibar Nationalist Party (ZNP) 184c
Zanzibar and Pemba Peoples' Party (ZPPP) 184c
Zapata, Emiliano 131b, 131c
Zaporozhye, Soviet Union 289c
Zaragoza, Spain 175c
Zaria, Nigeria 289c
Zauditu, Empress (Ethiopia) 62b
Zelaya, José Santos 140a
Zhdanov, Soviet Union 289c
Zhivkov, Todor 22b
Zimbabwe 155b
Zinc
  Australia 8b
  Congo (Kinshasa) 50c
  Germany 74b
  Greenland 226b
  Japan 109c
  Korea, North 115c
  Mexico 130a
  Morocco 133c
  Peru 148b
  Poland 151b
  South West Africa 234c
  Soviet Union 168b
  Spain 175c
  Sweden 180a
  Turkey 190a
  United Kingdom 194c
  Yugoslavia 215b
Zinder, Niger 140c
Zionism 105a–105b
Zloty 150c
Zog I, King (Albania) 3a
Zogolli, Ahmed bey *see* Zog I, King (Albania)
Zogu, Achmed *see* Zog I, King (Albania)
Zomba, Malawi 124b, 289c
Zuider Zee 246a
Zulu wars 203b
Zulus 17c, 155a
  Lesotho 118b
  South Africa 164b, 165a
  Swaziland 179a, 179b
Zürich, Switzerland 181c, 182c, 289c
Zürich, Lake 289c
Zwingli, Ulrich 182b